Windows™ 3.1
Revealed

Windows™ 3.1 Revealed

Robert Mullen, Paul Hoffman,
and Barrie Sosinsky

SAMS

A Division of Prentice Hall Computer Publishing
11711 North College, Carmel, Indiana 46032 USA

*Composed in New Century Schoolbook and MCPdigital by
Prentice Hall Computer Publishing.*

Printed in the United States of America

*Screen reproductions in this book were created by means of the
program Collage Plus from Inner Media, Inc., Hollis, NH.*

Publisher
Richard K. Swadley

Publishing Manager
Joseph B. Wikert

Managing Editor
Neweleen A. Trebnik

Acquisitions Editor
Linda Sanning

Development Editor
Jennifer Flynn

Production Editor
Katherine Stuart Ewing

Editors
Gayle Johnson
Becky Freeman
Fran Hatton
Cheri Clark
Gail Burlakoff
Bryan Gambrel

Technical Reviewers
Rob Caserotti
Sky Caserotti
Cathy Kenny
Bruce Wasserman

Editorial Assistant
Rosemarie Graham

Production Analyst
Mary Beth Wakefield

Book Design
Michele Laseau

Cover Art
Tim Amrhein

Production
Jeff Baker
Claudia Bell
Brad Chinn
Michelle Cleary
Scott Cook
Mark Enochs
Brook Farling
Audra Hershman
Carrie Keesling
Phil Kitchel
Bob LaRoche
Anne Owen
Cindy L. Phipps
Joe Ramon
Caroline Roop
Linda Seifert
M. Louise Shinault
Kevin Spear
Lisa Wilson
Allan Wimmer
Phil Worthington
Christine Young

Indexer
Johnna VanHoose

About the Authors

Robert Mullen lives in Amherst, New Hampshire, and has extensive experience in graphical user interface systems.

Paul Hoffman lives in Berkeley, California, and has written several books, including *Microsoft Word for Windows Made Easy* and *Microsoft Word 5.5 Made Easy.*

Barrie Sosinsky lives in Newton, Massachusetts, and has written numerous books, including *The Big Mac Book* and *Using Microsoft Works.*

For all the true friendship and loving support I received while working on this and other books, I would like to dedicate *Windows 3.1 Revealed* to Bets, my adoring wife, on this Valentine's Day, 1992.

R. T. Mullen

Cindy Cosgrove helped keep me sane during the arduous last weeks before the deadline.

Paul Hoffman

Friends don't let friends do DOS!

Robert A. Janukowicz
Customer Applications Manager
Optronics
An Intergraph Division

permission to duplicate granted by
Robert A. Janukowicz

vi

Acknowledgments

In the making of any book, there are many people who help get a book "to press." I would like to thank Jennifer Flynn for her patience with a new author, Kathy Ewing for her editing skills, Joe Wikert and Becky Freeman for their help with the figures in this book, and all of the good folks at SAMS for their help and generosity.

The authors gratefully acknowledge the help of many people in preparing this book. Special thanks to Cristi Gersage of Microsoft for providing evaluation products and to the folks of the Windows 3.1 beta project for their patience and resourcefulness. Special thanks also go to Teri Vanderboegh and Bill Horning of Hewlett-Packard for their help in providing a superb LaserJet IIIP printer for evaluation purposes.

The authors also express their thanks to the following contributors:

Ronald Hayden	Paintbrush and Terminal
Sharon Fisher	Networks
Peter Gofton	Programming Elements
Ben Wiseman	Recorder
Lolita Vlcek	Write
Hannah Raiden	Tables and Appendixes

Thanks also to the companies listed in the following Trademarks list that gave their time as well as beta or shrink-wrapped copies of their products.

Trademarks

All terms mentioned in this book that are known to be trademarks or service marks are listed below. In addition, terms suspected of being trademarks or service marks have been appropriately capitalized. SAMS cannot attest to the accuracy of this information. Use of a term in this book should not be regarded as affecting the validity of any trademark or service mark.

1-2-3 and Freelance are registered trademarks of Lotus Development Corporation.

386-MAX is a trademark of Qualitas, Inc.

Actor is a registered trademark of The Whitewater Group.

Adobe Illustrator is a trademark of Adobe Systems Incorporated.

Arts & Letters is a trademark of Computer Support Corporation.

AutoCAD is a registered trademark of Autodesk, Inc.

Bitstream is a registered trademark of Bitstream Inc.

Bitstream Fontware is licensed to Bitstream Inc. in the United Kingdom, France, and West Germany by Electronic Printing Systems Limited.

CompuServe Incorporated is a registered trademark of H&R Block, Inc.

Cricket Graph is a trademark of Cricket Software, Inc.

dBASE II and dBASE III are registered trademarks of Ashton-Tate Corporation.

dBASE III PLUS and dBASE IV are trademarks of Ashton-Tate Corporation.

DisplayWrite, DisplayWriter, Micro Channel, and PS/2 are trademarks of International Business Machines Corporation.

DynaComm is a trademark of Future Soft Engineering, Inc.

EPSON is a registered trademark of Epson Corporation.

FoxBase+ is a trademark of Fox Software, Inc.

GEM is a trademark of Digital Research Inc.

GEnie is a trademark of General Electric Company.

Harvard Graphics is a trademark of Software Publishing Corporation.

HotShot Graphics is a registered trademark of SymSoft Corporation.

Icons

Each chapter in this book can be identified by a specific icon. These icons were chosen directly from those available to Windows users, either by Microsoft or by the manufacturers of software programs.

The icons have been situated at the bottom of each page in conjunction with the page number so that you can use them to find information. The thumb tabs help identify chapters by their number and, used in conjunction with the icons, are designed to provide simple and quick locating of information. Following is a list of the chapters, their respective icons, and the name of the software from which each icon was derived.

Chapter	Icon	Software
1 The World of Windows		Microsoft Windows
2 Installing Windows		Microsoft Windows
3 Starting and Leaving Windows		Microsoft Visual Basic
4 Basic Windows Concepts		Microsoft Windows
5 Program Manager		Microsoft Windows
6 File Manager		Microsoft Windows
7 Control Panel		Microsoft Windows
8 Print Manager		Microsoft Windows
9 Clipboard Viewer		Microsoft Windows
10 Write		Microsoft Windows
11 Paintbrush		Microsoft Windows
12 Terminal		Microsoft Windows

Chapter	Icon	Software
13 Other Accessories		Microsoft Windows
14 Microsoft Excel		Microsoft Excel
15 Lotus 1-2-3 for Windows		Microsoft Windows
16 Microsoft Word for Windows		Microsoft Word
17 WordPerfect for Windows		Microsoft Windows
18 CorelDRAW!		Corel CorelDRAW!
19 Running Lotus 1-2-3 and WordPerfect for DOS		Microsoft Windows
20 Other DOS Programs and Windows		Microsoft Windows
21 Editing PIFs		Microsoft Visual Basic
22 Windows Operating Modes		Microsoft Windows
23 Windows Hardware Enhancements		Microsoft Windows
24 Memory Configuration for Windows		Microsoft Visual Basic
25 Changing Your Configuration		Microsoft Windows
26 Printers and Fonts		Microsoft Windows

Overview

Contents

Part II Basic Windows Programs

Part III Windows Accessory Programs

Part IV Using Other Windows Programs

Part V Running DOS Programs

Part VI Advanced Windows Techniques

28 Networking and Communications 883

Part VII Windows Programming

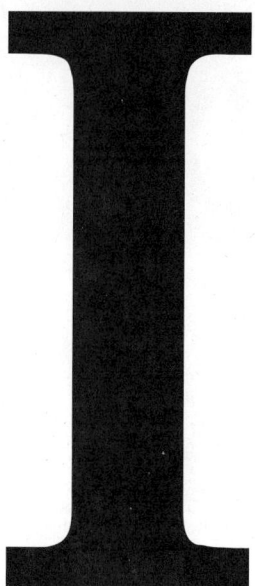

Refreshing the Basics

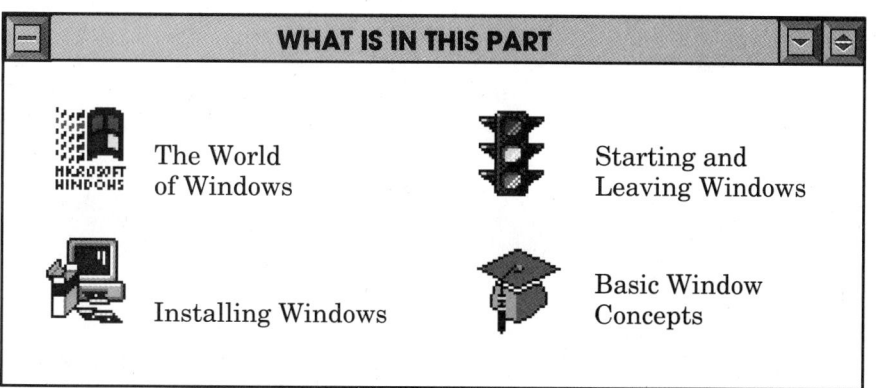

WHAT IS IN THIS PART

The World
of Windows

Starting and
Leaving Windows

Installing Windows

Basic Window
Concepts

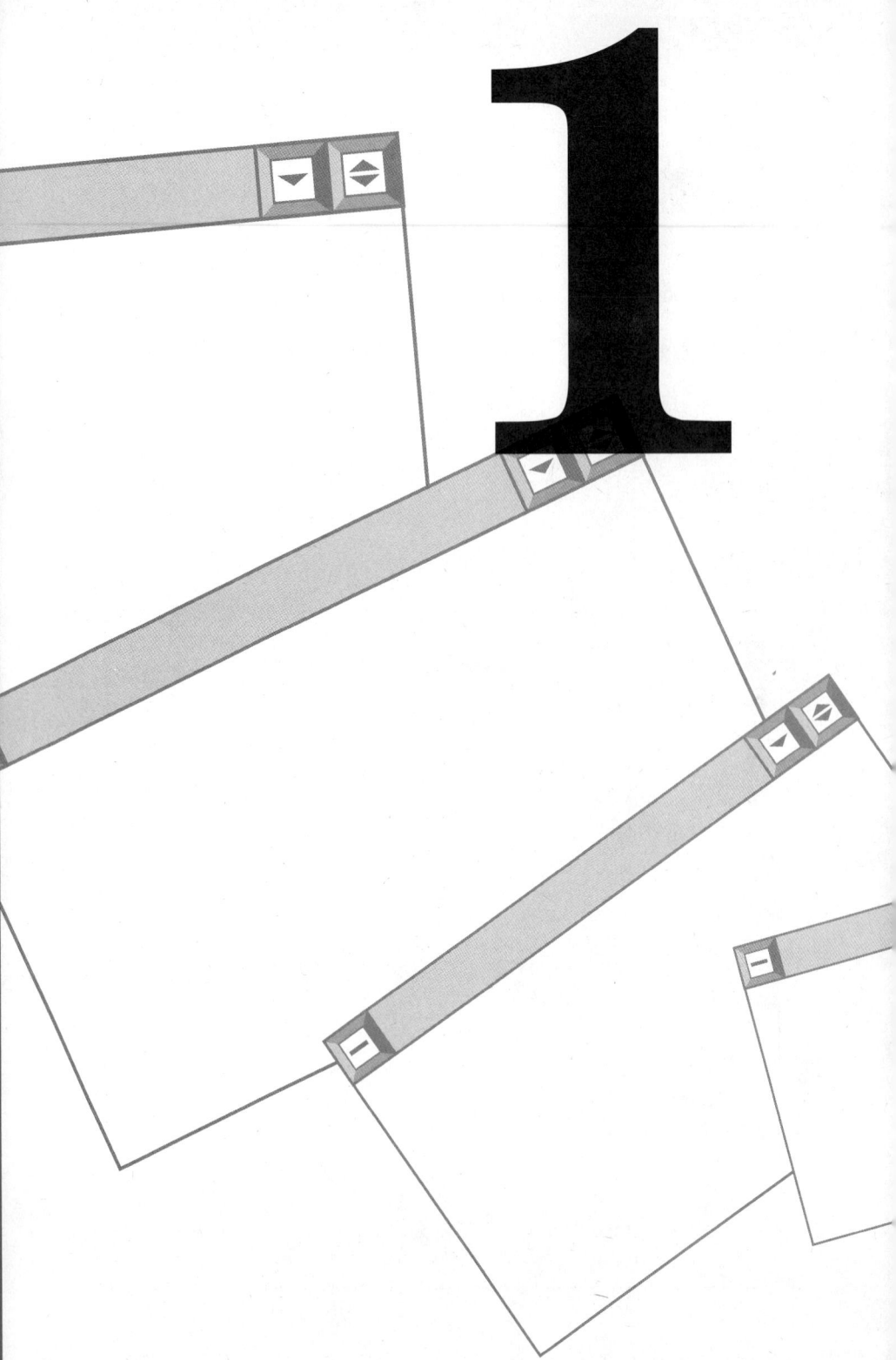

CHAPTER

1

The World of Windows

Microsoft Windows is unlike any other product available for the PC. Windows resembles an operating system, an integrated package, and a DOS extension, but it is much more than all of these. Windows is a GUI (*G*raphical *U*ser *I*nterface) combined with support of standardized methods.

Microsoft easily could have made Windows a full operating system, but decided instead to make it an add-on over MS-DOS. In fact, to be fully accepted by the using public, the Windows environment must accommodate older, character-based DOS applications. Clearly, the investment individual users have made in non-Windows software is too substantial to ignore. Windows not just accommodates, but actually enhances many character- or DOS-based applications that can benefit from the Windows memory management facilities.

What Is Windows?

Windows is called an operating environment. "Great," you say, "What is an operating environment?" The best way to define it without getting too technical is to say that operating environments such as Windows and OS/2 (for the PC) predefine the utilities that all applications share. You can call it user interface methodology. You don't have to care about how Windows works, because the goal of Windows application developers is to use the Windows environment to create applications with more visible continuity. This makes Windows applications easier to learn and use.

Metaphorically speaking, you could liken the ease of using Windows to that of using the basic tools in a familiar environment such as the kitchen. As soon as you have learned how to use a blender or a hand mixer, you have pretty much mastered them. Having become familiar with the tool, you do not need to relearn how to use a hand mixer to make a cake or to blend whipped cream. Even though you are making something new, the basic tool, the hand mixer, stays the same. Opening and saving files in Windows is an example of a similar sort of task that does not have to be relearned with each new application. If you can stick to the same tool to do the same sort of job, you can spend more time learning how to use new tools for other jobs. This is the greatest benefit of Windows: Learning more does not mean learning something over again.

Why Use Windows?

There are many reasons why Windows is sweeping the world:

▲ It's an easy-to-use, consistent GUI for virtually all programs.

▲ It is capable of multitasking (running several programs simultaneously). Graphics programs (Windows) and character-based programs (DOS) can be run concurrently.

▲ You can use Program Manager to switch easily between multiple programs.

▲ With Windows you can communicate and exchange data between programs without transferring or copying files.

▲ Because file- and disk-management facilities are ample and readily available, you don't have to close and open programs or use DOS commands to do standard file- and disk-maintenance chores.

▲ Windows can run applications that offer high-quality output.

▲ Many programs are included with Windows, such as a word processor and a drawing program.

When you buy a copy of Windows 3.1 (or get a copy with your computer), you get all these features in a single package. This is confusing to some people because MS-DOS, the most common operating system in the world, has few of these features. You should understand each of these features before delving into the nuts and bolts of using Windows. That understanding will give you a better idea of what you are doing. Also, when you know the philosophy behind Windows, you will find all aspects of Windows programs quicker and easier to learn.

Consistent User Interface

One major problem with PC software during the first 10 years of MS-DOS was that you had to learn a different method to interact with every program. A program's *user interface* is how you tell the program what you want to do. With some programs, you press the function keys (F1, F2, and so on, located at the top or to the left of your keyboard) to activate commands. With other programs, you press Ctrl- or Alt- key combinations. With still others, you press a special key, such as the / (slash) key, before entering commands. Other programs require a mouse. For the user, the variations among user interfaces have been and still are confusing.

To complicate matters even more, some companies copied user interfaces from popular existing programs so that people would learn to use their programs faster. The companies that wrote the original programs sued the newcomers, claiming that user interfaces are covered by U.S. copyright law. Many of these original companies won their cases, preventing other companies from copying their user interfaces. For example, Lotus Development Corporation won a landmark suit against the maker of a competitive tool, based on the similarities between the two programs. The situation encouraged a proliferation of different user interfaces, resulting in additional difficulties for computer users.

In 1984, Apple introduced the Macintosh computer—the first personal computer with a consistent user interface for all the programs that ran on it. Apple garnered much praise for the consistent user interface, even among PC users. Although the Macintosh has only about one-tenth as many users as the PC does, Microsoft recognized the advantages of Macintosh's consistent user interface. Microsoft's introduction of the standards that developers should use when creating programs for Windows made it clear that all Windows programs should look and act alike. The user interface Microsoft chose for Windows was very similar to the one Apple chose for the Macintosh. New text and graphics, or at least the most recent material, is displayed on screens just big enough to show them as overlays. The border placed around these "floating screens" that came to be known as windows defined the foreground display versus the background display. In this way, the Macintosh and now Windows permit a great deal of information to coexist concurrently. We no longer need to open and close programs and files whenever we need them. They can all stay open. Like the Macintosh, Windows uses an arrow tip as a pointer so that you know exactly where you are at all times. Figure 1.1 shows the arrow tip used as a pointer by Windows.

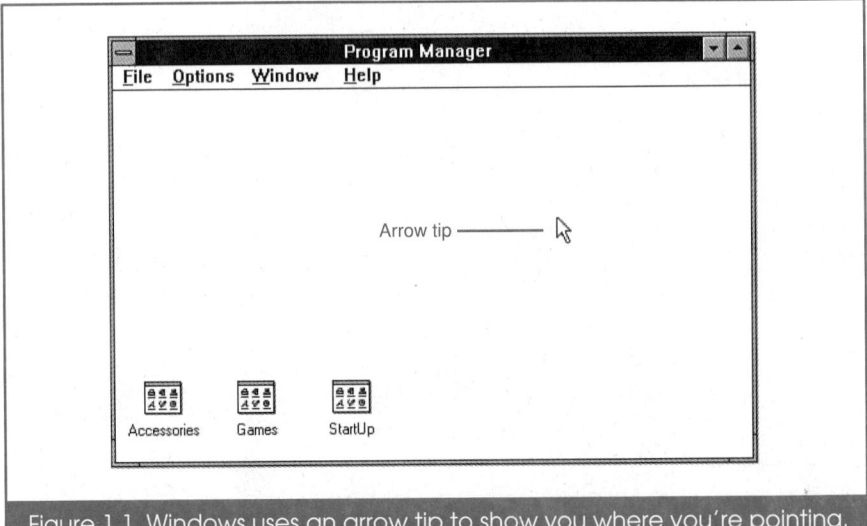

Figure 1.1. Windows uses an arrow tip to show you where you're pointing.

The primary advantage of this consistent user interface is having less to learn with a new program. After you know the general rules for Windows programs (covered in detail in Chapter 4, "Basic Windows Concepts"), you don't need to learn much more to be able to interact with other Windows programs. Thus, when you learn a word processing program, for example, you immediately start learning the features of the program without having to memorize any special keystrokes to run the program. In fact, (unless you replace the File Manager utility with an aftermarket product) whenever you click the File option in most Windows compatible program's menus, you will call up a subset of the Windows File Manager.

Another advantage is quality. With Windows administering the basic interface and I/O (Input/Output) handling functions, developers are freer to create more competent horizontal and vertical applications in less time. Even developers of DOS-based software are observing the emerging interface standards more and more when designing their interfaces. This means that applications which are neither graphics-nor character-based will become increasingly easy to learn, whether or not they are run from within Windows. These are just a few of the benefits of interface standardization.

Running Programs Simultaneously

Rarely can a busy person do only one task at a time. While you are writing a letter, the phone rings. You answer the phone, but you are thinking about the next sentence in your letter. If your keyboard is quiet, you may keep typing while you talk. And as you enter information in a database, you may remember something you want to add to your appointment calendar for next week.

Depending on your hardware, Windows makes doing several tasks simultaneously easy. Most Windows users can run many programs at the same time. When you use a database program, for example, your appointment book program can be running as well. You also can have your word processor and spreadsheet open simultaneously.

There are two advantages to having all these programs available simultaneously. First, you can move quickly between programs (as you move quickly among tasks in your mind). Second, you can integrate your work more easily. These two features are new to most people who have been using MS-DOS, but have been popular with users of Macintosh computers for almost a decade.

Before Windows, most PC users could run only one program at a time. To switch from your painting program to your word processor, you had to exit the painting program, go to MS-DOS, and then start the word processor. Leaving programs can be slow; starting other programs usually is even slower. You waste time watching one program end and another begin. With Windows, you switch between programs in less than a second.

Even with nongraphical desktop environments that juggled multiple DOS sessions simultaneously, data exchange between applications was virtually nonexistent. Again, a lack of standards was a problem, but Windows provides a solution—DDE (*D*ynamic *D*ata *E*xchange). The DDE is a standardized methodology software developers use to give their products the capability to talk to other DDE-compatible products without manually cutting and pasting with the Clipboard. This means instantly updating a selected spreadsheet or memo when you change data in a related data base. As long as developers meet the requirements set forth by the Microsoft DDE standards, developers can be virtually assured of compatibility with other developer's products.

When you use multitasking in 386-enhanced mode, integrating your work is much simpler if you can see simultaneously all the programs you are integrating. For example, assume that you want to include a picture in a written proposal. You start both the drawing and word processing programs, then use the drawing program to create an image. You make a copy of that image, switch to the word processing program, and drop the image in the desired place in your document. Then you realize that you need to make a slight change in the picture. You can make the change and replace the first image with the new one, noting the change as you put it in. This visual connection makes the integration process much easier. Modes and their meanings are discussed in Chapter 22, "Windows Operating Modes."

Program Manager

The main reason you have Windows is to run programs. The central program from which you run other programs is the Windows Program Manager. You see this program running when you first start Windows and again when you are about to leave Windows. In Figure 1.2, the programs located in the "Main" program group are made available by Program Manager.

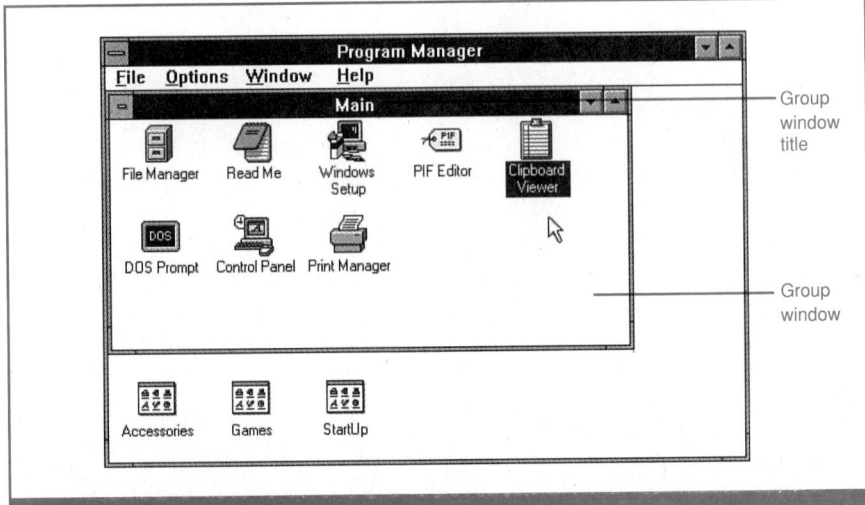

Figure 1.2. Program Manager organizes your programs into groups.

1

Because you'll mostly be running programs and switching among them, the main part of Windows logically should be the part that runs programs. In fact, a few other software companies sell programs that are useful replacements for the Program Manager. Using a different program manager is described in Chapter 25, "Changing Your Configuration."

One of the best features of Program Manager is its flexibility. You can easily change the way programs appear in Program Manager. You can rearrange the programs, add new ones, remove old ones, and so on. You also can configure how programs should be run, whether they should be run at startup, and what documents to open when a program starts. Chapter 5, "Program Manager," provides an extensive description of the Program Manager and what you can do with it.

Communication Among Windows Programs

In the not-so-distant past, PC programs communicated poorly with each other. Their communication often was obtuse. Typically, to move information from Program A to Program B, you had to save a file in Program A, exit Program A, run a conversion program on the file, and then open the converted file in Program B. Even if Program A could save a file that Program B could read directly, the file often had imperfections such as missing information or less formatting. These experiences were frustrating.

The Windows Clipboard is a buffer or holding area in your system's memory that contains one piece of data at any one time. You write to and read from the Clipboard with standard commands found in virtually every Windows program. Most of your interprogram communication is done through the Clipboard. We cover the Clipboard and Clipboard Viewer in detail in Chapter 9, "Clipboard Viewer." Figure 1.3 shows data being copied from Windows Write to Microsoft Excel. This was done using the Clipboard.

Under Windows, programs have many more direct methods for communicating with each other. With Windows, Microsoft gave programmers easy methods for passing information between programs as they run, so you don't even have to save information in files before transferring it. The two major methods for passing information are through the Clipboard and with a programming method called OLE.

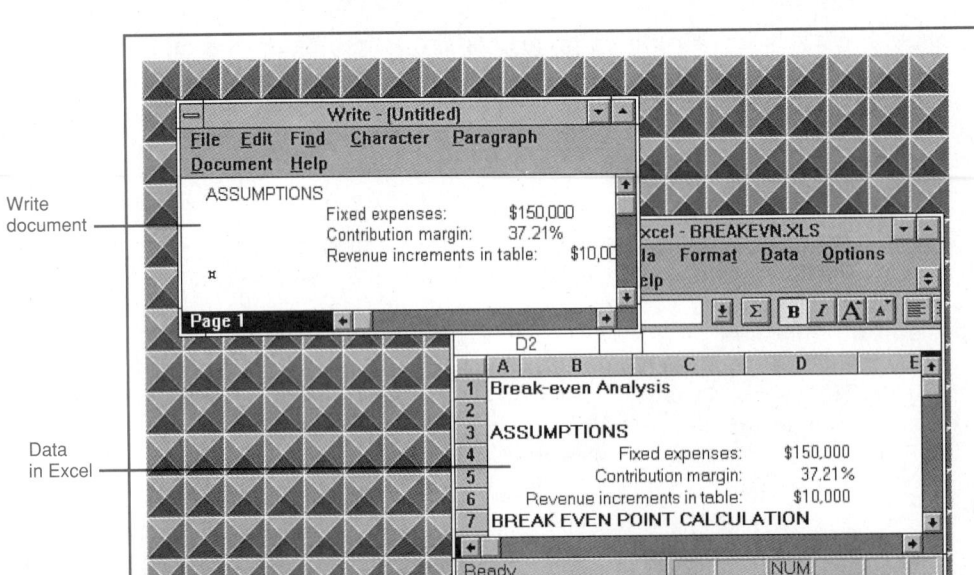

Write
document

Data
in Excel

Figure 1.3. Windows can exchange data transparently.

OLE, or Object Linking and Embedding, is a method for passing data directly between programs without having to use the Clipboard (see Chapter 31, "Introduction to Windows Programming Elements"). You can think of it as a telephone network on which one program can dial another program and pass on certain types of information. Many advanced Windows programs can be set up to use OLE, but this setup often requires the user to know advanced techniques.

File Manager

File Manager, shown in Figure 1.4 and described in Chapter 6, "File Manager," replaces the familiar MS-DOS commands such as DIR, COPY, MKDIR, and so on. If you have ever been frustrated with having to give the DIR command, another file command, the DIR command again, another command, and so on, you will appreciate File Manager. You can see any directory's list of files that stays on your screen instead of scrolling like they do in MS-DOS. Selecting files to copy and move is a snap, and you'll never have to remember command names again.

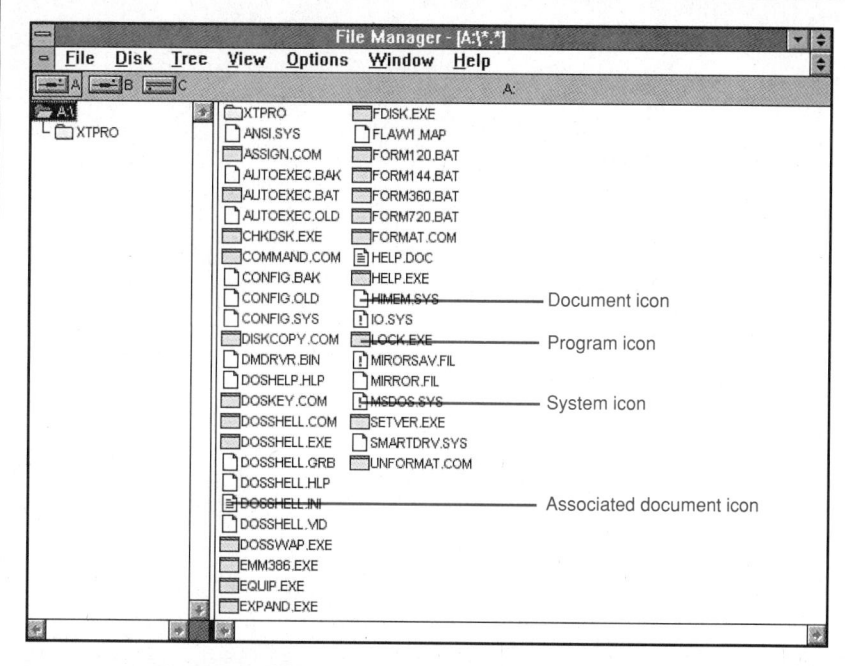

Figure 1.4. File Manager uses icons to differentiate between file types.

You can do more with File Manager. With a single command, you can change the way you see your files and directories. For example, you can view a list of files first in alphabetical order, then ordered by date, and then in alphabetical order again with a few keystrokes. You also can move files from one directory to another by typing a single command rather than many. Even if you use Windows for only one or two programs, you probably will find yourself running File Manager whenever you want to do things you used to do at the MS-DOS prompt.

File Manager can be essential because it makes tasks that were extremely tedious under MS-DOS seem natural. DOS requires that you type exact command syntax to get anything but an error message. In File Manager you can see and choose from the available options. Many Windows users utilize File Manager more than any other program except Program Manager. Although Windows's File Manager frequently disappointed Windows users before the release of Version 3.1, Microsoft's major rewrite of this utility has improved it immensely. Other companies also sell replacements for File Manager, as you will see later in the book. The utility's inner workings are described in Chapter 6, "File Manager."

Running MS-DOS Programs from Windows

You will not stop using all your MS-DOS software just because you have a copy of Windows. Many Windows users still use their favorite MS-DOS software, such as WordPerfect for DOS and 1-2-3. Windows makes it easy to run MS-DOS software and Windows programs at the same time. Depending on your hardware, you may be able to run more than one MS-DOS program at a time.

Because you can run most MS-DOS programs from within Windows, there is little incentive to run those programs from the MS-DOS prompt. You can set up Windows to run programs or batch files, and you can fine-tune the way Windows starts your MS-DOS programs so that you get as much memory as the programs need. A few programs do not work under Windows.

Warning: The most common kind of program that should never be run from Windows is a disk-compaction utility such as COMPRESS.EXE, included with PC Tools Version 7. COMPRESS.EXE or any programs that rearrange file locations on media to improve drive performance can create havoc and cost you lost data if you are using a disk-cache utility at the same time.

With few exceptions, however, you should run your character-based applications from within Windows. As soon as Windows 3.1 is properly configured (in concert with your hardware), enhancement to speed can be remarkable. FoxPro 2.0, Fox Software's database management system, is an excellent example of improved performance of a character-based application under Windows. FoxPro has a built-in programmer's editing utility that scrolls much faster when FoxPro is loaded from Windows 3.1. Even though FoxPro is designed to use any or all available memory, it does so much more productively from within the Windows environment.

Other Programs That Come with Windows

Most operating systems come with just a program launcher and a few file-management commands. Windows, on the other hand, comes with many useful programs that can help you in your daily work. You can buy hundreds of other programs, but the ones that come with Windows are enough to get most people started.

The programs that come with Windows include the following:

▲ Write, a word processor that can prepare letters, reports, and articles (see Chapter 10, "Write").

▲ Paintbrush, a painting program that can create color or black-and-white drawings (see Chapter 11, "Paintbrush").

▲ Calendar, an appointment calendar that helps you organize your time and alerts you when important events are planned. There is more on Calendar in Chapter 13, "Other Accessories."

▲ Cardfile, an organizational program you can use to keep and search for information (as you do with index cards). Cardfile is described in Chapter 13.

▲ Terminal, a communications program for connecting your PC to other computers through a modem (see Chapter 12, "Terminal").

▲ Calculator, a desk calculator that can replace that old pocket model. Calculator is described in detail in Chapter 13.

Tip: You can get many other Windows programs free. These programs, often called public domain or freeware, are available from many sources.

New Features in Windows 3.1

Windows 3.1 comes with several enhancements over previous versions:

▲ The TrueType scalable fonts included with Windows 3.1 provide true WYSIWYG (What You See Is What You Get) between your screen and supporting printers.

▲ The new File Manager is completely revised to resemble a multi-layered, configurable shell. Icons are assigned to files by type for easier file-display organization.

▲ With better network connections you can view all the files in a network printer's queue as well as files in a queue to which you are not connected. You can bypass Print Manager entirely and use the network queue.

▲ A built-in Screen Saver utility that entertains as well as saves your monitor from premature wear, called *burn in*.

▲ The Packager is a new utility that helps you create icons and place them in text and graphics.

It's Even Better with DOS 5.0!

With the advent of MS-DOS 5.0, device drivers and TSRs (*Terminate and Stay Resident* programs) can be loaded now in the XMA (high memory area). DOS can load much of itself into upper memory areas to dramatically increase available conventional memory. Not only does this increase execution speed, but memory address conflicts occur less often. Improved speed and reliability are just a few of the many improvements over previous versions of DOS. If you upgrade to MS-DOS 5.0 when you install Windows 3.1, you can tailor your system's overall performance even more. See Reference B, "MS-DOS 5.0 and Windows."

Moving On

This chapter has given you an overview of what Windows is and why it should interest you. The rest of this book explains in detail all the parts of Windows and how they work together.

If you have not yet installed Windows 3.1, you can do so as you read Chapter 2, "Installing Windows." If you have installed Windows (or someone else has installed it for you), you can skip to Chapter 3, "Starting and Leaving Windows."

Everyone should read Chapter 4, "Basic Windows Concepts," because it lays the groundwork for using Windows. Chapter 4 shows all the actions you can take when you use Windows and Windows programs. Chapter 5, "Program Manager," describes what is by far the most important Windows program. Chapter 6, "File Manager," shows how to use File Manager to make life easier for everyone.

2..

> **Tip:** Advanced Windows users may be saying, "I'll skip Chapters 4 through 6 because I already know how to use Windows, Program Manager, and File Manager." You can do what you will, but in these chapters, you probably will discover upgraded or significant new features that you have not yet seen. For example, if you are a keyboard user who knows only a little about the mouse, Chapter 4 will show you many actions that are easier and faster to do with the mouse than with the keyboard.

After reading those chapters on the fundamentals, you can pick and choose chapters according to your interests or you can read from start to finish. Remember that many reference charts, as well as many tips and warnings, are scattered throughout this book. Be sure to at least skim any chapter that discusses Windows features that interest you.

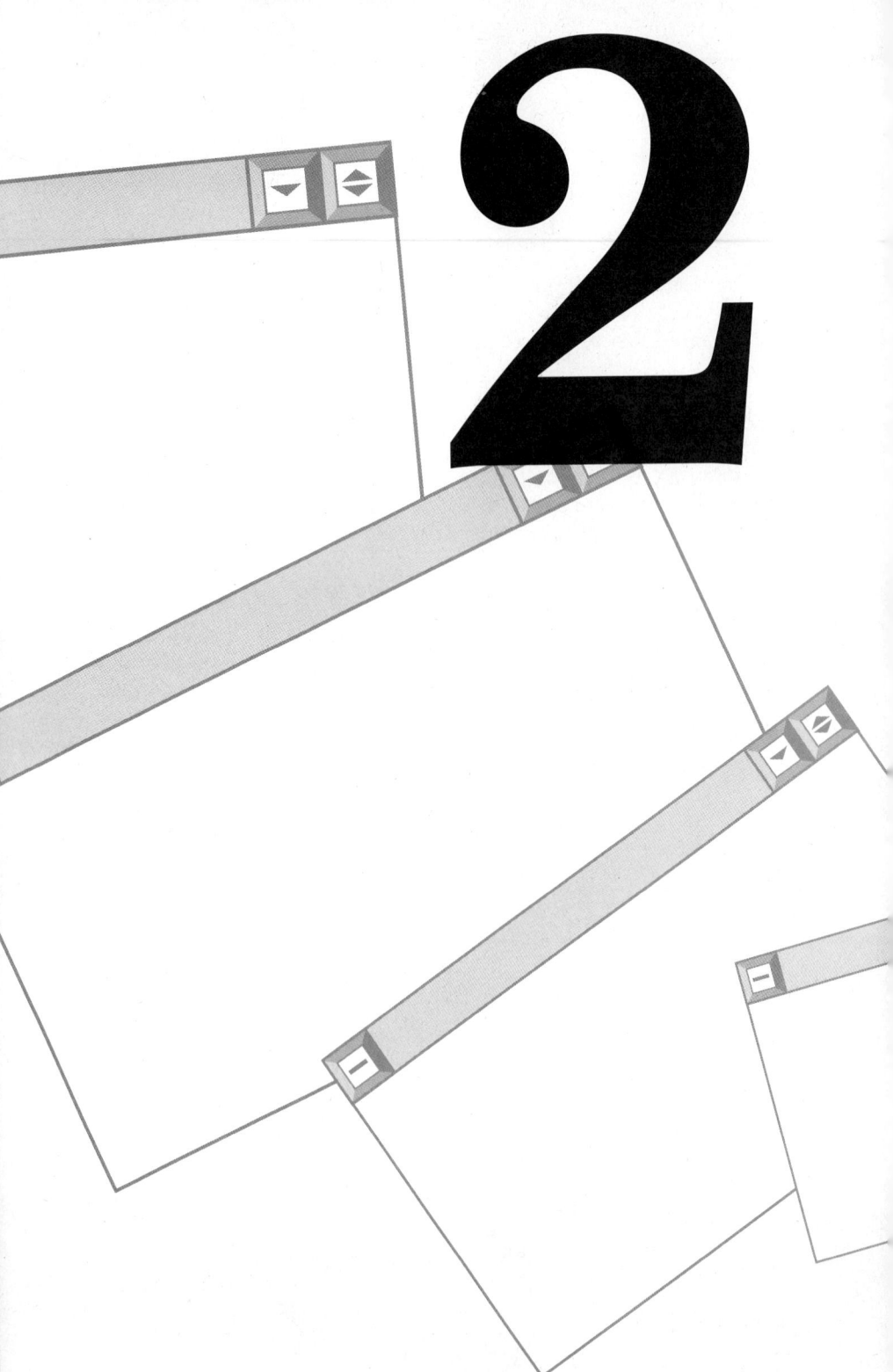

CHAPTER

2

Installing Windows

If you bought a computer with Windows 3.1 already installed on the hard disk and it appears to be operating correctly, you can safely skip this chapter. Some computer manufacturers and dealers include Windows on the hard disk of the computer so that you can simply turn on the computer and run Windows. Note, however, that you might want to return to this chapter later if you need to reinstall Windows—for instance, if you have to reformat your hard disk. Often problems with erratic Windows behavior can be fixed by reinstalling the program. Also, should you wish to add utilities such as printer drivers or additional fonts, using the installation procedure is one way to do it.

Microsoft sells Windows on both 5 1/4-inch and 3 1/2-inch floppies. If you have not yet bought your copy of Windows, be sure to buy the one that matches the type of diskette drive you have on your system. If you happen to get the wrong disk size for your computer, Microsoft includes a special mail-order form with Windows 3.1 so that you can send for what you need.

Installing Windows is very easy and straightforward. If you have installed other software on your computer, you may have come across installation programs that display cryptic messages and do not let you know how the installation is progressing. In fact, earlier versions of Windows were like this. Microsoft took heed of users' complaints and made the Windows installation procedure almost as easy as running Windows itself.

Hardware and Software Requirements for Windows 3.1

Windows 3.1 can run only on a PC that has the correct resources. If you do not have the correct resources (such as enough hard disk space), you cannot install Windows. Most computers sold today have the correct resources, but many older computers do not. In addition, some computers might be capable of running Windows but are so slow that doing so is counterproductive. This section describes the hardware and software you must have before installing Windows.

Warning: Windows Version 3.1 will not work on some older computers unless you update the BIOS (Basic Input/Output System), the software that runs the hardware in your PC. If your PC is more than a few years old, be sure to check with your computer's manufacturer before installing Windows.

The most common problem with running Windows on older computers is with systems based on the American Megatrends Inc. (AMI) BIOS dated earlier than September 1, 1988. You can tell whether you are using an AMI BIOS by restarting your computer. If you are using an AMI BIOS, the first line appearing on-screen when you reboot says American Megatrends Inc. Look at the bottom line of the screen as the computer is rebooting. You should see a code in the form of XXXX-NNNN-MMDDYY-XX. The MMDDYY part of the code is the date of the BIOS. If the date is before September 1, 1988, ask your computer manufacturer for an upgrade to a current version of the BIOS.

Software

The software requirements are the easiest ones to meet: You must be running MS-DOS or PC DOS Version 3.1 or later. Because Version 3.1 has been available for more than five years, most PCs are running 3.1 or later.

You can check your version of MS-DOS from the MS-DOS prompt with the VER command. MS-DOS responds with the version number:

```
C>VER
MS-DOS Version    3.10
```

Note: The only alternative to having MS-DOS/PC DOS Version 3.1 or later is to use DR DOS version 5 or later. DR DOS, an operating system from Digital Research, acts just like MS-DOS, but has some additional features. Some computers come with DR DOS installed, and you can buy it from many computer stores. Although Microsoft does not guarantee that Windows will always work correctly with DR DOS, many people run Windows successfully under DR DOS, and Digital Research representatives say they know of no compatibility problems.

2

Hard Disk

If you are not upgrading from an older version of Windows, you must have at least 6.5M (megabytes) free on your hard disk to install Windows. (A megabyte is 1,048,576 bytes, so 6.5M is about 6,815,744 bytes.) This amount is the minimum you need just to install Windows; you need up to another 2.5M of free space if you plan to use a printer or run Windows on a network. When Windows prints a document, it creates a file in the print spooler that is dispensed to the printer incrementally, as the printer can accept the file. This is an added file that Windows creates, not you. A twenty-five page document with a few pictures in it will take a few megabytes of extra space when it is being printed. You need to make sure you have enough space for Windows to use during printing and network operations. If you add an additional printer to your system—a special printer such as a typesetter or a plotter— or a printer that is out of date, you will need to copy a driver file (*.DRV) to your system in order for Windows to be able to print. Driver files can range in size from 5000 bytes to over 100,000 bytes (as in the case of some PostScript drivers).

If your system's CPU is an 80386 or higher, you can use part of your hard disk space as a *swap file*. A swap file is a permanent, unmovable storage location on your hard drive that Windows can use instead of creating temporary swap files. Permanent swap files enhance the performance of your system. When you have installed a permanent swap file, your Windows programs will "think" that you have much more *RAM* (random-access memory) than you actually do. If you have extra disk space after the 6.5M that Windows uses for files, and your computer has an 80386 or higher, you will want Windows to create a swap file. This will take up to four more megabytes of disk space. It's best to plan on having this additional space free. See Chapter 24, "Memory Configuration for Windows," for more on swap files.

Note: In this book, *CPUs* (central processing units) often are referred to as "80386 or higher." This phrase refers to the following CPUs:

▲ Intel 80386 family (currently the 80386DX and the 80386SX)

▲ AMD AM386 family

▲ Intel 80486 family (currently the 80486DX and the 80486SX)

▲ Intel 80586 family

As time goes on, more CPUs will be 80386-compatible and will work just like the 80386. All these chips will meet the criteria this book uses for "80386 or higher."

You can tell from the MS-DOS prompt how much hard disk space you have available by giving the CHKDSK command. When you give this command, MS-DOS displays information about the hard disk and memory, including the amount of free space on the hard disk.

If you're installing Windows on Drive C, you can check for available space. First make sure that you change to the \DOS directory, or that the \DOS directory is in your path, and type

```
C:\DOS>CHKDSK  C:
```

You will see something that resembles Figure 2.1. Your actual drive details will be different.

You are interested in the number of bytes available on the disk (shown as "bytes available on disk"). Figure 2.1 shows a disk drive with 112M remaining.

Even if you have more than one hard disk attached to your PC or you are on a network, you still must have at least 6.5M free on just one of the hard disks alone. Windows cannot be installed over several disk drives. You must install and leave Windows in the subdirectory named during the installation process. You can install Windows on any hard disk. You can locate Windows on the boot drive, and your programs on another drive, either logical or physical. This setup is convenient if you have partitioned your hard disk into smaller hard disks and do not have space on any one disk for all your files.

```
Microsoft(R) MS-DOS(R) Version 5.00
          (C)Copyright Microsoft Corp 1981-1991.

C:\ >chkdsk

Volume SOFTLAB SYS created 07-28-1991 2:45p
Volume Serial Number is 16FC-95B5

 71067648 bytes total disk space
  3287040 bytes in 3 hidden files
    81920 bytes in 30 directories
 49969152 bytes in 1287 user files
 17729536 bytes available on disk

     2048 bytes in each allocation unit
    34701 total allocation units on disk
     8657 available allocation units on disk

   655360 total bytes memory
   562032 bytes free

C:\ >
```

Available space on hard drive

2

Figure 2.1. Using the CHKDSK command to verify available disk space for Windows.

Warning: If you use hard disk partitioning software (that is, software that lets one physical hard disk look like many hard disks to MS-DOS), be sure to check with the disk partitioning software manufacturer before installing Windows. Also, be certain that you are using the latest version of the partitioning software before installing Windows.

RAM

You must have at least 1M of RAM to run Windows. Depending on the other software running on your PC, however, this minimum might not be enough. For example, if you are on a network and the network software requires lots of RAM, you might have to load some of these TSRs and drivers into the high memory area to free up space in the 0 to 640K memory area so that Windows can load and run. Generally, if you have 1MB of RAM, you can run Windows even if you are using RAM-hungry software.

Windows 3.1 can run on 1M of RAM, but it will run very slowly. You should strongly consider adding RAM to your system so that you have at least 2M. RAM is inexpensive (usually much less than $100 per megabyte, sometimes less than $50), and having extra RAM makes Windows run much faster and enables you to run more programs simultaneously.

Because of MS-DOS limitations, the RAM in your computer can have many names. The first 640K is called *base* or *conventional memory*. If you have more than 640K of RAM, it can be configured as either *extended memory* (the amount between 640K and 1M) or *expanded memory* (the amount over 1M). These terms are somewhat confusing, even to advanced PC users, but do not despair. They are fully described in Chapter 22, "Windows Operating Modes," along with full explanations of how to determine how much RAM you have and what type it is.

If you are running MS-DOS 5.0, you can check your memory resources by using EQUIP.EXE. First make sure that the DOS file EQUIP.EXE is in the current directory or PATH, or you will get a "nobody is home" message meaning that DOS cannot find the EQUIP.EXE file to run it for you.

```
C:\DOS>EQUIP
```

Some very valuable information about your system memory is listed. The number shown in parentheses before the expression Memory is your total conventional memory. The number given in parentheses before the expression Expansion Memory is your combined XMS and EMS memory (memory beyond 640K of conventional memory). Add the first two numbers given in parentheses to get your particular system's memory total. Figure 2.2 shows information learned about one particular system using the EQUIP command.

You must run CHKDSK.EXE and EQUIP.EXE on your own system to see your particular drive and memory details. For now, assume that any RAM you have over 640K should almost always be configured as extended memory (rather than expanded memory). Extended memory is the memory above the 1M mark. Expanded memory uses the area between 640K and 1M. Expanded memory is used only by certain programs that specifically require it. If you have more than 640K, you should read the manual that came with your computer to determine what type of memory you have. If your memory is expanded memory, the manual probably will instruct you to change to the extended memory that Windows requires by changing part of the CONFIG.SYS file that DOS reads when you boot your computer. Be sure to use expanded memory that conforms to the LIM 4.0 standard (not the earlier 3.2 standard) for best results. The LIM 4.0 standard is the most current set of definitions of how expanded memory should be handled by software developers. Memory is discussed in more detail in Chapter 24, "Memory Configuration for Windows."

```
C:\ >equip
Equipment Installed
( 640k)  -  Memory
( 7424K) -  Expansion Memory
   (0)   -  Math Coprocessor
   (0)   -  Monochrome Adapter
   (1)   -  Enhanced Graphics Adapter
   (2)   -  Floppy Disks
             A: High capacity diskette drive
             B: 3.5" micro diskette drive
   (1)   -  Hard Disks
             1:   68 Mb
   (2)   -  Parallel Ports
   (2)   -  Serial Ports
   (0)   -  Multiport Adapters

Operating system:  MS-DOS 5.00
ROM BIOS Version 4.26 (06/28/90)

C:\ >
```

Total conventional memory

2

Figure 2.2. Using the EQUIP command to verify memory capacity.

Tip: The only time you might want to configure memory to be expanded rather than extended is when you are running non-Windows programs that require expanded memory. Because these programs cannot use extended memory, you might want to allocate some of your extra memory to expanded memory. Note, however, that any such memory is not available to Windows, but only to programs that require expanded memory, such as CAD and spreadsheet programs designed to run without Windows.

Monitor and Display Adapter

Windows 3.1 can work with almost every standard PC monitor and display adapter. Windows comes with display drivers for many—but not all—display adapters. Setup shows you which displays are considered standard. If your display is not on the list, you have a nonstandard monitor or display adapter. If this is the case, you must have a display driver compatible with Windows Version 3.1 supplied by your display adapter manufacturer. For example, if you have a two-page display, Windows won't know how to use it unless you have a special display driver from the display manufacturer. If your display operates fine with Windows 3.0, it might run well with Windows 3.1. It's still best to check with the display adapter manufacturer on compatibility with Windows 3.1 before installing.

Even if you have a nonstandard monitor or display adapter but no Windows display driver, you might be able to run Windows. Most nonstandard displays come with software that enables you to make them act like standard displays. For example, your adapter might be able to act like a VGA adapter if you run its special software when you start up the computer. When you tell the adapter to act like a VGA adapter, you can run Windows and tell it you have a VGA adapter. In this case, you cannot access any special features of the adapter and monitor until you install a Windows 3.1-compatible display driver for those features.

Mouse

A mouse is really a must with Windows. You can work without it, but sooner or later you will run into a situation where you will need one, so it's best to plan on getting used to using one.

Even if you are a die-hard keyboard fan, you will find that using a mouse makes graphics programs much easier. Also, many people who used to swear they would never use a mouse have found that they now use a mouse about half the time when operating Windows. If your computer did not come with a mouse and you were thinking of running Windows without a mouse, consider buying one. Most mice cost less than $100, and some cost less than $50. Microsoft thinks so highly of mice that they sell the world's best-selling species. They even bundle it with a version of Windows.

It is the preference of all the authors of this book to use a mouse with Windows, especially when first learning a program. It greatly speeds up most operations. Later, as you become familiar with Windows, you can begin substituting keystrokes in place of mousing around. Learning Windows without a mouse will drive you nuts.

The mouse replaces the direction and Enter keys on the keyboard. Move it to the left and you get the same effect as pressing the left-arrow key, and so on. Most programs recognize the left mouse button as a substitute for the Enter key. The most powerful implementation of the mouse is in its capability to replace the cursor with a pointing symbol (which can be seen in Figure 1.1). Most pointing devices (including pens and trackballs) merely emulate a standard mouse.

Tip: Some popular Windows programs, such as Excel, require a mouse for some features. It will serve you well to get a mouse early on so that you will be ready if you buy a program that requires one.

Printer

You need a printer only if you intend to print your work. The Windows 3.1 disks include more standard printer drivers than Windows 3.0, and Windows has one of the most comprehensive lists of printer drivers of any program on the market. It is also the most supported program for third-party printer drivers. Use the third-party driver, if available; it is likely to be more up-to-date and compatible. Like nonstandard display adapters, most nonstandard printers come with Windows's *printer drivers.* If you incur any problems using one of the standard selectable Windows 3.1 printer drivers, get the printer manufacturer's Windows 3.1-compatible driver. Also, many off-brand printers act like or emulate other well-known printers, so you often can tell Windows that you are using the better-known printer with little trouble.

Windows enables you to have many printers attached to your computer. They can be attached to either the serial ports (such as COM1: and COM2:) or to the parallel printer ports (such as LPT1: and LPT2:). If you have many printers, be prepared to tell the installation program about each of them (and what port they are attached to) as you install Windows.

Modem

If you want to use Windows's Terminal program (or other such communications programs) to communicate with other computers, you must have a modem. A modem is an electronic device that connects your computer to other computers through phone lines. Modems transfer data files by listening for a dial tone, dialing the receiving computer's phone number, and when recognizing that the receiving computer is ready, sending the data over the established telephone connection. Using a modem enables you to access information sources and electronic mail systems worldwide as well. To do this, you must "pretend" that you are a computer terminal on, for example, the E-mail computer's system by using a communication program called a Terminal Emulator. Your computer essentially calls another computer and presents the impression that your personal computer is the same kind of computer that you are connected to. Your computer then emulates that system so that you can access data. The Terminal program included with Windows provides emulation services and transfers files via any modem that is compatible with the Hayes standard modems. Terminal is described in more detail in Chapter 12, "Terminal."

Network

If you are on a network that works with Windows, you can access data and files from other parts of the network while running Windows. You do not have to be on a network to run Windows. If you are, however, ask the network administrator about the network type so that you can tell the installation program about it. If you don't have this detail, do not try to install Windows.

Before You Install Windows

After you are sure that you have the right software and hardware to run Windows, you can run the installation program. Again, let's look at some of the requirements to do so:

▲ An IBM-compatible personal computer using an 80286 or higher processor

▲ At least 6.5M of hard disk space (a minimum of 9M is recommended)

▲ A video driver for your monitor that is compatible with Windows 3.1

▲ DOS 3.1 or later, installed as the bootable operating version of DOS

▲ At least 1M of memory

Removing Windows Version 2 or 3.0

If you have a copy of Windows Version 2 or 3.0 on your hard disk, you can install Version 3.1 in the same directory. The installation program will update the relevant files to bring your system up to Version 3.1. Unfortunately, it does not do a perfect job of updating. Many difficult-to-diagnose problems with Windows 3.0 were caused when the installation program did not fully update Version 2.

Although this procedure is not recommended by Microsoft, you probably should delete all your Windows old version files, remove the subdirectory, and install Version 3.1 on a disk that looks as though it has never had Windows on it. At the same time, you also should remove the HIMEM.SYS, EMM386, and SMARTDRV file notations from your CONFIG.SYS file, which was installed with either Version 2 or 3.0. They will be obsolete, and do not include all of the features and functionality of the latest and greatest versions.

If you have a file compression program such as LHARC or PKZIP and you have extra hard disk space, you might want to compress all the files into one archive file in case you ever need to go back to, for example, your old .INI files.

You can make your life easier by saving your PIF files to the root directory, then after installing Windows 3.1, copying them back to the Windows 3.1 directory. This saves your having to re-create them later. You are almost certain to need them, and you will not have to un-compress them. Keep compressed files in a special subdirectory until you are satisfied that there are no crucial problems with your upgraded Windows installation. You can always go after favorite icons and .INI files if you need them.

Delete all files in the \windows and \windows\system directories.

Even though you might have a tried-and-true driver set that worked great with an older version of Windows, some drivers simply do not offer the power, speed, and flexibility of current drivers that are designed to run with Windows 3.0 and 3.1. Note that you cannot run Windows Version 3.1 in either standard mode or 386-enhanced mode with any of the following Version 2 drivers:

▲ Display

▲ Mouse

▲ Sound

▲ System

▲ Communications

▲ Network

You will have to get a current driver from the manufacturer or supplier of your hardware if you expect your devices to operate properly.

> **Warning:** If you want to keep more than one version of Windows on your hard disk, you should also note the following:
>
> ▲ Never run Windows 3.1 when your current directory is the Version 2 or 3.0 directory, and vice versa. This can cause your PC to hang.
>
> ▲ Make sure that the PATH command in your AUTOEXEC.BAT file points only to the C:\windows directory with Version 3.1, not the directory for another version.
>
> ▲ Be sure to use only the version 3.1 HIMEM.SYS driver, even if you are running Windows Version 2. Windows 3.1 will not operate with an older version.
>
> ▲ Do not use FASTOPEN (in your CONFIG.SYS) if you intend to bounce between versions of Windows. FASTOPEN remembers the addresses of files you have used, and will go there first to get an older or a newer version of a Windows program file. You don't want to call up the Windows 3.0 version of File Manager if you are currently running Windows 3.1.
>
> ▲ If you are running Windows/386 Version 2, be sure to use the SMARTDrive and RAMDrive programs that come with it, not the ones that come with Version 3.1. This means that Windows 3.1 might have installed the Version 3.1 files in your AUTOEXEC.BAT and CONFIG.SYS files, and you might have a potential problem.

The rest of this book assumes that you either removed Versions 2 and 3.0 or never loaded them on your hard disk.

Preparing to Install Windows

There are two steps you should take before installing a Windows version or application program.

▲ At the DOS prompt, type CHKDSK/F followed by the drive letter to check the drive that will receive Windows. If CHKDSK finds no lost clusters, you are not prompted to take further action, and you can continue to the next step. If CHKDSK reports lost clusters, convert them to files when CHKDSK asks you to. Now look in your root directory for files with a file extension of .CHK. These files should be deleted. Be careful not to disturb any other files in your root directory.

▲ As soon as you have run the previous procedure, use a disk compaction or compression program if one is available. Compacting or compressing a hard disk is the process of placing parts of files that have been spread out across the hard drive into contiguous or adjacent areas on your hard drive. This process reorganizes the way files are stored on your disk drive so that files for a single directory are stored near each other on the disk. This process should be run periodically to improve speed and efficiency.

2

Most disk compaction utilities, such as the current versions of PC Tools and the Norton Utilities, offer several options when compacting or compressing a drive. If the option exists, use the most complete form of disk compression. If the utility supports it, use the directory sort option. Specify the \windows directory name as being the first in the directory order, then specify your DOS directory name next. Remember, Windows calls DOS to do much of its work. These utilities organize your directories so that disk read/write delay times are reduced. These utilities also get all the files reporting to a specified directory name back into the geographical neighborhood of those directories. The less time your hard drive spends getting to files, the better. This process can take as long as 30 minutes, depending on how your hard disk is organized now, but it's one of the essentials necessary to get Windows operating at maximum speed.

Warning: It is vitally important that you do not run the MS-DOS APPEND command before you install Windows. This command often is part of your AUTOEXEC.BAT file. To edit your AUTOEXEC.BAT file, use any word processing program that reads a standard ASCII text file. Open AUTOEXEC.BAT as you would any document file, and check your AUTOEXEC.BAT for any line that begins with the APPEND command. If there are such lines, comment them out (by typing REM in front of the line), save your changes, and restart your computer before installing Windows.

As the installation program runs, it will try to determine what type of hardware you have. If it cannot determine what type of hardware you have, it asks you about some of your hardware. For example, there is no way for the installation program to determine what type of printer you have. You should have the instruction manuals for your computer and other hardware handy in case Windows Setup asks you questions.

Running the Installation Program

This section walks you through the Windows 3.1 installation program. Although many of the steps are self-explanatory, you can make Windows run better the first time you use it if you follow the hints and suggestions presented here.

> **Tip:** Immediately before running Setup, you should reboot your PC. This helps memory-hogging programs to be emptied from RAM. If you have any utility programs (such as TSRs) that load themselves during the boot process, you should remove them from memory if you can. Many programs have special commands to do this removal. If Setup does not have enough memory, it might indicate a problem and terminate the installation process. To avoid this delay, reboot from a DOS system disk that doesn't have any AUTOEXEC.BAT or CONFIG.SYS files on it.

Starting the Setup Program

The Windows installation program is SETUP.EXE. To run the program, follow these steps:

1. Insert Disk 1 in your diskette drive.

2. Change the MS-DOS default prompt to the floppy drive you're using. For instance, if you are installing from the diskette in your A drive, type A: and press the Enter key.

3. Type the word SETUP and press the Enter key.

4. In a few minutes, you should see the words Welcome to Setup. If
   you want to learn more about the Setup program at this point,
   press F1. In fact, you can press F1 at any time during the installation to display more information about the screen you are seeing
   or the question Setup is asking you.

If You Make a Mistake

Some people get anxious when installing new software. Microsoft made
Setup as easy to use as possible, but you still might not feel comfortable
about going on at some point. If you want to stop the Setup program at
any time, simply press F3. You might have to start over when you run
Setup the next time, but at least you were able to stop when you
wanted to.

At a few points the F3 key doesn't do anything, such as when a dialog
box is open and waiting for your input. (A dialog box is an enclosed
space on your screen that says something to you, and then requires a
response from you.) In those cases, pressing the Esc key should make
the dialog box go away; when it does, try pressing the F3 key again.

Choosing a Directory for Windows

To continue with the installation program, press Enter. Setup then
checks your disks for earlier versions of Windows so that you can
replace them with the new version. Setup needs to know where you
want to install Windows. Usually this is a directory called \windows on
your C drive. Setup suggests this location, but you can select any disk
or subdirectory you want. To accept Setup's suggestion, simply press
Enter.

To change the directory or the disk drive, use the Backspace key to
delete letters. You also can use the left- and right-arrow keys (the ←
and → keys to the right of the main part of the keyboard) to move the
blinking underline in the prompt. When you have the directory name
and drive you want, press Enter.

Selecting Custom or Express Setup

At this juncture, you must make a choice. If you consider yourself
Windows-literate, choose Custom to gain control over what Windows

installs, as well as other important options that require you to make further choices. These choices usually are best left to the well-informed. If you choose Express, Windows asks you for diskette after diskette, installs everything that can be installed, and finally builds your program groups and fills them with icons. You are asked to decide only whether you want to run Windows immediately or exit to DOS as soon as the installation is complete.

If you choose Custom when prompted to choose between Custom and Express, you need to make choices regarding the programs included with Windows: if, how, and where your swap file is installed; which printer you want to install; and so on. Because the Express setup is something of a no-brainer, this section focuses on stepping you through the Custom setup process.

Specifying Your Hardware

Setup checks your hardware and makes judgements about what type of computer you are using, the type of monitor you have, and so on. Figure 2.3 shows the screen that enables you to choose a screen resolution, a network (if needed), and other items. Make any required changes to the list, and press the Enter key to continue.

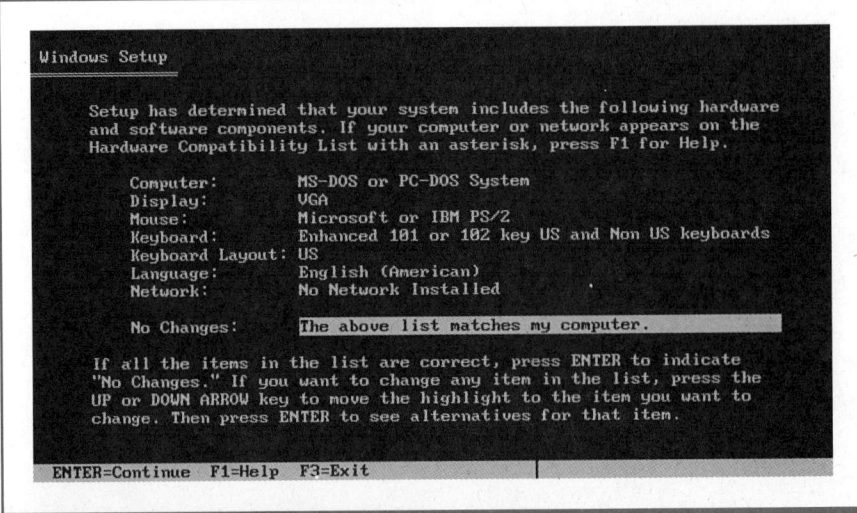

Figure 2.3. The hardware selection part of the Setup process.

Copying Files

Setup then copies many files to your hard disk. If you watch the lower-right corner of your screen, you can see the names of the files as each is copied. When windows changes to graphical mode (your mouse pointer becomes an arrow tip), the filenames appear in a dialog box along with a horizontal bar chart that displays the installation progress. This step usually takes quite a while because dozens of files need to be copied.

When Setup has copied as many files as it can from Disk 1, it prompts you to put in Disk 2. Remove Disk 1 from the drive and insert Disk 2, then press the Enter key. If you are installing from 3 1/2-inch floppies, Setup reads a few more files from the disk. If you are installing from 5 1/4-inch disks, Setup reads a few more files and might prompt you to insert Disk 3.

Setup then copies other files. As it does so, it shows a copy bar. The bar near the bottom of the window fills up as more files are copied. When Setup needs additional disks, it puts up a dialog box that tells you the name of the next disk to insert in the drive. After you put that new disk in, press the Enter key or click the OK button in the dialog box. This process repeats for as many disks as Setup needs to put the necessary files on your disk. You might be interested in the filenames as they appear in the dialog box, although they are not important.

After more files are copied, Setup makes your screen blank, paints a whitish-gray background, and pastes an hourglass icon and your mouse pointer onto it.

You then are presented with a dialog box that offers you the option of reviewing a short tutorial on the mouse. You can take time out from the installation to read the tutorial, or you can skip it entirely. One way or another, you now can use the mouse to click (press the left mouse button) the Continue button as soon as you are ready to go on with the installation of Windows. If you do not have a mouse, press Enter to continue.

Setting Up Components

A dialog box appears that gives you the options of setting up only the Windows programs that you can specifically ask for later, any printer(s) that you plan to use, and any applications that already reside on your hard disk(s). Figure 2.4 shows you what to expect when this dialog box presents itself.

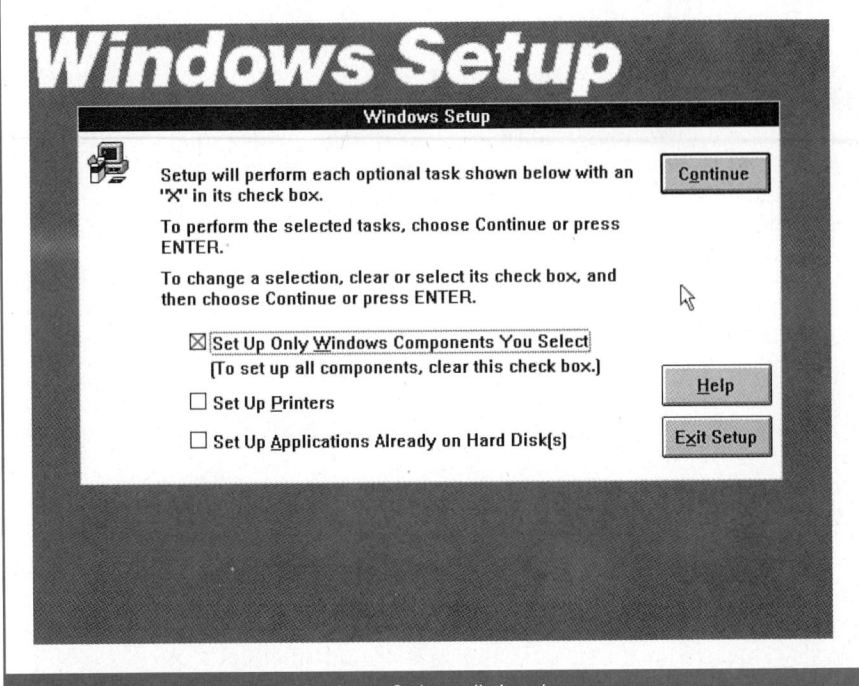

Figure 2.4. Yet another Windows Setup dialog box.

You can select/deselect any of these three options by clicking them:

▲ **W**indows Components: Deselect this check box to load only certain parts of the Windows program.

▲ **P**rinters: Deselect this check box if you do not want to install any printers now.

▲ **A**pplications: Deselect this check box if you do not want to have Setup search for applications to install.

If you choose to set up only certain Windows components, a far more complex dialog box, shown in Figure 2.5, appears.

You can select or deselect the copying of these files to your hard drive during the installation process:

▲ Read Me Files

▲ Accessories

▲ Games

▲ Screen Savers

▲ Wallpapers

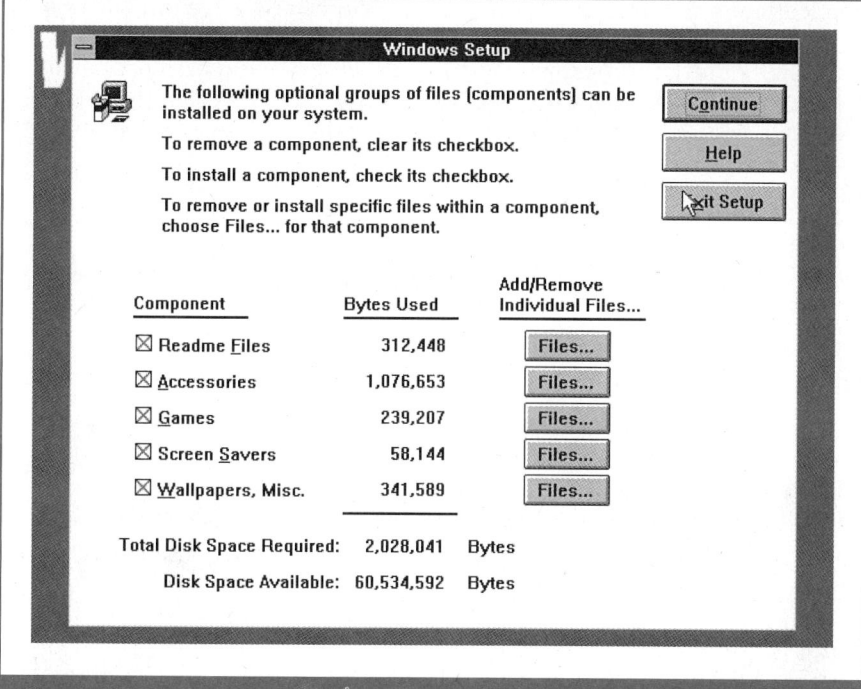

Figure 2.5. Component Setup dialog box.

You are given these options because they are not considered essential to Windows's operation, and you might be a little short of free drive space. You can install all files or individual files if you click the Files button provided for each option.

You might also have another screen saver program on hand—for example, one that you planned to use in lieu of the one included with Windows 3.1. If you want you can just click the Continue button and install these options later when you have had more time to think about the need for them. Figure 2.5 shows you this dialog box with all the options selected.

Virtual Memory

Virtual memory is your 386's capability to fool itself into thinking that part of your hard drive is actually part of its available RAM. When and if you run out of memory during a work session—for example, when you've loaded that colossal spreadsheet file, Windows and Windows applications turn to a dedicated space on your hard drive known as a swap file. You can select Temporary if you are absolutely out of hard drive space, but system speed will not be what it could be. Lost performance from system to system varies with the configuration, but you definitely will notice the added delays. This delay is more pronounced with slower systems.

If you can spare the space that Windows wants to use for virtual memory (a swap file), click the Continue button. Windows creates the unmovable file on the drive that was selected in the drop-down list box provided when you clicked the Continue button. The Virtual Memory dialog box is shown in Figure 2.6.

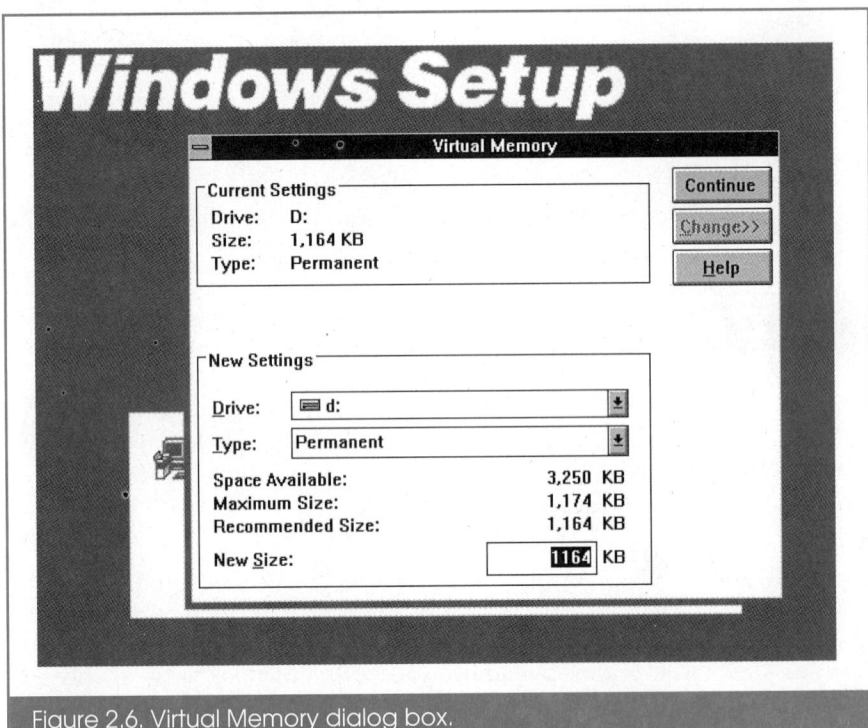

Figure 2.6. Virtual Memory dialog box.

Windows continues to copy files from the Setup diskettes to your hard drive. You are asked to insert diskettes 4 and 5, respectively. Remember, the disk numbers asked for by Windows at various points during the installation will differ depending on whether you are using 3 1/2" diskettes or 5 1/4" diskettes. Next you are prompted to install any printers that you plan to use.

Setting Up Printers

If you indicated that you wanted to install a printer, the next step is to tell Setup about the printers that are attached to your PC. Windows enables you to set up as many printers as you have attached to your PC or intend to attach in the future. Figure 2.7 displays the Install Printers dialog box.

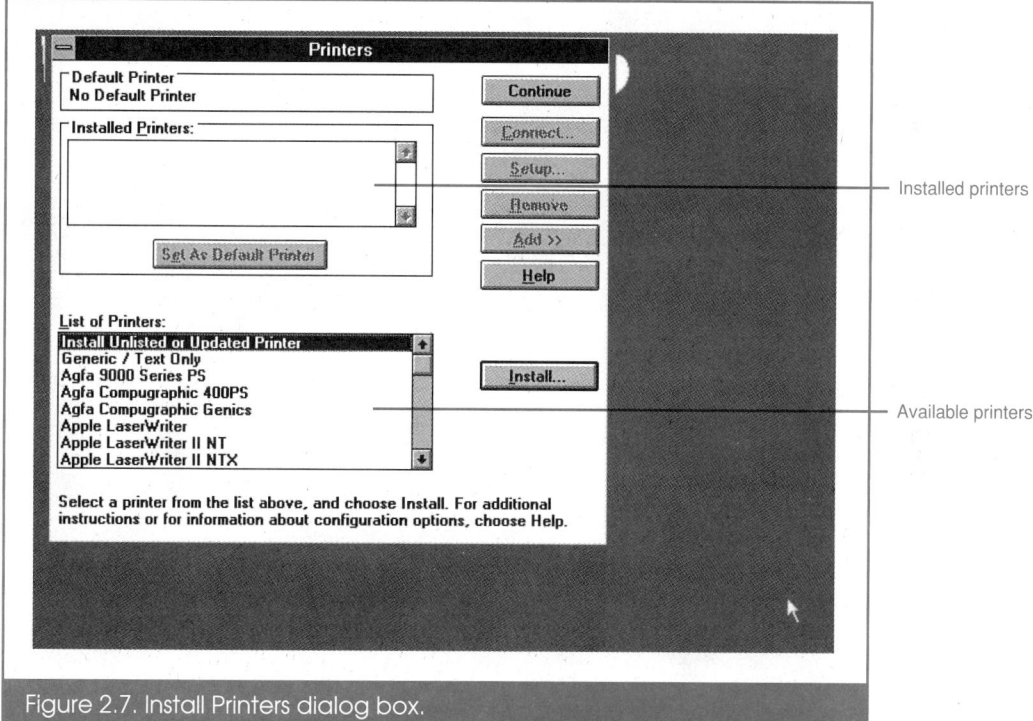

Installed printers

Available printers

Figure 2.7. Install Printers dialog box.

To install a printer, select it from the list at the bottom of the dialog box and click the Install button. If you are not familiar with how to use dialog boxes, press the Esc key on your keyboard to leave this dialog box. Later, after you are familiar with dialog boxes, you can come back and install the printers.

For example, assume that you have a Hewlett-Packard LaserJet III printer. Scroll through the list at the bottom until you see that printer, click it to select it, then click Install. Setup prompts you to insert a disk in your diskette drive so that it can copy the printer driver to Windows. Insert the disk and press Enter. After Setup copies the file, it adds the selected printer to the Installed Printers list at the top of the dialog box.

After installing a printer, you must configure it so that Windows knows what port the printer uses on your computer, the type of paper you are using, any font cartridges, and so on. Be sure that the printer is selected in the upper list, and click the **C**onnect button. You then see the dialog box shown in Figure 2.8.

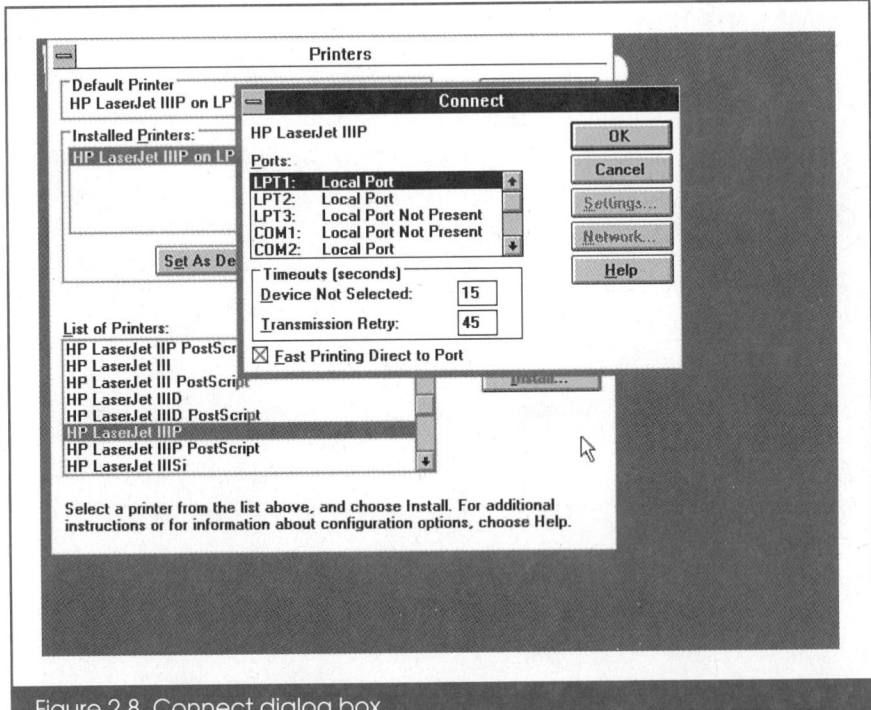

Figure 2.8. Connect dialog box.

In the Connect dialog box, select the port in the **P**orts list and click **S**ettings. You see another dialog box. Click the port name dedicated to the printer, and click the OK button.

You again see the Install Printers dialog box (shown in Figure 2.7). If you want to change any of the parameters for your particular printer, click the **S**etup button to see the available settings, make the appropriate choices that pertain to your particular printer, and click the OK button to return to the Install Printers dialog box. If you have more than one printer, follow the preceding steps for each. As you add printers, they appear in the Installed Printers list at the top of the Printers dialog box.

Now click the **C**ontinue button to go on with the installation of Windows 3.1.

Adding Your Applications

Program Manager can access programs other than just the ones that come with Windows 3.1. Setup looks for programs on your disks and automatically loads them into Program Manager. The dialog box shown in Figure 2.9 appears, displaying a list of available drives that it can search for programs not included with Windows 3.1.

2

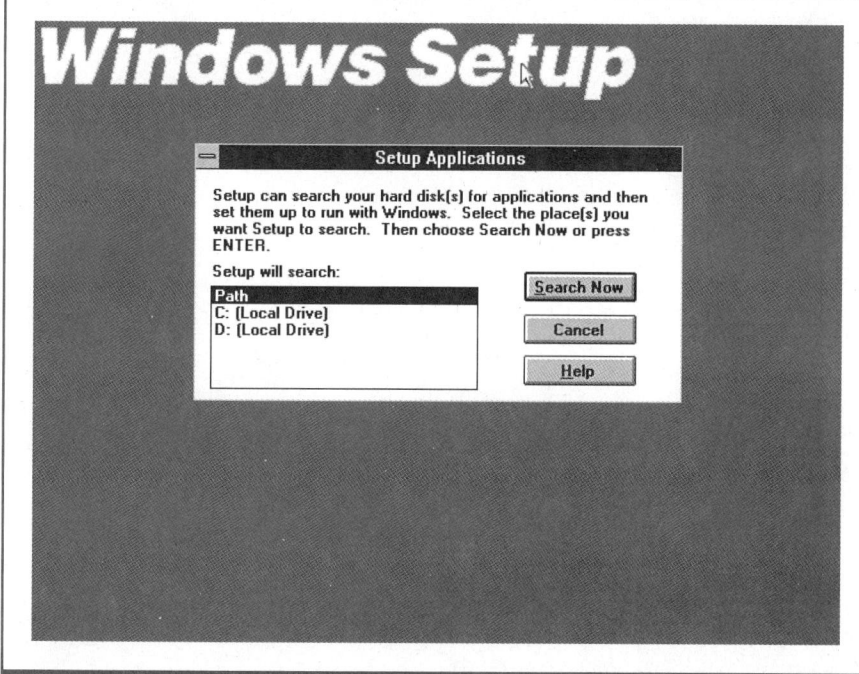

Figure 2.9. Setup Applications dialog box.

Tell Windows which drive has your programs. Setup can install programs that are represented in the PATH statement found in your AUTOEXEC.BAT file, or it can search a selected drive. Setup knows what you have for drives. Choose a drive or the path item, and click the **S**earch Now button. As Setup searches, it displays a copy bar so that you can tell how far it has gotten. Setup then sets up Program Manager with icons that represent all the program files found during the search process.

Changing CONFIG.SYS and AUTOEXEC.BAT

Next, Setup needs to change the system information that it runs each time you start your computer. These files, CONFIG.SYS and AUTOEXEC.BAT, are very important to Windows because they contain commands that affect both the memory configuration and the method by which you run Windows. Setup's dialog asks you what you want to do. The first choice, Make all modifications for you, is generally what you want. To have Setup do this for you, press Enter or click Continue.

If you are using a disk compression utility, Windows Setup notifies you that it is not changing the AUTOEXEC.BAT and CONFIG.SYS files because to do so might cause problems. Setup advises you to refer to the Windows 3.1 documentation so that you or another person can make the appropriate changes to these files.

Tip: If you are very familiar with the structure of your CONFIG.SYS and AUTOEXEC.BAT files, you can choose the second or third choices. This action rarely is necessary because the changes that Setup makes are innocuous. If you choose option 1, Setup makes the following changes to CONFIG.SYS:

▲ Updates the FILES parameter to 30.

▲ Adds the HIMEM.SYS and SMARTDRV.SYS drivers. If it finds any conflicting memory or cache drivers, it might remove them.

▲ Updates the RAMDRIVE.SYS driver.

▲ Determines whether you have a memory manager. If you don't and you are running with an 80386SX or higher CPU, it installs 386EMM.SYS. Otherwise, it lets you keep your current memory manager.

▲ Updates your mouse driver if you are using a Microsoft mouse.

▲ Finds and deletes drivers that it knows are incompatible with Windows.

▲ Adds or updates your EGA.SYS driver if you are using either a Mouse Systems mouse or an EGA display.

If you chose option 1, Setup makes the following changes to AUTOEXEC.BAT:

▲ Adds the requested Windows directory to your PATH statement.

▲ Deletes any old Windows directories from the PATH statement.

▲ Determines whether you have a directory for temporary files by looking for either TMP or TEMP environment variables. If there are none, Setup creates a directory under your Windows directory and sets TMP to that directory.

2

The Final Steps

Congratulations! You have finished installing Windows and are ready to start using it. Setup displays one last message, Windows 3.1 is now installed. If you want to start using Windows immediately, click the **R**estart Windows button or press Enter. If you want to run MS-DOS again, click the Return to **D**OS button.

Tip: Be sure to remove the last diskette you used from the diskette drive. You should store all the diskettes in a safe place for future use. You might need to reinstall Windows if you have hard disk problems. Also, you might buy a new printer or monitor later, and you might need to install the drivers from these diskettes.

Don't forget to send your registration card to Microsoft. This is the best way to get information from them about future versions of Windows.

Installing Devices After Installing Windows

You might need to add more devices after you have installed Windows with Setup. You can do this with the Setup program in Windows or from the Setup program at the MS-DOS prompt. This procedure is covered in detail in Chapter 25, "Changing Your Configuration." You will find that this procedure is as easy as setting up Windows.

In Case of Problems

Some PC hardware causes Setup to fail on occasion. If you are running Setup and your computer stops operating (the mouse and the keyboard seem to have no effect), you should try to determine whether you have hardware problems. Some common hardware problems are outlined in this section.

Setup first runs as a text program, then launches Windows itself for the remainder of the setup process. If Setup cannot run Windows after it has copied all the files, you might be able to determine the problem. You can tell that Setup is having a problem running Windows if it hangs in text mode with a message in the lower-right corner of the screen that says Copying EGALOGO.LGO or some other file with the .LGO extension. Note that this message does not indicate a problem with the file, but with the step after copying the file—namely, starting Windows for the first time.

If Setup cannot start Windows, you might have a hardware problem, such as the following:

▲ You are using a memory manager that is not compatible with Windows.

▲ You are running programs at the same time as Setup that conflict with running Windows.

▲ You specified the wrong display adapter.

▲ You are using an auto-switching display adapter that switches when it shouldn't.

▲ You specified the wrong network adapter, or your network is not working properly.

Try running Setup again, and be sure to specify the correct drivers for your system. If you still cannot get to the first step running under Windows, try specifying different hardware (such as no mouse and no network) to see whether these are the problem; you can always add the mouse and network later. You also might try to change the mode your display works in with a program that came with the display, then try setting up for that different display mode.

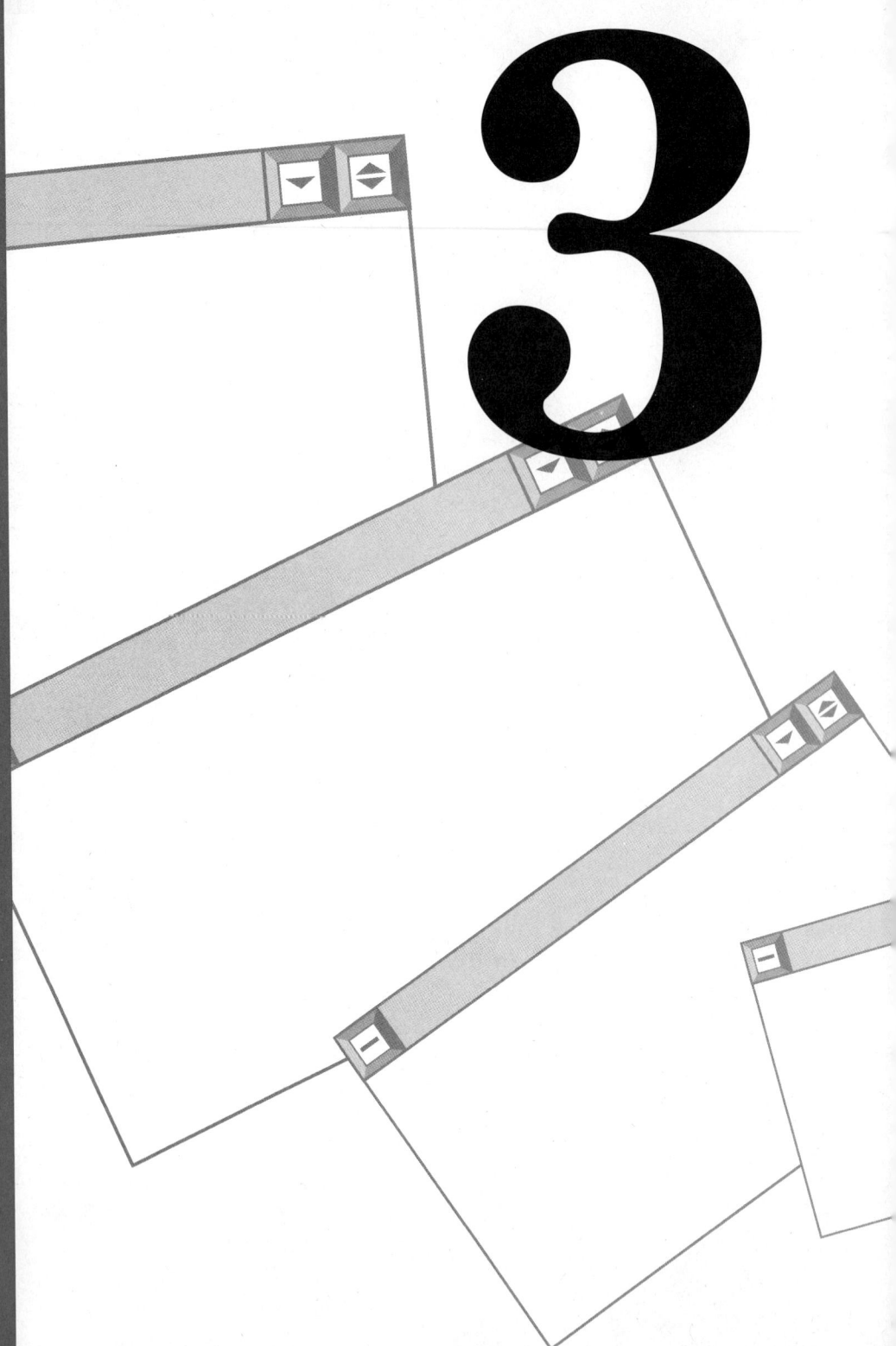

CHAPTER

3

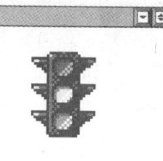

Starting and Leaving Windows

After you have installed Windows, starting the program is easy. From the MS-DOS prompt, enter the WIN command

```
C>WIN
```

Even with a very fast computer, Windows usually takes more than 10 seconds to start. When you start Windows with no other information on the command line, it automatically runs Program Manager. Your initial screen looks like Figure 3.1.

The rest of this chapter shows how to leave Windows, other ways to start Windows, and how to make Windows take best advantage of your hardware when you start it.

Options for Starting Windows

The easiest way to start Windows is with the WIN command. You can, however, add options to the WIN command to start Windows in more useful ways.

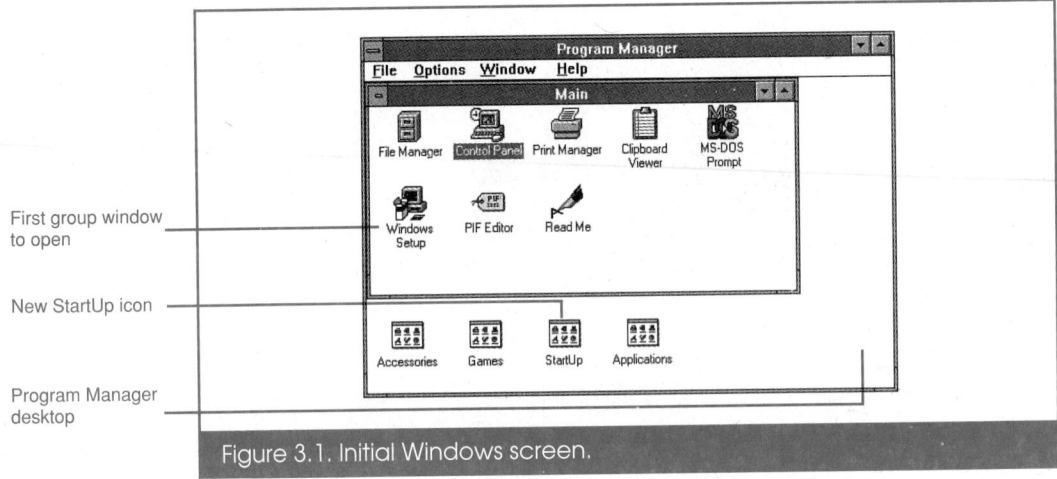

First group window
to open

New StartUp icon

Program Manager
desktop

Figure 3.1. Initial Windows screen.

Running Programs When You Start Windows

When you run Windows, you may know which program you want to run first. If you include the name of that program on the MS-DOS command line, Windows starts that program rather than Program Manager. (After you quit the program, you are at the Windows desktop and can open Program Manager.)

For example, if you want to start the Excel program and it is in the \EXCEL3 directory, you would enter

```
C>WIN \EXCEL3\EXCEL
```

You can even specify a document that you want the program to start with. For example, to start Excel and open a document called \ORDERS\BACKORD.XLS, enter

```
C>WIN \EXCEL3\EXCEL \ORDERS\BACKORD.XLS
```

Clearly, this is a lot to type each time you start Windows. If you run a particular program often, you may want to make an MS-DOS batch file that contains the complete command line. If you tend to use the same programs each time you start Windows, place those programs' icons in the StartUp program window, and Windows will load them for you.

Tip: When the program is in your MS-DOS path (usually set with the PATH= command in your AUTOEXEC.BAT file), you do not need to precede the command with its directory.

```
C>WIN EXCEL
```

Because all Windows's own programs are in the same directory as Windows, you do not need to give their path specification. For instance, to start Windows and go directly into the solitaire game (named "SOL" on the disk), you would enter

```
C>WIN SOL
```

3

Switches for Operating Modes and Memory Use

The second type of option you can add to the WIN command changes the way Windows deals with the operating mode it uses. These options are given as *switches*, which means that you enter them as a slash (/) followed by a single character. You do not use these switches most of the time because Windows usually chooses the best operating mode and memory use when it starts.

You can force Windows to use one of two operating modes by using the switches shown in Table 3.1. For example, to force Windows to run in standard mode, you would enter

```
C>WIN /s
```

Table 3.1. Switches for selecting operating modes.

Switch	Purpose
/s	Runs Windows in standard mode
/3	Runs Windows in 386 enhanced mode

You may be wondering what these operating modes are and why you would want to run in one mode versus another. Those topics are advanced and of little interest to most readers. They are described in great detail in Chapter 22, "Windows Operating Modes," because they would probably scare more people than they would help here. Windows looks at your system and starts itself based on your hardware configuration anyway. If you're ever curious about which mode Windows is currently running in, read the dialog box that opens when you select Help About when in the Program manager. On slower machines, running in Standard mode can reap some substantial performance benefits in the area of execution speed.

The only time most people need to think about these switches is when they want to run programs written for Windows version 2. Those programs can be run only in real mode, not in standard or 386 enhanced modes. Thus, if you want to run a Windows Version 2 program, you must use Windows Version 3.0 because Windows 3.1 does not run in real mode at all.

Starting Windows Without the Logo

When you start Windows, the first thing you see is Microsoft's logo. Although showing this logo takes almost no time, you may want to start Windows without it. To do so, include a colon (:) on the command line, as follows:

```
C>WIN :
```

You also can replace the logo screen with one of your own by using a paint program and a converter. Instructions for this procedure are described in Chapter 29, "Customizing Your Desktop."

Problems Starting Windows

Usually Windows starts just fine. In a few cases, however, you will see error messages when you start Windows. The following sections describe those problems and show you how to avoid them.

Windows Hangs When Starting in 386-Enhanced Mode

If you are running on a PC with an 80386 or 80486 CPU and a Super VGA video adapter, Windows may hang when you run it with the WIN command. (The system hangs if your video driver is incompatible with Windows; it is usually the high-resolution, high-number-of-colors monitors that can cause trouble.) If this is the case, yet Windows runs fine with the WIN /S command, you may need to add a line to one of the Windows startup files to force Windows to work correctly in 386-enhanced mode.

To add this line, follow the instructions for editing the SYSTEM.INI file given in Chapter 27, "Configuring with the WIN.INI and SYSTEM.INI Files." In the [386ENH] section of that file, add the following line:

```
EMMExclude=C400-C7FF
```

This command excludes an area of memory from use by Windows. Try running Windows again, using the MS-DOS WIN command. If Windows crashes again, try changing the line to

```
EMMExclude=C400-CBFF
```

3

This command excludes a different area of memory. This problem can also be caused by the use of a noncompatible video driver. If Windows locks up before it completes its startup process in either mode, use Windows Setup (from within Windows) to install the video driver supplied with your Windows 3.1 diskettes until you can acquire a bugless driver from the maker of your video card.

Windows Exits Before the First Screen

When you run Windows and it returns to the MS-DOS prompt before putting up Program Manager, two conditions (both easily remedied) are likely:

▲ If you moved the WIN.COM file to a directory other than the main Windows directory, Windows will not start. WIN.COM must be in the same directory as many of the necessary Windows files. Move WIN.COM back to the main Windows directory where Setup installed all the Windows files.

▲ If you installed Windows Version 3.1 on top of Windows Version 2 or Version 3.0, you may have some incompatible files from the old Windows version still on your hard disk. The Setup program does not always update old version files correctly. In this case, delete all the files in the main Windows directory and reinstall Windows.

Cannot Find File

When you start Windows, you may see an alert such as the one shown in Figure 3.2. Many situations, including the following, can cause this error:

▲ On the WIN command line, you named a file that did not exist.

▲ A program named in the LOAD= or RUN= lines of your WIN.INI file does not exist.

▲ Either the LOAD= or the RUN= line of your WIN.INI file is longer than 128 characters.

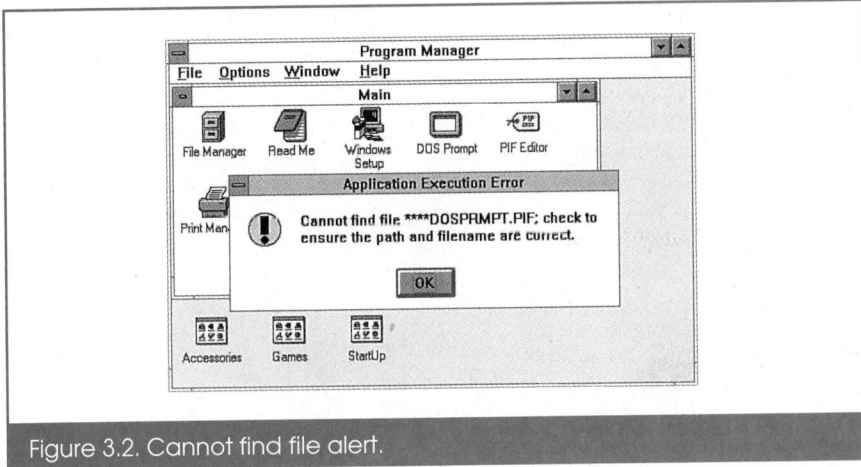

Figure 3.2. Cannot find file alert.

Editing the WIN.INI file is described in Chapter 27, "Configuring with the WIN.INI and SYSTEM.INI Files."

Program Group File Is Invalid or Damaged

If Program Manager has a problem reading one or more of the group files when Windows starts, you may see an alert similar to the one shown in Figure 3.3.

The following are some of the many reasons this message would be displayed:

▲ A Program Manager group file (one with the extension .GRP) has been deleted or is damaged. In this case, you should re-create the group by using Program Manager commands. See Chapter 5, "Program Manager," for more on program groups.

▲ The pathnames of the .GRP files are incorrect. This is common when you move Windows to another directory without updating the PROGMAN.INI file. See Chapter 27, "Configuring with the WIN.INI and SYSTEM.INI Files," for a description of how to update the PROGMAN.INI file when you move Windows files.

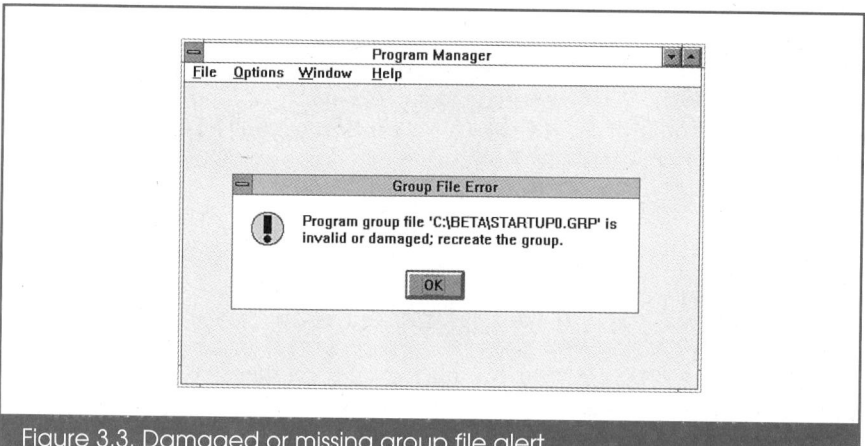

Figure 3.3. Damaged or missing group file alert.

Corrupt Swap File

If Windows has a problem reading your permanent swap file when you start, the program will advise you to re-create the swap file. Many situations can cause your swap file to become corrupt. Swap files are described in Chapter 22, "Windows Operating Modes."

In general, a re-create Swap file message is displayed if you created a permanent swap file and it was later deleted or damaged. In this case, you must follow these steps to re-create the swap file:

1. Open Windows Setup from within Windows.

2. Re-create a permanent swap file.

Share Violations Under DOS 3.3 and 4.01

If you get error messages when you start Windows indicating that you are having sharing violations, it is likely that you either did not run the MS-DOS SHARE.EXE program in your AUTOEXEC.BAT file or you have opened too many files for SHARE.EXE to handle. Due to the way that Windows works, you must run SHARE if you are using MS-DOS Version 3.1 or above before you start Windows. You may need to increase the number of file handles available to SHARE. If you are certain that SHARE has been run, you may want to modify your AUTOEXEC.BAT file to add the /L:100 option to the SHARE command, such as

```
SHARE /L:100
```

Share Violations Under DOS 5.0

If you are using DOS 5.0 and get share violation messages when starting, put SHARE.EXE in your CONFIG.SYS file. If you want all Windows applications to have access rights to all your data files, you must run SHARE when you boot the system. Before you edit the CONFIG.SYS file, be sure to check for an entry loading SHARE.EXE from the AUTOEXEC.BAT file. If you are running DOS 5.0, delete the AUTOEXEC.BAT entry relating to SHARE.EXE, then modify your CONFIG.SYS file to add the following syntax:

```
install=c:\dos\share.exe /f:4096 /1:25
```

where

> install tells DOS 5.0 to load a program as a TSR.
>
> = tells DOS 5.0 to look for a drive/dir/filename designation after the Install command.
>
> /f: asks DOS to allocate file spaces in bytes for the storage area used to record file-sharing information. The default is 2048. Increasing this value to 4096 is one way to avert future file-sharing hassles and related error messages.

/l sets the number of files that can be locked at one time. The unstated default is 20. Always increase this value to 25 or even 30 if you increase the /f: option to more than the default.

Tip: DOS 5.0 always looks for SHARE.EXE in drive C. If you have moved this and/or other DOS files to another drive, you may experience problems.

Starting Windows on Hewlett-Packard PCs

3

If you are running on a Hewlett-Packard PC in 386-enhanced mode, you may see the message

```
Unsupported DOS version
```

This message indicates that you are using generic MS-DOS rather than Hewlett-Packard's own version of DOS. You must use the Hewlett-Packard version in order to run Windows in 386-enhanced mode.

Leaving Windows

When you quit Windows, you return to the MS-DOS prompt. Remember that Windows is an environment, not a single program. As described in Chapter 1, "The World of Windows," an operating environment is a program that requires you to have a separate operating system (DOS). To exit Windows, you must exit from Program Manager. When you exit from other Windows programs, you return to Program Manager, not to the MS-DOS prompt.

When Program Manager shows in the front window, give the **Ex**it command in the **F**ile menu. If you do not know how to give commands from menus but you want to leave Windows, press Alt-F4. To learn how to give commands from menus, see Chapter 4, "Basic Windows Concepts."

When you close Program Manager, you are presented with a dialog box that prompts you as shown in Figure 3.4. Click OK or press Enter to leave. If you decide you want to continue running Windows, click Cancel or press the Esc key.

Any changes you have made to the way Program Manager looks—such as moving icons—are saved. The next time you run Windows, Program Manager will look the way it did when you left it.

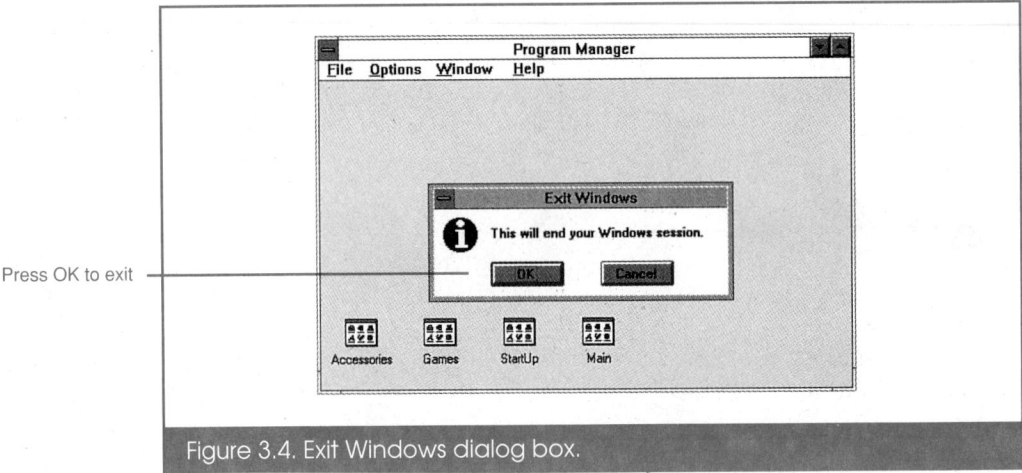

Press OK to exit

Figure 3.4. Exit Windows dialog box.

If you have made changes to Program Manager but do not want those changes saved, unselect the **S**ave Settings On Exit item from the **O**ptions pull-down menu. (To do this from the keyboard, press Alt-O, and then Alt-S.) Windows 3.1 still quits, but the next time you run Windows, Program Manager will not reflect any of the changes you made.

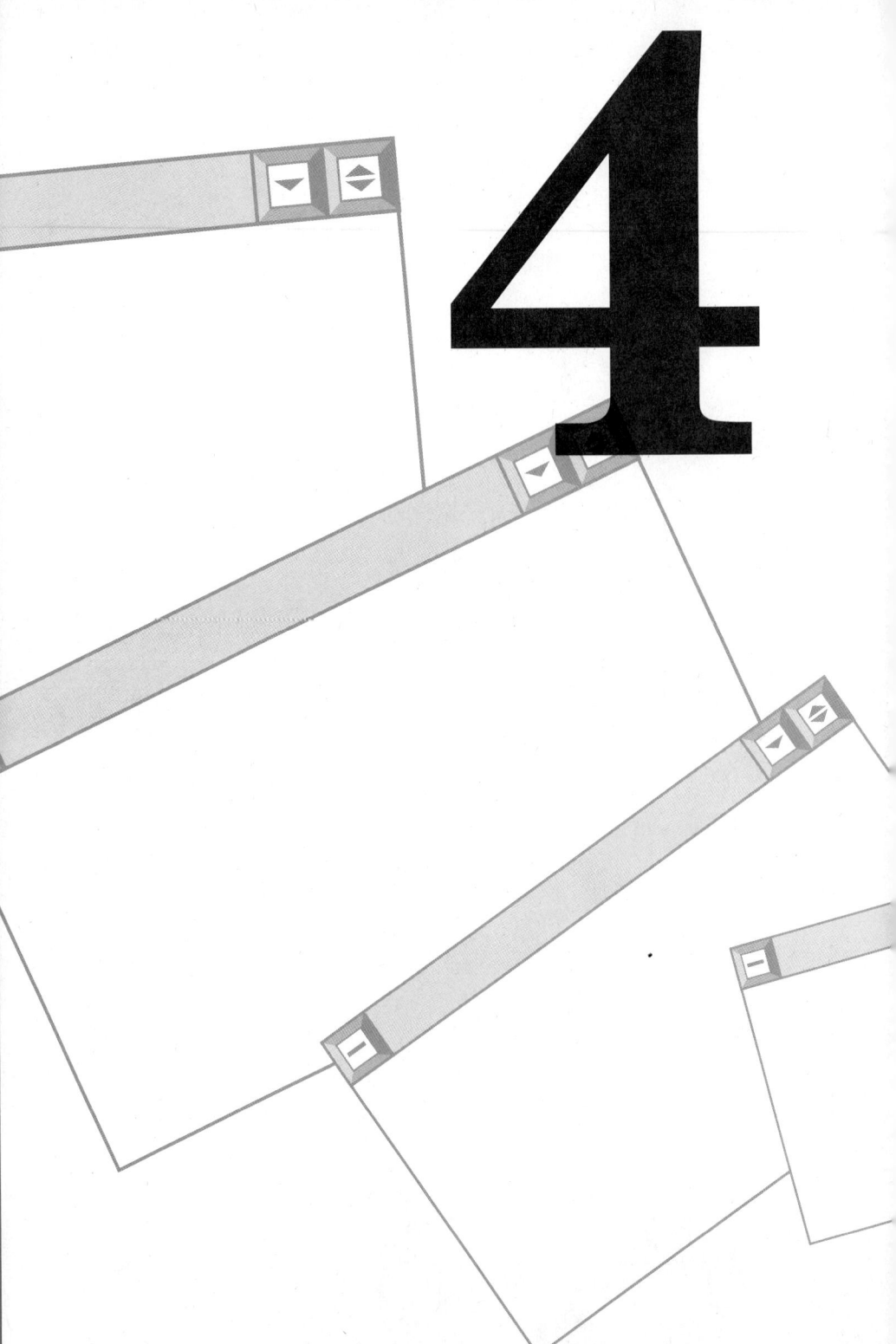

CHAPTER

4

Basic Windows Concepts

As you probably can guess, installing and starting Windows 3.1 is not nearly as interesting as using it. This chapter shows you the basics of how to use Windows and Windows programs and the ways you interact with Windows. After you finish this chapter, you will be able to start experimenting with Windows programs. (Of course, all the programs that come with Windows 3.1, and even a few that don't, are described in full detail later in the book.)

Before you start this chapter, you should have Windows running. If you decide to start any applications automatically on startup, you will move that program's icon into the StartUp group window. The StartUp group is discussed in more detail in Chapter 5, "Program Manager." Windows 3.1 StartUp group window makes it easy for you to activate programs when you start Windows, without having to click a program icon. Assuming that you haven't started fiddling with Program Manager, the first program that starts when you start Windows, your screen will look like Figure 4.1.

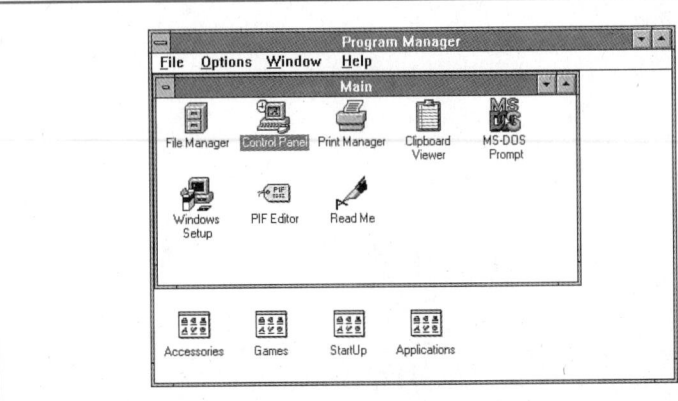

Figure 4.1. The Main Windows group.

Using Menus and Commands

The most common way to tell Windows what you want to do is by choosing a command from a menu. Every Windows program has at least one menu, and most have four or more. The *menu bar* is at the top of the program's window. As you can see from Figure 4.1, for example, the Program Manager menu bar has the following pull-down menus: **F**ile, **O**ptions, **W**indow, and **H**elp.

Menus hold lists of commands that usually are related in some way. For example, all the commands in the **W**indow menu in Program Manager (see Figure 4.2) relate to Program Manager windows. The first three commands are actions that arrange windows; the last four are actions that activate windows. Notice the solid line between the two groups: It is a visual cue that the groups of commands are related.

The standard way to refer to commands is by using the menu name, followed by the command name. Thus, the **T**ile command in the **W**indow menu usually is called the **W**indow **T**ile command. By telling you the menu in which the command is listed, this method makes finding the command easy.

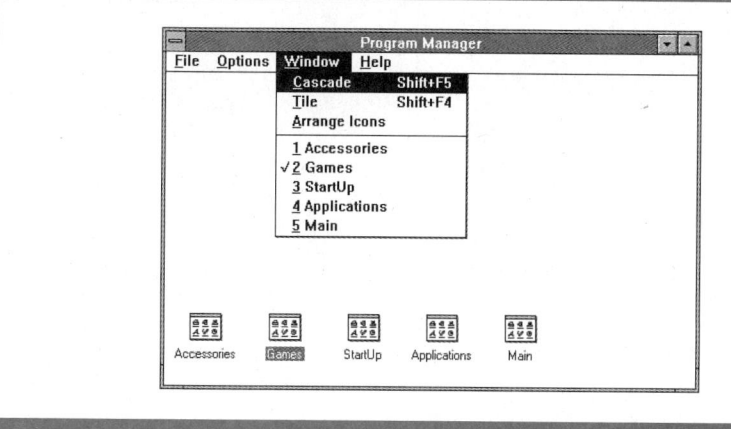

Figure 4.2. The Window menu.

Tip: Sometimes command names may be dimmed. You cannot execute dimmed commands. Programs dim the names of commands that make no sense in the current context. For example, if a command requires a window to be open and it isn't open, the program dims that command.

To execute a command, you select it from the menu. Like everything else in Windows, you can do this with either the mouse or the keyboard.

Giving Commands with the Mouse

If you have used a computer with only a keyboard for many years, the idea of using a mouse may be foreign to you. Many PC users don't know that people have been using mice with computers since well before the PC was invented—more than 15 years. The idea behind a mouse is that it helps you specify some actions more easily than you can with a keyboard. In many cases, you get the same result whether you use a mouse or a keyboard. Just choose whichever method is easier for you to remember and execute.

Tip: You, like many people, may prefer to have the mouse between your body and the keyboard rather than to one side of the keyboard. In recent years, health professionals have determined that the safest way to use a keyboard is with your arms parallel to the floor. Having your computer screen farther away from your eyes than the length of your forearms is good also. If you rest your arms on your desk when you type, you may find that moving to and from the mouse is easier if it is near your hand, just in front of the keyboard.

The Pointer

Using a mouse with a PC is surprisingly easy, even if you have never used one. The basic idea behind using a mouse is that you move a *pointer* on the screen by moving the body of the mouse in the direction you want the pointer to move. The normal Windows pointer is an arrow tip (see Figure 4.3). To move the pointer to the left on the screen, move the mouse to the left, and so on. As you can see, performing basic actions with a mouse is not very difficult. The action part of the mouse pointer is at the very tip of the arrow. Pressing the mouse button selects for action the pixel (picture element) to which that tip is pointing.

Of course, you must have a reason for wanting to move the pointer. In Windows, you use the pointer to point at things you want to work with. If you want to see a menu, you point at the menu; if you want to work with an icon, you point at that icon; and so on. You can move the pointer around the screen freely without worrying about going into the "wrong" places. Windows programs take action only when you click the mouse button, not just when you move the pointer.

As you move the pointer over different areas, Windows programs sometimes change its shape so that you get a better idea of what will happen. These different symbols tell you what is going on and what actions you can take. For example, you see an hourglass while the computer is processing and cannot be accessed.

To see the pointer change, move it near the right edge of the Main window in the Program Manager, like in Figure 4.3. Now move the pointer slowly to the right. When the arrow's tip is directly over the window border, it turns into a double-headed arrow, as shown in Figure 4.4. Windows presents a double-headed pointer to let you know you can stretch a window's border in either direction.

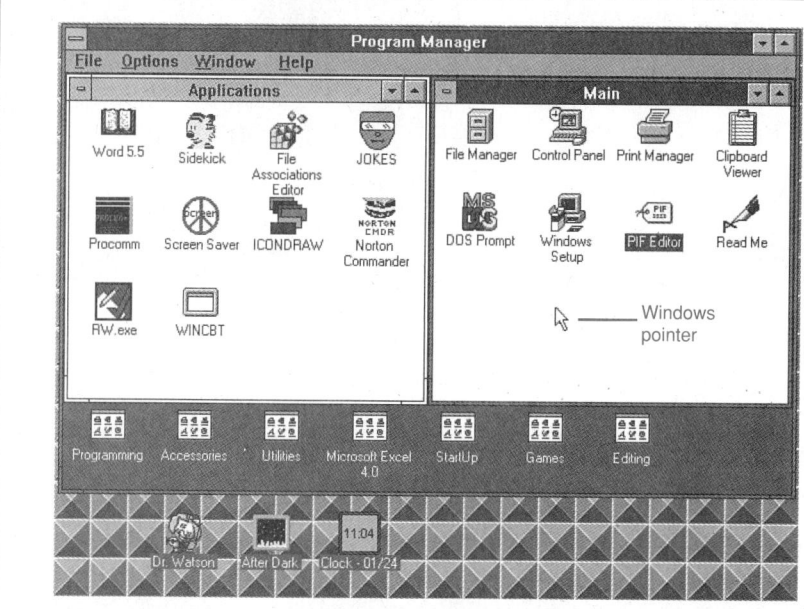

Figure 4.3. The normal Windows pointer.

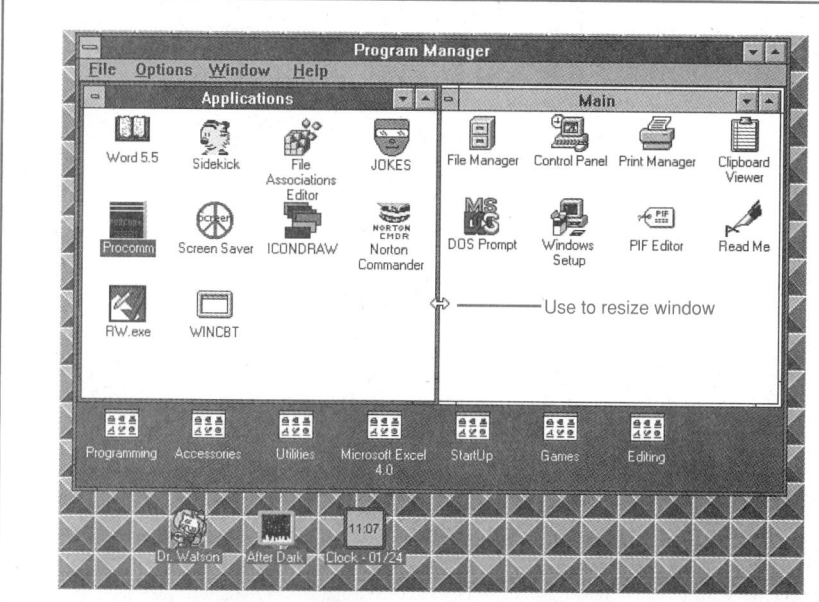

Figure 4.4. The pointer as a double-headed arrow.

When you move the pointer farther to the right, it reverts to the standard arrow.

Clicking, Double-Clicking, and Dragging

As soon as you point at something you want to act on, you take one of three actions with the mouse: You click once, you *double-click,* or you click and drag the mouse. The action you take depends on what you want to do. Almost every mouse used with the PC has two or three buttons, but because virtually every program uses only the left button, you do not have to spend time thinking about which button to use. Throughout this book, any reference to the mouse button means the left one, unless otherwise noted.

The three actions are similar:

▲ To click, simply press the mouse button and release it. You can do this at any speed.

▲ To double-click, press the mouse button, release it, press it again, and release it again. The time between the two clicks must be fairly short. You can adjust the maximum time allowed between clicks (for instructions, see Chapter 7, "Control Panel").

▲ To drag, press the mouse button and continue holding it down while you move the mouse. When the pointer is where you want it, release the mouse button.

Usually, remembering which of the three actions you want is easy. To select something without activating it, click it. To select and activate something in one motion, double-click it. To move something, drag it. Although these rules are not hard and fast, they apply often enough that remembering them should cover most situations.

A mouse is a relative pointing device. If you pick it up and set it down somewhere else, the pointer does not move on the screen. The only way to move the pointer is to move the mouse across a flat surface. This is quite different from graphics tablets that map directly to the screen. Pointing on a graphics tablet correlates to a position; moving to another position on the tablet puts you at a new position on the screen.

Tip: There are utilities for making the right and center buttons (if your mouse has them) useful. In fact, you can emulate the Enter key with the righthand mouse button with one popular mouse utility.

Issuing Commands

Selecting commands with the mouse is easy and direct. First, point at the menu in which the command resides and click the mouse button. This action opens and freezes the menu. When you are viewing the menu, simply point at the desired command and click the mouse again. This causes the command to execute.

Some people prefer to continue to hold down the mouse button after selecting the menu. In this case, you point at the menu, click and hold down the mouse button so that the menu drops down, then drag the menu down to the desired command. When you release the mouse button, the command is executed. (People familiar with the Apple Macintosh will notice a major difference here. On the Macintosh, you do not have a choice: You *must* continue to hold down the button after the menu drops down.) The process of holding down the mouse button and moving the mouse is often referred to as *click-dragging*.

If you choose a menu and then decide that you don't really want to give a command right now, simply move the pointer to the right of the last menu and click. This action makes the exposed menu disappear. You also can just click the menu name again to make that menu go away.

4

Giving Commands with the Keyboard

If you are familiar with the Apple Macintosh, you know that most actions can be performed on that computer only by using a mouse. When Microsoft developed Windows, the company determined that many people did not want to deal with a mouse, even though the mouse often is easier to use than the keyboard. Because some people think that the only way to deal with a computer is through the keyboard, Microsoft specified that almost all actions taken in programs should be able to be done with just the keyboard. If you use a portable computer on the road, you may be glad to know that you can use most Windows programs without a mouse—you don't have to carry around a mouse and then find space to use it in cramped areas.

The Basics of Using a Keyboard

More than half the actions you take require using the Alt key in combination with other keys. To give commands, for example, you activate a menu by holding down Alt and pressing the letter that's underlined in the menu name.

You use the Alt and Ctrl keys as you do the Shift key: while holding down Alt or Ctrl, you press another key. To type the Alt-Tab combination, for example, press Alt and then, while you continue holding it down, press Tab briefly. The Alt, Ctrl, and Shift keys can be used at the same time. For instance, to type a key combination such as Alt-Shift-F2, press Alt and, while you hold it down, press Shift; while holding down both of these keys, press F2 briefly. In combinations that include Alt, Ctrl, and Shift, you can press and hold those keys in any order before you press the letter or function key.

Using Menus

The most common way to drop a menu down using the keyboard is to press the Alt key and the underlined letter in the menu's name. Every menu option has one letter underlined.

To bring down the **F**ile menu, you would press Alt-F; to bring down the **O**ptions menu, you would press Alt-O; and so on. In most (but not all) menus, the first letter is underlined. Later in this book you will see menu bars in which the names of two menus begin with the same letter; in such cases, another letter is underlined in one of the menu names.

A less efficient way to bring down a menu is to press and release the Alt key or press F10. These actions highlight the leftmost menu on the menu bar. Then you can use the ← and → keys to move the highlight, pressing Enter after you have selected the desired menu. Although most people don't use this method, physically challenged people with severely limited coordination can use these key sequences to use Windows.

When a menu is displayed, you can select the command you want in any of several ways. Like the menu names, each command name has an underlined character. When you press that character, the command is executed—the most common way to issue commands. To give the **W**indow **T**ile command, for example, you press Alt-W and then T. You can keep holding down the Alt key between letters if you want to. For example, you can give the **W**indow **T**ile command by pressing Alt-W and then Alt-T.

After the menu is displayed, you can move the highlight with the ↓ and ↑ keys instead of using the underlined letter from the command name. When the command you want is highlighted, execute the command by pressing Enter.

> **Tip:** When you are selecting menus and commands, Windows cycles the selection from the left side of the menu to the far right side. Thus, if the leftmost menu name is selected and you press the ← key, Windows selects the rightmost menu. In a menu, if the last command is selected and you press the ↓ key, Windows selects the top command.

If you choose a menu and decide you don't really want to give a command right now, press Esc to make the menu disappear.

Keyboard Shortcuts

Many commands have single-key hotkeys. For these commands you do not need to use the Alt- key combinations. The short-cut keystrokes and keystroke combinations are listed at the right side of each drop-down menu. For example, notice that Shift+F4 is listed to the right of the **W**indow **T**ile command. You have another way to issue the **W**indow **T**ile command from the keyboard: Simply press Shift-F4. This is faster than pressing Alt-W and then T.

> **Tip:** The commands in some Windows programs have keyboard shortcuts that are not listed in the menu. This is unfortunate, because the best way to learn keyboard shortcuts is to see them in the menu. If you are running a Windows program that doesn't have many keyboard shortcuts listed in the menu, be sure to check the program's documentation to see whether there are unlisted shortcuts.

More About Commands and Menus

There are other common and basic menus that you will need to learn about.

Control Menus

Every program has an additional menu—its *control menu*—above and to the left of the menu bar. It looks like a small square with a hyphen centered in the box. This icon opens the program's *control menu*. The control menu for most programs usually contains similar commands (see Figure 4.5). Generally, the commands in this menu relate to the program's main window; they are described in this chapter's "Working with Windows" section.

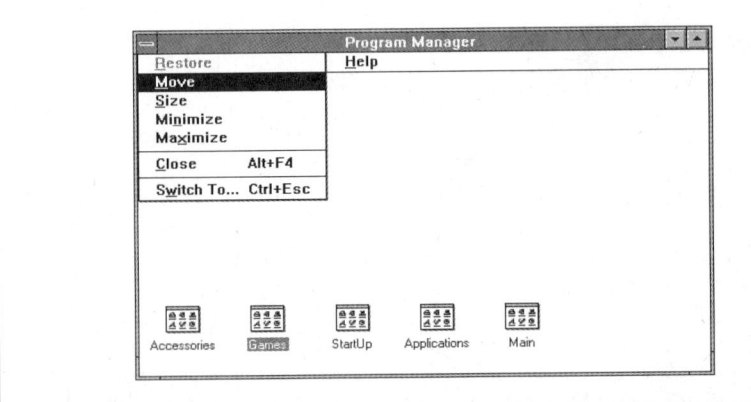

Figure 4.5. Control menu appears at a window's upper-left corner.

 You can display the control menu by clicking it with the mouse, just as you click commands in the menu bar.

 To access the control menu, press Alt-Spacebar. You can remember this key combination because the bar in the control menu looks like a space bar.

The only command that does not relate specifically to Windows is the Switch To command. When you have more than one program running simultaneously, you use this command to switch between programs. It is described in much more detail in Chapter 5, "Program Manager."

Most Windows programs create their own document windows, which also have control menus. For example, look at the Main window in Program Manager. At the left end of the menu bar is a box that looks like the main control menu, except that the bar in it is shorter (it represents a hyphen, not the space bar).

You can access a document window's control menu by clicking it.

To show a document window's control menu, press Alt--.

> **Tip:** You can issue the **C**lose command quickly in a control menu by double-clicking the Control window's icon. For document windows, this action closes the document; for program windows, it quits the program.

Ellipses

In some commands, an ellipsis (...) follows the command name. As you can see from Figure 4.6, which shows the **F**ile menu from Program Manager, some commands (such as **N**ew and **M**ove) have ellipses but others (such as **O**pen and **D**elete) do not.

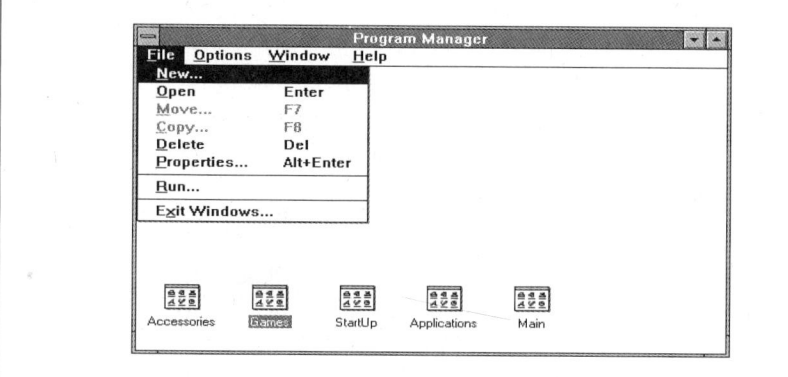

Figure 4.6. An ellipsis is three dots in a row after a menu command.

An ellipsis indicates that the command does not execute directly. Rather, issuing the command displays a *dialog box* from which you can make additional choices before the command executes. Dialog boxes are described later in this chapter, in the "Dialog Boxes" section. For now, be assured that whenever you give the name of a command that is followed by an ellipsis, you will be able to change the way the command executes (before it takes effect).

Check Marks

Some commands sometimes have check marks to the left of their names. For example, in the **W**indow menu shown in Figure 4.7, note the check mark to the left of the Games command.

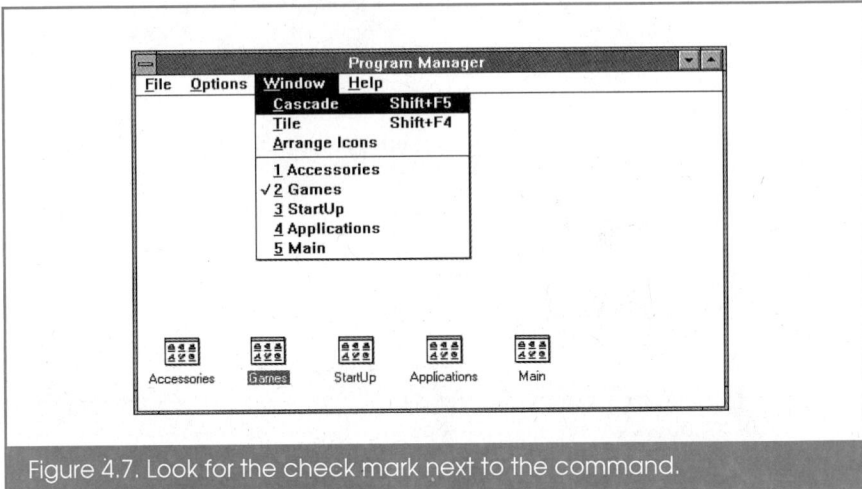

Figure 4.7. Look for the check mark next to the command.

A check mark indicates that a command is currently active or selected. When the command is inactive or unselected, the check mark disappears. In the **W**indow menu, a check mark appears next to the name of the window on top of all other open windows.

Check marks are on/off indicators. Sometimes they are called *toggles* because they are like the toggle switches used for electric lights. A command with a check mark next to its name is on; without the check mark, the command is off.

Working with Windows

This section describes how to handle the windows in Windows. Every Windows program runs in its own window. Most programs also open additional windows in their own window. You can think of these two types of windows as *program* and *document* windows. (They are referred to also as *parent* and *child* windows.)

Fortunately, you can handle program and document windows in the same way. The actions you usually perform on windows include moving them around the screen (called your *desktop*), making them larger and smaller, and switching between windows. When you are finished with a window, you close it. It is important to remember that document windows always appear only in their parent's window and that their size is limited by their parent. Program windows can be placed anywhere on the screen.

Program and document windows look very much alike. The parts of each type of window are the same, except that there is no menu bar at the top of document windows. Figure 4.8 shows the parts of a document window.

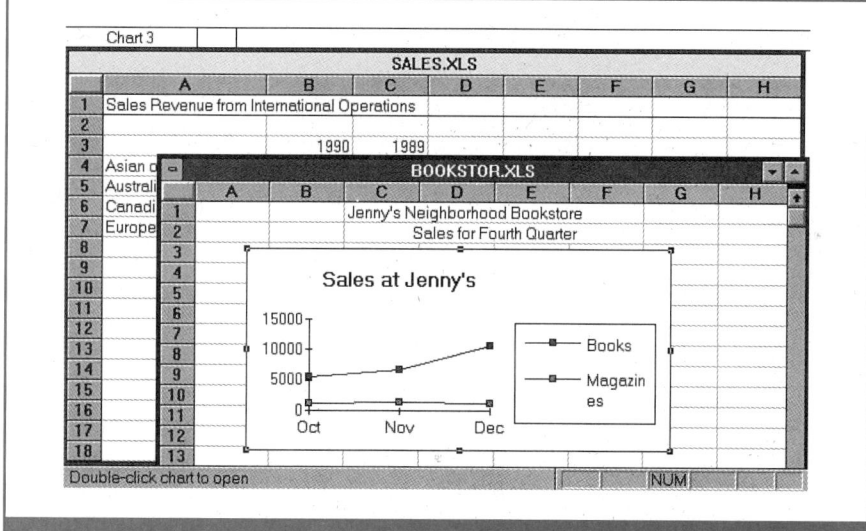

Figure 4.8. A typical document window.

Activating Windows

When a program opens many document windows, only one of them is *active* at any one time. When you take an action, it affects only the active window; the inactive windows just sit there until you activate them. You can tell which window is active by looking at the title bars. For most color combinations, the active window's title bar is darker than the title bars on inactive windows.

The method you take to activate a window depends on the program you are running. You will hear and see the term *Foreground* interchanged with the *Active* term. They both imply the same thing. The active window is always in the foreground.

 In almost every program, you activate a window by clicking any part of the window.

 Activating a window with the keyboard is generally done through the **W**indow menu.

Probably the simplest action you will take with a window is closing it. To close the active window, either use the Control **C**lose command or press Ctrl-F4.

Moving Windows

Often you will want to move windows on the screen so that you can see as much information as possible in the other windows. Moving windows is easy, especially when you use the mouse.

 To move a window with the mouse, simply click anywhere on the title bar and drag the window to a new location.

 To move a window with the keyboard, give the Control **M**ove command. The border of the window changes to a gray dotted line. Use the arrow keys to move the window to the desired location, then press Enter to finish moving. If you hold down the Ctrl key while pressing an arrow key, the window moves in smaller increments. This action gives you more accuracy in placing the window exactly where you want it.

You can move a document window anywhere in the window of the program that created it. You can move a document window off the edge of the program window so that only a small part of the document window shows. You can move a program window anywhere on the desktop.

Resizing Windows

Changing the size of windows is similar to moving them. When you resize a window, you move one of the edges in or out while the other edges remain fixed. This causes the window to change size. The double-headed pointer used for changing two edges of a window size is shown in Figure 4.9.

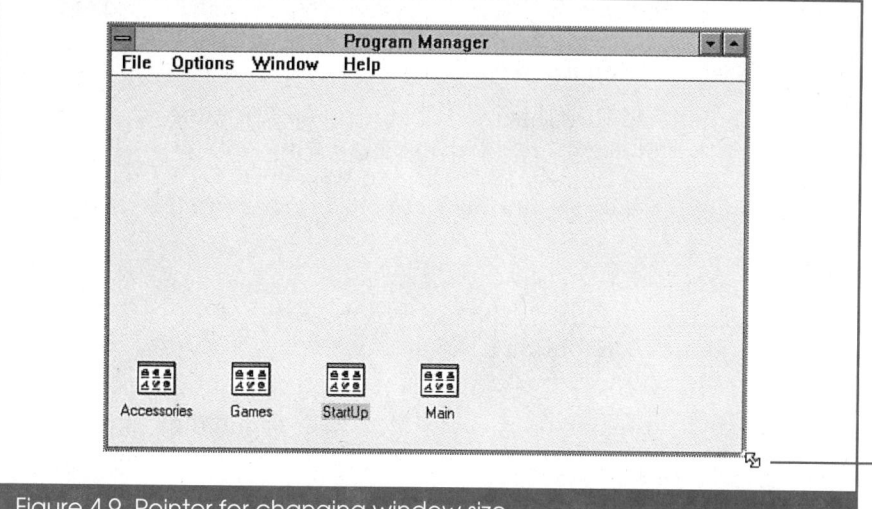

Figure 4.9. Pointer for changing window size.

With the mouse, point at the edge you want to move in or out. When you do this, the pointer changes to a double-headed arrow pointing left-and-right or up-and-down. Click and drag the edge to the desired new location.

To change the window size from the keyboard, first give the Control Size command. Next, press one of the four arrow keys to indicate which edge you want to move. Windows puts a double-headed arrow on that border. Using the arrow keys, move the border in the direction you want. Then press Enter to finish resizing. To resize the window in smaller increments, hold down the Ctrl key while pressing an arrow key (as you do when moving windows).

You can resize two edges at once. Resizing from a corner, as shown in Figure 4.9, is faster than resizing two edges in succession.

With the mouse, point at a corner rather than an edge, then click and drag. The two-headed arrow will point diagonally.

With the keyboard, press two arrow keys at once after giving the Control Size command. The two-headed arrow will point diagonally.

Maximizing and Restoring Windows

Moving and resizing windows can be tedious if what you really want to do is maximize the work area by making a window as large as possible.

For example, when you are working in a word processing program, you often want the program's window to be as large as the screen and the document window you are working in to be as large as possible.

Microsoft, realizing that this kind of moving and resizing is common, made it quick and easy to do. *Maximizing* a window is like moving the upper-left corner of the window to the far upper-left corner of the screen and dragging the lower-right corner as far down and to the right as possible.

 To maximize a window with the mouse, click the maximize button—the upward-pointing triangle in the upper-right corner of the window. The maximize and restore button and its companion, the minimize button, are shown in Figure 4.10.

 With the keyboard, give the Control Maximize command.

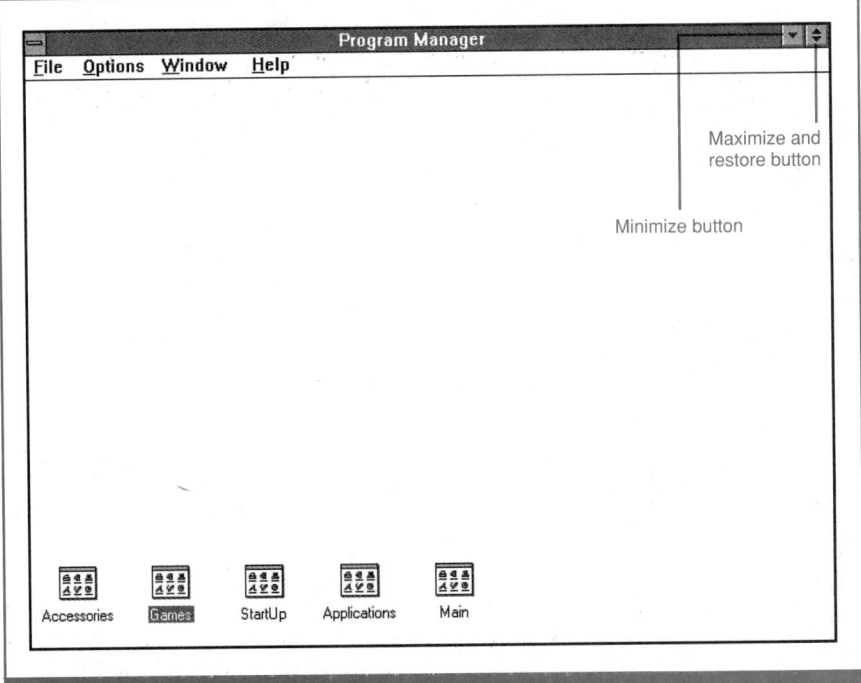

Figure 4.10. A maximized window.

When you maximize a window, Windows remembers the size and shape of the window before you maximized it. You can quickly *restore* the window to that size and shape with a single action, by clicking the double-headed triangle in the upper-right corner of a window.

In a maximized window, the maximize button changes to a restore button (with both upward- and downward-pointing arrows) like the one shown in Figure 4.10. You can restore the window to its original size by clicking this button with the mouse.

With the keyboard, give the Control **R**estore command. The Control **R**estore command is dimmed unless the window is maximized.

Minimizing Document Windows

Something else people often want to do is put windows out of the way without actually closing them. You want to make the window as small as possible while keeping it visible so that you can get at it easily. In Windows jargon, this is called *minimizing* the window.

Many Windows programs minimize document windows by turning them into icons and placing them at the bottom or right edge of the program's window. For instance, look at the Program Manager window in Figure 4.11. The Program Manager window is open, but there are two icons at the bottom of the desktop window. These are minimized programs. Note, however, that few Windows programs let you minimize document windows to icons within the program; they only let you close them.

To minimize a window with the mouse, click the downward-pointing arrow (the minimize button) near the upper-right corner of the window.

You can minimize from the keyboard with the Control **Mi**nimize command.

There is no standard way to open a minimized document window; it depends on the program you are running. Because Windows users become so familiar with Program Manager, many programs use it as a model for the way they open minimized windows.

In Program Manager, you can open a window represented by an icon by double-clicking the icon. You also can click the icon to bring up the window's control menu and then select **R**estore.

In Program Manager, press Alt-W and the ↓ keys to select the icon from the Window menu. In other programs you can select minimized icons by pressing the ← and → keys, and open icons by pressing Enter.

Although the actions for minimizing program windows are the same as those for minimizing document windows, the result is very different. For a discussion of minimized programs, see the "Running Programs" section later in this chapter.

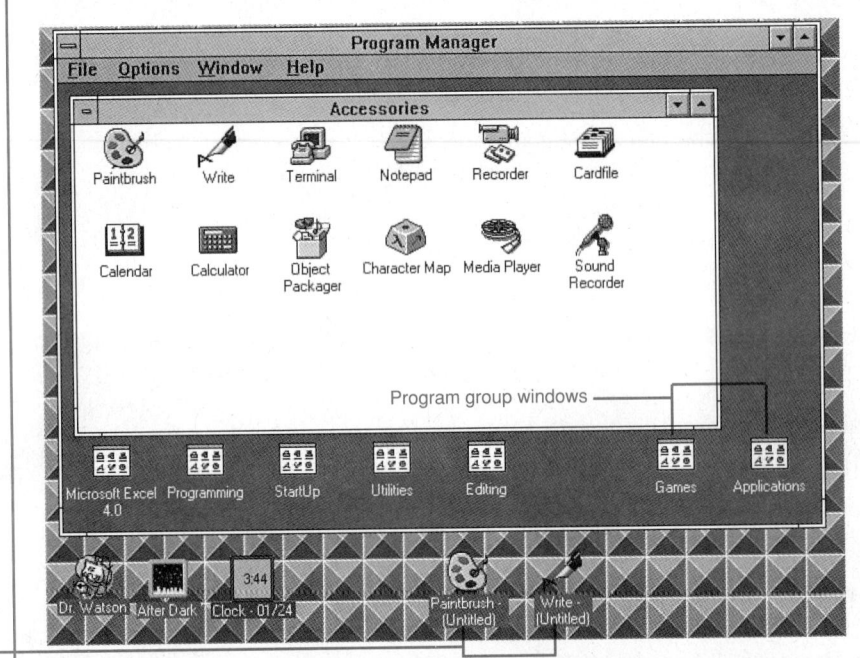

Figure 4.11. Minimized Write and Paintbrush document windows.

Scrolling in Windows

When a window is not big enough to show all its contents, *scroll bars* at the right and/or bottom edges of the window make it easy for you to see all the contents of the window by moving those contents under the window's frame. You use scroll bars only with the mouse, not with the keyboard.

To see how scroll bars work, select the Accessories window in Program Manager and, using the techniques you learned earlier, make it narrower. The result should look something like Figure 4.12. The new item along the side of the window is the vertical scroll bar. (If you make the window too short to show all the icons horizontally, you will see a second scroll bar along the bottom of the window.)

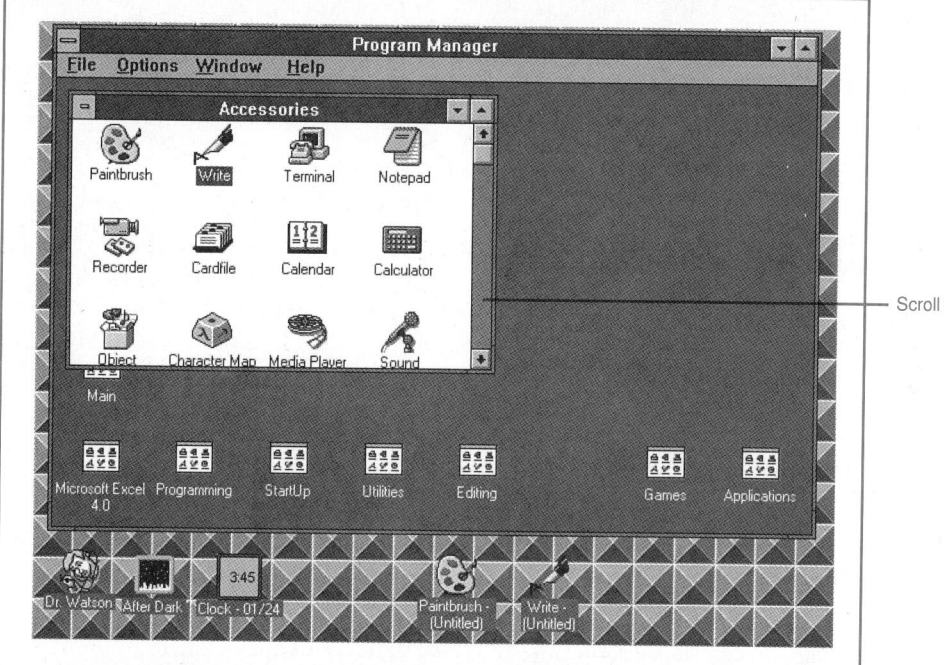

Scroll bar

Figure 4.12. Accessories window with scroll bar.

Using the scroll bar is easy. If you want to see items that are below or to the right of what you can see in the window, you scroll the contents of the window up or to the left by clicking the arrows at the end of the appropriate scroll bar. Because the position of the window remains fixed, the idea is to move the contents "under" the window so that you can see them.

To move the contents of the window up using the mouse, point at the downward-pointing arrow at the top of the scroll bar and hold down the mouse button. To move the contents down, use the upward-pointing arrow. You will see the contents of the window scroll smoothly past. You can move the contents of the window right or left in a similar manner, using a horizontal scroll bar.

As you scroll, you can tell where you are in the document by noting the position of the *scroll box,* the square that moves along the scroll bar. When the scroll box is at the top of the scroll bar, you see the beginning of the contents; when it is in the middle, you see the middle of the contents; when it is at the bottom, you see the end of the contents.

If you want to move faster, clicking in the gray bar between the arrows causes the contents to move a full window at a time. If the window contains a great deal of information, this is a fast way to view it. Some programs even move your position in the file relative to the point where you click on the scroll bar, not just one full window at a time.

You can even move a specific distance through the contents by dragging the scroll box. For instance, to quickly see a point three-quarters of the way into the document, click and drag the scroll box three-quarters of the way down the scroll bar.

With many Windows applications, when you scroll with the mouse, the item you have selected in the window remains the same until you finish moving the box and let go of the mouse button. Thus, you might not be able to see the selected item as you scroll.

 Scrolling with the keyboard is quite different from scrolling with the mouse. Unfortunately, each program has a different method for scrolling a window with the keyboard, and some (like Program Manager) don't give you any way to scroll (without a mouse) without selecting different items. Some programs, however, allow scrolling by use of the Page Up and Page Down keys.

Note that vertical scroll bars (the ones that move the contents up and down) and horizontal scroll bars act identically. If you use a word processor, you usually scroll vertically through your writing. If you use a painting program, you are likely to scroll both horizontally and vertically in your drawing.

Window Elements

There are many Windows screen objects that you will get to know as you work with Windows 3.1. Screen objects are elements of the Windows screen that serve a distinct purpose, but are only invoked when appropriate or required, like dialog boxes, for example.

Dialog Boxes

Many commands have associated *dialog boxes* from which you can choose options for the commands. In Windows, dialog boxes are the standard way to tell the program exactly how you want it to act. Because you interact with dialog boxes in the same way in each Windows program, you do not need to learn how to change settings. All you need to know is what type of settings you can make in each program.

Figure 4.13 shows a typical dialog box.

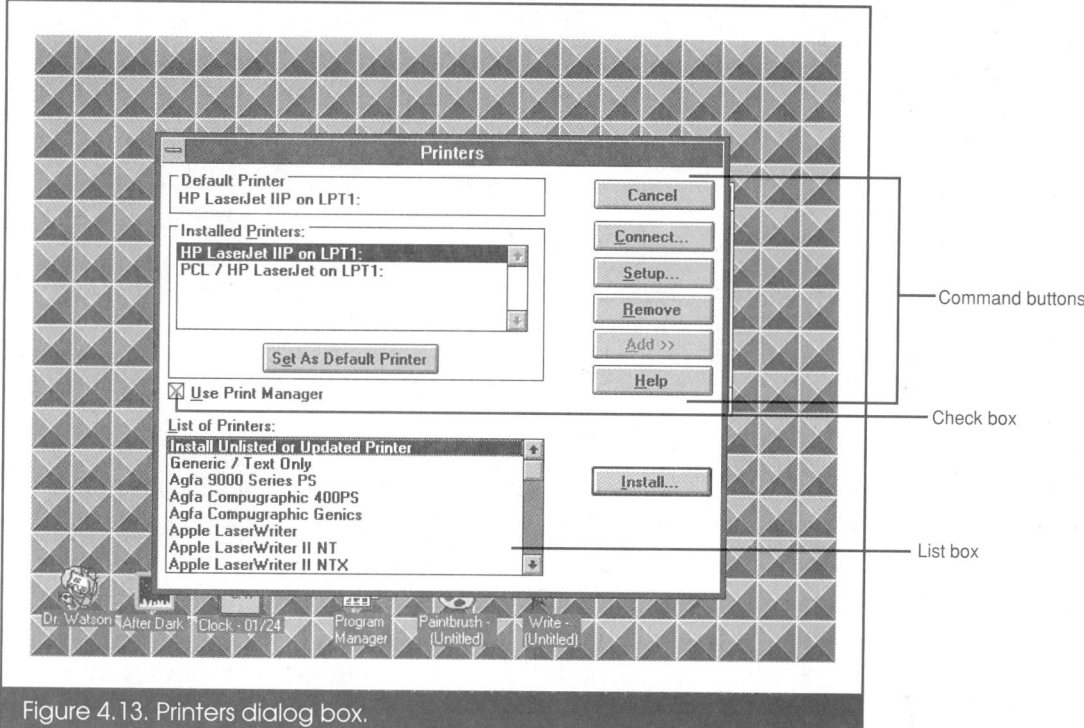

Command buttons

Check box

List box

Figure 4.13. Printers dialog box.

There are many ways to make choices in dialog boxes. For example, the Printers box uses a combination of *list boxes*, *command buttons*, and *check boxes*. You can make choices with either the mouse or the keyboard. Most people find that making choices with the mouse is much faster than with the keyboard, unless the dialog box has only a few buttons. The general rules are as follows:

Selecting items with the mouse is quick and easy. Most dialog items are selected by clicking them. All types of buttons are activated by clicking, and so are items in a list. You never need to double-click in a dialog box.

Selecting items with the keyboard is easy also. Like menus and commands, many items in a dialog box have an underlined letter. You can choose an item by pressing the Alt key and that letter. Choosing other items is possible but involves much moving around. To move from item to item, press the Tab key. Pressing Shift-Tab moves you in reverse order.

Command Buttons

The most common items you see in a dialog box are command buttons such as OK and Cancel (refer to Figure 4.14). You use these buttons after you have made all the choices you want in other parts of the dialog box and are ready to execute the command. Command buttons always either close the dialog box or bring up another dialog box so that you can make additional settings.

Many dialog boxes contain only a warning message and one button, the OK button. These dialog boxes are called *alert* dialog boxes because they are meant to tell you something. Clicking OK simply makes the dialog box go away.

Other dialog boxes contain text and only two buttons—OK and Cancel. One of the two buttons is highlighted; it is the one selected if you press Enter. The highlight appears differently on different screens, but generally is represented as a darker border around the button.

 To select a command button with the mouse, simply click the command button.

 To select a command button with the keyboard, type Alt and the underlined letter or use Tab or Shift-Tab to highlight the desired button, then press Enter.

 **Tip:** Every dialog box can be closed by pressing Esc. This is true even if a Cancel button is in the dialog box.

 **Warning:** Be sure not to double-click command buttons with the mouse. Windows acts on the first click. When the action is complete and the dialog box is gone, Windows acts as if you clicked the spot in the document under the command button you clicked. You usually do not want this to happen.

Check Boxes

You make on/off choices in a dialog box with check boxes, which are squares next to labels. A check box that contains an X is on; it is off when the box is empty. Figure 4.14 shows check boxes, two of which are on (selected) and one that is off (not selected).

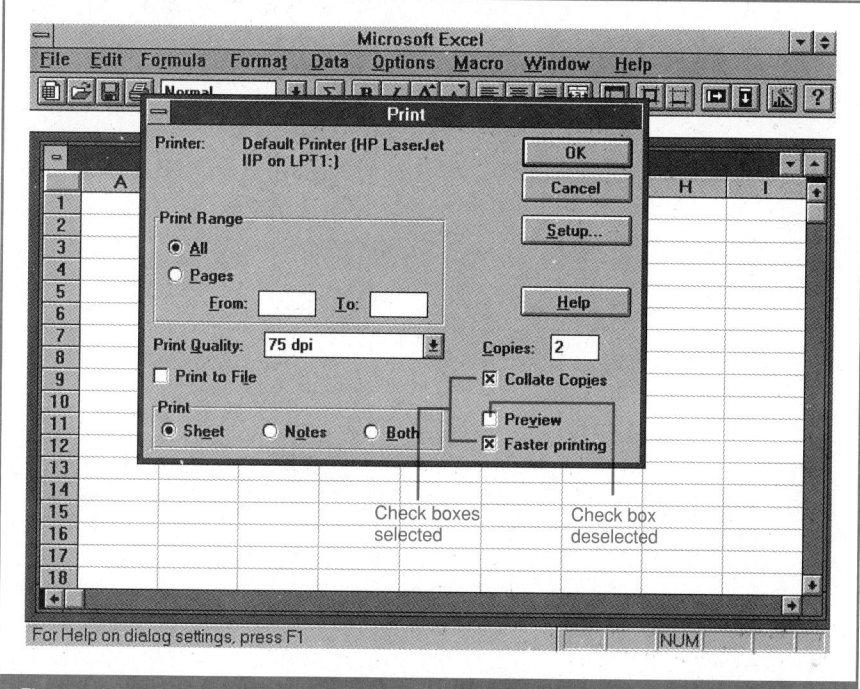

Figure 4.14. Check boxes.

Option Buttons

Option buttons appear in groups when you have to choose only one item from the group. Option buttons, sometimes called *radio buttons*, are the circles next to labels; they almost always occur as groups. The button for the selected item contains a dot, whereas the other buttons are empty. Remember that only one choice can be made from a group. Figure 4.15 shows a group of option buttons. Note that only one option is selected in each group.

You place the pointer over the desired button and click once.

If you are using the keyboard, you can choose the option from the group by using the direction and/or tab keys.

Tip: You can select check boxes and option buttons with the mouse by clicking anywhere in the button's text, not just directly on the square or circle. By clicking in the label, you don't have to aim the mouse as carefully.

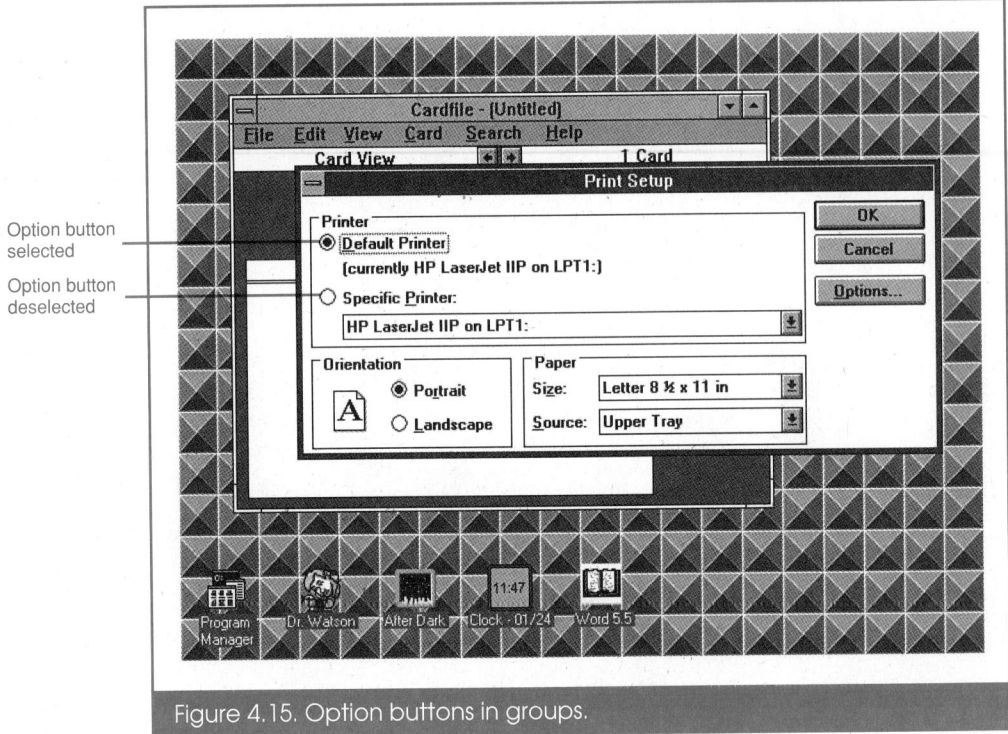

Option button
selected

Option button
deselected

Figure 4.15. Option buttons in groups.

List Boxes

Sometimes so many choices are possible for one item that showing all
the choices as option buttons would be unwieldy. For example, the list
of printers at the bottom of the Printers dialog box has dozens of
printers in it. In this case, you choose items from a list box. If all the
choices do not fit in the list box, the list box has a scroll bar like the
ones you saw earlier in this chapter. Figure 4.16 shows a typical list
box.

To choose an item from a list by using the mouse, make the item visible
with the scroll bar and then click it.

To choose an item with the keyboard, first activate the list with the Tab
or Shift-Tab keys. Next, use the ↑ and ↓ keys, and press the space bar
when you reach the desired item. Holding down the ↑ and ↓ keys causes
the list to scroll up and down. Use the Home and End keys to jump
quickly to the beginning or end of the list.

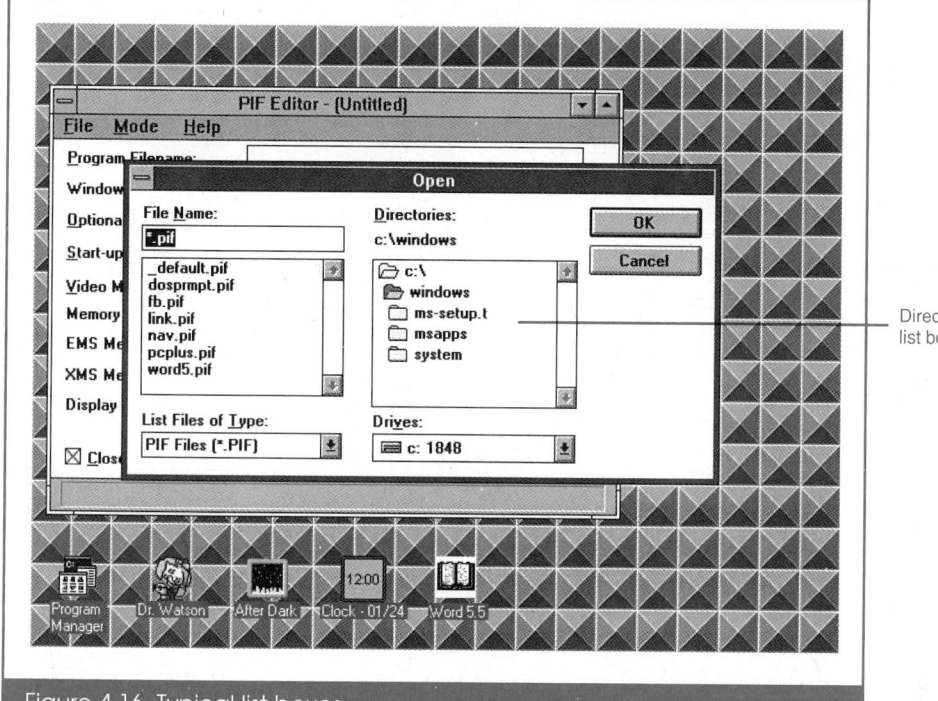

Directory
list box

Figure 4.16. Typical list boxes.

Some programers don't want to waste space in a dialog box with lots of
lists. Instead, they use drop-down list boxes. These are lists (they
resemble a menu) that you don't see until you select them. You would
see a drop-down list box used in lieu of a list box whenever the list
would be larger than the desired size of the dialog box. A long list of
fonts, for example, would best be presented by a drop-down list box.
Because the number of fonts would vary from system to system, the
drop- down list box makes the screen less cluttered. Expect to see the
use of this type of list become more popular with software developers as
time progresses.

To see the list with the mouse, click on the down-arrow button positioned to the right of the list element shown, then use the list as you
would a normal list box.

To see the list by using the keyboard, press Alt-↓, then use the ↑ and ↓
keys.

Key
board

Text Boxes

Some of the choices you make do not lend themselves well to the pre-defined choices you get with check boxes, option buttons, or lists. For example, you may want to enter the name of a file the program could not have predicted in a dialog box. In these cases, you use a text box (see Figure 4.17).

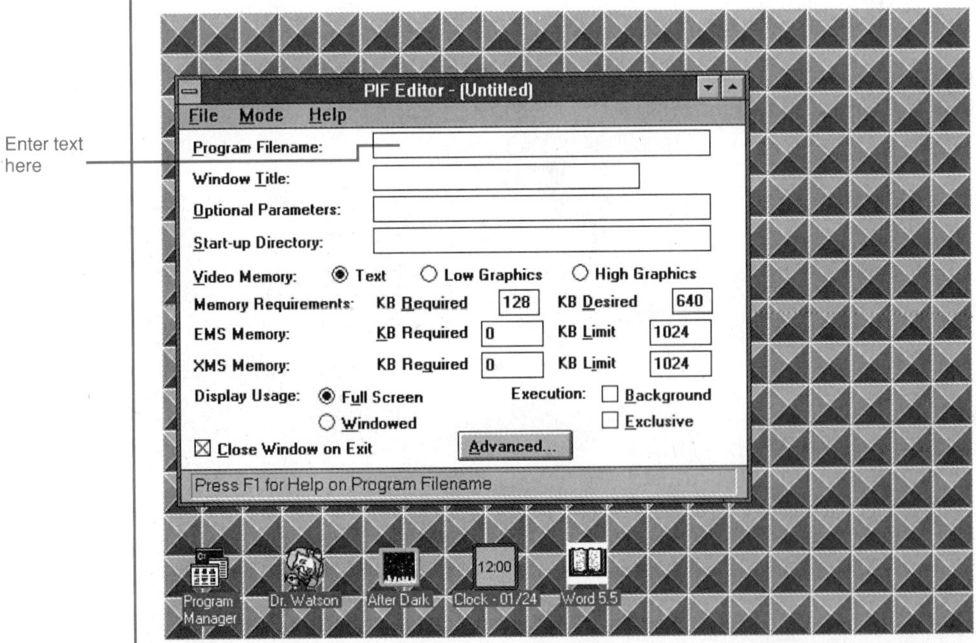

Enter text here

Figure 4.17. A text box.

When the text box is selected, a blinking *insertion point* at the beginning of the box indicates where your text will be inserted. If you already have text in the text box, you can move the insertion point to the location you want before you begin typing.

 To move the insertion point with the mouse, click at the desired location.

 To move the insertion point with the keyboard, use the ← and → keys. Press Home or End to move the insertion point to the beginning or end of the text in the text box.

Use the Backspace key to delete the letter to the left of the insertion point. You can remove blocks of text by selecting the desired characters and pressing Backspace or by typing new characters.

To select text with the mouse, click and drag over it.

To select text with the keyboard, hold down the Shift key and press the ← or → keys. Holding down the Shift key causes Windows to extend the selection. You also can press Shift-Home and Shift-End to extend the selection to the beginning or end of the text.

> **Tip:** Sometimes there is more text than can be shown in the text box, which causes text to extend beyond the right side of the box. To see the hidden text, select some of the visible text and extend the selection to the right. Windows scrolls the hidden text through the box.

4

Other Dialog Box Items

Programmers can add whatever features they want to dialog boxes. Most dialog boxes have only the items already mentioned, but a few have additional features. For example, Figure 4.18 shows one of the dialog boxes from the Control Panel. The scroll bar on the bottom right is used to set the speed at which the cursor blinks. The boxes on the left are text boxes combined with buttons that increase and decrease the numbers in the text boxes. These are called *spin buttons*. Other Windows programs may have other items that are described in the manuals for those programs.

A Look at Standard Dialog Boxes

Every program has its own dialog boxes. The look of these dialog boxes depends on the programmer who wrote the program.

Using the File Open Dialog Box

Figure 4.19 shows a typical **F**ile **O**pen dialog box. You see this dialog box when you want to open a document in the program. In the File

Name box you can type the name of the file you want to open. If you don't specify a drive and a directory in the File **N**ame box, Windows uses the directory shown next to the box. In this case, the directory is C:\.

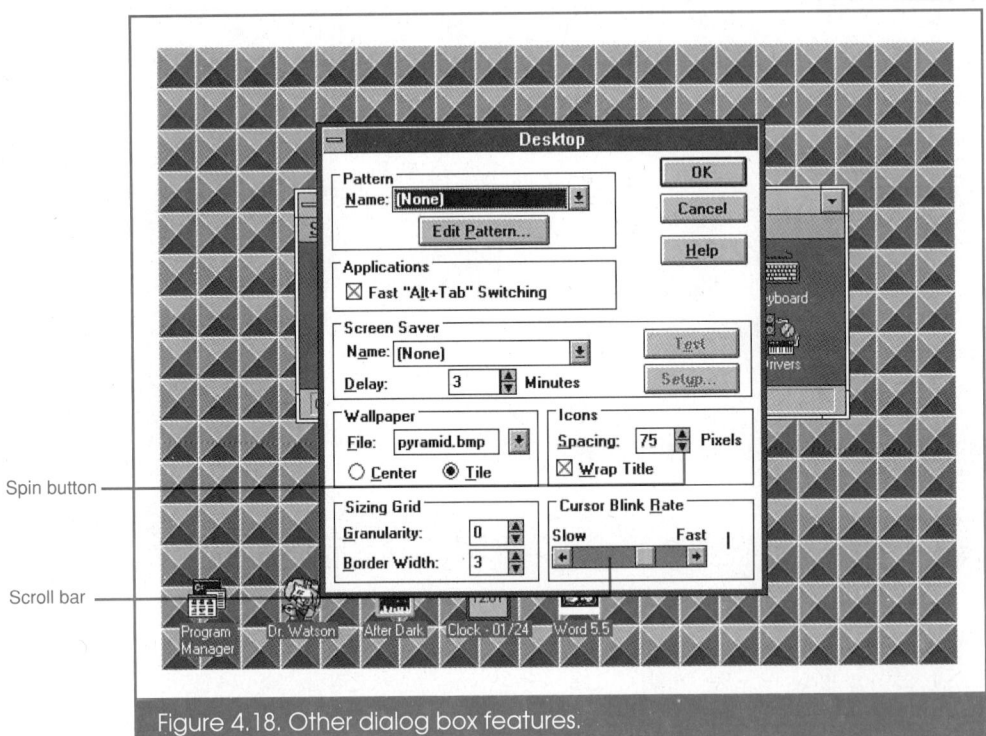

Spin button

Scroll bar

Figure 4.18. Other dialog box features.

With the two lists in the dialog box, you can navigate quickly through the directories on your disks to find the file you want. The Files list shows all the files that match the entry in the File **N**ame box. In this case, they are all the files in C:\ that match the specification *.WRI. You can change the specification in the File **N**ame box and click OK to see the list change. For example, changing the File **N**ame box to *.TXT and clicking OK changes the list to show on the files with a .TXT extension.

Starting with Version 3.1, Windows suggests the probable file-extension name and one or two others in a drop-down *pick list* near the bottom of the dialog box shown in figure 4.20. Windows remembers what you have selected in the immediate past and gives you the option of selecting again without having to enter data in a text field. Clicking the OK button always updates the **F**iles list, as long as you have a wildcard character in the filename.

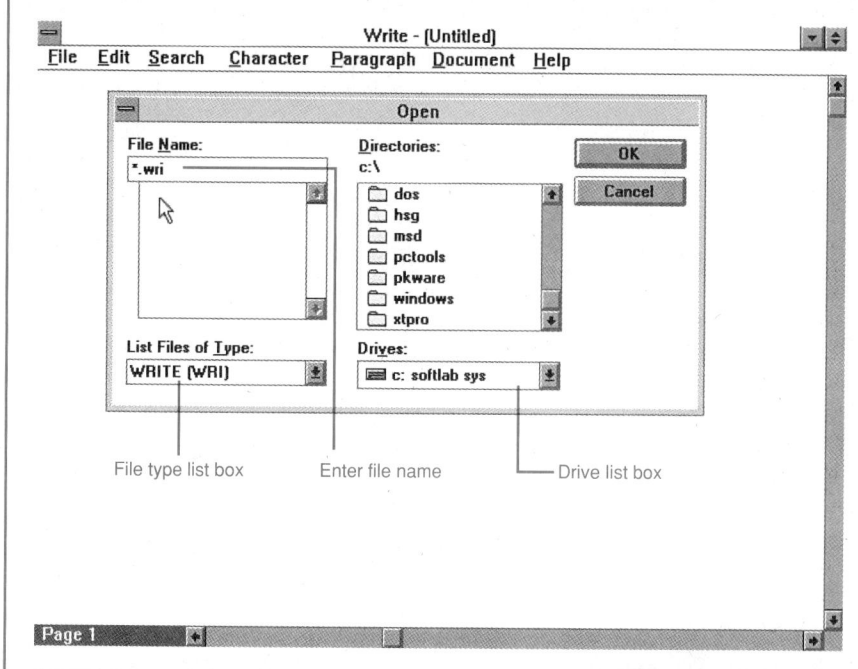

Figure 4.19. A typical File Open dialog box.

If you want to change the disk or directory in which to find the file, use the Directories list. All items in the Directories list are preceded by a file folder icon, indicating that they are not files, but directories, as shown in Figure 4.21.

To move to the directory one level higher in the directory tree, select a file folder icon that is located above the current directory and indented to the left. To change to a directory below the current directory, select a directory that is located below the current one and indented to the right. When you perform either of these steps, the File **N**ame search pattern remains the same and the **F**iles list changes to reflect the files that match the new directory.

To change to a different disk drive, select a disk drive using the Drives drop-down list box. To open the list, click the arrow to the right of the list. Select a drive from the list by double-clicking it. Of course, once you've saved a file using **F**ile **S**ave, Windows programs know where it should be saved next time. You will only see the **F**ile Save **A**s dialog box when the filename does not exist in the current directry. The **F**ile Save **A**s dialog box puts it there, once you make the selection.

Tip: In some programs you can list more than one wildcard file specifier at one time. There is no standard way to do this, but generally these programs separate the lists with commas. Check your program's documentation to see whether you can list more than one wildcard.

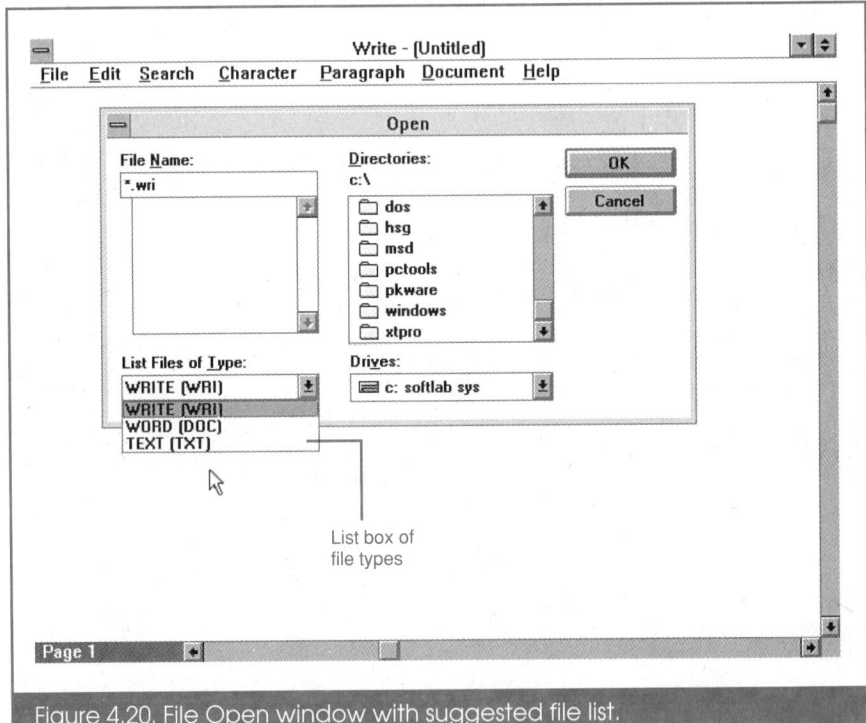

Figure 4.20. File Open window with suggested file list.

Using the File Save As Dialog Box

The **F**ile Save **A**s dialog box is similar to the **F**ile **O**pen command except that there is no **F**iles list. You would only see the **F**ile Save **A**s dialog box when you are saving a new file. Figure 4.22 shows a typical **F**ile Save **A**s dialog box. As before, you can type in the full path to the file or just the filename if the path specified in the dialog box is correct. If the path is not correct, use the **D**irectories list the same way you use the **F**ile **O**pen dialog box.

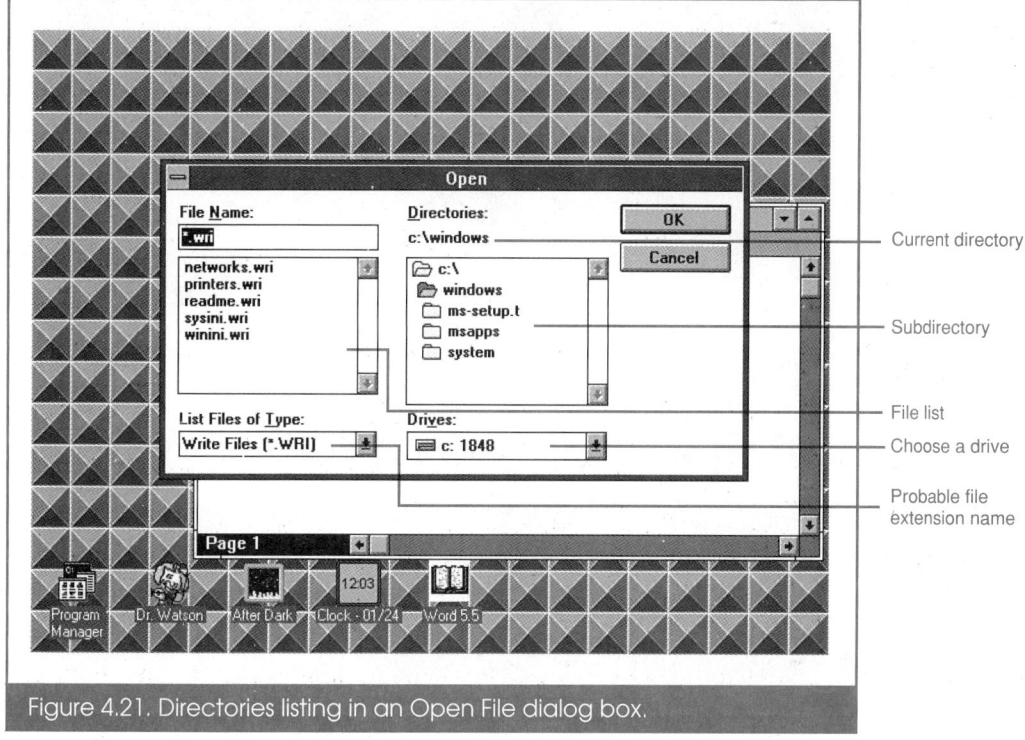

Figure 4.21. Directories listing in an Open File dialog box.

Additional Windows Features

The preceding sections show you all the typical methods to use when running Windows. You should note that although you will use these methods for the vast majority of your interaction, you may encounter other methods. Any company that writes Windows programs, including Microsoft, can add new features to the Windows interface for their programs. Many companies avoid the temptation in order to make their programs easier to learn, but others find that making little additions here and there makes the programs easier to use.

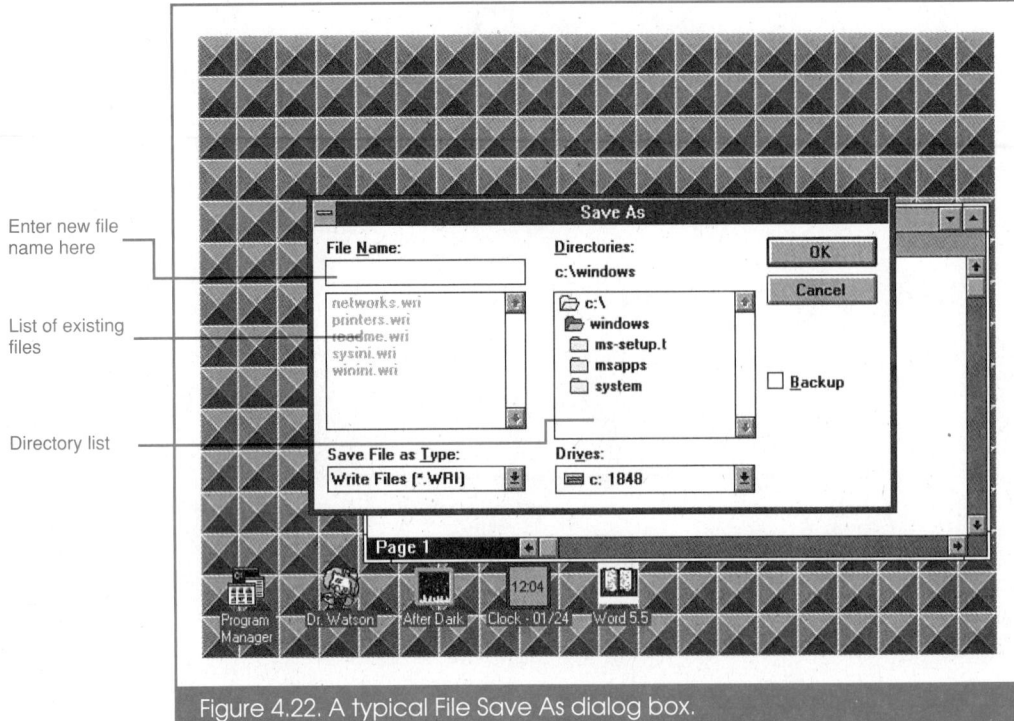

Enter new file
name here

List of existing
files

Directory list

Figure 4.22. A typical File Save As dialog box.

Some programs use *tool palettes* for choosing the type of tool you use in
the program. In a palette, you click a picture of a tool instead of choosing the tool's name from a menu. For example, Figure 4.23 shows the
Paintbrush program that comes with Windows. To use the tool palette
on the left, you click one of the pictures in the squares. If this palette
didn't exist, Paintbrush probably would have a Tools menu listing the
names of all the tools. Most people think that having a tools palette for
drawing programs is easier than making people pull down a menu
whenever they change the tool they are using.

In other programs, the palettes of tools are along the top of the windows, directly under the menu bar. For example, Figure 4.24 shows a
typical Microsoft Excel window. You can use the drop-down list box at
the left to choose from a list of styles. The buttons to the right of this
list are used to perform freguently used tasks without having to access
Excel's menu. For example, you could click a button to align selected
text to the right without having to choose the same command from the
Format menu.

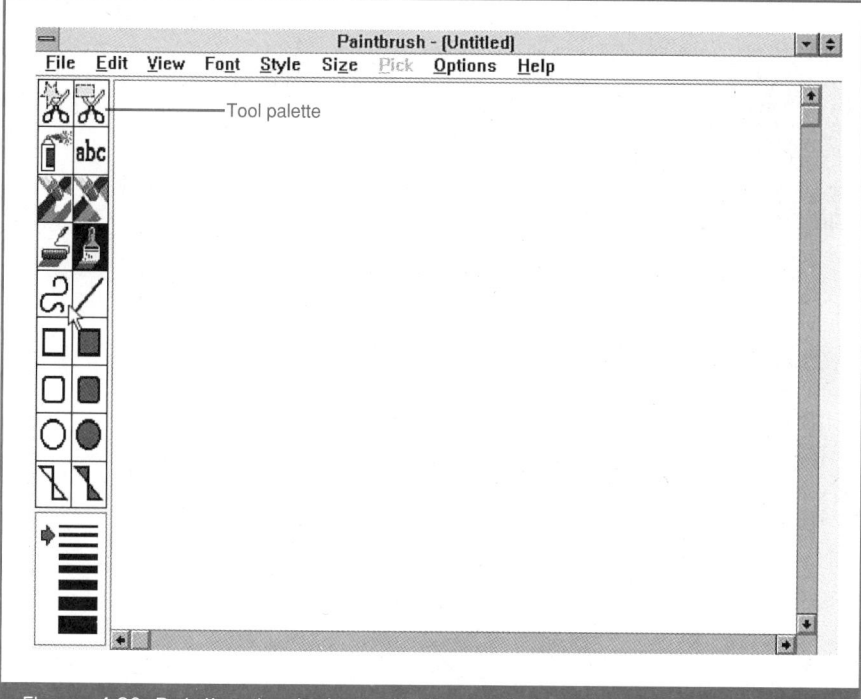

Figure 4.23. Paintbrush window with tool palette.

A few programs use *cascading menus*. These menus appear to the right of the regular menu when you select a command that has a right-facing triangle (see Figure 4.25).

To select a command from a cascading menu with the mouse, drag your way onto the desired option and let go of the left mouse button.

With the keyboard, use the → key to select the cascading menu, then use the usual keystrokes to select items on the menu.

Running Programs

After you first install Windows, the first program you see when you run Windows is Program Manager. It is the tool you use for starting other Windows programs such as File Manager, Windows programs you have bought, and non-Windows programs you may want to run. Chapter 5, "Program Manager," describes the program in detail.

Drop-down list —

Tool bar —

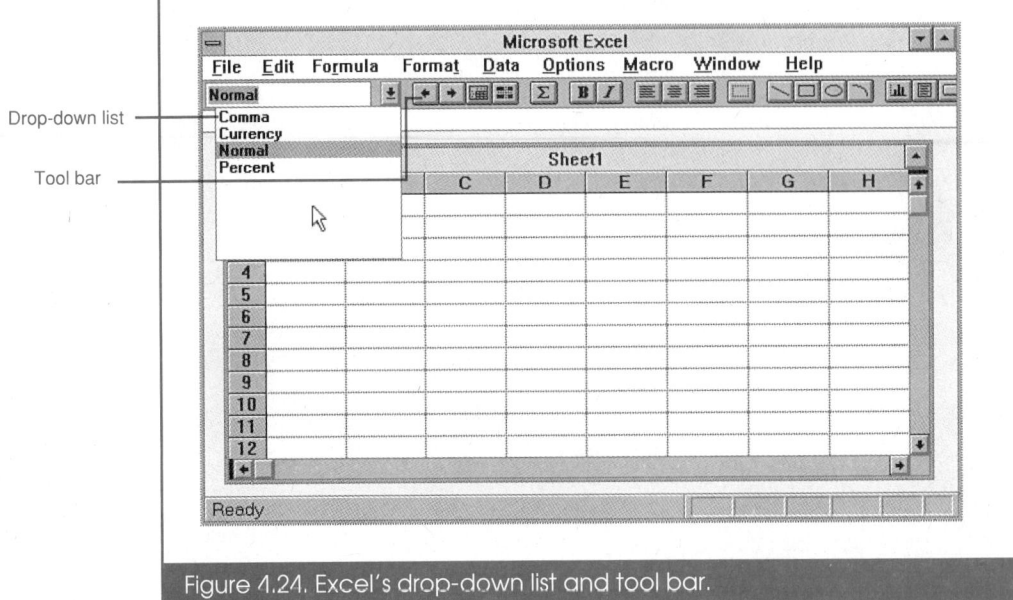

Figure 4.24. Excel's drop-down list and tool bar.

Cascade menu —

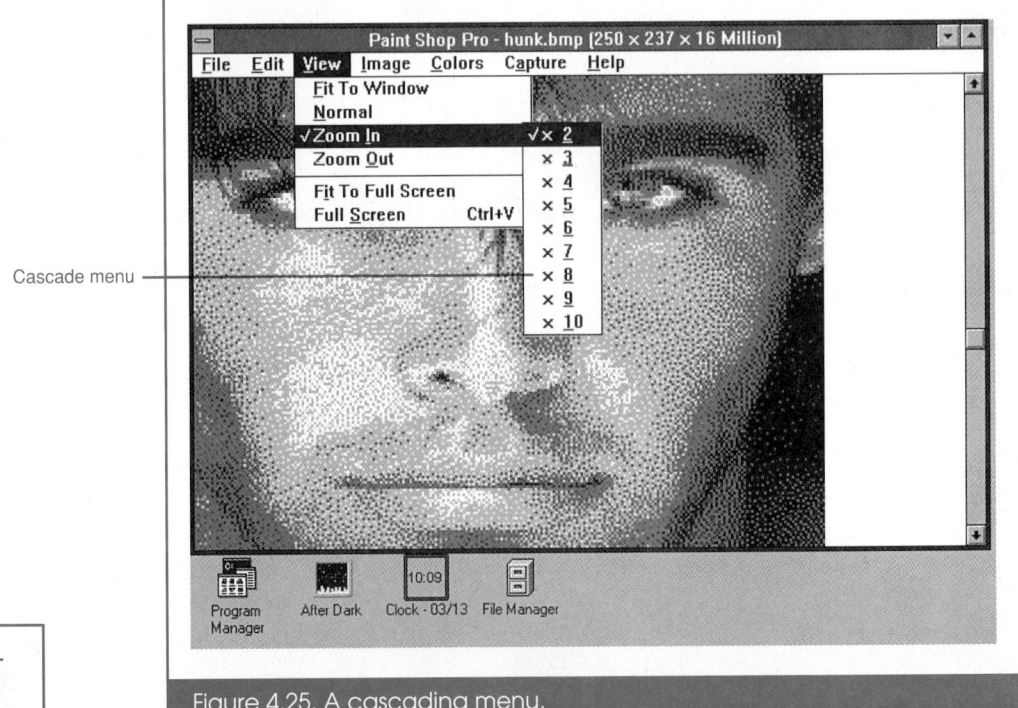

Figure 4.25. A cascading menu.

You do not need to know much about Program Manager to run programs, however. Basically, you find the icon for the program you want in Program Manager and double-click its icon to open it, using the techniques you learned earlier in this chapter. For example, to run the Paintbrush program, you locate its icon on the screen and double-click it. With the keyboard, use the **F**ile **O**pen command.

Active and Inactive Programs

Remember this extremely important concept: When you start a program, Program Manger does not "stop." It is still in memory. You can think of it as being in a layer behind the program you just ran. Many programs can run at the same time in Windows, depending on how much memory is available. Remember, there is a foreground (front) program as well as one or more background (back) programs. You can use Program Manager to switch between them.

Only one program is active at a time. You can have many *inactive* programs; inactive programs can still be doing background processing but are not available for changes unless you activate them.

4

Minimized Programs

You learned earlier in the chapter about how to minimize document windows. You can also minimize program windows when you are not using the program. It makes the programs easier to get to because they are arranged as program or file icons along the bottom of your screen.

To minimize a program with the mouse, click the minimize button (the downward-pointing arrow near the upper-right corner of the program's window).

You can minimize from the keyboard with the Control **Mi**nimize command.

Key board

After you minimize a program, its icon is displayed at the lower-left corner of the screen. For example, Figure 4.26 shows the screen with File Manager and Control Panel minimized.

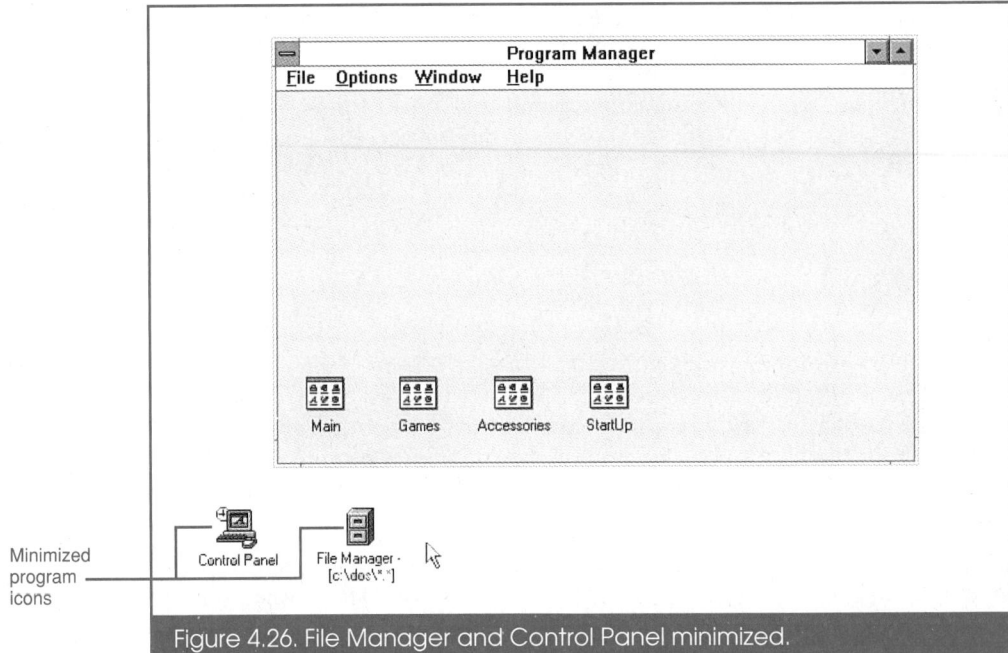

Minimized
program
icons

Figure 4.26. File Manager and Control Panel minimized.

Tip: In most circumstances, minimizing a program does not save any memory. Some programs are better than others about giving up memory when they are minimized. Try taking a look at available memory by selecting Help About from the Program Manager before you minimize a program, and then check it after you minimize. Subtract the second number from the first number and you will learn what has really been saved with that particular application.

Switching Between Programs

When you are running any program (including Program Manager), you can easily switch to other programs that are running. Windows gives you two ways to do this:

▲ Activating the program directly by double-clicking its icon.

▲ Using the Task List

To activate the program directly, if you can see part of the window of the program to which you want to switch, simply click anywhere in that window. If the program has been minimized, double-click the program's icon.

To activate the program directly, press Alt-Esc to cycle through the programs. Each time you press Alt-Esc, Windows makes the next program active. If the program has been minimized, press Alt-Esc until the program's icon is selected, press Alt-Spacebar to show the icon's control menu, and press Enter to give the **R**estore command from that menu.

The second way to switch programs is with the Task List. The Task List is a dialog box like the one shown in Figure 4.27. The items in the list are the programs that are running either as windows or as icons. The Task List is the easiest and quickest way to switch about when several programs are running.

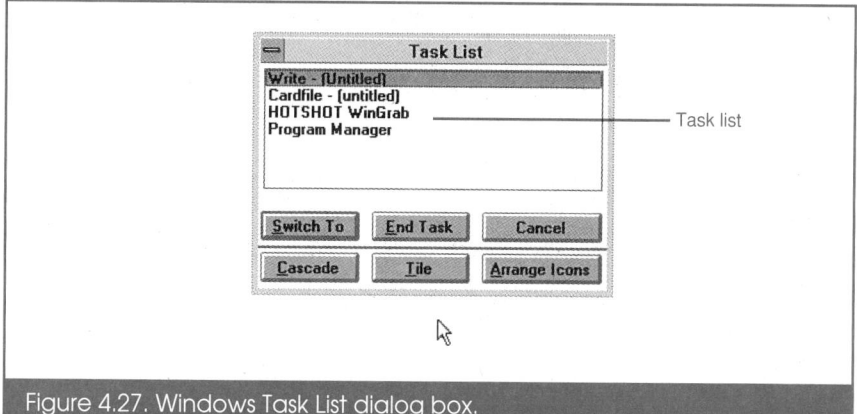

Figure 4.27. Windows Task List dialog box.

To bring up the Task List, double-click anywhere on the Windows desktop (not Program Manager's window background).

Press Ctrl-Esc to bring up the Task List. You also can choose the **S**witch To command in the active program's control menu.

You can use the six buttons at the bottom of the Task List window to perform various actions. Table 4.1 lists the actions these buttons perform.

Table 4.1. Task List buttons.

Button	Action
Switch To	Causes the selected program to become active
End Task	Closes the selected program
Cancel	Closes the Task List
Cascade	Rearranges the program windows, each partly covering the other
Tile	Rearranges the program windows so that they take up equal-sized rectangular areas of the screen
Arrange Icons	Rearranges the icons of minimized programs

Tip: The Task List is a handy way of stopping a program that has become "frozen." Bring up the Task List, select the program in the list, and click the **E**nd Task button.

Getting Help

Microsoft—realizing that even though Windows itself is easy to use, some programs would be difficult for some people—decided that there should be a standard way to get help at any time, so you could see your choices. With a single way to look for help, you are less likely to panic or run to the manuals, because you can get information quickly.

To run the Help program with the mouse, give the **Help Index** command.

To run Help from the keyboard, press F1. You can do this at any time in most programs.

Basic Use of the Help Program

The **Help** window is like other program windows. It has scroll bars, maximize and minimize buttons, and so on. Windows initially opens the **Help** window rather small; you may want to make it larger or even maximize it so that it fills the screen. If you resize the Help window, it opens to the new size the next time you ask for help.

To look at the **H**elp text and graphics in the window, scroll with the mouse or the keyboard. In **H**elp, you can scroll line-by-line with the ↑ and ↓ keys or screen-by-screen with the PgUp and PgDn keys. Two special types of words and phrases appear in **H**elp: *jump terms* and *definitions*.

Underlined text is called a jump term because selecting it causes you to jump to some associated text. To jump to the text associated with a jump term, click it with the mouse or select it by pressing Tab and then Enter. This takes you to a different part of the **H**elp text.

Text with a dotted underline is a definition; selecting this text opens a temporary window that defines the term. You select a definition by clicking and holding down the mouse button or by moving to the definition with the Tab key and holding down the Enter key. As soon as you let go of the mouse button or the Enter key, the definition window disappears.

When you are finished with **H**elp, give the **F**ile E**x**it command or press Alt-F4.

4

Navigating in Help

Help information is kept in many windows. You can scroll to the bottom of the initial **H**elp window and see only a fraction of the information available. To see more information, you follow paths of interesting topics or choose topics by searching for them.

The easiest way to navigate is to choose jump terms. When you choose a jump term, **H**elp shows you a different screen of information, with jump terms you probably want to see. For example, assume that you run **H**elp from Program Manager and you want information on the commands in the **O**ptions menu. To see an index of what is available for the **O**ptions Menu, select the Options Menu Commands jump term (see Figure 4.28). When you place the pointer over a Jump Term, the pointer changes from an arrow tip to a hand icon. The hand icon serves the same purpose as a normal pointer.

Sometimes when you jump to an area of **H**elp, such as `Organize Applications and Documents`, you will see additional topics to choose from—for example, `Moving a Program Item`. These screens can be thought of as levels within the **H**elp menu.

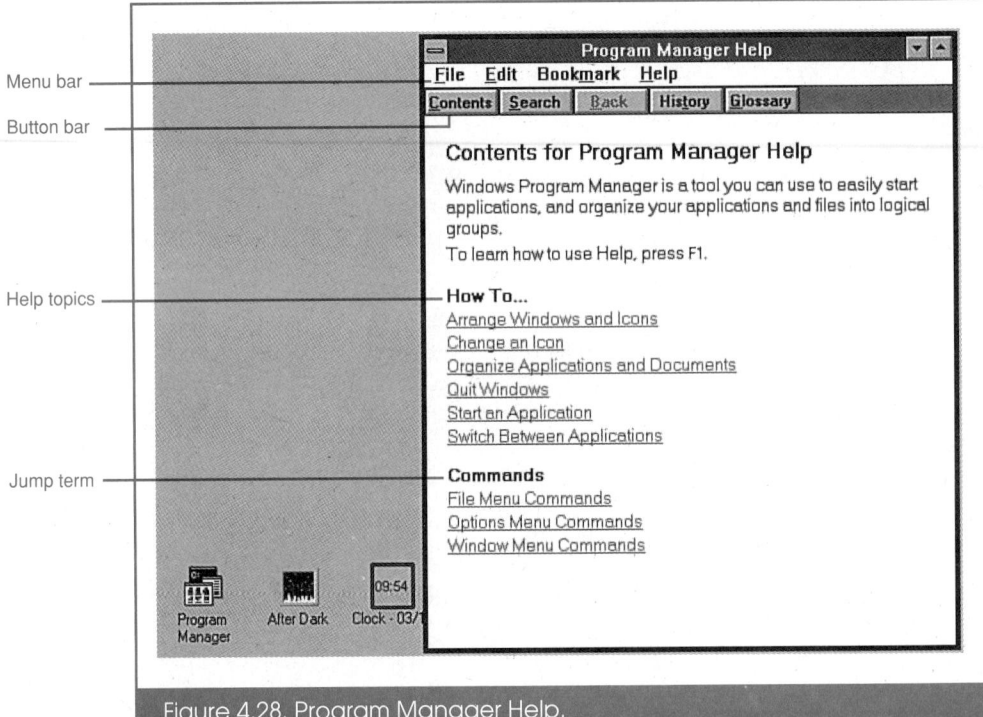

Menu bar

Button bar

Help topics

Jump term

Figure 4.28. Program Manager Help.

Help gives you an easy way to backtrack to where you were. The **Back** button at the top of the screen takes you back one step in the search process. You can press the **Back** button (or Alt-B) repeatedly to retrace your steps in the **Help** system. If you want to jump to the main index quickly, click the **Contents** button or press Alt-C.

A quick way to find what you want is to search for a word or phrase, using the **Search** button or Alt-S. This action brings up a dialog box like the one shown in Figure 4.29. You can scroll through the list of defined search topics to select the one closest to what interests you. When you select **Search**, the topics found are displayed by **Help** in the bottom part of the dialog box. You then select one of the topics and go to it directly.

Tip: Another way to look through **Help** for a program is to browse with the two browse buttons (or press Alt-R and Alt-O). These buttons show you the previous and next **Help** windows. Note that because the connections between windows usually are not very good, browsing does not give you much of a sense of order.

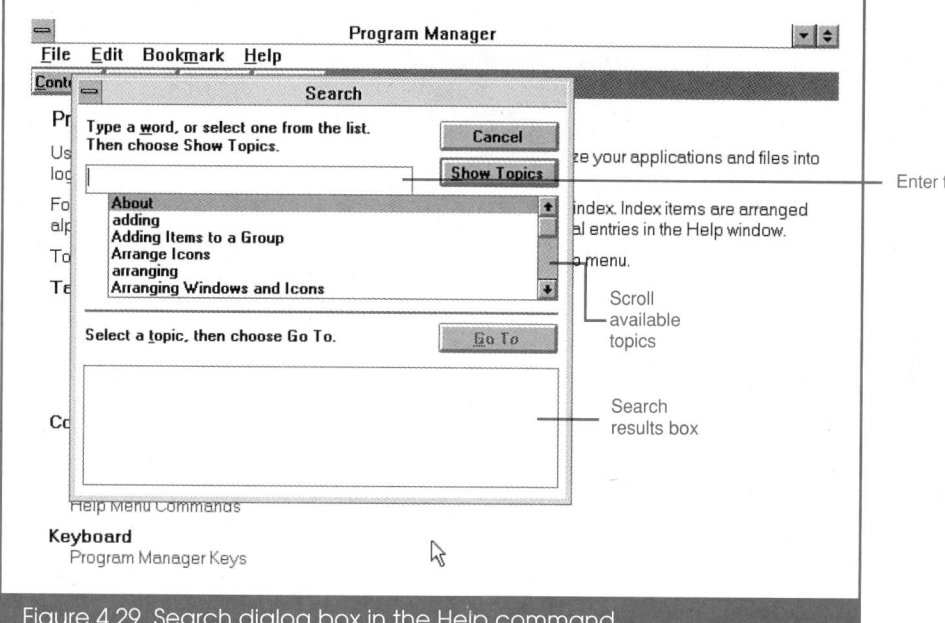

Figure 4.29. Search dialog box in the Help command.

Advanced Help Use

You may think that a help system should be as simple as possible and that the procedures just mentioned would be sufficient. Microsoft realized that advanced users also would be using **H**elp and provided additional features that most beginning users ignore. These features make **H**elp even more flexible and useful to people who are familiar with using Windows and who use **H**elp with other programs.

Frequently, you will want to add your own information to the **H**elp system. For example, if many people use the same computer, you may want to leave instructions about the way a particular procedure is followed at your company. You may want to leave notes to yourself also, but this is not as common as leaving notes for others. With the **E**dit **A**nnotate command, you can enter text that is associated with a particular **H**elp topic. Figure 4.30 shows the dialog box for the **E**dit **A**nnotate command.

After you enter the text, a paper clip icon appears next to the topic. Later, when you select the paper clip, **H**elp opens a window that shows the text you entered. You can tell people using your system to always look at the paper clips they come across when using **Help**, because these items are of special importance to your system. This feature of Help is especially useful to network administrators who can impart company policy regarding PCs to employees on the network.

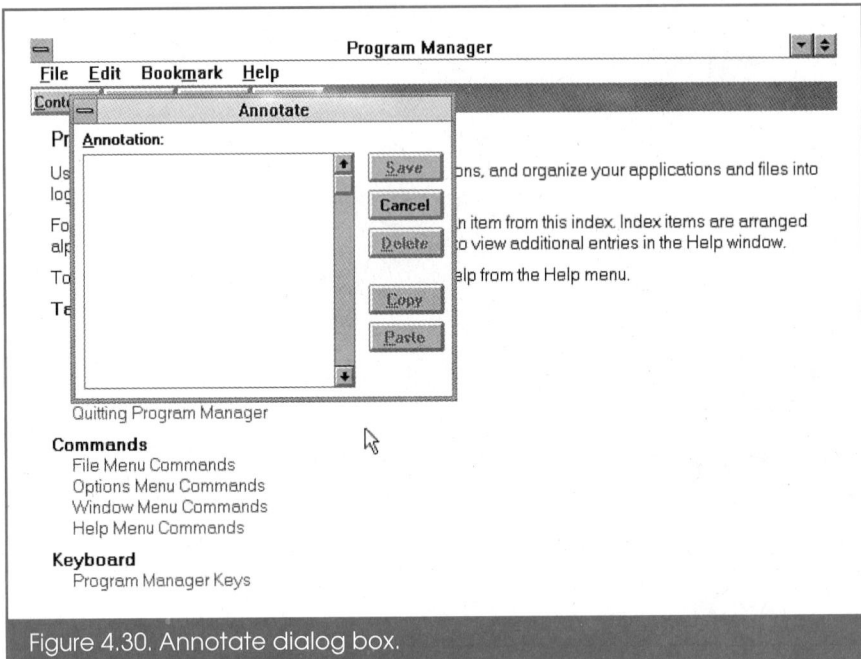

Figure 4.30. Annotate dialog box.

You may want to be able to come back quickly to certain places in a **Help** document. (If you were reading a book, you might put small bookmarks in those places.) You can use the Book**m**ark **D**efine command to place such a bookmark and give it any name you want. Later, you can look at the Book**m**ark menu and see the names of the book-marks you have defined. Selecting those commands causes **Help** to jump directly to those **Help** topics. For example, Figure 4.31 shows how to make a bookmark named Keyboard Entry in the Book**m**ark **D**efine command.

The Book**m**ark menu can hold as many as nine bookmark names. If you have more than nine bookmarks, the Book**m**ark **M**ore command has a list of all the bookmarks you can choose from.

You can use the **F**ile **O**pen command to open a different **Help** file than the one already open. In this way you can look at the **Help** information for many different programs without having to run those programs.

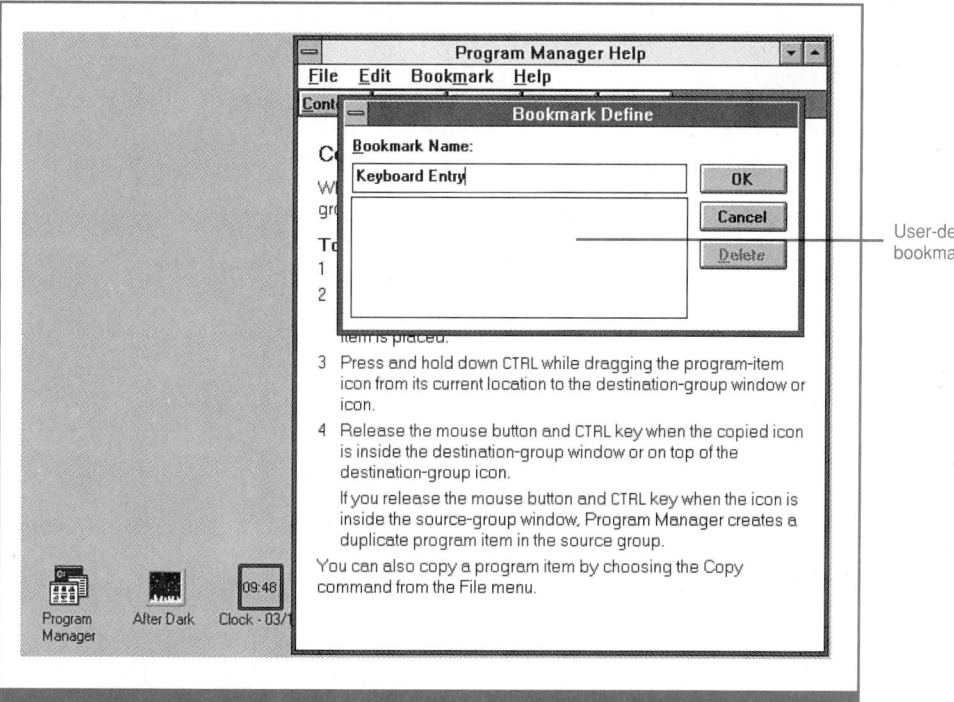

Figure 4.31. Defining with the Bookmark Define command.

You can print the current help with the **F**ile **P**rint Topic command. With the **F**ile **Pr**inter Setup command, you can pick a printer and the printing attributes you will use.

The **E**dit **C**opy command puts a copy of the current window in the Clipboard so that you can use it in other Windows programs. See Chapter 9, "Clipboard Viewer," for more information. A network administrator or IS person could use this feature to insert internal user support information, like the ADMIN's Name, Extension, and/or pager number to be used in the event of a down-system occurence.

Basic Windows Programs

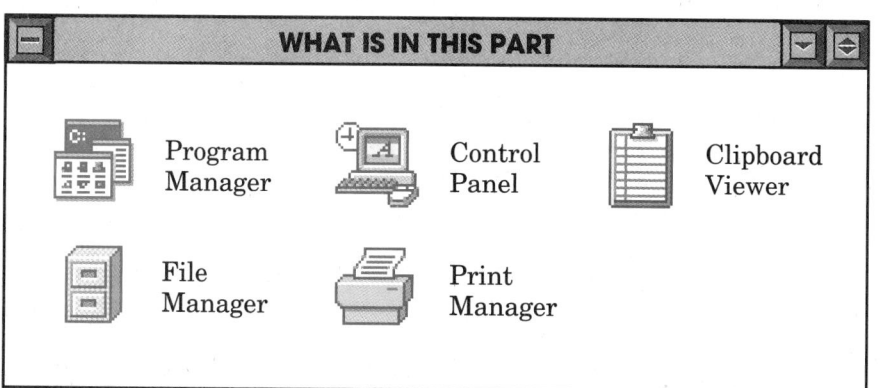

WHAT IS IN THIS PART		
Program Manager	Control Panel	Clipboard Viewer
File Manager	Print Manager	

P A R T

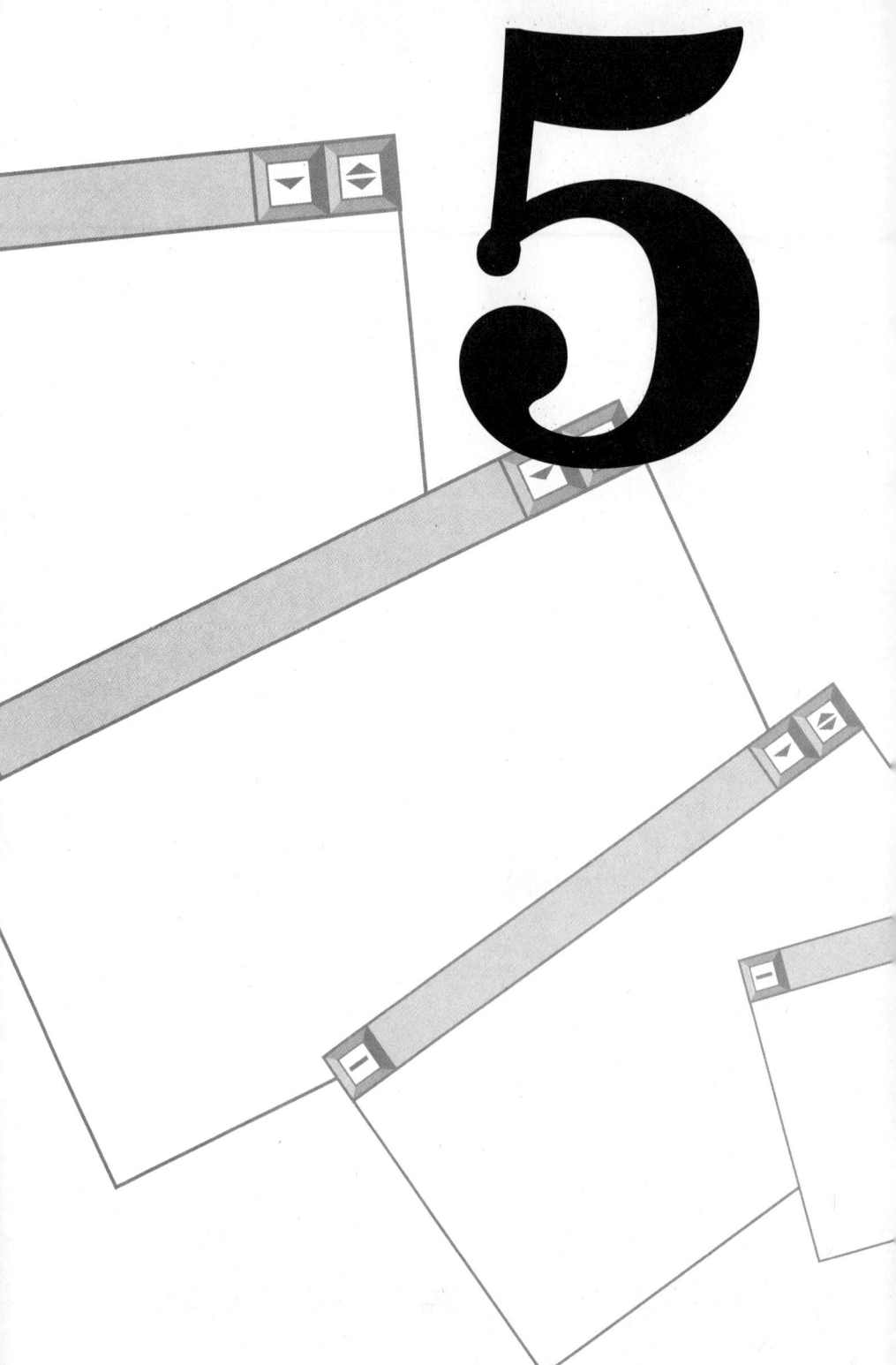

Program Manager

The primary task you perform with Windows is running applications. Windows itself would not be very interesting if it could not run programs. This chapter describes how you use several programs simultaneously within Windows. Although many people start by using Windows as a multitasking task switcher, the environment has many enabling capabilities that set it apart from other competent multitasking programs. The most common way to run programs is from Program Manager—the program that runs when you start Windows. The methods you use with Program Manager are the same as the ones you use with all Windows programs.

Although Program Manager is fine for most Windows users, it is not the last word in program management. Many companies have developed Windows programs that replace Program Manager by offering more flexibility and more information. Windows Express, from hDC Computer Corporation, is just such a program. With Windows Express you can arrange applications and files into folders displayed on the screen. More of these programs are described in detail in Chapter 30, "Windows for Advanced Users."

Tip: You can change Windows so that you do not see Program Manager when you start Windows. You may have bought a program, such as Norton Desktop for Windows, that replaces Program Manager, or you simply may want to run another program first. See Chapter 27, "Configuring with the WIN.INI and SYSTEM.INI Files," for information on how to cause some other program to be the first one run.

Introduction to Program Manager

Although Program Manager is just another Windows program, it deserves attention because it is like a control center for your Windows work. Most people use it as a central starting and stopping point for their work with Windows programs. Because you see it first when Windows starts, you probably associate it closely with Windows. It is just one view of the Windows environment; File Manager (discussed in Chapter 6, "File Manager") is another view.

Microsoft, recognizing that people would be using Program Manager a great deal, worked hard to make the Windows 3.1 Program Manager flexible. You can customize the look of Program Manager to suit your particular wishes and work patterns. This becomes especially important if you use many different Windows programs, because you can use Program Manager to keep each application's files and documents well organized and easy to manage.

As you read this chapter, remember that the main purpose of Program Manager is to make starting programs easier for you. Specifically, think about how you will use Program Manager to make your work easier by helping you organize your programs and the documents you use with them. No single style or placement of programs and icons is correct. Just work with windows and icons in the manner that makes the most sense to you. You can always change your arrangements later.

The Program Manager Window

Unless you have placed an icon in the StartUp group window, when you start Windows 3.1 you first see Program Manager with its Main window open. Figure 5.1 is something like the view you see right after you

use the Setup program to install Windows. The initial size of the Program Manager window is about one-half to three-quarters the size of your screen.

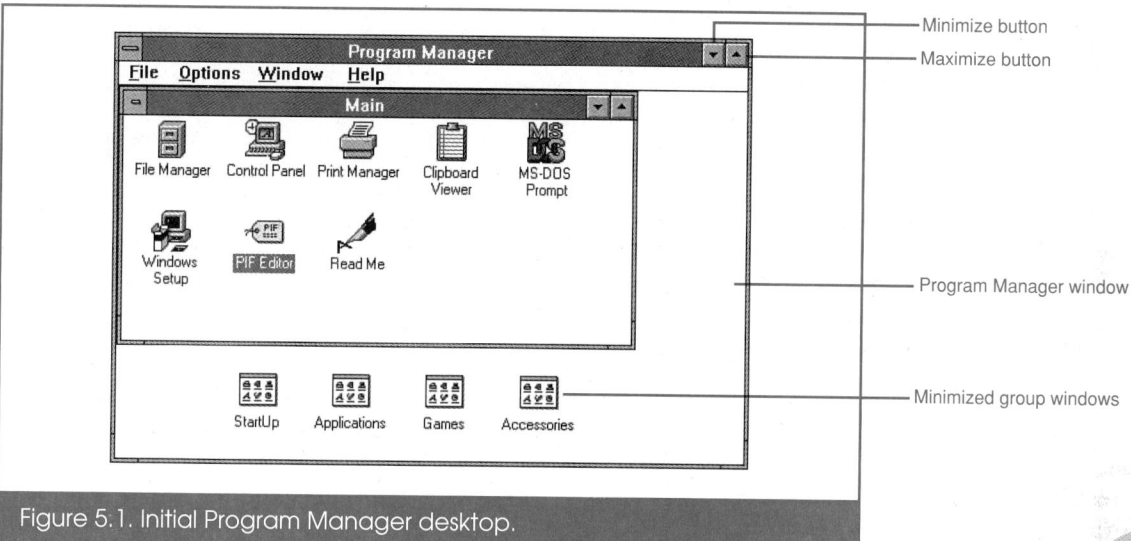

Figure 5.1. Initial Program Manager desktop.

When you install Windows, it creates the five icons listed in Table 5.1. These are called *program groups* because they hold related programs. At startup, the Main program group is open at first, but you can open the other windows easily. Each of the four icons below the Main window opens to reveal another window with a different grouping of programs.

Table 5.1. Initial Program Manager icons.

Icon	Contents
StartUp	Any icons in this group run on startup
Main	Primary programs that come with Windows
Accessories	Other programs that come with Windows
Applications	Programs that you work with
Games	Game programs that come with Windows

With the exception of the StartUp group, each program group consists of icons that represent programs or documents. For example, the icons in the Main program group represent the File Manager program, the

Control Panel program, and so on. The Read Me icon represents a document called README.TXT, which contains late-breaking information that didn't make it into the Windows manual. You can open README.TXT from within Notepad or by using any word processor.

You can open a window represented by an icon by double-clicking the icon. You also can click the icon to bring up the window's Control menu, then select the **R**estore command.

Press Alt-W and the ↓ key to select the icon from the **W**indow menu. Note that the windows are numbered. To open a window quickly from this menu, type its number.

Program Manager Menus

The commands in Program Manager are basic and easy to use. The commands in the **F**ile menu, shown in Figure 5.2, mostly relate to icons. You use these commands to create new icons, move them to different windows, and so on. Table 5.2 explains the **F**ile menu in more detail.

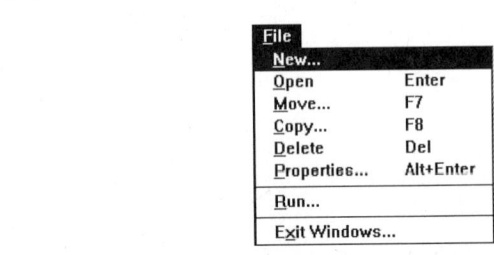

Figure 5.2. You control icons by using the File menu.

Table 5.2. File menu options.

Command	Function
New	Makes new groups or icons
Open	Opens the application that displays highlighted text
Move	Moves one icon from one group to another

Command	Function
Copy	Makes a copy of the highlighted icon in another group of your choice
Delete	Permanently removes an icon or a group
Properties	Changes details about choosing icons and the location of applications
Run	Brings up a text window so that you can enter a program name if you don't want an icon created
E**x**it Windows	Windows command used for leaving Windows

You use the **O**ptions menu, shown in Figure 5.3 and detailed in Table 5.3, to tell Windows some of your preferences.

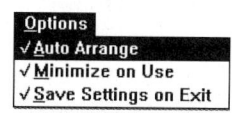

Figure 5.3. Preferences are maintained from the Options menu.

Table 5.3. Options menu selections.

Command	Function
Auto Arrange	Automatically keeps icons properly spaced
Minimize on Use	Causes the last program used to revert to an icon upon closing
Save Settings on Exit	Determines whether your changes to the environment will be saved on exit

The **W**indow menu, shown in Figure 5.4 and explained in Table 5.4, enables you to change the arrangement of windows and icons and to activate specific windows.

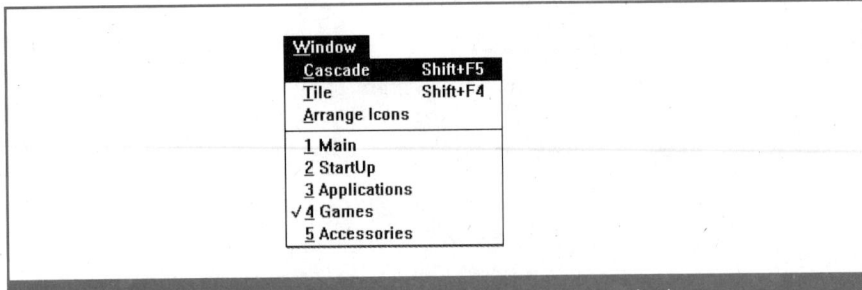

Figure 5.4. Use the Window menu to cycle between windows.

Table 5.4. Window menu options.

Command	Function
Cascade	Displays a set of windows below and to the right of each other
Tile	Divides the screen equally between visible windows
Arrange Icons	Spaces icons manually
Available groups	List of group windows names

The **H**elp menu gives you several ways to get help. The available selections are shown in Figure 5.5 and listed in Table 5.5. **H**elp is described in detail in the "Getting Help" section of Chapter 4, "Basic Windows Concepts."

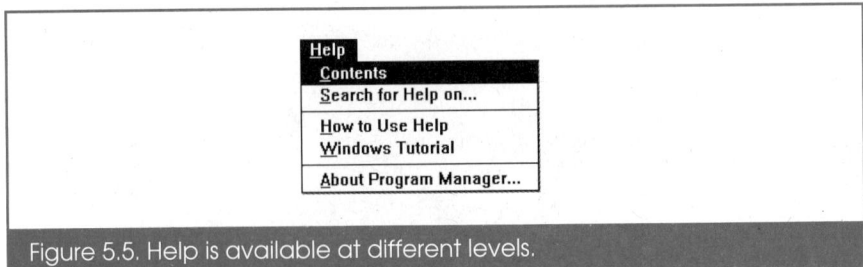

Figure 5.5. Help is available at different levels.

Table 5.5. Help menu options.

Command	Function
Contents	Displays a table of contents of topics covered by Help, arranged into two groups—How To and Menu Commands.
Search for Help On	Displays a detailed alphabetical list of topics, from which you can pick a topic.
How to Use Help	Provides tips and techniques for using Help.
Windows Tutorial	Presents a tutorial in two lessons—Mouse Basics and Windows Basics.
About Program Manager	Information about your copy of Program Manager, what mode it's operating in, how much memory is free, and how many of your system resources are available.

Arranging Your Windows

Moving windows in Program Manager is just like moving them in other Windows programs. You use the same methods you learned in Chapter 4, "Basic Windows Concepts." You can minimize, maximize, and resize windows.

Program Manager has two commands that help you arrange your windows if you do not want to move them by yourself. The **W**indow **C**ascade and **W**indow **T**ile commands rearrange all open windows automatically.

Figure 5.6 shows the result of cascading three open windows. The window that is active when you give the command remains the active window.

The **W**indow **T**ile command reshapes the windows so that they take up the entire Program Manager window, each with the same amount of window area. As you can see from Figure 5.7, this rearrangement usually cuts off your view of some of the icons. You must issue the **T**ile command every time you add windows to your display screen.

5

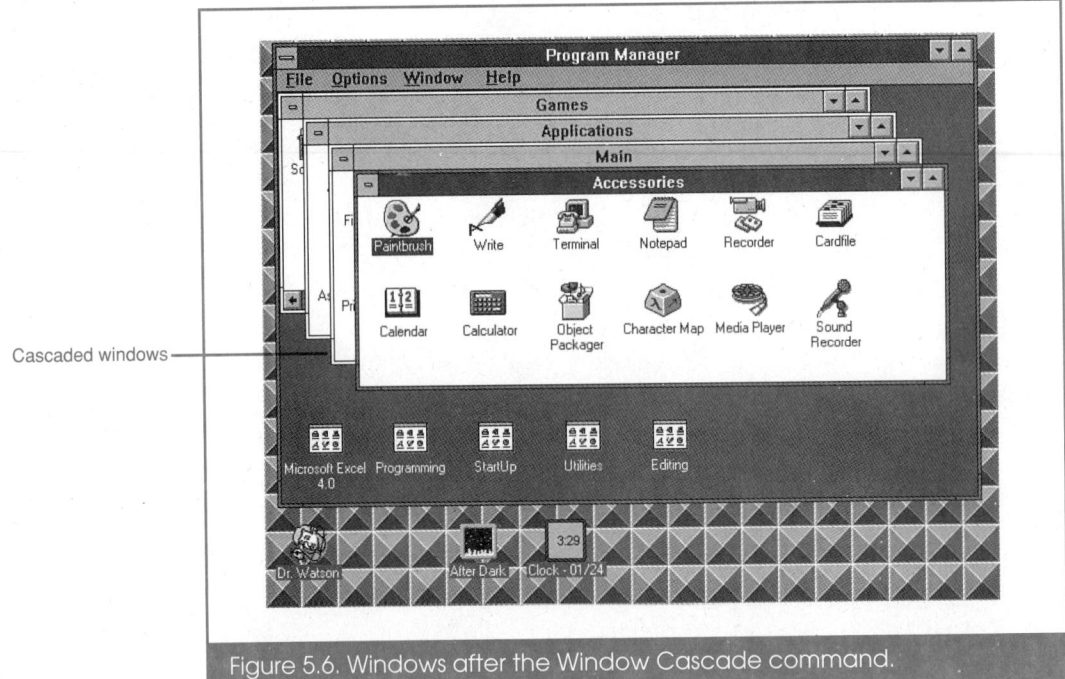

Cascaded windows ——

Figure 5.6. Windows after the Window Cascade command.

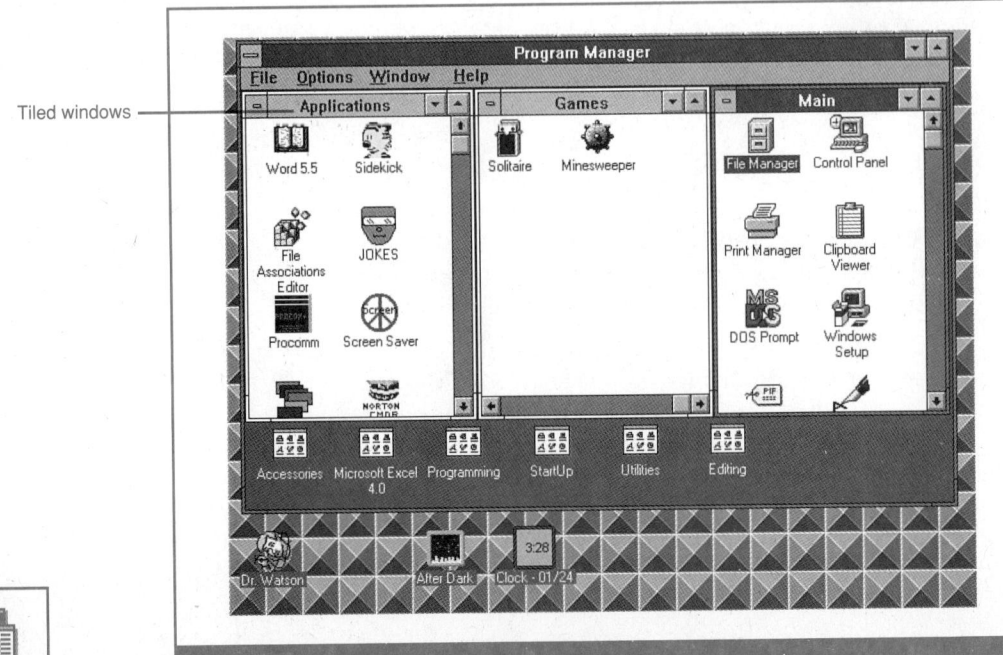

Tiled windows ——

Figure 5.7. Windows after the Window Tile command.

Running Programs

The most common way to run programs is to select programs that are represented by icons. When you install Windows, Setup installs all the icons it knows about. You will see later in this chapter how to install more icons.

Using Icons to Launch Programs

For you to launch a program from its icon, the icon must be in an open, active window. Running a program from its icon is referred to also as *opening* the icon. If the icon you want to select is not open, first open that window. Note that the actions you take are the same whether the icon represents a program, a document, or a program and many documents.

To run a program from its icon, simply double-click the icon. Or you can select the icon by clicking it (to highlight that icon) and then giving the **F**ile **O**pen command.

To run a program from the keyboard, select the icon in the window by using the ↑, ↓, ←, and → keys, then press Enter. Or select the icon and then use the **F**ile **O**pen command (press the Alt-F-O key combination).

5

After a program has been opened, the position of the program's window on the screen depends on how many programs you have run in this Windows session. Windows automatically moves each program down a bit on the screen. This makes finding the programs easier but also causes their windows to be progressively smaller.

Some programs remember their position on-screen when you last left them and open in the same location. If you maximize a program before quitting, it probably will be maximized when you start it again. (Note, however, that none of the programs that come with Windows has this feature.)

Using the File Run Command

You do not have to have an icon to run a program. If a program you want to run does not have an icon, use the **F**ile **R**un command. In the Command Line text-entry box of the **F**ile **R**un dialog box (see Figure 5.8), you enter the command line you would otherwise type at the DOS prompt.

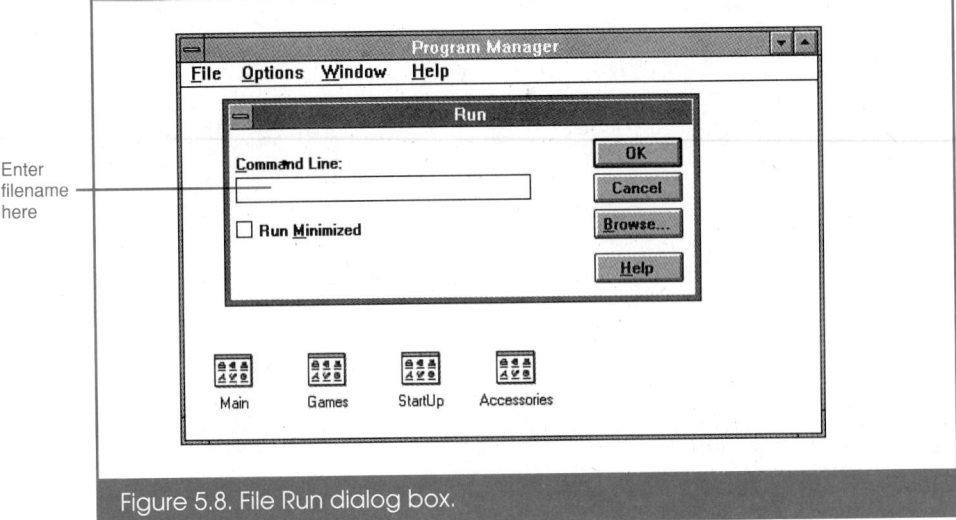

Figure 5.8. File Run dialog box.

File Run is a command-line dialog box that enables you to enter the name of a program to run, if, for example, you have just installed it on your hard drive and Windows does not know it is there. If the program you want to run is not in the main Windows directory or in your MS-DOS path, you can include the full path specification for the program. You can include any command-line options you want in the **File Run** command.

If you don't know what the exact filename spelling is or if you don't know where your program is lurking, you can click the Browse button to see a subset of File Manager. You can then proceed to look through your directories and files in order to find the program you want. When you do, double-click the filename and the Run text box will reappear with the filename inserted in the space provided for executable filenames.

You can run the program minimized by checking that option in the dialog box. When you check Run Minimized, the program loads but does not run until you double-click the appropriate icon at the bottom of your screen. Run Minimized makes a program readily available for future use by loading it into memory without your having to type it if you want to reuse a program that has no icon.

Running your programs minimized makes every program visible. You can see each application's minimized icon if it is minimized. You may not remember that you have an application open if it is hidden behind other windows. Minimizing applications that are not in the foreground can also help reduce screen clutter. Of course, you can arrange windows and icons to suit your personal preferences.

> **Tip:** Program Manager will not remember to keep an icon available after you have minimized and then exited Windows 3.1. You must *create* an icon to be sure that you have an icon available for that program when you start Windows again. Creating icons is discussed later in this chapter.

Customizing Your Icons

If Windows installs your applications at the end of the Setup program, it assigns an icon to each application. For Windows programs, the icon comes from the .EXE or .COM file that starts the application. For non-Windows applications, Setup assigns one of its default icons. You can customize the way these icons identify each program. Each icon has four characteristics you can control.

1. Visual: the look of the icon (the picture you see)

2. Textual: the name beneath the icon

3. Operational: the program and document that run when you open the icon

4. Geographical: the location of the icon (the window it is in and its position in the window)

The first three of these characteristics are set with the **F**ile **P**roperties command. The fourth characteristic is discussed later in this chapter in the section on windows and their contents.

An icon's appearance, name, and action can be modified easily by using the **F**ile **P**roperties command. For example, click the Read Me icon in the Main window and then issue the **F**ile **P**roperties command. The dialog box you see is shown in Figure 5.9. The title for this icon is the filename. The icon itself is assigned to the Notepad program. When you double-click this icon, Notepad is opened, and the README.TXT file is visible on-screen.

5

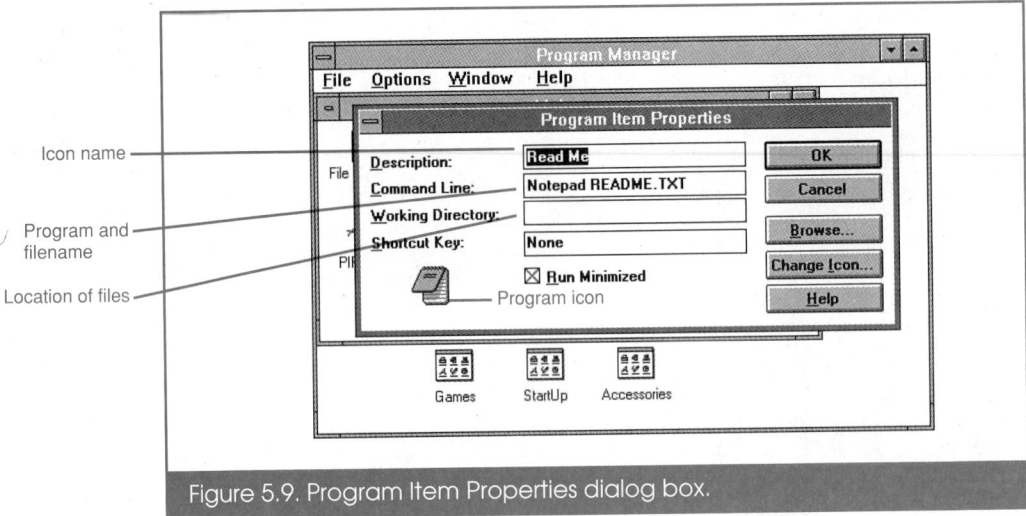

Figure 5.9. Program Item Properties dialog box.

Icon Name

The Description entry is the name that appears under the icon in the Program Manager window. The name can be up to 40 characters long. Generally, you want to use a descriptive name, one that tells you what will happen when you open the icon.

Command Line

The Command Line entry is where you enter the command you want executed when the icon is opened. The command line can be one of three types:

▲ *The name of the program*, such as EXCEL.EXE. If the program is in a directory that is not in your MS-DOS search path, you must include the path to the program file, such as C:\EXCEL3*EXCEL*. This is the most common type of command-line entry.

▲ *The name of the program and document*, such as C:\EXCEL3\EXCEL\ORDERS*BACKORD.XLS*. In this case, the most common argument is the name of one or more documents. In the example you saw earlier with the Read Me properties, NOTEPAD.EXE is the program name and README.TXT is the document to display.

▲ *Just a document name*. You can use just a document name if you are using Windows's extension-searching capabilities (see the section on extensions in Chapter 27, "Configuring with the WIN.INI and SYSTEM.INI Files"). Many programs have predefined file extensions; the Notepad program, for example, has files with the extension .TXT. If the extension of the document name you enter in the command-line entry box is in the list of known extensions, Windows runs the program associated with that extension.

Working Directory

The Working Directory is the place where your program saves files and looks for them when you need them. It's only the first place to look. If one of your directories is not in the path, Windows needs to know where to look for document or work files. You can specify a directory other than the one where the actual program resides. Some people organize their work files in separate subdirectories by task subject, like "Work" or "Home." You need to use the Working Directory text box to specify the name of the directory where work files reside.

Shortcut Key

5

The Shortcut Key text box is provided so that you can specify a keystroke or keystroke combination you want to use to bring a running application (either in a window or minimized to an icon) to the foreground and make it active. Take care to avoid assigning the same shortcut key to more than one program.

Browsing for Files

If you do not know the path to the program you want to use in the command-line entry, the **B**rowse button is handy. When you click that button, you see the dialog box shown in Figure 5.10. You can use the standard methods you learned in Chapter 4, "Basic Windows Concepts," to search through directories for the program you want. When you double-click the filename or click the OK button, Windows pastes the name you chose in the command-line text box in the Properties dialog box.

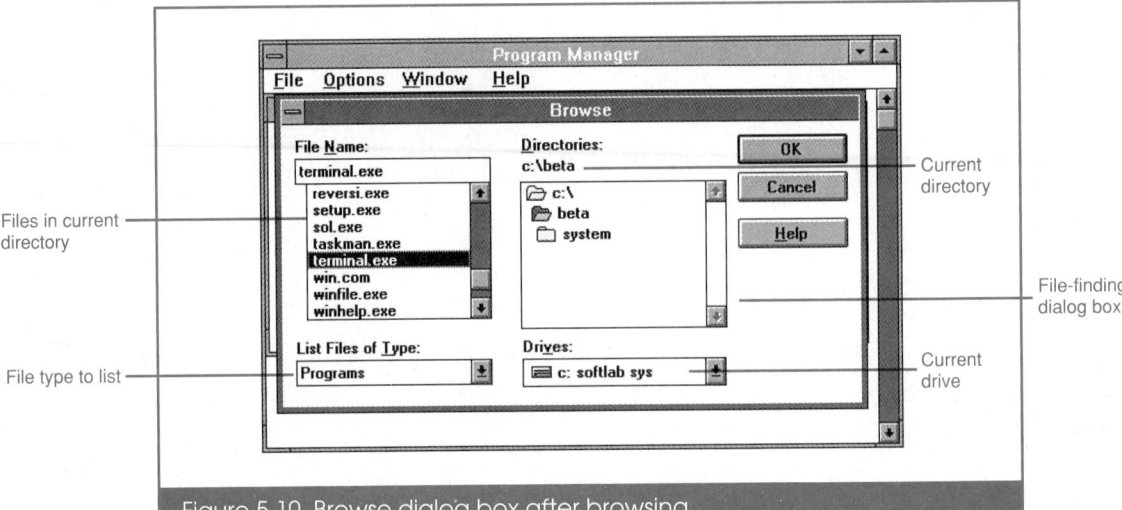

Files in current directory

File type to list

Current directory

File-finding dialog box

Current drive

Figure 5.10. Browse dialog box after browsing.

Tip: If you enter just a document name in the command-line entry, Windows starts the program with the program's directory location as the directory of the document. This is convenient if you are going to open documents and save them to that directory. If you like to organize *all* types of files by subject or perhaps by project name, it's best to enter the Drive and Directory names in the working directory dialog entry.

Selecting a Different Icon

When you add a new program, Windows chooses the first icon picture in the program file as the picture you see in Program Manager. Many programs come with more than one icon, however; you can choose the one you want to appear in Program Manager. To choose the picture you want, click the Change Icon button. For example, if you select the File Manager icon in the Main window, give the File Properties command, and click Change Icon, you see the dialog box shown in Figure 5.11.

Icons are displayed from left to right. If all available icons do not fit into the icon area, you can use the scroll bar to see more of them. To see icons that can be accessed by other means, click the Browse button. When you click the Browse button, you see the dialog box shown in Figure 5.12.

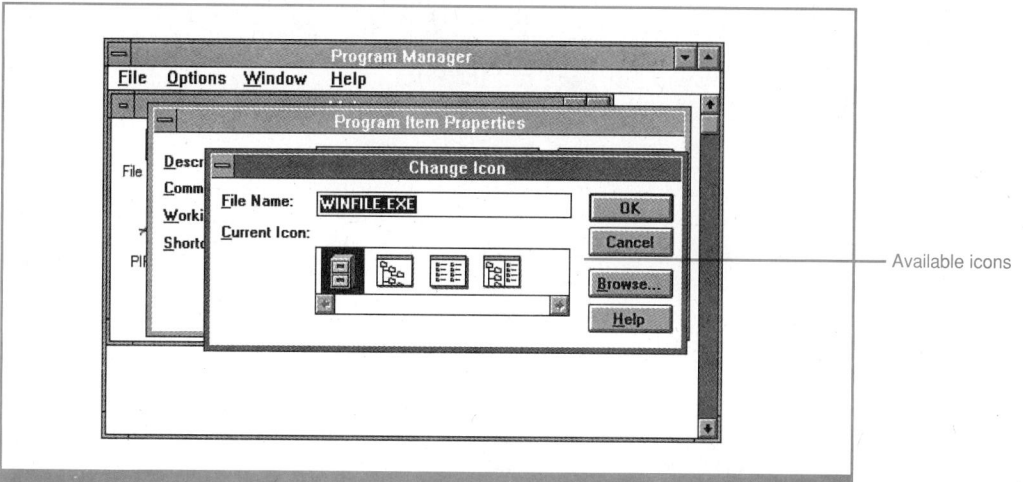

Available icons

Figure 5.11. Change Icon dialog box.

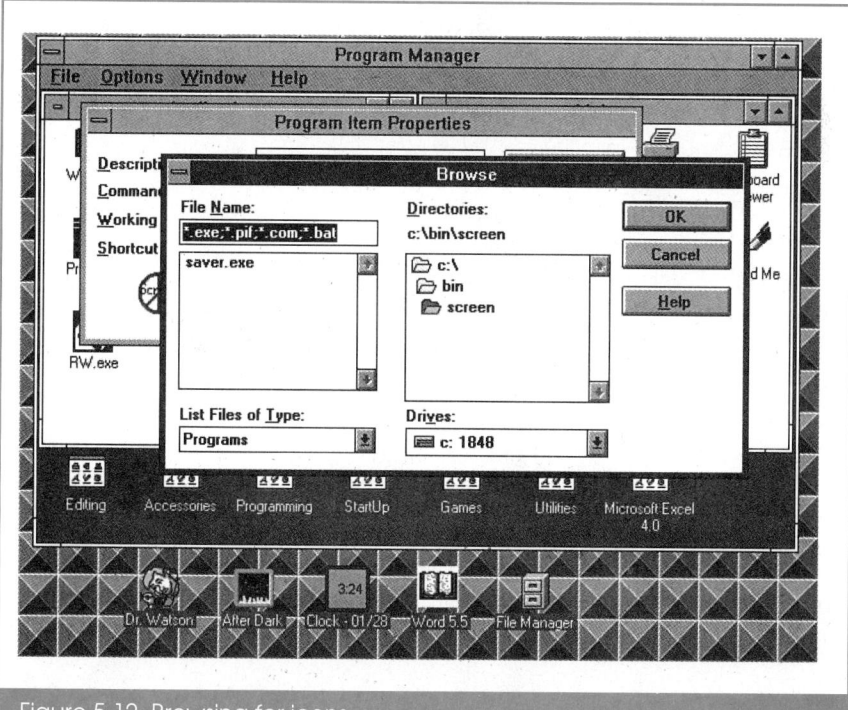

5

Figure 5.12. Browsing for icons.

You can choose to browse only files with an extension of .EXE, .DLL, or .ICO, sorted by these file types, or you can browse all files (*.*). Click the vertical scroll bar used to List Files of Type (at the dialog box's lower-left). .EXE (*executable*) files often contain embedded icons drawn for the specific .EXE file.

.DLL (*dynamic link library*) files can contain several icons. .ICO files are small files created to provide just one icon. The .ICO filename often indicates what sort of icon you may expect to see when you use it. If you run out of icons to access or just get bored with your choices, you may want to investigate several icon vendors at the shareware and private levels that offer libraries of premade icons for your applications. Several companies offer icon-creation tools for the hard-to-please user. hDC Computer Corporation sells an icon creation and editing tool called Icon Designer that is very popular.

Program Manager comes with many more icons than did PM for Windows 3.0. If you can't find an icon in PM that pleases, browse until you find the MORICONS.DLL file. This dynamic link library is host to many additional icons that are, in many cases, application-specific.

To change the icon associated with a program, choose the file you would like to browse through from the file list in the Browse dialog box. Click OK and you are returned to the Change Icon dialog box, shown in Figure 5.13.

Tip: Many free, shareware, and commercial icon packages are available. These packages consist of one or more files that contain dozens (often hundreds) of icons. To use any of these, simply enter the name of the file in the **F**ile Name section to choose the icon you want. Windows programs are also referenced in Reference C, "Windows Product Directory," at the end of this book.

Adding New Windows

The Windows Setup program is unlikely to provide enough group windows for you. You might want to have one window for each major project you are working on, or one window for each program and the documents you often use with that program. The number and arrangement of windows in Program Manager are strictly your decision.

You can add a new group or program window simply by giving the **F**ile **N**ew command and selecting the Program **G**roup option. You then see the dialog box shown in Figure 5.13.

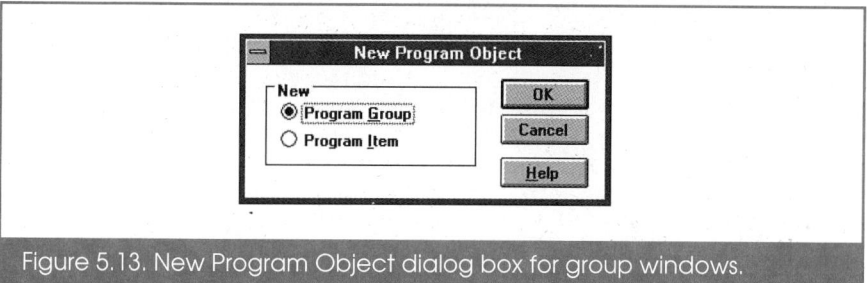

Figure 5.13. New Program Object dialog box for group windows.

The **D**escription text box enables you to enter a name for the window as it will appear in the title bar and under the minimized icon. The **G**roup File is the name of the file in which Windows keeps all the icon information. You do not need to give a group filename because Windows makes one up for you if you leave this option blank. When you click OK, Windows creates a new, empty window into which you can add program icons.

Changing a Window's Title

To change a window's title, use the **F**ile **P**roperties command. Before you give the command, however, you must minimize the window and then select it.

To change the window title, type over the description and click OK. Window titles, like icon titles, should be kept short.

Deleting Windows

Before you delete a program window, you must minimize it and then select it by single-clicking the icon. You then give the **F**ile **D**elete command or press the Delete key. Windows prompts you with a message: `Are you sure you want to delete group xxx?`. This program group will be deleted together with all of the icons contained.

Tip: If you want Program Manager to be out of the way when you run programs, give the **O**ptions **M**inimize on Use command. This causes the Program Manager window to be minimized whenever you run a program. Using this option also means, however, that you must actively open the Program Manager icon each time you quit a program if you want to run another one. If you are getting Out of Memory alert messages, use this tip to conserve RAM.

Adding New Icons

So far, you have seen how to change the properties of existing icons. Adding new icons to a window is easy. After making sure that the window in which you want the icon is the active window, give the **F**ile **N**ew command. That command's dialog box is shown in Figure 5.14.

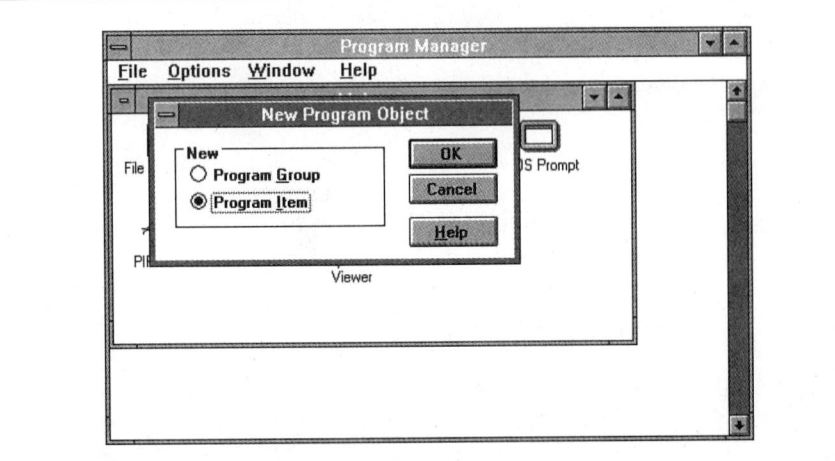

Figure 5.14. Adding new program items.

Tip: You can edit Program Manager icons with commercial and shareware icon editors such as IconEdit. These editors also enable you to create your own icons. For more on aftermarket icon vendors, see Chapter 30, "Windows for Advanced Users."

Because you want to add a new program item (that is, a new icon) to the window, click OK. When you do, you see an empty dialog box identical to the one displayed when you give the **F**ile **P**roperties command. Fill in the program description and the command line, choose an icon, and click OK.

For example, assume that you just bought a game called "My Aim Is True" and you want to add an icon for it to the Games window. Copy the program to your hard disk as instructed in the game's manual, then use the following steps.

1. Open the Games window. It does not matter if other windows are already open, because the Games window becomes the active window.

2. Give the **F**ile **N**ew command and click OK.

3. In the Description box, type the name of the game (My Aim Is True).

4. Click the **B**rowse button and find the directory in which you copied the game.

5. If you want to, use the Change **I**con button to choose an icon picture. Your dialog box now looks like Figure 5.15.

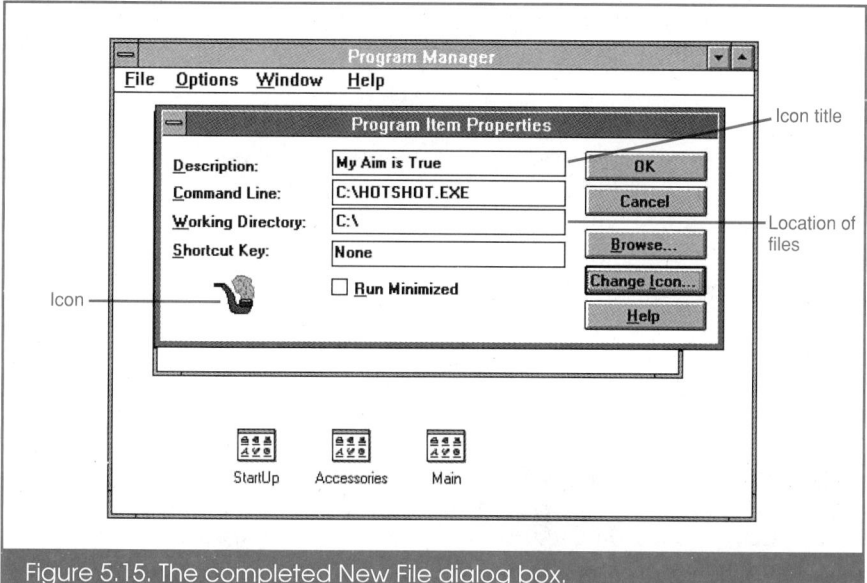

Figure 5.15. The completed New File dialog box.

6. Click OK. The icon appears in the Games window.

Tip: If you are running both Program Manager and File Manager, you can create new items (icons) in Program Manager by dragging filenames from File Manager to a Program Manager window. This is useful if you have a new directory with many programs and you want them to be in one of the group windows. Run File Manager, open the window for that directory, select the files, and drag them to the desired window in Program Manager. The file must be dragged *into a window*, not to the desktop. Program Manager automatically adds the icon for that file or program to the window. Windows fills-in the properties for you during the process.

Icons for Non-Windows Programs

Non-Windows programs do not come with icons. When you select a non-Windows program in the Command Line option, Windows version 3.1 gives you 47 choices for icons it keeps in the Program Manager file. This file (PROGMAN.EXE) is named in the File Name field when you select Change Icon for a non-Windows program or when you enter just a document filename. Windows provides you with a generic selection of icons that includes document, database, and communications icons, among others. Some of the 47 icons included with Windows are shown in Figure 5.16. To see them all, use the scroll bar.

You also can create an icon for a non-Windows program. The icon for a non-Windows program is stored in its *PIF* (Program Information File). The PIF contains information that determines how much of the system's resources and what types of resources are to be made available to the program named within. This gives you the advantage of being able to change the options for the program easily, in a single place. PIFs are described in Chapter 20, "Other DOS Programs and Windows," and in Chapter 21, "Editing PIFs."

Adding Program Icons
Later with Setup

You do not have to add program icons individually if you have many to add. You may recall from Chapter 2, "Installing Windows," that the Setup program found the initial programs for the program groups. You can run Setup again, this time from within Windows, to add more icons to your program-group windows.

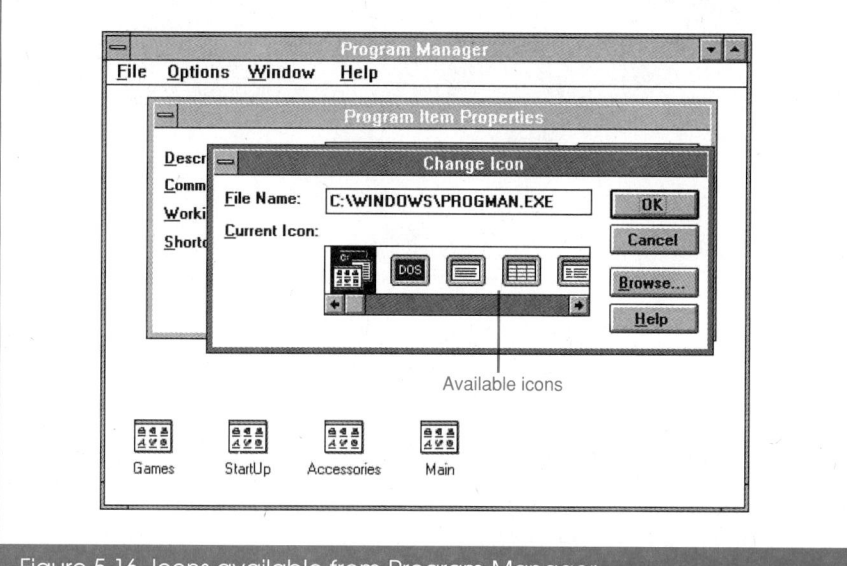

Figure 5.16. Icons available from Program Manager.

To add program icons not already in your windows, select the Windows Setup icon and open it. Your current Windows settings are displayed. These settings are described in detail in Chapter 25, "Changing Your Configuration."

Give the **O**ptions **S**et Up Applications command. A Setup Applications dialog box like the one shown in Figure 5.17 appears.

The following choices are presented in the Setup Applications dialog box:

▲ Search for applications. Tells Windows to look on all active drives for applications.

▲ Ask you to specify an application. Will allow you to specify a program to add.

When you click the OK button, Setup searches the selected disks and directories. When it is finished, you see the second Setup Applications dialog box, similar to the one shown in Figure 5.18. All the programs found are listed in the box on the left. The list on the right will include the programs you want to appear in the Applications window when you are done.

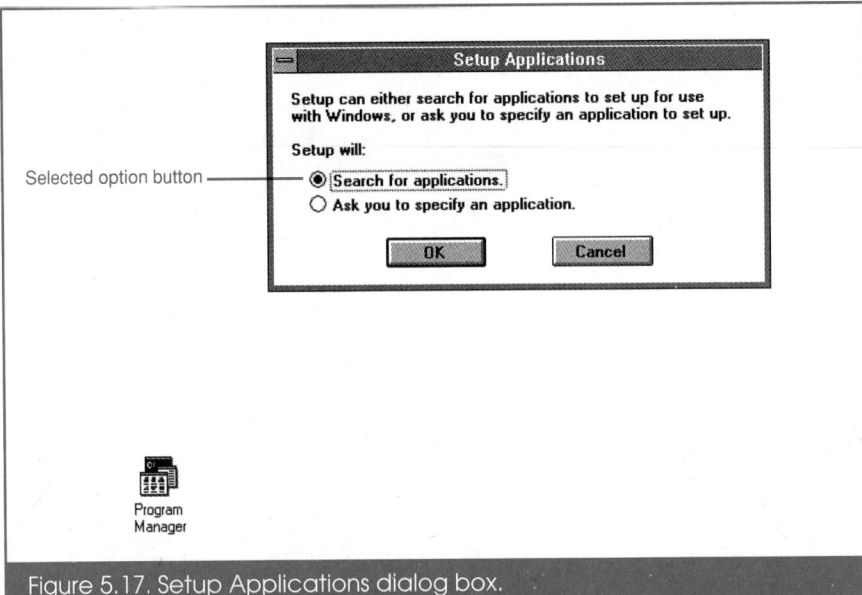

Selected option button

Figure 5.17. Setup Applications dialog box.

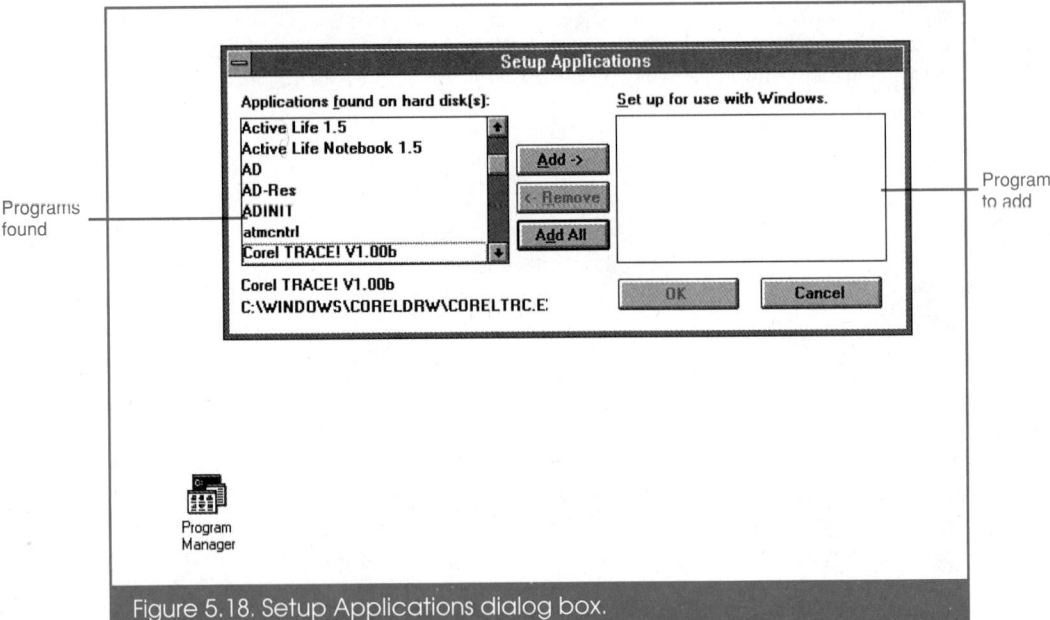

Programs found

Programs to add

Figure 5.18. Setup Applications dialog box.

You can move all the programs to the list on the right with the **Add All** button. You can move them individually in groups with the **Add →** button. To select several files from the list, simply click each file before clicking the **Add** button. If you accidentally add a program to the list on the right, you can move it back to the list on the left with the ← **R**emove button. When you click OK, Setup adds the programs you selected to either the Windows Applications window or the Non-Windows Applications window. After Windows finishes adding programs to the two group windows, you can complete the process by closing the next dialog box to exit Setup.

Warning: Setup often arranges added icons in an undesirable fashion. Be sure to check the Applications window after giving the **O**ptions **S**et Up Applications command, and give the **W**indows **A**rrange Icons command to arrange the icons in a better order.

You can click and drag the icons to the positions you want them on-screen.

To move an icon by using the keyboard, select the icon by pressing Alt-Tab. Then press the Tab key again to select the next icon. Use the **M**ove command on the **F**ile menu by pressing Alt-F-Ø. Then use the arrow keys to move the icon. Press Enter when the icon is where you want it on the screen.

If you want to set up an individual application and its icon, open Setup and choose **O**ptions **S**et Up Applications. Select Ask you to specify an application... and click the OK button. Enter the application path and filename in the text box provided. A list box with the heading Add to Program Group enables you to choose which group makes sense for your new application. If you don't know the filename and path, click the **B**rowse button to select a file from a drive and directory.

If you don't know the full filename and path, use the Browse dialog box to find your file. Double-click the filename, or click the filename to highlight it and then click the OK button. The filename and full path are pasted in the text box of the Setup Applications box. Now use the vertical scroll bar in the lower-left of the dialog box to select the program group that best accomodates your new program. If you choose the wrong file, you can click the **B**rowse button to start the process again, or click the Cancel button. When you are satisfied that the program path and filename and the destination program group are correct, click the OK button. In a message box, a horizontal bar graph depicts the progress of your file's icon-creation process. When the first Windows Setup box reappears, the task is complete. Select **Ex**it from the **O**ptions menu to exit and view your new icon in the chosen program group window.

> **Tip:** If you select a group name that already exists but currently is not in use, Windows re-creates a group with this "dormant" group name and automatically puts your application icon into that group. Even though you may re-create a group with a redundant title, the filenames will never be the same.

Windows enables you to install the *same* application repeatedly into any program group(s) if you want to do so. You can use this feature to create icons for individual documents. Popular form letters or company telephone directories can be maintained quickly and easily this way.

Arranging Icons

The arrangement of icons in your windows makes it easier for you to see your work. In the windows that Setup creates, the icons are in neat rows and columns. You can move the icons in windows to wherever you want them.

Moving Icons in a Window

In Chapter 4 "Basic Windows Concepts," you learned how to resize windows. You may not have noticed that when you change the size of the window, the icons for the closed windows do not move with the new borders. You can move the icons quickly to the new window bottom by selecting any of the closed windows' icons and giving the **W**indow **A**rrange Icons command.

 To move an icon with the mouse, simply click the icon and drag it to the desired location. You cannot use the keyboard to move individual icons.

You do not have to move the icons individually if you simply want them arranged in nice rows and columns. Windows can do that for you easily.

The **W**indow **A**rrange Icons command automatically spaces the icons in even rows. The default spacing is 75 pixels between rows, but you can change that value by opening Control Panel Desktop and selecting a value other than 75. You also can edit the WIN.INI file manually, as described in Chapter 27, "Configuring with the WIN.INI and SYSTEM.INI Files."

With Windows 3.1, if you enabled **O**ptions **A**uto Arrange from the Program Manager menu, icons spring back into the lineup if you drag them out of their usual place in the window. When you give the **W**indow **A**rrange Icons command, Windows arranges only the icons in the active window. Be sure that the window you want to rearrange is active. The active window will be in the foreground and will probably be colored differently from all of the inactive windows. If you have a minimized window selected when you give the command, Windows rearranges the icons of the minimized windows.

Copying Icons Between Windows

In many situations, you want a particular icon in more than one window. For example, if your windows are arranged by work project, you may want to have the icon for your word processor in every window. Or you may want to have the icon for a particular document in many windows if you modify that document when you work on different projects.

To copy an icon to another window with the mouse, start with both windows open. Select the icon in the origin window, hold down the Ctrl key, and drag the icon to the destination window.

To copy an icon to other windows with the keyboard, select the icon and give the **F**ile **C**opy command. Then, in the dialog box shown in Figure 5.19, select the desired group from the drop-down list and choose OK.

Moving Icons Between Windows

Instead of duplicating an icon in another window, you may simply want to move the item from one window to another. For example, a document in one project's window may now belong to another project. Moving an icon means moving the related file and/or program with it.

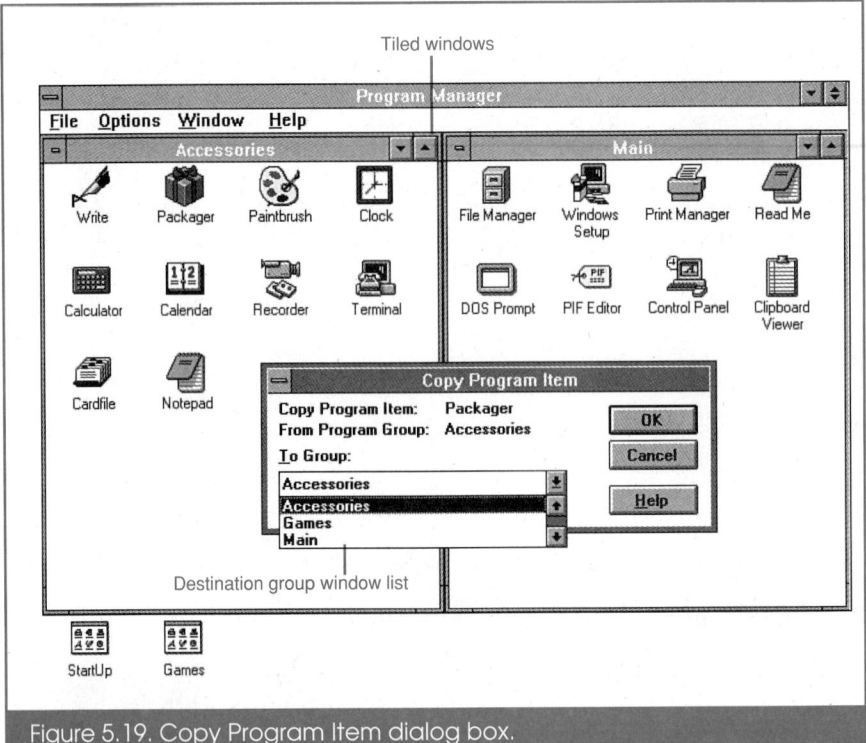

Figure 5.19. Copy Program Item dialog box.

 To move an icon to another window with the mouse, start with both windows open. Select the icon in the origin window and drag it to the destination window.

 To move an icon to another window with the keyboard, select the icon and give the **F**ile **M**ove command. Then, in the dialog box shown in Figure 5.20, select the desired group from the drop-down list and choose OK.

Deleting Icons

If you no longer need an icon, you can delete it by selecting it and pressing the Del key or by giving the **F**ile **D**elete command. Windows warns you before you delete the icon because you cannot restore an icon after you have deleted it.

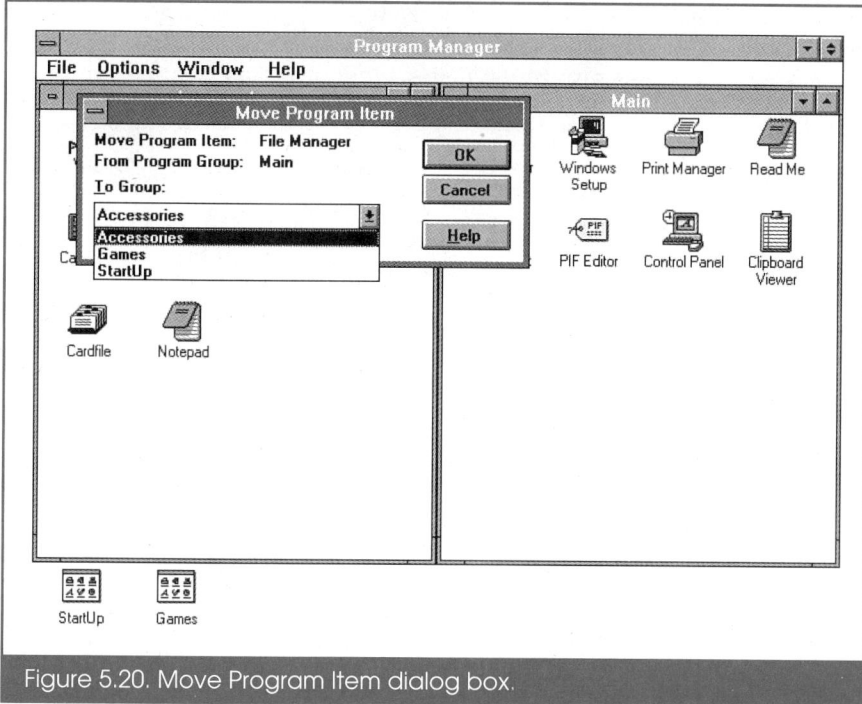

Figure 5.20. Move Program Item dialog box.

5

Sample Program Manager Layouts

Few people leave icons as Setup arranged them. Because each person's work is different, you probably will find your own preferred icon layout.

Tip: Generally, you should avoid creating windows that have scroll bars. Why force yourself to take two actions (scrolling and then selecting) when you don't have to? Squeezing your icons closer together is better than making yourself scroll.

If you think of your work as programs and their documents, you may want to create a layout in which each window is a program that includes the most common documents you would open. Linking or associating files to programs is done from File Manager, and is described in Chapter 6, "File Manager." In Figure 5.21, for example, the icons are arranged as programs in one window and as documents in the other.

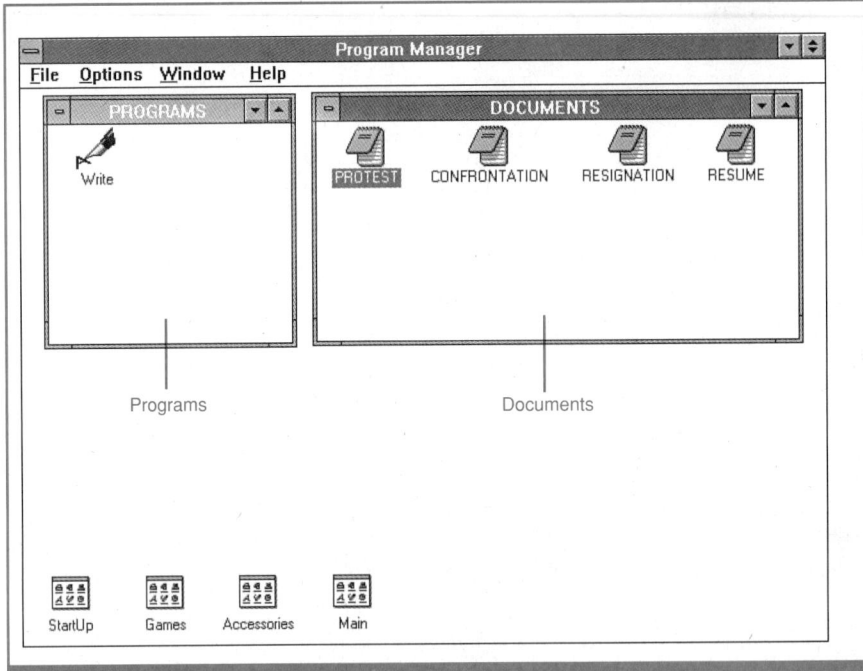

Figure 5.21. Windows with program icons separated from document icons.

If you think in terms of processes, you may want each window to be a step in a work process. You could, for example, create a window for a project that contains just programs and documents related to that project. Figure 5.22 shows steps in a process that must be performed in a particular order.

> **Tip:** Some people prefer to group their icons by importance. They put the most-used programs in one window, other common programs in another, rarely used programs in another, and so on. You also could have one large window with all your icons gathered into small groups.

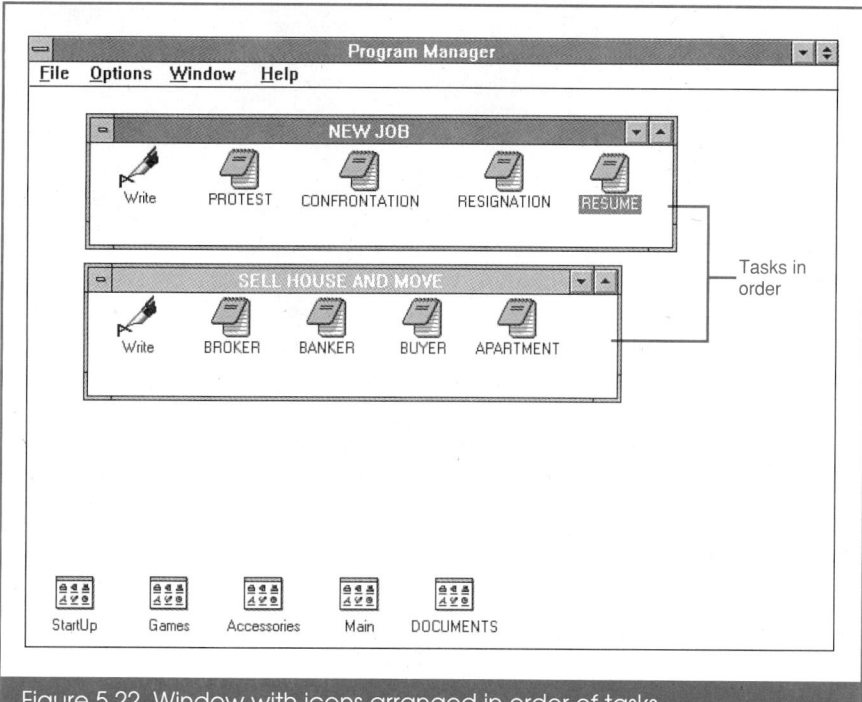

Figure 5.22. Window with icons arranged in order of tasks.

5

Files Used by Program Manager

In special files in the main Windows directory, Program Manager keeps the information about which windows to open and which icons are in those windows. Ordinarily, you do not need to worry about these files. If you have problems starting or running Program Manager, however, you usually can get around the problems by editing and deleting these files.

You may want to keep periodic backups of these files in case they become damaged. (You should keep periodic backups of everything on your hard disk.) Program Manager uses the PROGMAN.INI file and all files with the .GRP extension. Note that you should not set these files to be read-only, because Program Manager often changes them. If you do change the group-file attributes to read-only, when you exit Windows you will see an Alert dialog box that advises you of the attribute change and tells you that Windows cannot update the file properly. Click the Cancel button and open File Manager Properties to correct this problem.

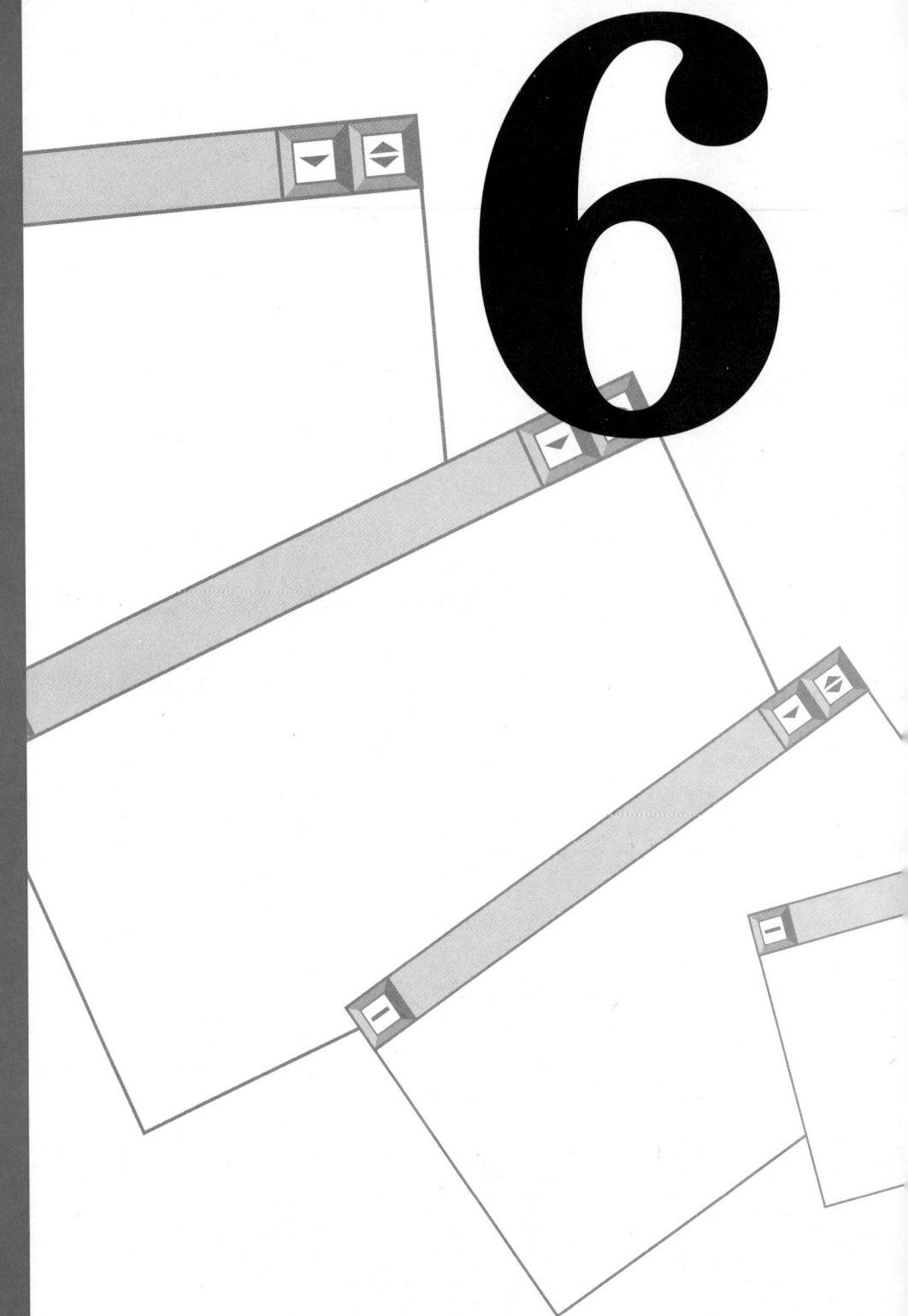

CHAPTER

6

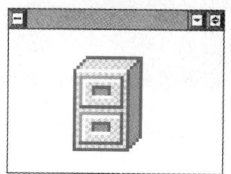

File Manager

I f you were familiar with MS-DOS before you started using Windows, you know that using DOS commands to manipulate files takes up much of your time. You often can spend too much time looking at lists of files in a directory, copying files between directories, renaming files, and so on. As you know, the amount of typing you sometimes have to do to issue the DOS commands from the familiar prompt (for example, C>) can be daunting. Even compared to the MS-DOS 5.0 shell, the Windows 3.1 File Manager is far more graphical than the MS-DOS shell. Because of its power and ease of use, Windows Version 3.1 File Manager could have been marketed alone as a Microsoft enhanced utility. The new File Manager is an improved version of the Windows 3.0 File Manager. You'll find out why as you continue reading this chapter.

Because of the complexity and tedium of typing commands in MS-DOS, Microsoft included with Windows 3.1 a much easier way of handling files—File Manager. The File Manager program displays your files graphically in windows, enables you to move them without having to type, and so on.

To understand the information in this chapter, you should know something about files and directories. You don't need to know much to use File Manager, but you should understand the following terms:

▲ *Files* are stored on a physical or virtual disk drive. A physical drive is a disk of some type; a virtual drive is a temporary one created in memory only. All *drives* have a name—a letter and a colon—such as `C:`.

▲ Every drive has a *root directory*. This directory, which has no directory name, is designated by the backslash character (\) following the drive letter (for example, `C:\`). Your DOS system files, AUTOEXEC.BAT and CONFIG.SYS, reside there (if the system boots from that drive).

▲ Files are stored in *directories* on the drive (for example, C:\WINDOWS).

▲ Directories can contain other directories, called *subdirectories* (`C:\WINDOWS\SYSTEM`, for example). Directories are sometimes referred to as Folders. The term *Folders* is a takeoff from the Macintosh and a direct metaphor for a folder stored within a drawer of a conventional filing cabinet.

You can start File Manager from Program Manager by double-clicking its icon in the Main window. When you start File Manager, you see one window opened. The last-viewed window with a *directory tree* portion is on the left and a file listing is on the right, as in Figure 6.1. Note that the directory tree and the directories shown in this chapter are for one computer; yours will, of course, look different.

The Directory Tree Window

Each window that File Manager creates contains a directory tree and a contents list, separated by a movable vertical bar. If your file- or directory names are very long, you can use this split bar to size the left or right window to help display all the text. A directory tree is a graphic representation of the directory and its relation to the drive and the other directories and subdirectories.

Although you can have only one directory tree and one file listing in each window created by File Manager, File Manager creates as many windows as your system memory allows. You can have many windows showing other directory trees. When you click a directory name, the file's contents list appears to the right of the split bar.

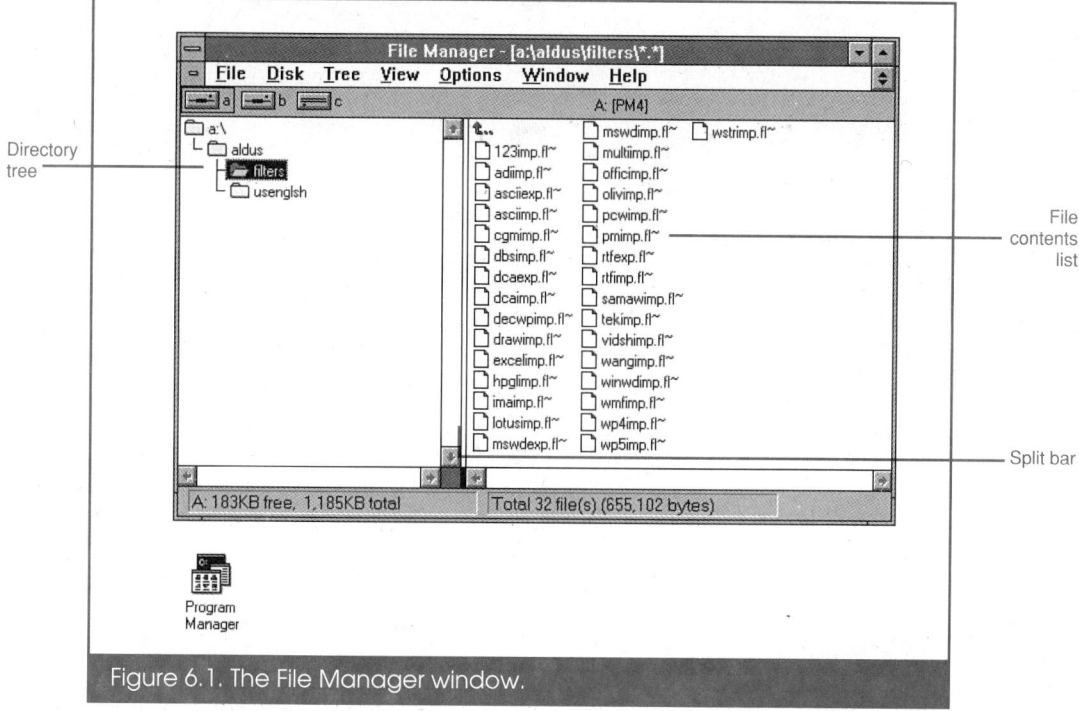

Figure 6.1. The File Manager window.

Changing Drives

Above the directory tree, the *drive icon bar* displays icons that represent each drive recognized by your system. Each drive's letter is to the right of the icon. Floppy drives are represented by pictures of each drive type. Floppy, hard, virtual network, and CD-ROM drives all have their own particular icons. Figure 6.2 shows two floppy drives and one hard drive. The drive tree and the related contents list represent the currently accessed drive and contents when you start File Manager. Click any other drive icon on the drive icon bar to view a directory tree and its contents list for the selected drive.

To change drives with the mouse, simply click the icon of the drive you want.

Press the Tab key to switch the dotted selection rectangle between the directories window and the drive icons on the drive icon bar. Press ← or → to select the desired drive, then press Enter. You can select a drive also by pressing Ctrl and the appropriate letter (Ctrl-D, for example, to select the D drive).

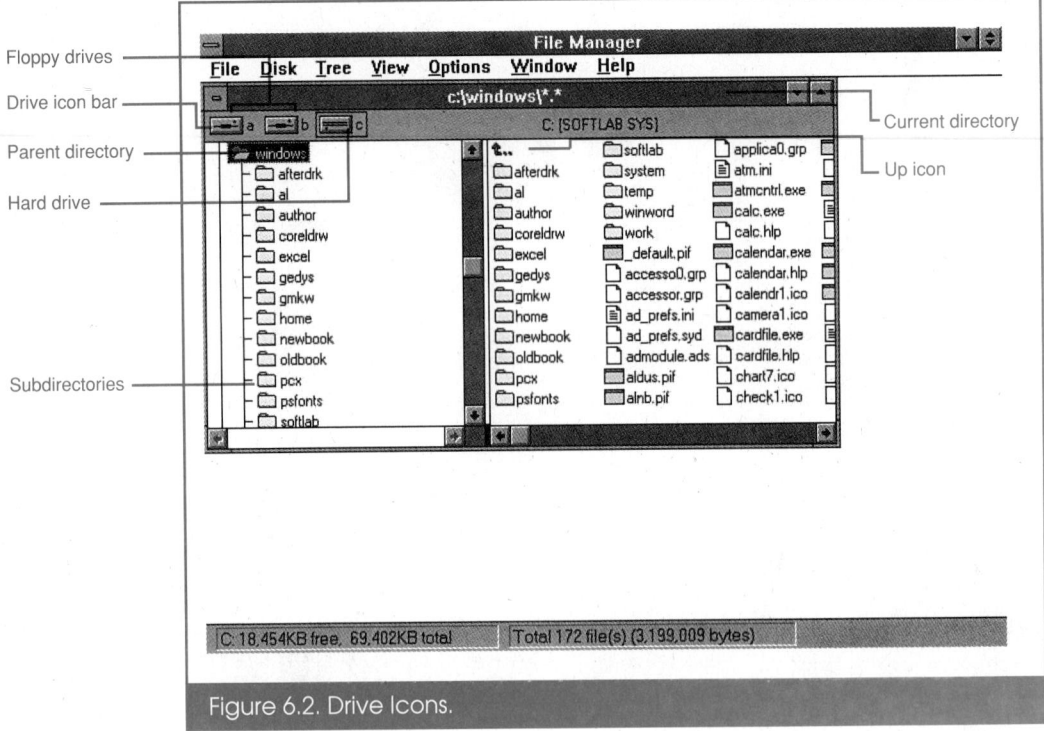

Figure 6.2. Drive Icons.

Changing Directories and Folders

The drive letter and volume label (if there is one) of the currently
selected drive are on the drive icon bar, to the right of the drive icons.
The name of the currently selected directory appears on the active title
bar above the drive icon bar. This information is useful when the
directory tree is so long that you cannot see which directory is selected.
In Figure 6.2, for example, the selected directory is C:\windows.

Each directory is represented by a folder icon. Folder icons (directories)
marked with a + symbol have directories below them. If there are too
many directories to fit in the window, you can use the scroll bar (to the
left of the split bar) to scroll through them.

Each subdirectory is displayed just below and to the right of its parent
directory (or another subdirectory), indicating deeper levels in the
directory tree. When you first start File Manager, you see only the first
level of directories. The currently open folder (or displayed directory) is

highlighted by an open-folder icon to the left of the directory name. You can view lower levels in the tree by clicking icons that look like closed folders.

To select folders from the keyboard, use the keys listed in Table 6.1. Or type the first letter of the directory's name, which takes you to the closest directory whose name starts with that letter.

Table 6.1. Selecting folder icons from the keyboard.

Key	Selects
↑	Directory above the current directory
↓	Directory below the current directory
Ctrl-↑	Directory on the same level but above the current directory
Ctrl-↓	Directory on the same level but below the current directory
←	Directory one level higher than the current directory
→	Directory one level lower than the current directory
Home	Root directory
End	Last directory in the list
PageDown	Directory on the next page
PageUp	Directory on the preceding page

Expanding Directories and Folders

You can ask File Manager to display hidden subdirectories by expanding them. You can expand directories (folders) in this way:

To expand a directory with the mouse, double-click the folder.

Key board

To expand a directory from the keyboard, select the folder and press the plus (+) key on either the main keyboard or numeric keypad. Or select the folder and give the **Tree Ex**pand One Level command.

If you want to expand simultaneously all the branches (subdirectories) under one folder (directory), select the folder and give the **T**ree Expand

Branch command. You also can press the asterisk (*) key. To see all the directories and branches expanded at once, give the **Tree Expand A**ll command or press the Ctrl-* keys at the same time.

If you don't know which directories are expandable, choose **Tree Indi**cate Expandable Branches. In Figure 6.3, a directory is expanded, with the **I**ndicate Expandable Branches option selected. A plus sign on a folder icon indicates that subdirectories under that directory are not currently visible. A minus sign is on the folder icon of each directory whose subdirectories currently are visible. This feature is designed to enable you to view all files under a selected folder or directory without having to view *all* subdirectories and files.

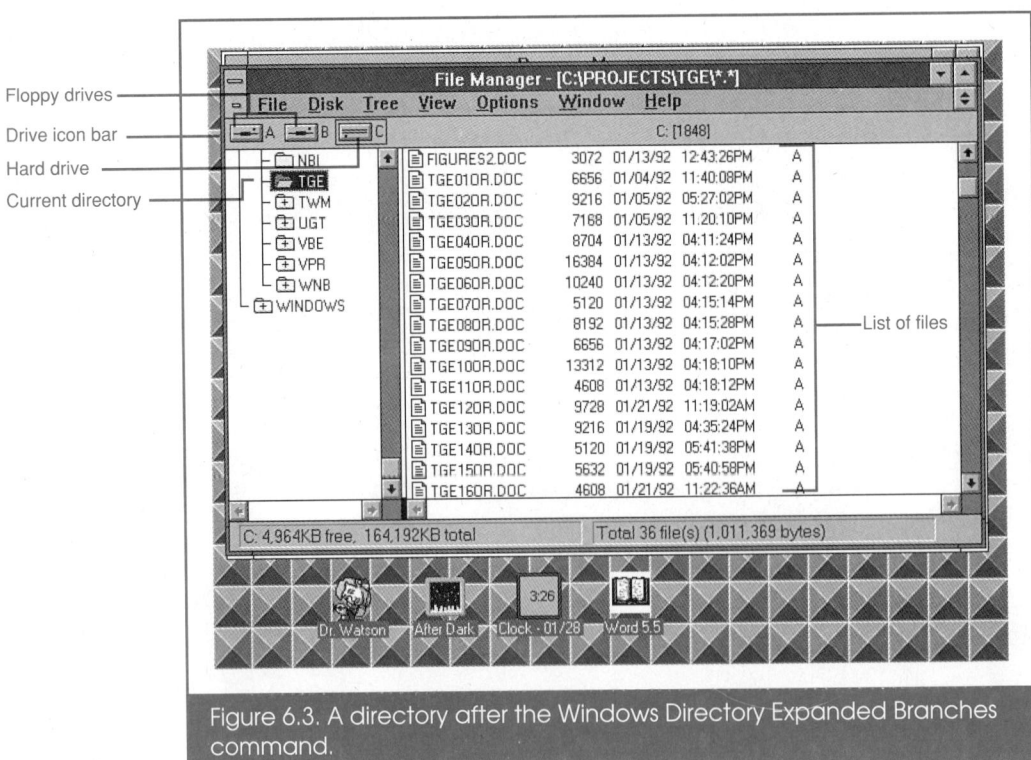

Figure 6.3. A directory after the Windows Directory Expanded Branches command.

You can collapse branches as easily as you expand them.

To collapse a folder (directory) that has been expanded with the mouse, double-click it, or select the folder and give the **Tree Expand B**ranch command.

To collapse a directory that has been expanded with the keyboard, use the arrow keys to select the folder and then press the minus (–) key on either the main keyboard or the numeric keypad. Or select the folder and give the **T**ree **C**ollapse Branch command.

6

Displaying Files in a Directory or Folder

You can see lists of the files in each directory. The display of filenames to the right of the split bar is called the *contents list*.

Figure 6.4 shows the icons used to identify file types. These file-type icons are listed between the vertical split bar and the filenames. Note that Windows 3.1 can identify which files are documents and so on by looking in the list in the [Extensions] area of the WIN.INI file. To learn how you can help Windows identify all your files, see Chapter 27, "Configuring with the WIN.INI and SYSTEM.INI Files."

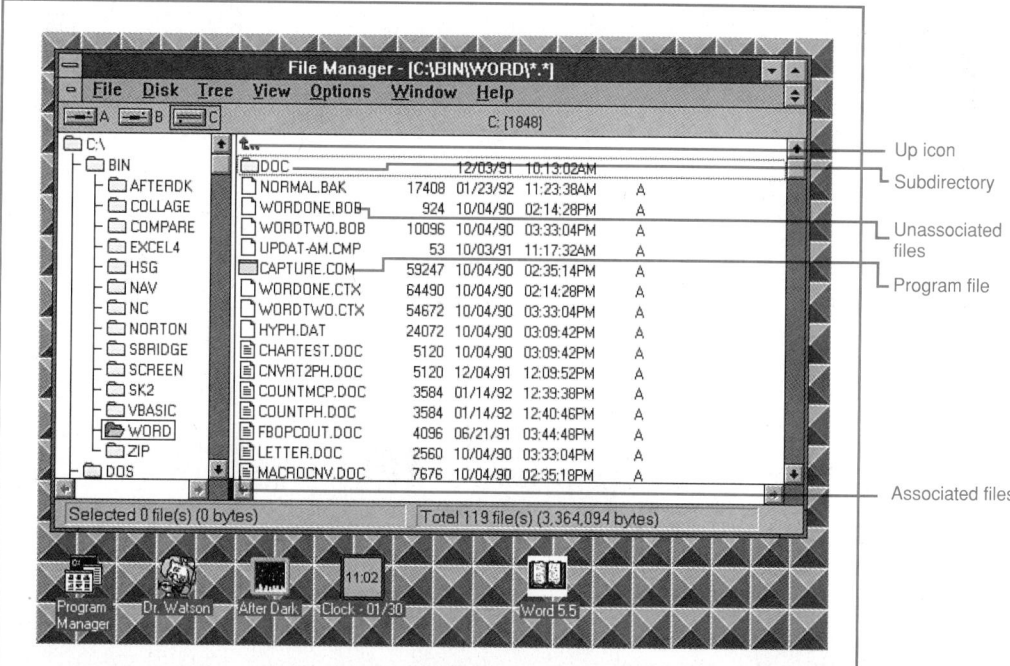

Figure 6.4. Icons identify the file type.

Icons that look like empty pages of text are files that Windows has not connected to a program. This process is called *associating* your files. The process is described later in this chapter.

Displaying Folder Contents

To see the files contained in a folder, you can use the mouse or the keyboard.

 To see the contents list for any folder, click the folder you want.

At the top of the contents list is the up icon. Double-click the up icon to see the contents list for the first folder at the next level *above* the current folder on the directory tree. If you continue to double-click the up arrow, you will find yourself at the root directory of the drive you're in.

 To see the file contents of a folder, use the arrow keys to scroll the folder tree. The file contents list will be updated, or refreshed, as you move among the folders.

Tip: Attention, keyboard shortcut users: You can bounce between the selected folder, the first file in that folder, and the drive icon by using the Tab and Shift-Tab keys.

Selecting Files in the Contents List

As you will see in this chapter's "Working Directly with Files" section, you can do things with files—copying and deleting them, for example. Selecting a single file or several files is quite easy.

Tip: The fastest way to select *all* the files in a directory window or all files of a similar type is with the **F**ile **S**et Selection command.

 To select a single file, simply click it. Holding down the Shift key causes all the files between the first selection and the next one you click to be selected. To select more than one file, but not all the files in between, hold down the Ctrl key as you click new files.

6

You can combine these two methods to select multiple groups of files with the mouse. Select the first group by clicking and using the Shift key. Next, hold down the Ctrl key while you click the first file in the second group. Press Ctrl and Shift as you click the last file in the second group. You can repeat this sequence to add other groups to the selection, or if you happen to make a mistake.

To select files with the keyboard, use the keys listed in Table 6.2. Also, typing the first letter of a file's name takes you to the closest file that starts with that letter.

Table 6.2. Selecting files with the keyboard.

Key	Selects
↑	Previous file
↓	Next file
←	File in previous column
→	File in next column
Home	First file in list
End	Last file in list
PageDown	File on next page
PageUp	File on previous page

Tip: You can set up Windows 3.1 so that only a list of your preferred files is visible in File Manager. If you tend to use .DOC or .TXT files, for example, you can tailor File Manager to appear at system startup and display only those files. You can do this by choosing **F**ile **A**ssociate after you have highlighted your preferred file type in the contents list. **F**ile **A**ssociate prompts you through the process.

Minimizing Directory Windows

You can end up with many windows open simultaneously in File Manager. Fortunately, there are ways to arrange the windows so that you can see many windows at the same time. This is useful not only for visually comparing the contents of windows, but also for carrying out some of the file actions you will see later in this chapter.

When you are not looking at a particular window, you may want to minimize it. Use the normal window-minimizing techniques to reduce windows you are not using. File Manager arranges the icons of minimized windows along the bottom of the File Manager window (see Figure 6.5).

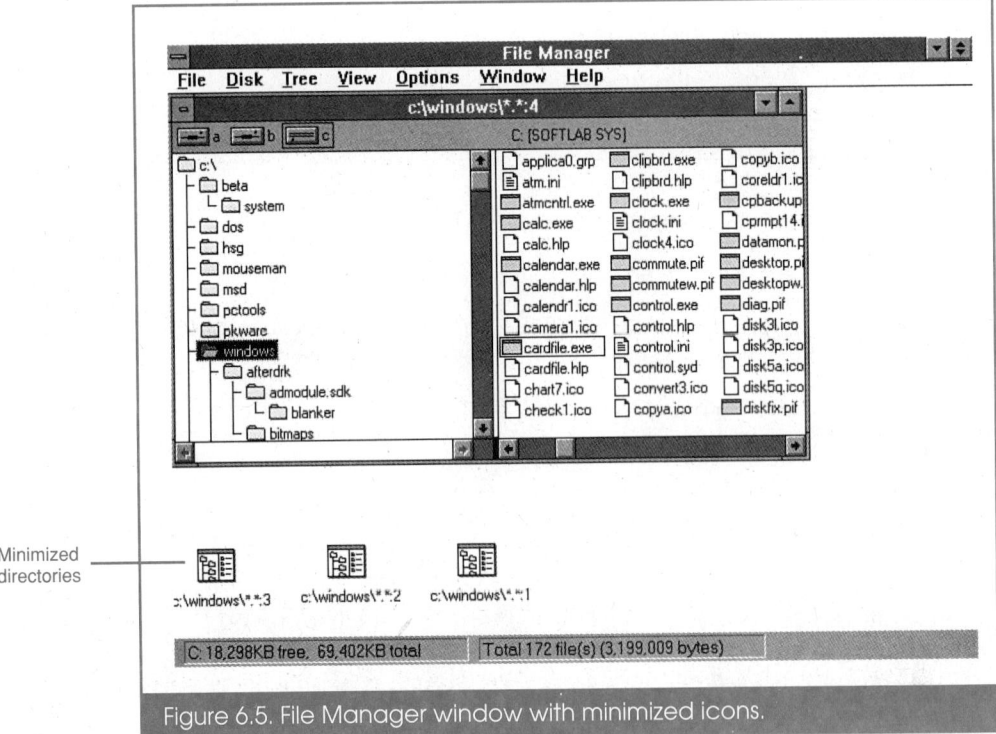

Minimized directories

Figure 6.5. File Manager window with minimized icons.

Tip: After you open a directory window, there really is no need to close it—just minimize it. If you want to look in that window again, picking it from the bottom of the File Manager window is much easier than having to look through the directory tree again.

Working Directly with Files

This section covers the tasks performed with files and directories, such as copying and deleting them. Copying and moving files and directories is easy when you use the mouse. Even if you use the keyboard, however, copying and moving selected files in Windows is much easier than in MS-DOS.

Copying and Moving Files with the Mouse

Copying and moving files in File Manager is easy. You simply select the files you want to copy or move and drag them to the destination window. You can even copy a file to the Clipboard if you have enough memory for the Clipboard to accept it. The Clipboard will hold your data until you erase it via the Clipboard Viewer, or you restart Windows. Click the appropriate check box in the File Copy dialog box, which is shown in Figure 6.6.

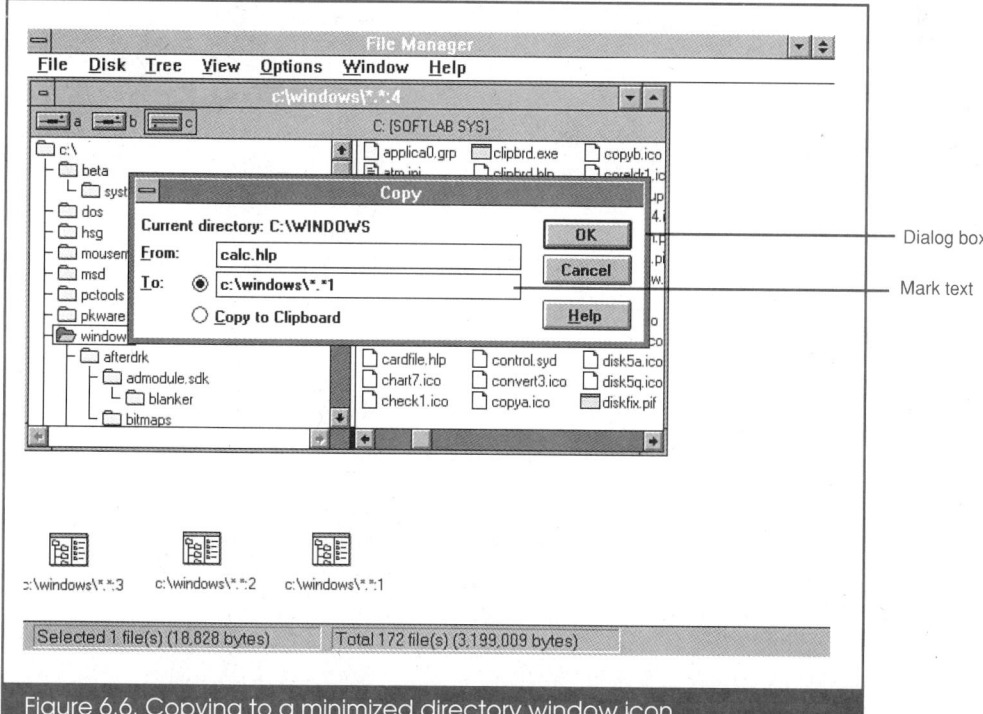

Figure 6.6. Copying to a minimized directory window icon.

Assume that you want to copy the calc.hlp file from the C:\windows directory to the C:\temp directory. You would select the file, hold down the mouse button, and drag the icon to anywhere in the C:\temp window. If **O**ptions **C**onfirmation is on, File Manager displays the following message: Are you sure that you want to copy the selected files into drive:\directory? To copy the file, press Enter or click OK.

 To copy files with the mouse, select the files and drag them to the destination. Dragging a file to a disk icon copies the file. Dragging a file to another point on the same drive moves the file. You have to use the **F**ile **C**opy option if you want to copy files to another point on the same drive. Correspondingly, you must use the **F**ile **M**ove option to move a file from one drive to another.

Moving files is just like copying files, except that you hold down the Alt key instead of the Ctrl key.

 To move files with the mouse, single-click the file of choice, hold down the mouse button while the pointer is positioned over the file, hold down the Alt key, and drag the file, placing the pointer and file icon(s) over the folder or drive icon that is the desired destination.

 **Tip:** The destination does not have to be active or open. You can drag to a drive icon, inactive window, or minimized icon. This saves space on the screen and reduces window clutter. For instance, if you are copying or moving files from the C:\windows directory to the C:\temp directory, open the C:\temp directory window, then minimize it so that your screen looks like Figure 6.6. You can then drag from the one open window to the minimized icon.

Copying and Moving Files with the Keyboard

Using the keyboard to copy or move files is almost as easy as using the mouse.

 To copy or move files with the keyboard, select the files and give the **F**ile **C**opy or **F**ile **M**ove command. The dialog box for the **F**ile **C**opy command is shown in Figure 6.7.

6

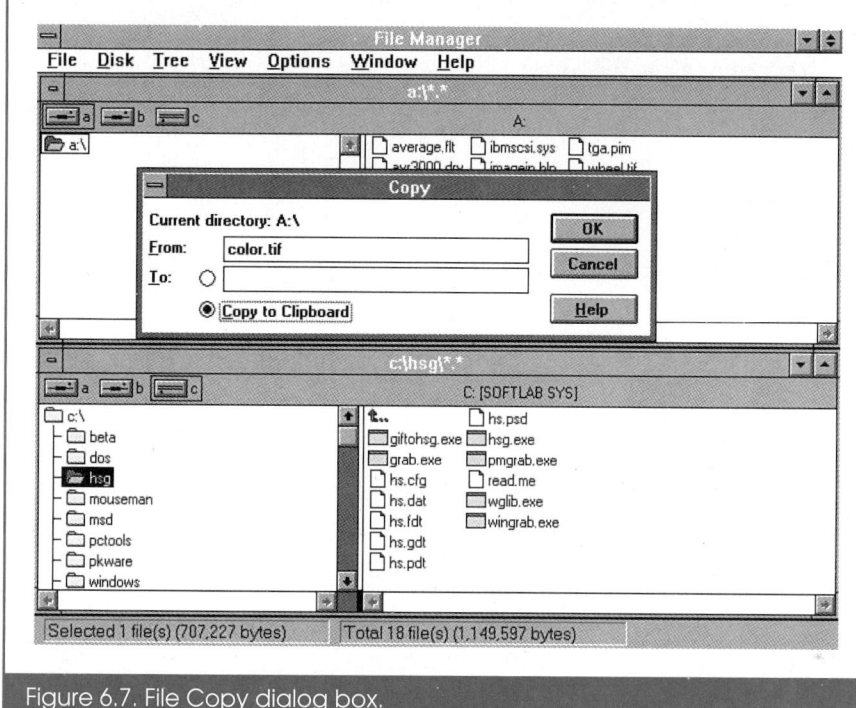

Figure 6.7. File Copy dialog box.

If you use the **F**ile **C**opy command instead of dragging the file with the mouse, File Manager fills in the **F**rom entry with the names of the files you have selected, separated by spaces. You can edit this entry if you want. To copy or move the files, type the name of the destination directory in the **T**o entry. You cannot rename a file during the **F**ile **C**opy process.

Copying and Moving Directories

Copying and moving directories is similar to copying and moving files. Note that you cannot copy or move more than one directory at a time. You can copy or move all subdirectories and files simultaneously by simply copying or moving the top-level directory. Click the desired directory icon and drag the folder icon onto the drive icon; Windows 3.1 re-creates the directory name on the destination drive and copies (not moves) all files to the new drive and directory.

Tip: With Windows 3.1 File Manager, automatically making backup diskettes for each directory is easier than ever. Simply place a blank diskette in a floppy drive, open File Manager, and drag the directory icon to the drive-letter icon on the icon bar. A dialog box opens, the directory is established on the floppy disk, and a dialog box displays the filenames as they are copied to the new directory on the floppy. Make sure that you have enough room on the floppy. Because Windows does not check destination drive capacity before copying, it will fail to copy all your files if space is inadequate.

Deleting Files and Directories

To delete one or more files or directories, select them and give the **F**ile **D**elete command, shown in Figure 6.8. If you have set confirmation on, File Manager asks for confirmation in a dialog box. (See the discussion of **O**ptions **C**onfirmation in the "Confirming File Operations" section.) You can edit the contents of the Delete text box before clicking the OK button or pressing Enter. If you do not want to see the confirmation dialog box when you delete a file or a directory, give the **O**ptions **C**onfirmation command and deselect the Confirm on File **D**elete check box.

Warning: File Manager will perform whatever task you require of it on any selected files. Selected files can be so far down the file contents list that you may not realize they are still selected. It's best to check the file contents list one last time before you do anything unrecoverable to a file or files.

Renaming Files and Directories

You can rename files and directories by selecting them and giving the **F**ile **Re**name command with either the keyboard or the mouse. If the name is in use, Windows displays the error message, `Cannot rename "xxxxxxxx.xxx": Source and destination are the same.`

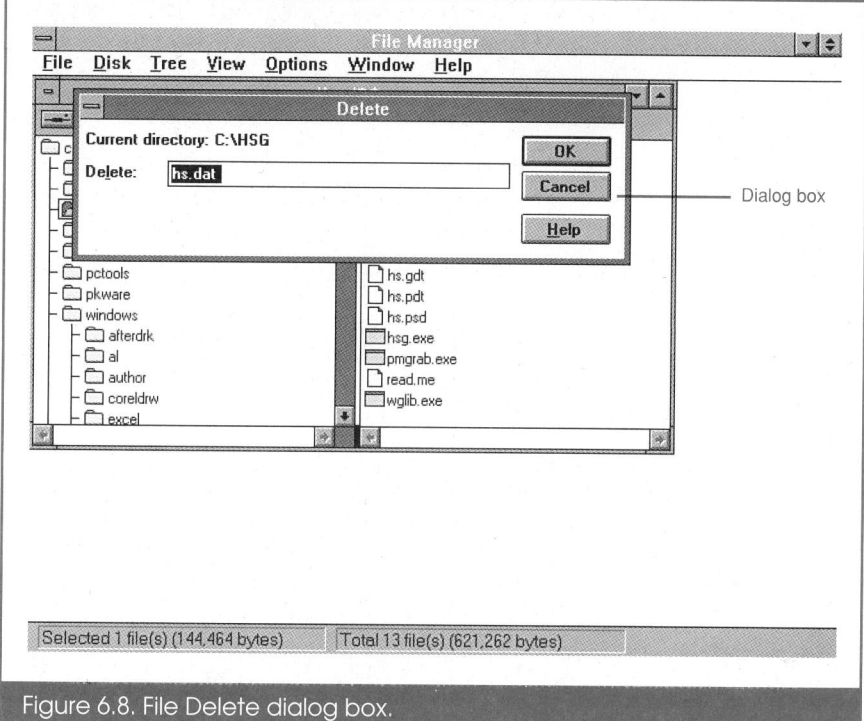

Figure 6.8. File Delete dialog box.

Changing File Attributes

DOS and Windows 3.1 recognize four file attributes that are set on or off with each file. File attributes are a system of classifying your files. There are essentially four classes of files, and they are identified with labels called attributes. For example, DOS will assign the Archive attribute (label) to any file with a filename extension of .BAK. .BAK files are created by your programs if you request that a backup copy of your file be made each time you save it.

Files are normally labeled with the Archive attribute unless a circumstance dictates that they be labeled differently. Critical files, say, ones that your computer needs to operate, cannot be changed or moved. These are the most sensitive files, and they are labeled with the System attribute. DOS creates two System files that are also Hidden. You can't see them when you use the DOS DIR command at the DOS prompt, because the Hidden attribute is set for these files, but they are there.

Making them Hidden helps keep them from being accidentally moved or deleted. Either action would render your previously bootable hard drive unbootable.

You can change the attributes if you want to by using the **F**ile Properties command:

▲ Read Only causes DOS to disallow modifications to this file, but the file can be moved and deleted.

▲ Archive tells DOS that modifications have been made to this file.

▲ Hidden hides the filename when files are displayed by the DOS DIR command. You can tell File Manager to display these hidden filenames by clicking the Show Hidden/System Files options in the View by File Type dialog box.

▲ System identifies the file as being essential and location-sensitive. Location sensitivity is established when the file is created. System files must not be moved, or your computer cannot find them when the machine boots up. This attribute also is set if in order to run, software has been written to look for a file at a specific location on a hard or floppy drive.

These attributes are either on or off for each file. Some attributes can be set along with others. You can have a read-only, system hidden file. You can have a file set with just the system or hidden attribute. You can set the attributes for files by selecting them and giving the **F**ile **P**roperties command. The dialog box for this command is shown in Figure 6.9. To change the attributes for a file, click the check boxes provided for each attribute.

Tip: If you are sharing a computer, you can prevent unauthorized modification of your files by using **F**ile **P**roperties and setting the Hidden and **R**ead Only attribute check boxes for all your files. Your files will not be visible when you refresh the window's content list or restart File Manager if you deselect the **V**iew **S**how Hidden/System Files check box before you close File Manager.

Warning: If you select a check box in the **F**ile **P**roperties command dialog box and then check it again, you might see a *shaded* check box in its place. The purpose of a check box is to provide an either/or option for a selection. Make sure that these check boxes are either checked or clearly without a check mark before you leave **F**ile **P**roperties. A shaded check box is recognized by Windows 3.1 as being unchecked.

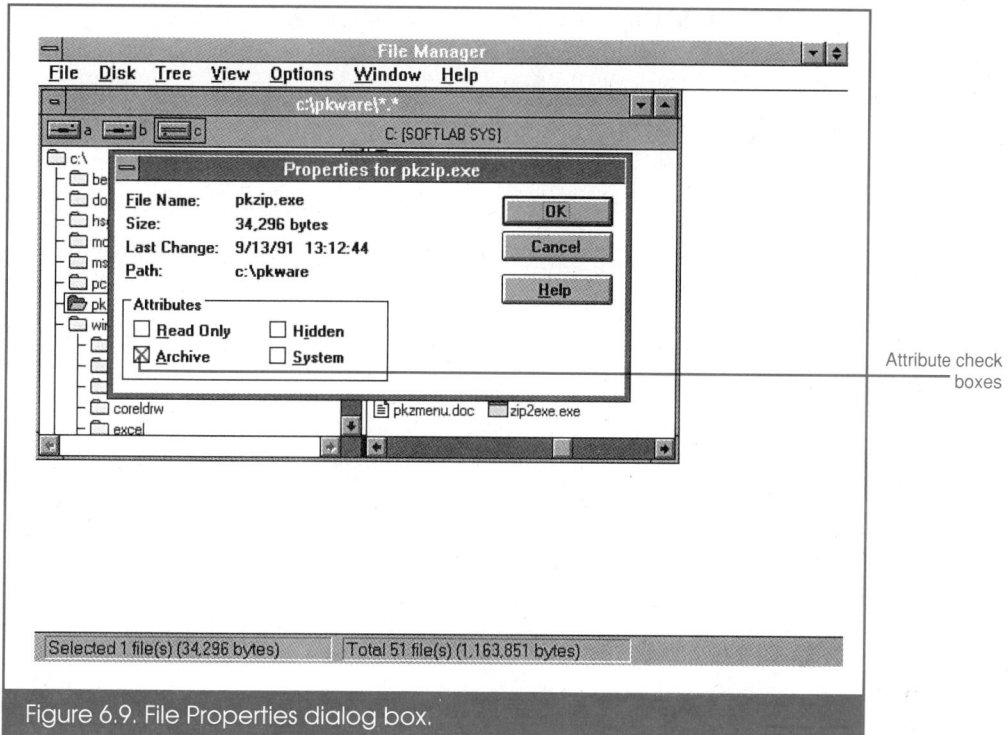

Figure 6.9. File Properties dialog box.

Running Programs and Documents

You can start a program from File Manager (rather than Program Manager) by double-clicking that program's file icon or by selecting it and using the **F**ile **O**pen command. These methods give you an easy way to start programs for which you do not have a Program Manager icon.

You can run programs also by using the **F**ile **R**un command. The advantage of using this command instead of clicking the file icon is that you can specify command-line options in the **F**ile **R**un dialog box (see Figure 6.10). Instead of entering a command line at the DOS prompt, you enter it in the **C**ommand Line text box.

If the program you want to run is not in the current directory or in your MS-DOS path, you must include the full path specification for the program. You can include any command-line options you want in the **F**ile **R**un command. If you want to run a program and load a file, select the filename you want to load and use the **F**ile **R**un command, as follows:

1. Choose **F**ile **R**un. If you have highlighted a file in the file contents list, the filename appears in the space provided for entering the command line. The cursor is placed at the end of the filename.

2. Press the Home key or use the mouse to place the cursor before the filename.

3. Type the program name (before the filename).

4. Press Enter or click the OK button to tell Windows to continue. Windows starts the program and loads the file.

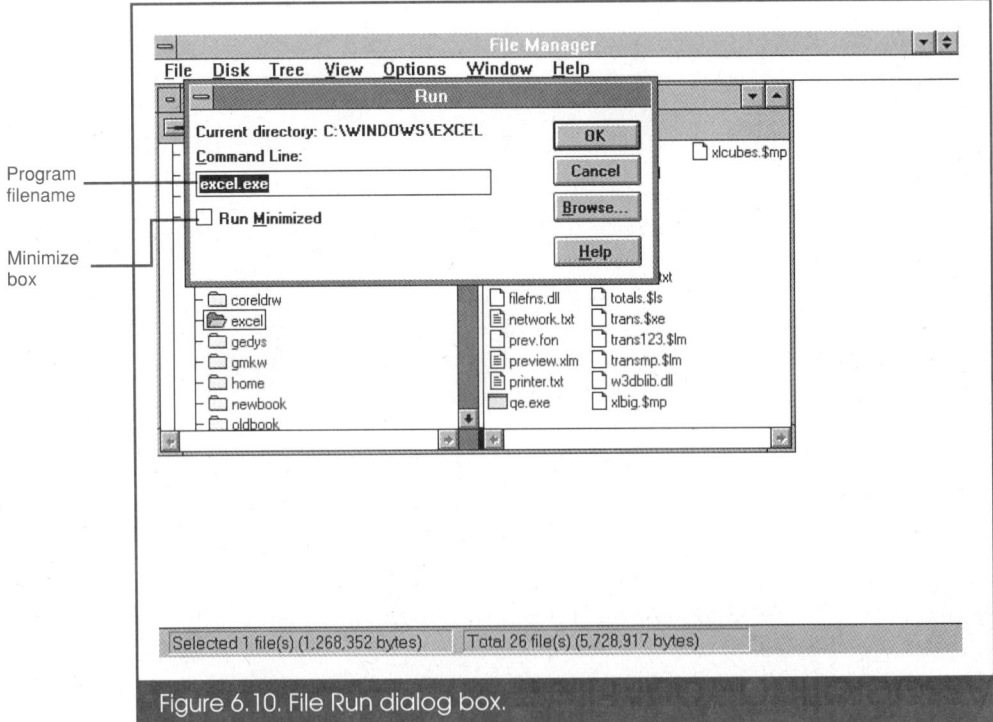

Figure 6.10. File Run dialog box.

Alternatively, you can highlight a program name on the file contents list and then type the name of the desired document file *after* the program name. You can enter as many command-line filenames and/or switches after the program name as your application will support.

You can load a program and minimize it for future use by clicking the Run Minimized check box in the **F**ile **R**un dialog box. The program will be loaded and ready but may not take up as much memory while it waits to be used. If you're curious about a program's memory usage when running compared to its usage in the minimized state, use Program Manager's **H**elp About dialog box to gain information about available memory before you minimize the program and then after it's minimized.

Associating Your Files

6

If you double-click a file with an extension (the part of the filename after the dot) of .EXE, Windows tries to run the program. If you double-click a file with an extension of .TXT, Windows runs Notepad and loads your file automatically as though you had created an icon to do just that. If Windows can associate the file extension with the application that uses the selected file, the program that can use the file will run and open the file. If not, this message is displayed: `No application is associated with this data file. Choose Associate from the File menu to create an association.` If you get this message and you want to run files of this type often, select **F**ile **A**ssociate and tell Windows what to do with this file type.

Most programs name your files with the program's preferred extension when you save the files. Windows knows which program to run in association with your selected files by looking at the `[Extensions]` section of the WIN.INI file. If you open your WIN.INI file with Notepad or SysEdit, you see the filename extensions that were associated during installation. Examples include Notepad and .TXT, and Word for Windows and .DOC, and so on.

File **A**ssociate enables you to update the WIN.INI file even further. It adds another line to that file for every added association. To learn how to modify the WIN.INI file without using the **F**ile **A**ssociate command, see Chapter 27, "Configuring with the WIN.INI and SYSTEM.INI Files."

To create an association between an extension and the program to run it with, select a file with the extension you want and then give the **F**ile **A**ssociate command. The dialog box is shown in Figure 6.11.

In the text box, type the name of the program you want to run when you select files with that extension. When a document is associated with a program, you can start the program and automatically open the document by double-clicking the document's file icon or by selecting it and giving the **F**ile **O**pen command.

For example, the .INI files in the main Windows directory are text files you can read with the Notepad program. Select any file with the .INI extension and give the **F**ile **A**ssociate command. Use the list box to browse the currently associated programs. In this case, look for Notepad on the list. In other cases, if the program that you wish to use to run the filename extension type is not on the list, you can click the Browse button to use a subset of File Manager to find the program file of your choice. Of course, the program must be located on one of your drives before you can associate it to a filename extension. Click the OK button when you're finished and Windows will update your WIN.INI file for you.

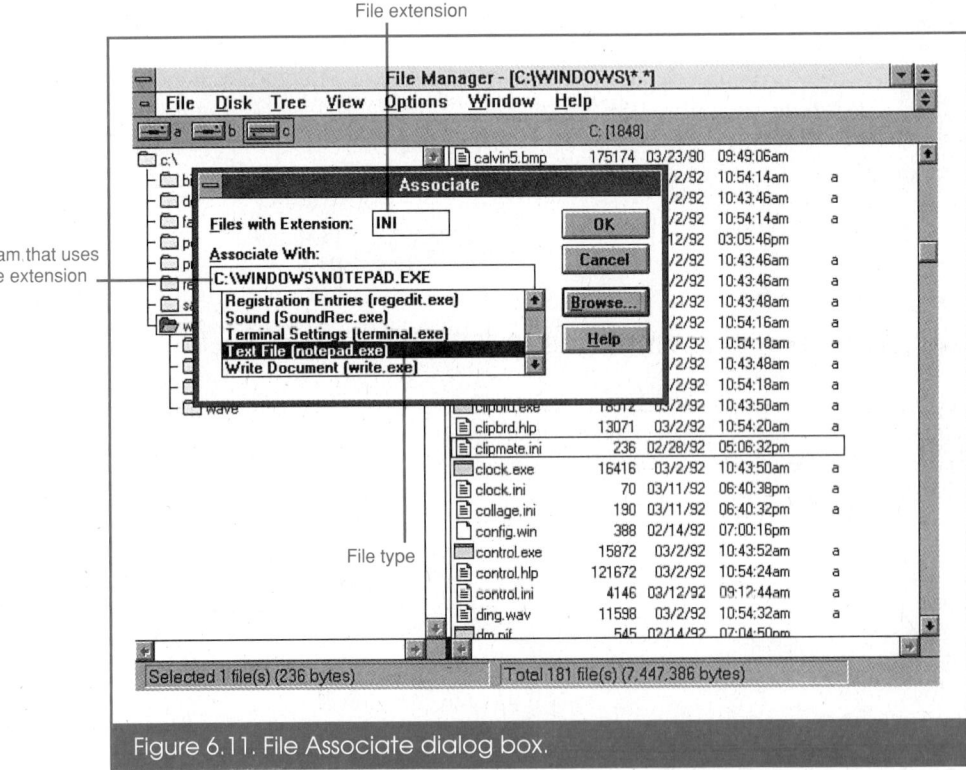

Figure 6.11. File Associate dialog box.

From then on, Windows will know which program to use when you click a file with the same filename extension. In the case of the .INI example, whenever you double-click a filename with the extension of .INI, Notepad will run and open your selected file.

It is unlikely that you will need to use this command, because Windows comes with most of the proper associations built in. Associations between most popular programs (such as 1-2-3, WordPerfect, and Microsoft Word) and their document files are built into the WIN.INI file. You can add your own associations by following the preceding instructions.

6

Printing Files

You can print files directly to an installed printer with one of these methods:

Click the file and drag it onto a minimized Print Manager icon.

To give the **F**ile **P**rint command, select the file and press Alt-F, then press P.

Key board

The **F**ile **P**rint dialog box is shown in Figure 6.12.

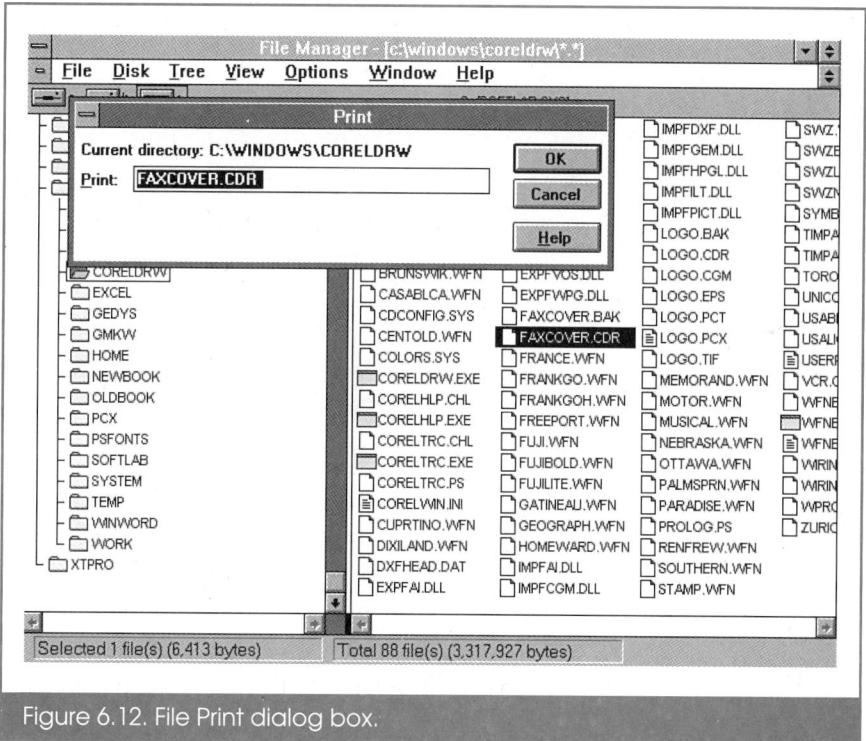

Figure 6.12. File Print dialog box.

If Windows knows which application normally uses the file, it opens that application and prints the file. If Windows does not know which application uses the file, it asks you to associate the file by using the **F**ile **A**ssociate command. Unlike Windows 3.1, previous versions of Windows would print only text (.TXT) files.

> **Note:** .TXT (text) files are in ASCII format (the format Notepad uses). ASCII files can handle only the 256 basic characters of the ASCII character set. The AUTOEXEC.BAT and CONFIG.SYS files are ASCII text files.

To learn a way to print multiple files with the **F**ile Searc**h**, **F**ile **S**et Selection, and **F**ile **P**rint commands, see the "Searching for Files" section later in this chapter.

Creating Directories

If you want to create a directory, select the directory under which you want the new directory created and then give the **F**ile Cr**e**ate Directory command. In this command's dialog box, shown in Figure 6.13, type the name of the new directory and then either click OK or press Enter. If you type a drive designation (for example, a:\) before the directory name, Windows creates the directory on that drive.

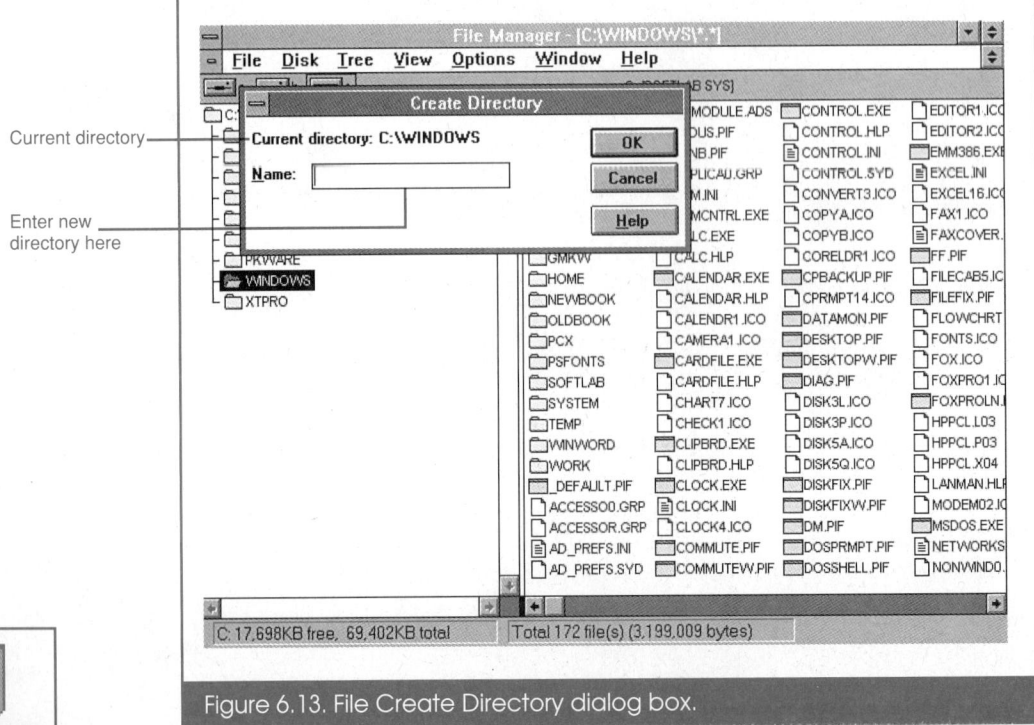

Figure 6.13. File Create Directory dialog box.

Searching for Files

The more files you have on disk, the less likely you are to remember where they are. You can look for the files by opening directory windows, but File Manager gives you a much more direct method—the **F**ile Sear**c**h command. That command's dialog box is shown in Figure 6.14.

6

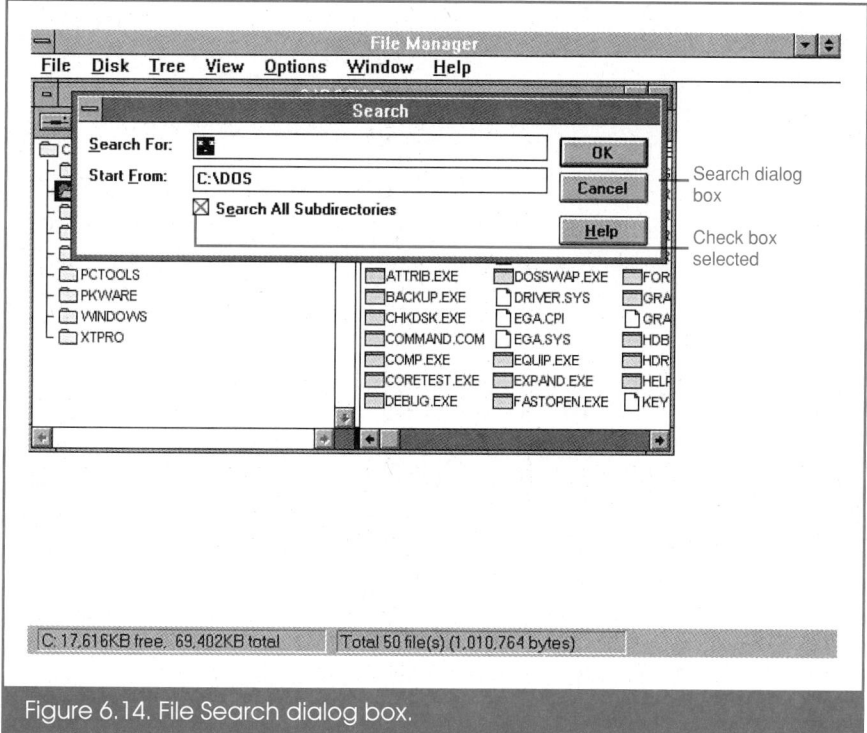

Figure 6.14. File Search dialog box.

Enter the name of the file in the **S**earch For text box. You can use the MS-DOS wildcard characters (* and ?) to replace unknown characters in the filename, or you can search for a specific name. If your file is on a 1.2G (gigabyte) Micropolis network hard drive, and you don't want to review hundreds of document files from all directories, you can specify a starting point. If you deselect the S**e**arch All Directories option, File Manager searches only in the current directory and related subdirectories.

When you click OK, File Manager searches for the specified files and shows a Search Results window similar to that in Figure 6.15. The icons in this list are just like the icons in File Manager's content listing.

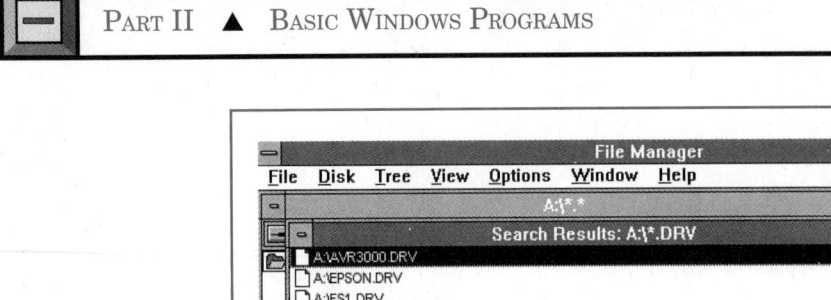

Figure 6.15. Search Results window.

You can treat this window like any other File Manager window. Assume that you want to delete or print all files with the extension .TMP. To do so, you would give the **F**ile Search command, specify *.TMP in the Search For text box, and then click OK. With the Search Results window active, you would give the **F**ile **S**elect All command, then the **F**ile **D**elete or **F**ile **P**rint command. If you double-click any of the filenames displayed in the Search Results window, the file is opened if you have previously associated that filename extension with a program.

You can use the **F**ile **S**et Selection dialog box as a *filter* for File Manager. A filter is a condition you set to limit what happens during a task. The **F**ile **S**et Selection command enables you to specify DOS wildcard substitutions (the * and ? characters) in a command-line text box so that you limit the display of filenames to that of your preference. You can specify any selection of files, such as program files only (*.EXE), all Word for Windows document files only (*.DOC), or all files beginning with the word Boss (BOSS*.*) to locate an important document fast.

MS-DOS Disk-Management Tasks

6

The commands in this section replicate some of the disk commands in MS-DOS. Not all MS-DOS commands have equivalents in File Manager. For example, Windows has no equivalent for the CHKDSK command. The most common disk-level commands, however, are available in the **D**isk menu.

Copying Entire Disks

You can make an exact copy of a diskette with the **D**isk **C**opy Disk command (which is the same as the DISKCOPY command in DOS). The source diskette (the one to be copied) and the destination diskette (the one receiving the files) must be the same size (either 3 1/2-inch or 5 1/4-inch) and type (high or double density), and a diskette must be in one or both floppy disk drives.

When you issue the **D**isk **C**opy Disk command, the dialog box shown in Figure 6.16 is displayed. Choose the destination drive and click OK or press the Enter key. If you are copying to the same drive (similar to DOS's DISKCOPY), File Manager reads the whole diskette, then prompts you to put the destination diskette in the same drive.

Changing Disk Volume Labels

To change the disk label on a hard disk or a floppy disk, use the **D**isk **L**abel Disk command. (This command is the same as the LABEL command in DOS.) The label can be up to 11 characters long and must follow MS-DOS file-naming conventions. The **D**isk **L**abel Disk dialog box is shown in Figure 6.17. File Manager puts the current label in the **L**abel text box so that you know what label you are changing.

Formatting Diskettes

You can format diskettes with the **D**isk **F**ormat Disk command. This command is the same as the FORMAT command in DOS, but safer. Unlike FORMAT, **D**isk **F**ormat Disk formats *diskettes only* (not hard disks). Be sure that File Manager's current drive is not the drive you want to format. Ncither DOS nor Windows gives you the option of formatting the drive from which Windows currently is running. In the **D**isk **F**ormat Disk dialog box (see Figure 6.18), choose the diskette and click OK.

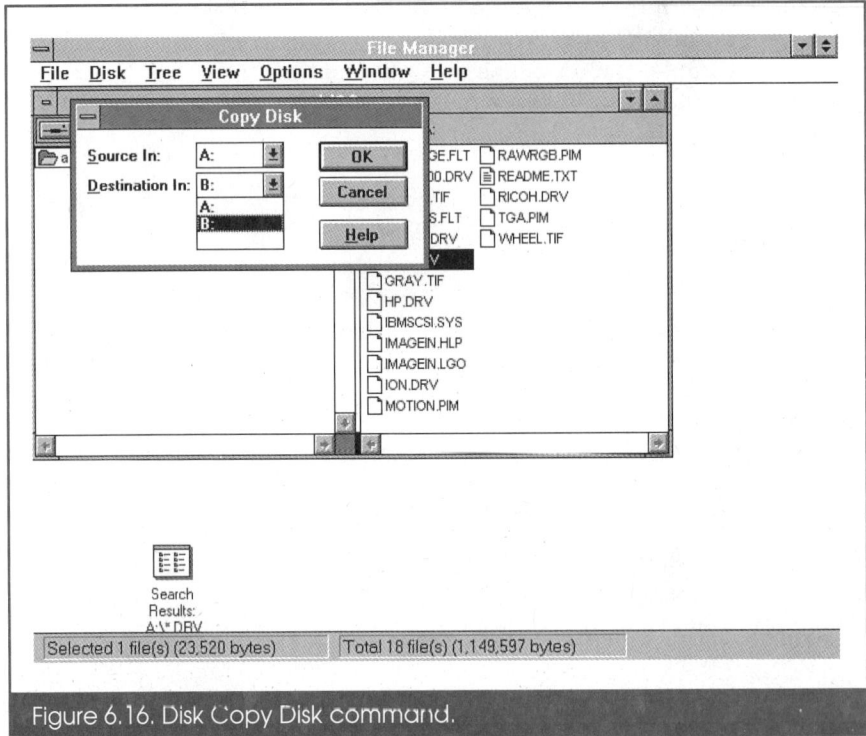

Figure 6.16. Disk Copy Disk command.

Warning: DOS and Windows always format the diskette to the maximum capacity of the drive unless you tell them otherwise. Be sure to select your actual media capacity when using a diskette of less-than-drive capacity. Failure to do so during the Format process produces a formatted diskette of reduced reliability.

If you have selected the **O**ptions **C**onfirmation Disk Commands check box, Windows asks whether you are sure you want to format the diskette. If the floppy disk drive is a high-capacity drive, you can choose to format the diskette as high- or low-density. If you choose to make the diskette a boot diskette, File Manager copies the necessary system files to it.

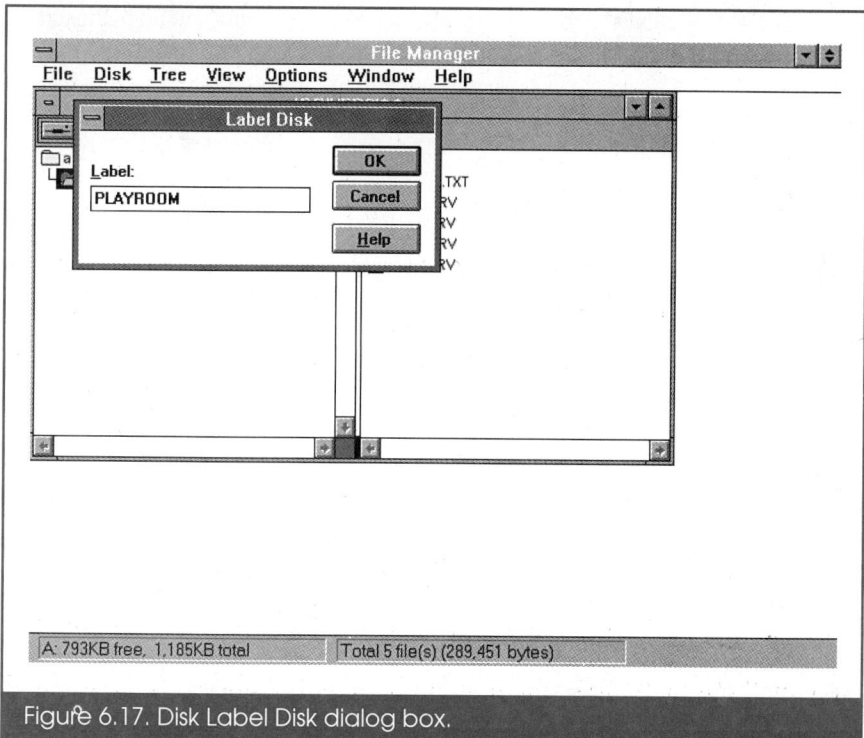

Figure 6.17. Disk Label Disk dialog box.

A faster method of formatting diskettes—cleverly called **Q**uick Format—is available from this dialog box. In the **Q**uick Format process, the *FAT* (File Allocation Table) is found and erased (as it is during normal formatting) but the disk is not scanned for errors. The **Q**uick Format option works only on previously formatted diskettes. It does not format a diskette with no FAT.

Type a label (up to 11 characters) in the text box. Then press Enter or click the OK button to complete the format process.

If you are making a "bootable" floppy diskette or system disk, use the **D**isk **M**ake System Disk command or the **D**isk **F**ormat Disk command and click the Make System Disk check box. You can use either of these options to create a system disk or diskette. If you make a system disk from the **D**isk **F**ormat Disk dialog box, Windows uses the DOS FORMAT x:/s command to make a formatted system disk. If you use the Make System Disk option and dialog box, Windows uses the DOS SYS command to copy the system files on your computer's boot drive to the destination drive. This function is useful if you want to upgrade a bootable floppy from an older version of DOS to a more current version.

The **D**isk **M**ake System disk command's dialog box is shown in Figure 6.19.

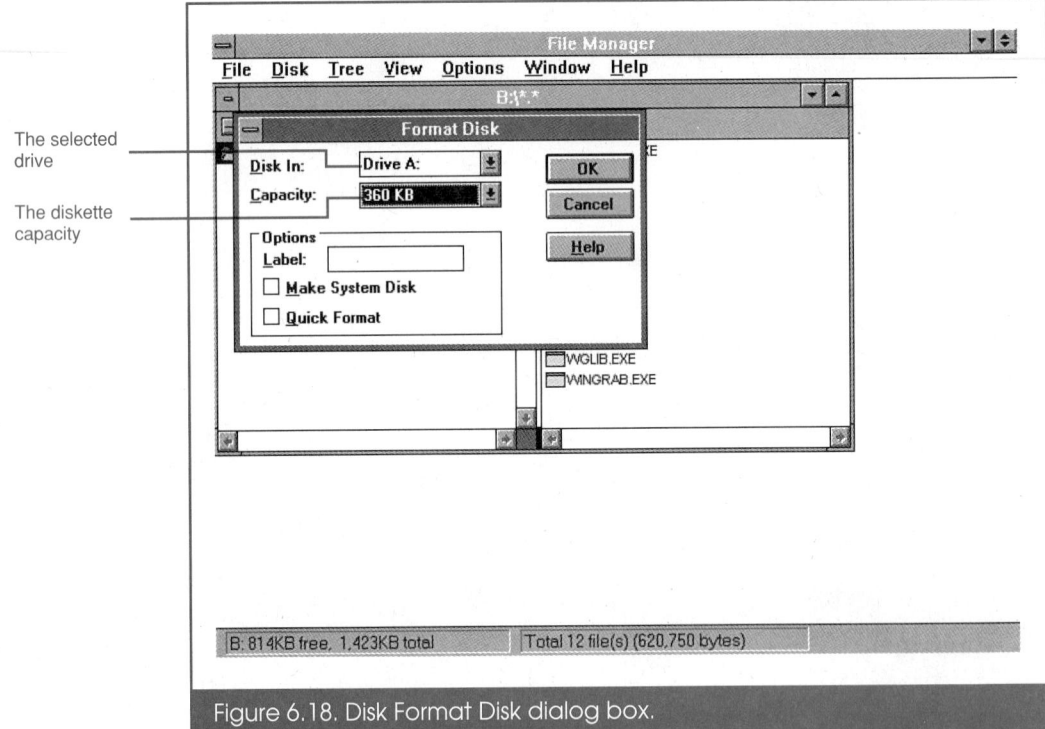

The selected drive

The diskette capacity

Figure 6.18. Disk Format Disk dialog box.

 **Tip**: Generally, the floppy diskette must have no files on it and must be free of errors before you format it. New disks usually are not a problem. Reformatted software-vendor demo disks often are the culprit. When magnetic media (diskettes, for example) are shipped, they can be damaged by other magnetic sources. It's not unlike attaching a diskette to a refrigerator with a little magnet. If you need absolute reliability, throw these freebies away. I have tried to save them, but have found that some diskettes won't reformat because of this sort of damage.

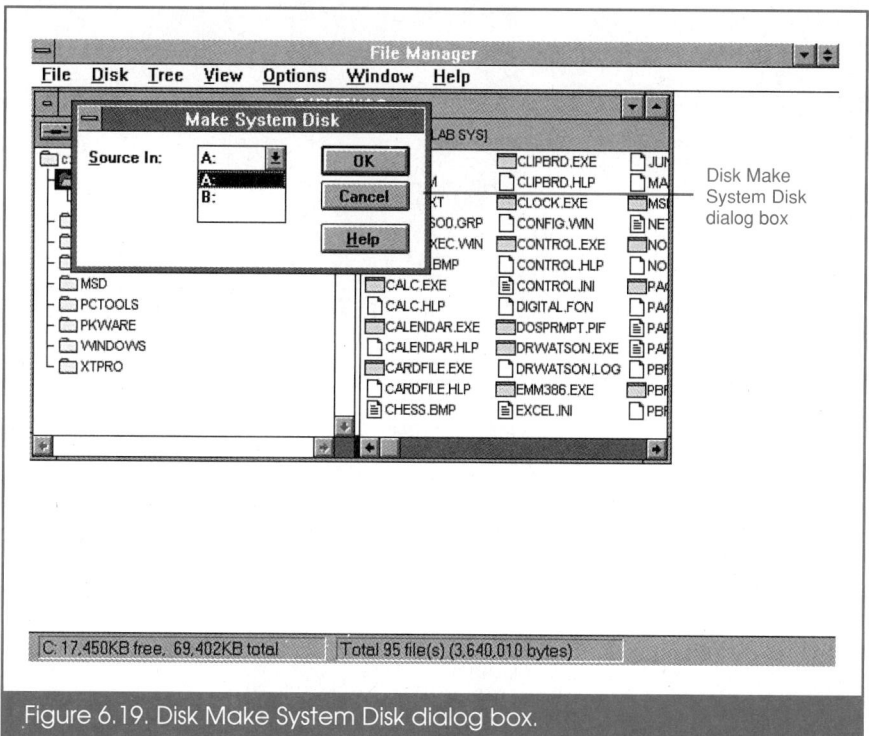

Figure 6.19. Disk Make System Disk dialog box.

View Menu

You can choose how much information is shown in the directory window, as well as the order in which the files are listed. The default is to show just the filename and to list the files in alphabetical order. The options available from the **V**iew menu, shown in Figure 6.20, enable you to change how you are viewing windows in File Manager.

Table 6.3 briefly describes each option.

Table 6.3. File Manager View options.

Option	Description	Hot Key
Tree and Directory	Displays both tree and files	R
Tree Only	Displays only the tree	E
Directory Only	Displays only the files	O

continues

Table 6.3. Continued

Option	Description	Hot Key
Split	Movable vertical window divider	L
Name	Displays only the filenames	N
All File Details	Displays everything about each file	F
Partial Details	Selects display of available details	P
Sort by Name	Sorts files by filename	S
Sort by Type	Sorts files alphabetically by extension name	B
Sort by Size	Sorts files (descending order) by size	Z
Sort by Date	Sorts files (descending order) by last save date	D
By File Type	Displays filtered list by selectable file type	T

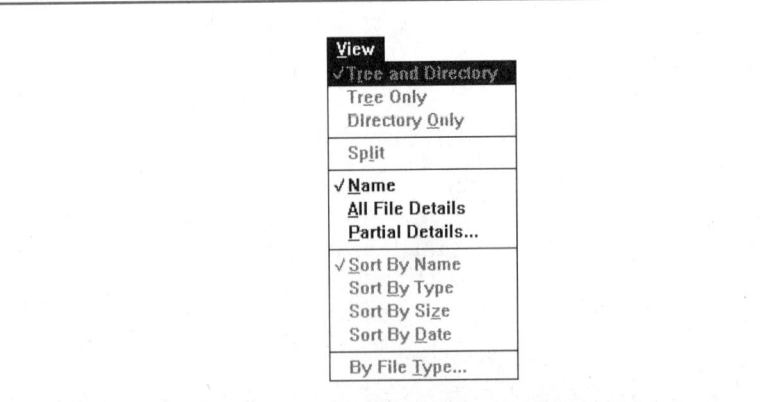

Figure 6.20. View menu.

6

Displaying File Information with View

The **V**iew commands can change the display so that each filename is displayed on a single line (see Figure 6.21). In addition to the filename, each line contains the following:

▲ The File Type icon

▲ Size of the file in bytes

▲ Date of last file save

▲ Time of last file save

▲ File attributes

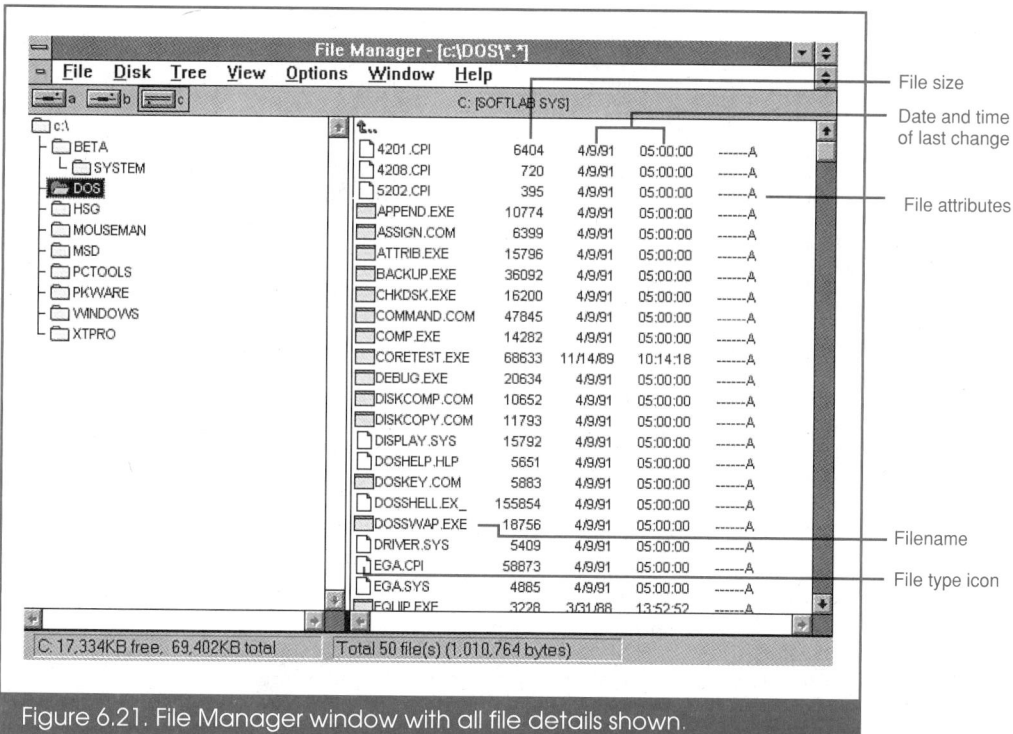

Figure 6.21. File Manager window with all file details shown.

You do not have to display all the information if you do not want to. Use the **V**iew **P**artial Details command to specify which of the last four options you want to see in the window. To make your choice the default (automatically in effect each time you run File Manager), check **O**ptions Save Settings on E**x**it.

Changing the Sort Order

Sorting by filename and by file extension are the two most common ways chosen for sorting filenames in the directory window. To change the order to "by extension," give the **V**iew Sort **B**y Type command. You can use the **V**iew Sort By commands also to sort by filename, type size, or modification date.

> **Tip:** Select Last **M**odification Date to rearrange the list so that the most recently modified file is first. If you keep all your correspondence in one directory, you easily can see your most recent letters first. You may find it helpful also in doing incremental backups.

Selecting the Type of Files to View

The **V**iew By File **T**ype command tells File Manager what type of files you want to include in the file content list. To filter out file types you don't want to see, give the **V**iew By File **T**ype command and then use the **V**iew By File **T**ype dialog box (see Figure 6.22) to choose the files you want to see. (You can choose to look at only program or document files, for example.) To make your choice(s) the default whenever you run File Manager, check Set System Default.

The **V**iew **N**ame option enables you to narrow the list of files shown in the window. Use the **V**iew Name option when you want a temporary way to limit the files you see, such as when you want to see only files that start with the letter W or only documents with the filename extension of .DOC. You can use the MS-DOS wildcard characters * and ? in the filename, also.

> **Tip:** Professional office support personnel may want to set the **V**iew By File **T**ype to list only .DOC or .TXT files if only these files usually are needed.

The **V**iew By File **T**ype choices enable you to exclude certain types of files. If you want to see only files that Windows knows to be programs or documents, for example, you deselect **O**ther Files. DOS has inherited the CP/M methodology of identifying files types by reading the filename extension. Whenever Windows looks at a file for file type, it uses the

6

filename extension to identify that file's purpose. An example would be a .COM or .EXE file. The .COM or .EXE filename extensions always denote executable or program files. This, by the way, is another great way of disguising private files on a public system. Change the name from .DOC (for example) to .EXE, and most people would not even consider reading your file. Rename the file back to it's original filename extension before trying to open it by double-clicking it from File Manager, though, or you will experience problems when Windows tries to execute the file.

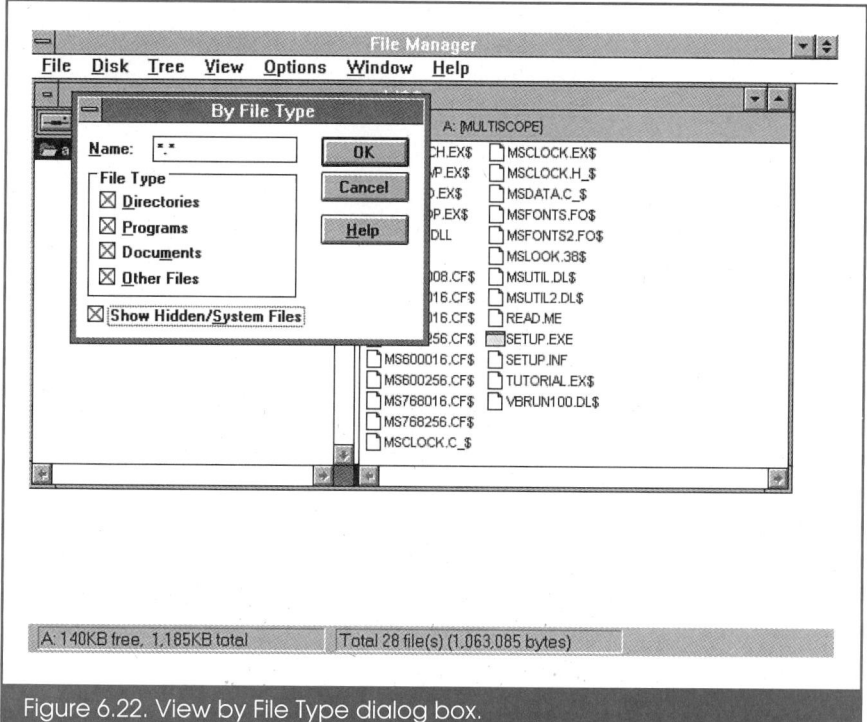

Figure 6.22. View by File Type dialog box.

If DOS were designed with the notion of identifying file usage by information contained in the file header like the Macintosh does, we could have variable file naming conventions, or really, no file naming coventions at all. You could be naming your files "My favorite Word Processor" instead of WORD.EXE. CP/M was the predecessor to DOS in the desktop computer world, and many of the people that had a hand in making CP/M popular in its day, also helped to pioneer the establishment of the Disk Operating System, or DOS.

Files that have the hidden or system attribute set "on" normally do not appear in the file list the first time you start Windows 3.1. If you select Show Hidden/System Files, you can see these files in the file contents list.

Tip: If other people use your computer, you probably should disable the Show Hidden/System Files option. Inadvertently moving or deleting hidden/system files can cause a great deal of trouble and cost you time. If your hidden/system files are moved or deleted, you must start your computer from a bootable floppy disk until you correct the problem.

Options Menu

Several general File Manager options are found in the **O**ptions menu, shown in Figure 6.23.

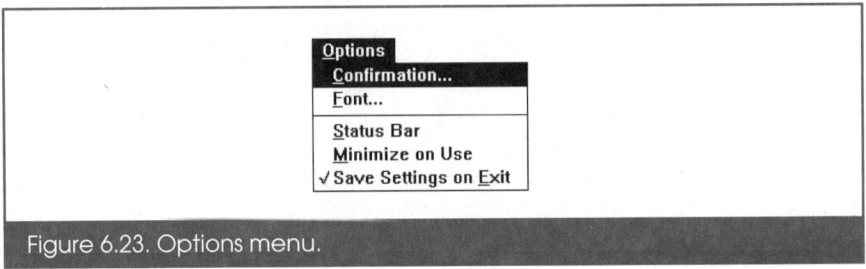

Figure 6.23. Options menu.

Confirming File Operations

The **C**onfirmation option, mentioned earlier in this chapter, controls whether File Manager displays a confirmation alert when you work with files in any way that can leave you in a lurch if you make a mistake. The **C**onfirmation option can be used to prevent display of the alert during the following operations: deleting a file or directory, replacing or moving files, and copying files.

If you do not want to see the confirmation dialog box when you use the mouse to perform certain file operations (such as copying or moving), give the **O**ptions **C**onfirmation command and deselect the appropriate check boxes. The **O**ptions **C**onfirmation dialog box, shown in Figure 6.24, tells File Manager whether to display a confirmation alert when you delete files, and so on.

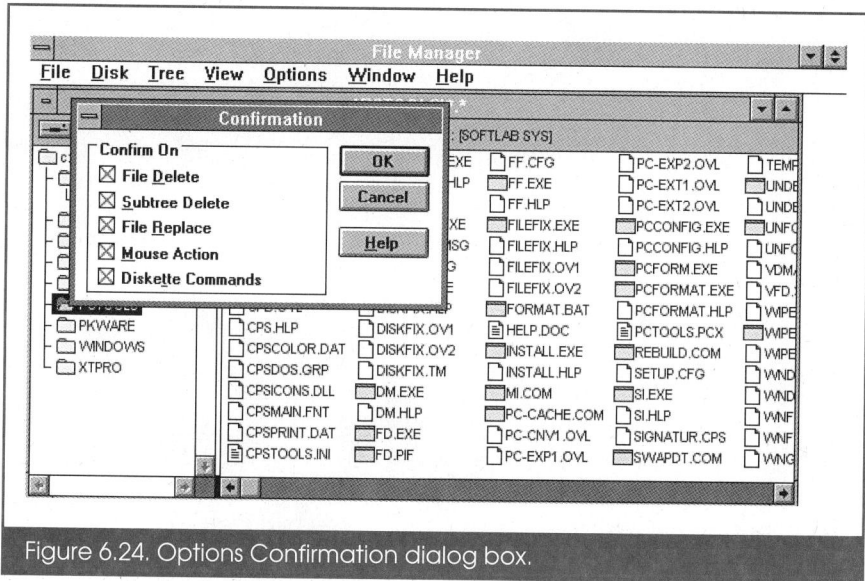

Figure 6.24. Options Confirmation dialog box.

When File Manager starts, all the options listed in Table 6.4 are selected.

Table 6.4. Options Confirmation options.

Option	Description
Confirm on File **D**elete	Displays an alert before deleting files
Confirm on **S**ubtree Delete	Displays an alert before deleting a subdirectory that is not visible when you delete a directory
Confirm on File **R**eplace	Displays an alert before replacing files on the disk with other ones you are copying or moving
Confirm on **M**ouse Action	Displays an alert before copying or moving files you dragged with the mouse
Confirm on Diskette Commands	Displays an alert before formatting or copying entire diskettes

If you do not want to receive the warning, Are you sure you want to copy the selected files into drive:\directory? when copying or moving files, for example, you simply deselect the Confirm on **M**ouse Action check box.

The Options Font Dialog Box

You can change the font used to display file and directory names in File Manager. As shown in Figure 6.25, in the **O**ptions **F**ont dialog box are three list boxes, three buttons, one check box, and a sample-text display box; descriptions of these are in the following list. When there are many choices, the list boxes can be scrolled.

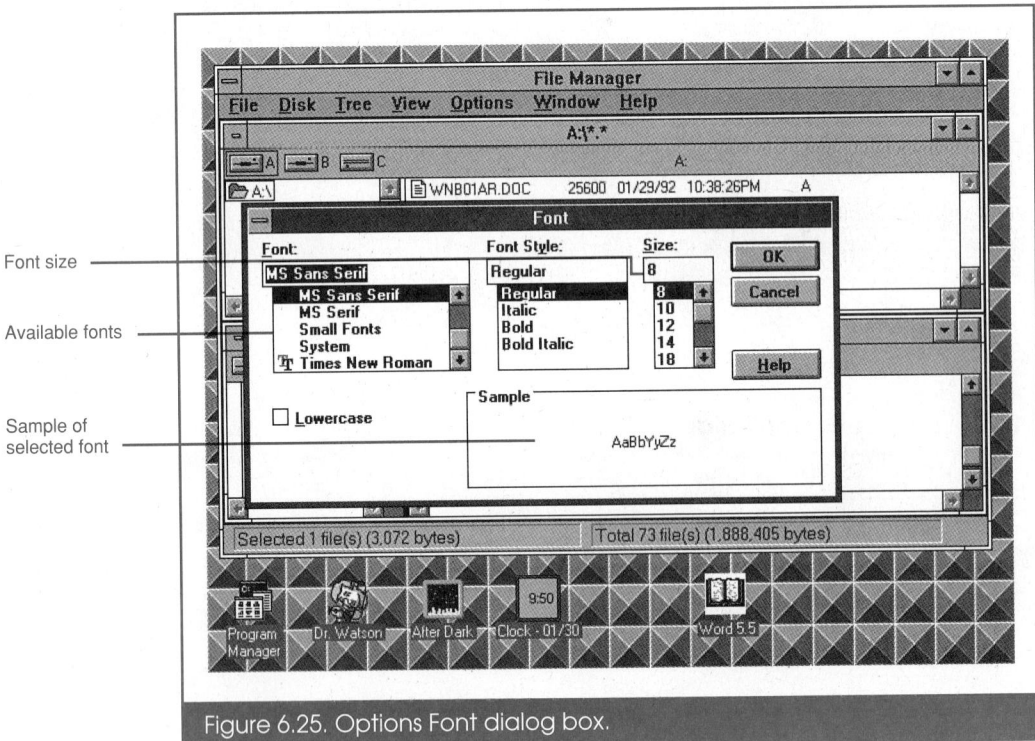

Figure 6.25. Options Font dialog box.

In the *Font list box*, the currently selected font is at the top of the list, followed by other available fonts. You can select and use only one font. When you select a font from the list, all text in the Disk Manager window changes to reflect the changed font.

6

The *Font Style list box* offers the styles available for the selected font. Regular, Bold, Italic, and Bold Italic are common.

The *Size list box* adjusts the character display size—that is, the size each character appears on-screen.

Lowercase check box. You can select or deselect the Lowercase check box, allowing only uppercase or lowercase to be used when displaying text in a window.

A sample of the currently selected font is displayed in the Sample box on the lower-right side of the Font dialog box. When you change any of the settings (other than the Lowercase setting), you see a corresponding change in the Sample box.

When you are satisfied with your changes, press Enter or click the OK button. Experimentation is the best way to determine which font configuration you prefer.

Other Options

You may use other options from time to time. For example, The **O**ptions **S**tatus Bar command tells File Manager whether to display the status bar at the bottom of the File Manager window.

As discussed earlier in this chapter, **O**ptions **M**inimize on Use causes File Manager to be reduced to an icon when you run a program from it. This option is useful when you are using File Manager to start programs and don't want to see the File Manager window after the programs are launched.

You can make your choices in this dialog box the default whenever you run File Manager by selecting **O**ptions Save Settings On **E**xit.

The Window Commands

You can manipulate windows within File Manager by selecting the **W**indow item from the File Manager menu. The options presented will let you work directly with windows to arrange and update them.

Making Multiple Windows

You can make multiple windows so that you can see several drives and directories simultaneously on-screen. Choose **W**indow **N**ew Window to create an exact copy of the currently active window. File Manager does not create an empty window, so it always recreates the window in the foreground, or the active window when it makes a new window.

Double-click a drive icon to create a new window for the drive.

The Cascade and Tile Commands

Two File Manager commands help you arrange windows: the **W**indow **C**ascade and **W**indow **T**ile commands automatically rearrange all open windows.

Figure 6.26 shows the result of cascading three open directory windows. The window that was in the foreground when you gave the command remains the active window.

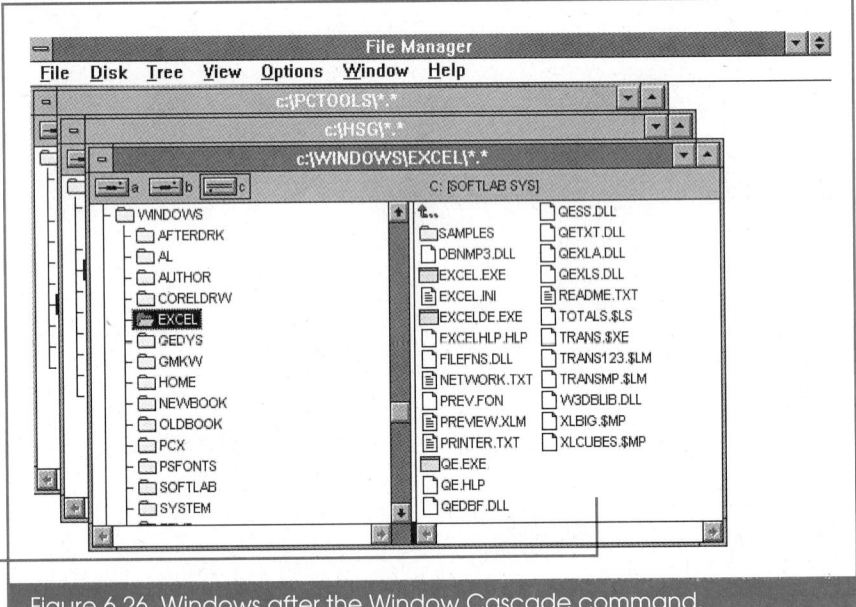

Figure 6.26. Windows after the Window Cascade command.

The **W**indow **T**ile command reshapes the windows so that they fill the entire File Manager window, each with the same area. As you can see from Figure 6.27, tiling more than three windows usually enables you to see only a few filenames. Thus, the command commonly is used for no more than two windows.

6

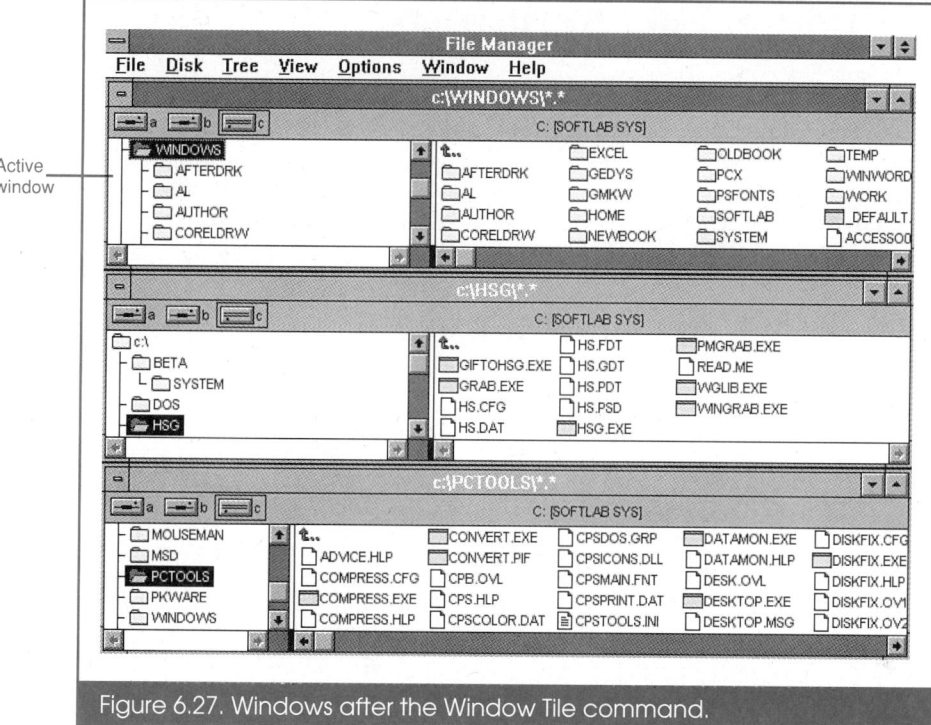

Active window

Figure 6.27. Windows after the Window Tile command.

Arranging Minimized Window Icons

You can arrange minimized window icons across the bottom of the File Manager window with the **W**indow **A**rrange Icons command. When you give this command, any minimized window icons are spaced evenly from left to right across the File Manager window. The effect of this command on minimized icons is similar to that of the **W**indow **A**rrange Icons command given from Program Manager.

Refreshing Windows

If you are running some non-Windows programs that add or delete files, the directory window may not be properly updated when you return to File Manager (but this is rare). To be sure that the directory window is up-to-date, give the **W**indow **R**efresh command.

Quitting File Manager

If you use the **F**ile E**x**it command to leave File Manager, and you have selected **O**ptions Save Setup on E**x**it, your settings are saved. If you opted not to save your settings, the current, unchanged settings will be used the next time you start File Manager. File Manager settings are saved in a file called WINFILE.INI in the main Windows directory.

Starting File Manager When You Start Windows

If you use File Manager a great deal, you may want to have it open when Windows starts. To do this, drag or copy the File Manager icon to the Startup Program Group.

A few people use File Manager more than Program Manager, sometimes using it (instead of Program Manager) to start programs. If you find yourself doing this, you may want to make File Manager your primary Windows program. You may want to change the shell= line in the SYSTEM.INI file to point to File Manager rather than to Program Manager (see Chapter 27, "Configuring with the WIN.INI and SYSTEM.INI Files").

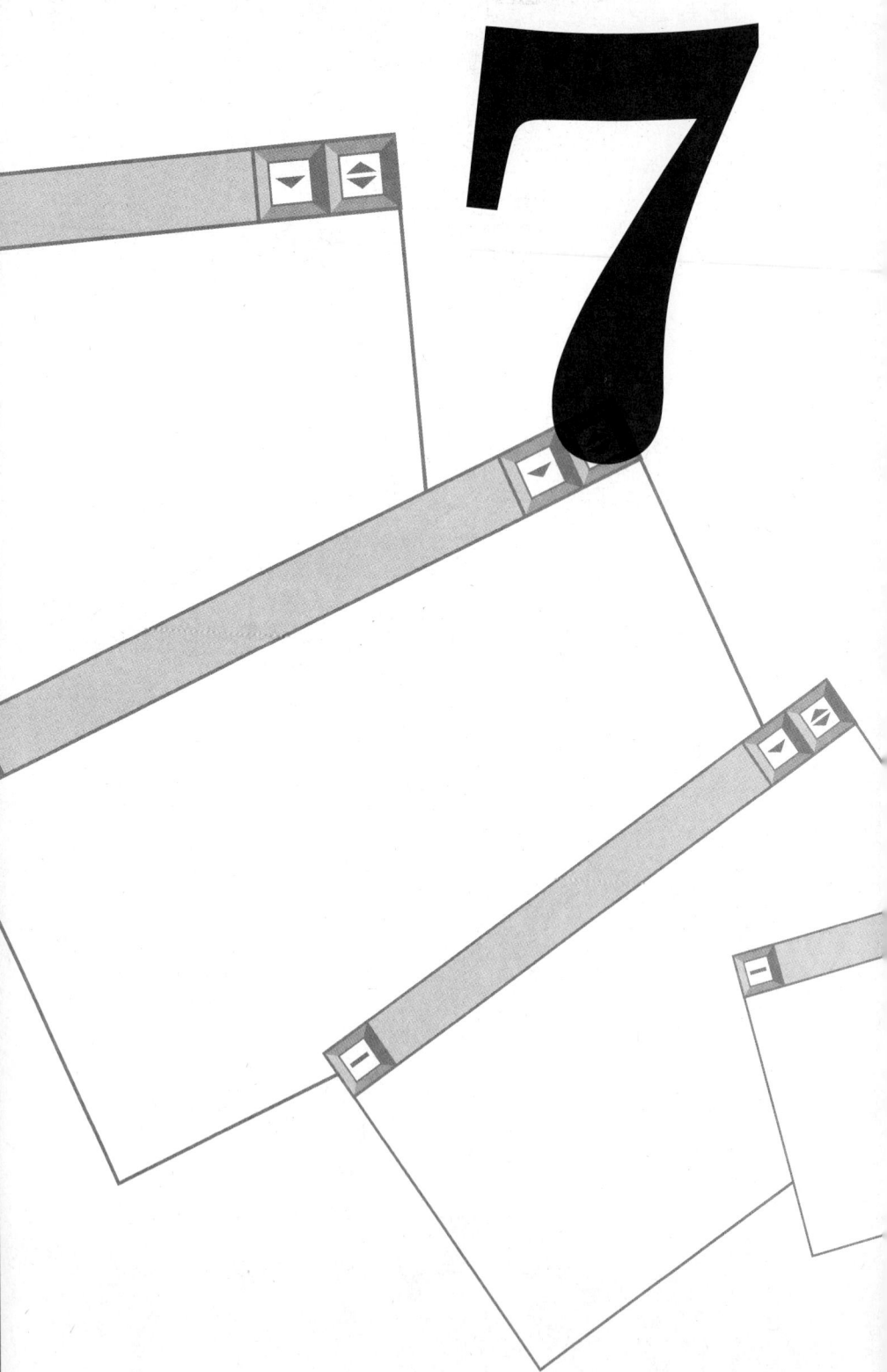

CHAPTER

7

Control Panel

Control Panel is the basic place where you change the way Windows operates and how it looks. Although you often have these choices in each program as well, Windows concentrates most of the choices into Control Panel so that you know where to go first when you want to change system settings.

Control Panel's window is shown in Figure 7.1. In it you can see icons that represent the basic items you change with Control Panel. To see the specific choices for each item, you open the icon. If you are part of a Local or Wide Area Network (LAN or WAN), a network icon also appears in the Control Panel Window.

To open a Control Panel icon's dialog box, do the following:

Double-click the icon.

Select the icon with the ← and → keys, then press the Enter key.

You also can select any of the icons from their equivalent commands in the **S**ettings menu, shown in Figure 7.2.

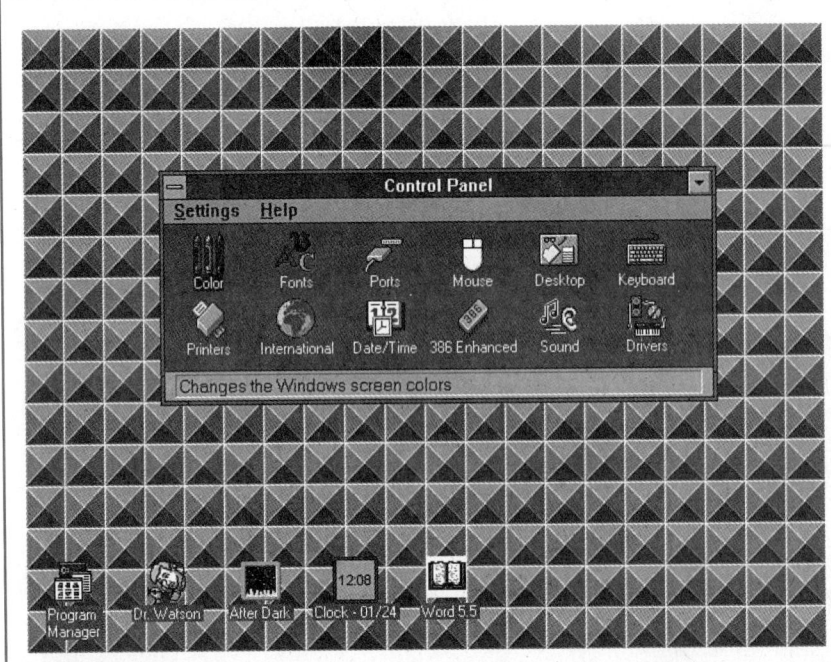

Figure 7.1. Control Panel window.

Files Modified by Control Panel

Before we discuss Control Panel and the items it can change, let's look at some files that store the changes you make in Control Panel. Windows uses these files to reference changes made here in Control Panel and in other places in the software. There are three major system files—WIN.INI, CONTROL.INI, and SYSTEM.INI.

When you make changes to any of the Control Panel settings, Windows stores those changes and remembers them the next time you run Windows. It writes the changes for most of the icons into the WIN.INI file in your main Windows directory. The WIN.INI file is a text file that you can edit if you want to. See Chapter 27, "Configuring with the WIN.INI and SYSTEM.INI Files," for a complete description of how to edit the WIN.INI file.

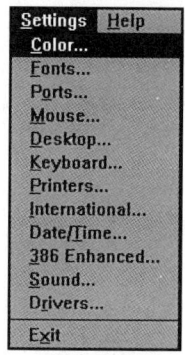

Figure 7.2. Control Panel Settings menu.

Some of the changes you make in Control Panel are stored in the file called CONTROL.INI in your main Windows directory. That file is also a text file that can be edited. The CONTROL.INI file also is described in Chapter 27, "Configuring with the WIN.INI and SYSTEM.INI Files."

The Color Option

The Color dialog box enables you to change the colors used by Windows for many of the items you see on the screen. Windows keeps *color schemes* that are groups of color definitions for items. You can choose a pre-made scheme or create your own schemes, giving them your own names. You also can edit the color choices in Windows's schemes.

> **Tip:** Because the figures in this book are in black-and-white, the illustrations in this section do not reflect what you will see as you use the Color icon. You should be sure to run Control Panel as you read this section so that you can see the variety of choices available to you.

Coloring Items

Figure 7.3 shows the dialog box for the Color icon. The Color **S**chemes section enables you to choose a color scheme from the drop-down list.

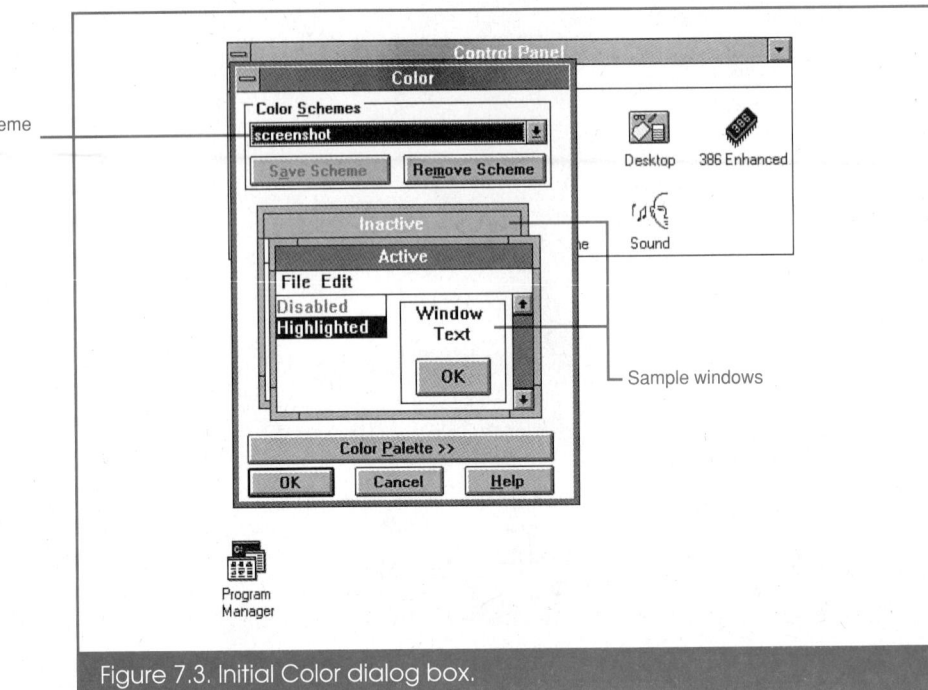

Choose a scheme
from the list

Sample windows

Figure 7.3. Initial Color dialog box.

The predefined color schemes are shown in Table 7.1.

Table 7.1. Predefined color schemes.

Color Scheme	General Design Feel
Windows Default	Plain
Arizona	Dark with earthy tones
Black Leather Jacket	Gray and purple tones
Bordeaux	Wine colors
Cinnamon	Shades of red tones
Designer	Grays and greens
Emerald City	Shades of green
Fluorescent	Garish and bright
Hot Dog Stand	Bold red and yellow
LCD Default Screen Settings	Grays and blue

Color Scheme	General Design Feel
LCD Reversed Dark	Olive, blue, black, and red
LCD Reversed Light	Gray-blues and white
Mahogany	Burgundy on gray
Monochrome	Washed-out gray
Ocean	Sea blues and greens
Pastel	Muted pastels
Patchwork	Festive polka dots
Plasma Power Saver	Fiery reds and blues
Rugby	Classic Ivy League colors
The Blues	Subdued blue-grays
Tweed	Shades of fall foliage
Valentine	Mixed pinks
Wingtips	Masculine browns

As you choose different color schemes, the area below the Color
Schemes section changes to show you the general pattern of your
new colors.

Creating and Editing Color Schemes

If you want to change some of the colors in a predefined color scheme,
choose the color scheme in the list that is most similar to the one you
want to create, and click the Color **P**alette » button below the color
samples. After selecting colors for screen elements, click on the Save
Scheme button to name and save your newly created color settings.
The window expands to show you the colors available, as shown in
Figure 7.4.

The Screen **E**lement drop-down list enables you to choose each element
on which you want to change the color. Choose an item from the list,
then choose a color either from the **B**asic Colors or the **C**ustom Colors

sections. You learn how to create your own custom colors in the next
section. Table 7.2 shows the elements listed in the Screen **E**lement list.

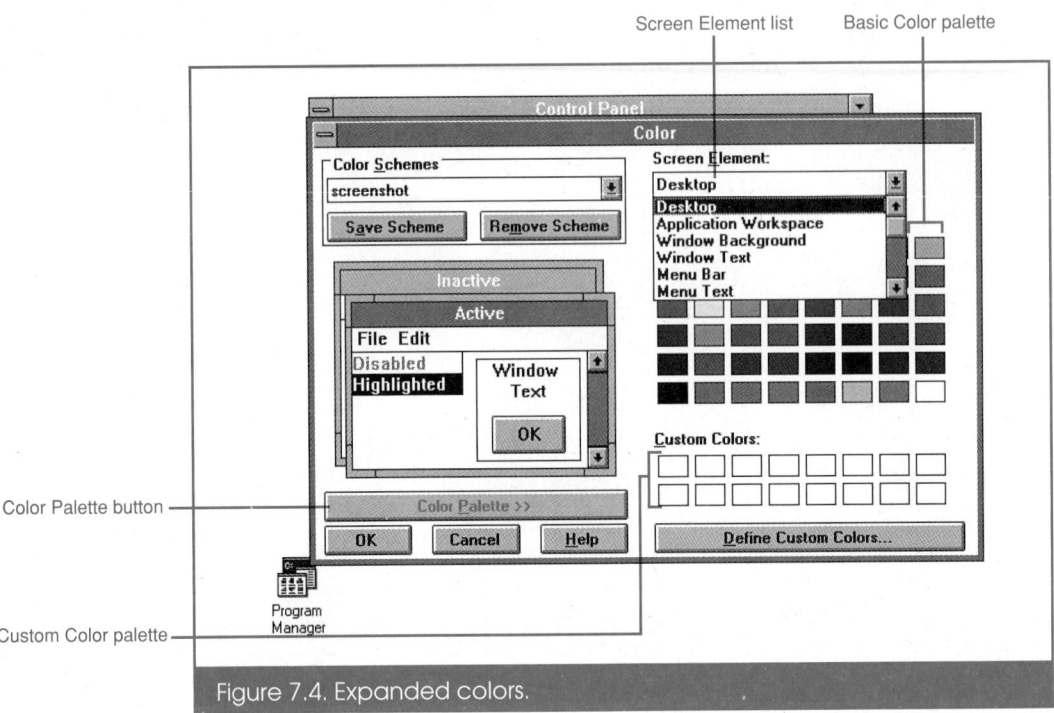

Figure 7.4. Expanded colors.

Table 7.2. Screen Element list.

Element	Screen Area
Desktop	Background for Windows
Application Workspace	Background for the program
Window Background	Window's background
Window Text	Window's text
Menu Bar	Menu bar background
Menu Text	Menu text
Active Title Bar	Active window's title bar
Inactive Title Bar	Inactive window's title bar
Active Title Bar Text	Active title bar text
Inactive Title Bar Text	Inactive title bar text

Element	Screen Area
Active Border	Active window's border
Inactive Border	Inactive window's border
Window Frame	Window's frame
Scroll Bars	Scroll bar
Button Face	Button surfaces
Button Shadow	Lower-right edge of buttons
Button Text	Text that appears on buttons
Button Highlight	Upper-left edge of buttons
Disabled Text	Menu options seen but not available
Highlight	Highlight bar on menus
Highlighted Text	Text on highlight bar

Creating Custom Colors

The **B**asic Colors section has many good colors to choose from, but it might not have all the ones you want for all the elements. Control Panel makes it easy to create your own colors and use them in any element. To create a custom color, select one of the 16 blank boxes in the **C**ustom Colors section and click the **D**efine Custom Colors button. You see the window shown in Figure 7.5.

A color is made up of the *hue* (the wavelength of the light in the color spectrum), the *luminosity* (the brightness of the color), and the *saturation* (the purity of the hue, from gray to the absolute color).

The large color patch (the *refinement area*) in the main part of the window shows the total selection of the colors that can be produced by your monitor. This area enables you to refine the color you want by moving the cross-shaped cursor. Moving up in the refinement area decreases the saturation (decreases the amount of gray). Moving to the right increases the hue. You can place the arrow pointer on the color patch, press and hold the left mouse button, and drag anywhere on the color patch and see the respective hues at the location in the Color | **S**olid box. The cross-shaped cursor will remain wherever your pointer is when you lift your finger off the left mouse button.

The vertical rectangle to the right of the color patch is the *luminosity bar*. When you move the triangular arrow up the bar, you increase the luminosity of the selected color. You must use the mouse to move the cursor and the arrow in the top part of the window. If you want to use the keyboard, you must enter numbers in the six boxes at the bottom of the window.

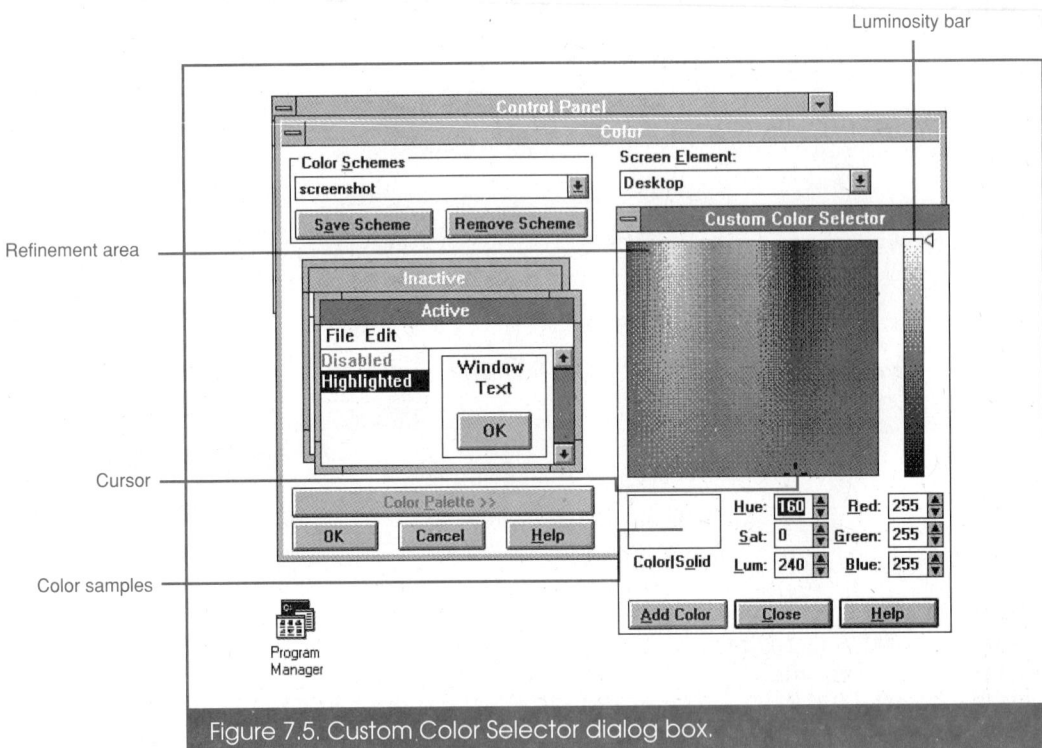

Figure 7.5. Custom Color Selector dialog box.

Note that the red, green, and blue values change as you change the value of the hue, luminosity, and saturation. The red, green, and blue values do not correspond to the color itself but rather to the interpretation of the adapter card and monitor you are using. Your video adapter card interprets color and your screen presents that color. Your video card might only be capable of displaying 16 colors at any one time. If you use the generic Windows drivers (VGA.DRV and SUPERVGA.DRV) you will get two resolutions, but you can still only display 16 colors at any one time. If you wish to work with other shades of the same basic color type, you must use a 256-color driver, and your video card must have at least 512K of video memory on it. Higher resolutions require more memory to display 256 or more colors. The classic dilemma for programmers is the yellow versus brown screen color attributes in character-based programs. Some video adapters display yellow as yellow, and some display it as brown. Because of the problems with video standard inconsistencies, there can be quite some variance in tones between two seemingly similar computers.

When you have created the color you want, click the **A**dd Color button. You can cancel the Custom Color Selector window by clicking the **C**lose button. When the Custom Color Selector window is open, you can create many custom colors simply by choosing a color, then clicking **A**dd Color.

> **Tip:** If you want to create a color that is similar to one of the colors in the **B**asic Colors area, click the color, then click the **D**efine Custom Colors button. The Custom Color Selector window opens with that color shown.

The Fonts Option

A font is a character of a particular style or typeface. Windows Setup installs a variety of fonts that work with many printers. The dialog box for the Fonts icon is shown in Figure 7.6. In Windows, fonts are stored as sets. That is, all the sizes of fonts for one typeface are in a single file. Thus, lines in the Installed Fonts list box display all the sizes for a particular typeface, such as Courier. As you select fonts in the list, Control Panel shows samples at the bottom of the dialog box.

TrueType fonts can be enabled by clicking the TrueType button. A dialog box opens that enables you to select from two check boxes. TrueType fonts are WYSIWYG (pronounced whizzy-whig). WYSIWYG means what-you-see-is-what-you-get. With true WYSIWYG, printed material is supposed to be identical to what you see on your screen before you print it. With TrueType fonts, characters appear on your screen exactly as they do in print. TrueType fonts are enabled when you install Windows 3.1. If you select the Enable TrueType Fonts option, you allow Windows to utilize the font of the same name that is located in the printer, rather than the TrueType font. If you select the Show Only TrueType Fonts in Applications check box, Windows uses the TrueType font rather than the font located in the printer, enabling the screen and printed characters' appearance to be virtually identical.

To install a font on the hard disk, click the **A**dd button. You see a standard browse box that prompts you for the font file that contains the fonts you want to add, as shown in Figure 7.7.

Installed fonts ——

Font Sample box ——

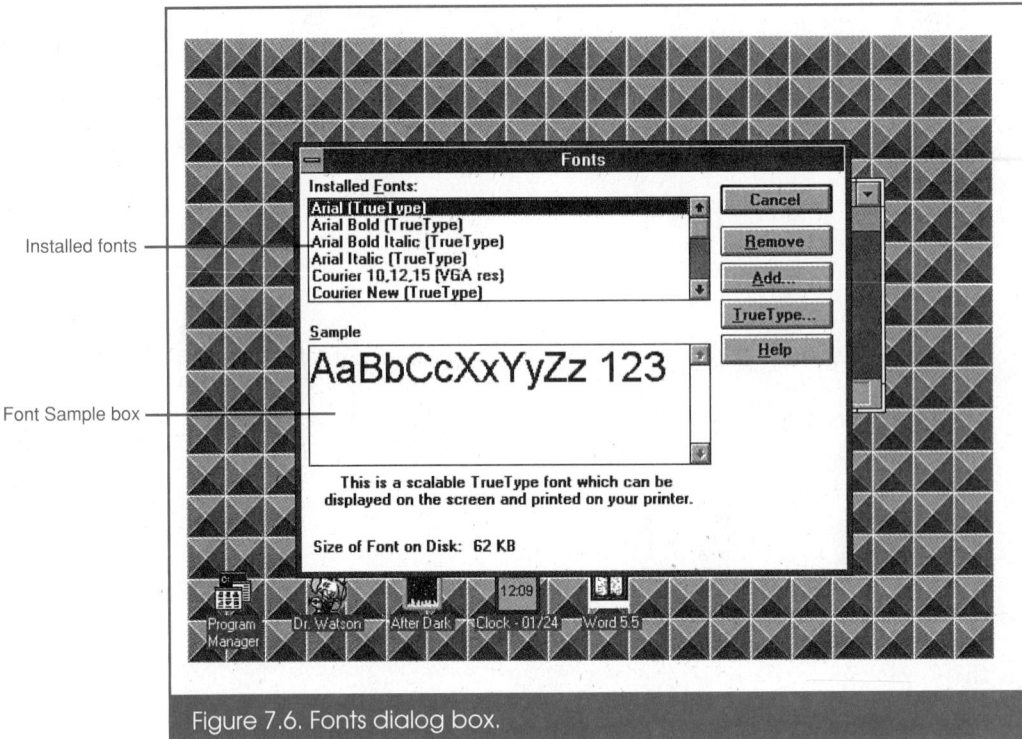

Figure 7.6. Fonts dialog box.

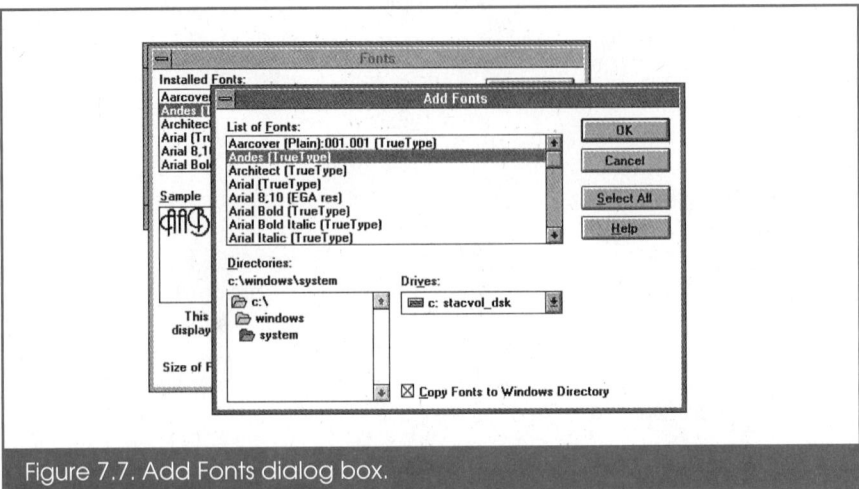

Figure 7.7. Add Fonts dialog box.

Tip: In the Add Fonts dialog box, you can select more than one file at a time. Use the file selection techniques discussed in Chapter 6, "File Manager," to select all the fonts between two selections or to select individual fonts. This makes it convenient to add many font files from a diskette at once.

To remove fonts, select the font from the available fonts in the list box and click (or tab to) the **R**emove button. A dialog box opens, asking you to confirm your desire to remove the selected font. A check box is provided if you also want to remove the font from the disk where it resides. When you remove the font from the disk, you delete the font file.

The Ports Option

The Ports icon enables you to configure the serial (COM:) ports on your PC. The initial window is shown in Figure 7.8. A COM port is your point of access for the computer. When you want to use external devices (other than printers) attached to your computer, you usually use a COM port. You need to tell Windows how your external devices are to access your computer with the port settings provided in the Ports dialog box.

When you select any of the ports and click the **S**ettings button, you see the window in Figure 7.9.

For each port, you can set the baud rate, number of data bits, parity, number of stop bits, and flow control (type of handshaking) the port uses. Check with the manual for the device attached to the port for information on the desired settings.

When you click the **A**dvanced button, the Advanced Settings for COM (1-4) dialog box opens. Normally, you cannot use all four COM ports (if your particular system has a total of four) simultaneously. You can assign interrupt levels for your ports and devices by first selecting the port address from the Basic I/O Port Address drop-down list box. Next, select the desired Interrupt Request Line (IRQ) opening the list box provides. If you aren't sure of the IRQ to use, don't change these settings now. See Chapter 25, "Changing Your Configuration," for more details before continuing with advanced settings. Some older printers and modems will not operate at the port's maximum baud rates. See your device's manual for details on how to set the Port settings.

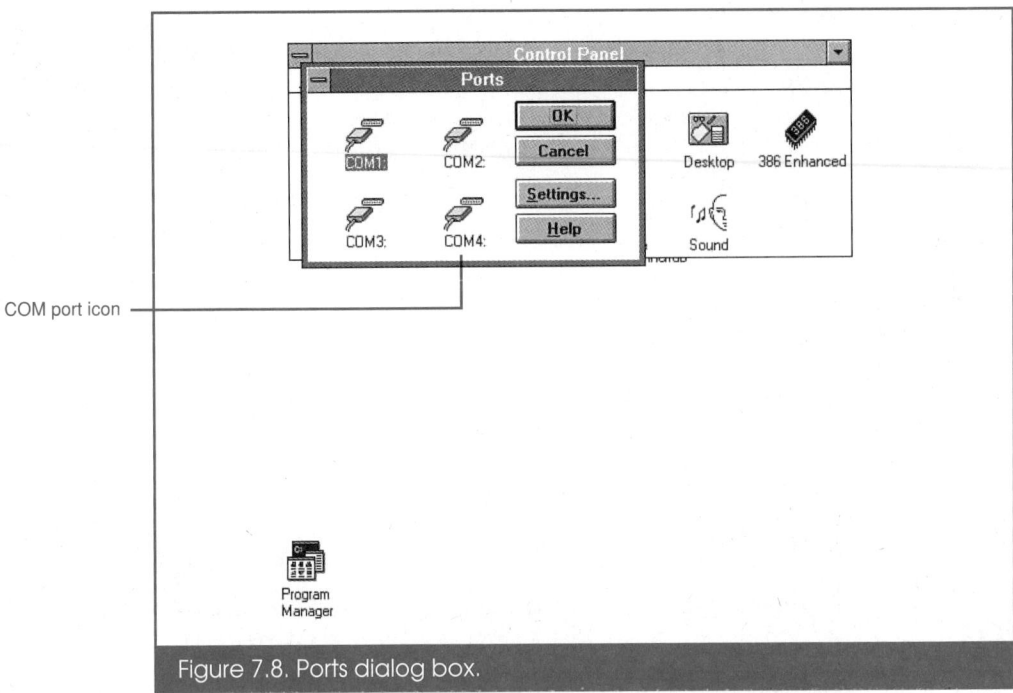

COM port icon

Figure 7.8. Ports dialog box.

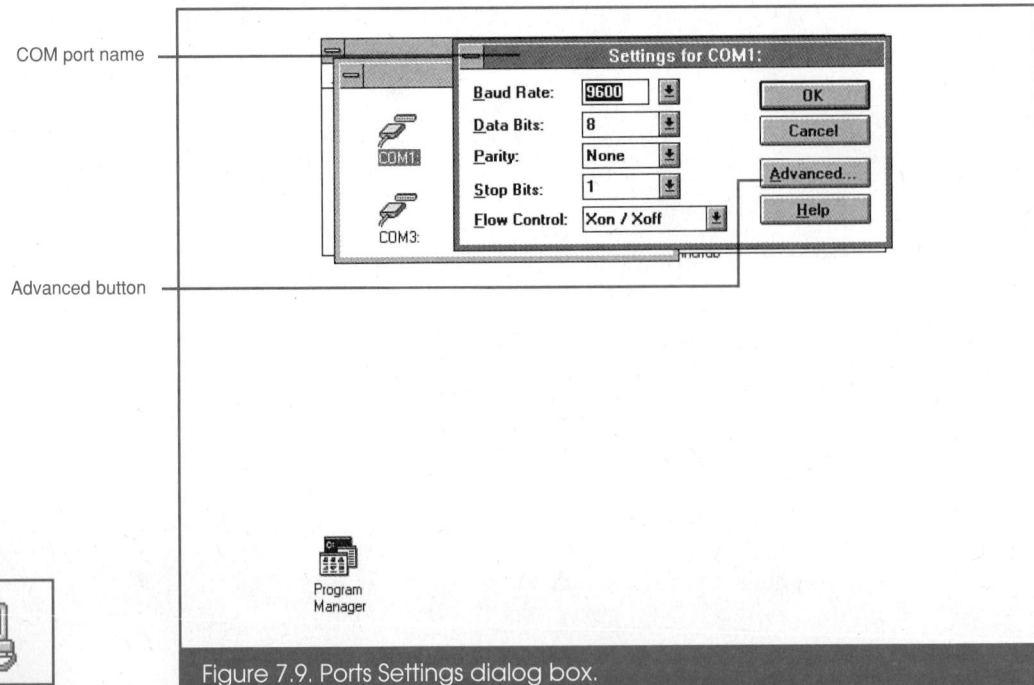

COM port name

Advanced button

Figure 7.9. Ports Settings dialog box.

Warning: Do not use Xon/Xoff handshaking on a port transmitting binary data because the port might lock up. Generally, you will choose None for the handshaking unless the device attached to the port expects hardware handshaking.

The Mouse Option

The Mouse icon can be used both to change how the mouse works and to test current settings. This window, shown in Figure 7.10, has three options: adjusting the tracking speed, adjusting the double-click speed, and swapping the buttons. All Windows applications use these mouse settings.

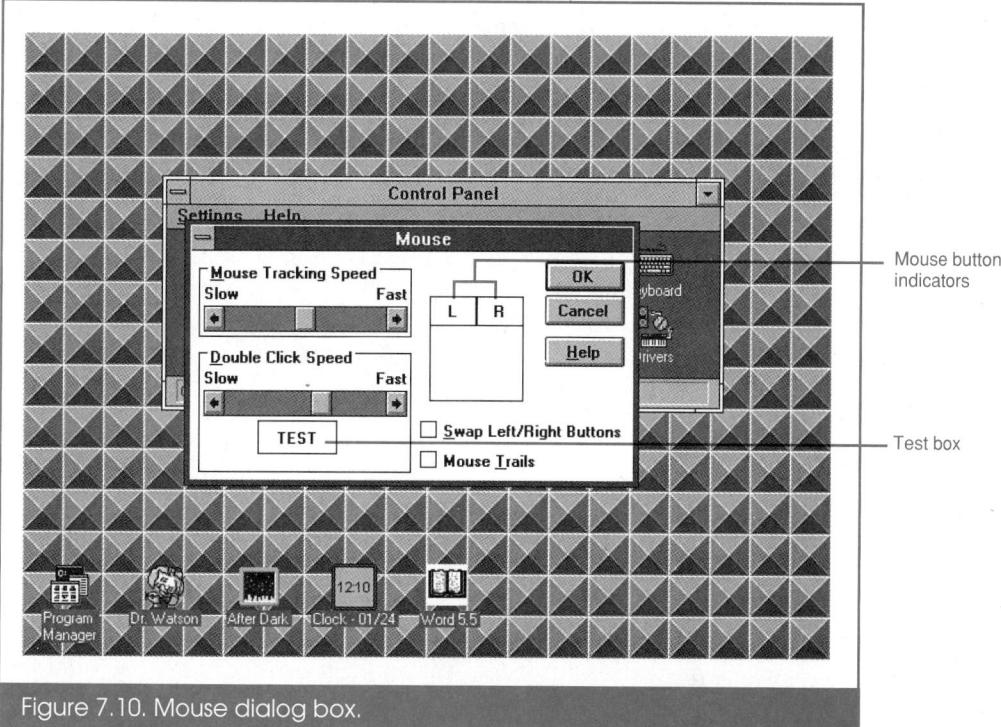

Figure 7.10. Mouse dialog box.

The tracking speed is the speed at which the cursor moves across the screen as you move the mouse on your desk. Although you adjust the mouse speed with the slider in the **M**ouse Tracking Speed section, the actual speed is not linear. If you move the mouse quickly, Windows actually accelerates the cursor so that you need only a small amount of desk space to move the cursor from one end of the screen to the other. If you move the mouse more slowly, you need more desk space. This fact is particularly noticeable if you choose a speed closer to the Slow setting in this section.

The double-click speed tells Windows how long to wait between two mouse clicks before it decides that they are two individual clicks and not a double-click. When you change the setting, you can test it by attempting to double-click in the rectangle marked TEST. When you successfully double-click, the color in the box reverses. Many people find that the default double-click speed is too slow; that is, two individual clicks often are mistaken for a double-click. If you find this to be true, move the thumb in the slider about halfway toward the fast end and double-click while adjusting until you are happy with the results.

Most mice are designed to favor right-handed people. If you are left-handed, you can use the right mouse button rather than the left for most actions. Selecting the **S**wap Left/Right Button button enables you to choose this feature. You can test how this feels by clicking in the window and watching the buttons on the mouse picture.

> **Tip:** Windows has its own mouse driver installed during setup. You need a separate mouse driver for using a mouse while you are not in Windows. Settings you apply to a mouse driver loaded when you are not in Windows do not stay in effect when you start Windows. Windows disables any loaded mouse drivers when Windows starts. You must load your non-Windows driver again after you leave Windows in order to emulate the direction keys in a character-based application such as Lotus 1-2-3 Version 2.2.

The Desktop Option

Because staring at your computer screen all day can be tedious, Windows enables you to change the way your screen looks. Some people pick one look and stay with it all the time. Others get bored and change looks every week. The Desktop icon in Control Panel enables you to choose the following:

▲ The look for the wallpaper behind windows (either a repeating pattern or a picture)

▲ A screen saver that uses static and moving bitmap images to keep your screen images from burning in or damaging your monitor

▲ The distance between icons in Program Manager, and optional title word wrapping

▲ The adjustment of an invisible grid to keep icons aligned

▲ The width around the borders of windows

▲ The cursor blink rate

Figure 7.11 shows the Desktop dialog box, where you can adjust the cursor blink rate or select a screen saver, among other things.

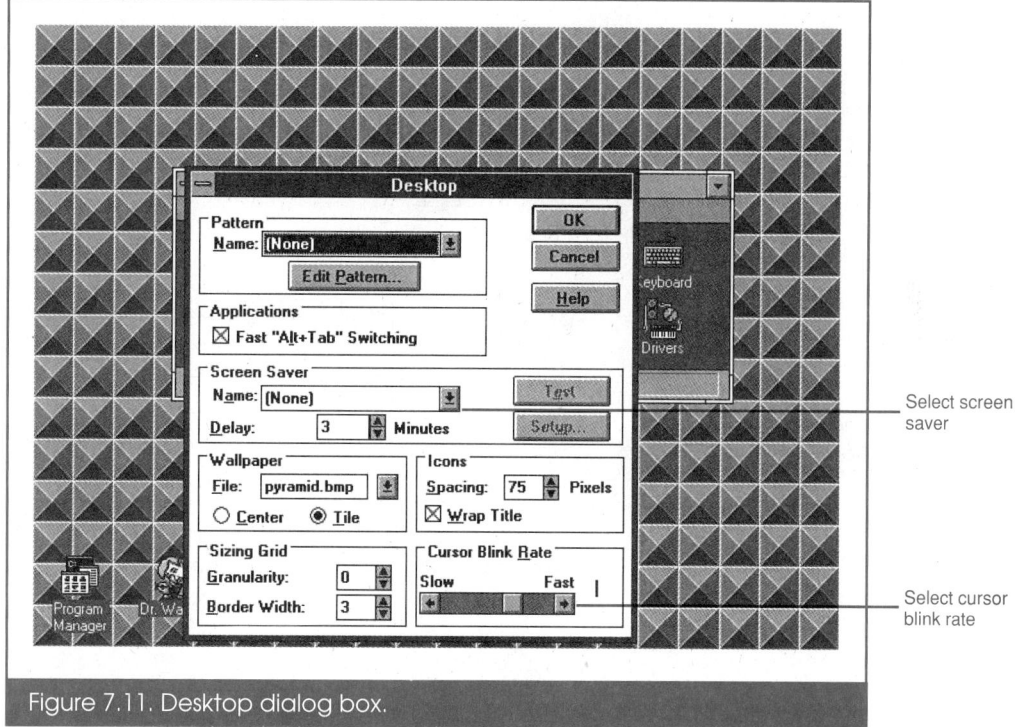

Figure 7.11. Desktop dialog box.

Screen Saver

Screen savers originally were just screen blankers that removed any image from the screen. They were told to remove any image if there was

no screen activity. Command line settings, typically embedded in your AUTOEXEC.BAT file, told it when to blank.

Open the **N**ame drop-down list box to select the screen pattern of interest. Select None if you don't want a screen saver. Select another, and click the **T**est button to see a sample of what you can expect. Set the delay time with the direction icon buttons next to the **D**elay text window or enter your preferred delay in minutes from the keyboard.

If the Setup button in the Screen Saver section is enabled, the appropriate Setup dialog box will be displayed. Each Setup dialog box offers you the ability to change characteristics of the screen saver of your choice.

Select the **P**assword Options Password Protected check box to assign a password to your screen saver. This option keeps unauthorized individuals from seeing what was on your screen when the screen saver took over the screen.

Warning: Print Manager can sense screen saver activity when operating in the background, and it interprets it as competition for system resources. If you set up Print Manager to print, for example, ten files, and your screen saver turns on, Print Manager can turn system resources over to the screen saver instead of printing your files.

Cursor Blink

You can set the speed of the cursor with the slider in the Cursor Blink **R**ate section. Many people find a rapidly blinking cursor to be annoying, even stressful. Setting the cursor to be very slow, however, can make it hard to find the insertion point when you are editing text.

Background Pattern

The background pattern is an eight-pixel-by-eight-pixel square that is repeated over the entire desktop. The pixels are in two colors—the ones you chose for Desktop Color and Window Text Color. If you like a regular pattern, you can choose from the list in the Pattern section or create one of your own.

Figure 7.12 shows the predefined patterns available in Windows. If you do not want a pattern, simply choose (None) from the top of the list.

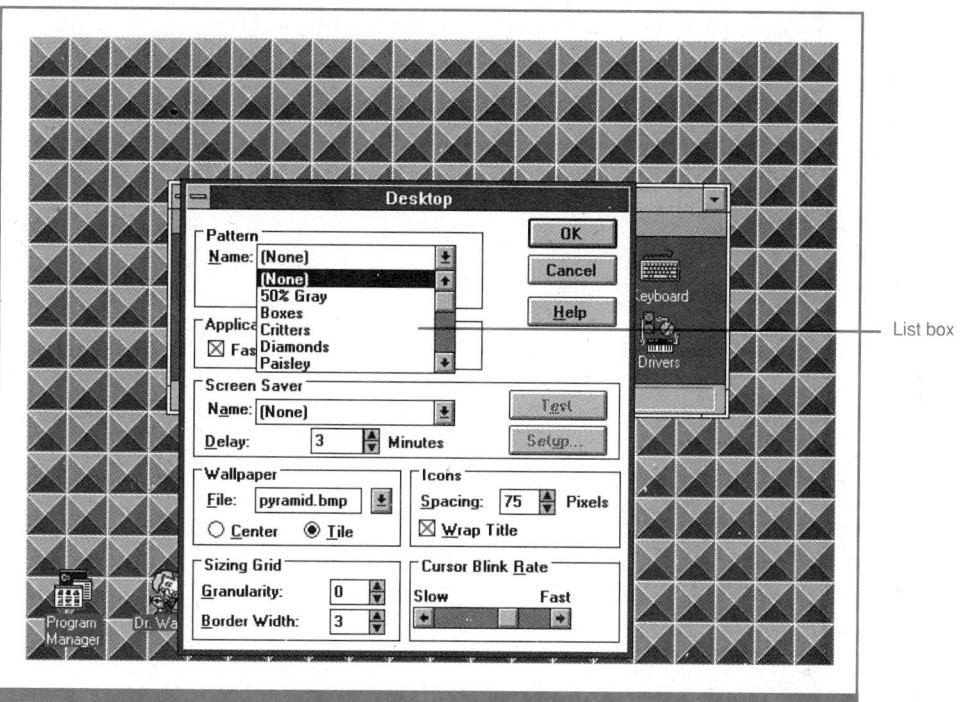

List box

Figure 7.12. Predefined patterns for the Desktop.

To create or edit a pattern, select any pattern from the list and click the Edit **P**attern button. You see the dialog box shown in Figure 7.13. You must use the mouse to edit the pattern. Enter a pattern name in the **N**ame box. If you enter a name that is not in use, you create a new pattern; if you use an existing name, you edit the pattern.

Click the middle of the large square to edit the pixel patterns. Change the pattern by "turning on" or "turning off" the individual pixels of the pattern by moving and clicking the mouse within the large square. The sample box on the left shows what the pattern will look like on your desktop. When you are finished adding to or changing the pattern, click the **A**dd or **C**hange buttons. You can use the **R**emove button to remove a pattern from the list.

Tip: Remember that the colors used in the pattern are regulated by colors chosen as the Desktop Color and the Window Text Color. If you choose a text color that is too similar to the background color, your pattern will look washed out or it will not seem to be there at all.

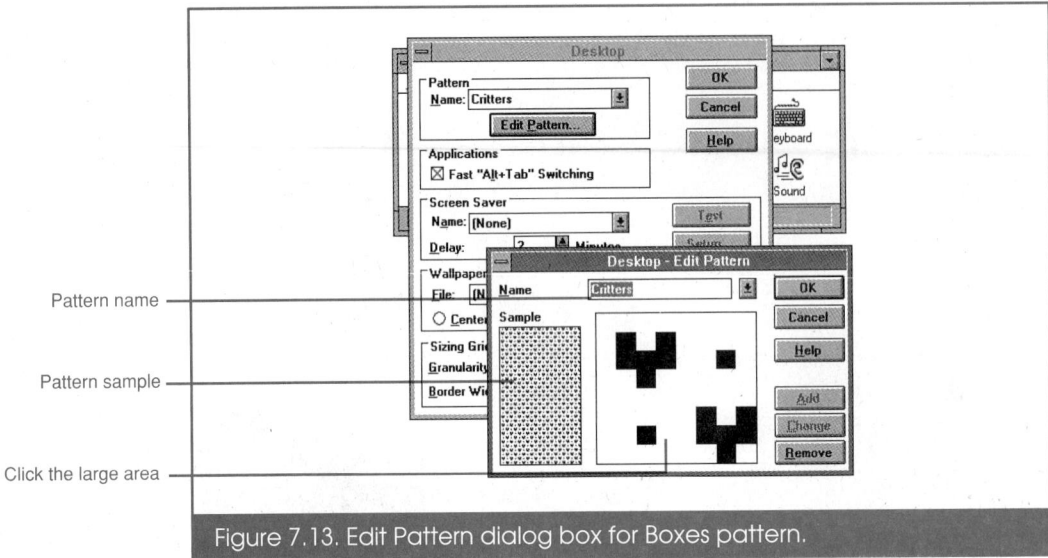

Pattern name

Pattern sample

Click the large area

Figure 7.13. Edit Pattern dialog box for Boxes pattern.

Wallpaper

If you want a more dramatic backdrop for Windows, you can use wallpaper—a single picture centered on your screen or a small picture that is repeated over and over. Windows comes with many sample wallpapers, and you also can create your own easily.

To use wallpaper, choose one of the wallpaper files from the **F**ile dropdown list. This list is of all the files with the extension .BMP in the main Windows directory. Choose **C**enter to make a single copy of the picture or **T**ile to cover the screen with copies of the picture. If you choose **C**enter, you will see the pattern you chose behind that one picture.

The sample wallpaper that comes with Windows has both small and large pictures. For instance, BOXES.BMP is a small box you need to tile in order to see. CHESS.BMP is a single large picture that covers the whole screen. You can create your own bitmap wallpaper with Paintbrush. See Chapter 11, "Paintbrush," for more details.

Warning: When you choose a wallpaper, you should choose either a very simple background pattern or the (None) option. The wallpaper you choose will cover the desktop, and the background pattern will be used very little. When you reduce programs to icons, their names appear over the background pattern, and it is often almost impossible to read the name of the icon on top of the background pattern. Wallpaper also uses a lot of memory. The busier it is, the more RAM it occupies.

7

Icon Spacing

You can place icons wherever you want in Program Manager windows. Many people, however, like them in neat rows and columns. When you use the **Window Arrange** Icons command, Program Manager rearranges the icons to be a certain number of pixels apart. This arrangement usually gives enough space for the icon names, except when the name is very long.

You can set the number of pixels between icons with the Icons **S**pacing setting. The default, 75, is good for most program icons but might be too close if you use long names on document icons. This value can be between 32 and 512. You can can set Windows 3.1 to word-wrap the icon titles if they conflict with adjacent icon tiles. Word wrapping works only if you allow Windows to find a space between words so that it knows it's OK to wrap.

Window Grid

If you want to arrange your windows on a fixed grid, you can change the **G**ranularity setting to a number from 0 to 49. Granularity is the number of eight-pixel units for the width of the grid. When you move or create a window, it will appear only on the grid. Because the unit is eight pixels and not one, it is unlikely that you will ever set this value above 2 (2 x 8 pixels wide). Most people do not care about aligning to a grid and probably will not change this number.

Border Width

You also can set the number of pixels in the border around windows. The default setting for the **B**order Width option, 3, is about the right size to choose when you want to resize a window. You can set this value to a number from 1 to 49, although it is unlikely that you will want to set it higher than 5. Setting this number at 1 makes it very difficult to resize a window with the mouse and saves only a little screen space.

The Keyboard Option

The Keyboard icon does not enable you to set much. Figure 7.14 shows the dialog box, which has two settings. The first is the speed at which a key repeats when you hold it down, and the second is the repeat rate itself. The default is the fastest speed, and most people prefer it.

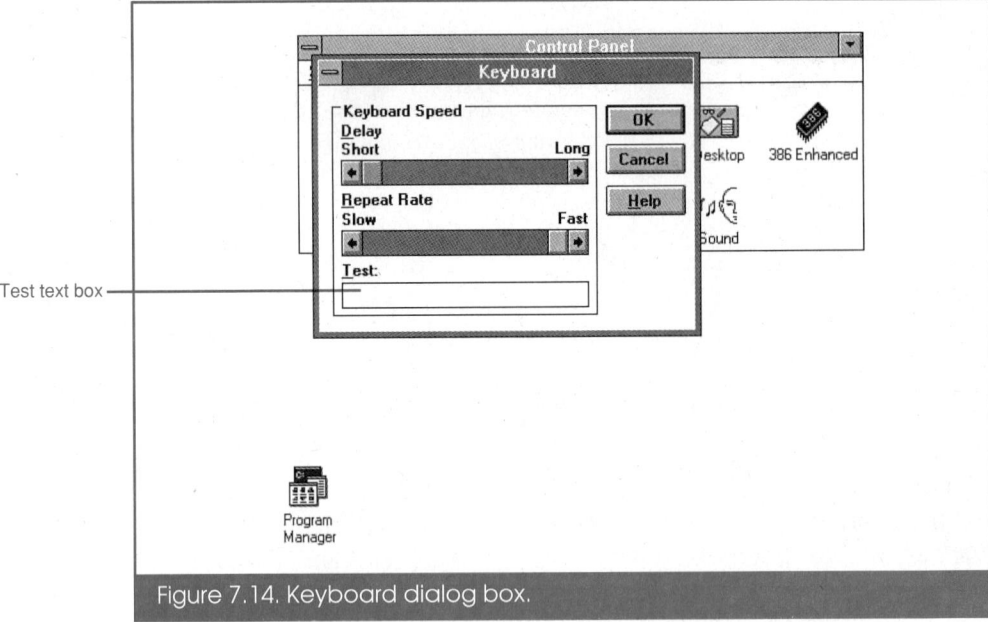

Figure 7.14. Keyboard dialog box.

Use the **T**est box to test the keyboard repeat rate.

The Printers Option

The options in this icon enable you to configure printers and add new ones, choose which printer is active, and choose whether to use Print Manager. Because printers are so important in Windows, and because they can be so complex, these options are described in Chapter 26, "Printers and Fonts."

The International Option

Windows 3.1 was designed to be used in many countries using many different languages. Because different countries have different ways of expressing the same thing, Control Panel enables you to specify the international parameters you want. Figure 7.15 shows the contents of the International window.

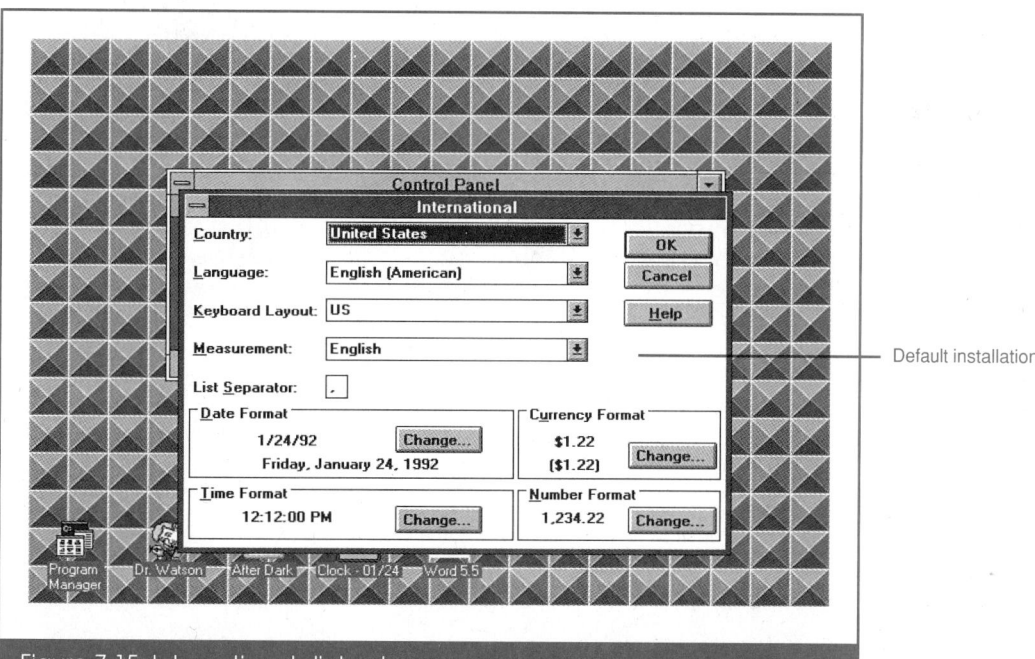

Default installation

Figure 7.15. International dialog box.

Most of the settings in the window are based on the country you choose. For example, when you change the country to Denmark, Control Panel automatically changes the measurement, date format, time format, currency format, and number format, as shown in Figure 7.16.

Parameters changed
to Denmark

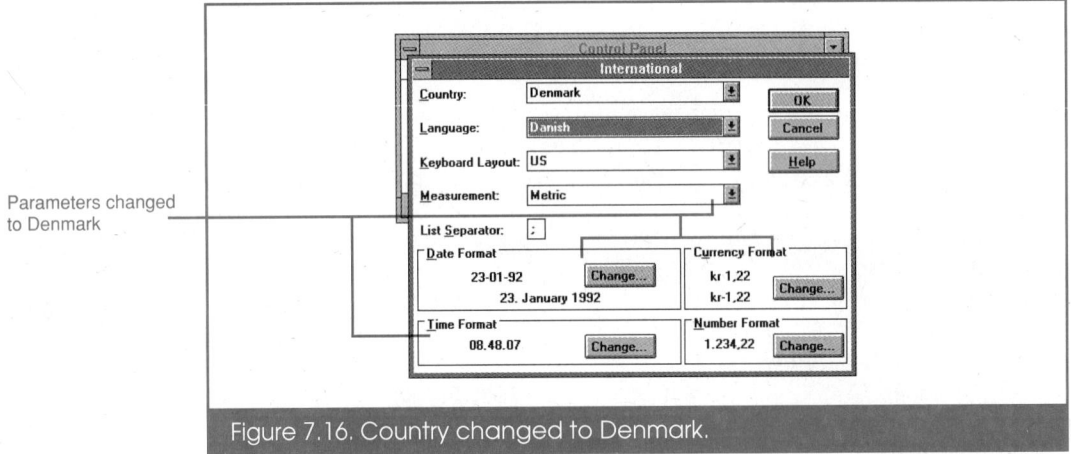

Figure 7.16. Country changed to Denmark.

Country

Use the **C**ountry list to choose the country you want. If you are internationalizing Windows for a country not on the list, choose Other Country at the bottom of the list. Some multilingual countries have more than one listing because the formats used by speakers of one language are different from the formats used by speakers of the other. For example, French-speaking Canadians use currency symbols that are different from those used by English-speaking Canadians.

The countries in the list include the following:

▲ Australia

▲ Austria

▲ Belgium (Dutch)

▲ Belgium (French)

▲ Brazil

▲ Canada (English)

▲ Canada (French)

- ▲ Denmark
- ▲ Finland
- ▲ France
- ▲ Germany
- ▲ Iceland
- ▲ Italy
- ▲ Mexico
- ▲ Netherlands
- ▲ New Zealand
- ▲ Norway
- ▲ Portugal
- ▲ South Korea
- ▲ Spain
- ▲ Sweden
- ▲ Switzerland (French)
- ▲ Switzerland (German)
- ▲ Switzerland (Italian)
- ▲ Taiwan
- ▲ United Kingdom
- ▲ United States
- ▲ Other Country

Language

You can choose any language supported by Windows for any country. You can even make choices that are not regular for a particular country, such as Finnish for the United States. The choice of language is important, because Windows 3.1 uses this choice when sorting words in alphabetical order. The choices of languages include the following:

- ▲ Danish
- ▲ Dutch

- ▲ English (American)
- ▲ English (International)
- ▲ Finnish
- ▲ French
- ▲ French Canadian
- ▲ German
- ▲ Icelandic
- ▲ Italian
- ▲ Norwegian
- ▲ Portuguese
- ▲ Spanish
- ▲ Swedish

Keyboard Layout

Many different layouts exist for PC keyboards. Because the characters on some of the keys differ, you must tell Control Panel which keyboard you are using. The choices include the following:

- ▲ Belgian
- ▲ British
- ▲ Canadian Multilingual
- ▲ Danish
- ▲ Dutch
- ▲ Finnish
- ▲ French
- ▲ French Canadian
- ▲ German
- ▲ Icelandic
- ▲ Italian
- ▲ Latin American
- ▲ Norwegian

▲ Portuguese

▲ Spanish

▲ Swedish

▲ Swiss French

▲ Swiss German

▲ US

▲ US-Dvorak

▲ US-International

7

> **Warning:** Some people switch back and forth between the US keyboard layout and another layout. The first time you switch to a non-US layout, you are prompted to insert a diskette. Unfortunately, each time after that when you switch to the other layout, you are prompted to insert the diskette again, even though the appropriate file was copied to your hard disk the first time.
>
> To prevent the prompt, you must edit the `keyboard.dll=` line of the `[keyboard]` section of the SYSTEM.INI file. This procedure is covered in Chapter 27, "Configuring with the WIN.INI and SYSTEM.INI Files." In that line, enter the name of the keyboard dynamic link library that was copied. You can keep a separate copy of the SYSTEM.INI file with this entry in it and simply copy the whole file to your main Windows directory when you want to use that keyboard.

Measurement

You can make Windows use metric or English measurements. Very few programs use this information, so changing it is of little value.

List Separator

The list separator is the punctuation mark used to separate a list of items in a sentence. This is almost always either a comma (,) or a semicolon (;). Most European countries use the semicolon, and most others use the comma.

Date Format

The date format is the way Windows displays dates on the screen. Many Windows programs use the date format you set here in their displays as well, so you should be sure to set this appropriately. There are two date formats: short and long. In the United States, the short format for a date might be "11/19/91" and the long one would be "Tuesday, November 19, 1991." In the short date format, you see only numbers, and the long date format has spelled-out names.

When you click the Change button in this section, you see the dialog boxes in Figure 7.17. You have numerous choices for each of the two date formats. The primary choice for both formats is the order in which the information appears: month-day-year (MDY), day-month-year (DMY), or year-month-day (YMD).

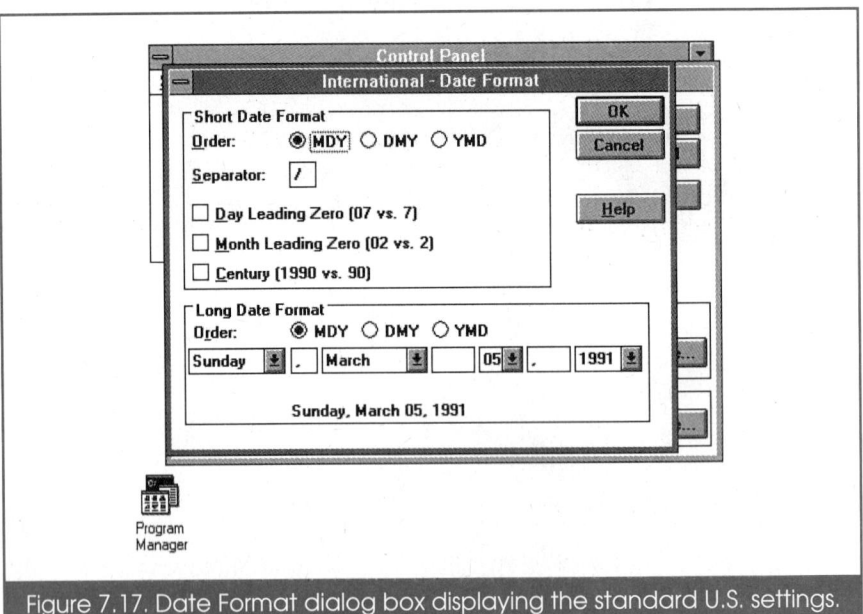

Figure 7.17. Date Format dialog box displaying the standard U.S. settings.

For the short date format, you can enter any character for the *separator* to put between the numbers. You also choose whether to have leading zeros for the day or month numbers less than 10, and whether to add the century (currently 19) before the year.

The long date format enables you to precede the date with the day of the week. If you choose to show the day of the week, you can spell out the whole word or just use the three-letter abbreviation (Monday or

Mon). For the month, you can choose from the number with no leading zero, the number with a leading zero, the three-letter abbreviation (Nov), or the full name (November). The day can be either the number with no leading zero or the number with a leading zero. You can choose whether to add the century before the year, and you can include a separator character between the day of week and the month, the month and the day, and the day and the year.

Although most Americans use the format suggested when you choose United States as the country, you might want to experiment with changing the format. For instance, using the three-letter abbreviations in the long format can make the date look less formal, yet still convey the information you want.

Time Format

The time format has fewer choices than the date format, as shown in Figure 7.18. You first choose whether you want to use 12-hour format or 24-hour format. If you use 12-hour, you choose what text you want after the time (such as AM or am for before noon). In either case, you can choose the separator you use in the time, usually a colon (:) or a comma (,). You also can specify whether to put a leading zero on hours before 10.

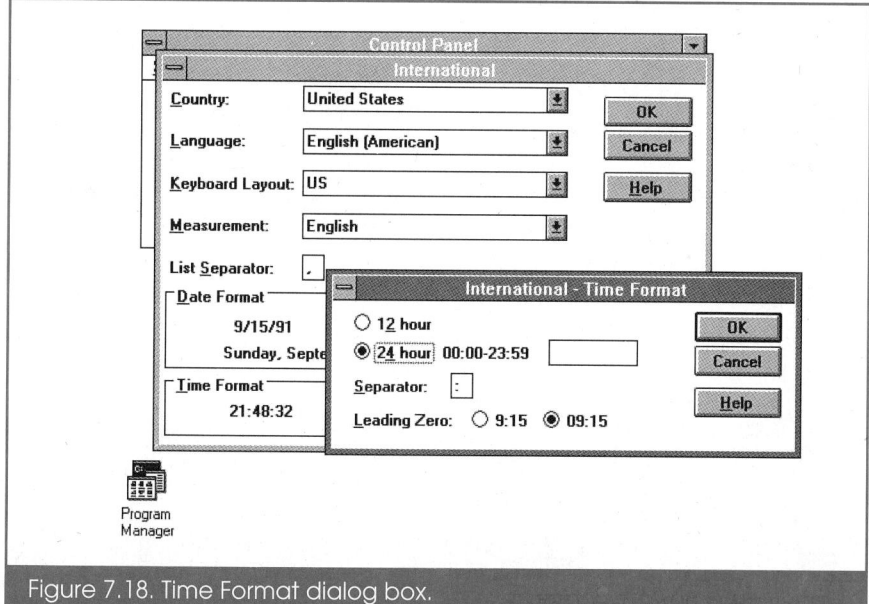

Figure 7.18. Time Format dialog box.

Currency Format

If there is one format item that people are picky about from country to country, it's how they write monetary amounts. Not only are there many different currencies (and thus many currency symbols), but there are also the questions of whether you place the symbol before or after the amount, whether there is a space between the symbol and the amount, and how to specify negative numbers. Fortunately, Windows 3.1 can handle almost all possible formats. The Change button in this section brings up the window shown in Figure 7.19.

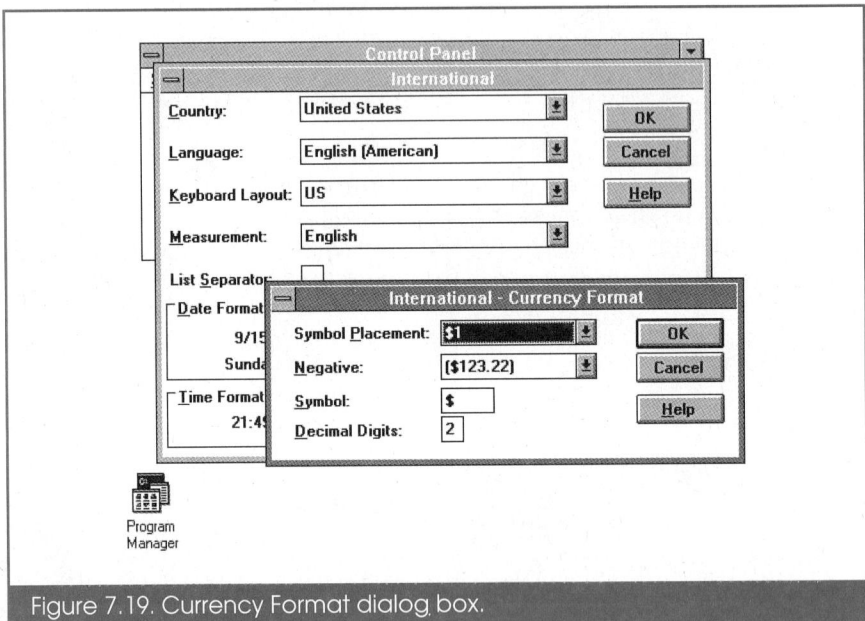

Figure 7.19. Currency Format dialog box.

The choices in Symbol **P**lacement are for positive values. They are shown in Table 7.3.

Table 7.3. Symbol Placement options.

Example	Meaning
$1	Symbol precedes number with no space
1$	Number precedes symbol with no space
$ 1	Symbol precedes number with space
1 $	Number precedes symbol with space

The **N**egative option has more choices, because you can denote negative values either by using a minus sign or by putting the value in parentheses. The negative choices are shown in Table 7.4.

Table 7.4. Negative options.

Example	Meaning
($123.22)	Symbol precedes number in parentheses
-$123.22	Minus sign precedes symbol, which precedes number
$-123.22	Symbol precedes minus sign, which precedes number
$123.22-	Symbol precedes number, which precedes minus sign
(123.22$)	Number precedes symbol in parentheses
-123.22$	Minus sign precedes number, which precedes symbol
123.22-$	Number precedes minus sign, which precedes symbol
123.22$-	Number precedes symbol, which precedes minus sign

You can set the **S**ymbol field to the symbol used for currency. This might be a character such as *$* or letters such as *mk*. If you are using the symbol for the British pound, (£), you type it by holding down the Alt key and pressing the numbers 1, 5, and 6 on the numeric keypad. To generate the symbol for the Japanese yen, (¥), hold down the Alt key and press the numbers 1, 5, and 7 on the numeric keypad.

You also can specify the number of digits following a decimal point to put in a currency amount. Some countries do not have fractional amounts, so for these countries the value would be 0.

Number Format

The number format enables you to describe precisely how regular numbers (not currency) are shown. Figure 7.20 shows the window for this section. The Windows default settings are shown.

You can specify the character that is used to separate thousands (usually a comma or a period) and the character used to precede the fractional part of a decimal (usually a period or a comma). You also can say how many digits are put in the fractional part and whether numbers less than 1 have a leading zero.

Figure 7.20. Number Format dialog box.

The Date/Time Option

The window for the Date/Time icon, shown in Figure 7.21, enables you to change the date and time for your PC. You can type numbers or you can use the arrows on the spin buttons to change the options.

Tip: When you change the date and time in this dialog box, they will be remembered by your PC at least until you reboot your system. On most PCs, they will be remembered after you reboot because the date and time are written to ROM (*Read-Only Memory*). On some PCs, however, you must run the PC's setup program to change the date and time.

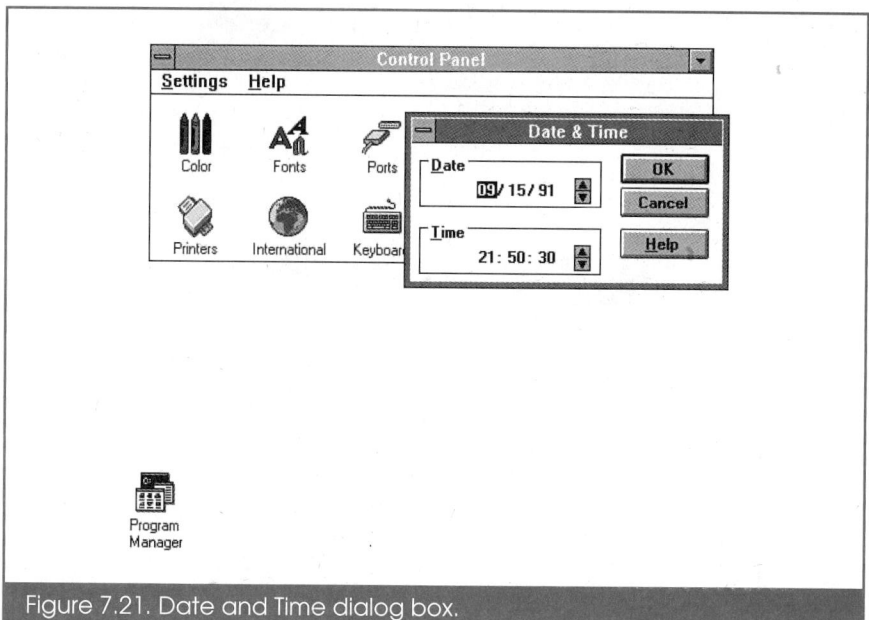

Figure 7.21. Date and Time dialog box.

The 386-Enhanced Mode Option

The settings for 386-enhanced mode generally are more technical than the settings in the other icons in Control Panel. All these settings relate to how Windows acts in 386-enhanced mode when you run non-Windows programs. Refer to Chapter 22, "Windows Operating Modes," for more detail on the subject. The defaults you see in Figure 7.22 are fine for most situations.

Device Contention

When non-Windows programs try to use the same hardware port, such as a modem or a printer port, Windows needs to know whether to let them share. The event that occurs when two devices compete for the same resource is called *contention*. You usually want to let them share, because you specified that they should use the ports when you ran the programs. However, you must be sure that two programs do not try to write to the same port at the same time, because the output will be garbled.

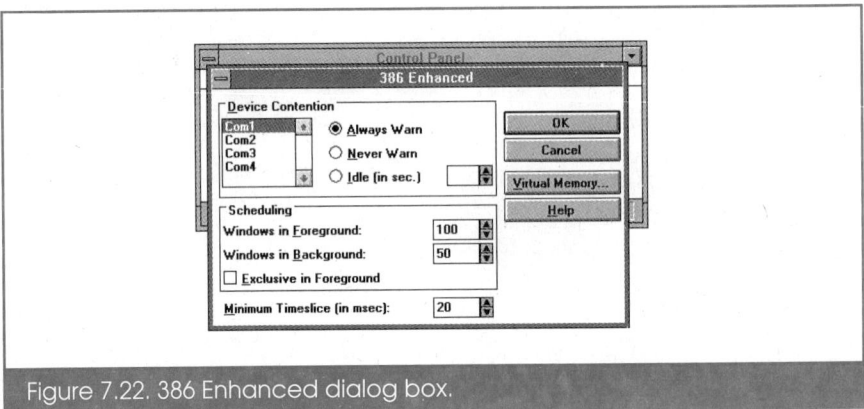

Figure 7.22. 386 Enhanced dialog box.

For each of the ports listed, you can choose how Windows will handle multiple requests for the port. The default choice, **I**dle, makes sure that the specified number of seconds has passed with no activity on the port before allowing the second program to use the port. You can change the amount of idle time, up to 999 seconds. This is generally the best choice because it's a good balance between safety and convenience.

The **N**ever Warn choice lets any non-Windows program use the port whenever it wants. This choice is the most convenient but the least safe because it might allow programs to read or write at the same time.

The **A**lways Warn choice puts up a dialog box with the message The COMx port is currently assigned to a DOS application. Do you want to reassign the port to Windows? when a second program tries to use the same port. This choice is the most restrictive, but it also is the safest.

Scheduling

Chapter 21, "Editing PIFs," explains how Windows decides how much CPU (central processing unit) time each non-Windows program gets. This *timeslice* is based on two settings you make in each program's PIF

(*Program Information File*). The setting in the Scheduling section tells how much CPU time all Windows programs will get relative to the non-Windows programs.

The two numbers for Windows in **F**oreground and Windows in **B**ackground are not absolute numbers: They depend on the settings you made in the non-Windows programs' PIFs. Setting the **M**inimum Timeslice to a certain number of milliseconds ensures that the Windows programs will get at least a small amount of time.

The **E**xclusive in Foreground option indicates that any Windows program running in the foreground will always get 100 percent of the CPU, regardless of the priorities set for the non-Windows programs. Select this only if you want to prevent your non-Windows programs from running in the background when you are running a Windows program.

Virtual Memory

Virtual memory is a term for an 80386 processor's capability to use hard drive space as backup, or auxiliary, memory. If you load several programs or very large spreadsheet files, for example, you could conceivably run out of memory. When this happens, Windows accesses your hard drive for space, copying parts of the program in the background to the swap file on the hard drive. This creates space in real system memory for the file or program space needed to run the application in the foreground.

This permanent swap file is kept in the same location on your drive, so Windows does not have to ask DOS to look for it whenever it is needed. It is primarily the look-up time that makes temporary swap files so inferior to permanent swap files. If you are using a disk caching manager, you already know how much time can be saved when you don't have to access your hard drive on every single occasion that you need to find or save data. Figure 7.23 shows you what Windows has to say about your system when the Virtual Memory dialog box opens.

If you do not create a permanent swap file, you will not be utilizing the full power of your 386, 486, or 586. You will experience unnecessary delays on occasion. Windows uses temporary swap files in standard mode, and also if you have not created a permanent swap file in 386-enhanced mode either during the Windows installation process or at some point thereafter. Figure 7.24 shows you the expanded Virtual Memory dialog box after you click the **C**hange» button.

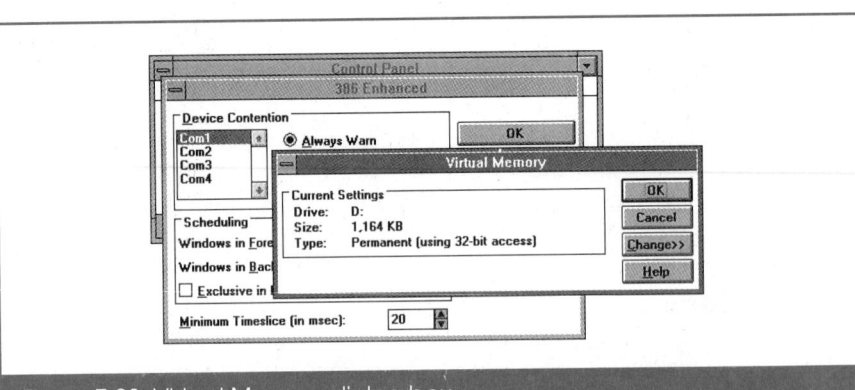

Figure 7.23. Virtual Memory dialog box.

Drive for swap file

Suggested swap file size

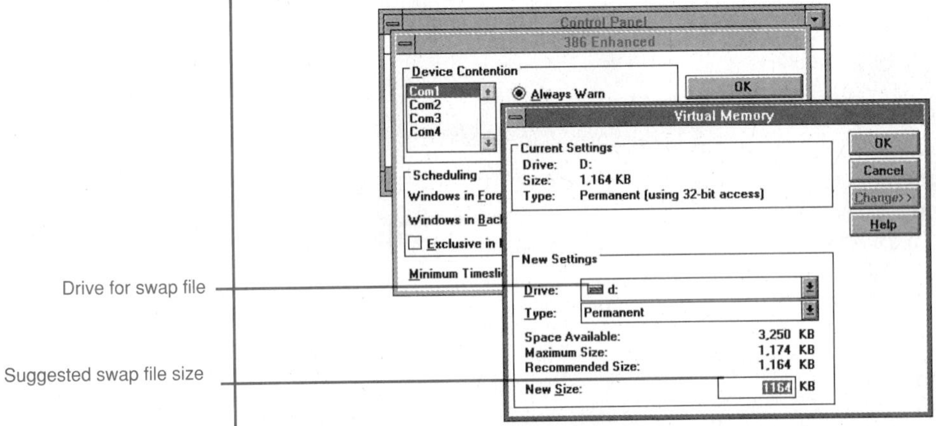

Figure 7.24. Expanded Virtual Memory dialog box.

Permanent swap files require at least 512K to be useful. The maximum for most systems is 2M. Let Windows recommend the optimum size, and create the swap file where you want it if you have enough space. If you don't have the space for the file size Windows recommends, cut down the size suggested to whatever works for you. Remember that because this swap file is a hidden file, you might not see it when you review files on the drive you specified during swap file creation. You must not move a swap file, because moving it destroys its usefulness. If you move it by mistake, create another one right away.

The Sound Option

The Macintosh has long been known for its capability to reproduce sounds stored in files, and to emit them whenever you might normally hear a system beep on a PC. Windows 3.1 comes with several .WAV files (sound files) that you can experiment with. A .WAV file contains digital information, like a recording.

Figure 7.25 shows the system events that can be used to trigger the playing of a .WAV file on your system speaker. The left list box contains system events, and the right list box contains your installed .WAV files.

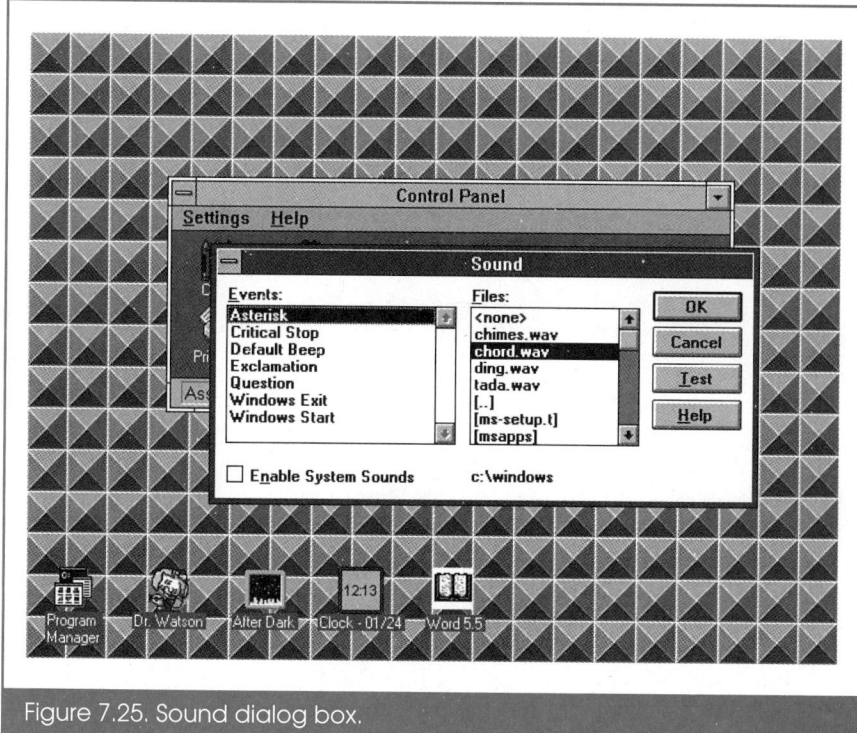

Figure 7.25. Sound dialog box.

If you click an event first, and then double-click a .WAV filename, you hear the file played, and you have assigned that .WAV file to the selected system event. Repeat the process for each of the system events, and you are finished.

The Drivers Option

The Drivers option enables you to add device drivers for multimedia hardware applications. If you are planning to use MIDI (*Musical Instrument Digital Interface*) equipment, or work with multimedia applications that directly access and use hardware devices such as audio gear, special multimedia video tape players, and some CD-ROM drives, you need to install the manufacturer-supplied driver for Windows 3.1 from the dialog box shown in Figure 7.26.

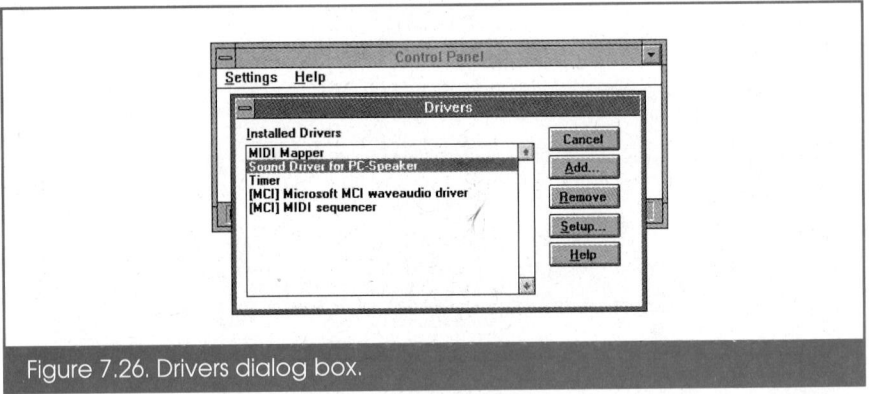

Figure 7.26. Drivers dialog box.

When you select a driver made to support your MPC hardware device, you can change the volume and pitch of the sounds made by your system at different points in day-to-day operation. Figure 7.27 shows you a dialog box with two sliding bars that enable you to change the volume and pitch of the speaker. You also can set the maximum length of play for all .WAV files. The default is three, but many .WAV files, especially the ones that contain famous quotes or lines from popular movies, can require up to ten seconds to complete the playing of the file. If your .WAV files seem to be cut short, raise the value of the number in the **L**imit Playback To text box and play the file again.

The Network Option

The options available in the Network icon depend on the type of network you installed. Depending on the brand of network and level of permission you have, this option might enable you to log on or off the network, send messages, and so on. Networks and the choices in this

dialog box are described in detail in Chapter 28, "Networking and Communications."

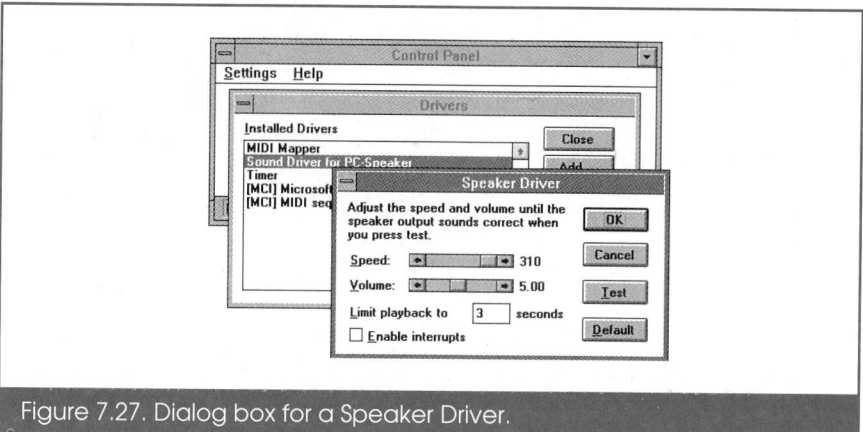

Figure 7.27. Dialog box for a Speaker Driver.

Other Configuration Changes

It would be nice if all the changes you made to the configuration of Windows appeared in Control Panel, but that is not the case. You should know about the other ways you change the appearance and performance of Windows so that you don't search through Control Panel in vain.

When you want to change your hardware configuration, such as changing the type of screen or network you use, you run the Setup program. Actually, there are two Setup programs—one you run from within Windows and one you run from MS-DOS. These are described in detail in Chapter 25, "Changing Your Configuration."

You also can change some of your hardware settings by editing the SYSTEM.INI file. This file is handled mostly by Setup, but you must put in many options yourself with a text editor. The SYSTEM.INI file is described in Chapter 27, "Configuring with the WIN.INI and SYSTEM.INI Files."

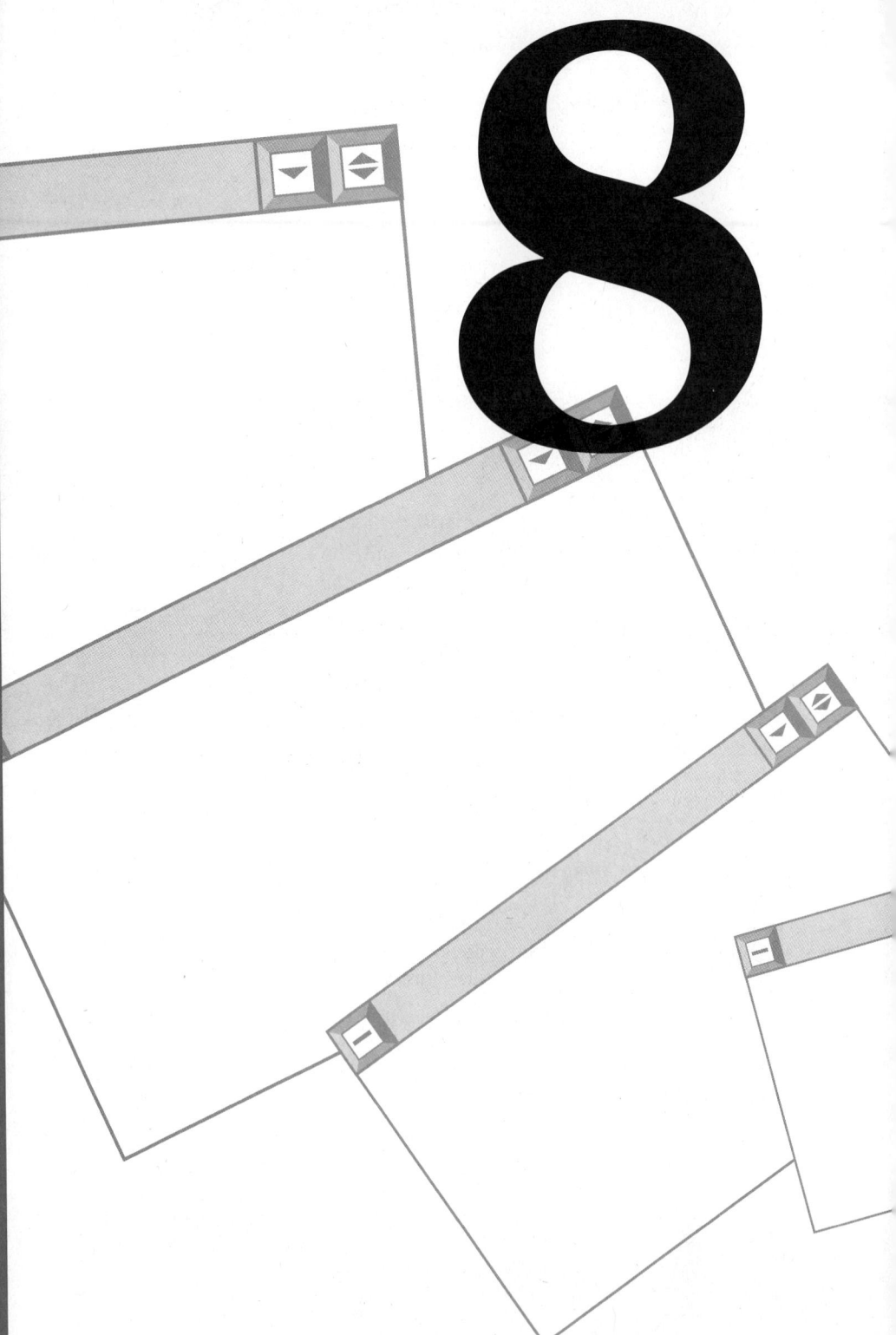

CHAPTER

8

Print Manager

In many MS-DOS programs, when you send a document to the printer you must wait until it is printed before you can start working again. Because this is tedious if you have long documents or a slow printer (or both), many companies sell *print spoolers*. Print spoolers are programs that receive multiple files to send to the printer as soon as the printer can process them. Printers take information one document at a time, but with a spooler operating in the background, you can print multiple files while you run your other programs.

Most print spoolers enable you not only to get back to your program faster, but also to send many documents to the printer simultaneously without having to wait for the previous job to finish. If you have ever been in a single line that feeds customers to four tellers at a bank, you already have a good understanding of queues. A group of files just waiting to be printed is stored in what is called a *print queue*. The print spool program takes care of sending the jobs from the queue in the correct order. See Reference C, "Windows Product Directory," for more about print spoolers you can buy.

Windows has its own print spooler, called Print Manager. Print Manager has many of the major features of commercial print spoolers (faster return to your program after printing, queueing multiple files) as well as some advanced features.

For example, you can use Print Manager to handle more than one print queue at a time. You can reorder the jobs in the queue if you have a document that needs to be printed sooner than others. Print Manager can handle most network printers. Print Manager uses system resources in memory and CPU access, but in almost unnoticeable amounts. After you have used a spooler on a 286 or 386 running in enhanced mode, giving up the resources seems a better deal than going without background multiple-document printing.

To send printer output to Print Manager, select the **U**se Print Manager check box option in Control Panel's Printer dialog box. If you don't select this option, Windows programs send the output directly to the printer, without using the Print Manager or any of its features. Unfortunately, sending output directly to the printer ties up your system. You must wait for DOS to release your computer for other tasks. Windows checks the **U**se Print Manager check box for you during Windows installation.

> **Warning:** When you close Print Manager (PM), any documents remaining in the queue are not printed; they are deleted from Print Manager. If you want these documents to be printed, you must resubmit the jobs, or simply minimize PM and let it continue to print the jobs undisturbed. If you must exit (either with the **V**iew E**x**it command or by quitting Windows), make sure that you know which documents have not been printed yet so that you can resubmit them later.

The Print Manager Window

When you double-click the Print Manager icon, you see a window like that shown in Figure 8.1. Using the commands on the **V**iew and **O**ptions menus, you can see the status of your print jobs at all times. If you have a network printer and a local printer attached to your PC and are using both of them at the same time, each queue is displayed separately in the same window. The Windows description for each printer is used as the available printer list header for the list of documents in each queue.

The first line is the name of the first printer and the device that connects the printer to your computer. This is the name given in the Printers icon of the Control Panel. The words to the right of the name indicate the status (Printing, Idle, or Paused). Each indented line under

the printer name indicates a job in the queue, the percentage of the document sent to the printer, and the size of the document in bytes. The job with the printer icon is the one being printed; those with numbers are the ones in the queue. The numbers represent their positions in the queue (the order in which they will print).

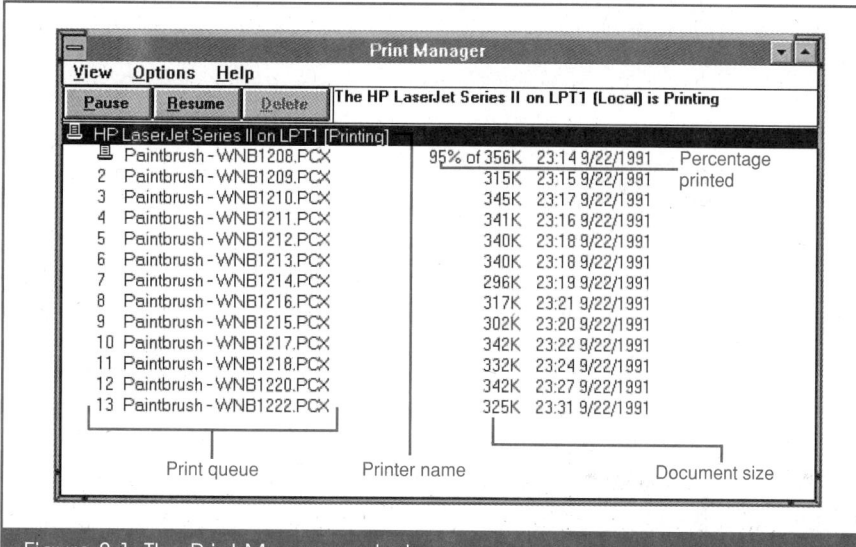

Figure 8.1. The Print Manager window.

Print Manager will advise you of your printer status should a problem arise during the printing of your documents. In the event of a problem, PM posts a message box in the center of your screen that conveys a suspected reason for the problem, and a suggestion as to how you might deal with the problem. Note that the message box may or may not change from posting-to-posting, depending on your printer. If your printer can communicate with Windows, this box may indicate that the printer is out of paper or that there is a paper jam. (This feature is new to Windows 3.1.)

Warning: Non-Windows programs never print to Print Manager; they always control the printer themselves. You should avoid having a non-Windows program and Print Manager printing to the same port. Some software will hang or at least give you an error message advising you of the conflict. See Chapter 20, "Other DOS Programs and Windows," for more information.

Stopping the Printer

The **P**ause and **R**esume buttons at the top left of the window enable you to stop and resume printing. You use these buttons when you want Print Manager to stop using the printer for a while. If there is more than one queue, select the queue you want to stop and then click the **P**ause button. Another way to pause and resume printing is to press Alt-P or Alt-R.

Changing the Order of the Queue

You can change the order of documents in the queue if they are not printing. (You cannot, however, move a document that is already printing to a different position in the queue.) By changing the order in the queue, you can advance the more important documents after you have sent them to print.

 To move a document in the queue, using the mouse, select the document's line and drag it to the new position.

 To move a document in the queue, using the keyboard, select the document's line and press Ctrl-↑ or Ctrl-↓ to move it to the new position.

Deleting Documents from the Queue

To delete a document from the queue, simply select the document and click the **D**elete button (or press Alt-D). This action works even if the document is being printed. If you delete the document being printed, Print Manager alerts you with the following message: `Terminate printing document: XXXXXXXX.XXX`.

Tip: Note that Print Manager tries (but may not be able) to reset your printer after stopping a document in the middle of printing. After you delete the document that was printing, it's a good idea to turn off your printer for a minimum of three seconds or reset it to clear the printer buffer. The other documents in the queue are safe.

Configuring Print Manager

You can adjust Print Manager to suit your system. Any changes to settings in Print Manager are retained the next time Print Manager is activated.

Suppressing Line Item Information

The first two options on the View menu display information on the document lines in Print Manager. These options—which show the time and date the document was sent from the program, and the size of the file—are the default when you install Windows. Figure 8.2 shows the View menu.

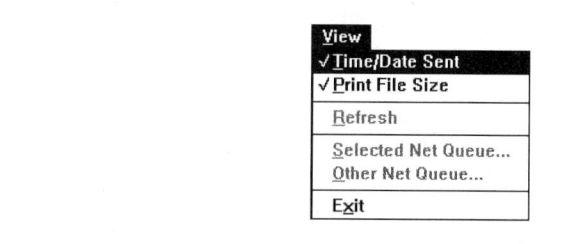

Figure 8.2. The View menu.

The information generated appears next to each line item in the queue. In the unlikely case that you do not want to see this information, giving the commands in this menu turns off the display.

Refresh

The **R**efresh command causes the screen to be repainted if you believe that changes are not reflected correctly on your screen. This command is useful when the printer has been shut off accidentally. To learn quickly what you lost, select **R**efresh.

Network Printers and Print Manager

Almost every network has its own print spooler for the network printers. When you print to a network printer through Program Manager, Print Manager quickly sends the entire job through to the network queue. Print Manager's capabilities with network printers depend on what type of network you have; some or all of network-related features might not be available. For more information, see Chapter 28, "Networking and Communications."

Queue List

Print Manager displays only your print queue to a network printer. If you want to see all the jobs in the network printer's queue, select the printer queue you want to view in the Print Manager window and give the **V**iew **S**elected Net Queue command. This command is available only if you told Windows during the Install or Setup process that you are on a network.

If more than one queue is on the network, you may be able to view the contents of the other queues with the **V**iew **O**ther Net Queue command (if it is available). You must enter the path in the text box provided to see the list of files in the queue.

If you are viewing more than one network queue at the same time, Print Manager updates the queue list periodically. You can force an update of the list by giving the **V**iew **R**efresh command (if it is available).

The Options Menu

If Print Manager needs to display a message (telling you that the printer is out of paper, for example), it needs to know whether you want to be interrupted while doing whatever you are doing in Windows. The **O**ptions menu is shown in Figure 8.3. Table 8.1 lists the items or settings that are available from the **O**ptions menu, and their meaning.

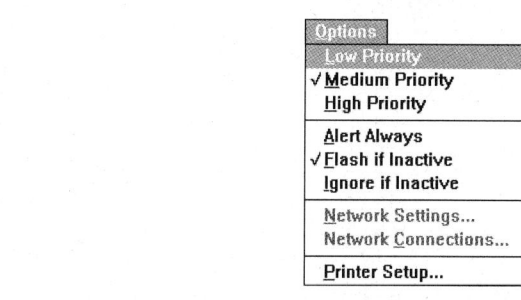

Figure 8.3. Options menu.

Table 8.1. Message options for Print Manager.

Command	*Meaning*
Alert Always	Display an alert when there is a problem
Flash If Inactive	Sound a beep and flash either the Print Manager icon or the title bar of the Print Manager window
Ignore if Inactive	Do nothing if Print Manager is minimized to an icon or in the background on the screen

Print Manager Priority

You can tell Print Manager how much of the system's resources it should take up when it is printing . If you give Print Manager low priority, your documents print slower but your programs run faster. Generally, you probably want to use medium priority; you may want to use high priority (faster printing but slower execution of other programs) if it does not degrade performance much or if you need your printed output very quickly.

Tip: If you are working with several large graphics files that eventually will be sent to the spooler (and if you can wait for the printed output), you can keep your program operating at high speed by setting Print Manager Priority to **L**ow while you work with the files. When you finish sending the files to the spooler, reset the priority in Print Manager to **H**igh; your queue will empty into the printer at the printer's maximum speed. If you arrange for the spool to fill (*full* means no more than 20 documents) and then reset the Priority to High before you leave your desk (for example, when you go to lunch), you avoid the printer noise and printer-sharing conflicts.

Network Options

The Network **O**ptions commands enable you to set the way Print Manager interacts with the network printers. **U**pdate Network Display tells Print Manager whether to update the queue for network printers. When this option is checked, Print Manager updates the list periodically (always updating it when you resume after minimizing Print Manager).

Warning: Some networks are slowed by several users concurrently or repeatedly updating their own video display of the shared network print queues. Deselect this option if you do not want to update the list, increasing network traffic.

The **P**rint Net Jobs Direct option tells Windows to pass network print jobs straight through to the network printer, bypassing Print Manager. If you use this option, which almost always is faster than going through Print Manager, you cannot take advantage of Print Manager features.

CHAPTER

9

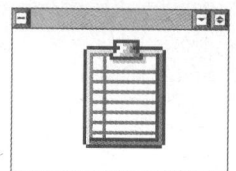

Clipboard Viewer

The Clipboard stores one piece of information while you run Windows. This information can be either text or graphics. The Clipboard is a temporary storage area or buffer that is assigned when you tell Windows to put something there. The information is in the Clipboard, and it stays in memory. Clipboard Viewer, on the other hand, is a small program that displays whatever you have put in the Clipboard buffer area. With Windows 3.1 many DOS programs can transfer data to and from the Clipboard. Clipboard Viewer is resident only when you run it. Clipboard Viewer can be closed or minimized without affecting the data in the Clipboard buffer.

The Clipboard has two common uses:

▲ To transfer information from one part of a program to another

▲ To transfer information from one program to another program

Warning: You may not be able to use the Clipboard with all DOS applications. Also, DOS applications can only transfer text information to the Clipboard. They cannot transfer graphical or text information from the Clipboard.

The most important fact to remember about the Clipboard is that it holds only one piece of information at a time. You cannot store two things on the Clipboard. You can store and retrieve the contents of the Clipboard in files, although often this is tedious.

As soon as you put an item in the Clipboard, it stays there until you put another item in the Clipboard or until you quit Windows. If you want, you can clear the Clipboard to free a small amount of Windows memory. When you first open Windows, the Clipboard is empty.

Remember that the Clipboard is managed by Windows itself, not by individual programs. This makes it much more universal; that is, all programs work well with the contents of the Clipboard.

Accessing the Clipboard Contents

Almost every Windows program has an Edit menu with three common commands: **E**dit **C**ut, **E**dit **C**opy, and **E**dit **P**aste. These commands work the same in every Windows program.

The **E**dit **C**ut and **E**dit **C**opy commands place the selected information in the Clipboard. The only difference between the two commands is that the **E**dit **C**ut command removes the information from the document when it puts it in the Clipboard, and the **E**dit **C**opy command leaves the selected image in the document. Generally, you use the **E**dit **C**ut command to move information and the **E**dit **C**opy command to duplicate it.

To put the contents of the Clipboard into your document, use the **E**dit **P**aste command. This command copies the Clipboard contents into the document at the currently selected point. Note that the **E**dit **P**aste command does not clear the contents of the Clipboard; they are still there for you to use again if you want to. Table 9.1 shows a summary of these actions.

Types of Clipboard Information

Two types of information can be stored in the Clipboard: text and graphics. When you use the **E**dit **Cut** or **E**dit **C**opy commands, Windows looks at the information you have selected in the program you are running and stores whatever it can.

Table 9.1. Accessing the Clipboard's contents.

Command	Action
Edit Cut	Removes the selected item from the document and puts it in the Clipboard
Edit Copy	Copies the selected item from the document and puts it in the Clipboard
Edit Paste	Copies the contents of the Clipboard and puts them in the current document

9

If you are using a basic text editor such as Notepad, you copy plain text to the Clipboard. If you are using a more advanced program, such as Write, you copy formatted text. Similarly, if you use a simple paint program, such as Paintbrush, you copy only a *bit map* of the picture—a copy of the pixels you see on the screen in their appropriate colors. If you use a more powerful program, such as CorelDRAW!, you copy many objects such as rectangles and circles, not just the bitmap. CorelDRAW! is detailed in Chapter 18, "CorelDRAW!"

While you are running a program, the Clipboard holds text with formatting information or graphics with objects. In fact, if you are using a program such as Write that enables you to have both text and graphics in a single document, you can have both text and graphics in the Clipboard at one time. The Clipboard is not famous for pasting perfectly formatted text when it is stored with graphics, though, so experiment with your system to determine the best attainable results.

Warning: As soon as you quit a program, the information in the Clipboard is reduced to either just text or just a bit map. All formatting and special objects are lost. In fact, even if the program is still running but you have switched to another program, that extra information still might be lost. In this case, you can transfer only pure text or a single bit map to another program. Again, this depends on what features the software manufacturer built into the program.

Tip: You can copy information from non-Windows programs to the Clipboard, although in a much more limited fashion than when you copy from Windows programs. Using the Clipboard from non-Windows programs is covered in detail in Chapter 20, "Other DOS Programs and Windows."

Clipboard Viewer Program

The Clipboard Viewer program in the Main window of Program Manager enables you to view the contents of the Clipboard. The program's window is shown in Figure 9.1. When there is nothing in the Clipboard, such as when you first start Windows, the Display menu is dimmed.

Clipboard Files

The File menu has three commands: **F**ile **O**pen, **F**ile Save **A**s, and **F**ile E**x**it. With the **F**ile Save **A**s command you can save the contents of the Clipboard in file on disk. Note that the contents saved are only pure text or a bit map, even if you can see more in the window when you give the command. The **F**ile **O**pen command can open either type of saved Clipboard file—text or bit map.

Clipboard files are useful for saving the contents of the Clipboard if you are about to replace them with other information. They are of limited value if you have to use them often, because you have to remember what is in each file by name; you can't "preview" the contents. Also, because the files save only text or bit maps, they aren't useful if you are putting complex information into the file.

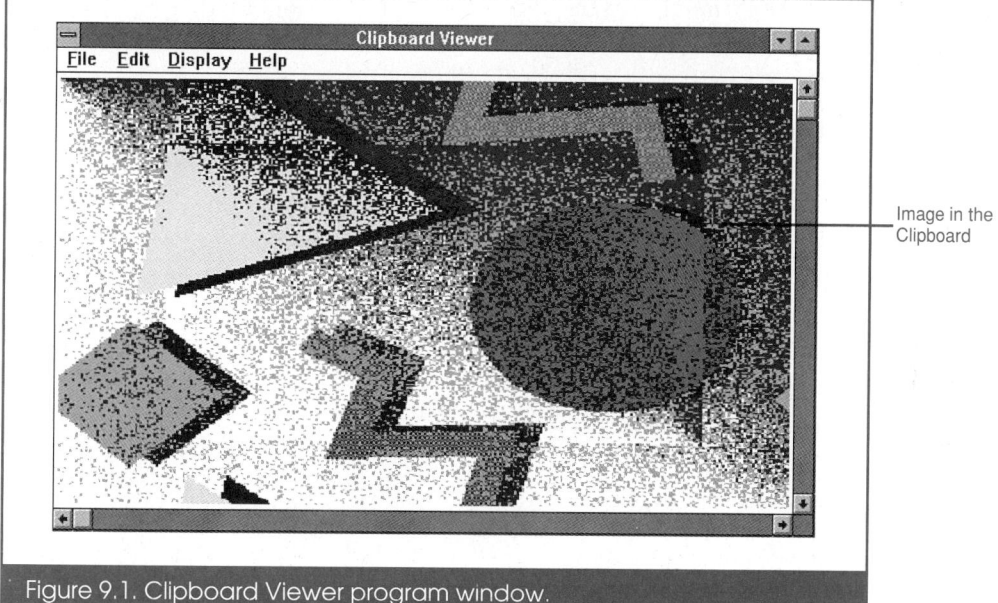

Image in the Clipboard

Figure 9.1. Clipboard Viewer program window.

The **F**ile **Ex**it command closes Clipboard Viewer. The data in the Clipboard is still intact, however, if you have not rebooted your computer or cleared the Clipboard.

Clearing the Clipboard

The **E**dit **D**elete command clears the contents of the Clipboard. This command rarely is useful because it doesn't hurt to leave the contents in the Clipboard until the next time you give an **E**dit **Cu**t or **E**dit **C**opy command. You might want to give the **E**dit **D**elete command if you are low on memory and you have a large picture or lots of text in the Clipboard. This action frees whatever memory has been allocated to your Clipboard image.

Display Options

Depending on the type of information you have in the Clipboard, there are many ways to display it. The **D**isplay menu changes based on the

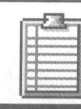

type of information in the Clipboard. For example, Figure 9.2 shows a typical **D**isplay menu for text information. When there is information in the Clipboard, the **D**isplay **A**uto command always is available. The default is **A**uto, which means that Windows looks at the Clipboard contents and determines what type of data is being stored there.

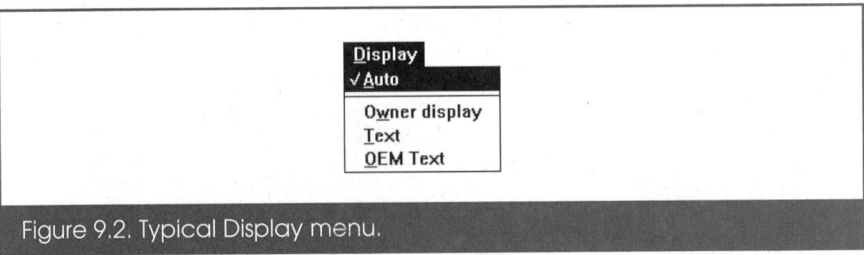

Figure 9.2. Typical Display menu.

When you have a simple bit map picture, you have only one other option in addition to **D**isplay **A**uto, and that is **D**isplay **B**itmap. If you have simple text, you have two options: **D**isplay **T**ext and **D**isplay **O**EM (Original Equipment Manufacturer) Text. The only difference between these two is the font that is used to display the text in the Clipboard window. The **D**isplay **T**ext command shows the text in the display font, which usually is a proportional font. The **D**isplay **O**EM Text command uses the OEM font, which usually is monospaced (every character takes up the same amount of space).

If you are running a program that handles formatted text or complex graphics, you might have additional choices in the **D**isplay menu. Generally, if the program works in full cooperation with Windows and the Clipboard, you will see the **D**isplay **O**wner Display command. This command makes the view in the Clipboard the same as the program that put the contents there. The view, therefore, retains formatting and special graphical characteristics.

Depending on the program, you might see other options in the **D**isplay menu. For example, Word for Windows uses a format for text called RTF (Rich Text Format). RTF is a file formatted with all the embedded format symbols (line feed, spaces, tabs, and so on) intact and in place. When you copy text in Word for Windows, the text is saved to the Clipboard in RTF format as well as text format, so that you see both choices on the **D**isplay menu.

Uses for the Clipboard

Whenever you want to transfer information from one program to another, you can use the Clipboard. As you saw earlier in this chapter, you might not be able to transfer all the information you want, but in most cases you can transfer at least all the text or a bit map between any two Windows programs.

For example, assume that Alicia is writing to the bank a letter that includes sales figures from her spreadsheet. She would have both the word processing and spreadsheet programs open at the same time. Figure 9.3 shows the letter as she is about to include the table of figures.

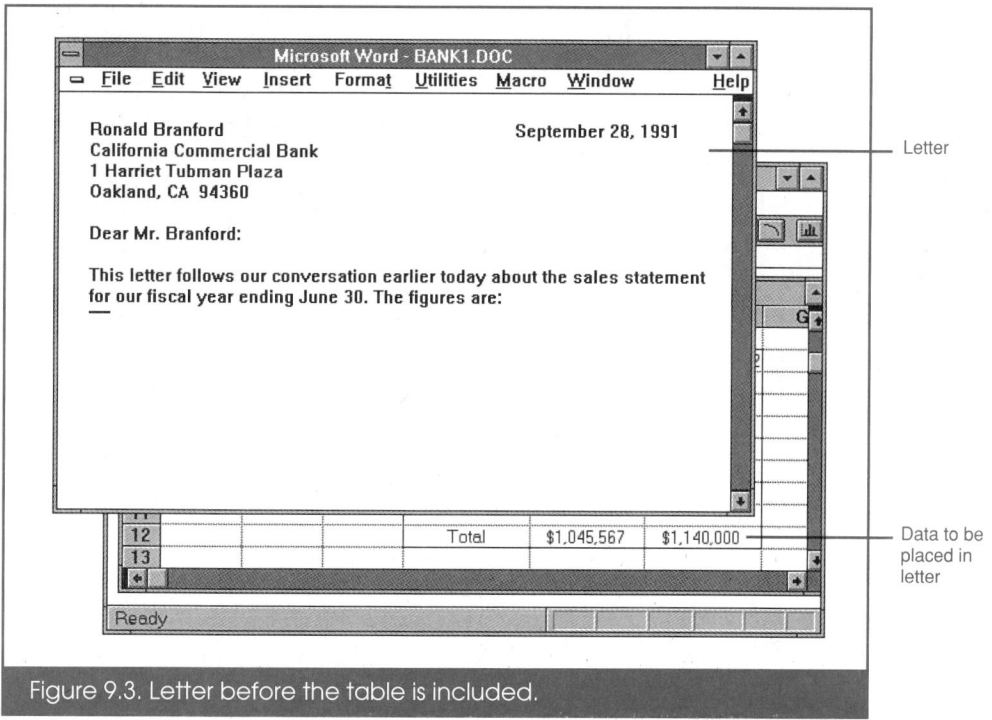

Figure 9.3. Letter before the table is included.

Next she switches to the spreadsheet program and selects (by whatever means her program allows) the information she wants in the letter. Figure 9.4 shows the information selected. She then gives the **E**dit **C**opy command in her spreadsheet.

She then switches back to her word processing program and gives the **Edit Paste** command. The results are shown in Figure 9.5. After the information is put in the letter, she can edit and format it just like text she has entered by hand.

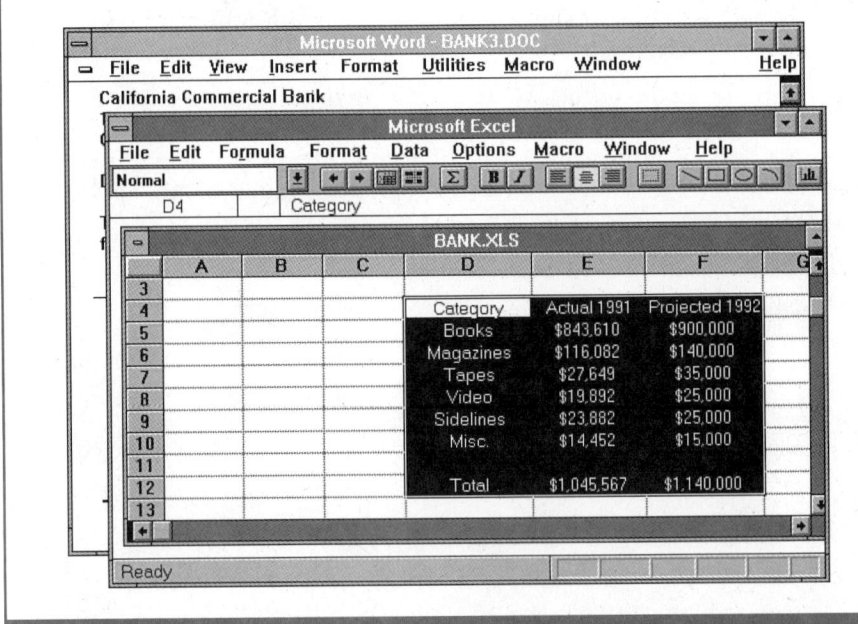

Figure 9.4. Spreadsheet information selected.

Tip: Most Windows programs are flexible as to the kinds of information you can move into and out of them. You should read the manuals for the programs you use to find out specifically how your programs work with the Clipboard.

Copying Screens to the Clipboard

You can copy a picture of the Windows screen to the Clipboard by pressing the PrintScreen key. (On some keyboards, this key may read

PrintScrn.) This action takes a picture of the entire screen, not just one window, and puts it in the Clipboard. If using the PrintScreen key doesn't work on your system, try pressing Alt-PrintScreen or Shift-PrintScreen. The screen image is saved to the Clipboard as a bit map image. Unless you have used a special program to change the keystroke assignment of the PrintScreen key, pressing the PrintScreen key will place a copy of what you see on your screen in the Clipboard, replacing any image already stored there.

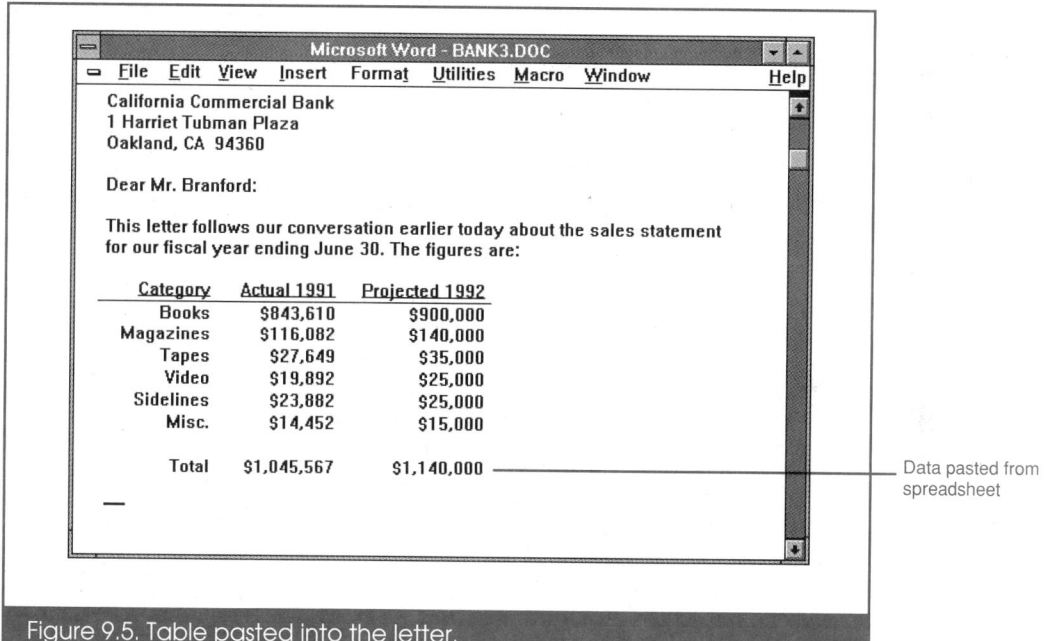

Data pasted from spreadsheet

Figure 9.5. Table pasted into the letter.

Note: The PrintScreen key has been remapped by Windows, but the printing function is still there. Some applications, such as Collage's Snap, have the ability to map the old print screen function to another key, enabling you to print what is on your screen with the press of a certain key.

If you are running in 386-enhanced mode, you can copy just the current window to the Clipboard by pressing Alt-PrintScreen. This is handy if you want a picture of just part of the screen. See Chapter 20, "Other DOS Programs and Windows," for more detail on the subject.

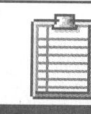

Tip: Many screen-capture programs such as HotShot Graphics are much more advanced than the screen-capture capabilities built into Windows. See Reference C, "Windows Product Directory," for more on these programs and their features.

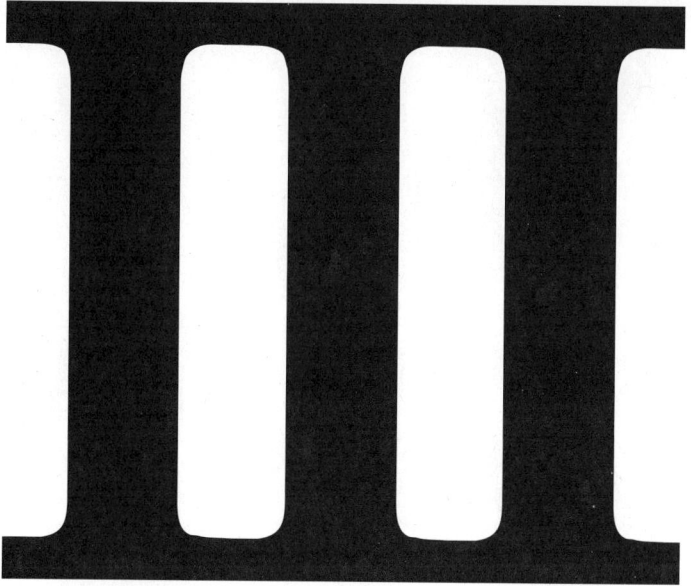

Windows
Accessory
Programs

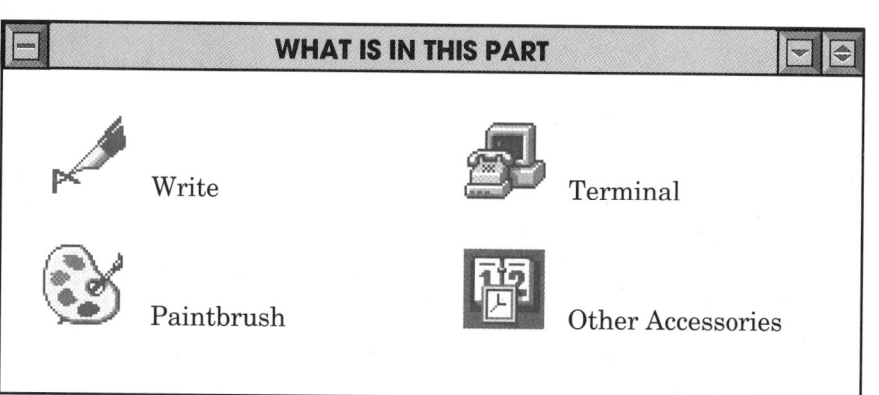

WHAT IS IN THIS PART

Write

Terminal

Paintbrush

Other Accessories

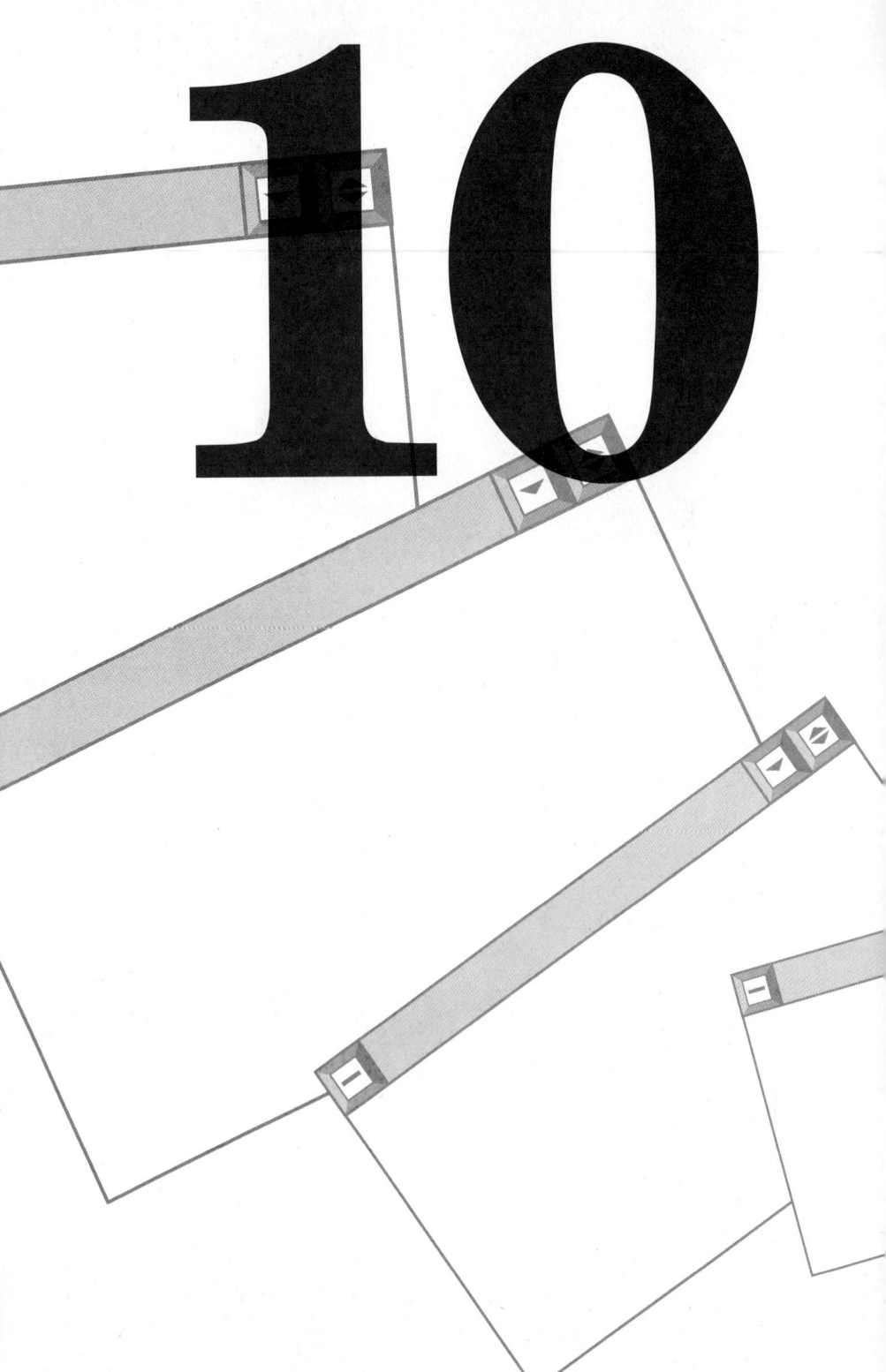

CHAPTER

10

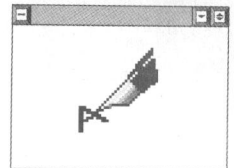

Write

The most common task for which PCs are used is word processing. Even people who crunch numbers all day usually need to present their results in written form. Many PC users do nothing but run a word processor. Because the word processor is the basis for many people's work, Microsoft included the Write word processor with Windows 3.1.

If you use a word processor often, you will recognize that Write is not a very powerful program. Because it uses the Windows user interface, however, even novices should find it easy to master. Even though it is simple to use, it has enough features to create professional-looking reports and signs.

Even though Write is lightweight compared to Word for Windows, Ami Pro, and WordPerfect for Windows, it can access the fonts in Windows almost as well as the big kids. Be sure to experiment with all the fonts and sizes. For your information, *font* is a term applied to any characters designed in a particular size and style. The height of a font is measured in *points*. One point is 1/72 of an inch. You will see that fonts are offered in point sizes incrementally, usually by values of 2 points (such as 6, 8, 10, 12, 14, and so on).

The techniques you use in Write are useful in many other Windows programs as well. For example, the steps used in editing text in Write are the same as the steps used in editing numbers in Excel (a spreadsheet program like Lotus 1-2-3). Also, the character formatting used in Write is available in most Windows programs. Even the concepts of alignment and indentation are applicable in many drawing programs.

If you plan to use Windows to write a great deal, you should consider getting a more powerful word processor than Write. Chapter 16, "Microsoft Word for Windows," and Chapter 17, "WordPerfect for Windows," describe two popular programs that have many more features than Write. Many other Windows word processors are available as well. See Reference C, "Windows Product Directory," for more on popular writing tools.

Figure 10.1 shows the initial Write window. The main part of the window is where your text appears. The insertion point is the thin I-beam symbol located in the text and marks the point where text appears when you type. The end mark (a four-pointed star) shown at the top of the window shows you where your text ends. The page status box at the lower-left of the window tells you what page you are viewing. The Write window has standard vertical and horizontal scroll bars for viewing different parts of your text.

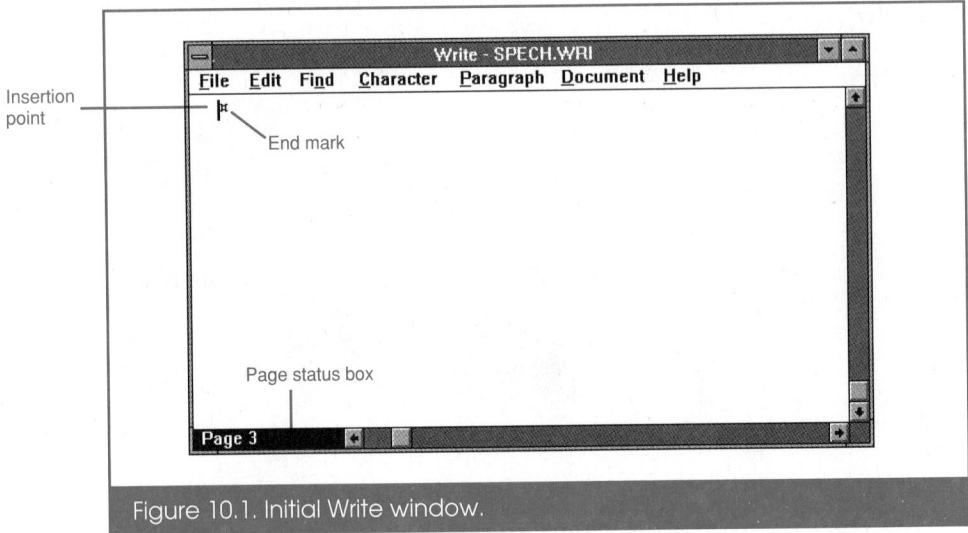

Figure 10.1. Initial Write window.

Introduction to Word Processing

If you have never used a word processor or have used one somewhat blindly, then knowing word processing concepts will help you create better documents and write more easily. The less time you need to think about the word processor, the more time you can spend thinking about your writing. Remember that Write is a low-end word processor: You do not need to learn many concepts in order to use it.

There are four basic actions in word processing:

Writing: the actual committing of text and graphics to a document or file

Editing: the amending of text and graphics in an existing document or file

Formatting: the determining of how your text and graphics will appear on the paper when they are printed

Saving and printing: naming, storing, and sending your file to an output device such as a printer

10

These actions do not happen one at a time. It is common to edit as you write, and you might even add formatting as you edit. Although most people tend to write, edit, and format at the same time, performing these tasks one at a time usually improves your writing because you concentrate on your words more in the first step. It is a good habit to save periodically as you use Write. Printing is almost always done at the end, after you have finished the other tasks.

In this section, Alicia Jacobs, manager of a bookstore, uses Write to create a press release about an author appearance. Later in the chapter are other examples of using Write for other business documents, such as letters and flyers.

Writing

The first step in creating a word processing document is to enter all the text. This is done simply by typing. As you type, you can correct mistakes by pressing the Backspace key. Any other changes you want to make—such as moving paragraphs, rewording awkward sentences, or reorganizing your ideas—is done in the editing phase.

Figure 10.2 shows the press release with just the first draft of the text entered.

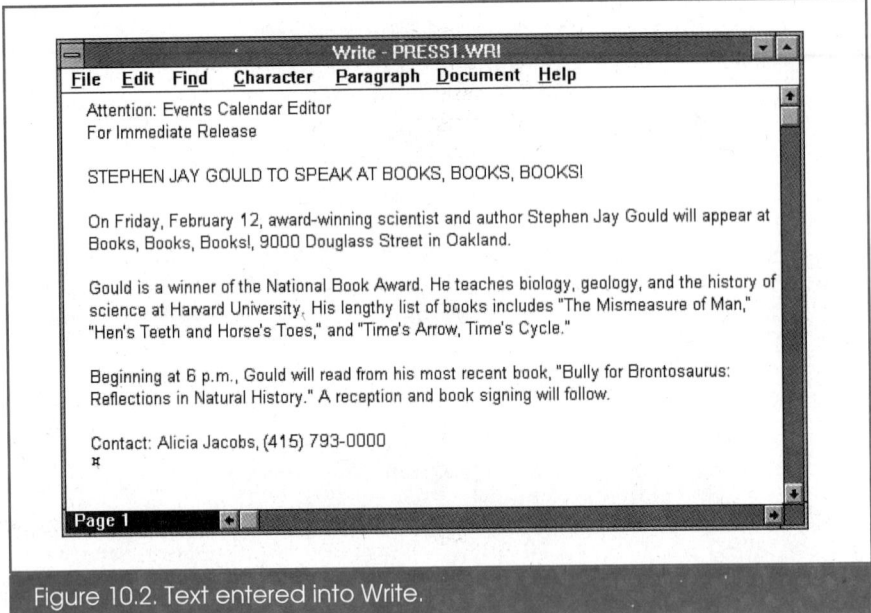

Figure 10.2. Text entered into Write.

Editing

Of course, nothing is perfect the first time you write it. On rereading, you might find grammatical errors, bad organization, or sentences and phrases that just look wrong. You also might think of things you want to add. All these actions are part of editing.

The following is a list of the four types of editing:

Adding. To add text, indicate the point where you want the text to be added by placing the insertion point at the desired location anywhere in the text, then type the new text. You can add text between two letters, or at the very beginning or the very end of the document. You can change the position of where text will be added at any time by using the mouse pointer and single-clicking on a location, or you can use the arrow keys if you have no mouse.

Removing. There are two ways to remove text. One way is to place the insertion point at the beginning of the undesirable text and drag the highlight so that it covers all of the text that you want to remove and then press Delete. You can also specify a position with the insertion point and remove letters to the left of that position one at a time with the Backspace key.

Changing. Changing text is the same as removing text, then adding new text. Thus, to change text, you select it, remove it, then add new text. You can also type over text of the same length by using the Overtype Mode. Press the **I**nsert key once, and you are in Overtype Mode. You will be typing over the top of existing characters on the screen. To get out of Overtype Mode, press the **I**nsert key again.

Moving. To move a block of text such as a word or a sentence, you must indicate the text to be moved and the desired location. Place the insertion point at the beginning of the text you want to move and select or highlight the text. Then use **E**dit **C**opy to place the selected text onto the Clipboard. Next, place the insertion point where you want the contents of the Clipboard to be pasted. Now use **E**dit **P**aste to place the contents of the Clipboard onto your document at the insertion point.

To reverse the last action you took, select **E**dit **U**ndo.

10

Formatting

After you decide that the words in your document are the way you want them, you can improve the look of the document with formatting. There are dozens of types of formatting, depending on the type of word processor you use. All Windows word processors have three levels of formatting: character, paragraph, and document.

Formatting changes the way your document looks. You can use formatting to make some parts of a document stand out, to make a document look more like an accepted or required norm, to give a document a certain feeling you can't achieve with words alone, and so on. The type of formatting you choose depends on the impression you want to make on the reader, similar to the way you choose words to create a certain tone or mood when you write.

Formatting in Write is broken down into these basic categories:

Character formatting. This changes the way characters look. The most common types of character formatting are character styles (such as bold and italic) and font choices. Unlike most MS-DOS word processors, Windows programs show you the style and fonts you are using as you make your changes.

Tip: The more you use Windows programs, the more you will run into the term WYSIWYG (what you see is what you get). The only way you can achieve true WYSIWYG is by using scalable fonts such as Microsoft's TrueType or the Adobe Type Manager. Scalable fonts create a font from a stored font outline to make the font you request if your printer does not have it built-in. Even though many programs say they are WYSIWYG without using scalable fonts, your printed results still are most likely to be dissimilar to your displayed document. If you use a scalable font manager, you gain WYSIWYG but you give up memory and speed. The general rule of thumb regarding today's up-and-coming scalable font managers is, "Don't use them unless you have at least 4M of RAM on your system." With Windows 3.1, this means deselecting the Use TrueType and TrueType Only check boxes in the Control Panel Font dialog box if you are using less than 4M of RAM.

Paragraph formatting. Changes how text is aligned with the margins and how lines within a paragraph appear. Common paragraph formatting includes indentation from the left margin for the first line of a paragraph or for the whole paragraph, *justification* of the paragraph (arranging text so that it is evenly spaced between the left and right margins), line spacing within a paragraph, and the amount of space above or below a paragraph.

Document formatting. These are settings that affect a whole document, not just some characters or paragraphs. The types of formatting that fall into this category vary from word processor to word processor. In Write, for example, you can set the margins only once for the whole document and you can have only one set of headers and footers. In other word processors, these settings can be changed within a document.

Figure 10.3 shows the press release with formatting added. Alicia added boldface character formatting to the heading to make it stand out, and she also justified the paragraphs against the left margin.

You choose the types of formatting to add to a document based on your own sense of design and aesthetics. Some people like to add much character formatting, and others prefer to keep their documents more plain.

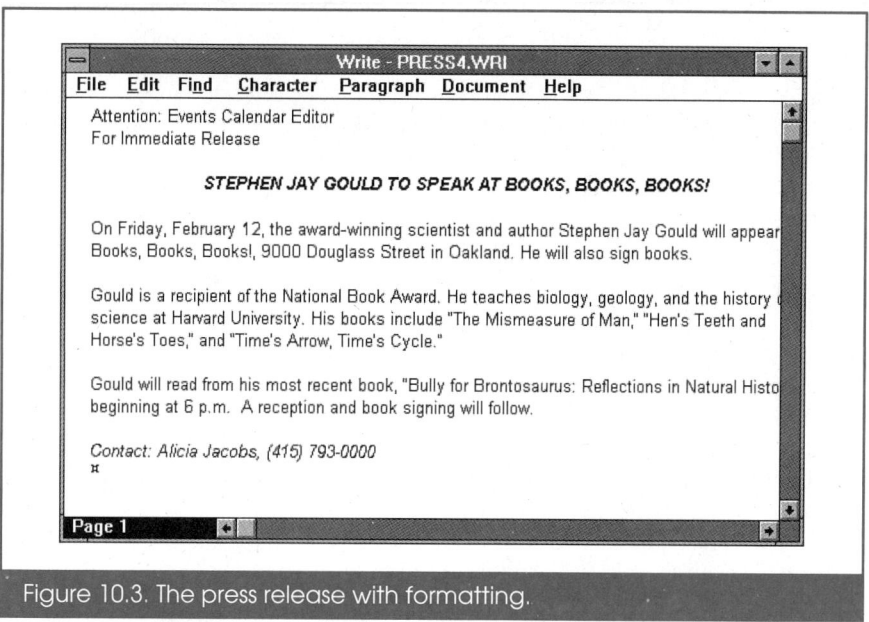

Figure 10.3. The press release with formatting.

Saving and Printing

10

After you enter, edit, and format a document, you will want to save it to disk. In fact, it is a good idea to save it to disk periodically as you work, before you are finished, in case your office has a power failure or something happens to your computer.

You can print your document at any time. Some people like to print drafts of their documents between each step of the writing process, although this can waste paper. Because Windows shows you almost exactly the way your document will appear when it is printed, there is little reason to print so often. When you print a multipage document, you can print all the document or just specific pages.

Entering Text

After you enter your text in Write, the most common thing you will do is edit it. Editing in Write is much like editing in other programs that run under Windows, so learning editing here will save you time when you use other programs.

Insertion Point

To enter text in Write, simply start typing. Text always appears at the *insertion point,* the blinking vertical bar in the window. You can think of it as a kind of cursor. The insertion point is always between two characters, between a character and a space, to the left of the first letter in the document, or to the right of the last letter in the document. As you saw earlier, the end of the document is noted by a bug-like character. When you start Write, there are no characters in the document, so the insertion point is just before the end-of-document marker.

For example, in Figure 10.4, the insertion point is between the letters *a* and *r* in the word *far.* You can move the insertion point without typing by using the pointer that looks like an *I-beam* ([I]). If you place the insertion point between the letters *a* and *r* and type the letters *ste,* the word becomes *faster.* Adding letters at the insertion point always moves the insertion point to the right.

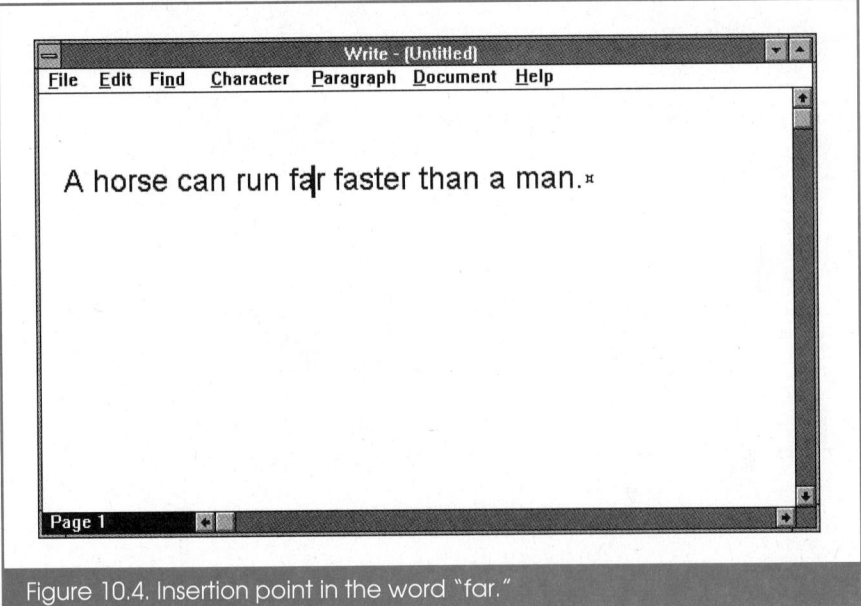

Figure 10.4. Insertion point in the word "far."

To move the insertion point with the mouse, simply click at the desired location. When you are pointing in the text area of the window, the pointer becomes an I-beam so that you can position it between letters more easily. If you click directly on a letter, Write puts the insertion point to the left or to the right of that letter, depending on which side of the letter you clicked.

When you use a small font, sometimes it is difficult to guess which line the insertion point is going to be on. Write uses the location of the middle of the I-beam to determine the line you want. If you also have a Macintosh computer, this can be confusing because the Macintosh uses a spot near the top of the I-beam. Experiment with clicking in different places on a line to see where the I-beam goes.

If you want to put the insertion point on a part of the document that is not showing on the screen, scroll up or down using the scroll bars. As you scroll, the insertion point stays where you left it while text scrolls by. The I-beam pointer stays visible so that you have a way to insert a new insertion point when you know where you want to type.

> **Tip:** To place the insertion point at the end of a line, click any-where to the right of the last letter on that line. To place the in-sertion point at the end of a document, point anywhere after the end-of-document marker and click.

Moving the insertion point with the keyboard is rather easy, although there are many keystrokes to remember when you want to move more than one character or line at a time. Table 10.1 shows the keystrokes arranged by movement, and Table 10.2 shows the keystrokes arranged by key. Use the table that makes it easier for you to remember the keystrokes. In the tables, "Keypad5" refers to the 5 on the keypad on the right side of the keyboard, and not to the numeric 5 at the top of the keyboard. To move to an area indicated with a "Keypad5," press the 5 on the numeric keypad (with the Num Lock off) and then press the arrow key.

Key board

10

Note that when you move using the keyboard, the insertion point is always visible on the screen. When you scroll with the mouse, you can scroll the insertion point off the screen.

Word Wrap

When you type text into Write that is longer than a line on the screen, Write automatically wraps the additional text to the next line. For example, Figure 10.5 shows a "before-and-after" view of typing text near the end of a line. While the word "greatly" is being typed, Write detects the end of the line and automatically drops the word to the next line.

Table 10.1. Keystrokes to move insertion point, arranged by movement.

Key	What It Moves To
←	Previous character
→	Next character
Home	Beginning of line
End	End of line
Ctrl-←	Beginning of previous word
Ctrl-→	Beginning of next word
Keypad5-←	Beginning of previous sentence
Keypad5-→	Beginning of next sentence
↑	Previous line
↓	Next line
Keypad5-↑	Beginning of previous paragraph
Keypad5-↓	Beginning of next paragraph
PageUp	Previous window
PageDown	Next window
Ctrl-PageUp	Top of window
Ctrl-PageDown	Bottom of window
Keypad5-PageDown	Next page
Keypad5-PageUp	Previous page
Ctrl-Home	Beginning of document
Ctrl-End	End of document

When you reach the end of a paragraph (even if that paragraph is just one line, such as the date in a letter), press the Enter key to go to the next line. This forces the line to end and the insertion point to go to the next line. You should always press the Enter key when ending a paragraph. Do not be tempted, as many beginners are, to press the Tab key or the Spacebar until the insertion mark goes to the next line. Write does not make formatting codes such as the paragraph mark visible to the user. It is very important to let Write word-wrap text in a sentence that is longer than one line, rather than pressing Enter at the end of each line you type.

Table 10.2. Keystrokes to move insertion point, arranged by key.

Key	What It Moves To
←, →	Previous or next character
Ctrl-←, Ctrl-→	Beginning of previous or next word
Keypad5-←, Keypad5-←	Beginning of previous or next sentence
↑, ↓	Previous or next line
Keypad5-↑,Keypad5-↓	Beginning of previous or next paragraph
PageUp, PageDown	Previous or next window
Ctrl-PageUp, Ctrl-PageDown	Top or bottom of window
Keypad5-PageDown,	Next or previous page Keypad5-PageUp
Home, End	Beginning or end of line
Ctrl-Home, Ctrl-End	Beginning of document

10

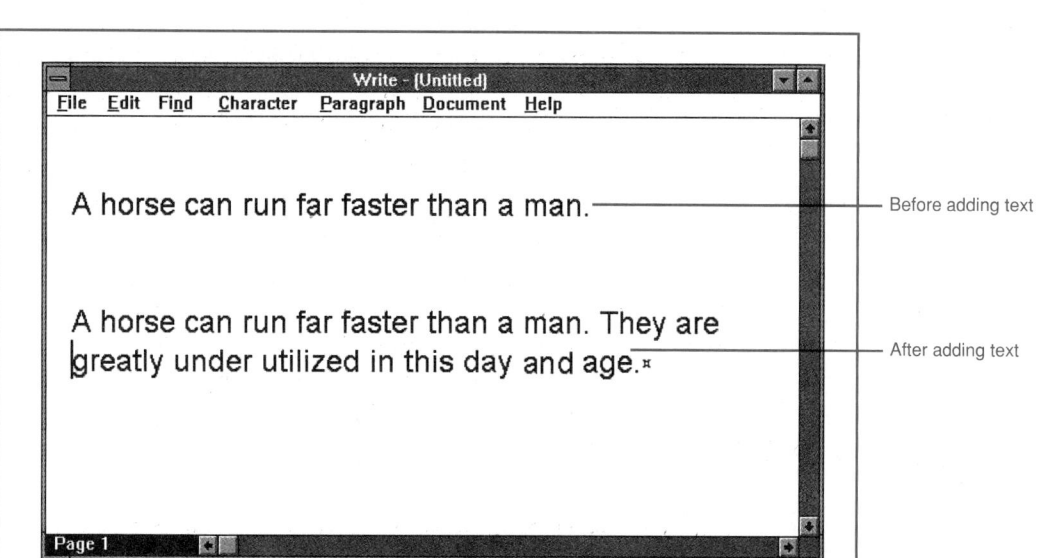

Before adding text

After adding text

Figure 10.5. Before and after a word is added near the end of the line.

Selecting Text

To act on text in your document, you must select it first. When you select text, it becomes highlighted. Most screens have dark letters on a light background, and highlighting appears as a black rectangle over light characters, as shown in Figure 10.6.

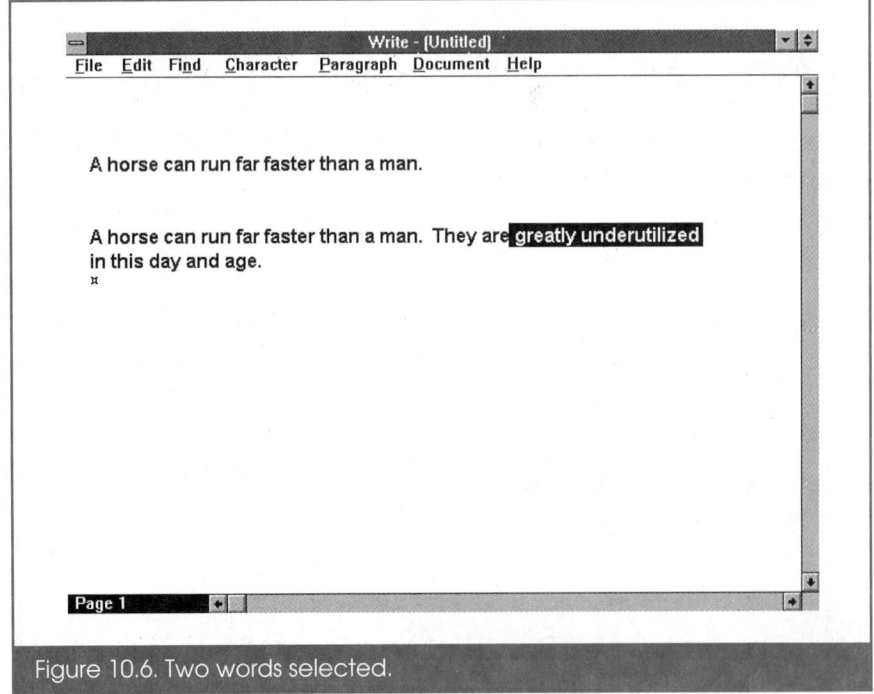

Figure 10.6. Two words selected.

You can select in any direction; that is, you can start your selection at the first or the last letter of the text you want to select. Note that you can select from one character up to all the characters in your document.

Selecting Text with the Mouse

To select text with the mouse, click and drag over the text. To extend a previously made selection to a new location, hold down the Shift key while clicking in the document.

To cancel the selection, click anywhere in the document. This action deselects the highlighted text and places the insertion point where you click.

You can use the mouse to select larger quantities of information quickly by pointing in the *selection area,* the white area at the far left of the window. Figure 10.7 shows the pointer in the selection area.

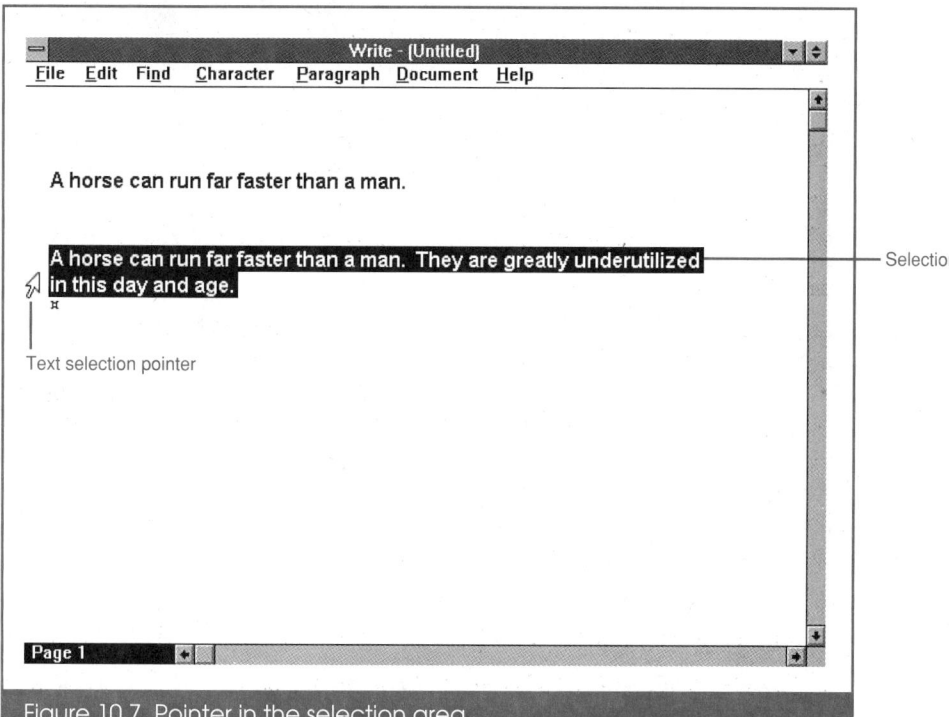

Figure 10.7. Pointer in the selection area.

You can use the selection area for three types of selections:

▲ Clicking in the selection area next to a line causes the line to be selected.

▲ Double-clicking in the selection area causes the paragraph to be selected.

▲ Holding down the Ctrl key and clicking in the selection area causes the entire document to be selected.

You can use the Shift key in combination with the preceding actions to extend the selection. For example, you can select two lines by clicking in the selection area next to a line, holding down the Shift key, and clicking the next line. If you don't use the Shift key to extend the selected area to the next line, and just click the next line in the same manner as the first, and the first selected line becomes deselected.

Tip: To select many lines or paragraphs, start the selection by clicking or double-clicking in the selection area, but keep holding down the mouse button. With the mouse button still down, drag the highlight area down or up, as well as left or right, while staying in the selection area. Write extends the selection without your having to use the Shift key.

Note that Write is one of the few Windows programs that has a selection area. Thus, these techniques do not work with many other programs.

Selecting Text with the Keyboard

You can select text using the keystrokes in Tables 10.1 and 10.2. You must hold down the Shift key as you use these keystrokes, however. The Shift key tells Windows that you want to create or extend the selection, not move the insertion point. For example, to select to the beginning of the previous word, you would press Shift-Ctrl-←.

Moving and Copying Text

Editing for good grammar usually consists of deleting words and phrases and replacing them with others. This is the most common task you perform when you edit your writing. The second-most common task is reorganizing sentences and paragraphs. Reorganization is common when you find topics that appear before the material that introduces them, or when you change your mind about where to mention particular concepts.

You use the Clipboard to move or copy text. It stores information, and you can put that information in another part of your document. The Clipboard is discussed in detail in Chapter 9, "Clipboard Viewer."

The most important fact to remember about the Clipboard is that it holds only one piece of information at a time. This information can be very long, such as dozens of paragraphs, but the Clipboard treats it as a single item. You cannot keep more than one **E**dit Cu**t** or **E**dit **C**opy image on the Clipboard at the same time. Whenever you put something in the Clipboard, the previous contents are lost.

To move text from one part of your document to another, you first highlight the text and use the Edit Copy command to move it to the Clipboard, then copy it from the Clipboard to the desired location. To move text to the Clipboard, select it and use the **E**dit Cu**t** command. The text disappears from your document, but it is safe on the Clipboard. Move the insertion point to the place where you want the text moved and give the **E**dit **P**aste command.

To switch the positions of the first and second paragraphs, you move the first paragraph so that it follows the second paragraph. The steps are as follows:

1. Select the first paragraph with the mouse or the keyboard. Also select the blank line after the first paragraph, as shown in Figure 10.8.

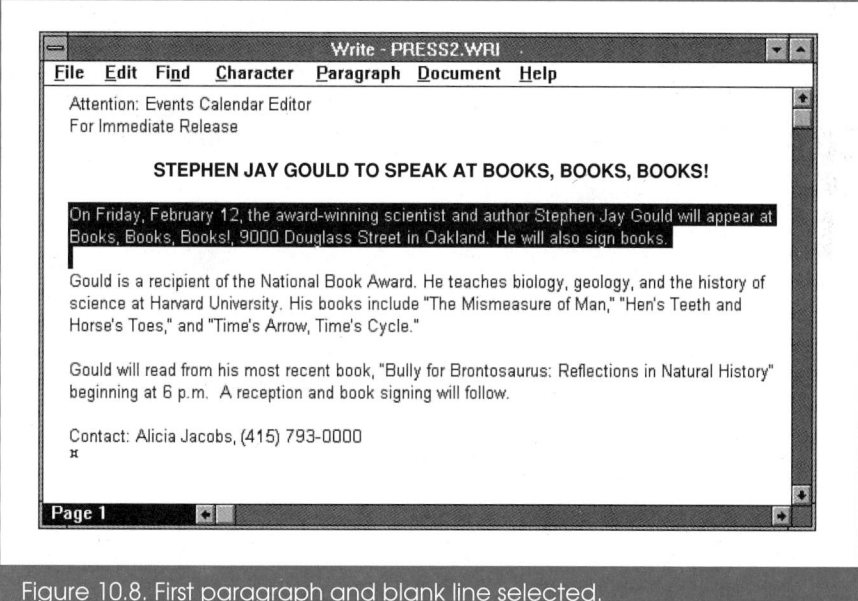

10

Figure 10.8. First paragraph and blank line selected.

2. Give the **E**dit Cu**t** command. The selected text disappears, as shown in Figure 10.9.

3. Move the insertion point to the desired location.

4. Give the **E**dit **P**aste command. The text you cut earlier appears at the insertion point, as shown in Figure 10.10.

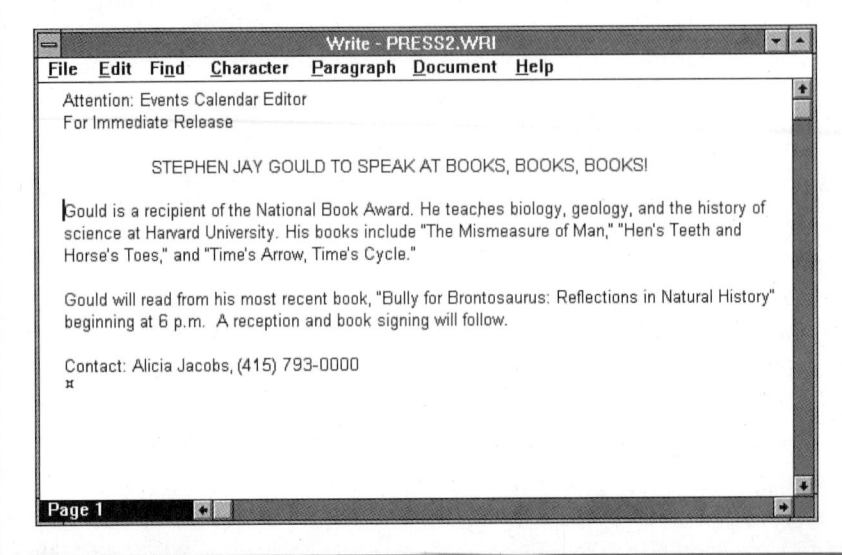

Figure 10.9. Paragraphs removed with the Edit Cut command.

Copied
paragraph

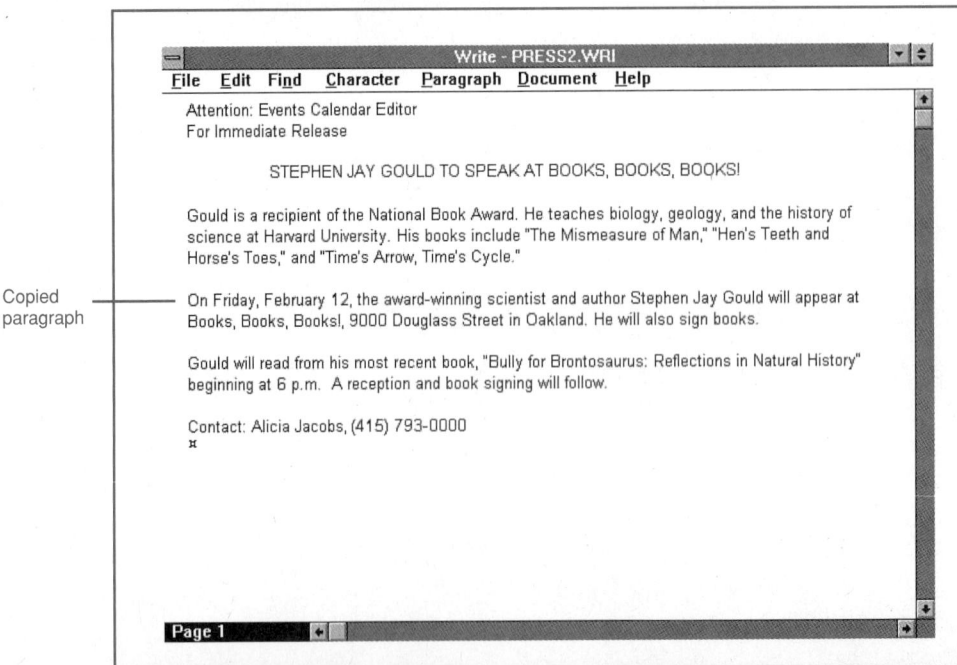

Figure 10.10. Paragraph copied from the Clipboard.

The Clipboard is useful for more than just moving parts of your document. When you give the **E**dit **P**aste command, the contents of the Clipboard do not disappear—they stay on the Clipboard. Thus, you can use the Clipboard to copy text, not just move it.

> **Tip:** If you know you are about to do a lot of cutting and pasting, it's always wise to save an original copy of your work. You can save it under another filename or in another directory, just in case you make mistakes that cause you to lose part of your original document during the learning process.

Figure 10.11 shows a request sheet kept at the cash register at Books, Books, Books! As you probably can imagine, typing the same three lines over and over would be tedious. Instead, Alicia typed the line once, selected it, moved the insertion point to the end of the document, and gave the **E**dit **P**aste command many times.

10

Write - EDITPAST.WRI

File Edit Find Character Paragraph Document Help

BOOKS,BOOKS,BOOKS! New titles special order request sheet.

Please list the Author Name,Book Title,Publisher and ISBN number on each line:

Barrie Sosinski "Beyond the Desktop" Bantam 0-xxx-xxxxx-x

——————————————————————— —— Original typed line

——————————————————————
——————————————————————
—————————————————————— —— Pasted lines
——————————————————————
——————————————————————

Your Name:_____

Your Phone:_____

Please leave this request sheet in the box provided. Someone will call you with price and availability.

Page 1

Figure 10.11. Example of copying text using the Clipboard.

Tip: If you want to check the contents of the Clipboard, run the Clipboard Viewer program from the Main window in Program Manager. You can leave this program running and/or minimized while you use Write. The contents of the Clipboard Viewer program window always reflect the current contents.

Opening and Saving Write Documents

Opening a document file is done when you want to work on a previously saved file. Write saves files on disk much like any other Windows program. You can save files in other formats so that programs that cannot read Write files can still read your documents.

Opening Documents

Write documents usually have a .WRI extension, although Write does not require this. To open a document that is on disk, give the **F**ile **O**pen command. The **F**ile **O**pen dialog box is shown in Figure 10.12. Opening files is covered in Chapter 4, "Basic Windows Concepts."

Although the dialog box prompts you with the .WRI extension, you can enter another extension or select a suggested extension from the contents of the drop-down list at the lower-left of the dialog box. Unless you select another drive and/or directory, only files in the current directory that match the file type you have selected will display. Write can open three types of files:

▲ *Write:* previously saved Write documents

▲ *Text-only:* documents from another word processing program

▲ *Microsoft Word:* Word for DOS and Word for Windows with a filename extension of .DOC

When you open a text-only document or a Microsoft Word document, Write asks whether you want to convert the file by displaying the message `Convert Text to Write format?` For Microsoft Word documents, you must convert. For text-only documents, you should convert only if the document has special graphics or international characters. These are described in Chapter 26, "Printers and Fonts."

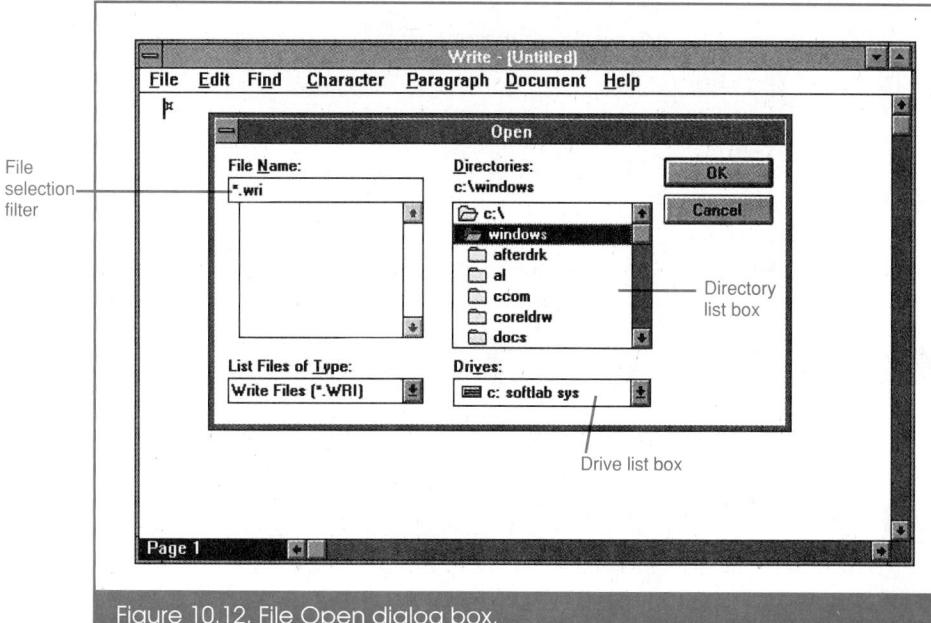

File selection filter

Directory list box

Drive list box

Figure 10.12. File Open dialog box.

10

Warning: Write preserves most character and paragraph formatting when you open a Microsoft Word document, but not all. Write does not recognize or preserve any formatting in a style sheet attached to the document. Do not save a Microsoft Word document that you open in Write in Microsoft Word format and expect all the formatting to reappear in Microsoft Word. Also, saving in Microsoft Word format deletes any pictures in your document, because Write does not include any graphics during conversion and will not save them. Sooner or later you might inadvertently trash days or weeks of work. For all these reasons, editing Word for DOS and Word for Windows documents with Write is not recommended.

Saving Documents

To save a document to disk, use the **File Save** or **File Save As** commands. The first time you save a file, these commands prompt you for the name of the file, as shown in Figure 10.13. Saving files is covered in Chapter 4, "Basic Windows Concepts."

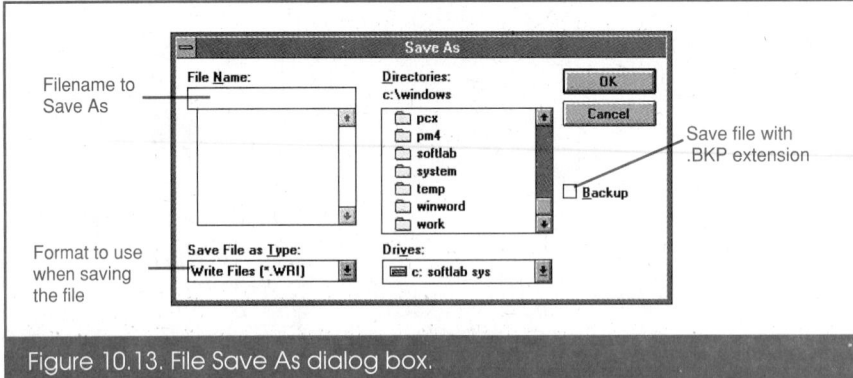

Filename to Save As

Format to use when saving the file

Save file with .BKP extension

Figure 10.13. File Save As dialog box.

Tip: You do not need to enter a file extension. Write adds the standard .WRI extension if you enter just a filename. The total size of the saved file in number of characters appears briefly at the bottom of the Write window as the file is saved.

If the file is already stored on disk, such as if you opened it or already have saved it in an earlier form, the **F**ile **S**ave command doesn't prompt you; it just saves the revised document to the name it already has. This is like saying, "Save the updates in the old file."

You can use the **F**ile Save **A**s command to save the file in a different directory. Simply choose a new directory or disk and click OK. You also can use the **F**ile Save **A**s command to change the name of the file by entering a new name in the File **N**ame section.

You also can use the **F**ile Save **A**s command to convert the file to a different format during saving. These options in the dialog box enable you to change the way Write normally saves files.

Selecting the **B**ackup check box causes Write to save a backup of the previous version of the file. This works only after the first time you select **B**ackup, and it saves only one previous version. The backup file has the same name as the file you are saving, but it has a file extension of .BKP.

The rest of the options involve the **S**ave File as **T**ype commands:

> *Word (.DOC)* converts the file to Microsoft Word format during saving. Graphics you created while editing the document during a Write work session are not converted. This command does not save all the formatting you use in Write.

Word/Text Only (.DOC) Format causes the file to be saved in a format that can be read by Microsoft Word for DOS (and any program that can read files that use this format, such as Word for Windows, WordPerfect, WordStar, DisplayWrite, and so on).

Text Only (.TXT) tells Write to save the file as a text-only file. These files can be read by many Windows programs, as well as by most non-Windows programs. For example, you can read text-only files with the Notepad program. Any formatting you use in the file is lost when you save it as text-only.

Tip: To stop making backup copies of a file, give the **F**ile Save **A**s command and deselect the **B**ackup check box. After that, when you choose **F**ile Save or **F**ile Save **A**s, the .BKP file created for your original will not be updated (overwritten) during each save.

Character Formatting

Because Windows handles fonts well, Windows programs such as Write can add formatting to characters easily. Write's character formatting is rather basic, but it is sufficient for most business and personal uses. The **C**haracter menu is shown in Figure 10.14.

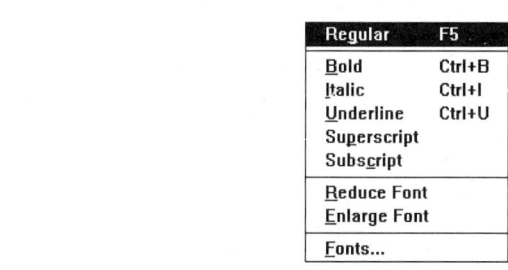

Figure 10.14. Character menu.

To add character formatting (such as bold or italic) to your document, simply select the desired characters and give the commands shown in the **C**haracter menu. If there is no selection (and thus the insertion point is blinking between two characters or spaces), giving character formatting commands tells Windows that the next characters you type at that position should have the specified formatting.

Tip: If you are having difficulty spotting the insertion point on your display and you have not changed the cursor blink rate since installing Windows 3.1, open Control Panel and the Desktop dialog box. Look for the Desktop Cursor Blink **R**ate section. Move the slider button toward the Fast end to increase the blink rate. A blinking cursor is displayed to the right of the slider as an example. Click the OK button or press the Enter key and leave Control Panel. Your cursor should now be more visible by virtue of its increased blink rate.

Tip: When you move the insertion point to a new location and begin typing, the characters you type will have the same formatting as the character immediately before the insertion point. This makes it easy to continue using character formatting that is already on text when you edit formatted text.

Character Styles

You can choose from three basic character styles: bold, italic, and underline. Write also gives you two positioning styles: superscript (such as 10^4) and subscript (such as 10_3). Of course, you can opt to use none of these styles, in which case your text is said to have *regular* character formatting. You apply this formatting using the first six commands in the **C**haracter menu.

When you first open Write, **C**haracter Re**g**ular is selected as the default, but you can change the way characters are presented. Text can have a combination of these styles (such as bold italic). You can have both superscript and subscript styles in the same document or even the same line, but you cannot have them both on the same character. Using multiple styles helps add emphasis and differentiation to text that you want to stand out. Figure 10.15 shows examples of the character styles, including some text with multiple styles.

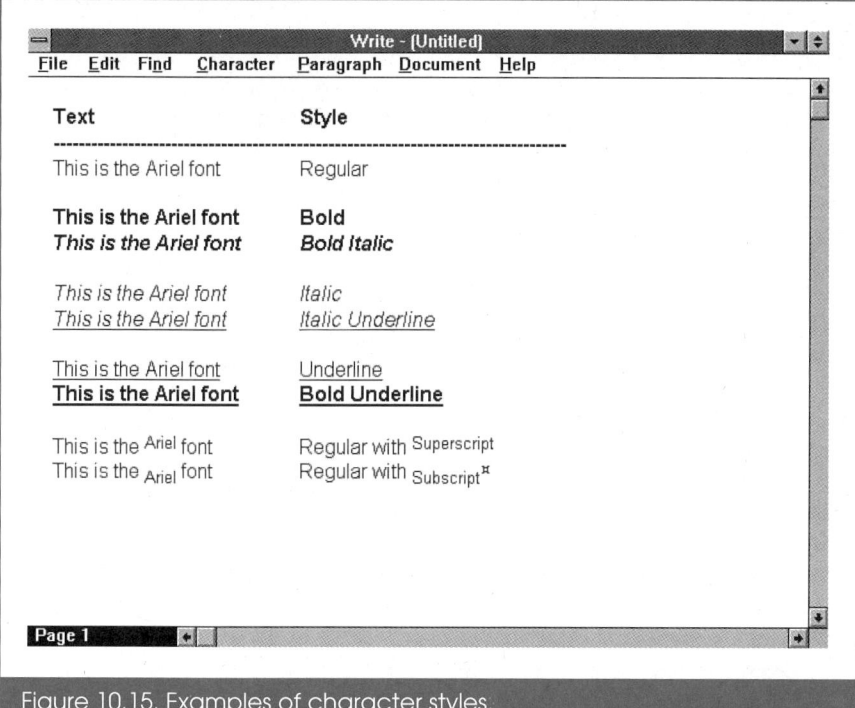

Figure 10.15. Examples of character styles.

10

Fonts and Sizes

Write can display text with any display fonts that are available to Windows. Fonts are described in detail in Chapter 26, "Printers and Fonts." That chapter explains which fonts appear in Windows programs and how to choose the best fonts for your printer.

The most general way to specify a font or a size is with the **C**haracter **F**onts command, shown in Figure 10.16.

Using the **C**haracter **F**onts command, you can change the font, the font size, and add any special formatting such as bold or italic. A sample of your choices will appear in the Sample box.

The **C**haracter **R**educe Font and **C**haracter **E**nlarge Font commands change the size of the selected characters. They decrease or increase the size based on the type of font, but the change usually is in 2-point increments.

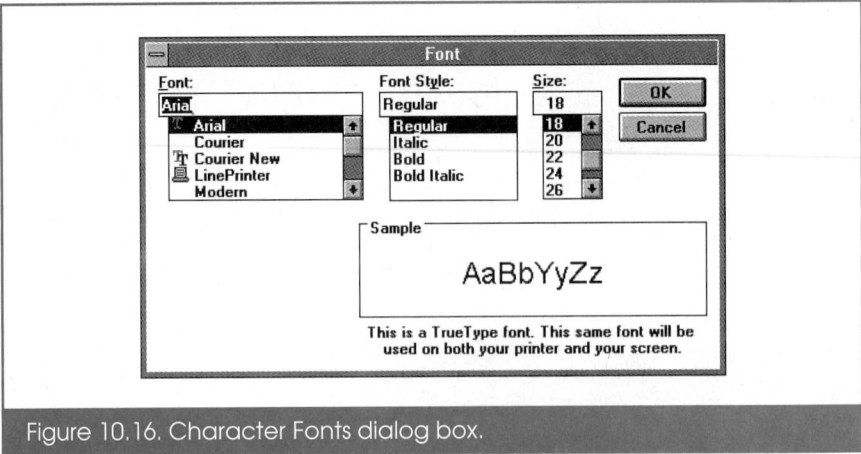

Figure 10.16. Character Fonts dialog box.

Figure 10.17 shows an example of using different fonts in a document. You can use as many as you want, but using too many fonts can make your documents look like an old-time circus poster.

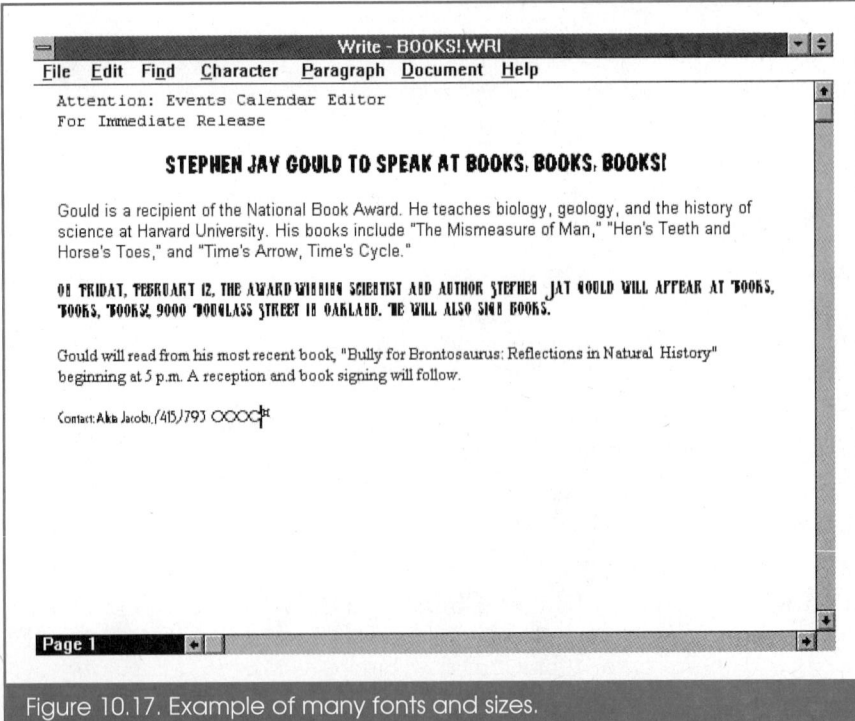

Figure 10.17. Example of many fonts and sizes.

Tip: When you specify that some text should have superscript or subscript style, Write automatically reduces the font size. Most business and technical writing shows superscripts and subscripts in the next-smaller font size. If you want superscripted or subscripted text to be the same size as regular text, you must give the **C**haracter **E**nlarge Font command after giving the positioning command.

Paragraph Formatting

Remember that in Write, a paragraph includes everything up to the point where you pressed Enter. You can quickly check whether some contiguous lines are part of a paragraph by double-clicking in the selection area. (Remember that double-clicking in the selection area selects a paragraph.)

Figure 10.18 shows the commands in the **P**aragraph menu. There are three types of paragraph formatting: alignment, line spacing, and indentation. These are shown in the three groups on the menu. A paragraph can have all three kinds of formatting.

10

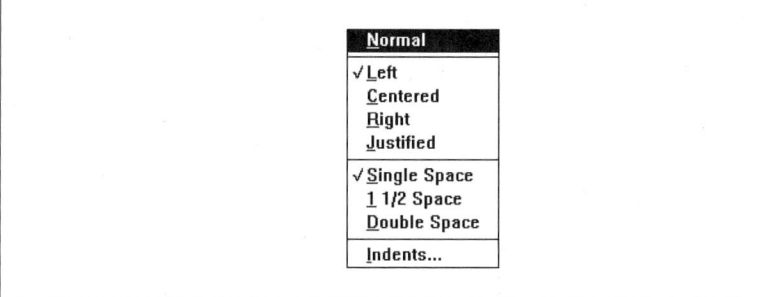

Figure 10.18. Paragraph menu.

The **P**aragraph **N**ormal command undoes any paragraph formatting that is on the selected paragraph. This means that the paragraph becomes left-justified, single-spaced, and has no indentation.

Alignment

Write enables you to specify how a paragraph will line up with the margins. You can align text with the left margin, the right margin, neither margin, or both margins. Table 10.3 describes the four types of justification.

Table 10.3. Types of alignment.

Name	Aligned with Left Margin	Aligned with Right Margin
Left	Yes	No
Right	No	Yes
Justified	Yes	Yes
Centered	No	No

The default, left justification, is what you often see in business documents. This book has left-justified alignment. Figure 10.19 shows examples of all four alignment styles.

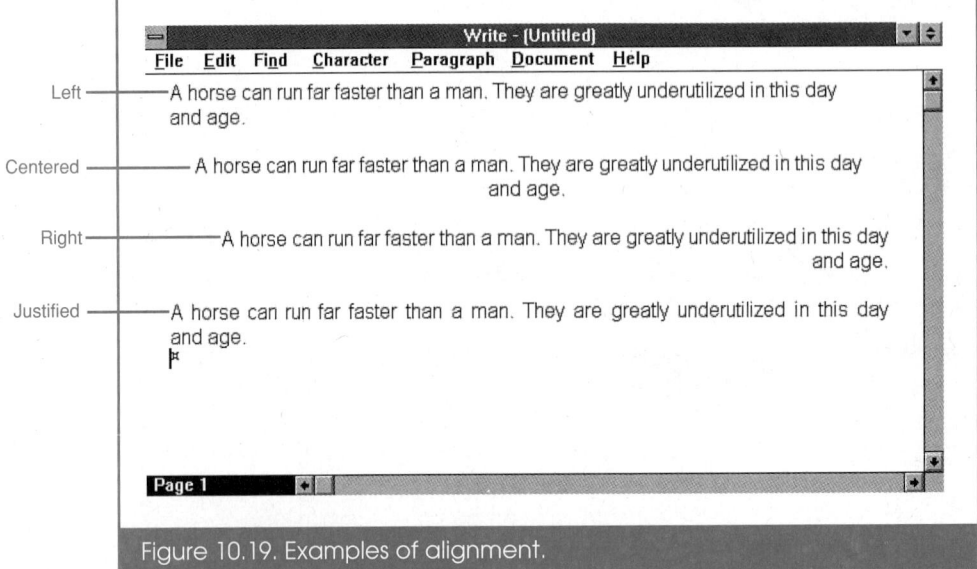

Figure 10.19. Examples of alignment.

Tip: It is not necessary to use justified alignment in your documents for them to look professional. Most of the fonts in Windows are proportional fonts. Thus, at normal size (less than 15 points), most fonts look good whether left-aligned or justified because the lines end very close to each other anyway. Justified text in an informal document or within narrow columns (such as newsletter layouts) sometimes looks unattractive.

Line Spacing

Most business documents are single-spaced. To make text easier to read, you might want to format your paragraphs as 1 1/2 spacing. Double-spacing rarely is used, except for editing a document on paper. With double-spacing, there is plenty of room between the lines for comments.

Indents

10

The margins in a document tell Write how the text is to be aligned. However, you might want some paragraphs to deviate from the margins. You also can select **P**aragraph **I**ndents to indent just the first line of a paragraph. Although you can indent the first line with a tab character (described later in this chapter in the section entitled "Tab Settings"), most people prefer to use **P**aragraph **I**ndents for this task. When you use **P**aragraph **I**ndents, Write senses the beginning of a new paragraph after you press the Enter key and automatically indents the first sentence of the new paragraph. This feature enables professional document creators to continue typing at high speed without having to press the Tab key occasionally.

The **P**aragraph **I**ndents dialog box is shown in Figure 10.20. You specify how far from each margin you want the selected paragraphs to be indented. The unit of measurement is either inches or centimeters, depending on the measurement setting you specify in the International icon in Control Panel or in the **D**ocument **P**age Layout command. Indentation is normally used only on the first line, when you are specifying indentation for a normal paragraph.

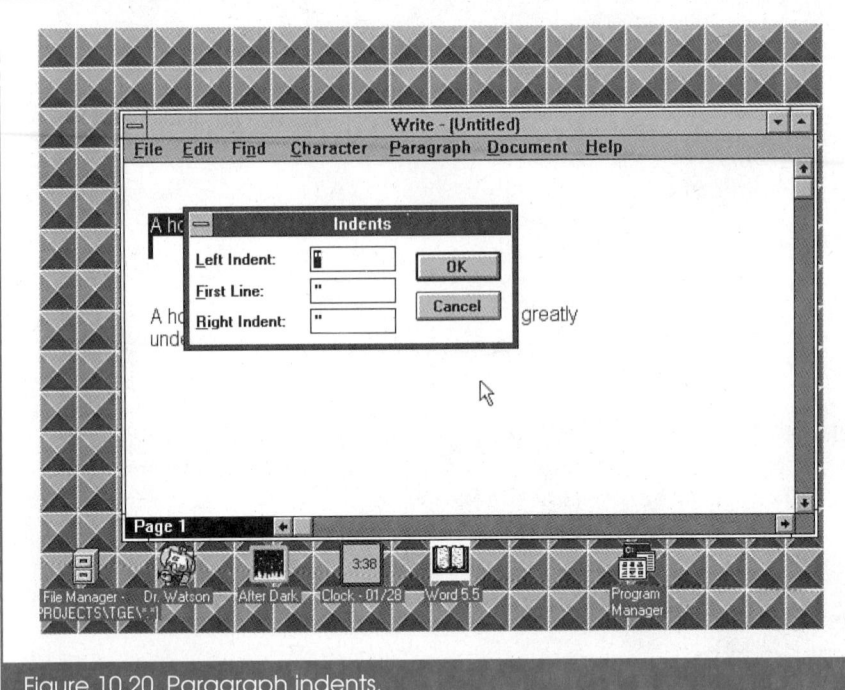

Figure 10.20. Paragraph indents.

Figure 10.21 shows examples of the same paragraph indented from each margin. The last paragraph uses a *hanging indent,* which means that the value for the **F**irst Line indentation is negative. Indentation generally is used sparingly. In academic papers, quotations often are indented equally from both margins. You also can use first-line indentation if you do not want to use tab characters to indent the first lines of paragraphs.

Using the Ruler

You do not have to use the **P**aragraph menu commands to add paragraph formatting to your document. Write's *ruler* is a graphical method of specifying and seeing paragraph formatting. To display the ruler, give the **D**ocument **R**uler On command. Figure 10.22 shows a document with the ruler displayed.

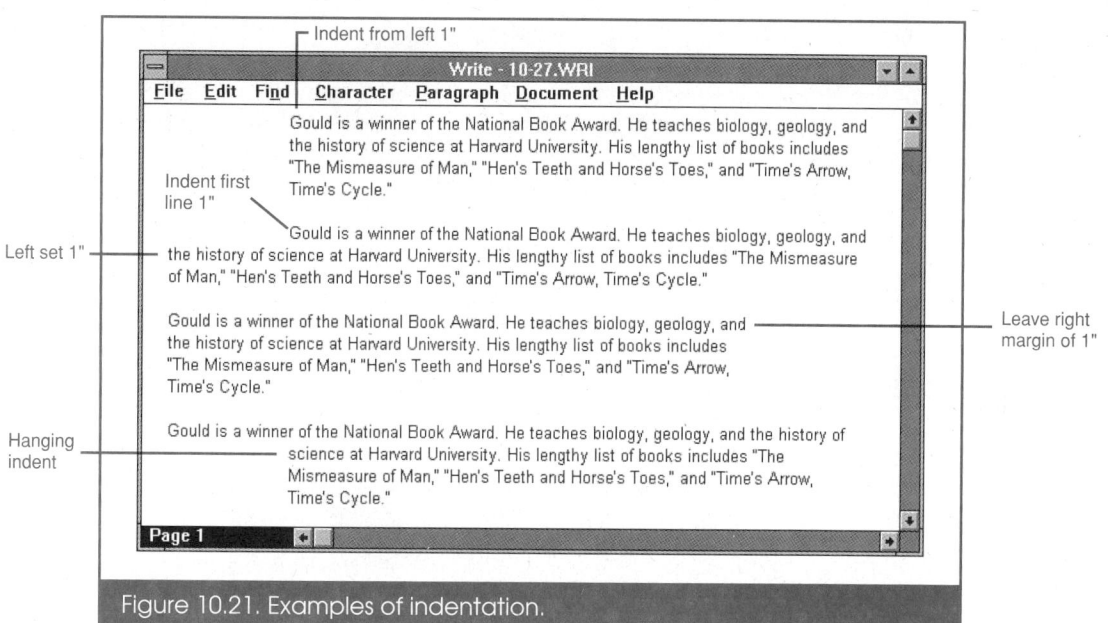

Figure 10.21. Examples of indentation.

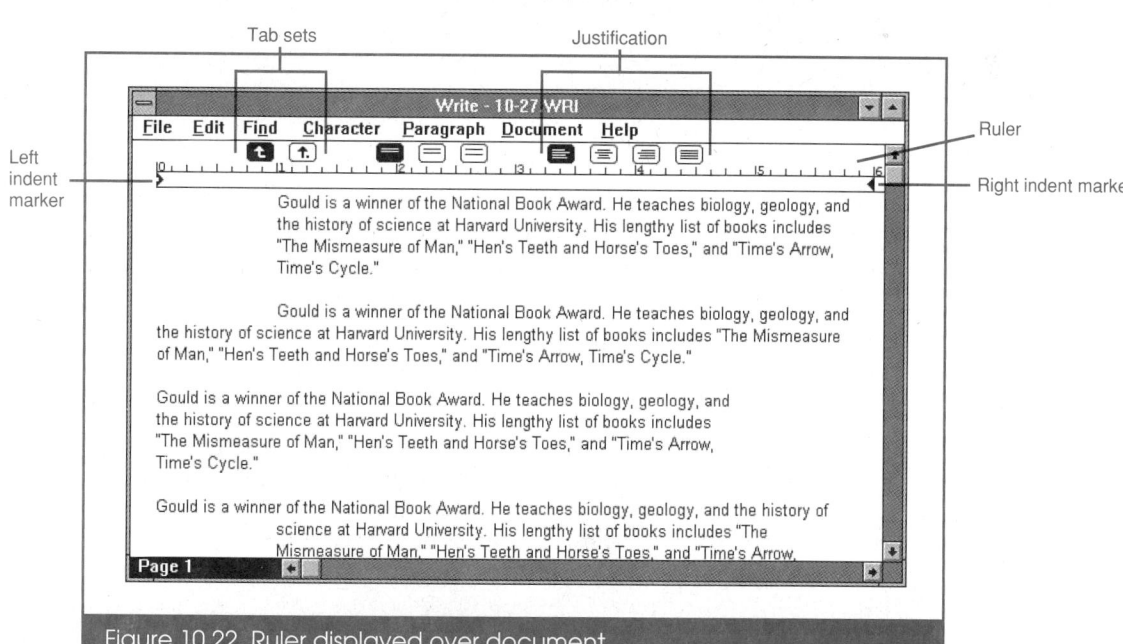

Figure 10.22. Ruler displayed over document.

10

When you scroll the document, the ruler stays at the top of the Write window. The settings on the ruler reflect the formatting for the paragraph you have selected. The set of icons at the left enables you to set tabs for the document, described later in this chapter. The middle set of icons shows the line spacing for the selected paragraphs, and the right set of icons shows the alignment of text on the page. The active icon will appear to be highlighted in much the same fashion as you see highlighted text. Click an icon that is not highlighted to change the settings created by these icon sets.

The indentation is shown beneath the number marks on the ruler. The triangle on the left is the left indent, the triangle on the right is the right indent, and the small square on the left is the first-line indent. When the first-line indent is 0, the first-line indent mark appears as a small white square over the triangle for the left indent. Indent markers can also be moved by clicking on them and dragging them with the mouse.

Copying Paragraph Formatting

Even though you cannot see paragraph marks, paragraph formatting is stored in a space at the end of the paragraph. The paragraph mark is like a space character, but it is wider. If you copy the paragraph mark to the ends of other paragraphs, they take on the same formatting as the original paragraph. Remember, you will be highlighting what *appears* to be a space.

You can select the paragraph mark with the mouse by clicking after the last character in the paragraph and dragging to the right for the width of one character.

You can select the paragraph mark with the keyboard by putting the insertion point at the end of the paragraph and pressing Shift-→.

Copy the paragraph mark by using the **Edit Copy** and **Edit Paste** commands. Because the paragraph mark holds the formatting for a paragraph, deleting the mark merges the paragraph with the one after it and causes the original paragraph to lose its paragraph formatting. For example, Figure 10.23 shows two paragraphs, the top one centered and the bottom one right-aligned.

If you select the paragraph mark at the end of the first paragraph and delete it, the text of the two paragraphs runs together, as shown in Figure 10.24, and the resulting paragraph is right-aligned because the remaining paragraph mark has right alignment.

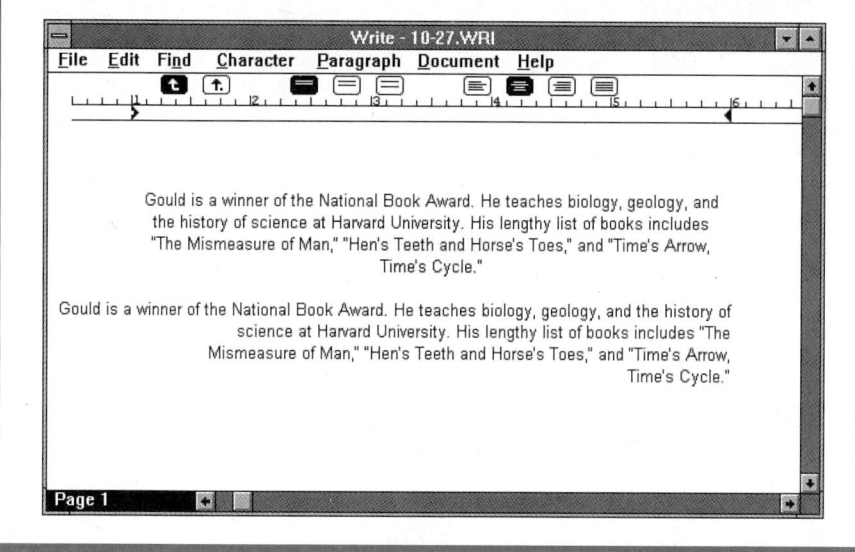

Figure 10.23. Example of paragraphs before deleting the paragraph mark.

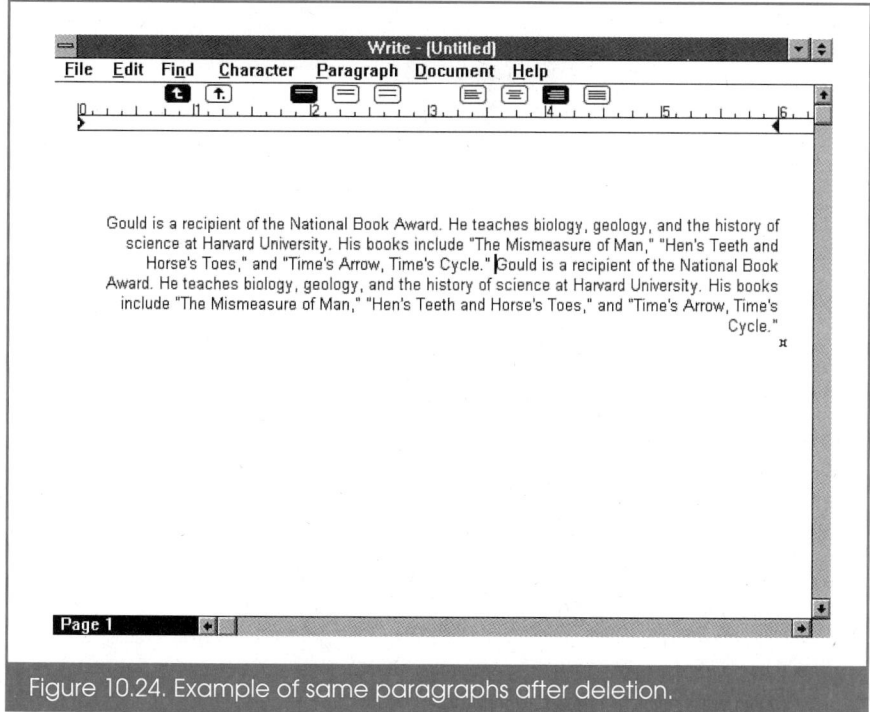

Figure 10.24. Example of same paragraphs after deletion.

10

Document Formatting

The document formatting commands act on the entire document, regardless of what characters are selected when you give the command. The **D**ocument menu is shown in Figure 10.25.

Header...
Footer...
Ruler On
Tabs...
Page Layout...

Figure 10.25. Document menu.

Headers and Footers

You can add text called headers and footers to the top and bottom of each page of text in your document. *Headers* (such as the name of a chapter) appear on the top of each page in your document. *Footers* (such as page numbers) appear at the bottom of each page. Most headers and footers are only one line long, but in Write you can create multiple-line headers and footers. When you give the **D**ocument **H**eader or **D**ocument **F**ooter commands, the Write window changes to that in Figure 10.26.

Enter the text you want to be a header or a footer in the main part of the window. You can use character and paragraph formatting on the text. In the dialog box, enter the distance from the top or the bottom of the sheet of paper that you want the header or footer to be. If you create headers or footers that are more than one line long, Write makes room on the page by decreasing the text area. Be sure that there is enough room between the edge of the paper and your margin.

Warning: Most printers cannot print near the edge of the paper. Some require at least .5 inches of white space. Be sure to take this into account when you set the distance for your header and footer.

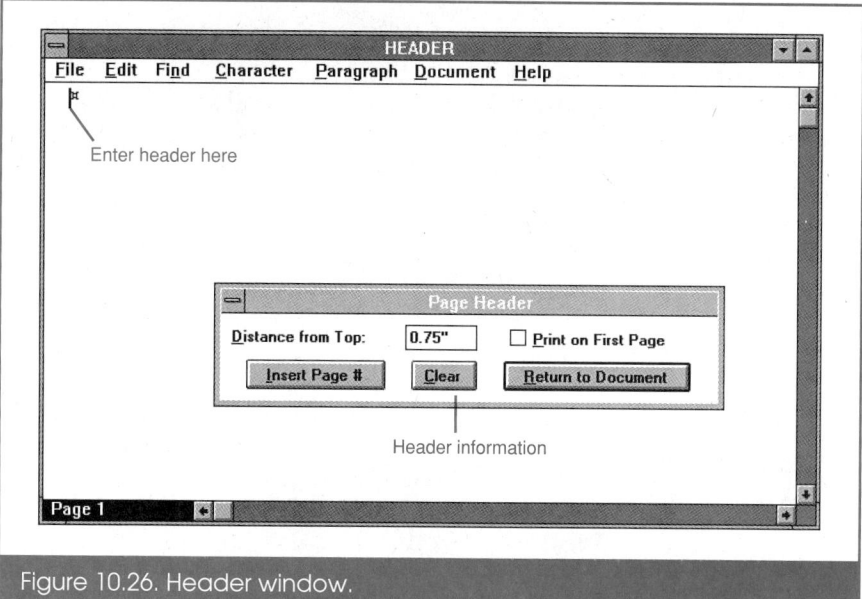

Figure 10.26. Header window.

If you are including the page number in the header or footer, you will want the page number to change with each page. Because the header or footer is the same for the entire document, you need a way to tell Word to put in the actual page number on each page. The **I**nsert Page # button in the dialog box inserts a special mark—signified by (page) on the screen—at the insertion point.

For example, assume that you want to create a footer that has some text and the page number. Give the **D**ocument **F**ooter command. Type Book Buyer's Survey, page and a space in the footer window. Then click the **I**nsert Page # button in the dialog box as shown in Figure 10.27. When you print your document, the footer reads Book Buyer's Survey, page 1, and so on.

Most documents with headers do not have one on the first page. To prevent Write from printing a header or a footer on the first page, be sure that the **P**rint on First Page option in the dialog box is not selected.

Tab Settings

On a typewriter, you can set the tab stops to cause the head to move to a marked position each time you press the Tab key. In Write, tab characters have the same effect. When you need to set tabs in your document, use the **D**ocument **T**abs command. The unit of measurement is either inches or centimeters, depending on the measurement setting you specify in the International icon in Control Panel or in the **D**ocument **P**age Layout command. The dialog box for this command is shown in Figure 10.28.

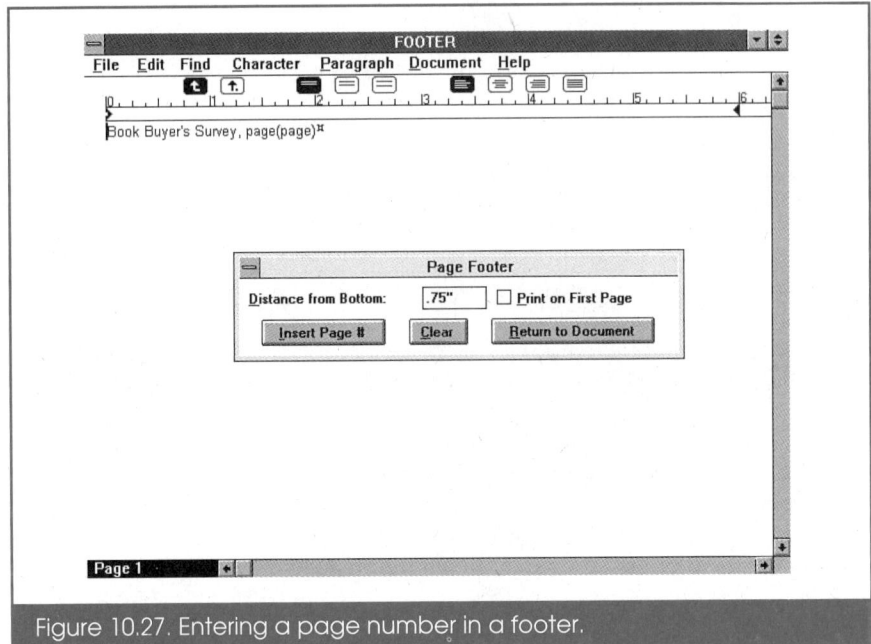

Figure 10.27. Entering a page number in a footer.

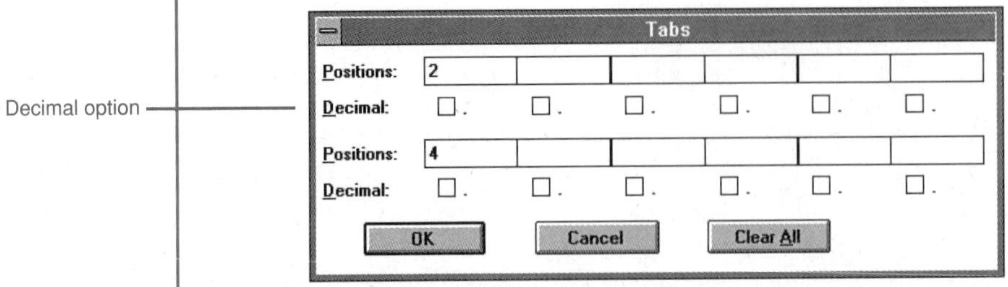

Decimal option ⎯

Figure 10.28. Document Tabs dialog box with tabs set at 2" and 4".

In the **P**ositions entry boxes, enter the positions where you want the tabs, with the first position in the first box. For example, if you are making a table with 3 columns, you might put one tab stop at 2 inches and another at 4 inches, as shown in Figure 10.28. Note that the Clear **A**ll button clears all the tabs you have entered.

> **Tip:** You do not need to put the tabs in order. Write sorts them for you.

To make text line up with the tab stops, simply press the Tab key. For instance, to fill in the table just described, you would type the text for the first column, press the Tab key, type the text for the second column, press the Tab key, type the text for the third column, and press Enter.

Write has two types of tabs: *normal tabs* and *decimal tabs*. Normal tabs line up the text so that it is left-justified. A decimal tab causes numbers with decimal points to line up along their decimal points. If you are creating a column of numbers with varying decimal digits, use a decimal tab. The numbers will align themselves along the tab at their decimal points. To make a tab a decimal tab, select the **D**ecimal option under the setting in the **D**ocument **T**abs dialog box.

For example, Figure 10.29 shows a column of numbers whose decimal points are aligned. Notice the decimal tab in the ruler at the top of the window.

10

You do not need to use the **D**ocument **T**abs command to set tabs when the ruler is visible. To set tabs on the ruler, click one of the two tab icons at the left side of the ruler. The left icon is for normal tab stops and the right icon is for decimal tabs. Then click the point on the ruler where you want the tab.

Margins

Before you print your text, you should set the margins—the distance from the edge of the paper that the text starts and ends. Use the **D**ocument **P**age Layout command, shown in Figure 10.30, for setting the margins.

This command also tells Write the number to use for the first page of your document when you print. This feature is very useful when you have one long document that you have split into many Write files.

The Measurements option changes all the units of measurement in Write, such as the margins, indentation, tab settings, and ruler. This option is set initially by the International icon in Control Panel.

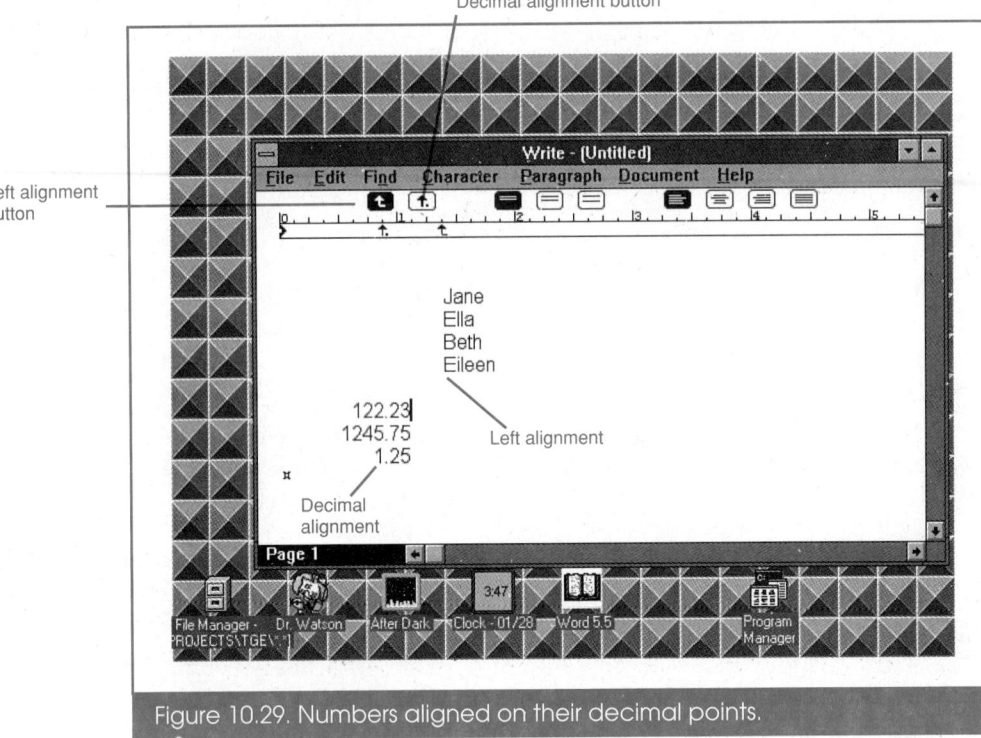

Figure 10.29. Numbers aligned on their decimal points.

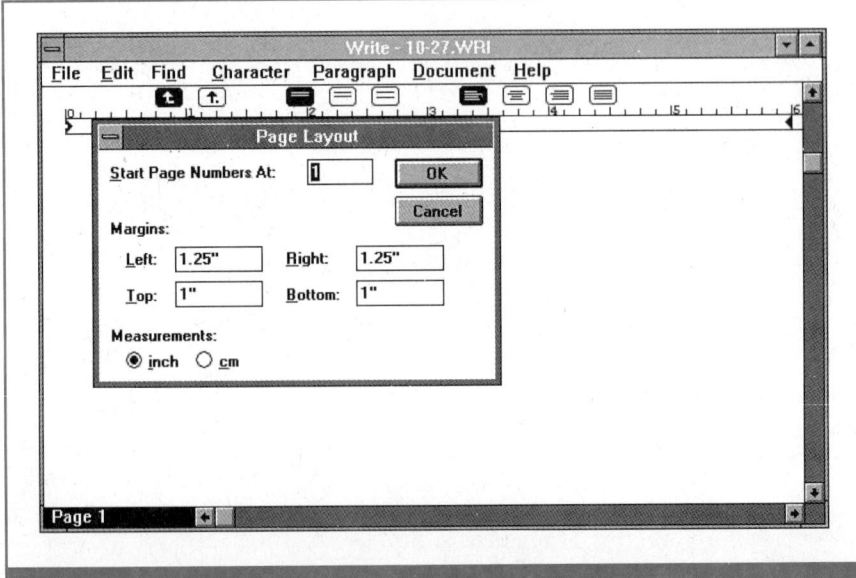

Figure 10.30. Document Page Layout command.

Searching and Replacing Text

In long documents, you cannot always find a desired location quickly just by scrolling. It is more convenient to search by context—that is, by a word or a phrase you know is in or near the location you want. The Find Find command helps you do this.

An even more common situation is wanting to change many or all of the occurrences of one word to another. For example, assume that you have written a report and you named a person who worked at your company, but that person leaves and is replaced by someone else. Write's Find Replace command enables you to change the name in the report easily.

Searching

The Find Find dialog box is shown in Figure 10.31. To use it, simply enter the text you want to find in the Find What field and click Find Next. When Write finds that text, it is selected in your document and the Find Find dialog box remains on the screen. If you want to find the next instance of that text, simply click Find Next again.

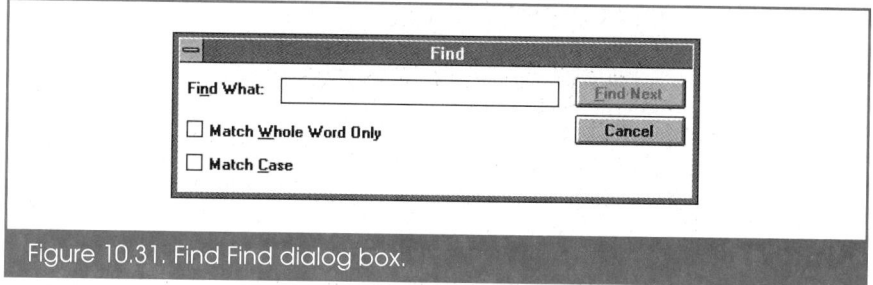

Figure 10.31. Find Find dialog box.

When you have found all the items you want, you can close the Find Find dialog box by pressing Esc or by double-clicking its control menu. You do not have to close it if you don't want to, however. If you simply click in the text, you can continue to work as the dialog box remains on the screen.

The two options in the Find Find command let you restrict the way Write looks for text.

> *Match Whole Word Only* specifies that Write will stop only when it finds the text you entered in the Find What as a whole word or a phrase of whole words. A whole word is one with a space

preceding it and a space following it. For example, if you enter *a* for **Fi**nd What and do not select Match **W**hole Word Only, Write stops at every word with an *a*. If you select Match **W**hole Word Only, Write stops only when *a* is a word by itself.

Match Case tells Write to find only text that matches the case of the text you typed. When this option is not checked, Write ignores the case of the words. This choice usually is what you want because the word might appear at the beginning of a sentence or in a capitalized heading.

If you want to repeat the last search quickly, give the **Fi**nd **R**epeat Last Find command or press F3. This command remembers the settings for **W**hole Word and Match **C**ase.

> **Tip:** If there are many occurrences of the text you are looking for, the **Fi**nd **F**ind dialog box might get in the way on the screen. You can move the dialog box by dragging it with the mouse or by using the **Move** command in the Control menu. Generally, you will want the dialog box as low on the screen as possible. Note that you can even drag it outside of the Write program window.

Replacing

The Find **R**eplace command works much like the Find **F**ind command, except that you are shown two entry boxes, as seen in Figure 10.32. Enter the text that you want to appear in your document in the Re**p**lace With field. The **W**hole Word and Match **C**ase options work the same as in the Find **F**ind command.

Figure 10.32. Find Replace dialog box.

The four buttons enable you to specify what the command will do next. You choose a button depending on the current selection and the extent of the desired changes.

Find Next does not change the selected text but finds the next occurrence.

Replace replaces the selected text and repeats the find.

Replace All searches the entire document and replaces every occurrence.

Close closes the Find Replace dialog box.

Special Characters

You can include special identifiers in the **Find Find** and **Find Replace** fields to look for things you usually cannot put in a dialog box. Table 10.4 shows the special identifiers and their meanings.

Table 10.4. Special identifiers for Find Find and Find Replace.

Identifier	Meaning
^p	Paragraph break (where you press Enter)
^t	Tab character
^d	Manual page break (described later in this chapter)
^w	Any kind of white space, such as space between words or a Tab character
^?	A question mark character
^^	A caret character
^-	An optional hyphen

For example, to search for the word *Finally* at the beginning of a paragraph, you would enter *^pFinally* in the **Find** What field.

You also can use the question mark to match any single character. This is like the question mark wildcard character used in DOS filename searches. For example, if you search for *p?re* with the **Whole Word** option selected, Write finds *pare*, *pore*, and *pure*. This feature is particularly useful when you are not sure of the spelling of a person's or a company's name.

Pages in Your Document

If you write any more than a single page, you will want to know before you print your document where page breaks occur. This action prevents page breaks from occurring just after a heading, for example, or in the middle of a table you want to keep together.

Warning: Don't forget to repaginate your document whenever you add or delete text. If you forget to repaginate, your page layout and numbers will be inaccurate.

Write does not automatically show you the page breaks as you enter text: You must ask it to do so with the **F**ile **R**epaginate command. This command checks the current contents of the file and all its formatting, as well as the type of printer that is selected, to determine where page breaks will occur. The dialog box is shown in Figure 10.33.

Page break marker ——

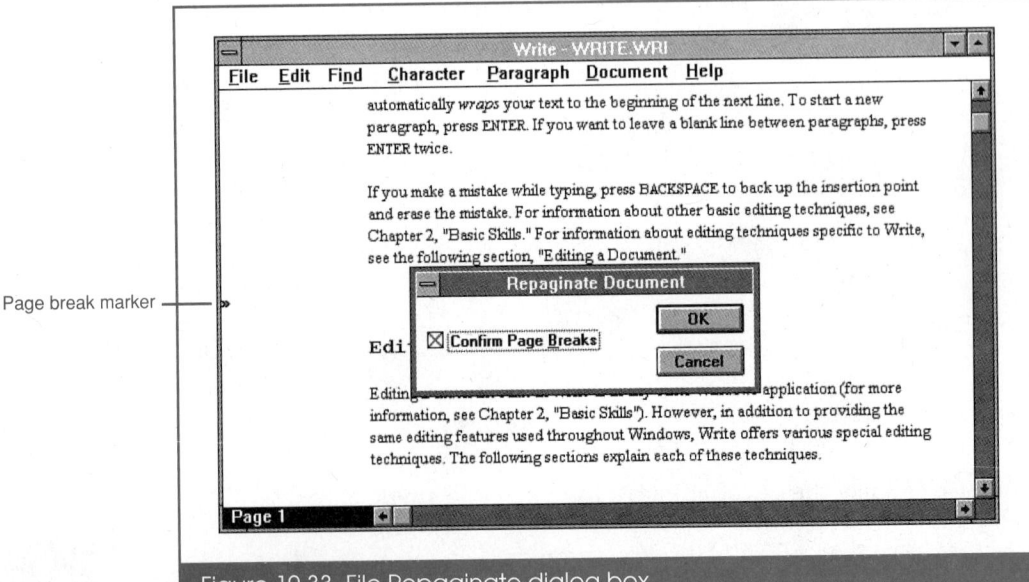

Figure 10.33. File Repaginate dialog box.

If you simply click OK, Write will determine all page breaks automatically. Page breaks are shown as a chevron (») in the selection bar, as shown in Figure 10.33. You can see the page number you are on in the information area at the lower-left corner of the window. The page number is for the page that appears at the top of the window.

If you select Confirm Page **B**reaks in the **F**ile **R**epaginate dialog box, you see the dialog box shown in Figure 10.34 at each page break.

Figure 10.34. Page Break Moving dialog box.

To move the page break to the desired location with the mouse, click the **U**p or **D**own buttons in the dialog box, then click **C**onfirm.

To move the page break to the desired location with the keyboard, press ↑ or ↓, then press Alt-C to confirm the choice.

Adding Your Own Page Breaks

If you will always want a page break at a certain position, you can enter a manual page break by pressing Ctrl-Enter. For example, in a document with chapters, you would want to put a manual page break at the end of each chapter. Manual page breaks appear on the screen as a dotted line, as shown in Figure 10.35.

Tip: You can delete a manual page break the way you can delete any other character. Simply select it and press the Backspace key.

Jumping to Pages

In a multipage document, you can jump directly to a desired page with the **Fi**nd **G**o To Page command, whose dialog box is shown in

Figure 10.36. Simply enter the desired page number and click OK. Remember that because Write does not repaginate as you enter or edit text, the page number will be the one you saw the last time you gave the **File R**epaginate command.

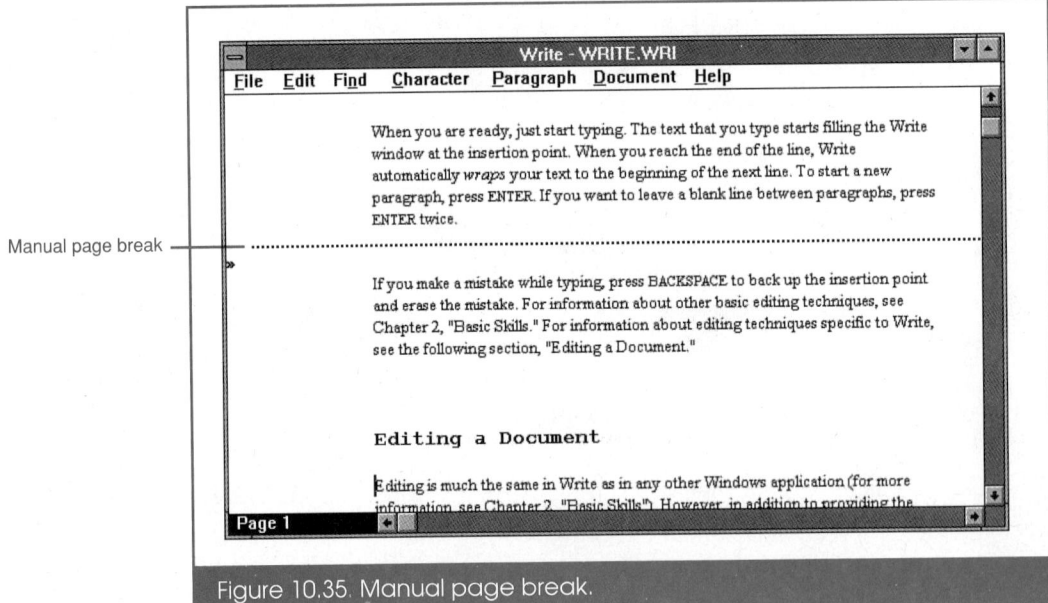

Manual page break ─

Figure 10.35. Manual page break.

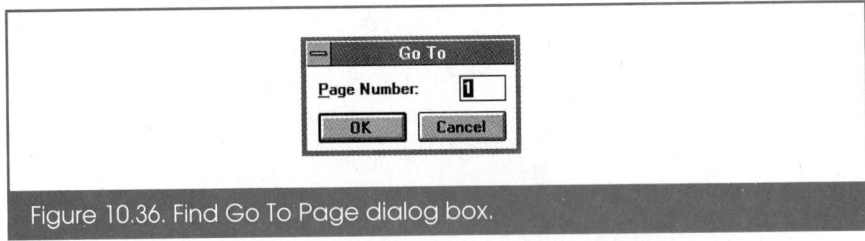

Figure 10.36. Find Go To Page dialog box.

Hyphenating Lines

Most people writing business documents use hyphenation to get as many words as possible on a line. However, if you put in hyphens with the hyphen key and then change printers, edit your document, or change the formatting, many of the words you hyphenated will appear

hyphenated in the middle of lines. If it is at the end of a line, Write always breaks a word with a hard hyphen—that is, one that you, the typist, enter with the hyphen key.

You can prevent this problem by using soft hyphens, which are visible only at the end of a line. When not at the end of a line, a soft hyphen is invisible. To enter a soft hyphen, put the insertion mark at the place that should be hyphenated and press Ctrl-Shift-hyphen. You can use as many soft hyphens in a word as you want.

Tip: You should use regular hyphens only for parts of your document that will always have hyphens, regardless of their position on the line. In all other cases, use soft hyphens.

Printing

Printing in Write is very easy. In fact, Write gives you printing options that other programs do not. Printing is covered in more detail in Chapter 26, "Printers and Fonts."

The **File Print** command prints the document on the default printer. Its dialog box looks like Figure 10.37. The name of the default printer appears at the top of the dialog box.

10

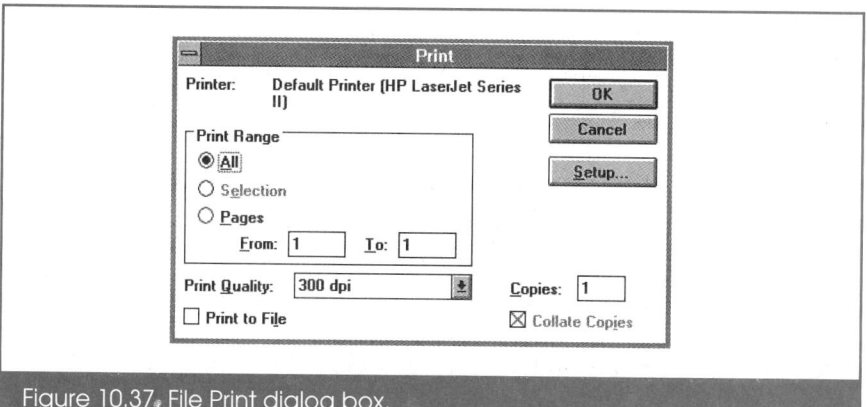

Figure 10.37. File Print dialog box.

The **C**opies option enables you to select how many copies of the document to print. With the **P**ages option you can decide how much of the document to print. If you want to print only a certain range of pages, enter those page numbers in the **F**rom and **T**o fields. If you want to print only one page, enter its page number in both the **F**rom and **T**o fields. If you want to print all pages starting at a certain page, enter that page number in the **F**rom field.

The Draft Quality choice appears only if your printer has high- and low-quality printing, such as a dot-matrix printer. In this case, selecting Draft Quality causes Write to use the lower- quality printing mode, which usually is much faster. Write knows that graphics cannot be reproduced properly on a printer operating in draft mode, and does not print them. It causes pictures to appear as empty rectangles (outlines of the graphic) on your printed output. If you use a laser printer such as a LaserJet II-compatible printer, you may have several choices in print quality available to you. Use **F**ile **P**rint Setup to access them.

If you have more than one printer installed in Windows and you want to switch printers, give the **F**ile **P**rint Setup command, shown in Figure 10.38. Choose the desired printer and click OK. From within the File Print dialog box, clicking the Setup button takes you to the Setup dialog box for that printer, also described in more detail in Chapter 26, "Printers and Fonts."

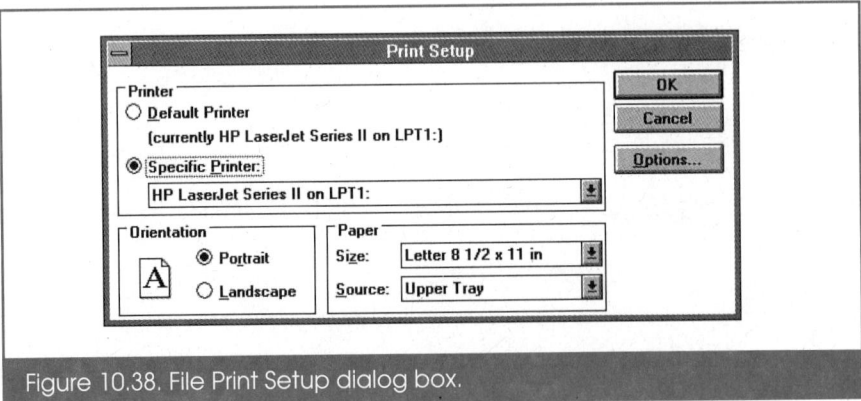

Figure 10.38. File Print Setup dialog box.

Tip: Always save your work to disk with the **F**ile **S**ave command before printing. If your printer locks up or jams (which is rather common), you might not be able to get back to Write. Of course, you should be saving your work to disk often anyway.

Pictures in Your Document

Although most people use just text in their writing, in many instances you might want to add pictures. Pictures can be used, for example, as letterheads or to enhance announcements. You should not go overboard with pictures in your text, of course, or your documents might seem too cute.

Entering Pictures

Write does not enable you to create pictures; you have to use another program, such as Paintbrush. The only way to enter a picture in a Write document is by pasting it from the Clipboard. You can use the Paintbrush program, described in Chapter 11, "Paintbrush," or any other DDE compliant paint program to create pictures and put them in the Clipboard. Note that if the picture has color, Write converts it to black-and-white, saves it as black-and-white, and prints it the same way—whether or not your printer can produce color hardcopy.

To insert a picture in a Write document, place the insertion point where you want the picture and give the **E**dit **P**aste command. Write left-justifies the insert of the picture as a paragraph.

10

> **Tip:** You can include pictures in the headers and footers of your document. A small picture on each page, such as the company logo or a "please recycle" symbol, can add class to a document. You can move, size, and justify it within the document using the **E**dit **M**ove Picture and **E**dit **S**ize Picture commands. Select the object and use the paragraph justification icons to move the graphic. Remember that Write considers a graphic image to be a paragraph.

Resizing a Picture

The size that the picture appears in your document depends on the default printer. If you have a high-resolution printer such as a laser printer, the picture might appear quite small. On a low-resolution printer, the picture will appear the same size as when you copied it from the paint program.

To resize a picture (or graphic), select it and give the **Edit Size** Picture command. This command puts a rectangle around the picture and changes the cursor to a square with a smaller square. In the lower-left corner of the window, the information box shows the size as multiples in the x (horizontal) and y (vertical) size of the original picture.

To resize a picture with the mouse, just move the cursor. As you do, the information box changes to reflect the current size. Click the mouse button when the picture is the size you want.

Key board

To resize with the keyboard, first press the direction key of the side you want to move—either → for the right side or ↓ for the bottom. To move the corner, press →, then ↓. Next, press the direction keys to move the sizing outline in and out until the picture reaches the desired size, and press the Enter key. If you like the picture where it is, save the file right away.

> **Tip:** When resizing a picture, it is almost always preferable to keep the x and y proportions the same. On some printers, however, you might want to make these proportions different if the picture comes out misshapen when printed. Also, some printers print pictures well only if the pictures are resized in whole-number increments. Other printers work fine with any size.

Placing a Picture on the Line

Because a picture is inserted as a paragraph, you can use the alignment commands in the **P**aragraph menu to move a picture across the screen. The **P**aragraph **C**entered command centers the picture, and the **P**aragraph **R**ight command moves it to the right margin. Also, because a picture is treated as a paragraph, you cannot paste pictures beside each other.

You can move the paragraph left or right across the page to an exact location with the **Edit M**ove command. This puts a rectangle around the picture and changes the cursor to a square with a smaller square. You can move the picture left and right with the mouse or press the ← and → keys.

 **Tip:** Because a picture is a paragraph, you cannot move it up and down on the page. You must remove it to the Clipboard and paste it in farther up or down the page.

10

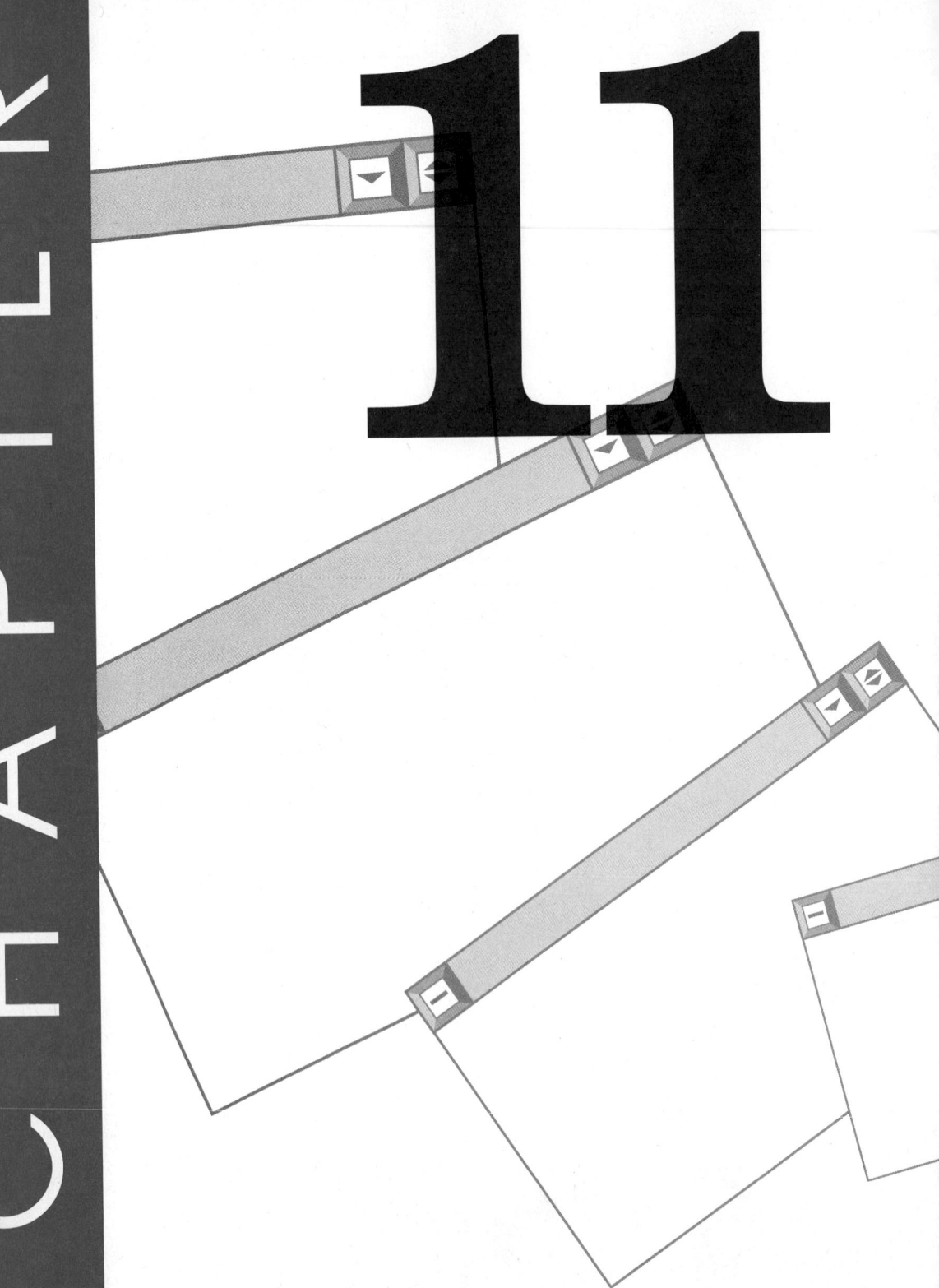

CHAPTER

11

Paintbrush

One of the advantages of Windows is that you can see graphics on the screen at all times. Many people therefore associate Windows with graphics and expect graphics in the output of Windows programs. The easiest way to produce graphics is with the Paintbrush program that comes with Windows.

Paintbrush is almost entirely mouse-driven; therefore, as with almost all competent paint programs, trying to use Paintbrush without a mouse is a real waste of time. Intelligent use of the keyboard in conjunction with a pointing device, however, can save you time and frustration and give your drawings a high degree of precision. Uses for the keyboard are discussed in relevant sections of this chapter.

General Paintbrush Concepts

Figure 11.1 shows the Paintbrush window. The drawing area takes up most of the space, with the drawing tools (toolbox) located on the left side of the window. The line-size box is in the lower-left corner, with an arrow pointing to the current line width. The *color palette* lies along the bottom of the window.

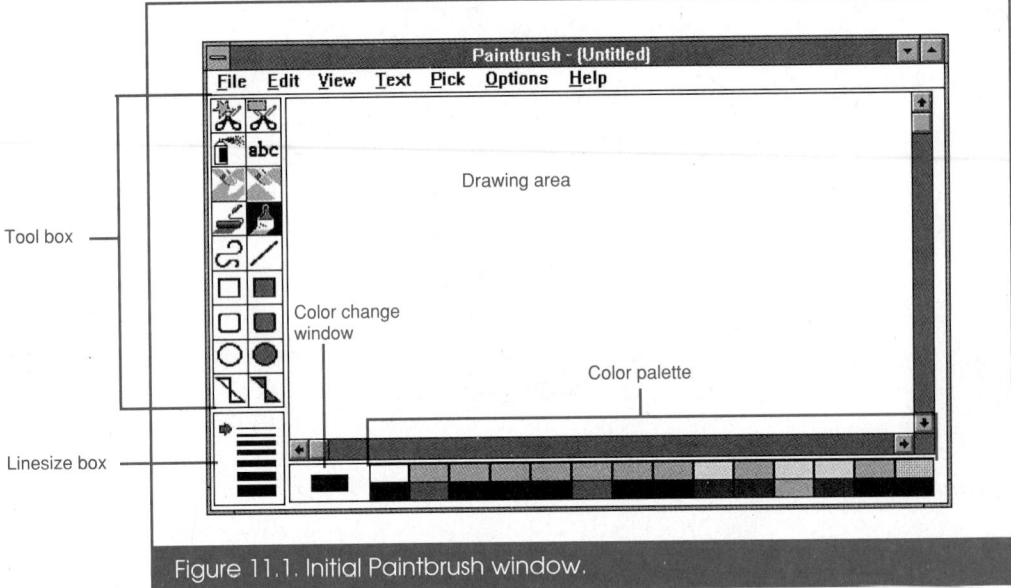

Figure 11.1. Initial Paintbrush window.

In this section, you can start drawing. Paintbrush is a hands-on program, so the best (and most fun) way to learn is to read the basics and then jump right in.

Drawing

The drawing tools are in the toolbox (see Figure 11.2). Although there are not many tools, and their uses are rather simple, they probably are all you need for most business and personal purposes.

When you first open the Paintbrush window, the cursor is set to the *brush* tool. You can start drawing right away by holding down the left mouse button and dragging the cursor across the drawing area. A black line appears, following the cursor's path.

You can select another drawing tool by clicking it in the toolbox. You can use different tools to draw in various styles and to help you with the more common tasks, such as drawing circles and squares. The shape of the cursor depends on the tool you have selected.

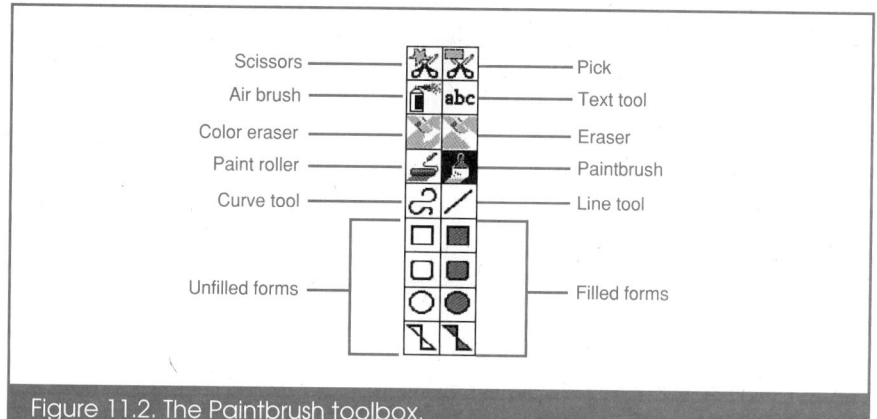

11

Figure 11.2. The Paintbrush toolbox.

If you have the patience, you can use the keyboard for drawing—but it is a slow process. To move the brush with the keyboard, use the arrow keys. The brush moves one pixel at a time in the direction of the arrow. You soon will find that there are many pixels in a small amount of space (72 per inch). To draw, press steadily on the Ins key while you use the arrow keys. Keyboard drawing is most useful when you need tight precision.

Key-board

For basic freehand drawing, all you need are the brush and airbrush tools. Try them by drawing a few lines with the brush, then clicking the airbrush to see what happens when you drag the cursor around.

Don't worry about making a mess. You can double-click the eraser to clear the drawing area completely.

Line Width

The line width can be changed through the line-size box shown in Figure 11.3. The arrow in the box points to the current line width, which can be changed by clicking the desired width or by dragging the arrow to it.

Figure 11.3. The line-size box.

Colors

The basic color functions are very easy to use. Available colors are displayed in the color palette along the bottom of the window. You can change both the current foreground and background colors, which are displayed in the box to the left of the palette. The foreground color is in the center of the box, with the background color in the border.

Paintbrush makes use of the right mouse button as well as the left. If you have a three-button mouse, just use the left and right buttons and ignore the middle one. When you are asked to left-click, press the left mouse button. When you are asked to right-click, press the right mouse button. Now try using both the left and right mouse buttons to manipulate the background and foreground colors.

Left-click one of the palette colors to change the foreground color, and right-click to change the background. Remember that when you use the **File New** command, the drawing area is completely filled with the background color you have set.

Advanced use of the background color and foreground color functions is discussed later in this chapter.

Brush

The brush is the basic drawing tool. After you select the brush, hold down the left mouse button and move the brush over the drawing area. Always be sure that you have selected a color before you begin to draw.

Changing the Brush Shape

You can change the shape of the brush by giving the **Options Brush** Shapes command or by double-clicking the brush tool. Figure 11.4 shows the different brush shapes.

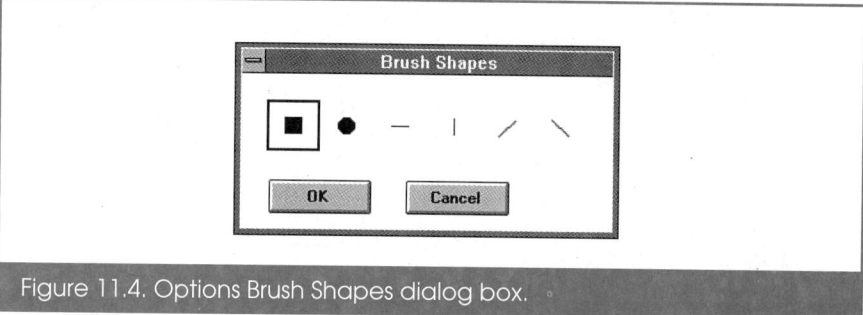

Figure 11.4. Options Brush Shapes dialog box.

To select a brush shape, click the shape. The selection box moves to the shape you have chosen. Click OK to get back to drawing.

Drawing Straight Lines

If you press the Shift key as you draw, you can draw only a perfectly horizontal or vertical line, depending on which direction you were going when you pressed Shift. The keyboard is extremely valuable here because creating a straight line when drawing freehand with the mouse is nearly impossible.

> **Tip:** When you use the Shift key, even if you move the brush away from the line, Paintbrush only adds to the line you were on when you started pressing Shift. To make the line longer after you have moved away from it, keep pressing Shift and move beyond the end of the line.

If you want only part of a line to be straight, draw freehand to that point, press the Shift key with your other hand (not the one you use for the mouse), and continue drawing. Release the Shift key and you are again in control of the direction. Figure 11.5 illustrates the use of the Shift key for drawing straight lines.

You always can erase what you have drawn by selecting the **Edit Undo** command. This command erases any changes since you last used the Clipboard or saved to a file what you have drawn.

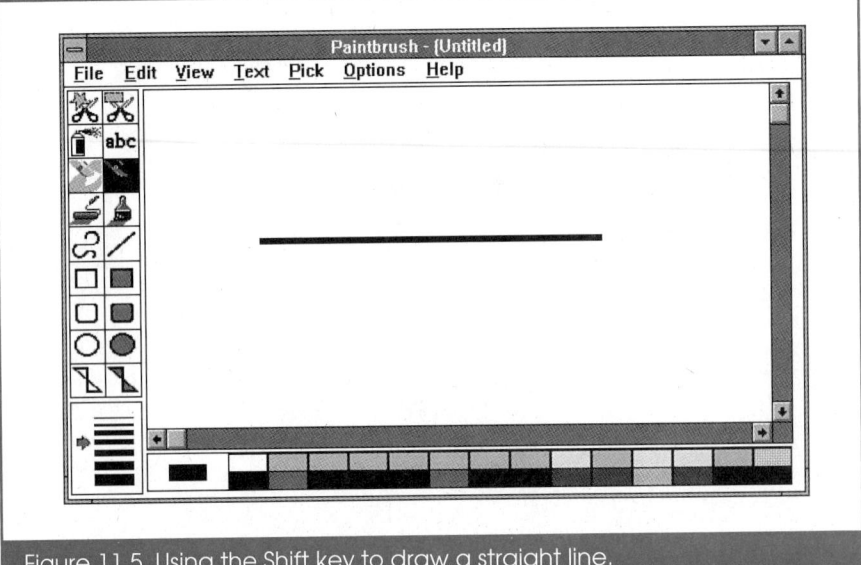

Figure 11.5. Using the Shift key to draw a straight line.

Airbrush

The airbrush tool does not have many uses, but is the most fun to play with. The best way to see what it does is to try it. Click the airbrush and drag it around. A spray of ink follows the airbrush, getting thicker and thinner depending on how fast you move. As you can see from Figure 11.6, the airbrush is perfect for graffiti.

Some paint programs have several airbrush options, such as adjustable paint speed and density. With Paintbrush, you use the line-size box to increase the size of the spray; that is the only option. To change the spray density, you simply slow down. By moving the airbrush slowly or keeping it still while pressing the mouse button, you allow the paint to build up, resulting in a thicker spray.

Tip: The Shift key can be used with the airbrush to create straight lines. The arrow keys can be used also, as with the regular brush.

Unlike the regular brush, the airbrush does not completely cover the colors it passes over. Unless you let the paint build up, some of the background color shows through, leading to some interesting color effects.

11

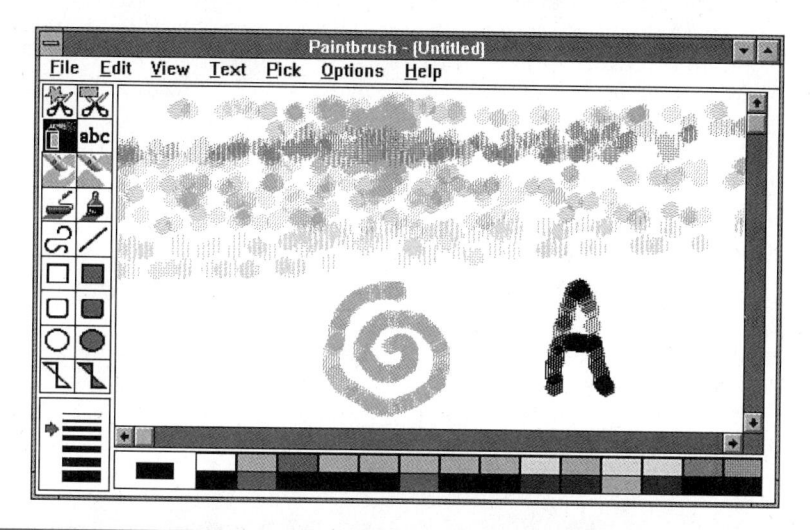

Figure 11.6. The airbrush at work.

Erasing

Erasing is as important as drawing. If you can erase, you don't have to start over whenever you make a mistake. The eraser can be used also as an artistic tool, especially because you can select a new erase width from the line-width box.

Before choosing to erase, you may want to use the **E**dit **U**ndo command. The **E**dit **U**ndo command removes everything you have done since selecting the current tool.

> **Tip:** If you accidentally undo more than you intended, immediately give the **E**dit **U**ndo command again. Your undo will be undone, restoring the drawing.

Regular Eraser

There is more than one way to erase. Double-click the eraser to completely clear the drawing area, filling it with the background color. If you have chosen blue as the background color and you double-click the eraser, for example, the entire drawing area becomes blue. When you double-click the eraser and you have made changes to the file, you see a dialog box with the message, Save current image XXXXXXX.BMP, which gives you a last chance to save the drawing, if the current or opened filename ends in .BMP. If you have not yet saved the file in one of the available formats, the expression (Untitled) will be substituted for the filename. If you have not made any changes, double-clicking the eraser is the same as giving the **F**ile **N**ew command.

For less drastic measures, click the eraser and drag it carefully over whatever you want to erase. Keep in mind that the eraser erases by covering the area under the cursor with the background color. If you want to erase with white, then white must be the currently selected background color. The size of the eraser depends on the line width. To erase large areas, save time by selecting a large line width with the eraser.

Warning: If you run Windows on a slow machine, a delay may occur between the time you drag the eraser over an area and the time the results of the erasure show in the window. If this happens, pause to allow the machine to catch up with you. Otherwise, you may erase much more than you intended.

Color Eraser

The color eraser affects whatever is in the foreground, rather than the background. If the foreground color is green, the color eraser changes only green. This means that you can either erase a single color (by setting the color eraser to the background color), or change it to another color (by changing the foreground color to one other than green, and then erasing with the new color). For example, suppose that you had a red box on top of a yellow circle, on a blue background. You could erase the red box only by selecting the color eraser, setting the foreground color to red, the background color to blue, and erasing. If you wanted the box shape to blend into the circle shape, you could choose the color eraser and set the foreground color to red, and the background color to yellow. The eraser would change the red box to a yellow one, blending the two shapes together.

11

Note that some colors are hybrids, made up of a mixture of colors. If one of the colors in the mixture matches the foreground color, the color eraser changes only the pixels that match, causing a new mixture to be created. Color mixtures are described later in this chapter, in the section about editing colors.

Detail Painting

Although the mouse provides a convenient and easy way to draw, it is not very precise. Even if you have a perfectly steady hand, an old mouse or a bad surface can make things difficult. Fortunately, you can edit pixel-by-pixel.

View Zoom In and View Zoom Out

The **V**iew Zoom **I**n command enables you to get much closer to your work. When you give the **V**iew Zoom **I**n command, the cursor changes to a rectangle. Move the rectangle over an area of the drawing and click the mouse. Your drawing is replaced by an enlarged representation of the area you selected, but with a grid drawn over it (see Figure 11.7).

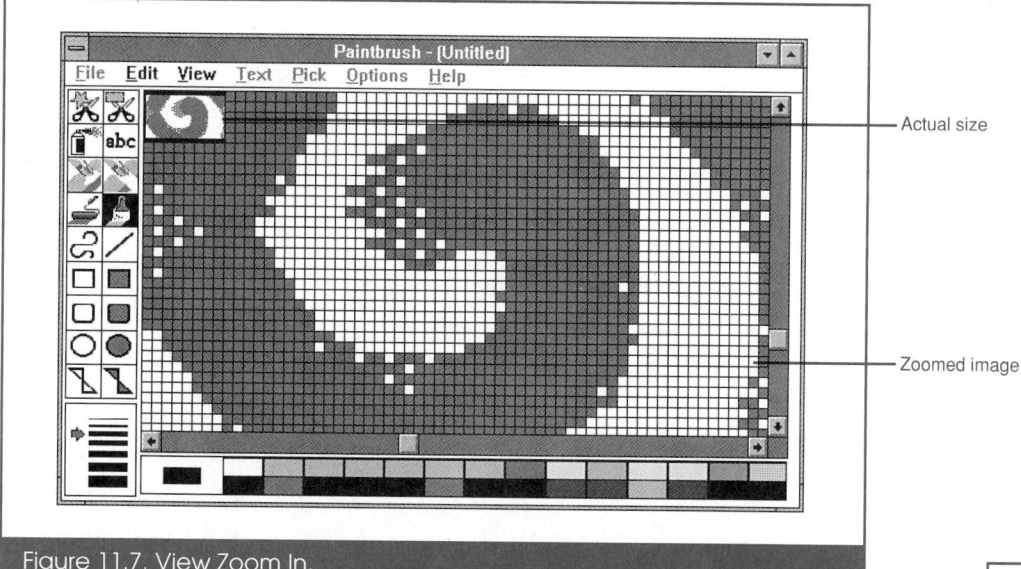

Actual size

Zoomed image

Figure 11.7. View Zoom In.

The rectangle in the upper-left corner shows the actual size of the area you have zoomed in on. Changes made in Zoom In mode show up in both the drawing area and the full-size view box.

Each square of the grid represents a pixel of your drawing. To change a pixel to the current foreground color, left-click it. To change it to the current background color, right-click. Changes you make are reflected in the smaller, complete image insert.

Warning: If you switch between Paintbrush and other windows, be careful where you click to activate the Paintbrush window while in Zoom In mode. Clicking anywhere on the drawing area not only activates Paintbrush, but also puts a pixel or two of the foreground color under the cursor. To avoid this problem, click outside the drawing area.

When working at the pixel edit level (Zoomed In), give the **View** Zoom **Out** command to return to the regular viewing mode. Other **View** commands, as well as another use for zooming out, are discussed later in this chapter.

Cursor Position

The cursor-position option is another valuable resource for detailed drawing. The cursor-position box gives you the cursor's X, Y coordinates so that you can carefully align different parts of your drawing. Give the **View Cursor** Position command to see the box.

The cursor-position box can be dragged to any position around the edge of the Paintbrush window, and can even be placed completely outside the window. It may not, however, be placed in the drawing area. The number on the box's left represents Y, the vertical position of the cursor; the number on the right is the horizontal position, X.

In Zoom In mode, the cursor position reflects the position of the last pixel changed, rather than the current position of the cursor.

Lines

The line tool is another way to draw a perfectly straight line at any angle. To use it, click the tool and move to the drawing area. Select the starting point by left-clicking, and drag the indicator line to the finishing point, as shown in Figure 11.8. Release the mouse button to create the line.

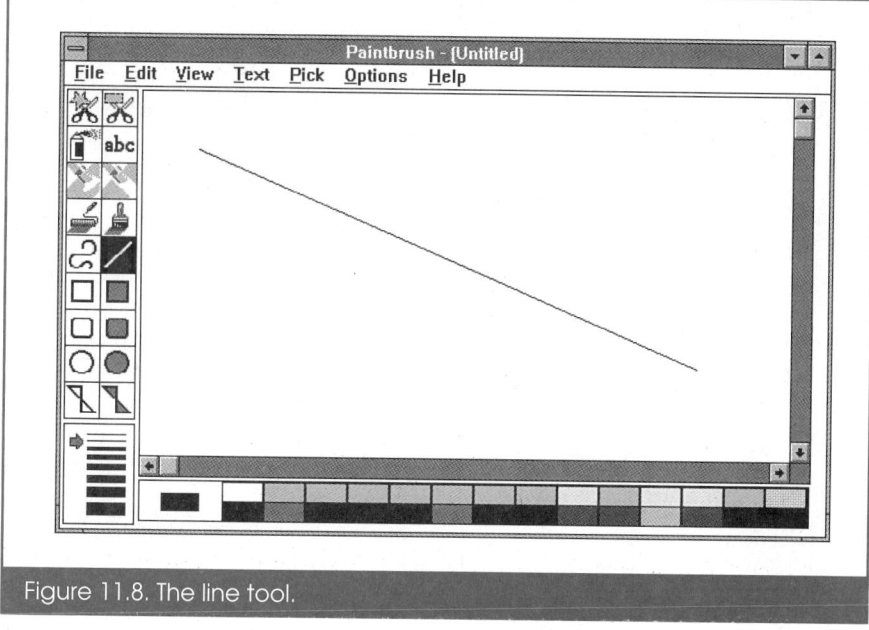

Figure 11.8. The line tool.

Tip: If you change your mind while creating a line, cancel the line by right-clicking before you release the left mouse button.

Holding down the Shift key causes the line tool to create lines in 45-degree increments only.

Curves

Curves are even more fun to create. You can smile and tell funny jokes while working with them. They can really enhance the professional look of your drawing.

Open Curves

An open curve is a curved line whose ends do not close to make the outline of a shape. To make a curve, follow these steps:

1. Click the curve tool and select a starting point for the curve. Next, as with the line tool, drag to an end point and release the mouse button. Now you have a line.

2. Left-click again and drag the cross hair around the drawing area. The "line" stretches out toward the cross hair, as in Figure 11.9, anchored at the two points you set.

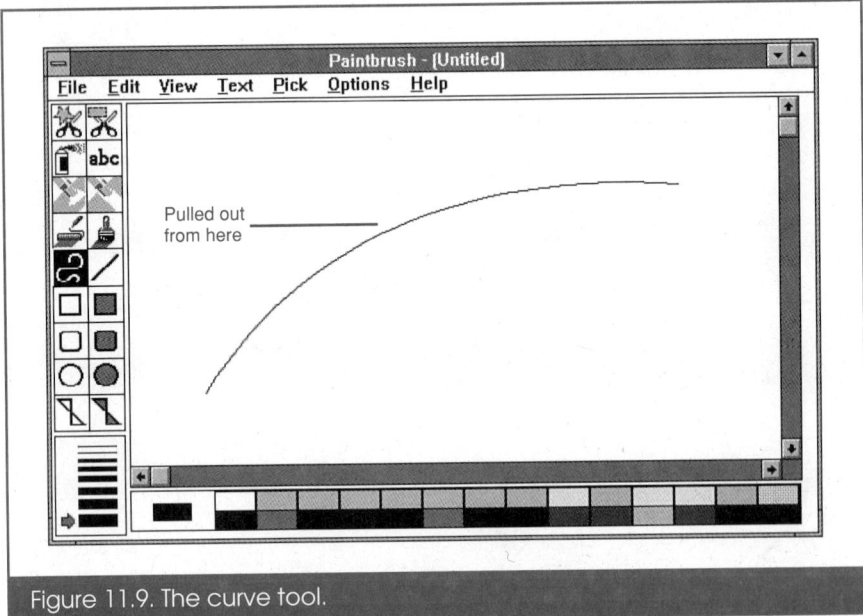

Figure 11.9. The curve tool.

3. Release the mouse button. You have a curve, but it is not set. If you are satisfied, click the second anchor point to set the curve as it is. If you want an extra curve in the line, press the left mouse button and drag again, as in Figure 11.10.

4. Release the mouse button to create the curve, or right-click to cancel the entire operation.

Closed Curves

Curves do not have to be open-ended. By getting creative with the extra curve option, you can twist a curve to fit your needs. Simply drag the curve back toward either of the line ends until the line gets a twist in it. Figure 11.11 shows shapes created by setting the first curve and then using the second curve to twist the line over itself.

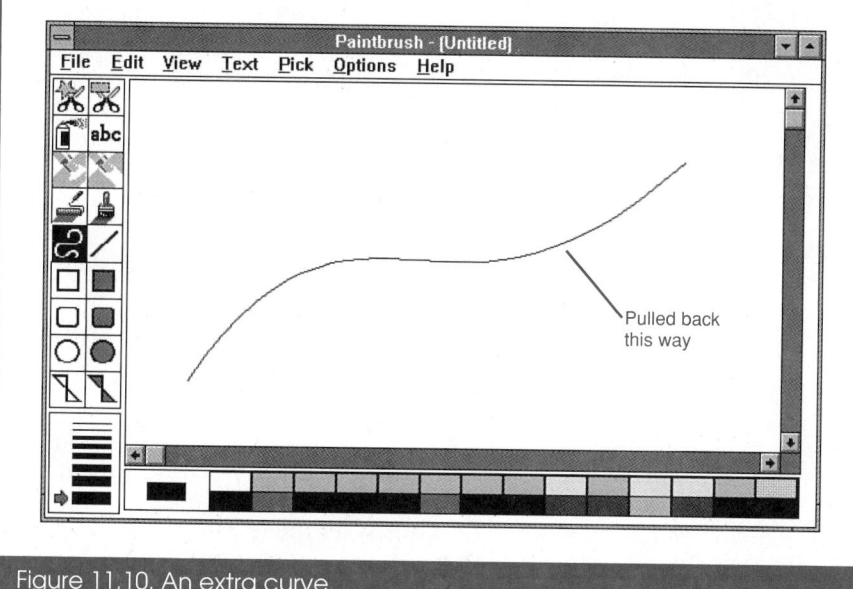

Figure 11.10. An extra curve.

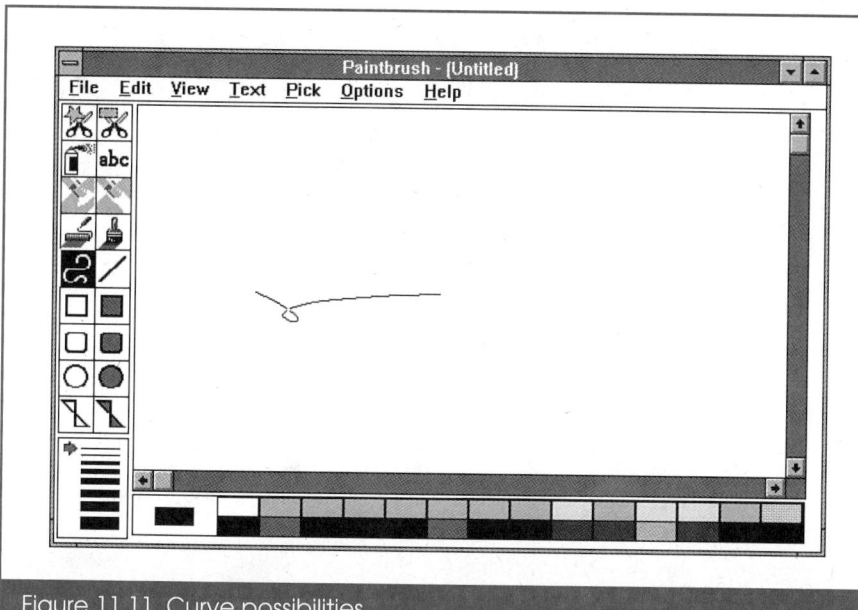

Figure 11.11. Curve possibilities.

Rectangles, Rounded Rectangles, and Ovals

The rectangle and oval tools all work similarly, enabling you to create common shapes easily. If you plan to do much work with Paintbrush, you should become familiar with them because they can save time and help you create drawings with a professional appearance. With the filled rectangle and oval tools, you can create filled (colored) forms.

Unfilled Forms

An unfilled form appears empty of color because it is filled with the background color. To create a rectangle or an oval, select the appropriate tool, click the anchor point in the drawing area, and drag the cross hair. The tool shape follows, stretching and growing according to the distance you move. Release the mouse button to have the shape actually drawn. To cancel the shape, right-click before releasing the left button. Figure 11.12 shows sample shapes created with these tools.

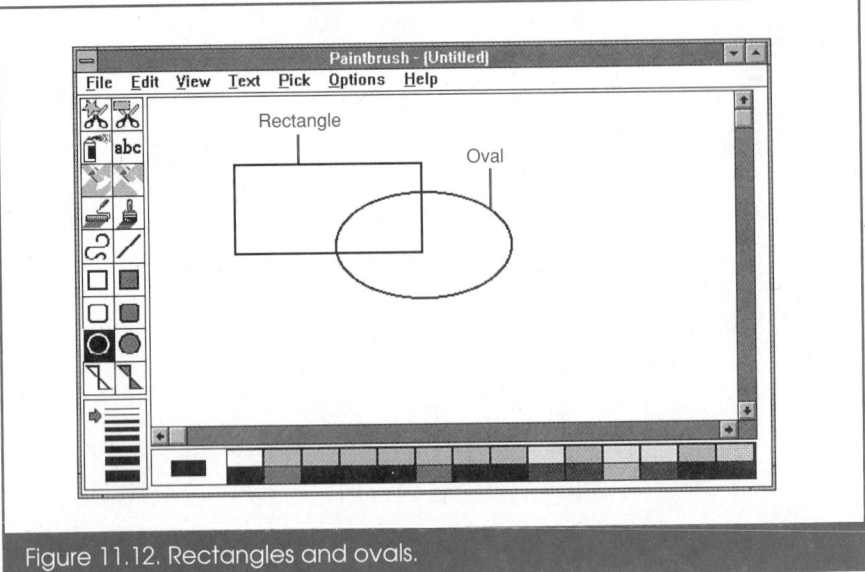

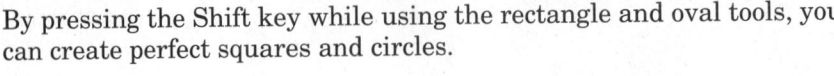
Figure 11.12. Rectangles and ovals.

By pressing the Shift key while using the rectangle and oval tools, you can create perfect squares and circles.

Filled Forms

The filled tools fill the shape with the current foreground color and create a border using the current background color.

The technique for drawing with filled tools is the same as for the regular rectangle and oval tools. Click an anchor point and drag the cursor until you get the shape you want, then release the mouse button. The shape fills automatically (see Figure 11.13).

11

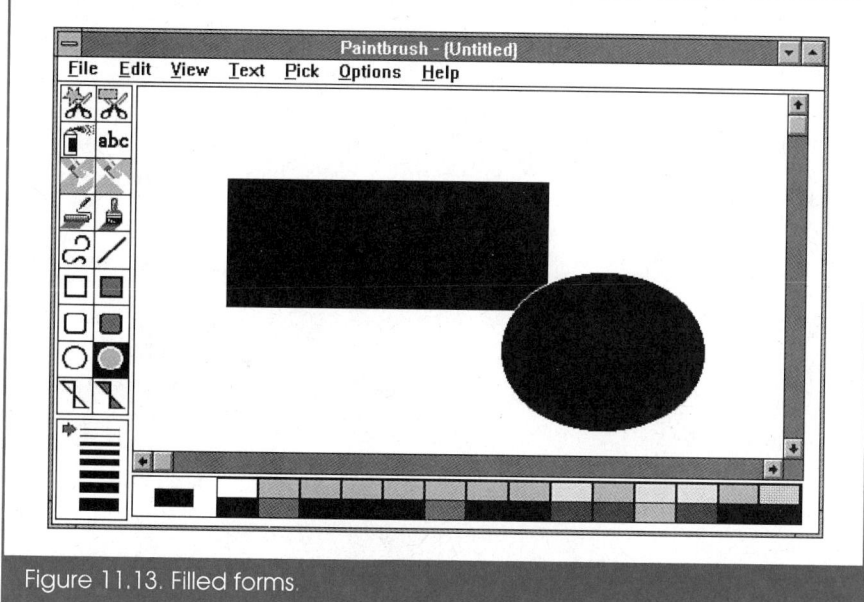

Figure 11.13. Filled forms.

Note that a completely solid figure with no border can be created by setting both the foreground and background to the same color.

Polygons

The polygon tool enables you to create a shape with as many points as you like, provided that the shape is closed (the first and last points must meet). This tool is quite flexible; with it, you can draw an entire figure at one time.

Using the polygon tool is like using the line tool several consecutive times, with each line connected to the last. When you have the figure you want, connect a line to the first point of the polygon, and the shape is drawn. Right-click to cancel the polygon at any time before connecting the last line. Figure 11.14 shows two figures, each drawn with one use of the polygon tool. Use of the filled polygon tool is illustrated also.

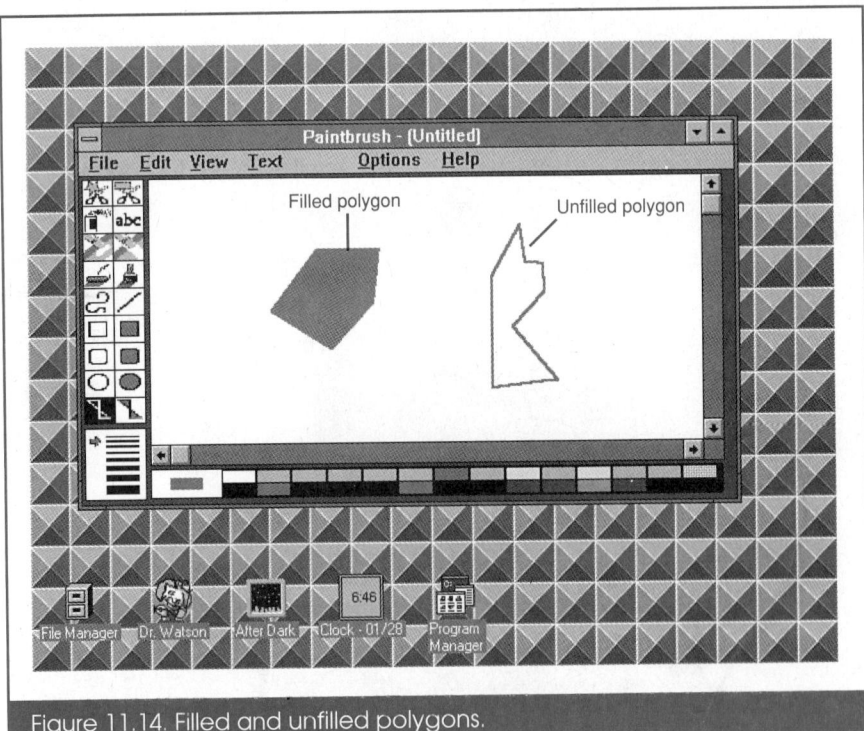

Figure 11.14. Filled and unfilled polygons.

Paint Roller

The paint roller is not a drawing tool. It is a color tool; that is, it fills enclosed areas with the current foreground color. (It also fills unenclosed areas, but this usually is done by accident, filling a shape that has a small break.)

To fill a square, for instance, move the roller inside the square and click. The foreground color fills the square. When you place the roller in the intersecting portion of two shapes and click, as in Figure 11.15, only the intersecting area is filled, provided that the area is completely enclosed.

11

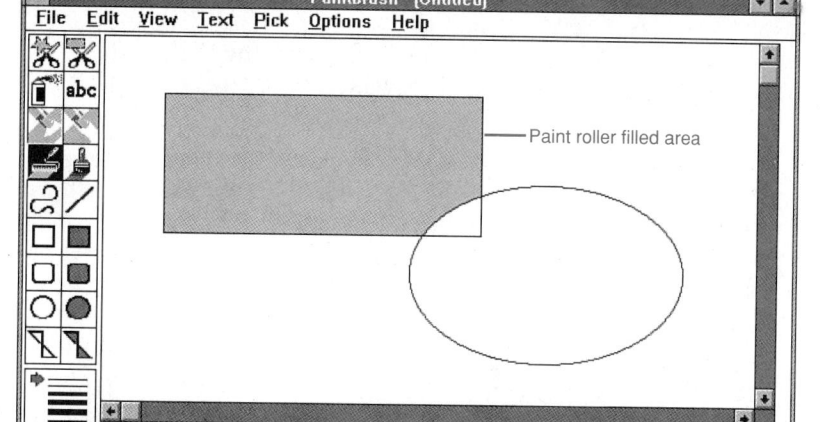

Figure 11.15. Using the paint roller.

Warning: Be sure that there are no gaps in the shape you are filling, or the rest of the drawing area will be filled with the foreground color also. Use the **V**iew **Z**oom command to look at the shapes in detail. Any gaps will be evident.

Tip: You can use the roller to "unfill" a figure, or replace the fill color with another color, by selecting another foreground color, clicking the roller, then clicking in the filled area.

Text Tool

Text can be used for titles or as part of your drawing. Paintbrush provides the ability to manipulate text, available through the **F**ont, **St**yle, and **Si**ze options. The current foreground color determines the color of the text.

Placing Text

Text can be entered anywhere in the drawing area. Click the text tool, move the cursor to the point at which you want the text to start, and click again. A text cursor (I-beam) appears, separate from the mouse cursor. This new cursor enables you to enter the text.

Type a few words, using the Backspace key to erase any mistakes. Because no real word processing functions are available (other than Backspace), try to type correctly the first time. Pressing Enter moves the text cursor down one line, aligning it with the first character of the first line of text. You can use Backspace and make other changes to the text until you select another tool or click another area with the mouse. When you save the image to a file, the text becomes a graphic object in the saved file.

Text Appearance

Although Paintbrush does not have many options for text editing, it compensates by offering many options for text appearance. Three menus are completely dedicated to text processing in Paintbrush. The first, the **Text** menu, is shown in Figure 11.16.

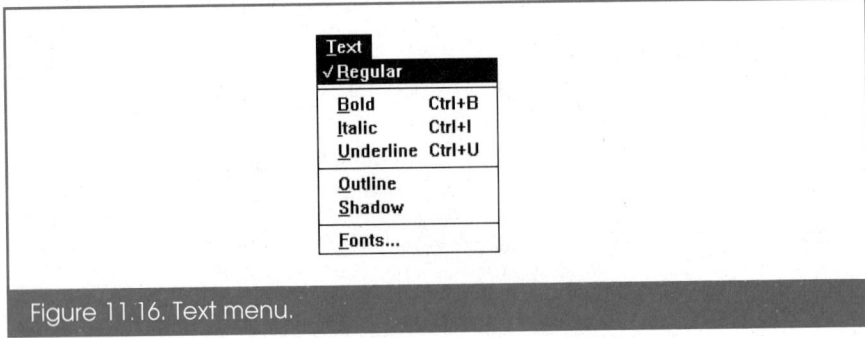

Figure 11.16. Text menu.

Table 11.1 lists the commands available from the **Text** menu.

Table 11.1. Text commands.

Command	Description
Regular	The basic text, printed in the current foreground color and the selected font, but with no special features.
Bold	Makes the text thicker and often easier to read. This style is good to have as a default for text near detailed art or headlines.
Italic	Italicizes the text, giving it a sleek, slanted look.
Underline	Draws a single thin line immediately below the text.
Outline	Puts a border of the current background color around the text, making the text stand out.
Shadow	Backs the text with a shadow of the current background color. The shadow will not be evident if the background color used when choosing this option is the same as the actual background color.
Fonts	Gives a choice of fonts, font styles, and point sizes.

The **Text F**onts dialog box shows the available fonts, including System, a font unique to Paintbrush. You can type in text and experiment by selecting different fonts. The text converts to any font you choose, until another tool is selected or another point is chosen with the mouse cursor. The style and size options work this way also, making it easy to adjust the text until you get just the look you want. The Font dialog box (see Figure 11.17) enables you to be creative with your text fonts.

Warning: If the foreground and background are set to the same color, or if the text is placed over an area that matches the background color, the outline and shadow options will seem not to work. Change the background color to fix this problem.

Size

The **S**ize list box enables you to control the size of the text. If you select an outline font, like TrueType, you can see text with a point size of up to 72.

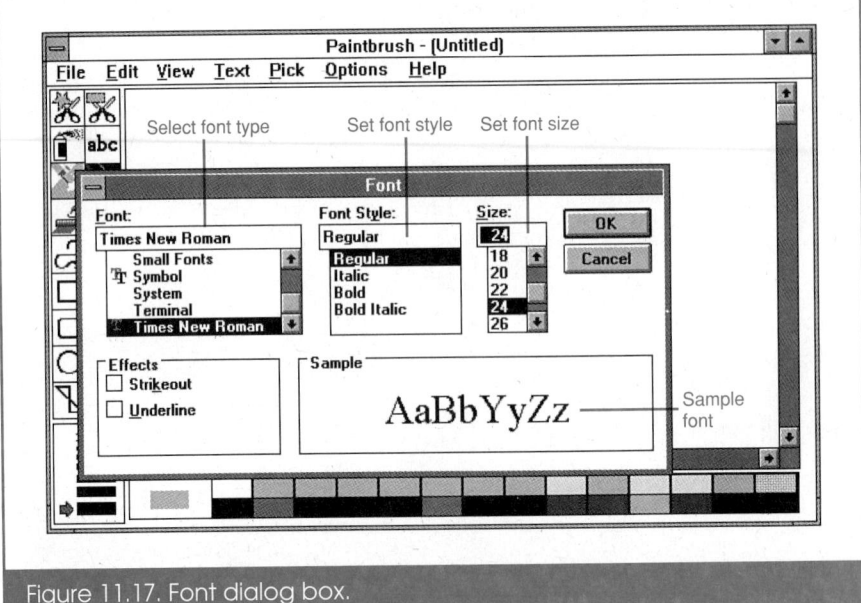

Figure 11.17. Font dialog box.

Sizes not available for the current font appear gray. A check mark is next to the current size, and asterisks mark the sizes that work best with your printer. Click one of the numbers to change the current text size. Because TrueType can be created at any size, all sizes appear in the drop-down list box.

Selecting Objects

Paintbrush, like a word processor, contains many functions for "editing" elements of your drawing. After you have drawn an object, you can flip it, move it, copy it to the Clipboard, and do just about anything else you can think of. Before you can do any of these wonderful things to a particular object, however, you must select the object. You select objects with either the pick or the scissors tool.

The Pick and Scissors Tools

You do most selecting with the Pick and Scissors tools. As in other applications such as CorelDRAW! and Micrographics Designer, these tools are used to outline the object or objects you want to manipulate.

11

The Pick tool (represented by the icon with the scissors on a yellow rectangle) provides a rectangular outline you can use to surround the desired area. After you select the pick, click an appropriate anchor point and drag the outline over the area to be selected.

The Scissors tool (identified by the icon with the scissors on a yellow star shape) is used for outlining irregular shapes. After you select the scissors, instead of dragging, hold down the left mouse button and draw around the area you want.

> **Tip:** When you have surrounded most of the area you want, using the scissors, releasing the mouse button causes the last outline point you drew to be connected automatically to the beginning of the outline.

You can perform the following operations only with the scissors and the pick:

▲ Move the outlined object by dragging it to another part of the drawing area. When you are done, click outside the area to complete the move.

▲ Move a copy of the outlined object by pressing Shift as you drag. This action leaves the original object in place.

▲ Move everything in the outlined area, including the background, by dragging while pressing the right mouse button.

Note that if you move an object, you leave behind a patch of the current background color. If you hold down the Shift key as you drag the selected object, you leave behind a copy of the object.

Pick Menu Items

The **P**ick menu, shown in Figure 11.18, remains gray until an area has been selected with either the pick or the scissors. The **P**ick menu provides nearly all the commands for manipulating images. These commands are listed in Table 11.2.

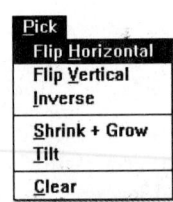

Figure 11.18. The Pick menu.

Table 11.2. Pick commands.

Command	Description
Flip **H**orizontal	Flips the outlined area, from right to left. This command is particularly interesting when used on text.
Flip **V**ertical	Turns the outlined area upside-down.
Inverse	Causes all colors in the outlined area to be reversed. Black becomes white, yellow becomes blue, green becomes purple, and so on.
Shrink + Grow	After you choose this command, the outline disappears, leaving you with a cross hair. Click an anchor point and drag the new outline to the place and size you want. Release the mouse button; the selected area is redrawn, shrinking or growing to fit inside the new outline.
Tilt	As with the **Pick S**hrink + Grow command, after you select **T**ilt you click an anchor point and create a new outline. When you move left or right, the outline tilts. When you release the mouse button, the selected area is redrawn at the new place and angle.
Clear	This is a toggle. When **Pick C**lear is set, the original image is replaced with the current background color whenever a **Pick** menu command is used. If **Clear** is not set, the original image stays in place and the **Pick** commands create a copy of the image, which is then tilted, shrunk, and so on.

Cut, Copy, and Paste

The **E**dit menu, shown in Figure 11.19, contains the **E**dit **C**ut, **E**dit **C**opy, and **E**dit **P**aste commands. The **E**dit menu commands are useful for sending and getting images from the Clipboard. If you are staying on the same "page" in Paintbrush, the pick and scissors perform the same actions with less trouble.

Edit	
Undo	Ctrl+Z
Cut	Ctrl+X
Copy	Ctrl+C
Paste	Ctrl+V
Copy To...	
Paste From...	

Figure 11.19. The Edit menu.

Select the area to be cut or copied with the pick or scissors. (If an area has not been selected, the **C**ut and **C**opy options are gray and unusable.) When an area has been selected, click the appropriate **E**dit option. A copy of the selected area automatically is placed on the Clipboard and the copy can then be pasted to other applications. You can see the contents of the Clipboard with the Clipboard Viewer.

To paste the cut or copied image to another portion of the drawing area, give the **E**dit **P**aste command. The outlined image appears in the upper-left corner of the drawing area. Drag the image to the desired area and click outside the outline to place it. See Figure 11.20 for an example.

Edit Copy To and Edit Paste From Commands

The **E**dit **C**opy To command copies the area selected with the pick or scissors to its own file. This feature is very useful when you want to save only a small drawing or a portion of the drawing area, because it enables you to save disk space.

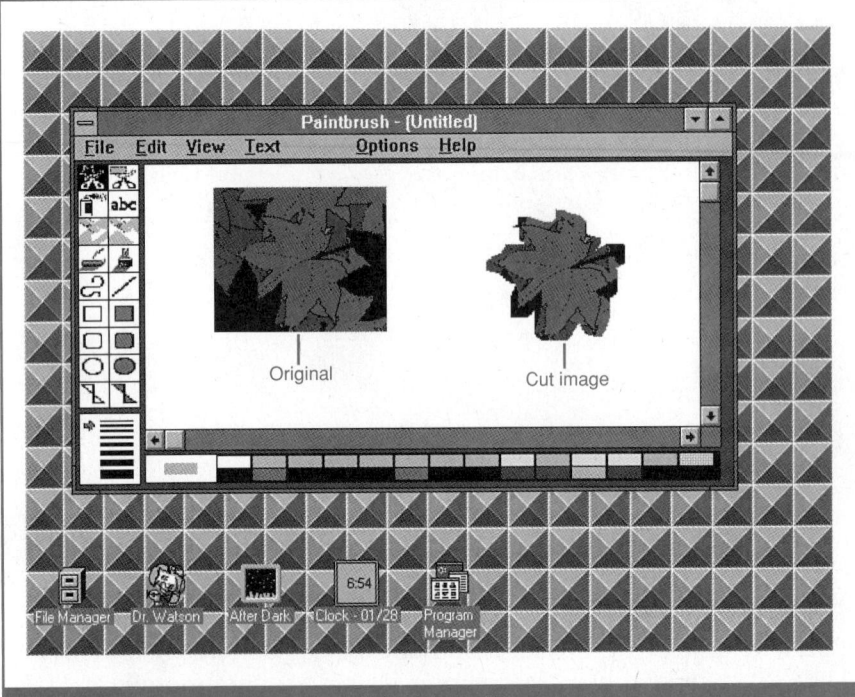

Figure 11.20. A leaf cut and copied from its original image.

Use the **E**dit Paste **F**rom command to copy a Paintbrush file into your current drawing. When you choose this command, you are prompted for the filename and the Paintbrush file format (covered later in this chapter), as shown in Figure 11.21. After you provide this information, the contents of the file appear, outlined in the upper-left corner. As with the **E**dit **P**aste command, drag the image to the desired area and click outside the outline.

Note that if the file you attempt to paste in is very large, you may run out of memory, and you will be prompted to close some windows.

Changing the View

The **V**iew menu, shown in Figure 11.22, enables you to see your drawing from different points of view. The commands are described in Table 11.3.

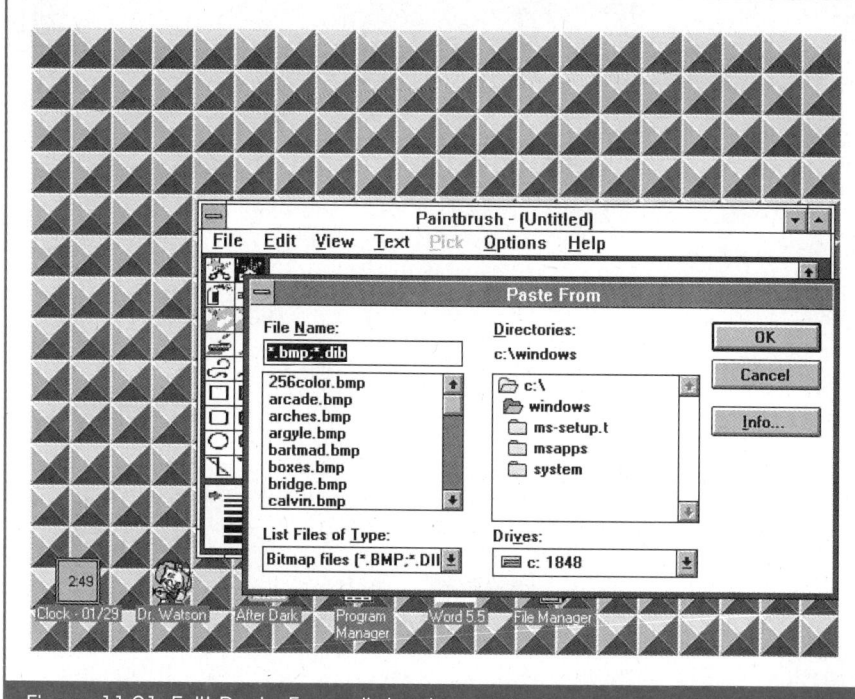

Figure 11.21. Edit Paste From dialog box.

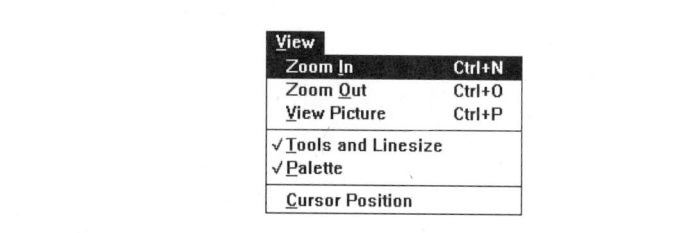

Figure 11.22. The View menu.

Table 11.3. View commands.

Command	Description
Zoom In	Enables you to see a pixel-by-pixel representation of part of the drawing area.
Zoom Out	Returns you to normal viewing mode after you have zoomed in. When you zoom out from the normal mode, you get a view of the entire drawing area reduced to fit the Paintbrush window.
View Picture	Fills the screen with a full-size picture of the drawing area. To return to the Paintbrush window, click anywhere on the screen.
Tools and Linesize	Controls whether the toolbox and linesize box appear in the Paintbrush window. This feature enables more of your drawing to show in the window. If you cause the toolbox and linesize box to be visible, a check mark will appear next to the menu option, denoting that these items should now be visible.
Palette	Controls whether the color palette appears in the window.
Cursor Position	Causes the current position of the cursor to be displayed.

Advanced Color Techniques

If you use Paintbrush often, you probably will find that the default color palette isn't always sufficient. Fortunately, customizing the palette to suit your needs is easy.

Editing Colors

You can access the **Options Edit Colors** dialog box, shown in Figure 11.23, through the **Options** menu or by double-clicking the color you want to change in the palette. If you choose the command from the **Options** menu, changes will be made in the current foreground color.

11

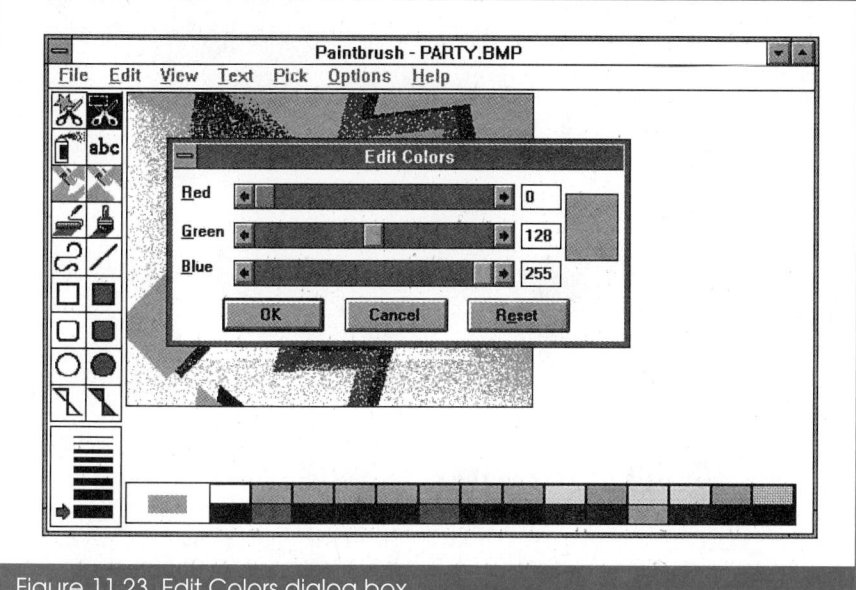

Figure 11.23. Edit Colors dialog box.

A sample of the color you are editing appears on the right side of the dialog box. All the colors are combinations of red, green, and blue. To change the current color, adjust the color combination by using the slider bar or by entering a number (from 0 to 255) in one of the text boxes. The numbers represent intensity levels for their respective colors.

The color in the **E**dit **C**olors box changes as you make adjustments. If you change your mind, click **R**eset to restore the original color. When you have created the color you want, click OK. Your color replaces the original in the color palette.

Saving Palettes

You can have as many customized color palettes as you want. After creating a palette you want to save, give the **O**ptions **S**ave **A**s Colors command. The dialog box shown in Figure 11.24 appears.

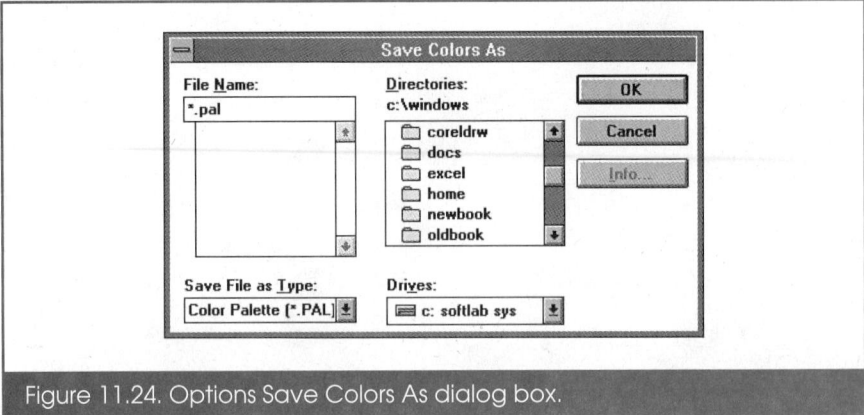

Figure 11.24. Options Save Colors As dialog box.

To load a color palette, choose the **O**ptions **G**et Colors command. Figure 11.25 shows the dialog box.

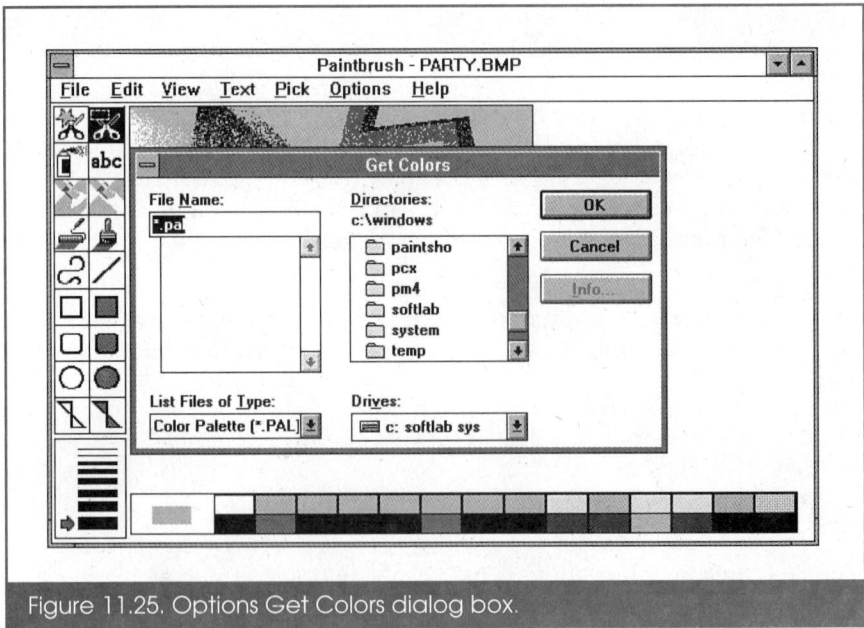

Figure 11.25. Options Get Colors dialog box.

Black and White

If you prefer to draw in black-and-white, or if you want to print your drawing on a noncolor printer, select Black and White in the **O**ptions

Image Attributes dialog box. (Image attributes are discussed in more detail later in this chapter.) When you give the **F**ile **N**ew command, the black-and-white palette will have replaced the color palette.

Paintbrush Files

11

This section describes the file formats available in Paintbrush and tells how to reduce the size of Paintbrush files.

Options Image Attributes Command

Figure 11.26 shows the **O**ptions **I**mage Attributes dialog box. This dialog box not only gives you the Black and White/Colors option discussed in the previous section, but also enables you to set the size of the drawing area.

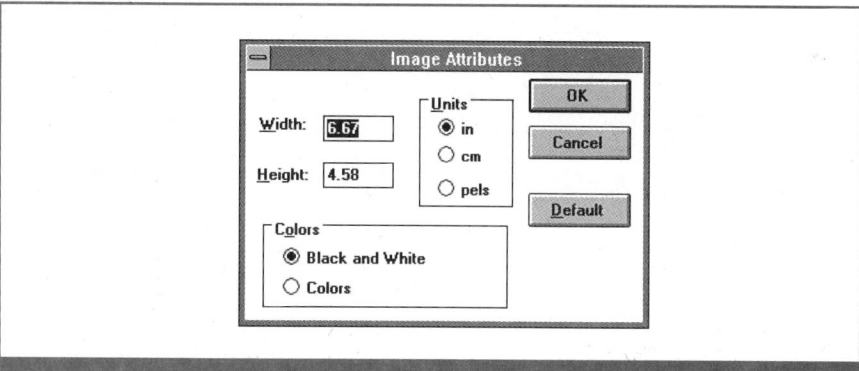

Figure 11.26. Options Image Attributes dialog box.

The size of the drawing area can be set in inches, centimeters, or pixels. In this context, the size of a drawing is the physical, or geographical size. Indicate the size in the **W**idth and **H**eight boxes, and the units in the **U**nits box. Reducing the drawing area can significantly reduce the size of the Paintbrush file.

The **D**efault option resets the attributes according to the memory available. If the default drawing area is too small, check for TSRs and/or close any unnecessary windows.

File Formats

There five file formats available. Which one to use depends on the drawing and what you want to do with it. When you give the **F**ile Save **A**s command you see the dialog box shown in Figure 11.27. The available file formats, listed at the lower-left of the dialog box, are explained in Table 11.4.

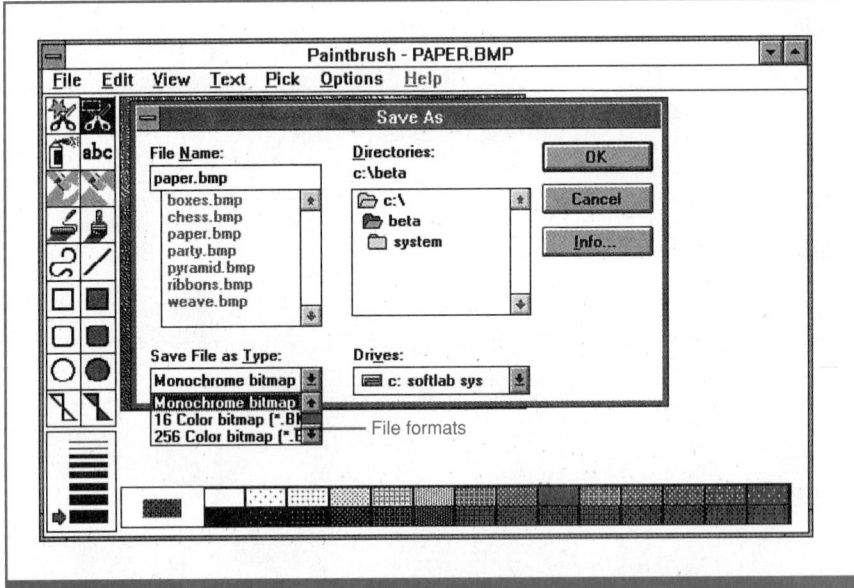

Figure 11.27. File format options.

Table 11.4. Paintbrush file formats.

Format	Description
PCX	A standard for many graphics programs; you can use it when you want to move a drawing between programs.
Monochrome bitmap	For black-and-white files. You can save a color drawing to a monochrome file, but the colors will be converted to black-and-white, sometimes in an undesirable way. Files saved in black-and-white (monochrome) and gray-level are always smaller in size than files saved in a color format.

Format	Description
16 Color bitmap	The standard Paintbrush format.
256 Color bitmap	For transferring a file to another graphics program that uses more than 16 colors.
24-bit bitmap	For transferring a file to another graphics program that uses more than 256 colors.

11

Info Button

The **F**ile **O**pen, **F**ile Save **A**s, **E**dit Copy **T**o, and **E**dit Paste **F**rom dialog boxes all have an **I**nfo button. When pressed, this **I**nfo button displays information about the format of the selected file (see Figure 11.28).

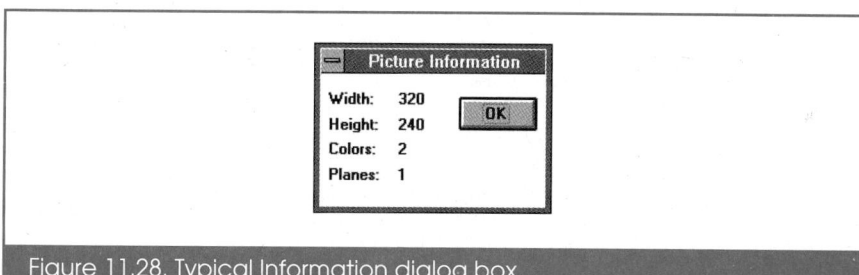

Figure 11.28. Typical Information dialog box.

Windows Wallpaper

Paintbrush files can be used also as Windows wallpaper. To do this, use the 16-Color bitmap file format and the file extension .BMP when you save the drawing. For information about using the file as Windows wallpaper, see the instructions in Chapter 7, "Control Panel."

Printing

You can print a Paintbrush file, although most printers will not do justice to your drawing. The **F**ile **P**rint dialog box is shown in Figure 11.29. Available options are listed in Table 11.5.

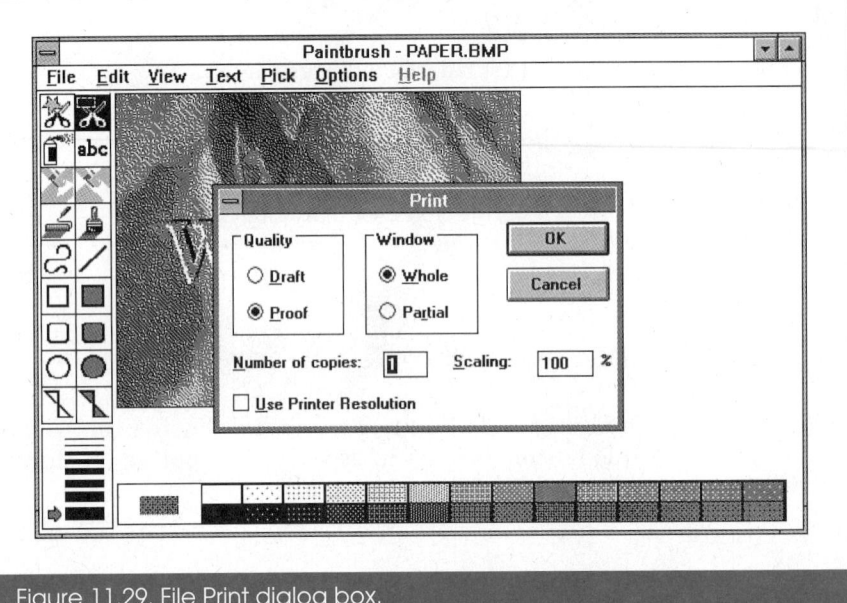

Figure 11.29. File Print dialog box.

Table 11.5. Print options.

Option	Description
Draft Quality	Prints at a higher speed without much regard for quality (if your printer supports this mode).
Proof Quality	Prints at the normal speed and quality.
Whole Window	Prints the complete drawing.
Pa**r**tial Window	Prints a portion of the drawing. When this option is selected, the complete drawing appears when you click OK. Drag a box over the area you want printed and release the mouse button to print. To cancel the box, right-click before releasing the mouse button.
Number of copies	The number of copies you want printed.
Scaling	What percentage size to print the drawing. Enlarges or reduces the drawing according to the percentage you enter.
Use Printer Resolution	Prints using a single dot for each pixel in the drawing.

File Page Setup

When you print an image, especially when it's intended to be viewed by others, it can be very useful to say something to the hardcopy viewer in the form of printed text. You can place a date, filename, or image title above or below the image on the hardcopy with the File Page Setup option. This option enables you to mark your drawing with a header and a footer, as well as set the margins. The dialog box is shown in Figure 11.30.

11

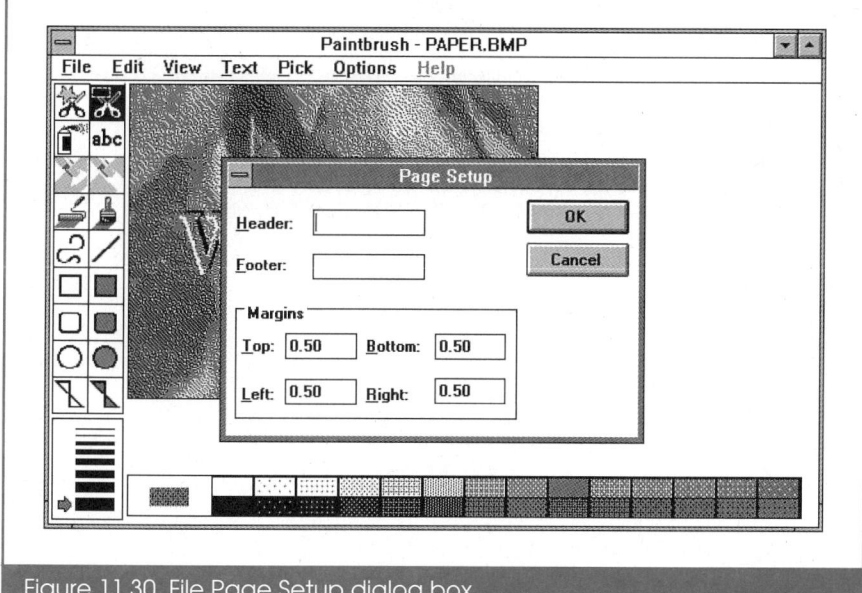

Figure 11.30. File Page Setup dialog box.

The text you type into the respective header and footer text boxes is placed in the header or footer and preceded by the ampersand (&) sign. Place a code (from the following table) before your text and the information substituted by the code will appear on the printed output as though you actually typed the data into the text box yourself. You don't see the codes on the printed output. Table 11.6 shows the codes and their uses.

Table 11.6. Use of codes in headers and footers.

Code	Will substitute this information
c	Center header/footer
d	Date
f	Filename
l	Left-justify header/footer
p	Page number
r	Right-justify header/footer
t	Time

The margins are set from the edge of the paper; for example, 0.50 is a half inch from the edge.

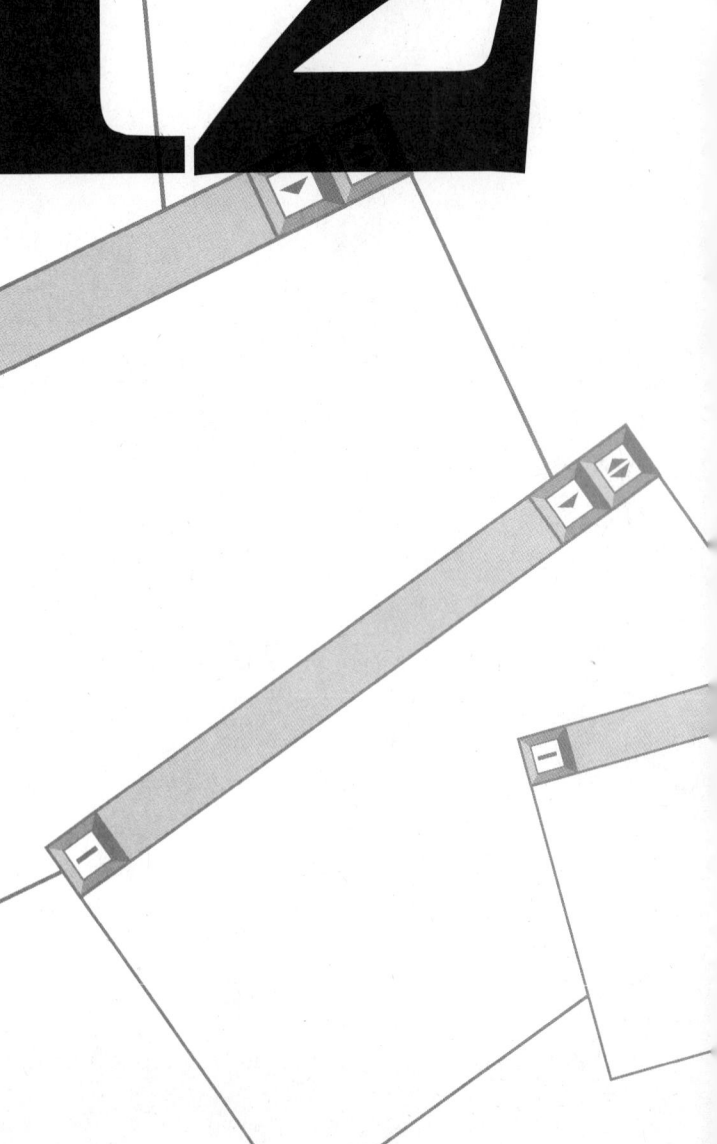

CHAPTER

12

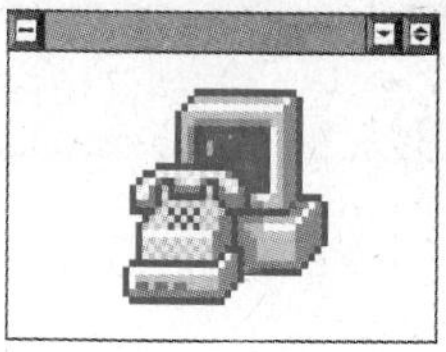

Ter

Leaser
+ Mrs. Sirenmenson
both
phoned

Debbie L
736-0154

Katherine
270-9069

The Termina ... r computer
to reach beyond ... nications
program, it give ... interact
electronically w...

To use Terminal ... your
computer to a te ... hardware
is li ... a wide
pri...

A... an control
t... not been
... nent;
... window in
...nhanced mode, and they often have many
features Terminal lacks.

The Essentials Before Going Online

Before you can use a modem, you must configure Terminal appropriately. The settings depend on the type of modem you have and the computer system you are calling. If you don't have specific information about the service you want to connect with, you may need to call its voice line. If the service doesn't have a voice line, or if you can't talk to someone human for other reasons, you can find the correct settings through a trial-and-error process.

All the basic settings necessary for going online are on the **S**ettings menu (see Figure 12.2). Fortunately, when you have determined the correct settings, you can save them to disk for future use.

Tip: Terminal is a bare-bones communications program. Many other programs have many more features. Chapter 30, "Windows for Advanced Users," describes these programs in detail.

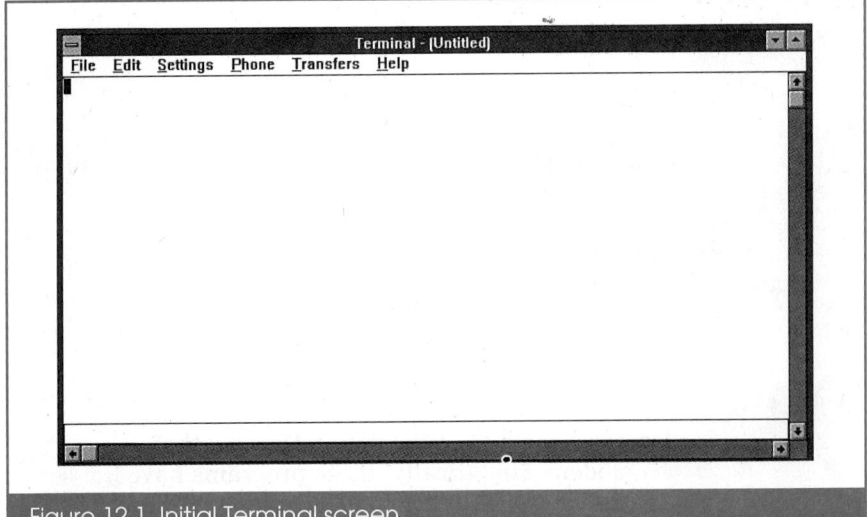

Figure 12.1. Initial Terminal screen.

Modem Commands

First, you need to tell Terminal what kind of modem you are using. The **S**ettings Mo**d**em Commands dialog box, shown in Figure 12.3, enables you to set the modem type to Hayes, MultiTech, or TrailBlazer. When you choose one of these, the appropriate modem commands are entered automatically into the Commands fields on the left of the dialog box.

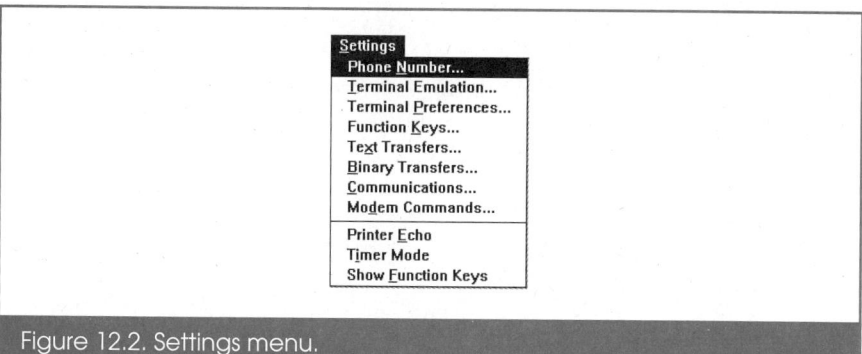

Figure 12.2. Settings menu.

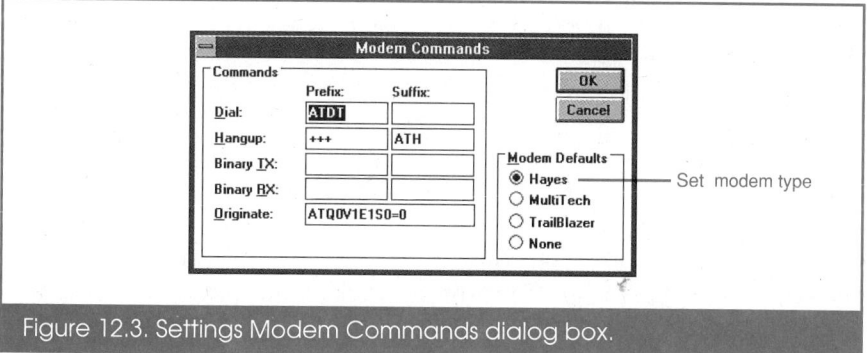

Figure 12.3. Settings Modem Commands dialog box.

Do not worry if your modem is not listed. The vast majority of modems act like one of these three brands. If your modem doesn't match any of the default choices and isn't Hayes-compatible, choose the None option, which makes the default commands disappear from the Commands box. Then, using your modem's manual, fill in the correct commands. The commands your particular modem uses will vary from modem-to-modem.

Tip: Change the **D**ial Prefix setting to ATD**P** if you have a rotary dial (pulse) phone.

Communications

The **S**ettings **C**ommunications dialog box, shown in Figure 12.4, determines exactly how your computer and the system you are calling communicate.

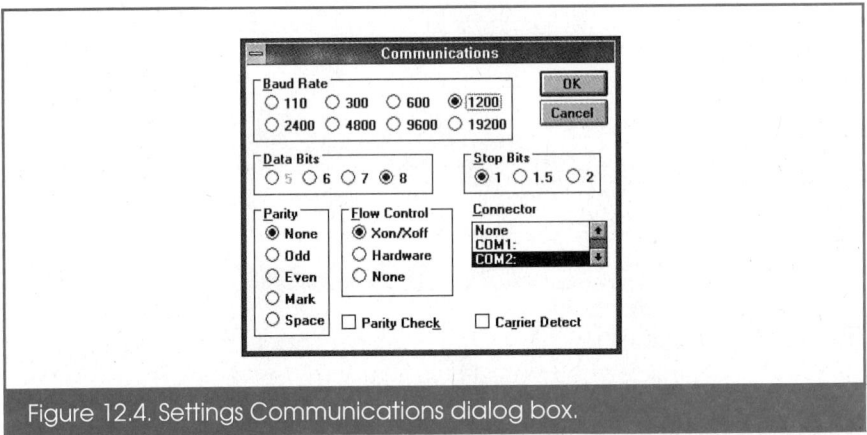

Figure 12.4. Settings Communications dialog box.

Before going any farther, you need to understand the terms *baud rate* and *connector*. These are the only important communications settings related to your computer.

The baud rate determines the speed at which computers communicate. The setting depends on your modem's capabilities and the maximum baud rate the remote system can handle.

The **C**onnector setting tells Terminal which serial port the modem uses. If you select a COM: port that is being used by a non-Windows program, or a CD-ROM drive, for example, you see an alert advising you to select another COM port.

The *parity*, *data bits*, and *stop bits* settings are completely dependent on the remote system. If you call another system and receive incomprehensible lines of characters, one of these settings probably is incorrect. Experiment with them to see whether you can find the correct configuration.

The communications settings for a system often are listed in a format such as

    E-7-1

or

    E, 7, 1

The first character represents the parity (even, in this case), the second represents the number of data bits (7), and the third the number of stop bits (1). Flow control also is dependent on the remote system, but rarely needs to be changed.

The Parity Check option attempts to determine which byte is causing a parity error, and prints a question mark at characters that are not transferred correctly. The Carrier Detect option tells Terminal to use your modem's carrier detection instead of Terminal's method. Although these settings are not dependent on the remote system, you probably will not find them useful.

12

Terminal Emulation

The term *Terminal Emulation* means that your PC can pretend to be a terminal that another type of computer (like a mainframe or a mini-computer) expects to work with. Different terminal emulations enable the on-line system to manipulate the output to your screen in different ways. Figure 12.5 shows the **S**ettings **T**erminal Emulation command. It is unlikely that you will need to change this setting, which is set to VT-100 emulation by default.

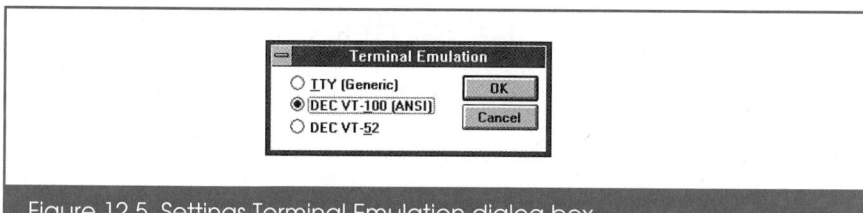

Figure 12.5. Settings Terminal Emulation dialog box.

Saving the Settings

After you determine the correct settings for an on-line system (including the phone number, covered in the next section), you can save them with the **F**ile Save **A**s command (see Figure 12.6).

It is customary to use the on-line system's name with an extension of .TRM for a filename. Whenever you want to call the same system in the future, use the **F**ile **O**pen command.

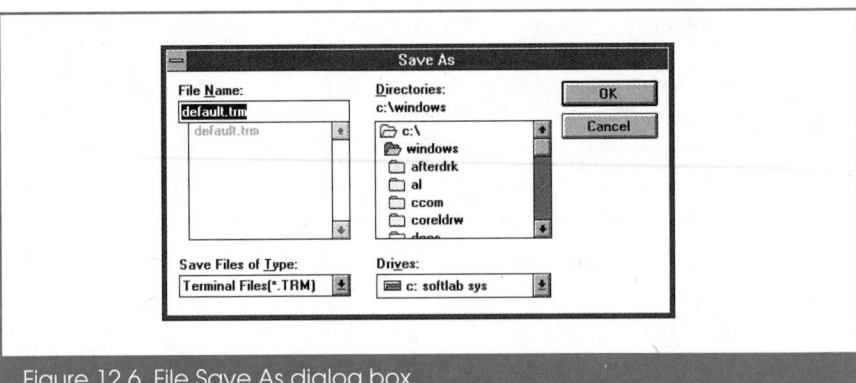

Figure 12.6. File Save As dialog box.

Connecting

With Terminal configured for the modem you are using and the system you are going to call—an on-line service like a bulletin board, for example—you are ready to make the phone call.

Using the Settings Menu to Make a Call

First, the phone number of the on-line system must be entered with the **S**ettings Phone **N**umber command (see Figure 12.7).

This dialog box can be accessed through the **S**ettings menu or when you give the **P**hone **D**ial command, if a number was not entered previously. You enter the dialable phone number in the text box provided. If you save the file by using the **F**ile **S**ave option, this phone number is saved and will be in the text box provided for the phone number whenever you open the **S**ettings Phone **N**umber dialog box. If you close the file without saving, you lose the phone number.

Tip: Be sure to use the **S**ettings Phone **N**umber command when you hang up from one on-line system and intend to call another. Otherwise, when you use the **P**hone **D**ial command, you will call the first phone number again.

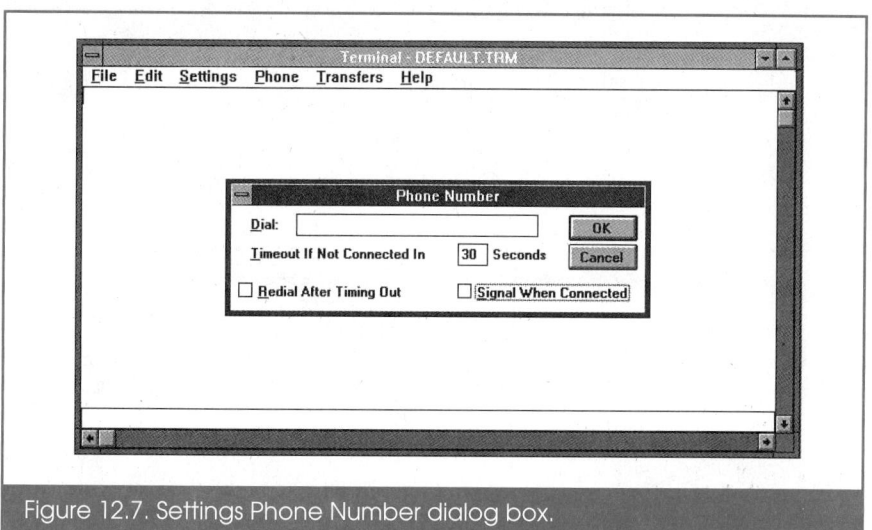

Figure 12.7. Settings Phone Number dialog box.

12

The other options in the command tell Terminal how to dial.

▲ The **T**imeout If Not Connected In setting determines how many seconds Terminal waits after dialing the number. If no connection is made in this time, Terminal hangs up. If you try to set the timeout for less than 30 seconds, you get the following error message: `Timeout if not connected has been reset to the minimum 30 seconds`.

▲ When **R**edial After Timing Out is selected, Terminal continually redials the number until a connection is established.

▲ The **S**ignal When Connected option causes your computer to beep when a connection is made. You can leave the computer or use the computer for another purpose, like word processing while Terminal redials a busy number.

Using the Phone Menu to Dial

You also can make the call with the **P**hone menu, shown in Figure 12.8, by using the **P**hone **D**ial command. If no phone number was entered previously, the phone number dialog box appears. Otherwise, Terminal starts the phone call and displays the dialog box shown in Figure 12.9.

Figure 12.8. Phone menu.

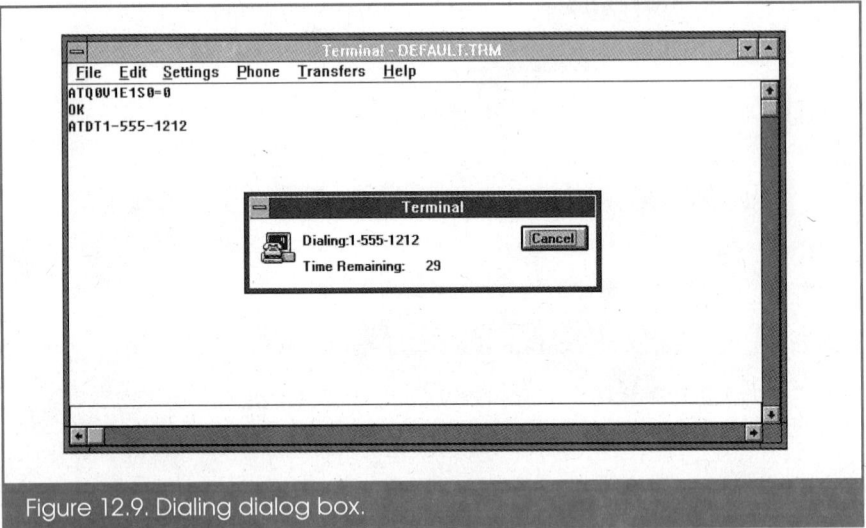

Figure 12.9. Dialing dialog box.

If Terminal has been configured correctly, lines of characters appear in the text area. These are commands being sent to the modem. If you change your mind and wish to cancel the call, click the Cancel button provided. You also can use the Phone Hangup command to cancel the call and disengage the modem.

Tip: If the word "ERROR" appears once or twice among the modem commands, you need to cancel the call and check the communications settings, particularly the data bits and parity.

At this point (assuming that the telephone number isn't busy) you are online. What happens now depends on your computer. If you receive garbled text, reread the "The Essentials Before Going Online" section and experiment with the settings described there.

Hanging Up

Whether you used the **S**ettings Phone **N**umber command or the **P**hone **D**ial command to make your call, you use the **P**hone **H**angup command to terminate it.

Exiting the remote system often causes the modem to hang up automatically. If you need to hang up before this, or if the remote system does not disconnect you, give the **P**hone **H**angup command.

> **Tip:** If the **P**hone **D**ial command is not dialing out correctly, the **P**hone **H**angup command often clears the modem and fixes the problem.

12

Terminal Preferences

The **S**ettings Terminal **P**references command, shown in Figure 12.10, establishes the look and feel for your online session.

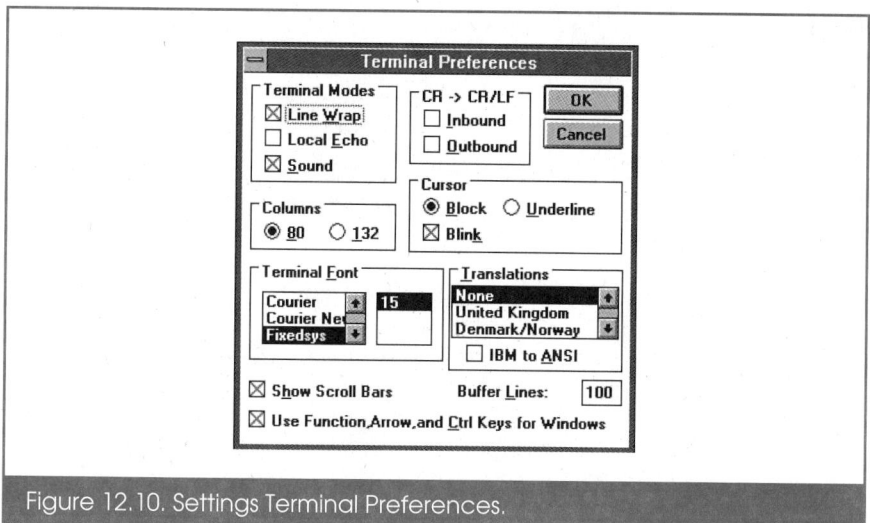

Figure 12.10. Settings Terminal Preferences.

Terminal Modes

The Line **W**rap option tells Terminal what to do with lines that are too long. Rather than allowing text to go past the main text area, this option (like a word processor) wraps the text to the next line.

The echo, also known as the *duplex,* determines whether Terminal should automatically display the text you enter or wait for the remote system to send back a copy of the characters your system sends to it. Local **E**cho rarely is set on.

> **Tip:** If the characters you type are displayed twice, such as "ttwwiiccee," turn off Local **E**cho. If characters you type aren't displayed at all, turn on the echo.

The **S**ound option enables the remote system to beep at you. If you turn off this option, you will not hear beeps from the other system. Another system might beep at you if you were accessing it in terminal-emulation mode and the remote system required an action from you for any reason.

Columns

The number of columns depends on your monitor; 80 columns is the usual setting. If you choose 132 columns but do not have enough space in your Terminal window, text runs off the screen even if line wrap is set.

Carriage Returns and Line Feeds

The CR → CR/LF options determine whether a line-feed character is added to carriage-return characters. The **I**nbound option is for the text you receive from the other computer; the **O**utbound option is for any text you send to the other computer.

> **Tip:** If all the text you receive is being displayed on one line and writing over itself instead of moving to the next line on the screen, change the **I**nbound option. If an extra blank line appears between every line of text you receive, turn off the **I**nbound option.

Cursor

The cursor can be a block or a line, and blinking can be toggled on or off. These settings are for your convenience only. They have no effect on the computer you are connected to.

Terminal Font

Both text font and text size can be set to your preference and changed at any time during an online session. The numbers in the box to the right of the fonts are the font sizes available. Note that you are limited to the fonts in this section; you cannot use other Windows fonts.

Translations

This setting adjusts the character set according to the standards of different countries. Because online systems are available worldwide, you may have to use a different standard for communications settings. Most countries, however, use the U.S. standard. Specify whether you want to use function keys with the Use Function, Arrow, and Ctrl Keys for Windows option.

Other Preference Options

The text area is a buffer that keeps a record of your online session. You can move around as you would in a word processor, by using the scroll bars to the right of and underneath the text area. The Show Scroll Bars option removes or replaces the scroll bars and changes the size of the text area accordingly.

The number of buffer lines determines how much of your online session is stored in the text area. When the buffer is filled, every new line pushes a line of text from the top of the buffer. If you set the line number higher than available memory can handle, Terminal resets the buffer to the highest possible number of lines. Information that has appeared on your screen during your communications session is saved to the buffer even though it scrolls out of sight. Just use the scroll bar to view anything that has scrolled out of sight.

12

Warning: Be sure that you have set the buffer large enough for your Terminal session if you want to scroll back. When information is pushed off the top of the buffer, you cannot get it back. The default setting is 100 lines of text, or a little more than 4 screens. Multiply the number of pages by 20 to get the anticipated line count. If the line count exceeds the default, change the setting. Remember, if you are operating in 800x600 or 1024x800 mode, your line count will be more per page. The best procedure is to load any text file available and check your video for the line count per page.

Other Settings

The last three commands in the **S**ettings menu round out the things you need to think about when you run Terminal.

Printer Echo

The **S**ettings Printer **E**cho command provides a hard copy of your online session by echoing to your printer everything that appears in the text area. The printer receives the information while you are online and tends to print whenever a page of text has been transmitted. Remember to turn off the printer echo when your online session is over.

Timer Mode

Many online systems charge by the minute. Terminal's timer helps you keep track of the time (and money) you spend online. Before you make a call, give the **S**ettings **T**imer Mode command. The timer starts immediately but resets to 00:00:00 when you first connect with a remote system.

To keep an eye on the timer during your session, give the **S**ettings Show/Hide **F**unction Keys command (discussed in detail in the next section). The timer is displayed in the lower-right function key box.

Tip: You can activate the timer also by clicking the lower-right function key box displaying the time.

Show Function Keys

Whenever you call an online system, you must go through the same log-in process, which frequently involves entering repetitive commands. Terminal's function keys store text and commands and reproduce them with a click of the mouse button, saving you time and the need to remember the exact format of a command. Figure 12.11 shows the **S**ettings **F**unction Keys dialog box.

12

Function Keys

	Key Name:	Command:
F1:		
F2:		
F3:		
F4:		
F5:		
F6:		
F7:		
F8:		

OK
Cancel

Key Level
◉ 1 ○ 2
○ 3 ○ 4

Selected key level

☐ Keys **V**isible

Figure 12.11. Settings Function Keys dialog box.

Enter the name of the function key in the left column. This name is displayed at the bottom of the Terminal window when the function keys are visible. Enter the desired text in the right column. Terminal outputs the contents of the command box when you click the function key. For example, to have a function key print your log-in ID, name the key something like "Login ID" and enter your log-in ID in the command box.

To enter a Ctrl character in the command, place a caret (^) before the character. The control character ^M is interpreted as a carriage return, the equivalent of pressing Enter. The command TIME^M types the word TIME followed by a carriage return. You can have the function key go through the entire log-in process while you drink a cup of coffee.

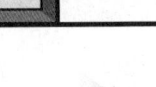

Tip: The control code ^$D# tells Terminal to pause # seconds before continuing with the rest of the function-key command. Use this code when you need the command to wait for the remote system to print the next prompt.

You can assign as many as 32 function keys by changing the key level. There are 4 levels (the use of levels is just a way to assign the same key to up to four commands; some autodial key assignments for pushbutton telephones store phone numbers the same way) and each holds up to 8 keys. To use other levels of functions while online, click the Key **L**evel box in the function key display, shown in Figure 12.11.

Turn on the function-key display with the **S**ettings Show **F**unction Keys command or the Keys **V**isible toggle in the Function Keys dialog box.

Editing the Terminal Buffer

You can use edit commands on the text in the Terminal buffer. The **E**dit menu, shown in Figure 12.12, provides the standard **E**dit **C**opy and **E**dit **P**aste commands, as well as commands unique to Terminal.

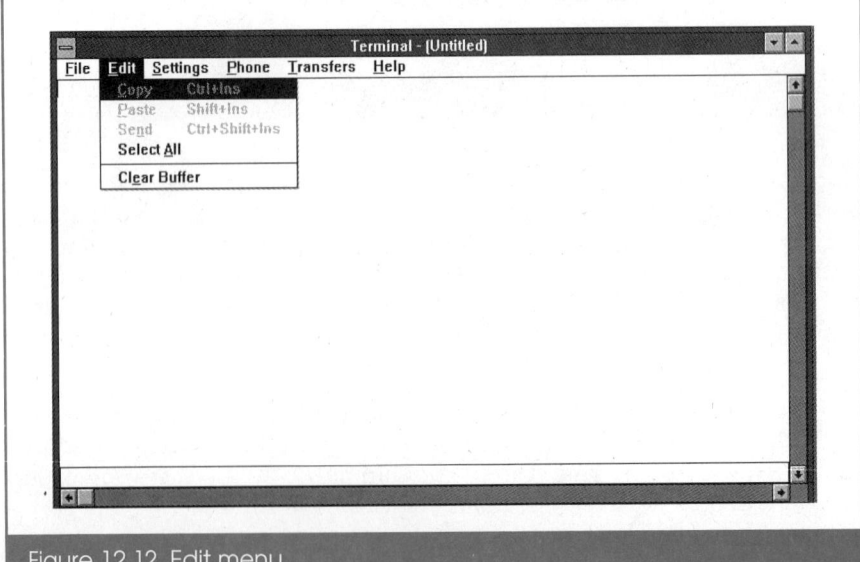

Figure 12.12. Edit menu.

To select text for editing, highlight it with the cursor. Table 12.1 lists the editing commands.

Table 12.1. Terminal editing commands.

Command	Description
Edit **C**opy	Copies selected text to the Clipboard.
Edit **P**aste	Sends the text in the Clipboard to the modem.
Edit Send	Sends the highlighted text (rather than text from the Clipboard) directly to the modem. Normally, lines of text are sent to the modem when you press the Enter key after you've typed some text.
Edit Select **A**ll	Highlights the entire Terminal buffer.
Edit Clear Buffer	Clears the Terminal buffer.

File Transfers

Transferring files from one system to another is one of the most valuable uses of a modem. Important files can be sent between the office and home, to a publisher (eliminating the need to send pounds of paper through the mail), or just to interested friends. There are two kinds of file transfers, *binary* and *text*, both of which are discussed in this section. Most of the transfer options are on the **T**ransfers menu (see Figure 12.13).

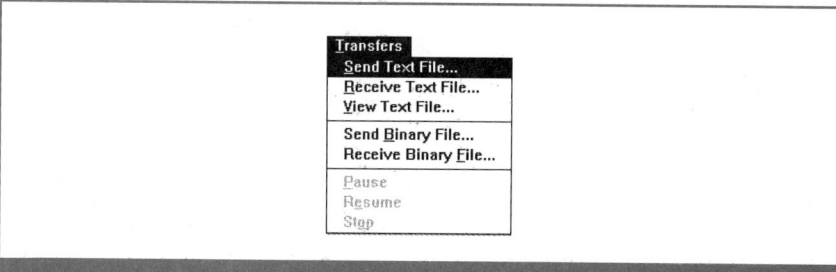

Figure 12.13. Transfers menu.

> **Tip:** Two terms are used a great deal in file transfers: *uploading* and *downloading*. As you may guess, these are opposites. According to Webster's *New World Dictionary of Computer Terms*, to upload means to "transfer data from a user's system to a remote computer system." In the same dictionary, download is defined as "the process of transferring data from a large central computer system to a smaller, remote computer system." It's not suprising that people cannot agree which term means which action. This set of definitions is gray at best because the terms were inherited from another context—the mainframe-dominated world of the '60s and '70s. For the sake of clarity in this book, the term *upload* means the act of transferring data *to* a remote system, and *download* means the transfer of data *from* a remote system.

Binary Transfers

If the file you want to transmit contains anything other than text characters, you must use a binary transfer. This is important if you are sending a program or a word-processed file that contains formatting codes. Always use binary transfers unless the remote system is not set up to accept them or you are sure that your file contains no special control codes or exotic characters.

Binary transfers use a high degree of error-checking to ensure that your file is not corrupted in the transfer process. When you send a binary file, you can be sure that any line-noise problems will not affect the file.

Two binary transfer protocols (**X**Modem and **K**ermit) are available in Terminal through the **S**ettings **B**inary Transfers command, shown in Figure 12.14. The computer to which you are sending the file must use the same protocol you are using. The differences between the two protocols are esoteric; all you need to know is which protocol the receiving computer is using.

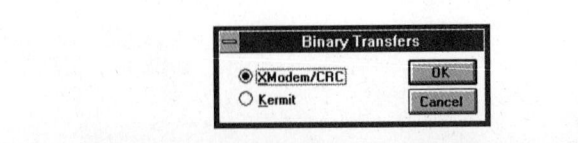

Figure 12.14. Settings Binary Transfers dialog box.

To send a binary file, you first prepare the remote system to receive a file with the appropriate protocol. The method for this depends on the remote system. Next, give the **T**ransfers Send **B**inary File command, shown in Figure 12.15, and select the file you want to send.

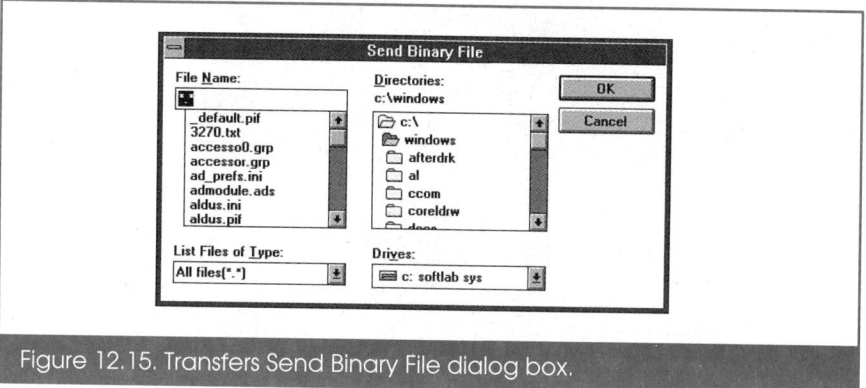

Figure 12.15. Transfers Send Binary File dialog box.

12

The transfer begins automatically when you select the file. Figure 12.16 shows the Terminal window during a transfer. Note the status at the bottom of the window.

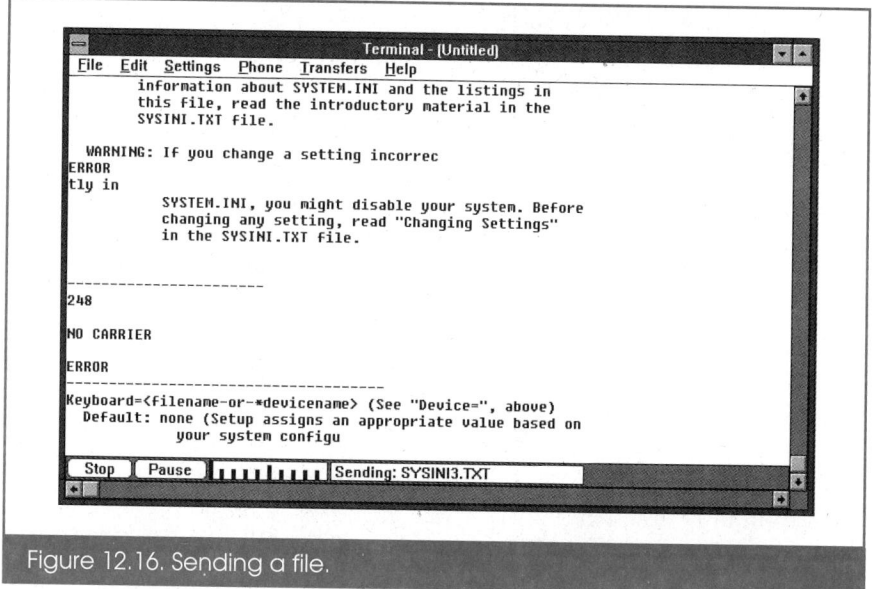

Figure 12.16. Sending a file.

If something goes wrong with the file transfer or if you click Stop during the transfer, the error `Binary transfer of file XXXXXXX.XXX failed on send` appears.

To receive a binary file, prepare the remote system to send the file and make sure that Terminal's binary protocol matches that of the remote system. Give the **Transfers Receive Binary File** command and enter the filename for your system. The filename you select does not have to match the name of the file being sent, because you are telling Terminal what name to save the file with on your own system. As you are receiving a binary file, you see the dialog box shown in Figure 12.17.

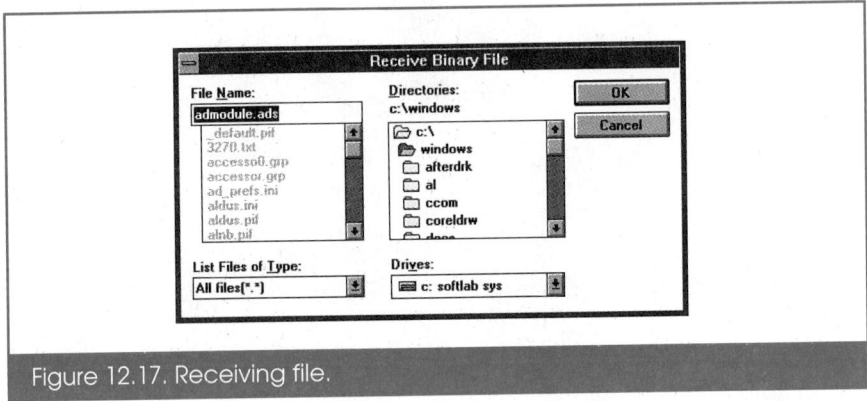

Figure 12.17. Receiving file.

Text Transfers

Text-file transfers use regular ASCII files which contain none of the special characters. Many word processors and applications can create ASCII or text files, which are easier to move between incompatible programs.

To send a text file, prepare the remote system and give the **Transfers Send Text File** command, shown in Figure 12.18. Choose the file and select whether you want a line feed added to or taken away from each carriage return in the file. The line-feed choices depend on what the receiving computer needs.

If the remote system is unable to handle the speed of the text transfer, use the **Settings Text Transfers** command, shown in Figure 12.19, to slow the pace.

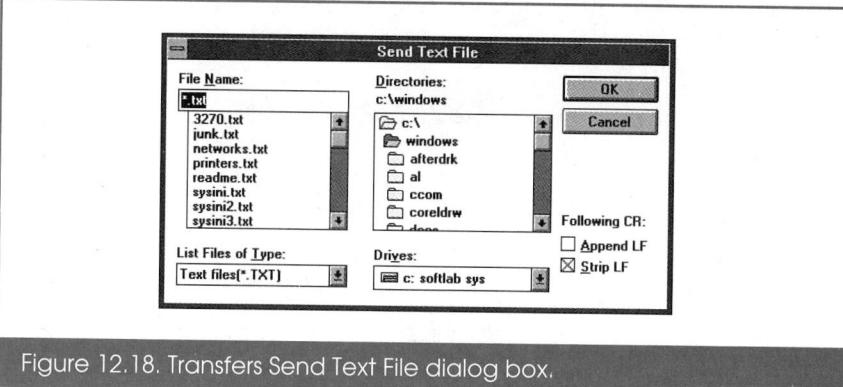

Figure 12.18. Transfers Send Text File dialog box.

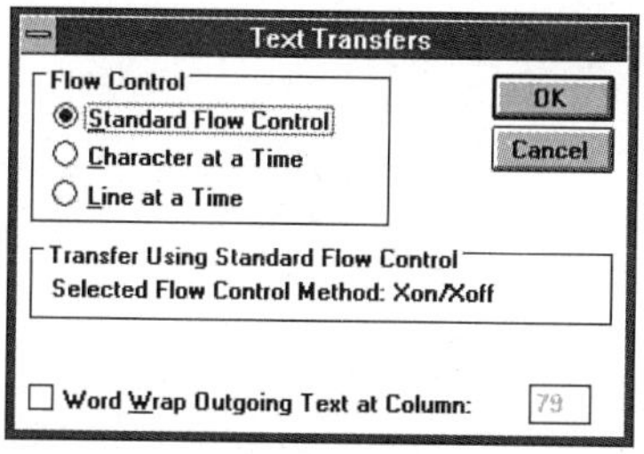

Figure 12.19. Settings Text Transfers dialog box.

The text transfer slows down if you choose either the **C**haracter at a Time or **L**ine at a Time options. You can set the text also to be word-wrapped as it is transmitted.

To receive a text file, give the appropriate commands to the remote system and select **T**ransfers **R**eceive Text File, shown in Figure 12.20. Enter the filename and determine whether you want to use any of the options explained in Table 12.2.

Table 12.2. Transfers Receive Text File options.

Option	Description
Append File	Adds the file to the end of an existing file.
Save **C**ontrols	Saves limited formatting codes that can be transmitted in a text file.
Table **F**ormat	Converts two or more consecutive spaces into a tab character.

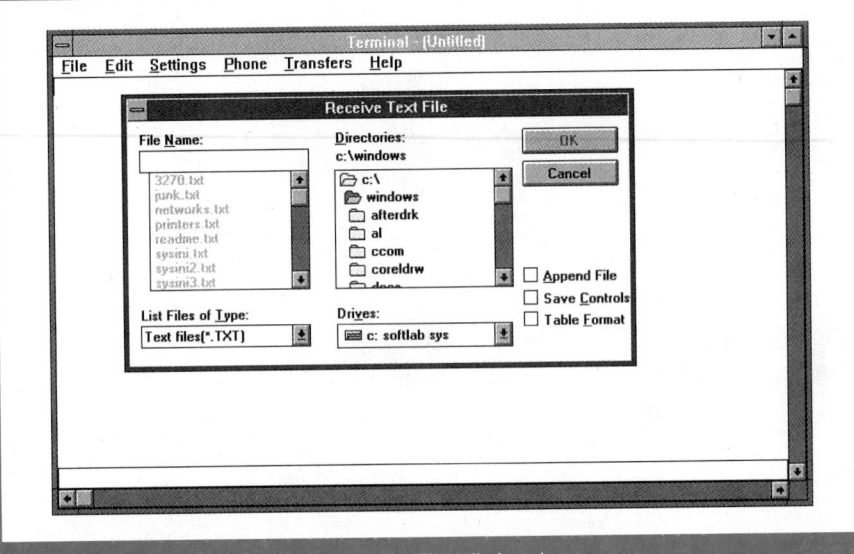

Figure 12.20. Transfers Receive Text File dialog box.

View Text File

Use the **T**ransfers **V**iew Text File command to look at the contents of a file on your system. You can use this command to preview a file before transferring it or to check a file you have received.

CHAPTER

13

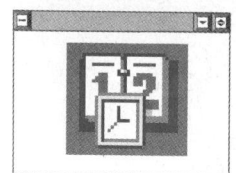

Other Accessories

The other programs in Program Manager's Accessories window are minor tools for helping you with your daily work. Most of them can be learned quickly and used for odds-and-ends tasks.

Notepad

The Notepad is useful for limited editing of text files. Notepad is like a subset of Write but often is much quicker for editing text files. Because Notepad uses only the lower ASCII character set, Notepad is very fast. Like Write, it can handle just one single document at a time. Many Notepad concepts are covered in detail in Chapter 10, "Write," and are not repeated here. All of the basic Windows concepts apply (working with the mouse to highlight text, for example), so the learning curve is a lot less vertical than you might otherwise expect when picking up a new program.

Tip: Windows comes with many text files you can edit to improve your system's performance. You can use Notepad to edit these files. SysEdit, another utility that comes with Windows, enables you to edit the four most common system files: WIN.INI, SYSTEM.INI, AUTOEXEC.BAT, and CONFIG.SYS. For more information on SysEdit, see Chapter 25, "Changing Your Configuration."

Figure 13.1 shows the initial Notepad window with a file open. You move the insertion point and select text just as you do in Write. Notepad only offers you the system font that Windows uses when it posts dialog boxes and messages. If you want to use other fonts you will have to use Write or another word processor.

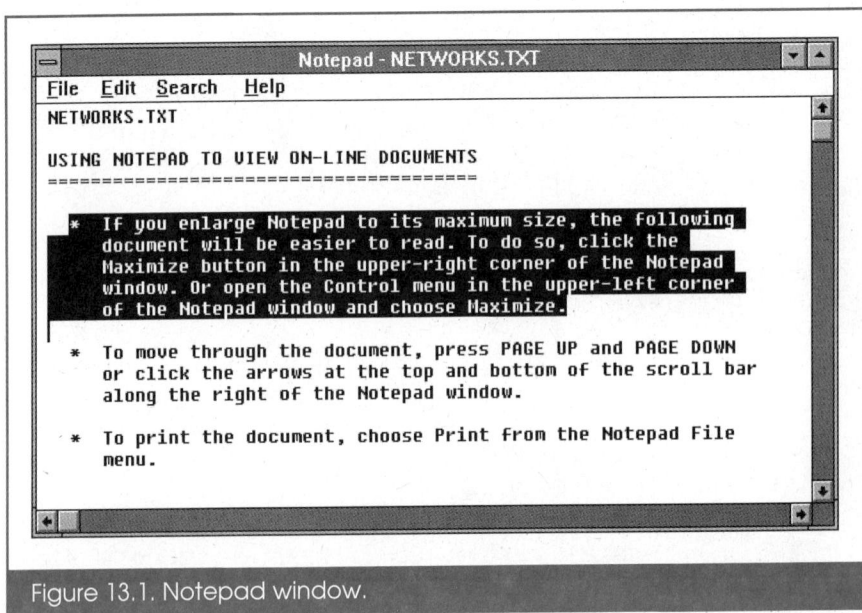

Figure 13.1. Notepad window.

File Menu

The File menu, shown in Figure 13.2, is fairly standard for Windows programs. The commands in the File menu are similar to those for Write, except for the File Save As command, which does not enable you to choose any options for the file format.

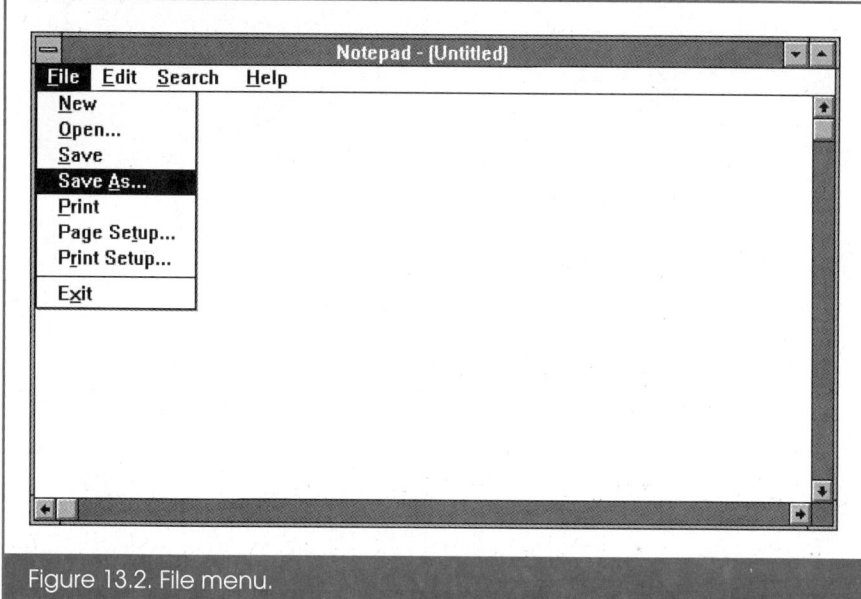

Figure 13.2. File menu.

You can use the **F**ile Page Se**t**up command, shown in Figure 13.3, to specify the text for a header and a footer, as well as the margins. You can enter regular text for the header and footer, or you can use the special symbols shown in Table 13.1.

Figure 13.4 shows how you indicate that you want the date and time in the header aligned with the margins, for example, with the page number centered in the footer.

Using the Clipboard

Notepad supports the **E**dit **C**ut, **E**dit **C**opy, and **E**dit **P**aste commands for interacting with the Clipboard. The **E**dit De**l**ete command deletes the selected text without copying it to the Clipboard.

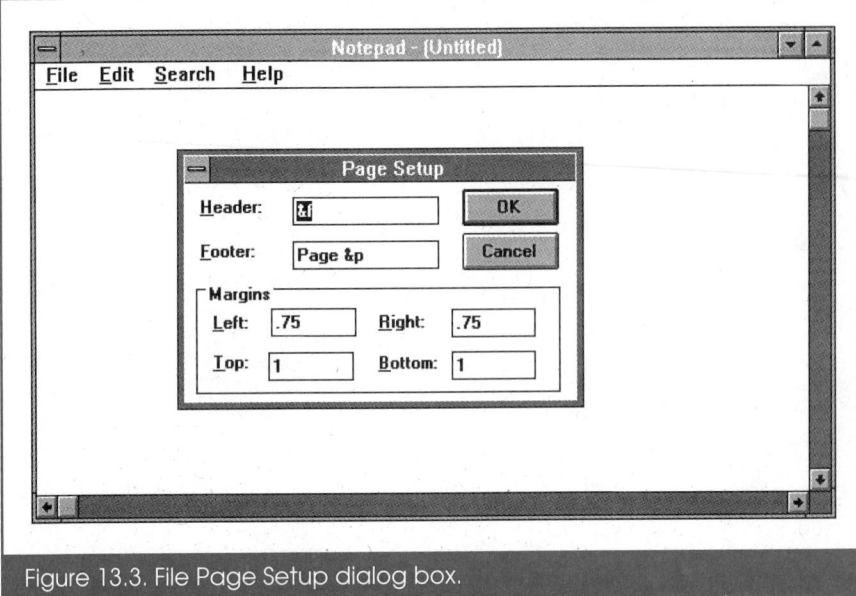

Figure 13.3. File Page Setup dialog box.

Table 13.1. Symbols for File Page Setup.

Symbol	Description
&d	Today's date
&t	The time
&p	Page number
&f	Filename
&l	Causes text following it to be left aligned
&r	Causes text following it to be right aligned
&c	Causes text following it to be centered

The **E**dit Select **A**ll command is a handy way to select the entire document without having to scroll through it. If you want to append the contents of one document to the end of another document, for example, open the first document, give the **E**dit Select **A**ll command, followed by the **E**dit Copy command. Then open the second document and give the **E**dit **P**aste command.

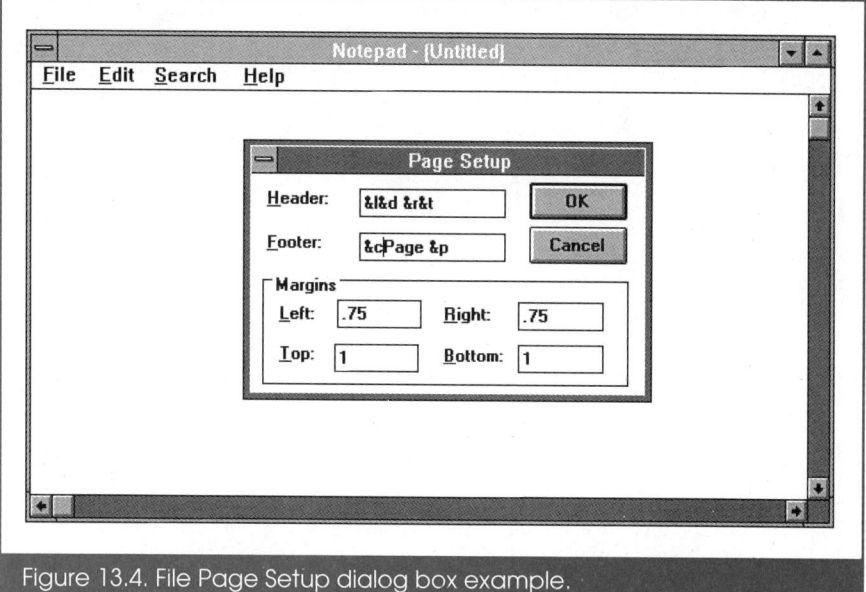

Figure 13.4. File Page Setup dialog box example.

Wrapping Long Lines

If the lines in your text file are longer than the lines in the window, you can use the **E**dit **W**ord Wrap command. Note that this command works only on small files; in very long files, Notepad does not wrap lines. Figure 13.5 shows the narrower window that results from giving the **E**dit **W**ord Wrap command.

Adding the Date

The **E**dit Time/**D**ate command puts the current date at the insertion point (see Figure 13.6). You might use this command if you are keeping a log of your activities, for example, or if you are preparing electronic mail. You can use the F5 key also to perform this task.

Searching for Text

The **S**earch **F**ind command, shown in Figure 13.7, enables you to look for text. In the Fi**n**d What field, type the text you want to look for; then

click OK. Selecting the Match **C**ase check box tells Notepad that you want to find only text that matches the text you typed (both upper- and lowercase). You can specify also the direction in which to search.

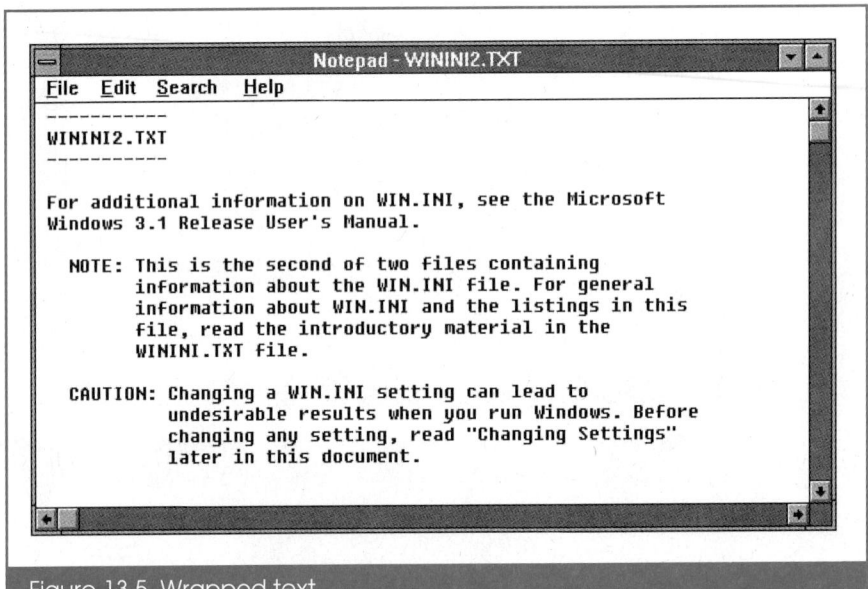

Figure 13.5. Wrapped text.

Use F5 to insert date and time

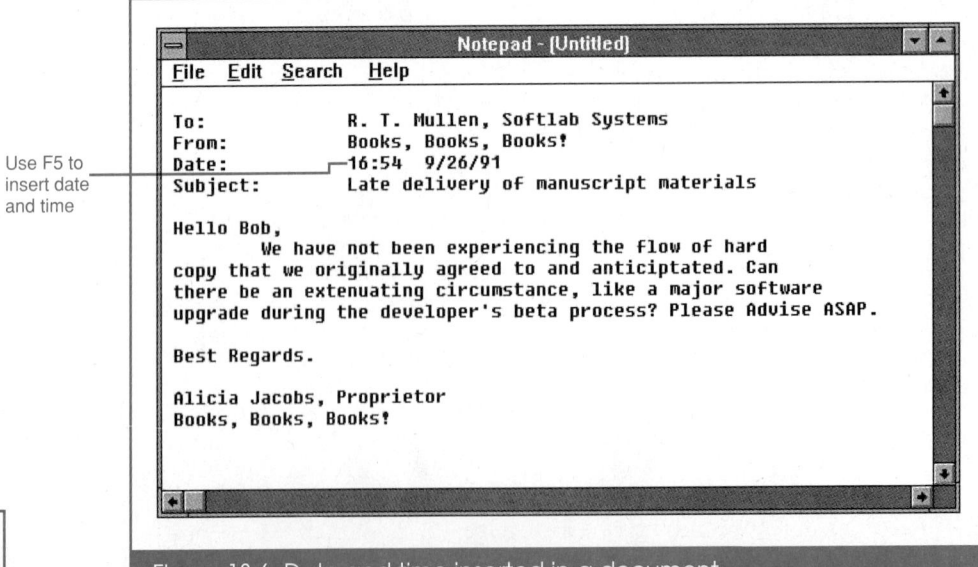

Figure 13.6. Date and time inserted in a document.

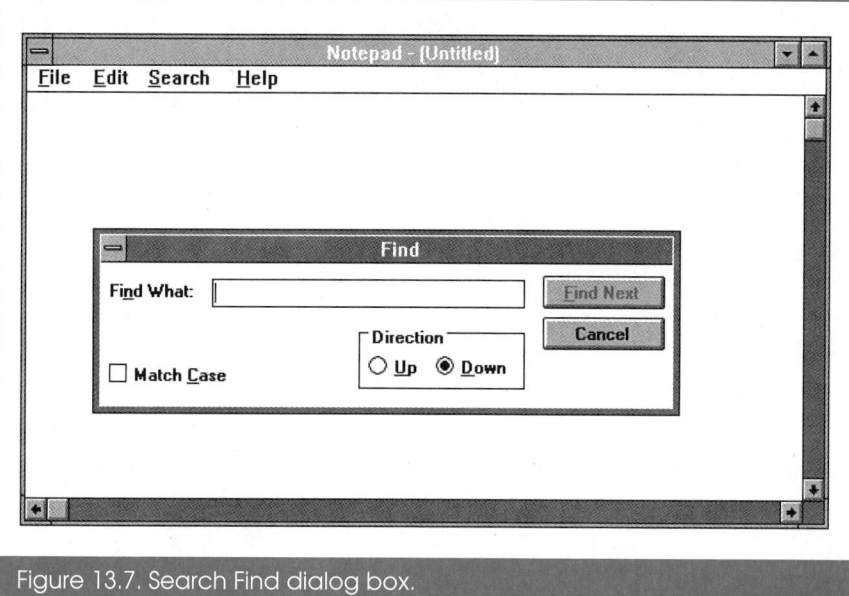

Figure 13.7. Search Find dialog box.

To repeat a search without opening the **Search F**ind dialog box, give the **Search Find N**ext command or press F3.

Tip: If you find that you use one of the tools often and you wish it were a more complete product, you should see whether commercial programs that do more are available. Recorder is only mediocre at recording, for example, but a much better macro recorder called Tempo is available. Chapter 30, "Windows for Advanced Users," lists many of these programs. Hundreds more are available as shareware and commercial software.

Calendar

Calendar, shown in Figure 13.8, is useful for keeping track of appointments and meetings. You can use it also as an electronic wall calendar. You can change from a military clock by using the **O**ptions **D**ay Settings Command.

When you first open Calendar, the date given will be today's date if your computer's clock is running and set correctly. To switch to the month view shown in Figure 13.9, give the **V**iew **M**onth command or double-click in the status line.

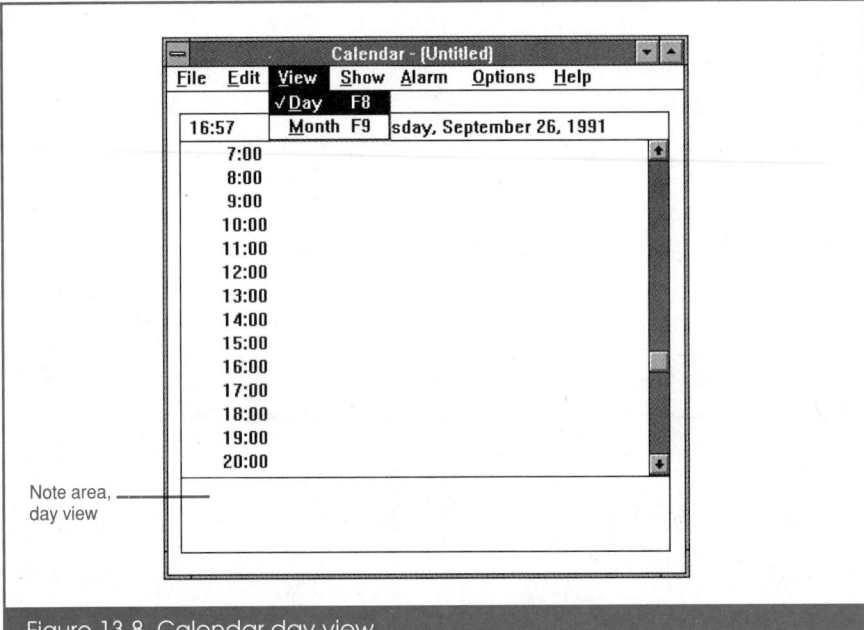

Note area,
day view

Figure 13.8. Calendar day view.

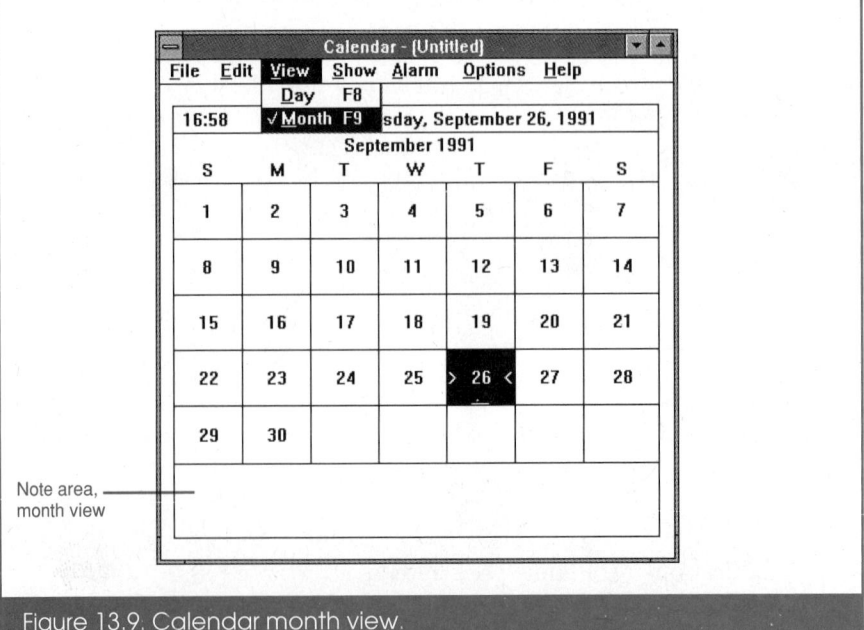

Note area,
month view

Figure 13.9. Calendar month view.

Warning: If you start Calendar from its icon, it opens with no calendar file. You must open your own calendar file to see dates and appointments you have already saved on disk. This action is described later in this chapter.

Entering Appointments and Notes

In **D**ay view, you can enter text on any line, next to the hour. If the time you want is not visible, use the scroll bar on the right or press the ↑ and ↓ keys. You can use the PageUp and PageDown keys also.

At the bottom of each day's window is an area for notes. You might put someone's birthday there, for instance, because the birthday is not associated with any particular time of day. Figure 13.10 shows an example of how the note area can be used. To move to the note area, click there or press Tab.

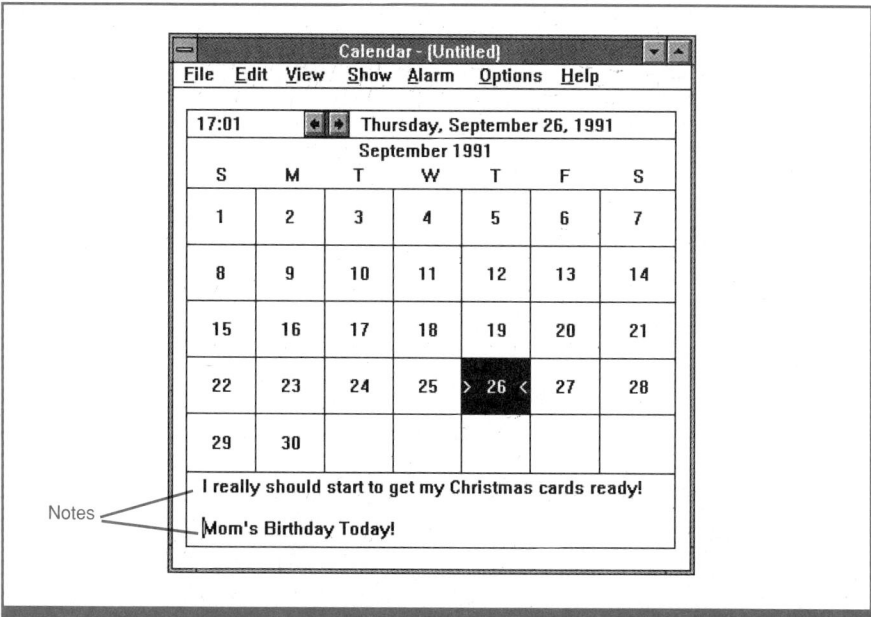

Figure 13.10. Example of using note area.

Expanding the Day View

With the **O**ptions **D**ay Settings command, shown in Figure 13.11, you can add to the day view additional spaces for appointments. If you are one of the many people who need to show their appointments with greater accuracy, you will likely choose to have lines for every 15 or 30 minutes.

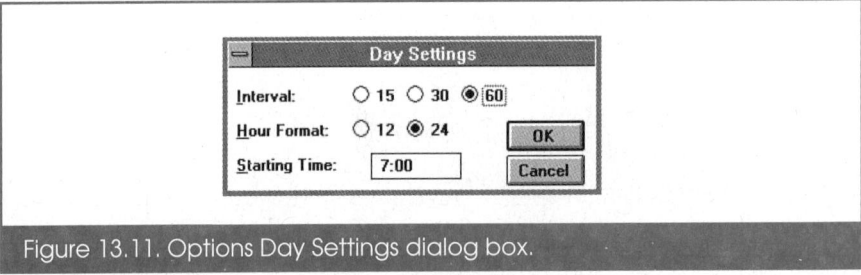

Figure 13.11. Options Day Settings dialog box.

You can use this command also to specify the hour format and to set the time initially displayed when you open a day view.

Adding Times Not Shown

You may have appointments that fall between the times shown, even if you choose to have a line for every 15 minutes. Using the **O**ptions **S**pecial Time command, shown in Figure 13.12, you can enter any time on the current day's calendar. Then you can enter information for that time.

Figure 13.12. Options Special Time dialog box.

To remove a time you added, simply put the insertion point on the message area for that time, give the **O**ptions **S**pecial Time command again, and click the **D**elete button.

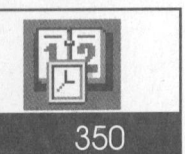

Viewing Different Days

Clearly, you need to be able to move from one date to another, to enter new appointments and to look at your current appointments.

To move to the previous and next day's appointments:

With the mouse, click the left and right arrows at the top of the day.

With the keyboard, give the **S**how **P**revious and **S**how **N**ext commands, or press Ctrl-PgUp or Ctrl-PgDn.

To jump to today's page, give the **S**how **T**oday command. To go to a specific date, give the **S**how **D**ate command (see Figure 13.13). You can enter the date in several formats, including 1/15/92 or 1-15-92.

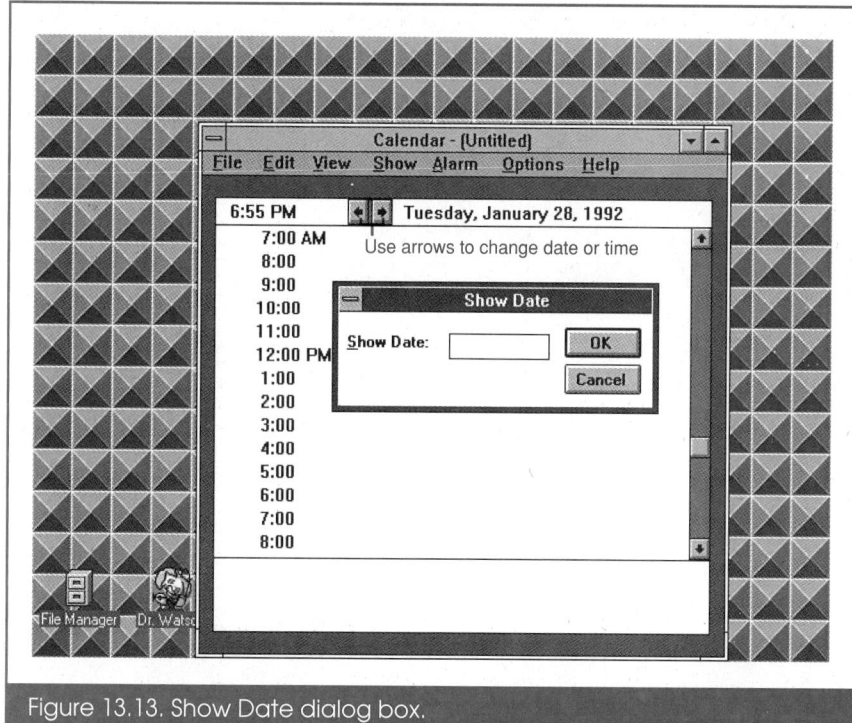

Figure 13.13. Show Date dialog box.

Viewing Different Months

In month view, you can move around in the desk calendar as you can in day view.

Clicking the left and right arrows at the top of the month takes you to the previous and next month's page.

 With the keyboard, give the **S**how **P**revious and **S**how **N**ext commands or press Ctrl-PgUp or Ctrl-PgDn.

To jump to this month's page, give the **S**how **T**oday command. To go to a specific month, give the **S**how **D**ate command. Note that you must enter the date in the same format as before (as 1/15/92 or 1-15-92, for example). You cannot enter just the month and year.

Setting Alarms

You can set alarms in day view so that Calendar reminds you of an appointment or other event. This is very useful when you are absorbed in a project or are working on many tasks at once. To set an alarm, put the insertion point on the line for the time you want and give the **A**larm **S**et command. You see a small bell to the left of that time on the day view, as shown in Figure 13.14.

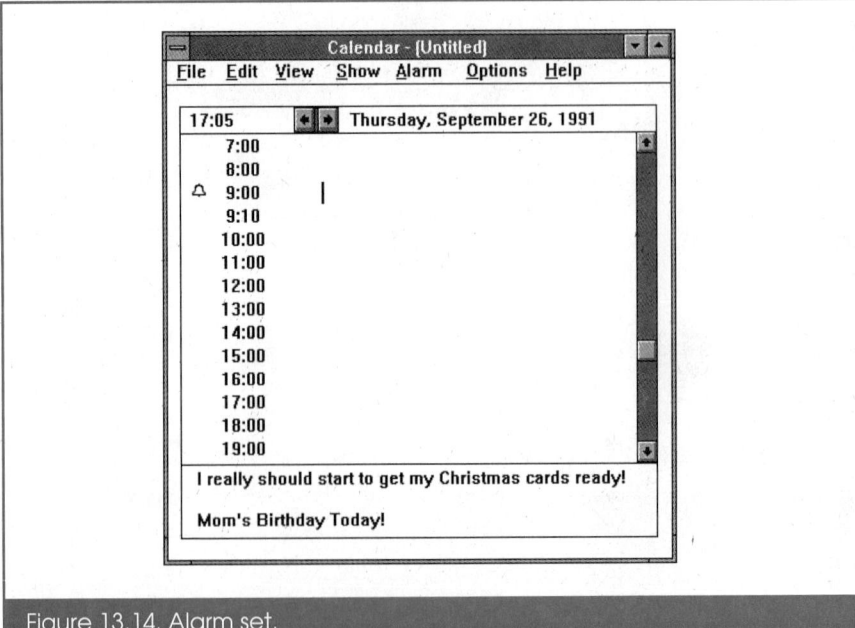

Figure 13.14. Alarm set.

If you set an alarm and later want to turn it off, put the insertion point on any part of that line and again give the **A**larm **S**et command. The bell icon disappears.

The way Calendar tells you about your alarm depends on the current state of the Calendar program. The active state would occur when Calendar is active or in the foreground, the inactive state would be when Calendar is in the background, and the closed state would be when Calendar is minimized to an icon. Calendar works well even if you are working with a DOS program in a window. Of course, 386-enhanced mode is required to run Calendar and a DOS program in a window simultaneously. Table 13.2 shows the Calendar states and how you can tell that an alarm has gone off. One way or another, you must leave Calendar running in order for you to be alerted by alarms.

13

Table 13.2. Alarm actions.

State of Calendar	Action
Active	You see a dialog box with the event's message
Inactive	The Calendar program's title bar flashes
Closed (an icon)	The Calendar program's icon flashes

Warning: If Calendar is not running when an alarm is set to go off, you will not know. You must have Calendar running to see your alarms. If you rely on alarms, you should run or load Calendar whenever you start Windows.

You can vary the way Calendar gives you alarms. The **A**larm **C**ontrols command, shown in Figure 13.15, lets you specify how early to alert you about the alarms and whether to use sound. The **E**arly Ring option tells how many minutes before an alarm is set to go off you should be warned. If you turn off the **S**ound option, Calendar only flashes or puts up a dialog box. If you are using Windows 3.1's multimedia capabilities, you can arrange to hear a .WAV file instead of your system's usual "BEEP" sound. The alarm will sound four times. If you turn the alarm off after it has been set and rung early, it does not go off again at the actual set time. To remove all alarms you may have set for a particular day, just select the **E**dit **R**emove option, and the little bells next to the alarm times you set for an entire day will disappear.

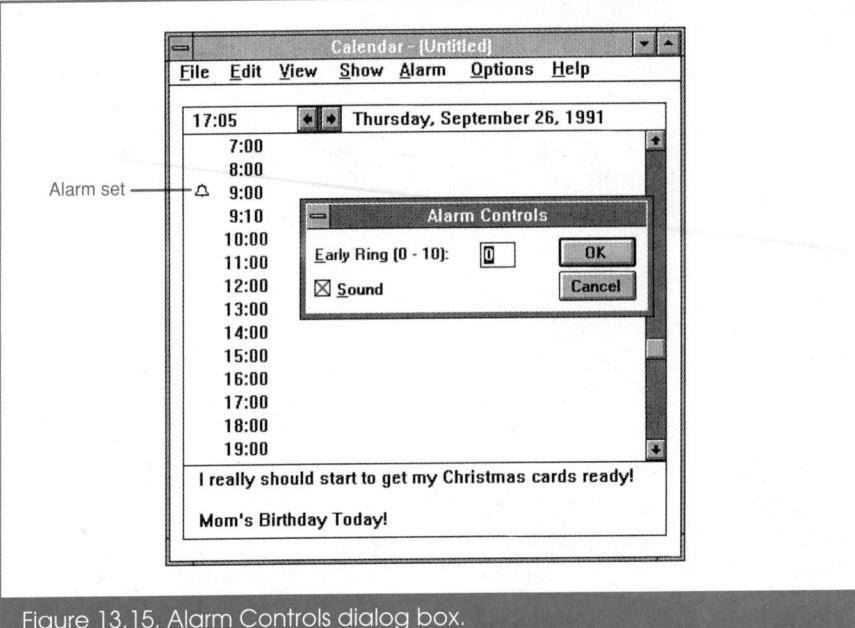

Alarm set

Figure 13.15. Alarm Controls dialog box.

Marking Dates in Month View

In month view, the current date is enclosed in greater and less than signs (> <). You can mark other days with marks that signify different things, such as regular meetings or games. Select a day and give the **O**ptions **M**ark command (see Figure 13.16).

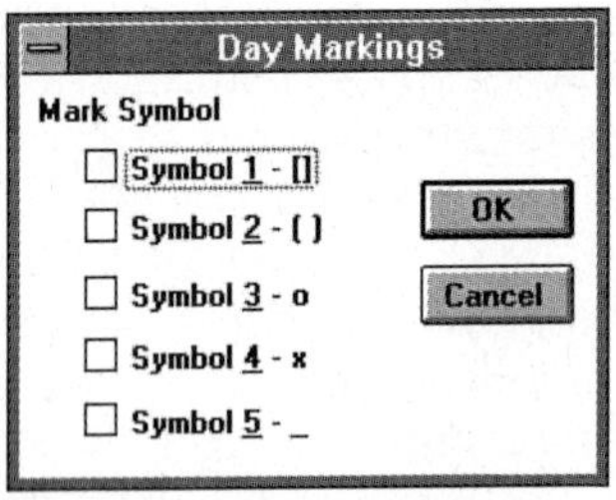

Figure 13.16. Day Markings dialog box.

Generally, you should keep one set of symbols for each type of mark you use. Note that a particular day can have many marks. The month page shown in Figure 13.17, for example, has two types of marks, in addition to the marks for today.

Figure 13.17. Examples of marks in use.

Removing Old Days

If you want to delete a certain day's appointments from your calendar, give the **E**dit **R**emove command shown in Figure 13.18. **E**dit **R**emove only removes the appointment and alarms for one day, unless you enter other dates in the To and From text boxes in the Edit Remove dialog box. Enter the range of dates in the **F**rom and **T**o text boxes, and click on the OK button.

Printing Your Calendar

You can print your Calendar with the **F**ile **P**rint command, shown in Figure 13.19. Enter the dates for which you want to print your appointments.

13

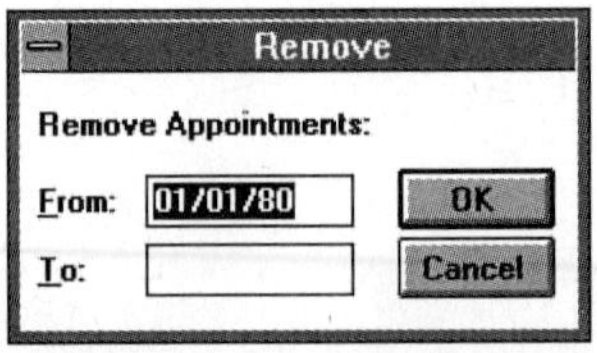

Figure 13.18. Edit Remove dialog box.

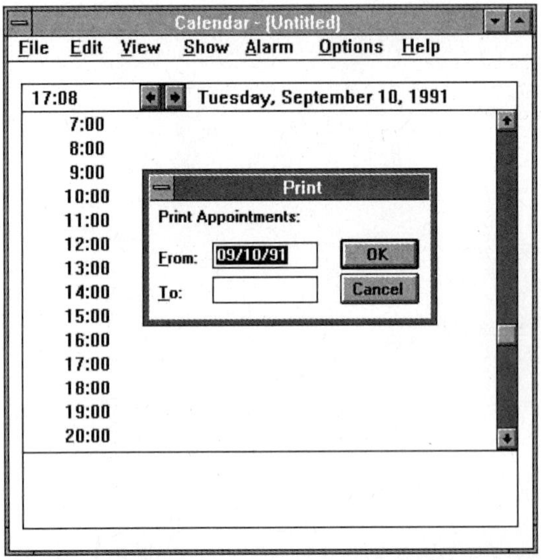

Figure 13.19. File Print dialog box.

Before you print, use the **F**ile Page Se**t**up command, shown in Figure 13.20, to set the header and footer for the printed page, as well as the margins. You can enter regular text for the header and footer, or you can use the special symbols listed in Table 13.1.

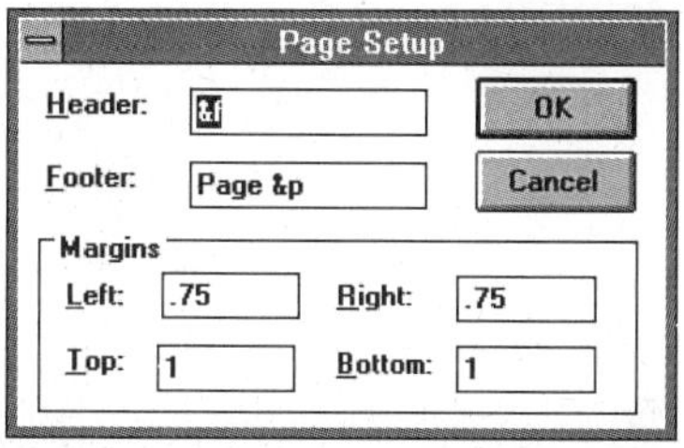

Figure 13.20. File Page Setup dialog box.

Figure 13.21 shows how to indicate that you want the date and time in the header aligned with the margins, with the page number centered in the footer.

13

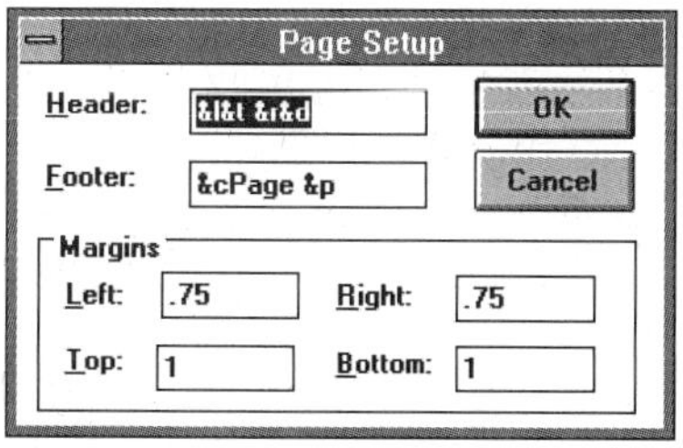

Figure 13.21. File Page Setup dialog box example.

Calendar Files

The **File New**, **File Open**, **File Save**, and **File Save As** commands are similar to the commands in other Windows programs. Calendar uses the .CAL extension for calendar files.

> **Tip:** When you start Calendar, you almost always want to use your regular Calendar file. To open this file automatically, change the properties of the Calendar icon using the **File Properties** command in Program Manager. This action is described in Chapter 5, "Program Manager."

The **F**ile **O**pen command, shown in Figure 13.22, can open a file for reading only when you select the **R**ead Only option. This is useful when you are looking at someone else's calendar on a network, for example.

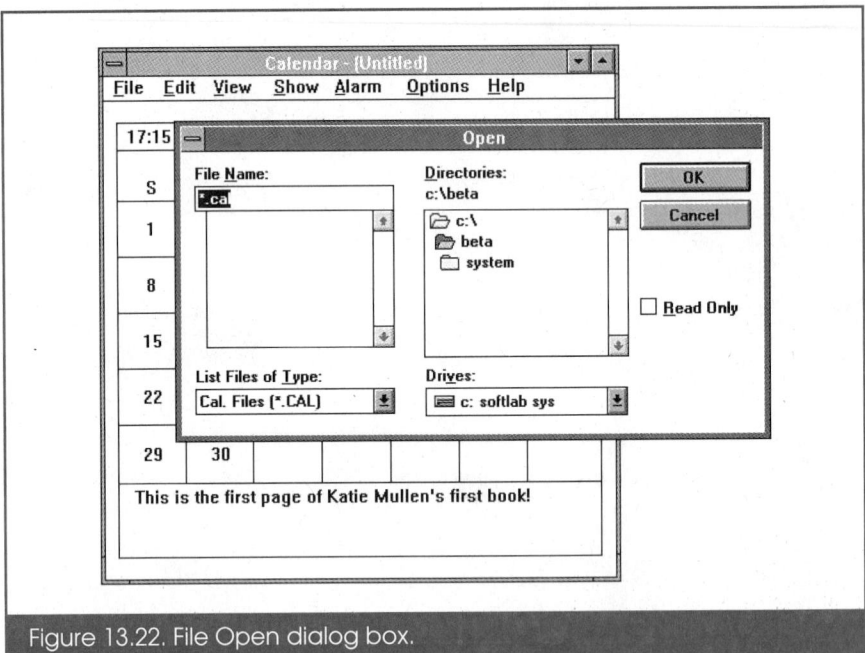

Figure 13.22. File Open dialog box.

Cardfile

The Cardfile program is useful for keeping bits of unorganized information. You can keep many files of related information or put all your information into one large file. Finding cards with the information you want is quick and easy.

Figure 13.23 shows the main Cardfile program window. Each card has an index line and an information area. You use the index to find quickly the cards you want. If you are using Cardfile for names and addresses, for example, you should keep the name in the index line. Cardfile enables you to search for information from either the index or the information area.

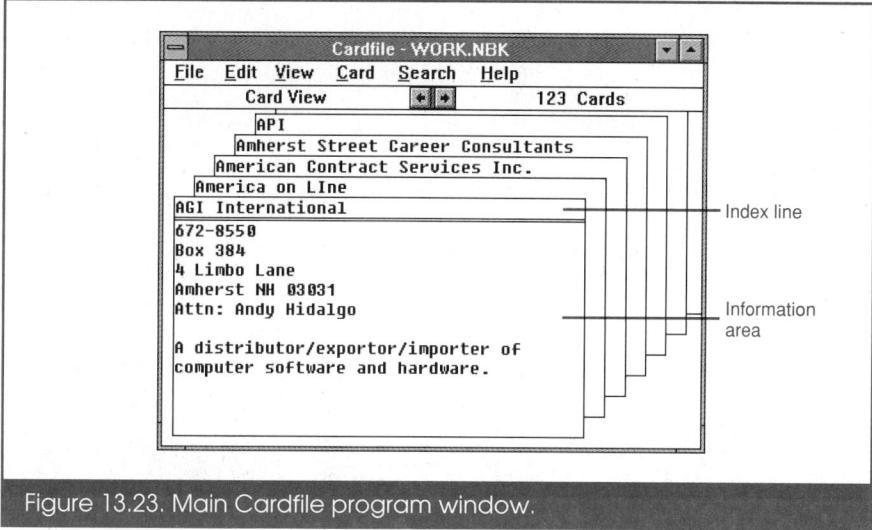

Figure 13.23. Main Cardfile program window.

13

The information in a card usually is text but can include pictures also.

Adding New Cards

When you start Cardfile, you are presented with a blank card. You can fill in the information by putting the insertion point in the information area and typing. Generally, you will want to fill in the index also.

Double-click the index line.

Give the **E**dit **I**ndex command.

Figure 13.24 shows the dialog box for editing or entering a new index.

You add a new card in much the same way, except that you always edit the index first. Give the **C**ard **A**dd command, shown in Figure 13.25, to add another card to your Cardfile.

Editing the text in a card is the same as editing in other Windows programs. In addition to selecting, overtyping, and so on, you can select text and use the **E**dit **C**opy, **E**dit **C**ut, and **E**dit **P**aste commands to copy or move text in a card or between cards.

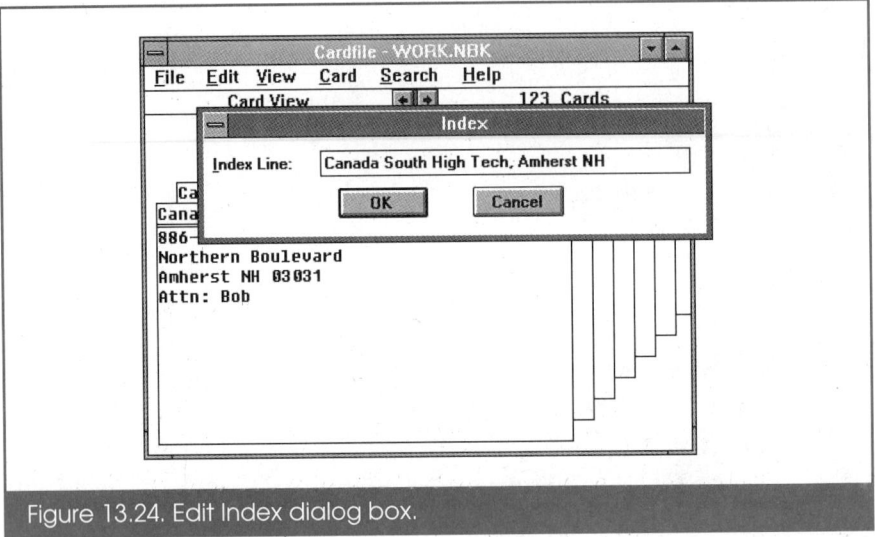

Figure 13.24. Edit Index dialog box.

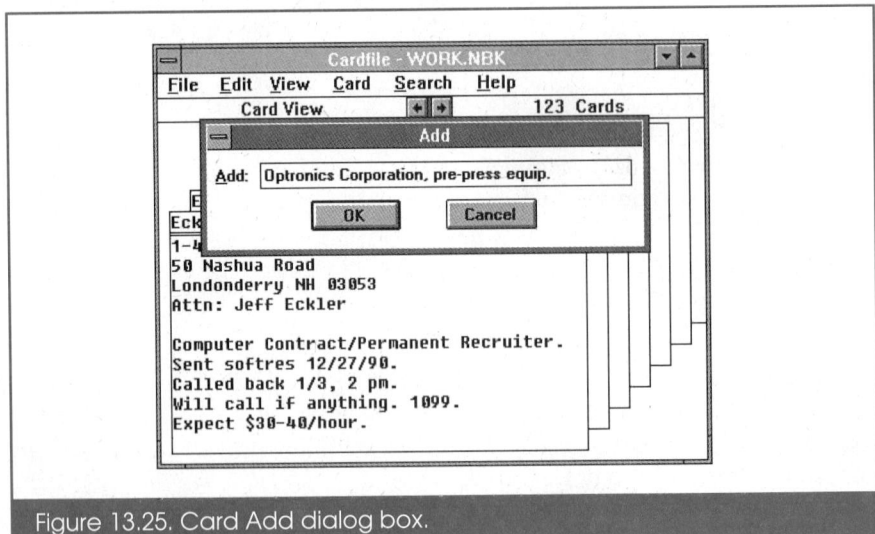

Figure 13.25. Card Add dialog box.

Selecting Cards

You can search for a particular card by looking through the cards one at a time, or by letting Cardfile search for a card that contains specific words or characters. To look through cards one at a time, do the following:

Rifle through the cards by clicking the left and right arrows near the top of the window.

Use the key combinations shown in Table 13.3 to move through the cards.

Table 13.3. Key combinations for selecting cards.

Key	Action
PgUp	Cycles cards back
PgDn	Cycles cards forward
Ctrl-Home	Shows first card
Ctrl-End	Shows last card

13

Finding Cards

You can choose a specific card with the **S**earch **G**o To command, shown in Figure 13.26, if you know part of what is in the index. Type whatever characters you remember in the **G**o To field and click OK.

To find cards by the text they contain, use the **S**earch **F**ind command (see Figure 13.27). Enter the text you want to search for and click OK.

To look for every occurence of the same string of text, select the **S**earch **F**ind Next button from the Search Find dialog box. By selecting the Direction **U**p or Direction **D**own option buttons, you can search toward the beginning or toward the end of the cardfile. And you can ask Cardfile to look specifically for upper- or lowercase text—just select the Match **C**ase check box.

Use these arrows
to move between cards

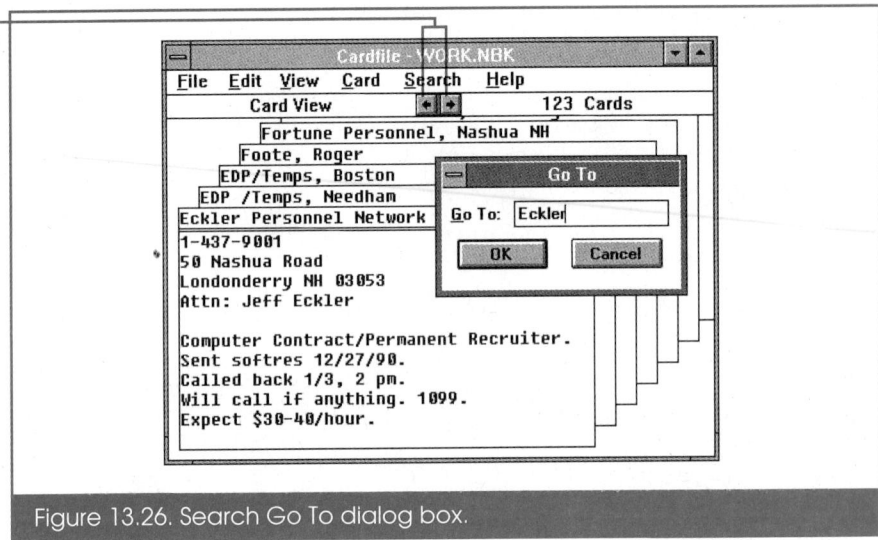

Figure 13.26. Search Go To dialog box.

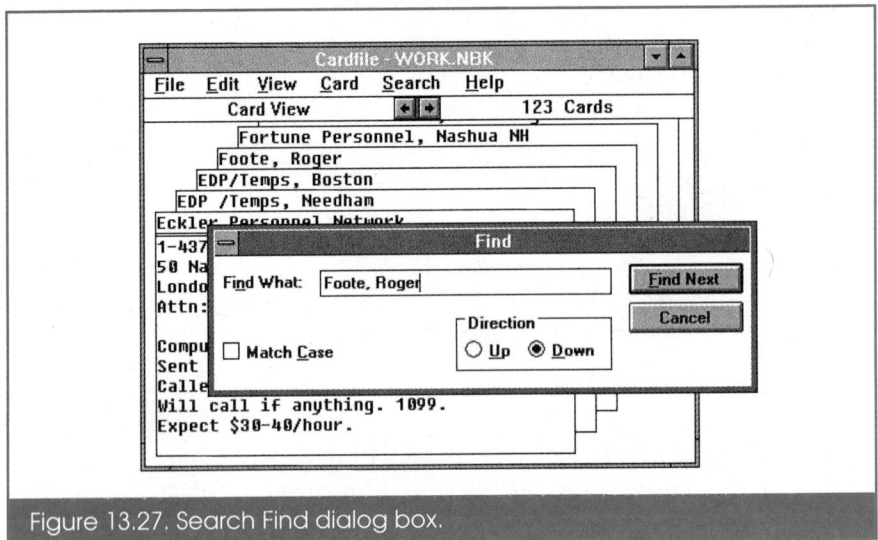

Figure 13.27. Search Find dialog box.

Managing Cards

You can duplicate a card with the **C**ard Du**p**licate command. This command is handy when a card contains a great deal of information, most of which you want to use in another card. Duplicate the card, change the index on the new card (if you want), and make any changes to the information area.

To remove a card, give the **C**ard **D**elete command. This command permanently deletes the card from the file.

If you make a mistake when editing a card, give the **E**dit **R**estore command. This command deletes your changes and returns the card to its unedited state.

13

Card Files

The standard extension for Cardfile files is .CRD. You may want to keep different files for related types of information, or keep all your information in one large file.

> **Tip:** The **F**ile **M**erge command enables you to combine two files. Simply open one of the files, give the **F**ile **M**erge command, choose the second file, and click OK to bring the information from the second file into the first file.

> **Warning**: Windows 3.1 converts Windows 3.0 Cardfile files to the 3.1 Cardfile format. Windows 3.0 cannot read a 3.1 card file after conversion. Be sure to save your original card file to another filename to be used for conversion if you intend to open the same card file under Windows 3.0 later.

Printing

The **F**ile **P**rint command prints the current card, and the **F**ile Print All command prints all cards in the file. Before you print, use the **F**ile Page Se**t**up command, shown in Figure 13.28, to set the margins, header, and footer for the printed page. You can enter regular text for the header and footer, or you can use the special symbols shown in Table 13.1.

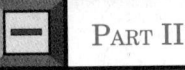

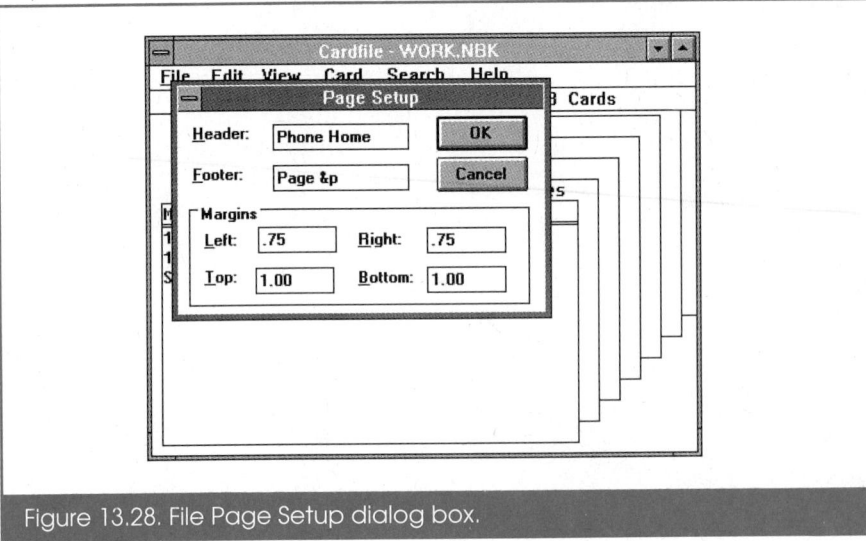

Figure 13.28. File Page Setup dialog box.

Figure 13.29, for example, illustrates how you would indicate that you want the date and the time in the header aligned with the margins, with the page number centered in the footer.

Figure 13.29. File Page Setup dialog box example.

Automatic Dialing

Most people use cards for names and telephone numbers. If you have a modem in your PC, you can use the phone number in a card to dial the modem. This option is useful if your modem enables you to pick up the phone connected through the modem after it has dialed a number for you.

Cardfile is very good at finding telephone numbers in cards. To dial a
telephone number in a card, give the **C**ard Aut**o**dial command, shown
in Figure 13.30. As you can see, Cardfile finds the telephone number
and puts it in the **N**umber field (you can change this number if you
want). The Pre**f**ix field enables you to prefix the telephone number with
a number to dial first, but only if the **U**se Prefix option is selected. Click
OK to dial the number.

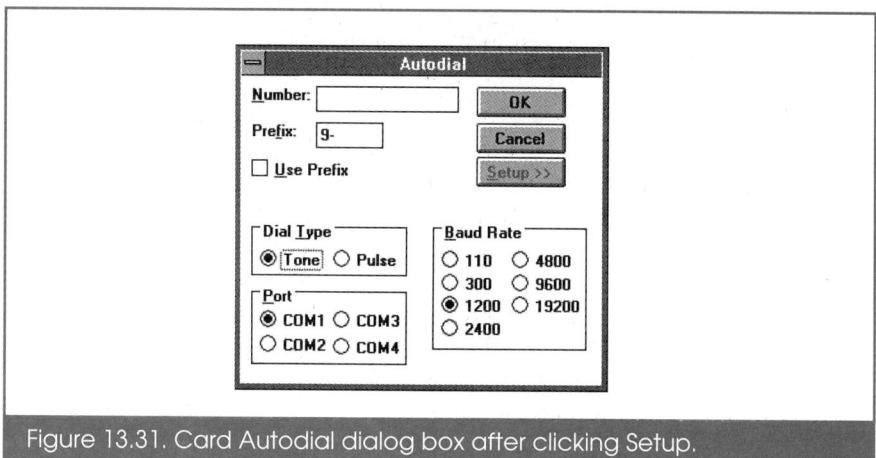

Figure 13.30. Card Autodial dialog box.

13

As you can see from Figure 13.31, the **S**etup button expands the dialog
box so that you can set parameters for the modem (such as the way to
dial, the serial port, and the baud rate). These parameters are described in more detail in Chapter 12, "Terminal."

Figure 13.31. Card Autodial dialog box after clicking Setup.

Pictures in Cards

You can include pictures in cards by pasting them from other programs such as Paintbrush. To do this, first copy a picture to the Clipboard using any Windows program's **E**dit **C**opy command. Open or switch to Cardfile, open the file and card you wish to add the picture to, and give the **E**dit Pictur**e** command. You will then see a small rectangle, shown in Figure 13.32. Give the **E**dit **P**aste command to paste the picture from the Clipboard into the card.

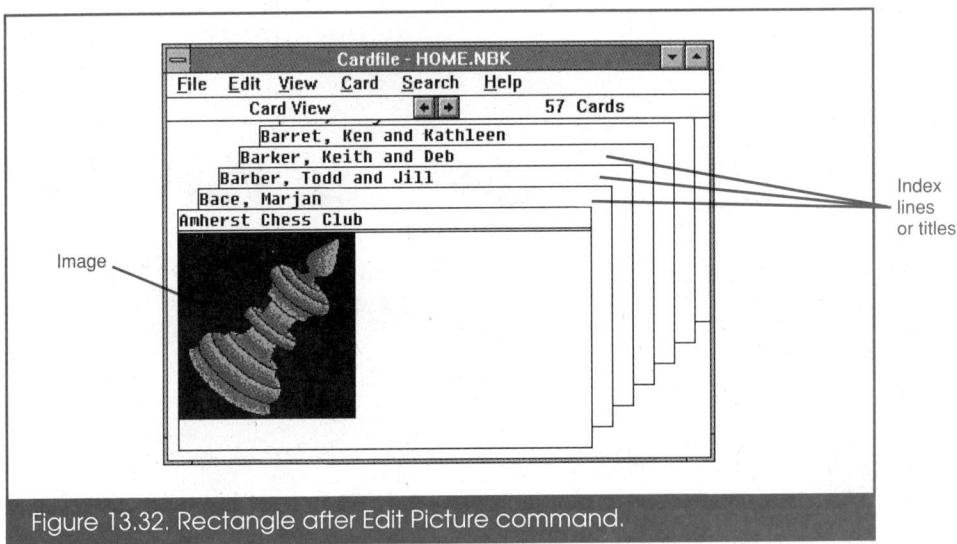

Figure 13.32. Rectangle after Edit Picture command.

Windows 3.1 offers OLE (*o*bject *l*inking and *e*mbedding), a new and fully implemented feature that saves a great deal of time when you want to cut and paste between applications. Essentially, the OLE process enables you to change other pictures you have cut and pasted while you are changing the original picture. If you copy any selected picture to the Clipboard, then paste it into a file currently opened by an application that supports OLE, you can simultaneously change the pasted picture as you make changes to the original.

To get a feel for the power of this new feature, follow these simple steps (note that these steps involve the use of Paintbrush, discussed in Chapter 11, "Paintbrush"):

1. Open Paintbrush as you normally do.

2. Open Cardfile as you normally do.

13

3. Arrange both application windows so that you can see them on-screen at the same time.

4. Open any file in Cardfile, or make a new file with one card in it.

5. Click Paintbrush again and give the **F**ile **O**pen command.

6. Select the PARTY.BMP file from the **F**ile **O**pen dialog box. You see the bitmap pasted into the Paintbrush workspace.

7. Select the rectangular cut tool from the Paintbrush dialog box.

8. Use the mouse pointer to select an area of the picture by dragging all or a portion of the bitmap to any size you want.

9. Select **E**dit **C**opy from the **E**dit menu in Paintbrush.

The following steps involve the use of Cardfile:

10. Click any area of the Cardfile window.

11. Place the insertion point wherever you want and select **E**dit **Pictur**e.

12. Select **E**dit Paste **L**ink from the Cardfile menu.

13. The bitmap PARTY.BMP is pasted below and to the right of the Cardfile insertion point.

The following steps involve the use of Paintbrush:

14. Click the Paintbrush workspace area to activate Paintbrush and deactivate Cardfile.

15. Again, use the cut tool to select a portion of the bitmap image. This time, for best results (and the sake of this little demonstration), select only a section of the center of the bitmap.

16. Select **E**dit Cu**t** from the Paintbrush menu.

OLE automatically updates the picture in Cardfile to reflect the changes you made to the same image in Paintbrush. Both applications involved in this process must be able to use OLE.

Imagine how useful OLE could be if you needed to make last-minute changes to an image already inserted into a finished, time-sensitive PageMaker document. (PageMaker is a desktop publishing program.) PageMaker cannot make many of the changes that need to be made to images; these changes must be made with the application that created the picture, such as CorelDRAW! or Micrographics Designer. Imagine if the image were inserted into the PageMaker document in several places, as in the recurring page header of a newsletter. OLE can save a

great deal of work by helping you change images inserted into documents that are open in other running programs. You simply change the image with the original creation program. After pasting an image in the card, you can drag the picture anywhere in the card with the mouse or use the direction keys to position it. To lock the picture in place, give the **E**dit Te**x**t command.

Viewing Just Indexes

Windows 3.0 calls the heading line at the top of your cards Titles. Windows 3.1 refers to the top line as the Index line. The **V**iew Menu enables you to choose how you see your cards. The **V**iew **L**ist command changes the cards to list mode (see Figure 13.33). The List mode shows you a list of only the Index lines. This mode is a quick way to see an alphabetical list of your cards, but because you cannot see the information in the cards, it is not used often.

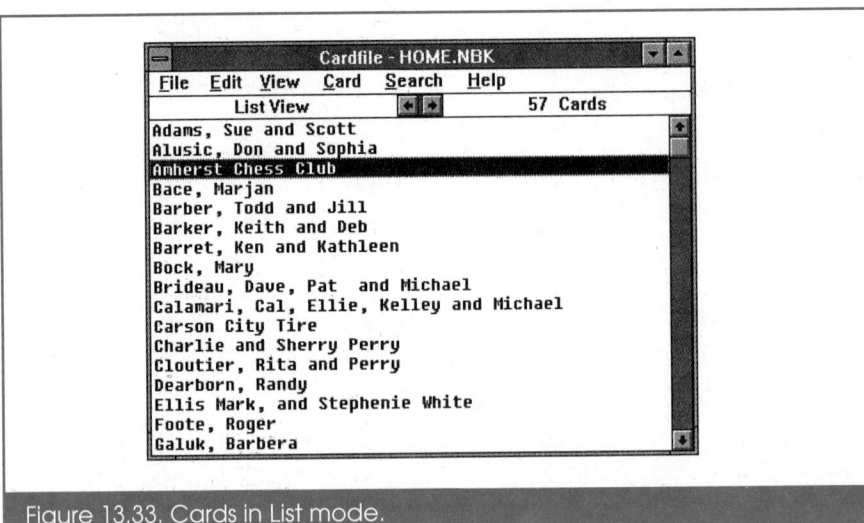

Figure 13.33. Cards in List mode.

Recorder

The Windows Recorder program is a simple accessory that enables you to create your own programs. The Windows Recorder will only launch DOS-based applications. The Recorder cannot preform tasks within

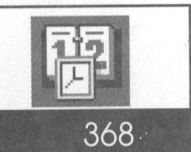

DOS-based applications. These small programs, called *macros,* may be as simple as the characters in a name and address block or as complex as a series of commands to open and transfer data between applications. You create these programs by storing the keystrokes you use to run your applications.

Recorder is extremely simple to use, but not very powerful. With some practice and patience, however, you can create macros to simplify and standardize some of your regular computer tasks.

> **Tip:** Other macro recorders are available. See Chapter 30, "Windows for Advanced Users," for more information on commercial macro recorders.

13

Why Use Macros?

By design, Recorder is best at automating simple, short tasks. Although you can create extremely long macros (64K is the limit), you cannot edit them, view them, or fix them. The following are some suggested applications in which you may want to write your own small macros:

- ▲ Projects in which you need to switch between devices, such as between a laser printer and an impact printer. Instead of having to work your way through the setup dialog boxes each time you switch, you simply record the sequence as a macro once, and then run the macro to do the task for you.

- ▲ Transferring data. If you routinely write telephone messages in Notepad and transfer them to a large database or Cardfile, you can use a macro to do the job.

- ▲ For certain projects, you may want to set up your desktop with tiled windows or some other combination of options. This can be done once and stored as a macro. Then you can run that macro to re-create the desktop when you need it.

- ▲ You can use macros to store standard blocks of text, such as address blocks, company logos, and so on, and then play them back, or paste them into other application's documents.

What Recorder Can Do

Recorder's major features include the following:

- ▲ One macro can open and run another macro. You can link as many as five macros into one large one.

- ▲ You can program demonstrations that play back continuously. You can even select whether these demos can be interrupted by a simple command or stopped only by turning off the computer.

- ▲ Recorder can record all the movements and clicks of the mouse— but using this method is not a good idea. When you include mouse movements in a macro, any change in the window size, position, or even the screen resolution can make the macro run (play back) with unpredictable results. Fortunately, you can use an Alt-*alpha* (Alt plus a letter key) key combination to activate any Windows command menus.

What Recorder Cannot Do

Recorder is easy to use because its capabilities are strictly limited. Some of Recorder's limitations include the following:

- ▲ Macros do not run with non-Windows applications. Therefore, you can create macros only for Windows applications such as Windows Write and Windows Terminal, or Windows-based applications such as Microsoft Excel and Microsoft Word for Windows.

- ▲ You cannot edit a macro after you have created it. The macro works very much like a filmstrip loop that you can play back but cannot change. Because of this "feature," you should break complex macros into a series of simpler and smaller macros that you can isolate and replace.

- ▲ With Recorder (unlike some other macro packages), you cannot view the individual steps in a macro or move step-by-step through the macro.

- ▲ Macros cannot be paused to wait for you to enter data from the keyboard or to make a menu selection. You can work around this by breaking the task into several small macros. Run the first macro, which will end at an insertion point where you can enter the needed information. Then run the second macro.

An Example of Using Recorder

The best way to understand what Recorder can do for you is to look at a practical example. Here, Alicia Jacobs, owner of a bookstore, uses Recorder to create and print a notice to a customer that the book he or she ordered has arrived and is ready to be picked up. When the books arrive, Alicia needs to send a personalized letter to notify the customer. Because she must do this several times a day, she uses the Recorder application to save time. Without using Recorder, Alicia would have to open the Cardfile and Windows Write applications and switch back and forth between them. By using Recorder, she has to do this only once.

The first task is to create a form-letter document in Write. Save the file (see Figure 13.34) in a directory as RESRVLTR.WRI.

13

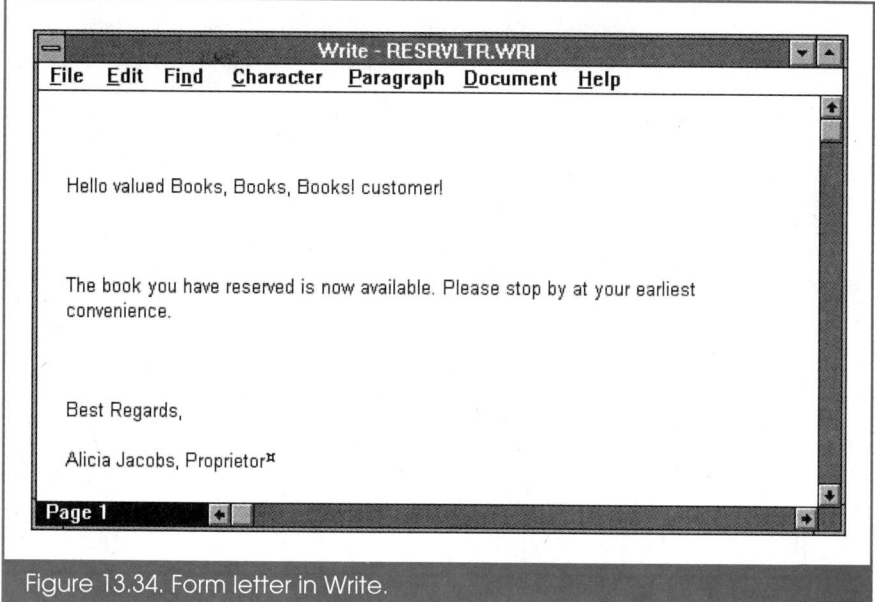

Figure 13.34. Form letter in Write.

Next, she creates a Cardfile file with the names and addresses of customers and the books they have ordered (see Figure 13.35).

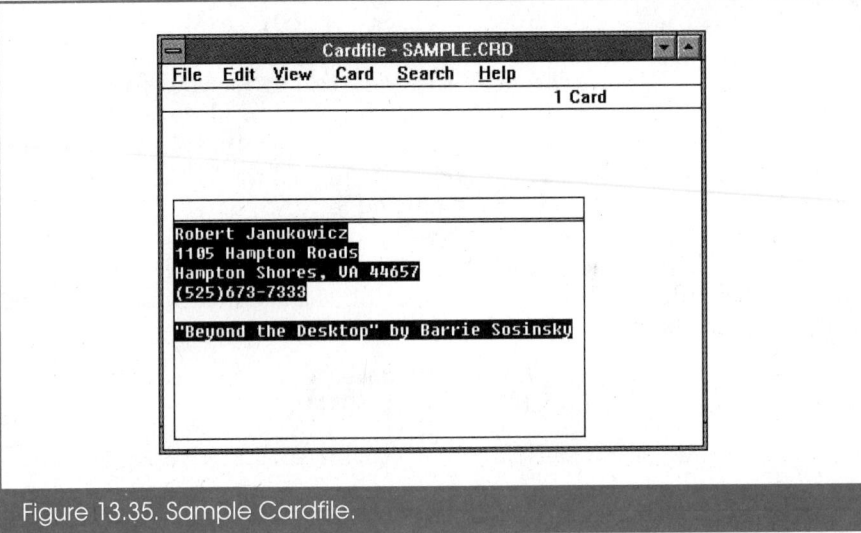

Figure 13.35. Sample Cardfile.

Preparing to Record a Macro

To create a macro that will copy information from Cardfile into a standard letter format and then print the letter, she uses the following steps:

1. Open the Cardfile and select the card with the customer's name and book order.

2. Select the customer's name, address, and book title.

3. Go to the Applications window in Program Manager.

4. Run Recorder.

5. Select **M**acro Re**c**ord. The **M**acro Re**c**ord dialog box is shown in Figure 13.36.

6. Under Record Macro **N**ame, give the macro a name you can recognize easily, such as "Your book order is ready." The name can have as many as 40 characters.

7. In the Shortcut **K**ey entry, type the letter **B** (for book) and select Ctrl.

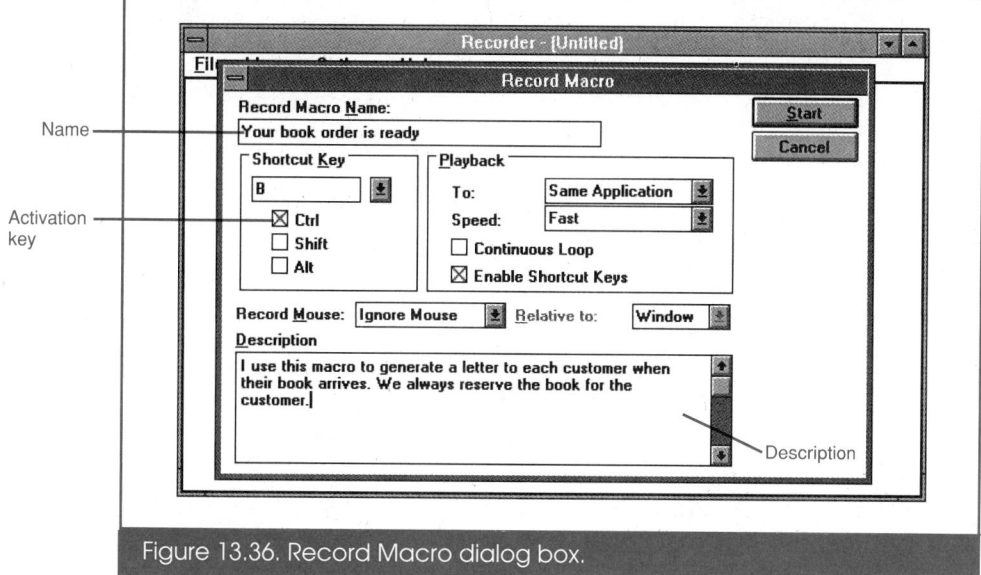

Name ——

Activation key ——

Description

Figure 13.36. Record Macro dialog box.

Tip: When you assign shortcut keys, do not use combinations with Alt and another key. Because Windows uses Alt and another key to access its own functions, Windows might run its own function rather than the macro you expected.

8. In the **P**layback section, choose Same Application for the To option (because this macro runs only from Cardfile) and Fast for the Speed option.

9. Select Enable Shortcut keys. This option lets you specify custom shortcut keys to be used in executing your macro.

10. In the Record **M**ouse section, select Ignore Mouse. This option ensures that no actions or selections made by the mouse are recorded in the macro.

11. In the **D**escription text box, tell what the macro does and which files are required. Alicia might type a long description here.

13

Tip: Although you may find it easier to skip over the description while you are creating a macro, a sentence or two describing the files used and where to find them can spare you from a great deal of searching later. Also, writing a detailed description is good practice and will be appreciated when other people try to use your macros. If many people are developing macros on your particular computer, you may want to design a standard format indicating who wrote it, what it does, which files are required, and any warnings.

12. Click the **Start** button to start recording the macro. The Recorder icon flashes at the bottom of the screen.

Warning: Be sure not to use the mouse until you stop recording. Because you selected Ignore Mouse, the macro will not record any actions activated by the mouse. Use the Alt-key combinations to select and run all commands.

Recording Actions

Because the recorder is now on, all actions you take become part of your macro. Be careful to record only those actions you want to repeat.

1. To return to Cardfile, bring up the Task List window (see Figure 13.37) by pressing Ctrl-Esc. Then choose Cardfile by typing the letter c and pressing Enter.

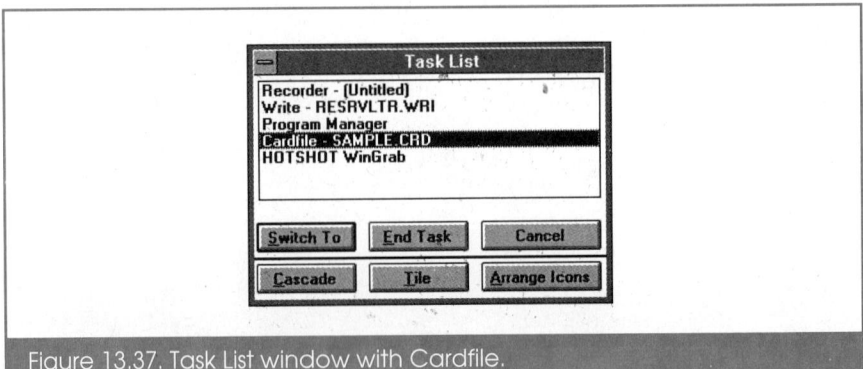

Figure 13.37. Task List window with Cardfile.

2. The Cardfile window comes to the front, with the text selected earlier still highlighted. Give the **E**dit **C**opy command to copy the data.

3. Press Ctrl-Esc to bring up the Task List window, select Program Manager by typing **p**, then press Enter.

4. To open the form letter, give the **F**ile **R**un command. Enter the following in the text box provided:

   ```
   C:\WINDOWS\WRITE.EXE \LETTERS\RESRVLTR.WRI
   ```

5. Click on the OK button and to run Write which also opens the letter.

6. To paste the data copied from Cardfile, give the **E**dit **P**aste command. The letter is now ready to be printed.

7. Print the letter by issuing the **F**ile **P**rint command.

The macro recording is now done. Stop the macro by pressing Ctrl-Break. When the Macro Recording Suspended dialog box appears, as in Figure 13.38, select the **S**ave Macro option button. If you make a mistake during the procedure, you can choose **C**ancel Recording. Note, however, that selecting the **C**ancel Recording option button erases the entire macro—you will have to start over. You can select the **R**esume Recording option button if you are not finished recording at this time.

13

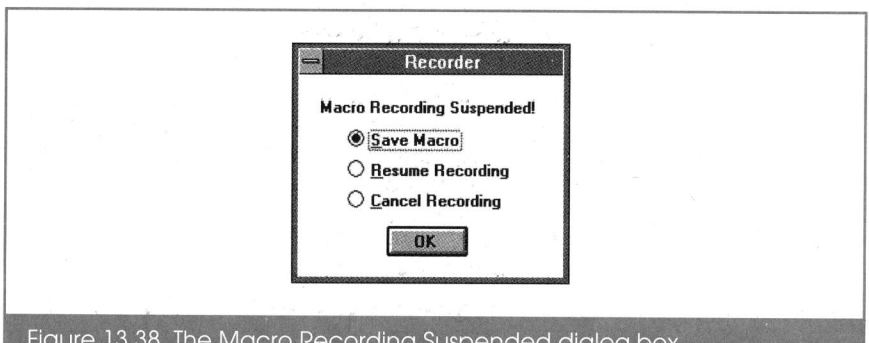

Figure 13.38. The Macro Recording Suspended dialog box.

Steps After Recording

Now that you have finished recording your macro, you need to clean up. In this case, you want to close the Write window. Do not save the newly

inserted data in RESRVLTR, because you will use RESRVLTR as a template. Because you are no longer recording, you can use the mouse again if you want to.

You also need to save the macro you have recorded to disk. Double-click the Recorder icon (still displayed at the bottom of the screen) and give the **F**ile **S**ave or **F**ile Save **As** command to open the **F**ile Save **As** dialog box shown in Figure 13.39. Give the macro file a name. (Recorder automatically adds the extension .REC.) You can use this file to store other macros also.

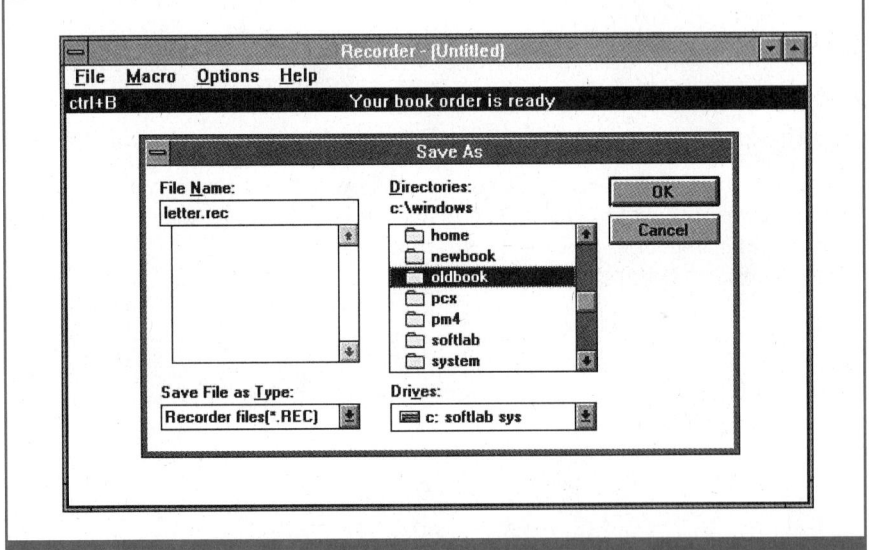

Figure 13.39. File Save As dialog box.

Running a Macro

Running a macro is easy. First, set up the environment for the macro by selecting the right text and so on. Open Recorder, then open the necessary macro file (if it is not open already). Then run the macro by selecting the macro you want and giving the **M**acro **R**un command or by pressing the macro's key combination.

In the case of the macro Alicia recorded, for example, the following steps run the macro:

1. Open Cardfile, select the appropriate card, and highlight the customer, address, and book title.

2. Click the Program Manager window and open Recorder.

3. Give the **F**ile **O**pen command and select the LETTERS.REC macro if that is not the current macro file.

4. Press Ctrl-Esc to bring up the Task List window. Type **c** for Cardfile and press Enter.

5. Press Ctrl-B.

The macro opens the Write template, inserts the data from Cardfile, and then prints the letter.

Special Key Combinations

You can assign a macro to any of the keys on the keyboard, not just the alphanumeric key set. To assign a macro to these other keys, use the drop-down list in the Shortcut **K**ey section of the **M**acro Re**c**ord dialog box (see Figure 13.40). This list includes all the nonalphanumeric keys (such as Home, Caps Lock, and function keys, F1 through F16).

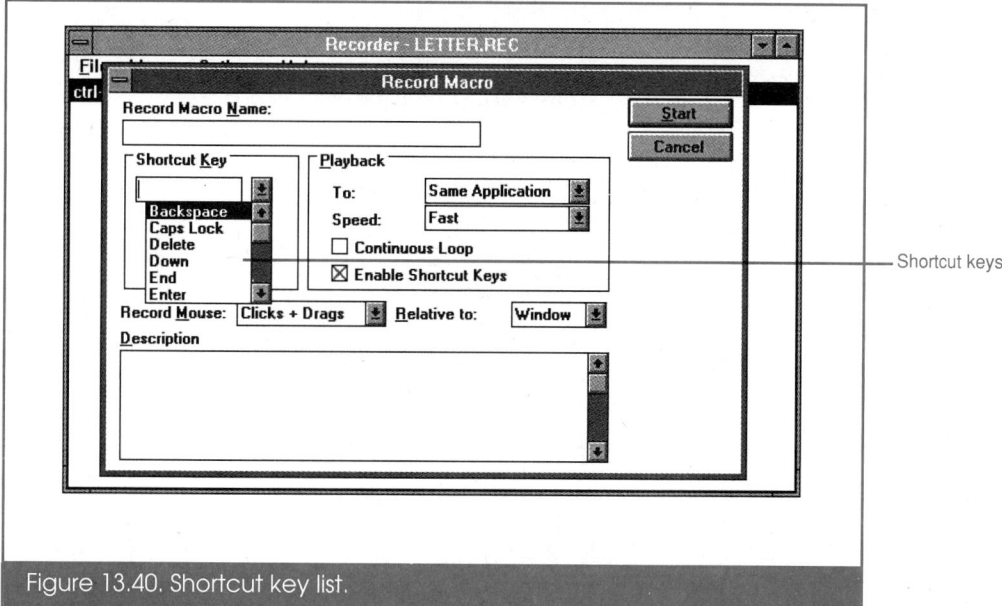

Figure 13.40. Shortcut key list.

Be careful not to reassign to a macro any function key you use for other purposes. Table 13.4 lists three key combinations you should not use.

Table 13.4. Recorder key combinations not to use for macros.

Key	Use
Ctrl-Break	Stops macro recording
Ctrl-Esc	Brings up the Task List
Alt-Esc	Brings up the Switch To function

Managing Macro Files

Collections of individual macros are stored in files with the .REC extension. They act like any other file in Windows. You can create new ones and open, save, or delete them, but Recorder will not let you edit them.

You also can merge .REC files with the **F**ile **M**erge command. When you merge files, be sure that the same shortcut keys have not been assigned in both files; if they have, Recorder will remove them from the second file. If the files do have duplicate keys, rename one set before you merge the two files. If you do not do this, the macros are not deleted, but you can run them only by name, through the **M**acro **R**un command. To merge two Recorder macro files, open the first macro, give the **F**ile **M**erge command (see Figure 13.41), select the second file to be merged, and click OK.

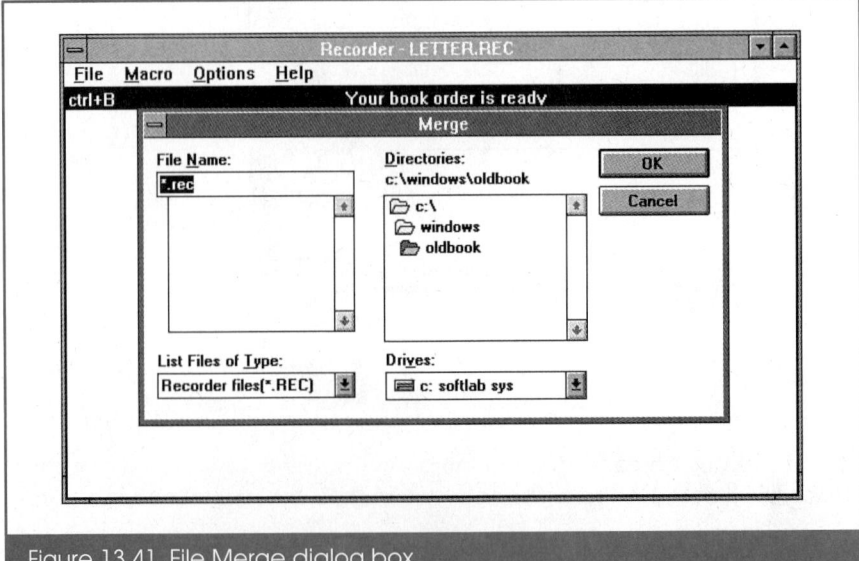

Figure 13.41. File Merge dialog box.

Macro Properties

After you have recorded a macro, you can alter its properties with the **Macro Properties** command, shown in Figure 13.42. From this dialog box, you can control the filename to save, shortcut key, and playback options. Note that you cannot change how the mouse properties are used, as you could when you recorded the macro.

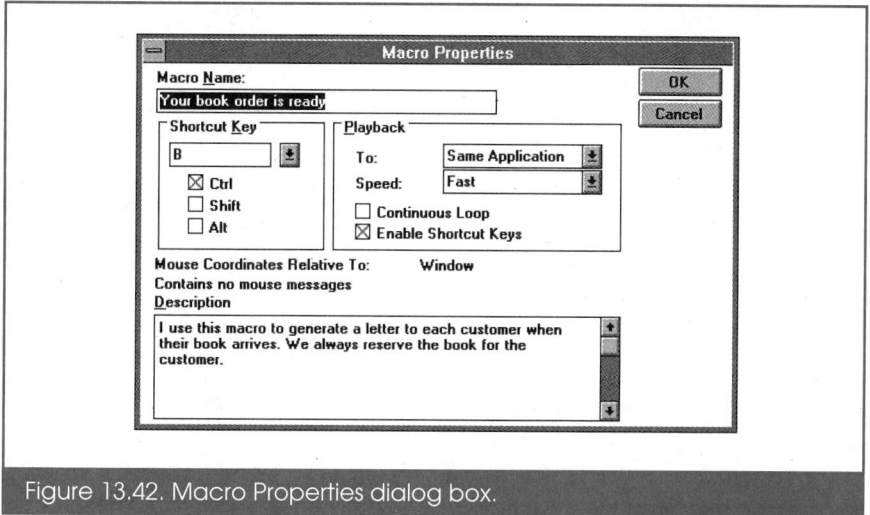

Figure 13.42. Macro Properties dialog box.

13

Options

The **O**ptions menu, shown in Figure 13.43, controls important features that affect how you record and play back macros.

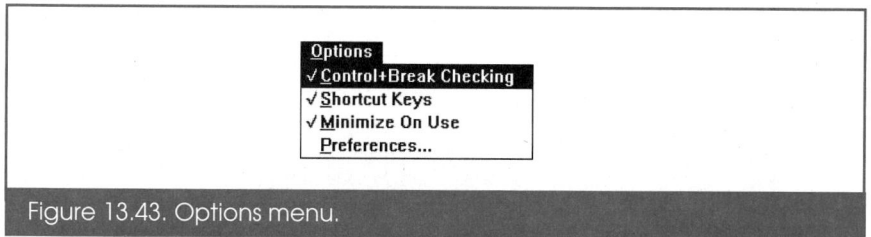

Figure 13.43. Options menu.

If you select the **C**ontrol+Break Checking option, you can stop a macro while it is running by pressing Ctrl-Break. This feature can stop a runaway macro and is particularly useful when you first start using Recorder.

The **S**hortcut Keys option enables you to run a macro by using a short key sequence instead of having to choose the macro by name from the Recorder .REC file. This is almost always what you want. When the **M**inimize On Use option is selected, the Recorder window shrinks to an icon when you run a macro.

The **O**ptions **P**references command opens the Options Default Preferences dialog box, shown in Figure 13.44, which enables you to set defaults for recording new macros. Note that the options contained in the Options Default dialog box do not force new macros to have these properties, but any new macros you create will have those properties automatically set in the **M**acro Re**c**ord dialog box.

Figure 13.44. Options Default Preferences dialog box.

Normally, Recorder plays back the sequence of keystrokes as fast as the computer can execute them. But when you are running a demonstration, you may want the viewer to see the sequence of events, and you will need time between actions. You can run a macro at your system's best speed, or you can run a macro at the speed at which it was recorded. Use the Macro Properties dialog box to select Recorded Speed from the Playback Speed drop-down list. The macro will then play back at the speed at which you entered it. If you waited 25 seconds on the first screen of a demo before bringing up the second screen, for example, the macro waits 25 seconds before bringing up the second screen when the macro is played back. To make the demonstration repeat in a continuous loop, select Continuous Loop in the **M**acro Re**c**ord dialog box.

Calculator

Calculator is a surprisingly handy program. Although many people dismiss the Calculator program because it seems to be little more than a cheap hand-held calculator, the program is very useful.

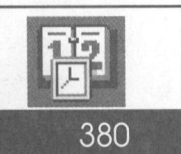

Note: When you see the term *standard mode* mentioned in this text, do not confuse it with Windows's standard operating mode. The word *standard* is meant to label or convey the concept of a normal or standard calculator—one with which you probably are familiar.

Figure 13.45 shows the Calculator program as it starts. When you give the **V**iew **S**cientific command, however, you get a much more complete calculator, shown in Figure 13.46. It is not clear why Microsoft hid scientific mode, because this mode has more features.

13

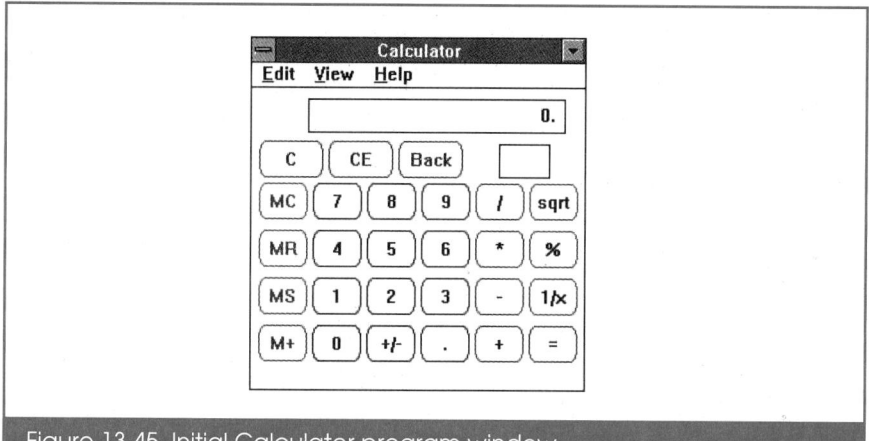

Figure 13.45. Initial Calculator program window.

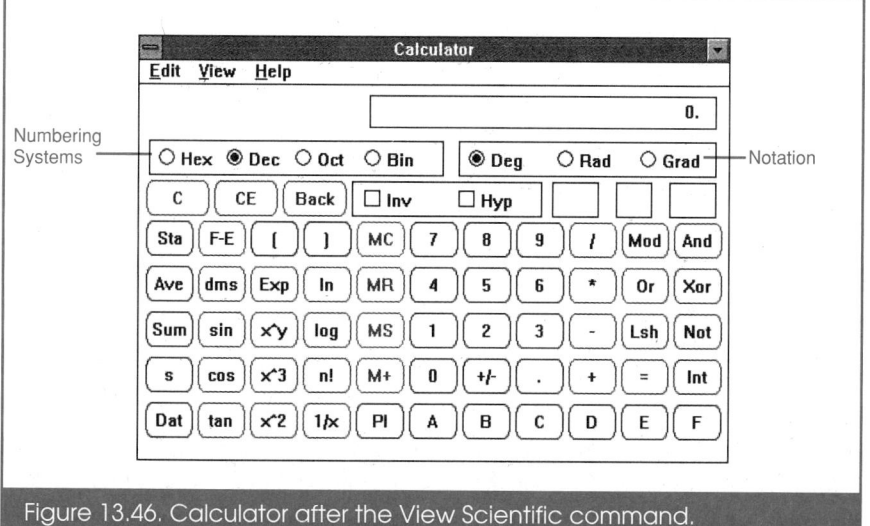

Figure 13.46. Calculator after the View Scientific command.

Performing Calculations in Standard Mode

In Standard Mode, you perform calculations as you would with a standard calculator. You can click the buttons or use the keyboard, as shown in Table 13.5. Note that if you want to enter numbers from the numeric keypad, you must press the Num Lock key first.

Table 13.5. Keyboard equivalents for buttons in Standard mode.

Button	Keyboard Equivalent	Description
C	Esc	Clears current calculation.
CE	Delete	Clears the entry.
Back	←	Backspaces one character in the entry, deleting one character in the string from right to left.
MC	Ctrl-C	Sets memory to 0.
MR	Ctrl-R	Recalls the value in memory.
MS	Ctrl-M	Stores the current value in memory.
M+	Ctrl-P	Adds the current value to memory.
/	/	Division.
*	*	Multiplication.
−	−	Subtraction.
+	+	Addition.
sqrt	@	Square root.
%	%	1/100.
1/x	r	Inverse.
=	= or Enter	Equals.
+/−	F9	Toggles between negative or positive value.
.	. or, depending on your international settings	Inserts decimal separator.

Performing Calculations in Scientific Mode

The functions in the **S**cientific view are similar to those on advanced calculators. Table 13.6 shows the keyboard equivalents and the meanings of the buttons that are different from the ones in **St**andard mode.

Table 13.6. Keyboard equivalents for buttons in Scientific mode.

Button	Keyboard Equivalent	Description
Sta	Ctrl-S	Starts the statistics box, described later in this chapter.
Ave	Ctrl-A	Average.
Sum	Ctrl-T	Total.
s	Ctrl-D	Standard deviation of the population.
Dat	Insert	Inserts current number in statistics box.
F-E	v	Switches between scientific and normal format.
dms	m	Switches between degrees and degrees/minutes/seconds format.
sin	s	Sine.
cos	o	Cosine.
tan	t	Tangent.
(	(	Starts grouping.
Exp	x	Sets exponent. To enter 43x–2, for example, type 43, click Exp or press x, then type –2.
x^y	y	x raised to the y power.
x^3	#	Cube of x.
x^2	@	Square of x.
)	)	Ends a grouping.
ln	n	Natural log.
log	l	Log base 10.

continues

13

Table 13.6. Continued

Button	Keyboard Equivalent	Description
n!	!	Factorial.
PI	p	Pi.
Mod	%	Modulo.
Or	|	Or.
Lsh	<	Binary left shift. In Inv mode, this becomes a binary right shift.
And	&	And.
Xor	^	Exclusive Or.
Not	~	Binary inverse.
Int	;	Integer portion. In Ins mode, this becomes the fractional portion.

Number Systems

Calculator can handle numbers in four formats in each of these number systems:

▲ Hexadecimal

▲ Decimal

▲ Octal

▲ Binary

To convert a number from one format to another, select the first format, enter the number, and then enter the format you want. To enter hexadecimal numbers, you can use the letter buttons in the bottom row or the equivalent letters on the keyboard.

If you choose decimal notation, the second set of buttons enables you to choose a notation for trigonometric functions. You can choose to show numbers in degrees, radians, or gradients. In the other three notations, you use the second set of buttons to show the numbers in three forms:

▲ Dword shows the number as a 13-bit form

▲ Word shows the lower 16 bits

▲ Byte shows the lower 8 bits

Table 13.7 shows the keyboard equivalents of the number system buttons.

Table 13.7. Keyboard equivalents of number system buttons.

Button	Key	Notes
Hex	F5	
Dec	F6	
Oct	F7	
Bin	F8	
Deg	F2	Works only on decimal mode.
Rad	F3	Works only on decimal mode.
Grad	F4	Works only on decimal mode.
Dword	F2	
Word	F3	
Byte	F4	

13

Statistics

Because statistics manipulate groups of numbers, Calculator needs to collect numbers before it can act on them. To collect numbers, click the Sta key to see the Statistics Box, shown in Figure 13.47.

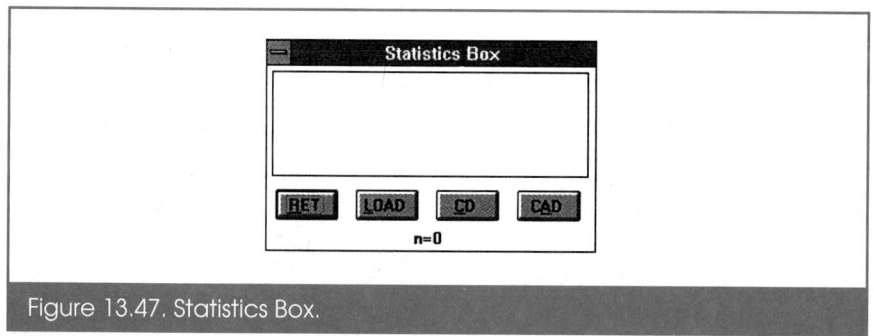

Figure 13.47. Statistics Box.

To enter a number in the statistics group, enter it in the main Calculator window and click Dat. Clear the number with the CE button, enter

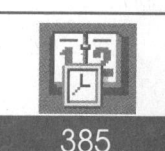

the next value, click Dat, and so on. When you click Sta, you see the numbers entered into the Statistics Box, as shown in Figure 13.48.

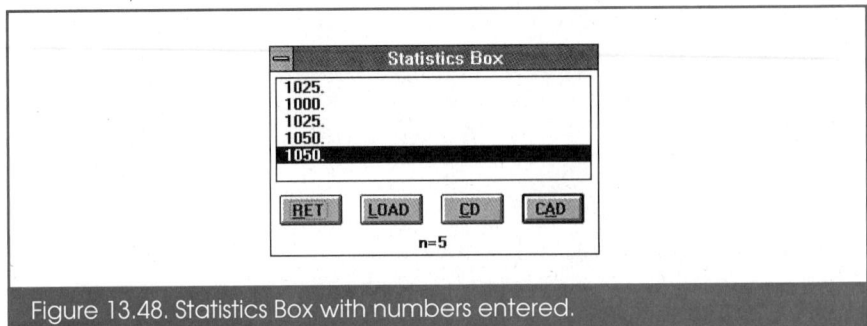

Figure 13.48. Statistics Box with numbers entered.

The four buttons in the Statistics Box enable you to control how it works, as described in Table 13.8.

Table 13.8. Statistics Box buttons.

Button	Purpose
RET	Brings main Calculator window to the front
LOAD	Makes the number selected in the Statistics Box the current number in the main Calculator window
CD	Clears the number selected in the Statistics Box
CAD	Clears all numbers from the Statistics Box

Inv and Hyp

The Inv and Hyp options change the way many other buttons work. These options are used primarily for the sin, cos, and tan trigonometric functions, to make them inverse and hyperbolic functions. You can turn on these options with the i and h keys, respectively.

The Inv option affects other buttons also. With this option on, the x^2 button calculates the square root, the x^3 button calculates the cube root, and the x^y button calculates the yth root. It also causes the PI button to display 2*pi rather than pi.

Performing Calculations from the Clipboard

You can perform calculations from other Windows programs by putting them into the Clipboard and pasting them into the Calculator. For example, if the Clipboard contains "43.91*17=" and you give the **Edit Paste** command, Calculator calculates the product. Because some characters cannot be put into the Clipboard, you must use the character equivalents shown in Table 13.9.

Table 13.9. Equivalents for keys from the Clipboard.

Button	Clipboard Character
MC	C
MR	R
MS	M
M+	P
C	Q
Dat	\

13

Clock

Clock is a simple program that shows the time as a standard analog or digital clock. It shows the time when the clock is in a window and when it is minimized to an icon.

The analog version is shown in Figure 13.49, with the digital version in Figure 13.50. You can switch between the two with the **S**ettings **A**nalog and **S**ettings **D**igital commands. And you can open the control menu from the clock display window to select Always on **T**op, an option that keeps the Windows Clock visible and on top of any number of layers of windows or icons.

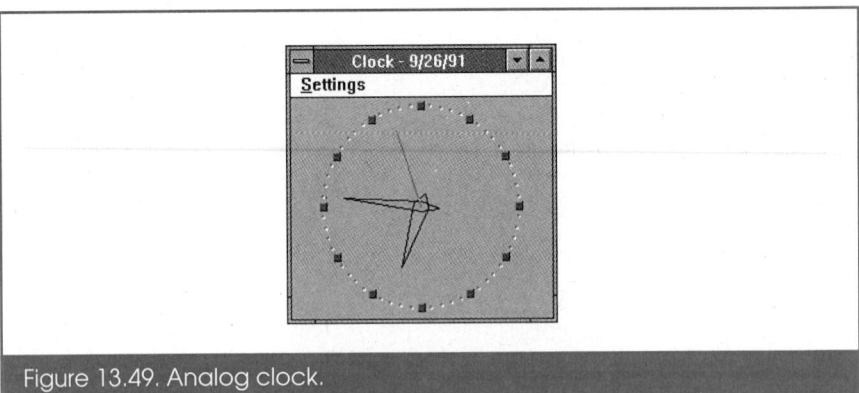

Figure 13.49. Analog clock.

Figure 13.50. Digital clock.

On the digital clock only, the font can be changed as well. Simply select Set **F**ont from the Clock **S**ettings menu to see the Font dialog box. Select a font, review it in the sample text box, and click the OK button when you find one you like.

With the **N**o Title option on the **S**ettings menu you can enable or disable the title bar and menu when the clock is displayed. You also can select or deselect the date and seconds display options to suit your taste. The Clock will be colored according to the colors you have selected for your windows, window borders, and so on. Clock provides you with no independent way of customizing colors for the clock displays.

Tip: If you want a small clock displayed at all times, you can copy the clock icon to the Startup group window and check the Minimize check box for that icon in the File Properties dialog box. You can run the clock as a minimized icon by inserting a command on the `load=` line of your WIN.INI file, or you can place it in your Startup group window in Program Manager. This action also loads Clock as an icon that still keeps time if you have checked the Run Minimized check box in the File Properties dialog box in Program Manager. See Chapter 27, "Configuring with the WIN.INI and SYSTEM.INI Files," for more information on changing the WIN.INI file.

13

Minesweeper

Windows 3.1 includes a new game called Minesweeper. The idea is to use your "foot" (the click of the mouse) to "step" on various squares, until you have discovered where all the bombs are. If you step on a bomb, the game is over and you lose. The number of bombs (and the size of the mine field) is determined by the level at which you play (beginner, intermediate, or expert). You can even create your own custom mine field. The minesweeper screen is shown in Figure 13.51.

The trick in playing Minesweeper is to figure out where all the bombs are without stepping on one or using too much time. When you step (click with the left mouse button) on a square, one of three things happens:

▲ A bomb appears and you lose.

▲ A number from 1-7 appears.

▲ Several surrounding blank squares appear, the exposed area being bordered by either bombs or squares with numbers.

If the square shows a number, it indicates that there are exactly that number of bombs in the surrounding squares. For example, in Figure 13.51, the square with the number 2 indicates that there are two bombs in one of the eight squares that touch it. Combining that knowledge with the numbers shown in other squares can give you an idea of where the bombs must be.

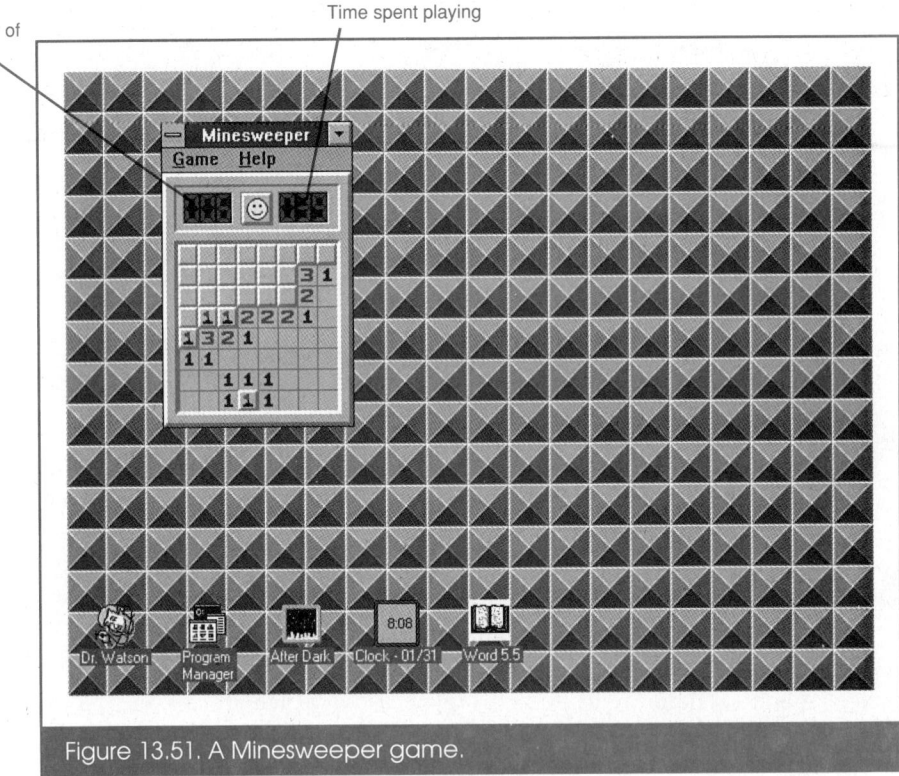

Figure 13.51. A Minesweeper game.

Marking Squares and Stepping

To step on a square, simply click the left mouse button. Use the mouse to mark squares to avoid. Listed below are the marking options:

Mark	Meaning	How to mark the square
?	Possible bomb	Double-click with the right mouse button.
Flag	Definite bomb	Click once with the right mouse button.

If you are not certain about a square, mark it with a question mark. Once you have uncovered enough of the surrounding squares, place either a flag on that square, or remove the question mark by double-clicking again, or stepping on the square.

Warning: The number of bombs will be reduced by using the flag marker, even if there is not a bomb located there.

Setting the Playing Levels

You can set the different playing levels with the **G**ame menu, shown in Figure 13.52.

13

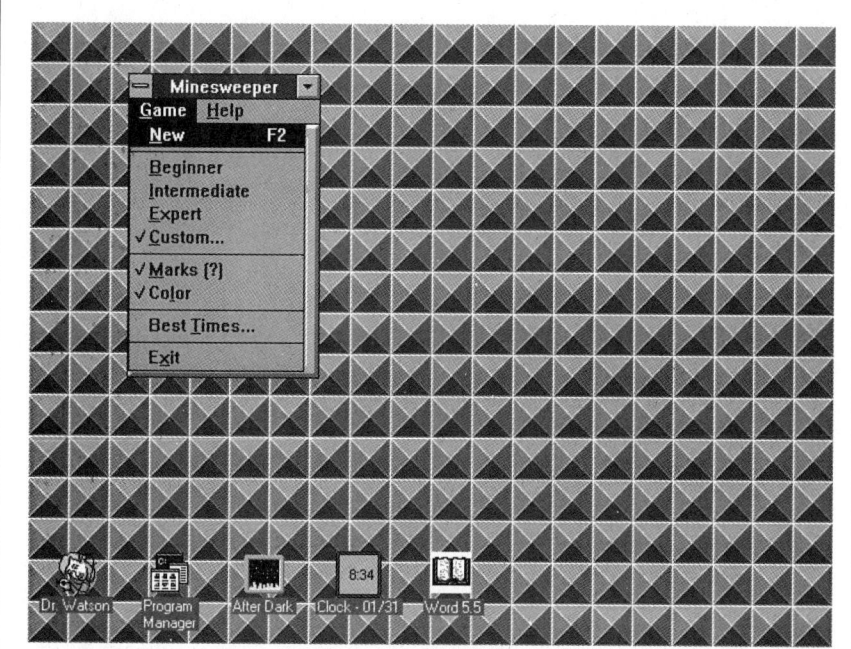

Figure 13.52. The Game menu.

Choose from **B**eginner, **I**ntermediate, **E**xpert, or **C**ustom. A brief description of each option is shown below.

Mines		Size of Playing Area
Beginner	10	8 x 8
Intermediate	40	16 x 16
Expert	99	16 x 30
Custom	Set by the user.	Set by the user.

You can also see a list of the best players by using the Best Times command. Figure 13.53 shows Minesweeper at the end of a game.

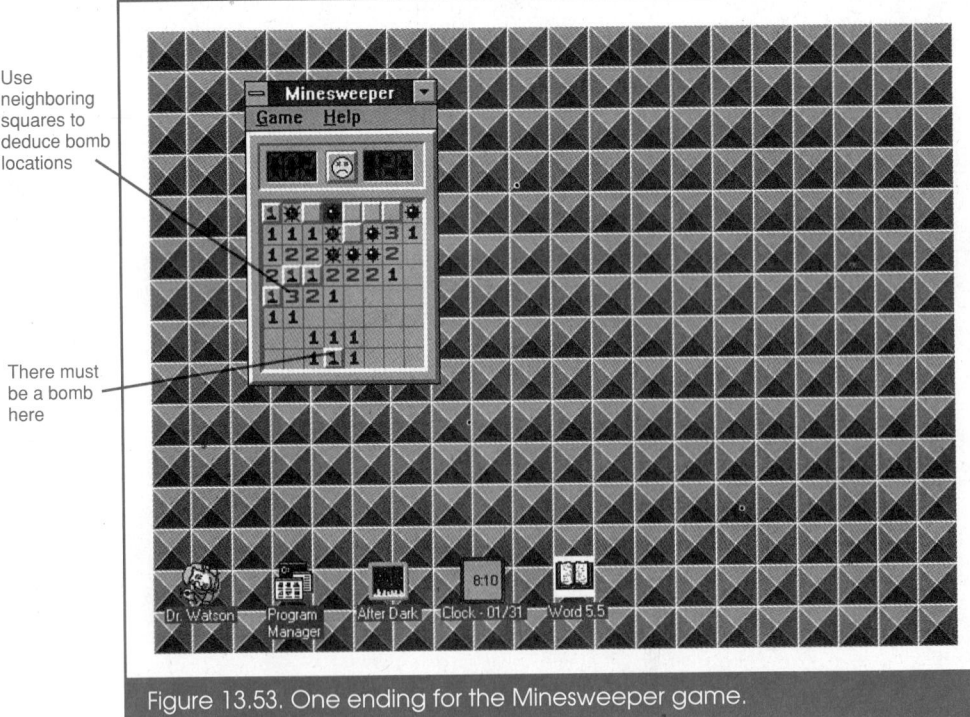

Use neighboring squares to deduce bomb locations

There must be a bomb here

Figure 13.53. One ending for the Minesweeper game.

Solitaire

The Solitaire game enables you to play a standard game of solitaire by yourself. Many people have accused this program of being the most

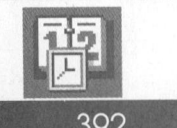

addictive part of Windows. Playing Solitaire is also a great way to become proficient with a mouse. The object of the game is to make stacks of each suit in the suit stacks area at the top of the window, starting with Aces and building up to Kings (see Figure 13.54).

To play the game, you deal cards from the playing deck (by clicking on it), and either place them (if allowed) on the stacks in the deck area, or on the stacks in the table area. Cards placed on the stacks in the table area must alternate from red to black, and must be placed in descending order. To start a game, give the **Game Deal** command.

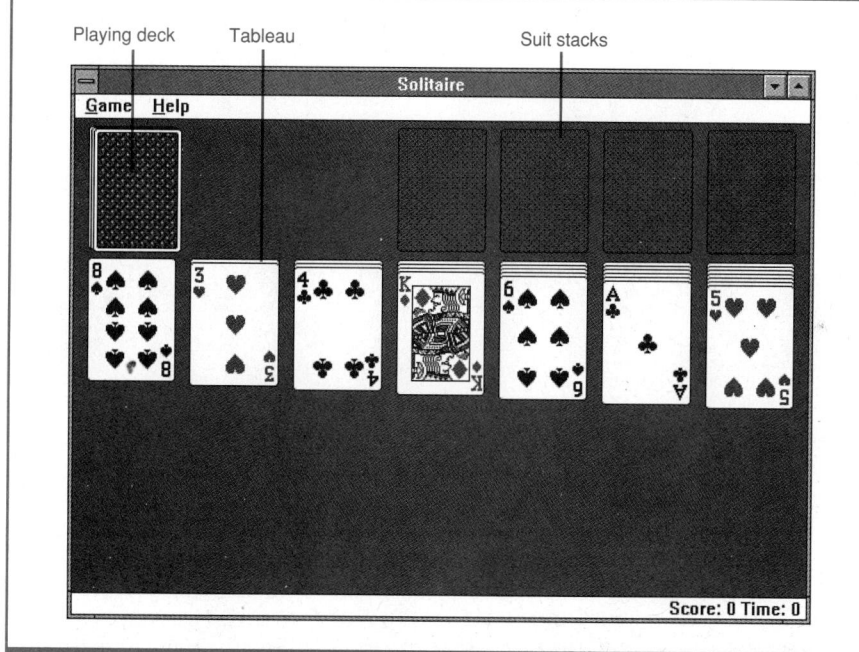

Figure 13.54. Solitaire opening.

To move a card with the mouse, drag it to the desired location. You can drag cards that are not on the top of the stack. To turn over a face-down card, click it.

To move a card with the keyboard, use the ← and → keys to select the card at the bottom of the stack. Press Enter. Then press ← and → again to move to the destination, and press Enter again. You can turn over a face-down card by selecting it and pressing Enter.

Key board

13

Scoring Options Available with Solitaire

Many scoring options are available. The **G**ame **O**ptions command, shown in Figure 13.55, lists the different ways you can play. The **D**raw options tell how many cards are turned over from the deck each time. Table 13.10 lists the **S**coring options.

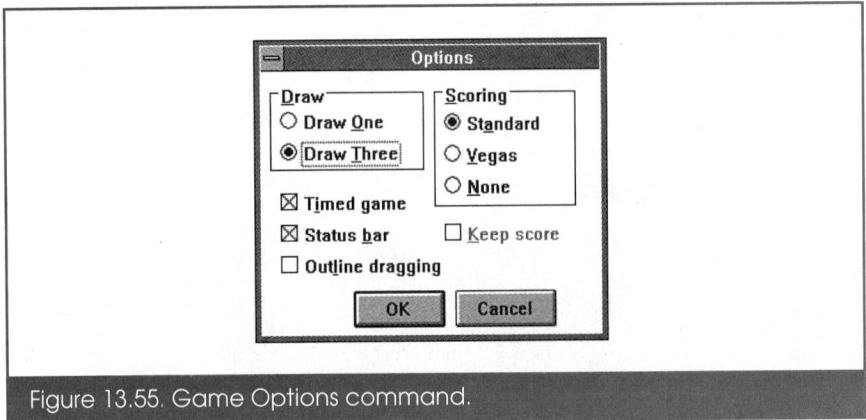

Figure 13.55. Game Options command.

Table 13.10. Scoring options.

Option	Description
Standard	You get 10 points for each card placed on an ace stack, 5 points for each card moved from the deck to the playing field, 15 points for moving a card from the ace stacks back to the playing field, and −15 points for each round through the deck after the first three (in Draw **T**hree) or −100 points for each round through the deck after the first (in Draw **O**ne).
Vegas	You earn $5 for each card moved to an ace stack (each deck costs $2).
None	No scoring

If you want to take your time, deselect the Timed Game option. If you are playing a timed game, you can pause it without a time penalty by minimizing the Solitaire program.

The Status **b**ar option tells you whether to display the status line at the bottom of the window. Turn this option off only if you do not want to follow your progress. The Outline dragging option tells whether you want to see only an outline rather than the card face when you drag cards.

The **G**ame De**c**k command, shown in Figure 13.56, enables you to choose the type of deck you use.

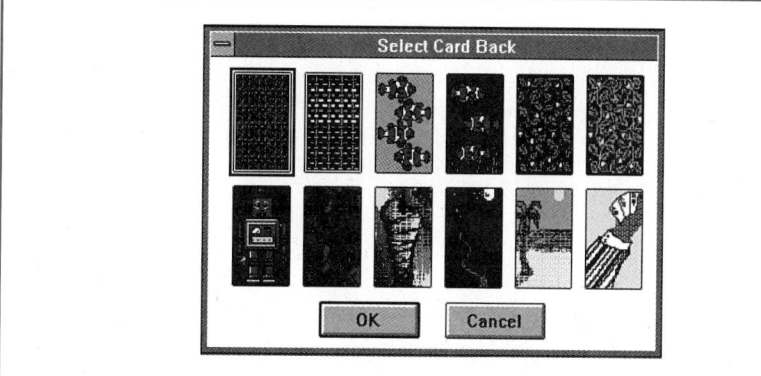

Figure 13.56. Select Card Back dialog box.

13

IV

Using Other Windows Programs

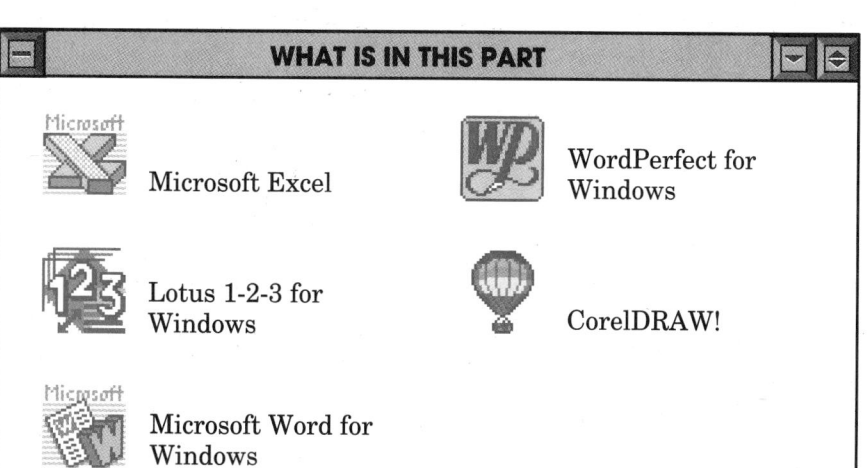

	WHAT IS IN THIS PART		
Microsoft Excel		WordPerfect for Windows	
Lotus 1-2-3 for Windows		CorelDRAW!	
Microsoft Word for Windows			

P A R T

CHAPTER

14

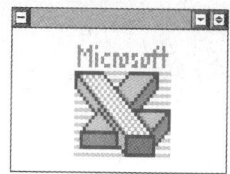

Microsoft Excel

Excel was the first major spreadsheet to run under Windows. Excel's origins are on the Macintosh, where it holds the vast majority of the spreadsheet market for that machine. Since Windows Version 3 was released, Microsoft has had some competition in the Windows spreadsheet market from other major software companies, but Excel Version 3.0 is still the standard against which other Windows spreadsheets must compete.

This chapter describes the parts of Excel that use Windows to its fullest. It is a visual tour of Excel's most important features. Because Excel started as a graphical spreadsheet, it has advantages over spreadsheets that started as character-based and had to have the Windows interface pasted on top. By using Windows's graphics capabilities and advanced linking to other programs, Excel makes analysis and understanding of data much easier.

Tip: Excel relies on the mouse more heavily than Windows in general does or other Windows programs do. In fact, some actions, such as using the tool bar, require you to use the mouse.

Quick Introduction to Excel

When you start Excel, you see a screen like Figure 14.1. As you can see from the window called Sheet1, the Excel program window contains document windows. There are three types of Excel documents: worksheets, charts, and macros.

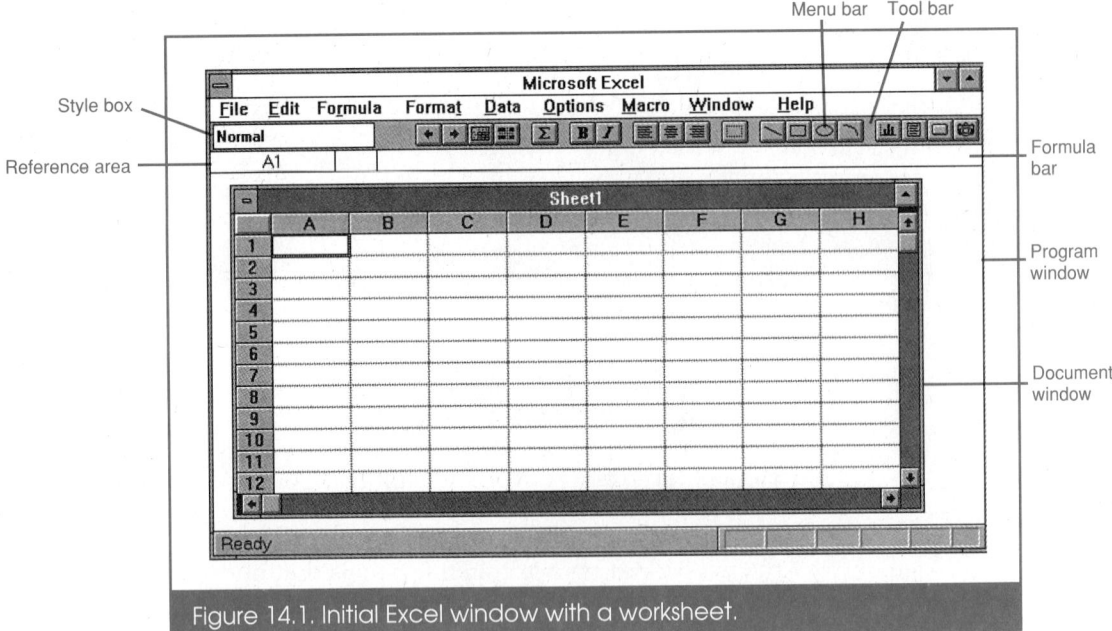

Figure 14.1. Initial Excel window with a worksheet.

Under the menu bar in the Excel program window are two additional lines. The first is the *tool bar,* which consists of a drop-down list of style names and many buttons for common tasks. The next line has the *reference area* and the *formula bar.* Figure 14.2 shows each part of the tool bar, and the following list describes the uses of the tool bar's parts.

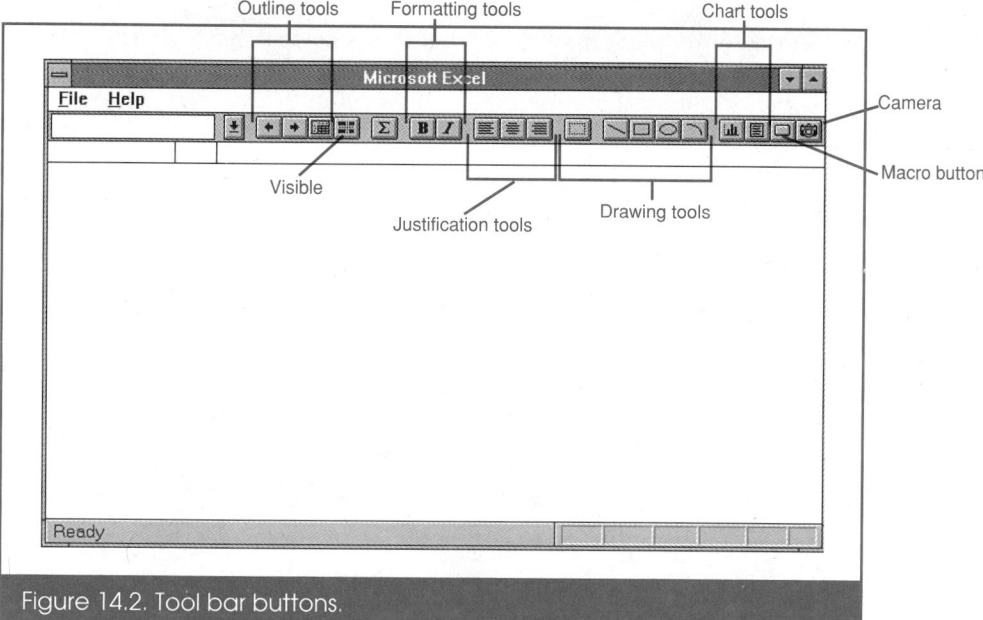

Figure 14.2. Tool bar buttons.

14

Outline tools helps you create an outline of your worksheet data.

Visible cells selects only visible cells, not hidden ones.

Autosum automatically creates a sum of rows or columns based on the location of the current cell.

Formatting tools adds bold and italic to text.

Justification tools aligns text left, right, or center.

Drawing tools draw objects on your worksheets.

Chart tools creates charts from your tools.

Macro button assigns a macro to a button and places that button on your worksheet.

Camera takes a picture of worksheet data or charts and places that picture wherever you like.

Worksheets

A worksheet consists of rows and columns of cells where you enter numbers and text. Columns run down the worksheet and are identified by their column headers, which are letters. Rows run across the worksheet and are identified by their row headers, which are numbers. A cell is identified by the intersection of its column and row. For example, the cell in the third column and the second row is cell C2 because it is in column C and row 2.

Note that the column letters and row numbers in the worksheet window are not just labels. Clicking one of them selects the entire column or row. This makes formatting a block of cells very quick, because most columns and rows hold related information. For example, Figure 14.3 shows column B selected.

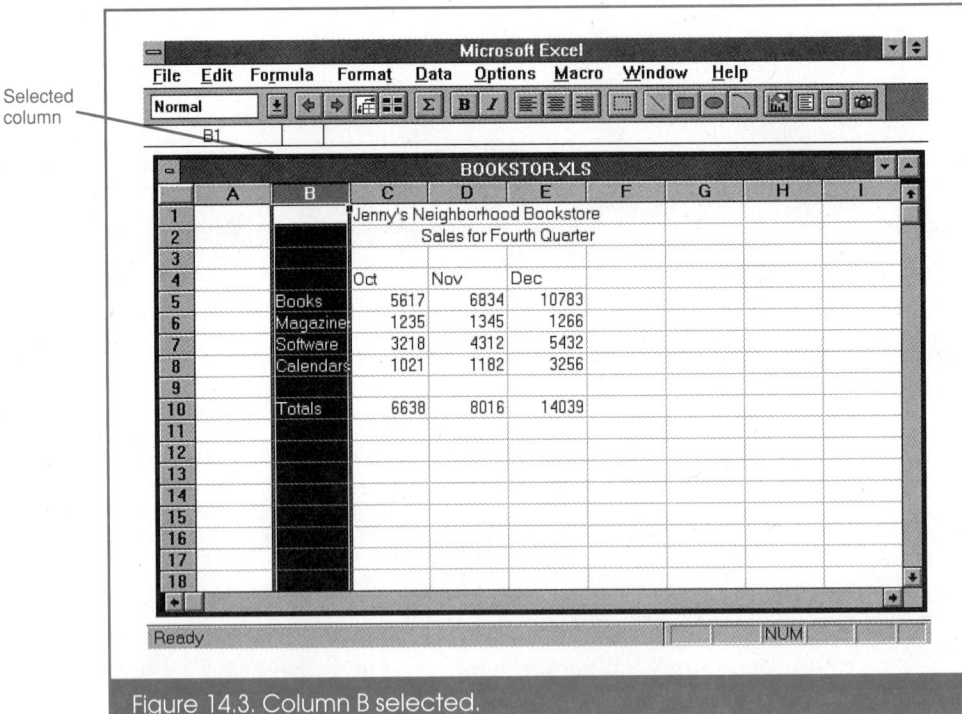

Figure 14.3. Column B selected.

Charts

When you want to see a graphical display of data, you select the data and create a chart. Figure 14.4 shows a typical chart. All the parts of the charts can be customized, as you will see later in this chapter.

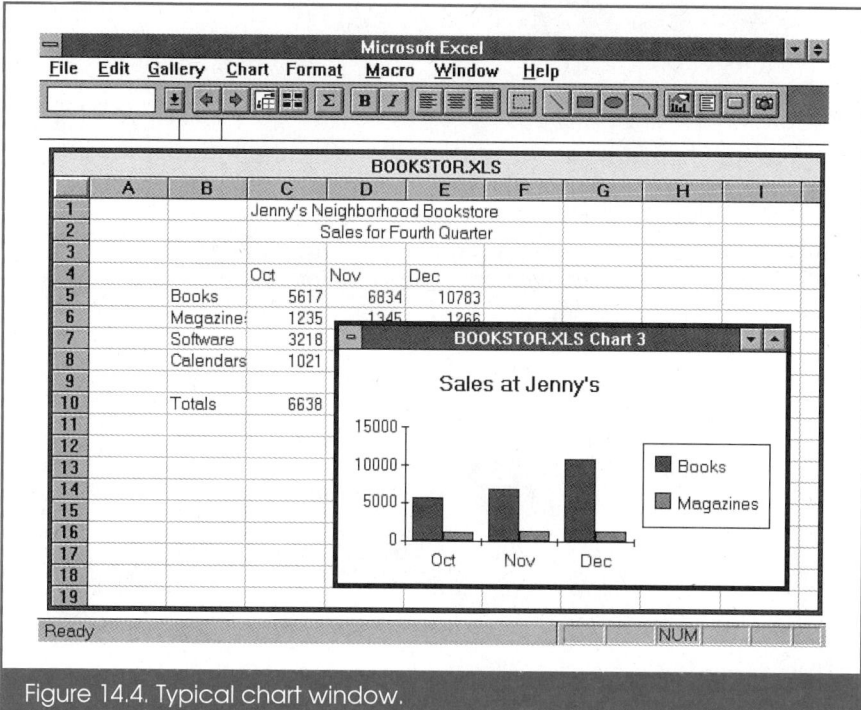

Figure 14.4. Typical chart window.

Note that charts do not have to be in their own windows. You can have a chart in a worksheet, as shown in Figure 14.5. This enables you to see both your figures and the graphical analysis of them at the same time.

Macros

Macros are programs that run within Excel. As you will see later in this chapter, macros can be simple step-savers or complex programs that link Excel with other Windows programs. Macro windows look just like worksheets with rows and columns.

Information in Cells

You can enter whatever you want into cells. The three types of information you can put in Excel cells are the following:

▲ Text

▲ Numbers

▲ Formulas

Text and numbers are fairly easy to figure out, but formulas are where Excel gets its power. A formula enables you to combine the contents of cells in many ways. Without formulas, Excel would be just a table display tool. Because formulas can get quite long, Excel does not try to display them in cells. Instead, only the value or result of the formula appears in the cell; the formula itself appears in the formula bar near the top of the window.

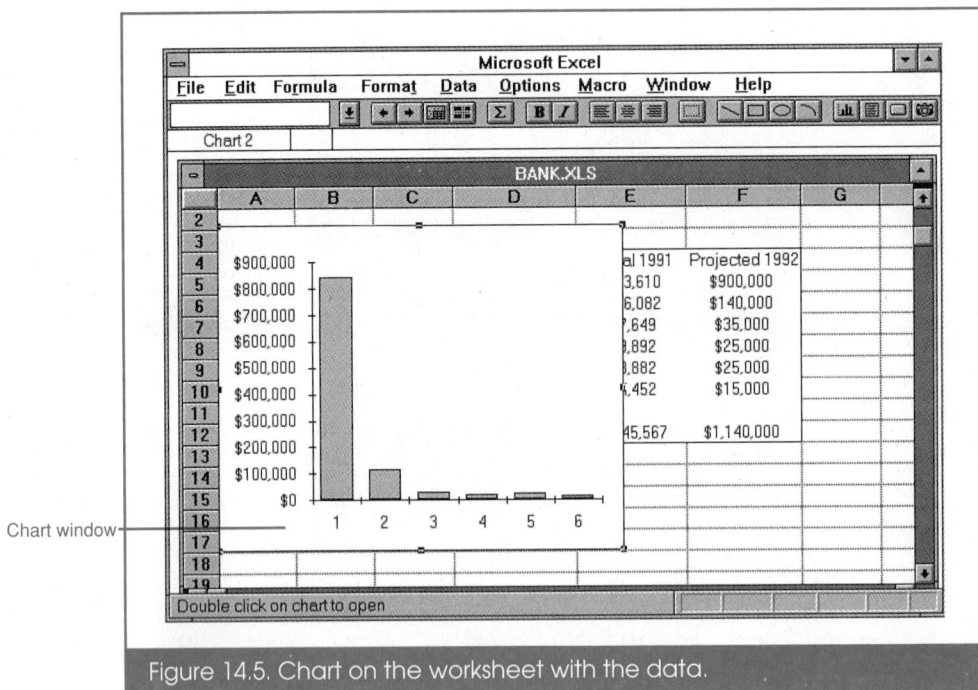

Figure 14.5. Chart on the worksheet with the data.

Numbers

When you enter a number into a cell (or you generate a number from a formula), Excel stores that as a pure number with 15 digits of precision. The number displayed on the screen probably will have fewer digits shown, of course. When it displays a number, Excel looks to the cell's

number formatting to determine how to display that number. Number formatting is described later in this chapter. It is important to remember that the number you see in a worksheet is a representation of a much more accurate number stored internally.

Formulas

When people think of spreadsheets such as Excel, they usually think of the "number-crunching" part—the formulas. Generally, you enter a group of numbers and perform one or more calculations on them. In Excel, you enter formulas into cells just like you enter numbers. The cells show the result of the formula, however, not the formula itself.

Figure 14.6 shows an example of this difference. Notice that the selected cell, C10, has a value that is the sum of the values above it. You can see the formula, =SUM(C5,C8), in the formula bar near the top of the window. This formula says to add the values of the cells C5 to C8. The result is displayed in cell C10.

14

Selected cell

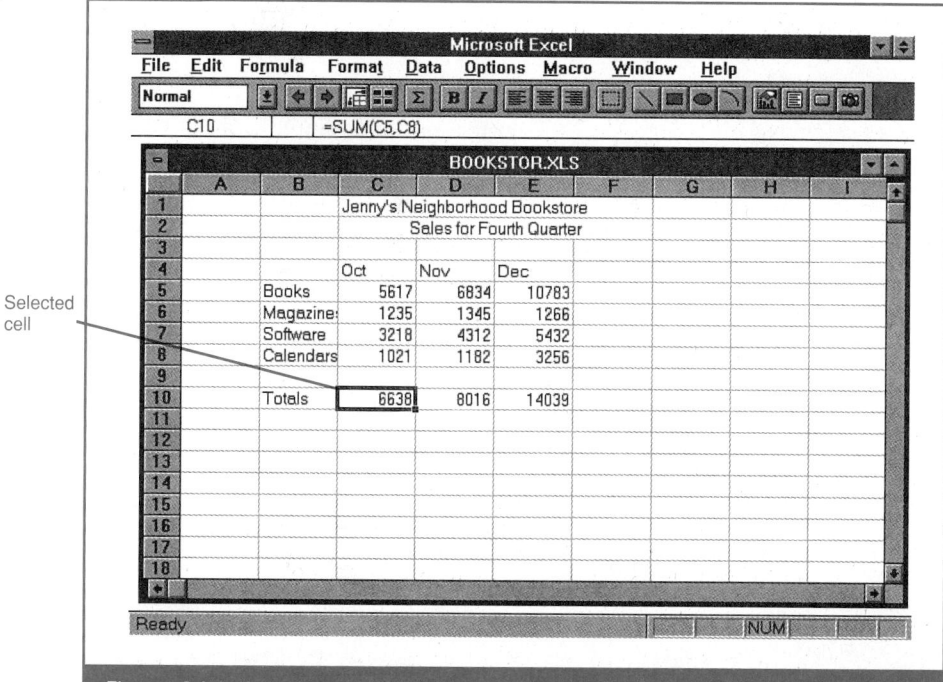

Figure 14.6. Formula shown in formula bar; value shown in cell.

Formatting Values in Cells

Because most visual and printed output comes from the worksheet, Excel enables you to format the contents of cells in many different ways. This flexibility makes it easy to produce spreadsheets that are clear and easy to read both on-screen and on paper.

Selecting Cells

All cell formatting is performed on whatever cells are selected at the time. Table 14.1 shows the methods for selecting cells with the mouse, and Table 14.2 shows how to select cells with the keyboard. As you can see, Excel gives you a great deal of flexibility in selecting cells so that formatting is quicker.

Table 14.1. Selecting with the mouse.

Action	Selection
Click a cell once	Selects a cell
Drag through an area of cells	Selects a range
Drag through a row	Selects a row or a column or a column heading
Ctrl-Shift and double-click	Selects a range based on the location of the current cell
Click gray rectangle in upper-left corner of worksheet	Selects an entire worksheet
Hold down Ctrl while dragging through another selection	Creates a multiple selection

Table 14.2. Moving and selecting with the keyboard.

Action	Movement or Selection
← → ↑ ↓	Moves to a cell in the chosen direction and selects it
Shift-direction key	Enlarges the selection by one cell in the chosen direction

Action	Movement or Selection
Ctrl-direction key	Moves the cursor over one block of data in the chosen direction
Ctrl-Shift-direction key	Enlarges the specified range by one block of data in the chosen direction
Home	Moves the cursor to the beginning of the active cell's row
Shift-Home	Enlarges the specified range to the beginning of the row
End	Moves the cursor to the end of the active cell's row
Shift-End	Enlarges the specified range to the end of the row
Shift-Spacebar	Selects rows that contain the selected cell or range
Ctrl-Spacebar	Selects columns that contain the selected cell or range
Ctrl-Shift-Spacebar	Selects the entire worksheet
Ctrl-Home	Moves the cursor to the cell at the upper-left corner of the worksheet and selects it
Ctrl-Shift-Home	Enlarges the selection to the active cell at the upper-left corner of worksheet
Ctrl-End	Moves the cursor to the active cell at the lower-right corner of the worksheet and selects it

14

Basic Text Formatting

Excel supports all font formatting you have seen in other Windows programs. The Format Font dialog box is shown in Figure 14.7. In addition to font, size, and style, Excel can add color to characters. Like character styles, color is a good method for highlighting text that you want to stand out. Note that the Format Font dialog box shows a sample of the format you are applying to the selected cells.

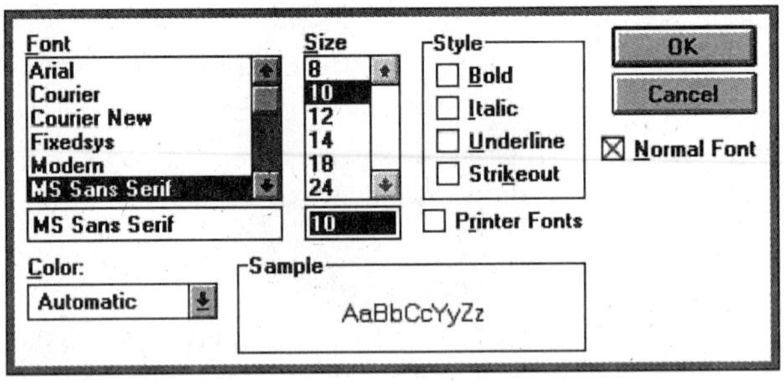

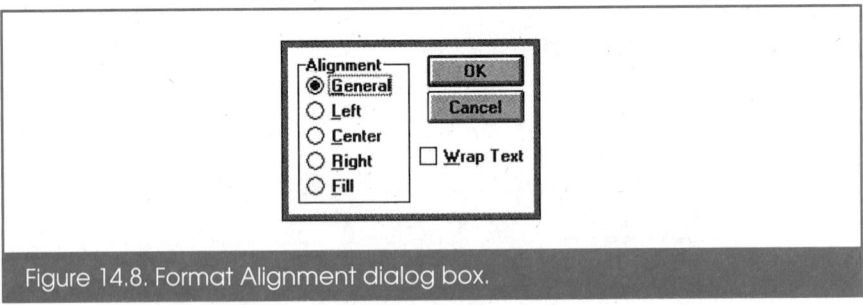

Figure 14.7. Format Font dialog box.

You also can specify how the value in the cell is aligned with the cell edges with the Format Alignment command, shown in Figure 14.8. General alignment, the default, aligns text values against the left edge and numbers on the right edge. The Wrap Text option enables you to have text that runs more than one line wrap within the cell. Excel automatically adjusts the height of the cell to accommodate the wrapped text.

Figure 14.8. Format Alignment dialog box.

Because you often add basic text formatting and alignment to cells as you edit, Excel has buttons on the tool bar for these tasks.

Borders and Patterns

Every cell can have whatever type of border you want. You can use the Format Border command, shown in Figure 14.9, to put boxes around cells or to add lines for tables. You also can choose the color for the lines.

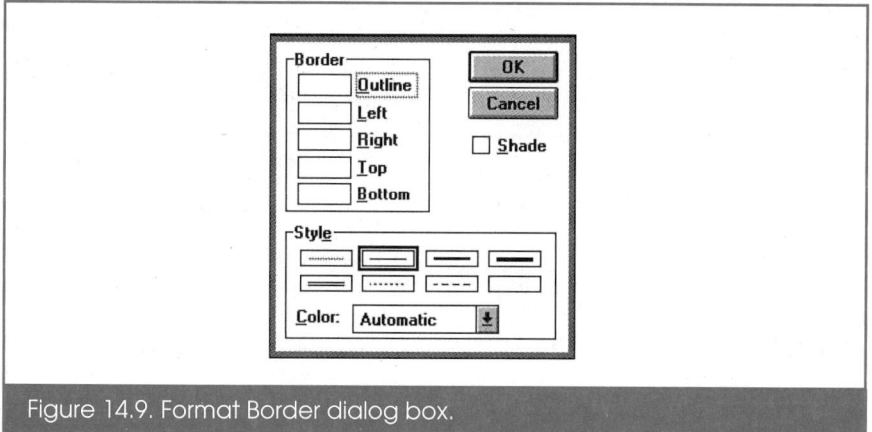

Figure 14.9. Format Border dialog box.

The Format Patterns command tells Excel how to shade cells. The dialog box, shown in Figure 14.10, has three choices for the selected cells. The pattern is the type of shading, such as levels of gray or stripes. The foreground and background are the colors you want to use in the cells.

14

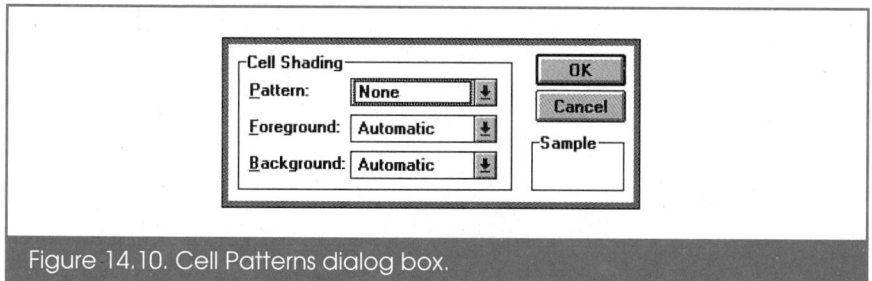

Figure 14.10. Cell Patterns dialog box.

Number Formatting

You normally do not think of numbers as being "formatted," but in fact they are. For example, the numbers 5,245.230 and 5.24523e4 represent the same number but appear in a different format. Of course, most Excel worksheets have lots of numbers. Microsoft made Excel extremely flexible in formatting numbers.

The Format Number command, shown in Figure 14.11, lists many predefined formats you can choose from. You do not need to use any of these definitions, however. You can enter your own format in the **F**ormat field.

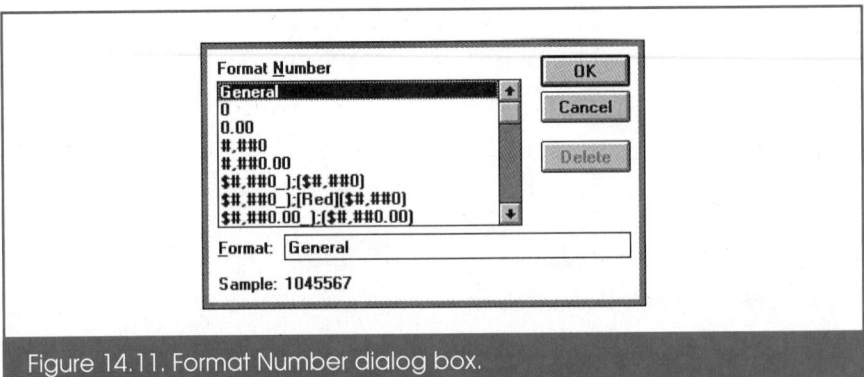

Figure 14.11. Format Number dialog box.

A format describes how Excel will display a cell if it contains a positive number, a negative number, or text. For example, you can specify that you want positive numbers shown normally but negative numbers shown in parentheses. You can specify an exact number of decimal places to show, use scientific notation, use currency signs, and show various time and date formats. You can even change the color of numbers based on their values, such as showing negative values in red or values over a certain amount in blue.

Cell Styles

You do not have to add all of the aforementioned formatting to cells individually. Instead, you can define cell styles that combine all of the formatting into a single format. Then you can select cells and specify a style for them. Thus, if you have a few sets of formats you use often, you can cut down your formatting time by defining them as styles.

To define or view a style, use the Forma**t S**tyle command, shown in Figure 14.12. To view the formatting for a style, choose it from the **S**tyle Name drop-down list.

To change the definition of a style or to add new definitions, click the Define » button. The dialog box changes to that shown in Figure 14.13. Each style can consist of one of the six types of cell formatting (protection is not really formatting, because it locks or hides the value of the

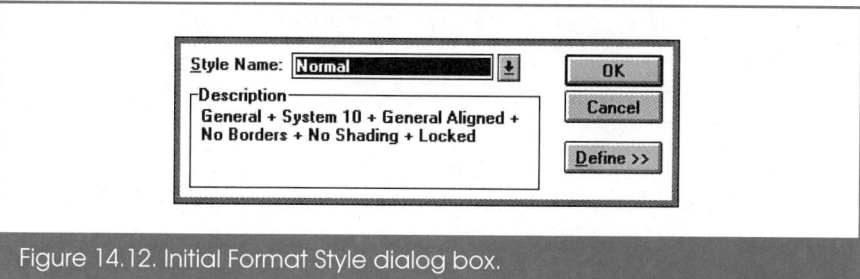

Figure 14.12. Initial Format Style dialog box.

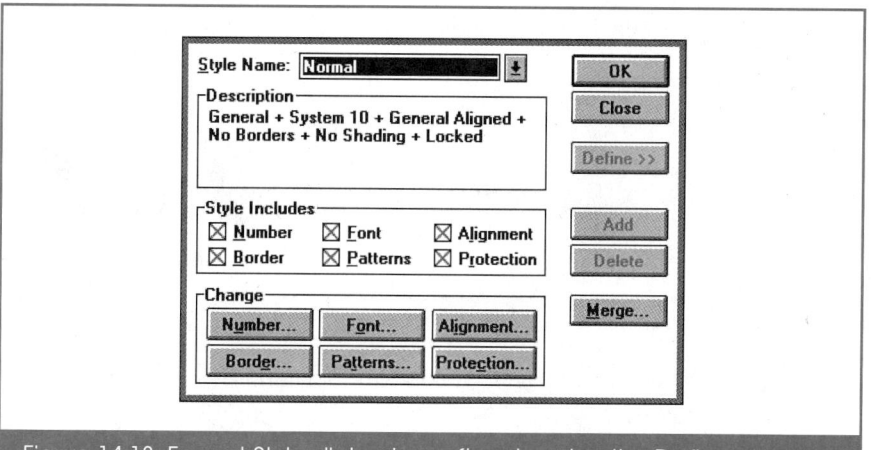

Figure 14.13. Format Style dialog box after choosing the Define » button.

14

cell). From this dialog box, you can change the formatting for each style. You also can quickly merge styles from other worksheets with the **M**erge button.

Cell styles are more than just a convenience feature. You might have a company presentation style for spreadsheets (such as for headings, currency formats, date formats, and so on), and you can implement it as a standard style sheet. When people create new worksheets, they don't have to look up the styles in a book; they can just apply them. If you use good style names, people will know exactly what to use in each part of the worksheet.

You do not have to use the Forma**t S**tyle dialog box to give selected cells a style. Instead, use the drop-down list at the left of the tool bar to apply styles.

Adding Graphics to Worksheets

Although the basic purpose of a worksheet is to calculate and display values, it also is used as a presentation tool. As you saw earlier, you can add charts to your worksheet so that the data and its graphical representation are together. You also can add graphical items such as lines and circles.

To add graphical items, use the buttons on the tool bar. Figure 14.14 shows examples of each of the four basic types of objects (line, rectangle, oval, and quarter arc) and of a text box.

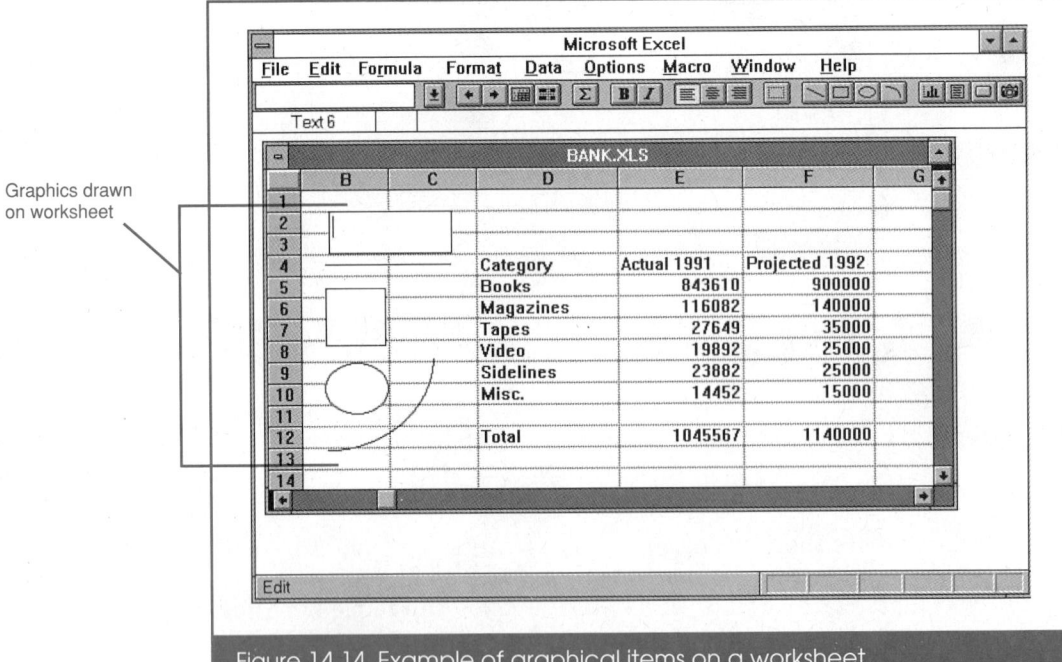

Graphics drawn on worksheet

Figure 14.14. Example of graphical items on a worksheet.

Tip: A text box is a good method for creating a floating label for information in the worksheet. It does not have to align with the cell grid, and you do not need to worry about its value changing or being shifted as you expand or edit the worksheet.

You can format the graphical items with the Format Patterns command. Select the item and give the command, or simply double-click the item. The Format Patterns command for a rectangle is shown in Figure 14.15. The dialog box is the same for ovals, except that ovals do not have the Round Corners option. It is also the same for quarter arcs, except that quarter arcs do not have either the Shadow or the Round Corners options.

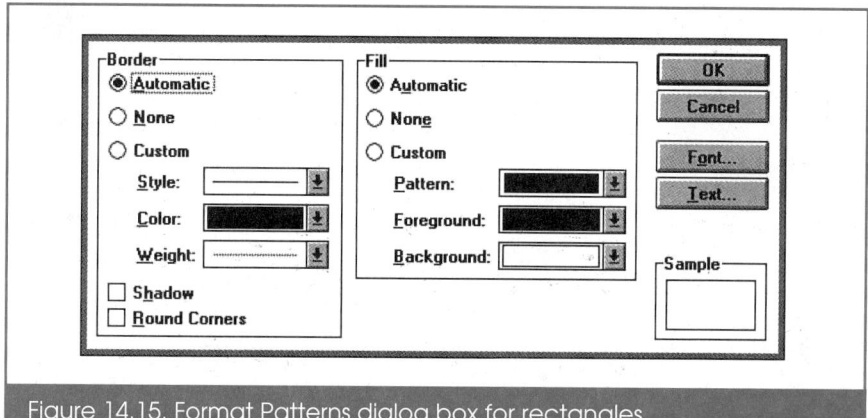

Figure 14.15. Format Patterns dialog box for rectangles.

Figure 14.16 shows the Format Patterns dialog box for lines. Note that you can make lines into arrows. Using arrows in a worksheet is another good method for highlighting cells that you want to emphasize. You can choose the type of arrow head (none, open, or closed triangle), the width of the head, and the length of the point. Like cell borders, you also can select the line style (hairline, dotted, and so on), the color, and the thickness of the line.

You also can paste pictures from the Clipboard onto a worksheet. For example, if you are making a presentation, you might want to include a company logo, as in Figure 14.17. You might also use a picture as a backdrop for a chart that you have in a worksheet.

Worksheet Display Options

You can change the look of more than just cell contents. Excel enables you to change the way that the entire worksheet looks. This enables you to create attractive screen displays before you print your documents.

413

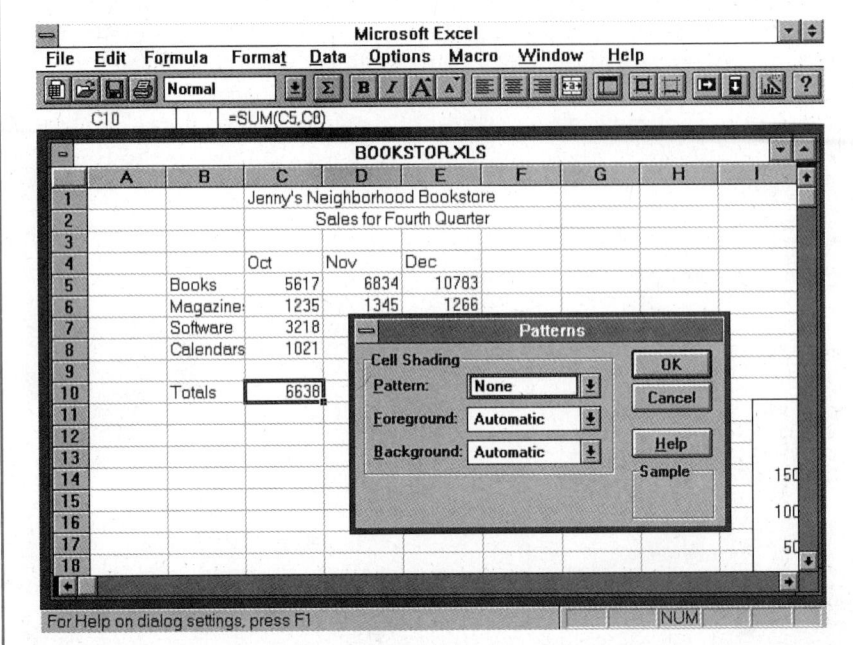

Figure 14.16. Format Patterns dialog box for lines.

Column Width and Row Height

The most common changes you make to a worksheet are to change the column widths and row heights to match the data in the worksheet. Using different column widths is like changing the column size in a table. Sometimes you want wide columns for an airy feeling, and other times you want tight columns so that it is easy to scan across a page.

You can change the column width or row height with the mouse by clicking between the heading cells and dragging the dividing line to the desired location. You also can use the Format Column Width or Format Row Height commands. The Format Column Width command is shown in Figure 14.18. (The Format Row Height dialog box is almost identical.)

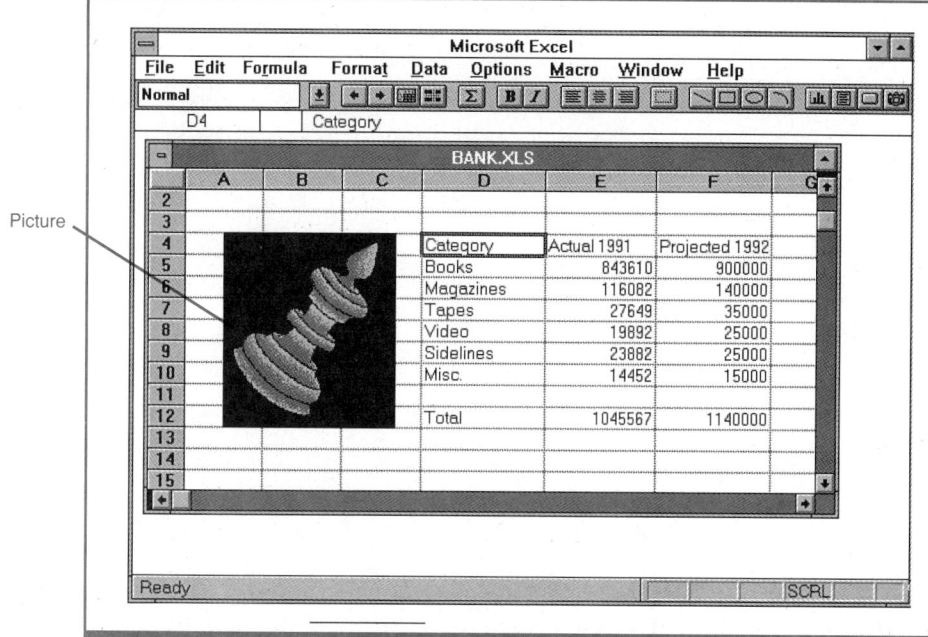

Figure 14.17. Example of a picture pasted in a worksheet.

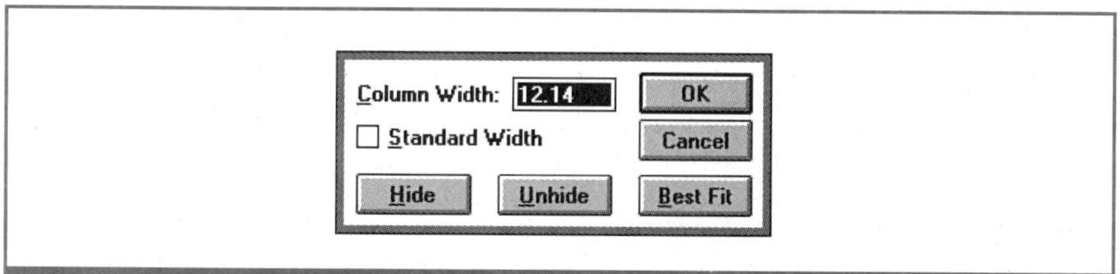

Figure 14.18. Format Column Width dialog box.

You can specify the width in the **C**olumn Width entry as the number of characters in the Normal style's font. If you want a tight fit around the values in a column, click the **B**est Fit button. This action sets the width just wider than the longest value of the selected cells.

You can choose a row height taller than normal characters. In this case, if you have more text in a cell than will fit in the column width and you have selected the **W**rap Text option in the Forma**t** Alignment command for that cell, Excel wraps the text like a word processor would. Figure 14.19 shows an example of text wrapped in a cell.

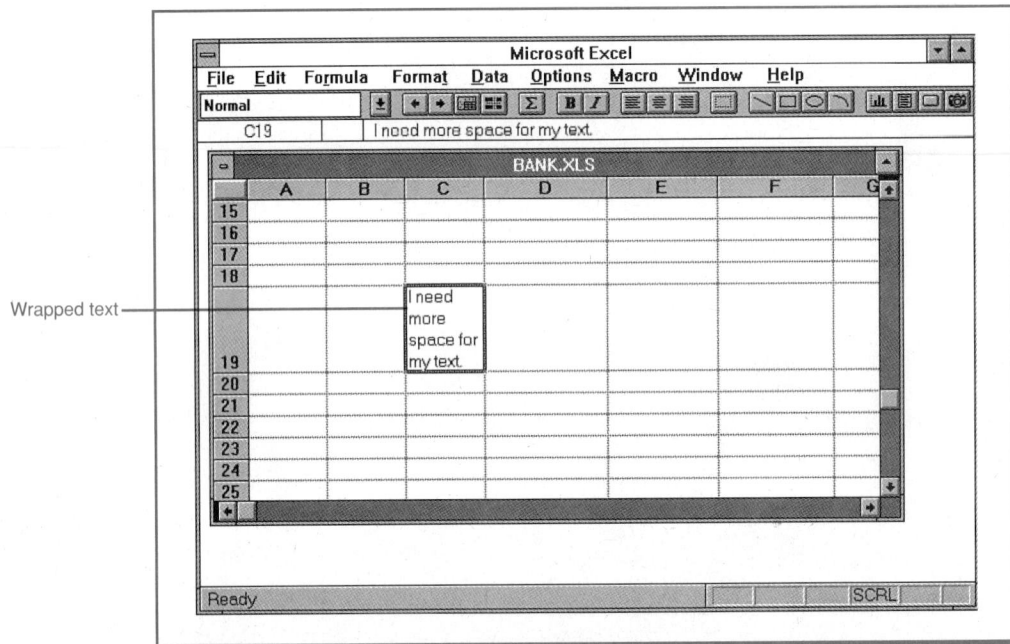

Figure 14.19. Text wrapped in a cell.

Worksheet Display

You can change many of the ways that a whole worksheet is displayed on the screen by using the **O**ptions Display command to open the dialog box shown in Figure 14.20. These options affect only the selected worksheet, so you might need to set them for every worksheet you create. Table 14.3 describes each option.

The most common display change you will make is to hide the grid lines by unselecting the **G**ridlines option. If you don't turn off the gridlines, they will be printed by default. Figure 14.21 shows a worksheet without grid lines. Gridlines are useful for entering and formatting your worksheet but often are distracting when you are using the worksheet for a presentation. Remember that, after you remove the grid lines, you still can add lines to connect the cells visually using the Forma**t B**order command. If you've made borders with the Forma**t B**order command, they will print regardless of whether you disable the gridlines before you print.

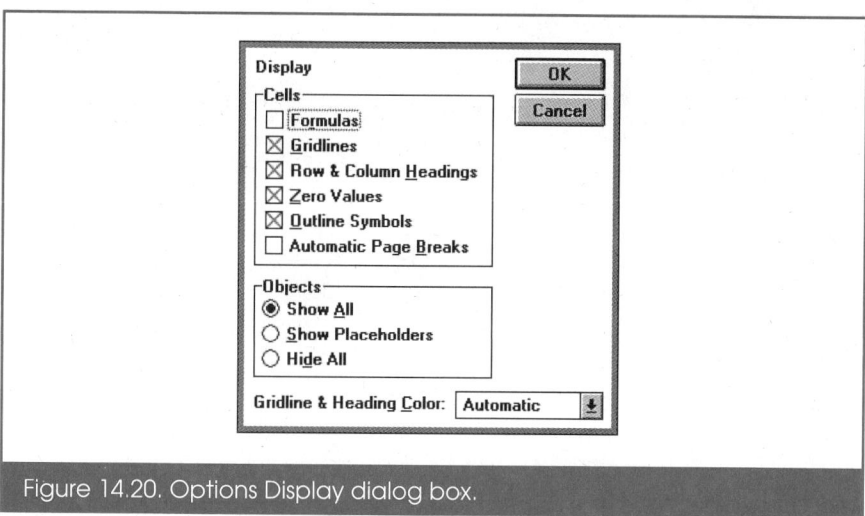

Figure 14.20. Options Display dialog box.

14

Table 14.3. Options Display options.

Option	Displays
Formulas	The formulas (instead of the results of the formula) are displayed in the cell.
Gridlines	The grid in the document window.
Row & Column Headings	The headings at the top and left of the window.
Zero Values	Numbers that are zero; if not selected, zeros show as blanks.
Outline Symbols	Outline controls (described later in this chapter).
Automatic Page Breaks	Page boundaries.
Objects	All graphical objects, gray rectangles (placeholders), or none.

Turning off the row and column headings gives you more screen space, although it makes it a bit more difficult to use Excel. This option is useful when you need all the space on your screen for a presentation.

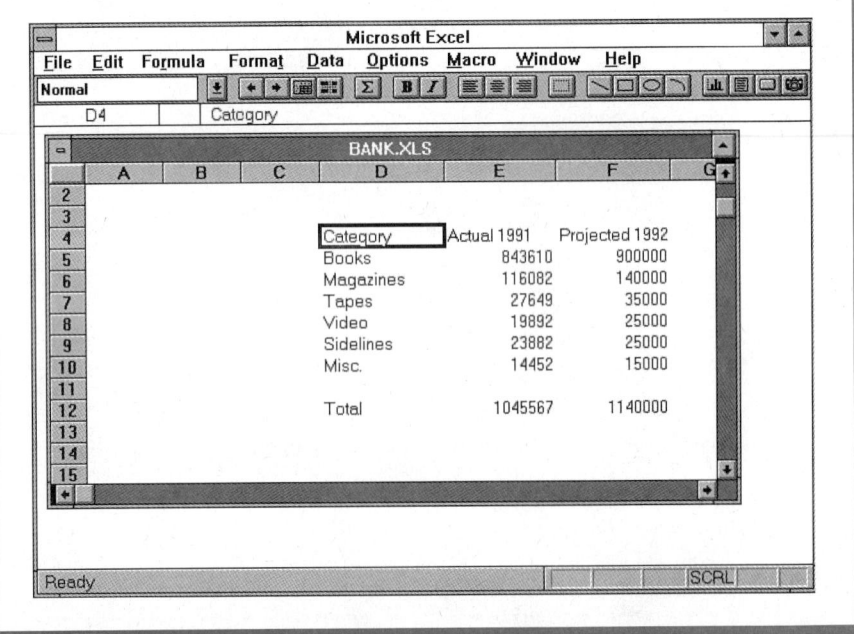

Figure 14.21. Worksheet without grid lines.

Workspace

There are also some display options in the **O**ptions Workspace command, shown in Figure 14.22. Setting these options affects all
worksheets, as well as the look of the program window. They are
described in Table 14.4.

Charts

Excel's charts can reside either in their own window or on a worksheet
as a graphical element. When the active window is a chart, the menus
and commands available are different than when the active window is a
worksheet.

Creating a chart is simple. To create a chart in its own window, select
the data for the chart in a worksheet and give the **F**ile **N**ew command.
In that command's dialog box, shown in Figure 14.23, select Chart and
click OK.

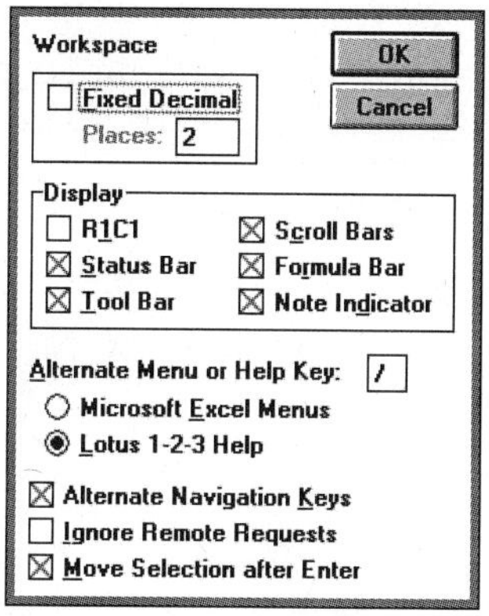

Figure 14.22. Options Workspace dialog box.

Table 14.4. Display options in the Options Workspace command.

14

Option	Displays
R1C1	Cell references in formulas
Status Bar	The information line at the bottom of the program window
Tool Bar	The tool bar below the menu bar
Scroll Bars	Scroll bars on worksheet and macro windows
Formula Bar	The formula bar below the tool bar
Note Indicator	A small square that identifies cells that have notes

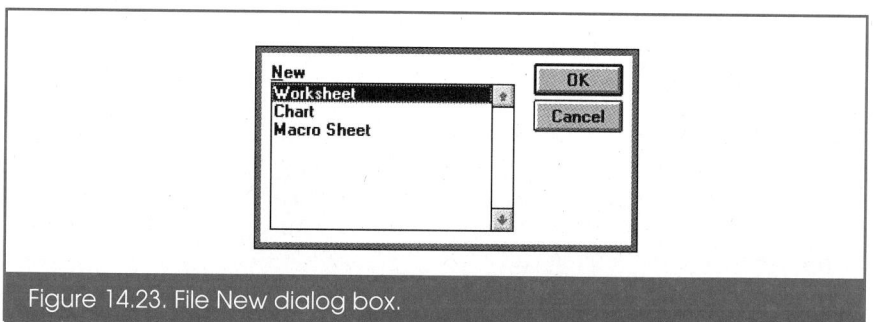

Figure 14.23. File New dialog box.

To create a chart on a worksheet, select the data for the chart, click the chart button in the tool bar, and drag over the area where you want the chart to be displayed. To edit that chart, simply double-click it; Excel opens a chart window with the chart so that you can access all the chart-specific menus.

Types of Charts

The charts available in Excel are shown in the **G**allery menu, shown in Figure 14.24.

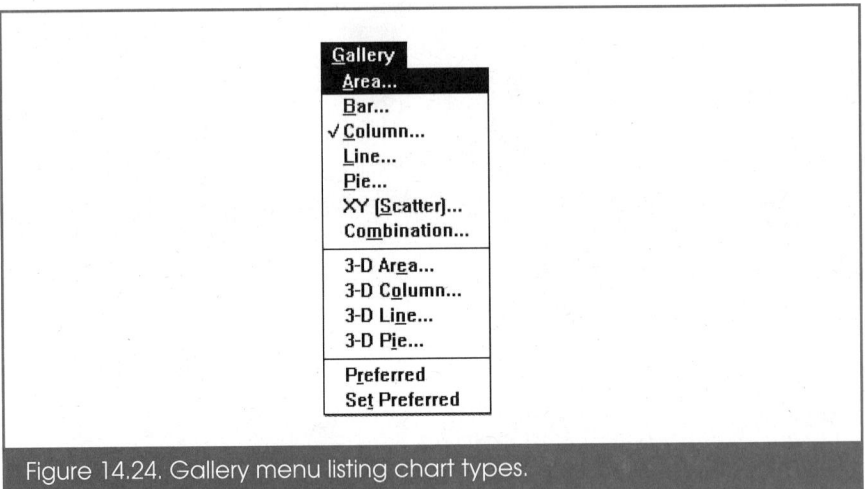

Figure 14.24. Gallery menu listing chart types.

For each type of chart, there are many layouts. You can see the layouts by giving the command for the chart's type. For example, Figure 14.25 shows the **G**allery 3-D **C**olumn dialog box.

You can use any chart type for any data you have. To change to a different type, select that type from the **G**allery menu and choose the desired layout.

Specific chart types are better for some types of data than for others. For instance, a line chart is better for data that is in a series. Using a line chart for data that is not in a series can be confusing. Figure 14.26 shows a line chart used for categorical data. Your eye naturally moves along the line, but because the categories are not in a series, there is no sense in the line.

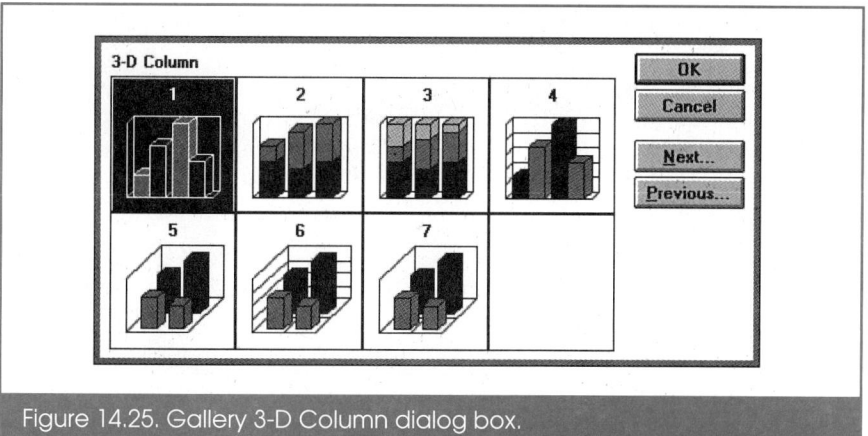

Figure 14.25. Gallery 3-D Column dialog box.

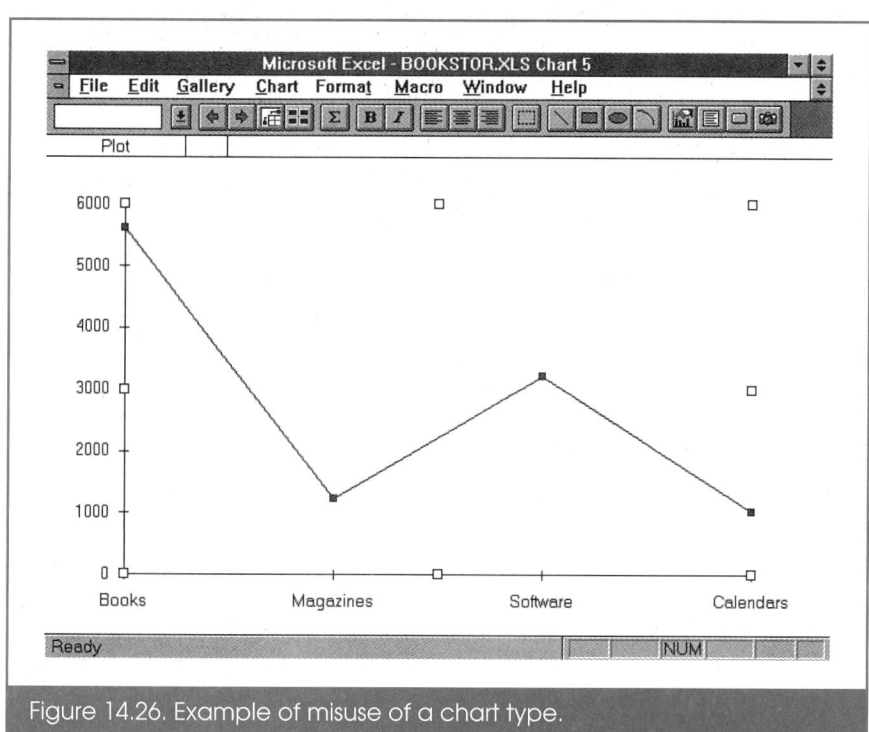

Figure 14.26. Example of misuse of a chart type.

Adding Graphics

You can add graphics to your chart to highlight or elucidate parts of your data. Note, however, that you cannot add rectangles, ovals, and quarter arcs as you can in a worksheet. The most common form of graphical additions are those pasted from the Clipboard from, say, another application.

The **C**hart Attach Text command enables you to add text to particular parts of the chart, as shown in Figure 14.27. If you resize your chart, the attached text moves with the item to which it is attached.

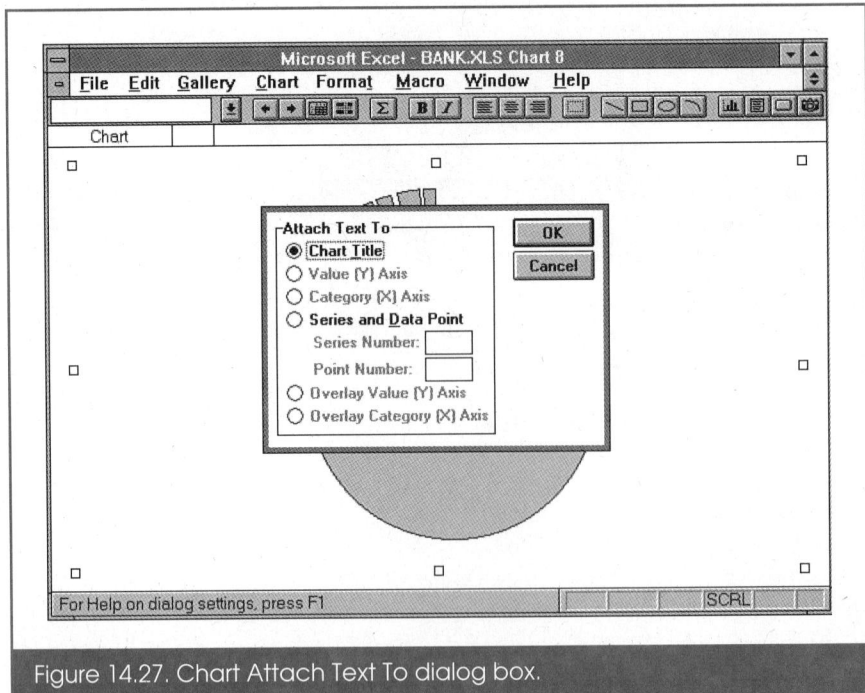

Figure 14.27. Chart Attach Text To dialog box.

You also can add free-floating text as you can in the worksheet. You can add arrows to point out specific features of the chart using the **C**hart Add Arrow command.

Legends

Some charts need legends to make them understandable. For example, in Figure 14.28, the bar on the left in each group represents the actual

1991 sales and the bar on the right represents the projected 1992 sales. Without a legend, the chart would be almost meaningless.

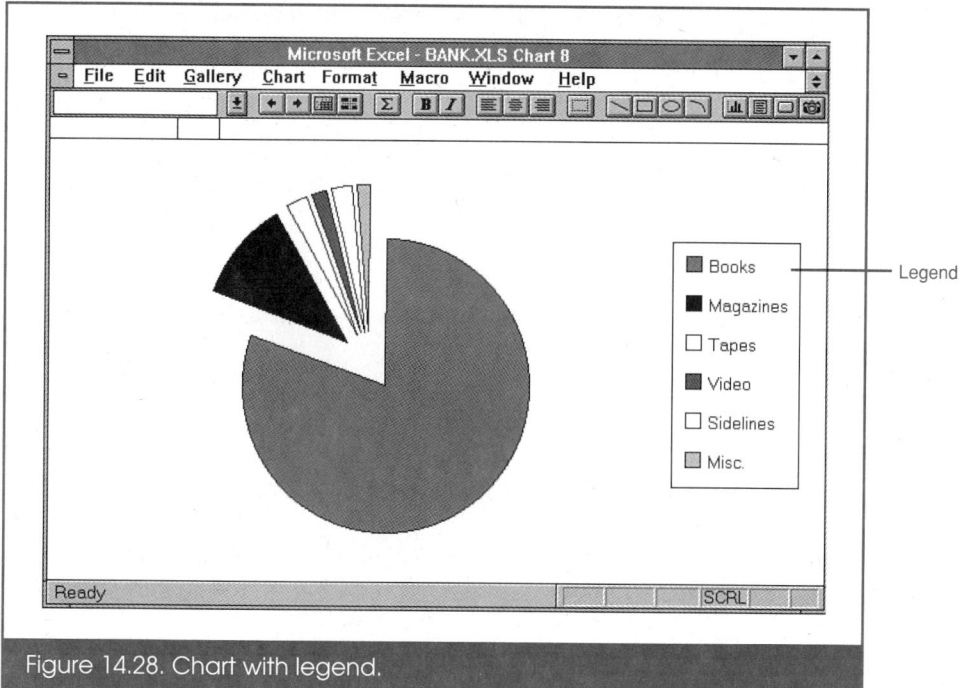

Figure 14.28. Chart with legend.

14

The Forma**t** Legend command, shown in Figure 14.29, enables you to place the legend in different locations with respect to the chart. Putting the legend on the right is by far the most common choice. You also can place the legend wherever you want it simply by dragging it with the mouse.

Formatting

Figure 14.30 shows the Forma**t** menu for charts. The commands available depend on the chart object that is selected. The options are similar to the options for formatting graphical items in a worksheet.

In general, the Forma**t** **P**atterns command is used for all coloring, shading, border, and other visual changes. When you double-click a nontext chart item such as a wedge of a pie chart or a column, you see the Forma**t** **P**atterns dialog box. A typical Forma**t** **P**atterns dialog box is shown in Figure 14.31.

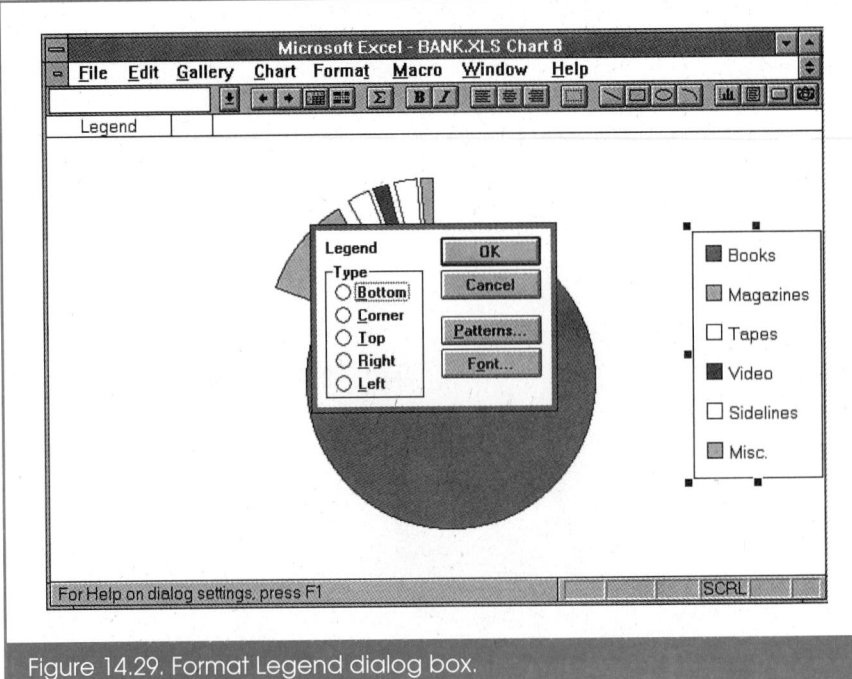

Figure 14.29. Format Legend dialog box.

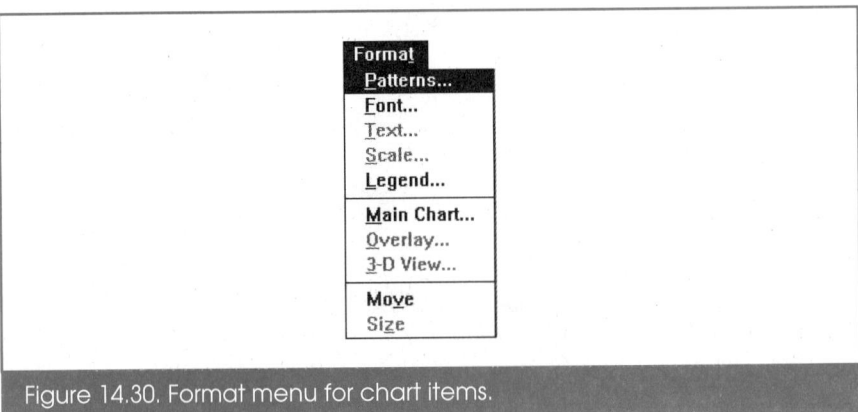

Figure 14.30. Format menu for chart items.

As you saw earlier, Excel has four types of three-dimensional charts. These charts give the illusion of depth using perspective. You can use the Format **3**-D View command to change the perspective from which the chart is drawn. The dialog box in Figure 14.32 shows how you can control the perspective by changing the elevation and rotation of the

axes. If you deselect Right Angle Axes, you also can change the perspective, enabling you to rotate in all three dimensions. As you change the values with the buttons or by entering values in the fields, the sample in the middle of the dialog box changes to preview what your chart will look like.

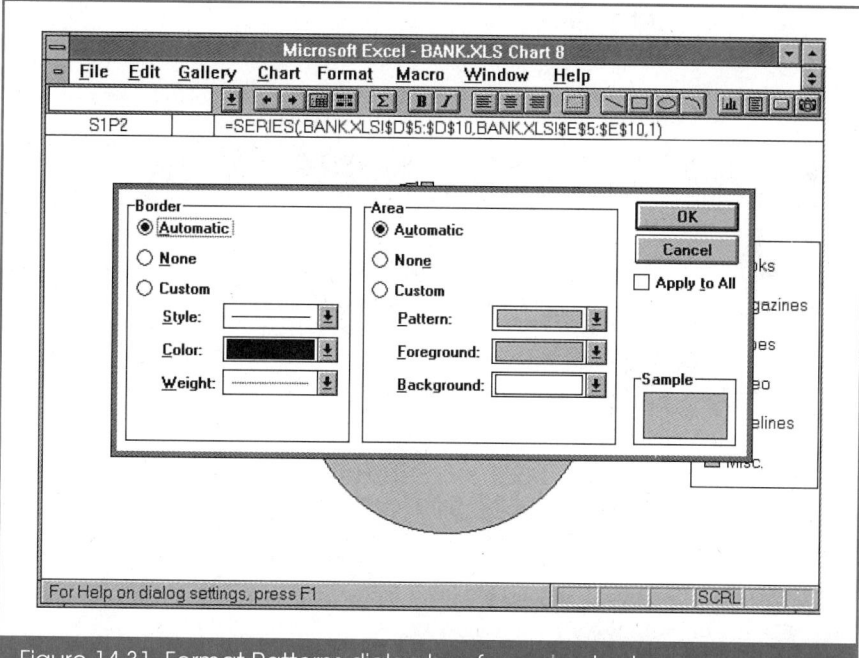

Figure 14.31. Format Patterns dialog box for a pie chart.

The Forma**t** **F**ont command gives you standard choices about font, size, and character styles. The Forma**t** **T**ext dialog box command, shown in Figure 14.33, enables you to change the orientation of the selected text. This is particularly handy for text on axes because short category names often look better in one orientation than in another. The options shown here will vary, depending on the type of text selected.

Axes and Grid Lines

Excel gives you a great deal of flexibility as to how the axes and the grid behind a chart are shown. Figure 14.34 shows the **C**hart Axes command. Deselecting any of the three axes removes the labels from that axis.

14

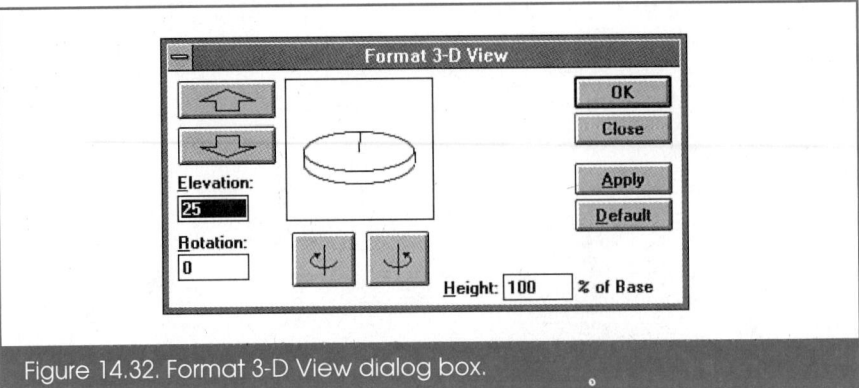

Figure 14.32. Format 3-D View dialog box.

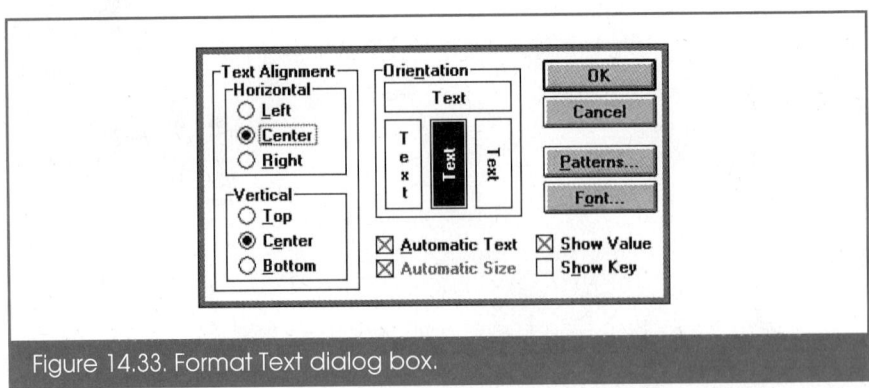

Figure 14.33. Format Text dialog box.

Similarly, the **C**hart Gridlines dialog box shown in Figure 14.35 enables you to add horizontal and/or vertical gridlines behind your chart.

The Forma**t S**cale dialog box, shown in Figure 14.36, tells Excel how you want your axes to look and where they should cross. For example, you do not have to have the axes meet at the ends; changing the first option in this dialog box causes the vertical axis to cross the horizontal axis at different locations.

Overlay Charts

So far, all the charts you have seen have had only one chart type, such as a column chart. If you are charting many columns or rows of data, you can combine two chart types into one, called an overlay chart. For example, Figure 14.37 shows a typical overlay chart with the line representing number of customers and the columns representing actual sales.

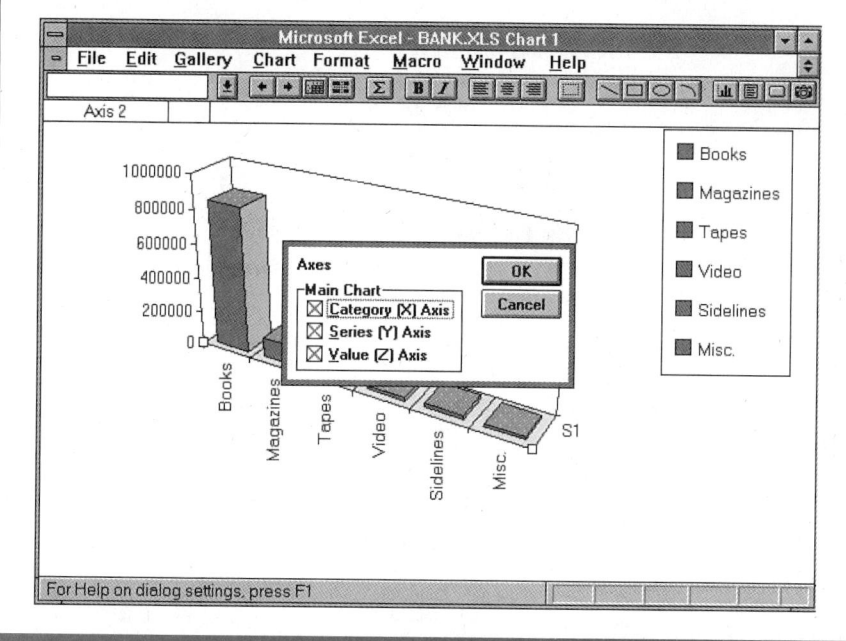

Figure 14.34. Chart Axes dialog box.

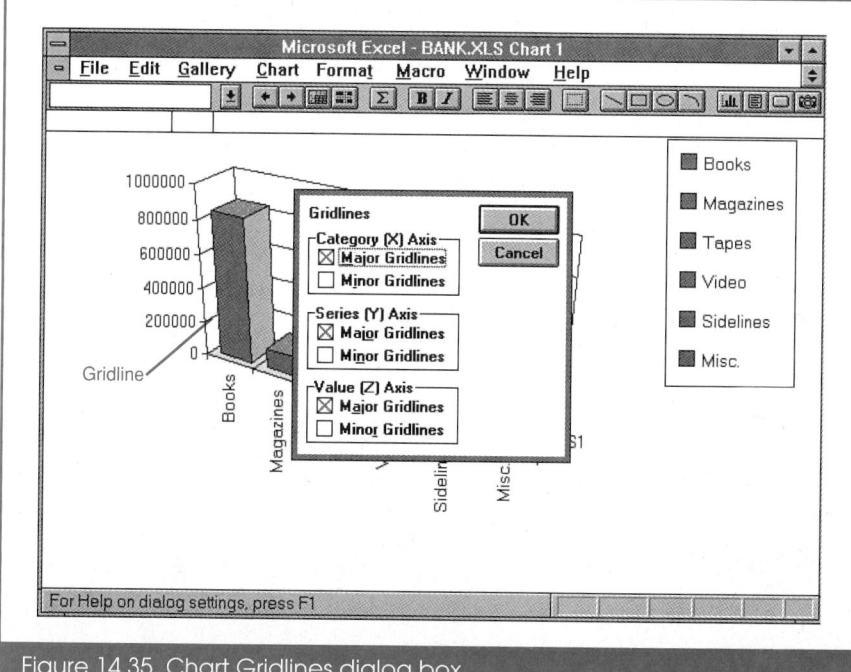

Figure 14.35. Chart Gridlines dialog box.

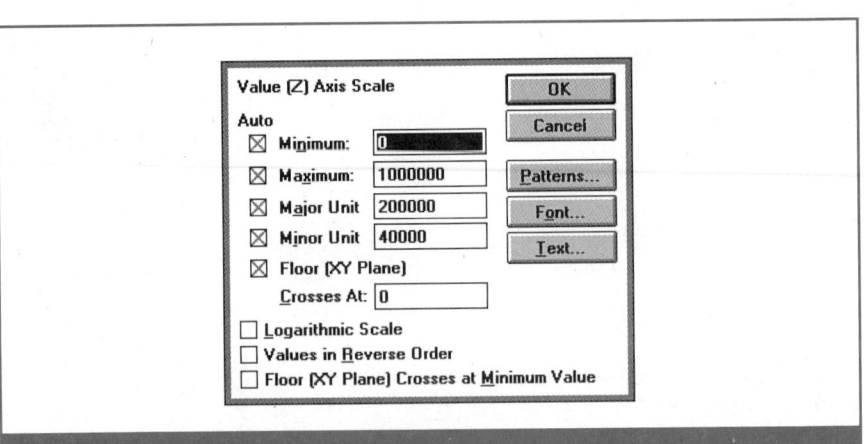

Figure 14.36. Format Scale dialog box.

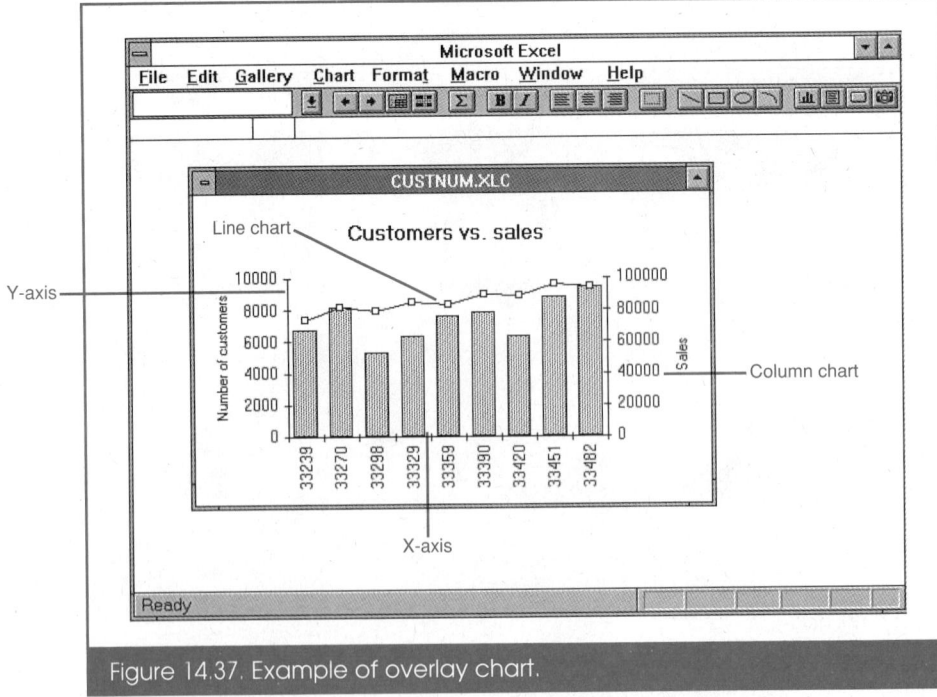

Figure 14.37. Example of overlay chart.

Note that you can have two different value axes (the y-axis in this case) for the second chart. In fact, you can have two category axes (x-axes) if the two charts have different category values. Figure 14.38 shows the

Gallery Combination choices. As you will see in the next section, you can choose many types of charts when you create overlay charts.

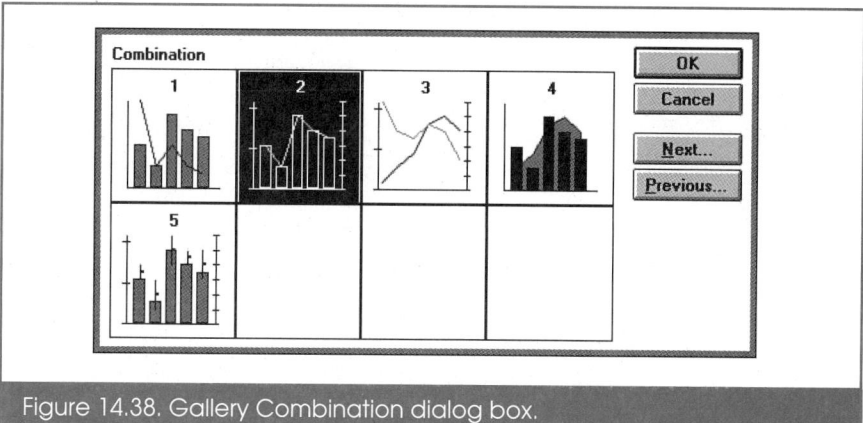

Figure 14.38. Gallery Combination dialog box.

14

Customizing Charts

The choices you see in the **G**allery dialog boxes are only suggestions. You can change many of the options, such as spacing, after you have created the chart. The Forma**t M**ain Chart dialog box, shown in Figure 14.39, shows the choices for column charts. You can even use this command to change the chart type, using the Main Chart **T**ype drop-down list at the top of the dialog box. The Forma**t O**verlay Chart command opens a similar dialog box.

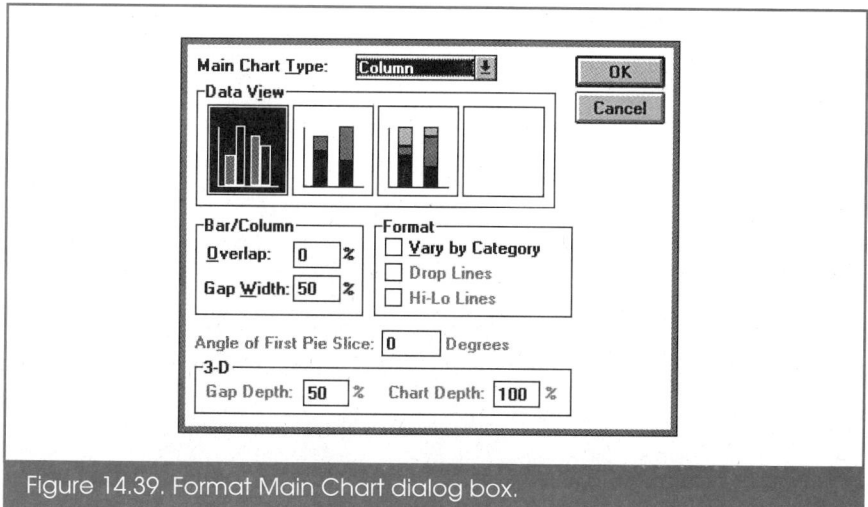

Figure 14.39. Format Main Chart dialog box.

Outlines

Many worksheets contain cells that summarize other cells. For example, Figure 14.40 shows a simple worksheet with two levels of totals.

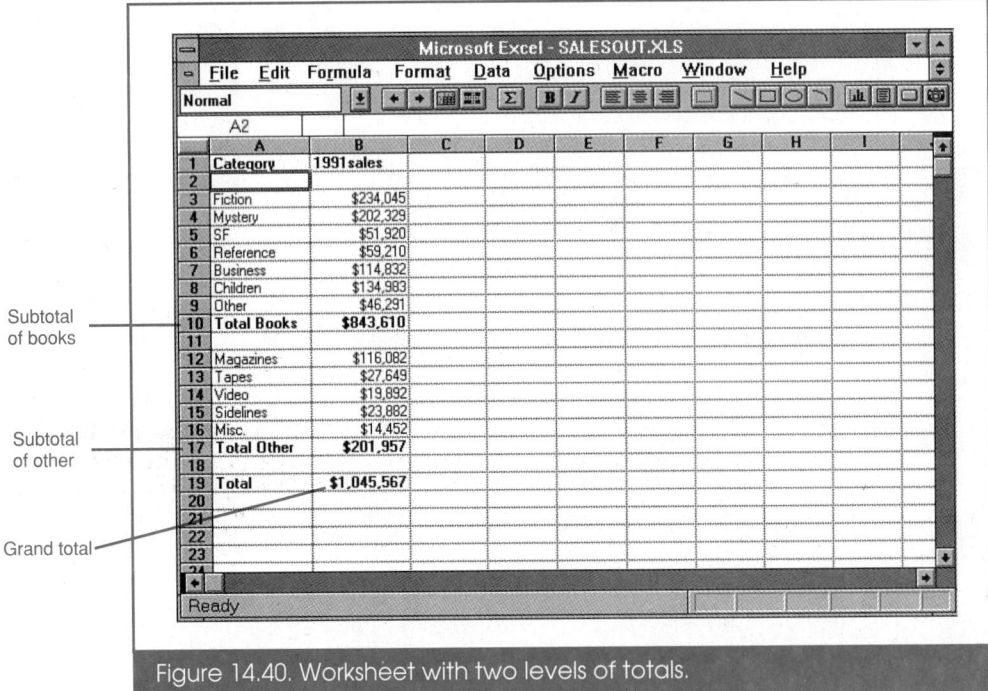

Subtotal of books

Subtotal of other

Grand total

Figure 14.40. Worksheet with two levels of totals.

The total in row 10 is for books, the total in row 17 is for other products, and the grand total on line 19 is for the two totals. You can imagine that you might want to see three different reports out of a table like this:

▲ All items

▲ Just the subtotals

▲ Just the grand total

If you have ever used an outline processor such as the one in Word for Windows, you know that it enables you to hide details and look at the big picture level by level. Excel's outline feature acts the same way. The outline feature automatically hides rows that contain lower levels of information, so you can see your information at whatever level you want.

To create an outline, simply click the outline button on the tool bar. If your information is not already in an outline, Excel automatically figures out what the levels are and creates an outline for you. It adds outline tools in the margin, as shown in Figure 14.41. Note that if you have levels of information in both vertical and horizontal directions, there are outline tools along the top as well.

Outline levels
Level indicators

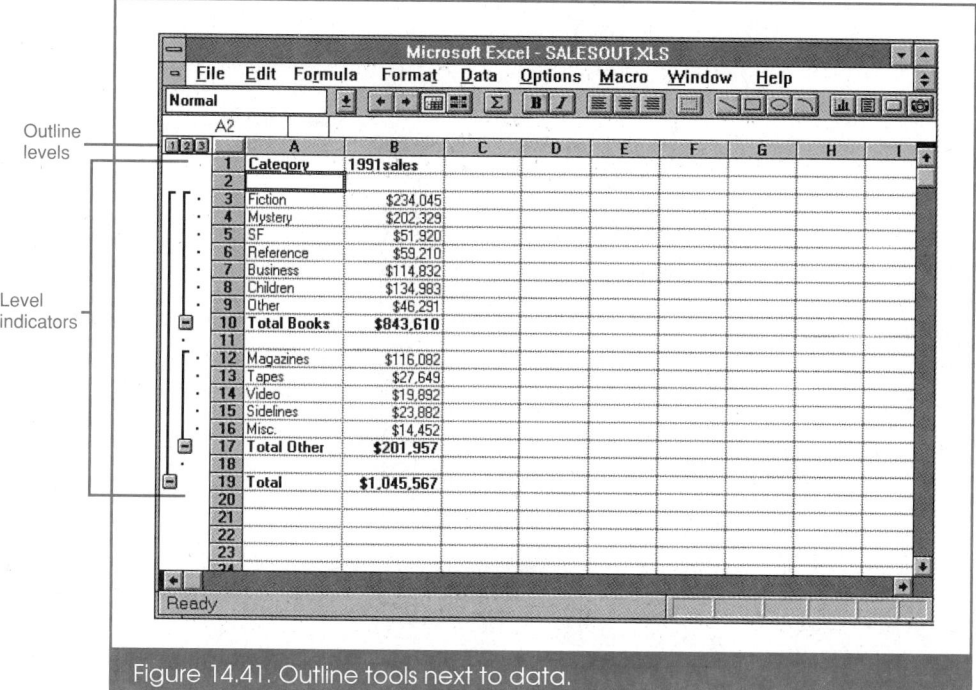

Figure 14.41. Outline tools next to data.

14

The numbered buttons at the top of the outline enable you to quickly choose the level you want to display. The higher the number, the more levels that are displayed. Clicking one of these buttons collapses the display to just that level. For example, clicking the 2 button shows just second level headings, such as Figure 14.42.

The vertical brackets with minus-sign buttons at the bottom show the exposed levels; the minus-sign buttons enable you to collapse some headings while leaving others open. For instance, Figure 14.43 shows just the other sales figures collapsed by clicking the button next to line 10. The button turns into a plus sign, which expands that level when clicked.

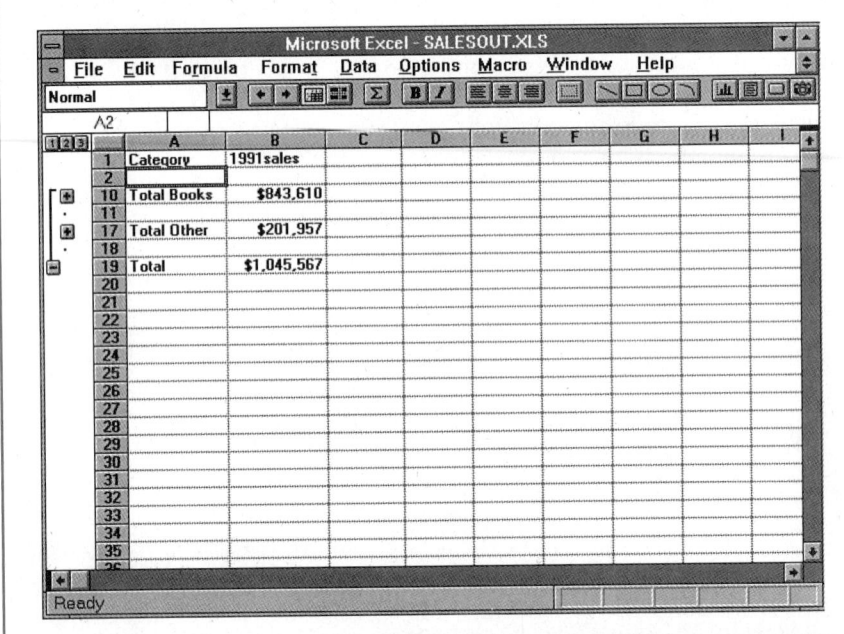

Figure 14.42. Just second-level heading shown.

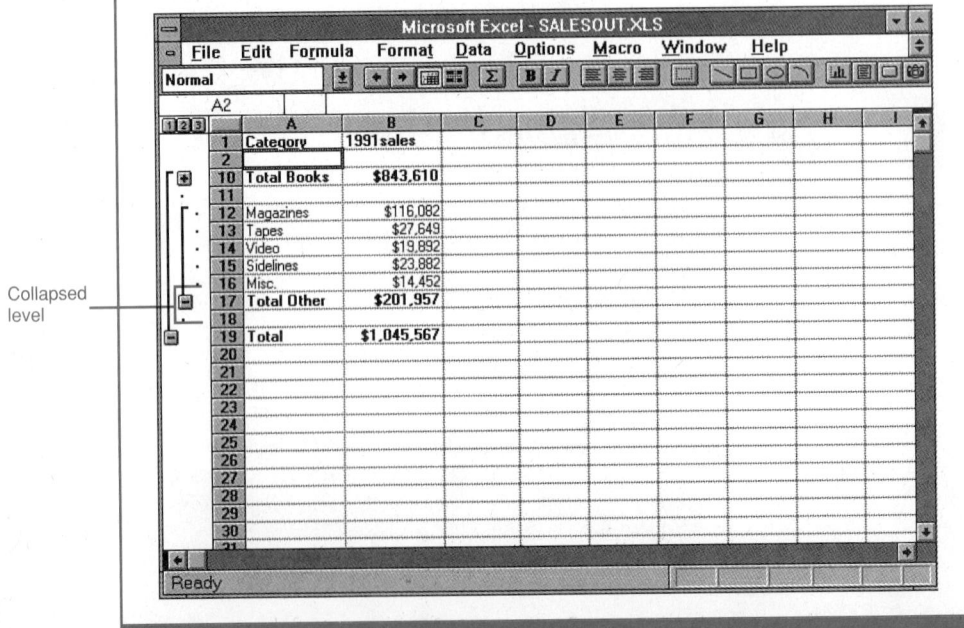

Collapsed level

Figure 14.43. Other sales items collapsed.

If you do not want to view your worksheet as an outline, simply click the outline button in the tool bar again.

Linking Excel to Other Programs

Excel can, of course, pass information back and forth through the Clipboard. You also can pass information to and from Excel with links that are automatically updated using OLE (Object Linking and Embedding). Both methods are discussed in this section.

Copying Cells From Excel

Excel copies to the Clipboard in a more advanced fashion than many other programs by using Microsoft's Rich Text Format (RTF). If you are pasting from the Clipboard into another program that can use RTF, such as Word for Windows, you retain all the formatting that you had. RTF stores information about the formatting of cells, their width, and so on. For example, Figure 14.44 shows a small table selected in Excel.

14

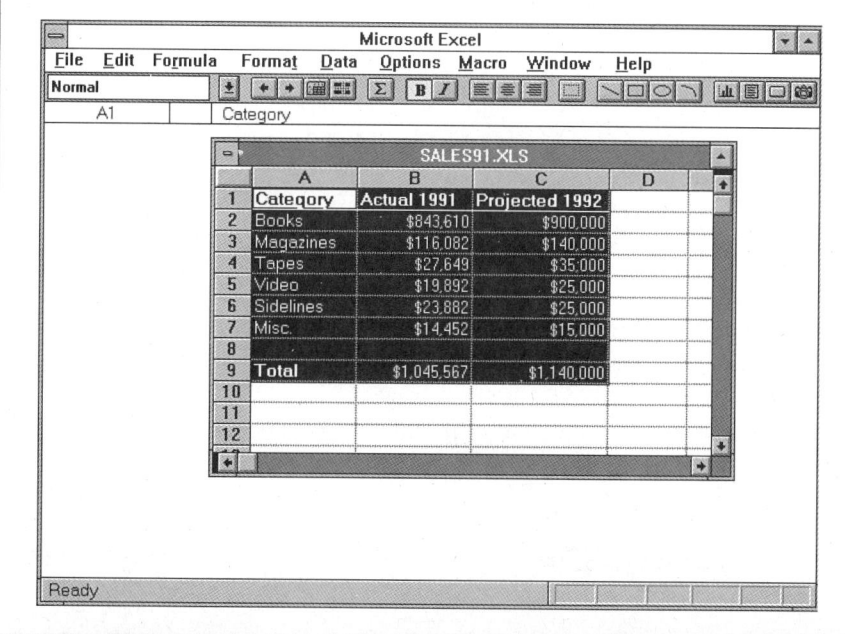

Figure 14.44. Cells selected in Excel.

When you copy a table to the Clipboard and paste it into a word processing program that does not use RTF, such as Write, you get a plain table such as Figure 14.45. However, when you paste into a program that does use RTF, such as Word for Windows, you get a real table with all the formatting, such as Figure 14.46.

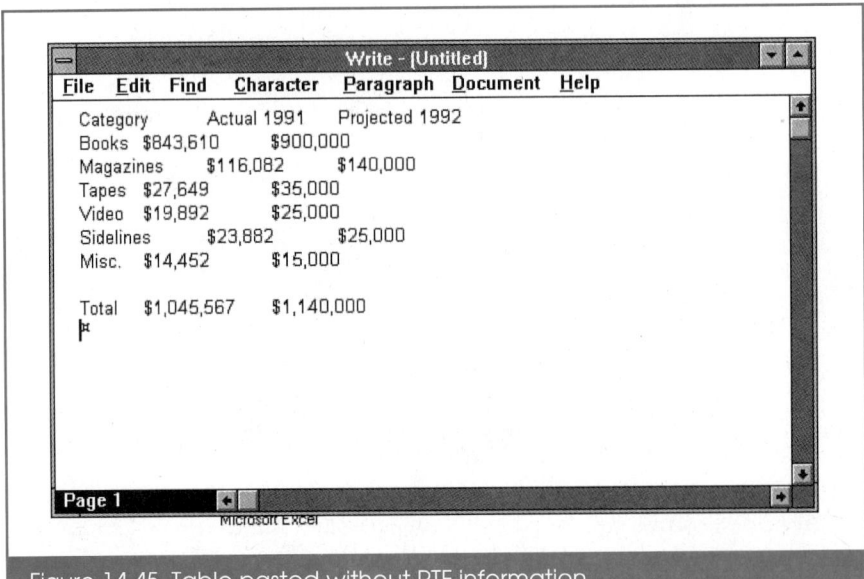

Figure 14.45. Table pasted without RTF information.

Copying Charts From Excel

You can copy charts from Excel using the Clipboard as well. Excel uses the Windows Metafile format, which gives much more information about the chart than the standard bitmap picture. A standard bitmap does not contain anything other than what the name implies—a map of bits. Thus, if you copy a chart into a paint program such as CorelDRAW! that uses the Windows Metafile standard, you can edit each part of the chart as a separate object.

Copying Cells to Excel

Excel can read the Clipboard in a wide variety of formats. Almost any format can be used so that Excel will be able to separate items in the

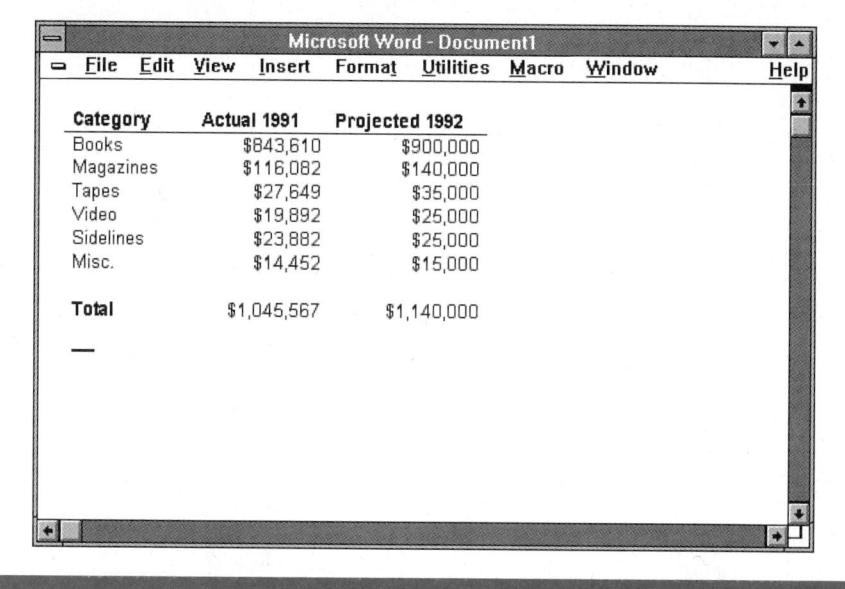

Figure 14.46. Table pasted with RTF information.

Clipboard into cells properly. Few of these formats can pass formatting information, however. The formats for cell information that Excel can read include the following:

▲ BIFF (Excel's own format)

▲ RTF (from other programs that support RTF)

▲ WK1 (from programs that emulate Lotus 1-2-3)

▲ Plain text

▲ Values separated by commas

▲ SYLK (an old format from early spreadsheets)

▲ DIF (another old format from early spreadsheets)

Copying Pictures to Excel

Excel can read pictures that are in the Windows Metafile format or the more common bitmap format. You can copy pictures onto worksheets just like a graphic object. This is useful for things such as company logos or icons.

Excel and Object Linking and Embedding (OLE)

You can link to and from Excel with active links, a method for making sure that you always have the most current information whenever you access it. For example, if you use active linking to copy a table from Excel to another program that uses OLE, each time that program opens the document with the table, it checks the file from which the table came and instantaneously recopies the information if you have changed it.

This has a radical effect on the way documents interact. Instead of your having to remember to look for the latest information when you are ready to finalize a document, Excel can do that for you automatically. You do not even need to know which data was linked and which was native to the file. Excel (or the other program) does that for you.

Excel Macros

Excel's powerful macros enable you to reduce the number of steps you have to take for repetitive actions. You can create simple macros by recording steps you take, but these usually are only for very basic steps. Creating useful macros requires programming in the Excel programming language.

Teaching the intricacies of the Excel programming language is well beyond the scope of this book. In fact, few books on Excel discuss Excel macro programming in much depth because the language is rather arcane. However, if you use Excel much, it is to your advantage to look into learning the macro language because macros can greatly reduce your work.

Using These Macros

This section contains many macros that automate different tasks in Excel. Even if you do not know about macro programming, you can copy them and use them in your work. The steps for copying macros are simple.

Figure 14.47 shows a simple example macro that reports the amount of free memory your computer has. This macro is useful if you have multiple applications open and linked, and your computer runs out of memory.

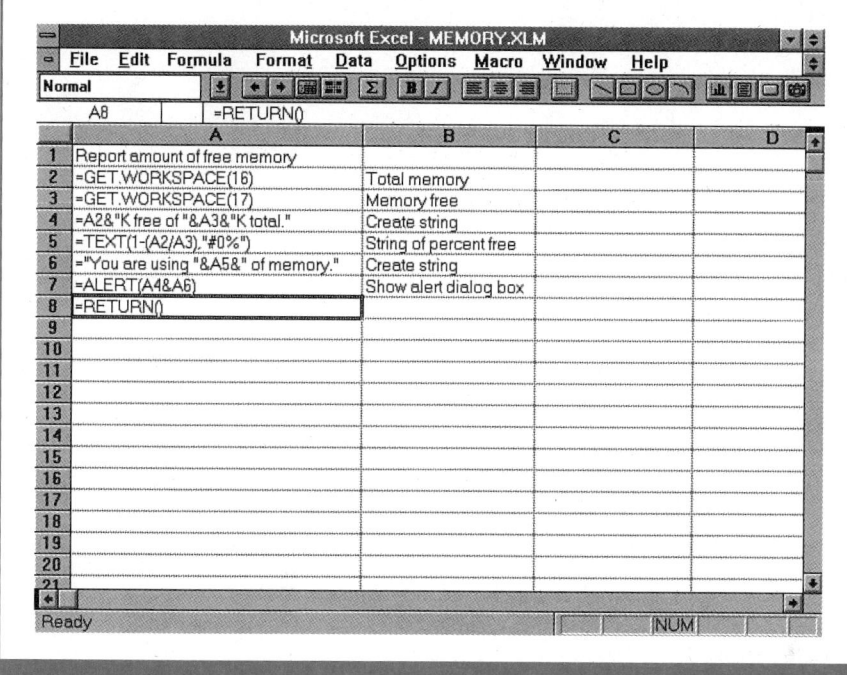

Figure 14.47. Macro to report free memory.

If you want to use this macro, follow these steps:

1. Open a new macro sheet with the **F**ile **N**ew command. Select Macro Sheet in the list and click OK.

2. Copy the macro instructions in column A into your macro sheet. The comments in column B help you understand the macro, but they are not required.

3. Select all the lines you entered. In this case, you would select A1 to A8.

4. Give the Fo**r**mula Define Name command. You see the dialog box shown in Figure 14.48.

5. Click the **C**ommand option at the bottom of the dialog box. In the Ctrl+ option, enter M to indicate that you want to run this macro when you press Ctrl-M. Click OK.

To use this macro, the macro sheet must be open. If you have many macros that you use often, you can put them all into one macro sheet and then have to open only one file to have access to all the macros.

14

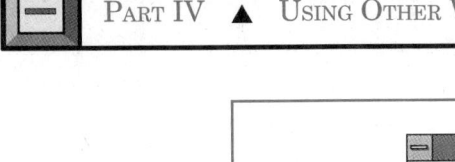

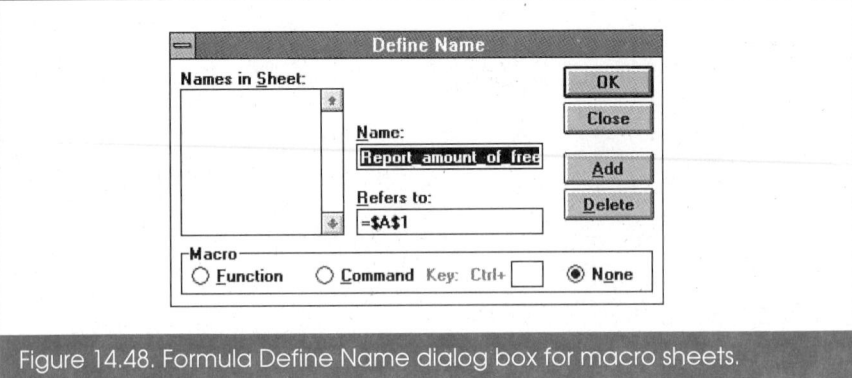

Figure 14.48. Formula Define Name dialog box for macro sheets.

Running Macros

Normally, you run macros by pressing their Ctrl-key equivalent or by giving the **M**acro Run command. Excel also enables you to put buttons on a worksheet to run macros. You can make worksheets that have just buttons and use them as quick ways of getting at the macros. This button bar can be like a second tool bar. Figure 14.49 shows a horizontal button bar near the top of the window.

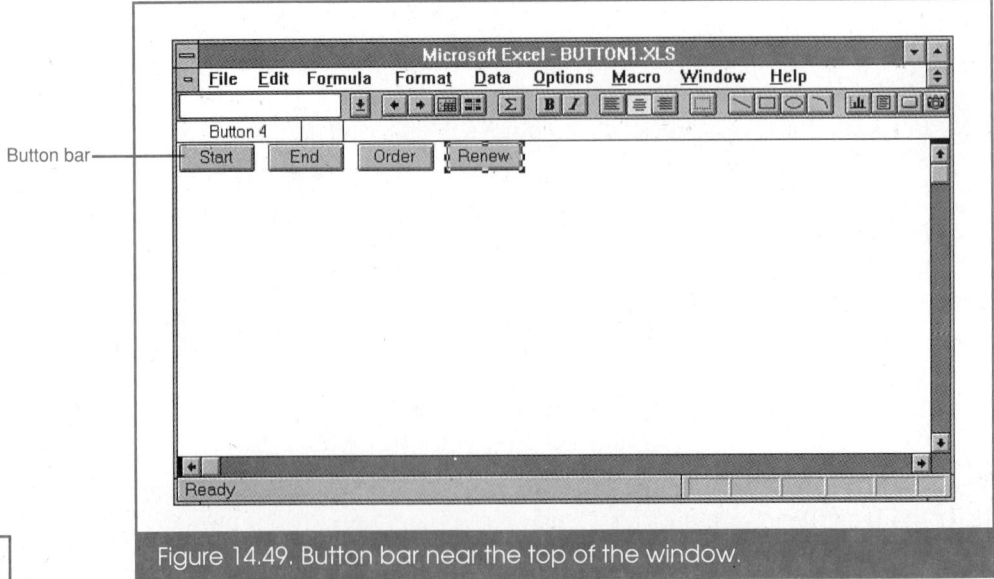

Figure 14.49. Button bar near the top of the window.

Because vertical space in Excel often is more precious than horizontal space, you might want to make a button bar down the side of the window, as shown in Figure 14.50.

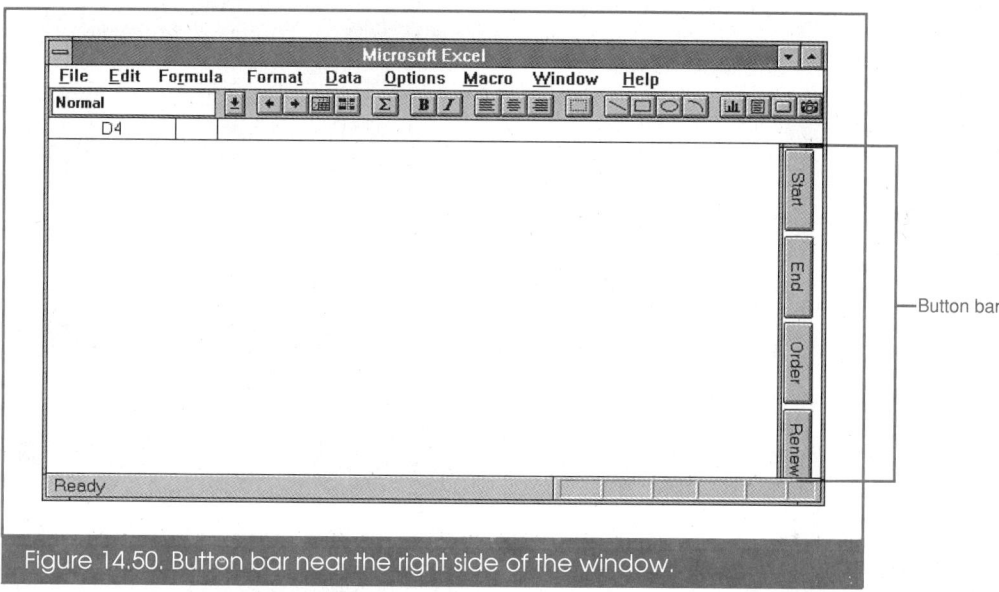

Figure 14.50. Button bar near the right side of the window.

14

File Save All Macro

Some Windows programs have File Save All commands that save all open documents. Excel doesn't, but the macro in Figure 14.51 performs this task. It is faster than many File Save All commands in that it saves only documents that have been changed and thus need saving.

Center-Aligning Text Macro

The **G**eneral format of the Forma**t** Alignment command always aligns text with the left margin of the cell. In many worksheets, you want to use the **G**eneral format but much of the text is centered in the cells. The macro in Figure 14.52 looks in each cell in the selection and, if it is text, changes the alignment to center.

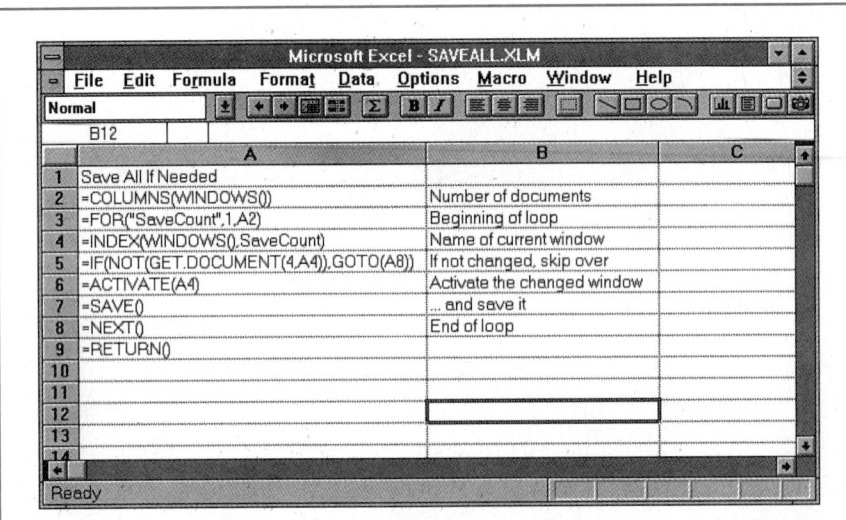

Figure 14.51. SAVEALL.XLM macro to save all documents.

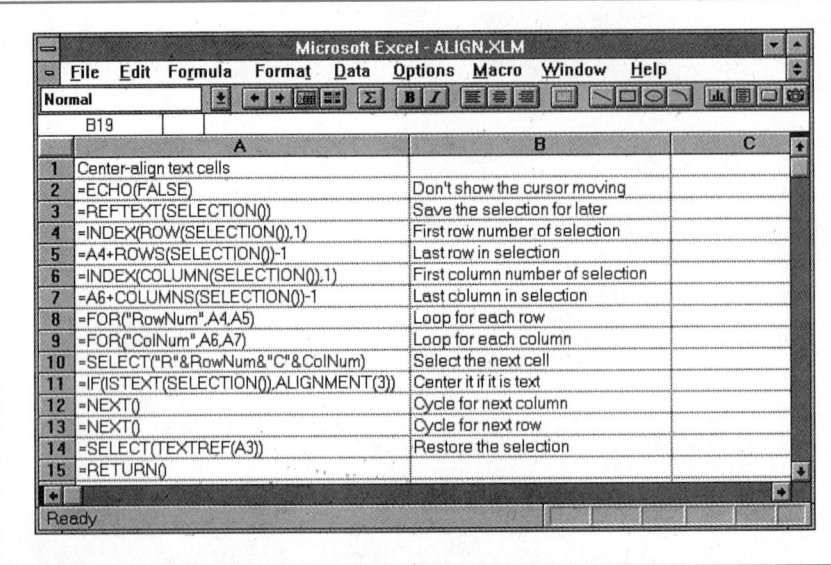

Figure 14.52. ALIGN.XLM macro to center text.

Convert Names to Last-Name-First Macro

Excel enables you to write functions that work just like Excel's internal functions. You can use all the power of the macro language in your functions. Figure 14.53 shows a function that takes a name that is in regular form (such as "Alicia L. Jacobs") and returns it in last-name-first order ("Jacobs, Alicia L."). It also recognizes standard family names such as "Jr." In the macro, "Family" is defined as the range A21:A24.

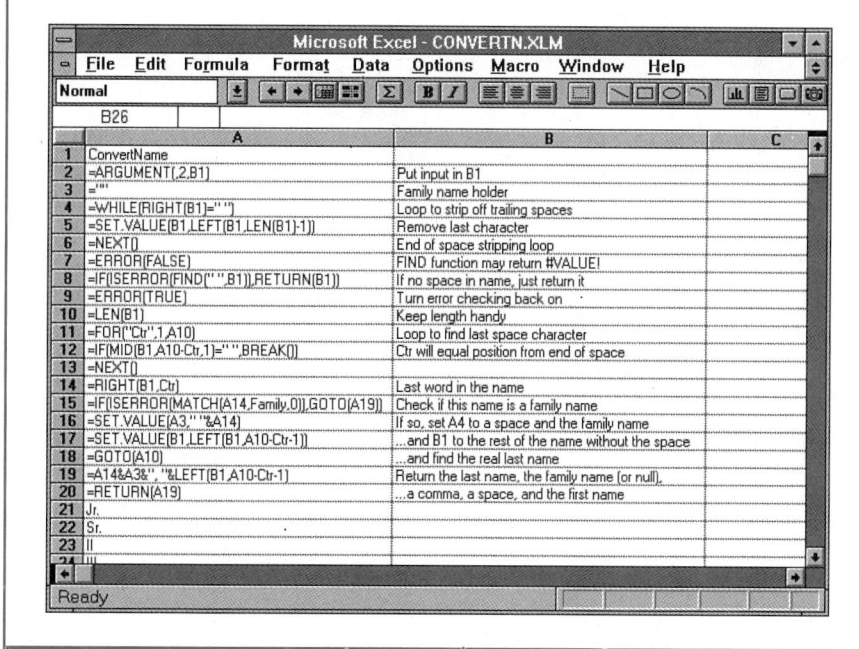

Figure 14.53. CONVERTN.XLM macro to convert name order.

14

Cascading Windows Macro

Excel's **Window** Arrange All command acts like the **Window** **T**ile command in Program Manager: It changes the size and shape of each window to tile them. This is rarely what you want if you have more than two windows open, and even then, it is unlikely that you will want Excel to change the size of the window you have created. The macro in Figure 14.54 is a better version of **W**indow Arrange All because it cascades windows instead of tiling them.

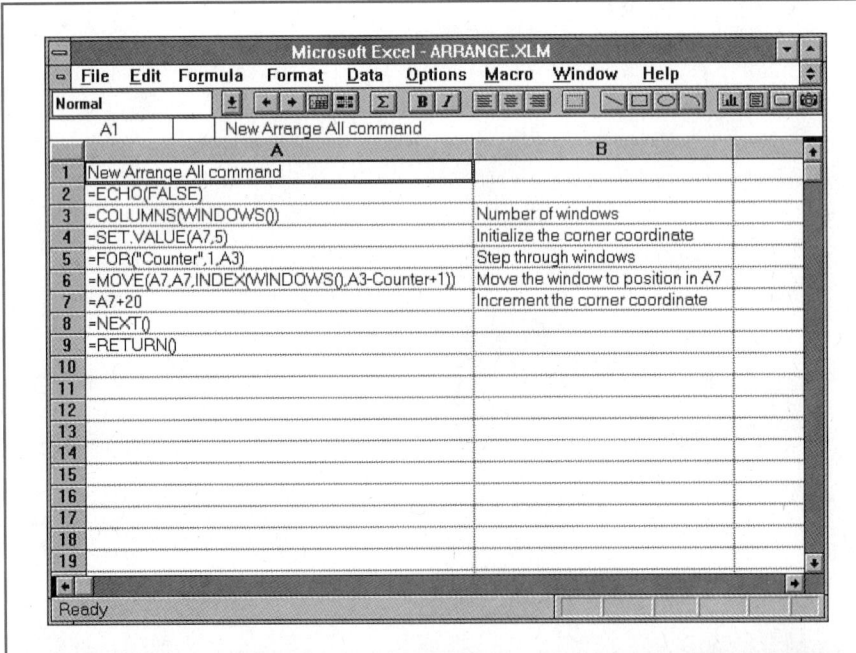

Figure 14.54. ARRANGE.XLM macro to cascade windows.

Better Window New Window Macro

Excel's **W**indow New Window command opens a second view into the current window. Unfortunately, it does this by cascading a new window. Unlike when you are using the **W**indow Arrange All command, you usually want to see as much of a new view of a window as you can and you don't want it to hide the original view. The macro in Figure 14.55 is a better version of the **W**indow New Window command because it opens the second window and tiles these two views (without tiling other open windows).

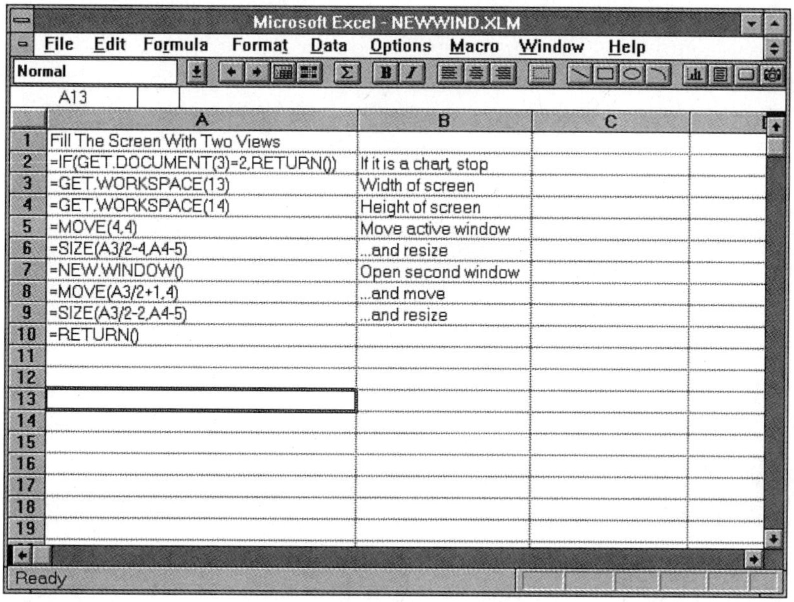

Figure 14.55. NEWWIND.XLM macro to open a second view.

Unhiding All Windows Macro

If you are using Excel for presentations, you might want to have some worksheets available but not visible. Excel enables you to hide these windows with the **W**indow Hide command. To unhide windows, however, you must use the **W**indow Unhide command, which enables you to unhide only one window at a time. If you have hidden many windows, this can be tedious. The macro in Figure 14.56 unhides all hidden windows at once.

Adding Notes to All Cells Macro

Excel enables you to attach notes to cells as a way of documenting your work. Notes can be very useful if someone else looks at your worksheet when you are not there. Most people, however, usually are lax about using notes. The macro in Figure 14.57 opens each cell and enables you to enter a note for it. Of course, you won't want to put notes on every cell, so you can click OK in the dialog box for the cells you want to keep empty. If there already is a note on the cell, the macro skips over it. You can use this macro while you are putting the final touches on a worksheet.

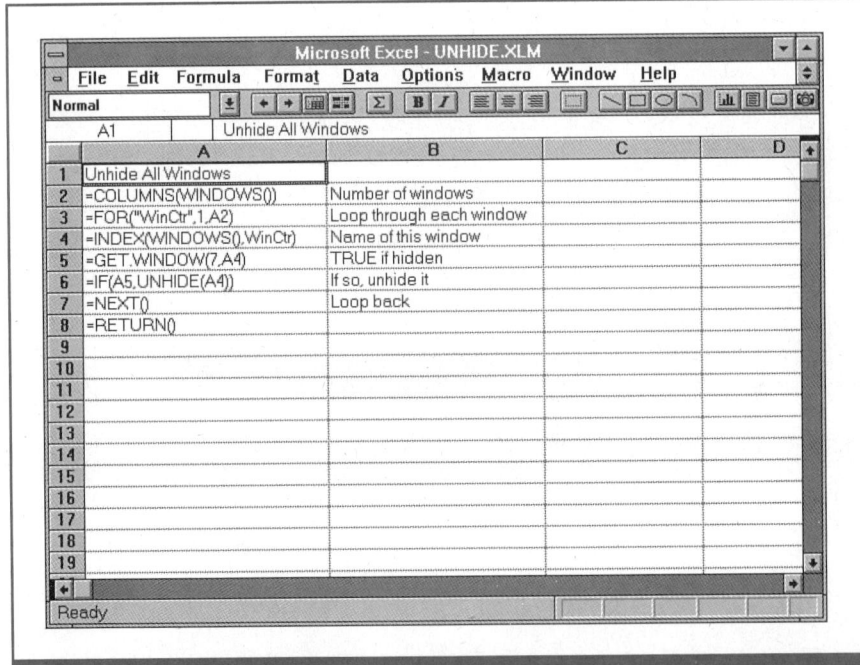

Figure 14.56. UNHIDE.XLM macro to unhide all windows.

Adding the Same Note to Many Cells Macro

Another common desire with Excel's notes is to add the same note to many cells at once. Unfortunately, there is no easy way to do this with the Formula Note command. The macro in Figure 14.58 prompts you for the note, then adds it to every cell that was selected when you ran the macro. The selection must be rectangular.

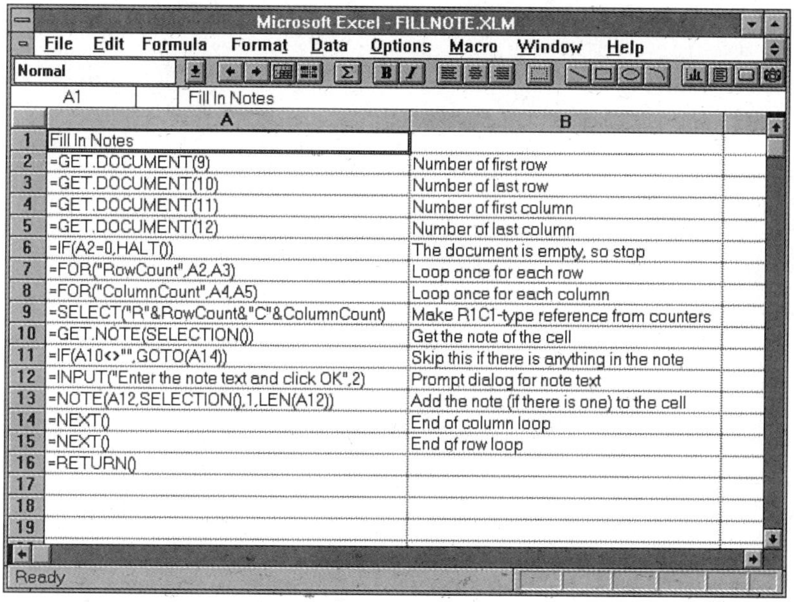

Microsoft Excel - FILLNOTE.XLM

	A	B
1	Fill In Notes	
2	=GET.DOCUMENT(9)	Number of first row
3	=GET.DOCUMENT(10)	Number of last row
4	=GET.DOCUMENT(11)	Number of first column
5	=GET.DOCUMENT(12)	Number of last column
6	=IF(A2=0,HALT())	The document is empty, so stop
7	=FOR("RowCount",A2,A3)	Loop once for each row
8	=FOR("ColumnCount",A4,A5)	Loop once for each column
9	=SELECT("R"&RowCount&"C"&ColumnCount)	Make R1C1-type reference from counters
10	=GET.NOTE(SELECTION())	Get the note of the cell
11	=IF(A10<>"",GOTO(A14))	Skip this if there is anything in the note
12	=INPUT("Enter the note text and click OK",2)	Prompt dialog for note text
13	=NOTE(A12,SELECTION(),1,LEN(A12))	Add the note (if there is one) to the cell
14	=NEXT()	End of column loop
15	=NEXT()	End of row loop
16	=RETURN()	

Figure 14.57. FILLNOTE.XLM macro to fill in notes in a worksheet.

Modifying the Same Attributes of Many Charts Macro

When you add graphics to a chart, you can select only one of them at a time. If you want to change them all to have consistent formatting, you must select the first one, change the formatting, select the next one, and so on. The macro in Figure 14.59 shows a simple way to select each item of a certain type and change the formatting. In this case, it selects each arrow and changes the length of the arrow head. You can modify the contents of A4 and A6 to choose other item types and to set other pattern characteristics.

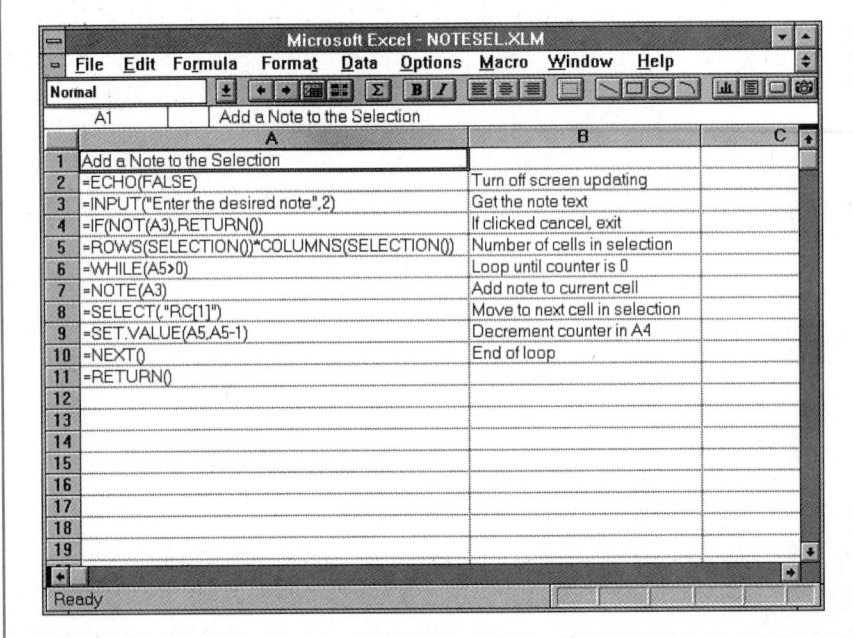

Figure 14.58. NOTESEL.XLM macro to add one note to all cells in a selection.

Checking Excel Names Macro

Most people use Excel's name feature to name ranges of cells. You also can use names to create functions, although this is considered to be a bad practice by many programmers. The macro in Figure 14.60 looks at all the names in a worksheet and alerts you if any of them are not for ranges.

Command Summary

This section is a command summary for Excel 3.0.

Microsoft Excel - ARROWS.XLM
File Edit Formula Format Data Options Macro Window Help
Normal
A1
Make Arrows Short
A
B
C
Make Arrows Short
=ERROR(FALSE)
Turn off error checking
=1
Initialize counter
=SELECT("Arrow "&A3)
Select the arrow
=IF(ISERROR(A4),RETURN())
Stop if A4 gets #VALUE!
=PATTERNS(1,,,,1,1,2)
Automatic line, narrow, short, and open head
=SET.VALUE(A3,A3+1)
Increment counter
=GOTO(A4)
Loop
=RETURN()
Ready

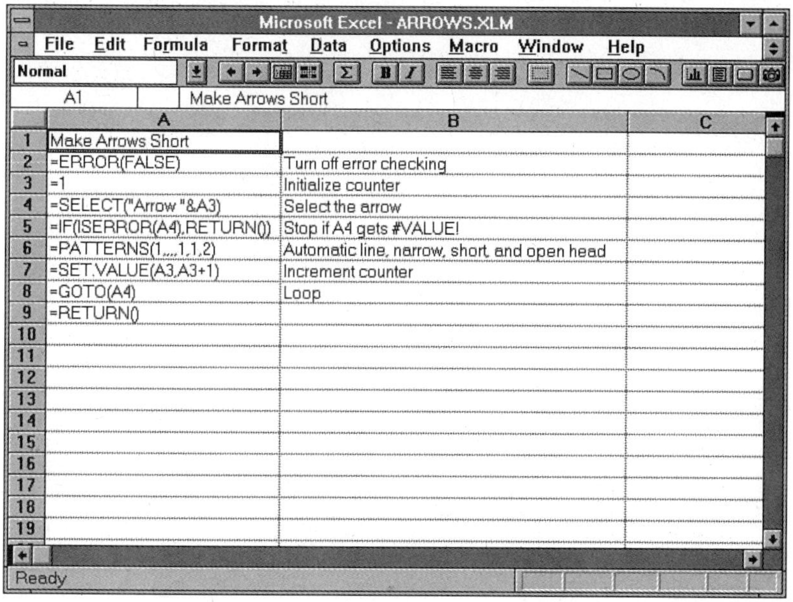

Figure 14.59. ARROWS.XLM macro to change item formatting.

File Menu

This is the command summary for the **F**ile menu.

File **N**ew	Begins a new worksheet, chart, macro sheet, or template.
File **O**pen	Opens an existing document or enables you to import information from a different application. Also used for changing directories.
File **C**lose	Closes all windows of the current document.
File **L**inks	Opens documents linked to the current document, or changes those links.
File **S**ave	Saves changes made to the current document.
File Save **A**s	Saves a new document or a new version of an existing document in the file format and with the filename you choose. It is also used for saving a file in a different directory.

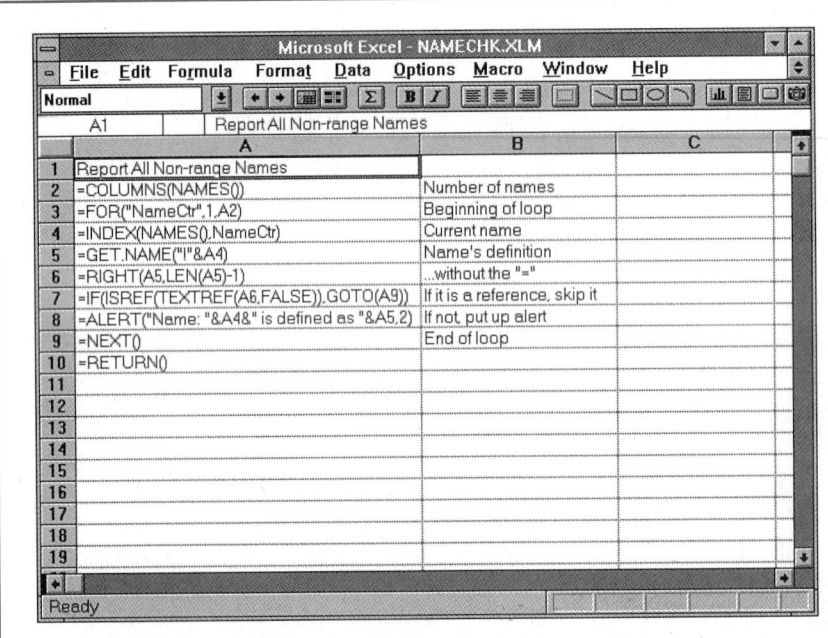

Figure 14.60. NAMECHK.XLM macro to check for nonrange names.

File Save Workplace	Begins a workspace file containing a list of the open documents, their positions on the screen, and the current workspace options. It also saves chart preferences.
File Delete	Removes the specified document from a disk.
File Print Preview	Enables you to view the document as it will appear when printed.
File Page Setup	Controls the appearance of items such as margins, headers, and footers on the document's printed pages.
File Print	Prints the current document according to your chosen specifications.
File Printer Setup	Identifies the specified printer and enables you to select options for it.
File [list]	Lists the four most recent files you've opened.
File Exit	Enables you to exit from Microsoft Excel.

Edit Menu

This is the command summary for the **E**dit menu.

Edit Undo	Reverses certain commands or actions.
Edit Repeat	Repeats the most recent command you've chosen.
Edit Cut	Moves a selection onto the Clipboard.
Edit Copy	Copies a selection onto the Clipboard.
Edit Paste	Pastes a copied or cut selection into the formula bar, a chart, a worksheet, or a workgroup.
Edit Clear	Deletes the data, formats, or both from the specified worksheet cells. If the active document is a chart, it erases chart data sets or formats.
Edit Paste Special	Pastes specified attributes of copied cells into the current selection on the active worksheet or workgroup. If the current document is a chart, it pastes a series of data from a worksheet or another chart into the current chart.
Edit Paste Link	Pastes copied data into the selection and creates a link with the data source.
Edit Delete	Deletes selected cells from a worksheet and shifts surrounding cells to fill the space.
Edit Insert	Inserts a range of cells equivalent in size and shape into the specified range, and rearranges the selection to accommodate new cells.
Edit Fill Left	Copies the contents and formats of cells in the right column of a selected range into the remaining cells in the selection. Fill Left appears only when you hold down Shift and select the **E**dit menu.
Edit Fill Right	Copies the contents and formats of cells in the left column of a selected range into the remaining cells in the selection.
Edit Fill Up	Copies contents in bottom row into the above remaining cells.
Edit Fill Down	Copies the contents and formats of cells in the top row of a selected range into the remaining cells in the selection.

14

Edit Fill Workgroup	Inserts the contents of the current sheet's selection to the same specified location on all sheets in the workgroup.

Formula Menu

Commands for the Formula menu are outlined in this section.

Formula Paste Name	Enters the specified name into the formula bar.
Formula Paste Function	Enters the chosen function into the formula bar.
Formula Reference	Changes the specified references in the formula bar from relative to absolute, absolute to mixed, and mixed to relative.
Formula Define Name	Makes a name for a cell range, value, or formula.
Formula Create Names	Uses text in the range to name the rows and columns.
Formula Apply Names	Looks for formulas in specified cells and replaces cell references with defined names.
Formula Note	Enables you to delete, add, view notes, or edit for specific cells on the current worksheet.
Formula Goto	Scrolls the worksheet and selects the cells or names area of your choosing.
Formula Find	Looks for selected cells or an entire worksheet for specified characters and chooses the first cell containing those characters.
Formula Replace	Finds and replaces characters in specified cells or in the entire worksheet.
Formula Select Special	Selects cells with the characters you've specified or selects all objects.
Formula Show Active Cell	Scrolls the worksheet until the current cell can be viewed.
Formula Outline	Makes an outline from an existing worksheet or cell range.

| Formula Goal Seek | Changes the value in a cell until a formula reaches the desired value. |
| Formula Solver | Runs the separate Solver Program that comes with Excel. |

Format Menu

This is the Format menu command summary.

Format Number	Enables you to specify how numbers, currency, dates, and times are displayed in the chosen cells.
Format Alignment	Aligns the contents of chosen cells and enables you to activate text wrapping.
Format Font	Changes the font for the specified text, text boxes, or cells on the current worksheet.
Format Border	Enables you to change the borders by adding or removing solid border lines, shading, or both in the chosen cells.
Format Patterns	Enables you to alter the appearance of cells or objects.
Format Cell Protection	Enables you to decide whether cells will be locked or their formulas hidden when protecting the document.
Format Object Protection	Sets whether objects or specified text in a text box is locked when you protect the document.
Format Style	Enables you to specify cell styles.
Format Row Height	Alters the height of selected rows.
Format Column Width	Alters the width of chosen columns.
Format Justify	Distributes text evenly throughout the chosen range.
Format Bring to Front	Puts the specified objects in front of all other objects.
Format Send to Back	Puts the chosen objects behind all other objects.
Format Group	Forms a group of several objects into one object.

14

| Format Object Placement | Enables you to determine whether an object is linked to the underlying cells and repositioned with them if their position is changed or their size is altered. |

Data Menu

The commands found in the **D**ata menu are summarized here.

Data Form	Displays a database form for viewing, changing, adding, and deleting records.
Data Find	Finds records in the database that correspond to the criteria you specify.
Data Extract	Copies all records from the database into an extract range according to the criteria you specify.
Data Delete	Erases from the database all records that correspond to the criteria you specify.
Data Set Database	Defines the chosen range of cells as a database.
Data Set Criteria	Defines the chosen cell range as the criteria range.
Data Set Extract	Defines the specified cell range as an extract range for extracting records from a database.
Data Sort	Sorts selected rows or columns.
Data Series	Enables you to fill a cell range with one or more series of dates or numbers.
Data Table	Makes a data table using the input formulas and values on a worksheet.
Data Parse	Enables you to distribute the contents of one column into several columns.
Data Consolidate	Consolidates the contents of various ranges on several sheets into one range.

Options Menu

This is the **O**ptions menu command summary.

| **O**ptions Set Print Area/ Remove Print Area | Specifies the parameters of the current worksheet you would like to print. |

Options Set Print Titles/ Remove Print Titles	Creates titles in the printed document from selected text in rows and columns.
Options Set Page Break	Sets manual page breaks.
Options Remove Page Break	Deletes manual page breaks.
Options Display	Enables you to change many of the options for the screen display.
Options Color Palette	Enables you to modify every color in the color palette for a document and copy the color palette onto another document.
Options Freeze Panes	Keeps a pane visible in the worksheet at all times.
Options Protect Document	Enables you to turn on a worksheet's cell and window protection.
Options Calculation	Enables you to change when and how formulas are calculated in open documents.
Options Calculate Now	Calculates all open charts, macro sheets, and worksheets.
Options Workspace	Enables you to change the option settings that correspond to the entire Microsoft Excel session.
Options Short Menus	Enables you to shorten the menu so that only a limited number of commands are displayed.
Options Full Menus	Enables you to lengthen a shortened menu.

14

Macro Menu

These are the commands for the **M**acro menu.

Macro Run	Enables you to run a macro.
Macro Record	Starts recording a macro.
Macro Start Recorder	Restarts recorder after pausing.
Macro Set Recorder	Sets the range into which you will record.
Macro Relative Record	Changes the style of references for macros.

| **M**acro Assign to Object | Assigns a macro to a button or other object in the worksheet. |

Window Menu

This is the **W**indow menu command summary.

Window New Window	Opens another window for the current worksheet or macro sheet.
Window Show Info	Enables you to view the Info window for the current worksheet or macro sheet.
Window Arrange All	Tiles all open windows for viewing them simultaneously.
Window Workgroup	Creates a workgroup of various worksheets and macro sheets so that a command issued once can act on each sheet in the workgroup.
Window Hide	Hides the current window.
Window Unhide	Brings back a hidden window to view.
Window 1,2,3...9	Displays a list of all the open windows and enables you to select the one you would like to activate.
Window More Windows	Enables you to view a list of all the open and unhidden windows when there are more than nine windows open, and activates the one you select.

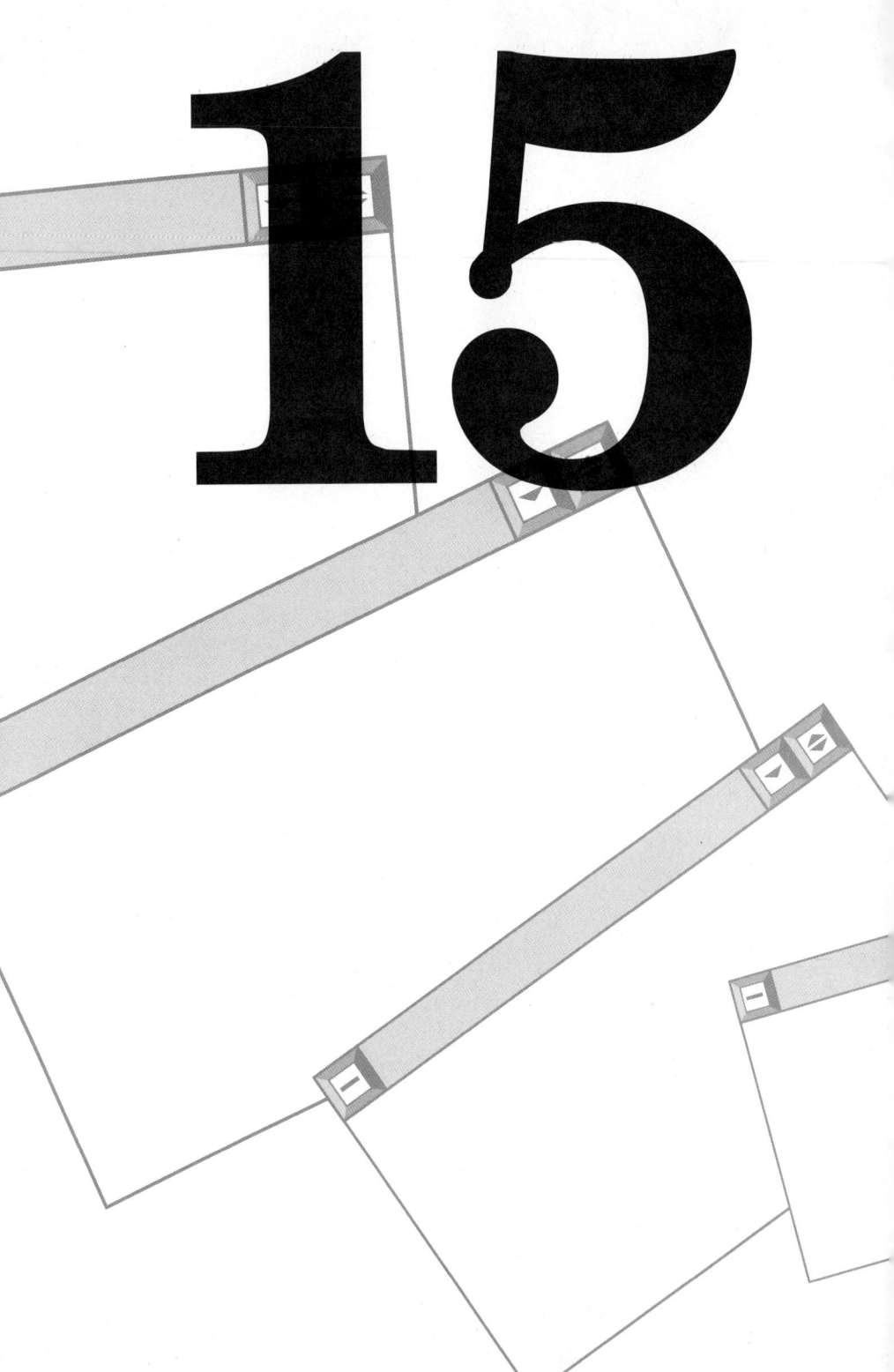

CHAPTER

15

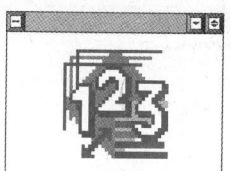

Lotus 1-2-3 for Windows

To say that Lotus Corporation has been making well-accepted spreadsheet management software for many years is something of an understatement. Since the founding days of Jonathan Sachs and the original 1-2-3 program in April of 1982, many spreadsheet users have migrated to 1-2-3, to the tune of about 73 percent of total market share at the character-based application's peak. 1-2-3 for Windows appears to utilize more of a three-dimensional interface than its contemporaries. Dialog boxes are well-shaded and icon buttons usually are multicolored. Lotus obviously has tried to adhere to current standards as much as possible. Many of the SmartIcons are familiar to users of Excel and Word for Windows.

Lotus began shipping its first 1-2-3 product for the IBM PC on January 26, 1983. In the summer of 1991 (more than eight years and six major revisions later), Lotus finally released a GUI (Graphical User Interface) 1-2-3 for Windows. This chapter is about the Windows version.

Note: Because this book is primarily about Windows 3.1 and products designed to operate under Windows, we refer to 1-2-3 for Windows as simply 1-2-3. If a discussion specifically refers to a non-Windows-based Lotus 1-2-3 version, we use the "1-2-3 for DOS" descriptor to maintain clarity. Unless otherwise stated, when we say 1-2-3, we are referring to Lotus 1-2-3 for Windows.

Lotus 1-2-3 for Windows Features

These are some of the features that are discussed later in the chapter:

▲ Lotus has preserved its popular original menuing system for the die-hard 1-2-3 for DOS user. You can use 1-2-3 without a mouse, essentially pretending that you are using 1-2-3 for DOS. You simply press the slash key to bring up traditional 1-2-3 menus.

▲ Lotus has included Adobe Type Manager, a font-enhancement product designed to improve printed output.

▲ The application is fully DDE- (*D*ynamic *D*ata *E*xchange) compliant: You can seamlessly exchange data between many Windows products and 1-2-3 for Windows.

▲ Included are Solver and Backsolver, two analytical add-on products that provide sophisticated analysis support for your spreadsheet data.

▲ DataLens is a data collection tool add-on that enables the user to access and utilize popular database files in dBASE III, III+, Paradox, and SQL formats. It's also included with 1-2-3 Version 1.0.

▲ A concept of initiating tasks that Lotus calls "SmartIcons" has been developed as a superset of the traditional icon bar (Excel uses an icon bar). SmartIcons is a concept of assigning often-used functions to a button, called a SmartIcon. See Figure 15.1 for a look at the SmartIcon icon bar.

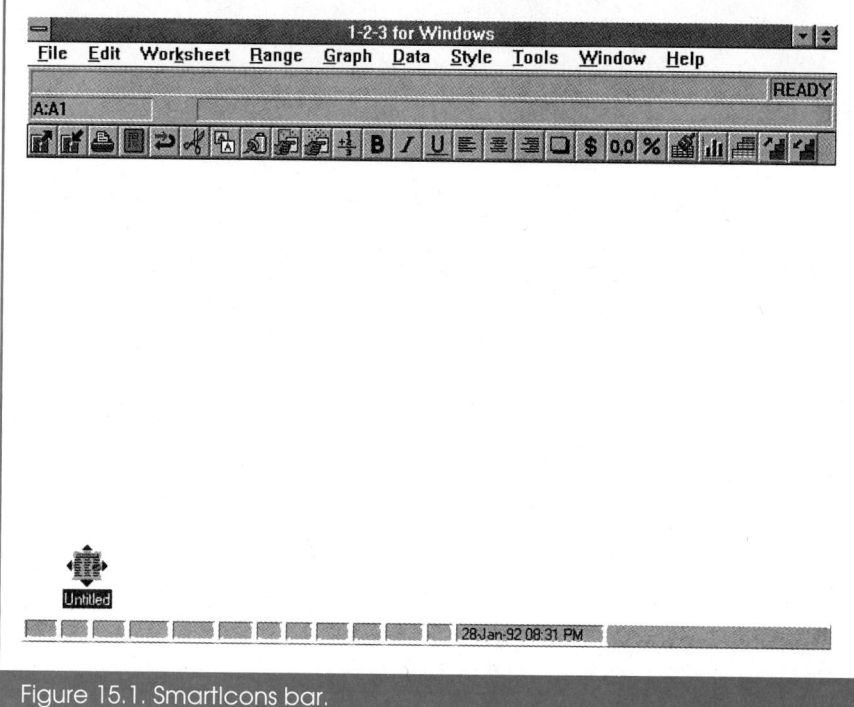

Figure 15.1. SmartIcons bar.

15

System Requirements

The hardware and software requirements for running 1-2-3 are the following:

Hardware Requirements

- ▲ An 80286, 80386, 80486, or 80586 that is Microsoft-certified for use with Windows versions 3.0 or higher.

- ▲ An EGA, VGA, or IBM 8514 monitor.

- ▲ A mouse or other pointing device is strongly recommended, but not required.

- ▲ A minimum of 2M (megabytes) of system RAM (*R*andom-*A*ccess *M*emory).

- ▲ At least 5M of available hard disk space to hold 1-2-3 for Windows. This space does not include space taken by files you create for your data.

Tip: Even though 1-2-3 requires only 2M of RAM, you no doubt will run into RAM shortages as soon as you load screen savers, font managers, and other memory-intensive utilities or applications. If you are reviewing this book in order to decide on the software and hardware you need to upgrade to 1-2-3 for Windows, consider buying a system with *at least* 8M of RAM and a hard drive with a random access rate of no more than 18 milliseconds. Spreadsheet files tend to get big and get saved more often than other types of application files, requiring lots of hard disk involvement. In a nutshell, the more you can spend on your system, the greater your productivity.

Software Requirements

▲ Microsoft Windows 3.0 or later.

▲ DOS 3.11 or later.

The Components of a 1-2-3 Screen

Each 1-2-3 screen is made up of objects that form the 1-2-3 application screen. When you start 1-2-3, you see the screen shown in Figure 15.2.

The Menu Bar

The menu bar contains all the drop-down main menu titles. Any of these menus can be selected with the mouse or the keyboard.

Click the menu item to bring down the full menu for that title.

Hold down the Alt or F10 key and press any underlined letter found in any of the menu names. For example, pressing Alt-F opens the **F**ile menu. Press the ↓ key to position the highlight over the command of your choice. Press the Enter key to execute that command.

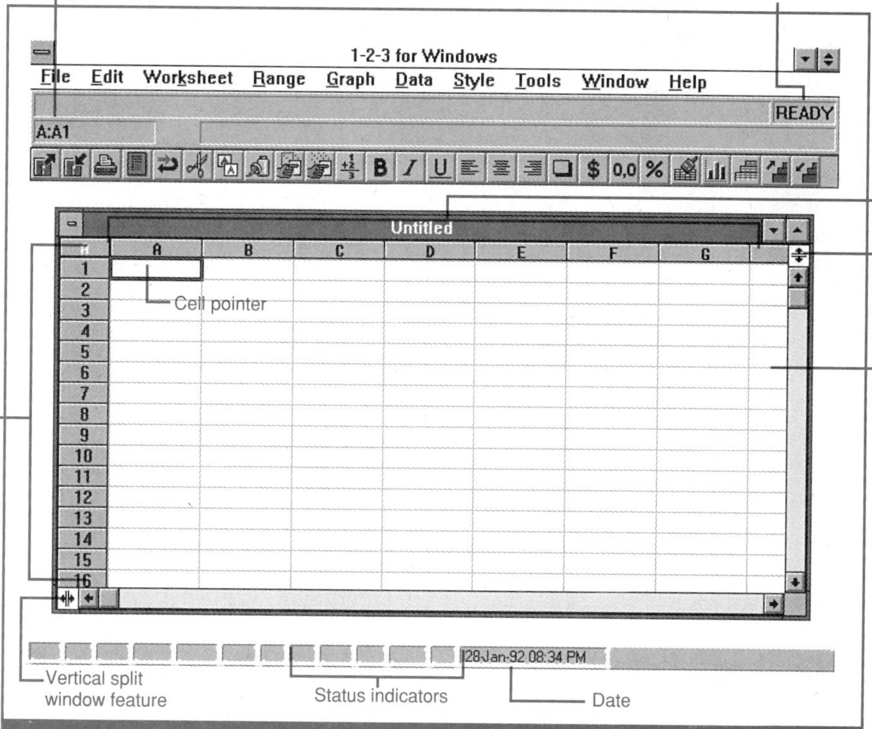

Figure 15.2. The components of a 1-2-3 screen.

SmartIcons

The fifth line on the initial 1-2-3 screen contains SmartIcons. SmartIcons are simply shortcut and task icons located on individual buttons. Lotus calls this horizontal bar area the SmartIcon palette. SmartIcons are detailed later in this chapter.

The Status Bar

The status bar is located at the base of the 1-2-3 screen or window, and it displays useful information. When 1-2-3 executes a command, it tells you so in the status bar. The date and time also are displayed there. If your keyboard does not have LEDs (*L*ight-*E*mitting *D*iodes) that dis-

15

play the status of your Num Lock, Insert, Scroll Lock, and Caps Lock keys, you are in luck. 1-2-3 displays the status of these keys in the status bar.

Running 1-2-3

This section is dedicated to the process of starting and using 1-2-3.

Getting Set Up

When you start 1-2-3, the screen elements described in the previous section are visible, along with an empty worksheet or spreadsheet. Before you begin to work with worksheets or spreadsheets, you should set some of the 1-2-3 defaults from the **T**ools menu.

Note: 1-2-3 documentation and software refer to spreadsheets as *worksheets* in both the text and the actual displays on your screen. You need to get used to this exchange of definitions. Just think of a worksheet as a spreadsheet throughout this chapter and you will do fine.

Select **T**ools **U**ser Setup to open the Tools User Setup dialog box, shown in Figure 15.3.

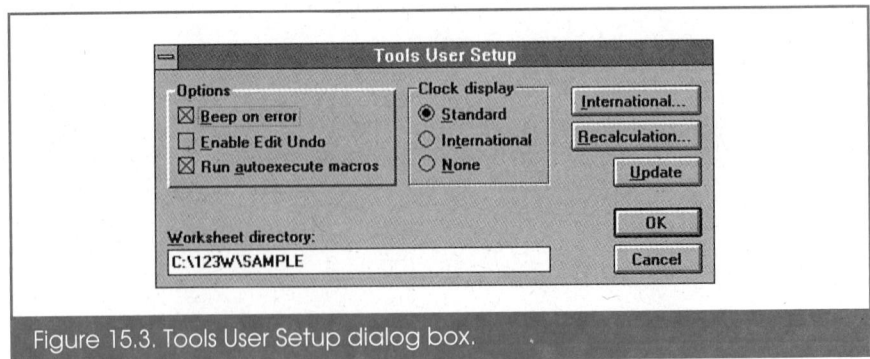

Figure 15.3. Tools User Setup dialog box.

The Tools User Setup dialog box provides you with several options. If you don't set these options or preferences to suit yourself, 1-2-3 always

starts using the default preferences determined during the installation process. Use Table 15.1 to review each option and decide how you want 1-2-3 to run each time you start it.

Table 15.1. Tools User Setup dialog box options.

Option	Explanation
Beep on error	You might not want to hear a loud beep every time you err.
Enable Edit Undo	Activates the **E**dit **U**ndo option in the **E**dit menu.
Run **a**utoexecute macros	1-2-3 can run macros from the startup point if you prefer.
Clock display **S**tandard	Choose this to see Lotus's idea of standard date and time format (for example, 30-Sep-91 09:05 AM).
Clock display In**t**ernational	Choose this to see the alternative date and time format (for example, 9/23/91 9:00).
Clock display **N**one	Enables/disables the clock display on the status bar.
Worksheet directory	1-2-3 looks for files in the directory named in this text box.

Opening a File

To open a file, select **F**ile **O**pen from the 1-2-3 main menu bar. For the sake of people familiar with 1-2-3 for DOS, 1-2-3 for Windows displays a message related to each highlighted menu option in the title bar area. The **F**ile **O**pen dialog box appears in the center of the display, as shown in Figure 15.4.

The filename currently highlighted in the **F**iles list box is pasted after the directory name in the File **n**ame text box. The directory name used is based on your input in the Tools User Setup dialog box, discussed earlier in this chapter. You can stay in the same directory, or you can select another directory, and then double-click a preferred file displayed in the **F**iles list box.

15

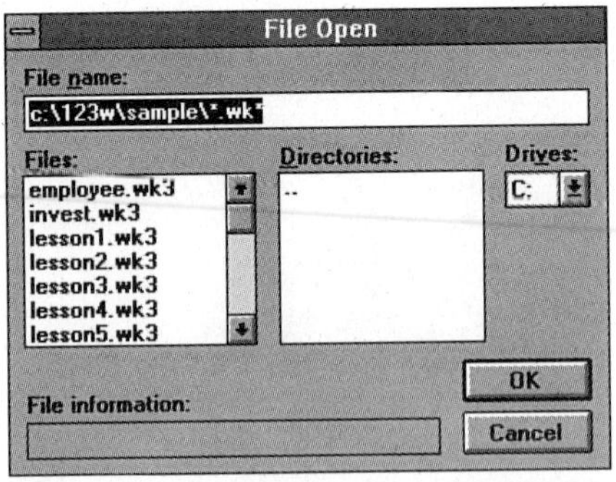

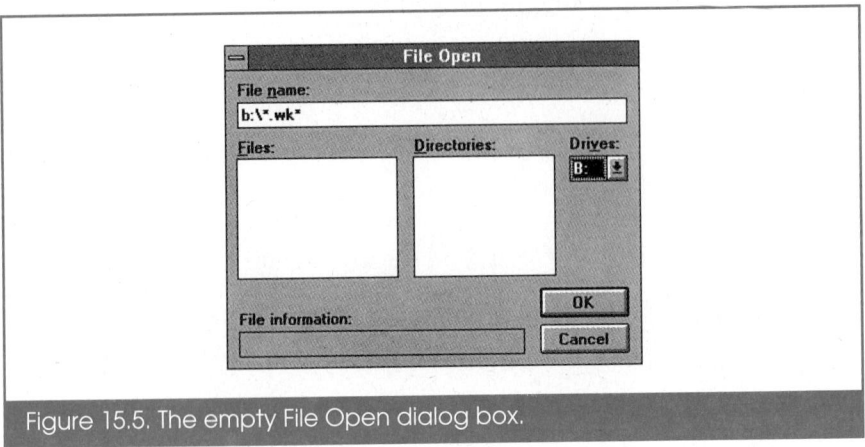

Figure 15.4. File Open dialog box.

If your files are located on another drive, use the Drives drop-down list box to select the drive. 1-2-3 displays the available drive names. Select one, and give 1-2-3 a few seconds to read and display the selected disk drive contents. If you don't have a disk in the drive selected, you do not see an alert box as you might expect. 1-2-3 simply displays empty text and list boxes if it finds no disk or files on a selected disk. The empty File Open dialog box is shown in Figure 15.5.

Figure 15.5. The empty File Open dialog box.

1-2-3 now displays the normal 1-2-3 screen. You should see a window in the workspace area of the screen that contains a display of the worksheet you selected, as in Figure 15.6.

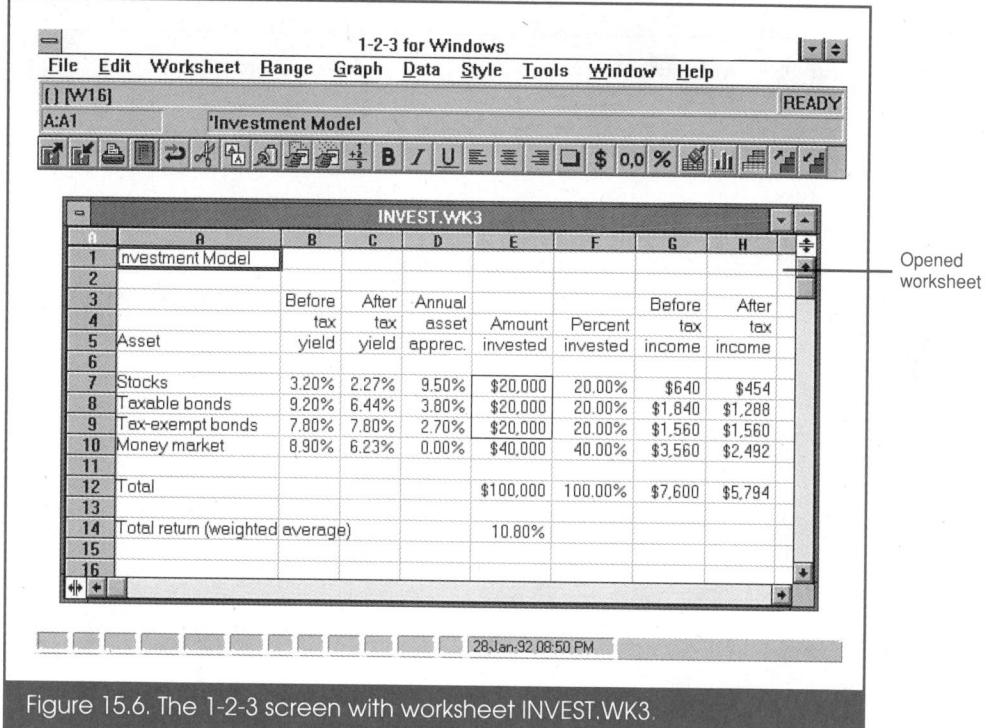

Figure 15.6. The 1-2-3 screen with worksheet INVEST.WK3.

Navigating the 1-2-3 worksheet is like most other Windows-based spreadsheets. To select a cell in which to edit or enter data, use the pointer to select a cell, and click.

The Split Screen Feature

The split screen feature enables you to keep two distant parts of one spreadsheet on the screen at the same time. The vertical split screen icon is located just above the vertical scroll bar on the screen. The horizontal split screen icon is located to the left of the horizontal scroll bar. Experiment with this feature to create the correct environment for you. An example of the use of the split screen feature is shown in Figure 15.7.

15

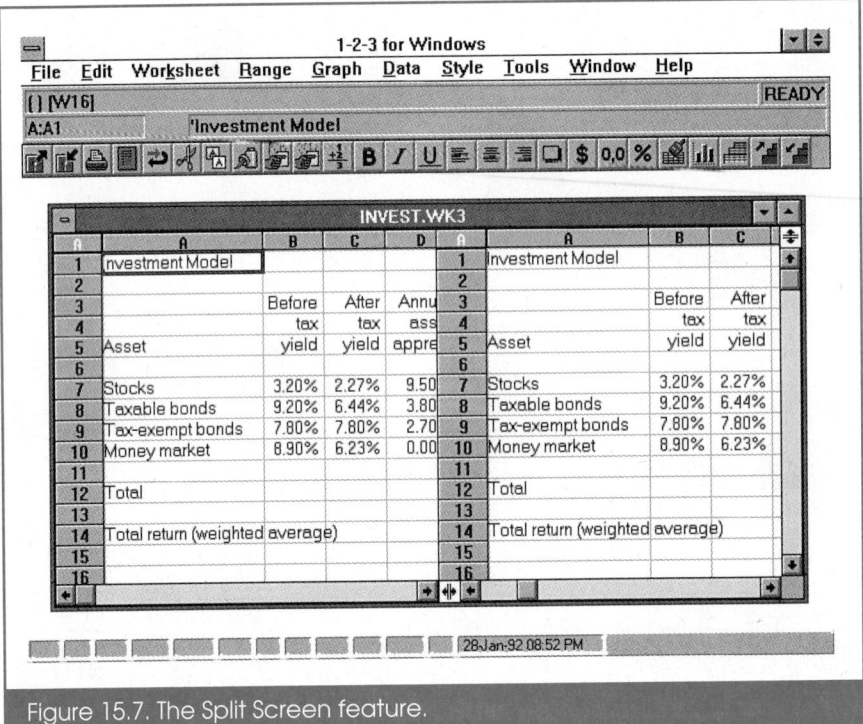

Figure 15.7. The Split Screen feature.

Window Display Options

You can change the overall screen display options by opening the Window Display Options dialog box, shown in Figure 15.8.

This dialog box enables you to configure the colors for each area on the spreadsheet by object type. You can change the colors of the cell contents, the worksheet frame, and so on. You can further customize your color settings by clicking the **P**alette button at the lower-right of the Window Display Options dialog box. A new dialog box opens. The Window Display Options Palette dialog box is shown in Figure 15.9. To save your color selections and return to the Window Display Options dialog box, click the OK button in the lower-right corner of the dialog box. You now see the previous dialog box. Save all your color preferences by clicking the **U**pdate button, or click the **R**estore button to revert to the settings in place when you first selected **W**indow **D**isplay Options from the menu. Clicking OK will allow you to change the settings for this session only. 1-2-3 utilizes your display preferences whenever you restart 1-2-3.

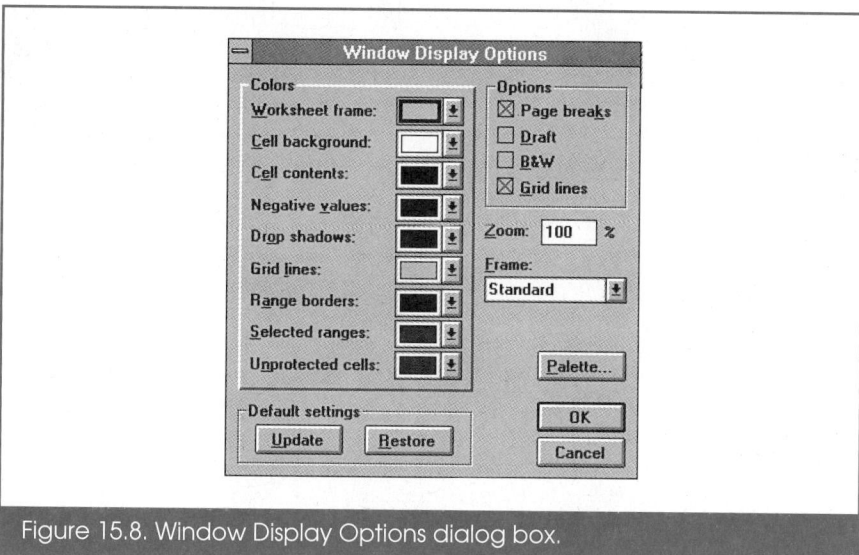

Figure 15.8. Window Display Options dialog box.

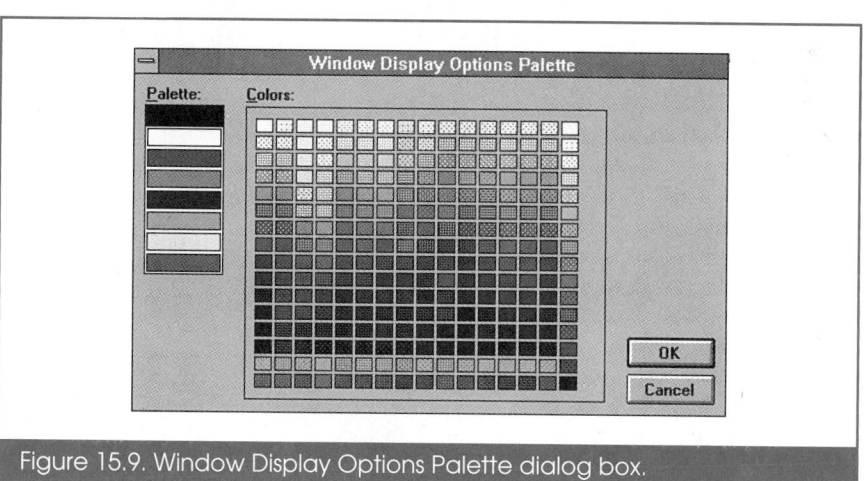

Figure 15.9. Window Display Options Palette dialog box.

Using SmartIcons

SmartIcons are designed to handle worksheet tasks for you. In this
sense they are in many cases shortcut buttons that are both
customizable and creatable. You can arrange SmartIcons to run across
the upper area of the display, across the left or the right side of the

screen, or across the bottom of the screen. Alternatively, you can arrange for the SmartIcons to float in a rectangular block arrangement anywhere you choose to drag and leave the SmartIcon palette.

This is the default 1-2-3 positioning of SmartIcons unless you change the default setting. Figure 15.10 shows SmartIcons across the upper portion of the display, the default position.

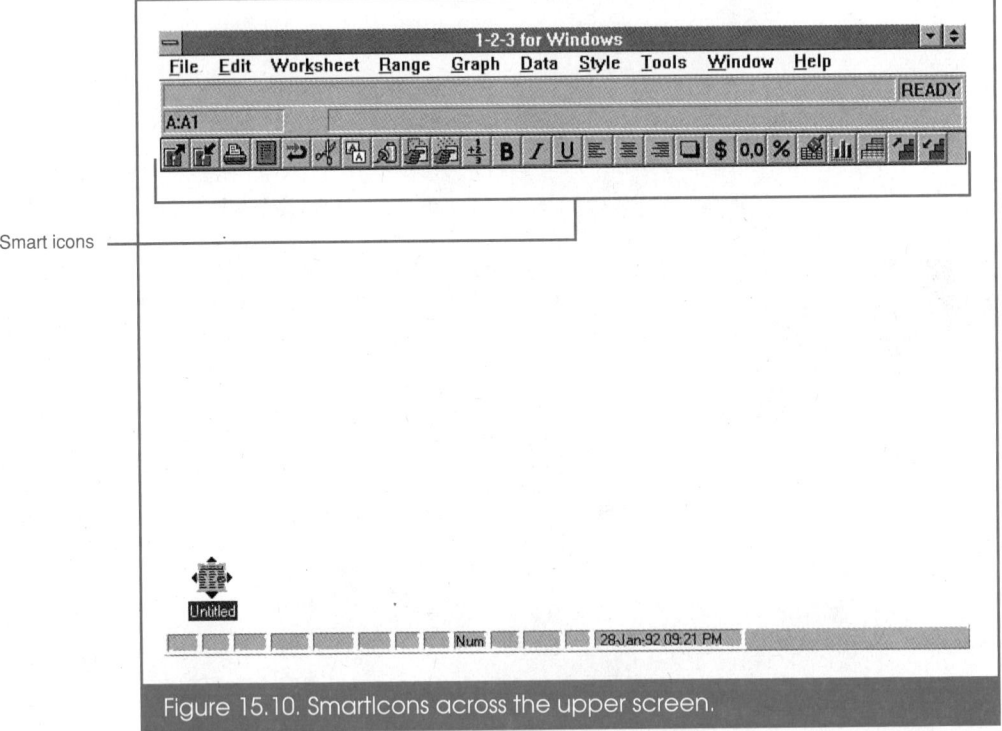

Smart icons

Figure 15.10. SmartIcons across the upper screen.

Tip: If you want to know what a SmartIcon does before you click it, position the pointer over the icon of interest and hold down the right mouse button to see a brief description in the title bar area. Release the right mouse button to cancel the inquiry.

Figure 15.11 shows SmartIcons displayed vertically on the left side of the screen.

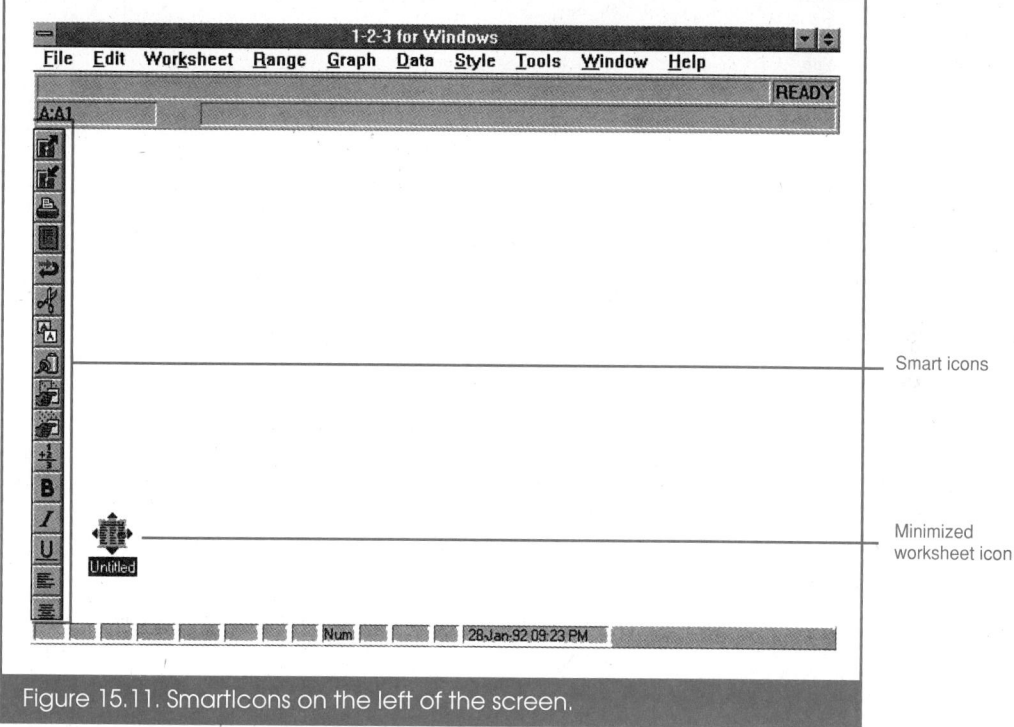

Smart icons

Minimized
worksheet icon

Figure 15.11. SmartIcons on the left of the screen.

You can arrange to float the SmartIcon display as shown in Figure 15.12, by clicking the Float button in the Tools SmartIcons dialog box.

There is a SmartIcon display for graphics tasks as well. Click the SmartIcon that shows a small vertical bar chart to open a graph window. The SmartIcon bar is replaced with the graphic SmartIcons that always appear when you have a graph window in the foreground. Close the graph window using the window's control menu to re-create the worksheet SmartIcon palette and return to the worksheet.

You can write a macro and assign a custom SmartIcon to it. You then can add that SmartIcon to the SmartIcon palette with all the other SmartIcons. Figure 15.13 shows the Tools SmartIcons Customize dialog box.

Smart icons ──────────

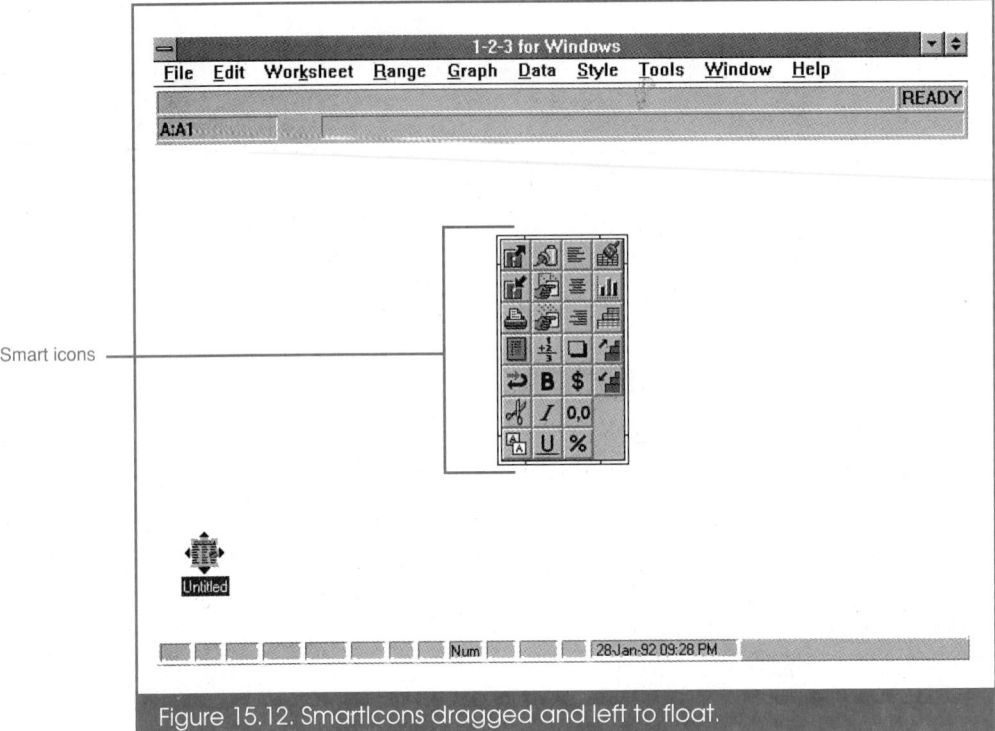

Figure 15.12. SmartIcons dragged and left to float.

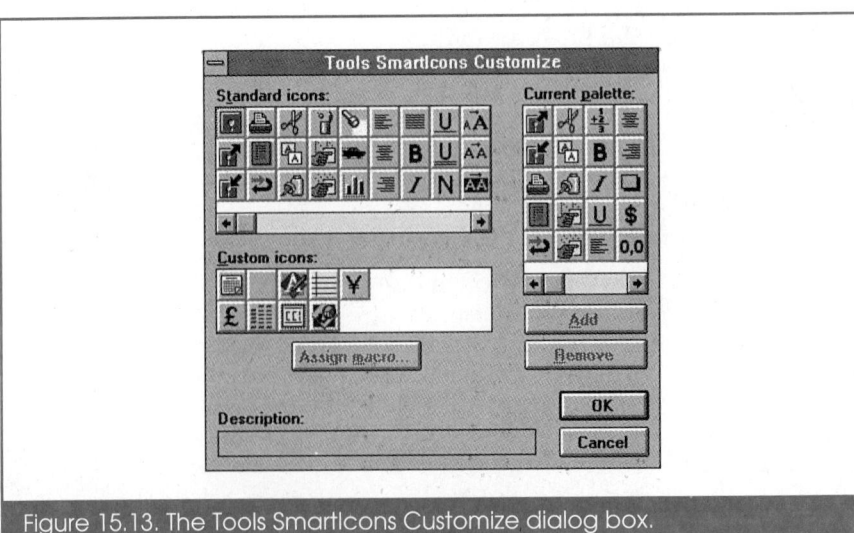

Figure 15.13. The Tools SmartIcons Customize dialog box.

3-D Worksheets

A single 1-2-3 file can contain 256 worksheets. Each worksheet can contain 256 columns and 8192 rows. Figure 15.14 shows the first worksheet in a file containing several worksheets. Within the file, topics are assigned or organized into worksheets of their own.

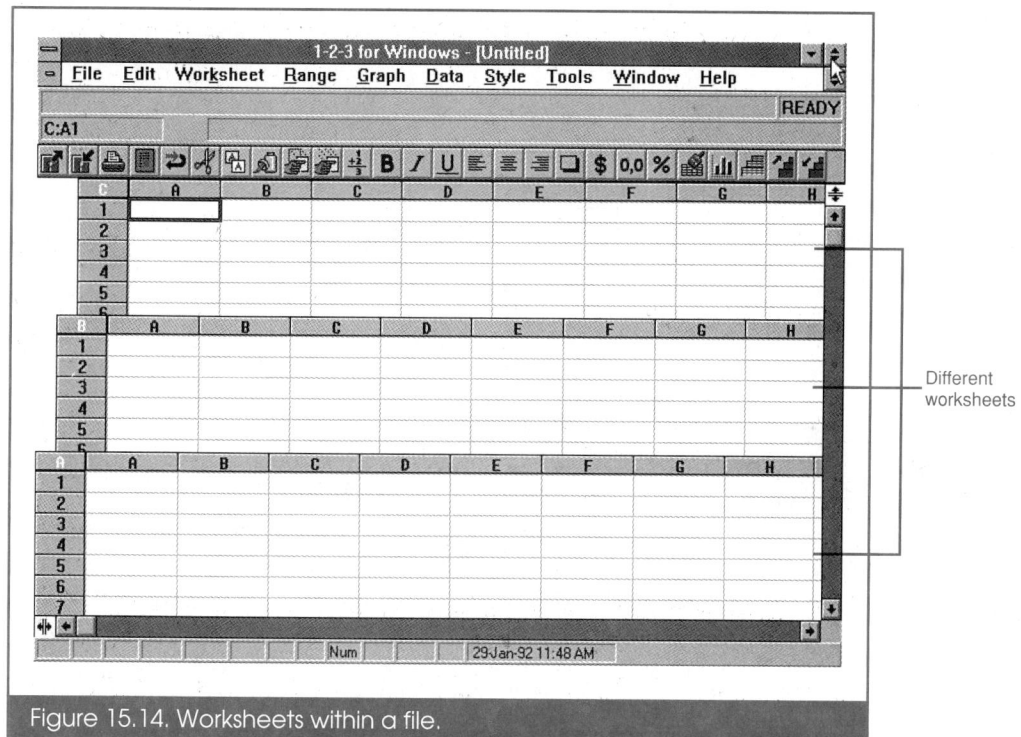

Figure 15.14. Worksheets within a file.

15

Copying Between Files

1-2-3 enables you to open multiple files that contain multiple worksheets. You can cut and paste between open worksheets just as if you were using any modern Windows product. DDE is fully implemented. You can use DDE to change data that occurs in completely separate applications simultaneously and without switching between windows.

Named Style

If you have ever worked with elaborate formatting of text with a competent word processor, you will appreciate the value of 1-2-3's Named Style feature. It's a way of assigning sophisticated formatting requirements to a style name. You assign color, alignment, date formatting, and so on to a name in the Style Name dialog box, as shown in Figure 15.15.

Figure 15.15. Style Name dialog box.

It works like style sheet functions do within Word for Windows. Instead of assigning paragraph and indentation parameters, you select preferred foreground and background colors, cell alignment, or number formatting. Apply the Name style to a cell or cells, and you convert the selected cell(s) to respect all of the presaved preferences you have named.

Graphs

1-2-3 makes slick graphs and enables you to use very competent drawing tools within your graphs. You can draw lines, ellipses, boxes, and curved lines, all by clicking the SmartIcon that represents the related function.

A full set of two-dimensional and three-dimensional graphs can be selected, as shown in Figure 15.16.

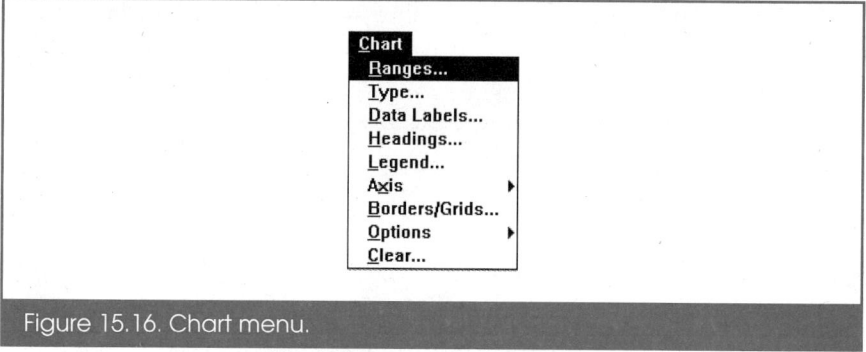

Figure 15.16. Chart menu.

More than 200 graph style combinations are available. You can use the drawing tools to create arrows that draw attention to an aspect of a chart. Virtually all these functions are available by simply clicking a SmartIcon. The SmartIcon palette for graphs works the same way that the SmartIcon worksheet palette does.

You can always press and hold down the right mouse button to read a brief description of any SmartIcon function. The description appears in the title bar at the top of the screen.

Font Management

As well as accessing all the fonts your system has to offer any Windows application, 1-2-3 offers some unique font management features normally found only in high-end page layout programs. For example, when you are working with a graph and you want to insert a string of text and make it stand out just a bit, open the Style Font dialog box.

You can choose each font from the list box provided. The Style Font dialog box is shown in Figure 15.17.

Adobe Type Manager

You can add hard or prebuilt fonts to a printer by purchasing just such a font in the form of a font cartridge, or you can arrange a software-based solution such as ATM.

ATM is included with 1-2-3 Version 1.0. ATM is a utility that creates soft fonts, or software-based fonts, as opposed to hard fonts or prebuilt bitmap fonts. Soft fonts are generated from a library of font outlines stored within files that ATM installs on your hard disk. The result is a smoother outside edge on each character printed. Hard or prebuilt fonts reside in programs stored on printer hardware.

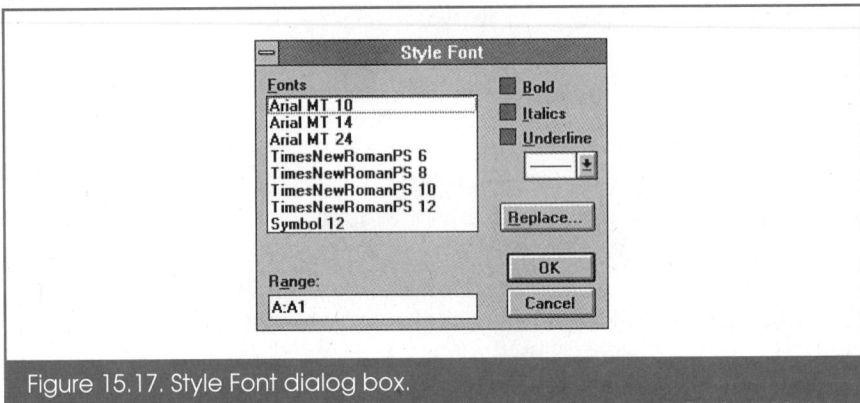

Figure 15.17. Style Font dialog box.

The Pros and Cons of Using ATM

The real benefit of ATM is measured by the frequency of use of larger character sizes (24 points or greater) versus the amount of memory space that ATM requires. If you make many large words, ATM makes a better-looking printed character than standard vector fonts (such as those used by Windows 3.0). ATM is great with large characters. You will really notice the difference.

Because ATM uses a portion of memory to re-create each character "in its own image," it downloads these reformed fonts to the printer each time you print a document using ATM. If you have the memory to spare, ATM causes little or no loss in printing speed. You can configure ATM to use more memory to increase its operating speed if you need to.

If you do not have gobs of memory (one "gob" is 4M of RAM on your system) and cannot spare ATM the extra room it needs to really perform, the speed of your applications can suffer, because ATM might need additional memory to quickly redisplay your characters on the screen.

Because ATM also downloads a font to your printer every time it prints a document, if you have minimal printer memory (for example, 512K RAM) it takes a little longer to print a long document. Figure 15.18 shows the ATM dialog box.

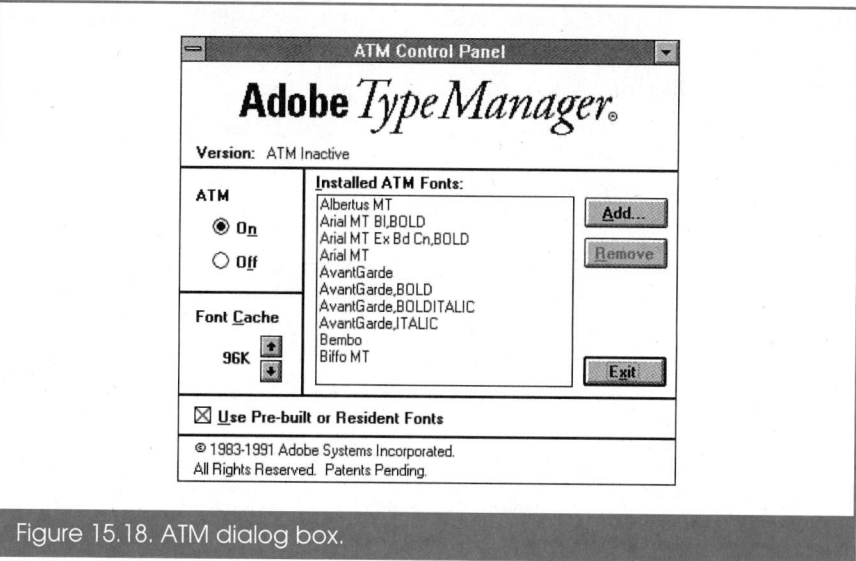

Figure 15.18. ATM dialog box.

ATM is considered by many to be the best of the best. It's nice to get a useful product that usually costs $50 or more by mail order, bundled with an application at no extra cost.

Even though it comes free (this term is subjective) with 1-2-3, you really should compare the quality of ATM's printed output against that of TrueType before deciding to give ATM a permanent place in your work station. If you can spare the space on both your drive and in system memory, ATM can in many cases improve the quality of your printed output.

Solver

The Solver feature of 1-2-3 is essentially an analysis tool. In business statistical analysis, it would be referred to as a simulation modeler. Simulation modeling tools enable you to build a scenario with data (usually numbers) in order to learn "what-if" outcomes based on numbers that change over the course of the simulation.

For example, let's say that you build a worksheet that includes values for sales, cost of sales, inventory aging costs, sales volumes in dollars (seasonal smoothed), and overhead costs. Let's also say that you want to learn the correct product mix to manufacture to balance the costs against the sales dollars, creating a profit. Solver changes just the numbers that you say can realistically be changed, using the constraint parameters you provide.

A simpler example to illustrate the power of Solver is one familiar to many of us: *How to know how much to spend on the purchase of a house.* You would build a worksheet that included payment data, income figures, down payment amount, and so on. What makes using Solver so different is that you then tell Solver what the constraints are.

You plug in a limitation (in dollars, for example) to each number you have entered (such as maximum payment per month, one of my personal favorites). Solver returns a true or false statement in the form of *1 for true* and *0 for false*. This type of formula is referred to as being *logical* in nature: Either it works or it doesn't. If you tell Solver which cells it can adjust so that all the logical formulas return the true (1) statement, it seeks an adjustment to the cell values that will help it to meet all criteria for all the named cells—that is, to return a true value for each logical formula you have devised. Solver does this for a virtually unlimited number of formulas and values in a specified cell or cells.

Solver also displays its progress in finding a solution to the problems that you construct in the Solver Progress dialog box, shown in Figure 15.19.

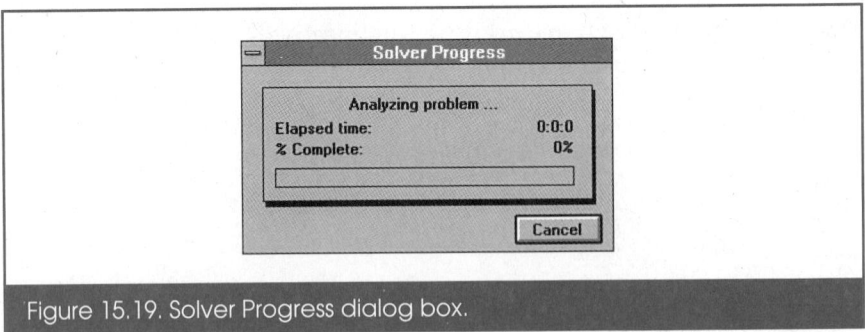

Figure 15.19. Solver Progress dialog box.

Backsolver

Backsolver is a tool to reverse-engineer a problem evidenced by the outcome of a series of formula calculations in a worksheet. If you enter a lot of real data on your personal living costs, for example, and then you enter your net income amount and calculate how much is left, you might uncover a problem. You might not be able to balance your budget. You either can make more money instantly, or you can do what

most of us do: Change the cost figures so that they do not exceed the income figures. *The trick is to know which numbers can be changed and by how much.*

Backsolver can do this for you. You can specify which cells and how much they can be affected. You then can change the negative number at the bottom of the budget worksheet to an even zero, and Backsolver will go through your worksheet and make the cuts that you believe are realistic. It will do this until it meets the end criteria. Some people call this "balancing your budget."

Solver and Backsolver actually perform very elaborate tasks using several worksheets. The limitations to what can be done with Solver and Backsolver are most likely to be perceived by you well before they are realized by 1-2-3.

DataLens

DataLens is a collection of drivers that enable you to work directly with a dBASE, Paradox, or SQL database. 1-2-3 considers a driver to be an interface that works with one of the three database types supported. In software development circles, the term more commonly used is *front end*. DataLens is no more than a very simple front end for the three types of external tables, or database files, that 1-2-3 can access directly.

15

Early 1-2-3 for DOS versions could only convert database files (in various formats) to 1-2-3 worksheets and back again to the appropriate database file format when you were finished working with the data from within 1-2-3. Each DataLens driver is a front end designed to provide a simple interface for these popular database file formats.

Tip: With dBASE files, you must open the associated *index* file that has been created and used to organize the dBASE data file. An index file keeps the database file sorted correctly based on criteria established when the index file was created. You must update the index file. If you open just the database file (filename with an extension of .DBF), you will not be able to save your changes or additions to the database file as organized by the associated index file (filename with an extension of .NDX. or .MDX). What this means is that the next time you look for your latest changes to the dBASE database file, you might not see it listed in its proper place in the order. You will have to actually start dBASE or the dBASE clone to reindex the file and correct the order.

DataLens directly reads, adds, edits, or deletes information in a database file. You can create a table or a database file from within 1-2-3. You can read and work with the data in that file from within 1-2-3 in a *real-time* (instant update) fashion, but you cannot perform elaborate functions directly with the table or database file. 1-2-3 is not designed to replace the database management system.

> **Warning:** 1-2-3 does not recognize data stored in a database's memo fields. 1-2-3 displays blank cells in place of that data, because memo fields can contain data strings of varying length. Some database management systems store memo field information in separate-but-related files not callable by 1-2-3 via the DataLens feature.

Command Summary

This section is a summary of the commands found in the menus of 1-2-3 for Windows.

File Menu

This is a summary of the **F**ile menu commands.

File **N**ew	Opens a new, empty worksheet.
File **O**pen	Opens an existing worksheet.
File **C**lose	Closes the active file.
File **S**ave	Saves the active file.
File Save **A**s	Saves the active file using a specified name.
File Com**b**ine From	Retrieves data from disk for insertion into the current worksheet file.
File **I**mport From	Retrieves text data on disk for insertion into the current worksheet file.
File **E**xtract To	Copies a range of data to the worksheet file on disk.

File **Ad**ministration	Manages reservation settings, creates a table of file information, and recalculates linked formulas.
File Pre**v**iew	Displays print range as it should be printed.
File Pa**g**e Setup	Makes headers, footers, borders, margins, and other page settings.
File **P**rint	Prints a worksheet or a chart.
File Printer Setup	Changes printer configuration.
File E**x**it	Leaves 1-2-3.

Edit Menu

This is a summary of the **E**dit menu commands.

Edit **U**ndo	Releases recent changes stored in the buffer and clears those changes.
Edit Cut	Removes highlighted data from the screen and stores it in the Clipboard.
Edit **C**opy	Copies highlighted data to the Clipboard.
Edit **P**aste	Places the contents of the Clipboard within the open window.
Edit Cl**e**ar	Removes highlighted data from the screen.
Edit Clea**r** Special	Removes highlighted data and formatting from an entire range.
Edit Paste **L**ink	Creates a new link to the current worksheet file without using the Clipboard.
Edit Link **O**ptions	Adds, edits, and deletes linked data in another application.
Edit **F**ind	Finds and/or replaces specified characters.
Edit **M**ove Cells	Transfers data to another range of cells without the Clipboard.
Edit **Q**uick Copy	Transfers data to another range of cells in the same worksheet file or another worksheet file without the Clipboard.

15

Worksheet Menu

This is a summary of the Worksheet menu commands.

Worksheet **G**lobal Settings	Changes default settings.
Worksheet **I**nsert	Inserts blank columns or rows in a worksheet.
Worksheet **D**elete	Deletes columns, rows, or worksheets.
Worksheet **H**ide	Hides columns or worksheets.
Worksheet **U**nhide	Redisplays hidden columns or worksheets.
Worksheet **C**olumn Width	Sets the width of one or more columns.
Worksheet **R**ow Height	Sets the height of one or more rows.
Worksheet **T**itles	Freezes or unfreezes rows and columns.
Worksheet **P**age Break	Inserts vertical or horizontal page breaks in printed worksheets.

Range Menu

This is a summary of the **R**ange menu commands.

Range **F**ormat	Changes how data is displayed within a range.
Range **N**ame	Creates, lists, and deletes range names.
Range **J**ustify	Rearranges data in a column to fit as specified.
Range **P**rotect	Prevents changes to unprotected cells.
Range **U**nprotect	Makes changes in a cell and over-rides global protection.
Range **T**ranspose	Copies a range of data and updates formulas.
Range **A**nnotate	Moves the cell pointer to a cell.

Graph Menu

This is a summary of the **Graph** menu commands.

Graph New	Creates and names a new graph.
Graph View	Displays a graph for the current file.
Graph Add to Sheet	Adds a graph to the current worksheet.
Graph Name	Deletes graphs not yet saved and lists saved graphs.
Graph Import	Copies a .PIC or a .CGM graph to the current file.
Graph Size	Resizes a graph.
Graph Refresh	Updates all graphs in the current file.
Graph Go To	Moves the cell pointer to a cell containing a graph.

Data Menu

15

This is a summary of the **Data** menu commands.

Data Fill	Enters a sequence of values in one range.
Data Sort	Arranges data in a table or a range.
Data What-if Table	Creates a table showing how values have changed along with formula changes.
Data Distribution	Creates a frequency distribution based on values in a range that fall within specified intervals.
Data Matrix	Multiplies or inverts a matrix made up of a range of data.
Data Regression	Performs regression analysis.
Data Parse	Separates long labels into separate columns.
Data Query	Goes to a specified record in a table.

Data **C**onnect to External	Connects 1-2-3 to an external table or database.
Data **E**xternal Options	Exchanges data between 1-2-3 and an external table or database.

Style Menu

This is a summary of the **S**tyle menu commands.

Style **F**ont	Changes fonts and text attributes.
Style **A**lignment	Organizes labels so that they are all displayed in a uniform fashion.
Style **B**order	Adds a dark outline or a shadow around a range.
Style **C**olor	Selects color for ranges and shows negative values in red.
Style **S**hading	Adds shading effects to a range.
Style **N**ame	Assigns a style name to a cell and its formatting.
1,2,3...8	Displays currently named styles.

Tools Menu

This is a summary of the **T**ools menu commands.

Tools **B**acksolver	Finds a value within a cell that causes a formula in another cell to evaluate to a predetermined value.
Tools **S**olver	Finds solutions to what-if problems.
Tools **U**ser Setup	Changes display and configuration defaults.
Tools **M**acro	Starts, displays, and records macros.
Tools **A**dd-in	Starts an add-in application or utility.

Window Menu

This is a summary of the **W**indow menu commands.

Window **S**plit	Divides a worksheet horizontally or vertically to create two worksheet panes.
Window **D**isplay Options	Changes the current worksheet color, gridline, and frame display settings.
Window **T**ile	Concurrently displays all open worksheets in windows of the same size.
Window **C**ascade	Displays each open window slightly to the lower-right of each other.
1 through *n*	Lists the names of as many as nine worksheet, graph, and transcript windows.

15

CHAPTER

16

Microsoft Word
for Windows

Word processing is familiar to almost everyone who uses a computer.
Almost everyone writes, even if it is just short memos or letters to their
parents. A word processor makes writing easier and faster for most
tasks, and greatly simplifies more advanced tasks that would otherwise
require many repetitive actions.

Word for Windows 2.0 (WFW) is an advanced word processor that takes
advantage of many of Windows's graphical features. The
first version of Word for the PC appeared in 1983 and was
soon followed by Word for the Macintosh. Word for
Windows takes many of its user interface features from
Word for the Macintosh and its advanced writing tools
from Word for the PC.

The initial WFW screen is shown in Figure 16.1. The
information window at the bottom-left tells you
what page you are on and the section number.

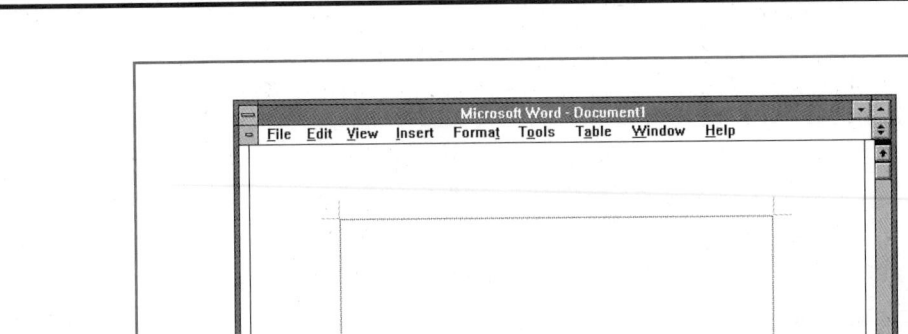

Page and
section number

Figure 16.1. Initial Word for Windows screen.

System Requirements for Installing Word for Windows

This section describes the system requirements you need to install Word for Windows.

Hardware

A PC with an 80286 or higher processor. If you're buying a system especially for using WFW, buy a machine with the highest processor speed you can afford. It will mean less waiting for WFW when you become more proficient.

One megabyte of RAM. Even more RAM is a dramatic improvement. If you want to make charts and graphs using the utilities included with WFW, you must have at least 2M of RAM. Most users consider 2M to be a minimum if you work with large documents, anyway. If you are just buying a system, now is the time to get at least 2M of RAM. In most modern systems, if you buy only 1M of memory, you must replace the first megabyte when you expect to add additional memory. This is because you usually have to fill a minimum number of memory module sockets just to make

16

the system work. Best to buy your first system with at least 2M (if not 4M) of memory to avoid wasting money in the future.

EGA video monitor and card or higher. Again, if you are buying hardware to accommodate WFW, VGA is now the same price as EGA. VGA performs much better and is easier on the eyes.

One hard disk. If you install the full-blown version of Word for Windows 2.0, you need about 18M of space to use the program to its full potential. Word installs a charting, graphing, and equation-editing set of programs in a separate directory called MSAPPS. This set of programs takes about 4M out of the 18M required. You can install WFW in a minimal working fashion, with none of the icing, and take up about 5M to 6M of hard drive space. Whether you install the minimum number of files or the maximum, you'll need yet more space to store the files you create and/or edit.

One double-sided diskette drive. WFW comes with diskettes that require high-density drives, in both 3 1/2-inch and 5 1/4-inch sizes.

A mouse or other pointing device. It's true that you can create documents and print them without a mouse. If you really want to take advantage of the new features included with WFW 2.0, however, you need some way of pointing to an icon on the toolbar. You can buy a good mouse for about $30 these days (street price), and you won't have to waste time learning keystroke combinations when you should be learning how to make slicker documents and presentation materials.

Software

Windows 3.0 or higher. Windows 3.1 runs WFW much faster than Windows 3.0. If you need to choose, and you can supply the needed hardware, choose Windows 3.1.

DOS 3.1 or higher. You need this version of DOS or higher just to run WFW. If you need to make a choice when you buy WFW, buy DOS 5.0. The memory management strength of DOS 5.0 is clearly unparalleled in earlier versions of DOS. Most systems intended to run in an office environment utilize hard drives larger than 32M. Most DOS versions before 5.0 do not enable you to partition a hard drive larger than 32M anyway, so if you don't want to get stuck with four separate logical drives on your 120M hard drive, make sure that DOS 5.0 is installed on the system.

This tidbit of advice will come in handy when you start loading several large Windows applications. For example, one 120M drive is easier to organize than is one drive partitioned to appear as four separate drives.

Major Features of Word for Windows 2.0

Word for Windows 2.0 has added several new features since the last revision of Word for Windows. Microsoft says that Version 2.0 is the first *major* revision of Word for Windows, and this impressive list of new and improved features supports the statement:

▲ Customizing the toolbar. You can add, delete, and create custom buttons that do just what you want them to do.

▲ Easy-access drawing and charting. When you click the Chart or Draw buttons on the toolbar, WFW opens a full-featured charting or drawing program. You might remember the charting program from Excel. They are virtually identical. You can assign this feature to a toolbar button.

▲ Print Merge Helper is a utility designed to make graphical the layout of mail merge documents and envelope printing and therefore much simpler.

▲ The WordPerfect Help utility offers very specific help for WordPerfect converts. You have the option of installing this added help utility when you install Word for Windows 2.0.

▲ You no longer have to use the cut-and-paste method to move text in a document. You simply select the text, place the insertion point somewhere inside the selected text, and click and hold down the mouse button while dragging the selected text to its new place in the document. Release the mouse button and the text is placed perfectly in its new home (drag and drop). All formatting is preserved.

▲ File **F**ind is a file preview utility that gets a little of its power from File Manager. You can browse through a group of files, reviewing as you go without actually opening files with Word for Windows. You can review files much faster this way, waiting until you find the file you really need before you have WFW open it. You can assign this feature to a toolbar button.

488

▲ Envelope Generator is a real, live envelope printing utility that sends labels to your printer in the form of text. You can assign this feature to a toolbar button.

▲ Zoom is a feature that enables you to focus on a very small part of your document or to back all the way out so that each page appears to be at arm's length. You can assign this feature to a toolbar button.

16

▲ You now can shade text with gray levels or colors (to take advantage of your color printer) to make strikingly clear presentations with the kind of emphasis that only color and shading can provide.

▲ Integrated grammar checking enables you to check your sentences and paragraphs for grammatical accuracy. The grammar checker also questions misspellings it finds in a body of text. This utility actually explains why it suggests a change and tells you how to go about changing something.

▲ You now can choose for use as a bullet any dingbat or character from any character set available to Windows. This feature usually is seen only in high-end desktop publishing applications.

Features Beyond Windows Write

As discussed in Chapter 10, "Write," the Write program that comes with Windows has some basic word processing features. Word for Windows is a superset of those features. Not only does it do everything that Write does more completely, but it also has dozens of features that Write doesn't have (such as a spelling checker, footnotes, a table of contents creator, and so on).

Table 16.1 describes all of Write's major features and the extensions that Word for Windows has made to them. The rest of this chapter describes these features, as well as the many features that do not exist in Write (or, in many cases, in other popular Windows word processors).

Table 16.1. Write features and their extensions in Word for Windows.

Write Feature	Word for Windows
One document open at a time	As many as nine documents in separate windows.
Import text and Word files	Import from more than a dozen formats.
Export text and Word files	Export to more than a dozen formats.
Manual repagination of pages	Also automatic repagination.
Must print to see exact layout	Preview printing on the screen.
Paste text or pictures	Paste-linked information from other programs.
Pictures are paragraphs	Pictures act like characters. They can be on the same line with other text.
Search forward	Also search backward.
Go to page numbers	Also go to hidden marks in your text.
Character, paragraph formatting	Also section formatting and document formatting.
Bold, italic, underline	Also small caps, hidden, underline, and double underline.
Fixed superscript and subscript	Variable distance superscript and subscript.
Line spacing for paragraphs	Also spacing before and after a line.
No header on first page	Different header on first page; also different headers for even and odd pages.
Page numbers in headers/footers	Choose page number format.
Tab set for entire document	Different tabs for each paragraph.

Formatting

Most beginning and intermediate word processing users use formatting features more than any other features. Word for Windows shines in this respect. In all three types of formatting (character, paragraph, and document), Word for Windows is very flexible in its features. It also supports *section* formatting, such as for different chapters in a document.

Character Formatting

Figure 16.2 shows the Forma**t** **C**haracter command. Note that characters can be in color and that you can specify the amount of vertical offset for superscript and subscript characters. You also can see a sample of your selections before you apply them. This can be a real time-saver if you are changing an entire document at once.

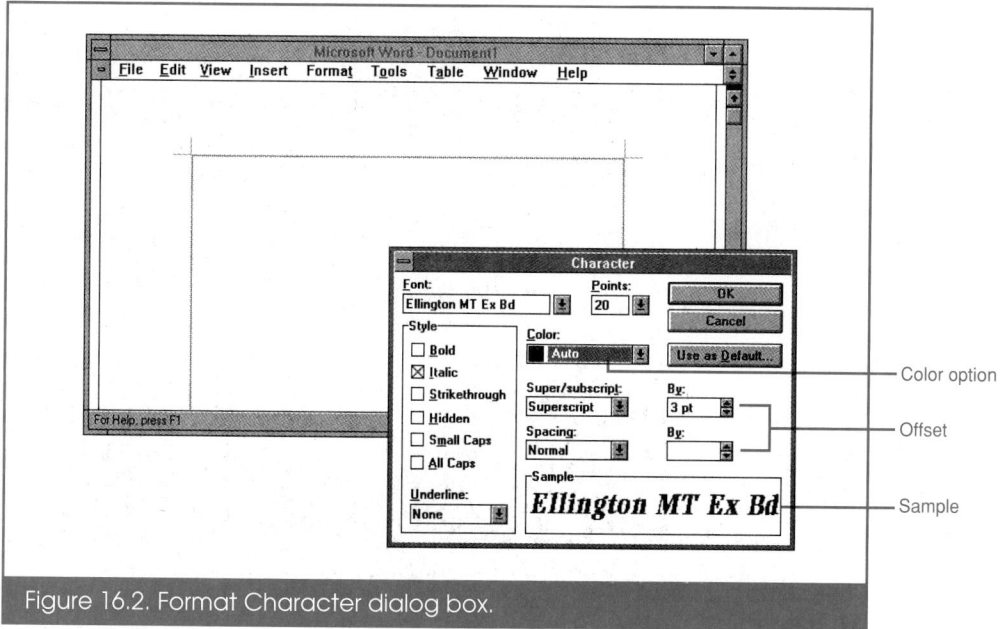

Figure 16.2. Format Character dialog box.

Paragraph and Border Formatting

Paragraph formatting is used mostly for improving documents to make them look more professional. Figure 16.3 shows the Format Paragraph dialog box. The spacings before and after a paragraph are important options because most documents have blank space between paragraphs. Using these options, you can ensure that a regular amount of space always appears between paragraphs. Using blank paragraphs, such as Write requires, means that a page might start with a blank line. Unlike Word for Windows Versions 1.0 and 1.1a, you now get to see an example of how your text will look *before* you apply the selections. An example of the page with the paragraph formatting changes is shown in the lower-right corner of the dialog box.

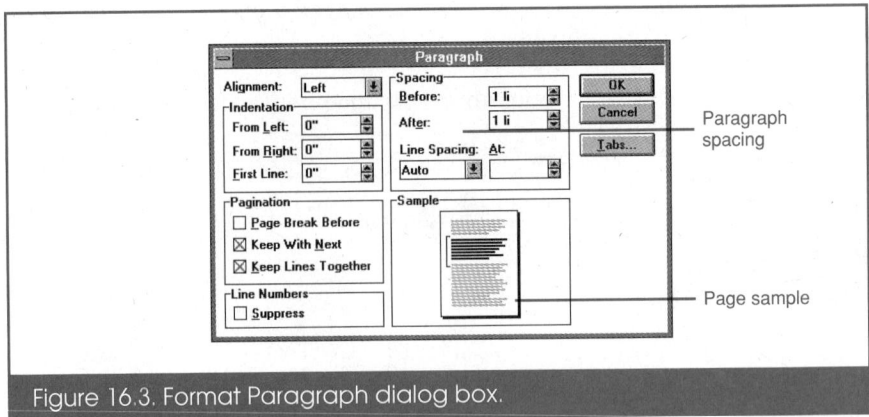

Figure 16.3. Format Paragraph dialog box.

Keeps are methods for making sure that paragraphs appear together on a page no matter what. The **K**eep Lines Together option keeps the selected paragraphs together, and the Keep With **N**ext option keeps the paragraph with the next paragraph regardless of that second paragraph's formatting. You want to use keeps with section or paragraph headings so that a heading does not appear at the bottom of a page and the first paragraph on the next page. It is also common to use keeps in small tables.

You can put borders around paragraphs to emphasize them or to make tables. Your choices for borders are boxes (around the page or the paragraph) using several selectable border styles or shadow. If you use a border, you can choose nine different ways it is done. You also can shade areas of text, and you can place a shadow behind your document pages to really ice the cake. Of course, like most WFW formatting

options, you get to see what your changes will look like before you actually apply them to your document.

Tabs Formatting

16

You can have many different sets of tabs, such as for different tables. Figure 16.4 shows the Format Tabs dialog box.

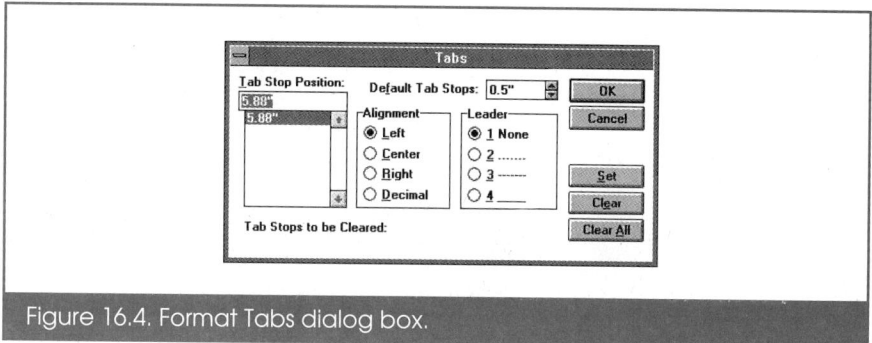

Figure 16.4. Format Tabs dialog box.

You can enter many positions and choose a type of alignment and a leader character for each. Leader characters are those little dots or dashes you see between items and their relative page numbers in a table of contents. The results of the settings in Figure 16.4 are shown in Figure 16.5.

Most word processors position paragraphs on the page one paragraph after another. This is normal, because most writing consists of flowing text. Often, however, you want to position a paragraph out of normal alignment. For instance, you might want to put a quotation in a box by itself in the middle of a page, or you might want to have a graphic with text flowing around it at the bottom of a page. You can put special text in a frame to make it stand out. You use the insertion point to place text in a frame. Figure 16.6 shows text inserted in a frame for special emphasis.

Section Formatting

Many word processors have only character, paragraph, and document formatting. Word also has *section formatting* and column formatting. You can break a document into many sections and give each section its own formatting. Figure 16.7 shows the Format Section Layout dialog box.

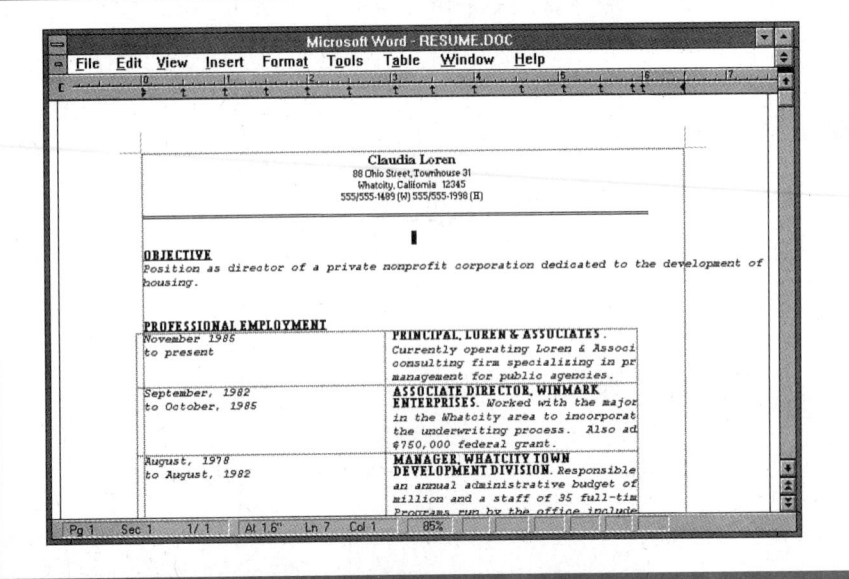

Figure 16.5. A sample formatted document.

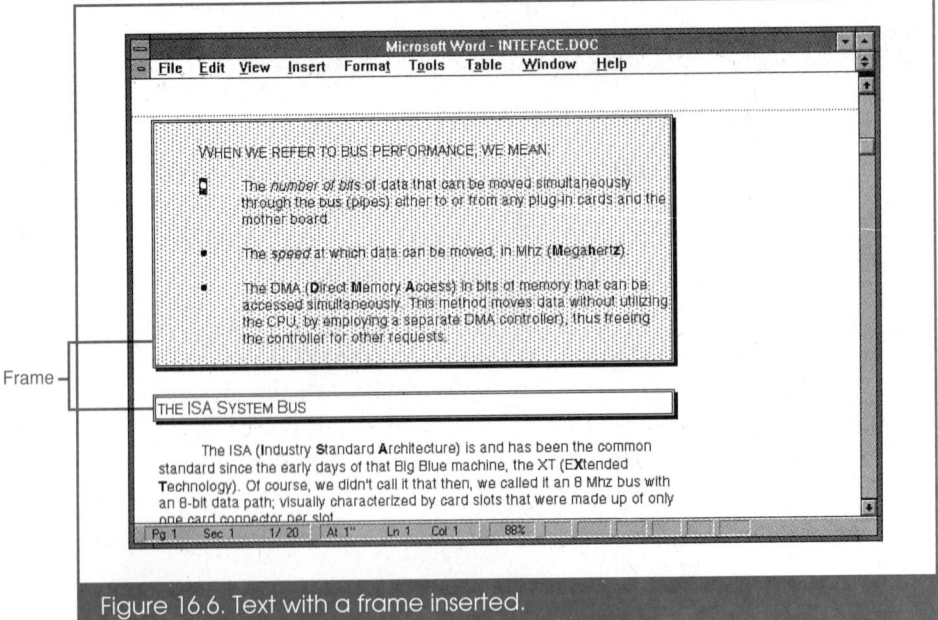

Figure 16.6. Text with a frame inserted.

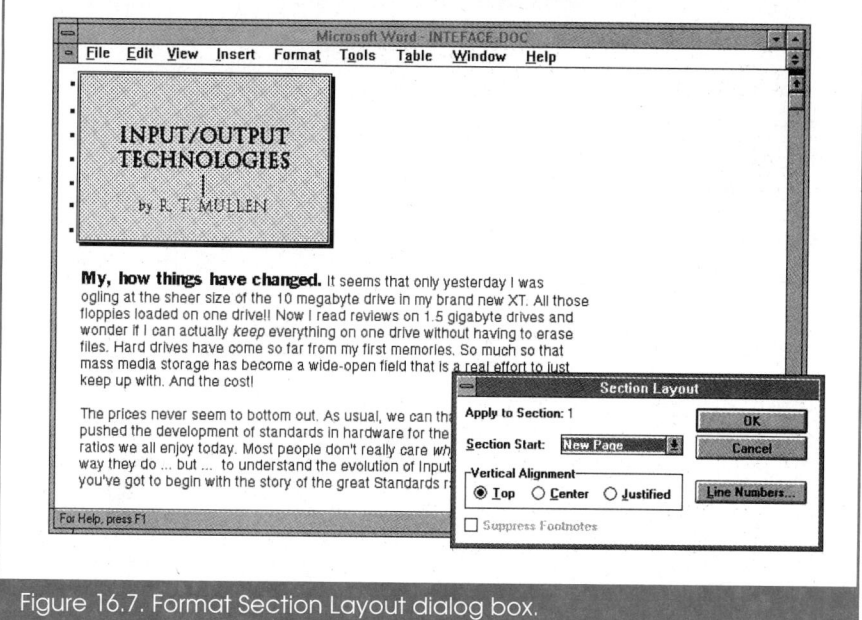

Figure 16.7. Format Section Layout dialog box.

You can have more than one column on the page, similar to newspapers. Many newsletters use multicolumn formatting. You can specify how each section starts: with no break, in a new column, on a new page, on the next even page, or on the next odd page. If you choose to have no break, you can have a page that has two columns in part of the page and three in others. This gives Word for Windows 2.0 many of the features found only in desktop publishing programs.

You can also number lines by section. This generally is useful only for lawyers who use it in pleadings and depositions. It is also occasionally used in drafts of contracts.

You also can align the pages in the section. Normally, you simply start at the top margin and fill down the page. The Center option causes the page to be centered vertically, such as for announcements or resumes. If you want to spread the lines out so that they always start at the top margin and go all the way to the bottom margin, choose the Justified option.

Document Formatting

Word for Windows's document formatting includes many options that help you get your printed output exactly right on the page. You also can specify how footnotes are handled in the document. Figure 16.8 shows the Format Page Setup command.

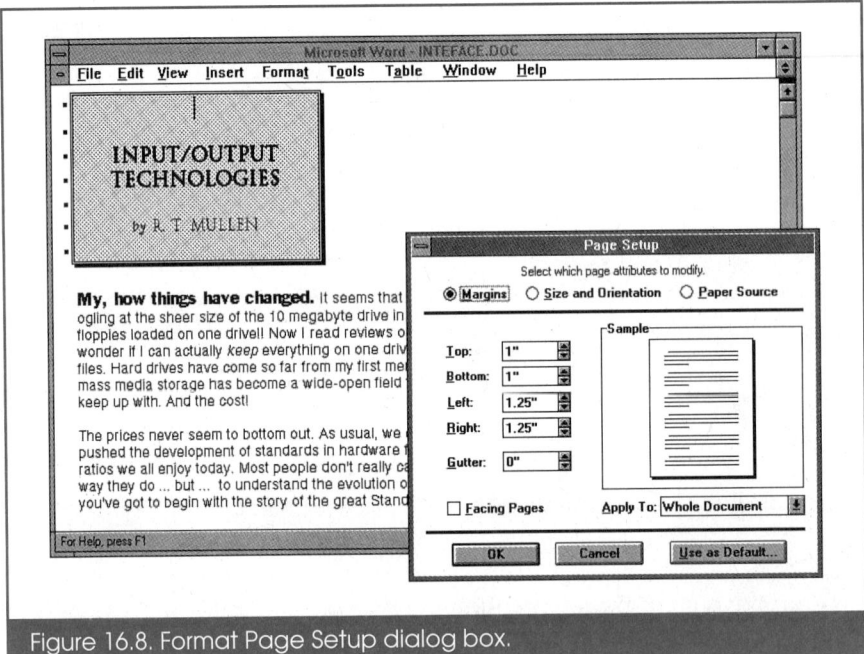

Figure 16.8. Format Page Setup dialog box.

When you are planning to create a document that will be bound, you should take advantage of the WYSIWYG method of managing this element of the page layout features. The *gutter margin* is the open space that is used in documents that are meant to be copied on two sides of a sheet and bound in a book. Binding takes a little off the right side of even-numbered pages and a little off the left side of odd-numbered pages (for instance, look at the center of this book). The *gutter* is the amount to add to these pages so that the text still appears to be even when the book is opened. It is also useful for documents that will be three-hole-punched.

Word for Windows 2.0 enables you to put footnotes throughout a document. The numbers appear in the text as you would expect. You can specify where the footnotes themselves should appear: at the bottom of the page, beneath a group of text, at the end of each section, or at the end of the document. Your choice usually depends on what others in your field do. For instance, academic humanities books often have footnotes at the end of each chapter (section), and legal journals usually have them at the bottom of the page. You can place footnotes in a document by using the Insert Foot**n**ote command from the main menu.

Visual Formatting Aids

16

The plain Word for Windows screen shows only your text with the formatting applied. If you are willing to sacrifice a bit of screen room, you can enhance your formatting capabilities by showing the *ribbon, ruler, and toolbar*.

Figure 16.9 shows the program window with the ribbon displayed. The settings there show the character formatting for the current selection. You also can use the buttons in the ribbon to apply formatting. For example, to change the font on some words, select them and choose the font from the list.

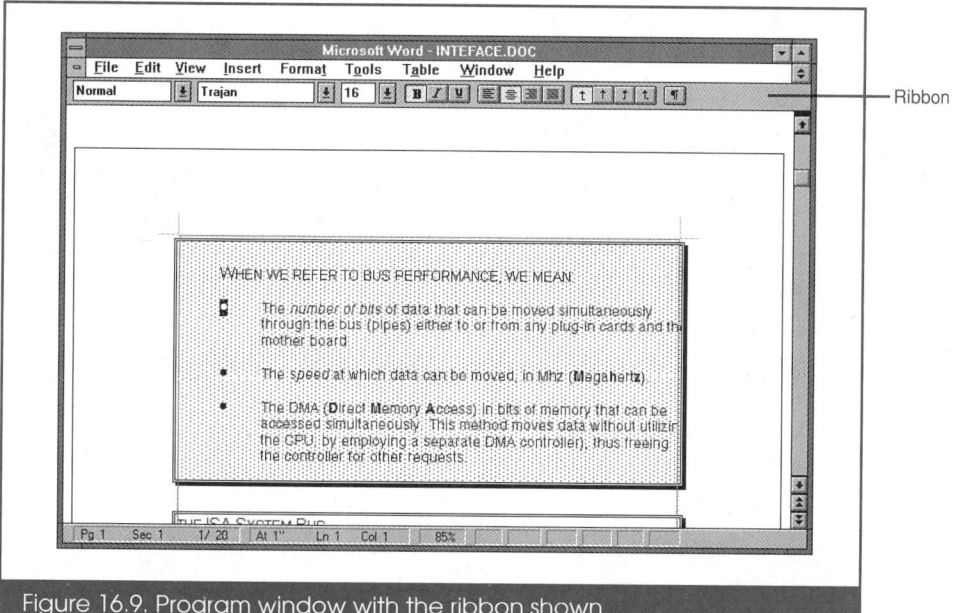

Figure 16.9. Program window with the ribbon shown.

The ruler can appear in each document window. It shows the paragraph formatting, including tabs, indentation, and so on. Like the ribbon, you also can apply formatting with the ruler by selecting the paragraphs and then selecting the desired tabs and indents in the ruler.

The toolbar is one of the most noticeable features of WFW 2.0. You can create and assign either commands or macros to buttons that are displayed between the menu and the ribbon. Figure 16.10 shows you the **To**ols **O**ptions Toolbar dialog box. Here you make changes to the toolbar, such as where your assigned buttons appear on the toolbar, what they do, and which buttons you want to use.

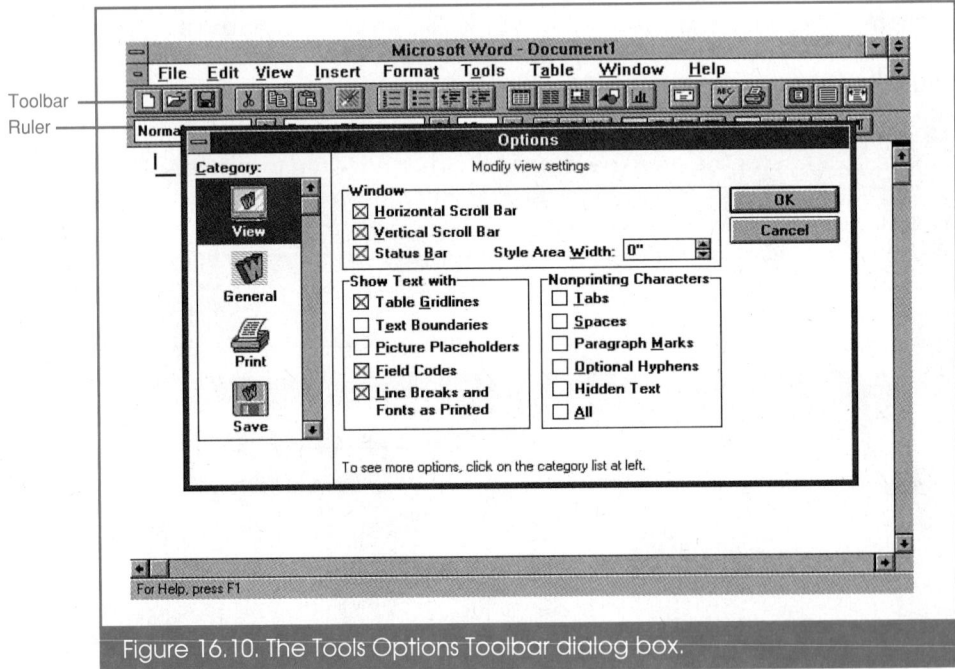

Figure 16.10. The Tools Options Toolbar dialog box.

Style Sheets

Changing the formatting of a long word processing document can be a formidable task. For example, assume that you have written a 50-page report and you decide that you want to use a new font for the headings. You would have to search for each heading, select it, and change the font. Because this type of action is common, Word for Windows 2.0 has simplified the process significantly with *style sheets*.

A style sheet is a collection of formatting instructions for elements of your document. Each element is a paragraph. A style sheet for a report might have the following elements:

16

▲ Title

▲ Chapter heading

▲ Secondary heading

▲ Table

▲ Normal paragraph

▲ Table of contents entry

▲ Index entry

For each style, you could define any character and paragraph formatting. For example, the formatting for a secondary heading might be centered, boldface, italic, with two blank lines after.

To create or modify a style sheet, you open the Format Style dialog box, shown in Figure 16.11. To change or add styles, you click the **D**efine» button to reveal more of the dialog box, shown in Figure 16.12.

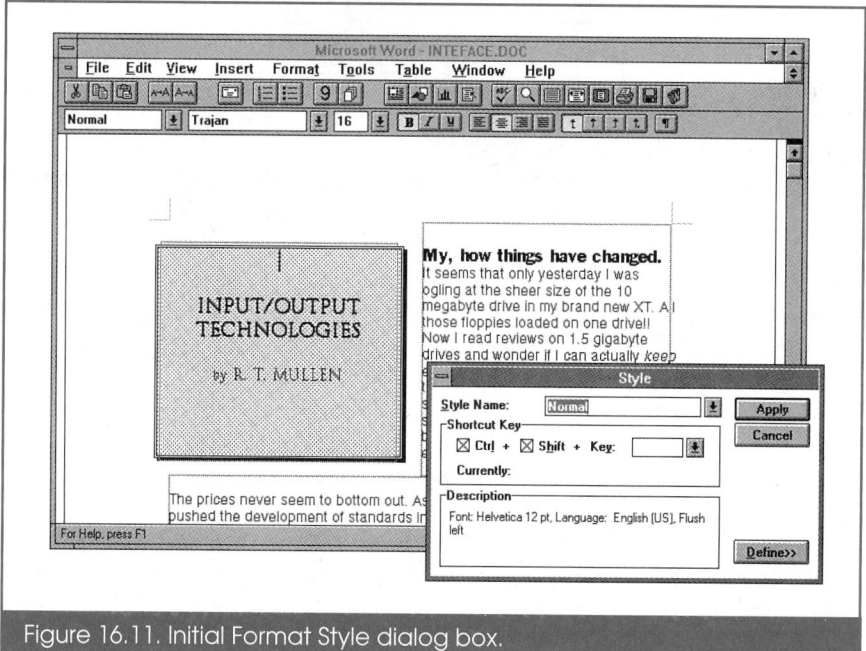

Figure 16.11. Initial Format Style dialog box.

The current formatting for the style is shown under the style list. To change the formatting, click on the Cha**n**ge formatting button. When

you have the formatting you want, click the OK button. To add a style, type a new name in the **S**tyle Name text box and click the **D**efine» button.

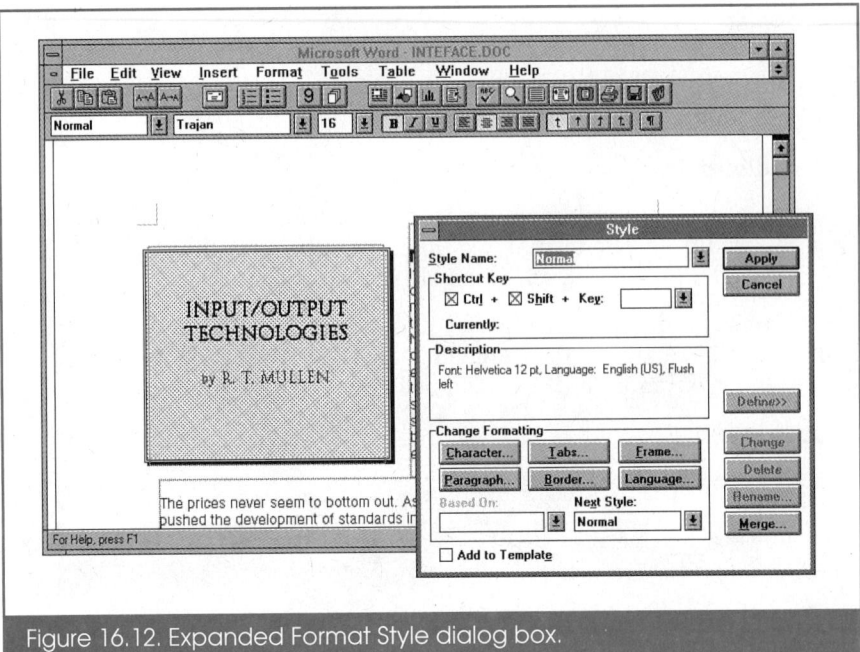

Figure 16.12. Expanded Format Style dialog box.

After you have defined all the styles you need, you can apply them to the paragraphs in your document easily. Simply select the paragraph, give the Forma**t** St**y**le command, shown in Figure 16.13, and choose the desired style. If you have the ribbon open, you can apply the style by selecting it from the ribbon. You also can press Ctrl-S and type the name of the style.

After you have specified styles for the paragraphs in your document, it is easy to change the formatting universally. Simply give the Forma**t** St**y**le command again, choose the style, change the formatting, and click the Apply button. Word for Windows 2.0 changes all the paragraphs that have that style.

The Based **O**n field in the Forma**t** St**y**le dialog box makes universal changes even easier. Each style can be based on another style. For example, in the default styles, all the heading styles are based on the Normal style. If you change part of the Normal style, Word for Windows automatically makes the same changes in all the heading styles. For

example, if you get a new font for Windows and you want to change all the styles of a particular type to use that font, if they are based on one style, you can change just that one style and have all the related styles change too.

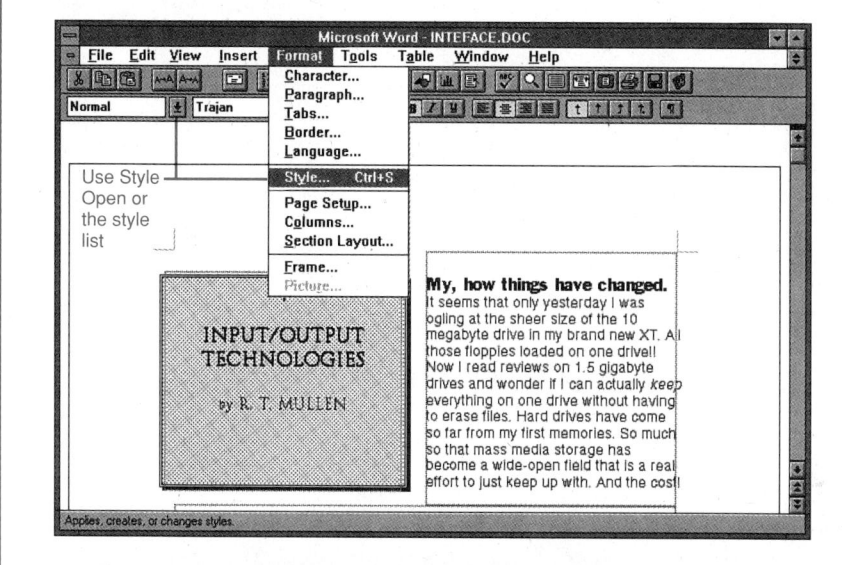

Figure 16.13. Style option on the Format pull-down menu.

Tables

The bane of most people who prepare reports is formatting tables. Most word processors do not help much because they only enable you to set tab stops. If any column in your table has multiple lines, such as in Figure 16.14, simple tab stops won't work. It is not uncommon for people to create tables in a spreadsheet such as Excel and paste them into their word processing documents.

Word for Windows's table feature makes creating tables easy. Tables are made up of *cells* that can hold any amount of text, including many paragraphs. With this flexibility, making tables becomes much faster, and you do not need to worry about the amount of text you are showing. Figure 16.15 shows the Table Insert Table dialog box.

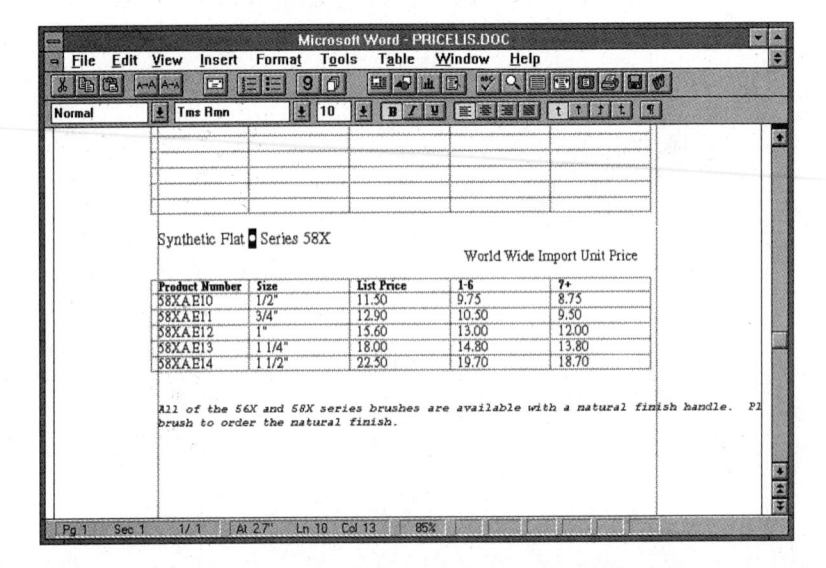

Figure 16.14. Table with entries that have more than one line.

You specify the initial number of columns, rows, and width, although you can add to or subtract from them at any time. If you have paragraphs selected when you give this command, you can select Convert Text to Table from the Table menu. Figure 16.15 shows you the available selections when you open the Table Insert Table dialog box.

You can create an empty table ready to be filled by just highlighting blank page space and then using the Convert Text to Table option from the Table menu. Figure 16.16 shows you what a newly created, empty table looks like. As soon as you have created the table, you can simply enter text into the cells as normal. If you want to add rows, simply move the insertion point into the last cell in the last row and press the Tab key.

Changing the width of columns is also easy. Generally, you want to keep the columns close together so that the reader can easily see what the rows are. However, you might want to keep them far apart until you have entered all the text, and then select them and make them the proper size for the text. You can change the rows and columns with the Table Row Height and Table Column Width options found on the Table pull-down menu, shown in Figure 16.17.

16

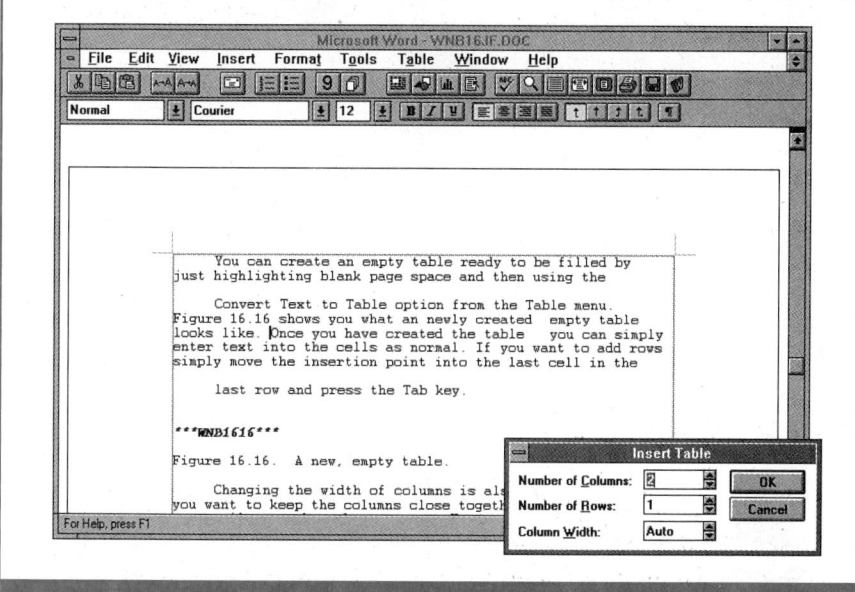

Figure 16.15. The Table Insert Table dialog box.

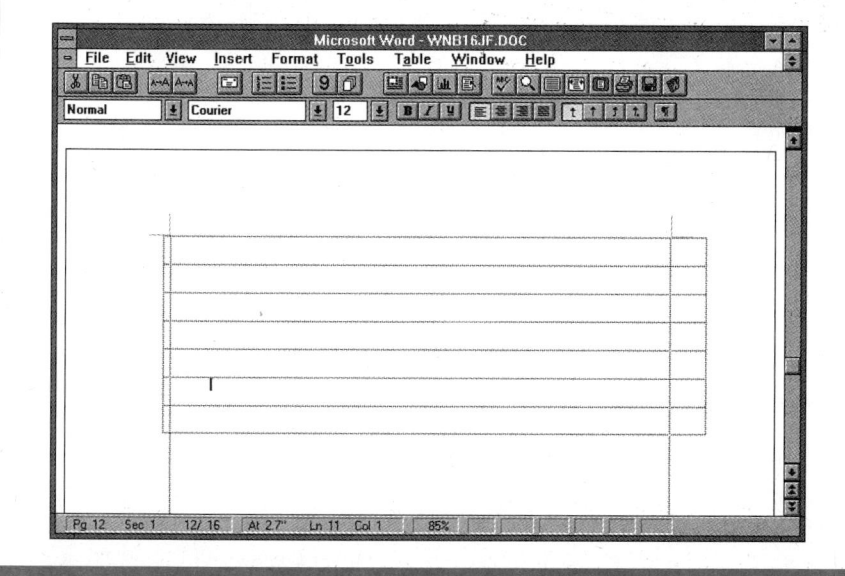

Figure 16.16. A new, empty table.

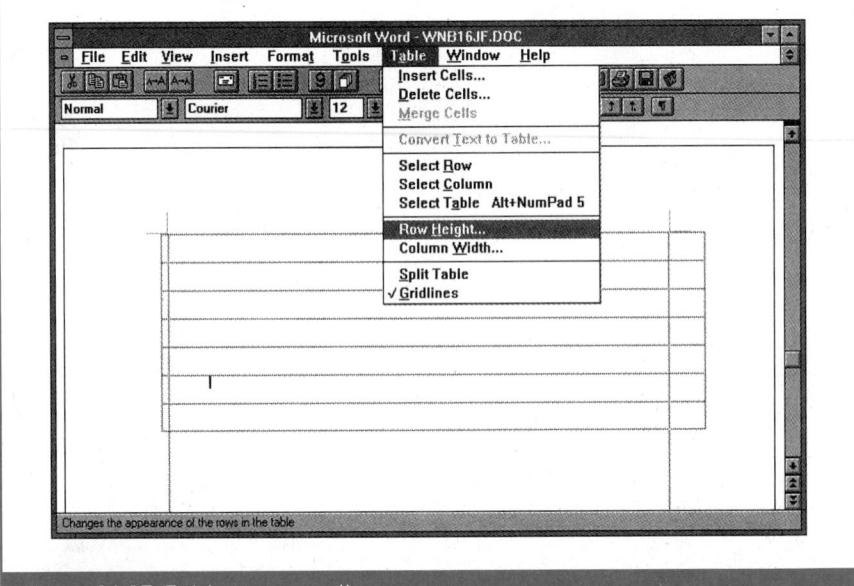

Figure 16.17. Table menu options.

Pictures

Like other Windows programs, Word for Windows can handle both pictures and text. Its picture-handling capabilities go well beyond simply pasting pictures from the Clipboard, however. Because Word for Windows treats pictures as characters, you can easily mix them with text.

When you select a picture in a document, it is displayed with *handles* that look like small dark rectangles. You can click these handles and drag them with the mouse to scale the picture. You also can open the Format Picture dialog box, shown in Figure 16.18, to crop and scale the picture. You can go on to frame the picture by clicking on the Frame button in the Format Picture dialog box.

If you have a picture on disk as a TIFF, a .PCX, or any one of the many popular file formats, you can insert it in your document without using the Clipboard. The Insert Picture dialog box enables you to open a graphics or a picture file and place it as if it were pasted from the Clipboard. The Insert Picture dialog box also gives you the ability to preview a picture before you place it in your document, as shown in Figure 16.19. The Insert Frame option pastes a blank frame as a placeholder. You can use this if you do not have the picture ready but want to hold a space for it.

Microsoft

16

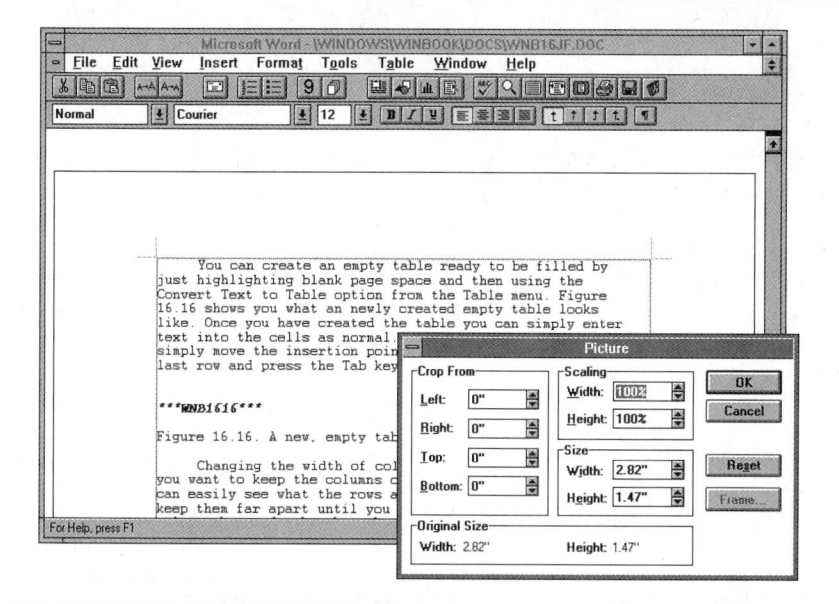

Figure 16.18. Format Picture dialog box.

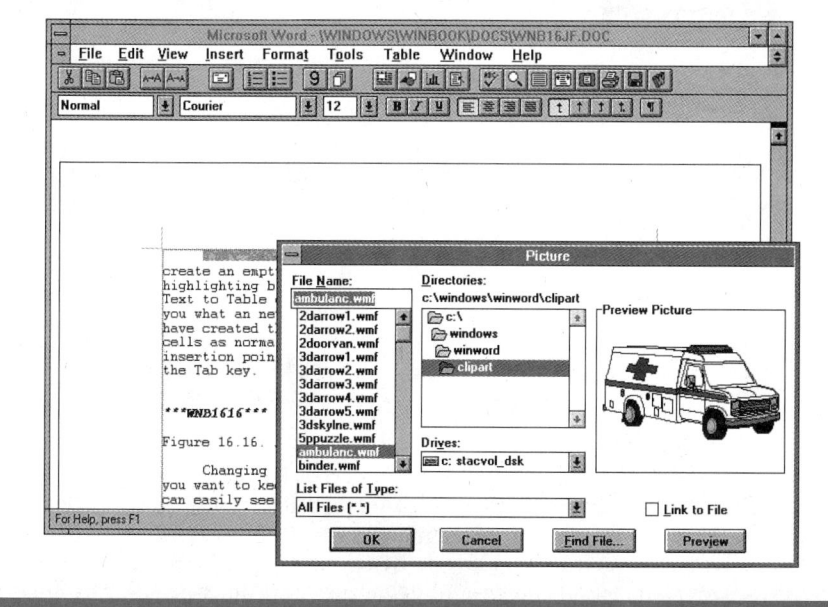

Figure 16.19. Insert Picture dialog box.

Linking Word for Windows to Other Programs

Because you often use a word processor as a collection point for various information sources, it should be able to create documents that have data from many programs. It should also be able to distribute information to other Windows programs in a form they can use with ease. Word for Windows handles both of these tasks well.

Using the Clipboard

Word for Windows can copy to and from the Clipboard like other Windows programs. You can copy either text or graphics. Word for Windows copies to the Clipboard in a more advanced fashion than many other programs by using Microsoft's Rich Text Format (RTF). If you are pasting from the Clipboard into another program that can use RTF, such as Excel, you retain all the formatting. RTF stores information about the formatting on cells, their width, and so on.

Converting Files

The **F**ile **O**pen and **F**ile Save **A**s commands in Word for Windows have automatic translation built into them. When you install Word for Windows, you have the option of installing translators that can read and/or write documents from a large number of Windows and non-Windows programs.

The programs and formats that Word for Windows can read from and write to are shown in Table 16.2.

Word for Windows and Object Linking and Embedding (OLE)

You can link to and from Word for Windows with *active links,* a method for making sure that you always have the most current information whenever you access it. For example, if you use active linking to copy a table from Word for Windows to another program that uses OLE, each time that program opens the document with the table, it checks the file

16

from which the table came and recopies the information if you have changed it.

Table 16.2. Word for Windows conversions.

Format Name	Used With
DCA/RFT	IBM DisplayWrite and DisplayWriter format
dBASE	Versions II, III, III+ and IV
Lotus 1-2-3	Versions 2.x, 3.0, and 1-2-3 for Windows
RTF	Rich Text Format
Windows Write	.WRI files
Word for Windows	1.x
Word for DOS	Versions 4.0, 5.0, and 5.5
Word for Macintosh	Versions 4.0 and 5.0
Microsoft Works	Windows and DOS 2.0 versions
BIFF	Excel Versions 2.x and 3.0
Multiplan	Versions 3.0 and 4.2
WordPerfect	Version 4.1, 4.2, 5.0, and 5.1
WordStar	3.3, 3.4, 4.0, 5.0, and 5.5
Text only	Various formats (with and without line breaks)

This has a radical effect on the way documents interact. Instead of your having to remember to look for the latest information when you are ready to finalize a document, Word for Windows can do that for you automatically. You do not even need to know which data was linked and which was native to the file. Word for Windows (or the other program) does that for you.

You also can use one-time, inactive links if you want. If you are worried that someone will incorrectly change the contents of the file with the information, a one-time link is much safer than an active link.

Customizing Your Screen

The screens you have seen so far all have shown the document in Word for Windows's normal editing mode. There are other modes that you will use at different times.

▲ *Normal* view puts all text in a single font and shows graphics as only outlines. This makes Word for Windows run much faster, which can be a blessing on slower PCs or if you have very complex documents that take a long time to display.

▲ *Page layout* shows you exactly how your document will look when printed, with all margins and borders. This is handy for checking layout.

▲ *Draft* view shows you your text using the system font, which is proportionally spaced. This mode is very fast. Draft view is also useful when you have characters that are very small and difficult to read.

▲ *Normal* view text looks very much like DOS-based word processing that uses only the ASCII character set. Characters are monospaced and do not appear as they might when printed.

You can edit in both draft view or page layout. You also can choose to show or hide various elements of a document with the **O**ptions View selection in the **To**ols pull-down menu, shown in Figure 16.20. The first set of options, such as Tabs and Spaces, causes Word for Windows to make those characters visible on the screen so that you can see what characters were used in your document. Figure 16.21 shows an example of text changed by selecting the All check box in the **To**ols **O**ptions dialog box.

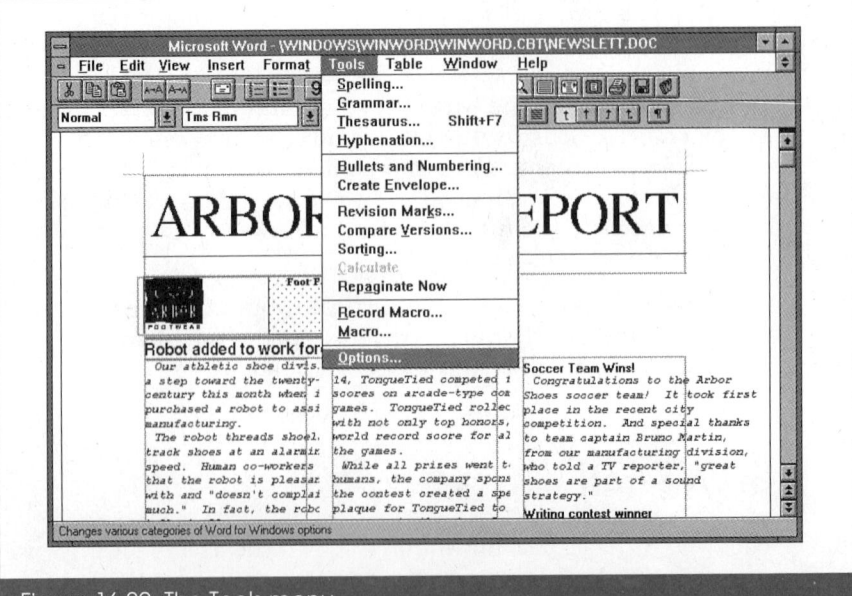

Figure 16.20. The Tools menu.

16

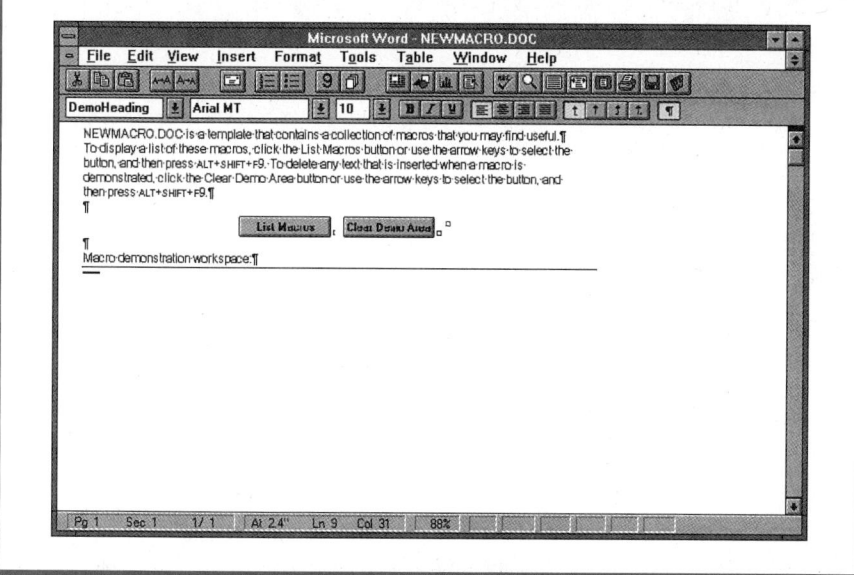

Figure 16.21. Example of the All option selected.

Macros

The macro language in Word for Windows is very similar to the popular BASIC language; in fact, it's called WordBASIC. The structure is very much like Microsoft's Visual BASIC, which is described in Chapter 30, "Windows for Advanced Users." Beyond the normal features of BASIC, WordBASIC gives you access to every command and action in Word for Windows.

When you create an outline, Word for Windows uses the styles "heading 1," "heading 2," and so on. When you save these files as text only, there is no way to see what the indentation should be. This style macro finds each heading and inserts the appropriate number of tab characters before it so that the text-only file is indented.

You can run Word for Windows macros from the **Macro Run** command or by assigning them a toolbar button. When you click these buttons, the macros associated with them run.

Command Summary

This is a summary of the menu commands for Microsoft Word for Windows. Use the following as a quick reference for this program.

File Menu

File **N**ew	Starts a new document.
File **O**pen	Opens a document or template that exists on your disk.
File **C**lose	Closes all windows that contain the active document.
File **S**ave	Saves the current document.
File Save **A**s	Saves the current document on disk, enabling you to change the file name, directory, file format, fast save on or off, and annotations locking.
File Sav**e** All	Saves all current documents and templates and the global glossary and macros.
File **F**ind File	Helps you search for a particular document. Displays a dialog box that you can use to create, edit, sort, print, and review the summary information for a list of documents.
File Summary **I**nfo	Displays the current document's summary information for viewing and editing.
File **T**emplate	Opens dialog box to select templates.
File Print Previe**w**	Displays a whole page with all contents in place. Enables you to do limited formatting.
File **P**rint	Prints the active document.
File Print **M**erge	Enables you to print form letters and to print with merged contents of another document.
File Print Setup	Enables you to choose the printer on which to print, as well as change the settings for that particular printer. When used with some laser printers, enables you to change the font cartridge.
File E**x**it	Quits Word without exiting Microsoft Windows. Performs the same action as the Close command on the Word Control menu.

File **1,2,3,4**   Lists the last four documents you opened or saved so that you can access them quickly without searching and without changing directories. (If a file has been deleted, it may still appear on the list. Word displays the message that it cannot locate the file.)

16

Edit Menu

Edit **U**ndo   Reverses the last editing or formatting action.

Edit **R**epeat   Repeats the most recently carried out editing or formatting command.

Edit **C**ut   Removes the selection from the document and places it on the Clipboard.

Edit **C**opy   Copies the selection to the Clipboard.

Edit **P**aste   Copies the contents of the Clipboard into the document at the indicated point.

Edit Paste **S**pecial   Enables you to paste, link, and paste without formatting.

Edit Select **A**ll   Selects the entire document.

Edit **F**ind   Locates text or formatting in the current document.

Edit **R**eplace   Locates and replaces text or formatting in the current document.

Edit **G**o To   Moves the insertion point to a new place in the document.

Edit Gl**o**ssary   Enables you to create or insert glossary text.

Edit **L**inks   Enables links for reviewing and updating.

Edit O**b**ject   Opens a selected object for editing purposes.

View Menu

View **N**ormal   Displays the current document without page boundaries.

View **O**utline   Displays the current document's outline in the active window.

View **P**age Layout	Enables you to view the current document as it will appear when printed. While you are using View Page, you can also edit and format.
View **D**raft	Displays text using the system font for speed advantage.
View **T**oolbar	Enables/disables button bar.
View **Ri**bbon	Displays the icons that represent the basic character formats together with the current font and style.
View **R**uler	Displays the icons that represent the basic paragraph formats.
View **H**eader/Footer	Opens the Header/Footer window for editing.
View **F**ootnotes	Displays the Footnote window for editing.
View **A**nnotations	Displays a pane containing annotations with references.
View Field **C**odes	When it is on, codes inside the fields are displayed. When it is off, the results of the field as text or graphics are displayed.
View **Z**oom	Opens dialog box to select magnitude of zoomed view.

Insert Menu

Insert **B**reak	Inserts a page, column, or section break.
Insert Page **N**umbers	Inserts a page number.
Insert Foot**n**ote	Inserts a footnote reference at the point selected.
Insert Book**m**ark	Defines a name for the selection.
Insert **A**nnotation	Inserts an annotation reference at the insertion point.
Insert Date and **T**ime	Pastes the date and time at the insertion point.
Insert Fiel**d**	Inserts a field in which control codes can be contained for inserting text, graphics, or numbers.
Insert **S**ymbol	Places a special character in the text.

16

Insert Index **Entry**	Inserts an index entry, all of which are compiled into an index.
Insert Index	Compiles index entries and inserts an index.
Insert Table of **Contents**	Collects headings or table of contents entries and inserts a table of contents.
Insert File	Inserts the contents of a selected file at the insertion point. It has the capacity for subsequent updating if the user desires to maintain a link.
Insert **Frame**	Places a frame in the document at the insertion point.
Insert **Picture**	Inserts a picture at the insertion point.
Insert **Object**	Inserts an equation, object, chart, or drawing at the insertion point.

Format Menu

Format **Character**	Controls the type style of characters such as font, point size, and italics.
Format **Paragraph**	Controls paragraph formatting such as alignment, indentation, and line spacing.
Format **Tabs**	Controls tab stop setting and clearing, tab stop alignment, and type of leader character.
Format **Border**	Opens dialog box to select border options.
Format **Language**	Selects language for current use.
Format **Style**	Displays names and formatting definitions of styles for review, redefinition, and application.
Format Page Set**up**	Opens dialog box for setting margins and other page layout parameters.
Format **Co**lumns	Opens dialog box for editing settings for columns.
Format **Section** Layout	Controls page formatting within sections such as section start, line numbering, and number and spacing of columns.
Format **Frame**	Enables editing of formats for frames.
Format **Pictur**e	Displays picture sizing and cropping controls.

Tools Menu

Tools Spelling	Checks spelling and assists in correcting spelling and typing errors.
Tools **G**rammar	Checks proper use of words and phrases.
Tools **T**hesaurus	Displays a list of alternative words for the selection.
Tools **H**yphenation	Hyphenates the text to reduce gaps in justified text.
Tools **B**ullets and Renumbering	Numbers or renumbers paragraphs, selects bullet types.
Tools Revision **Mar**ks	Marks changes made to document.
Tools Compare **V**ersions	Compares a selected document with the current document and in the current document, inserts revision marks beside paragraphs that have been altered.
Tools Sorting	Rearranges paragraphs alphabetically or numerically.
Tools **C**alculate	Performs math on numbers in the selection.
Tools Rep**a**ginate Now	Paginates the document when background pagination is turned off. When the background pagination is turned on, this command paginates the entire document immediately and ignores any further keyboard or mouse actions.
Tools **R**ecord Macro	Displays a dialog box for naming the macro, and then records typing, commands, and operations to build a macro.
Tools **M**acro	Runs a selected macro.
Tools **O**ptions	Adjusts some Word operations according to your preference.

16

Table Menu

Table **I**nsert Table	Inserts a new table into the text.
Table **D**elete Columns	Deletes selected columns.
Table **M**erge Cells	Changes selected cells into one cell.
Table Convert Text to **Ta**ble/ **Ta**ble to Text	Converts selected text to a table or a selected table to text.
Table Select **R**ow	Selects the current row.
Table Select **C**olumn	Selects the current column.
Table Select **Ta**ble	Selects the entire current table.
Table Row **H**eight	Enables changing of row height.
Table Column **W**idth	Enables changing of column width.
Table **S**plit Table	Places a row of text above the current row in the table.
Table **G**ridlines	Enables/disables viewing of table gridlines.

Window Menu

Window **N**ew Window	Opens a new window in the current window.
Window **A**rrange All	Arranges all windows in nonoverlapping tiles.
Window [List]	Brings up a list of up to nine open documents that can be selected for rapid activation.

Help Menu

Help **I**ndex	Lists all Help topics.
Help **G**etting Started	Displays lessons for starting with Word for Windows.
Help **L**earning Word	Displays lessons for learning Word for Windows.
Help **W**ordPerfect Help	Help for WordPerfect converts.
Help **A**bout	Copyright and system information.

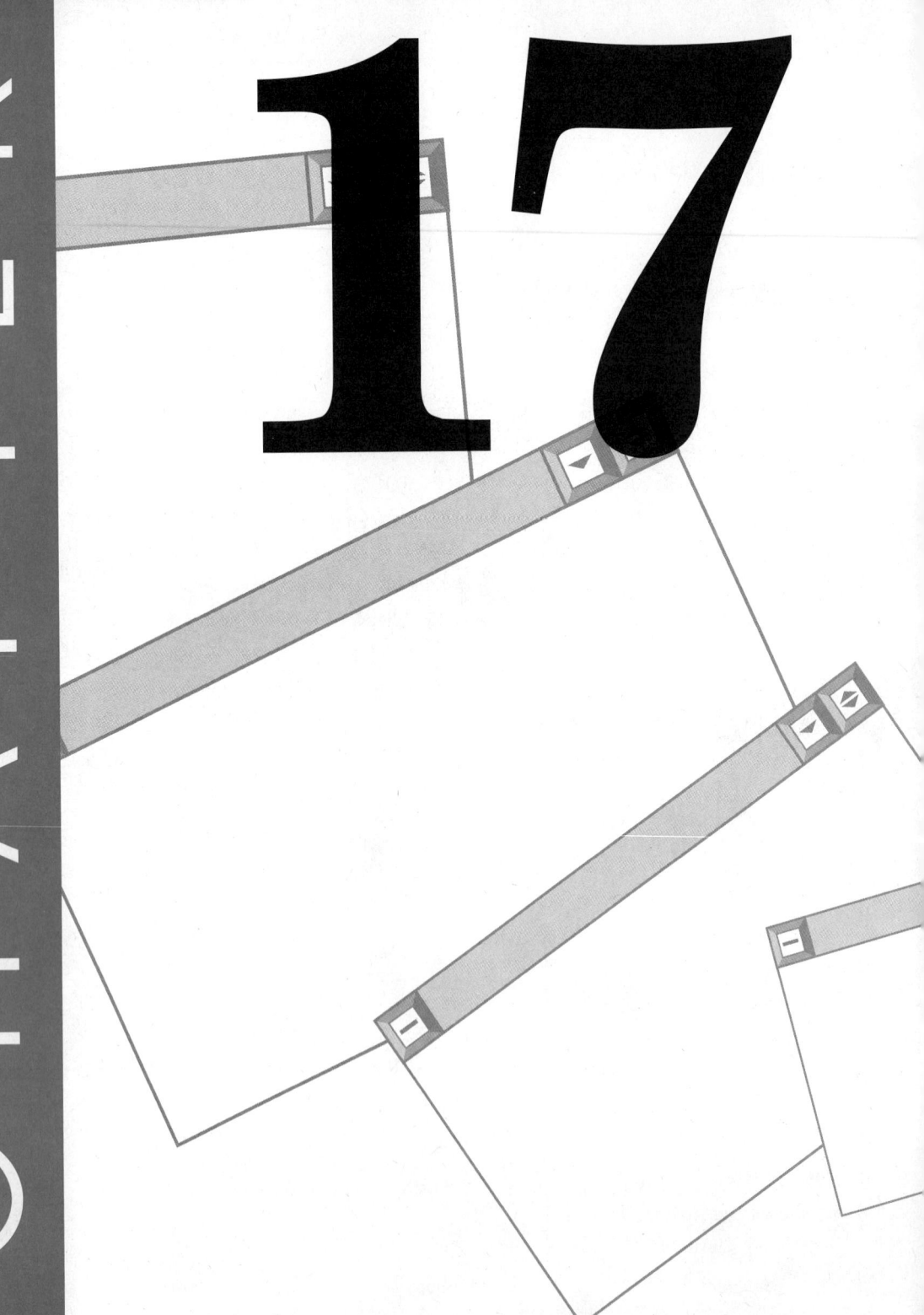

CHAPTER

17

WordPerfect for Windows

WordPerfect for DOS has been the word processor of choice for the serious user for many years. Even now, the application holds more than 50 percent of the marketplace—quite a feat in a world full of contenders. Now WordPerfect Corporation has unleashed the power of its DOS-based application in the Windows environment with WordPerfect for Windows (WPW) Version 5.1.

This chapter describes the features of WPW that make it stand out from the crowd. Even though WPW is set up so that a die-hard keyboard user can get along without a mouse in many situations, sooner or later you will have to use a mouse, so plan on it.

Setting Up for a Work Session

When you open WPW for the first time, you see the application window with menu items across the top, just below the title bar. An empty document window is open that shows only a title bar and an empty document. Figure 17.1 shows the initial WPW screen.

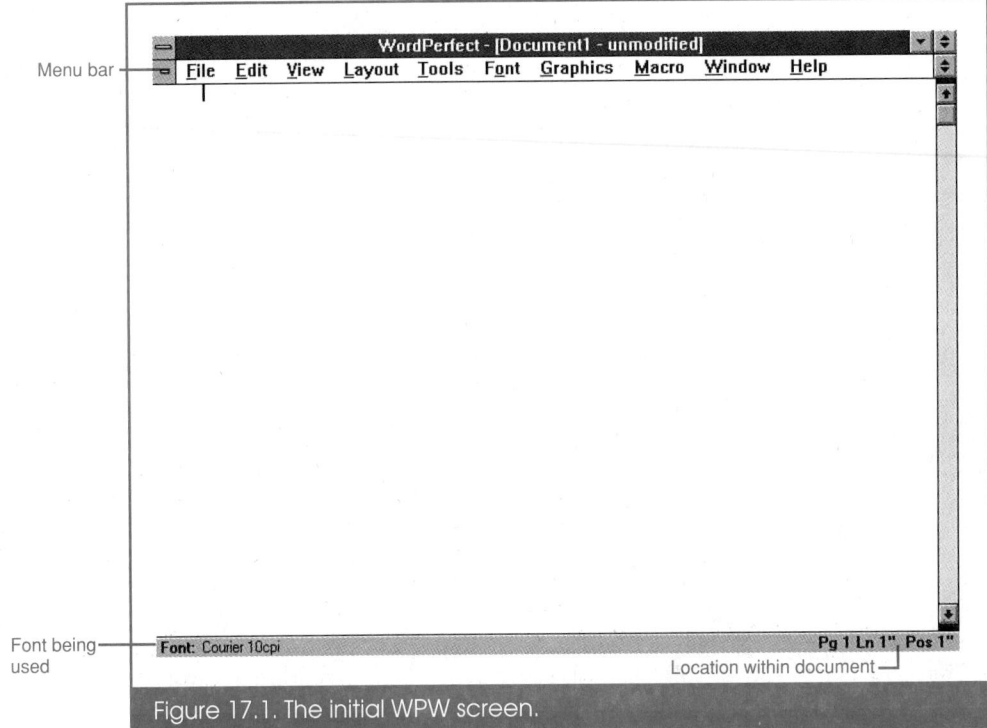

Menu bar

Font being used

Location within document

Figure 17.1. The initial WPW screen.

WPW enables you to view and work with a menu button arrangement that the WordPerfect Corporation has dubbed the *button bar*. Figure 17.2 shows the WPW application window with the button bar enabled. The button bar is a customizable display of buttons that work the way you would expect a macro function to operate. In other words, instead of giving (or designing a macro to give) the menu commands to open a file (**F**ile **O**pen), with the button bar visible, you simply click the appropriate function—in this case, the Open button. The most common menu commands are found on the button bar, enabling people who use the mouse to edit documents more quickly. Use the **V**iew **B**utton Bar command to display the button bar.

If you want to see a ruler displayed, you can make that happen, and set it as a preference for future work sessions. The ruler is displayed within each document window, just below the title bar (or button bar, if displayed). Text formatting buttons allow you to change text by simply pressing a button. Each button has its own dedicated function. When the ruler is displayed, so are the text formatting buttons, as seen in Figure 17.3.

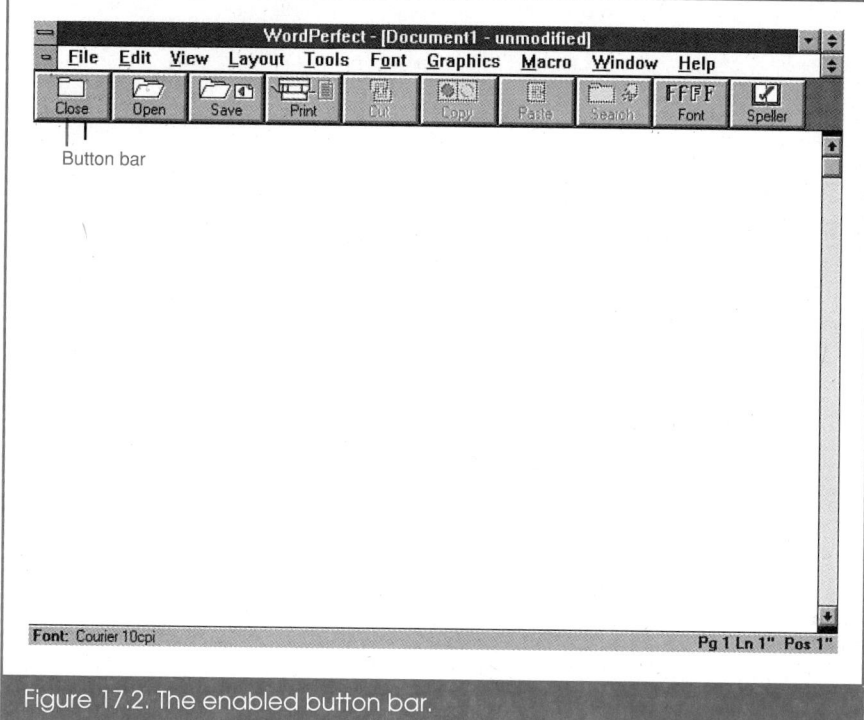

Figure 17.2. The enabled button bar.

17

The status bar at the base of the application window shows you the document style, the page number, and the location of the pointer on the page (in inches).

Making a New Document

To make a new document in WPW, you simply start typing. In this respect, WPW is not unlike other word processors. It uses the default layout, font, and style until you tell it otherwise.

For example, assume that you want to make a list of tunes you would like to add to your CD collection. You might type a list, as shown in Figure 17.4.

It's a pretty basic document. When you first open WPW, the default document type is *letter*, the tabs are set at *one-half inch* increments, and the margins are set to *0*.

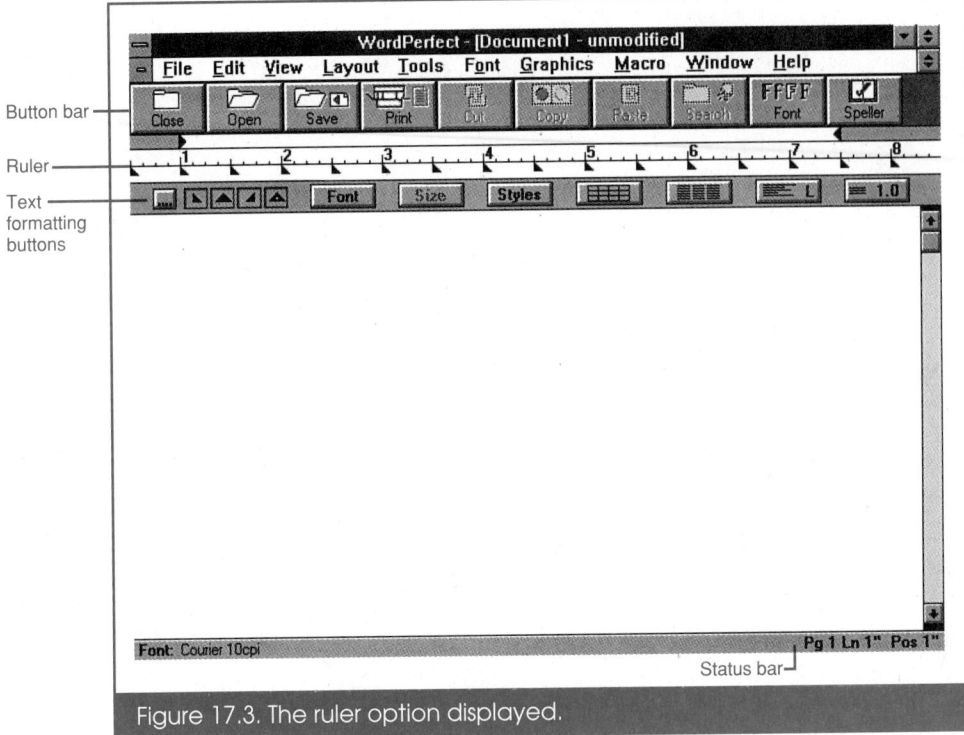

Figure 17.3. The ruler option displayed.

Setting Margins

If you want to move the margins, click the left or the right margin indicator and drag it to the desired point on the ruler. The left margin indicator is circled in Figure 17.5.

Setting Tabs

If you want to reset the tabs, simply click and drag the tab symbol to your preferred positions. Tabs are indicated as the triangular symbols under the numbered ruler line within the document window. Figure 17.6 shows these tabs. You can reduce the number of tabs by dragging them to a location where a tab already exists, and placing the dragged tab marker so that it overwrites another tab marker. WPW gives you a tab every half-inch as a default. This can be changed to suit your needs. You can also remove tabs by dragging them off of the ruler.

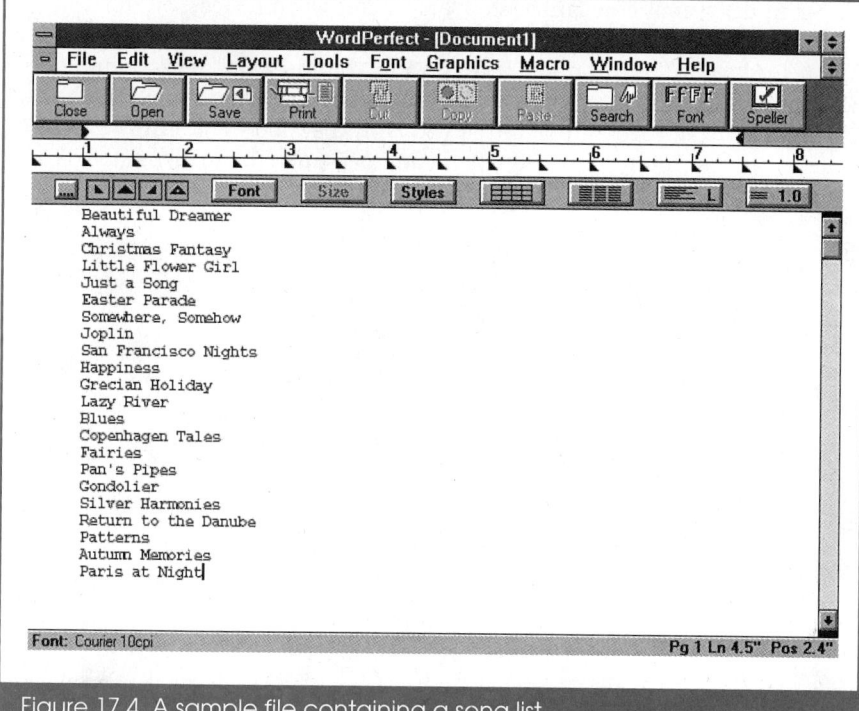

Figure 17.4. A sample file containing a song list.

Selecting Text

You select or highlight text as you would with any Windows-based product. Simply click at the top left of the text and/or graphics you want to work with, drag the insertion point to the lower-right side, and release the mouse button. This function is not new or awfully interesting. Highlighted text is shown in Figure 17.7.

Draft Mode

Draft mode is a viewing tool intended primarily for WP for DOS users. The characters are monospaced (like the DOS version), the default screen colors are white-on-blue (like the DOS version), and the attributes for each character are highlighted with the same color-coding method that WP for DOS uses. Virtually any word processor will run faster in draft mode because (in draft mode) word processors do not have to use as much of the system resources (memory, CPU involvement, and so on) manipulating text and attributes on the screen. Of course, your printed document will reveal proportionally spaced characters with all the screen attributes you would expect from a WYSIWYG editing environment. Using draft mode does not affect the printed output in any way.

Left margin indicator

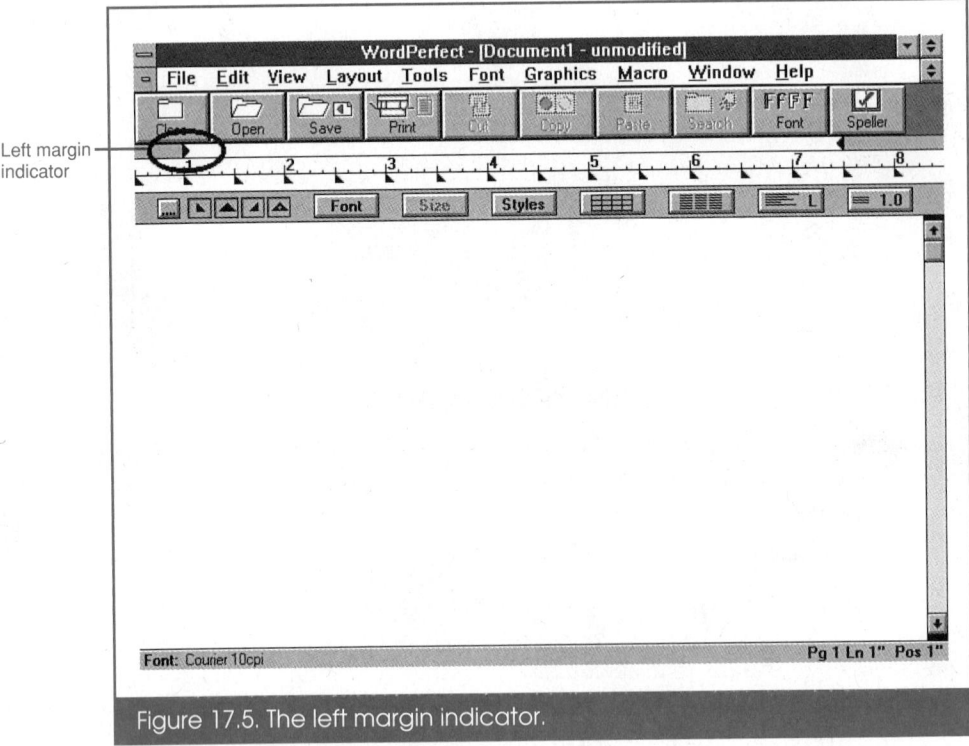

Figure 17.5. The left margin indicator.

You can change the color schemes to suit your taste. In fact, you can match the familiar color settings if you are a WP for DOS user. Figure 17.8 shows what you can expect when you switch to draft mode from the View menu.

Changing the color configuration of draft mode is simple. You can select the individual colors for the character attributes and also the predefined display color settings if you have a monochrome, LCD, or plasma screen.

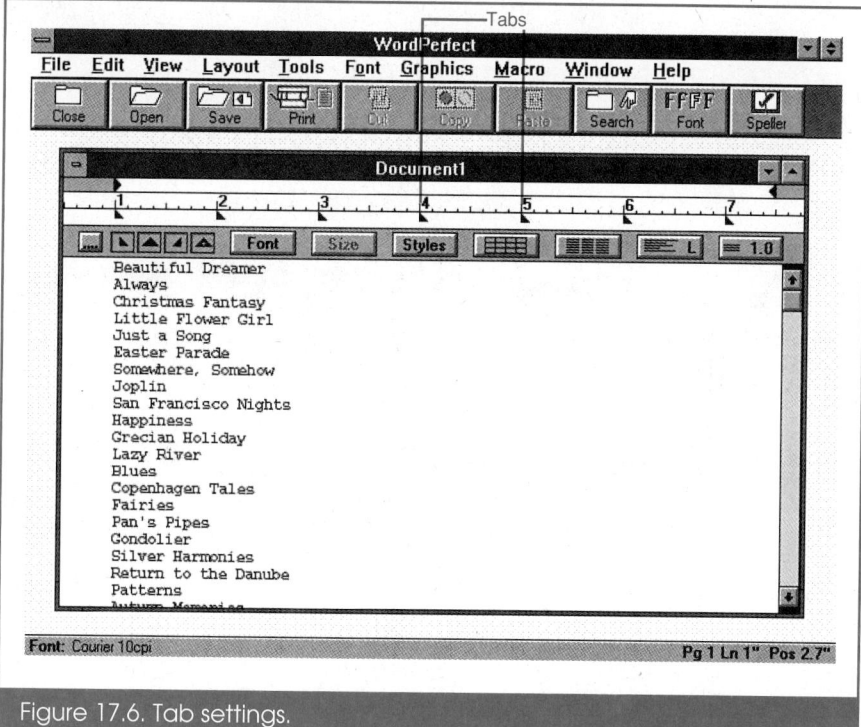

Figure 17.6. Tab settings.

Edit Go To

The **Edit G**o To feature is one of the niceties of WPW. You have several options from which to choose. The first is the standard **G**o To Page Number with the familiar text box for the entry of the desired page number. This is where familiarity might end. The Go To dialog box is shown in Figure 17.9.

If you click the Last Position button, WPW sends you back to the last position that it remembers you asking for the last time you used the **G**o To option.

When you are working with normal text, you can click the **P**osition button in the Go To dialog box to select **G**o To Page Number, **T**op of Current Page, and **B**ottom of Current Page.

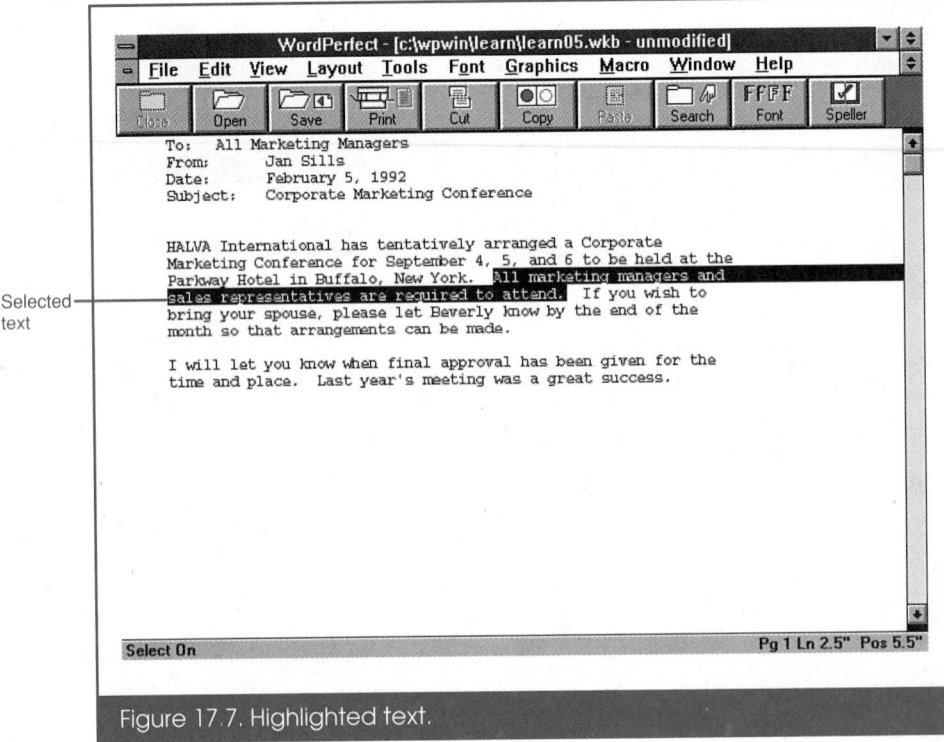

Selected text

Figure 17.7. Highlighted text.

When you work within a table, you can go to the following:

▲ Page Number

▲ Cell

▲ Top of Cell

▲ Bottom of Cell

▲ First Cell

▲ Last Cell

▲ Top of Column

▲ Bottom of Column

▲ First Column

▲ Last Column

▲ Previous Column

▲ Next Column

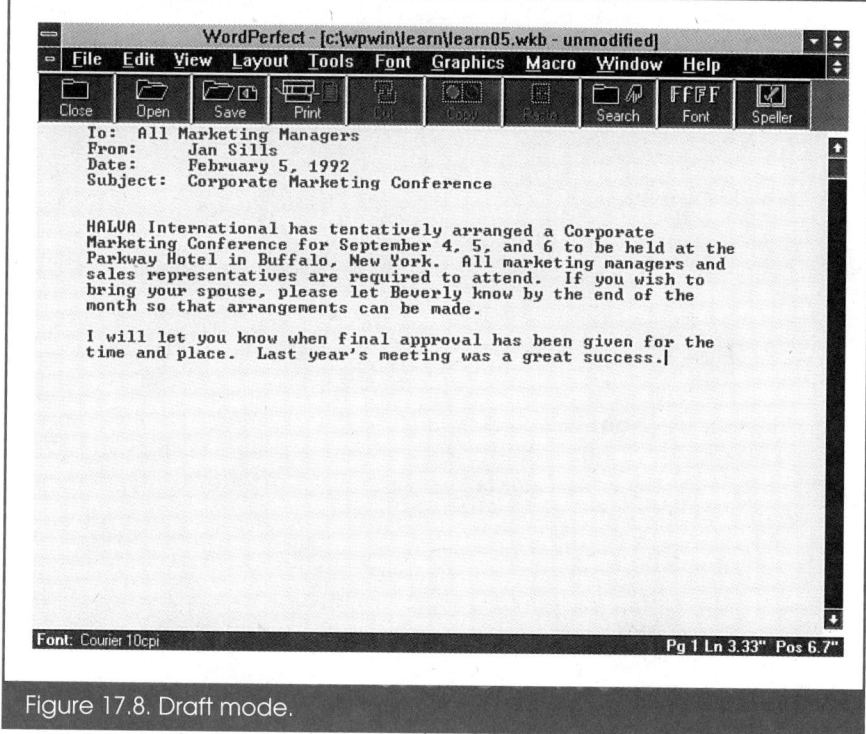

Figure 17.8. Draft mode.

There are also seven effective options from which to choose when you work within columns.

Working with Your Text

Working with text is relatively straightforward. You highlight text that you want to manipulate, and then give commands via the menu or button bar to complete the task.

Selecting Fonts

You can change the font in use by selecting Font Font from the menu, clicking the font button (it says FONT and shows four typefaces of the letter F), and selecting one of the fonts assigned to the Font button located on the ribbon at the top of each document window.

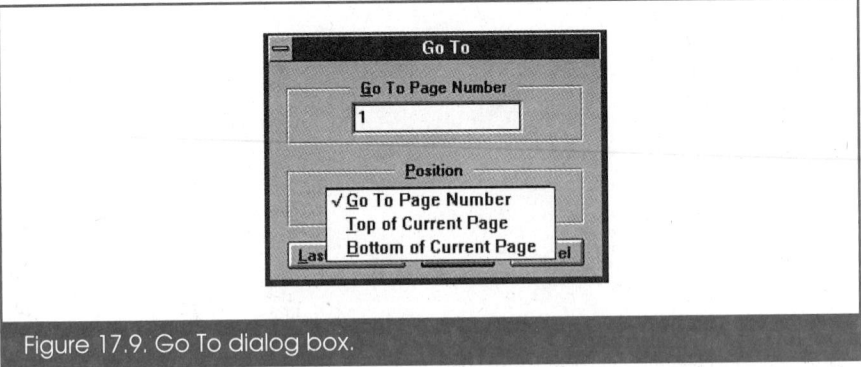

Figure 17.9. Go To dialog box.

When you use the **F**ont selection available from the main menu bar, you can select one of many likely options from the list. When you select **F**ont **F**ont from the menu bar (or use the Font Button), a dialog box like the one in Figure 17.10 opens.

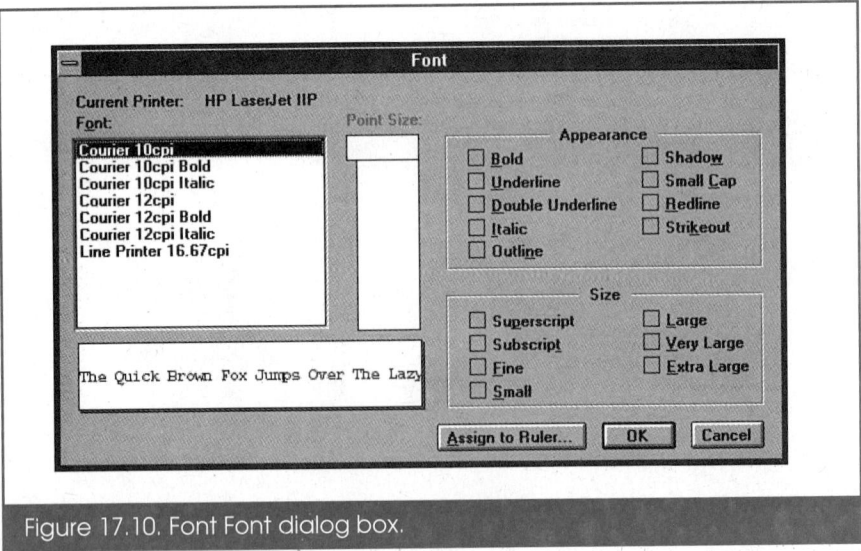

Figure 17.10. Font Font dialog box.

The list of fonts that are available to you from your system might be different, but the overall concept is the same from machine to machine.

You select the desired font from the font list to the left, you select the font size in points from the list box in the center of the dialog box, and then you select any additional attributes you might want to apply to your highlighted text.

You then can assign the font style to the ruler found at the top of every document window. This is really quite handy if you tend to use just a few fonts or type styles, and don't want to go through the selection process every time you want to apply that special font.

The assignment of fonts to the ruler is limited to the inclusion of fonts and size settings, but you can change the size of any assigned font by clicking the Size button on the window ruler.

Selecting a Style for Your Document

17

A style is a collection of text formatting information that is saved to a file. The information is made up of tab settings, font choice, indenting, paragraph formatting, point size, line spacing, and so on.

If you wanted to use a lengthy quote in a document, for example, you would create a style named "Long Quotes" so that you would not have to manually reformat each line of text in the quote itself. Instead, you would simply assign the style to the text.

WPW comes with a small starter library of styles. Figure 17.11 shows the basic styles that come with WPW. There is no limit to the number or type of styles you can create with WPW. You also can use styles created with WP for DOS, or import several other word processors' style sheets.

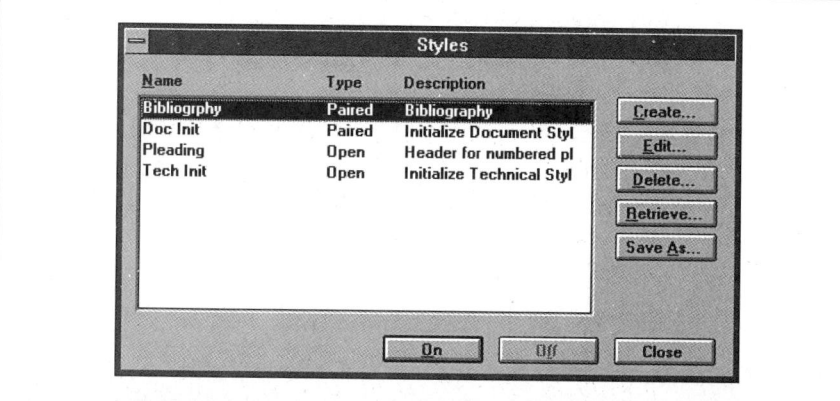

Figure 17.11. Styles dialog box.

Inserting Special Characters

You can insert special characters into your text by giving the WP Characters command from the **Fo**nt menu. This option gives you the ability to insert characters from several languages and character sets into your text.

An interesting use for this feature is to insert symbols into a bulleted list in lieu of the bullets themselves. You might use Japanese language symbols if you were writing about something related to that culture or language.

You also can insert boxes, typographic symbols (such as dingbats), and simple icons. Figure 17.12 shows the list of symbols available to you.

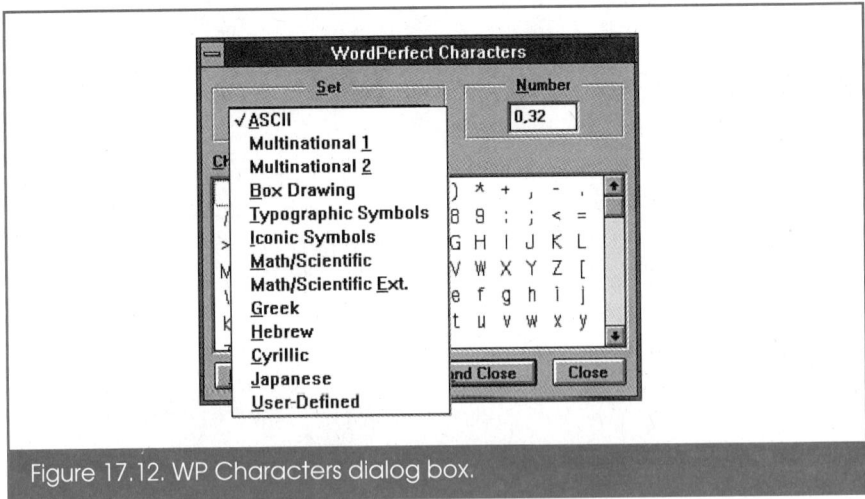

Figure 17.12. WP Characters dialog box.

Numbering Pages

Page numbering with WPW is the easiest and slickest in the business. When you select the page numbering option from the **L**ayout **P**age menu, a dialog box such as that shown in Figure 17.13 opens. Several options are available. WPW gives you two sample pages to look at while you go through the selection process. You can put page numbers in many places on a page.

17

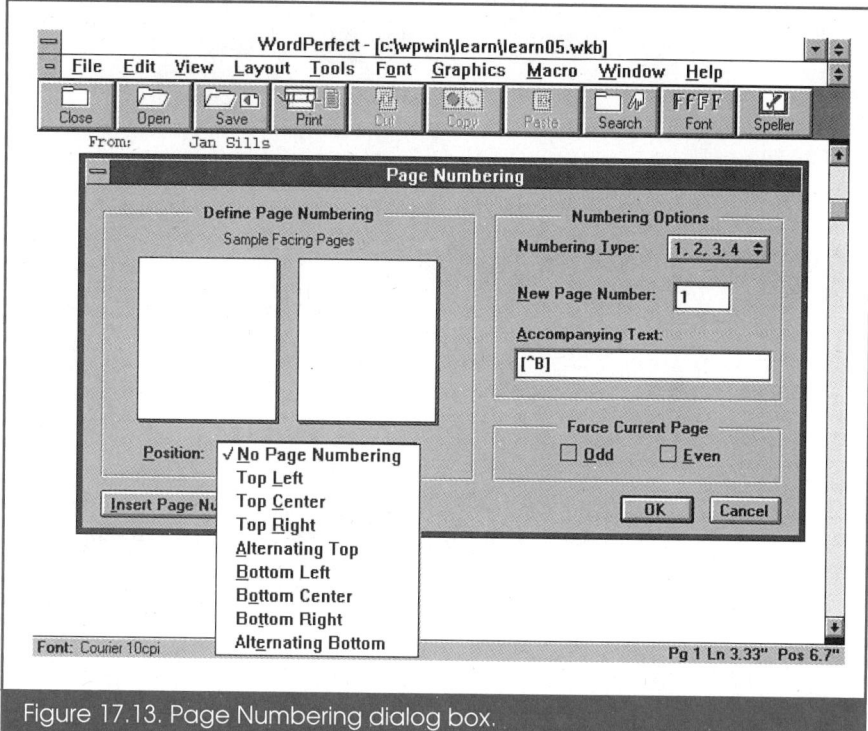

Figure 17.13. Page Numbering dialog box.

You can use Roman numerals or numbers, and you can even add text to
them. Just type the desired text before or after the [^B]. This is a
function name that substitutes your number format choice on the
sample pages and final pages of text. You can look at your choices
before you go back to your document. This is a real time-saver.

Defining Columns

If you are creating a document that eventually will become a newsletter
or a magazine column, you will want to use the Layout Define Columns
function. The way WPW handles column sizing and margins is very
graphical in nature.

When you open the Define Columns dialog box, shown in Figure 17.14,
you select the number of columns for your document. WPW then
measures how much space is needed and calculates the appropriate
margins based on the distance between the columns and the page size.
You can make your life easier if you select Newspaper from the short
list of radio button selections.

Define Columns

Number of Columns

2

Type
● Newspaper
○ Parallel
○ Parallel Block Protect

Options
☒ Evenly Spaced
☒ Columns On

Margins

	Left	Right
1:	1"	4"
2:	4.5"	7.5"
3:		
4:		
5:		

Distance Between Columns
0.5"

OK   Cancel

Figure 17.14. Define Columns dialog box.

WPW makes a judgment as to how much margin space is needed and lays out the page for you. You can change any one of the margins or the space between the columns and WPW changes the rest of the settings for you.

The result is very fast and tidy column formatting. WPW also saves your settings with your document, so the next time you open it, you don't have to re-create the column layout settings to match the existing layout.

Spelling It Right

The WPW Speller is revolutionary in one major way. The spelling module is a stand-alone executable file that can be opened from Windows itself, without running WPW at all. This means that you can spell check your WPW documents from Windows without opening WPW at all. By minimizing the Speller window, you can conveniently move between the Speller, a WPW document, and Windows.

As you can see in Figure 17.15, WPW Speller will check an entire page or just one word, with all of the functionality of popular third-party specialty programs.

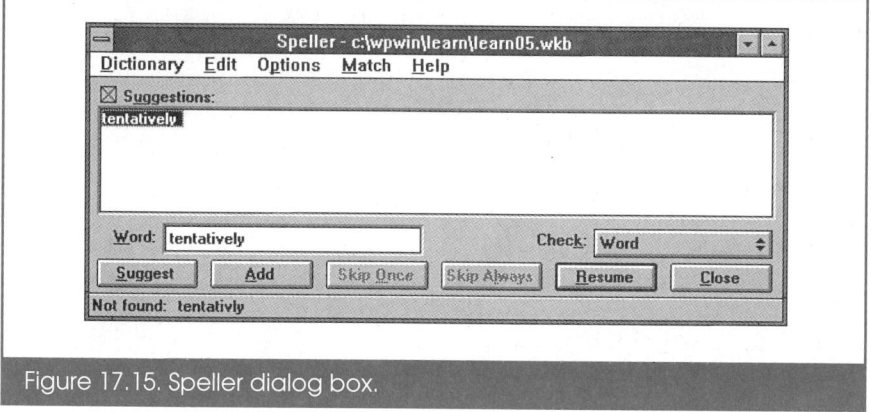

Figure 17.15. Speller dialog box.

17

Thesaurus

The WPW Thesaurus is a stand-alone module as well. You can use it to check synonyms, antonyms, and so on. Of course, it can be of great service when you are using a Windows application that has no thesaurus of its own. Both the Speller and the Thesaurus have their own icons that can be added to any Program Manager group window.

This feature of WPW is very straightforward and graphical. Figure 17.16 gives you an image of what Thesaurus looks like.

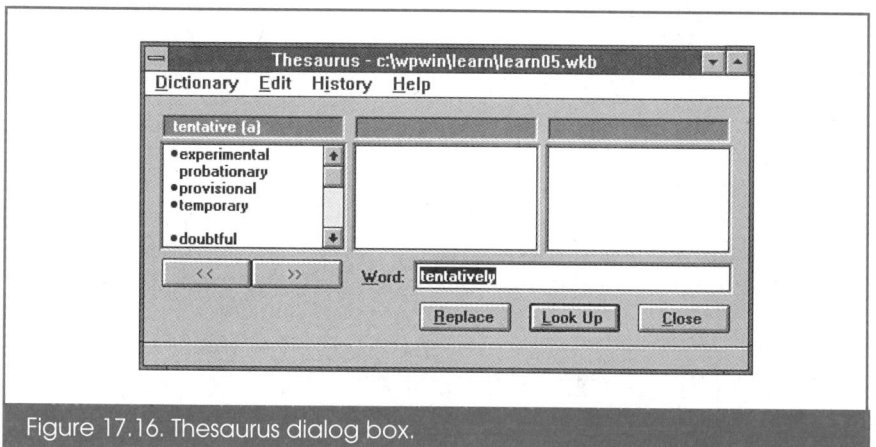

Figure 17.16. Thesaurus dialog box.

Drawing Graphics Lines

You can add lines to your document by using the **Graphics Line** option from the **Graphics** menu. This function creates a line and places it on the page where you want it. It makes horizontal and vertical lines.

This feature is really useful when you want to separate a header from a body of text, or a figure on the left side of a page from text on the right. You can specify the length of the line, the thickness, how dark you want it to be, where you want it placed in respect to the page size, and how you want it placed on the page (centered and so on). Figure 17.17 is the Create Horizontal Line dialog box.

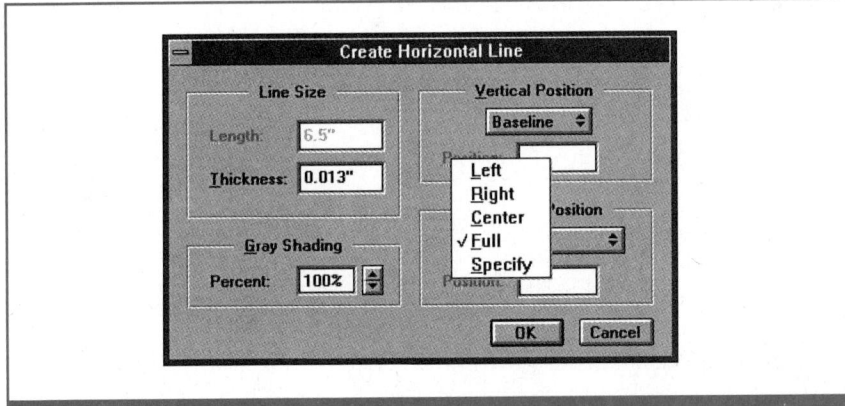

Figure 17.17. Create Horizontal Line dialog box.

Making a Footnote

Footnotes are great for listing sources of your information, or for defining details in your text. You can create footnotes with WPW by selecting **Layout Footnote Create** from the main menu. This action opens a footnote window that prompts you to type the text you want to use for a footnote. WPW adds a number before the footnote text and places a corresponding number in the body of the document text to be used when you want readers to refer to the footnote.

Inserting Dates

The Date feature of WPW places the current date into your document. WPW places the date where you want it and/or updates it every time

you open the document. Figure 17.18 shows the Document Date/Time Format dialog box.

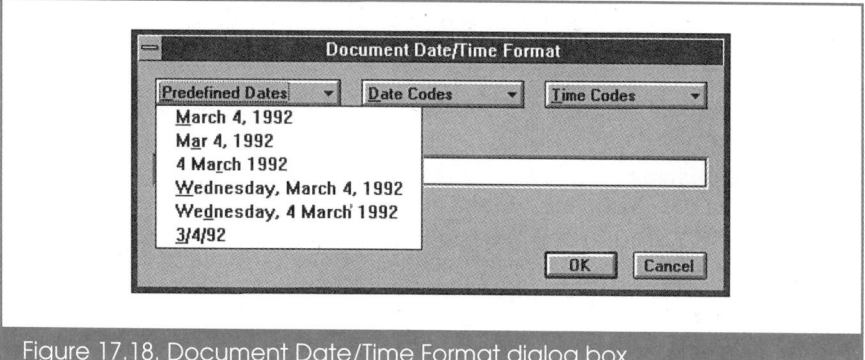

Figure 17.18. Document Date/Time Format dialog box.

17

Typesetting

You use Layout Typesetting to change the way your text looks in print. You change all the options associated with typesetting by opening the Typesetting dialog box, shown in Figure 17.19.

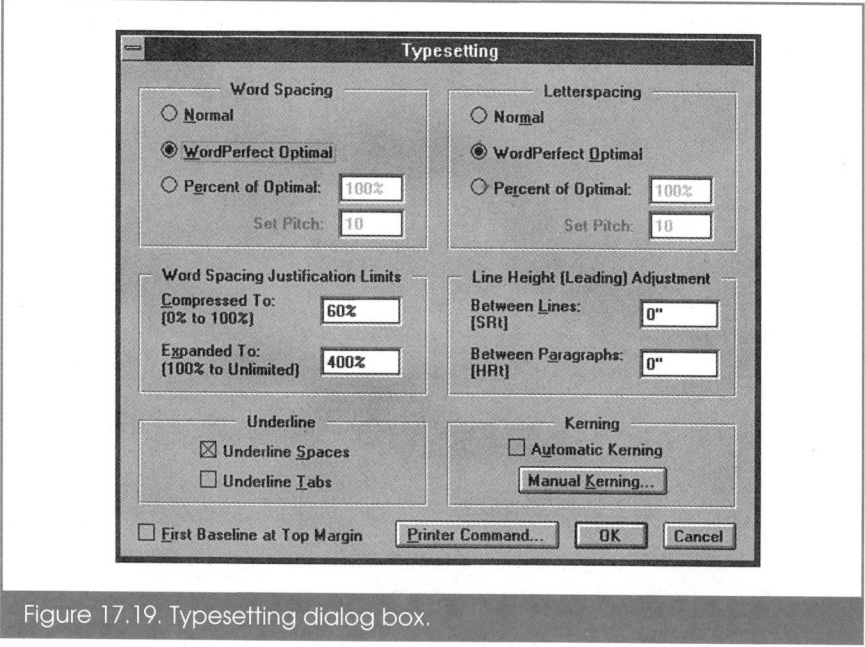

Figure 17.19. Typesetting dialog box.

Some of things you can do with your text by using the typesetting feature include the following:

- ▲ Kerning (adjusts the distance between characters)
- ▲ Line height options
- ▲ Justification limits
- ▲ Printing options
- ▲ Letter spacing
- ▲ Word spacing
- ▲ Underlining

Adding Graphics to Documents

One of the best things about the new generation of word processors is their capability to work directly with graphics images inside your document. You can insert graphics files, clip art, and frames for text to get professional results that were available only to desktop publishing practitioners two years ago.

WordPerfect for Windows flexes its new muscle with some standard means and a few more sophisticated features that make WPW unique.

Inserting Graphics into Your Text

WPW creates and inserts five types of graphical boxes. These include the following:

- ▲ Figures: images, diagrams, and charts
- ▲ Text: quotes, sidebars, and text aside from the body
- ▲ Equations: mathematical and scientific
- ▲ Tables: maps, WPW tables, statistics, and so on
- ▲ User: all other user-defined purposes

You can change the appearance of your graphical images without leaving WPW. The Figure Options dialog box, illustrated in Figure 17.20, shows how simple it is to shade, change the border, and change

the positioning of your inserted graphical images. Correspondingly, if you change any other type of image, such as a text box, the title of the dialog box would be Text Box. You have the same flexibility when you change any type of graphical insert.

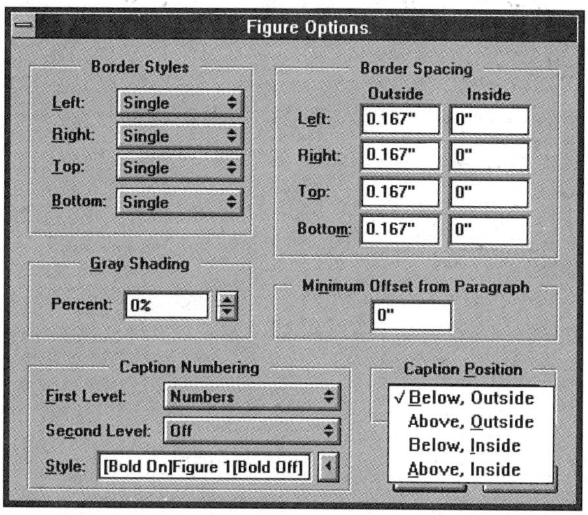

Figure 17.20. Figure Options dialog box.

WPW also provides a utility called Caption Editor. This feature enables you to create and edit textual captions for your figures. The Caption Editor can be accessed from the Figure Editor. Figure 17.21 shows the Caption Editor.

The WPW Graphics Editor

You can create, modify, and save a graphics image to a file or insert it in a document without leaving WPW. If you want to create a figure, for example, you open a subapplication called Figure Editor from the Graphics menu.

The title changes with the item you select from the **G**raphics menu, but the functionality remains the same. In fact, using one editor to work with five types of images makes the learning curve much less vertical for new users. The Graphics Editor is shown in Figure 17.22.

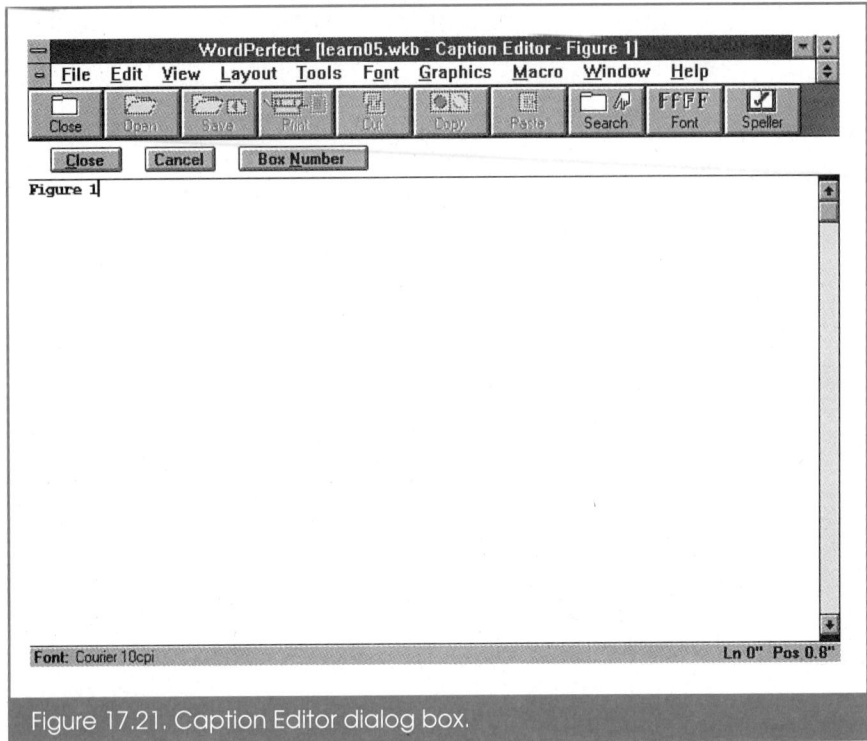

Figure 17.21. Caption Editor dialog box.

Outlining Images

With the Figure Editor, you can take a color image and render it into an outlined monochrome image for insertion into a document intended for monochrome printing. An example of an image before rendering is shown in Figure 17.23. An example of the same image after outline rendering is given in Figure 17.24.

Mirroring Graphics Images

You can actually create a mirror of an image within the Figure Editor. Figure 17.25 shows an image before mirroring, and Figure 17.26 shows the same image after mirroring.

17

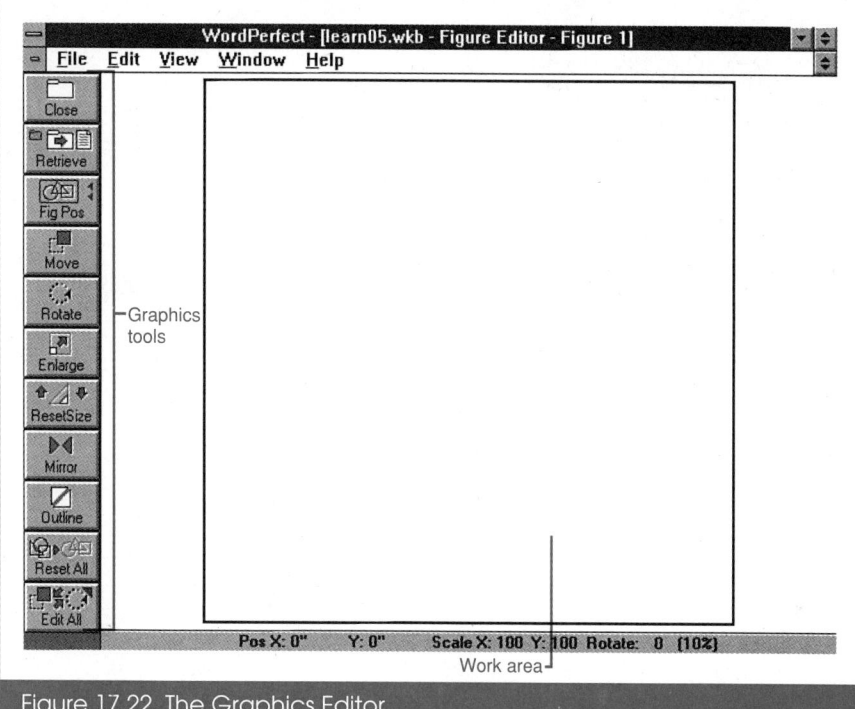

Figure 17.22. The Graphics Editor.

Rotating Pictures

Images can be rotated for maximum effect with the Figure Editor. In many cases, it's best to use the same image as a pointer, for example, within your document.

To make this point, I've used the Fat Pencil graphical file, or clip art file, for Figures 17.27 and 17.28. The image is shown before and after rotation. You could include this graphic in your corporate procedure to place emphasis on a sentence or a phrase, or simply as an icon to mark the beginning of a word or a paragraph.

If you don't like the position of the graphical image within the graphics file itself, you can rotate it to gain the best implementation within your own documents. You can save the file after you've rotated the image, or save it the way it was before you worked with it.

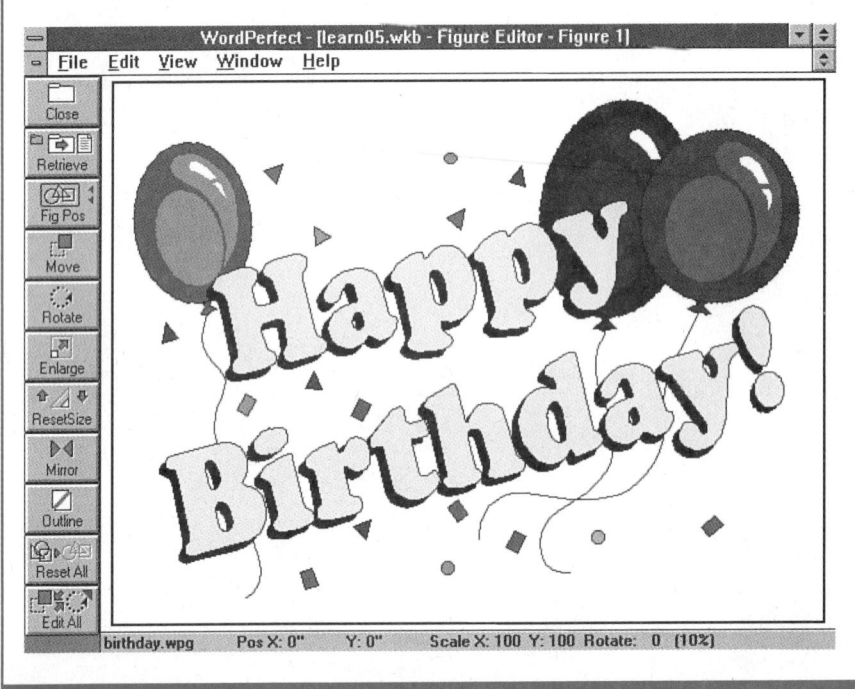

Figure 17.23. An image not yet outlined with the Figure Editor.

If you are editing a document that already includes graphical images, you also can edit those images by double-clicking the image itself. When you do this, the Figure Editor automatically opens with your figure in place as though you retrieved it manually. You then can work directly with the image before reinserting it into your document. Creating and editing images to be used in documents works the same way as soon as you've opened the Figure Editor and retrieved the image in any way you want.

Using WPW's Graphics Library

WPW comes with a graphics library of 36 image files. You can review them without actually inserting them into your document by viewing them from the dialog box that comes up when you ask to retrieve a graphics file. You can select any file from the list box and retrieve it, or view any file if you're not sure which one you really need. Figure 17.29 shows the Figure Retrieve dialog box, with the View feature engaged.

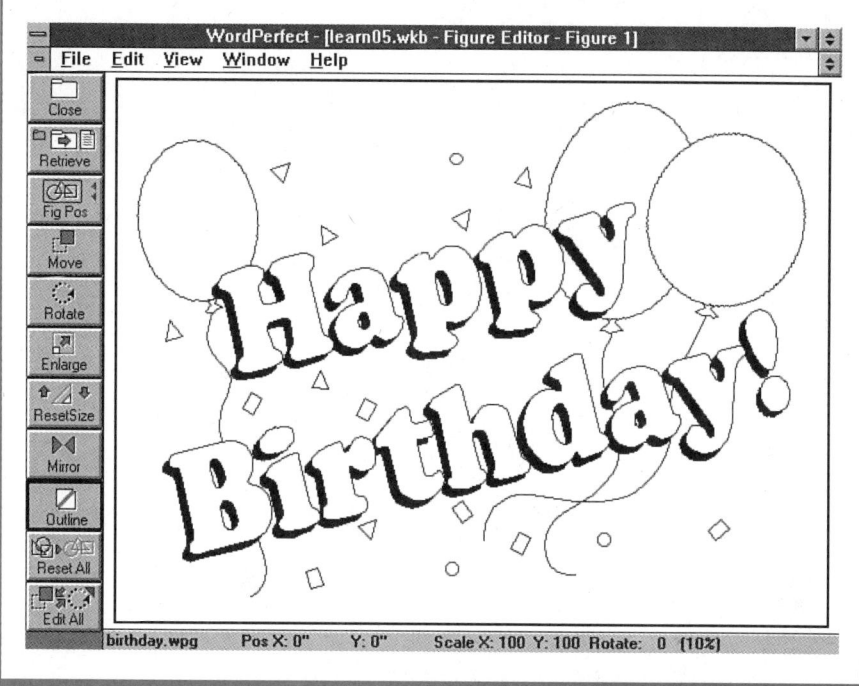

Figure 17.24. The same image after outline rendering.

17

Using WPW File Manager

The WPW File Manager included with WordPerfect for Windows can be run from WPW, or it can be used as a stand-alone utility from the Windows Program or File Manager because it has its own icon just like the Speller and Thesaurus and is fully executable all by its lonesome. It's easy to run WPW File Manager if you like it more than the utility you are currently using.

Note: The WPW File Manager discussed in this chapter is not to be confused with the Windows File Manager utility. The two are similar in name only.

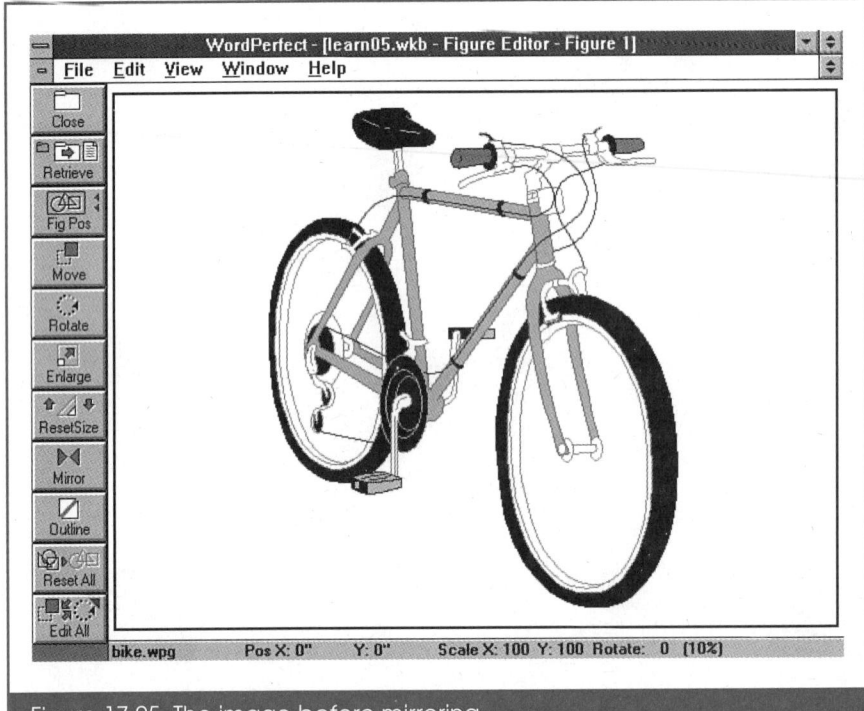

Figure 17.25. The image before mirroring.

The Navigator Windows

The WPW File Manager opens a separate small window for each drive, directory, and subdirectory file listing. WPW File Manager opens these windows from left to right.

If your files are organized several subdirectories deep, you can scroll or "navigate" your way through the windows by clicking the arrow or direction buttons located on the left side of the WPW File Manager window. You keep your place throughout this process because WPW places "pointing hand" icons to keep you advised of your position. Figure 17.30 shows you how these hand icons point to your point of entry into subsequent windows from the initial frame.

17

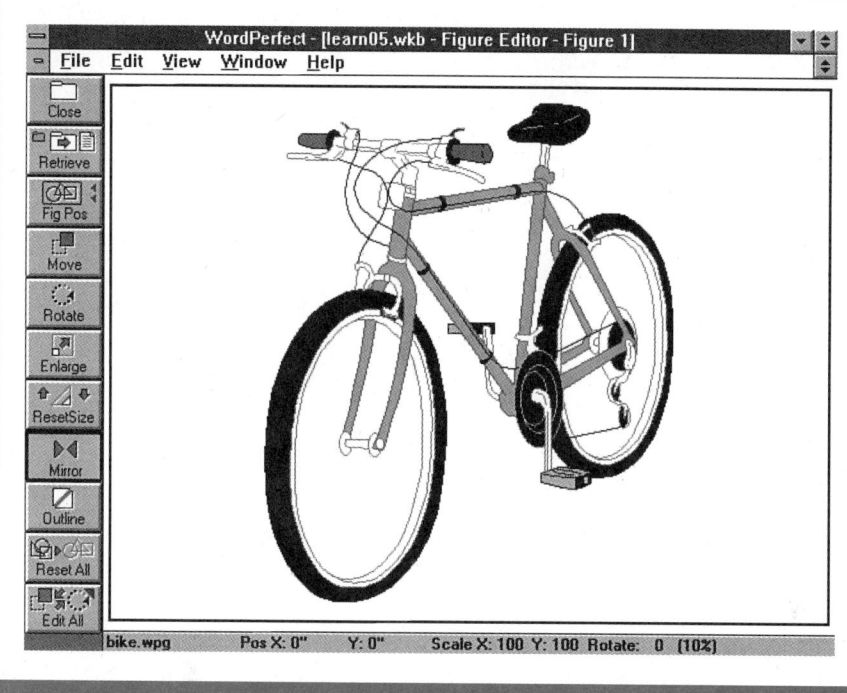

Figure 17.26. The same image after mirroring.

If you click the title bar for each Navigator window, you'll find that it's actually a button that opens a list box of the files found in that subdirectory's window. The file listing can be reorganized to suit your needs by simply clicking and dragging the header name buttons. Moving the buttons themselves enables you to change how wide the listed columns are. Figure 17.31 shows the File List window.

The Info Features

There are four Info message boxes that give you various information about current system condition and events:

▲ System: details about hardware and the DOS version

▲ Windows: version, video mode, free memory, and more

▲ Printers: installed, driver names, and ports

▲ Disk Info: drive, volume, bytes used, and bytes free

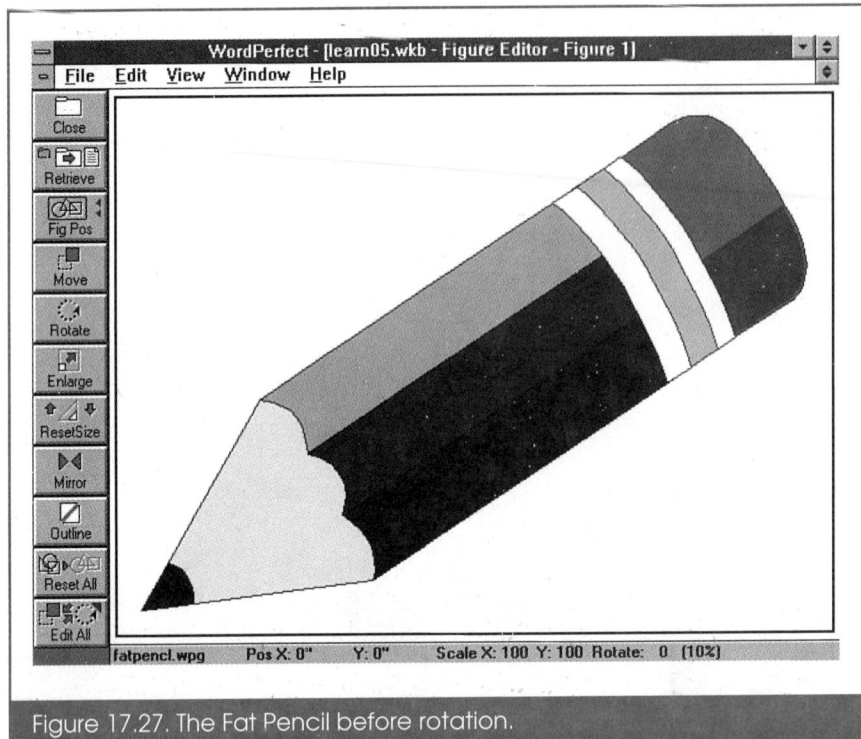

Figure 17.27. The Fat Pencil before rotation.

The Info features included within WPW File Manager can be of great service, especially if you are importing or exporting large documents with many graphics inserted. Figure 17.32 shows you the Info Disk Information dialog box. There may be nothing more aggravating than finding out that you don't have enough room on a floppy disk after you have started the process of saving to that floppy. A quick check with the Info Disk Information message box can spare you that trouble.

Changing WPW File Manager Fonts

Changing screen fonts is as slick and easy as the rest of WPW. You simply bring up the dialog box dedicated to that purpose from within WPW File Manager and select the font, point size, and attribute you want to use.

WPW File Manager recognizes and utilizes Adobe Type Manager and other font management utilities as well as the WPW fonts, Windows vector fonts, and outline fonts. Seamlessly integrated into the font management process, these totally unrelated font utilities appear to users of WPW as though they are all of the same type or make.

17

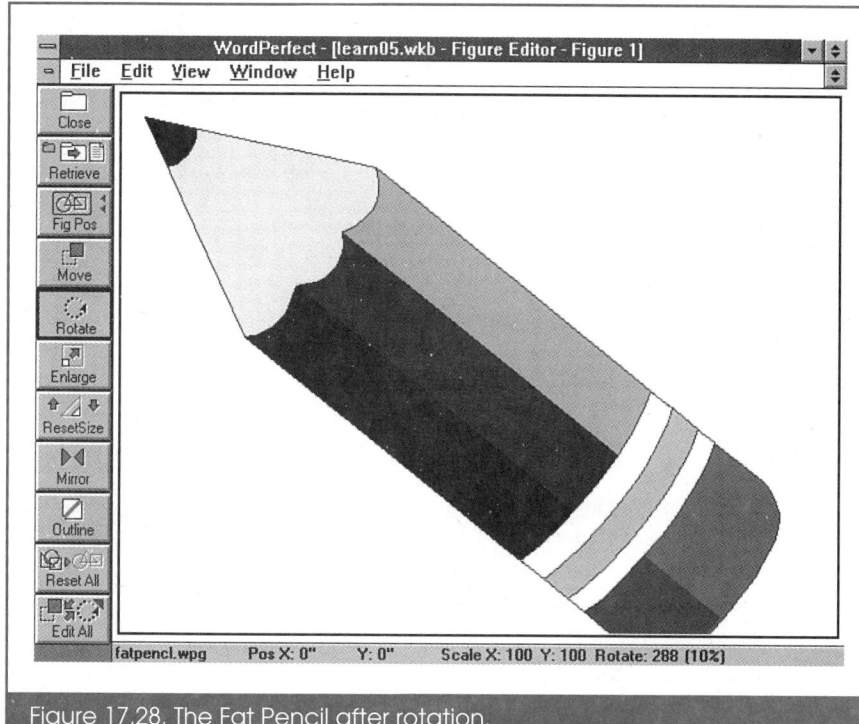

Figure 17.28. The Fat Pencil after rotation.

By selecting the application for your font selection in the Apply Font To drop-down list box found within the Font dialog box, you can assign your font selection to just one of the WPW File Manager windows or to all of them.

A text box is provided at the base of the dialog box so that you can actually see an example of your font choices before you save them. WPW saves your font assignments so that they remain intact the next time you use WPW File Manager. Figure 17.33 shows you what your choices are when you are ready to assign the fonts you selected.

Figure 17.29. Figure Retrieve and View dialog boxes.

Using Viewer

Viewer is a file-reading utility built into WPW File Manager. You can read the contents of any file. When WPW File Manager Viewer cannot directory-read the file of your choice, it loads the program associated with the extension of the filename you have selected. If you prompt WPW to show you a file with the filename extension of .PCX, WPW asks you if you want to use PC PaintBrush or another application to view the file. WPW then loads PC Paintbrush and the file of your choice. Figure 17.34 is an example of Viewer displaying an ASCII text file named CONFIG.SYS.

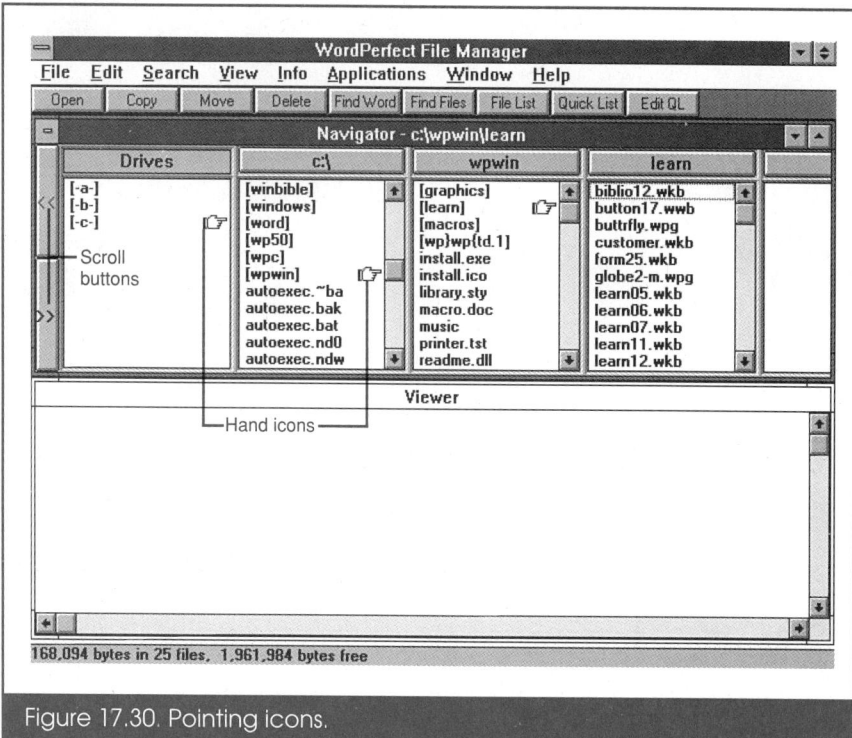

Figure 17.30. Pointing icons.

17

You can view the contents of an ASCII or binary file, then you can execute that file by double-clicking the filename. You can even run DOS- or character-based programs from WPW File Manager in this fashion.

Saving Your Document

When you are ready to save your work, you have two choices initially. You can save the open file to the original filename (and format), or you can save the file with a new filename or in one of several formats provided.

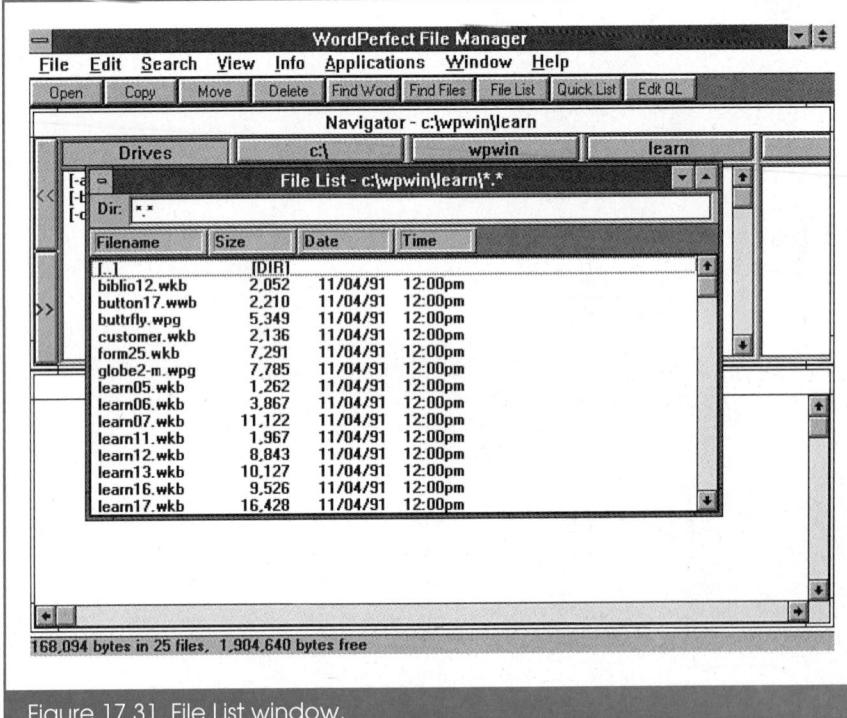

Figure 17.31. File List window.

By using the **F**ile Save **A**s command from the menu or by clicking an
icon you've created, you can save a file using any name you devise, in
any subdirectory, and with any one of many popular file formats that
WPW supports. WPW actually performs a file conversion process when
you save a file to another format. Figure 17.35 shows you what to
expect when you open the Save As dialog box and invoke the drop-down
list box showing only a partial list of available file formats.

In Closing

WordPerfect for Windows may well have the market cornered in the
features and power department. The way it handles graphics, text, and
files is not to be outdone by any other maker of high-end document
generation software.

17

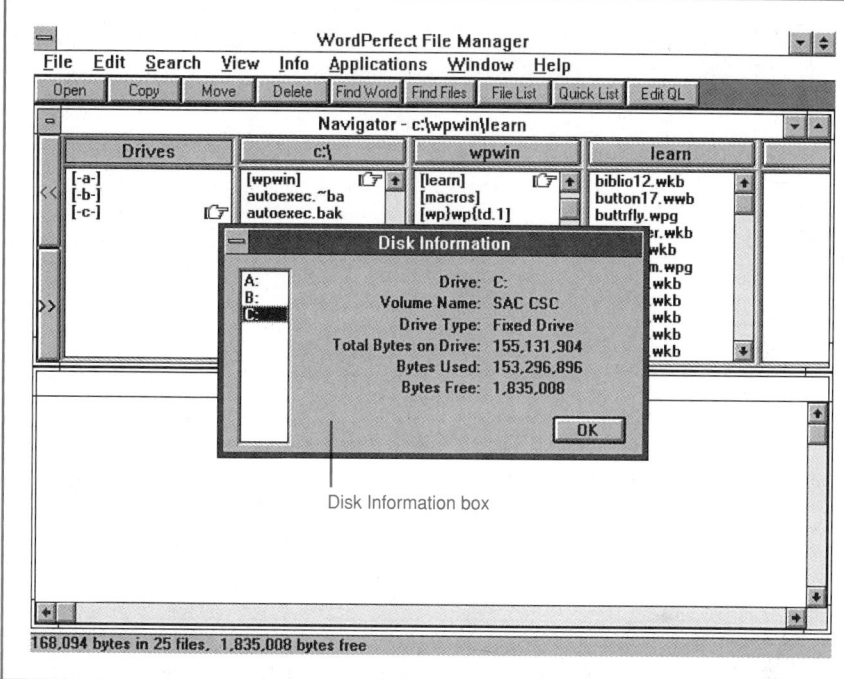

Figure 17.32. The Info Disk Information message box.

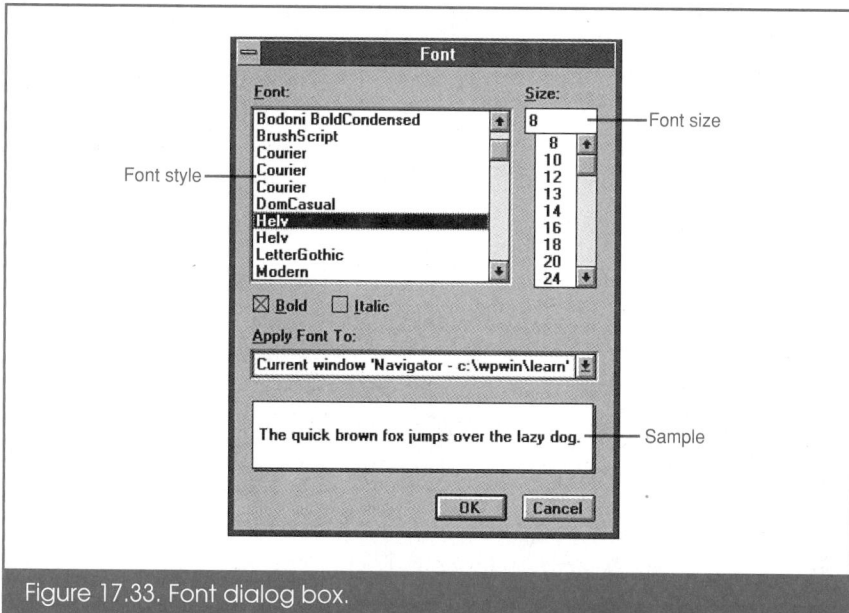

Figure 17.33. Font dialog box.

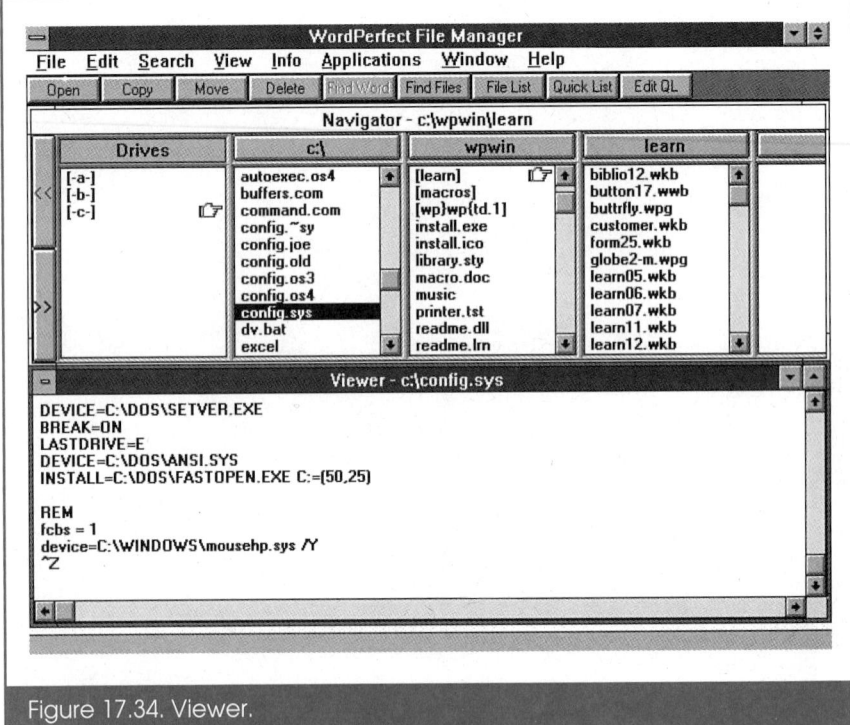

Figure 17.34. Viewer.

As the big five word processing applications edge toward being more like desktop publishing packages, you can expect to see programs such as WPW actually stepping over that line in more categories than ever before.

For current WordPerfect for DOS Version 5.1 users, the migration to the Windows environment should pose less difficulty with the release of WPW. WordPerfect Corporation virtually ensured the success of this new product by utilizing the file format of Version 5.1 for DOS.

Command Summary

This section is a command summary for WordPerfect for Windows.

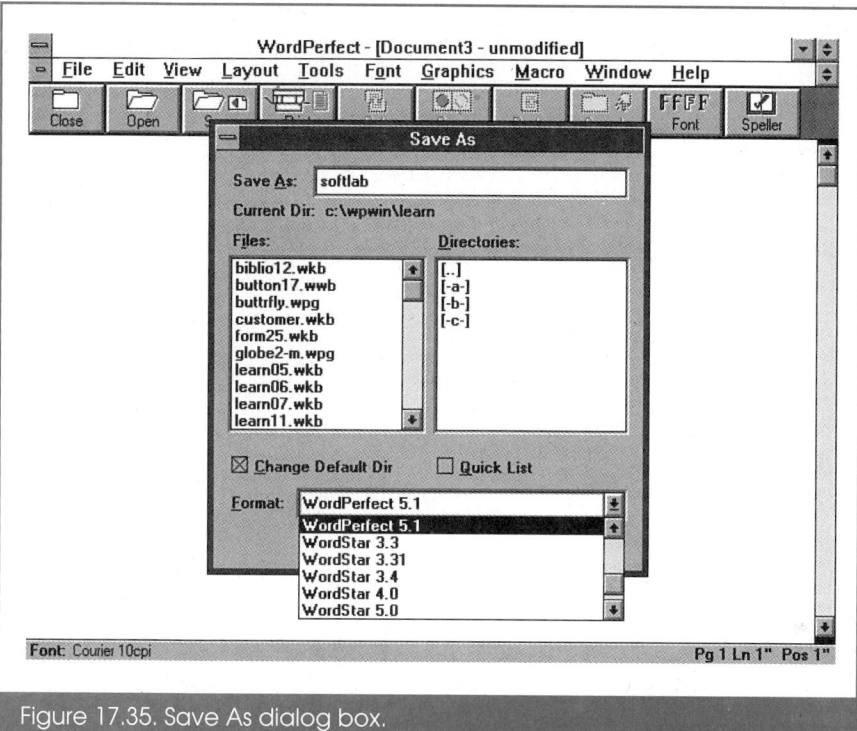

Figure 17.35. Save As dialog box.

File Menu

This is the command summary for the **F**ile menu.

File **N**ew	Begins a new document.
File **O**pen	Opens an existing document or enables you to import information from a different application. Also used for changing directories.
File **R**etrieve	Brings a file into the existing window.
File **C**lose	Closes all windows of the current document.
File **S**ave	Saves changes made to the current document.
File Save **A**s	Saves a new document or new version of an existing document in the file format and with the filename you choose. It is also used for saving a file in a different directory.

17

File Pass**w**ord	Sets or removes a document password.
File **M**anager	Invokes WordPerfect's File Manager.
File P**r**eferences	Changes initial document settings.
File **P**rint	Prints the current document according to your chosen specifications.
File Print Preview	Enables you to view the document as it will appear when printed.
File **S**elect Printer	Enables you to choose an available printer and to select options for it.
File E**x**it	Enables you to exit from WordPerfect for Windows.
File [list]	Lists the most recent files you've opened.

Edit Menu

This is the command summary for the **E**dit menu.

Edit **U**ndo	Reverses certain commands or actions.
Edit U**n**delete	Reverses the most recent deletion.
Edit Cut	Removes a selection onto the Clipboard.
Edit **C**opy	Copies a selection onto the Clipboard.
Edit **P**aste	Pastes a copied or cut selection into the current document.
Edit **A**ppend	Adds selected text to contents of the Clipboard.
Edit **L**ink	Opens the DDE access menu.
Edit Select	Selects a group of words.
Edit C**o**nvert Case	Converts a group of words to upper- or lower-case.
Edit **S**earch	Searches for an occurrence of text.
Edit Search Ne**x**t	Searches for a second occurrence of text.
Edit Search Previous	Searches for a previous occurrence of text.
Edit **R**eplace	Replaces existing text with new text.
Edit **G**o To	Places you in the desired page of a document.

View

This is the command summary for the **V**iew menu.

View **R**uler	Makes the ruler visible on the screen.
View Reveal **C**odes	Shows all text formatting codes.
View **D**raft Mode	Switches to high-speed viewing mode.
View **G**raphics	Hides or shows graphics in a document.
View Co**m**ments	Hides or shows comments in a document.
View **B**utton Bar	Displays button bar on the screen.
View Button Bar **S**etup	Opens dialog box used to manage the button bar.
View Short **M**enus	Displays only partial menu options.

Layout

This is the command summary for the **L**ayout menu.

Layout **L**ine	Changes the line format.
Layout **Pa**ragraph	Changes the paragraph format.
Layout **P**age	Changes the page format.
Layout **C**olumns	Manages columns in a document.
Layout **T**ables	Changes the layout of a table.
Layout **D**ocument	Changes the format of a document.
Layout **F**ootnote	Creates, edits and places footnotes.
Layout **E**ndnote	Creates, edits and places endnotes.
Layout **A**dvance	Moves text to a new place in a document.
Layout Typesett**in**g	Makes changes to typesetting features.
Layout **J**ustification	Sets text justification.
Layout **M**argins	Sets document margins.
Layout **St**yles	Creates and names a group of text formats.

17

Tools

This is the command summary for the **Tools** menu.

Tools Speller	Invokes the Speller utility.
Tools Thesaurus	Invokes the Thesaurus utility.
Tools Word Count	Displays word count of open document.
Tools Language	Selects language used to create text.
Tools Date	Selects and insert date in document.
Tools Outline	Creates and manages outlines.
Tools Sort	Sorts text by selectable criteria.
Tools Merge	Manages merge options for documents.
Tools Mark Text	Marks text that relates to addenda.
Tools Define	Defines text used for addenda.
Tools Generate	Creates and edits text for addenda.
Tools Document Compare	Compares two versions of a document.
Tools Master Document	Expands or compresses master documents and/or subdocuments.
Tools Spreadsheet	Imports and manages spreadsheet data.
Tools Comment	Inserts comments into a document.
Tools Line Draw	Invokes line-drawing utility.

Font

This is the command summary for the **Font** menu.

Font Font	Chooses from available fonts.
Font Color	Chooses color for available fonts.
Font Normal	Changes selected text to normal.
Font Bold	Changes selected text to bold.
Font Italic	Changes selected text to italic.
Font Underline	Applies single underline to selected text.

Font **D**ouble Underline	Applies double underline to selected text.
Font **R**edline	Lines-out text with thin red line.
Font Stri**k**eout	Lines-out text with a thin line using the current text color.
Font Subscrip**t**	Causes selected text to shrink and be placed slightly below normal text.
Font Superscript	Causes selected text to shrink and be placed slightly above normal text.
Font **S**ize	Changes the size of selected or new text.
Font **O**verstrike	Combines standard keyboard characters to make new characters.
Font **W**P Characters	Opens the special character utility. Used for inserting special characters, (example: Hebrew) into the text of a document.

17

Graphics

This is the command summary for the **Graphics** menu.

Graphics **F**igure	Creates and edits graphics figures.
Graphics Text **B**ox	Creates and edits text boxes.
Graphics **E**quation	Creates and edits equations.
Graphics **T**able Box	Creates and edits table boxes.
Graphics **U**ser Box	Creates and edits user boxes.
Graphics **L**ine	Creates and edits vertical or horizontal lines only.

Macro

This is the command summary for the **M**acro menu.

Macro **P**lay	Plays back commands in an existing macro.
Macro **R**ecord	Records commands for a new macro.

Macro Stop	Halts the recording of commands for a new macro.
Macro Pause	Pauses during the recording of commands for a new macro.
Macro Assign to Menu	Places an existing macro into the Macro menu.

Window Menu

This is the command summary for the **W**indow menu.

Window Cascade	Causes all document windows to be overlayed downward and to the right during display.
Window Tile	Causes all windows to divide up the workspace area between themselves for purposes of display.
Window 1,2,3...	Displays a list of all the open windows and enables you to select the one you would like to activate.

Help

This is the command summary for the **H**elp menu.

Help Index	Displays a list of Help options.
Help Keyboard	Gives advice on using the keyboard.
Help How Do I	Provides instructions for simple, common tasks.
Help Glossary	Supplies dictionary of definitions.
Help Using Help	Gives tips on using Help.
Help What Is	Displays help on specific topic of your choosing, using the mouse or keyboard.
Help About WordPerfect	Displays version, license and user information.

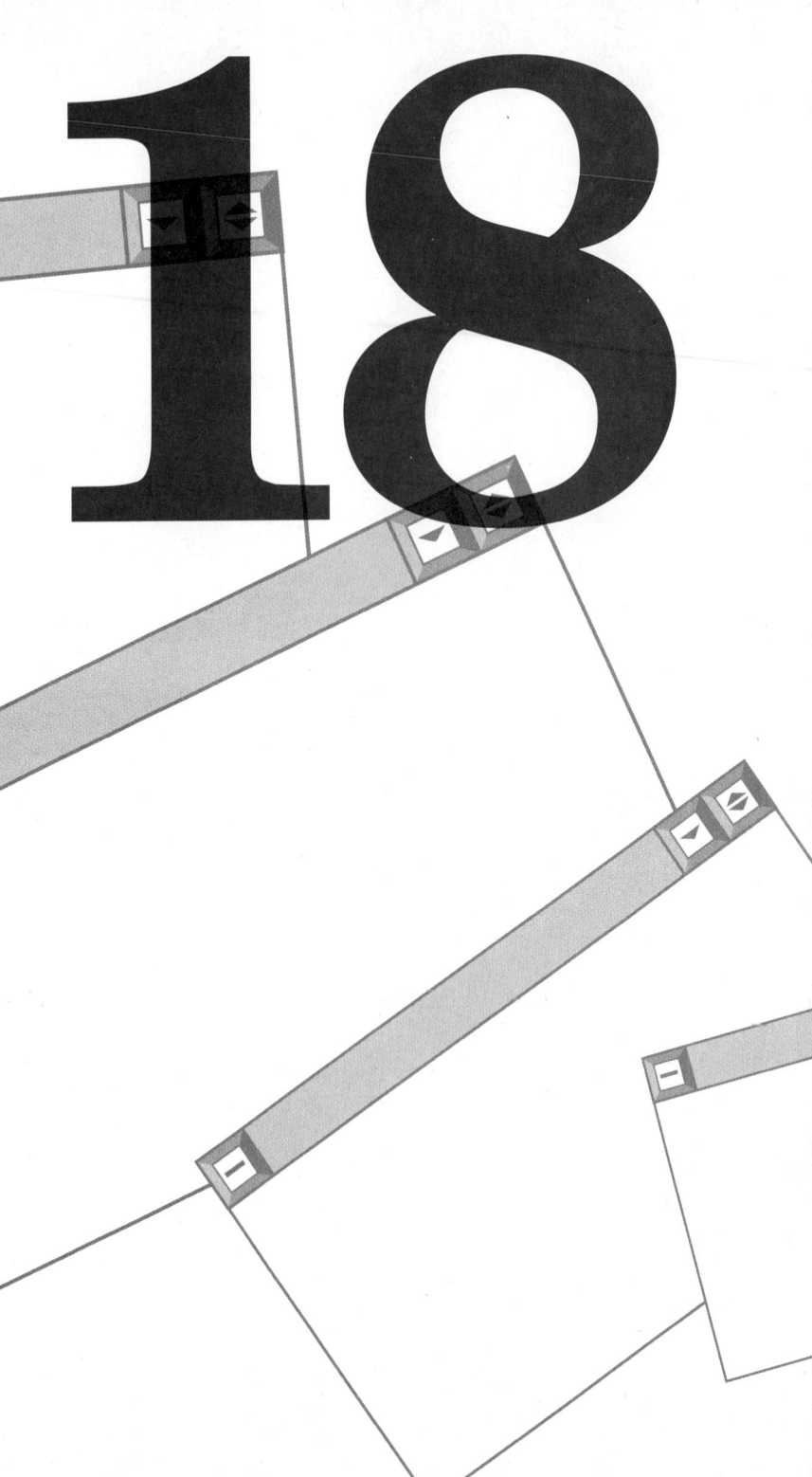

CHAPTER

18

CorelDRAW!

Not many of us are artists. In fact, most of us are shaky with pencil and paper and do not have much sense of design. Yet we often need to create pictures. As the PC revolution began to take hold about a decade ago, programs that helped people with limited art ability started to become popular. When the Apple Macintosh was released in 1984, it came with MacPaint, a black-and-white program that made it almost inconsequential for anyone to add art to his or her work.

Windows comes with the Paintbrush program (described in Chapter 11, "Paintbrush"), but that program is of limited usefulness. Although it uses color, it has fewer features than MacPaint did almost a decade ago. Many software companies, however, offer much more advanced programs for Windows. The most popular of these is CorelDRAW!.

CorelDRAW! is a huge package and much more than a painting program. In fact, it isn't a painting program at all. Early in the development of graphics programs, a split was formed in the market between painting programs and drawing programs.

▲ Painting programs enable you to draw on a pixel-by-pixel basis. All actions, such as adding rectangles or erasing dots, are always done on pixels. For example, when you draw a rectangle with a painting program, you can erase a few pixels from the rectangle to open it. However, there is no easy way to change the color of its border or round its corners.

▲ Drawing programs create shapes as objects, which are independent and modified individually. For example, when you draw a rectangle in a drawing program, you can select it and give commands to change the color of its border or round its corners. You cannot, however, remove pixels from it.

Each approach has its advantages. With painting programs, it is easier to create small drawings that are exactly what you want. You need to do much more planning ahead with a painting program, however. The output of drawing programs is almost always much nicer on laser printers because a drawing program can directly control the printer much more accurately than a painting program can. Sketching is easier in painting programs; finalized pictures are easier to produce in drawing programs.

Paintbrush is a painting program; CorelDRAW! is a drawing program. Some programs have elements of both styles, but CorelDRAW! only creates drawings. It can, of course, read bitmaps from painting programs and include them in its documents. Because every copy of Windows comes with Paintbrush, you can use it when you need fast pixel-level editing. However, when you see the difference between the two in output and flexibility (when you need to reduce a picture by 27 percent or change the gray tone, for example), you will find drawing programs such as CorelDRAW! to be much more valuable.

Introduction to CorelDRAW!

Like Paintbrush, CorelDRAW! uses tools for drawing and selecting. Figure 18.1 shows the main CorelDRAW! window. Note that there are only eight tools in the palette on the left of the screen. The theory of using the program is that you make simple choices first, and can easily modify them later. Because CorelDRAW! is a drawing program, you do not need as many tools as you would for a painting program such as Paintbrush.

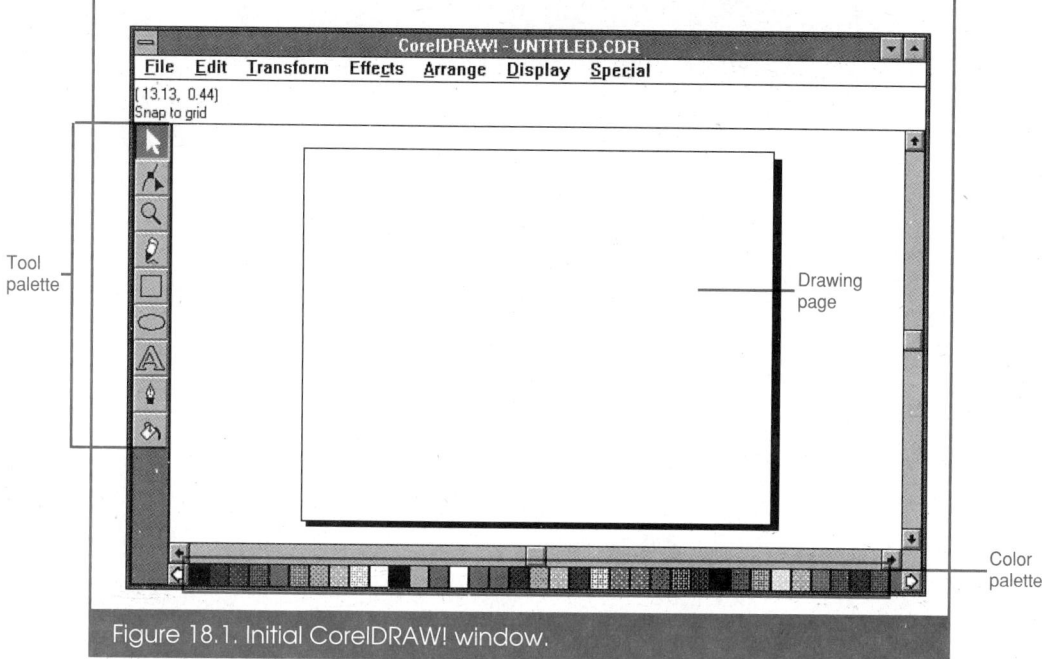

Figure 18.1. Initial CorelDRAW! window.

18

The box in the center of the window is the drawing page. It determines the area to be printed. You can place objects outside the drawing window or overlapping it. Only the parts that are in the rectangle appear when a document is printed.

Almost everything in CorelDRAW! is done with the mouse. Although there are dialog boxes for changing sizes and shapes, almost all actions that draw objects or reshape them directly are done with only the mouse.

System Requirements for Installing CorelDRAW!

CorelDRAW! has software and hardware requirements that must be taken into consideration.

Hardware Requirements

▲ An 80286 PC or higher

▲ A hard drive with at least 2 megabytes free for program files

▲ An EGA video display or higher

▲ A printer supported by Windows 3.0 or higher

▲ A mouse or tablet supported by Windows 3.0 or higher

Software Requirements

▲ DOS 3.1 or higher

▲ Microsoft Windows 3.0 or higher

Major Features of CorelDRAW!

This version of CorelDRAW! offers some outstanding capabilities.

▲ Choose from 153 fonts

▲ Fit text to curves

▲ Manipulate paragraph and multicolumn text

▲ Create three-dimensional perspectives from two-dimensional images

▲ Includes an extensive free clip-art library

▲ Includes WFNBoss, a typeface converter

▲ Includes Corel Trace, an image tracing utility

▲ Includes a convenient tutorial videotape

▲ Comes with a typographic ruler for sizing text and images

Objects

An object is created by the object tools (the pencil, rectangle, oval, and text). You also can paste objects from the Clipboard. Each object has

many properties, such as the width of the lines in the object, the fill pattern, the colors, the size, and so on. When you select an object by clicking on it, CorelDRAW! puts handles around it, such as in Figure 18.2.

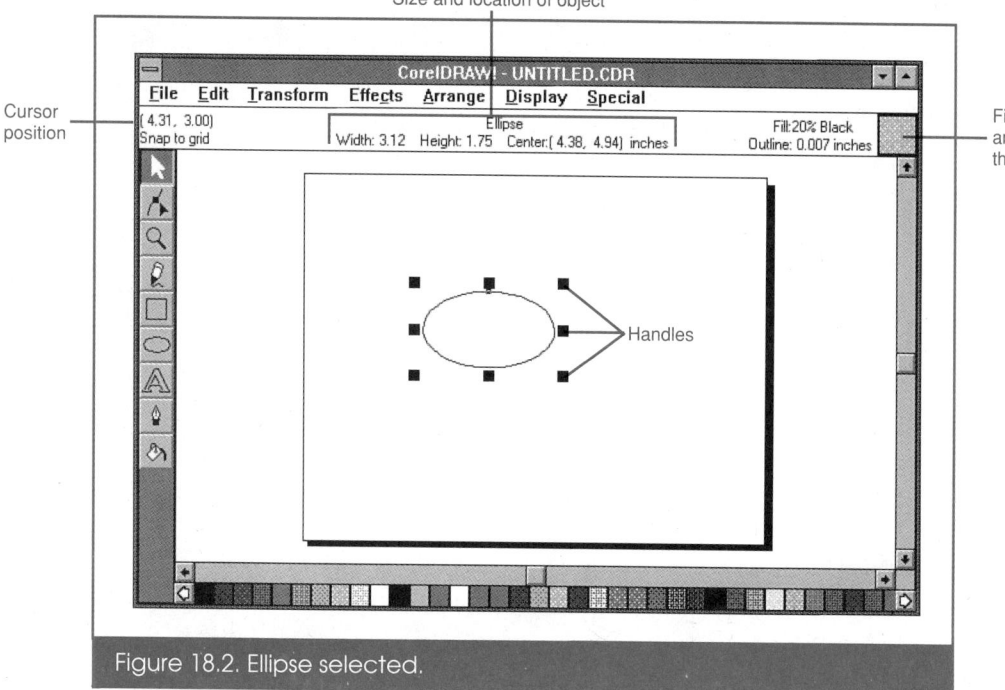

Figure 18.2. Ellipse selected.

Note the amount of information in the message area near the top of the window. The numbers in the upper-left corner are the position of the cursor. The main section in the middle tells you the type of object selected, its size, and its location. The information on the right describes the fill pattern and the thickness of the outline.

Previewing Your Drawing

Note that the ellipse shown in Figure 18.2 has a fill pattern shown in the message area but not in the picture itself. In editing mode, (you know CorelDRAW! is in editing mode because an object has handles attached to it) CorelDRAW! does not draw the fill pattern, enabling you to see the picture more quickly and see other objects more easily. You can, of course, preview your drawing using the **D**isplay Show **P**review command. This command splits the window into two windows—the editing window on the left and the preview window on the right, as shown in Figure 18.3.

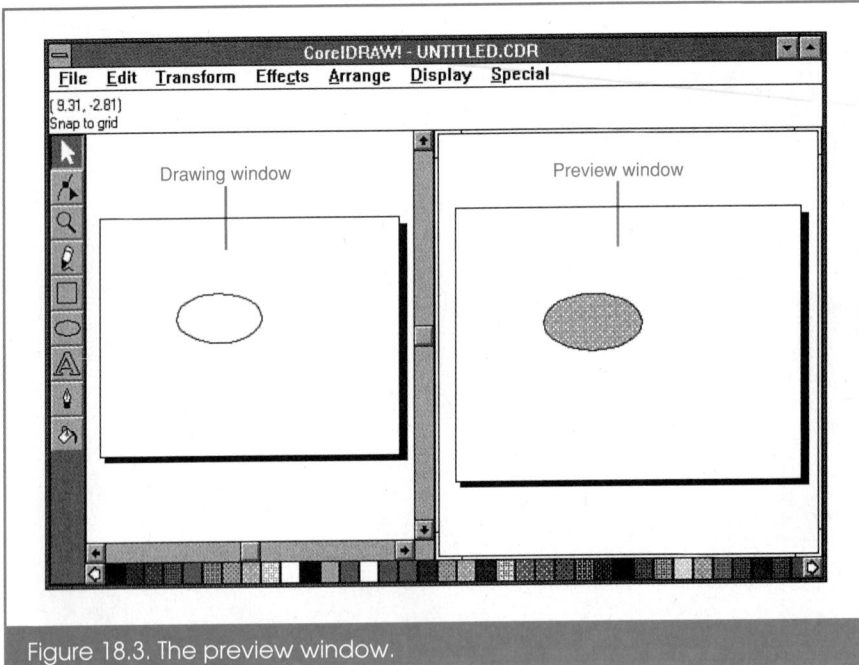

Figure 18.3. The preview window.

You use the preview window when you want to see the fills and line thicknesses. You also can look at how well the colors you are using go together. You can change the size and shape of the preview window, and even do a full-screen preview. With the magnifying glass tool in the preview window, you can focus in on one part of the preview of the document.

Arranging Objects

Objects can be on top of or beneath other objects. This enables you to create different shapes by hiding parts of an object under another one. For example, Figure 18.4 shows a rectangle with a hole in it. It was made by drawing a large rectangle with a fill pattern, then drawing a smaller rectangle with a white pattern and putting it on top of the large rectangle. You can specify to CorelDRAW! which object you want on top or on bottom, which helps you create stacks of objects. You can bring objects in the background "up front" by using the **A**rrange To **F**ront command.

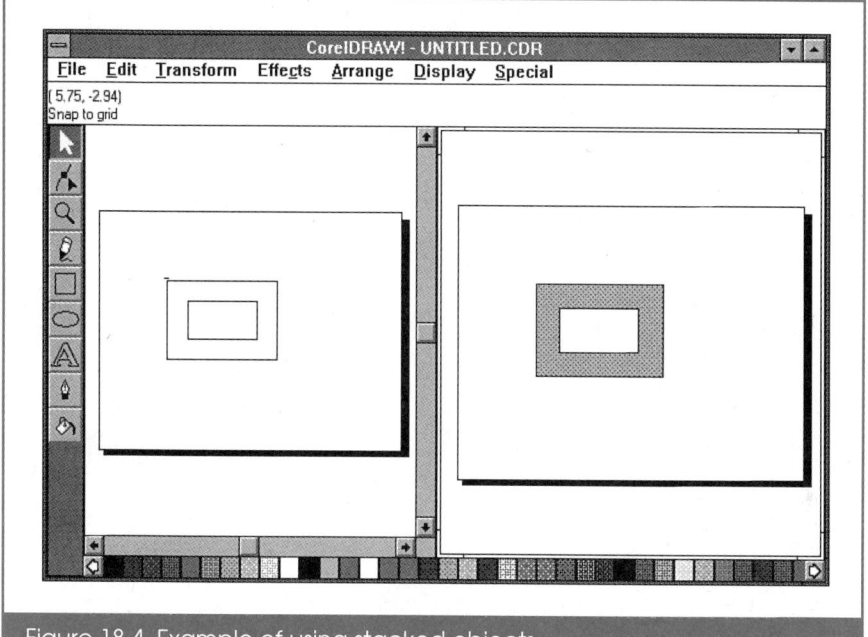

Figure 18.4. Example of using stacked objects.

You also can use object stacking to give text interesting backgrounds. Figure 18.5 shows two objects—a piece of text and a rectangle with a gradient scaling. The rectangle is behind the text; if it weren't, you would see only the first "Books," because the rest would be hidden.

Grouping Objects

You can tell CorelDRAW! to treat multiple objects as a single group. For example, in the simplified house sketch in Figure 18.6, you probably would group the four small rectangles and one large rectangle that make up the window so that it would be easier to move the entire window. You can select an entire group of objects by selecting the **E**dit Select **A**ll command.

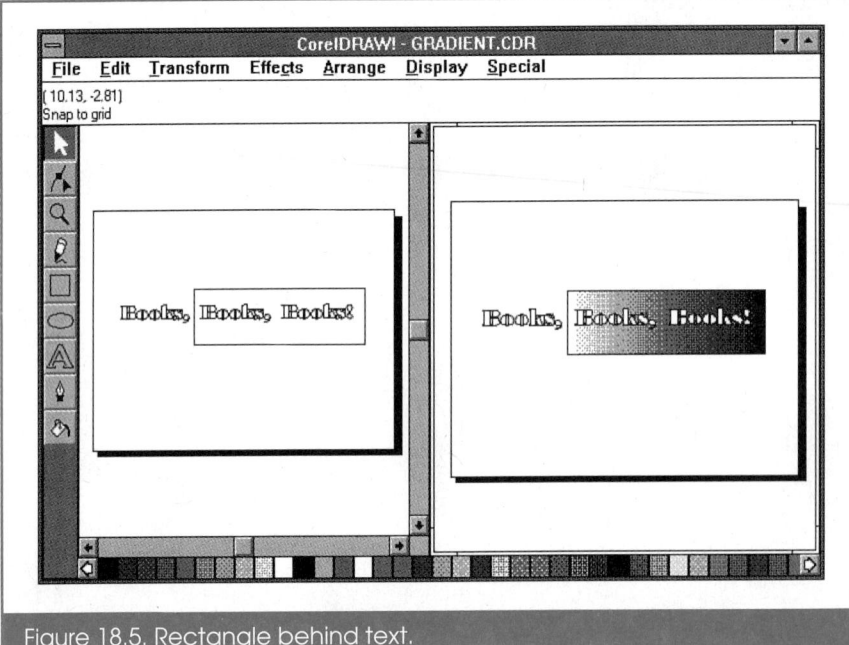

Figure 18.5. Rectangle behind text.

Figure 18.6. An example of grouping.

Aligning Objects

Often you draw two or more objects and want them aligned along a particular line. For example, you might draw two rectangles of different sizes and want them to line up along the same bottom line, or you might want their centers aligned. The **Arrange Align** command, shown in Figure 18.7, offers you the eight possible choices for alignment.

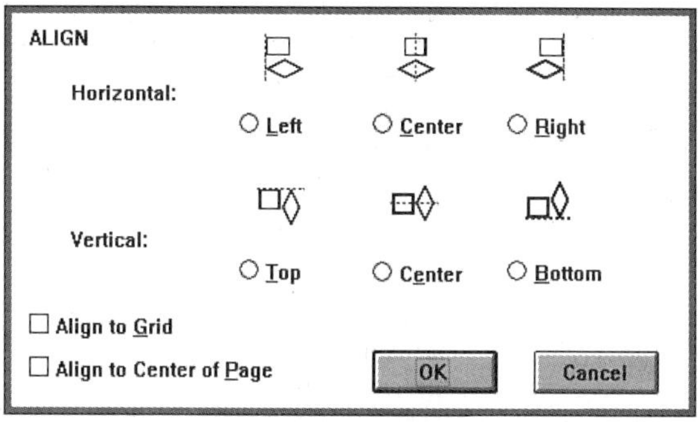

Figure 18.7. Arrange Align dialog box.

The **Align** to **Grid** option aligns the objects to a CorelDRAW! grid you define; this option is handy when you are drawing forms or using fixed-size objects. Grids are described later in this chapter. The **Align** to Center of **P**age option centers the objects not only with each other, but also to the center of the paper. This is a good way to start a drawing when you want to be sure that the main parts are centered on the page.

Drawing Tools

At first, eight tools might not seem like enough for a program as powerful as CorelDRAW!, but they are very well designed and compact. The tools are used for making the most common changes, and other, less common changes are made by selecting and using the commands described in this chapter. The drawing tools are the six bottom tools on the tool palette.

Rectangle and Ellipse

The rectangle and ellipse tools are the most basic drawing tools. Table 18.1 shows the shapes they draw, depending on the keys you hold down.

Table 18.1. Rectangle and ellipse keys.

Key(s)	Draws
No key	Rectangle or ellipse from corner
Ctrl	Square or circle from corner
Shift	Rectangle or ellipse from center
Ctrl-Shift	Square or circle from center

Drawing Lines with the Pencil

The pencil tool draws both straight lines and curves. Rather than a line tool, CorelDRAW! uses the pencil tool for both actions. This means that you have to change tools less often than with other programs.

To draw a line with the pencil tool, you click at one corner, then click at the other. To draw lines that are connected at the ends, start by clicking, then double-click at each corner; when you are done, click once. You can restrict the line to angles of 15-degree increments by holding down the Ctrl key while drawing.

If you are drawing closed shapes with the pencil, you will appreciate CorelDRAW!'s auto-join feature. If you are drawing a line near the first point in your shape, the end of the line jumps to that point, making it very easy to close the shape exactly.

Drawing Curves with the Pencil

Drawing curves is very different. To sketch a curve initially, just click and drag over the desired curve. If you are like most people, your first attempt won't be great. In a painting program, you would have to go back and erase the pixels that were wrong or out of the desired range and put in new ones. In CorelDRAW!, changing a curve is much easier, because it uses Bézier curves, a method that enables you to change the shape of a curve with very little effort.

Figure 18.8 shows a freehand curve. When you then select the shape tool, you see small squares on the curve. These nodes define the shape of the curve. Note that you do not have to put the nodes in; CorelDRAW! does that after you drag over the desired shape. Moving one of the points stretches the curve in that direction. For example, Figure 18.9 shows the result of dragging one of the nodes up and to the right.

18

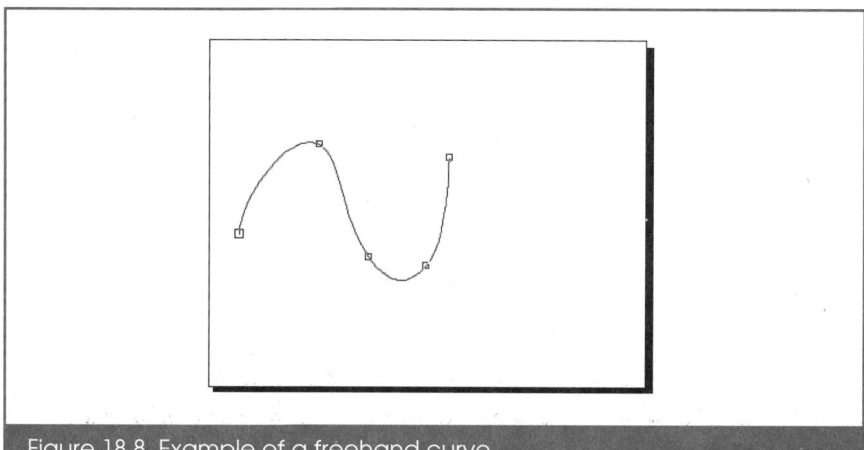

Figure 18.8. Example of a freehand curve.

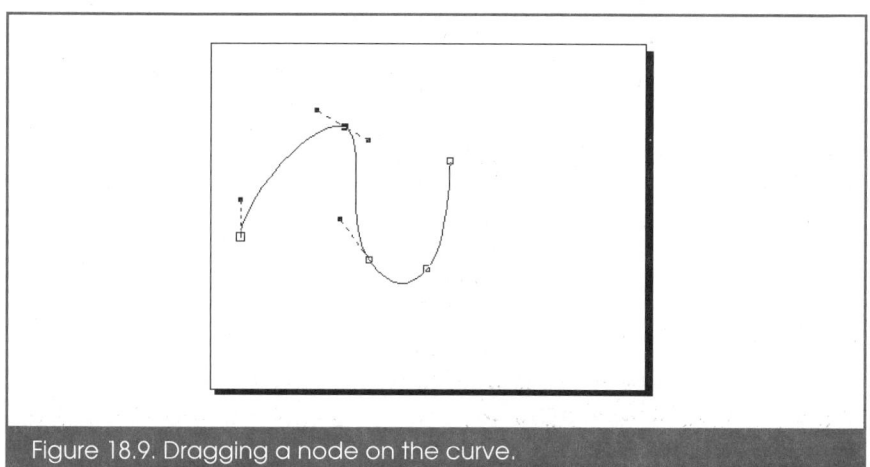

Figure 18.9. Dragging a node on the curve.

If all you could do was drag nodes, it would be difficult to get the curve exactly the way you wanted. However, notice the two sets of squares that appear next to the selected node. The position of these control points determines the flatness of the curve near the node. For example, look how the flatness of the curve changes in Figure 18.10 after the control point is dragged to a different angle.

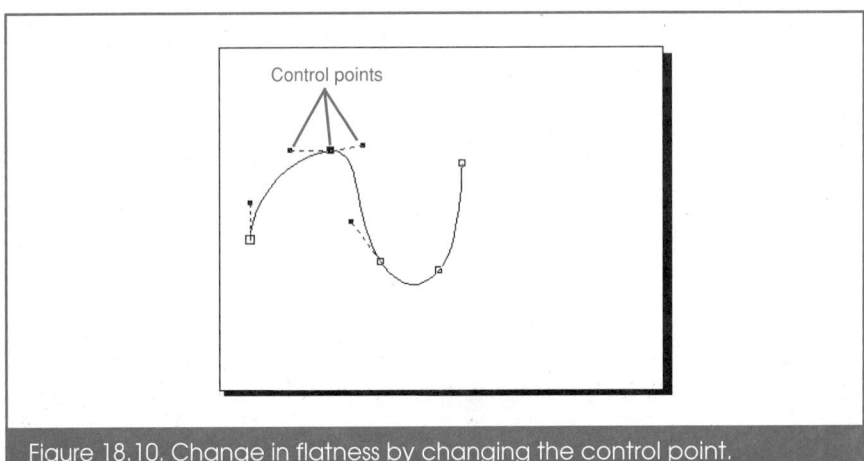

Figure 18.10. Change in flatness by changing the control point.

Moving the control point closer to or farther from the node gives you even more control over the shape. The farther away the control point is, the farther away from the node the curve is. This is shown in Figure 18.11.

Text

CorelDRAW!'s text tool differs from most other graphics programs in that you do not edit directly on the screen. Instead, you select the text tool and click where you want the text to appear. When you do, you see the large dialog box shown in Figure 18.12. You then type the text you want (up to 250 characters) in the box at the top of the screen. When you drag to form a box with the text tool, you can enter up to 4000 characters.

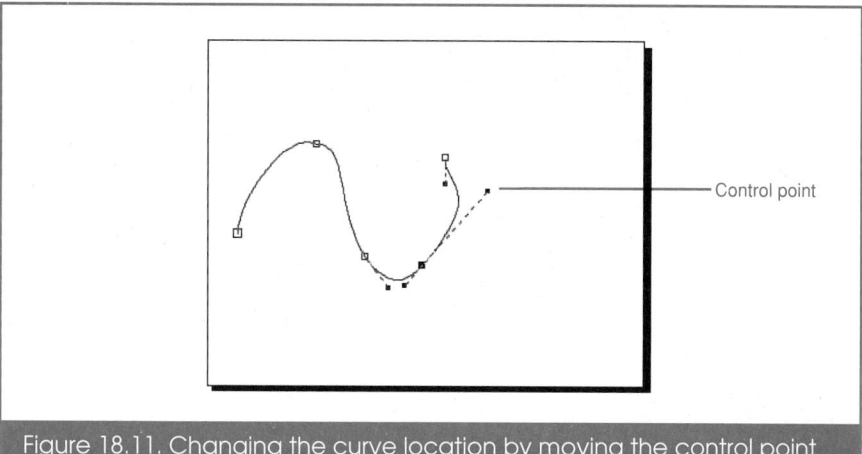

Figure 18.11. Changing the curve location by moving the control point away.

18

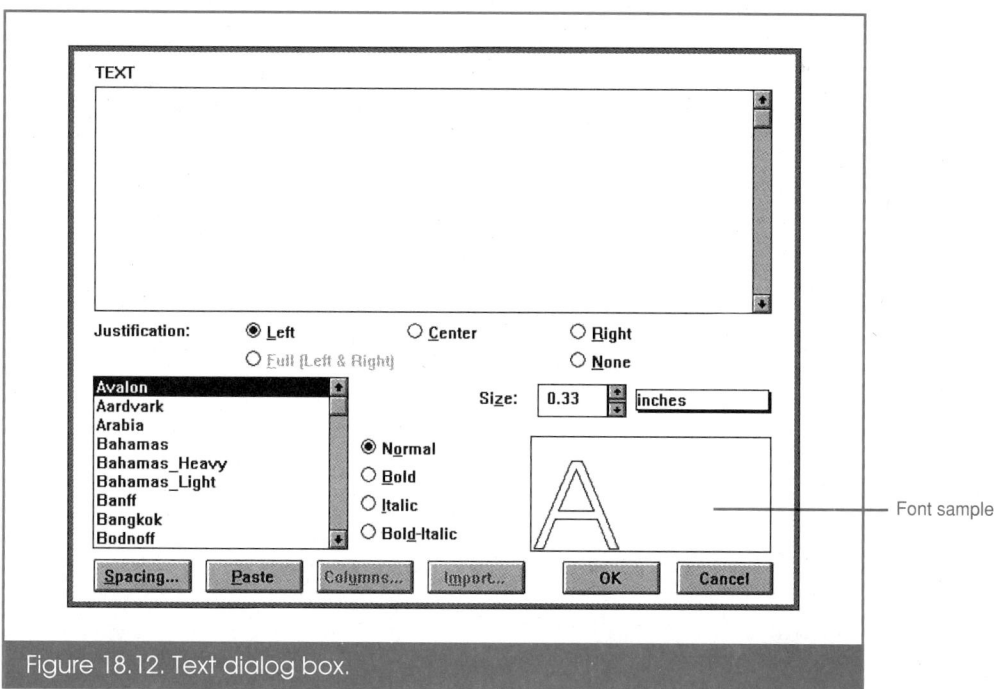

Figure 18.12. Text dialog box.

After entering the desired text, you can choose the alignment for the text, the font, the font style, and the font size. You can specify the size in points, inches, millimeters, or picas. The text can be from less than 1 point up to 1440 points, and you can use fractional sizes. As you change the font and style, CorelDRAW! shows you a sample in the window at the lower-right of the dialog box.

Tip: Note that CorelDRAW! does not use standard Windows fonts; it uses only fonts that come with CorelDRAW!. Fortunately, it comes with 153 of its own fonts, as well as a font converter that enables you to bring fonts in from these other formats:

▲ Adobe Type 1
▲ Agfa Compugraphic
▲ Bitstream
▲ DigiFont
▲ PostScript Type 3
▲ ZSoft Type Foundry

The Columns button works with paragraph text, enabling you to create columns as in newspapers. This button enables you to use CorelDRAW! as a rudimentary desktop publishing tool.

Tip: If the text you want is in the Windows Clipboard, simply click the **P**aste button. If you have text in a text file, you can read it in with the **Im**port button. These buttons give you easy access to text you have created in other Windows programs.

You also can modify the default amount of space between characters with the **S**pacing button. That button's dialog box is shown in Figure 18.13. Note that you also can change the spacing between any two letters after you create the text, as described later in this chapter.

Symbols

When you hold down the Shift key as you click the text tool, you access almost 3000 symbols that come with CorelDRAW!. The dialog box you see is shown in Figure 18.14.

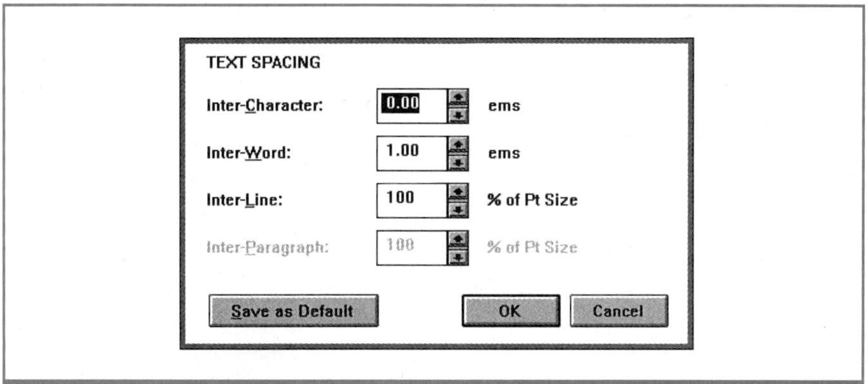

TEXT SPACING

Inter-Character: `0.00` ems

Inter-Word: `1.00` ems

Inter-Line: `100` % of Pt Size

Inter-Paragraph: `100` % of Pt Size

[Save as Default] [OK] [Cancel]

Figure 18.13. Text Spacing dialog box.

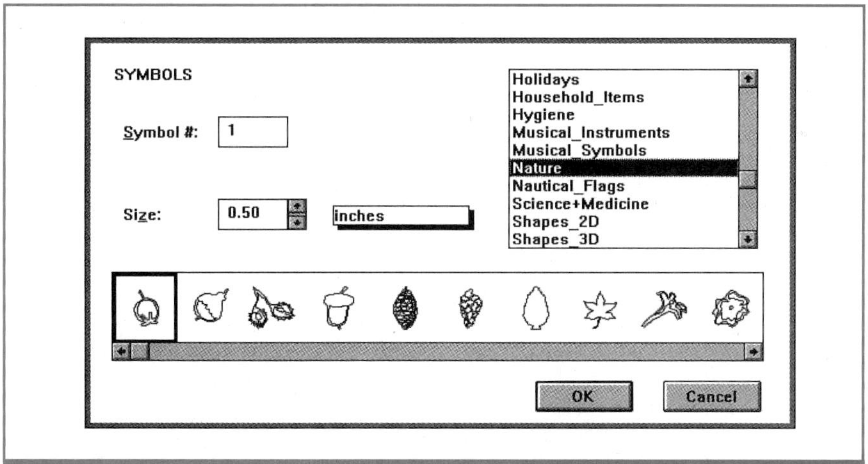

18

SYMBOLS

Symbol #: `1`

Size: `0.50` `inches`

Holidays
Household_Items
Hygiene
Musical_Instruments
Musical_Symbols
Nature
Nautical_Flags
Science+Medicine
Shapes_2D
Shapes_3D

[OK] [Cancel]

Figure 18.14. Symbols dialog box.

Choose the symbol library from the list on the right and pick the symbol from the horizontal list. Each library has more than 50 elements. Fortunately, CorelDRAW! comes with a booklet showing all the symbols. Shrinking or enlarging symbols in your document does not affect their printed quality.

Outline

Every object has an outline, which you can change with the outline tool. The outline tool has submenus that appear to the side when you click it. You can choose an option in the menu by clicking it.

Figure 18.15 shows the submenu for the outline tool. The top row determines the thickness of the outline and the bottom row determines the pattern of the outline (not the fill of the object). The first choice in each row enables you to create custom thicknesses and outline patterns. The second choice in each row indicates no outline and a white fill. The other choices in the menu are common choices for thickness and outline patterns.

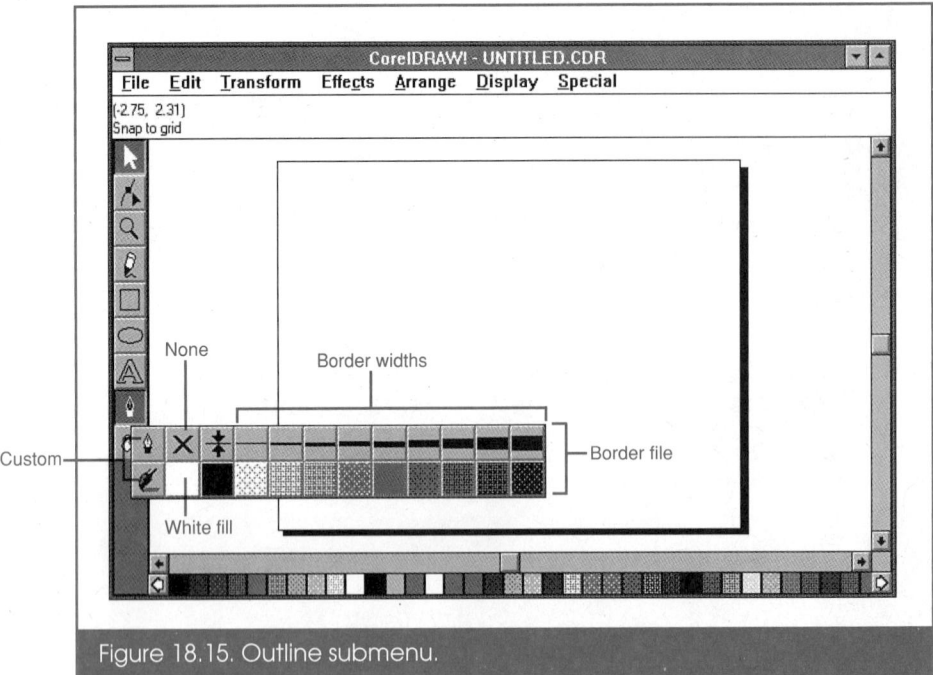

Figure 18.15. Outline submenu.

You can create a custom outline by clicking the first submenu item. The dialog box is shown in Figure 18.16. You might use the choices here to slightly round the corners on a rectangle or to make the line segments more visible, or you might use them to make text or curves appear as if they were drawn with a calligraphy pen.

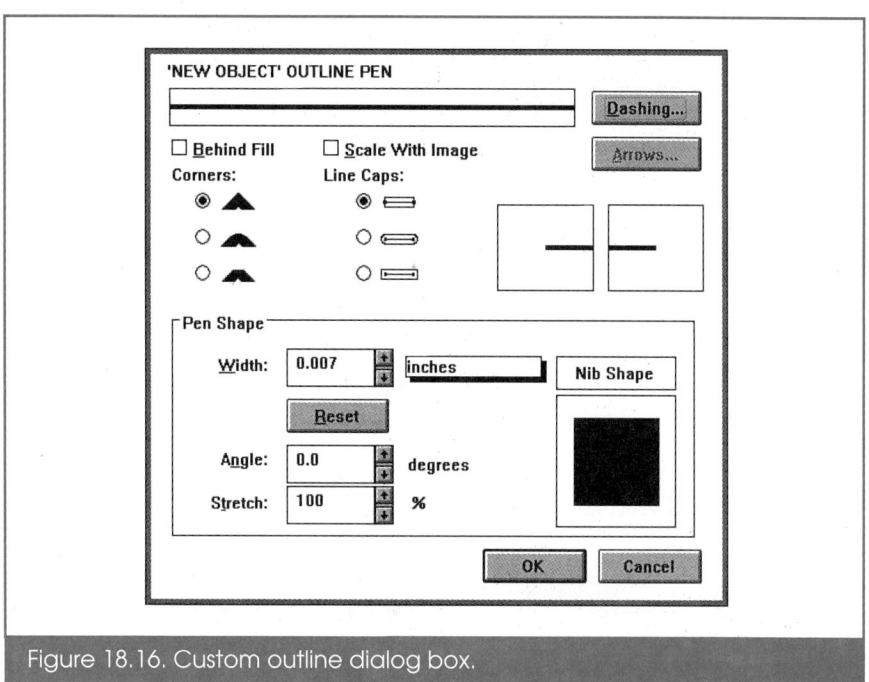

Figure 18.16. Custom outline dialog box.

With the **D**ashing button you can choose from a variety of dash patterns for the line. The Arrows dialog box, shown in Figure 18.17, enables you to make lines into a wide variety of arrows.

The outline pattern choices enable you to choose only shades of gray. With the Custom Outline Pattern dialog box you can choose any color.

Fill

Like the outline tool, the fill tool has a submenu that appears to the right when you click it. Figure 18.18 shows the fill tool's submenu.

The bottom row is common shades of gray used for fills. The second choice in the top row (the X) indicates no fill, and the next two choices indicate white and black fills. Note that having no fill is different from having a white fill. No fill means that the object is transparent, and a white fill blocks out anything behind it. The remaining four choices in the top row enable you to specify many custom fills.

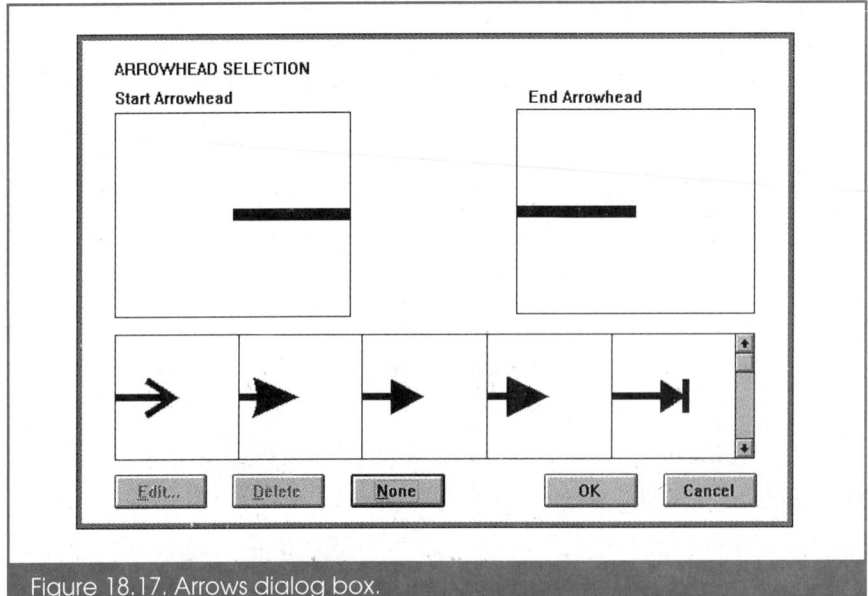

Figure 18.17. Arrows dialog box.

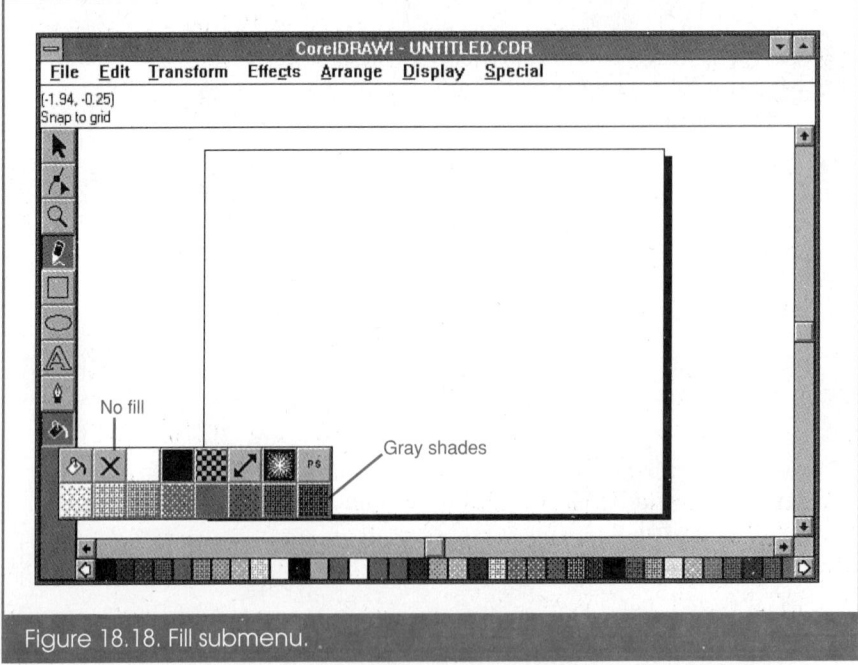

Figure 18.18. Fill submenu.

The Bitmap Fill Pattern Option

The Bitmap Fill Pattern option (accessed with the Fill button) enables you to choose among the many bitmap patterns that come with CorelDRAW!. The dialog box is shown in Figure 18.19. If you want a pattern other than those that come with CorelDRAW!, you also can create your own patterns by importing them from TIFF or .PCX files, using the buttons at the bottom of the dialog box. You can create your own bitmaps with the Create button. The patterns can be 18-by-18, 32-by-32, or 64-by-64, which gives you plenty of resolution for patterns.

18

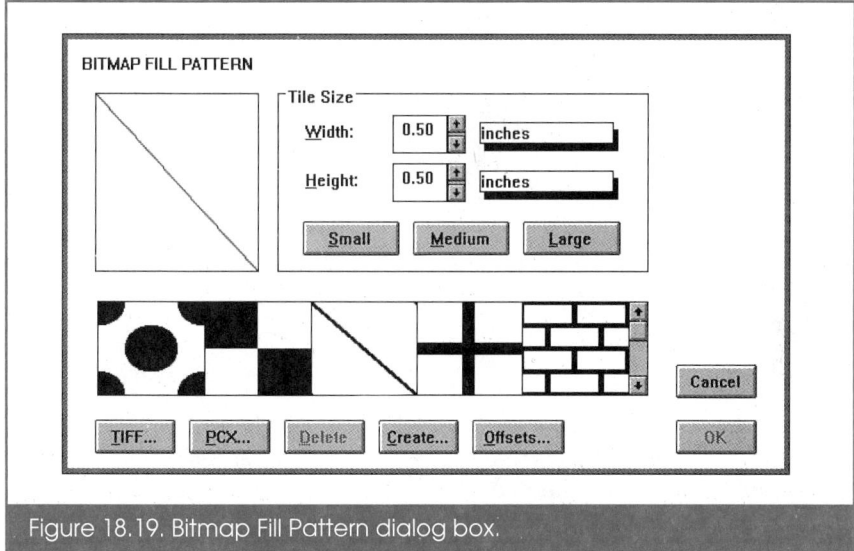

Figure 18.19. Bitmap Fill Pattern dialog box.

The Tile Size options in this dialog box enable you to specify the size of the pattern. CorelDRAW! will reproduce the pattern at any size so that you can get more or fewer of the pictures in your object. The **O**ffsets button enables you to specify where the pattern starts and how to offset each column of patterns. You also can color your patterns.

The Vector Fill Pattern Option

The Vector Fill Pattern option is like the Bitmap Fill Pattern option, except that it enables you to use vector pictures as fills. You first select a vector pattern fill from disk, then you see the dialog box shown in Figure 18.20. The options in this dialog box are the same as for the pixel pattern fills. You can use the vector patterns that come with CorelDRAW! or create your own with the **S**pecial **C**reate Pattern command.

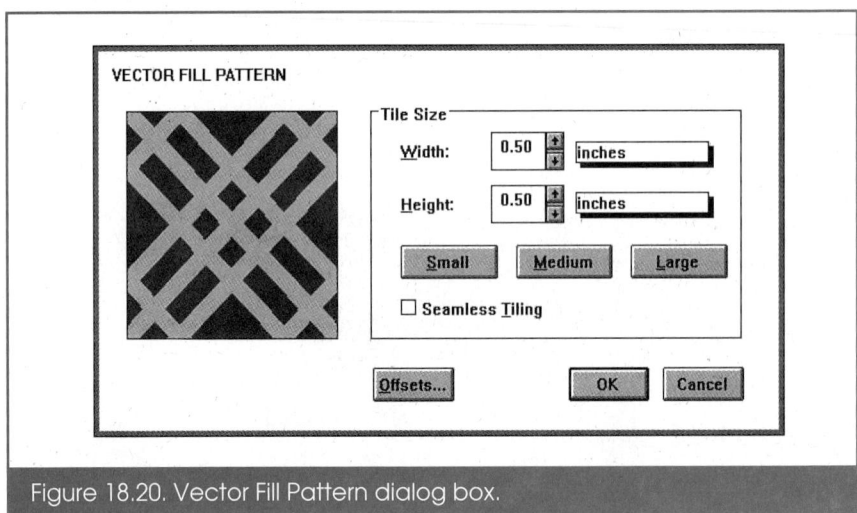

Figure 18.20. Vector Fill Pattern dialog box.

Fountain Fill

The Fountain Fill option is one of the most interesting features of CorelDRAW!. Click on the paint bucket icon, and then click on the pattern to the far right of the menu that presents itself. The dialog box is shown in Figure 18.21. You can specify linear or radial fills for your objects. These sort of fill patterns usually have only been available if you pasted an imported bitmap image into your drawings. The color choices specify the two colors for the fill.

The **A**ngle option tells the angle for tilted linear fills. In the Fountain Fill Options dialog box, shown in Figure 18.22, you can reduce the area for the fountain and offset the beginning of the radial fill. You also can optimize the fountains for PostScript printers. Figure 18.23 shows examples of objects with many fountain fills using these options.

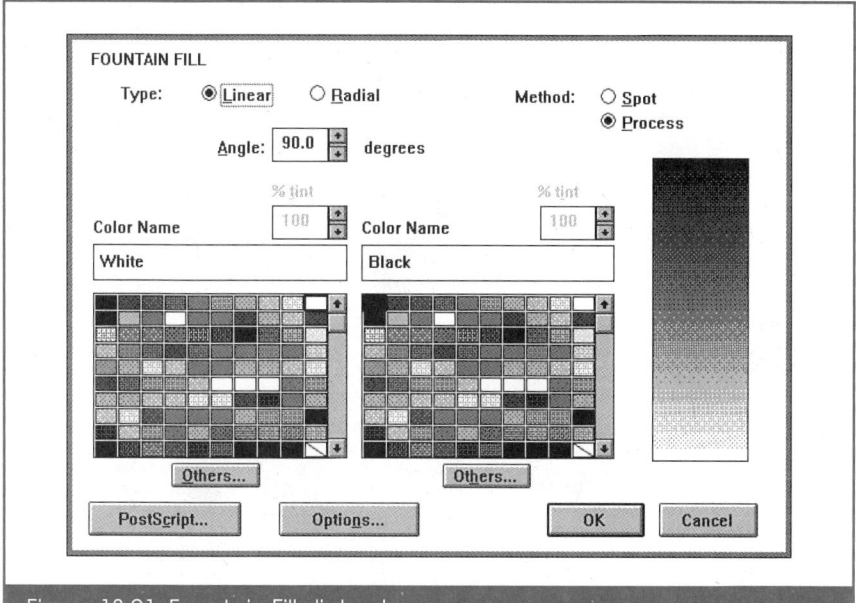

Figure 18.21. Fountain Fill dialog box.

18

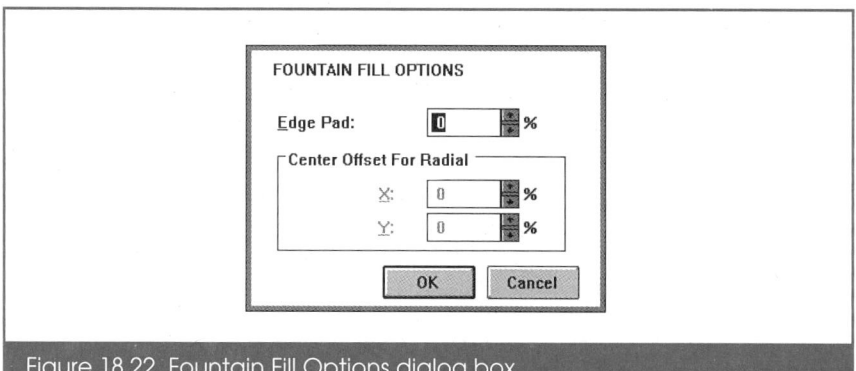

Figure 18.22. Fountain Fill Options dialog box.

Figure 18.23. Examples of fountain fills.

PostScript Fill

If you have a PostScript printer, the PostScript fill option, shown in Figure 18.24, enables you to choose fills made up of PostScript code. These textures give a sophisticated vector pattern, but only affect output produced on a high-resolution, PostScript printer.

Colors and Patterns

Both the outline and the fill tools enable you to choose the colors for your fills. (Of course, the dialog boxes in this section will make more sense in color.) CorelDRAW! supports both process color, in which you define your own color mixes, and spot color, which uses the Pantone color matching system.

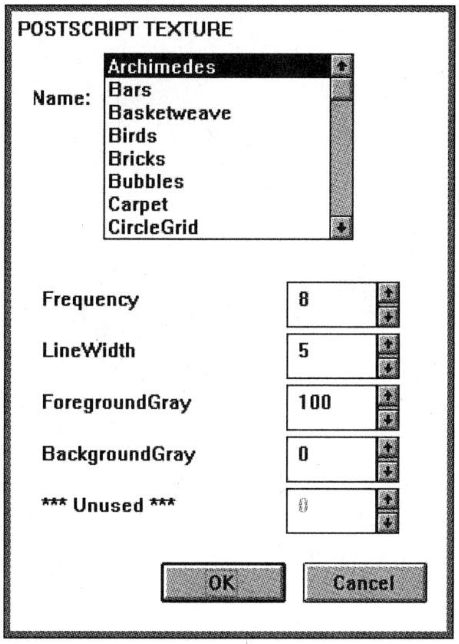

Figure 18.24. PostScript Texture options.

Process Color

You can blend the amount of cyan, magenta, yellow, and black in the colors you use in your drawings. This task is called processing color. The dialog box for these choices is shown in Figure 18.25. Simply pick a color from the palette of 99 colors and click on the OK button. Each color has a name that appears in the Color Name box. CorelDRAW! comes with additional palettes containing 255 colors for an even wider selection.

Of course, you can select more than just these 99 colors. Clicking the **O**thers button brings up a second dialog box that enables you to select your own color. You can use four different color schemes to choose the color (**C**MYK, **R**GB, **H**SB, and **N**amed). In the first three modes, you can select a color by pointing at it in the visual selector, or by specifying values for the components of the color.

18

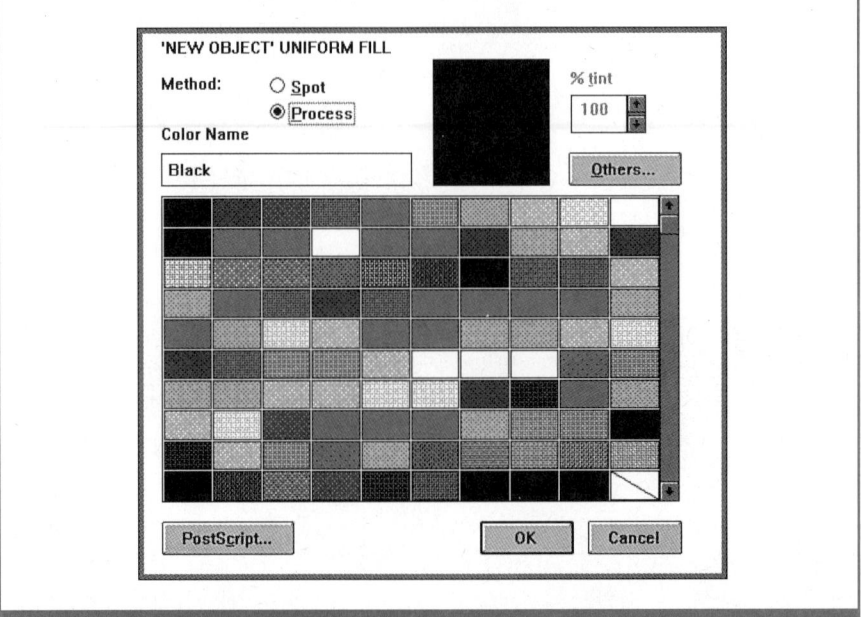

Figure 18.25. "New Object" Uniform Fill dialog box.

CMYK

The default mode, CMYK, enables you to specify the amounts of cyan, magenta, yellow, and black in the color, as shown in Figure 18.26. This is the most popular way of describing color when you use four-color printing. Use the sliders to specify values from 0 to 100. If you want to select the color manually, use the large box in the color selector, which has the shades of cyan and magenta, with an implicit black, and the narrow band, which specifies the amount of yellow.

RGB

If you are producing color for a computer display, you might prefer to use the RGB (red, green, blue) dialog box, shown in Figure 18.27. In this dialog box, you specify the amount of red, green, and blue in the color. Most computer displays are controlled using these values. Use the sliders to specify values from 0 to 100. Selecting manually from the large box varies the amount of red and green, and the narrow band varies the value of blue.

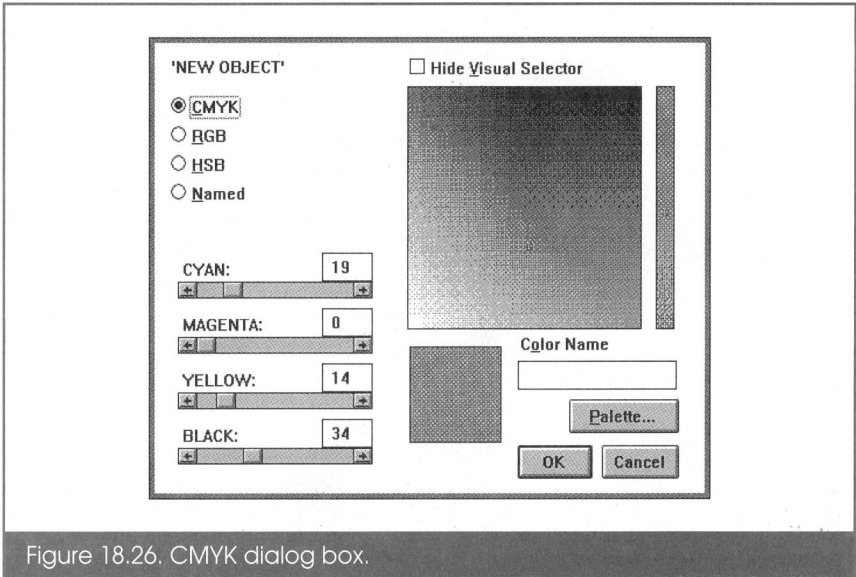

Figure 18.26. CMYK dialog box.

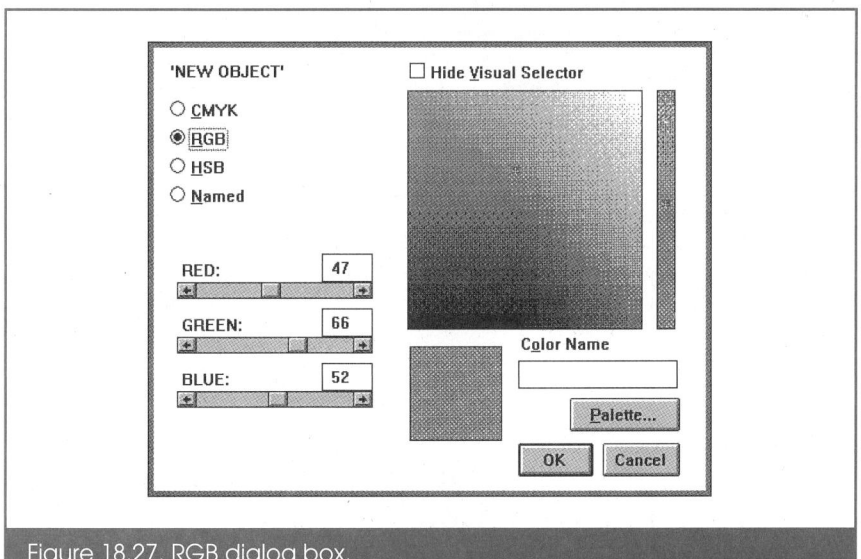

Figure 18.27. RGB dialog box.

18

HSB

HSB is a more recent color specification that defines a color by its
hue, saturation, and brightness. The dialog box for this is shown in
Figure 18.28. Hue is the value of a color in its purest state and is
defined by a value from 0 to 360, saturation is the amount of gray in
a color, and brightness is the amount of white added to a color. Both
saturation and brightness are changeable in a range from 0 to 100.
When you select manually, the angle around the wheel is the hue, the
distance from the center is the saturation, and the narrow band is
the brightness.

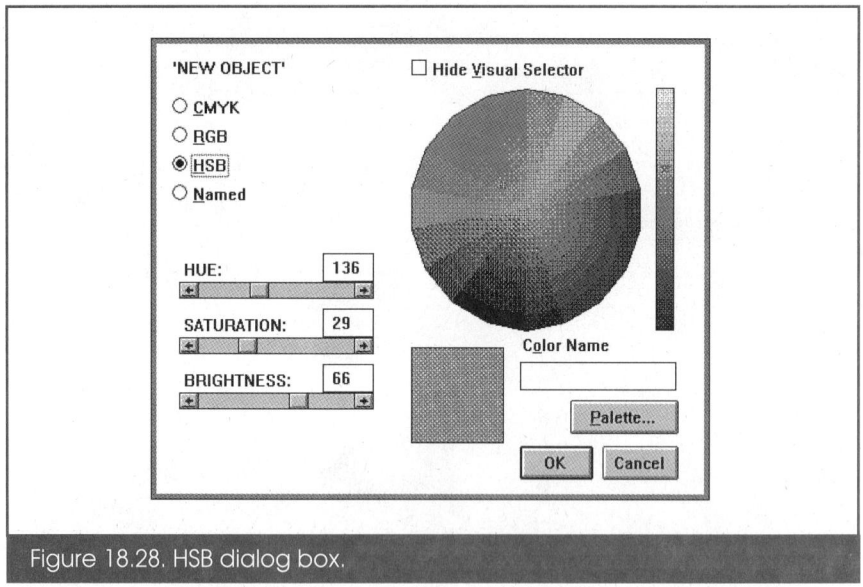

Figure 18.28. HSB dialog box.

Named

Of course, you might not want to find the perfect color. The Named
option puts up the alphabetized list of names shown in Figure 18.29.
You can pick an appealing-sounding name and use that for your color.

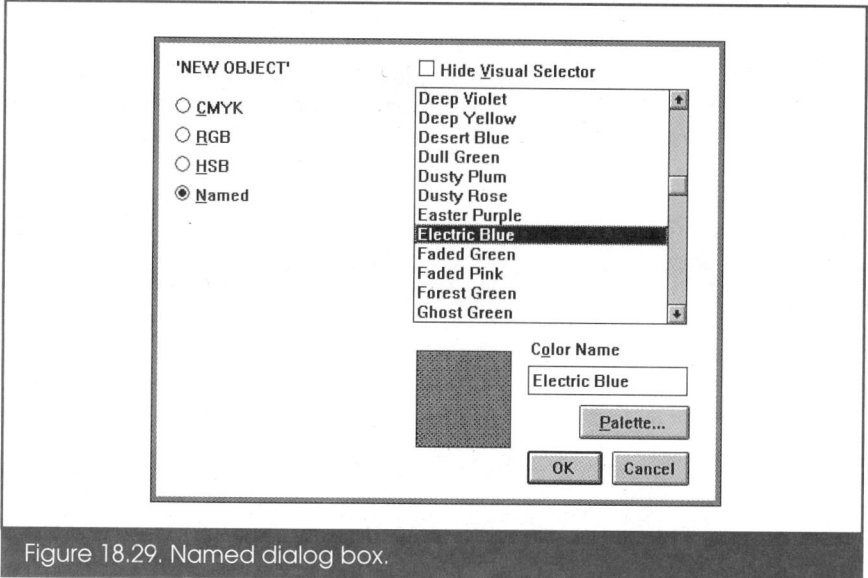

Figure 18.29. Named dialog box.

18

Pantone Color

Many printers use the Pantone system for matching colors to the printed output. The Pantone system is the printing industry's international standard that accurately defines all colors. The Pantone system is something of the Who's Who in the color definition sense. A color dictionary, if you will. You can choose the desired Pantone-matched color from the Main Spot color dialog box, shown in Figure 18.30.

If you would rather pick by name, click the **O**thers button and choose the name from the list shown in Figure 18.31. The list includes both the Pantone word names and the Pantone number system names.

PostScript Controls

If you have a PostScript printer, you can change the screen used to print to one of the CorelDRAW! custom screens. The really unique aspect of PostScript is that a PostScript (EPS) file is a conversion from another format into a collection of vectors with specific shapes. If you are printing an EPS file to a PostScript compatible output device, the EPS file will be produced at the best output capability of the output device, not the monitor or (in some cases) the typesetter. Check your printer's documentation to see whether your printer is PostScript compatible. The PostScript dialog box, shown in Figure 18.32, also enables you to change the frequency and angle of the screen. When the frequency and angle of an image is on the screen, you can arrange the way halftones are printed. If your image displays unpleasant patterns when printed, you can reduce this unwanted effect (called moiré) by changing the frequency and angle elements. CorelDRAW! lets you change these two elements to improve the quality of your printed materials. These screens can have a big effect on the way your printed output looks, because a large screen adds effects similar to patterns.

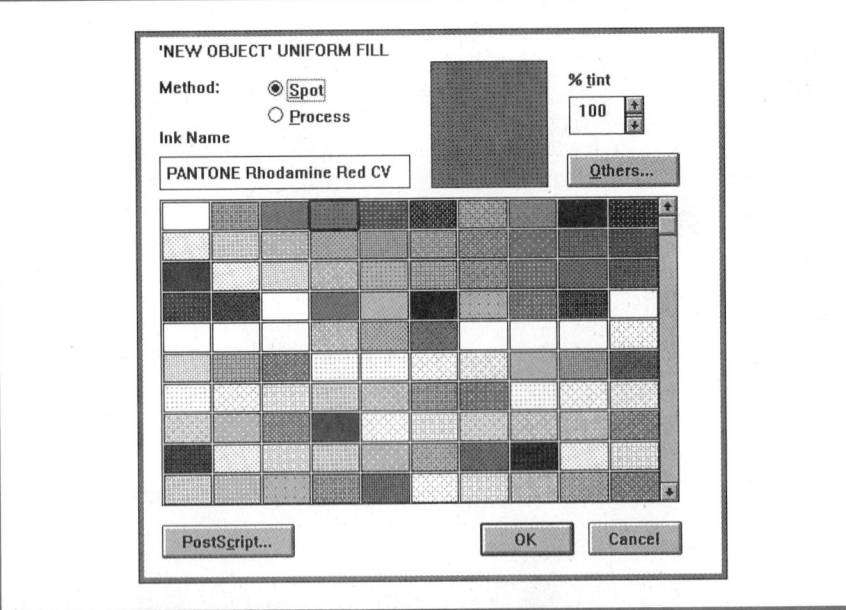

Figure 18.30. Main Spot color dialog box.

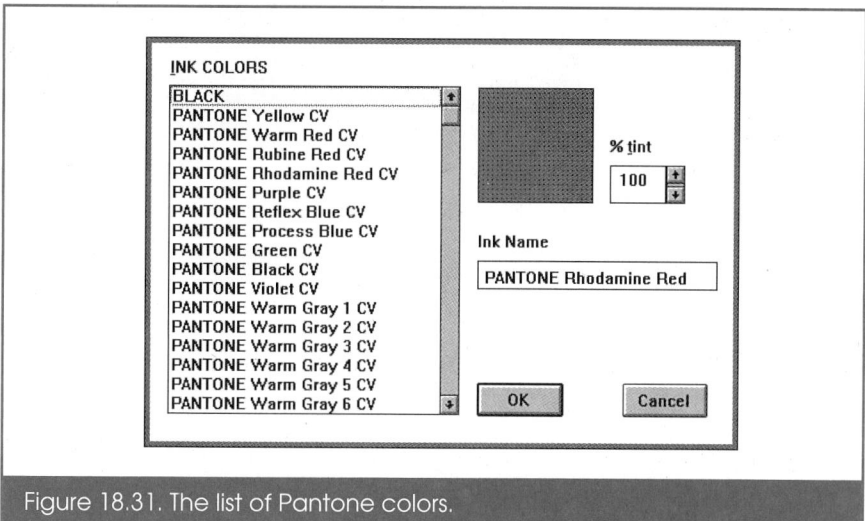

Figure 18.31. The list of Pantone colors.

18

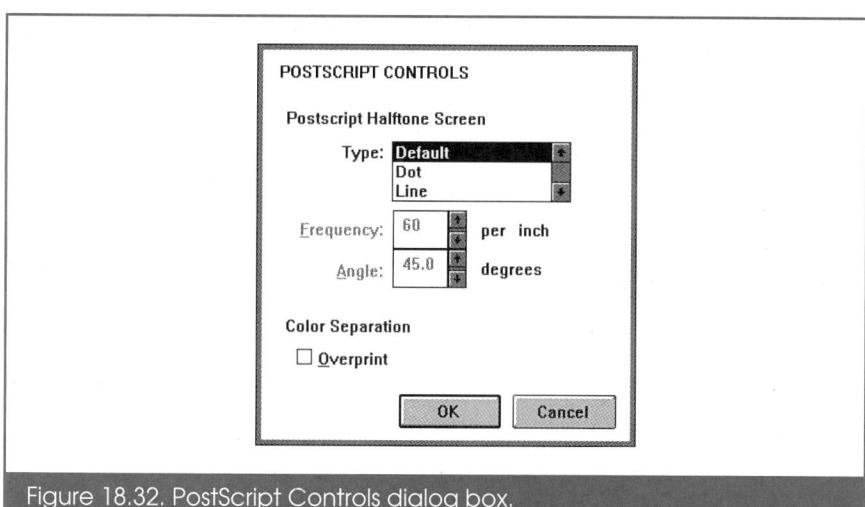

Figure 18.32. PostScript Controls dialog box.

Transformations and Effects

You can change the location and shape of an object in literally dozens of ways. Some changes are simple to do, such as dragging an object around with the mouse. Others are more obscure but still useful, such as stretching just one corner of some text.

Pick Tool

When you select an object with the pick tool (the top tool in the tool palette), the object gets eight handles, as shown in Figure 18.33. If you then click the border of the object, you can drag it to a new location. If you hold down the Ctrl key as you drag the object, you can drag the object only horizontally or vertically.

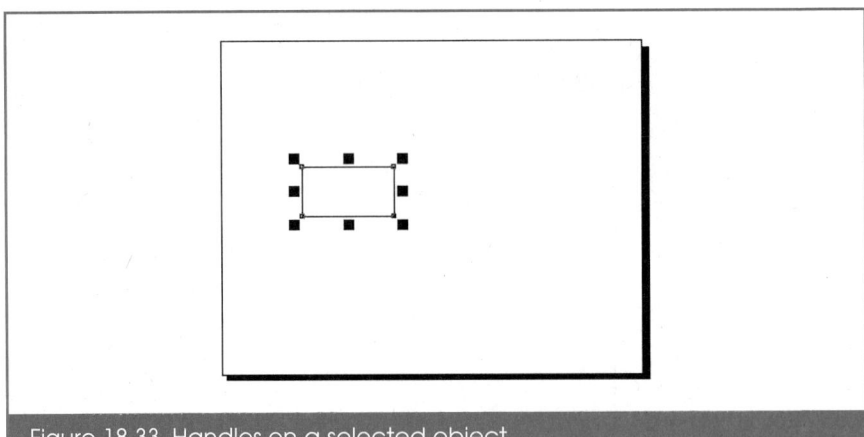

Figure 18.33. Handles on a selected object.

If you drag any of the handles on the sides of the object, you stretch the object in that direction. Dragging the handles on the corners scales the object in the same proportion horizontally and vertically. Holding down the Ctrl key while you drag a handle restricts the stretching and scaling to 100 percent increments. Holding down the Shift key causes the stretching and scaling to happen in both directions as you drag.

You also can rotate and skew objects with the pick tool. If you click the object after it is selected, the handles turn to arrows, as shown in Figure 18.34. Dragging the corner arrow handles rotates the selection. Dragging the side arrow handles skews the object. Figure 18.35 shows examples of rotated and skewed objects.

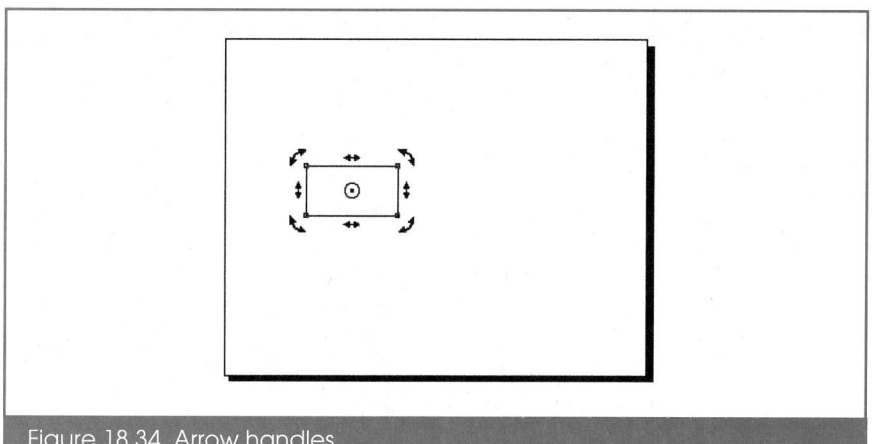

Figure 18.34. Arrow handles.

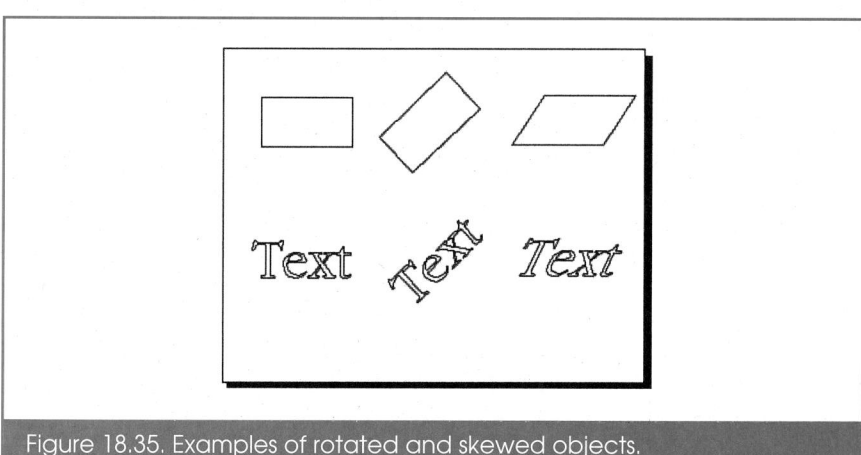

Figure 18.35. Examples of rotated and skewed objects.

18

Shape Tool

The shape tool, the second tool in the tool palette, enables you to modify the shapes of objects. You already saw how to use the shape tool with curves (dragging nodes and moving control points). You also can use it with other CorelDRAW! objects to change shape attributes.

On rectangles, the shape tool rounds the corners. On ellipses, it opens the ellipse into an arc of any length. However, using the shape tool on text shows the greatest changes. When you select text with the shape tool, you see two spacing icons, as shown in Figure 18.36. Dragging the icon on the left changes the spacing between the lines; dragging the icon on the right changes the spacing between letters.

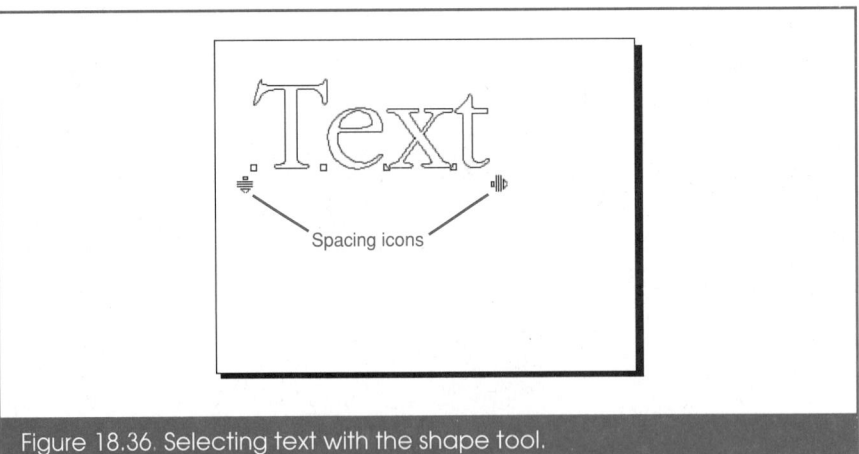

Figure 18.36. Selecting text with the shape tool.

Dragging the white handles to the left of each letter enables you to change the position of the letter horizontally and vertically. You can use this for manual kerning (the moving of text characters to optimize the space between them) of characters in text. For example, notice how much more tightly the characters in Figure 18.37 are kerned than in the previous figure.

Transform Menu

The **Transform** menu enables you to perform many of the mouse actions you have already seen from dialog boxes. These actions include

moving, rotating, and stretching an object. This menu enables you to specify exact positioning and alteration. The **Transform Clear Transfor-mations** command removes all the transformations you make to the object after it is first created.

Figure 18.37. Tighter kerning.

18

For example, the **Transform R**otate & Skew command, shown in Figure 18.38, gives you the same capability as the pick tool with the arrow handles. In this case, you might use the **Leave Original** option to create a shadow of the object you are rotating or skewing.

Effects Menu

The commands in the **Effects** menu are also transformations. However, they are more advanced than the simple transformations you have seen so far. They enable you to stretch objects by their corners, blend two objects into one, and extrude the object in three dimensions.

Envelopes

An envelope is a shape in which you can fit your object. The **Effects Edit Envelope** command has a submenu, shown in Figure 18.39. You can select an envelope from that menu, then stretch your object within the screen. The last option, which looks like the shape tool, enables you to create your own envelope with a Bézier curve.

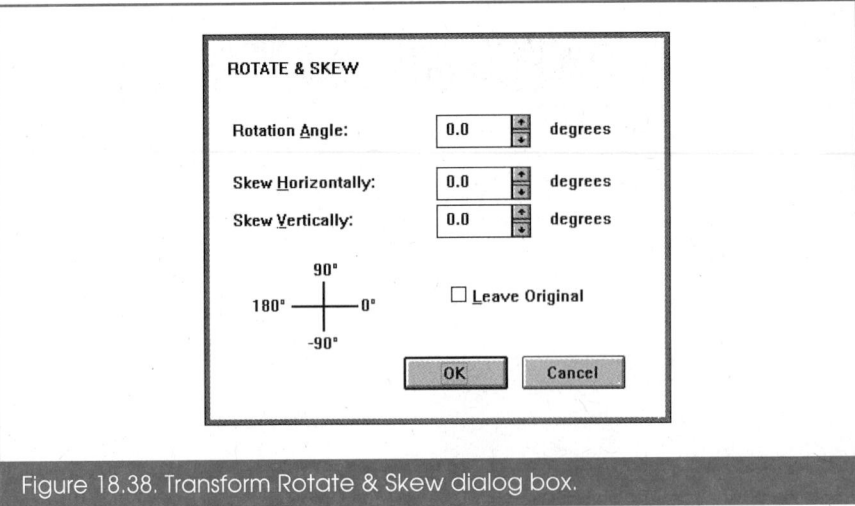

Figure 18.38. Transform Rotate & Skew dialog box.

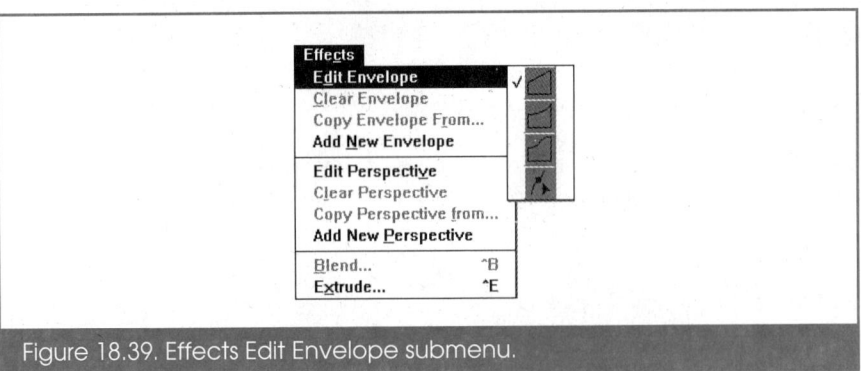

Figure 18.39. Effects Edit Envelope submenu.

For example, if you select the second choice with the rising curve, any of the corners you drag cause the line along which you drag to be curved. This is shown in Figure 18.40. You can drag as many corners as you want this way.

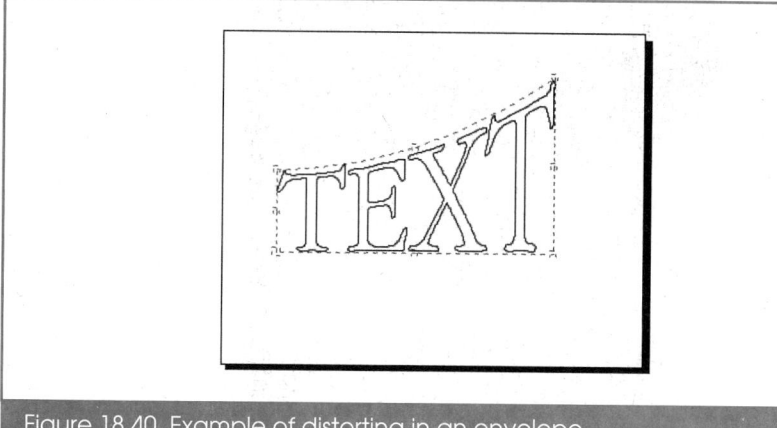

Figure 18.40. Example of distorting in an envelope.

18

The **Effects Clear** Envelope command removes the envelope effects. The **Effects** Add **New** Envelope command adds a second copy of the envelope to the object so that you can perform the transformations twice, doubling their effects. The **Effects** Copy Envelope **From** command enables you to copy an envelope from another object and use it for your transformations.

Perspective

You can add perspective to objects with the **Effects** Edit Perspective command. CorelDRAW! supports both one- and two-point perspectives. When you give the **Effects** Edit Perspective command, you can move the corners of your object along perspective lines, as shown in Figure 18.41.

The X that appears is the vanishing point you choose. You can drag the vanishing point around (rather than the corners) so that the vanishing points are at particular spots in your drawing. This action gives all the objects in your drawing the same vanishing points, and thus the same perspectives.

The **Effects Clear** Perspective command removes the perspective effects. **Effects** Add New **P**erspective adds a second copy of the perspective to the object, so that the bounding box is in the same perspective as the object. The **Effects** Copy Perspective From command enables you to copy a perspective from another object and use it for your transformations.

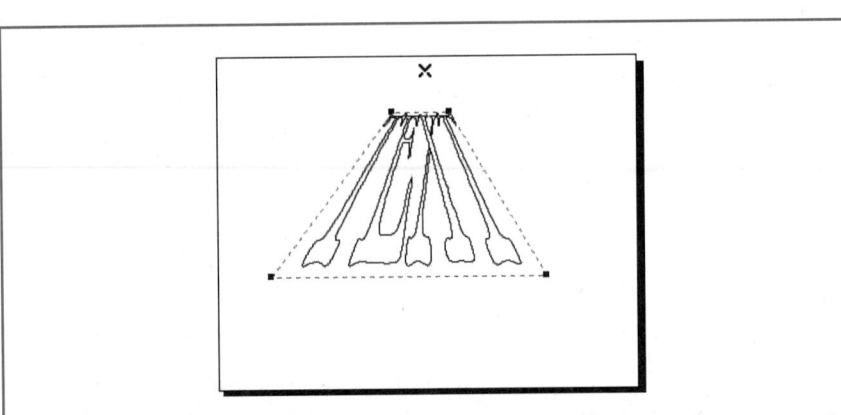

Figure 18.41. Example of perspective.

Blending Objects

You can blend the shape of one object into another with the **Effects Blend** command, shown in Figure 18.42. This command enables you to make smooth transitions between two objects of any type. You can set the number of steps in the transition and whether to rotate the objects as you blend them.

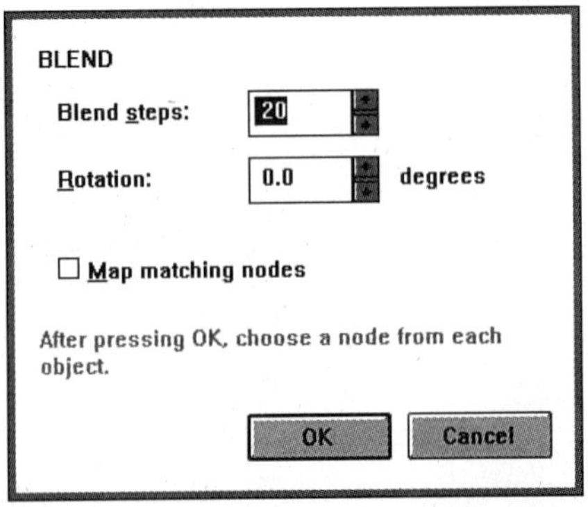

BLEND

Blend steps: 20

Rotation: 0.0 degrees

☐ Map matching nodes

After pressing OK, choose a node from each object.

OK   Cancel

Figure 18.42. Effects Blend dialog box.

For example, Figure 18.43 shows two symbols from the CorelDRAW! library (a bus and a car) being blended. You can use the blending feature with colored objects as well, and CorelDRAW! will blend their colors at the same time it blends their shapes.

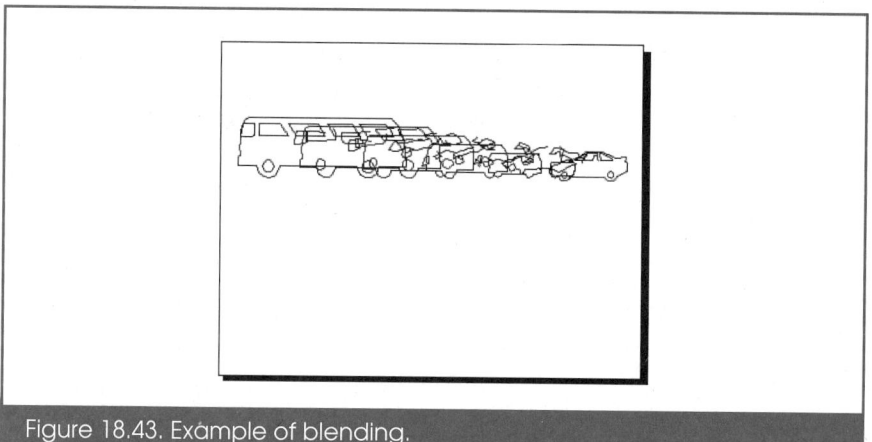

Figure 18.43. Example of blending.

18

Extruding

Because the third dimension is very important in many designs, CorelDRAW! makes it easy for you to extrude objects. Extrusion turns a two-dimensional object such as a box or a line into a three-dimensional one. The Effects Extrude dialog box is shown in Figure 18.44.

You can extrude either in perspective or in parallel, depending on the **P**erspective choice. Normally, you extrude in perspective so that the object looks visually correct. For example, Figure 18.45 shows the results of extruding a curve and some rectangles.

Display Options

There are many ways you can see your work in CorelDRAW!. The zoom tool, the second from the top in the tool palette, has a submenu that enables you to choose the way you narrow or widen your focus. The submenu is shown in Figure 18.46.

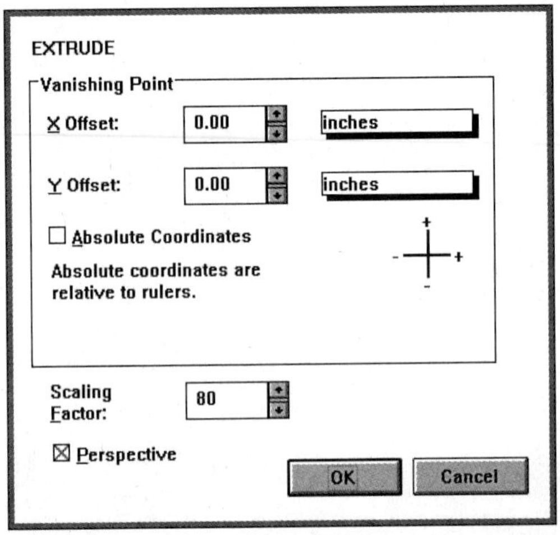

EXTRUDE

┌─ Vanishing Point ─────────────────────────┐

X Offset: [0.00] [±] [inches]

Y Offset: [0.00] [±] [inches]

☐ Absolute Coordinates

Absolute coordinates are
relative to rulers.

Scaling
Factor: [80] [±]

☒ Perspective   [OK]   [Cancel]

Figure 18.44. Effects Extrude dialog box.

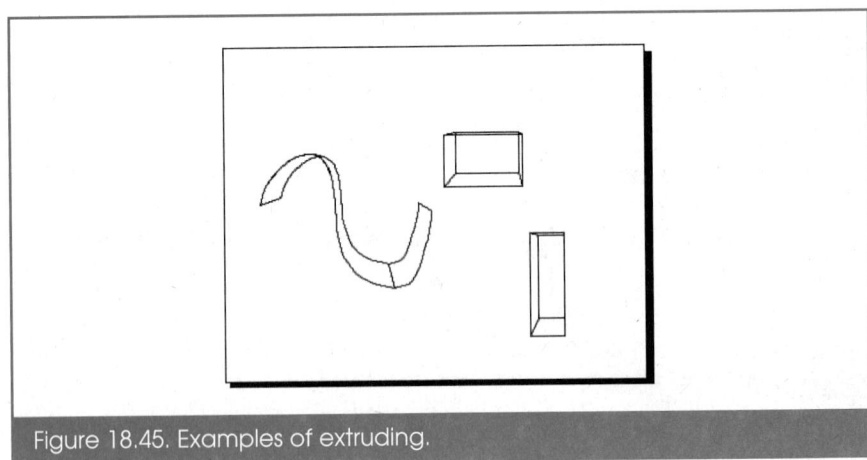

Figure 18.45. Examples of extruding.

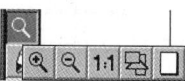

Figure 18.46. Zoom tool submenu.

From left to right, the options are the following:

▲ The magnify option enables you to drag over a region to magnify.
You can magnify up to approximately 10 times.

▲ The reduce option reduces the view to the previous magnification
or by a small amount.

▲ The 1:1 option shows the screen at the same resolution as the
printed page.

▲ The fit in window option shows all of the active drawing in the
window. This option is useful when you have just a small drawing.

▲ The show page option goes back to the original page view.

Grids

You often want objects lined up with each other. You can use the
Arrange Align command described earlier, but there is a way that you
can have objects line up automatically as you create them. You can
make a grid on the screen with the **D**isplay Grid Setup command shown
in Figure 18.47. After you create the grid, choosing the **D**isplay Snap to
Grid command causes all new objects to align with the grid. In fact, any
object you move also is placed on the grid.

If you want to align objects along a line, it is often easier to use the
Display Guidelines Setup command, shown in Figure 18.48. This
command enables you to specify a few horizontal and vertical guidelines that objects jump to when you move them near the guidelines.
You can set up a guideline and move the objects you want without
worrying about the placement of other objects in your drawing as you
continue to create them.

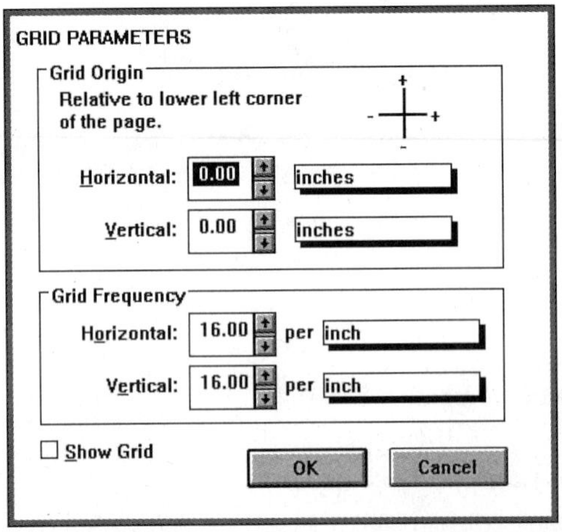

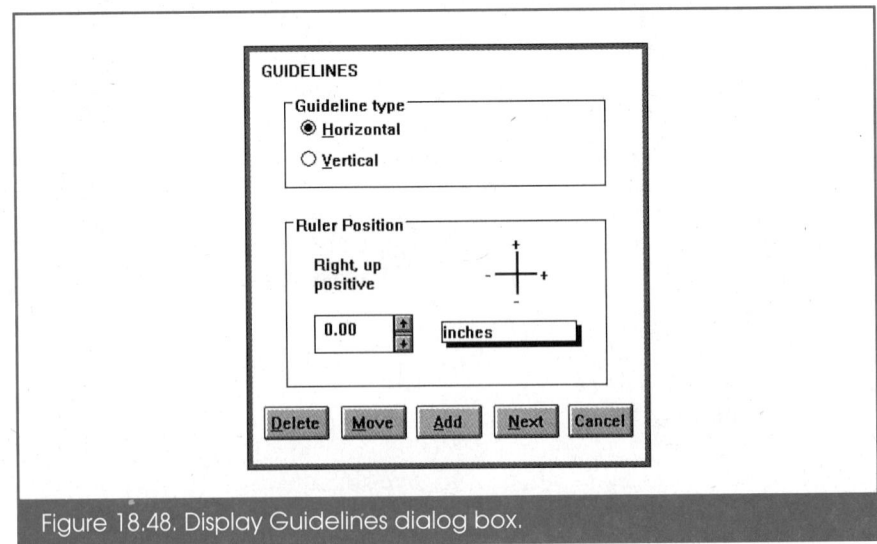

Figure 18.47. Display Grid Parameters dialog box.

Figure 18.48. Display Guidelines dialog box.

Previewing

You have seen how the **D**isplay Show Preview command splits the
screen so that you can preview your work at the same time you make
formatting changes. The preview window's optional tool palette has
three tools, as shown in Figure 18.49. The zoom tool is just like the
zoom tool in the main window, with the same submenu. The other two
tools enable you to specify whether the preview window is next to or
below the main window.

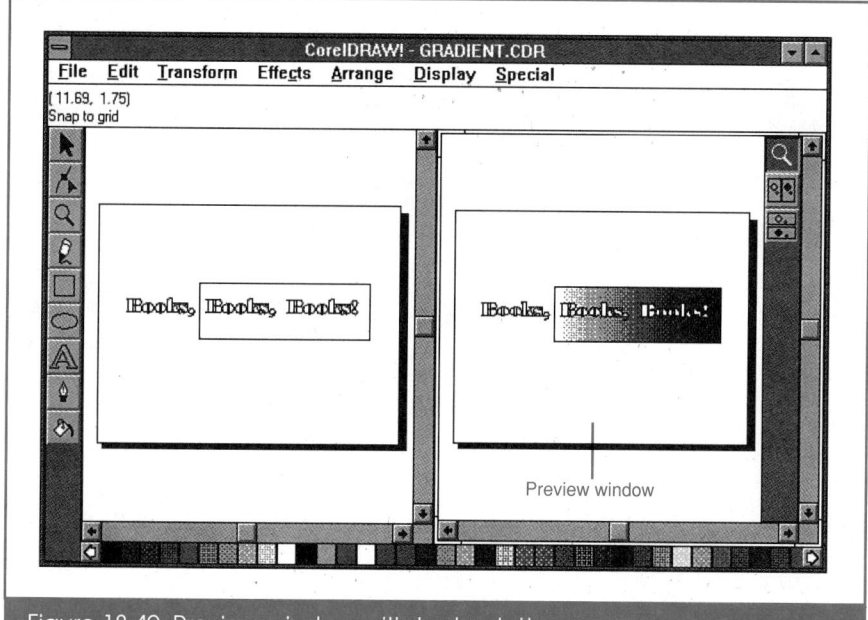

Figure 18.49. Preview window with tool palette.

You can change the size of the preview window simply by dragging its
corner. It starts out at half the size of the full screen, but most people
prefer to have a much smaller preview window, such as in Figure 18.50.
If you want a larger preview, you can use the **D**isplay Show Full Screen
Preview command, which temporarily makes the entire screen a
preview (until you press any key).

18

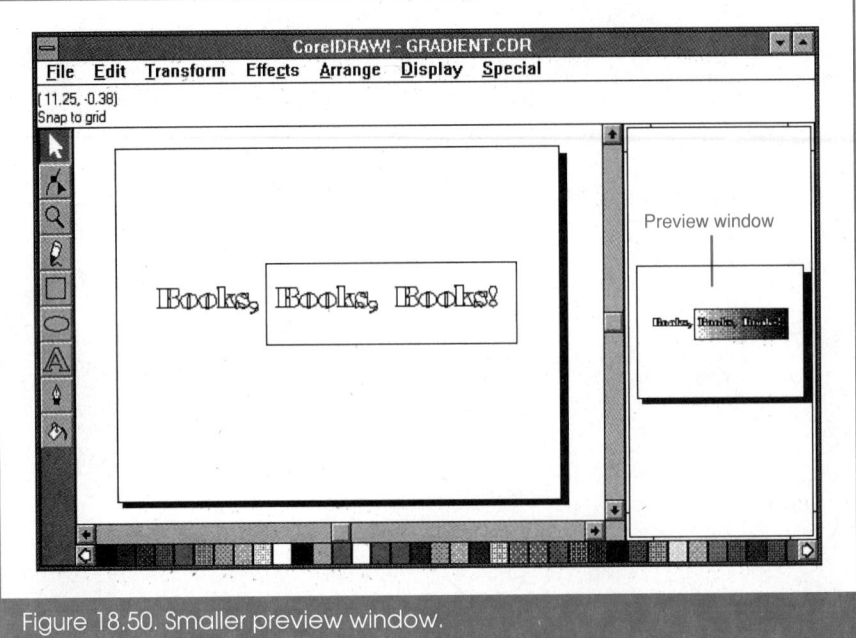

Figure 18.50. Smaller preview window.

Other CorelDRAW! Programs

The CorelDRAW! package comes with three programs that supplement the main CorelDRAW! program you have seen so far. These three programs include the following:

▲ WFN Boss converts fonts to and from the CorelDRAW! WFN font file format. This program also enables you to create symbols (like dingbats) that are used with the main CorelDRAW! symbol library. If you often use certain pictures in your work, such as a company logo or signage, converting these to symbols makes them easily accessible.

▲ Corel Trace converts bitmap images into outline objects. These objects act just like curves you create, so you can modify the shape when you put the image into a document. This is an advanced tracing program with many options concerning tracing methods and detail searching.

▲ Mosaic enables you to store and retrieve documents on disk easily. If you have many images, it is easy to forget where they are or what is in a file just by looking at its filename. Mosaic enables you to assign keywords to documents and search for the documents on the keywords. You also can see small sketches of the contents of the files. With Mosaic, you can organize your files into libraries and annotate them.

Communicating with Other Programs

18

CorelDRAW! uses the Clipboard in a fairly standard fashion. It can import graphics and text from the Clipboard, and the pictures it puts on the Clipboard can be used by many other Windows programs. CorelDRAW! uses its own picture format that has bitmaps that can be read by other programs. However, CorelDRAW! has a better method for communicating with other programs—by importing and exporting files.

The **F**ile Import command can read files from a wide variety of sources. Depending on the type of file, it reads a file either as a single large bitmap or as objects that can be independently manipulated. The file formats that CorelDRAW! can read are the following:

▲ .PCX and .PCC files from Paintbrush

▲ TIFF files

▲ Windows bitmaps (.BMP)

▲ Adobe Illustrator (.AI)

▲ Encapsulated PostScript files

▲ GEM picture files

▲ Graphics metafiles (.CGM)

▲ Macintosh PICT files

▲ Hewlett-Packard-compatible plotter files (HPGL format)

▲ AutoCAD files (DXF files)

▲ .PIC files from Lotus 1-2-3

▲ Mainframe art files in GDF format

You can export in many of the same formats and a few additional formats.

The file formats that CorelDRAW! can save in are the following:

- ▲ .PCX files for Paintbrush
- ▲ TIFF files
- ▲ Windows Metafile
- ▲ Adobe Illustrator (.AI)
- ▲ Encapsulated PostScript files
- ▲ GEM picture files
- ▲ Graphics metafiles (.CGM)
- ▲ Macintosh PICT files
- ▲ Hewlett-Packard-compatible plotter files (HPGL format)
- ▲ AutoCAD files (DXF files)
- ▲ .PIC files for Lotus 1-2-3
- ▲ Mainframe art files in GDF format
- ▲ WordPerfect graphics (.WPG)
- ▲ SCODL (specialized printer)

You can even export and import CorelDRAW! files as text. The **S**pecial Extract command creates a text file that contains a readable version of all the steps it takes to create the drawing. You can use this command to make a text file and then edit the text in it. For example, you can translate the words into another language. The **S**pecial Merge Back command reads this file and creates a picture from it.

Command Summary

This section is a summary of the commands found in CorelDRAW!'s menus.

File Menu

This is the command summary for the **F**ile menu.

File **N**ew	Begins a new document.
File **O**pen	Opens a document that exists on your disk.
File **S**ave	Saves the current document.
File Save **A**s	Saves the current document, enabling you to change its name or add a new name.
File **I**mport	Enables you to bring in a document from another source.
File **E**xport	Enables you to save your document in a format readable by other graphics programs.
File **P**rint	Prints the document according to your specifications.
File Print Mer**g**e	Inserts text into a document at the indicated point or replaces specified text before sending the information to the printer, giving you the option of having the printed text vary from copy to copy.
File Page Se**t**up	Defines the specifications of page size and orientation.
File **C**ontrol Panel	Connects you with the Windows Control Panel.
File E**x**it	Exits CorelDRAW!, with the option of saving your most recent changes.

Edit Menu

This is the command summary for the **E**dit menu.

Edit **U**ndo	Reverses your last action.
Edit **R**epeat	Repeats the last operation on the selected object.
Edit Cut	Removes the selected object from the document and places it onto the Clipboard.
Edit **C**opy	Copies the selected object onto the Clipboard.
Edit **P**aste	Copies the contents of the Clipboard onto the document at the insertion point.

18

Edit **C**lear	Deletes the selected object from the document.
Edit **D**uplicate	Makes a copy of the chosen objects and inserts them into the document.
Edit Copy **St**yle From	Copies one or more of the selected style attributes from one object to another.
Edit **T**ext	Enables you to edit text as well as specify all the text formatting.
Edit **C**haracter Attributes	Enables you to edit character formatting, including individual character attributes within a text string.
Edit Select **A**ll	Selects all objects in the document.

Transform Menu

This is the command summary for the **T**ransform menu.

Transform **M**ove	Moves an object or a copy of an object to a specified distance or an exact location.
Transform **R**otate & Skew	Enables you to rotate and skew an object to your exact specifications, with the option of leaving a copy of the original object.
Transform **S**tretch & Mirror	Gives you the option of mirroring, stretching, and scaling an object to your exact specifications.
Transform **C**lear Transformations	Clears all Rotate & Skew and Stretch & Mirror commands, leaving the object in its original state. It also clears any Envelope and Perspective commands executed from the Effects menu.

Effects Menu

This is the command summary for the **E**ffe**c**ts menu.

Effe**c**ts **E**d**i**t Envelope	Enables you to manipulate the shape of an object or text, restore an object to its original form, and copy an object.

Effects Perspective	Makes one- and two-point perspectives of an object, adds a new perspective, and enables you to edit a perspective, return a perspective to its original form, and copy a perspective form.
Effects **B**lend	Creates a series of objects between two objects that are a blending of their shapes, with the option of rotating them as they are being blended. It also enables you to create highlights and airbrush effects.
Effects **E**xtrude	Enables you to make a shape into a "three-dimensional" object.

18

Arrange Menu

This is the command summary for the **A**rrange menu.

Arrange To **F**ront	Makes the selected object appear on top of the other objects.
Arrange to **B**ack	Makes the selected object appear behind the other objects.
Arrange **F**orward One	Moves the selected object forward one position in the drawing order.
Arrange **B**ack One	Moves the selected object back one position in the drawing order.
Arrange **R**everse Order	Reverses the drawing order of the selected objects.
Arrange **G**roup	Enables you to group selected objects so that they can be treated as one item.
Arrange **U**ngroup	Enables you to disassemble previously grouped objects.
Arrange **C**ombine	Combines the selected objects into a single curve. (This is quite different from the Arrange Group Command.)
Arrange Brea**k** Apart	Splits a curve that has been put together with the Arrange Combine command.

Arrange Convert to Curves	Changes the selected shape or text string into a single curve/line so that you can customize its shape. As soon as this command is used, the only way to return the object to its original state is to use the Undo command immediately afterward.
Arrange Align	Precisely aligns the specified objects.
Arrange Fit Text to Path	Makes the selected text string follow the shape of the outline of the other chosen object.
Arrange Align to Baseline	Aligns all the characters in a line of text to a baseline.
Arrange Straighten Text	Aligns a line of text to its baseline, returning all character vertical positioning attributes to their original state. This does not affect the text string spacing options.

Display Menu

This is the command summary for the Display menu.

Display Snap to Grid	Turns the Snap to Grid command on or off, forcing the cursor to remain on the grid points and enabling you to create aligned or equally-sized or equally-spaced objects.
Display Grid Setup	Displays the gridlines in the work window.
Display Snap to Guidelines	Enables you to align objects on nonprinting lines that can be put anywhere in your work area. Takes precedence when used simultaneously with the Snap to Grid command.
Display Guidelines Setup	Enables you to place, erase, or move guidelines without using the mouse.
Display Show Rulers	Displays the rulers at the edges of your window. Enables you to see the current position of your cursor and enables you to determine the zero points on the ruler.
Display Show Status Line	Displays or hides the status line.

Display Show Color Palette	Displays either the spot color palette or the process color palette.
Display Show **P**review	Enables you to see how the printed document will appear, while simultaneously providing you with an editing window.
Display Show **F**ull Screen Preview	Enlarges the preview window to fill the screen.
Display Show Preview **T**oolbox	Displays the optional preview toolbox and scroll bars. This enables you to control the preview window independently of the editing window.
Display Show Preview Selected **O**nly	Displays only selected objects in the preview window.
Display Show **A**uto-Update	Gives you the option of having the preview window automatically updated each time you make an editing change.
Display Show **B**itmaps	Shows or hides the bitmap display in the editing window.
Display Show **R**efresh Wire Screen	Enables you to redraw an object in the editing window.

18

Special Menu

This is the command summary for the **S**pecial menu.

Special **Ex**tract	Converts a drawing to a text file description of all the elements in the drawing.
Special **M**erge-Back	Converts an extracted drawing back into a picture.
Special Create **P**attern	Enables you to make customized bitmaps and vector fill patterns that will be added to those already in the fill tool.
Special Create **A**rrow	Enables you to make a customized arrow head or line-ending shape.
Special **Pr**eferences	Enables you to specify how CorelDRAW! will perform certain operations.

V

Running DOS Programs

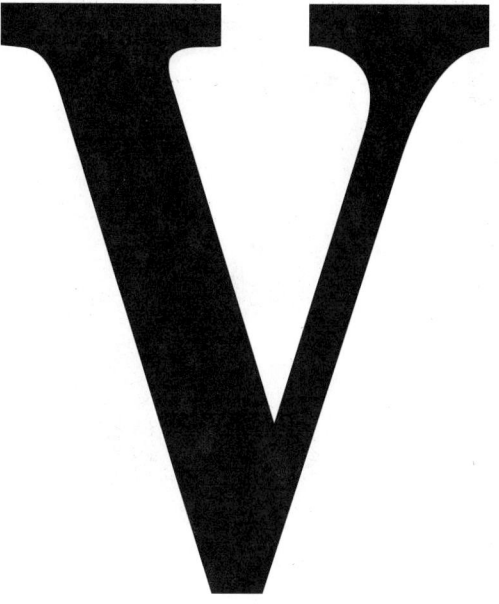

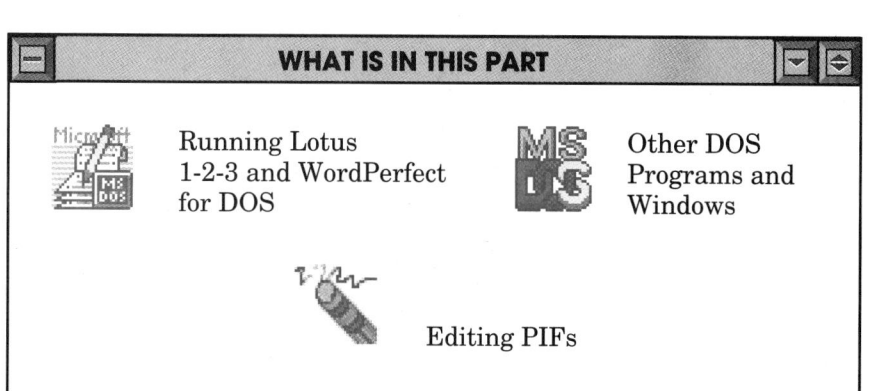

WHAT IS IN THIS PART

Running Lotus
1-2-3 and WordPerfect
for DOS

Other DOS
Programs and
Windows

Editing PIFs

Running 1-2-3 for DOS, Version 3.1

A PIF file is sort of like a batch file. It contains parameters that tell Windows what a program's needs really are. In some cases, without a PIF file tailored to a particular program's requirements, the program will not run at all from Windows. Make sure you use this PIF file. With a PIF file tailored to 1-2-3's needs, you can successfully run Version 3.1 of 1-2-3 for DOS.

Tip: Version 3.1 of 1-2-3 for DOS works with Windows 3.1 better than it does with Windows 3.0. The description in this section is for Windows 3.1 only. If you have not updated to Windows 3.1, you should do so as soon as possible.

If you do not have access to the PIF, you can create your own with the PIF Editor. Figure 19.1 shows the standard mode setting; Figure 19.2 shows the main 386-enhanced mode settings, and Figure 19.3 shows the advanced 386-enhanced mode settings.

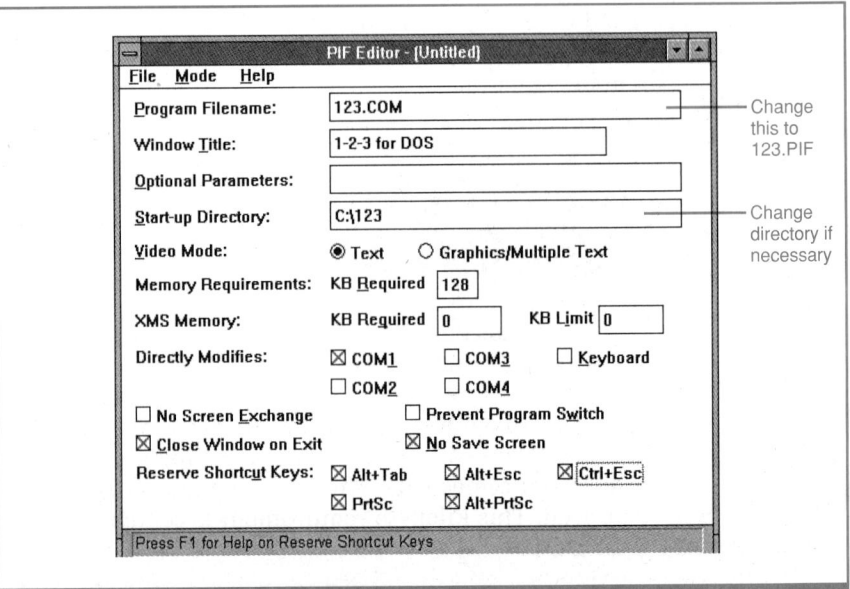

Figure 19.1. Standard settings from 123.PIF.

V

Running DOS
Programs

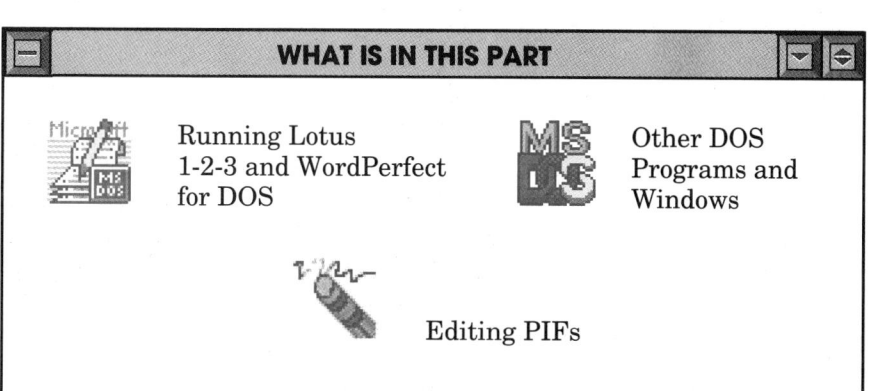

WHAT IS IN THIS PART

Running Lotus
1-2-3 and WordPerfect
for DOS

Other DOS
Programs and
Windows

Editing PIFs

Running
Lotus 1-2-3 and
WordPerfect
for DOS

This chapter describes the PIF settings for the two most common programs, Lotus 1-2-3 for DOS and WordPerfect for DOS. It also gives you tips on how to avoid problems with those programs when running them in Windows.

Running 1-2-3 for DOS, Version 2.2

You do not have to do anything special to run 1-2-3 Version 2.2 for DOS in Windows. As a general rule of thumb, remember to use the PIF file instead of the executable filename that comes with the software—if the manufacturer supplies one. The PIF that comes with Windows requires 310K, but 384K is desired. This kilobyte requirement is compatible with 1-2-3 Version 2.2 for DOS.

Running 1-2-3 for DOS, Version 3.1

A PIF file is sort of like a batch file. It contains parameters that tell Windows what a program's needs really are. In some cases, without a PIF file tailored to a particular program's requirements, the program will not run at all from Windows. Make sure you use this PIF file. With a PIF file tailored to 1-2-3's needs, you can successfully run Version 3.1 of 1-2-3 for DOS.

Tip: Version 3.1 of 1-2-3 for DOS works with Windows 3.1 better than it does with Windows 3.0. The description in this section is for Windows 3.1 only. If you have not updated to Windows 3.1, you should do so as soon as possible.

If you do not have access to the PIF, you can create your own with the PIF Editor. Figure 19.1 shows the standard mode setting; Figure 19.2 shows the main 386-enhanced mode settings, and Figure 19.3 shows the advanced 386-enhanced mode settings.

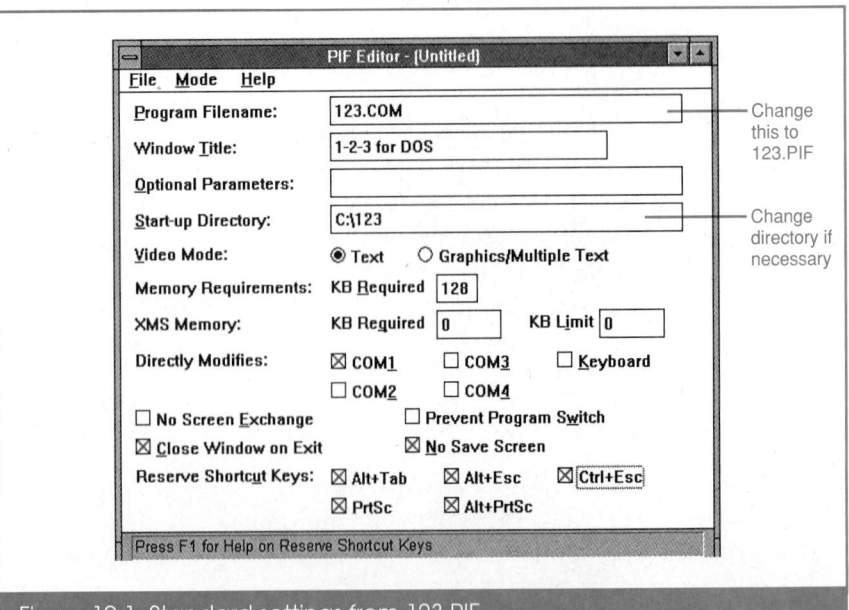

Figure 19.1. Standard settings from 123.PIF.

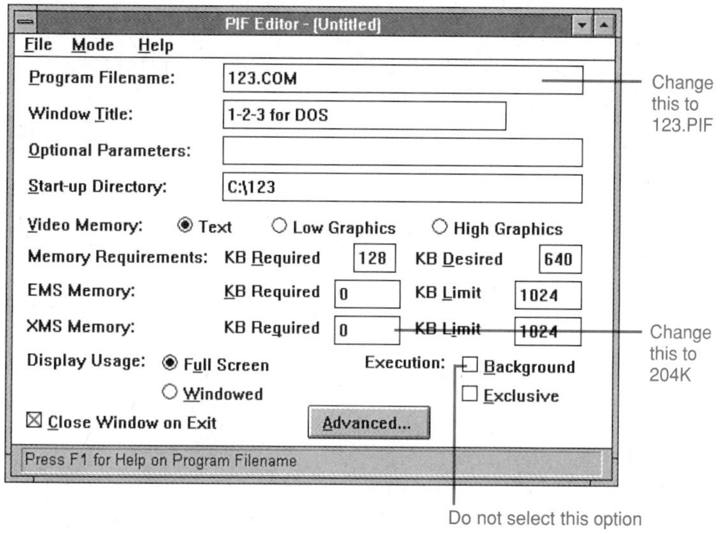

Figure 19.2. Main settings from 123.PIF for 386-enhanced mode.

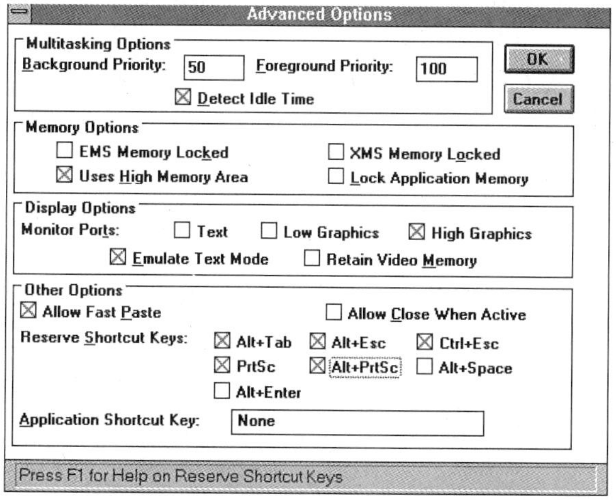

Figure 19.3. Advanced Options from 123.PIF for 386-enhanced mode.

The most important settings to notice are

▲ The program name in the PIF file is always C:\123R3\123.EXE. If you installed 1-2-3 for DOS in any other directory, be sure to change this setting to reflect the correct directory.

▲ The amount of conventional memory required in standard mode is 128K.

▲ The amount of conventional memory required in 386-enhanced mode is 204K, and 235K is desired. Change the PIF default to reflect these numbers. Conventional memory is defined as all memory on your system below the 640K mark. If you require much more for 1-2-3, your other DOS-based programs may not have enough conventional memory to run properly.

▲ Your PC must have 256K of extended (XMS) memory to run 1-2-3 for DOS. Extended memory is defined as memory above the 1 megabyte mark, managed by a memory manager. The limit on extended memory of 1024K is suggested, but you can change it.

▲ You should only set the XMS limit to the amount of memory that you really need. Switching will be slower if you set the limit higher than you need. This higher limit causes all the XMS memory to be written to or read from the disk each time you go in or out of 1-2-3 for DOS, even if you aren't using this application. You might want to try this value at different points to see what setting works best with your system.

▲ Do not select **B**ackground in the 386-enhanced mode options. Version 3.1 will not run in the background. The background versus foreground setting determines whether the program will run with only half of the systems resources, versus all of the systems resources and subsequent attention of the central processing unit.

▲ Note that the extended and expanded memory settings in the PIF file are independent of the 123MEMSIZE discussed in the section, "Setting Memory Aside," later in this chapter. Do not increase or decrease the 123MEMSIZE numbers.

Using 123.PIF

The best way to start 1-2-3 for DOS is from the PIF file. When you install 1-2-3, 123.PIF and 123.ICO are installed in the same directory with the other 1-2-3 for DOS files. Use the methods described in Chapter 5, "Program Manager," to create an icon for this PIF rather than for the program. When Program Manager asks you to fill in the program

name in the text box provided in the Properties dialog box, enter the name and location of the PIF file instead of the program name. If you don't substitute the PIF filename for the program name as described in the last sentence, the PIF you create will reside on your hard drive, unused.

Figure 19.4 shows a popular version of the 123.ICO icon file.

Figure 19.4. Some 1-2-3 for DOS icons.

19

Minimum Requirements

To run Version 3.1 of 1-2-3 for DOS in Windows, you need enough RAM and hard disk space for both programs. 1-2-3 uses different memory management schemes depending on the Windows operating mode you are using (See Table 19.1 for a list of these schemes).

Table 19.1 shows the required RAM space for each operating mode. In Table 19.1, the *RAM* heading represents the minimum amount of RAM (conventional and extended memory) you need to start 1-2-3 from Windows. These requirements are described in more detail in Chapter 24, "Memory Configuration for Windows."

Table 19.1. Minimum RAM required for 1-2-3 for DOS, Version 3.1.

Mode	RAM
Standard	1.5M
386 enhanced mode	2M

Running in Standard Mode

1-2-3 for DOS, in essence, keeps its own application swap space on hard disk. You can decide how much memory 1-2-3 has available and where it stores temporary files.

There are two ways to specify the amount of memory available in standard mode. Both methods involve setting two MS-DOS environment variables: 123VIRTSIZE and 123SWAPSIZE. Set these variables before you run Windows, preferably in your AUTOEXEC.BAT file.

123VIRTSIZE

The 123VIRTSIZE variable determines the total RAM space for the 1-2-3 for DOS program. If there isn't enough RAM memory available from Windows, the program creates its own temporary swap file on the hard drive, thus creating more memory. For example, if you want to be sure to have 1500K of memory for 1-2-3 for DOS, use the following MS-DOS command:

```
SET 123VIRTSIZE=1500
```

The default amount for 123VIRTSIZE is 1131K. 123VIRTSIZE holds a maximum of 32767K. Of course, there must be enough space on the hard disk for the file or 1-2-3 cannot start.

123SWAPSIZE

A second environment variable, 123SWAPSIZE, sets the absolute size of the temporary swap file, regardless of how much RAM memory is available when you start the program. Thus, if you always want the swap file to be 2048 kilobytes, use the following MS-DOS command:

```
SET 123SWAPSIZE=2048
```

When 123SWAPSIZE is set to 0, no swap file is created. The maximum size of 123SWAPSIZE is 32M minus the amount of memory 1-2-3 for DOS uses. Of course, there must be enough space for the file or 1-2-3 for DOS can't start.

Choosing Between 123VIRTSIZE and 123SWAPSIZE

If you use both 123VIRTSIZE and 123SWAPSIZE, 1-2-3 for DOS ignores 123VIRTSIZE and creates the swap file based on the number set in 123SWAPSIZE. It makes sense to use one or the other of these variables, not both. If you use both settings, you are wasting your time and cluttering your AUTOEXEC.BAT file unnecessarily.

Use 123VIRTSIZE if you want a consistent size for your work space; use 123SWAPSIZE if you want a consistent size for the swap file. Unless you are lacking in hard disk space, use 123VIRTSIZE because 1-2-3 for DOS is more predictable with this variable. 123SWAPSIZE is practical when you have a limited amount of hard disk space.

123SWAPPATH

Use 123SWAPPATH, another MS-DOS environment variable, to decide where the program will write the temporary file. Be sure this variable is set to your local hard disk if you are running on a network.

If you have more than one hard disk, set 123SWAPPATH to the fastest hard disk. The directory you specify must exist, and you must specify a hard disk drive, not a diskette drive. For example, to write the swap file to C:\123SWAP, use the following command:

```
SET 123SWAPPATH=C:\123SWAP
```

19

Tip: Swapping is more efficient if your hard disk is not fragmented. If you have an unfragmenting utility such as PC Tools or Norton Utilities, use the utility on the disk that you are swapping. Swapping also is more efficient if the swap file is the only file in the directory. You might want to set up a special directory for the swap file.

Running in 386-Enhanced Mode

Unlike standard mode, 1-2-3 for DOS doesn't use its own swap file in 386-enhanced mode. Instead, it receives the extra memory it needs directly from Windows. If Windows doesn't have enough RAM, Windows simulates RAM with a Windows swap file (assuming you have set one up). Strongly consider using a swap file with Windows because 1-2-3 for DOS will have more memory with which to work. The Windows swap disk is described in Chapter 24, "Memory Configuration for Windows."

Setting Memory Aside

To tell 1-2-3 how much memory it should request from Windows, use the MS-DOS environment variable 123MEMSIZE. This variable specifies

the number of extra kilobytes of memory that you request. For example, if you want 1024 kilobytes of extended memory, you give the following MS-DOS command:

```
SET 123MEMSIZE=1024
```

Running in a Window

> **Warning:** Running 1-2-3 for DOS in a window works with many systems, but not all. Some users have reported that their systems lock up when they quit 1-2-3 if it is in a window, or even if it has been in a window during the session. Use care when running 1-2-3 in a window and save your work before you enter **W**indowed mode.

When 1-2-3 for DOS starts, it displays a graphics-based screen unless you have the video driver set to CGA for Windows. Thus, you have to use the driver if you intend to run 1-2-3 in a window on start-up. Even with this driver, you can't run the WYSIWYG program to view printed output or graphs on the screen.

To switch your 1-2-3 for DOS video driver to CGA for Windows:

1. Run the 1-2-3 for DOS INSTALL program.

2. Select Change Selected Equipment from the main menu.

3. Select Modify Current DCF from the next menu to change the driver configuration file.

4. The next screen is labeled Modify Current DCF. Select Change Selected Display so you can change the monitor. Press Enter.

5. Use the ↑ and ↓ keys to select CGA for Windows and press Enter. This takes you back to the screen labeled Modify Current DCF. Select Change Selected Display and press Enter.

6. You should now have two displays marked with numbers: the original display marked with a 1 and the CGA for Windows display marked with a 2. Use the ↑ and ↓ keys to select the adapter that is marked with a 1. Press Delete. If you see a second screen, such as one that reads "Select a VGA screen display mode," press Delete again.

7. You should now be back at the Modify Current DCF screen. Press Enter to return to the previous menu. Select Save Changes and press Enter. Save the file with the same name you used before.

You are prompted to insert diskettes into your disk drive so that the program can copy the necessary files for the CGA for Windows driver.

1-2-3 for DOS Starting Errors

If there is not enough space for the 1-2-3 for DOS swap file, you see the following message:

```
VM error[27]: Not enough disk space for swap file
```

This message also shows the name of the swap file it is trying to create. If you see this message, it means there is not enough hard disk space for the file you are trying to create. Either free up your hard disk space or change the 123VIRTSIZE setting so 1-2-3 for DOS uses less disk space (see the section called "Choosing Between 123VIRTSIZE and 123SWAPSIZE," earlier in this chapter).

In standard mode, be sure the 123SWAPPATH variable is set with a specification for a hard drive and an existing directory. If either of these is not true, you will see the following message:

```
VM error[26]: Cannot create swap file. Make sure the
123SWAPPATH statement in your AUTOEXEC.BAT file contains
only existing directories and no diskette drives.
```

If you are running in 386-enhanced mode but your memory is low, you might see an error message such as

```
Cannot load driver file
```

or

```
Cannot initialize resident segments
```

Both of these errors indicate that there was not enough memory to start 1-2-3 for DOS. Free some memory using the methods shown in Chapter 20, "Other DOS Programs and Windows."

19

Running WordPerfect 5.0 and 5.1 for DOS

WordPerfect 5.1 comes with a PIF for Windows. That file, called WIN30-WP.PIF, is on the first utilities disk from which you loaded WordPerfect. You have to load the utilities to retrieve the file. If you do not have access to the file, you can create your own file with the PIF Editor. Figure 19.5 shows the standard mode settings, Figure 19.6

shows the main 386-enhanced mode settings, and Figure 19.7 shows
the advanced 386-enhanced mode settings.

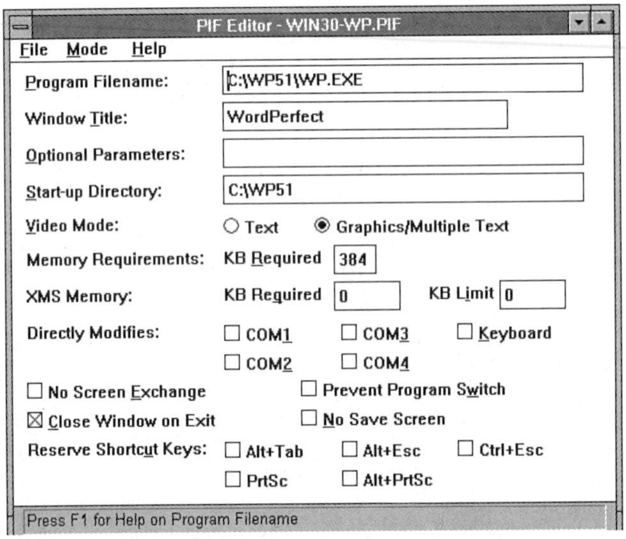

Figure 19.5. Standard settings from WIN30-WP.PIF.

The most important settings to remember are

▲ The minimum amount of conventional memory required is 384K
  in standard mode and 358K in 386-enhanced mode.

▲ The Graphics/Multiple Text is used in standard mode and High
  Graphics is used in 386-enhanced mode.

The other settings are standard.

WordPerfect ignores the Start-up Directory field if the internal setting of
WordPerfect for DOS is selected. Thus, no matter what you put in the
PIF, WordPerfect for DOS uses its internal setting. To avoid this problem:

1. Run WordPerfect for DOS.

2. Press Shift-F1 for the Settings menu.

3. Press 6 for the Location of the Files menu.

4. Press 7 for the Documents choice.

5. Remove any entry in this choice.

This causes WordPerfect for DOS to use the directory you specify in the PIF.

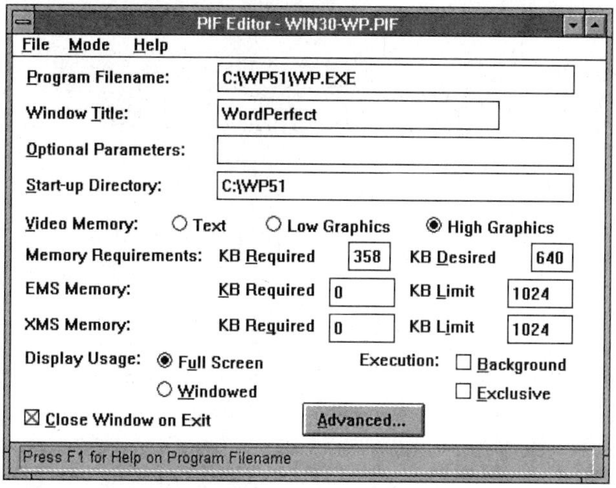

Figure 19.6. Main settings from WIN30-WP.PIF for 386-enhanced mode.

19

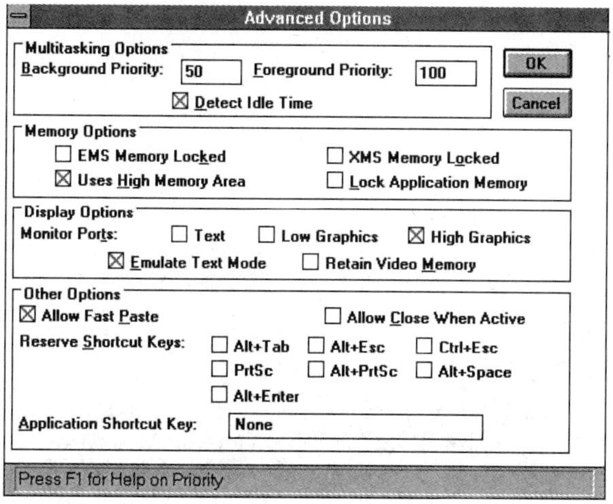

Figure 19.7. Advanced settings from WIN30-WP.PIF for 386-enhanced mode.

Running in Windowed Mode

You can run WordPerfect for DOS in a window in 386-enhanced mode, but you lose the capability of previewing your pages. Remember that you can run combination-based programs like WordPerfect for DOS only if you keep them in text mode. When you enter preview mode in **V**iew, you use your PC's graphics mode, which cannot be used within a window.

Hints for More Reliable Use

Some Windows users have had occasional problems with WordPerfect for DOS crashing under Windows 3.x. If you are having problems with WordPerfect under Windows 3 or 3.1, the following guidelines (based on anecdotal wisdom and trial and error) should help the programs interact better.

▲ Be sure to use the most current version of WordPerfect for DOS available. Earlier versions had problems with expanded memory that caused Windows to crash.

▲ Change the minimum amount of conventional memory required to 512K. Try this first, it seems to clear up most problems. If that option doesn't work, try starting WordPerfect for DOS with the /32 option. This option forces WordPerfect for DOS to use LIM 3.2 expanded memory. For example,

```
WP.EXE /32
```

▲ Some people receive reliable results by setting the video memory settings to Text.

▲ Start WordPerfect for DOS with the /R option (which loads menus into extended memory) only if WordPerfect is stored on a network. If WordPerfect is on your local hard drive, using the /R option can crash the system.

▲ If you have problems switching to or from WordPerfect for DOS in 386-enhanced mode, select the **L**ock Application Memory and Retain Video **M**emory options. Note that this option might prevent you from running other non-Windows programs due to lack of memory.

▲ If you have problems reading from your floppy drives in WordPerfect in 386-enhanced mode, or WordPerfect for DOS begins to run extremely slow after reading from or writing to a

floppy drive, you are having some device conflicts. Add the following line in the [386Enh] section of your SYSTEM.INI file:

```
HIGHFLOPPYREADS=FALSE
```

You also might have to add the EMMExclude line, as described in Chapter 27, "Configuring with the WIN.INI and SYSTEM.INI Files." If neither of these works, try adding the line

```
IRQ9Global=YES
```

▲ If WordPerfect for DOS hangs when you start it or operates sporadically when you run it, try starting WordPerfect for DOS with the /NE option. This option prevents the application from using any expanded memory, making the application run slower but more reliably.

▲ Follow the suggestions at the end of Chapter 20, "Other DOS Programs and Windows."

19

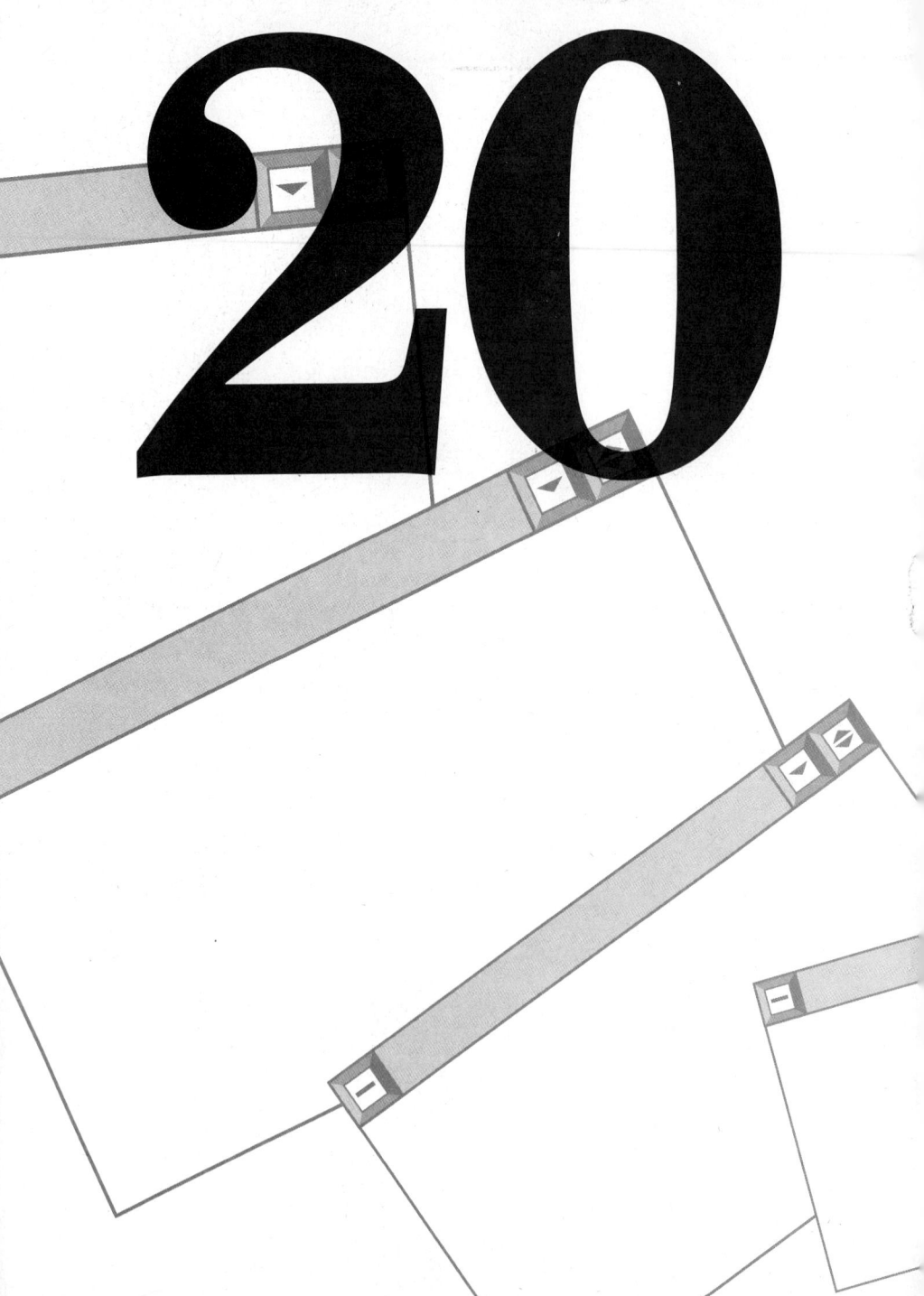

CHAPTER

20

Other DOS Programs and Windows

Just because you run Windows doesn't mean that you will never want to run your old MS-DOS programs again. In fact, one of the most popular features of Windows 3.1 has nothing to do with its user interface: It is the ability to run MS-DOS programs without having to leave Windows. You can run more than one MS-DOS program at the same time, and, if your PC has an 80386 or an 80486 CPU, you can run each program in its own window.

Programs that run under MS-DOS but are not written for Windows are called non-Windows programs. There are three types of non-Windows programs:

▲ Text-based programs run on any adapter, even one that does not support graphics. These programs display only letters and numbers, not lines, circles, or other drawings. Some text-based programs have special modes that require graphics, but those programs require a graphics adapter. Common text-based programs include Word-Perfect, 1-2-3, Microsoft Word, and Paradox.

▲ Graphics-based programs require graphics adapters and include art programs, design programs, presentation programs, and so on. Common graphics-based programs include Harvard Graphics, AutoCAD, and Freelance.

▲ Combination-based programs can be run either in character mode or in graphics mode. Note that many text-based programs have graphics modes. When you run those programs in character mode, Windows treats them like text-based programs. However, when you try to switch into graphics mode, Windows begins to treat them like graphics-based programs. Many common programs such as WordPerfect, Lotus 1-2-3, and Microsoft Word are combination-based.

Windows treats all three types of programs basically the same. Some graphics-based programs, however, do not run well under Windows, especially ones with their own menu systems. As Windows grows in popularity, the number of programs that do not work well with Windows likely will decrease. Note, however, that many non-Windows graphics-based programs from major software manufacturers, even Microsoft, do not work well under Windows. For example, Microsoft's Flight Simulator can cause Windows to crash.

If you run in 386-enhanced mode (as described in Chapter 22, "Windows Operating Modes,"), you need to know the difference between text-based programs and graphics-based programs because some limitations apply to graphics-based programs. When using combination-based programs, you must be careful not to change from text mode to graphics mode.

You can run memory-resident or TSR (*Terminate and Stay Resident*) programs under Windows the way you run other non-Windows programs. These programs, such as Borland's SideKick, usually are used for small tasks, many of which are replicated in the programs that come with Windows.

Running Non-Windows Programs

Most people run their non-Windows programs from Program Manager because they already are familiar with running Windows programs. However, you also can run non-Windows programs from File Manager or with the **File Run** command in either program.

Icons in Program Manager

When you first install Windows, the Setup program creates a program group for all of your programs called "Applications." You will find some of the non-Windows programs on your hard disk in that window. Setup installs only non-Windows programs it knows about, which is probably many fewer than you have on your hard disk. If you want, you can create a separate group such as the one shown in Figure 20.1.

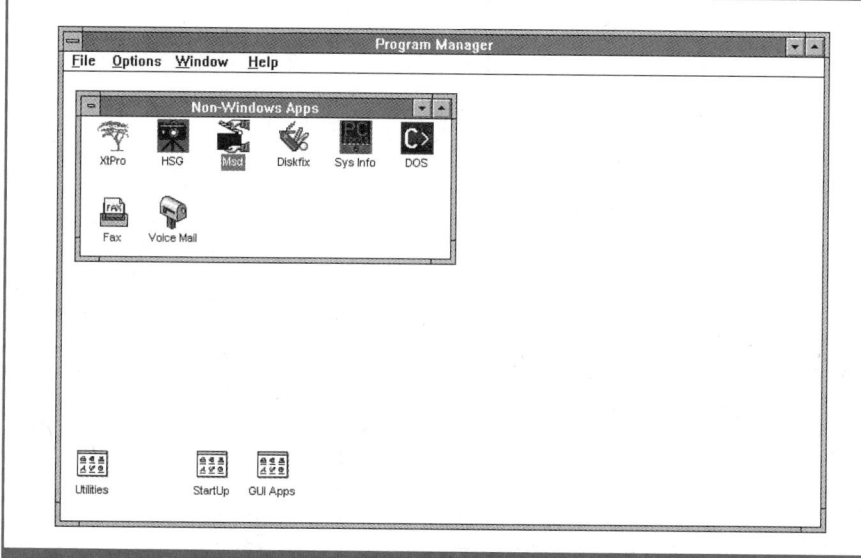

Figure 20.1. Typical non-Windows applications window.

You generally will find that Setup does not add all of your non-Windows programs to this window. It also does not add any batch files that load executable programs to the window. Chapter 5, "Program Manager," shows how to add more programs to this window and other windows.

You run non-Windows programs the way you run Windows programs—from Program Manager. The usual method is to run programs from their icons in program group windows.

With the mouse, double-click the desired icon to run the program.

With the keyboard, use the direction keys to select the desired program and press the Enter key.

20

Running from File Manager

If you use File Manager more than Program Manager, you might want to start your non-Windows programs directly from File Manager. You can start any non-Windows program, including batch files, from File Manager. You can start programs with the extensions .EXE, .COM, .BAT, and .PIF. Table 20.1 shows the different types of non-Windows programs.

Table 20.1. Types of non-Windows programs.

Extension	Type of Program
.EXE and .COM files	Standard MS-DOS programs. Almost every commercial program comes as either an .EXE or a .COM file.
.BAT files	Batch programs written in the MS-DOS batch command language. These often are files you write yourself, although some commercial programs come with batch files.
.PIF files	Program information files that tell Windows how to run non-Windows programs. The PIF has over a dozen options that help you control how Windows runs a program. These files are associated with specific .EXE, .COM, and .BAT files on your disk. When you run the .PIF from File Manager, Windows runs the associated program.

A typical File Manager window with .EXE, .COM, and .BAT programs is shown in Figure 20.2.

With the mouse, double-click the desired filename to run the program.

With the keyboard, use the direction keys to select the desired file and press the Enter key.

Using the File Run Command

Both Program Manager and File Manager have **File R**un commands. The dialog box for the **File R**un command in Program Manager is shown in Figure 20.3. To run a program, type the full filename, including path and extension. If you select the Run **M**inimized option, the program runs as a minimized icon. This means that the program is loaded into memory, then is reduced to an icon at the bottom of your desktop. You can switch into the program instantly by clicking the icon.

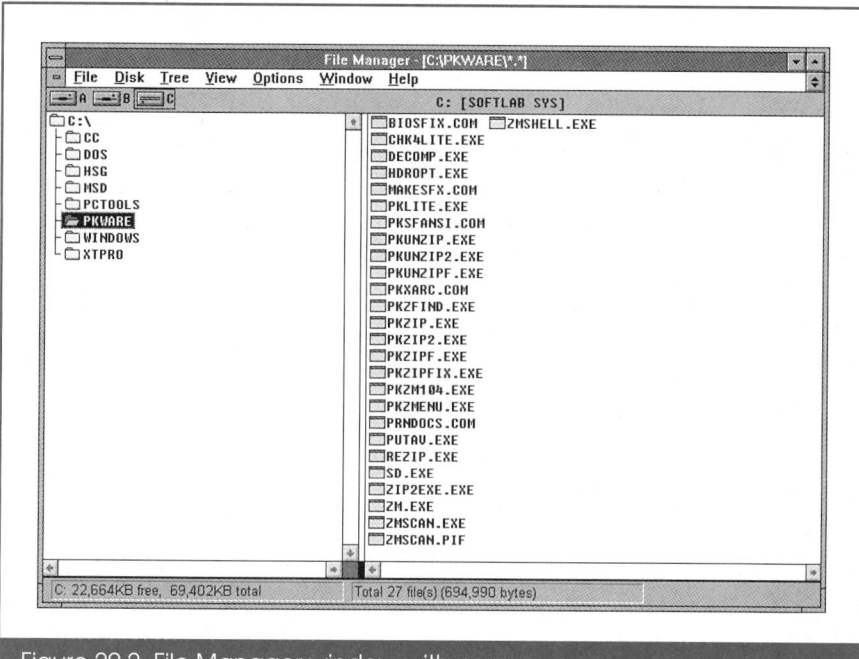

Figure 20.2. File Manager window with programs.

Often you will want to open a document automatically when you run a non-Windows program. To do so, enter a space after the program name and enter the document name. Figure 20.4 shows an example of running the Notepad program and opening the BOOK4.TXT file.

Using the DOS Prompt Icon

When you use the DOS prompt icon in the Main window of Program Manager, you can run programs from the MS-DOS command line. The DOS prompt icon puts up a window with a standard MS-DOS prompt. You then can run programs as you normally would in MS-DOS.

When you are finished with the MS-DOS session, you must give the EXIT command at the MS-DOS prompt. Otherwise, the MS-DOS session will continue indefinitely. This is the only way to finish a DOS-prompt session.

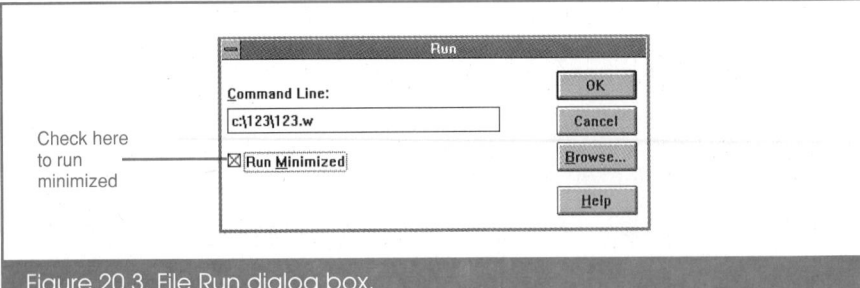

Check here
to run
minimized

Figure 20.3. File Run dialog box.

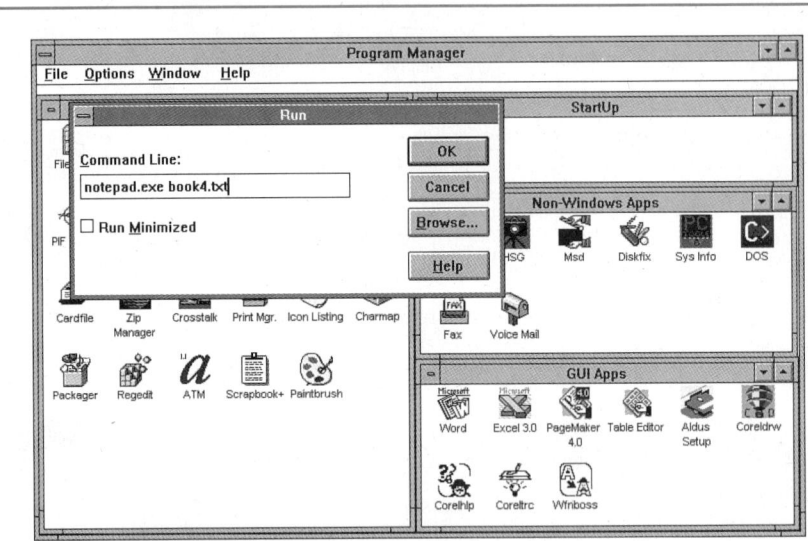

Figure 20.4. Command line to open the BOOK4.TXT file.

Warning: When running a DOS-prompt session, be sure not to delete or alter any file that Windows is using. Doing so can cause your PC to crash. Also, be sure not to run commands that change the parts of the disk that Windows uses.

In general, you should not delete any files in the Windows directory while running Windows, because this action can cause unpredictable results. This fact is particularly true when you run non-Windows programs, because Windows will expect all files to be available when you return to MS-DOS and will crash if they are not there.

The DOS prompt icon works fine as it is, but advanced users might want to change the way MS-DOS runs when it starts up. Figure 20.5 shows the default Program Manager properties for the DOS prompt icon. Setup simply places the current command processor in the **Command Line** option of the properties.

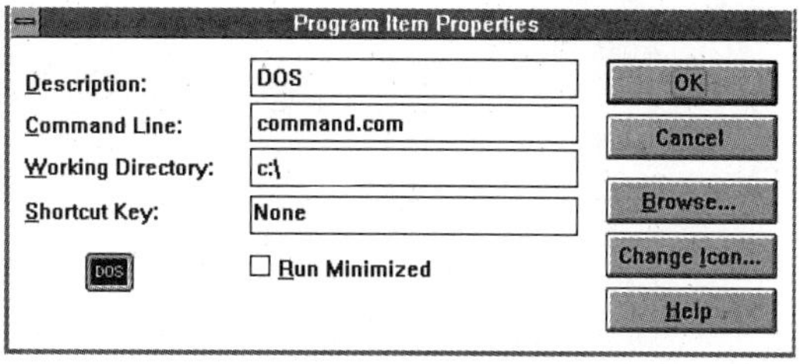

Figure 20.5. Properties of the DOS prompt.

You can create your own equivalent of the DOS prompt that has different features than the minimal ones provided by the DOS prompt. The following sections show advanced users how to add such features.

Increasing Environment Space

Often you will see the following error message when you start an MS-DOS session or run a batch file in an MS-DOS session:

```
Out of environment space
```

Environment space is where MS-DOS stores environment variables. Unless you specify how much you want, MS-DOS gives you a very small amount. When you start an MS-DOS session, that session gets a copy of all the environment variables, (such as PATH and SET) but only a fraction of space to add variables to. The rest of the environment space you allocated before running Windows is truncated.

You can increase the amount of environment space by giving program parameters to COMMAND.COM. The best way to do this is in the PIF for the icon you use to start the MS-DOS session. Creating and editing PIFs is described in Chapter 21, "Editing PIFs." Use the /E parameter in the Optional Parameters section of the PIF to reserve space. The /E parameter is used to set the size of the environment area.

20

For example, Figure 20.6 shows a PIF that reserves 1024 bytes of environment space for the MS-DOS session. A setting of –1 allocates as much Expanded Memory to a program as it requests, but this could cause the system to slow down.

Figure 20.6. PIF for reserving environment space.

Tip: The argument you use for the /E parameter depends on the version of MS-DOS you use. In MS-DOS version 3.2 or later, you specify the number of bytes in the /E parameter. In MS-DOS Version 3.1, you specify the number of units of 16 bytes, not the number of bytes.

Changing the MS-DOS Prompt

Often when you run the DOS prompt, you forget that you are running from within Windows. Forgetting this can result in many problems.

▲ You might try to run Windows again, which might cause your computer to lock up. You might see a message such as

```
Sharing error on Drive C:
```

or

```
Cannot run second instance of Windows. Exit this instance of
Windows and run from the original version of Windows.
```

▲ You might restart your computer, thinking that it is safe, instead of returning to Windows and quitting from Windows first.

▲ You might give a command that should not be given when you are in Windows. These commands are listed near the end of this chapter.

To remind yourself that you are in Windows and not in MS-DOS, you should add something to your MS-DOS prompt. For example, you might want to keep the same prompt but add Windows: to the beginning.

To automatically add a reminder to your prompt, follow these steps:

1. Create a batch file that contains these three lines:

```
@echo off
prompt Windows: %prompt%
%COMSPEC%
```

You can use the Notepad program to create the file. Of course, you can change the text that appears at the beginning of the prompt. The %prompt% keyword in the second line appends your current prompt after the text you add. The %COMSPEC% variable is used by DOS to find the COMMAND.COM file.

2. Save this batch file to disk. The file is called WINDOS.BAT.

3. Run the PIF Editor as described in Chapter 21, "Editing PIFs."

4. Enter the information shown in Figure 20.7. The dialog box you see might look different, depending on the operating mode you run in. However, the information you change in the dialog box is the same regardless of the mode. The two optional parameters are fairly important additions to the COMMAND.COM command. /E:500 indicates that you want an environment space of 500 bytes. If you have an /E parameter in your CONFIG.SYS file, the one here should be larger (because you are adding text to the PROMPT string). The /C parameter tells MS-DOS to run the batch file you just created to change the prompt.

5. Save this PIF to disk. The file is called WINDOS.PIF.

6. Create an icon in any of your program groups for this new PIF. The properties definition for the icon should look like Figure 20.8.

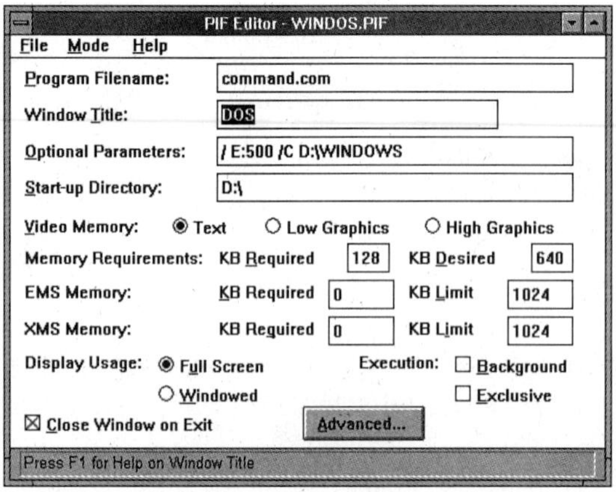

Figure 20.7. PIF for WINDOS.BAT.

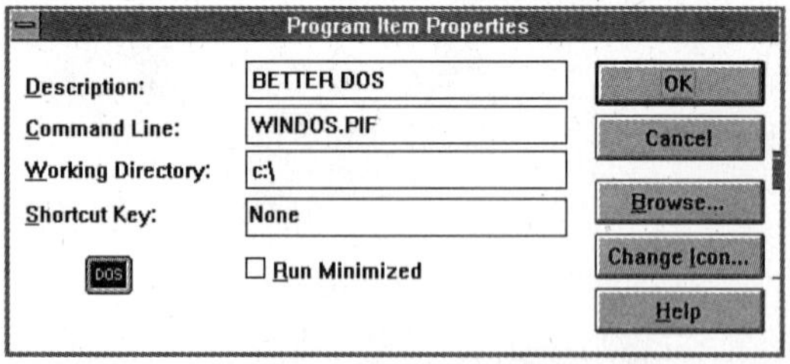

Figure 20.8. Properties for new icon.

Whenever you run the MS-DOS prompt from this icon, you will automatically get the new prompt.

Of course, you can add whatever you want to the batch file. For example, if there is a TSR you want to run only when you are starting DOS programs from Windows, you should add it to the batch file.

Differences Between Operating Modes

The way you view non-Windows programs and the way Windows treats these programs depends on the operating mode you use (standard or 386-enhanced). Operating modes are described in detail in Chapter 22, "Windows Operating Modes." For now, you need to know only which operating mode you run in. The fastest way to find out is with the **H**elp **A**bout Program Manager command. The mode is shown below the copyright notice, as shown in Figure 20.9.

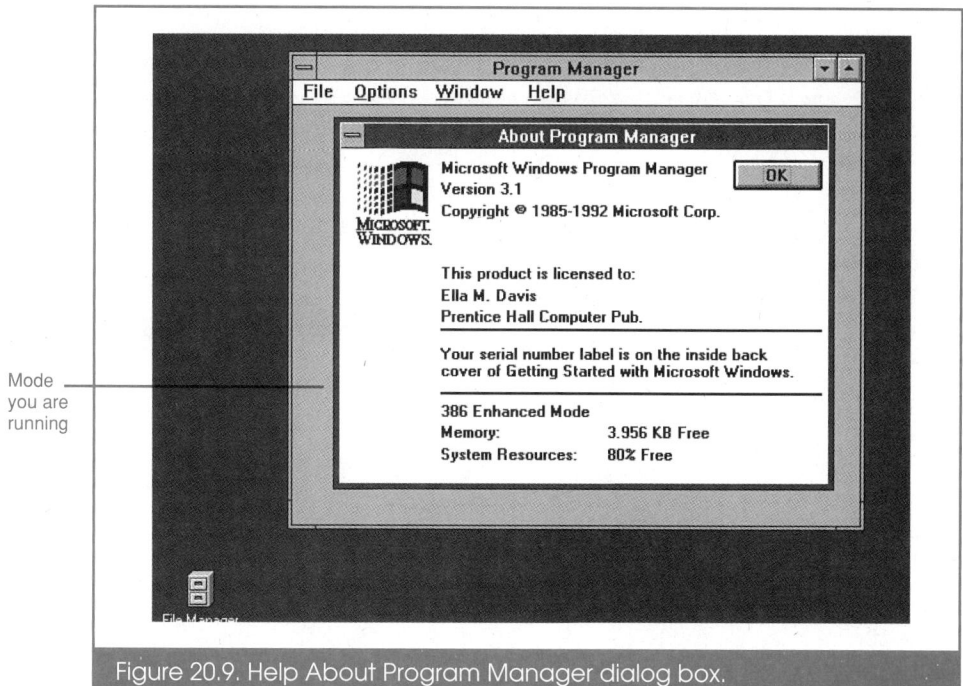

Mode you are running

Figure 20.9. Help About Program Manager dialog box.

Standard Mode

In standard mode, all non-Windows programs run full-screen; that is, you cannot run a non-Windows program in a window.

When you run or activate any non-Windows program, Windows suspends other Windows programs, meaning that information coming to them from your PC or devices is ignored. This can be a problem if you are running Windows programs that use a network or a modem, for example.

386-Enhanced Mode

In 386-enhanced mode, you can run many non-Windows programs in their own resizable windows. Also, when you run non-Windows programs, Windows continues to run other Windows programs in the background.

If you run in 386-enhanced mode, you can specify that text-based non-Windows programs run in their own windows rather than full-screen. Note that you cannot run graphics-based non-Windows programs in their own window: They must run full-screen. The mouse still is controlled by Windows alone, and is used to copy text from the window, as described later in this chapter.

When you run a combination-based program in a window, you must not switch to graphics mode. In WordPerfect, for example, the page preview mode is graphics-based and should be avoided if you are running in a window. Even if you do not switch to graphics mode, Windows might give you an error alert when you quit the program, as described in the next section.

To tell Windows 3.1 that you want a program to start in its own window in 386-enhanced mode, use the PIF Editor, described in Chapter 21, "Editing PIFs," on the program's PIF. You see a dialog box similar to Figure 20.10. Change the Display Usage choice from **Fu**ll Screen to **W**indow and save the changes to the PIF.

Even if you started the program in full-screen mode, you can change it to a window by pressing Alt-Enter while the program is running. Alt-Enter switches between windowed and full-screen mode regardless of whether you started the program in windowed mode.

If you are in windowed mode, you can switch to full-screen mode with the mouse.

1. Give the Settings command from the control menu in that program's window. You see a dialog box similar to Figure 20.11.

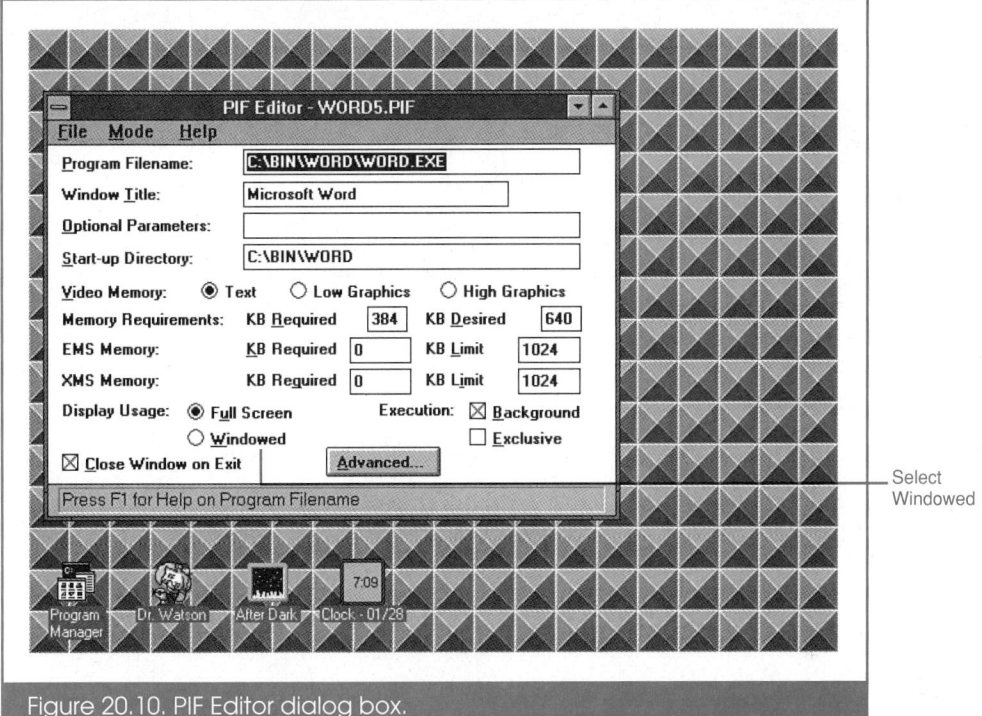

Figure 20.10. PIF Editor dialog box.

Select
Windowed

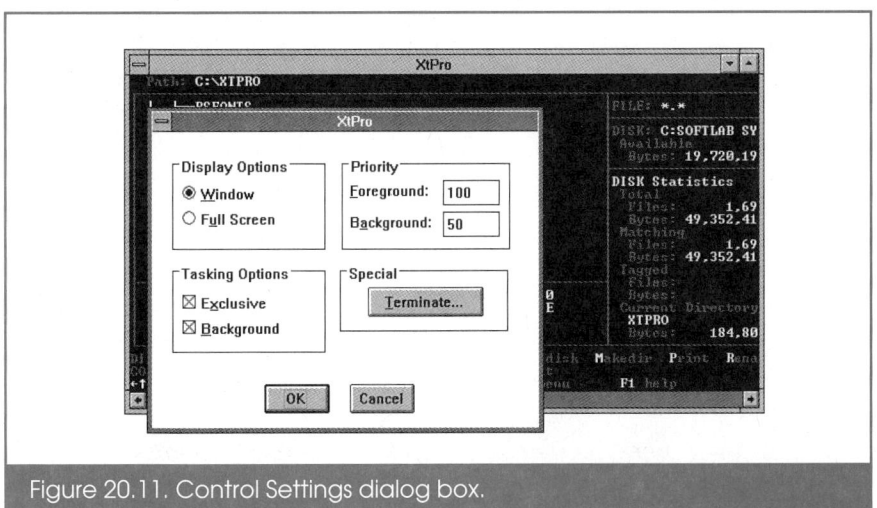

Figure 20.11. Control Settings dialog box.

2. Change the Display Options setting from **W**indow to **Fu**ll Screen.

3. Click OK.

Problems Switching into or Out of Windowed Mode

Changing to windowed mode works for many text-based programs, but it does not work for graphics-based programs. It also does not work for some combination-based programs such as Microsoft Word 5.5 or Microsoft Works 2.0. Even if you can start the combination-based program successfully, you might have problems when you quit the program.

If Windows detects a graphics-based element in a program you are starting in a window or a program you are switching to windowed mode by pressing Alt-Enter, you see a dialog box with the following message:

```
You cannot run this application in a window or in the back-
ground.
You can display it in a window, but it will be suspended until you
run it full screen. Check the PIF settings to ensure they are correct.
```

If you see this dialog box, click OK and switch back to full-screen mode.

If Windows shows the alert when the program is exiting, click OK. After you take the steps just mentioned, you might see an inactive window. You must close this inactive window from its control menu. Until you do, each time you press a key, Windows will beep at you.

Click the window's control menu and choose **C**lose.

Press Alt-Spacebar, then C.

Starting TSRs

It is common for people switching to Windows to be dependent on many TSR programs they use under MS-DOS. These TSRs fall into two general categories:

▲ Background device handlers such as network programs and mouse drivers

▲ Pop-up utilities available at all times

Background Devices

Background device handlers are almost always loaded in your AUTOEXEC.BAT and CONFIG.SYS files when you start your PC. You don't need to "start" them when you run Windows because they are already running. Most of these devices are useful to you even when you are not running Windows, so you might want to judge whether you really need them.

If you run Windows in 386-enhanced mode and there are special device drivers you need only when running Windows, you can use a special file to load them only during Windows. This situation is not common; it usually comes up only when you are using a device such as a main-frame network connection that you access only from within a Windows program.

If you have such a device and run Windows in 386-enhanced mode, you should not put the device driver in your CONFIG.SYS file because this wastes RAM for all your MS-DOS programs. Instead, create a file called WINSTART.BAT in your Windows directory that contains the name of the device driver program. You can do this with the Notepad program or another text editor. The device's documentation should have instructions for the exact command line to use in this file. The WINSTART.BAT file is loaded only when you start Windows in 386-enhanced mode, so the device doesn't waste RAM when you are not running Windows.

20

Pop-Up Utilities

Windows treats pop-up utilities like other MS-DOS programs. Thus, you should start them from within Windows the same way you start other non-Windows programs. Be sure to create a PIF for the utility, as described in Chapter 21, "Editing PIFs." As soon as you have loaded a pop-up utility in memory, it stays in memory until you quit Windows.

After you have started a pop-up utility, you activate it the same way you would activate it under MS-DOS—by pressing its special key combination. The only exceptions to this rule are utilities that use keystrokes used by Windows, such as Alt-Tab and Ctrl-Esc. If you have trouble activating a pop-up utility because it conflicts with Windows keystrokes, follow these steps:

MS
DS

1. Run the PIF Editor.

2. Open the PIF file for the utility.

3. In the Reserve Shortcut Keys section, choose the key that you need to activate the utility. If you run in 386-enhanced mode, you must click the **A**dvanced button to see this section. Choosing a key tells Windows not to use that key for itself when that program is running. For example, Figure 20.12 shows how to reserve the Alt-Enter key for your TSR.

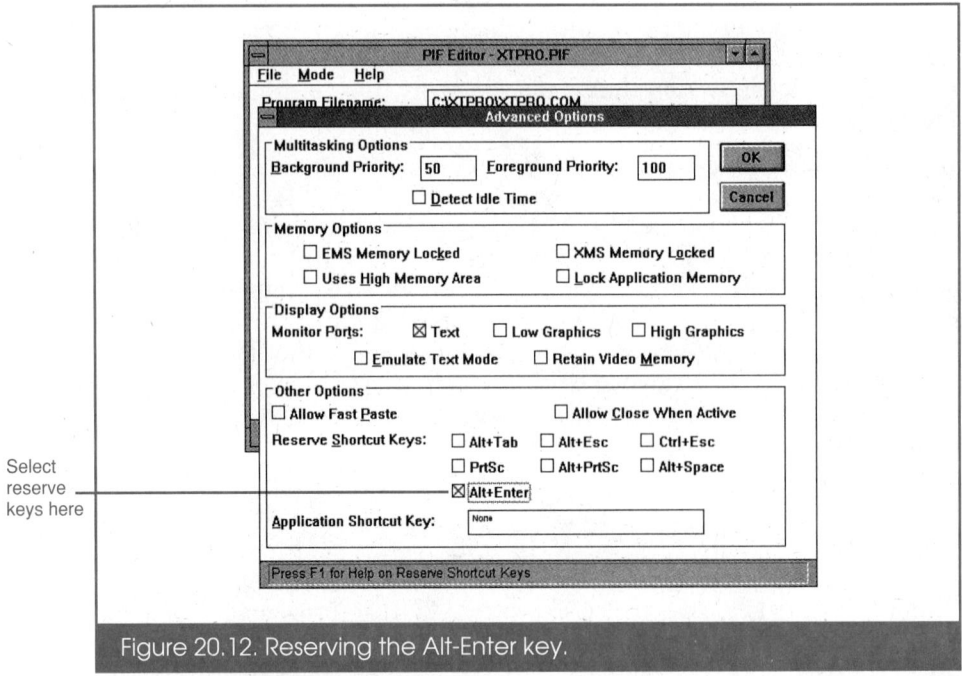

Select
reserve
keys here

Figure 20.12. Reserving the Alt-Enter key.

4. Save the changes to the PIF.

5. Quit from Windows.

6. Restart Windows to effect the changes.

Switching Between Programs

Non-Windows programs act the same as Windows programs after you have started them. You use the same actions to switch between programs. To switch to or from a non-Windows program, press Alt-Esc or use the Task Manager. For more information on these, see Chapter 5, "Program Manager."

Passing Data to and from Non-Windows Programs

Windows is weakest in passing information to and from non-Windows programs. As with Windows programs, you use the Clipboard to transfer information (as discussed in Chapter 9, "Clipboard Viewer"). The type of information you can put on the Clipboard or retrieve from the Clipboard is very limited, however.

The information you can copy to the Clipboard depends on the mode you run in and what type of non-Windows program you are running. Note that if you run in standard mode and your program is graphics-based, you cannot copy anything from that program to the Clipboard.

20

> **Tip:** A few non-Windows programs such as Microsoft Word can read from and write to the Windows Clipboard. Be sure to check the documentation for any non-Windows programs you use to see whether it supports their own transferring of information to and from Windows.

Copying Pictures of the Screen

When you run a text-based non-Windows program in any mode and you are running full-screen, you can copy a bit-mapped picture of the entire screen to the Clipboard by pressing the PrintScreen key on your keyboard. If the PrintScreen key does not copy the screen to the Clipboard, try Shift-PrintScreen or Alt-PrintScreen.

If you run in 386-enhanced mode and your non-Windows program is graphics-based, you can copy a picture of the screen to the Clipboard by pressing PrintScreen. Pressing the PrintScreen key when you are running Windows causes the image on your screen to be saved to the Clipboard—it does not print on your printer. You can look at the image by running Clipboard Viewer, and you can print it if you paste the contents of the Clipboard (your screen image) into any application (like Windows Write) that will accept the Clipboard's contents into a document.

In either case, you can paste the results of your copying into any Windows program that can handle graphics. You cannot paste the graphic back into a non-Windows program.

Copying Text in 386-Enhanced Mode

If you run in 386-enhanced mode and you are running in a window, you can copy a bit-mapped picture of the entire window to the Clipboard by pressing Alt-PrintScreen. Note that you cannot copy the text on the screen as text in the Clipboard if you run in standard mode.

If you run in 386-enhanced mode and are running in a window, you can copy text from your program to the Clipboard. This is a convenient way to copy text information to Windows programs. To do this, you must use commands from the **E**dit cascading menu in the window's control menu. The control menu with the **E**dit menu is shown in Figure 20.13.

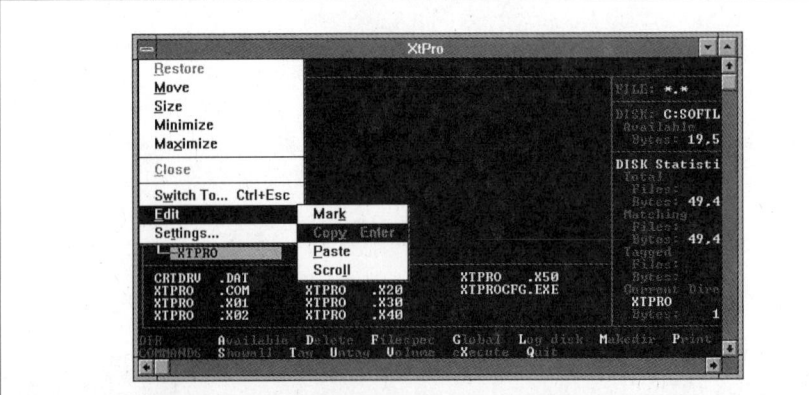

Figure 20.13. Edit menu in the Control menu.

To copy text to the Clipboard with the mouse, follow these steps:

1. Use the mouse to select the text you want to copy to the Clipboard.

2. Select the window's control menu.

3. Select the **E**dit cascading menu.

4. Give the **C**opy command.

To copy text to the Clipboard with the keyboard, follow these steps:

1. Press Alt-Spacebar to open the window's control menu.

2. Use the ↓ key or press E to show the **E**dit cascading menu.

3. Select the Ma**r**k command. A blinking rectangle appears in the window. You use this pointer to select the text you want.

4. Use the direction keys to move the pointer to one corner of the desired selection.

5. Hold down the Shift key and move the pointer to the opposite corner of the desired selection.

6. When you have made the selection, display the **E**dit menu again (with Alt-Spacebar, E) and click on the Copy Enter command with the mouse, or press C.

20

Pasting Text into Non-Windows Programs

You can paste text from the Clipboard to your non-Windows program using the control menu for the program's icon or, if you run in 386-enhanced mode and are using a window, from the window's control menu. You can paste text only into non-Windows programs; Windows does not enable you to paste if the Clipboard contains a graphic.

When Windows pastes text into a non-Windows program, it does so by typing the contents of the Clipboard. To the program, it is as if you were typing at the keyboard. Any line ends are typed into the program as return characters.

To paste text from the Clipboard into a full-screen program, follow these steps:

1. Make sure that the insertion point in your program is at the place where you want Windows to start "typing."

2. Press Alt-Esc to minimize the program and return to Windows.

3. Give the **Paste** command using the mouse or the keyboard:

Click the program's icon at the bottom of the screen to open the icon's control menu. Choose **Paste** from the menu.

Press Alt-Esc until the program's icon is selected. Press Alt-Spacebar to open the control menu, then press P to select **Paste**.

If you run in 386-enhanced mode, **Paste** is in the **Edit** cascading menu.

The steps for pasting to a non-Windows program running in a window are similar, except that you do not need to minimize the program. Simply select the **Paste** command from the window's control menu.

> **Tip:** If you run in 386-enhanced mode and you have trouble pasting into a non-Windows program, the program's PIF might be set to "fast paste" mode. Most programs have no trouble with this mode, but some do. Quit from the program, change the paste mode as described in Chapter 21, "Editing PIFs," and try pasting again.

Memory Considerations

Many situations might keep Windows from starting a non-Windows program due to lack of memory. Note that this problem is different from not having enough memory to run a Windows program. That topic is covered in Chapter 24, "Memory Configuration for Windows."

There are two ways to get a program running in a low-memory situation:

▲ Free memory in Windows.

▲ Reduce the amount of memory the program needs.

Freeing up Windows memory is described in detail in Chapter 24, "Memory Configuration for Windows."

As discussed in Chapter 21, "Editing PIFs," you can set the amount of memory a program needs in its PIF. You should be careful when reducing this amount because although most programs will start all right, they will crash later if they have too little memory.

If you run in 386-enhanced mode, you often can reduce the memory requirement for a program simply by running the program in full-screen display rather than in its own window. You can change the setting for this in the program's PIF, described in Chapter 21, "Editing PIFs."

You also can change whether a program runs full-screen as it is running. If the program fails to run successfully and displays an empty window, you can make the program run full-screen by using the Settings command in that window's control menu. Figure 20.14 shows the dialog box for a typical program. Simply change the Display Options setting from **W**indow to F**u**ll Screen and click OK.

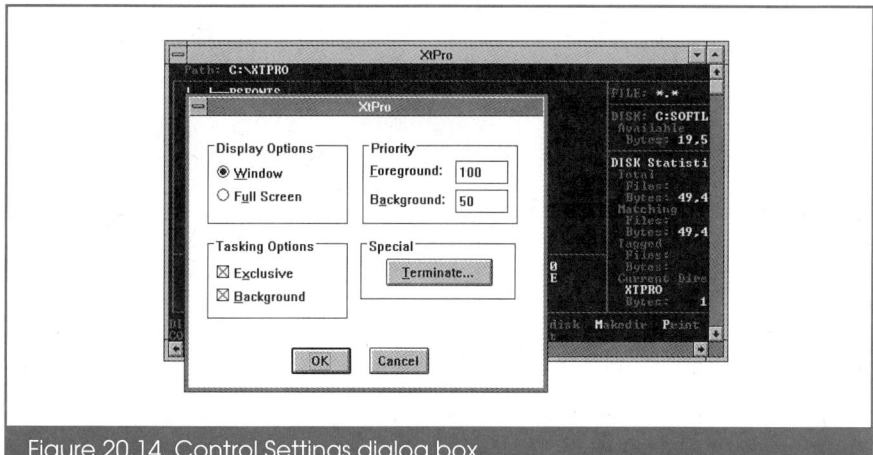

Figure 20.14. Control Settings dialog box.

Error Messages for Non-Windows Programs

There are dozens of error messages you might see when running Windows, but only a few of them relate to running non-Windows programs. This section lists the most common ones you might see and explains what they mean and how to avoid them.

20

System Integrity Violation

A non-Windows program that causes protected RAM errors will cause Windows to stop the program and display this message:

```
This application has violated system integrity and will be
terminated; close all applications, exit Windows, and reboot
your computer.
```

This means that the non-Windows program has scrambled memory that might be used by other programs. You should try to quit from other programs that are running, although it is likely that your system might lock up as you do so.

Warning: If you have unsaved documents in any of the other applications, you should not save them because that could save scrambled information to disk. Instead, save unsaved documents to files with new names and, as soon as you have started your programs again, check the new file to see whether it is in good shape.

Protected-Mode Programs

Some non-Windows programs, such as Borland's Paradox 3.5, use a form of memory handling called protected-mode memory. If you try to run one of these programs from 386-enhanced mode, you see this message:

```
Error: You have attempted to run a protected-mode application
in 386 enhanced mode. To run the application, exit and run
Windows using the WIN /S command.
```

In this case, first you should try to run Windows in standard mode with the MS-DOS command WIN /S.

Some non-Windows programs use a form of memory handling called VCPI (Virtual Control Program Interface). If you try to run one of these programs from 386-enhanced mode, you see the message just discussed, or possibly a different message. In this case, first you can try to run Windows in standard mode with the MS-DOS command WIN /S.

You still can run this program after you get the alert. When you click OK, Program Manager minimizes the icon. Simply double-click the icon or switch to it with Alt-Tab. The program then runs without trouble.

You should not run VCPI programs in 386-enhanced mode. Windows does not prevent you from running these programs after it has given you the warning, however. If you do not want Windows to warn you about running VCPI programs, you can modify your SYSTEM.INI file to add the following line in the [386ENH] section:

```
VCPIWarning=false
```

See Chapter 27, "Configuring with the WIN.INI and SYSTEM.INI Files," for more information on editing the SYSTEM.INI file.

Cannot Return to Windows

When you run a non-Windows program from standard mode, Windows creates a program swap file for every non-Windows program you run. These program swap files are temporary and are used only when you switch to or from the program. Windows normally places these files in the main Windows directory, but you can specify another directory to put the files in.

If you see the message

```
Cannot return to Windows /c start Windows again
```

after you quit from a non-Windows program, it means that Windows cannot find the swap file it needs. Windows looks for the swap file by checking the value of the SwapDisk parameter in the SYSTEM.INI file. If you want, you also can specify a directory for the swap files on the desired disk. See Chapter 27, "Configuring with the WIN.INI and SYSTEM.INI Files," for a description of editing the SYSTEM.INI file. For example, you might see the line

```
SwapDisk=D:
```

In general, you should choose the disk with the fastest access time that has more than a few megabytes free. If Windows runs out of program swap space, it does not let you run any more non-Windows programs.

Cannot Find File

Occasionally you might see the not terribly informative error message

```
Unable to open XXXXXXXX.XXX;
check to ensure the path and filename are correct.
```

20

This message usually is caused by having an invalid path or filename in the **P**rogram Filename field of a PIF you are starting. Use the PIF Editor to change the field to a valid program or batch file.

This error also might be seen if Windows cannot open the file because Windows does not have enough file handles. This can happen if the FILES= parameter in your CONFIG.SYS file is too low. If you are sure that the file in the PIF exists, edit your CONFIG.SYS file to increase the number of files available, restart your computer, and try running Windows again.

The following message is a second, more complete alert:

```
Cannot find file XXXXXXXX.XXX (or one of its components); check to
ensure the path and filename are correct and that all required
libraries are available.
```

You will see this warning if the name in the properties for an icon in Program Manager is invalid. To fix this problem, select the icon, give the **F**ile Properties command, and change the program name.

No Association Exists

If you installed Windows Version 3.1 in the same directory that you had a copy of Windows Version 2 located, you might see the dialog box with the following message when you try to start a non-Windows program from a PIF:

```
No application is associated with the data file. Choose
Associate from the File menu to create an association.
```

This message indicates that the installation program did not correctly update your WIN.INI file. In that file, there is a line that begins

```
programs=com exe bat
```

You should edit that line so that it reads

```
programs=com exe bat pif
```

See Chapter 27, "Configuring with the WIN.INI and SYSTEM.INI Files," for more information on editing the WIN.INI file.

Warnings and Limitations

Despite all its improvements over Version 3.0, Windows 3.1, still leaves us with some things to be desired. Absolute simplicity is still to be achieved by our friends at Microsoft. Until Windows and DOS are in effect, combined as they are in OS/2, we will have to live with the problems of using a graphical environment that has to deal with an underlying disk operating system. This section contains advice both weak and strong about some pitfalls to reckon with.

Dangerous Commands

Unfortunately, there are many MS-DOS commands you should never run *while* you are running Windows. These commands can cause unpredictable results for many reasons. In fact, some can cause you to lose files from your hard disk. The dangerous commands, utilities, and programs you should never run while running Windows include the following:

▲ The FORMAT command.

▲ The FASTOPEN command.

▲ The SHARE command.

▲ The APPEND command.

▲ The JOIN command.

▲ The SUBST command.

▲ Any utilities such as the Norton Utilities Disk Doctor or PCTools Fixdisk that change the low-level structure of a disk. This is an even greater problem if you are running SMARTDRV.EXE and Windows.

▲ Any disk unfragmenting or compression program such as Norton Speed Disk or PCTools Compress.

20

Changing Options While a Program Runs in 386-Enhanced Mode

You saw earlier how to change a non-Windows program running in 386-enhanced mode from full-screen to windowed. The Settings command in the window's control menu looks like Figure 20.15. The meanings of the Priority and Tasking Options settings are described in Chapter 21, "Editing PIFs."

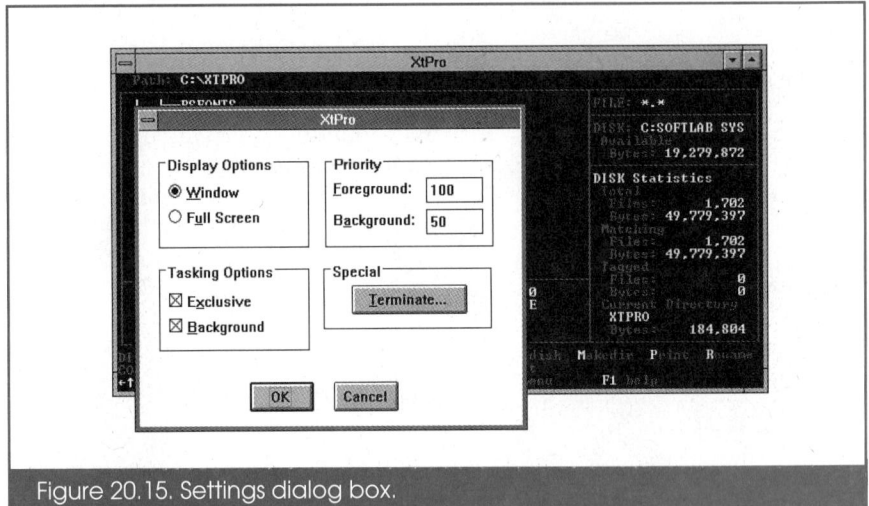

Figure 20.15. Settings dialog box.

Although Windows enables you to change the priorities and tasking options while running non-Windows programs, changing them can cause programs to crash. It is a much better idea to quit all non-Windows programs, change the options in the program's PIFs, then run the programs again.

The Terminate button enables you to stop a non-Windows program in a window if you cannot stop it from the program itself. When you select this button, Windows displays the dialog box shown in Figure 20.16. The warning is a good one because quitting a program in this fashion can cause serious memory problems and leave files open on your disk.

You should use the Terminate button only as a last resort. After you use it, you should quit Windows immediately in case the non-Windows program which you quit left memory unstable. To be especially cautious, you should reboot your computer as well.

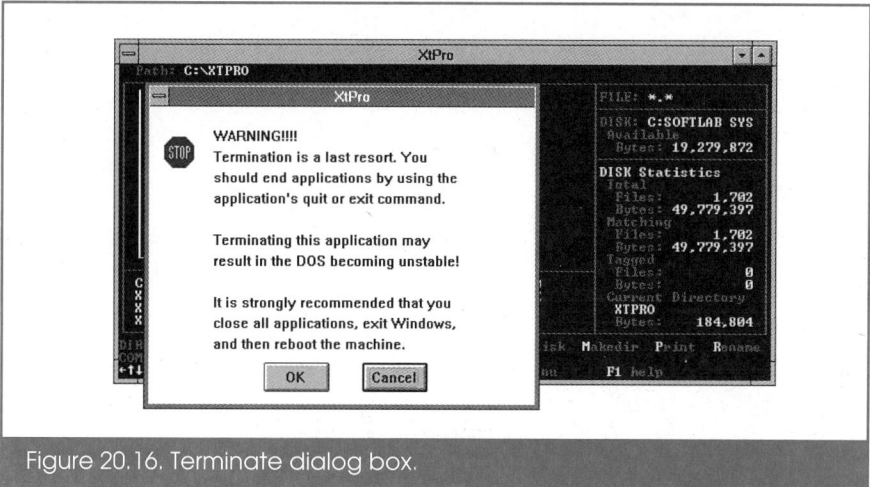

Figure 20.16. Terminate dialog box.

Losing the Video Image of the Program

20

When running a non-Windows program full-screen, you might not be able to see the characters on the screen anymore. This can happen for many reasons, some of them preventable. Occasionally this happens for no predictable reason and there is nothing you can do but quit the program and run it again.

If you use a screen-saving program such as Intermission or After Dark and the screen for the non-Windows program disappears after the screen-saving program stops, there probably is a conflict between the two programs. Sometimes this problem can be alleviated by changing the picture that the screen-saving program uses, but other times the conflict is unavoidable.

If you lose the screen image when your non-Windows program switches between two video modes, such as when it changes from text to graphics mode, there is not enough memory for both modes. If you run in standard mode, you cannot do anything about this situation. If you are running in 386-enhanced mode, you can change the program's PIF to use High Graphics for the video mode and select the Retain Video **M**emory option. If you are running in standard mode, be sure that the video mode in the PIF is set to Graphics/Multiple Text.

If you use an EGA monitor and run in standard mode, your non-Windows programs might use a custom EGA palette. Switching to and from these programs can cause strange colors to appear on your screen. If you have this problem, you must use the EGA.SYS driver that comes with Windows. It is copied to your main Windows directory automatically if you have an EGA monitor. Be sure that the driver is added to your CONFIG.SYS program with a line such as

```
DEVICE=C:\WINDOWS\EGA.SYS
```

Switching from Non-Windows Programs

Many things can prevent you from switching from a non-Windows program when you press Alt-Tab, Alt-Esc, or Ctrl-Esc. This section should help you determine what is keeping you from switching.

The most common reason for not being able to switch using one of the key combinations is that the program's PIF has reserved the combination for itself. Quit the program and edit the PIF as described in Chapter 21, "Editing PIFs," to check whether any of the combinations are reserved.

The next most common reason is that the program's PIF specifies the wrong video mode for the program. Quit the program and change the PIF to the correct video setting.

Two other PIF settings can prevent you from switching from the program. As you might imagine, setting the Prevent Program Switch option in the PIF would keep you from switching. The Directly Modifies options act the same as the Prevent Program Switch option because you cannot switch from a program that directly modifies hardware until that hardware is "cleared" by quitting the program. In either of these two cases, you cannot leave the program without quitting.

Warning: If a PIF that comes with a non-Windows program has the Prevent Program Switch or a Directly Modifies option set on, do not edit the PIF to turn off these options. The program probably will run but might cause Windows to act unpredictably or crash.

Another reason you might not be able to switch is that the program uses a video mode Windows does not know about. If Windows cannot save the contents of the screen, it does not switch from the program. This situation is rare because Windows knows about almost every video mode used in almost every common PC program.

> **Tip:** A few older MS-DOS programs steal all keyboard input from other programs, even Windows. In this case, you can never use the Alt-Tab, Alt-Esc, or Ctrl-Esc keys to switch from the program. You must quit the program in the normal fashion first. If a DOS program remaps the keyboard for its own keystroke combinations, some of the Windows keystroke combinations will be superceded when you are running the DOS program.

Running Extended Memory Programs

Two standards for programs, DPMI and VCPI, use extended memory. These are described in Chapter 24, "Memory Configuration for Windows." DPMI programs run fine under Windows. Non-Windows programs that were written exactly to the VCPI standard might run well in standard mode, but there is no guarantee. Check the documentation for DOS-based programs that you intend to run, or contact the customer support group for the company that sells the DOS-based program you want to run to learn if your program uses one of these standards.

20

General Safety

Although all non-Windows programs are supposed to work fine under Windows, often they do not. Your computer can crash, forcing you to reboot your system or at least quit the program unexpectedly. The following tips, although inconvenient, should reduce the number of problems you have running non-Windows programs.

▲ Run only one non-Windows program at a time. Making Windows juggle more than one program can cause the two programs to conflict.

▲ Do not run non-Windows programs when backing up your hard disk with a Windows backup program. Some programs, such as WordPerfect 5.1, have problems when Print Manager has been used during a Windows session.

▲ Do not run non-Windows programs from Windows in the background in 386-enhanced mode. Many programs will crash, sometimes locking up your entire system.

▲ Minimize Windows programs before running a non-Windows program. This gives the program more memory and reduces the chance that a Windows program will do something unexpected in the background.

▲ Use HIMEM.SYS for your extended memory management. Even though some commercial products are better, most program manufacturers have tested their non-Windows programs only with HIMEM.SYS. HIMEM.SYS is described in Chapter 24, "Memory Configuration for Windows."

▲ If you do not need to access files on the network while you run non-Windows programs, boot your system without the network software. This gives the programs more memory and reduces the chance of a device problem.

CHAPTER

21

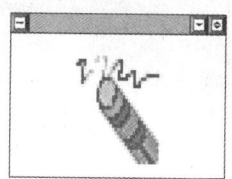

Editing PIFs

In some cases, PIF (*Program Information Files*) are required in order to run your DOS-based programs. This is especially true of memory hogs, like many of the executive word processors. PIF files can improve the performance of DOS-based programs that don't need the special treatment the PIF files offer. In fact, once you get used to Windows 3.1, you will start looking for ways to speed up the programs you use, above and beyond things you can do to improve general system performance.

PIF files are a great way to hone your application's ability to maximize the resouces inside your computer. PIF files are particularly adept at improving the way programs react to each other when they are competing for your system's resources in memory as well as getting attention from the central processing unit.

If you ever want to consider yourself a "power user," you must learn to use PIFs for all of your DOS- or character-based programs, and for many of your Windows or graphical-based programs.

What Is a Program Information File?

A PIF is a file that stores data about a program. Essentially, you can think of it as a compiled .INI file that handles operating details for the program. The PIF is used to determine how much of a resource (in this case, memory, ports, and so on) the program gets to use, and how strongly it is allowed to compete with other programs for additional needed resources.

Windows uses a PIF every time it runs a non-Windows program. If there is no PIF for the program, Windows uses the PIF stored in the file called _DEFAULT.PIF in the same directory as Windows. You can change the values of the settings in a program's PIF to make the program run better. Note that many non-Windows programs come with PIFs from their manufacturers that have already been set to the best settings based on the manufacturer's experience with Windows.

Each PIF has options for two modes. Standard options cover standard mode, and 386-enhanced options cover 386-enhanced mode. Almost all the settings in the PIF for the same program can be different for the two modes. Only the program name and the window title are the same.

Locating PIFs

When you start a non-Windows program, Windows first looks in the directory of the program for a file with the same name as the program with the extension .PIF. If Windows finds the file, it uses that as the PIF. If that file doesn't exist, Windows looks in the same directory as Windows for a file by that name and uses it if it is found. If there is not a PIF in either directory, Windows uses _DEFAULT.PIF. You can keep a PIF file anywhere, really, but you will have to provide the full pathname so Windows can find it in the Program text box provided in Program Manager's Properties dialog box. Some people use this last method so they can store PIFs in a subdirectory kept just for PIFs.

Warning: This example is extremely important: If you are running the program BOOKSELL.EXE from the directory c:\invprogs, Windows looks first for c:\invprogs\booksell.pif, then looks for c:\windows\booksell.pif. If neither is found, it uses c:\windows_default.pif. You must place each PIF where Windows can find it or you will have created the PIF for naught.

21

Running the PIF Editor

Run the PIF Editor from the Accessories window of Program Manager. It puts up a simple window that looks like a standard Windows dialog box. The window you see depends on the mode you are running in. Figure 21.1 shows the dialog box for standard options. Note that standard mode is covered by one dialog box.

PIF Editor - [Untitled]

File   Mode   Help

Program Filename: |

Window Title:

Optional Parameters:

Start-up Directory:

Video Mode: ● Text   ○ Graphics/Multiple Text

Memory Requirements: KB Required   128

XMS Memory: KB Required   0   KB Limit   0

Directly Modifies: ☐ COM1   ☐ COM3   ☐ Keyboard
                       ☐ COM2   ☐ COM4

☐ No Screen Exchange   ☐ Prevent Program Switch
☒ Close Window on Exit   ☐ No Save Screen
Reserve Shortcut Keys: ☐ Alt+Tab   ☐ Alt+Esc   ☐ Ctrl+Esc
                        ☐ PrtSc   ☐ Alt+PrtSc

Press F1 for Help on Program Filename

Figure 21.1. PIF Editor dialog box for standard options.

If you are running in 386-enhanced mode, the dialog box has two parts. Figure 21.2 shows the dialog box you see when you run the PIF Editor. There are more options for 386-enhanced-mode PIFs. Clicking the **A**dvanced button at the bottom of the dialog box brings up a second dialog box, shown in Figure 21.3.

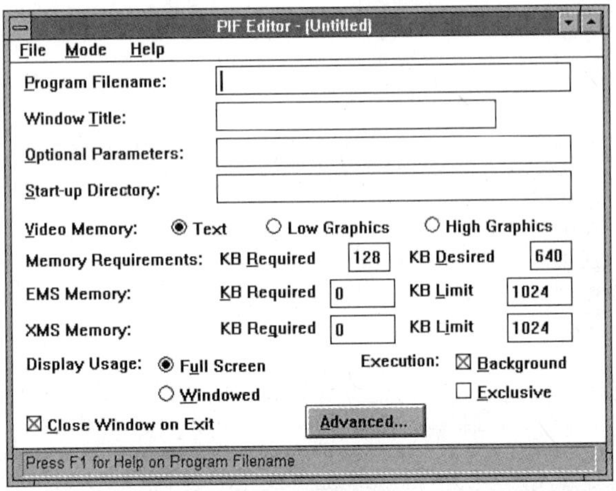

Figure 21.2. Initial PIF Editor dialog box for 386-enhanced mode.

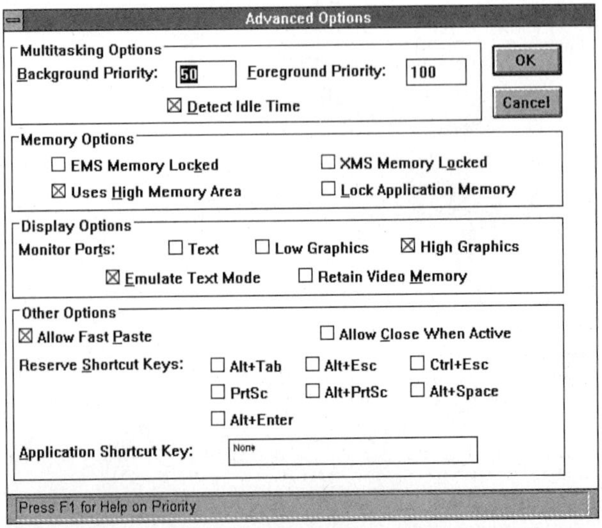

Figure 21.3. PIF Editor Advanced dialog box for 386-enhanced mode.

Related items in 386-enhanced mode appear in both dialog boxes. In this chapter, the items are described by topic, not by position in the dialog box. They are marked as appearing in the "main" or "advanced" dialog boxes.

21

> **Tip:** Note that many of the settings for the two modes are similar but that they have some important differences. In this chapter, the settings that are identical are covered first, then the settings for standard mode, then the settings for 386-enhanced mode. If you need to know about both modes, you should read the material carefully and not assume that the information is the same as for the other mode.

Changing the Mode

The PIF Editor initially displays the mode that you are running in. Because every PIF has two sets of options, it is important to make settings for both modes if you will run the non-Windows program in both modes. It is also very important to make settings for both sets of options if you are going to give the PIF to someone else or put it on a network, because you have no idea what mode that person will be in when he or she uses the PIF. You create a PIF filename when you save the PIF. You can change each PIF filename slightly so that you know which PIF is for standard mode and which PIF is intended to run in 386-enhanced mode.

To change the mode, select the desired mode (Standard or 386-Enhanced) from the **M**ode menu. When you change modes, the PIF Editor displays this alert:

```
Windows is not running in standard mode. The PIF information you
enter may not be appropriate. Are you sure you want to switch
to this mode?
```

Simply click OK or press the Enter key.

PIF File Menu

The PIF Editor's **F**ile menu is similar to those in many Windows programs. Figure 21.4 shows the **F**ile menu. The **F**ile **N**ew command starts a new PIF, and the **F**ile **O**pen command opens a PIF that already exists on disk. The **File Save** and **File Save As** commands save PIFs to disk. Use the **File Exit** command to leave the PIF Editor.

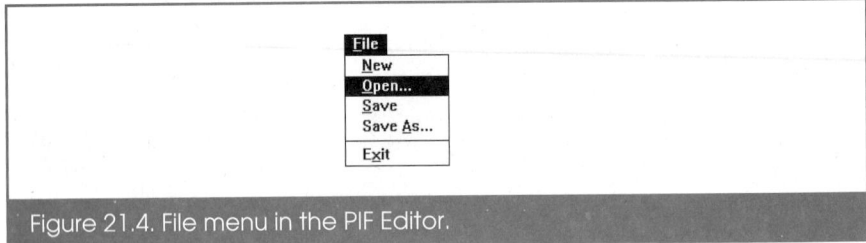

Figure 21.4. File menu in the PIF Editor.

Default PIF

The _DEFAULT.PIF file comes with fairly standard settings. As you can see from Figure 21.5, however, the program filename is one that does not come with Windows. You can edit the _DEFAULT.PIF file just like other PIFs if you don't want to create a special PIF for just one DOS program that you may use. You will learn what each of the settings mean starting in the next section.

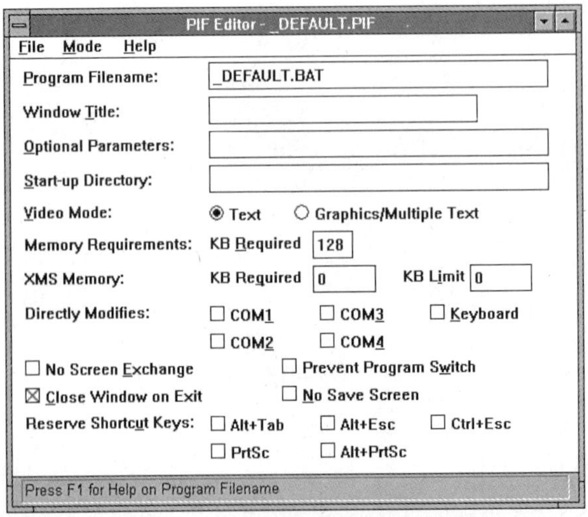

Figure 21.5. Standard settings for _DEFAULT.PIF.

Basic PIF Settings for Both Modes

These settings are used in both standard and 386-enhanced modes:

- ▲ **P**rogram Filename
- ▲ Window **T**itle
- ▲ **O**ptional Parameters
- ▲ **S**tart-up Directory

21

Program Filename

Enter the name, including the path, of the file with which the PIF is associated; for example, C:\123\123.EXE. You must enter something in this field. Enter only the filename, not any arguments you use with the program. You can enter the names of .COM, .EXE, or .BAT programs.

This field is used only when you run the PIF from File Manager or when you make a Program Manager icon that is associated with the PIF rather than with the program. You do this from Program Manager's File Properties dialog box. Use the PIF file name instead of the program name. In these cases, Windows needs to know what you want the PIF to run, and it looks in this field.

Window Title

This field is optional. If you leave it blank, Windows uses the filename of the program for the minimized icon or the window title.

Optional Parameters

Use this field to enter any parameters you normally would put on the MS-DOS command line. If you are using the PIF to cause the program to always start by opening a document, you would enter the document name here. You also would use this field for any parameters such as /S that you would use with the command. This field is optional; if you use it, it can be up to 62 characters long.

You might want to change the parameters you give to the program each time you run it. It would be tedious to have to edit the PIF each time to change the parameters. Instead, enter a single question mark for the **O**ptional Parameters. This causes Windows to display a dialog box similar to the one shown in Figure 21.6 when you start the program. Type the parameters you want in the dialog box (or don't enter anything if you want no parameter) and click OK.

Figure 21.6. Dialog box for prompted parameters.

Start-Up Directory

Enter the path name of the directory you want the program to start in. Entering a path here causes the program to start as if you had run the program from the named directory. For example, if your PIF looks like Figure 21.7, the WP program will act as if you had given the MS-DOS command C:\WP51\WP MARTYL from the directory c:\letters\cpa.

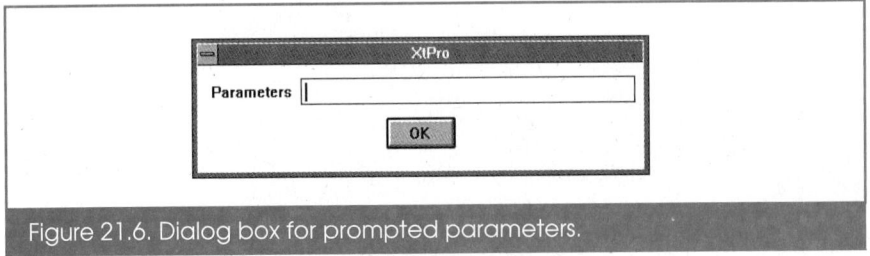

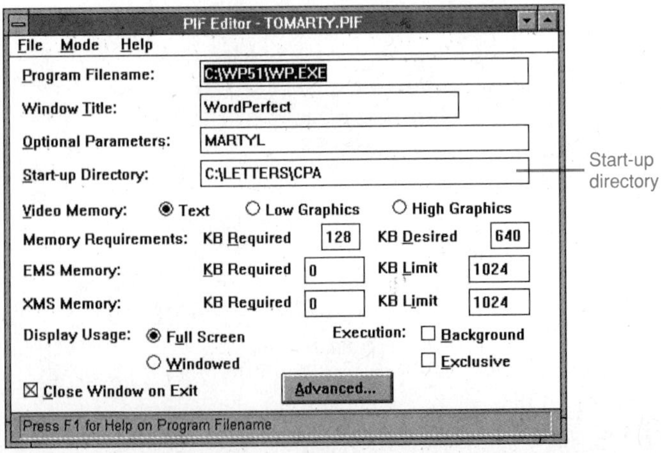

Figure 21.7. Example of a start-up directory.

21

> **Warning:** Some older MS-DOS programs require that you run the program from the program's home directory, not from any other directory on your hard disk. This is not common, but if your program requires this, you must put the name of the program's home directory in the **S**tart-up Directory field in order for the program to run correctly.

Standard Mode Video and Memory

In standard mode, Windows needs to know what type of video adapter you are using and the amount of memory the non-Windows program needs in order to run the program. This information is necessary because Windows has to move aside and give as much memory as possible to the program. By setting these options correctly for the program you are running, you leave the most memory possible for the program and are more confident that the program will run correctly.

The settings for Windows standard mode video and memory are shown in Figure 21.8.

Figure 21.8. Video and memory options for standard mode.

Video Mode

You need to tell Windows which type of video you are using so that it can set aside the proper amount of memory for the program. Text mode takes less memory than graphics mode. If your program uses only text mode, it can run on a plain monochrome display adapter (MDA) without any graphics support. If your program uses any graphics, even if it uses graphics only part of the time, such as in a special preview mode (like the page preview feature of many word processors), you must select the Graphics/Multiple Text option.

It is usually safer to choose the Graphics/Multiple Text option if you are not sure whether the program has a graphics component to it. Windows reserves more memory for these programs than for text-based programs so that if the program turns out to be text-based, it will have enough graphics memory. Some text-based programs, however, need all the memory they can get. Because choosing the Graphics/Multiple Text option takes away memory from the program, this might keep the program from running due to too little memory.

> **Tip:** If you are using a Hercules monochrome graphics adapter or an adapter that is compatible with the Hercules standard, you should choose the Graphics/Multiple Text option. Many programs use the Hercules adapter's graphics modes even if they are displaying only text. Choosing the Graphics/Multiple Text option assures you that your program can use all of the card's capabilities.

Memory Requirements

This option tells Windows the least amount of memory that the program needs. It has nothing to do with how much memory Windows will give: Windows always gives the maximum amount of conventional memory available to the program. However, this maximum amount might not be enough. If the documentation for your program tells you how much memory is absolutely required (as compared to desired) in order for the program to run, enter that number here.

Tip: Note that the documentation for many programs specifies the amount of memory that your PC should have in order to run the software. This number is not the amount of memory required. Generally, the number required is 128K less than the amount of memory that is required for your computer. (The rest of the memory goes to MS-DOS and some assumed overhead for device drivers.)

21

Warning: Note that the default amount provided by the PIF Editor, 128K, is archaic. Very few modern MS-DOS programs require less than 256K, and many, in fact, require 384K or more. When editing PIFs, you should be careful to set this option as required by the program. Many non-Windows programs do a very poor job of checking for low memory conditions as the program is running and have a tendency to crash when there is just enough memory.

XMS Memory

There are many types of memory, as described in Chapter 24, "Memory Configuration for Windows." XMS memory is memory that conforms to the current industry standard for extended memory. (Extended memory is the memory over 1M.) This standard is catching on with many software developers, and major programs such as Lotus 1-2-3 Version 3.0 and 3.1 use it. Note that this is different from the expanded memory standard often called "LIM EMS 4.0." (Expanded memory managers can access the memory between 640K and 8M, if your applications require it.) LIM EMS 4.0 is a weighty acronym for the Lotus-Intel-Microsoft Expanded Memory Specification, Version 4.0. The three manufacturers (LIM) got together to create some kind of standard for memory management, because there were no clear standards due for implementation by ANSI (American National Standards Institute) at that time.

The KB **R**equired is the amount of XMS memory that the program needs in order to run. Few programs absolutely require XMS memory, so this setting usually is 0. Setting this option to anything other than 0 causes switching to this program or away from this program to be very slow.

The KB Limit is the maximum amount of XMS memory you want to give to this program. Set this to –1 to give the program all the XMS memory it wants, or set it to some value to limit the amount it can use.

Warning: Note that many programs take all the memory they can get and thereby leave other programs with none available. Also, the more XMS memory the program uses, the slower switching to and from the program will be. Use this option judiciously, or you will be closing windows to gain available memory more often.

Leave both these settings at 0 to prevent the program from using any XMS memory. This makes switching to and from the program faster but limits the amount of memory the program has access to.

Standard Mode Program Switching

The remaining options in the standard mode PIF relate to how Windows switches to and from a non-Windows program. In a perfect world, Windows could just switch in and out without worrying about what the program is doing. This cannot be the case, however, because many non-Windows programs do things that would adversely affect other non-Windows programs as well as Windows programs you might be running.

Windows runs best when you do not run any non-Windows programs, because Windows programs conform to very tight operating standards. These standards make it much easier for Windows to make assumptions about what can and cannot be done when switching between programs. Because there are no such standards for non-Windows programs, you need to pay attention to the most common things that can prevent Windows from switching to and from the programs.

Warning: If your program comes with a PIF that has any of these options set, be sure not to change those settings unless specifically instructed to do so by the company that made the program. Changing these settings can cause unpredictable results with Windows and the other programs you are running.

The settings for standard mode switching are shown in Figure 21.9.

21

PIF Editor - TOMARTY.PIF

File   Mode   Help

Program Filename:	C:\WP51\WP.EXE
Window Title:	WordPerfect
Optional Parameters:	
Start-up Directory:	C:\LETTERS\CPA
Video Mode:	● Text ○ Graphics/Multiple Text
Memory Requirements:	KB Required 128
XMS Memory:	KB Required 0 KB Limit 0
Directly Modifies:	☐ COM1 ☐ COM3 ☐ Keyboard
	☐ COM2 ☐ COM4

☐ No Screen Exchange   ☐ Prevent Program Switch
☒ Close Window on Exit   ☐ No Save Screen
Reserve Shortcut Keys: ☐ Alt+Tab   ☐ Alt+Esc   ☐ Ctrl+Esc
                         ☐ PrtSc   ☐ Alt+PrtSc

Press F1 for Help on Program Filename

— Miscellaneous options

Figure 21.9. Switching options for standard mode.

Directly Modifies

If a non-Windows program directly modifies one of the serial ports (often called COM ports) or the keyboard without using standard MS-DOS calls, Windows will not let you switch from that program. This is because there is no way Windows can know what the state of the ports or the keyboard would be while you were running the program. Thus, selecting any of these options prevents you from switching from this program without quitting.

If other non-Windows programs or Windows programs use any serial ports, those programs could crash or receive unexpected results if you switched from this program. Of course, almost every Windows program uses the keyboard, so any untraceable use of the keyboard could have serious effects on other programs.

You might wonder how this situation comes about. Programmers have two options when they want to communicate with hardware on your PC:

▲ Use MS-DOS programming calls that go through the operating system.

▲ Use instructions that communicate with the hardware without going through the operating system.

The first method is safer and the one that is preferable. If the programmer uses the first method, Windows has no problems, and none of the choices here need to be selected. The second method, however, makes the program run faster; thus, many programmers use the second method. If you are using a program that was written using the second method, you must indicate that by selecting the appropriate choices in this section of the PIF. Most reputable software developers tell you whether they are handling hardware directly, either in the documentation or during installation of the software. These days, most of the handling of hardware in this direct fashion is done by software programs that work closely with a video card, for example.

Tip: Selecting the **K**eyboard option in this section prevents any of Windows's task-switching or screen-saving keys from having any effect. If you are sure you never want to switch away from this non-Windows program, you can select the **K**eyboard option to give your program a little more memory.

No Screen Exchange

If you never want to copy a picture of the screen to the Windows Clipboard, select No Screen **E**xchange. This option frees up a small amount of memory for your program. When this option is selected, the PrintScreen and Alt-PrintScreen keys have no effect on Windows, and they take whatever actions they would have in your program.

Prevent Program Switch

This is the generic way of preventing you from switching from your program. Selecting Prevent Program **S**witch prevents you from switching back to Windows without quitting the program. A positive side effect of this option is that it gives your program a little more working memory.

Close Window On Exit

Normally you want this option selected. It is used to determine what happens when you quit the program. If you deselect this option, you must press any key on the keyboard to return to Windows.

▲ If your program is text-based or combination-based and was in text mode when you quit, Windows puts up the message Press Any Key To Exit in the lower-right corner of the screen.

▲ If your program is graphics-based, you see a black screen with no words on it.

In either case, press any key to return to Windows.

> **Tip:** Note that changing this option for standard mode also changes it for 386-enhanced mode.

No Save Screen

This option determines whether Windows saves the image on the screen when you change programs. Some character-based or text-based programs have the capability to save their own screens within the memory Windows allocated to them. If you select this option, Windows saves the screen in order to make it available when you switch back from another application. This takes additional memory. If you can potentially run short on memory when you are switching between programs, don't check this box. Try not to use this option, especially if you are being asked to close windows to create memory. Most modern text-based programs manage their own screen solutions without the need for help from Windows.

Reserve Shortcut Keys

Many non-Windows programs use shortcut key combinations such as Ctrl-C and Alt-R. Some use the same shortcut keys as Windows uses, namely Alt-Tab, Alt-Esc, and Ctrl-Esc. For example, XyWrite uses the Alt-Tab key combination to bring up a tab table. Some programs also use PrintScreen and Alt-PrintScreen, which also conflict with Windows.

If you want those key combinations to be used by the non-Windows program rather than by Windows, use this section of the PIF to reserve them for the program. Note that setting these in the PIF affects only the current program, and that other programs will still use these keys in the normal Windows fashion.

> **Tip:** Do not select all three of the switching keys (Alt-Tab, Alt-Esc, and Ctrl-Esc) unless you do not want to be able to switch from the program. If you select two of the three switching keys, you still can use the third to switch to other applications or back to Program Manager. If you select all three keys in the PIF, you will not be able to leave the application without quitting.

386-Enhanced Mode Memory

The Memory Requirements choices for conventional memory from the main dialog box are shown in Figure 21.10. The Memory Options area of the advanced dialog box, used to control the use of memory outside of conventional memory, is shown in Figure 21.11.

Memory Requirements

There are two options for setting the amount of conventional memory: the amount required and the amount desired. The amount required tells Windows the least amount of memory that the program needs. The amount required has nothing to do with how much memory Windows will give: Windows will give up to the maximum amount of conventional memory specified in the amount desired.

If the documentation for your program tells you how much memory is absolutely required (as compared to desired) in order for the program to run, enter that number here. Setting this option to –1 prevents Windows from checking the amount of conventional memory that is free. This is a very dangerous choice.

21

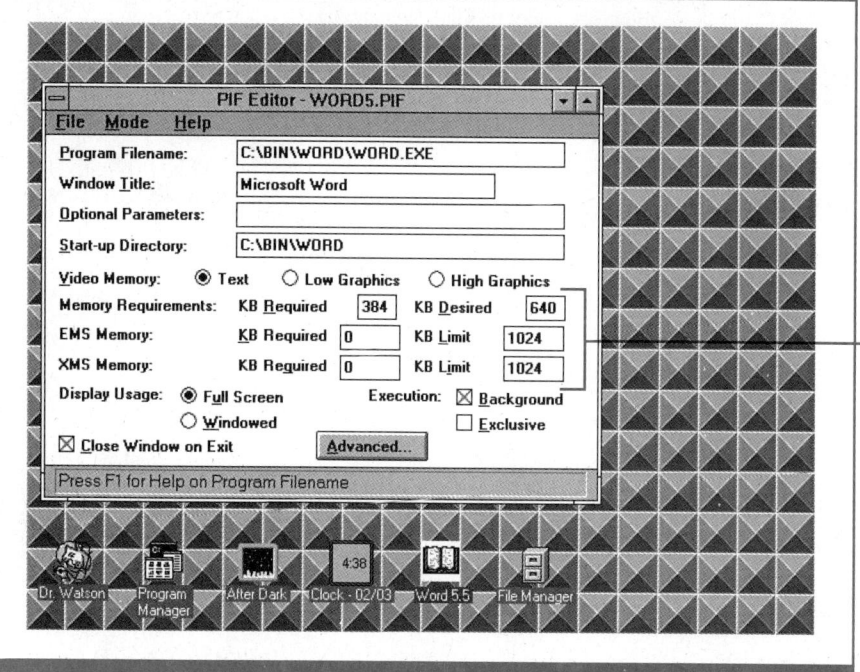

Used to set
memory requirements

Figure 21.10. 386-enhanced mode memory requirements options.

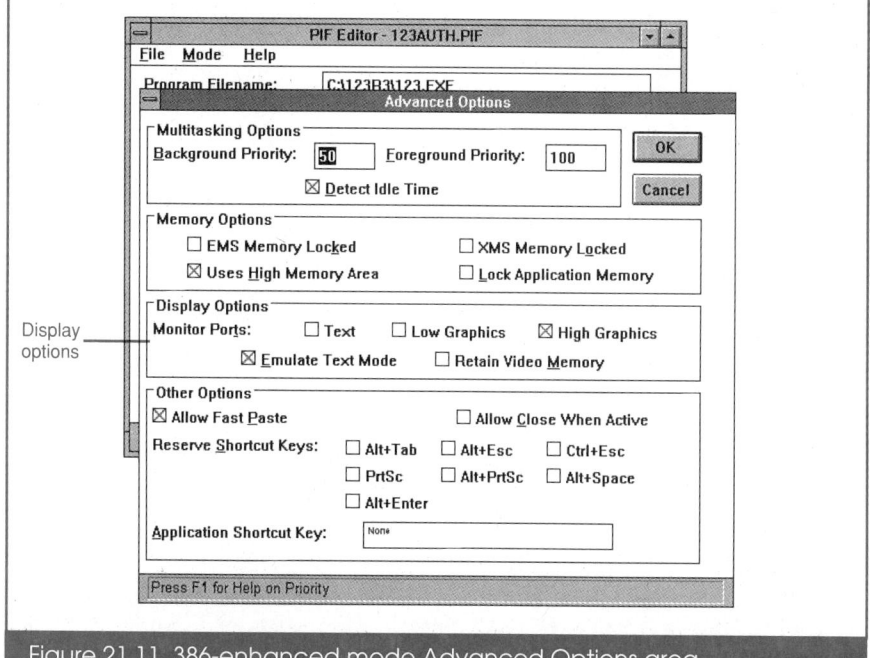

Display
options

Figure 21.11. 386-enhanced mode Advanced Options area.

Tip: Note that the documentation for many programs specifies the amount of memory that your PC should have in order to run the software. This number is not the amount of memory required. Generally, the number required is 128K less than the amount of memory that is required for your computer. (The rest of the memory goes to MS-DOS and some assumed overhead for device drivers.)

Warning: Note that the default amount provided by the PIF Editor, 128K, is archaic. Very few modern MS-DOS programs require less than 256K, and many, in fact, require 384K or more. When editing PIFs, you should be careful to set this option as required by the program. Many non-Windows programs do a very poor job of checking for low memory conditions as the program is running and have a tendency to crash when there is just enough memory.

KB **D**esired is the limit of conventional memory (under 640K) you want to give to the program. The only time you would want to set this less than 640K is when you are running out of memory for Windows and you want to save the memory for other programs. Generally, you will leave this option set to 640K.

EMS Memory

Many non-Windows programs can use expanded memory (the memory between 640K and 1 M) to enhance their speed and the number of features they offer (expanded memory sometimes is called LIM memory). Note that "expanded memory" is different from "extended memory," as described in Chapter 24, "Memory Configuration for Windows." Extended memory is the memory over 1M. Many older non-Windows programs need expanded memory (here called EMS memory) and cannot use the extended memory that Windows uses. Thus, Windows must simulate expanded memory for them. Use the two EMS Memory choices to specify the amount of simulated expanded memory you want to make available to the program. Note that this EMS memory is simulated and is thus slower than using actual EMS memory.

21

KB **R**equired is the amount of EMS memory that the program needs in order to run. Few programs absolutely require EMS memory, so this setting usually is 0. Set this number above 0 only if the program's documentation says that a certain amount of extended memory must be present in order to run.

KB **L**imit is the maximum amount of EMS memory you want to give to this program. Note that many programs take all they can get and thereby leave other programs with none available, so you probably should put a limit on the amount you are willing to allocate to this program. The default value of 1024K is reasonable: It is similar to running the program not under Windows on a PC with 2M of RAM installed.

Locking a program's EMS memory prevents Windows from swapping the memory to disk. This makes the program run faster but usually causes other programs to run slower. Some programs, however, require this option to be set in order for them to run under Windows without crashing.

XMS Memory

XMS memory is memory that conforms to the current industry standard for extended memory. This standard is catching on with many software developers, and major programs such as Lotus 1-2-3 version 3.1 use it. Note that this is different from the expanded memory standard, often called "LIM EMS 4.0." XMS, or extended memory is all memory located above the 1 megabyte mark, assuming you have more than 1 megabyte of memory.

KB Re**q**uired is the amount of XMS memory that the program needs in order to run. Few programs absolutely require XMS memory, so this setting usually is 0. Setting this option to anything other than 0 causes switching to this program or away from this program to be very slow.

KB L**i**mit is the maximum amount of XMS memory you want to give to this program. Note that many programs take all they can get and thereby leave other programs with none available, so you probably should put a limit on the amount you are willing to allocate to this program. The default value of 1024K is reasonable: It is similar to running the program not under Windows on a PC with 2M of RAM installed.

Locking a program's XMS memory prevents Windows from swapping the memory to disk. This makes the program run faster but usually causes other programs to run slower. Some programs, however, require this option to be set in order for them to run under Windows 3.1 without crashing.

Uses High Memory Area

This option tells Windows whether to try to use the memory in the high memory area (also known as the HMA). The high memory area is 64K of memory that has special meaning to 80286 and higher CPUs. It is described in Chapter 24, "Memory Configuration for Windows."

If a program is using the high memory area, Windows will never try to use the high memory area for your non-Windows programs, regardless of the setting. If you are not using such devices and you have this option checked, Windows lets your program use the high memory area as normal XMS memory.

The only time you would want to turn this option off is if you thought that some hardware or a device would use the high memory area after you were already running Windows. This is rare.

Lock Application Memory

This option locks the program's conventional memory and prevents Windows from swapping it to disk. This makes the program run faster but usually causes other programs to run slower. A small number of programs, however, require this option to be set in order for them to run under Windows without crashing.

386-Enhanced Mode Display

The option for full-screen or windowed operation is in the main dialog box, as shown in Figure 21.12. The other display options are in the Advanced dialog box in the Display Options area, as shown in Figure 21.13.

Display Usage

As described in Chapter 20, "Other DOS Programs and Windows," you can open a non-Windows program in 386-enhanced mode in its own

21

window under certain conditions. The Display Usage choices specify whether the program starts in full-screen mode or windowed mode. You can switch between the two modes after the program has begun.

PIF Editor - TOMARTY.PIF

File   Mode   Help

Program Filename: `C:\WP51\WP.EXE`

Window Title: WordPerfect

Optional Parameters: MARTYL

Start-up Directory: C:\LETTERS\CPA

Video Memory: ◉ Text   ○ Low Graphics   ○ High Graphics

Memory Requirements: KB Required   128   KB Desired   640

EMS Memory: KB Required   0   KB Limit   1024

XMS Memory: KB Required   0   KB Limit   1024

Display Usage: ◉ Full Screen   Execution: ☐ Background   ⟵ Usage options
               ○ Windowed   ☐ Exclusive
☒ Close Window on Exit   Advanced...

Press F1 for Help on Program Filename

Figure 21.12. 386-enhanced mode Display Usage options.

PIF Editor - 123AUTH.PIF

File   Mode   Help

Program Filename: C:\123R3\123.EXE

Advanced Options

┌Multitasking Options──────────────────────────────┐
Background Priority: 50   Foreground Priority: 100   OK
                  ☒ Detect Idle Time   Cancel

┌Memory Options────────────────────────────────────┐
   ☐ EMS Memory Locked   ☐ XMS Memory Locked
   ☒ Uses High Memory Area   ☐ Lock Application Memory

┌Display Options───────────────────────────────────┐
Monitor Ports: ☐ Text   ☐ Low Graphics   ☒ High Graphics   ⟵ Advanced display options
          ☒ Emulate Text Mode   ☐ Retain Video Memory

┌Other Options─────────────────────────────────────┐
☒ Allow Fast Paste   ☐ Allow Close When Active
Reserve Shortcut Keys: ☐ Alt+Tab   ☐ Alt+Esc   ☐ Ctrl+Esc
                    ☐ PrtSc   ☐ Alt+PrtSc ☐ Alt+Space
                    ☐ Alt+Enter

Application Shortcut Key: None

Press F1 for Help on Priority

Figure 21.13. 386-enhanced mode Display Options area.

Monitor Ports

A few programs use nonstandard methods for displaying text and graphics. In general, most programs use standard methods for displaying information and are not much of a problem for Windows. If a program you are using uses one of the nonstandard methods, Windows has to monitor the program's interaction with the displays. Because this monitoring slows down the program, it shouldn't be done unless necessary. Due to the way that high-resolution graphics adapters were designed, Windows generally needs to monitor the high-resolution ports (but not always).

If the display of the non-Windows program is garbled, has unexpected colors, or does not appear, you probably need to monitor the ports. If it is a text-based program with these problems, select Text; if it is a CGA graphics-based program with these problems, select Low Graphics.

Windows needs to know how much video memory the program needs when you start the program. This is the minimum amount of video memory that the program will get. If you are running the program and it switches into a higher video mode that requires more memory, Windows will allocate more memory to it if there is more memory available. If there is no more memory available, the program crashes or the display is partially or totally lost. Thus, it is important to choose the highest video setting that you might use during a session. The three video modes are shown in Table 21.1.

Table 21.1. 386-enhanced mode video modes.

Mode	Description
Text	If your program uses only text mode, it can run on a plain monochrome display adapter (MDA) without any graphics support. This mode takes less memory than either graphics mode, about 16K.
Low Graphics	This mode usually is for old-style graphics, commonly called CGA graphics. Few new PCs come with CGA graphics anymore, but many older systems and many laptop PCs use CGA graphics. This mode takes about 32K of memory.
High Graphics	This mode corresponds to EGA and VGA graphics, the current standards for PCs. This mode takes about 128K of memory.

Tip: If your program is graphics-based and seems to be updating the screen especially slowly, you might want to try deselecting the High Graphics option. Also, turning off these options makes running non-Windows programs a little faster. However, this may prevent you from being able to switch away from this program under Windows.

21

If there is any chance that your program will switch into EGA or VGA mode and you might run short of memory because you are running many other programs, you should select High Graphics in the PIF so that enough memory is put aside for the program.

Tip: If you are using a Hercules monochrome graphics adapter or an adapter that is compatible with the Hercules standard, you should choose the High Graphics option. Many programs use the Hercules adapter's graphics modes even if they are displaying only text. Choosing the High Graphics option assures you that your program can use all of the card's capabilities.

Warning: Windows uses the setting for Video Memory only to determine the minimum amount of memory the program needs to start. Windows might not save the amount you tell it if the program starts in a lower mode. In order to reserve enough memory in the higher mode, you also must set the Retain Video **M**emory option, described in the following section.

Retain Video Memory

When you start a program, Windows looks at the **V**ideo Memory setting and compares it to the type of video the program is using. If the program is using a lower mode than you specified in the **V**ideo Memory setting, Windows can return that extra memory to the memory pool to be used by other programs. This usually is not a problem, because when your program switches to a higher mode, Windows gives your program more memory if it is available. Character-based programs intended to run from DOS can switch between video types in order to display ASCII text and then display charts or graphs, for example.

If there is no more memory available, the program crashes, or the display is partially or totally lost. To prevent this, you need to prevent Windows from taking away unused video memory by setting the Retain Video **M**emory option. This option locks the amount of memory you set in the **V**ideo Memory option and prevents Windows from taking it away if it isn't being used when you are in a lower mode.

Emulate Text Mode

This option makes almost all text-based programs run faster, because it helps Windows display text quickly. Generally, you should leave it selected. (It has no effect on graphics-based programs.)

However, if you are running a text-based or a combination-based program and text is missing from the screen, text appears scrambled, the cursor appears in the wrong place, or the cursor doesn't appear at all, you should turn this option off. This action rarely is necessary.

386-Enhanced Mode Multitasking

The options that allow a non-Windows program to continue running in the background or prevent other programs from doing so are in the main dialog box, as shown in Figure 21.14. The other options for multitasking are in the Advanced dialog box in the Multitasking Options area, as shown in Figure 21.15.

Note that the **B**ackground, E**x**clusive, and **B**ackground and **F**oreground options also are available from the Settings command in the control menu if you are running the non-Windows program in windowed mode. This dialog box is shown in Figure 21.16.

Background Execution

When you switch from a non-Windows program to another program in 386-enhanced mode, the program can keep running. For example, if you are running a telecommunications program that is receiving data, you don't want that program to be suspended when you switch. You want it to keep running so that it can continue to receive data. Similarly, many non-Windows database management systems and spreadsheets can continue to process data in the background if you select this option.

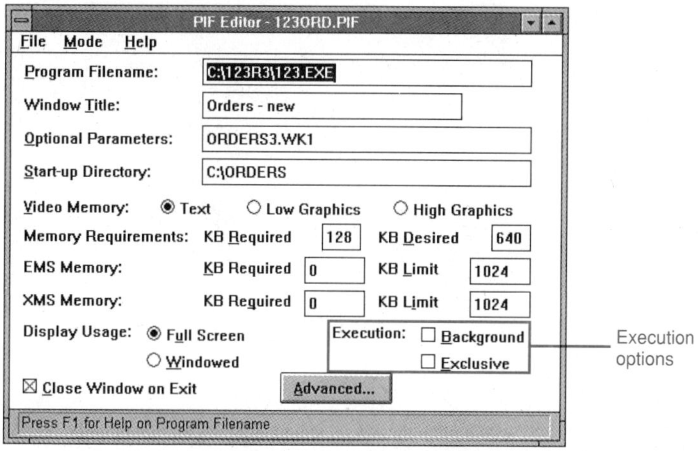

21

PIF Editor - 123ORD.PIF

File   Mode   Help

Program Filename: C:\123R3\123.EXE

Window Title: Orders - new

Optional Parameters: ORDERS3.WK1

Start-up Directory: C:\ORDERS

Video Memory: ● Text   ○ Low Graphics   ○ High Graphics

Memory Requirements: KB Required   128   KB Desired   640

EMS Memory: KB Required   0   KB Limit   1024

XMS Memory: KB Required   0   KB Limit   1024

Display Usage: ● Full Screen   Execution: ☐ Background
                 ○ Windowed   ☐ Exclusive

☒ Close Window on Exit   Advanced...

Press F1 for Help on Program Filename

Execution options

Figure 21.14. 386-enhanced mode execution options.

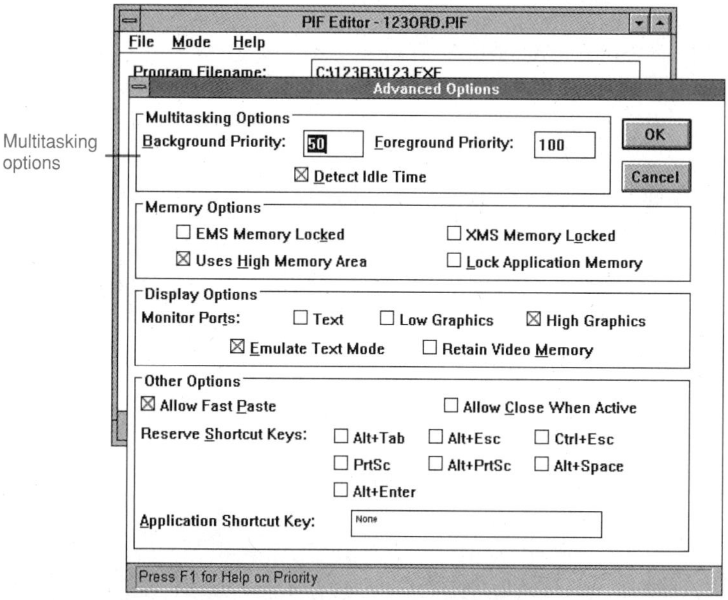

PIF Editor - 123ORD.PIF

File   Mode   Help

Program Filename: C:\123R3\123.EXE

Advanced Options

Multitasking Options
Background Priority: 50   Foreground Priority: 100   OK

☒ Detect Idle Time   Cancel

Memory Options
☐ EMS Memory Locked   ☐ XMS Memory Locked
☒ Uses High Memory Area   ☐ Lock Application Memory

Display Options
Monitor Ports: ☐ Text   ☐ Low Graphics   ☒ High Graphics
                 ☒ Emulate Text Mode   ☐ Retain Video Memory

Other Options
☒ Allow Fast Paste   ☐ Allow Close When Active

Reserve Shortcut Keys: ☐ Alt+Tab   ☐ Alt+Esc   ☐ Ctrl+Esc
                         ☐ PrtSc   ☐ Alt+PrtSc ☐ Alt+Space
                         ☐ Alt+Enter

Application Shortcut Key: None

Press F1 for Help on Priority

Multitasking options

Figure 21.15. 386-enhanced mode Multitasking Options area.

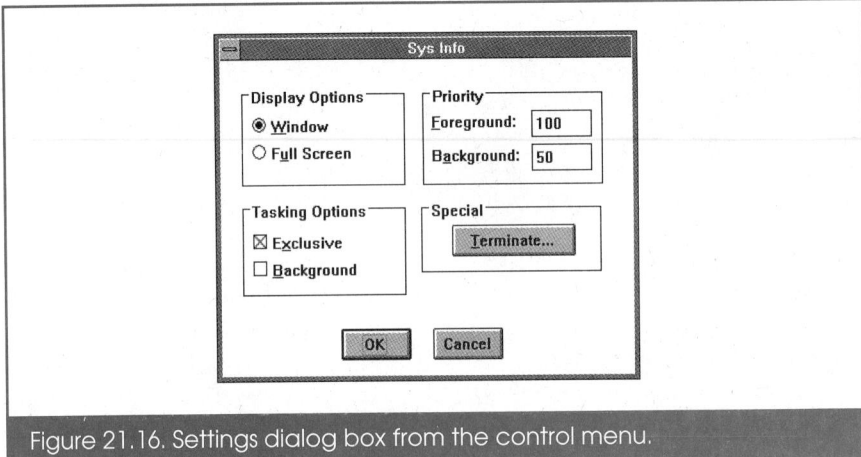

Figure 21.16. Settings dialog box from the control menu.

Exclusive Execution

If you select exclusive execution, all other programs (both Windows and non-Windows) are suspended when this program is active. This is true even for other non-Windows programs that have **B**ackground execution selected. Setting this option gives an application more memory and processor time, although not so much as to make you want to set the option for all non-Windows programs.

In general, you should set this option only for programs that would be adversely affected by other programs taking system resources in the background. For example, your telecommunications program might lose characters if it multitasks with other programs. If so, you should set the E**x**clusive option in its PIF or switch to Exclusive mode in the Settings command in the control menu if the program is in windowed mode.

Foreground and Background Priorities

A program's priority is the relative amount of processor time the program gets when you are multitasking. Priorities are relevant only when you are running multiple non-Windows programs that can run in the background. If you are not ever going to be in this situation, you can safely skip this section.

21

Tip: When you deal with priorities of non-Windows programs, you also should think about how much priority you want to give to Windows programs running at the same time. These priorities are set in Control Panel and are described in Chapter 7, "Control Panel."

Every program has two priority numbers: the foreground and the background priorities. The foreground priority is the relative amount of processor time the program gets when it is running in the foreground, and the background priority is the relative amount of processor time the program gets when it is running in the background.

Priorities can have any value from 0 to 10,000. Note that priorities are relative, not absolute. To determine how much processor time a program will get, add up the priorities of each program running and divide the relevant priority by the sum.

For example, use the example programs in Figure 21.17 to calculate the relative processor time for three programs running at the same time. Note that each program must have the **B**ackground option set. The program running in the foreground, A, has a foreground priority of 75; program B has a background priority of 50, and program C has a background priority of 25. The sum is 150, so A gets half (75/150) of the processor time as it runs in the foreground, B gets 33% (50/150) as it runs in the background, and C gets 16% (25/150) of the processor time as it runs in the background.

Note that when you switch between these programs, the amount of processor time changes. For example, when B is running in the foreground, the total priorities are 175 (100 for B, 50 for A, 25 for C). Therefore, B gets 57%, A gets 29%, and C gets 14%.

Tip: If you want to be sure that a program gets as much processing time as possible when it is in the foreground, you can set the foreground priority to 10,000. It is better, however, to use the **Ex**clusive option described earlier than to set the foreground priority to its highest.

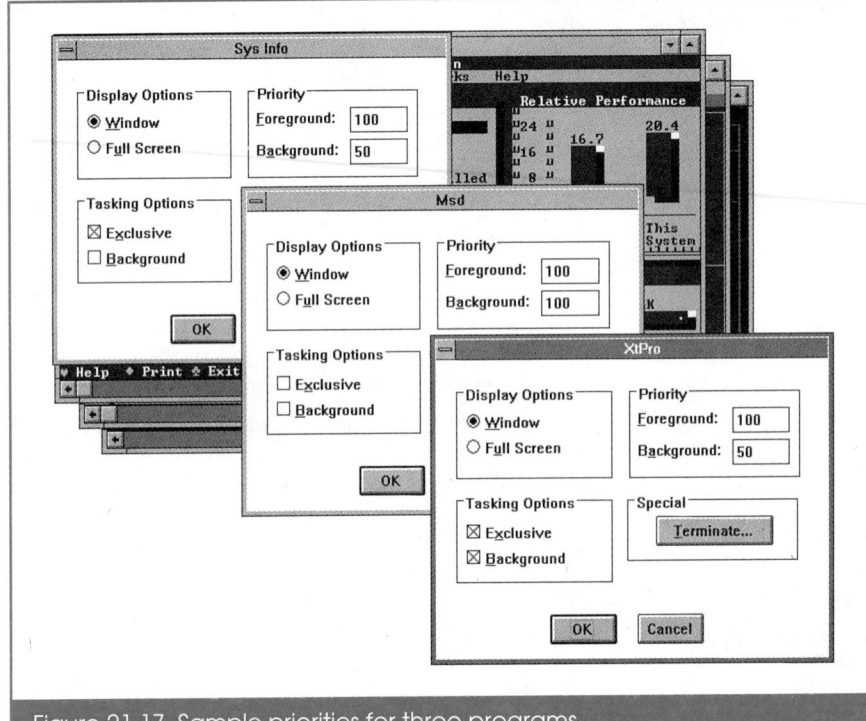

Figure 21.17. Sample priorities for three programs.

Detect Idle Time

Normally, you want Windows to give unused processor time to other resources. Windows can detect when a program is idle and locate most of its processor time away from it toward other programs. As soon as the program is no longer idle, it gets back its full processor allocation. This helps the entire system run more smoothly.

This option should be deselected only in cases where the program seems to be running much slower than expected. This slowness might be due to Windows's guessing incorrectly about when the program is idle. If deselecting this option speeds the program up, you should keep it deselected in that program's PIF. In general, however, you will want to enable this option by selecting the check box provided.

386-Enhanced Mode Program Switching

The options discussed in this next section pertain to those of us who switch between programs in 386-enhanced mode.

21

Close Window on Exit

You normally want this option selected. It is used to determine what will happen when you quit from the program. If you deselect this option, you must press any key to return to Windows.

▲ If your program is text-based or combination-based and is in text mode when you quit, Windows puts up the message Press Any Key To Exit in the lower-right corner of your screen.

▲ If your program is graphics-based, you see a black screen with no words on it.

In either case, press any key to return to Windows.

> **Tip:** Note that changing this option for standard mode also changes it for 386-enhanced mode.

Allow Close When Active

This option enables you to quit from Windows even if this program is running. This rarely is safe because most programs open files when they run, and leaving the program without closing the files can cause you to lose information. You should select this option only for programs that do not write to files, and only when you think that you will leave Windows without wanting to (or being able to) quit from the program.

Allow Fast Paste

Pasting to a non-Windows program in 386-enhanced mode is covered in Chapter 20, "Other DOS Programs and Windows." Most programs can take "fast" pasting, and Windows almost always can detect those that can't and uses a slower pasting mode. You should deselect this check box only if you have tried pasting to the program and had some characters lost or nothing pasted.

> **Tip:** Remember this caveat: Selecting this option dedicates additional memory (possibly unused) whether or not the application needs it.

Reserve Shortcut Keys

Many non-Windows programs use shortcut key combinations such as Ctrl-C and Alt-R. Some use the same shortcut keys as Windows uses, namely Alt-Tab, Alt-Esc, Ctrl-Esc, Alt-Spacebar, and Alt-Enter. For example, XyWrite uses the Alt-Tab key to bring up a tab table. Some programs also use PrintScreen and Alt-PrintScreen, which also conflict with Windows.

If you want those key combinations to be used by the non-Windows program rather than by Windows, use this section of the PIF to reserve them for the program. Note that setting these in the PIF affects only the current program, and that other programs will still use these keys in the normal Windows fashion.

> **Tip:** Do not select all four of the switching keys (Alt-Tab, Alt-Esc, Ctrl-Esc, and Alt-Enter) unless you do not want to be able to switch from the program. If you select three of the four switching keys, you will still be able to use the fourth to switch to other applications or back to Program Manager. If you select all four keys in the PIF, you will not be able to leave the application without quitting.

Application Shortcut Key

If you want to bring a particular non-Windows program to the foreground, you might find it tedious to cycle through all of the running programs with the Alt-Esc key combination or to bring the Task List

21

forward with the Ctrl-Esc key combination. Windows enables you to specify a key that will always bring a non-Windows program to the foreground. Whenever you press this key (whether you are running a Windows or a non-Windows program), the program will come to the foreground.

As you might imagine, you want to pick a key combination that is not important to any of the other programs you are using. The key combination must include the Alt key, the Ctrl key, or both. You are restricted from using a combination that includes the following keys:

▲ Backspace

▲ Enter

▲ Esc

▲ PrintScreen

▲ Spacebar

▲ Tab

To assign a shortcut key combination, follow these steps:

1. Put the insertion point in the **A**pplication Shortcut Key field.

2. Press the desired key combination.

3. Click OK.

The PIF Editor spells out the key combination in the text entry box. To delete a key combination, put the insertion point in the field and press Shift-Backspace.

Tip: You probably should not use Alt and a letter as the key combination, because doing so would preclude you from choosing a menu in a Windows program that had that combination. The best keys to use are those that rarely are used by either Windows programs or non-Windows programs. Good choices for key combinations include the following:

▲ F11, F12, and combinations that include them, such as Ctrl-F11

▲ Alt and a number, such as Alt-9

▲ Ctrl or Alt and keys from the numeric keypad, such as Ctrl-1

Getting the Most from PIFs

PIFs can be powerful in the hands of the knowledgeable. If you are so
inclined, you can continue to fine-tune your system's performance after
you have made all of the global improvements that you can make. One
of the ways to work on bettering your Windows environment is to use
PIFs to optimize individual program performance.

Creating Multiple PIFs

You might want to have many PIFs for one program and run the
program from the PIF. This is most common when you want different
command-line options when running the program at different times.
Conversely, you might want the program to start with a different startup directory in different circumstances.

Any time you want a different PIF setting for a program you use often,
simply create additional PIFs and run from the PIF rather than from
the program. For example, assume that you want to start 1-2-3 in two
ways:

▲ Open the file ORDERS3.WK1 and have the default directory be
c:\orders.

▲ Open the file AUTHORS.WK1 and have the default directory be
c:\books\old.

You would create two PIFs. The first might be called 123ORD.PIF and
is shown in Figure 21.18. The second might be called 123AUTH.PIF
and is shown in Figure 21.19.

Next, you want to create Program Manager icons for each of these PIFs.
Give the File New command, select Program Item, and fill in the
properties dialog box with a description of the icon and the name of
the PIF (not the program). Figure 21.20 shows the dialog box for
123ORD.PIF; the PIF file for 123AUTH.PIF would look similar.

Changing _DEFAULT.PIF

The file _DEFAULT.PIF is just like any other PIF file. You can change
the options in it for both modes just like you do other PIF files. The only
time you would do this is when the settings that Microsoft assigned are
not what you want for the non-Windows programs that do not have
PIFs.

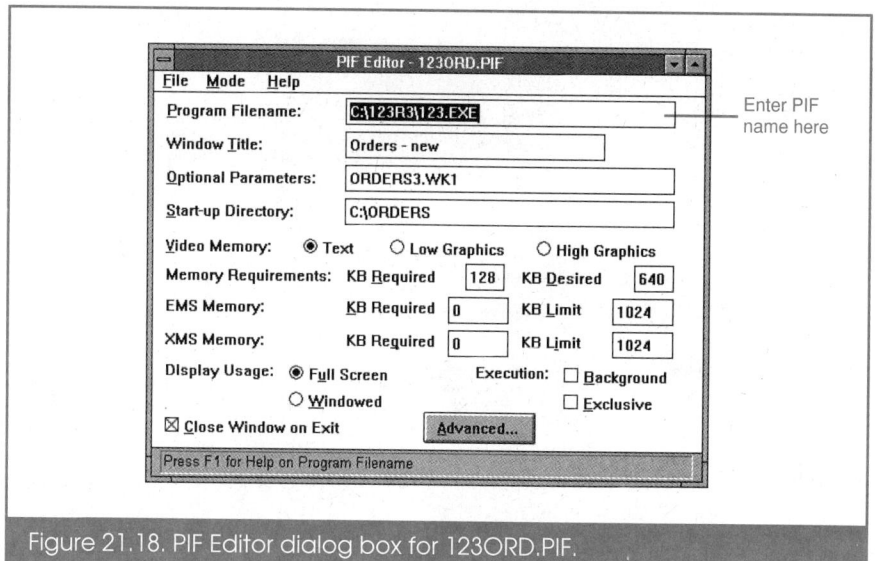

Figure 21.18. PIF Editor dialog box for 123ORD.PIF.

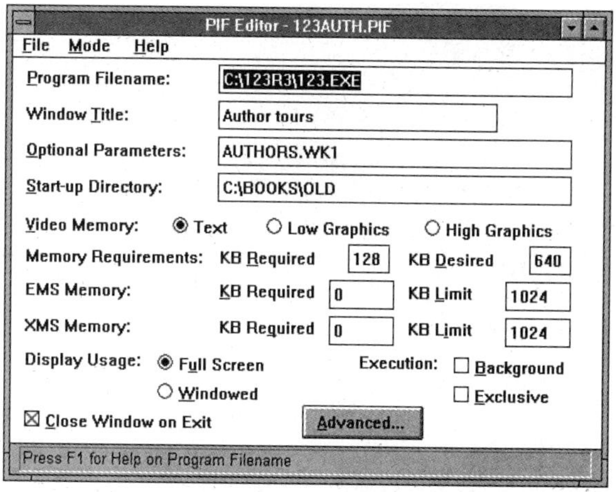

Figure 21.19. PIF Editor dialog box for 123AUTH.PIF.

21

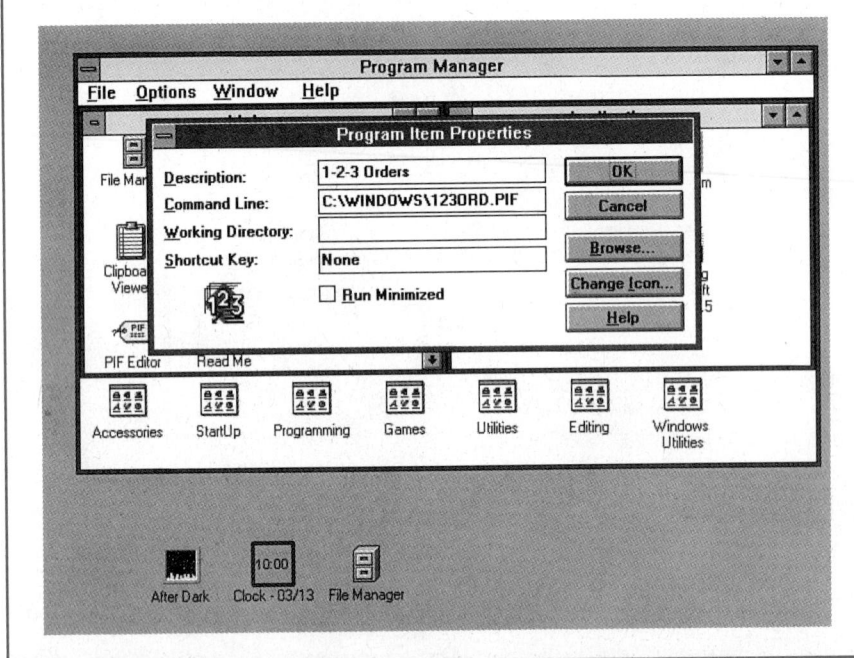

Figure 21.20. Program Item Properties dialog box for 123ORD.PIF.

Note that changing _DEFAULT.PIF does not change the choices that
the PIF Editor displays when you start it or when you give the File
New command. Those settings are fixed and cannot be changed. If you
want to start your PIFs with different settings than those offered by the
PIF Editor, you must make a template PIF file, open it with the File
Open command, then save it under the name you want when you have
made your settings. You should use File Manager to change the template to read-only after you have made the settings you want so that
you don't accidentally write over it.

VI

Advanced
Windows
Techniques

| ─ | **WHAT IS IN THIS PART** | ▼ | ⬍ |

Windows Operating
Modes

Printers and Fonts

Windows Hardware
Enhancements

Configuring with
the WIN.INI and
SYSTEM.INI files

Memory
Configuration for
Windows

Networking and
Communications

Changing Your
Configuration

Customizing Your
Desktop

Windows for
Advanced Users

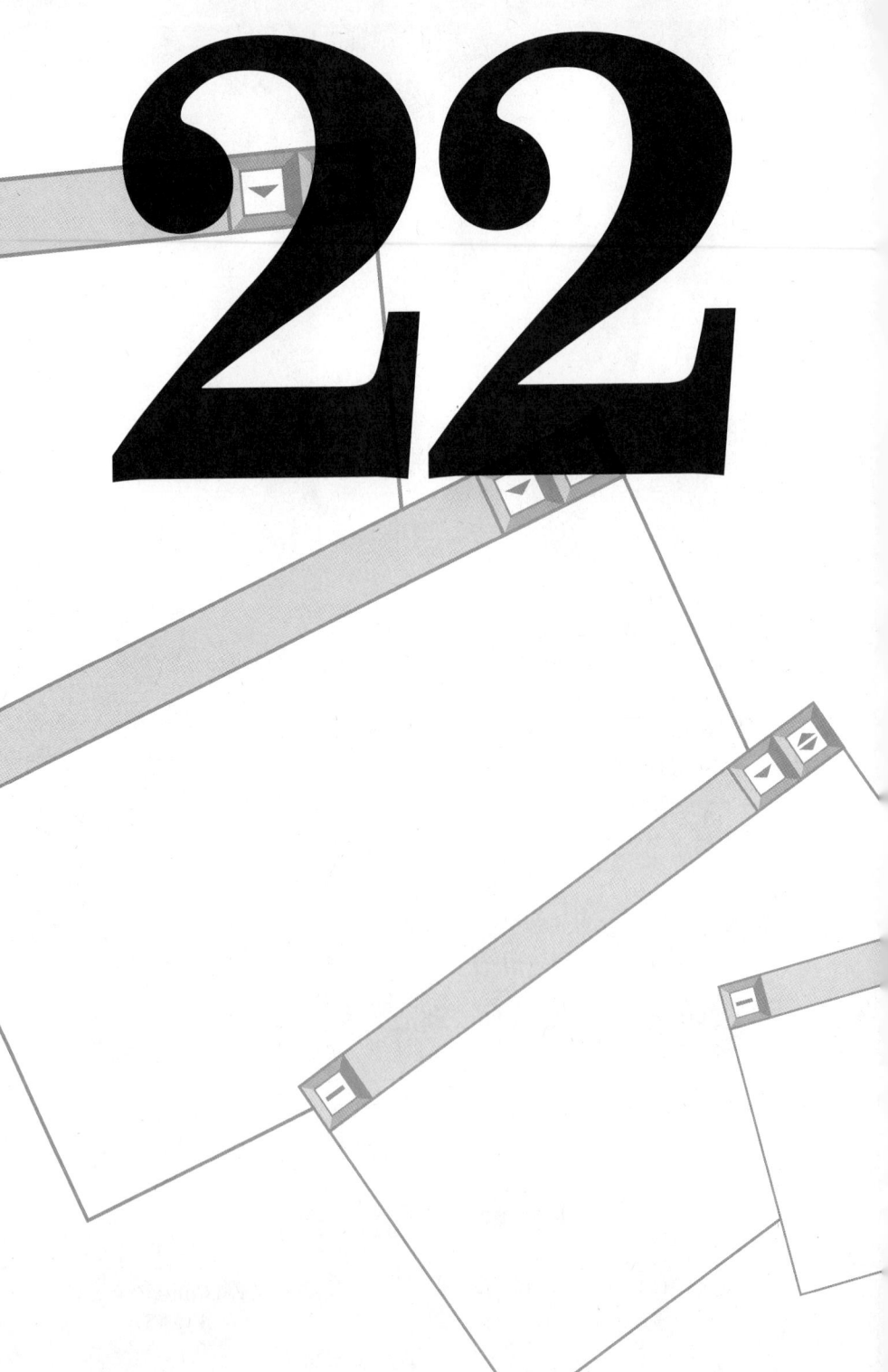

CHAPTER 22

Windows Operating Modes

One of the most difficult Windows concepts for most PC users is that of operating modes. When Microsoft first developed Windows, there was no need for different modes. As the technology in the PC progressed, however, Microsoft wanted both to keep up with the technology but not to leave early Windows users behind. They did this by allowing Windows Versions 2x and 3.0 to run in three different modes.

Windows Version 3.1 does not run on 8086 or 8088 processors. Windows 3.0 was (and still is) immensely more successful than even Microsoft marketing would have expected at the product's inception. Microsoft will continue to support the 8086 and 8088 user with Windows 3.0 for what is expected to be a year or more.

Introduction to CPUs

To understand modes, it helps to understand the different ways that a CPU (*C*entral *P*rocessing *U*nit) operates. This may seem a bit esoteric to the person who simply wants to run Windows without becoming a propeller-head, but it is in fact useful so that you can get the most out of

Windows and understand why you might have to switch operating modes for particular tasks. If you intend to use more advanced PCs in the future, understanding these differences will help you use Windows and other programs better.

Early CPUs

When the IBM PC was developed, the two CPUs available for the task were the Intel 8088 and 8086. There were many other CPUs from other vendors, but IBM chose Intel because they produced the best personal computer CPUs at the time.

These two chips are almost identical except that the 8086 runs faster due to the way it can address more memory outside the chip. Internally, both chips process data 16 bits at a time. The 8086 can read 16 bits of data in a single step; the 8088 can only read 8 bits. This means that the 8088 has to read two 8-bit chunks in order to process it as a 16-bit chunk.

These early CPUs could only run in one mode, *real* mode (supported by Windows Version 3.0 and not 3.1). In fact, real mode could be called "original mode" because other modes supersede it. Real mode lets the CPU control the computer in a simple, direct fashion.

The basic limitation of real mode is that it can only read or write up to one megabyte of memory. This means that no matter how much memory you put into your computer, the CPU in real mode can only see the first megabyte of it. As you can imagine, this becomes increasingly frustrating to people who work with computers that could access much more memory.

Some companies designed a kludge (a programmer's pseudonym for a type of "band-aid" or "make-shift method") to allow real mode CPUs to use more memory than the 1-megabyte maximum, but the enhancement method was slow, unreliable, and very limited due to the non-standardized memory management methodologies of the time. This memory access limitation, among other reasons, inspired Microsoft to discontinue support of real mode in Version 3.1.

Note: The technical reason that a CPU in real mode can only see the first megabyte of RAM is that the addresses it uses to read and write RAM are only 20 bits wide. A 20-bit address can only go from 0 to 1,048,576.

386 Enhanced

The 80286

In 1984, Intel introduced the 80286. This chip was much more advanced than the preceding chips. It had special features that made it easier to run advanced operating systems. These features included more advanced CPU instructions and a second operating mode that gave the CPU more control over multiple programs, making it much faster at executing instructions and more efficient with common operations.

With the release of Windows 3.0, the 80286 could run in two execution modes: real mode and protected mode. In real mode, the 80286 acted just like earlier CPUs. In protected mode, however, it had many more features. The feature that made it most interesting was that it could read and write up to 16 megabytes of RAM. This made using more memory much faster and easier. Through another feature called *virtual memory,* you could access over 1000 megabytes of additional memory that resided on disk.

You might think that people would be very excited about protected mode and start writing all of their programs for it. Due to an unfortunate design choice on Intel's part, this wasn't the case. The 80286 always started in real mode, and you could send a special signal to put it in protected mode. Once there, however, you could not get back to real mode. Thus all the programs that people had written for the real mode 8088 and 8086 were inaccessible from protected mode. Still, some programmers started thinking about how they could use the 80286 to access more memory.

Note: Protected mode CPUs can address up to 64 megabytes of memory because the addresses they use to read and write to RAM are 24 bits wide.

Advanced CPUs: The 80386 and Higher

In 1986, Intel started shipping the 80386, a big improvement over the 80286. It took a few years for this expensive chip to become commonplace, but people who have used one will probably never go back. Not only is the 80386 flat-out faster than the 80286, it has many advanced

features that finally let software developers create software with much less hassle. The 80386 uses 32-bit addresses and can use up to 4 gigabytes (4096 megabytes) of RAM at one time.

To be compatible, the 80386 has both real and protected modes that make it act like an 8086 and an 80286. It adds a third mode, virtual 8086 mode, that gives it the ability to run many real-mode programs at the same time. This capability is behind Windows' ability to run lots of non-Windows programs in 386-enhanced mode and still switch rapidly between programs. The 80386 also cures the blunder that Intel made with the 80286: you can switch between modes any time you want.

Intel also redesigned the way that the CPU looked at memory. In the earlier chips, all memory was boxed in 64K segments. This meant you had to do fancy programming if you had more than 64K of data that you wanted to use at one time, and it slowed down some memory operations. In the 80386, Intel removed the segmenting so that you could access as much data as you wanted at any time. This also helps Windows in 386-enhanced mode.

In 1988, Intel introduced the 80386SX. To software, the 80386SX is the same as an 80386. Thus, anything you can do in Windows with the 80386, you can do with the 80386SX. The hardware is somewhat different. The 80386SX uses a 16-bit bus rather than a 32-bit bus and is therefore slower in many areas (although still faster than the 80286).

In 1991, AMD, a competitor of Intel's, released the AM386, a clone of Intel's chip. The AM386 runs Windows programs just like the Intel chip. The politics and legal disputes behind the AM386 could fill books, but the gist is that this chip will run Windows and other MS-DOS programs just as well as the Intel chips.

The 80486, announced in 1990, is very similar to the 80386 , but it runs much faster and has an internal mathematical coprocessor. Any program (including Windows itself) that uses the special mathematical functions, which on the 80386 requires a separate mathematical coprocessor, run significantly faster. All CPU functions of the 80486 are exactly the same as for the 80386 and the software will see these two chips as identical. In 1991, Intel announced a less expensive version of the 80486 called the 80486SX, which has the speed advantages of the 80486, but no internal math coprocessor.

In mid-1991, Intel announced the 50 MHz 80486 and the launching of the development program for the upcoming 80586 family of processors, to be available mid-to-late 1992. We already see 33 MHz and 40 MHz 80486 machines in virtually every walk of life.

386 Enhanced

You will often see this expression regarding CPU compatibility: "Compatible with 386 and higher." New processors are being developed and released so often now that software developers are clinging to the expression in an effort to avoid the appearance of obsolesence in their documentation. For the record, the 80486 and 80586 are designed to be completely compatible with software developed to use the full strength of the 80386, and are by definition, 80386 compatible.

Introduction to Operating Modes

22

Now that you understand how more advanced CPUs can do more advanced processing, you can see why Microsoft put the option for more than one operating mode into Windows. If they restricted Windows to the simplest mode that could be run on all CPUs, it would run slowly and not be able to take advantage of many advanced features of the more modern CPUs. On the other hand, if they required that you had the most recent CPU so that you could always use all of the features, many people would not be able to use Windows since there are still tens of millions of PCs that have less powerful CPUs.

Operating modes depend not only on the CPU but also the amount of RAM memory you have. It takes a certain amount of RAM just to load the many advanced features of Windows and to help Windows when it comes time to switch between programs.

Table 22.1 shows the two operating modes that Windows 3.1 uses. The order of the table corresponds to increasing CPU power and speed. Unlike Windows 3.0, Windows Version 3.1 does not support what was called the real mode. This means that as of Version 3.1, Windows requires an 80286 CPU processor or higher to run.

Table 22.1. Windows operating modes.

Mode	Description
Standard mode	Works with 80286 CPUs or higher and must have at least 1 megabyte of RAM
386-enhanced mode	Works with 80386 CPUs or higher with at least 2 megabytes of RAM

When you start Windows without telling it what mode you want to start in, it checks for the highest mode your PC can handle and starts you in that mode. You cannot switch modes while you are in Windows: you must quit and start in the desired mode. This is because Windows must analyze your configuration and save it to an .INI file.

To see which operating mode you are running in, use the Help About Program Manager command in Program Manager. Figure 22.1 shows a typical dialog box for this command. In this case, the system is running in 386-enhanced mode.

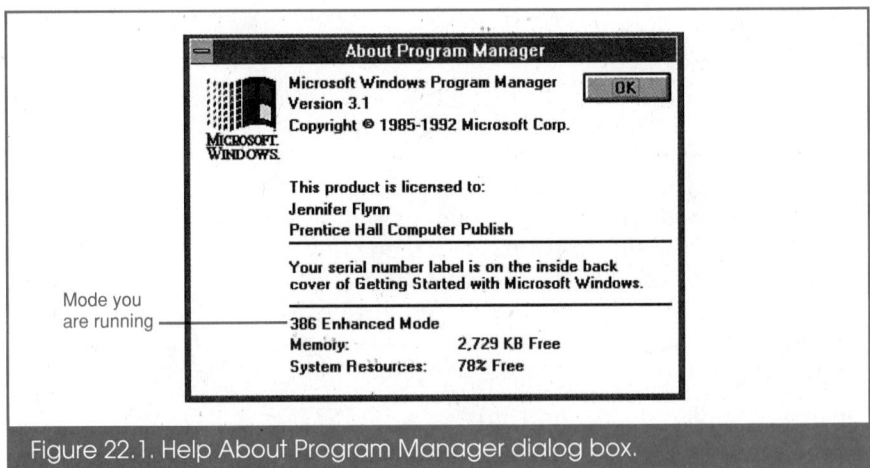

Figure 22.1. Help About Program Manager dialog box.

Standard Mode

When Windows 3.0 was released, Microsoft assumed that most people who wanted to run Windows had the 80286 CPU and only 1 megabyte of RAM. Their assumption was that if people had larger memory capacities in their PC, they would prefer to run OS/2, a more advanced operating system. They (being Big Blue) strongly misjudged the market and only a tiny fraction of people with these more powerful computers run OS/2. Many of them, however, are happy to run Windows on their systems. At the same time as the OS/2 release, Intel started an advertising campaign that denigrated the 80286 and made statements that computer users would only be happy if they had systems with 80386SX CPUs or better.

To run Windows 3.1 in standard mode, you must have an 80286 or better CPU and 1 megabyte of RAM. You may also want to use standard mode even if you have an 80386 or higher CPU, for reasons described later in this chapter.

386-Enhanced Mode

If you have an 80386SX, 80386, 80486, or the upcoming 80586 CPU, you can use 386-enhanced mode and take advantage of the features unique to those CPUs. This is almost always the best mode to run in if you have one of these CPUs and more than 3 megabytes of RAM. Running non-Windows programs is almost always better in 386-enhanced mode, because Windows 3.1 has much more control over the programs.

Choosing the Best Operating Mode

There are a few hard-and-fast rules about what mode to use when running Windows. You can usually figure out which mode is best by looking at the type of CPU you have and the types of programs you intend to run. Even then, there will be programs that will make you want to change modes.

Some of the rules have more to do with the amount of RAM you have than the type of CPU. Because many advanced Windows programs require lots of RAM, having a particular type of CPU doesn't assure you that you can run in a particular mode.

These are the absolute rules that determine the mode to use when running Windows:

▲ You need an 80386 or higher and at least 1 megabyte of RAM to run in 386-enhanced mode (all others need not apply).

▲ All 80286 CPUs must run in standard mode, regardless of the processor's speed.

22

386 Enhanced

When to Run in Standard Mode

As we said earlier, if you have an 80286 with 1 megabyte or more of RAM, you must run in standard mode.

If you have an 80386 or higher, but less than 3 megabytes of memory, and you are planning to run only Windows programs, you should run in standard mode. This may seem like you are hamstringing your snazzy, high-powered CPU, but these systems actually run faster in standard mode than in 386-enhanced mode. If you run non-Windows programs (even DOS Prompt), however, you will lose the speed advantage.

If you have an 80386 or higher and some of your non-Windows programs have problems running in 386-enhanced mode, you should run in standard mode, regardless of the amount of RAM you have. This is slower than running in 386-enhanced mode, but at least you will be able to run your programs.

When to Run in 386-Enhanced Mode

If you have an 80386 or higher and 3 megabytes or more of memory, you should be running in 386-enhanced mode. You will see a great improvement in speed when switching between programs in this mode. You also have many more options for running non-Windows programs.

Although you can run in 386-enhanced mode if you have as little as 1 megabyte of extended memory, running with less than 2 megabytes of extended memory can cause Windows to run very slowly due to constant disk swapping. There is almost never a reason to run in 386-enhanced mode unless you have 3 or more megabytes of extended memory.

Starting Windows in Particular Modes

When you start Windows from the MS-DOS command line and do not include any switch, Windows uses the following logic to choose the operating mode.

1. If your computer has an 80386-CPU or better, and it has 2 or more megabytes of memory, Windows starts in 386-enhanced mode.

386 Enhanced

2. If your computer has an 80286 CPU and it has 1 or more megabytes of memory, Windows starts in standard mode.

As you saw in Chapter 3, "Starting and Leaving Windows," you can
specify from the Windows command line the mode you want to start in.
Table 22.2 shows the options for starting Windows.

Table 22.2. Switches for selecting operating modes.

Switch	Purpose
/S	Runs Windows in standard mode
/3	Runs Windows in 386-enhanced mode

22

Warning: Note that you can use the /3 switch if you have an
80386 CPU or higher, but less than 2 megabytes of memory. You
can start in 386-enhanced mode with as little as 1 megabyte of
RAM, but your system will have significant performance problems
and may be unstable.

386 Enhanced

699

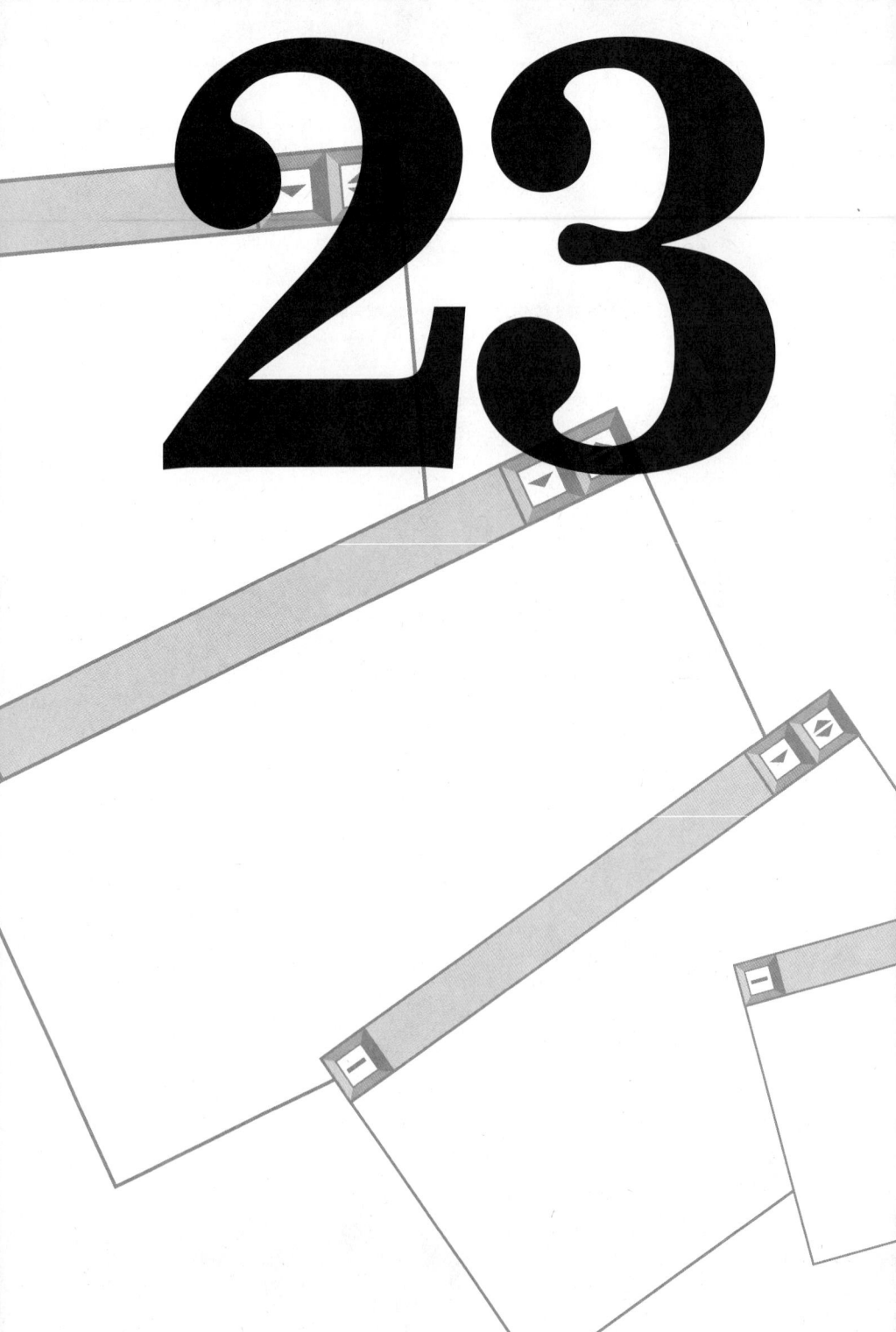

CHAPTER

23

Windows Hardware Enhancements

Windows hardware enhancements can best be defined as any additional hardware that improves an aspect of Windows. All of the enhancements described in this chapter will directly improve your perception of the performance of your system, and enhance some aspect of Windows.

Performance is the key. Each type of device is working within the maker's performance goals. Video card makers talk about their product's incredible speed and the diversity of the color palette choices; so much so that even Carl Sagan might have a hard time nutshelling the quantity of the colors now available. Caching controller board makers bark about how fast they can deliver information to and from your fixed media.

Rather than talk about any maker's product specifically, this chapter will break out the classes of products by what they really do for us.

Processor Accelerator Boards

Processor clock speed is extremely important to Windows performance. The faster the processor of any type, the faster Windows runs. Processor accelerator boards accomplish their task by displacing your system processor with a higher-speed processor. This more muscular chip is normally found mounted on a board that fits into one of your system bus slots. Essentially, you unplug your current processor chip and plug it into the add-on board, then connect the add-on board to the motherboard processor socket using a ribbon cable supplied with the accelerator board. Of course, you need to then plug the add-on board into a free system slot.

Some processor accelerator board makers require you to perform a setup procedure to install a *driver* file into your CONFIG.SYS or AUTOEXEC.BAT file before the product can be used. A driver is a software file that describes your new hardware product to your computer (and Windows) so that it can be properly integrated into the system.

Tip: The cost of many of the brand-name products of this class actually can be more expensive than upgrading your entire motherboard. If you have an 80286 machine and you simply want to use Windows in 386-enhanced mode, you can get a replacement motherboard for your system for what is often cheaper than an add-on speed enhancement product. This is especially true if the price for the product approaches the manufacturer's list price.

It takes more technical know-how to replace a motherboard (even to make the proper selection), but you'll get several benefits from migrating to the 80386 architecture. The memory management benefits (among others) of a 386 motherboard may make the add-on board's single attribute of increasing processor speed pale by comparison.

Video Enhancement Products

There are many products available that were formerly only purchased by so-called high-end users. The CAD/CAM and Desktop Publishing

industries have improved video device price/performance ratios enough so that the average user can now buy a product that was five times the price only two years ago.

Warning: Make certain the supplier providing the product can guarantee that the device and driver are both indeed Windows 3.0 and/or 3.1 compatible, *and* will refund your money if it turns out to be incompatible. There are many products out there that work well in a non-Windows environment, but have not been upgraded to perform with Windows 3.1. There is always a lot of inventory that seems like a great buy until you get it home and find out that the product is of a design or version level that has been discontinued before the advent of Windows 3.0.

It's best to read the text (.TXT) and information (.INF) files that came with your Windows package to see which hardware devices and drivers are incompatible regardless of a supplier's assurances.

23

Video accelerator products process video instructions with a dedicated processor, which often has been specially programmed to transfer data using burst mode technology. These dedicated half-card video processing boards can run at the speed of a 50 MHz 80486. Because they are *dedicated* video processors, they can process instructions within a 64-bit, on-board data path.

TV Tuner products allow you to collect standard television cable signals so you can view standard TV programming within a window. Most often offered by multimedia board manufacturers as a part of an integrated multimedia solution.

Stereo Audio, although not a video enhancement, is an added benefit of many multimedia boards. You can receive stereo TV or stereo FM signals with additional available software.

Still Frame Compression cards allow the user to compress graphic files to drastically reduce the space that they occupy on a hard disk. If you do a lot of file transfer via modem, these boards can pay for themselves within a year. File size reduction ratios of up to 24 to 1 (ex: 10M to 420K) can be accomplished. These cards can be capable of compressing a 1M graphic file in less than one second.

Multimedia imaging hardware provides facilities to display still or moving images within a window. Capture moving images from a VCR or camera and display them in a window on your monitor. You can save images to a database to support a presentation that changes the display of these images as the presentation progresses. There are many uses for multimedia hardware beside the obvious training and presentation management applications:

▲ Stockbrokers use these boards to view CNN with stock quotations at the same time.

▲ E-Mail users leave pictures with their messages.

▲ Bank ATMs run ads while you wait for your transaction to be completed.

Motion Compression boards allow the display of moving images direct from a hard drive using motion compression techniques. Up until 1992, motion images were much too large to be stored on a PC hard drive.

Video Controllers now offer resolutions of 1280 by 1024 operating from a standard AT compatible machine. Resolutions of 1280 by 1024 is more than twice the resolution of today's VGA standard of 640 by 480. This high-resolution level requires a vertical refresh rate of at least 72 MHz to be usable, and you really want at least a 17" monitor to run such a card. If you can afford it, you can place a lot more windows on your screen and they will still be readable. Controllers can now offer up to 64M of onboard memory dedicated to the task of displaying video *fast*. Some boards employ dedicated processors or controllers such as the Intel i860 (more often seen in high end workstation architecture) and are capable of executing 67 MIPS (*M*illion *I*nstructions *P*er *Sec*ond). These specifications sort of redefine my idea of fast.

Memory Add-On Boards

Memory add-on boards have been around for a long time. They range all the way back to the early personal computer days when you were able to add 128K or even 256K of memory, *if* you could afford it.

These days, 32M capacities for memory add-on boards (RAM) cards are not unheard of. Today's cards usually emulate expanded memory using the LIM 4.0 (*L*otus-*I*ntel-*M*icrosoft) standard. Price/performance ratios vary with configuration, maximum memory capacity, and the actual speed of the board.

The early add-on boards and 8-bit memory boards are simply too slow to be of any real value in a fast paced environment.

LaserJet Enhancement Devices

There are two general classes of hardware that are popular for improving LaserJet performance.

Cartridges as add-ons can be an expensive proposition. There are pros and cons for hard fonts versus soft fonts. A soft font is software based, and is usually resident on your computer, not your printer. Hard fonts are permanently located on chips that have been installed inside printer cartridges. Soft fonts cost less but take up disk space. Most soft or outline fonts also download the font to the printer with every page of a document, making the printing of long documents a wait-and-see event. If you have waited up to half an hour for a twenty-page document to print, you may want to consider a hard font cartridge versus downloadable soft fonts for your printer.

Traditionally, cartridges offered by large printer manufacturers have been a bit pricy, and third party vendors have risen to the opportunity and undercut the Big Guys—the way of the world, it seems. The print quality of hard fonts and the printing speed that results make the investment tempting, even at two- to three-hundred dollars per cartridge.

There is a new generation of cartridges being offered that accept soft fonts once from your document processor, and save them to rewritable memory *in the cartridge.* Instead of downloading the soft font to the printer with every page, the cartridge accepts the font once and stores it for future use. You can buy cartridges of different font capacities: up to 1.5M, so the cartridge can hold more than one font.

These newer font cartridges save their contents when you power-down the printer and the computer. There are some compatibility issues regarding some soft font maker's products, but overall, if you use soft fonts at all, this is the best approach.

Data Storage Products

Data storage devices have developed into a great deal more than just a slow hard drive and dumb controller. Drives now think for themselves and act like others if need be. This section describes some of the things that are happening in the world of data storage devices. By today's definition, hardware that will retain data for recall is a storage device.

A lot has changed since the days of the early Shugart interface. First there was MFM, then RLL, then came early SCSI and ESDI, IDE and now SCSI-1 and SCSI-2. Like most hardware enhancement concepts, this one also is centered on isolating critical functions and dedicating resources for that function's exclusive use. In the case of controllers, speed coupled with memory are the focal points of performance with most of today's manufacturers.

Cached Controllers

The confusion that has occurred when people talk about caching in regard to data storage has become widespread. To clarify, essentially three caching methods are commonly used today.

The first such method involves using system RAM to set up and maintain a disk cache, a buffer (a bucket of dedicated, available memory) that gives you instant access to its contents. It does this without requiring the drive to work with your system at exactly the same time that you need it. This software-based cache simply acts as a go-between for the drive and your requests, so that the system is freed up sooner than it would be without the cache. The cache works with the drive at the drive's speed, and it works with you and your system at your system's RAM speed. The effect is that your system can disengage from the drive much sooner than it normally could. The software-based RAM cache updates the hard drive as soon as the drive can handle and complete the transaction, while you go on to other things.

The second method is called read-ahead caching. This method relies on the concept of dedicated quantities of RAM located on the drive itself, prompting a "look ahead" when the drive is accessed. The look-ahead buffer loads more data into itself based on data that is located on the hard drive *nearest* your requested data.

These drives store in RAM the next few sectors located on the drive itself, awaiting requests for that data. Since DOS tries to store data in contiguous sectors, the data you may well ask for next is quite often in the cache already. So the effect is that you really access the *memory* on the drive, not the retrieval mechanics of the drive. The result is *very* fast data access, on the average.

The third means of using memory caching when accessing data storage devices is through the use of caching controllers. These boards, exotic by yesterday's standards, have larger banks of memory chips located on the controller board itself. The concept is that if you make the memory cache big enough to accommodate the largest file sizes you can transact, you will always offload or onload large files to and from the cache, not the drive.

In this respect, the hard cache on the controller is not unlike the software-based cache solution. The biggest difference is that you don't have to allocate system memory for the purpose. Most systems have memory size constraints that make the caching disk controller much more attractive.

In general, and this depends on whether you are using any form of disk caching now, you will experience a 25- to 75-percent increase over current performance.

When completing redundant tasks such as large database packing or reindexing, the difference between no cache and a hard drive controller with a 4-megabyte cache will be a realized improvement, finishing the job up to three times faster. There are actually some database management tasks out there that will experience increases in speed of up to *five times* the normal period span required to complete the task.

Windows would like you to use a disk cache size of 2M. It will tell you so during the install process. With this type of cached controller, you can free this memory for use with your applications. Just think! You may be able to do away with the dreaded `Close one or more applications and try again` message when you try to run those chunky programs concurrently!

Coprocessing Intelligent Controllers

State-of-the-art coprocessing controllers means arbitrating SCSI. SCSI means *S*mall *C*omputer *S*ystems *I*nterface. Arbitrating means that the board decides the order in which devices (hard drive, CD-ROM, and so on) get attention from the system processor and memory banks. These boards actually talk to devices that want to access the main system bus and dole out the bus access based on which one of the devices asks for it first! This facet of the SCSI-2 standard is particularly valuable to network users who place multiple demands on their systems, often using several data storage devices simultaneously.

If two drives ask to talk to the system at exactly the same time, these state-of-the-art I/O boards will check the head position in relation to the data location of each requesting drive. This determines which drive will complete its task first. The controller then provides access to the drive that will accomplish its needs and then release the system *soonest*.

23

The controller effectively makes the best judgement for the overall system. Its goal is to go to that level of detail if required, to free up the system as soon as possible for other tasks.

Current maximum drive capacity of these boards can be up to 16.8 gigabytes. By using an 80386 or higher processor dedicated to the purpose of I/O task management, throughput rates of 6 megabytes per second are achieved. Throughput rates measure how much data can pass between the system bus and a device, such as a hard drive, over the period of one second.

Now, these boards are not for the faint of heart. They are very expensive, and are primarily designed to support EISA servers. *Extended Industry Standard Architecture* motherboards are something of a clone of IBM's MCA (*Micro Channel Architecture*) boards. But like all other hardware advancements that seem to be above the heads of the average user, we will all be pricing these boards when they drop below a thousand dollars; as virtually all hardware items in the PC world eventually must.

Mass Media

In the world of microcomputers, a mass media device is typically described as a data storage device that will hold 500 million characters or more: 500M. Now, in the mainframe world, the classic definition of mass media is a device that will hold up to 500 *billion* characters. Yes, that's 500 gigabytes!

Hard drives that hold around 1.2 gigabytes are becoming standard fare with network system operators (SysOps) because they are perhaps the most cost-effective solution for today's network mirroring needs.

Disk mirroring is a technique that is used by many manufacturers of sophisticated server hardware. The method is to copy the same data to locations on two separate drives to provide guaranteed availability even in the event of a single drive's failure. The concept is part of the *Fault Tolerance* thought process that has become popular with data management groups working within financial and medical institutions. Of course, Fault Tolerance requires you to maintain two drives for one drive's worth of data. The hard drives that will hold all of this data have become fast and cost effective, even for the average user.

Even though sophisticated business-based users benefit from the sheer size of mass storage devices, at great expense, the single user gets to take advantage of the boon of recent technological advances.

A 1.5 gigabyte SCSI drive will fit into a desktop computer in the full-height slot formerly occupied by the 10M drives of yesteryear.

CD-ROM

If your principal requirement is only to *access* large volumes of data while staying on a budget, CD-ROM has evolved into a reliable and reasonably fast solution to your needs. The modern CD-ROM drive typically works with CD-ROM disks that hold 600M of data. At a street cost of about $500, you can install a high-quality drive with at least some of the symptoms of state-of-art technology. The drives can be installed internally or externally, at additional cost.

You can even put your company's parts catalogs or policy and procedures on CD-ROM just like General Motors does. In fact, two Japanese manufacturers have released rewritable drives for under $4000 that let you create your own CDs. These disks have a capacity of up to 650M and offer access times of around 30 milliseconds.

For the desktop publishing type, CD-ROMs have been made available that contain a wealth of clip art and images. With the advent of Microsoft Windows 3.1 MPC (*M*ultimedia *PC*) extensions and its capability of manipulating sound and moving imagery, a new standard will be in place that will assure the opening of a broad range of multimedia software and hardware.

Tip: If you're incensed over an offer you've seen that includes a CD-ROM drive and seemingly thousands of dollars of CDs, think again. The buy is great, but the drive is probably outdated technology. In translation, this means immeasurably slow drive access times.

The CDs are indeed a good buy, but remember how slow your old XT drive used to be? The originals yanked data off the platter (sometimes) at a speed of around 110 milliseconds. Imagine a CD-ROM drive that is *six times* the wait—600 milliseconds. That's the average access time of the bargain CD-ROM drives included with most package deals. Buy the CDs but leave the dinosaurs to the Flintstones.

Removable Media Drives

A Removable Media drive unit is nothing more than a hard drive with a platter or platter pack that is removable. You treat the drive and disk sort of the same way you treat a CD drive. The rest of the differences are major, though. Access times are fast approaching 19 milliseconds.

Tip: Many people use these drives to preserve privacy on a public machine. If you are sharing a machine at the office, you may find that using one of these drives when other employees use their own cartridges can protect confidential information like engineering designs and employee records from prying eyes.

Removable Disks are available in sizes of around forty and eighty megabytes for two of the most popular units.

Tip: Project-based organizations have found that arranging their program files on an internal hard drive and their data files on a removable drive will increase overall system data storage capacity. It helps keep project related data organized. It also eliminates the need for storing backup data on floppies. It is more costly to use a cartridge than a diskette, but the transfer rates and access times of hard drives and removable media drives are far more desirable than those of floppy disk drives.

Hard Card Drives

Well, those days of slow, expensive and unreliable hard cards are virtually gone. If you are short of drive bay space or you just want to add another drive without the hassle that usually goes with installing a hard drive, there's hope yet.

Today's hard cards have not only gotten better, they have gotten BIG! Seagate makes a 420 megabyte hard card. Interestingly enough, in cost it's just about four times the price of a conventional 100 megabyte hard drive.

The speed of hard cards is no longer an issue, either. Some manufacturers offer an effective access time of *9 milliseconds* by using a 64K disk

cache (for an explanation of read-ahead caching see the "Cached Controllers" section in this chapter).

These cards are actually hard drives that are mounted sideways on a long 8- or 16-bit card. You plug it in in much the same way you plug in a modem or game port board.

The upside of this concept is that installing a second or third hard drive is much easier with a hard card. It does cost more than a conventional drive, byte for byte, but not drastically so. For example, a very fast 105 megabyte hard card costs about 16% more than the traditional configuration.

The downside is that these hard cards take at least two slots worth of case space. They are two to three inches thick in some cases.

23

> **Warning:** Make sure you have *at least* two slots available (side by side) before you buy one of these hard cards. Even though the hard card board will normally plug into only one slot, it will take more than one slot of space. Unless the maker states it as such, the hard card will take *at least* two slots worth of space. You must specify that you want a "one-slot card" if you really only have one slot of space to spare.

If you have the slots to spare, the hard card is looking better all the time.

Tape Backup Units

Tape backup units have evolved from the days when mainframe operators spent sleepless nights running reports and backing-up and archiving system data to keep it from getting lost. Some companies actually saved their noncritical data in printed-report form to keep the cost down. Of course, if you needed the data, you had to enter it again.

Nine-track reels of tape never became popular on the desktop computer because they do not allow for fast storage and retrieval of data. The same holds true for cartridge-based units. To get at data from a tape drive of any type, you may have to race from one end of the tape to the other, a concept that does not provide the speedy data access times that we all want.

So the role of the tape drive has been relegated to that of the backup-storage device. When you hear someone speak of tape backup units, they are most likely talking about the cartridge variety. People (or a backup software program responding to the system clock) usually copy the contents of critical data to these tape units at regular intervals to preserve the data in the event that data is somehow lost or damaged on the hard drive.

The nice thing about tape backup units is that you can buy tapes relatively cheaply, and archive them if the hard drive is larger in capacity than the tape drive. You can in effect take a snapshot of a project and its data at any time and retrieve it later.

Tip: You can arrange the directories on your hard drive so that only data files are copied during the backup process. Thus, you can get away with a smaller and less expensive tape backup unit. Using this method you would also need less tapes.

These units can be found in either stand-alone or internal configurations. Tape drive units offer capacities of 20M, 40M, 120M, and even 250M for internal units.

CHAPTER

24

Memory Configuration for Windows

In the early days of the IBM PC, there was just one type of RAM, and there was only 64K of it. Within a few years, companies were making PCs with up to 640K of memory, an incredible amount at the time. Programs could use almost all of that memory for any purpose.

The 640K limit is enforced by MS-DOS, not by the PC. Even the earliest of CPUs could access up to 1M of RAM. MS-DOS, however, reserved everything between 640K and 1M for itself and for housekeeping areas.

As software became more hungry for memory, hardware companies had to come up with schemes to allow software to use more memory. The technical solutions they came up with to go above 640K probably have caused more confusion and consternation among PC users than any other issue. There are now many types of RAM, and programs can access only some types and not others.

This chapter describes the types of RAM and describes how to set up your computer to use the types Windows 3.1 can use best. It also describes how to save memory so that your programs have as much as possible. If you are running in standard or 386-enhanced mode, you can even get Windows to use the hard disk as though it were RAM and give your computer even more capabilities.

Introduction to RAM Types

The type of memory you have depends on how much memory is in your system and what type of memory management software you are using. Most PCs can have up to 16M of RAM in them, although the vast majority have less than 4M. Figure 24.1 shows the types of memory based on their addresses.

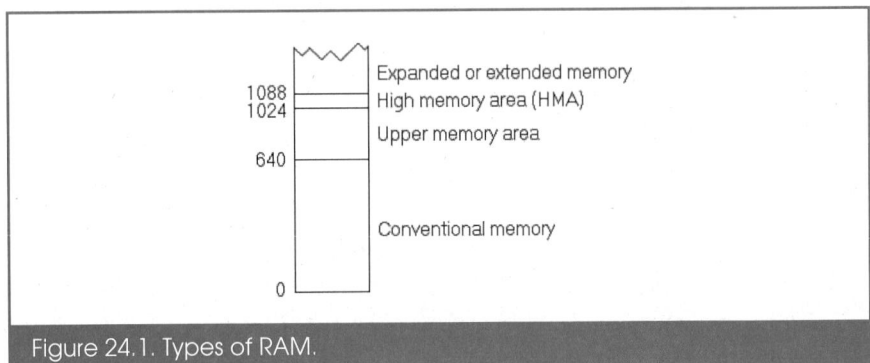

Figure 24.1. Types of RAM.

Tip: The names used in this chapter are standard but are not the only names. In fact, even Microsoft uses different definitions for the types of memory. For example, some people count the upper memory area as part of expanded or extended memory and do not have special names for them. Do not be surprised if you come across definitions that are different from the ones described here.

Conventional Memory

Because Windows requires at least 640K of RAM in your system, every Windows user has the full 640K of conventional memory. Note that not all of that 640K is available to programs: MS-DOS takes some memory for itself, and any "memory-resident" or TSR (terminate-and-stay-resident) programs also take up memory. TSRs were more popular during the time when applications like Borland's Sidekick was one of the few ways you could keep yourself organized in the DOS-based, pre-Windows world. The TSR of today is usually a memory manager of some sort. The amount of memory MS-DOS takes depends on the version of MS-DOS you are running.

It is typical to have about 550K of conventional memory free after you start MS-DOS. This is the amount of conventional memory any program, including Windows, has to work with. Some TSRs and device drivers can reduce this number to as low as 450K, which is often too little for many programs.

Upper Memory Area

Most PCs built since 1989 come with 1M of RAM or more. With any PC, you can increase RAM either by adding it on the motherboard of the PC or by using a memory card. When you add memory to a system with 640K of conventional memory, you start adding to an area called the upper memory area (this is also sometimes called *high* memory, but that term is often confused with the HMA or *high memory area*, which is different). Some of this area is reserved for use by the system's BIOS and video memory, although some of the area is unused. If you are using expanded memory, at least 64K of the upper memory area is reserved by the expanded memory manager. This 64K area is called the EMS page frame. Expanded memory is described in the next section.

24

Depending on the memory manager you choose, you might or might not be able to access the unused part of the upper memory area. HIMEM.SYS, the memory manager that comes with Windows and with MS-DOS Version 5, does not try to use this area. Similarly, most of the memory managers that come with PCs also ignore this area.

Commercial memory managers such as QuarterDeck's QEMM and Qualitas 386MAX can use some of the upper memory area by moving TSRs and device drivers from your conventional memory to the upper memory area. Most of these programs run just as well in the upper memory area as they do in regular memory. Using programs such as these leaves more conventional memory for your programs.

Expanded Memory

The first solution that companies came up with for how to add memory to a system was expanded memory. Expanded memory can be accessed in any type of PC. Expanded memory is created by swapping data between the page frame area of upper memory and conventional memory. Due to the way it is accessed, expanded memory is slower than its counterpart, extended memory. Expanded memory is sometimes called LIM (*L*otus-*I*ntel-*M*icrosoft) memory or EMS (*E*xpanded

*M*emory *S*pecification) memory. You need to use an expanded memory program to allow programs to access the memory. You can have up to eight megabytes of EMS memory in a PC. This memory can be either on the system board or on an add-on board that plugs into one of your motherboard's slots. Memory that is on an add-on board is usually a lot slower because slots only allow 16-bit access to memory. Memory attached to the motherboard through proprietary add-on boards available through a manufacturer (such as DTK) offer 32-bit access to add-on memory.

In the "old days" previous to motherboards being made to handle more than four megabytes of memory, you were doomed to poor memory performance because your only option to add memory was through a 16-bit memory board. The fact that these "old days" were previous to Windows (and extended memory) may have caused misconceptions about the inferior speed of expanded versus extended memory. Back then, even slow memory was better than not enough if you were trying to work with a certain spreadsheet program or very large spreadsheets, for example. The only non-Windows programs that can get value from expanded memory are those specifically written to use it. If the program was not written to work with EMS, it will not even know that the EMS memory is there. For a program, EMS can be accessed only in 16K chunks. Changing which parts of EMS memory were in the chunks is slow due to the way the data is read from EMS and put into the upper memory area. Because of this, not many non-Windows programs used EMS.

If your system uses expanded memory and memory management software, they must conform to the LIM 4.0 standard for Windows to be able to use it. Many expanded memory add-on boards and software conform to the LIM standard, but some comply only with LIM 3.2.

In standard or 386-enhanced mode, Windows ignores the expanded memory. However, non-Windows programs that use expanded memory can use it in any of the three modes.

Warning: Be sure that the programs you are running expect the type of expanded memory your computer supports. Programs that expect LIM 3.2 memory might crash if you are using LIM 4.0 memory. The reason for this is that in LIM 3.2, the four 16K chunks had to be in one block so that programs could treat them as 64K. In LIM 4.0, they can be in different places. Programs that don't check can read and write to parts of memory that can cause your program to crash.

Extended Memory

With the advent of the 80286 CPU, programmers had a direct way of accessing up to 16M of memory directly. The memory above the 1M point, which is inaccessible to programs running on the 8088 and 8086, is easily used by the 80286 and later CPUs. Because this memory is a simple extension to conventional memory and the upper memory area, it was called *extended memory*. You can have up to 15M of extended memory in your PC. If you have an 80286 or higher, you should try to have as much extended memory as possible.

Programs can use the same extra memory simultaneously. Thus, programs access the memory through an extended memory manager.

There are two standards for programs that use extended memory: DPMI and VCPI. The DPMI (DOS Protect Mode Interface) specification is the newer of the two and is fully supported by Windows. When a program wants to use extended memory, it gets it from a managed pool that Windows knows so that there is no conflict. Unfortunately, few DPMI programs exist; Lotus 1-2-3 Version 3.1 is one of the few. More programs are being written to this standard so that they can successfully run under Windows.

24

Many popular programs, such as Borland's Paradox 3.5 and Fox Software's FoxBase+, use the VCPI (Virtual Control Program Interface) specification. This is the older standard and Windows does not use it. Because of this, using VCPI programs can cause parts of Windows to use the same memory and probably crash your system. You should never use VCPI programs in 386-enhanced mode, but you might be able to use them in standard mode. Check your program's documentation to find out what its memory requirements are before you configure your memory as either expanded or extended memory.

If your CPU is an 80386 or higher, you can use part of your extended memory as expanded memory with the EMM386.EXE driver that comes with Windows 3.1 and with MS-DOS Version 5. This is useful only if you are running non-Windows programs that require expanded memory. The EMM386.EXE driver is described later in this chapter.

High Memory Area

The high memory area (sometimes called the *HMA*) is the first 64K of extended memory, starting just after the upper memory area. This area is treated as special by some devices such as networks and high-speed disk drives. Devices sometimes use the 64K in the high memory area as a safe place to keep data that needs to be accessed quickly. MS-DOS Version 5 can also use this area and thus make more space available to standard MS-DOS programs.

As you saw in Chapter 22, "Windows Operating Modes," the CPU has to go into protected mode to access memory above 1M. However, CPUs can get at the high memory area without going into protected mode. This is valuable because going into protected memory is slow, especially on an 80286. The high memory area was thus considered a "special" area of memory. Expanded memory managers all know about the high memory area and give access to it only if the program requests HMA memory specifically.

Determining Your Current Memory Use

To see how much of each type of memory you have in your system, use the **Help About** Program Manager command in the Program Manager program. This also tells you the operating mode you are running in. The possible lines in the memory part of the dialog are described in Table 24.1. Figure 24.2 shows a typical dialog box.

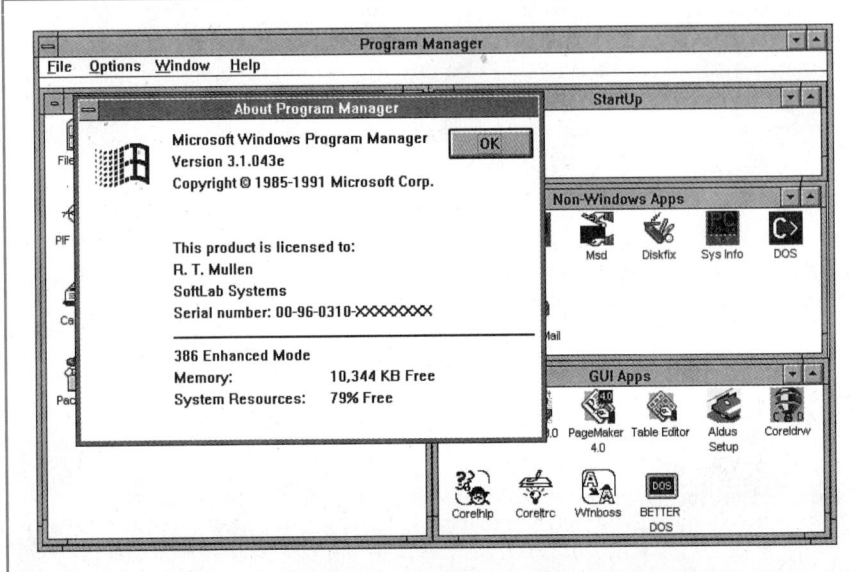

Figure 24.2. Help About Program Manager dialog box.

Table 24.1. Description of memory information in the Help About Program Manager command.

Type of Memory	Description
Amount of memory free	The memory available to programs. In standard mode, this is conventional and extended memory. In 386-enhanced mode, this is conventional, extended memory, and swap disk space.
Free system resources	The percentage of the 64K system resources area available. System resources and their limitations are described later in this chapter.

A better way to see your actual RAM use is MS-DOS's MEM command. This command is available only in MS-DOS Version 4 or later. Typical output of the MEM command might look like this:

```
Type Exit to close this DOS prompt
Microsoft(R) MS-DOS(R) Version 5.00
Copyright Microsoft Corp 1981-1991.

C:\ >mem

    655360 bytes total conventional memory
    655360 bytes available to MS-DOS
    386512 largest executable program size

   7602176 bytes total contiguous extended memory
         0 bytes available contiguous extended memory
         0 bytes available XMS memory
           MS-DOS resident in High Memory Area
```

This indicates that the PC has 640K of conventional memory (655360 bytes).

Specifying Memory Setup in Your CONFIG.SYS File

When you run Setup to install Windows, it changes your CONFIG.SYS file to include calls to Microsoft's two memory management programs. Often, you don't need to worry about these changes because the standard settings are just fine. However, it is useful to understand what is happening in your CONFIG.SYS file so that you can fine-tune the settings or use replacements to the programs. The contents of your CONFIG.SYS file and methods for changing them are described in Chapter 25, "Changing Your Configuration."

The memory managers and disk caching programs that come with Windows 3.1 are device drivers, meaning that you run them by including their names in the CONFIG.SYS file. That file is a text file that runs commands using an individual line per command. Figure 24.3 shows an example of a typical CONFIG.SYS file. In that file, note the lines that begin with device=. Those lines load device drivers.

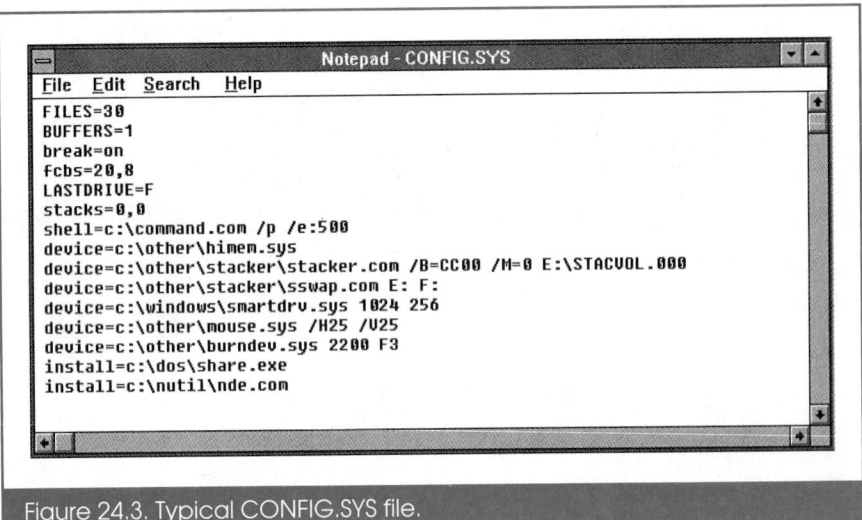

Figure 24.3. Typical CONFIG.SYS file.

A device driver line consists of three things:

▲ The notation device= or devicehigh= at the beginning of the line

▲ The name of the device driver file, including a disk letter and directory path

▲ Arguments used by the driver

For example, look at the following line:

```
device=C:\WINDOWS\SMARTDRV.SYS 1024 256
```

C:\WINDOWS\SMARTDRV.SYS is the name of the device driver file, and 1024 256 are the arguments used by the driver.

HIMEM Memory Manager

One of the first devices that should appear in your CONFIG.SYS file is the extended memory manager. Windows comes with an extended memory manager, HIMEM.SYS, which conforms to the XMS memory standard. HIMEM.SYS manages extended memory (memory over the one megabyte mark). Windows programs only use extended memory. DOS-based programs only use expanded memory. When you load devices and/or DOS into the Upper Memory Area via your CONFIG.SYS file, you need another file called EMM386.EXE loaded, as described later in this chapter.

HIMEM.SYS should be the first device in your CONFIG.SYS file unless the instructions for the other devices say they should come before an extended memory manager.

> **Tip:** The version of HIMEM.SYS that comes with Windows 3.1 is newer than the one that comes with MS-DOS Version 5.0. You should always use the most recent version of HIMEM.SYS. This section documents the version of HIMEM.SYS that comes with Windows 3.1.

24

Generally, you will use HIMEM without arguments, so the line in your CONFIG.SYS file will look like this:

```
device=C:\WINDOWS\HIMEM.SYS
```

HIMEM can include seven possible arguments, shown in Table 24.2. You can use any combination of these.

Table 24.2. Arguments to HIMEM.

Argument	Description
/A20CONTROL:	Tells HIMEM whether to take control of the A20 pin on the CPU. The default is ON. If you set this to OFF, HIMEM takes over the A20 line only if the A20 was not in use when HIMEM was loaded. The A20 pin on the CPU provides direct access to the system's extended memory.

continues

Table 24.2. Continued

Argument	Description
/CPUCLOCK:	Tells HIMEM whether to affect the clock speed of your PC. HIMEM occasionally changes the clock speed of the computer, although it is difficult to detect this. Setting this to ON corrects the problem but slows HIMEM.
/HMAMIN=	Minimum amount of high memory area memory a program must request to get access to the area. Because only one program can use the high memory area, you can use this setting to ensure that a program that wants lots of high memory area memory gets it. This is rarely used. It is also ignored if you are running in 386-enhanced mode.
/INT15=	Sets aside the number of kilobytes for the interrupt 15 interface. You can use any value above 0, but any value below 64 is automatically rounded down to 0 (which is also the default). It is unlikely you will ever need to use this option, because only older programs utilized this interrupt, and most software developers have abandoned the technique in favor of using one of the more current memory XMS memory managers.
/MACHINE:	Tells HIMEM the type of machine you are using so it can adapt to the peculiarities of how the system handles the CPU. If you use this argument, you include a machine number or name, as shown in Table 24.3. For example, /MACHINE:4 is the same as /MACHINE:HPVECTRA. You can shorten /MACHINE: to /M: if you want.
/NUMHANDLES=	Maximum number of extended memory block handles to be allocated. This can be between 0 and 128, and defaults to 32 if you do not give this argument. A general rule of thumb is that you should allocate 16 handles for each megabyte of extended memory. However, this isn't usually necessary for Windows because it allocates memory in large blocks and the default of 32 should be plenty in most cases.

Argument	Description
/SHADOWRAM:	Set this to ON or OFF to enable or disable ROM shadowing. The ROM in PCs is much slower than RAM, and many newer PCs run faster because they copy parts of ROM into RAM to get the speed increase. Normally, HIMEM tries to turn this shadowing off to gain more memory, but most PCs do not allow it (you must change the setting when you turn on your computer). Use the /SHADOWRAM:ON command to prevent HIMEM from disabling shadow ROM.

Table 24.3. Machine numbers and names for the /MACHINE argument.

Number	Name	Computer
1	AT	IBM PC/AT or 100 percent compatible
2	PS2	IBM PS/2 or 100 percent compatible
3	PTLCASCADE	PC with a Phoenix Cascade BIOS
4	HPVECTRA	Hewlett-Packard Vectra model A or A+
5	ATT6300PLUS	AT&T model 6300 Plus
6	ACER1100	Acer model 1100
7	TOSHIBA	Toshiba model 1600 and 1200XE
8	WYSE	Wyse 12.5 MHz 80286-based system
9	TULIP	Tulip SX
10	ZENITH	Zenith with ZBIOS
11	AT1	IBM PC/AT, second variant
12	CSS or AT2	CSS Labs clones with alternative delay
13	PHILIPS or AT3	Philips clones with alternative delay
14	FASTHP	HP Vectra, second variant

24

When HIMEM is loading, you see a message on your screen, such as

```
HIMEM: DOS XMS Driver, Version 3.0 - 05/24/91
XMS Specification Version 3.0
Copyright 1988-1991 Microsoft Corp.

Installed A20 handler number 1.
64K High Memory Area is available
```

Tip: The handler number is the number specified in the /MACHINE argument. If you encounter problems with HIMEM, such as it doesn't load or Windows says you have no extended memory when you are sure you do, try giving a different number in the /MACHINE argument. Note that some of these arguments might lock up your system, so you might need to have a boot floppy available.

Commercial Memory Managers

Windows works with extended memory managers other than HIMEM. In fact, the two major commercial memory managers for the 80386, QEMM/386 by Quarterdeck Office Systems and 386MAX by Qualitas, do everything that HIMEM does and much more. By the time you read this, there might be others that compete with HIMEM.

HIMEM has one major advantage over the commercial memory managers: it's free. On the other hand, that might not be a good enough reason to use it because the other memory managers give you some big advantages. Commercial memory managers free up conventional memory and are often much faster than HIMEM.

The most important way commercial memory managers free up conventional memory is to put device drivers and some TSR programs into the unused parts of the upper memory area. This results in a net increase in conventional memory not only when you run MS-DOS, but also when you run non-Windows programs in Windows.

With the advent of MS-DOS 5.0's LOADHIGH and DEVICEHIGH commands (these DOS commands load TSRs and device drivers into the normally underutilized upper memory area), some of the value of the commercial memory managers is negated, at least in their current versions.

Depending on your PC and the type of drivers you use, this savings can be significant. If you are running on a network, using a commercial memory manager can save more than 50K. A typical savings is around 35K, which is still quite valuable when you are talking about programs that might crash if not given enough RAM.

The commercial memory managers are often faster than HIMEM in giving programs the memory they request. They also do it using less memory than HIMEM requires, especially if you are using EMM386.EXE. If you are using both HIMEM.SYS and EMM386.EXE, you might be able to replace them both with a single commercial memory manager that is more flexible. Commercially available memory managers like QEMM 386MAX compare the size of each file you load into the Upper Memory Area with contiguous sections of memory in the UMA. It attempts to place as many device drivers in the UMA as can be arranged. EMM386.EXE will load as many as can be loaded in the order that you requested the load to be executed, making UMA utilization potentially less effective.

24

Disk Caching Programs

When you read information from a disk drive, the computer must wait for the head in the drive to go to the right part of the drive, then wait for the platter to spin around to the right location, and then wait while all the information is read. Although this happens very quickly (especially relative to floppy disks), if your program has a lot to read, it can slow down your work.

A disk caching program is one that helps cut down the number of times the computer has to wait. It keeps copies of the information on the hard disk in RAM in your system. If a program asks the computer to read some information from disk that is already in the disk cache, it gets the information from the cache in an instant instead of having to wait. The more RAM you give a caching program, the more likely it is that the information you are reading will be in the cache.

The slower your hard disk, the more valuable a disk caching program is. Most PCs built before 1988 have slower disk drives (particularly the ones built before 1985), and even modern laptop computers have slow disk drives. If you have the extended or expanded memory to spare, a disk cache program can make your system respond much faster.

Modern disk cache programs are perfectly safe to use because they speed up only reading from the disk, not writing to it. Older cache programs also sped up writing to the disk but turned out to be unsafe in some circumstances. The reputation old cache programs got for being unsafe is no longer deserved.

Using a disk cache program greatly speeds up Windows because Windows uses the disk often when you switch between programs. A nice feature of disk caching programs is that they help speed up all programs, not just a specific program like Windows.

SMARTDrive

Windows 3.1 comes with a free disk caching program, SMARTDrive. You load SMARTDrive in your CONFIG.SYS file on a line after HIMEM.SYS. The two main arguments you use with SMARTDrive are the default amount of memory and a minimum size it can be shrunk to. A typical CONFIG.SYS line is

```
device=C:\WINDOWS\SMARTDRV.SYS 1024 256
```

The first of the two arguments tells SMARTDrive the amount of memory to use for the cache in kilobytes. This can be between 128 and 8192 (8M) but it is of little value if it is below 256. If you don't include any arguments, SMARTDrive uses 256K.

The second argument tells how little you are willing to shrink the cache if Windows wants more memory. This is very valuable because Windows 3.1 does its own equivalent of disk caching. Without this feature, running SMARTDrive would take longer under Windows. You can set this to any size up to the size from the first argument, but it is likely you will want to set this to 128 (the default is 256). This is because other programs that run under Windows read from the disk and those reads should still be cached for best performance.

Table 24.4 gives suggested values for setting SMARTDrive, depending on the amount of extended memory you have. In general, you should give about 25 precent of your extended memory to a disk cache under normal circumstances, and up to 35 precent for disk-intensive programs. Note that you might want to change this percentage depending on the programs you run on your system other than Windows.

Table 24.4. Suggested SMARTDrive arguments.

Amount of Extended Memory	Arguments
2M	512 128
3M	768 256
4M	1024 256
5M	1280 256

Tip: Don't hand too much memory to SMARTDrive thinking it will greatly speed things up. There is a diminishing return on disk cache RAM that depends heavily on how often the disk needs to search. For example, if allocating 1M to SMARTDrive gets you 50 percent better disk response, allocating 2M might get you only 60 percent better response.

SMARTDrive generally uses extended memory because it is faster. If you have both extended system memory and expanded memory on a 16-bit memory board in your PC and want SMARTDrive to use the expanded memory instead, add the /A argument to the command line.

Warning: SMARTDrive is incompatible with some commercial disk-partitioning programs. It works fine if you partition your disk with the MS-DOS command FDISK, but it can cause damage if you are using other partitioning programs. Often, it detects the partitioning program when it starts, and it gives the error message

SMARTDrive: Incompatible disk partition detected.

Tip: You must use SMARTDrive (or an equivalent caching program) if you are running in 386-enhanced mode and are using a drive controller that is a bus master such as a SCSI bus controller. This is due to the need for double-buffering by such a system. Bus master cards go around your system's DMA controller and use fixed addresses that do not work in 386-enhanced mode. For more information about how SCSI bus masters work, see Chapter 23 "Windows Hardware Enhancements."

continues

> SMARTDrive provides the necessary double-buffering by causing all reads and writes to go through it instead of going to the erroneous fixed address. If you need to turn off SMARTDrive's double buffering, add the /B- argument, such as
>
> ```
> device=C:\WINDOWS\SMARTDRV.SYS 1024 256 /B-
> ```

Other Caching Programs

There are more than a dozen popular disk caching programs. Many of them are somewhat faster and more flexible than SMARTDrive, but, of course, they are not free. Some are written like SMARTDrive so that they give up extra memory when Windows is running. If you find that running SMARTDrive improves the speed of running Windows, you might want to investigate a commercial disk caching program.

Setting Up a Swap File in 386-Enhanced Mode

If you are running in 386-enhanced mode, you can make it look to programs as though you have a large amount of RAM by creating a Windows *swap file*. When Windows uses a swap file, it can access the swap file like it accesses data in RAM. If you have 5M on your hard disk free, for example, you can use it as a swap disk and it seems to Windows as though you added 5M of RAM.

The only drawbacks of using a swap file are that it is much slower than RAM and it takes up space on your hard disk. When you use a swap file, any program (including Windows) that needs information from the area of memory the hard disk is emulating causes your PC to read from the hard disk. This takes significantly more time than reading from RAM. (In fact, using a swap file is almost the opposite of using a disk caching program.) Also, if you are very tight on hard disk space, you might not be able to spare it for Windows.

On the other hand, hard disk space is much less expensive than RAM. For the price you would pay for 6M of RAM, you can buy a 50M hard drive. If you use 10M of that drive for a swap file, it is unlikely you will ever need more, and you have 40M of extra hard disk space.

Permanent and Temporary Swap Files

The two types of swap files are useful in different situations. A permanent swap file is kept on disk all the time, even when you are not running Windows. A temporary swap file is kept only during your Windows session. When you start Windows in 386-enhanced mode, it checks for a permanent swap file; if it does not find one, it creates a temporary swap file for you.

The advantage of using a permanent swap file is that it is faster than a temporary swap file. Windows reads from and writes to the file without going through MS-DOS and thus can access data faster. The disadvantage of a permanent swap file is that it occupies hard disk space that could be used by other programs. You must weigh the speed versus space loss when you decide what kind of swap file to use.

A permanent swap file is kept as a pair of hidden files on your disk. These files, called SPART.PAR and 386SPART.PAR, must consist of contiguous blocks on the disk. If your disk is fragmented—meaning that only small holes are free for data, so large files have to be in discontiguous parts of the disk—you cannot create a permanent swap file, although Windows can create a temporary swap file. Many commercial disk maintenance utilities such as Norton Utilities and PC Tools Deluxe have programs that compact the hard disk to reduce fragmentation.

If not much hard disk space is available for a permanent swap file, remember that Windows will create a temporary swap file for you. Although this is slower than a permanent swap file, it still gives you access to more memory for your programs.

24

Creating a Permanent Swap File

Unfragment your hard drive before you create a permanent swap file.

First, check the drive for fragmentation by

1. Running CHKDSK/F before you compress. Convert fragmented sectors to files if prompted.

2. Deleting any files in the drive's root directory with a file extension name of .CHK.

Tip: Compact your hard disk if you have a disk maintenance utility that does this. You should do this immediately before creating your permanent swap file.

Now you are ready to create a swap file. The Windows 3.1 Setup program creates a permanent swap file for you. If you did not create a permanent swap file during the Windows 3.1 installation process, (there will not be a System/Hidden file named 386SPART.PAR located in the root directory of your boot drive) you can still create one. You can create a permanent swap file, delete the current swap file, or change the current swap file's size. To access the Windows 3.1 utility that creates a permanent swap file, follow the steps outlined here:

1. Start Control Panel in your preferred fashion.

2. Double-click the 386 Enhanced icon.

3. Single-click the **V**irtual Memory button on the dialog box displayed.

4. If you have a permanent swap file, information about it will be displayed in the Current Settings area of the dialog box. If not, you should create one that is not less than 512K in size and not more than 2M in size. If you are using a disk compression utility like Stacker, you should create a permanent swap file on the disk that is not compressed. To create a permanent swap file, click the Change button. Select the desired drive. Now select Permanent from the Type drop-down list box.

5. Windows shows you the maximum size for a swap file. The number it uses also happens to be the amount of free space on the drive you selected.

6. Windows will suggest the size of your swap file based on how much memory you have and how much drive space is free.

7. Note that the recommended size and the new size are the same. Unless you change the new size amount, Windows will create a new swap file with the new size amount. Click the Use 32-Bit Disk Access check box if you have an 80386 processor or higher to fully utilize your computer's performance potential.

8. Click the OK button and Windows will do the rest.

The Virtual Memory dialog box is shown in Figure 24.4. Your basic options are to select the file size, choose a drive on which you want to create Virtual Memory, create the file, and quit the program. Don't forget to tell Windows that the file type you want is Permanent.

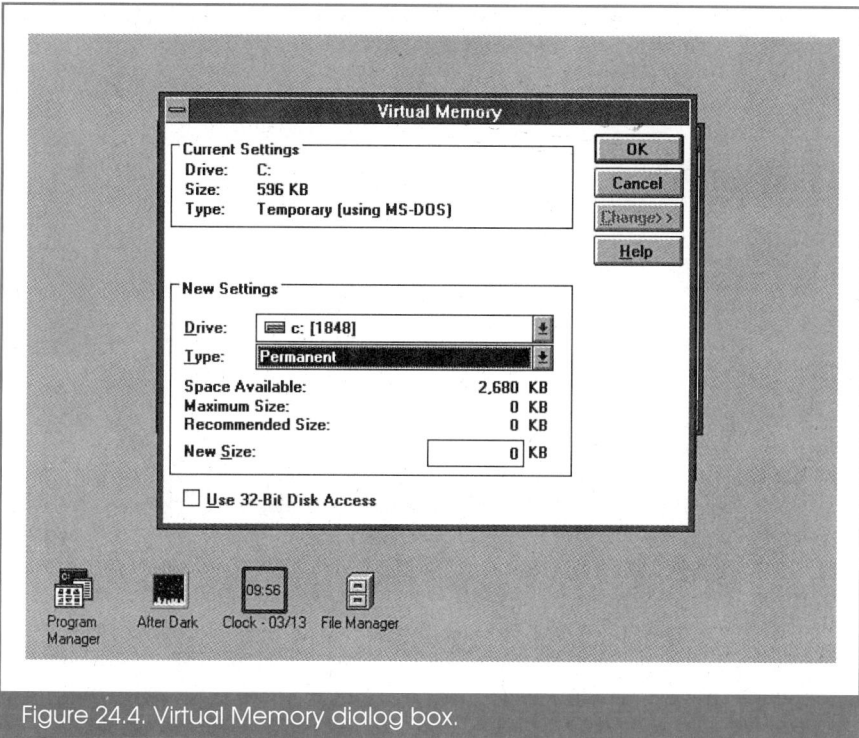

Figure 24.4. Virtual Memory dialog box.

24

The Virtual Memory dialog box after permanent swap file creation is shown in Figure 24.5.

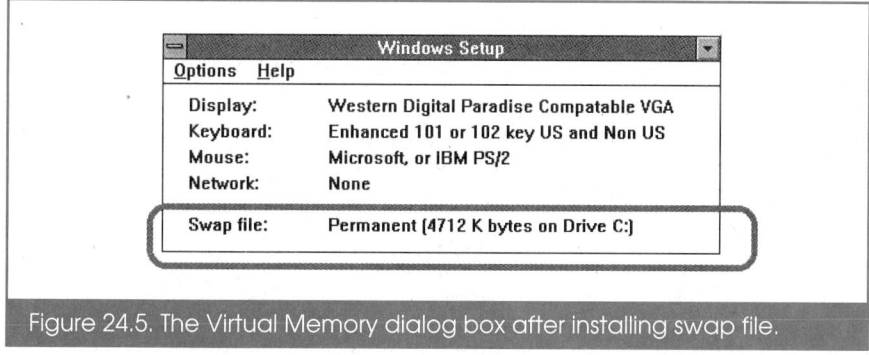

Figure 24.5. The Virtual Memory dialog box after installing swap file.

Changing the Size of Your Permanent Swap File

When you change the size of your swap file, you should delete an existing one first. You have to run the 386 Enhanced program and then the Virtual Memory program to delete and re-create the permanent swap file. When you are working within the Virtual Memory dialog box, click the **T**ype button. Select None. Click the OK button and exit the dialog box. From the 386 Enhanced dialog box, again click on the Virtual Memory button to get back into the Virtual Memory dialog box. Click the **T**ype button. You see three selections in a drop-down list box, shown in Figure 24.6:

▲ Temporary

▲ Permanent

▲ None

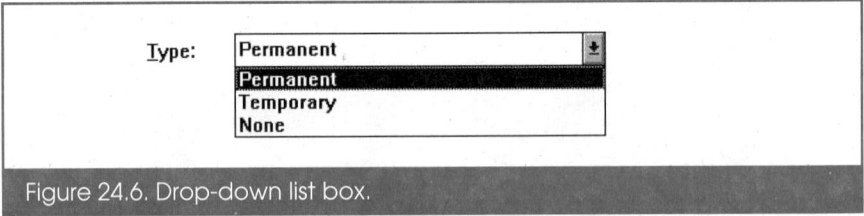

Figure 24.6. Drop-down list box.

Select Permanent. Follow the same steps you used to change the swap file size to create the new swap file.

Deleting the Permanent Swap File

You have to run the 386 Enhanced program and Virtual Memory programs to delete the permanent swap file. Again, you must start the Control Panel and 386 Enhanced programs while running Windows. From the Virtual Memory dialog box, simply choose None instead of the Permanent or Temporary type and click OK.

> **Tip:** If your hard disk backup program only enables you to back up the entire disk, you might want to delete a large permanent swap file before creating the backup. Most backup programs, however, enable you to exclude particular files. You should exclude the swap file because it never contains any useful information you could use later.

Problems with Using a Permanent Swap File

If the permanent swap file is not present or is damaged when you start Windows, you will see an alert box to that effect.

This usually indicates that one of the two swap files (SPART.PAR in the Windows directory or 386SPART.PAR on the disk you chose) has been corrupted, moved, or deleted. Windows will start in 386-enhanced mode, but with a temporary swap file. You should follow the steps shown previously to create a new permanent swap file using the Setup program.

24

Using a Temporary Swap File

Although using a permanent swap file is faster than using a temporary swap file, a temporary swap file is still a much better option than not using a swap file at all. When you start Windows in 386-enhanced mode, if you do not have a permanent swap file, Windows creates a temporary swap file called WIN386.SWP with 1M. If it later wants more memory, it simply extends the file as needed.

Normally, Windows puts the temporary swap file in the main Windows directory. You might want to change the drive Windows uses for the file if you have more than one hard drive. For example, you might want Windows to use a drive that has more free space on it or one that is faster than the one that has the main Windows directory.

To specify the desired drive for the temporary swap file, edit your SYSTEM.INI file. See Chapter 27, "Configuring with the WIN.INI and SYSTEM.INI Files," for a description of editing the SYSTEM.INI file. Add the following line to the [386Enh] section of the file:

```
PagingDevice=drive
```

Of course, you should be sure to indicate the drive you want, such as the D drive. For example:

```
PagingDevice=D:
```

Warning: When choosing a drive for your temporary swap file, be sure not to indicate a drive on a network because this causes Windows to run slowly or crash.

You can also limit the amount of hard disk Windows uses for the temporary swap file. In the [386Enh] section of the SYSTEM.INI file, edit or add one or both of the following lines:

```
MinUserDiskSpace=size
MaxPagingFileSize=size
```

Include the number of kilobytes you want for either or both options. The MinUserDiskSpace option tells Windows how much disk space to leave when it is creating a temporary swap file. MaxPagingFileSize is the largest the temporary swap file gets.

Tip: If you do not have a hard disk and Windows seems particularly slow in starting, this is because creating a large temporary swap disk takes a long time. You should unfragment your hard disk and create a permanent hard disk, or create a RAMDISK that can hold the required permanent swap file.

You are running Windows from a networked, diskless workstation. See the next section in this chapter for more on this technique.

Using a RAM Drive

In the mid-1980s, RAM drives were a popular method for speeding up programs if you had extra RAM. A RAM drive acts like a disk drive but is much faster. It uses the same principle as a disk cache except that you both read from and write to the RAM drive. The advantage of RAM drives is that you can specify them just like regular disk drives in programs. The very large disadvantage is that when you turn off the computer or experience a power loss, everything in the RAM drive is lost.

There is rarely any need to use a RAM drive in Windows. Because Windows already uses RAM in the most efficient manner, using a RAM drive is redundant (and therefore slower). If you instead use SMARTDrive, you get better performance. The only time using a RAM drive is of much value is if your PC has no hard disk but is attached to a network. In this case, you can set up a RAM drive for holding temporary files that would normally be written out to the network.

Windows comes with a device driver called RAMDrive that you can use to create a RAM drive. Note that you can use RAMDrive outside of Windows for non-Windows programs that can be improved by using a RAM drive.

To use RAMDrive, enter a line in your CONFIG.SYS file, such as

```
device=C:\WINDOWS\RAMDRIVE.SYS 310 /E
```

Be sure to enter the line after the line for HIMEM. The contents of your CONFIG.SYS file and methods for changing them are described in Chapter 25, "Changing Your Configuration."

24

> **Tip:** The RAMDRIVE.SYS driver line must come after the HIMEM.SYS driver line in your CONFIG.SYS file. Otherwise, MS-DOS does not load RAMDrive.

The full syntax for the RAMDrive command is

```
device=[drive][path]RAMDRIVE.SYS [disksize]
        [sectorsize] [filelimit] [/E ¦ /A]
```

In the syntax, *disksize* is the number of kilobytes the RAM disk will be. If you don't specify a size, RAMDrive uses 64K. The *sectorsize* is the number of bytes for each sector; this can be 128, 256, 512, or 1024. The default sector size is 512. You can limit the number of files and directories that can go in the root of the RAM disk; the default is 64.

You can also specify whether to create the RAM disk in extended memory (/E) or expanded memory (/A). If you don't specify either, RAMDrive takes the memory from your conventional memory, which is rarely what you want it to do.

EMM386.EXE

If you have an 80386 or higher and need to run programs that use expanded memory, you can use the supplied EMM386.EXE driver to emulate expanded memory.

Tip: The version of EMM386.EXE that comes with Windows 3.1 is newer than the one that comes with MS-DOS Version 5.0. You should always use the most recent version of EMM386.EXE.

Warning: If you are running a commercial memory manager like QEMM or 386MAX, do not use EMM386.EXE. It can conflict with the memory manager's allocation. Instead, if you need to allocate expanded memory, use the memory manager's own commands.

To use EMM386.EXE, enter a line in your CONGIG.SYS file, such as

```
device=C:\WINDOWS\EMM386.EXE 1024
```

The command tells where the EMM386.EXE file is (normally, in the directory in which you installed Windows) and how much memory to emulate as expanded memory (in this case, 1024K of memory). This is the way you will generally use EMM386.EXE.

Tip: The EMM386.EXE driver line must come after the HIMEM.SYS driver line in your CONFIG.SYS file. Otherwise, DOS does not load EMM386.EXE.

Advanced users might want to use other EMM386.EXE arguments. Because these arguments are all very technical, it is unlikely that anyone but an advanced user would be interested in them; you can safely skip to the next section.

The full syntax for loading EMM386.EXE is

```
device=[drive][path]EMM386.EXE [AUTO ¦ ON ¦ OFF] [amount]
       [W= {ON ¦ OFF}] [Mf ¦ FRAME=mmmm ¦ /Pmmmm] [Pn=mmmm]
       [I=mmmm-nnnn] [X=mmmm-nnnn] [B=mmmm] [L=n] [A=n]
       [Hnnn] [D=nnn] [RAM] [NOEMS]
```

Active Status

The AUTO/ON/OFF options tell MS-DOS the state of the PC when EMM386.EXE returns to MS-DOS. AUTO, the default, indicates that

EMM386.EXE is inactive except when the PC is in virtual mode (the mode that gets expanded memory) and there is at least one expanded memory handle in use. This means that expanded memory support is available only when a program requests it. ON means to keep the driver active all the time, and OFF means to keep the driver inactive all the time.

Amount of Expanded Memory

As already stated, the amount in the command line is the number of kilobytes to allocate for expanded memory. If this number is not included, EMM386.EXE allocates 256K. If you give an argument that is greater than the amount of memory available, EMM386.EXE uses all the available memory.

Weitek Coprocessor

24

The W argument tells whether to enable support for the Weitek coprocessor. Set this to ON only if you have a Weitek coprocessor in your PC. A Weitek coprocessor is a numeric (math) coprocessor designed to replace the Entel 80287 and 80387 coprocessors. Coprocessors are used to improve the speed of certain programs such as computer aided design (CAD) programs.

Frame Location

The EMS (expanded memory) page frame is located in upper memory, as described earlier in this chapter.

If you want to specify exactly where the page frame is, you can use the M option, the FRAME= option, or the Pn= option. Note that the location you specify must have four contiguous 16K pages. If you do not give one of these options, EMM386.EXE starts looking for pages starting at E000 and keeps looking down until C000. However, if you want to give an exact page so that EMM386.EXE doesn't conflict with some other program, you can give it by frame number or by segment base.

The M option uses frame numbers as shown in Table 24.5. Use frame numbers 10 through 14 only if you have configured your conventional RAM to be 512K. It is unlikely you will ever use frame numbers 10 through 14.

Table 24.5. M option base addresses.

Argument	Address
M1	C000
M2	C400
M3	C800
M4	CC00
M5	D000
M6	D400
M7	D800
M8	DC00
M9	E000
M10	8000
M11	8400
M12	8800
M13	8C00
M14	9000

The FRAME= option takes an address of the desired segment base in hex. For example, you would specify that the frame should start at D400 with the argument

```
device=C:\WINDOWS\EMM386.EXE FRAME=D400
```

The Pn option enables you to specify the location for each page. You have to specify all four pages if you use this option, and thus it is rarely used. For example, the following line would define the pages that each start on segment bases:

```
device=C:\WINDOWS\EMM386.EXE P0=E000 P1=DC00 P2=D800 P3=D400
```

If you are letting EMM386.EXE search for free pages, you can specify a range in which it will not look with the X= option. For instance, to prevent it from searching in C000 to D000, give the command

```
device=C:\WINDOWS\EMM386.EXE X=C000-D000
```

You can include an entire range with the I= option. This forces EMM386.EXE to use the specified range, such as

```
device=C:\WINDOWS\EMM386.EXE I=D000-E000
```

You can specify the lowest segment that EMM386.EXE will look in with the B= option. The values can be as low as 1000 and as high as EC00. For example, to cause it to look down to 2000, use the command

```
device=C:\WINDOWS\EMM386.EXE B=2000
```

Minimum Available

The L= option enables you to specify the minimum amount of extended memory available after you load EMM386.EXE. This option specifies memory in kilobytes. You can use this as a safety valve to ensure that you have enough other memory available. For example, request 1024K of expanded memory, but to be sure 512K of extended memory is still available, use the command

```
device=C:\WINDOWS\EMM386.EXE 1024 L=512
```

24

Fast Alternate Sets

The A= option tells how many fast alternate register sets to allocate. In memory, alternate registers are similarities of a CPU's data registers. The default is 7. The minimum is 2, and the maximum is 254.

Number of Handles

Use the H switch to specify the number of handles used to reference pages you want to allocate, between 1 and 255. The default is 255. For instance, to allocate only 127, use the command

```
device=C:\WINDOWS\EMM386.EXE H=127
```

DMA Buffering

EMM386.EXE should buffer DMA (*Direct Memory Access*) operations. The D= option enables you to specify how many kilobytes of memory to allocate for DMA buffering (between 16 and 256). This should be the largest DMA transfer EMM386.EXE will possibly see. You do not need to use this option unless you get an error message from EMM386.EXE specifying that you should.

Kinds of Access

The RAM option tells EMM386.EXE to access both expanded memory and the upper memory area. The NOEMS option causes EMM386.EXE to control only the upper memory area.

Understanding EMM386 Memory Use

EMM386.EXE is not very efficient at allocating memory. The driver itself takes 48K of your extended memory. This, on top of the 64K reserved for HIMEM, can gobble 112K of memory. Most commercial memory managers can do the same work in about 10K.

> **Warning:** Depending on the arguments you use, EMM386.EXE can take up part of your conventional memory for large-frame EMS page handles. This usually occurs only when you have little extended memory to work with but can significantly cut the amount of conventional memory you have available for programs. Be sure to check the amount of conventional memory you have left after you load EMM386.EXE with the MS-DOS CHKDSK command or, if you are running MS-DOS 4.0 or later, the MEM command. If EMM386.EXE is taking too much memory but you still want to have expanded memory, you should strongly consider buying a commercial memory manager such as Quarterdeck's QEMM-386 or Qualitas's 386MAX.

Choosing a Frame Size

Windows can access your expanded memory in two ways: in small-frame or large-frame modes. If you are running large Windows programs, small-frame EMS is more efficient because it is designed for programs that do not do much memory switching. If you are running many Windows programs at the same time and are switching between them, you should use large-frame EMS.

The /E argument followed by a number tells Windows how much conventional memory must be free in order to use large-frame mode. If there isn't that much conventional memory, Windows starts in

small-frame mode. For example, to use large-frame mode unless there is less than 540K of conventional memory available, give the command

```
C>WIN /R /E 540
```

To guarantee that Windows starts in small-frame mode, give a number that is so high that the test always fails, such as 641 (no computer has more than 640K free).

Large-Frame Bank Line

In large-frame mode, EMS memory is split into two regions: *global* and *banked.* Global EMS memory is available to all programs; banked EMS memory is available to only one program at a time. The line between these two types of memory is the *bank line.* Global memory is below the bank line and banked memory is above it.

Some programs that use expanded memory need particular amounts of both types of memory, so you might need to move the line to make a sufficient amount available. If a program runs out of one or the other type of memory, it will probably give you an error message that indicates what type of memory it ran out of.

If you move the bank line down, more banked memory is available but there is less global memory. Moving the bank line up reverses that, giving you more global and less banked memory. The /L argument followed by a number tells Windows to move the bank line up or down. You can move the bank line from its default position by up to 16K.

For example, to move the bank line down by 8K, giving you 8K more banked and 8K less global memory, start Windows with the command

```
C>WIN /R /L -8
```

Memory Problems

You might encounter many problems that deal with the computer's memory. You might have too little memory, or there might be problems with many programs trying to use the same memory. Windows is usually good about letting you know when you run out of memory, but not always. This section describes the memory problems you might encounter when running Windows. Note that Chapter 20, "Other DOS Programs and Windows," describes the memory problems you might encounter when running non-Windows programs and how to solve them.

System Resources

When running Windows programs, you might see an error message telling you that you are low on memory. Many programs have ways of finding out how much free memory is available, and you should next check the value there. If you find that there seems to be plenty of free memory, you might be running out of *system resources,* a special area of memory that Windows uses to store windows and graphics objects.

The system resources area is a 64K chunk of memory maintained by Windows. To see the percentage of how much of that 64K is in use, use the **Help** **A**bout Program Manager command in the Program Manager program. Figure 24.7 shows an example of this command. Note that the system resources area is listed as percent free: The lower the number, the closer you are to running out of system resources.

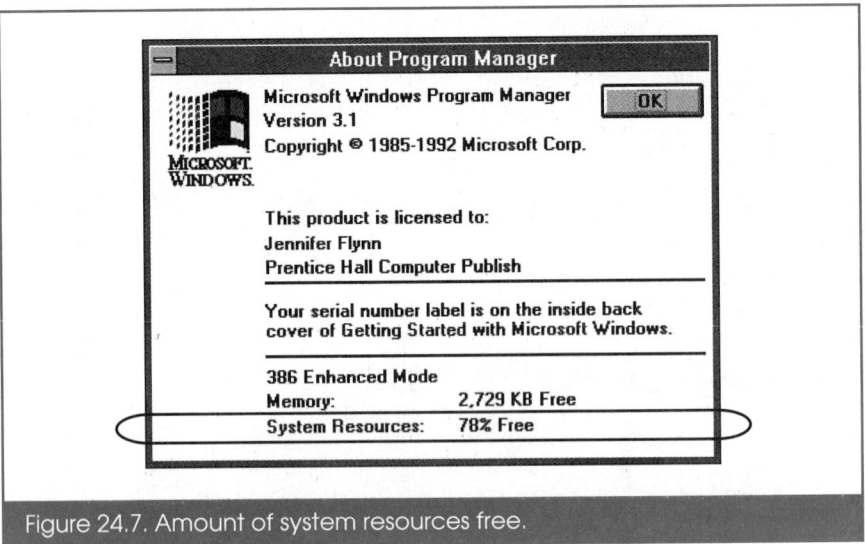

Figure 24.7. Amount of system resources free.

It is an unfortunate fact, but Windows has an absolute limit of 64K for system resources: you cannot increase this amount no matter how much memory you have. The technical reason behind the decision was to make Windows slightly faster, but the result is that you might run out of system resources long before you run out of other memory. The information kept in the system resources area includes

- ▲ Window size and location
- ▲ Window attributes
- ▲ Line types in use
- ▲ Graphical fill patterns
- ▲ Brush shapes
- ▲ Other graphics items

The only way to free up space in the system resources area is to close windows or quit from programs that use lots of graphics. If you are running out of system resources while running in Program Manager, you should reduce the number of program groups you have, because each group has its own window that takes a certain amount of memory regardless of the number of programs and their icons in each group.

> **Tip:** As it turns out, Program Manager eats up more system resources than most other Windows programs because of the number of windows and icons you have. If you have persistent problems with running out of system resources, you probably want to minimize Program Manager when you are not using it. The easiest way to do this is to give the **O**ptions **M**inimize on Use command in Program Manager. This causes the Program Manager program window to minimize immediately after you start a program from it.

24

EMMExclude

Windows in 386-enhanced mode uses the memory areas in the upper memory area if they are not already in use by devices such as your video board. This procedure frees RAM that would otherwise be wasted. However, it means that Windows has to be correct about what areas are not in use or else a memory conflict will occur.

If you are using an enhanced VGA adapter or a nonstandard video display adapter and you have problems running Windows in 386-enhanced mode, that might be because Windows is trying to use memory that the adapter thinks belongs to it. You can test this by specifying in your SYSTEM.INI file that you do not want Windows to use parts of that memory. See Chapter 27, "Configuring with the WIN.INI and SYSTEM.INI Files," for more information on modifying your SYSTEM.INI file.

In the [386Enh] section of the SYSTEM.INI file, you want to include a line that looks like

```
EMMExclude=start-end
```

in which *start* and *end* are memory addresses in hexadecimal notation. For example, some enhanced VGA adapters use addresses C400 through C7FF. Windows often detects this, but if it doesn't, your system can crash or your screen might appear incorrect. You should try clearing up the problem with the line

```
EMMExclude=C400-C7FF
```

(Note that the addresses use the number *0,* not the letter *O.*)

If that line does not clear up the problem, you can try expanding the range to include all the usable area in the upper memory area to see whether it is some other address. For testing purposes only, try the line

```
EMMExclude=A000-EFFF
```

If this clears up the problem, some parts of the upper memory area need to be excluded, but you have to find out by testing. Do not leave the entire range A000-EFFF excluded because this slows down Windows significantly.

> **Tip:** Some network adapters and other hardware drivers use some parts of the upper memory area. Windows is not very good at checking for many hardware adapters, so you must check the technical sections of your hardware documentation. Look for references to them using hexadecimal addresses between A000 and EFFF (or, more precisely, A000:0 and EFFF:F). If you find such addresses, try mapping them out with the EMMExclude line.

Stacks

Most programs use special data blocks called *stacks* to help them run efficiently. Stacks help keep well-written programs from using RAM unnecessarily. However, you need to allocate enough stacks in your CONFIG.SYS file for all programs. This is particularly true when you run Windows in 386-enhanced mode. If you receive error messages that talk about "stack overflow" or "out of stack space," you might have to change the amount of stack space allocated when you start the computer.

If you are running MS-DOS Version 3.2, your CONFIG.SYS file should have the following line in it:

```
STACKS=9,192
```

If you are running MS-DOS Version 3.3 or later, the line should read

```
STACKS=0,0
```

Allocating memory to stacks is redundant, because Windows handles this memory management chore for DOS. The DOS Stacks default allocation is disabled with this statement.

Freeing Windows Memory

The most common way to free memory while running Windows is to close other programs that are running. This usually frees many hundreds of kilobytes at a time. If you ran a program earlier and are sure you don't want to use it again in this Windows session, activate the program and quit it.

Another common method of freeing memory is to minimize running programs to icons. This recovers most of the memory the program is using and gives you easy access to the program later without having to restart it. This is covered in Chapter 5, "Program Manager."

In some cases, clearing the Clipboard can free a great deal of memory. If you have stored a large or complex picture, or a great deal of text, in the Clipboard and you no longer need it, you should clear the Clipboard. Run the Clipboard program from Program Manager and check the contents to be sure you want to lose them. If so, give the **E**dit **D**elete command. This is covered in more detail in Chapter 9, "Clipboard Viewer."

If you are using SMARTDrive or some other disk caching program, you might want to reduce the size of the cache to give more space to Windows as described earlier in this chapter.

Terminate-and-stay-resident programs (TSRs) can take up a great deal of conventional memory. If you can, reduce the number of TSRs you use when you boot your PC. Programs like Quarterdeck's Manifest can help you pinpoint which TSRs are taking up the most space in memory.

24

If you can't reduce the number of TSRs, you can load them more intelligently. You should always try to load TSRs in your CONFIG.SYS file rather than your AUTOEXEC.BAT file. If they must be loaded in your AUTOEXEC.BAT file, you should load them before you give the PATH, PROMPT, or SET commands. Loading TSRs after these commands causes them to take up more space in memory because of the way MS-DOS loads the environment with them.

If you are running Windows in 386-enhanced mode and there are TSRs that you need only when running Windows, you can use a special file to load them only during Windows. If you have such a TSR and are running Windows in 386-enhanced mode, you should not put the device driver in your CONFIG.SYS file because this wastes memory for all your MS-DOS programs. Instead, create a file called WINSTART.BAT in your Windows directory that contains the name of the device driver program (you can do this with the Notepad program or another text editor). There should be instructions for the exact command line to use in this file in the documentation for the device. The WINSTART.BAT file is loaded only when you start Windows in 386-enhanced mode so that the device doesn't waste RAM when you are not running Windows.

Of course, if you are using DOS 5.0, you can load TSRs in the upper memory area by using the DEVICEHIGH or LOADHIGH commands. See your DOS manual for the correct application of these commands for your environment.

Many people have fancy wallpaper for their desktops. Using wallpaper takes up memory, however, and you might want to forego the aesthetic value of your desktop to save memory. To remove the wallpaper from your desktop, run Control Panel as described in Chapter 7, "Control Panel." Choose the Desktop icon to open the dialog box shown in Figure 24.8. In the File option of the Wallpaper box, select the first choice (None) and click OK.

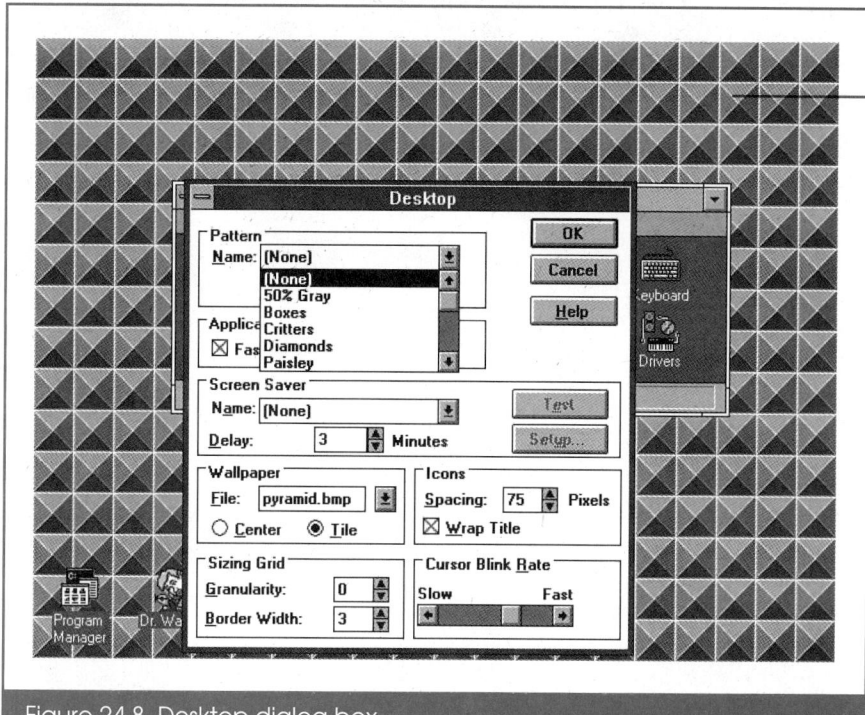

Wallpaper design

Figure 24.8. Desktop dialog box.

24

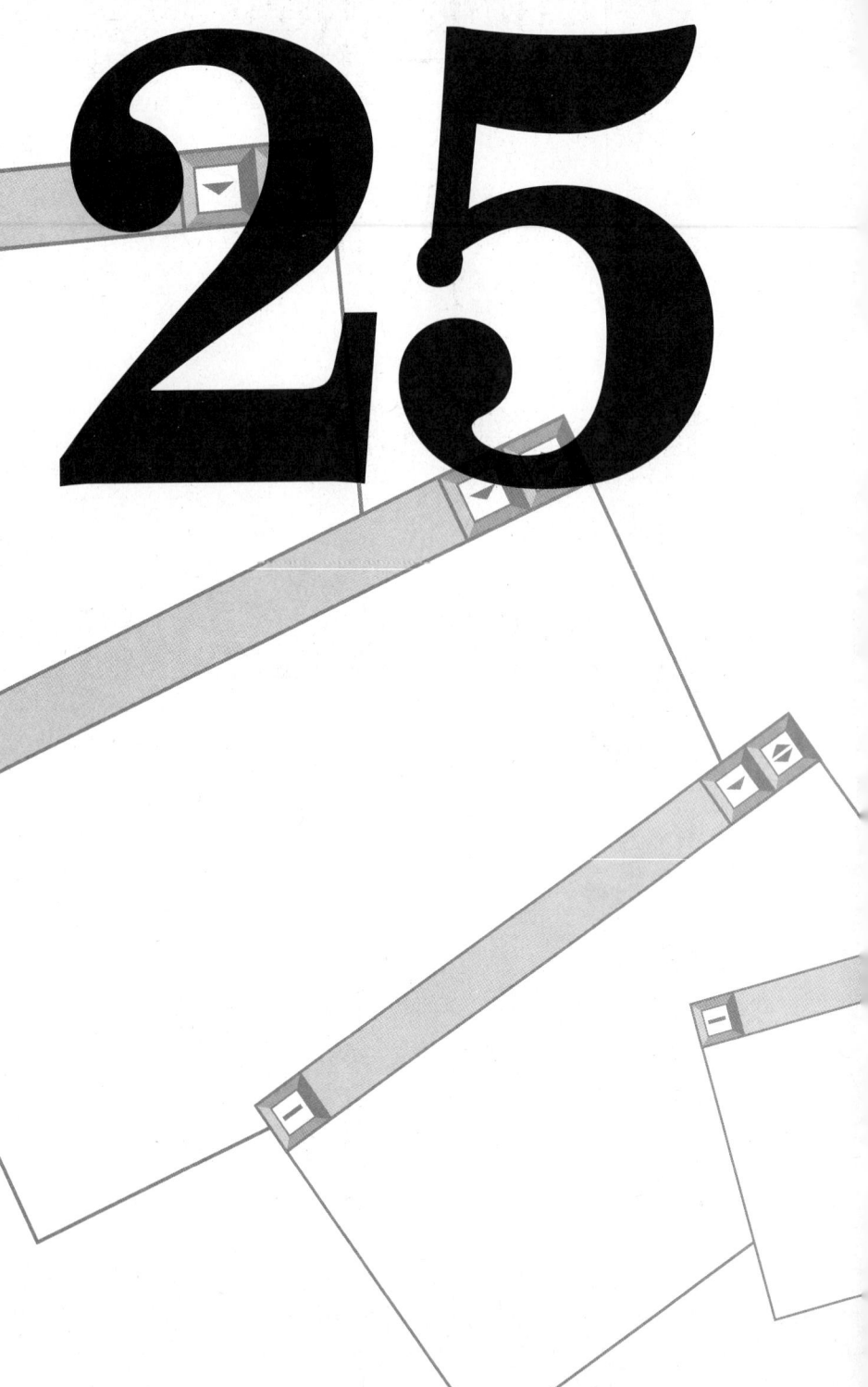

CHAPTER

25

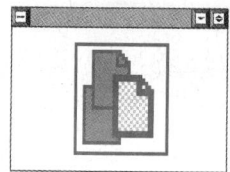

Changing Your Configuration

It is likely that after you set up Windows 3.1 you will want to change it. You will find things to add to Windows, discover tips in other chapters of this book that can help you run Windows faster or more reliably, and so on. You can change Windows in many different ways depending on the thing you want to change.

This chapter covers the most common ways people change Windows. The four methods covered here are

▲ Running Setup from within Windows

▲ Running Setup outside of Windows

▲ Changing the AUTOEXEC.BAT file

▲ Changing the CONFIG.SYS file

Other ways to fine-tune Windows are covered in later chapters. These involve the editing files Windows looks at when it starts. The two most frequently modified files are WIN.INI and SYSTEM.INI. The WIN.INI and SYSTEM.INI files are covered in Chapter 27, "Configuring with the WIN.INI and SYSTEM.INI Files." Other files, such as CONTROL.INI and PROGMAN.INI, are described in the same chapter.

The Two Setup Programs

Chapter 2, "Installing Windows," showed how to use the Setup program to put Windows on your hard disk the first time. You need to run Setup again if you want to change installed hardware or Windows devices. The changes you might want to make are to the

- ▲ Computer system motherboard
- ▲ Graphics adapter
- ▲ Keyboard
- ▲ Mouse
- ▲ Network

You can also use Setup to quickly add programs to windows in Program Manager. This process is covered in Chapter 5, "Program Manager."

Setup can be run in two ways: from within Windows and from MS-DOS.

- ▲ Run Setup from within Windows if you are changing a device, if you are adding a device that Windows knows about, or if you want to add programs to Program Manager.

- ▲ Run Setup from MS-DOS to change motherboards or copy and install some device drivers on your hard drive.

Changing and Adding Devices

The Setup program icon in Program Manager is in the Main window. When you run this program, you see a dialog box similar to Figure 25.1. This tells you the current settings for the four device types.

You cannot change the displayed options from the main window. To change options, give the **O**ptions **C**hange System Settings command. The dialog box for that command is shown in Figure 25.2. Each of the four settings has its own drop-down list box that contains all the devices Windows knows about for each type.

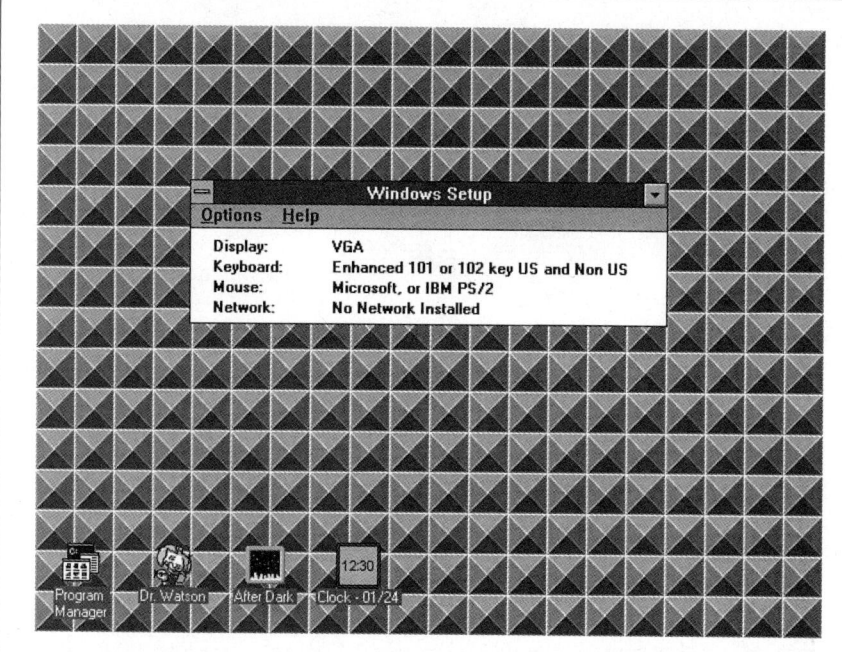

Figure 25.1. Windows Setup dialog box.

25

For example, to change devices from a standard VGA monitor to monochrome VGA, click the downward-pointing arrow to the right of the Display choice, or press the Alt-↓ keys. The drop-down list box is shown in Figure 25.3. Choose VGA with Monochrome display by clicking it or scrolling to it and pressing the Alt-↓ keys again.

If you select a device that Windows did not copy to your hard disk when you installed Windows, you see a dialog box like the one shown in Figure 25.4. Insert the specified disk in your disk drive and click OK. If your disk drive is a different letter than the one indicated, edit the drive letter before clicking OK.

You might have to insert more than one disk, especially if you change displays. This is due to Windows's loading in new fonts and color patterns.

After you have changed the device, you see the dialog box shown in Figure 25.5. You have to choose one of these two; you cannot change another device first. Choose the left button to start Windows immediately or the right button to quit from Windows with your new setting in place.

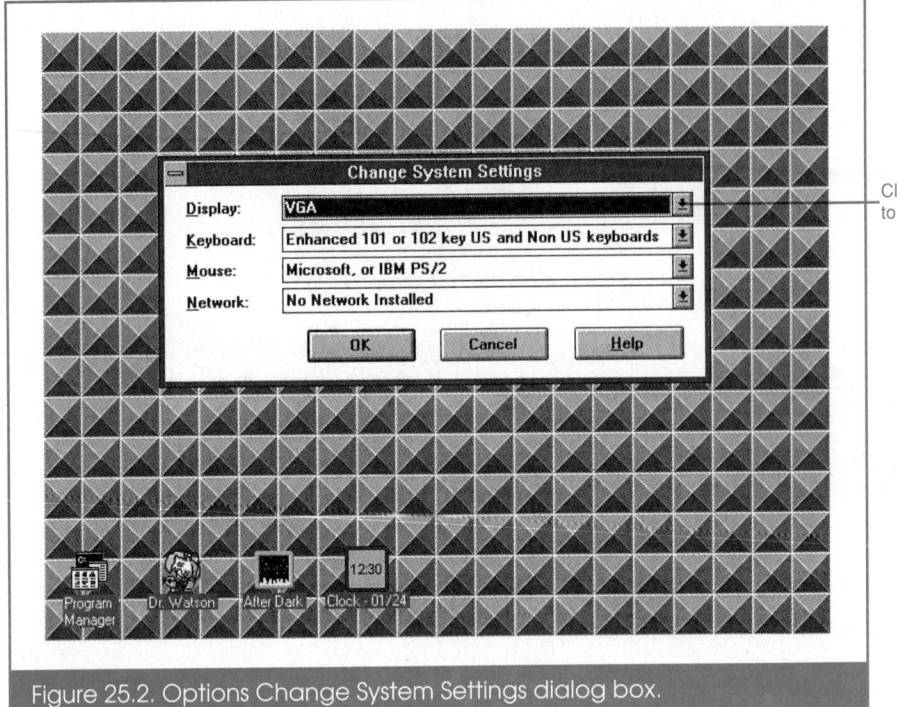

Click here
to reveal list

Figure 25.2. Options Change System Settings dialog box.

Warning: Because you have to restart Windows or quit from Windows to use your changes, you should quit from any programs you are running before changing system settings with Setup.

If you later switch back to a device you had already installed, you do not need to insert diskettes again. The device driver you used to use will be resident unless you have taken steps to delete it.

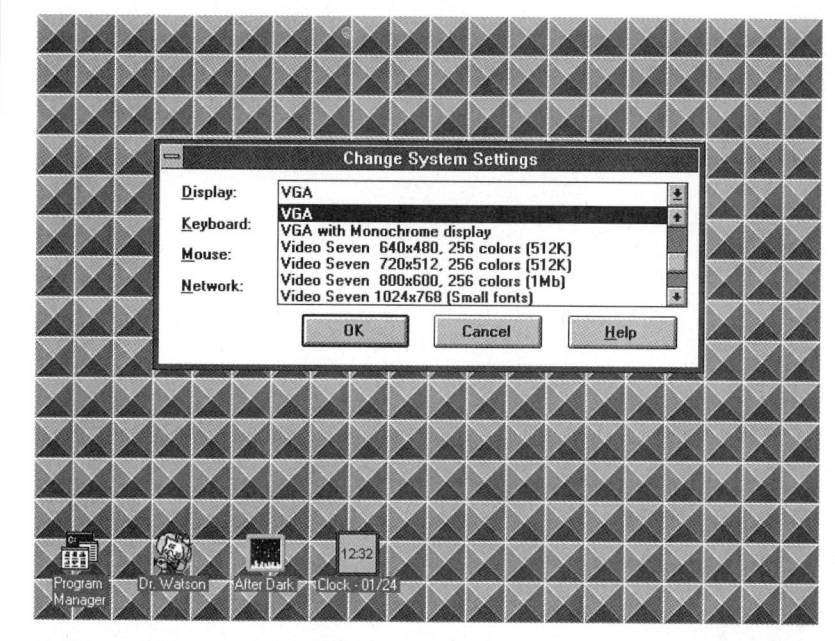

Figure 25.3. Drop-down list box for Display.

25

Tip: When you tell Setup you want to install a new driver, it looks at the SETUP.INF file it has stored on the hard disk. This file includes, among many other things, the disk numbers of the various drivers. The SETUP.INF file for Windows distributed on 3 1/2-inch disks is different from the SETUP.INF file for 5 1/4-inch disks because the two sizes of disks are different. If you installed from 3 1/2-inch disks, you need those disks to add new drivers. If you no longer have the same disks from which you installed Windows, you can get around this problem. Insert the first disk of your current diskette set and copy the SETUP.INF file from this diskette to the \system directory under the main Windows directory. You can copy SETUP.INF without decompressing it because it is stored on the first disk in decompressed form.

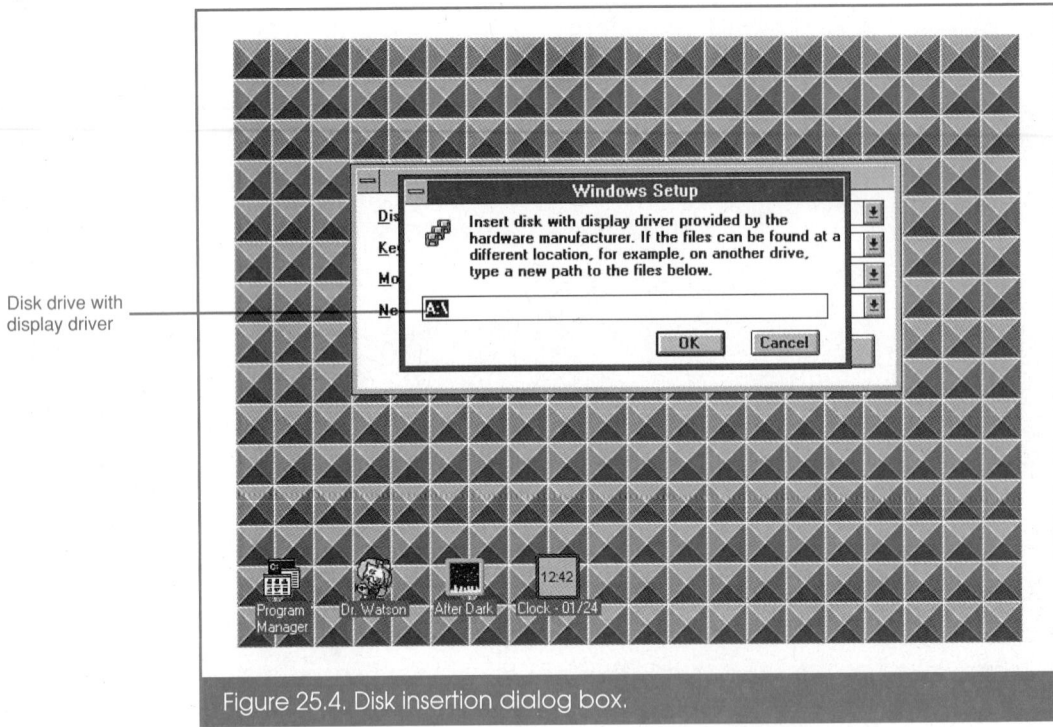

Disk drive with
display driver

Figure 25.4. Disk insertion dialog box.

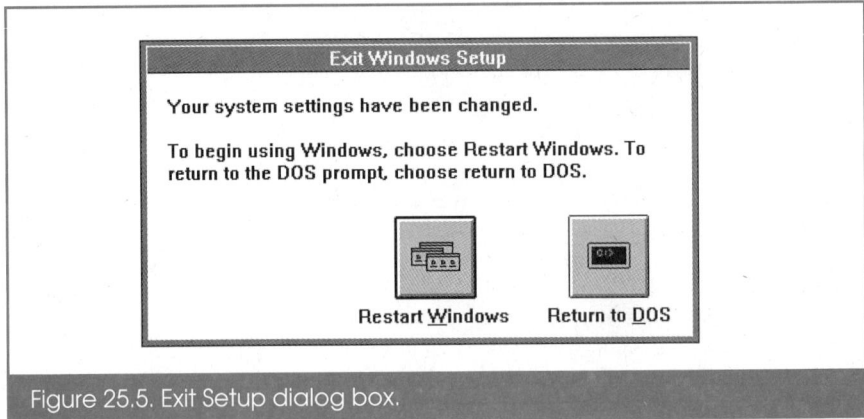

Figure 25.5. Exit Setup dialog box.

Adding and Removing Windows Components

You can add Windows components that might not have been added during the installation process. If you want, you can add or delete the following items:

- ▲ README files that contain last-minute changes to the manual

- ▲ Accessories like Write and Terminal

- ▲ The Minesweeper and Solitaire games

- ▲ The Screen Saver files

- ▲ The Wallpapers

These files are not considered critical to Windows's correct operation. They do, however, take up valuable disk space. To remove or add any of these files, choose **A**dd/Remove Windows Components from the **O**ptions menu. Simply select or deselect the check boxes located to the left of the items on the previous bulleted list. Windows keeps you abreast of the file-size totals as you make changes. Click the OK button when finished.

25

Adding Devices Windows Does Not Know About

Microsoft included drivers for all the devices that it knew worked correctly with Windows 3.1 when it was released. Of course, some devices did not exist at the time Windows was released or did not have completed Windows drivers. You can still install these devices, but it is somewhat difficult to do so in a way in which you can easily switch devices. You can now install a device Windows does not know about from the Setup program in Windows.

Adding a Device

To add a device Windows doesn't know about, be it video or a pointing device, you need only open Setup by clicking the Setup icon from the

Main Group, choose **O**ptions, **C**hange **S**ystem **S**ettings, and you see a dialog box like the one shown in Figure 25.6.

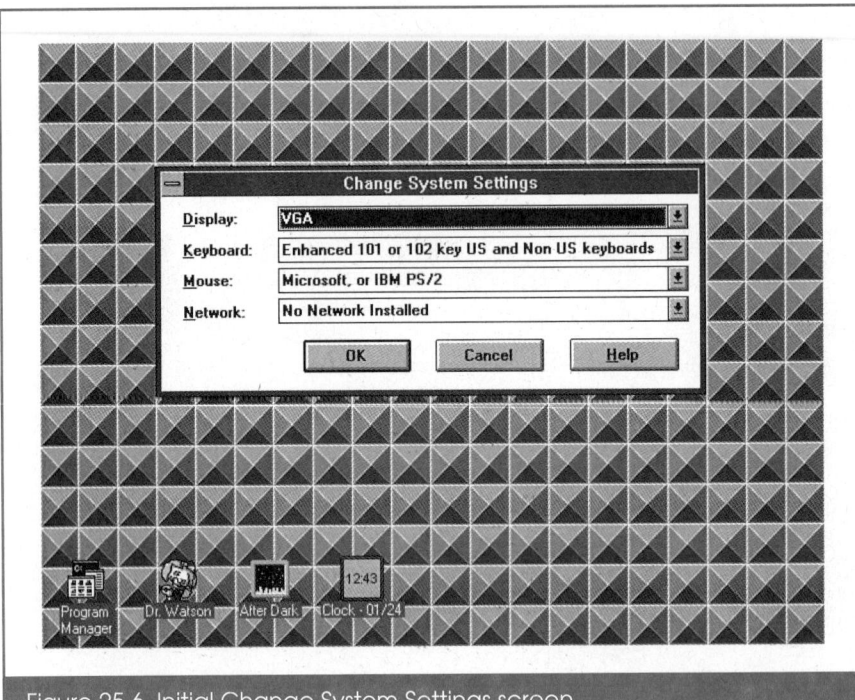

Figure 25.6. Initial Change System Settings screen.

Click the arrow to the right of the list box, and Setup shows you a screen with the choices for that type of hardware, such as are shown in Figure 25.7 for displays. This is the hardware Windows knows about.

Scroll to the bottom of the list to the choice Other (Required disk provided by a hardware manufacturer) and press Enter. Windows prompts you for a diskette, as shown in Figure 25.8.

Insert the diskette in the drive and press Enter. Setup reads the device drivers and any other files it needs. It then tells you it has successfully loaded the driver, and you exit to MS-DOS. When you start Windows the next time, that device will use the new driver.

Modifying the SETUP.INF File

When you install a new device that Windows does not initially know about, Setup copies the information from the manufacturer's diskette to

your Windows directory on your hard disk. It does not, however, update Windows's SETUP.INF file in the SYSTEM subdirectory. Although the device will work fine, if you switch to another device in Windows's Setup program, you have to reinstall the files when you switch back to your new device because SETUP.INF was not updated.

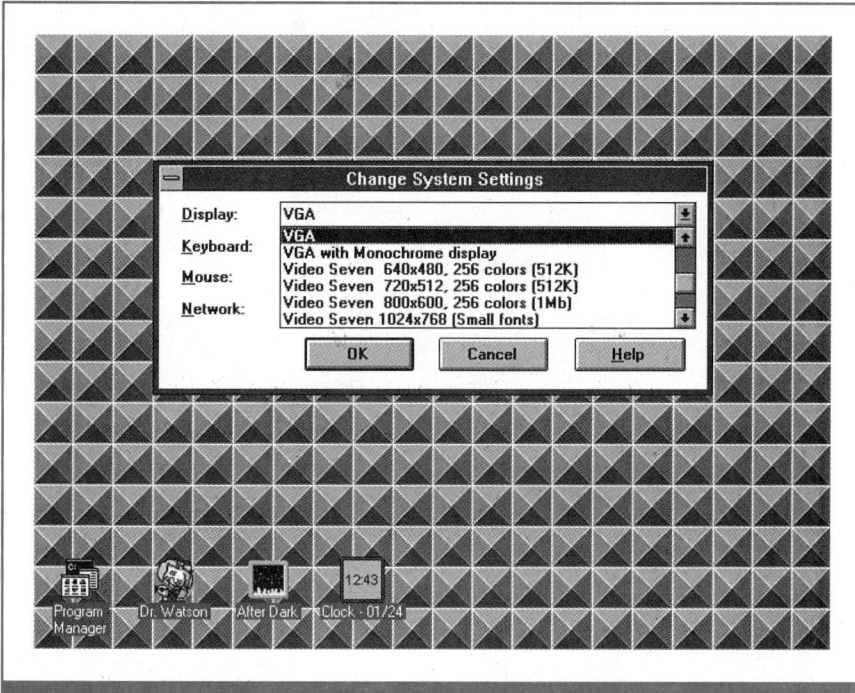

Figure 25.7. Choices for specific hardware.

This section shows you how to change the SETUP.INF file so that you do not need to reinstall files to switch devices. If you install a new device that Windows does not initially know about but you never change that driver, you do not need to worry about the information here. However, if you switch between devices (such as different video mode for a new monitor), this procedure makes switching drivers much faster.

This discussion assumes that you received the driver files from the hardware manufacturer with a file called OEMSETUP.INF or with instructions on how modify SETUP.INF. The OEMSETUP.INF file has information in it to make modifying SETUP.INF much easier. Without this information, you need to know an incredible amount of technical detail about the hardware.

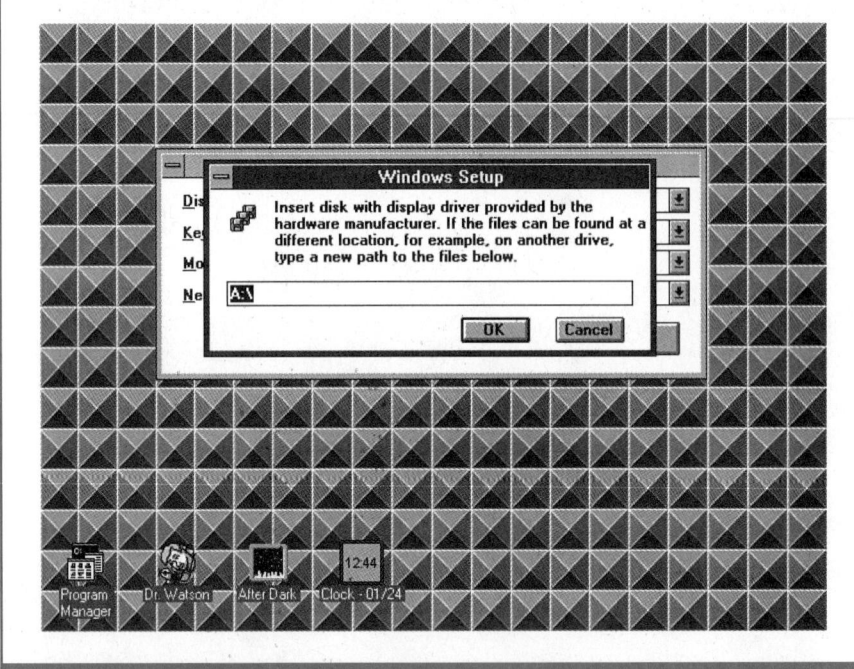

Figure 25.8. Prompt for diskette.

Before you edit your SETUP.INF file, you should make a backup copy of the file on your hard disk and one on a floppy diskette, and then follow these steps:

1. Run File Manager.

2. Open the directory in which you stored Windows.

3. Open the SYSTEM directory under the main WINDOWS directory.

4. Select the SETUP.INF file.

5. Give the **F**ile **C**opy command.

6. In the **T**o field of the dialog box, enter SETUP.ORG (ORG stands for "original"). The dialog box now looks like Figure 25.9.

7. Click **C**opy.

8. SETUP.INF is still selected. Give the **F**ile **C**opy command again.

9. In the **T**o field, enter A:SETUP.INF.

10. Place a diskette in drive A and click OK. Keep this diskette with your Windows distribution diskettes.

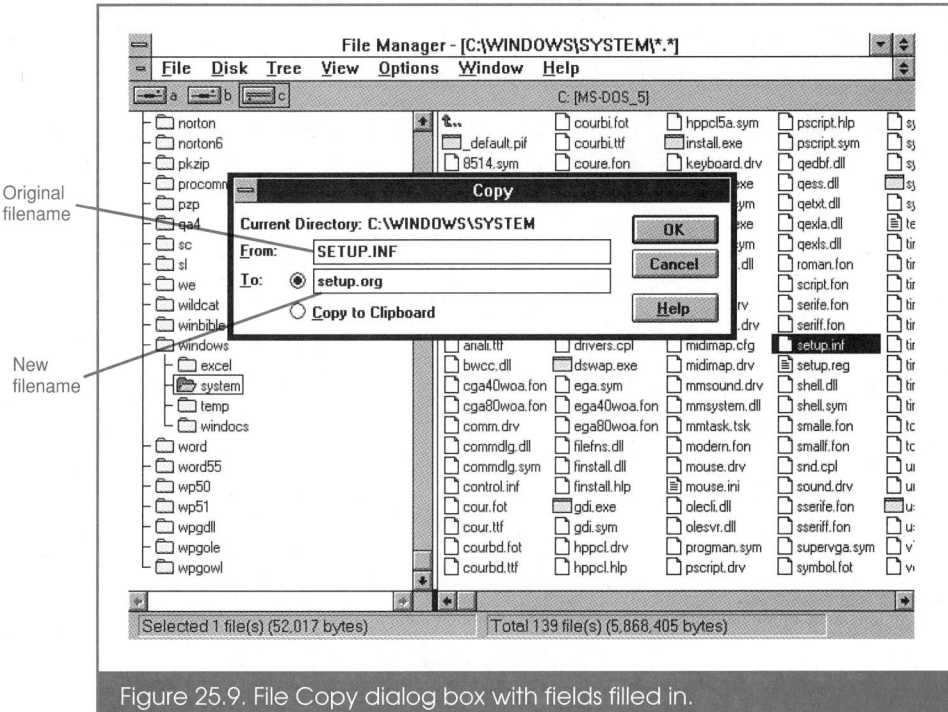

Original filename

New filename

Figure 25.9. File Copy dialog box with fields filled in.

Warning: It is very important to back up your SETUP.INF before modifying it. If you make a mistake when editing it, both of the Setup programs might exhibit strange behavior and you might not be able to use parts of Windows until you recover the file from your backups.

The SETUP.INF file is a plain text file that can be edited with the Notepad program or any other text editor you have. It is long (over 1,000 lines long) and has lots of information used by many parts of Setup. In the file, each section has a header that has a name in square brackets, such as

```
[dialog]
```

The four headings you are interested in here are shown in Table 25.1. Additional information about editing the SYSTEM.INI file can be found in Chapter 27, "Configuring with the WIN.INI and SYSTEM.INI Files."

Table 25.1. Headings for device drivers in SETUP.INF.

Device Type	Heading
Graphics adapter	[display]
Keyboard	[keyboard.types]
Mouse	[pointing.device]
Network	[network]

The general instructions for updating your SETUP.INF file so that you do not have to keep reinstalling device drivers are

1. Run Setup from MS-DOS as described in the previous section to copy the needed driver files to your hard disk. Keep the diskette in the disk drive.

2. Run Windows, then run Notepad.

3. Open the OEMSETUP.INF file on the diskette with the drivers.

4. Find the section with the heading of the device type (such as [display] for graphics adapters).

5. Copy (using **E**dit) to the Clipboard the line that describes the device you just installed.

6. Open the SETUP.INF file in the system subdirectory in the main Windows directory.

7. Find the same section heading.

8. Put the insertion point at the bottom of the list of devices and paste the line from the Clipboard.

9. Save your changes to SETUP.INF.

When you run Setup from within Windows and give the **O**ptions **C**hange System Settings command after this, you see the device you installed in the list of devices.

For example, assume you are adding a video driver for a new large-screen monitor. You would take the following steps:

1. Back up your SETUP.INF file by copying it to another name on the hard disk and copying it to the diskette. Keep the diskette in the disk drive.

2. Run Setup from MS-DOS to copy the video driver files to your hard disk.

3. Run Windows, then run Notepad.

4. Open the OEMSETUP.INF file on the diskette with the drivers. Figure 25.10 shows the top part of that file.

Top of file

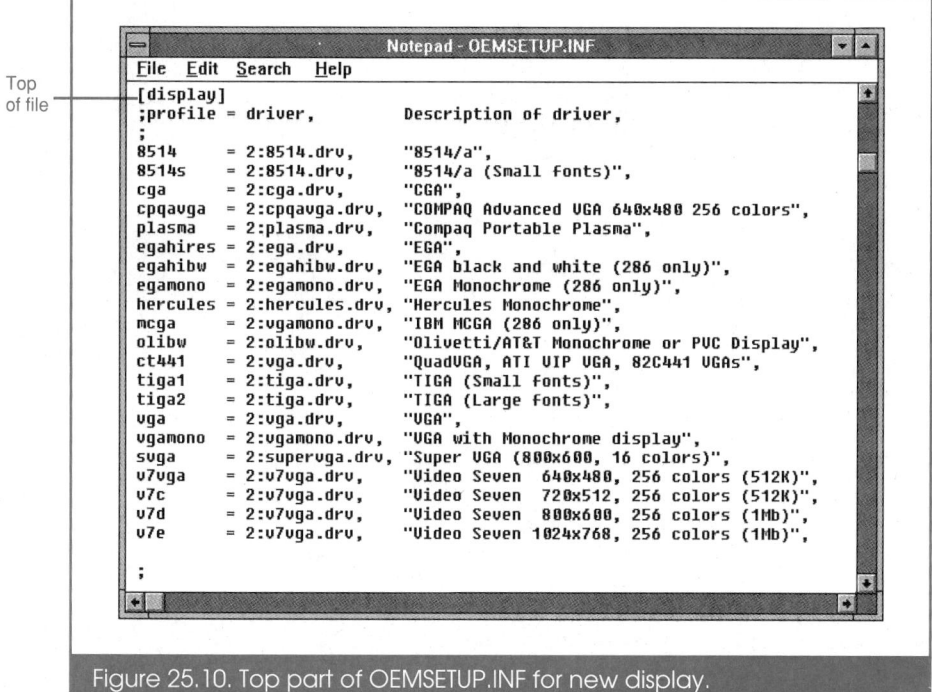

Figure 25.10. Top part of OEMSETUP.INF for new display.

5. Select the line under the [display] heading, as shown in Figure 25.11.

25

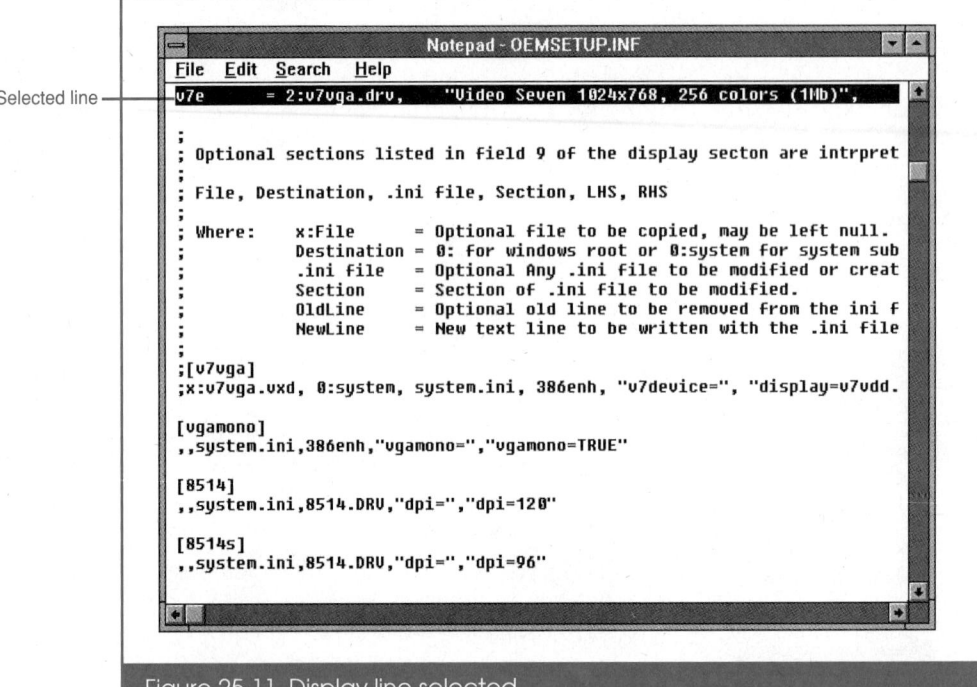

Selected line ⟶

```
                    Notepad - OEMSETUP.INF
 File  Edit  Search  Help
 v7e       = 2:v7vga.drv,    "Video Seven 1024x768, 256 colors (1Mb)",
 ;
 ;
 ; Optional sections listed in field 9 of the display secton are intrpret
 ;
 ; File, Destination, .ini file, Section, LHS, RHS
 ;
 ; Where:    x:File       = Optional file to be copied, may be left null.
 ;           Destination  = 0: for windows root or 0:system for system sub
 ;           .ini file    = Optional Any .ini file to be modified or creat
 ;           Section      = Section of .ini file to be modified.
 ;           OldLine      = Optional old line to be removed from the ini f
 ;           NewLine      = New text line to be written with the .ini file
 ;[v7vga]
 ;x:v7vga.vxd, 0:system, system.ini, 386enh, "v7device=", "display=v7vdd.

 [vgamono]
 ,,system.ini,386enh,"vgamono=","vgamono=TRUE"

 [8514]
 ,,system.ini,8514.DRV,"dpi=","dpi=120"

 [8514s]
 ,,system.ini,8514.DRV,"dpi=","dpi=96"
```

Figure 25.11. Display line selected.

6. Give the **E**dit **C**opy command.

7. Give the **F**ile **O**pen command and select the SETUP.INF file in the system subdirectory under the main \windows directory. Figure 25.12 shows the top of a typical SETUP.INF file.

8. Give the **S**earch **F**ind command and search for [display]. Notepad scrolls to that heading, as shown in Figure 25.13.

9. Scroll to the bottom of the list under that heading and put the insertion point on the blank line.

10. Give the **E**dit **P**aste command to put the line at the end of the list, as shown in Figure 25.14.

11. Give the **F**ile **S**ave command and quit from Notepad.

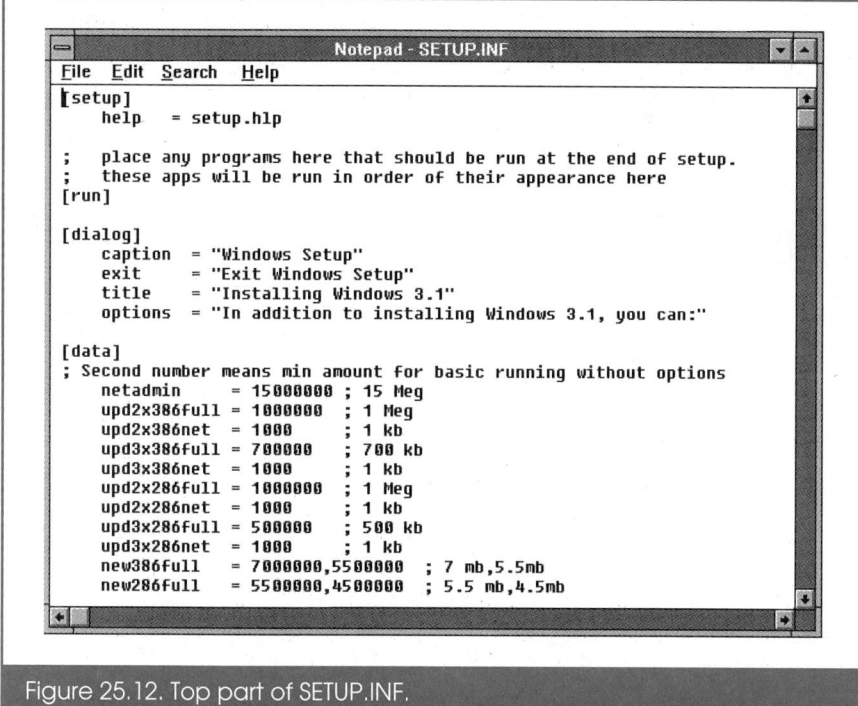

Figure 25.12. Top part of SETUP.INF.

25

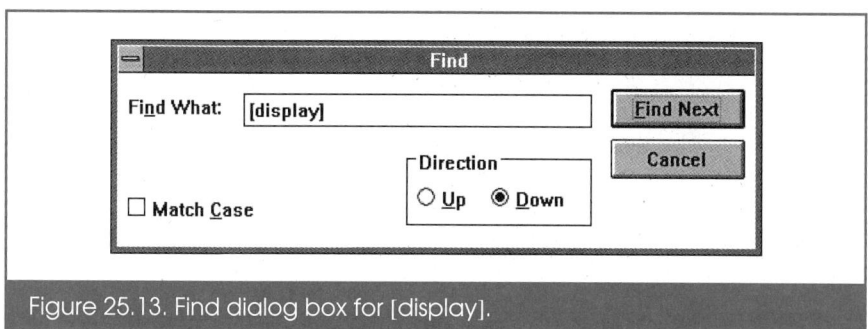

Figure 25.13. Find dialog box for [display].

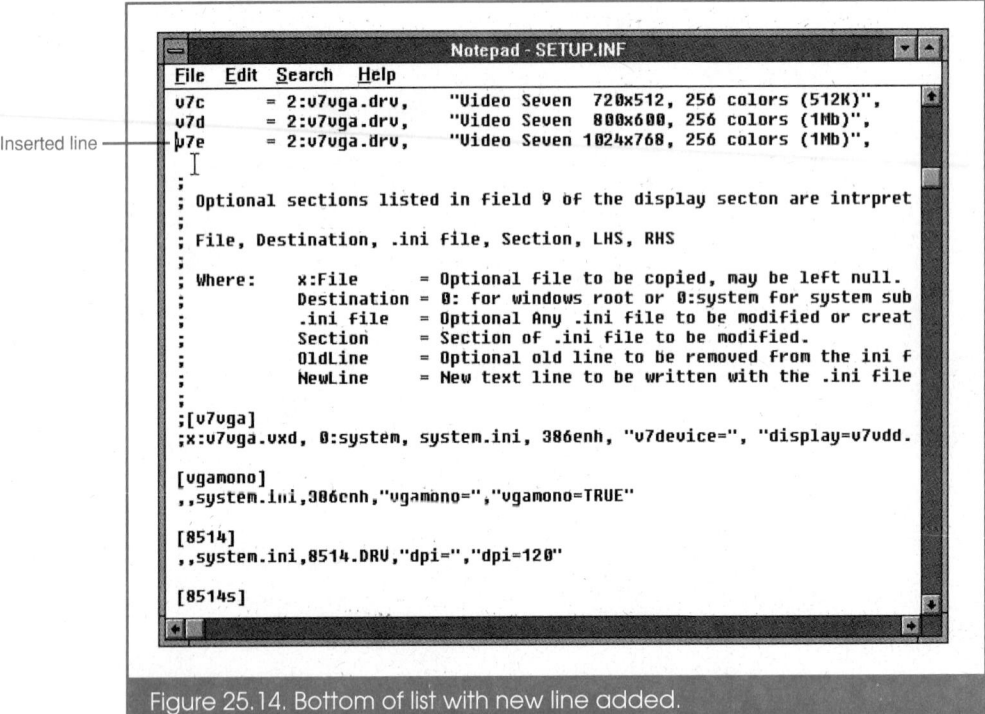

Inserted line

Figure 25.14. Bottom of list with new line added.

Modifying SETUP.INF for Network Installation

You can modify other parts of SETUP.INF if you are installing Windows on a network. This is covered in detail in Chapter 28, "Networking and Communications." For example, you can

▲ Cause Setup to copy more files than it does presently, such as files used at your company

▲ Prevent Setup from copying some files you do not want copied

▲ Specify different sets of files to be created in the initial Program Manager windows

▲ Change the startup directory for files as they are initially installed in Program Manager

Using SysEdit

You can use Notepad to edit text files, but it is not always convenient. You can see only one file at a time, and you have to open the files individually with the **F**ile **O**pen command. If you edit your AUTOEXEC.BAT or CONFIG.SYS files often, you will probably want to use SysEdit, a utility that ships with Windows.

SysEdit is a very simple text editor that automatically opens four files:

▲ SYSTEM.INI

▲ WIN.INI

▲ CONFIG.SYS

▲ AUTOEXEC.BAT

You can edit the files and save the changes to disk quickly.

SysEdit is kept in the \system subdirectory under the main Windows directory. You can run it by giving the **F**ile **R**un command in Program Manager and typing SYSEDIT.EXE or by creating an icon for it.

Figure 25.15 shows the SysEdit window. As you might expect, you can maximize the windows for the files. You can also scroll horizontally or vertically.

25

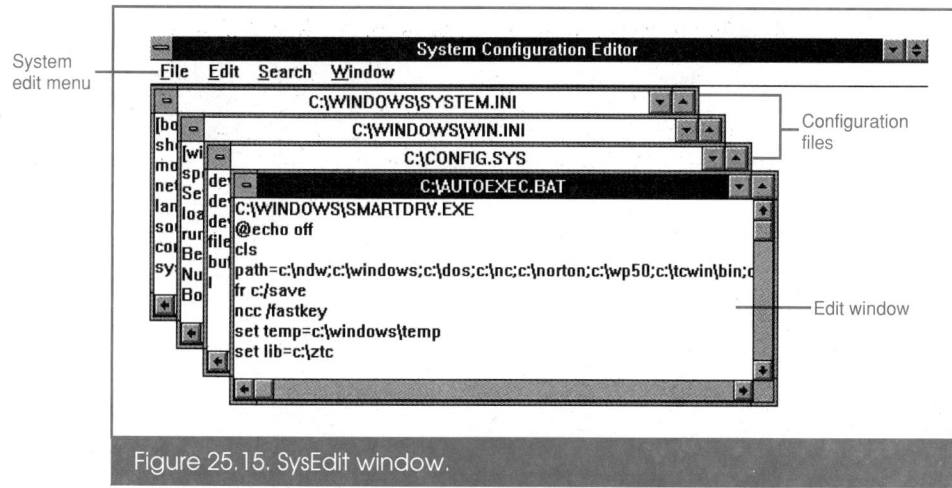

Figure 25.15. SysEdit window.

The menus are very simple. The **F**ile menu, shown in Figure 25.16, has five commands: **S**ave, **P**rint, P**r**int Setup, E**x**it, and **A**bout. If you exit after making changes in any of the files without saving them, SysEdit prompts you. The **E**dit menu has the standard **U**ndo, Cu**t**, **C**opy, **P**aste, and **C**lear commands, as well as Select **A**ll to select all the text in the file. The **S**earch command has a **F**ind command, a **N**ext command to repeat the last Find, and a **P**revious command to repeat the Find but going backward. The **W**indow command enables you to arrange the four windows and make one active.

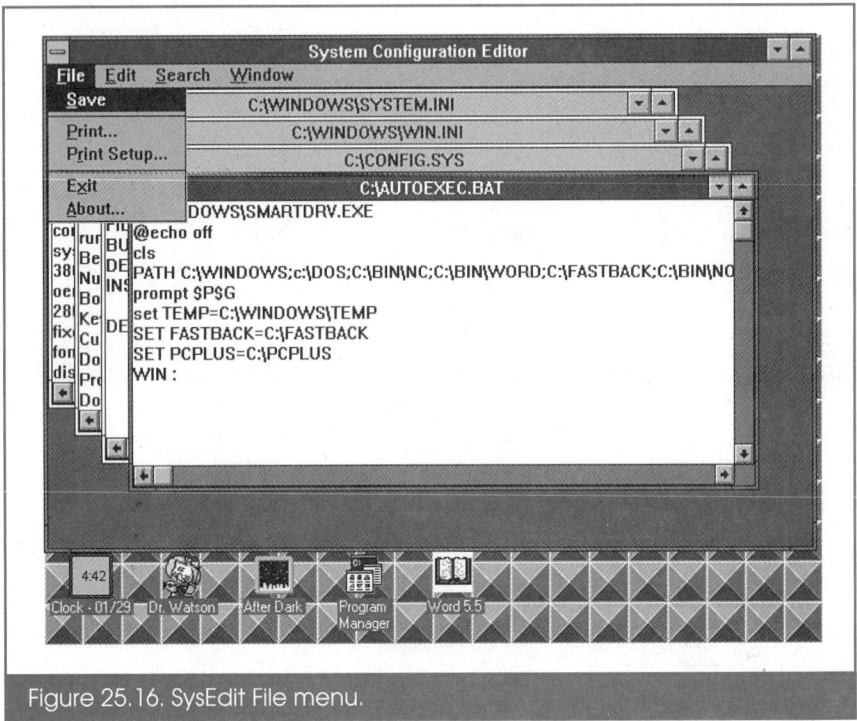

Figure 25.16. SysEdit File menu.

Changes Made to Configuration Files by Setup

When you run Setup to install Windows, it changes parts of your AUTOEXEC.BAT and CONFIG.SYS files to be consistent with

Windows. Those changes, detailed in Chapter 2, "Installing Windows," basically consist of removing things that Setup knows conflict with Windows and adding commands to make Windows run better.

The changes Setup makes to AUTOEXEC.BAT are fairly minor. It updates the PATH command and adds a TEMP variable if you do not already have one.

The changes to CONFIG.SYS are more extensive. Setup looks for programs that might conflict with Windows, such as disk partitioning software, extended and expanded memory managers, caching programs, and RAM drives. If you have any of these programs when you install Windows, Setup either replaces them with its own programs or warns you. You can find the names of programs that conflict with Windows by looking in SETUP.INF in the following headings:

```
[compatibility]
[lim]
[diskcache]
[ramdrive]
```

Keeping Multiple Configurations on Disk

Changing Windows through Setup can be slow and difficult to automate. However, after you have established the Windows environment you want, you can save the files that Windows uses to save the settings and use them later to reproduce the environment.

For example, two people might use Windows on the same PC but have different preferences for the way Windows looks (such as a different wallpaper and different Program Manager groups) and have different programs they want automatically run when they start. They also might have different graphics adapters they want to use. As another example, you might have two very different environments for two different projects you work on and you might want to switch environments quickly.

It is simple to automate the process of switching environments. Basically, you keep multiple copies of the files Windows uses to set the environment, and you copy the files into the main Windows directory before you start Windows. Table 25.2 shows the files and their use. The files are quite small; all the files together usually take up less than 50K of disk space.

Table 25.2. Windows environment files.

File	Purpose
CONTROL.INI	Settings for Control Panel colors and patterns
PROGMAN.INI	Settings for Program Manager
SYSTEM.INI	Settings for devices and modes
WIN.INI	Settings for starting Windows
*.GRP	Program Manager group windows

The easiest way to automate the process is to keep copies of all these files for each environment in a separate subdirectory. When you want to run Windows with a particular environment, use a batch file to copy them to the main Windows subdirectory and start Windows.

Assume that two people, Alicia and Roger, each use the PC. Here are the steps they would take to make switching environments easy:

1. Set up two directories under c:\windows for the environments. These would be c:\windows\alicia and c:\windows\roger. You can use the **F**ile **C**reate Directory command in File Manager to do this, as described in Chapter 6, "File Manager."

2. Let Alicia set up Windows the way she wants. She would create the Program Manager groups, set Control Panel, and choose the devices from Setup that she wants to use.

3. Quit from Windows.

4. Give the following MS-DOS commands to copy the files to Alicia's directory:

```
C>COPY CONTROL.INI C:\WINDOWS\ALICIA
C>COPY PROGMAN.INI C:\WINDOWS\ALICIA
C>COPY SYSTEM.INI C:\WINDOWS\ALICIA
C>COPY WIN.INI C:\WINDOWS\ALICIA
C>COPY *.GRP C:\WINDOWS\ALICIA
```

5. Run Windows again. This time, Roger would set up Windows the way he wants.

6. Quit Windows.

7. Give the following MS-DOS commands to copy the files to Roger's directory:

```
C>COPY CONTROL.INI C:\WINDOWS\ROGER
C>COPY PROGMAN.INI C:\WINDOWS\ROGER
C>COPY SYSTEM.INI C:\WINDOWS\ROGER
C>COPY WIN.INI C:\WINDOWS\ROGER
C>COPY *.GRP C:\WINDOWS\ROGER
```

8. Run Windows again and then use the Notepad command to create the first short batch file, shown in Figure 25.17.

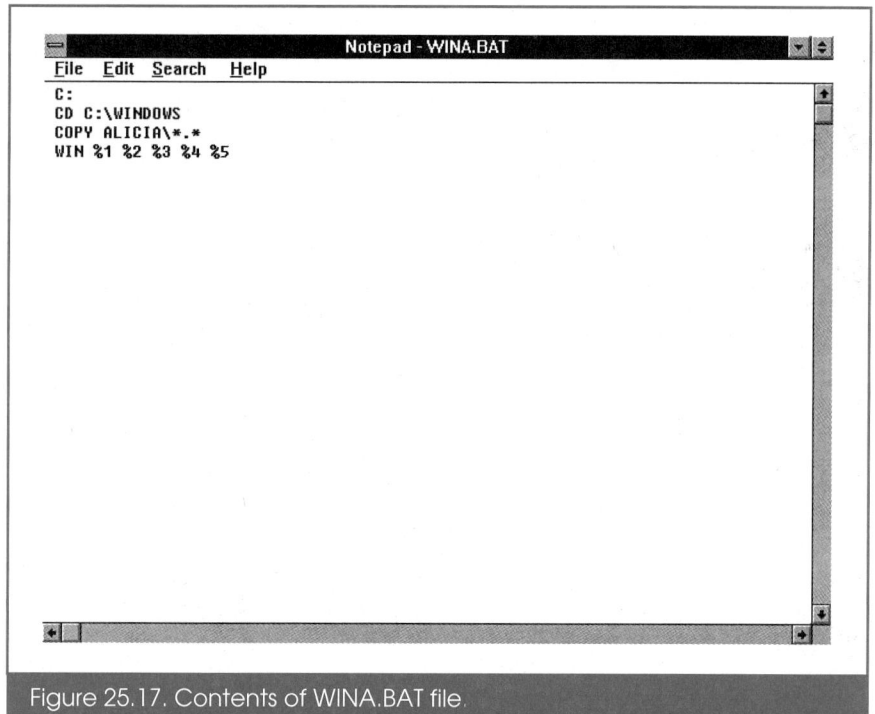

Figure 25.17. Contents of WINA.BAT file.

9. Give the **F**ile **S**ave command and name the batch file WINA.BAT. They would make sure the batch file is in the c:\windows directory.

10. Edit the batch file slightly to create the second batch file, shown in Figure 25.18.

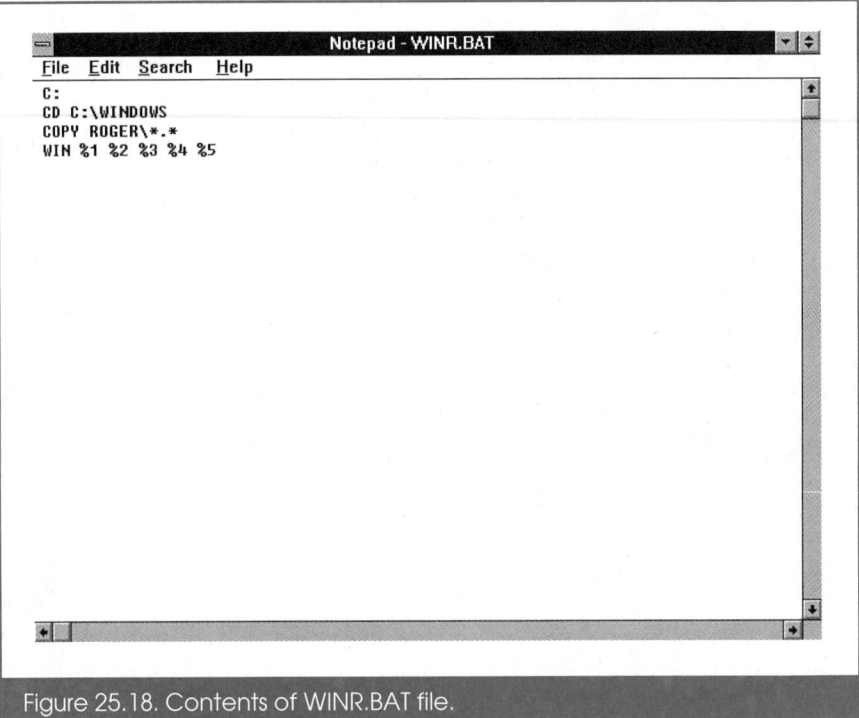

Figure 25.18. Contents of WINR.BAT file.

11. Give the **F**ile Save **A**s command and name the batch file WINR.BAT.

Now, when Alicia wants to run Windows, she gives the MS-DOS command WINA to copy the files and to start Windows with the new environment. Roger starts Windows with the WINR command.

It is important to remember that the batch files are copying over whatever files are already on the hard disk. This means that any changes either person makes to the files will be lost unless the changed files are copied to the respective subdirectory. For instance, if Alicia adds an icon in one of the Program Manager windows, she has to remember to copy the changed file to her subdirectory.

Figure 25.19 shows a short batch file called SAVEENV that copies all the relevant files to a subdirectory. You can create it with Notepad. To run the batch file, you give the command SAVEENV followed by the name of the directory you are saving the files to. For instance, Alicia would give the command

        C>SAVEENV ALICIA

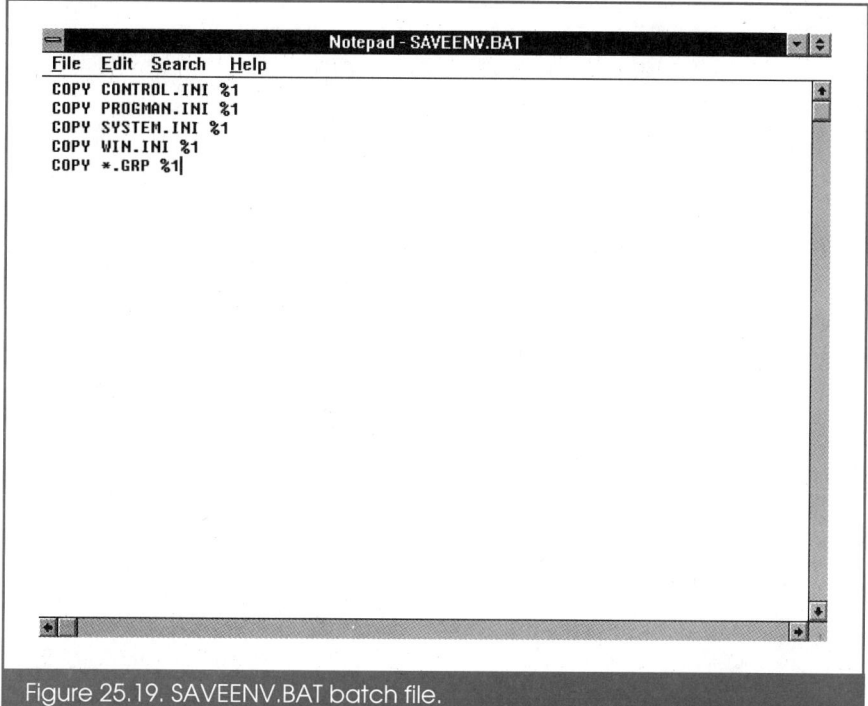

Figure 25.19. SAVEENV.BAT batch file.

25

26

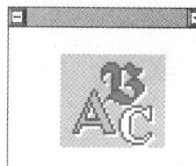

Printers and Fonts

Windows 3.1 comes with many printer drivers that enable you to print both text and graphics. Chapter 2, "Installing Windows," briefly discusses printer drivers; they are described in much more detail later in this chapter. Windows also comes with many high-quality fonts. Fonts are character sets that can be displayed on the screen and printed on the printer. Fonts are one of the more confusing aspects of using Windows. Modern printers have special features that improve print quality. Printers and fonts have become tightly related and thus are covered together in this chapter.

If you have installed your printer for Windows and have not had any problems, you probably do not need to read this chapter. The Setup program does a very good job of guessing what you need and making the necessary choices for you. When you print a document in a Windows program, you get pretty much what you expect, because it is just like what you see on the screen.

This chapter covers font and printer basics, as well as methods you can use to enhance the quality of your printed output. It also explains the differences between types of fonts and printers. You can buy commercial fonts and font-handling programs to help you get better-looking printed output. Your printer also has many options that you can set to give you more flexibility, and a few options that improve the look of your documents.

Early Printers and Fonts

Ten years ago, most printers attached to PCs had only one font style in them. Letters and reports that were printed on these printers looked fairly dull because everything looked the same. If you were lucky, some of the letters came out in boldface because of the printer's overtyping on the page to make the letters darker. A few "advanced" printers had multiple fonts, but they often were not supported by most common software.

Within a few years, multiple fonts were all the rage for printers and software. As people discovered how much easier it was to read documents in which the headings looked different from the main text, software and hardware companies rushed to meet the demands of people preparing these documents. Now, it is uncommon to find even the least expensive printers without the capability to create a few different fonts.

As the printer market matured, the words that were used with fonts and printing changed. Unfortunately, many terms were misused or used in conflicting fashions. Each manufacturer could use its own vocabulary, making documentation difficult to understand. This section describes fonts as they are used in Windows. In other software or on other computers, the terminology used here might be somewhat different.

The New Breed of Printers

There is a new kind of LaserJet-compatible printer slated to replace the now obsolete LaserJet II compatibility standard. It's a printer that is more intelligent than others. It converses with Windows in ways never accomplished before. It can use all manner of fonts, including the new scalable outline fonts, and it will do so as quickly as other printers utilize their onboard hard fonts. Even without the optional PostScript cartridge, the print quality is crisper than the 300 dpi resolution LaserJet II-compatible printers provide. PostScript is a page description language that enables a printer to produce professional quality output. PostScript is described later in this chapter.

This new compatibility standard is that of the LaserJet III series from Hewlett-Packard. Lest you assume that the previous paragraph is a paid advertisement, think again. Our evaluation of the LaserJet IIIP left us optimistically checking street prices (it's what you do when you spend your own money, yes?). One of the interesting things we learned

26

when pricing HPs LaserJet III printers is that the street prices are somewhat higher than other makers of 300-dpi laser printers, but the aftermarket add-ons like memory cards and font cartridges are sold in a competitive marketplace. The HP machines cost a little more when you buy them, but when you add memory or a PostScript cartridge, you have several choices. You don't have to buy HP-brand cartridges, so there are a lot of opportunities to save money when purchasing accessories and options for the machines.

There are so many HP LaserJets that a huge market exists for add-on manufacturers, and dozens of makers have gotten on the bandwagon. The result is that you can find 1M add-on boards for the LaserJet III at around a third to one-half the cost of memory add-on boards for machines costing two-thirds the price of the LaserJet machine. A bargain today can become an expensive proposition tomorrow. In a nutshell, if you want to expand any part of your laser printer in the future, for reasons of cost alone, you are best advised to purchase a Hewlett-Packard LaserJet printer to begin with.

The price for expansion items is more competitive on HP machines, but what about the performance? The best way to judge whether the HP LaserJet III is for you is to print the same file using the same font on different printers. You should definitely try to do this using a single computer if at all possible to maintain the apples-to-apples comparison. Series III machines can scale fonts right inside the printer. Scaling fonts to huge point sizes appears to be flawless and fast. The larger the point size, the more perfectly formed the character seems.

Most laser printers use common primary parts, called engines. HP uses the Canon engine, as do most other makers of laser printers. This fact alone makes the HP machine as reliable as any on the market. The Canon engine has been on the market longer and has been sold in higher quantities than any other engine.

WordPerfect users gain an additional bonus when using the LaserJet III series of printers. WordPerfect and Hewlett-Packard agreed on the selection of a set of fonts that have proven to be the most commonly requested by WordPerfect users.

HP has developed a font management application called Intellifont for Windows that maximizes the font handling capabilities of the HP LaserJet III printers. Intellifont provides the power to print exactly what you see on the screen. It matches your screen fonts to your printer to ensure accurate output.

Cartridges are available to meet just about every need imaginable. You can even buy foreign language character sets so that you can correctly print unique characters only used in a few European languages.

We found that the LaserJet IIIP that we evaluated was indeed the quietest and produced the highest quality output of all the other laser printers evaluated in this class. Not all laser printers are created equal.

Font Basics

A font is a description of how to display characters. For example, Figure 26.1 shows the same information in two different fonts. Notice how the letters are formed differently, and because they are different, how they evoke a different feeling. A font, then, is a design for letters.

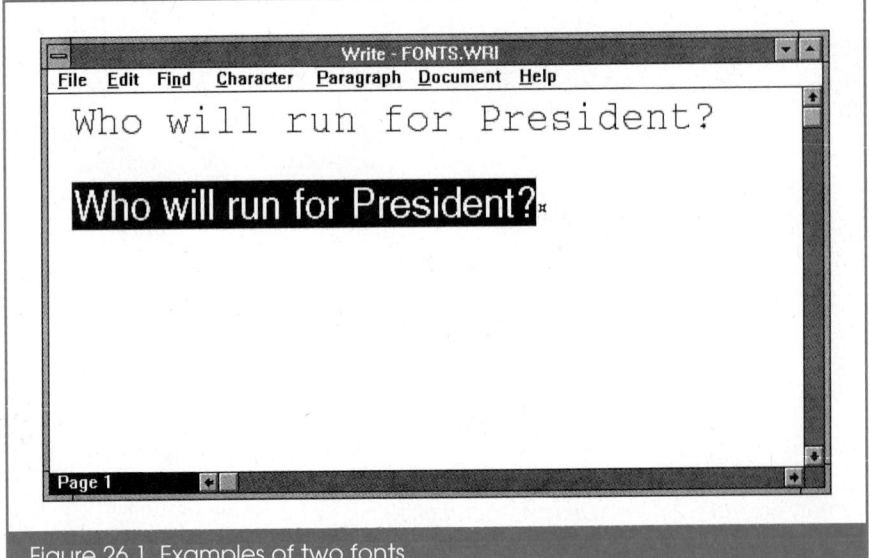

Figure 26.1. Examples of two fonts.

Font Names and Sizes

Each font has a name so that you can identify it easily. When you install Windows, it installs seven standard fonts plus other fonts that might be appropriate for your printer. These standard fonts have names such as *Courier*, *MS Serif*, and *Modern*. In the Fonts icon of Control Panel, you can see a list of all the fonts you have installed. Opening that icon shows the dialog box in Figure 26.2.

26

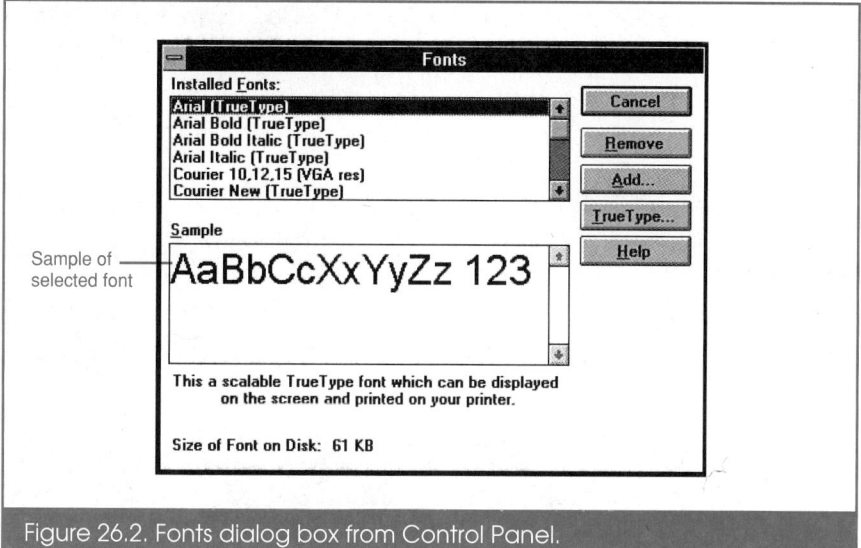

Figure 26.2. Fonts dialog box from Control Panel.

Characters can be displayed in many sizes. Until about ten years ago, printers displayed characters in only one size. Later, some printers could vary the size of the characters. In business correspondence, you rarely use different-sized characters. In reports or brochures, however, using different character sizes helps emphasize parts. For example, Figure 26.3 shows an example of using a larger font to make headings easier to see.

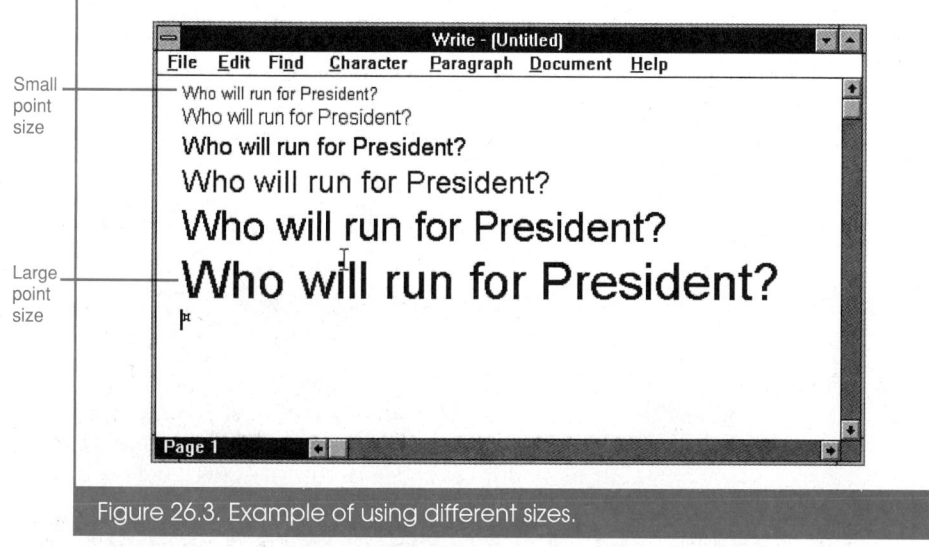

Figure 26.3. Example of using different sizes.

Character sizes are measured in *points*. A point is 1/72 of an inch. The measurement goes from the top of a capital letter to the lowest point on a descender on a lowercase *y* or *g* character. Most character sets in normal typing are between 8 and 15 points tall.

Warning: Because of differences between font manufacturers, the point sizes stated in Windows are approximate. Two fonts that are both 14 points might have different line heights. In fact, some 15-point fonts are actually taller than some 16-point fonts. Do not rely on the stated point sizes when deciding what size to use: Look at the output.

When you add fonts to Windows and restart Windows, all programs can access that information to know which fonts are available. Programs know which fonts are available by looking in the [Fonts] section of the WIN.INI file, described in Chapter 27, "Configuring with the WIN.INI and SYSTEM.INI Files."

Most Windows programs enable you to choose from available fonts and sizes. For example, Write enables you to choose any font and font size you want from its **C**haracter **F**onts command, shown in Figure 26.4.

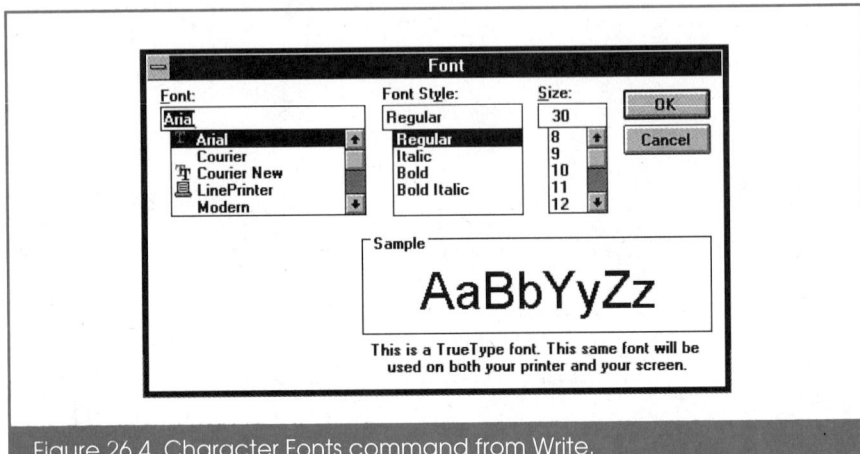

Figure 26.4. Character Fonts command from Write.

In Windows, what is referred to as a "font" is actually a font set. A font set is a file that describes a single font in many sizes. Thus, the font called *Courier* might actually be a font set that contains descriptions of how to draw characters that look alike in three different sizes. As you

will see later in this chapter, some fonts are available in all sizes from 4 to 127 points, but others are available only in particular fixed sizes.

Boldface and Italic

Most Windows programs enable you to display fonts in their normal mode as well as in boldface and italic. A font displayed in boldface is a thicker, darker version of the font. A font in italic looks like the original font but is slanted to the right. You can also make fonts both boldface and italic at the same time. Figure 26.5 shows examples of boldface and italic used in writing.

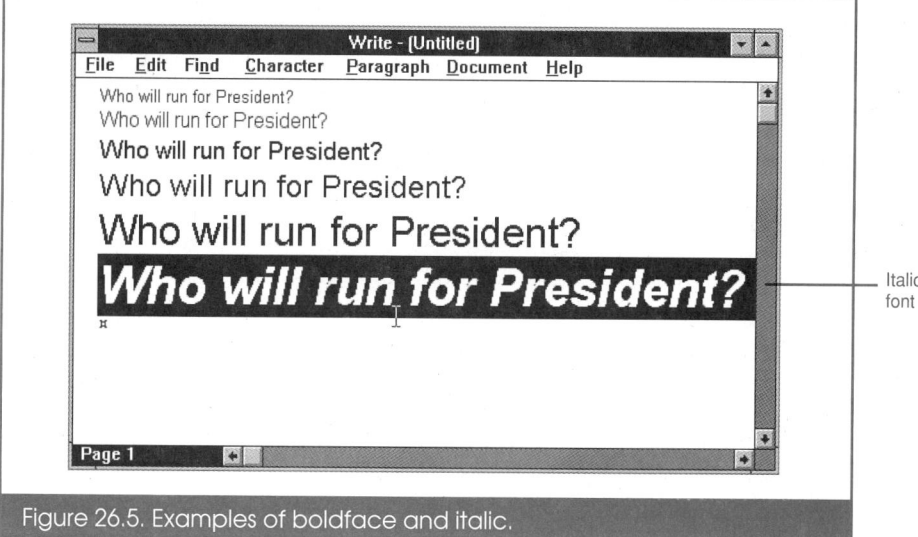

Figure 26.5. Examples of boldface and italic.

The method you use to make some characters boldface or italic depends on the program you are running. Generally, you select the characters you want to change and give a command called Bold or Italic from a menu, or possibly from a dialog box in which you are choosing the font.

Warning: When you display boldface and italic characters, Windows changes the original characters using a formula to make them fatter or slanted. This works well for some fonts but looks terrible in others. Typographic systems use special fonts that are designed boldface and italic instead of using formula transformations.

Font Families

Fonts come in two basic designs: those that have tiny lines at the ends of characters and those that do not. These tiny lines are called *serifs;* fonts that use them are called serif fonts, and those that do not are called *sans serif* fonts. Figure 26.6 shows examples of each.

Windows 3.1 has five font families into which it associates each font. A family is a group of fonts that have a similar appearance. Some families are characterized by serifs or the lack of them (sans serif). The family names and information about each family are shown in Table 26.1.

Table 26.1. Font families.

Family Member	Distinguished by	Font Name
Roman	Serifs	Roman
Modern	Sans Serifs	Modern
Decorative	Symbols	Symbol
Swiss	Sans Serifs	Arial
Script	Handwritten effect	Script

The family designation is important only when Windows 3.1 is substituting one font for another when displaying it on the screen. For example, if you add a printer font that has no screen display font, Windows substitutes on-screen a font from the same family because the two fonts often look similar.

Warning: Do not change the order of the lines in the [Fonts] section of the WIN.INI file. When substituting fonts, most programs look for the first font that matches the family type of the font being substituted. If you change the order of the lines, you might get unexpected results and different line lengths if a different family member is chosen.

Other Font Terms

When you use fonts in Windows 3.1, Windows needs to know only the font name, size, and whether you want boldface or italic. You can use other typographic guidelines to classify fonts. These might help you choose the font you want to use in your work.

Most fonts are *proportional* fonts, meaning that each letter can have a different width. Almost every book and magazine uses proportional fonts. Notice how in this book the letter *i* is narrower than the letter *o* and how some capital letters are much wider than others.

Fonts in which every letter is the same width are called *monospaced* fonts. These often look like typewriter printing. It is unlikely that you will use monospaced fonts in your work because monospaced fonts are rarely as easy to read or as friendly as proportional fonts. Figure 26.7 shows examples of proportional and monospaced fonts.

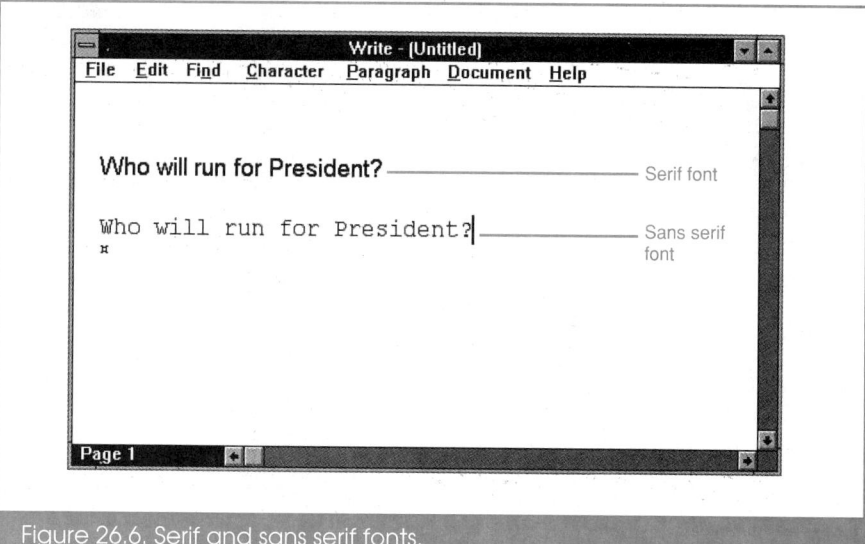

Figure 26.6. Serif and sans serif fonts.

Letters in a font can be narrow or wide. These are known as *compressed* and *expanded*. You use compressed fonts when you want to get as many letters in a particular amount of space as you want, and you use expanded fonts when you want to make it easy to read text quickly. If you buy commercial fonts, you will find that you can get examples of many popular fonts in the expanded and compressed forms.

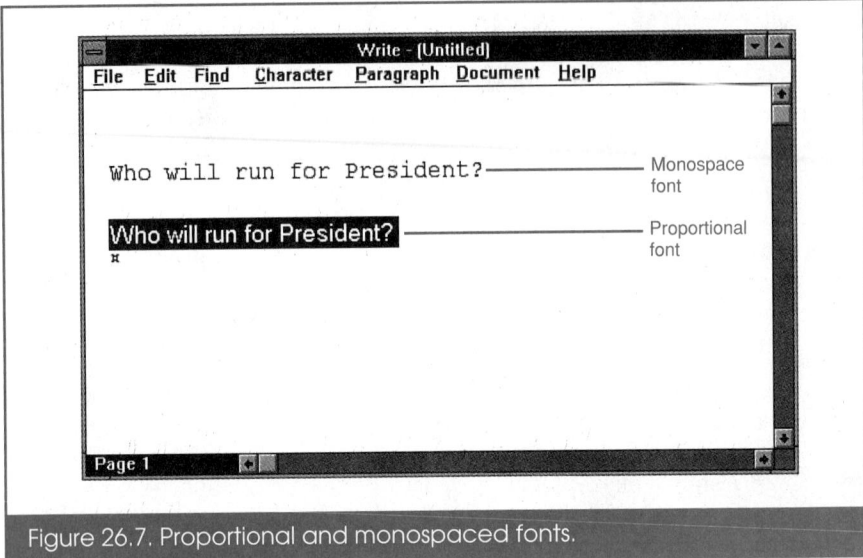

Figure 26.7. Proportional and monospaced fonts.

Raster and Stroke Fonts

Windows supports two types of fonts that have very different purposes. Understanding the difference helps you choose the best fonts for your printed output. Although the difference is somewhat technical, it is worth knowing, especially if you have a laser printer or some other modern printer.

The two types of fonts are *raster* fonts and *stroke* fonts. The names come from the way Windows stores the information in the font file telling how each character looks.

▲ Raster fonts (also called *bit-mapped* fonts) are stored as dot-for-dot images of the characters. These fonts come in specific sizes. The file contains a picture of how each character looks at each size. If you try to draw a character from a raster font in a size that is not in the font file, Windows interpolates from another size with often very ugly results. Each font file usually contains between three and seven sizes for a particular font.

▲ Stroke fonts (also called *vector* fonts or *outline* fonts) are stored as a description of how to draw the lines that make up the character, not as the actual dots for each size. Windows interprets the lines

26

into dots at the specified font size. The line-drawing instructions work at any size because they are descriptions of how to draw the lines in the characters relative to the font height. You can display stroke fonts in any size from 4 to 127 points.

Table 26.2 describes how these two fonts differ in Windows.

Table 26.2. How raster fonts and stroke fonts are stored on disk.

Raster Font Description	Stroke Font Description
Point at 0,0	Start at 0,0
Point at 0,1	Thin line to 0,2
Point at 0,2	Start at 1,1
Point at 1,1	Thick line to 1,4
Point at 1,8	Start at 5,1

Because raster fonts are exact pictures of the dots needed to display or print a letter, Windows can use them much faster than stroke fonts. On the other hand, stroke fonts are much more flexible because you have more than just a few choices for font size. TrueType fonts are stroke fonts.

Another difference between the type of fonts is their *device dependence,* the need for different fonts on different devices like VGA adapters, EGA adapters, dot-matrix printers, laser printers, and so on. Raster fonts are very device dependent because the dot size and shape on each device is different. For instance, the dots on dot-matrix printers are bigger than the dots on laser printers. If you had only one size of raster fonts, they would appear huge on the dot-matrix printer. On the other hand, stroke fonts are device independent because the lines that make up the letters are easily tailored by each device's driver.

Raster and Stroke Fonts Installed by Windows

Setup installs fonts with Windows 3.1, as shown in Table 26.3 and Table 26.4. If you install a printer, Setup may install more fonts. The basic fonts are available to all programs, but not all programs use them. (For example, Notepad uses only Courier.) These fonts are shown in Figure 26.8.

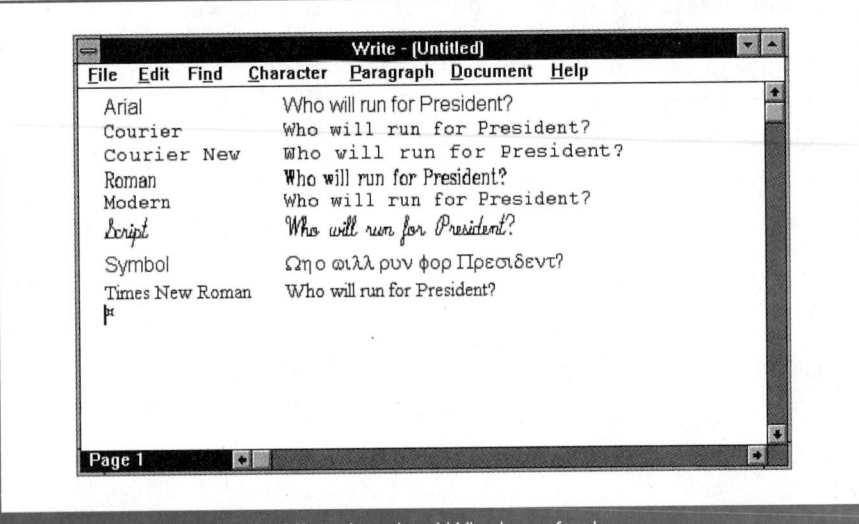

Figure 26.8. Examples of the standard Windows fonts.

Table 26.3. Windows fonts.

Font Name	Type	Sizes in VGA Mode	Description
MS Sans Serif	Raster	8, 10, 12, 14, 18, 24	Proportional
MS Serif	Raster	8, 10, 12, 14, 18, 24	Proportional
Symbol	Raster	8, 10, 12, 14, 18, 24	Symbols and Greek characters
Small	Raster	Used to preview documents	Proportional
Courier	Raster	10, 12, 15	Monospace thin
Modern	Raster	All	Proportional, narrow, sans serif
Symbol	Stroke	All	Symbols and Greek characters
Arial	Stroke	All	Proportional
Roman	Stroke	All	Proportional, serif
Script	Stroke	All	Proportional, cursive
Courier	Stroke	All	Proportional
Times	Stroke	All	Proportional

Table 26.4. TrueType fonts.

Font Name	Type	Size	Description
Arial	Stroke	All	Proportional, sans serif
Arial Bold	Stroke	All	Proportional, sans serif
Arial Bold Italic	Stroke	All	Proportional, sans serif
Arial Italic	Stroke	All	Proportional, sans serif
Courier New	Stroke	All	Monospace, thin
Courier New Bold	Stroke	All	Monospace, thick
Courier New Bold Italic	Stroke	All	Monospace, thick, slanted
Courier Italic	Stroke	All	Monospace, slanted
Times New Roman	Stroke	All	Proportional, serif
Times New Roman Bold	Stroke	All	Proportional, thick
Times New Roman Bold Italic	Stroke	All	Proportional, thick, slanted
Times New Roman Italic	Stroke	All	Proportional, slanted
Symbol	Stroke	All	Symbols and Greek characters

Size Differences

You get different sizes for the raster fonts for different types of graphics adapters. If you install a custom graphics adapter, the fonts that come with the Windows driver might have different sizes than the ones you were using before. Some programs also come with their own fonts.

To make things even a bit more confusing, the font sizes you see in the Fonts dialog box in Control Panel might be different from the font sizes you see in a dialog box in other Windows programs. If you are using a dot-matrix printer, Windows matches the font sizes of the raster fonts as closely as possible to the sizes available on the printer. This often causes the font sizes to be different from what you expect from the Fonts dialog box in Control Panel.

You should have no such problems with stroke fonts. You can choose any size and know that it will appear on the screen and on the printer in the correct size.

 **Tip:** Most Windows programs list the sizes for fonts in their character formatting dialog boxes. However, you can usually type a number for a size that is not in the list. For stroke fonts, these customized sizes look fine on the screen and when printed. For raster fonts, the results often are ugly but might be all right for you when printed. You should expect to experiment with the look of the printed output when you use sizes that are not listed.

Fonts Specific to Printers

You can use most fonts with most printers, but the results might be varied. When you use a font that is not best suited for a printer, Windows guesses what to do. It usually, but not always, shows you on the screen lines that look like the lines you will see when you print.

Note that when you use a printer-specific font in a Windows document, the characters you see on the screen might look different from the characters you see when you print. Windows does not display the same fonts as the printers use; it simply displays its own fonts scaled and adjusted so that the lines on the screen are the same as the lines on the printer. This is done for efficiency: the fewer fonts Windows has to keep in memory, the faster it runs and the more memory you have available.

This section describes how Windows handles internal, or hard fonts, located inside printers and their cartridges. You can always use the standard Windows fonts with these printers, but the output usually takes much longer and often is less attractive. You should experiment with the internal fonts on the printer if you have not already done so; you might be surprised at how much better the output looks.

Fonts for Dot-Matrix Printers

Most dot-matrix printers (and printers that act like them, such as many ink-jet printers) use their own monospace internal fonts. Windows installs fonts for these, usually under the name *Courier* or some variant of it. Dot-matrix printers usually have only one or two font heights for their built-in fonts. Some dot-matrix printers use proportional fonts, and Windows often installs the proper fonts for these as well. Remember, the printer's device driver contains information about the printer's capabilities. A printer's fonts are located in the printer. Device drivers

contain a list of what Windows can expect to find inside the printer as far as fonts go.

When you select a font (like Courier) from the front panel of a printer, and then send a document that calls out the use of Helvette instead of the Courier font, the printer prints the Helvette font. Printers that can print graphics will print any TrueType or ATM font, albeit very slowly and loudly.

26

The names for the internal fonts are often similar to *Roman 5cpi*. In this case, *cpi* stands for *characters per inch*. A smaller number means wider characters. Standard characters for most dot-matrix printers are either 10 or 12 characters per inch. Figure 26.9 shows the Character Fonts dialog box for Write when a dot-matrix printer is the default printer.

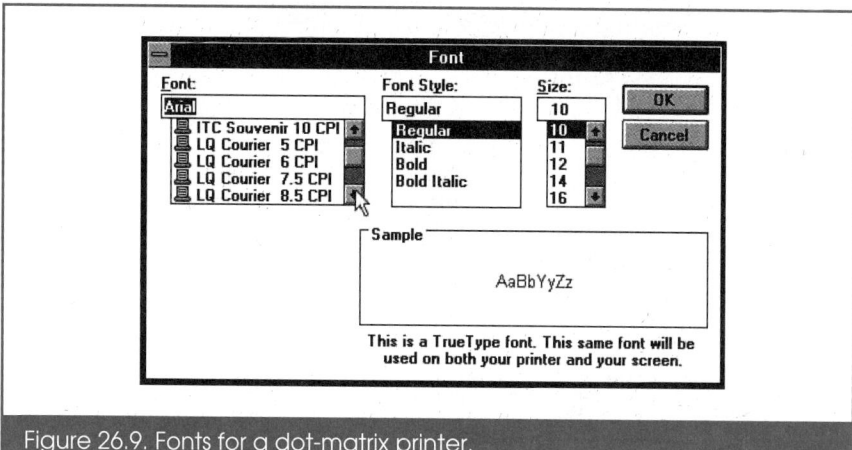

Figure 26.9. Fonts for a dot-matrix printer.

Fonts for LaserJet II and Compatible Printers

The Hewlett-Packard LaserJet II revolutionized the PC industry by being the first low-cost laser printer to achieve wide acceptance. Many other manufacturers made laser printers that emulated the LaserJet II and could thus work with programs that knew about the LaserJet II. Not only was the LaserJet II low cost, but it also was flexible. It came with some fonts built in, and you could add cartridges or download fonts from software.

One disadvantage of the LaserJet II's fonts is that they are fixed size and they can be displayed in only one direction. Windows can print its stroke fonts just fine on the LaserJet II but cannot display the raster fonts, like LinePrinter. The LaserJet II driver comes with just the two standard fonts on the LaserJet II: Courier and LinePrinter. Figure 26.10 shows the Character Fonts dialog box for Write when a LaserJet II is the default printer. If Windows cannot display or print a printer's particular font, it substitutes the requested font with a font from the same font family.

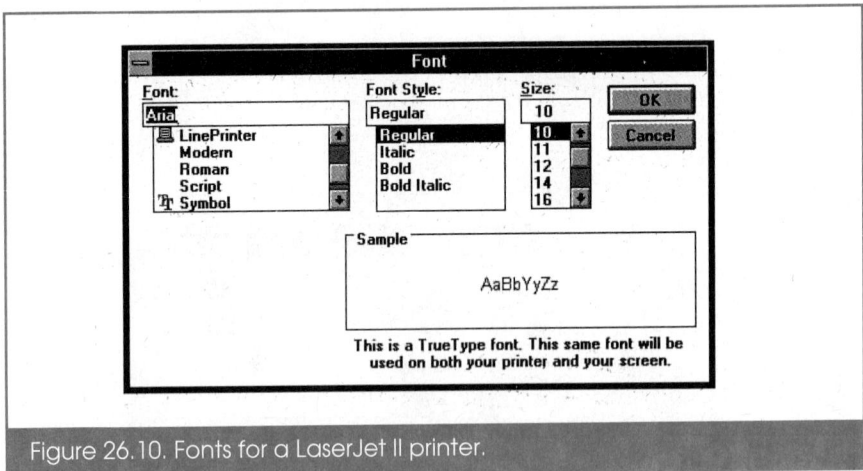

Figure 26.10. Fonts for a LaserJet II printer.

If you have standard cartridges, you can specify them in the Setup command as described later in this chapter. You can specify up to two cartridges. When you do, the fonts for those cartridges also appear in Fonts dialog boxes.

You can also install soft fonts with the LaserJet II. Most of the commercial soft fonts have their own programs for installing in Windows. The standard method for copying soft fonts is also described later in this chapter in the discussion on adding printers.

If you have nonstandard font cartridges or soft fonts that do not have Windows installation instructions, you can still install them. You need to go through some extra steps, however, and the installation is not as easy as it is for most other Windows software. This method is also described later in the chapter.

Fonts for LaserJet III and Compatible Printers

The LaserJet III printer series has all the features of the LaserJet II plus one major improvement: it can handle scalable fonts. These internal scalable fonts produce excellent type that rivals other scalable font technologies. Figure 26.11 shows the Character Fonts dialog box for Write when a LaserJet III is the default printer. Scalable fonts are fonts that can be "scaled" to any size.

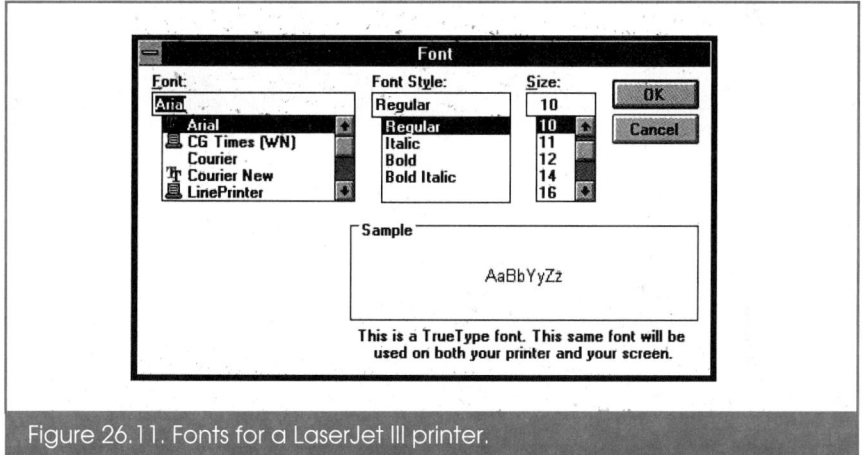

Figure 26.11. Fonts for a LaserJet III printer.

Like with the LaserJet II, you can install additional soft fonts and cartridges using the printer setup commands described later in this chapter. The steps for installing scalable soft fonts and cartridges are the same as for installing fixed fonts.

Fonts for PostScript Printers

Almost every PostScript-compatible printer comes with many fonts installed. Because all PostScript fonts are scalable, you can use any Windows font at any available point size. Figure 26.12 shows the Character Fonts dialog box for Write when a PostScript printer is the default printer.

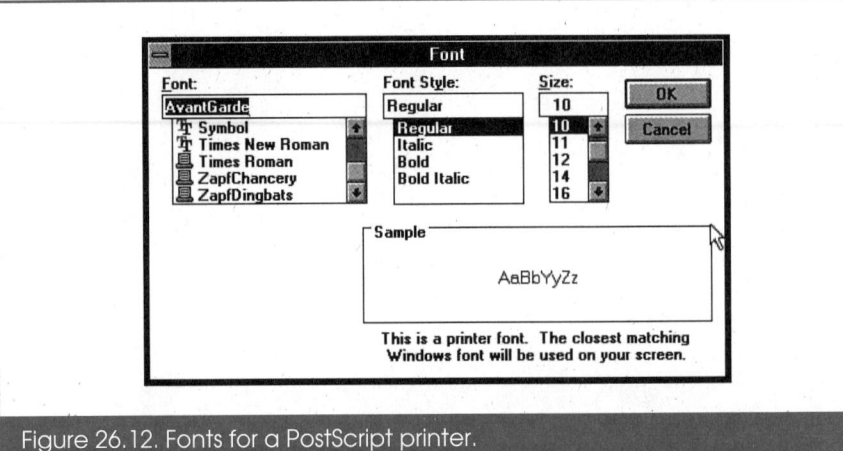

Figure 26.12. Fonts for a PostScript printer.

Installing Screen Fonts

You can add two types of fonts to Windows: screen fonts and printer fonts.

▲ *Screen fonts* are like Windows standard fonts: They can be displayed either on the screen or on printers. Most screen fonts you add to Windows are decorative or headline fonts.

▲ *Printer fonts* are fonts that work only with a particular printer. They might be the screen equivalents of fonts in a printer cartridge or soft fonts that you load into the printer from the hard disk.

This section describes how to install screen fonts. Installing printer fonts is described later in this chapter in the section on how to set up the printer.

Many screen font packages come with their own installation program. If yours did, you should use that rather than the Windows installation because there might be special requirements for installation. If the program does not come with an installation program, use the Fonts icon in Control Panel. (Control Panel is described in Chapter 7, "Control Panel.")

The Fonts dialog box for Control Panel is shown in Figure 26.13. The list at the top shows all the fonts that are already installed, and the box at the bottom shows a sample of how the font looks.

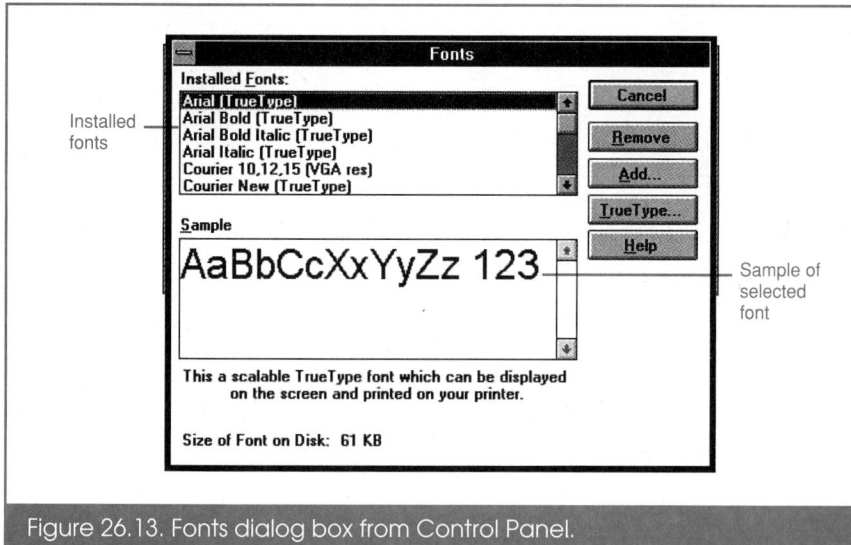

Figure 26.13. Fonts dialog box from Control Panel.

To add screen fonts, click the **Add** button. You see the dialog box shown in Figure 26.14. Select the disk and directory that contains your screen font and click OK. When you are finished, the fonts appear in the Fonts list and are accessible in other programs that you start after you quit the Fonts dialog box.

Tip: Installing fonts can be very slow. If you are installing fonts from a diskette or over a network, you should first copy the desired font files to the hard disk and install from the hard disk. This is usually much faster than installing from a slow device like a diskette or network.

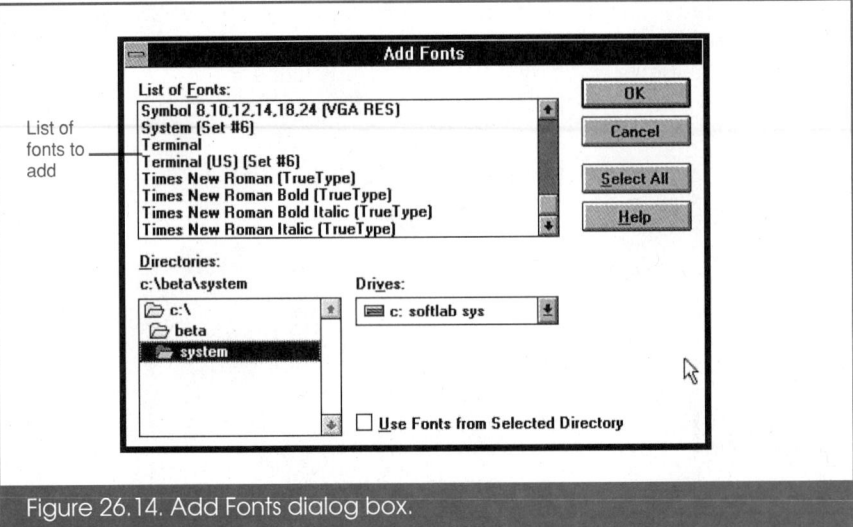

Figure 26.14. Add Fonts dialog box.

Using Other Font Managers

The font manager that comes in Windows is good but not terribly efficient. It is also not compatible with other font systems in other MS-DOS programs. There are many popular low-cost alternatives to the Windows font manager: Adobe Type Manager (commonly referred to as *ATM*), Bitstream FaceLift, Zenographics SuperPrint, ZSoft SoftType, and Atech Publisher's Powerpak.

These packages have much in common. They install as drivers in Windows so that they work in the background. After you have installed them, they work invisibly and well with all Windows programs. All five programs produce characters on the fly, meaning that they use all stroke fonts, not raster fonts. All the fonts come out in very high resolution on all types of printers. You no longer see jagged characters on the screen regardless of the size of characters you are using (just as you do not now with the stroke fonts). Each of these font managers is represented by an icon in the group window where it was installed. The most popular package, ATM, is actually a set of drivers that replace the SYSTEM.DRV in your SYSTEM.INI file. This is how ATM works so well, transparently. It is invoked whenever you are running Windows. You can turn it off, but you have to leave and restart Windows in order for ATM to uninstall itself. These programs are usually TSRs or

*T*erminate and *S*tay *R*esident programs. They load and remain in memory as long as your system is powered up and you are using Windows

Each package comes with many fonts of a much wider variety than the standard Windows fonts. In addition, the companies each sell dozens of additional fonts that work with the font manager so that you can choose fonts that exactly suit your purpose. Some packages also make printing much faster than Print Manager. See Reference C, "Windows Product Directory," for more on available font management software.

Adobe Type Manager

Adobe Type Manager is the best known of the three packages. Adobe invented the PostScript language for printers and has extensive experience in creating high-quality fonts for the computer industry. ATM enables you to use any commercial PostScript Type 1 fonts from Adobe or the numerous other companies that make Type 1 fonts. You do not need a PostScript printer to use these fonts. Any HP Laserjet II compatible printer will do.

You can get more information by writing or phoning Adobe Type Manager, Adobe Systems, 1585 Charleston Rd., P.O. Box 7900, Mountain View, CA 94039-7900, (415) 961-4400.

Bitstream FaceLift

Facelift uses Bitstream's Speedo format for fonts. Because this technology has been popular with manufacturers of non-Windows software, the fonts you use with FaceLift can also be used in many other programs, and vice versa. Facelift also has features to make printing on Hewlett-Packard laser printers faster than with other font managers. If you use the same size of typeface often, you can create a bit map of that size and download it to the printer for faster access.

You can get more information by writing or phoning Facelift, Bitstream, 215 First St., Cambridge, MA 02142, (800) 522-3668.

Zenographics SuperPrint

SuperPrint is more than just a font manager. The font manager is unique in that it handles many font types automatically. It reads Adobe Type 1 fonts, Speedo fonts (and the older Fontware format from Bitstream), Agfa Compugraphic IntelliFont fonts, and Hewlett-Packard soft fonts. Although it is a bit slower than ATM and FaceLift in creating screen fonts, it adds a much faster print spooler that replaces Print Manager. If you are using a Hewlett-Packard LaserJet, you will find SuperPrint to be significantly faster than other font managers because it creates immediate soft fonts when you print. This means it can send a print job to the printer much faster because less information is being printed.

You can get more information by writing or phoning Zenographics, 4 Executive Circle, Suite 200, Irvine, CA 92714, (714) 851-6352.

Zsoft SoftType

SoftType supports its own type format (called URW), but it can coexist with ATM if you have that package as well. SoftType comes with interesting additional software that enables you to define your own font styles such as shaded, gray, rotated, and so on. Zsoft sells its own fonts, and other publishers support the URW format as well.

You can get more information by writing or phoning SoftType, ZSoft, 450 Franklin Rd., Suite 100, Marietta, GA 30067, (404) 428-0008.

Atech Publisher's Powerpak

Atech's format is the least common of the five font managers, but the package comes with a font importing utility so that you can convert other fonts to Atech's format. Thus, if you have access to Adobe Type 1 or Type 3 format fonts or Bitstream's fonts, you can use them with the Publisher's Powerpak. It also comes with more fonts than the other two packages, and the additional fonts are generally less expensive.

You can get more information by writing or phoning Publisher's Powerpak, Atech Software, 5964 La Place Court, Suite 125, Carlsbad, CA 92008, (800) 748-5657.

26

TrueType

Microsoft has announced that all versions of Windows beginning with 3.1 will come with a new printing technology called *TrueType*. TrueType, developed by Apple Computer, first became available early in 1991 with the introduction of the Macintosh system software version 6.0.7. TrueType uses font outlines to show smooth outlines on the screen and printer regardless of the size of font you are using.

TrueType works much like Adobe Type Manager, described previously, except that it can generate slightly better-looking characters at small sizes on dot-matrix printers. Because TrueType is available free on the Macintosh, many font companies have already released hundreds of high-quality TrueType fonts, just like they have PostScript Type 1 fonts. The most obvious difference to Windows users between TrueType and other font managers is that TrueType comes as part of Windows but you must buy the other font managers.

Beyond TrueType, other printing technologies might appear in the future. Because Windows has a huge audience in the PC market, it is likely that most major printing technologies will become available on Windows fairly quickly. Because alternative type managers are already fairly inexpensive, you probably will not have to spend much for these other printing technologies.

Characters in Fonts

Each font can have as many as 256 characters. Each character has a numeric code from 0 to 255. The first 127 character codes have standard representations that everybody has agreed on for decades. This standard, called ASCII, means that in every font, the code for the letter *a* is 97, the code for * is 42, and so on. This also means that in every font, a 97 is always shown as the letter *a* (in whatever style the font looks like), 42 is always shown as * (in whatever style the font looks like), and so on.

From 128 to 255, however, things change. The characters that usually appear for these codes (often called *high-order characters*) are international characters, symbols, and special graphics characters. There are many conflicting standards for how characters match up to the codes in high-order characters. The standard Microsoft chose for Windows is the ANSI standard. However, most commercial fonts do not conform to the ANSI standard for correlation between the characters and the codes.

Figure 26.15 shows the code mapping for the ASCII/ANSI standard for codes 0 to 127. As you can see, the codes from 32 to 126 are the standard characters you see on the keyboard. Figure 26.16 shows the code mapping for the ANSI high-order characters. The characters above 127 are characters that are not commonly found on keyboards but that are useful in writing, especially in other languages. In these tables, the characters represented by dark thin rectangles are not supported by Windows but might have representations in some ANSI-compatible fonts.

0	16 ▮	32 space	48 0	64 @	80 P	96 `	112 p
1 ▮	17 ▮	33 !	49 1	65 A	81 Q	97 a	113 q
2 ▮	18 ▮	34 "	50 2	66 B	82 R	98 b	114 r
3 ▮	19 ▮	35 #	51 3	67 C	83 S	99 c	115 s
4 ▮	20 ▮	36 $	52 4	68 D	84 T	100 d	116 t
5 ▮	21 ▮	37 %	53 5	69 E	85 U	101 e	117 u
6 ▮	22 ▮	38 &	54 6	70 F	86 V	102 f	118 v
7 ▮	23 ▮	39 '	55 7	71 G	87 W	103 g	119 w
8 ▮	24 ▮	40 (	56 8	72 H	88 X	104 h	120 x
9 ▮	25 ▮	41)	57 9	73 I	89 Y	105 i	121 y
10 ▮	26 ▮	42 *	58 :	74 J	90 Z	106 j	122 z
11 ▮	27 ▮	43 +	59 ;	75 K	91 [	107 k	123 {
12 ▮	28 ▮	44 ,	60 <	76 L	92 \	108 l	124	
13 ▮	29 ▮	45 -	61 =	77 M	93]	109 m	125 }
14 ▮	30 ▮	46 .	62 >	78 N	94 ^	110 n	126 ~
15 ▮	31 ▮	47 /	63 ?	79 O	95 _	111 o	127 ▮

Figure 26.15. ASCII/ANSI character chart for 0 to 127.

If a font is not ANSI-compatible, the high-order character codes might not display or print characters the way you expect. For example, the internal fonts in most dot-matrix printers are not ANSI compatible. If they are characters for a specific printer and there is a Windows driver for that printer, they might print as expected because Windows translates the codes you enter to the ANSI codes as you print. If you are using non-Windows fonts and high-order characters, you have to experiment to be sure they display and print as you want.

128 I	144 I	160	176 °	192 À	208 Ð	224 à	240 ð
129 I	145 ´	161 ¡	177 ±	193 Á	209 Ñ	225 á	241 ñ
130 I	146 ´	162 ¢	178 ²	194 Â	210 Ò	226 â	242 ò
131 I	147 I	163 £	179 ³	195 Ã	211 Ó	227 ã	243 ó
132 I	148 I	164 ×	180 ´	196 Ä	212 Ô	228 ä	244 ô
133 I	149 I	165 ¥	181 µ	197 Å	213 Õ	229 å	245 õ
134 I	150 I	166 ¦	182 ¶	198 Æ	214 Ö	230 æ	246 ö
135 I	151 I	167 §	183 ·	199 Ç	215 ×	231 ç	247 ÷
136 I	152 I	168 ¨	184 ‚	200 È	216 Ø	232 è	248 ø
137 I	153 I	169 ©	185 ¹	201 É	217 Ù	233 é	249 ù
138 I	154 I	170 ª	186 º	202 Ê	218 Ú	234 ê	250 ú
139 I	155 I	171 «	187 »	203 Ë	219 Û	235 ë	251 û
140 I	156 I	172 ¬	188 ¼	204 Ì	220 Ü	236 ì	252 ü
141 I	157 I	173 -	189 ½	205 Í	221 Ý	237 í	253 ý
142 I	158 I	174 ®	190 ¾	206 Î	222 Þ	238 î	254 þ
143 I	159 I	175 ‾	191 ¿	207 Ï	223 ß	239 ï	255 ÿ

Figure 26.16. ANSI character chart for 128 to 255.

Setting Up Printers

Chapter 2, "Installing Windows," discusses the basic steps of installing a printer. After the printer is installed, you need to make many choices relating to that printer, such as which port it is connected to, the resolution you want to print at, and so on. All these choices, and the ability to add printers to Windows, are made from the Printers dialog box in Control Panel. The initial dialog box is shown in Figure 26.17.

Standard Items

The Installed Printers list box lists all the printers that you have installed so far. Each line in this list tells the type of printer, the port that it is connected to, and whether it is active. You can install many printers on the same port; of course, only one printer can be using the port at one time. The printer that has access to the port is the active printer, and all other printers assigned to that port are inactive.

The Default Printer is the one that any Windows program will access when it prints. Some programs enable you to change the default printer from within the program, but most do not.

Figure 26.17. Printers dialog box.

To make a printer the default printer with the mouse, click the **Set As Default** button.

To make a printer the default printer with the keyboard, select the printer in the Installed Printers list and press the Tab key to highlight the **Set** as Default button. Press the Enter key to set the selected printer to be the default device.

The Use Print Manager option tells Windows whether you want to use Print Manager, the print spooling program that comes with Windows. For more information on Print Manager, see Chapter 8, "Print Manager."

Printer Actions

The three buttons at the right of the Printers dialog box enable you to perform all the other actions that relate to printers. Table 26.5 explains the use of the buttons.

Table 26.5. Printer action buttons.

Button	Purpose
Cancel	Closes the current dialog box for Printer Setup.
Connect	Opens dialog box to enable you to assign ports, files, and so on to a printer.

26

Button	Purpose
Setup	Changes the setup for the printer selected in the Installed Printers list. This includes the port to which the printer is attached, the length of time Windows will wait for the printer, the specific brand of printer you are using, and other printer-specific information.
Remove	Use this button to remove a printer from the list.
Add »	Adds a printer to the Installed Printers list. This enables you to add new printers or to duplicate printers that are already installed for different setups such as a different port or layout.
Help	Provides help support.

Adding a New Printer

When you click the **A**dd » button, the Printers dialog box expands as shown in Figure 26.18. This additional list includes all the printers that Windows knows about. Choose the printer you want from the list and click the **I**nstall button.

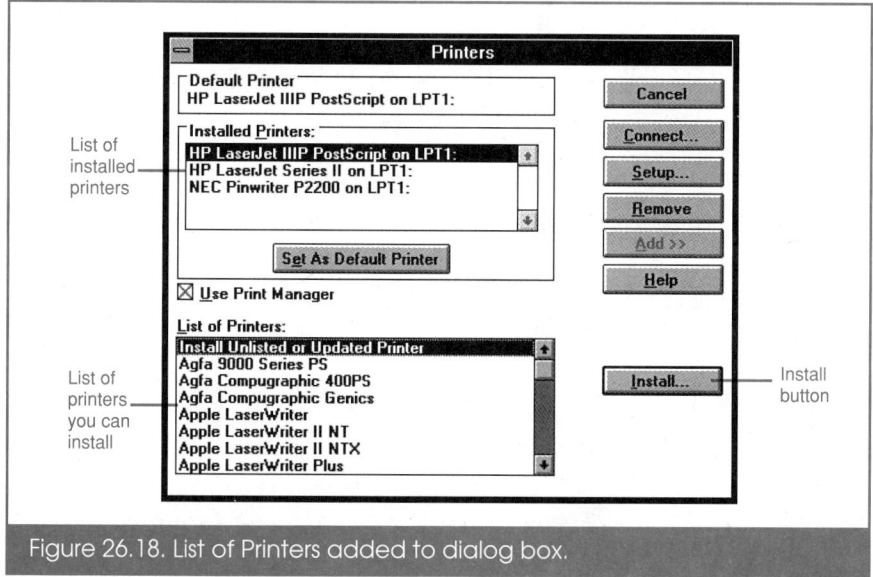

Figure 26.18. List of Printers added to dialog box.

If the printer is one that you have not already installed, you see the prompt shown in Figure 26.19. Insert the appropriate diskette and click OK. For some printers, you might have to insert more than one diskette.

Figure 26.19. Prompt for the diskette.

Tip: If you have a printer that is compatible with a major brand such as Epson, be sure to check the entire printer list before choosing the compatible model. Some compatible printers have their own drivers that work better than choosing the major brand.

Warning: If you do not see any list of printers when you click the **A**dd » button, you might have one of two problems:

▲ Very little memory is available in Windows. If you are low on memory, Control Panel cannot make the list of printers.

▲ The SETUP.INF file in the main Windows directory is damaged or missing. You can copy the SETUP.INF file from the first disk of the Windows setup disks to replace the SETUP.INF in the main windows directory.

Warning: After you install a new printer, it is usually not configured in any way. You must configure the printer using the methods in the next section.

26

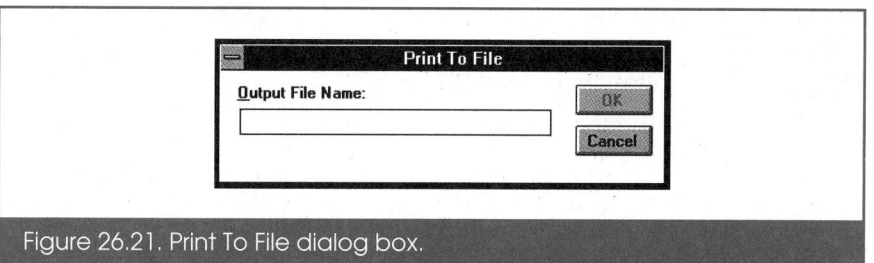

Figure 26.21. Print To File dialog box.

If you have a standard name for the print file you want to save, a better method is to enter that name in the [ports] section of the WIN.INI file as described in Chapter 27, "Configuring with the WIN.INI and SYSTEM.INI Files." When you add this line, the filename appears in the Setup dialog box, as shown in Figure 26.22. Simply select that as the port for the printer, and the output is directed to it.

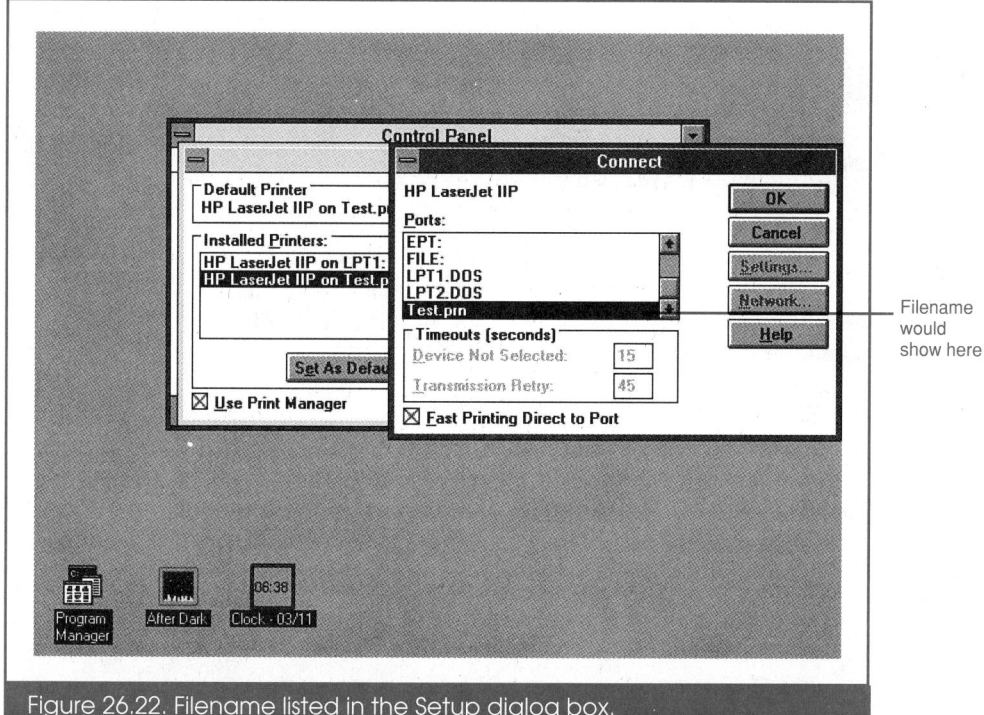

Figure 26.22. Filename listed in the Setup dialog box.

You should use a short filename for a port that is a filename. If the name is too long, it does not appear completely in the Setup dialog box or in the Print To File dialog box.

Warning: If you print a second document to the port that is a filename, the output of the first document is deleted. You cannot append printed documents to a port that is a filename.

Warning: If you add a filename to the [ports] section, be sure to add it to the end of the list, not the beginning of the list. Control Panel assigns printers to ports on the relative position of the port in the list. If you add a line at the beginning, all other printers become assigned to the wrong ports.

Removing or Updating a Printer

If you want to remove a printer from the list of available printers, select it in the main Printers dialog box, and click the **R**emove button. Control Panel asks you whether you really want to remove the printer.

To update a printer driver, such as if you receive a better version of the driver from the printer manufacturer, first remove the printer. Then select the Install Unlisted or Updated Printer line from the list of available printers, as shown in Figure 26.23.

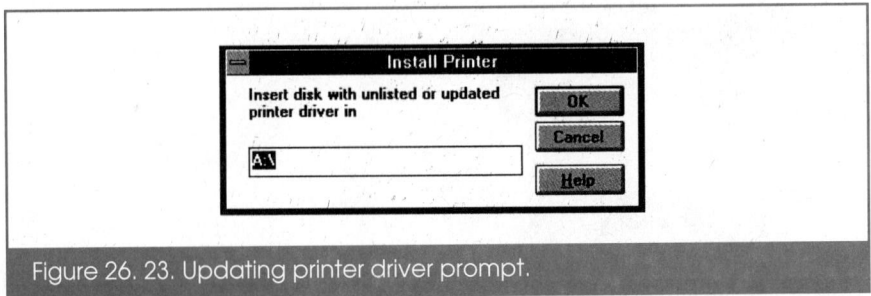

Figure 26. 23. Updating printer driver prompt.

Setup then asks you to insert the disk containing the device driver in a disk drive and begin the copy process.

Timeouts

Windows has two methods for detecting whether the printer is working. It first looks at whether the printer responds to an initial message. If it doesn't respond in a certain amount of time, Windows tells you it cannot print to the printer. After it starts sending data to be printed, the printer might tell Windows it is busy. If the printer stays busy for too long, Windows tells you.

The default value for the Device Not Selected option, 15 seconds, is usually enough for you to turn on the printer if it is off and to have it warm up. The default value for the Transmission Retry option, 45 seconds, is long enough for many printers but not for all. If you are printing a complex graphics image, for example, the printer might take many minutes to interpret it. This is particularly true for most PostScript printers. You might want to increase the time for the Transmission Retry option to 600, or ten minutes, if you get the device busy error message too often.

Tip: Print Manager uses different methods for determining whether the printer is working. It also uses different dialog boxes depending on the printer and how you have set it up.

Printer-Specific Settings

After you have selected a printer and port, you should generally tell Control Panel about specific settings for that printer. These settings, which are different for each printer type, modify the way information is sent to the printer. In many cases, they also modify the way the printer works, such as the direction it prints (portrait or landscape) on the page.

The Setup dialog box for each type of printer is different because different types of printers have different features. For example, the Setup dialog box for LaserJet II printers has a list of cartridges you might have inserted in the printer, but the Setup dialog box for PostScript printers does not have such a list.

The following sections describe the setup options for the three most common types of printers used with Windows 3.1: Epson dot-matrix printers (and compatibles), Hewlett-Packard LaserJet printers (and compatibles), and PostScript printers.

Common Choices

Some fields appear in the Setup dialog box for many printers. They are described here.

All printers (except the Generic printer described later) have the Printer field in the Setup dialog box in common. The Printer option is the brand and model of printer. Although most printers claim to be compatible with a standard, there are often slight differences. By choosing the correct model from this list, you can usually avoid problems that appear due to slight incompatibilities.

The *resolution* is the number of dots per inch the printer uses when printing graphics or characters that are not in the printer's internal fonts. The more dots per inch, the better the quality of the output but the longer it takes to print. The resolution is shown with the horizontal resolution first, then the vertical resolution. For printers on which the horizontal and vertical resolutions are the same, only the single number is listed.

The *orientation* of the paper is how the printer prints across a page. Portrait orientation indicates that the paper is taller than it is wide, as in formal portraits. Landscape orientation indicates that the paper is wider than it is tall, as in a landscape painting. For example, this book is in portrait orientation.

Some Setup dialog boxes have Help or Info buttons. These are usually dialog boxes that tell you who wrote the driver, but some have valuable information about how to set up the printer. You should always check the information in those dialog boxes before clicking OK.

Epson-Compatible Dot-Matrix Printers

Figure 26.24 shows the Setup dialog box for the Epson 9-pin printers. These are the most common type of inexpensive dot-matrix printers available in the U.S. market. The choices in this dialog box enable you to specify how the printer prints and the type of paper you are using.

The Printer field lists all the Epson models that have 9 pins. Choose the printer you have from that list.

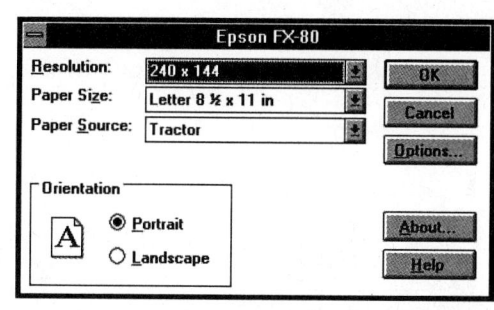

Figure 26.24. Setup dialog box for Epson 9-pin printers.

Tip: Note that if you are using an Epson-compatible printer, you should choose the printer type carefully because some printers from other manufacturers do not exactly correspond to a particular Epson printer. If you have problems printing, you might want to choose a different printer from the Printer list to see whether that clears up the incompatibility.

Some models, such as the JX-80, can take color ribbons. If you have a color ribbon, be sure to select the Color option.

The Paper **S**ource option tells how the paper is fed into the printer. Most of the time you use the tractor option. If you have added a standard sheet feeder, select one of the other choices.

When printing characters from the printer's internal character set, you can choose either Letter mode (high quality, slower printing) or Draft mode (lower quality, faster printing). Note that these settings have no effect on some printers: you must put the printer in the proper mode by setting switches, usually on the front or top of the printer.

The paper width and height tell Windows the type of paper you are using. This information is used to tell Windows programs the total paper size and thus the margins it should use when printing. The No page break option tells Windows that it should print without advancing at the end of a page.

Figure 26.25 shows the dialog box for Epson 24-pin printers. The choices are similar to the 9-pin printers with a few additions.

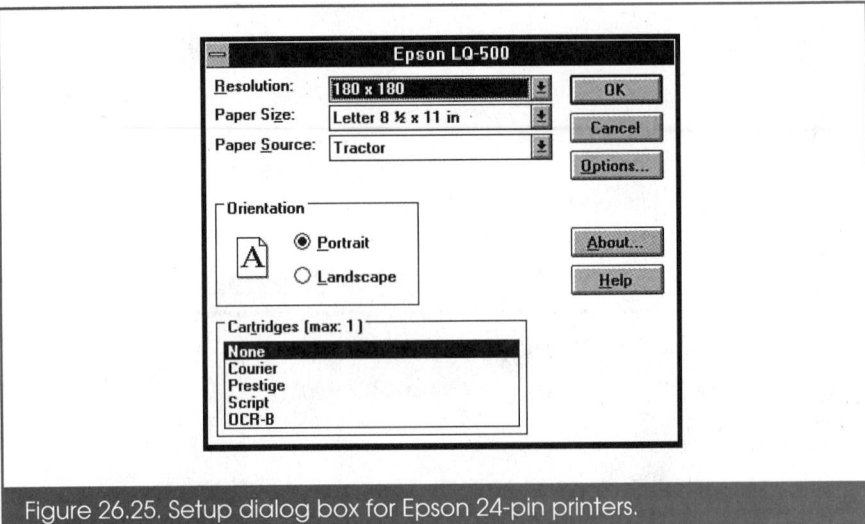

Figure 26.25. Setup dialog box for Epson 24-pin printers.

For some models in the list, such as the LQ-850, you can set the amount of margin at the top and bottom of the paper. Figure 26.26 shows this dialog box. The defaults, .5 inches, are usually fine, but you might want to leave more room if you have special letterhead or less if you are using forms that have information close to the top or bottom of the page.

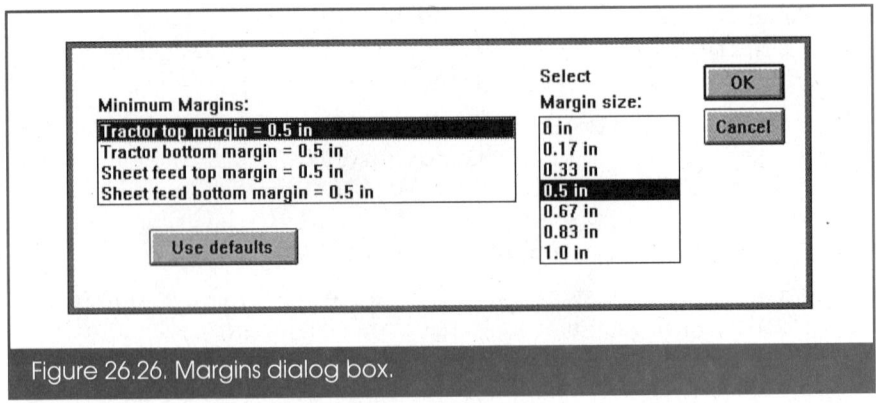

Figure 26.26. Margins dialog box.

The Other LQ Fonts list enables you to choose the default font for the printer. These are usually much nicer-looking fonts than the standard Courier font.

26

Hewlett-Packard LaserJet Printers

The Setup dialog box for the Hewlett-Packard LaserJet II is shown in Figure 26.27 (the dialog box for the LaserJet III is almost identical). The Printer list includes not only printers made by Hewlett-Packard but numerous other compatible printers as well.

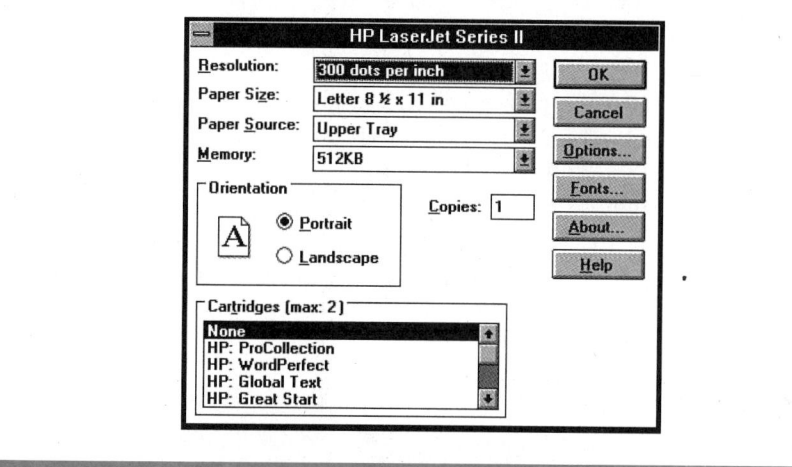

Figure 26.27. Setup dialog box for Hewlett-Packard LaserJet II printers.

Tip: If you have a LaserJet printer with a PostScript cartridge, you must set up the printer as a PostScript printer, not as a LaserJet. See the instructions later in this chapter for a description of the PostScript Setup dialog box.

Many models of laser printers can have more than one paper tray or can take paper trays that hold different types of paper. The Paper **Source** option enables you to specify the tray or tray type. This is also where you specify that you want to feed paper manually and be prompted for each sheet. For some models, the options here are Upper Tray, Lower Tray, and Manual feed; for others, they are Upper Tray, Manual feed, and Envelope.

The Paper Size list tells Windows the type of paper you are using. This information is used to tell Windows programs the total paper size and thus the margins it should use when printing. The sizes are given both by their common names (such as Letter and Legal) and by the actual measurement (such as 8 1/2 x 11 in).

The memory setting is very important because Windows acts differently if it knows that you have more or less memory. Be sure the memory listed matches the memory in your printer.

The **C**opies option tells Windows how many copies to print. Note that the copies are uncollated; that is, they come out with all the copies for one page, then all the copies for the next page, and so on. It is much more efficient to specify the number of copies in the Setup dialog box than to give the print command many times. You can override this setting each time you print from any windows application that gives you the option to do so.

If you install cartridges into the printer, you must tell Windows about them so that it can make the fonts for those cartridges available to your Windows programs. You can select up to two cartridges (the number the printer can hold) from the list, depending on how many your model of printer can handle.

If you select the LaserJet IID or the LaserJet 2000, the **O**ptions button is active. This enables you to set the duplex printing options for these printers, as shown in Figure 26.28.

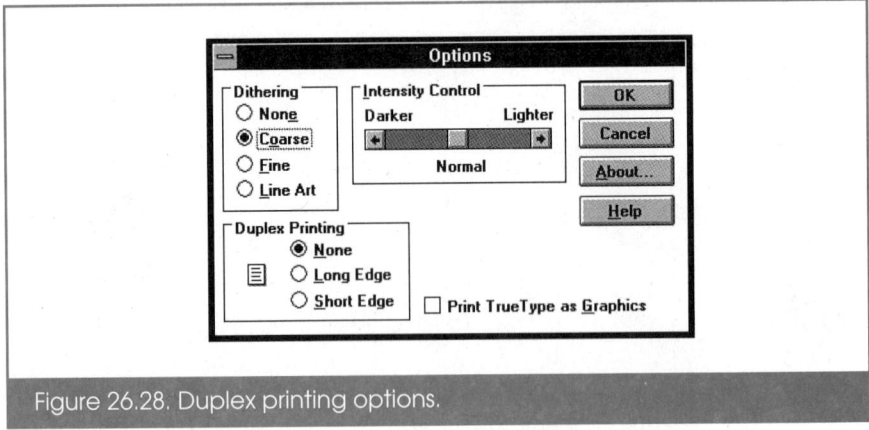

Figure 26.28. Duplex printing options.

Most soft fonts come with their own Windows installation programs. Most cartridges are listed in the Setup dialog box, but some are not. Of those that are not, many come with Windows installation programs. If you can, you should use these installation programs. If you can't, you can still install the fonts.

In the Setup dialog box, click the **F**onts button. You see a dialog box like Figure 26.29. The list on the left is the fonts you have installed.

26

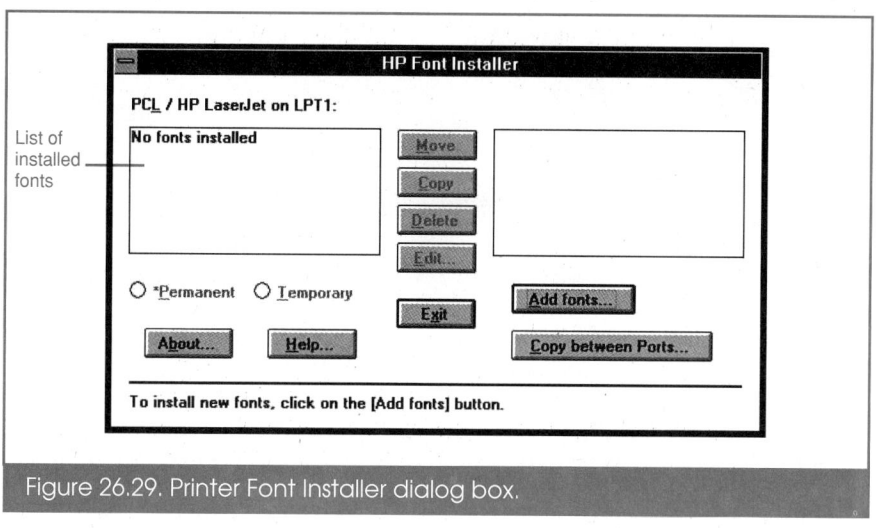

Figure 26.29. Printer Font Installer dialog box.

To add a soft font or cartridge:

1. Click the **A**dd fonts button. You are prompted for the fonts you are installing as shown in Figure 26.30. Type the drive name or the directory name if you have already copied the fonts to the hard disk.

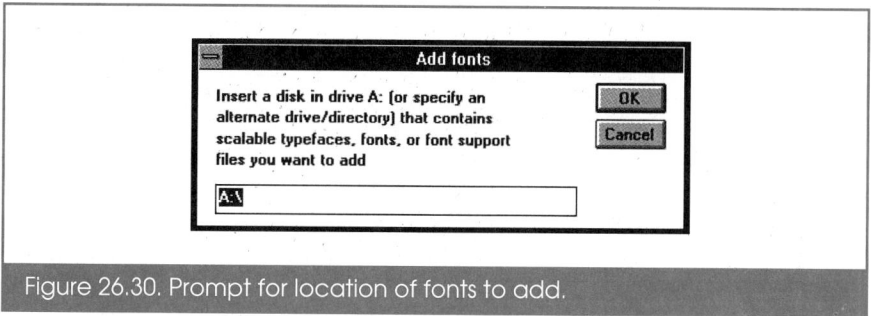

Figure 26.30. Prompt for location of fonts to add.

2. The installer scans the drive and directory you specify for fonts. The fonts it finds are displayed in the list on the right. Select the fonts you want to add.

If you installed a cartridge, you must now go back to the Setup dialog box and choose the cartridge. After you do that, the fonts in the cartridge will be available in your Windows documents.

PostScript Printers

The Setup dialog box for PostScript printers is shown in Figure 26.31.

Figure 26.31. Setup dialog box for PostScript printers.

Tip: If your printer is not listed in the Printer list but you have a driver for that printer, click the Add Printer button to install the new driver. This is usually necessary only for very new PostScript printers.

Many models of laser printers can have more than one paper tray or can take paper trays that hold different types of paper. The Paper Source option enables you to specify the tray or tray type. This is also where you specify that you want to feed paper manually and be prompted for each sheet. The options might include Upper Tray, Lower Tray, Manual Feed, Auto Select, Large Capacity, Envelope, and so on. For printers with a single paper source, such as a phototypesetter, the choice is Upper Tray.

The paper size list tells Windows the type of paper you are using. This information is used to tell Windows programs the total paper size and thus the margins they should use when printing. The sizes are given both by their common names (such as Letter and Legal) and by the actual measurement (such as 8 1/2 x 11 in).

You can cause the print on the printer to be smaller or larger than normal with the Scaling size. For example, to print at half size, specify 50 for this option.

26

The Copies option tells Windows how many copies to print. Note that the copies are uncollated; that is, they come out with all the copies for one page, then all the copies for the next page, and so on. It is much more efficient to specify the number of copies in the Setup dialog box than to give the print command many times. Normally, the Windows application you are using offers you the same option when you print a document.

If you are using a color PostScript printer, be sure to select the Color option in the check box provided.

The **O**ptions button brings up the dialog box shown in Figure 26.32. These are options that rarely need to be changed.

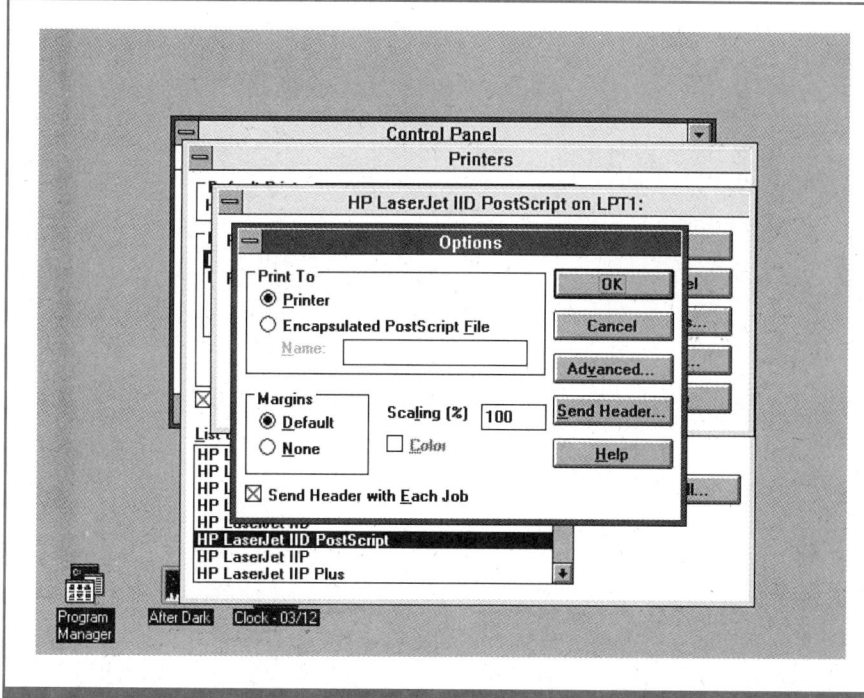

Figure 26.32. PostScript Setup Options dialog box.

The Print To section enables you to specify that the file will be printed as an encapsulated PostScript file (often called an EPS file) instead of being sent to the printer. This is useful if you want to import the output from one program to another in EPS format. An EPS file has a graphical image of the output as well as the PostScript instructions for creating it.

Warning: Note that this is different from capturing the output with the methods described earlier in this chapter. An encapsulated PostScript file does not have the header necessary to print a file on a PostScript printer and thus cannot be sent to the printer directly.

The Job Timeout section tells the printer how long to wait for text from the PC before assuming there is an error. If you set this to 0, it will never get such an error. Setting this to any other value causes the printer to generate an error if it takes too long to get information from the PC.

The Margins option enables you to specify whether to use the printer's default margins (which are usually .25 to .5 inches from each edge of the paper) or to use the actual edge of the paper. This is useful if you need to line up the output exactly relative to the edge of the paper and the program is being fooled by the printer's default margins.

The Send Header section tells Windows whether to download the PostScript header file each time you start a print job or to assume that the header is already loaded in the printer. If the printer is attached only to your PC, you can set this to Already downloaded to prevent the computer from sending the header file each time you print and thus save yourself time.

To send the header file only once each time you turn on the printer, you must download the header file yourself. Create the header file by clicking the Send Header button in the Options dialog box. You see the dialog box shown in Figure 26.33. Select File and click OK. When prompted, enter a path and filename for the header file. (You can also use the Header dialog box to send the header to the printer immediately.)

To send the header file to the printer, use the MS-DOS copy command, such as:

```
C>COPY C:\WINDOWS\PSHEAD.TXT LPT1:
```

Of course, you must use the name of the header file you created and the port to which the printer is attached.

Warning: The header files (files which contain PostScript instructions) for different printers are different. Be sure you have the correct printer set up when you create a header file.

26

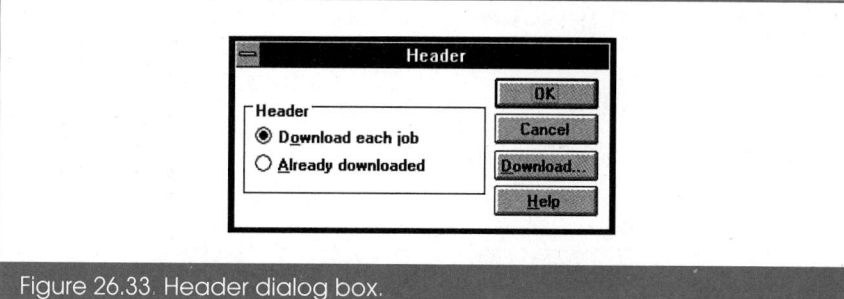

Figure 26.33. Header dialog box.

The Handshake button displays the dialog box shown in Figure 26.34. This is used only if the printer is attached to a serial port (such as COM1:). This dialog permanently changes the way the printer communicates with the PC. In general, hardware handshake is better than software handshake. Read the printer's manual to be sure this option works with your particular model of printer. After choosing this, open the Ports icon of Control Panel, choose the port you have the printer attached to, and set the flow control to Xon/Xoff if you selected software control or Hardware if you selected hardware control.

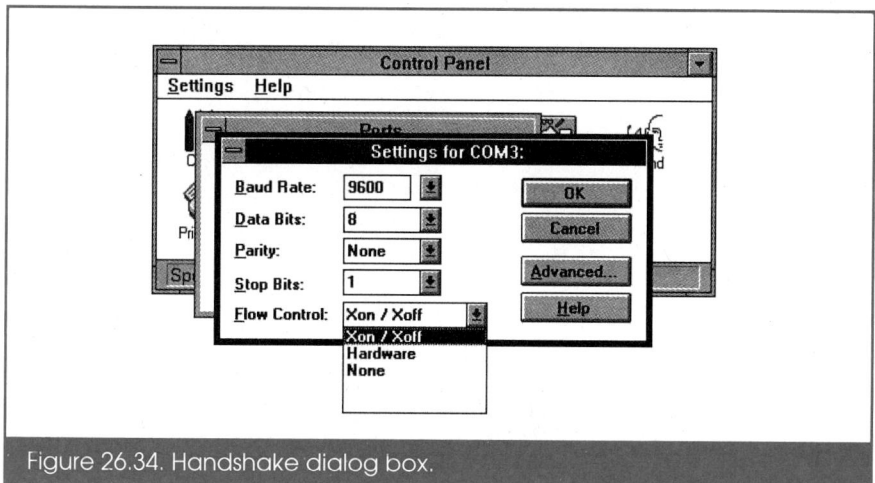

Figure 26.34. Handshake dialog box.

Generic Printers

If you have a printer not supported by Windows, you can use the Generic/Text Only driver. The Setup dialog box for that driver is shown in Figure 26.35. This driver enables you to set the standard printer settings such as paper size, but it also enables you to enter the special control codes that most printers use to control how the printer operates.

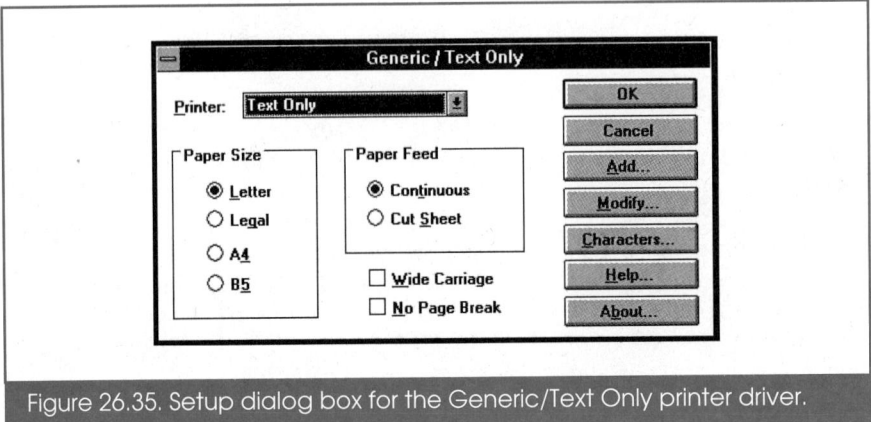

Figure 26.35. Setup dialog box for the Generic/Text Only printer driver.

To configure the control codes, you must know the codes required by the printer. These are listed in the printer's manual, usually in an appendix. To enter control codes, click the **Add** button. You see the dialog box shown in Figure 26.36. Give the driver a name (such as the manufacturer and model of the printer).

To enter the codes, select the option you want to modify and type the codes. You can type codes in two ways:

▲ If the codes are letters or Ctrl-key sequences, type them directly.

▲ If the codes have ASCII values above 127, you have to enter those values by holding down the Alt key, pressing 0 (zero) on the numeric keypad, and then typing the three-digit decimal value of the code. Be sure to hold down the Alt key continuously while pressing the four numbers on the numeric keypad.

If the manual has only the hexadecimal values for the codes, you must first convert them to decimal with the Calculator program in the Accessories window of Program Manager.

26

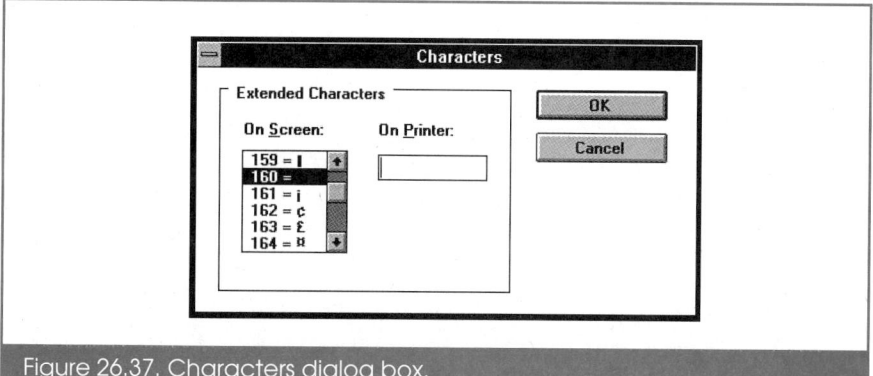

Figure 26.36. Add dialog box.

You can also translate screen characters to the appropriate printer
characters with the **C**haracters button in the Setup dialog box. The
Characters dialog box is shown in Figure 26.37. To set up a translation,
you select the screen character that corresponds to a printer character
and enter the printer character's equivalent code in the On **P**rinter box.
For example, if the printer uses code 204 for the cent sign (which is
screen character 162), select the line with 162 in the list and type Alt-0
and 204 (while still holding down the Alt key) in the On **P**rinter entry.

Figure 26.37. Characters dialog box.

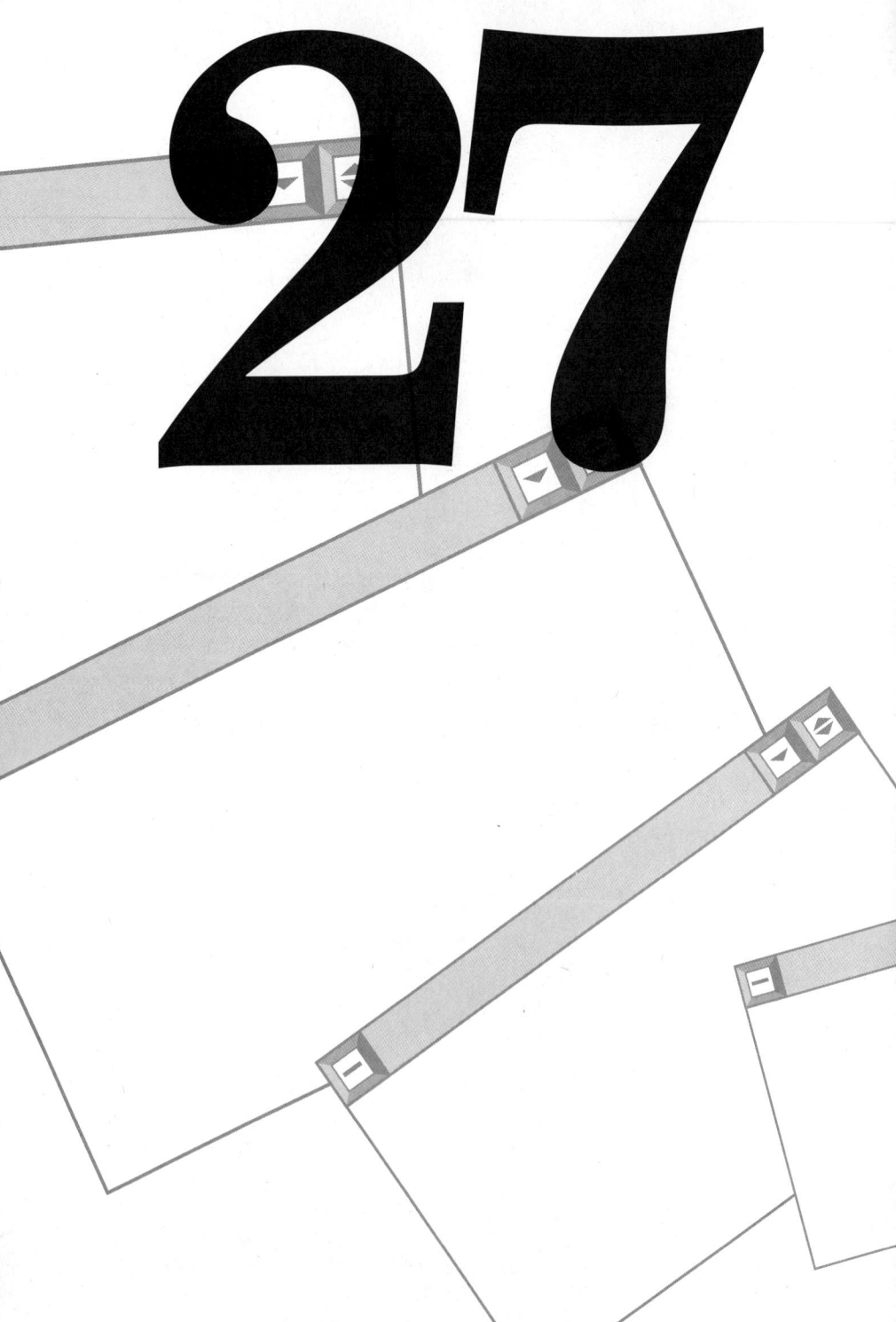

CHAPTER 27

Configuring with the WIN.INI and SYSTEM.INI Files

Windows uses the WIN.INI file as a guide to the way you want Windows to look when you start. As you change Windows, the WIN.INI file is kept up-to-date with your changes. Many Windows programs also store their startup information in WIN.INI. You can change the WIN.INI file with Control Panel or by editing it directly. Note that Chapter 7, "Control Panel," describes how to use the Control Panel program; part of this chapter describes how those changes are remembered by Windows.

Some of the settings in WIN.INI can be changed only by editing the WIN.INI file, not with Control Panel. If you want to change WIN.INI yourself, you can use any text editor. The SysEdit command, described in Chapter 25, "Changing Your Configuration," is a very handy way to do this and have access to the SYSTEM.INI file at the same time.

Although the WIN.INI has most of the startup settings, the SYSTEM.INI file also has startup settings. The settings in SYSTEM.INI mostly relate to hardware.

Although we have endeavored to cover every aspect of each setting that can be found in the four Windows .INI files, many of the settings you can find on your system will have been created by applications for their own use, and will not be covered in this chapter.

How to Read WIN.INI

The WIN.INI file is a plain text file. It starts off short (about 70 lines) but grows longer as you run Windows programs. Because some settings are not stored in WIN.INI until you change them in Control Panel, WIN.INI gets longer the first few times you modify the way Windows looks. Incidentally, all the information in this section applies to the SYSTEM.INI file as well.

In the file, each section has a header that has a name in square brackets, such as:

```
[Desktop]
```

Under each heading is a series of lines in the form

```
[keyword]=[value]
```

Here, *keyword* is a word or phrase WIN.INI recognizes, and *value* is the value you want to set that keyword to. For example, one of the first lines in the WIN.INI file is

```
Spooler=yes
```

in which Spooler is the keyword and yes is the value. (As you might guess, this line tells Windows that you want to use the print spooler in Print Manager.)

A few notes on the lines in WIN.INI and SYSTEM.INI:

▲ The capitalization of the keywords is not important. Thus, you could have entered the previous example as

```
spooler=yes
```

▲ The capitalization of the values might or might not be important, but it is always safer to follow the capitalization that is already in the file or in this book. This is particularly true for values that are in quotation marks.

▲ Usually, one or more blank lines appear before a new heading. These are optional but they help you read the file.

▲ The headings in WIN.INI and SYSTEM.INI can appear in any order. The lines under the heading can also appear in any order.

▲ You can put lines in WIN.INI and SYSTEM.INI that are ignored by Windows when it starts. Simply put a semicolon (;) at the beginning of the line. For example:

```
;The next line defines the main printer port
LPT1:=
```

▲ You should not put a space before or after the equal sign, although this is not strictly required. Some programs reading WIN.INI or SYSTEM.INI might have problems reading lines that have spaces around the equal sign.

▲ Some yes-or-no settings are specified with yes and no values; others are set with 0 and 1. Be sure to check the setting type before editing WIN.INI or SYSTEM.INI.

▲ Most filenames appear in lowercase instead of the normal uppercase. The case does not matter for filenames.

27

Warning: Before you edit your WIN.INI file, you should be sure to make a backup copy. Use File Manager or the MS-DOS COPY command to make a file called WININI.OLD that you can use if the changes you make to WIN.INI cause Windows not to work correctly.

The headings that appear in the WIN.INI file when you first install Windows are shown in Table 27.1. Other headings are added by programs that store their information in the WIN.INI file. For example, Word for Windows creates a heading [Microsoft Word].

Table 27.1. Headings in WIN.INI file.

Heading	Use
[windows]	General settings
[Desktop]	Settings for icon spacing, background color, and wallpaper
[Extensions]	Associations between file extensions and programs
[intl]	Country and language settings
[ports]	Settings for output ports
[fonts]	List of all installed fonts
[FontSubstitutes]	Specifies a font to be used in place of another
[TrueType]	Sets TrueType font name and enabling settings
[mci extensions]	Associates files with devices
[networks]	Network settings and connections
[embedding]	Used in object linking and embedding programs

continues

Table 27.1. Continued

Heading	Use
[Windows Help]	Settings for Windows Help windows
[sounds]	Sound files related to system events
[PrinterPorts]	Output devices
[devices]	Output devices (used only by Windows Version 2 programs)
[programs]	Additional paths used to find associated files
[colors]	Color settings for displaying all windows

The rest of this section is organized by heading in the order in which the headings appear in the .INI files. Within each heading, the keywords are organized alphabetically.

Windows

The [windows] section has general Windows settings, such as programs to load when you start Windows and settings for the mouse. A typical [windows] section looks like this:

```
[windows]
Spooler=yes
load=c:\windows\blankscr.exe
run=
Beep=yes
NullPort=None
BorderWidth=3
CursorBlinkRate=530
DoubleClickSpeed=452
Programs=com exe bat pif
Documents=
DeviceNotSelectedTimeout=15
TransmissionRetryTimeout=45
swapdisk=
KeyboardDelay=2
KeyboardSpeed=31
ScreenSaveActive=0
ScreenSaveTimeout=120
DosPrint=yes
```

```
MouseSpeed=1
MouseThreshold1=7
MouseThreshold2=0
MouseSpeed=2
Modem=COM2,T,3
NetWarn=1
Prefix=
UsePrefix=0
Device=HP LaserJet Series II,HPPCL,LPT1:
```

27

Spooler

This specifies whether information sent to the printer is passed to Print Manager. The default value is yes, indicating that Print Manager is active. This value is set from the Printers section of Control Panel.

For example, to turn off spooling to Print Manager, use the line

```
Spooler=no
```

Load

You can automatically load programs as icons when you start Windows. This makes them easily available to you. Also, some programs, such as screen savers and screen-capture programs, load themselves into memory when they are loaded as icons. To use this line, add the names of the programs you want loaded. You can change this value only by editing WIN.INI.

For example, if you have a screen-saving program BLANKSCR.EXE in the c:\main directory and also want to run the CLOCK.EXE program, you might have a line like this:

```
load=c:\main\blankscr.exe clock.exe
```

Tip: Note that you can place any icon in the Startup group window to load a program without using the load= command line in the WIN.INI file. If you don't want to keep a Startup window visible, use the load= command in the WIN.INI file instead.

In 386-enhanced mode, if you load a non-Windows program and the PIF for that program does not specify that it can run in the background, the program does not load until you select its icon. In standard mode, the program loads as you start up.

Tip: The `load=` line is different from the `run=` line. Use `load=` to load programs without running them in their own windows; use `run=` to start the programs running. Generally, you use `load=` for small utilities that run in the background (with icon minimized) and `run=` for regular Windows programs.

Run

You can automatically start running programs when you start Windows. This is handy if you run certain programs every time you run Windows and you have enough memory to do so. To use this line, add the names of the programs you want to run.

Tip: With Windows 3.1 you can also run programs without editing the WIN.INI file by placing the program's icon in the Startup group window. Make sure the check box provided for Run Minimized is *not* selected (if it is, the program will only *load* and minimize to an icon).

For example, if you always run Excel when you run Windows, you might have a line like this:

```
run=c:\excel3\excel.exe
```

In another example, people who like to run File Manager automatically when they start Windows would have a `run=` line like this:

```
run=winfile.exe
```

If you have more than one program listed in the line (separated by a comma), the last one on the line is the active program after Windows has started them all. You can also use the StartUp group window to run programs automatically during startup. See Chapter 5, "Program Manager" for more on how this is done.

Tip: The `load=` line is different from the `run=` line. Use `load=` to load programs without running them in their own windows; use `run=` to start the programs running. Generally, you use `load=` for small utilities that run in the background and `run=` for regular Windows programs.

Beep

Set Beep to yes to sound a warning tone when you do something incorrect or to no to inhibit the beep. In a room with many people, it might be polite to turn off the warning tone. The default is yes. This value is set from the Sound section of Control Panel.

For example, to turn off the tone, use

```
Beep=no
```

NullPort

You can set the name of the port to be used when a printer is installed but not connected to any port. You should never need to change this unless you are really bored. The default value is None. You can change this value only by editing WIN.INI.

BorderWidth

You can set the number of pixels in the border around windows. The default, 3, is about the right size for pointing at when you want to resize a window. You can set this value from 1 to 49, although it is unlikely you will want to set it higher than 5. Setting BorderWidth to 1 makes resizing a window with the mouse very difficult and saves only a little screen room. This value is set from the Desktop section of Control Panel.

For example, to make the window border slightly wider, try the setting

```
BorderWidth=5
```

CursorBlinkRate

Use this setting to specify how many milliseconds elapse between each time the insertion point blinks. The default is 530, and you can set this between 200 and 1200 milliseconds. This value is set from the Desktop section of Control Panel.

For example, you can make the cursor blink very slowly with the line

```
CursorBlinkRate=1000
```

DoubleClickSpeed

You can set the number of milliseconds that can elapse between two mouse clicks, after which they are considered two clicks rather than a double-click. The default, 452 (or about half a second), is often too long for advanced mouse users but sometimes too short for novices. This value can be between 100 and 900, although few people can double-click faster than 175 milliseconds. This value is set from the Mouse section of Control Panel.

For example, to allow a fairly long time between clicks and still have the action count as a double-click, use the line

```
DoubleClickSpeed=750
```

Programs

This setting tells Windows the extensions on files that make them programs. For example, .COM is an MS-DOS program. The default value for this line, com exe bat pif, rarely should be changed. You can change this value only by editing WIN.

Documents

List document extensions here that do not exist in the [Extensions] section to make them recognized by File Manager. This changes icons for these documents from the generic plain icon to one with stripes. If you tend to visually sort icons for file types instead of reading filenames when using File Manger, this trick can be very helpful. For example, to make File Manager recognize files with the .DLL or .FON extension as documents, use the line

```
Documents=dll fon
```

DeviceNotSelectedTimeout

This setting tells Windows how many seconds to wait for a response from a printer (the default is 15 seconds). Note that this value is only the default for new printers, not the value for all printers. The value for a particular printer is listed in the [PrinterPorts] heading. You can change this value only by editing WIN.INI. It is unlikely you will change this because you set the value for each printer as you install it.

For example, to cause Windows to default to 20 seconds for new printers, use the line

```
DeviceNotSelectedTimeout=20
```

TransmissionRetryTimeout

This setting tells Windows how many seconds to keep trying to retransmit information to the printer if a transmission was initially unsuccessful (the default is 45 seconds). Note that this value is only the default for new printers, not the value for all printers. The value for a particular printer is listed in the `[PrinterPorts]` heading. You can change this value only by editing WIN.INI. It is unlikely you will change this because you set the value for each printer as you install it.

For example, to cause Windows to default to 30 seconds for new printers, use the line

```
TransmissionRetryTimeout=30
```

27

Swapdisk

If your WIN.INI file has this line in the `[windows]` section, you can ignore it. It is a remnant from earlier versions of Windows.

KeyboardSpeed

When you hold down a key on the keyboard, Windows repeats the key. This setting tells Windows how fast it should reproduce the letter. The default is `31`, the fastest repeat rate; the slowest rate is `0`. This value is set from the Keyboard section of Control Panel.

For example, to slow down the repeat rate to half its normal speed, use the line

```
KeyboardSpeed=16
```

ScreenSaveActive

This setting indicates whether the Windows 3.1 screen-saver utility is enabled. It looks like this:

```
ScreenSaveActive=0    Where 0 is off and 1 is on
```

ScreenSaveTimeOut

This setting determines how long the *enabled* Windows screen saver waits between periods of keyboard or mouse activity before engaging (ScreenSaveActive must = 1).

MouseSpeed, MouseThreshold1, and MouseThreshold2

As you change the speed setting in the Mouse section of Control Panel, Windows changes how fast the cursor moves across the screen by changing how it accelerates. This is specified in WIN.INI in three settings: MouseSpeed, MouseThreshold1, and MouseThreshold2.

MouseSpeed has three possible settings: 0, 1, and 2. The meanings of these values are shown in Table 27.2. It is difficult to predict how MouseSpeed will be set.

Table 27.2. Values of MouseSpeed.

Value	Meaning
0	The cursor does not accelerate when you move the mouse.
1	The cursor accelerates to twice its normal speed when you go faster than the value in MouseThreshold1. The default value is 5.
2	The cursor accelerates to twice its normal speed when you go faster than the value in MouseThreshold1 and four times its normal speed when you go faster than the value in MouseThreshold2. MouseThreshold1 and MouseThreshold2 are the number of pixels the pointer can move between mouse interrupts before Windows accelerates the pointer, as determined by MouseSpeed. The default value is 10.

For example, if you want the mouse to move at a medium speed, include the lines

```
MouseSpeed=1
MouseThreshold1=7
MouseThreshold2=0
```

SwapMouseButtons

This setting tells Windows whether you want to use the right mouse button rather than the left for normal clicking. The normal value is no, meaning that you want to use the left button. This value is set from the Mouse section of Control Panel.

For example, to switch the left and right mouse buttons, use the line

```
SwapMouseButtons=yes
```

27

Device

The device specifies the name and connection for Windows's default printer. The format of the line is

```
Device=devicename,drivername,port
```

In this case, the *devicename* is the name from the [PrinterPorts] section. The *drivername* is the name of the disk file that has the printer's device driver (minus the .DRV extension), and the *port* is the port to which this printer is attached. This value is set from the Printers section of Control Panel.

For example, the default printer might be specified as

```
device=HP LaserJet III,HPPCL5A,LPT1:
```

NetWarn

This setting tells Windows whether to display a warning message if the network you are using stops working. This warning lets you know that Windows has disabled all networking actions. Set this to 1 to enable the message or 0 to disable the message (the default is 1). You might want to set this to 0 if you are running on a network that crashes often and you use the network services in Windows only occasionally. This value is set from the Network section of Control Panel.

For example, to turn off the warning, use the line

```
NetWarn=0
```

Desktop

The settings in [Desktop] affect the appearance of the desktop, such as the pattern, wallpaper, and icon placement. A typical [Desktop] section looks like this:

```
[Desktop]
Pattern=
Wallpaper=(None)
TileWallpaper=0
WallpaperOriginX=0
WallpaperOriginY=0
GridGranularity=0
IconSpacing=75
```

All values in this section (except WallpaperOriginX and WallpaperOriginY) are set from the Desktop section of Control Panel.

Pattern

The desktop pattern is an 8-by-8 square of pixels repeated over the entire backdrop of the desktop. It consists of pixels in two colors set in the [colors] section: Background and Windows Text. You can choose from a set of preselected patterns, edit a pattern, or create your own pattern.

The value in this line is not the name of the pattern you see in Control Panel but a numerical representation of the pattern. Each pattern consists of pixels that are in the Background color and the Windows Text color. Pixels in the Background color have a value of 0; pixels in the Windows Text color have a value of 1. The binary pattern for each row is converted to a decimal number that is used in the line.

For example, Figure 27.1 shows the Diamonds pattern you see after clicking the Edit Pattern button in the Desktop section of Control Panel. The first row has a value of 32 because one bit, the third from the left, is turned on, giving a binary value of 00100000. The second row has a value of 80 because the pattern is 01010000, and so on. The values equated with the selected pattern are stored in the WIN.INI.

The line in WIN.INI that defines the diamond pattern is

```
Pattern=32 80 136 80 32 0 0 0
```

It is unlikely you will ever want to set this line yourself. It is much easier to simply create a pattern in the Desktop section of Control

Panel. You can see examples of the number equivalent of all the patterns in the CONTROL.INI file described later in this chapter.

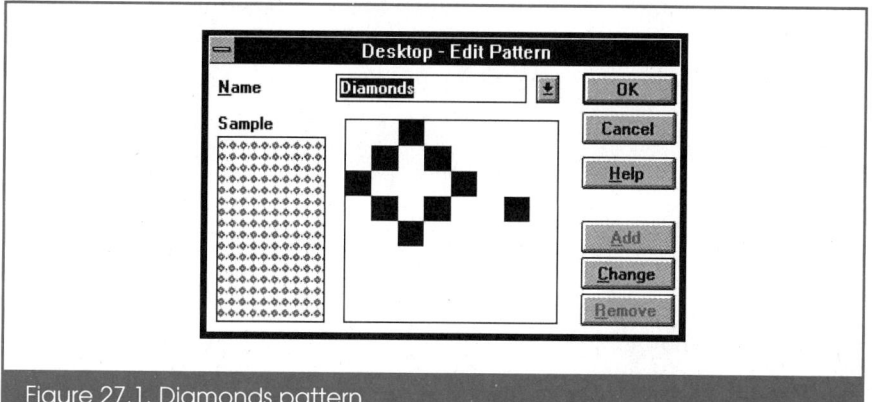

Figure 27.1. Diamonds pattern.

Wallpaper

You can specify the name of the wallpaper file you want to use with this line. If you do not want to use wallpaper, set this to (None) or remove the line. Wallpaper files are in Windows's bit-map format and usually have the extension .BMP. If the file is in the main Windows directory, you do not need to specify a path name.

For example, to specify BOOKS.BMP as the wallpaper file, use

```
Wallpaper=BOOKS.BMP
```

TileWallpaper

This setting tells Windows whether to tile the wallpaper you have specified. A value of 1 tiles the wallpaper, and 0 centers it.

For example, to specify that the wallpaper should be tiled, use the line

```
TileWallpaper=1
```

GridGranularity

If you want to arrange your windows on a fixed grid, you can change this setting to a number from 0 to 49. When you move or create a window, it appears only on the grid. The value is the number of eight-pixel units for the grid. Because the unit is eight pixels and not one, it is unlikely you will ever set this value above 2. Few people care about window grid alignment at all, and most people will probably not change this number.

For example, to change the grid granularity to 1, use the line

```
GridGranularity=1
```

IconSpacing

When you use the **W**indow **A**rrange Icons command in Program Manager, it rearranges the icons to be a certain number of pixels apart. This usually gives enough space for the icon names except where the name is very long. The default spacing, 75, is good for most program icons but might be too close if you use long names on icons with documents. This value can be between 32 and 512.

For example, to add more space between icons when you arrange them with the **W**indow **A**rrange Icons command, use the line

```
IconSpacing=120
```

WallpaperOriginX and WallpaperOriginY

When you tile wallpaper, Windows initially uses the upper-left corner of the screen as the origin for tiling. You can change this origin with these values. You can change them only by editing WIN.INI.

For example, to move the origin up and to the left by four pixels, use the lines

```
WallpaperOriginX=4
WallpaperOriginY=4
```

Extensions

When you select a nonprogram file in File Manager or you create an icon for a document in Program Manager, Windows looks at the [Extensions] section in WIN.INI for the extension on the file. If it finds an extension, it runs the associated program. A typical [Extensions] section looks like

```
[Extensions]
cal=calendar.exe ^.cal
crd=cardfile.exe ^.crd
trm=terminal.exe ^.trm
txt=notepad.exe ^.txt
ini=notepad.exe ^.ini
pcx=pbrush.exe ^.pcx
bmp=pbrush.exe ^.bmp
wri=write.exe ^.wri
rec=recorder.exe ^.rec
```

27

Lines in this section have the following format:

```
ext=program arguments
```

Here, *ext* is the extension you want to make an association for. The *program* is the name of the program you want to run when you select any file with that extension. Note that the program can be either a Windows program or a non-Windows program. The *arguments* are the arguments you want to include with the program name.

The arguments you want to use almost always include the name of the document you selected so that the program starts with that document. The special character ^ is the name of the document without any extension. Thus, the line

```
pcx=pbrush.exe ^.pcx
```

indicates that when you select a file called BACKCOV.PCX, Windows should give the command

```
PBRUSH BACKCOV.PCX
```

You can add any extensions to the list you want. For example, if you have text files on your disk with the extension .TEX, you might want to add the line

```
tex=notepad.exe ^.tex
```

If you use Excel (which can read Lotus 1-2-3 files), and you want to open Excel when you select 1-2-3 files with the .WK1 extension, add the line

```
wk1=c:\excel3\excel.exe ^.wk1
```

Tip: You can use the **F**ile **A**ssociate command in the File Manager program to add lines to the [Extensions] section. See Chapter 6, "File Manager," for more information on the **F**ile **A**ssociate command.

> **Warning:** Do not place the line
>
> ```
> hlp=winhelp.exe ^.hlp
> ```
>
> in the [Extensions] section. Although this enables you to launch help files from File Manager, it prevents some Windows programs that have their own help systems (such as Excel) from working properly.

International

Windows was designed to be used in many countries speaking many different languages. Because different countries have different ways of expressing the same thing, Windows enables you to specify the international parameters you want.

Two types of values are in the [intl] section: strings and numbers. The keywords that start with the letter *s* have string values, and the keywords that start with *i* have numbers.

If you chose the United States as your country when you set up Windows, your [intl] section probably has only one line:

```
[intl]
sCountry=United States
```

However, if you chose a different country or a different language, you probably have many lines. For instance, people from Denmark would have the following for their [intl] section:

```
[intl]
sCountry=Denmark
iCountry=45
iDate=1
iTime=1
iTLZero=1
iCurrency=3
iCurrDigits=2
iNegCurr=5
iLzero=1
iDigits=2
```

```
iMeasure=0
s1159=
s2359=
sCurrency=kr
sThousand=.
sDecimal=,
sDate=-
sTime=.
sList=;
sShortDate=dd-MM-yy
sLongDate=dd. MMMM yyyy
```

27

All values in this section are set from the International section of Control Panel.

iCountry

This is the country's numeric code. A 1 means the United States and 2 means Canada. The rest of the countries' codes are the same as their international telephone codes. You can find these codes at the front of your telephone directory.

For example, to set the country code for Australia, use

```
iCountry=61
```

iCurrDigits

This number is the number of digits to put after the decimal separator in the country's currency.

For example, Italians do not use fractional lire. Thus, the line would be

```
iCurrDigits=0
```

iCurrency

You can specify one of four formats describing where to put the currency symbol relative to the currency amount in positive values. Note that the currency symbol is set with sCurrency. The values are described in Table 27.3.

Table 27.3. Values for iCurrency.

Value	Meaning	Example
0	Symbol precedes number with no space	$35
1	Number precedes symbol with no space	35$
2	Symbol precedes number with space	$ 35
3	Number precedes symbol with space	35 $

For example, to specify that you want the currency amount to go before the currency symbol without a space in positive numbers, use

```
iCurrency=1
```

iDate

Short dates are those that use all numbers. There are three popular orders for showing short dates. Table 27.4 shows the values for iDate to describe the order. The separator used in the date is set with sShortDate.

Table 27.4. Values for iDate.

Value	Meaning	Example
0	Month Day Year	08/18/92
1	Day Month Year	18/08/92
2	Year Month Day	92/08/18

For example, to specify year/month/day ordering for short dates, use the line

```
iDate=2
```

Warning: This value is not used by Windows version 3 and is supplied only so that Windows version 2 programs can form a date correctly. To set the order for short dates, use the sShortDate line described later in this section.

iDigits

This number is the number of digits to put after the decimal separator in regular numbers (not currency).

For example, to show three digits, the line would be

```
iDigits=3
```

iLZero

The custom in some countries is to use leading zeros before a decimal point; other countries do not use leading zeros. Setting iLZero to 0 gives you no leading zeros; setting iLZero to 1 gives you leading zeros. Note that the character used for decimal numbers is set with sDecimal.

For example, to indicate that you want the number .369 indicated as 0.369, use the line

```
iLZero=1
```

27

iMeasure

You can specify that Windows uses metric measurements (0) or English measurements (1) in this line. Very few programs use this information.

For example, to specify that you are using metric measurements, use the line

```
iMeasure=0
```

iNegCurr

You can specify one of eight formats describing where to put the currency symbol relative to the currency amount in negative values. Note that the currency symbol is set with sCurrency. The eight formats are described in Table 27.5.

Table 27.5. Values for iNegCurr.

Value	Meaning	Example
0	Symbol precedes number in parentheses	($35)
1	Minus sign precedes symbol precedes number	−$35

continues

Table 27.5. Continued

Value	Meaning	Example
2	Symbol precedes minus sign precedes number	$-35
3	Symbol precedes number precedes minus sign	$35-
4	Number precedes symbol in parentheses	(35$)
5	Minus sign precedes number precedes symbol	-35$
6	Number precedes minus sign precedes symbol	35-$
7	Number precedes symbol precedes minus sign	35$-

For example, to specify that you want the currency amount to go before the currency symbol without a space in positive numbers, use

```
iNegCurr=
```

iTime

This specifies whether you are using a 12-hour clock (0) or a 24-hour clock (1). Note that this sets only the number format; sTime sets the separator.

For example, to have 2:30 PM displayed as 14:30, use the line

```
iTime=1
```

iTLZero

This specifies whether you want a leading zero on times whose hour number is less than 10. A value of 0 indicates not to use a leading zero; a value of 1 indicates using a leading zero.

For example, to display 2:30 as 02:30, use the line

```
iTLZero=1
```

s1159

This string is used to indicate times before noon. The default is AM, but you can set it to other values such as am or one appropriate for the country.

For example, to show prenoon times with am, use the line

```
s1159=am
```

If you want to not have any string after the time, such as if you are using 24-hour time, include the keyword without a value

```
s1159=
```

s2359

This string is used to indicate times before midnight. The default is PM, but you can set it to other values such as pm or one appropriate for the country.

For example, to show pre-noon times with pm, use the line

```
s2359=pm
```

If you want to not have any string after the time, such as if you are using 24-hour time, include the keyword without a value

```
s2359=
```

sCountry

This is the name of the country for which you have Windows set, such as United States or Canada.

sCurrency

You can set the symbol used for currency. This might be a character such as $ or letters such as mk. If you are using the symbol for the British pound, £, you type it into the WIN.INI file by holding down the Alt key and pressing the numbers 1, 5, and 6 on the numeric keypad. To generate the symbol for the Japanese yen, ¥, hold down the Alt key and press the numbers 1, 5, and 7 on the numeric keypad.

For example, to set the currency string for Germany, use the line

```
sCurrency=DM
```

sDecimal

This is the punctuation mark used to separate the decimal part of a number. It is almost always a period or comma.

For example, to set the decimal mark to a comma, use the line

```
sDecimal=,
```

sLanguage

This is the name of the language you are using with Windows. Table 27.6 lists the values for the different languages. Note that Microsoft might add languages to this list in the future.

Table 27.6. sLanguage values.

Language	Value
Danish	dan
Dutch	dut
English (American)	usa
English (International)	eng
Finnish	fin
French	frn
French Canadian	fcf
German	ger
Icelandic	ice
Italian	itn
Norwegian	nor
Portuguese	por
Spanish	spa
Swedish	swe

sList

This is the punctuation mark used to separate items in a list, which is almost always either a comma or a semicolon.

For example, to set the list separator to a semicolon, use the line

```
sList=;
```

sLongDate and sShortDate

You specify the format in which dates should be shown using *date pictures*. These are combinations of symbols that represent the various ways of showing the month, day, and year in words and numbers. You also include punctuation marks such as commas and slashes in the date picture. Table 27.7 shows the values you can use in a date picture.

27

Table 27.7. Date picture formats.

Format	Example	Picture
Month, digit, no leading zero	3	M
Month, digit, leading zero	03	MM
Month, word, abbreviation	Mar	MMM
Month, word, full	March	MMMM
Day, digit, no leading zero	9	d
Day, digit, leading zero	09	dd
Day, name, abbreviation	Mon	ddd
Day, name, full	Monday	dddd
Year, two-digit	92	yy
Year, four-digit	1992	yyyy

For example, the default long date format is dddd, MMMM d, yyyy. This would display a date such as Monday, March 9, 1992 on the screen. The default short date format is M/d/yy, which would display 3/9/92 on the screen.

The International section of Control Panel can generate only certain combinations of pictures. If you want a picture that you cannot generate with Control Panel, you must modify WIN.INI yourself. For example, you might have the line

```
sShortDate=ddd:dd/MM/YY
```

sThousand

This sets the punctuation mark used to separate thousands in numbers with more than three digits. This is almost always a comma or a period.

For example, to set the thousands separator to a period as is used in many European countries, use the line

```
sThousand=.
```

sTime

This sets the punctuation mark used to separate the parts of a time specification. This is almost always a colon or a period.

For example, to set the time separator to a period as is used in many European countries, use the line

```
sTime=.
```

Ports

This section lists the hardware ports available for printing and specifies their default settings. The Printer section of the Control Panel command uses this list to determine the ports available for attaching a printer.

A typical [ports] section looks like this:

```
[ports]
; A line with [filename].PRN followed by an equal sign causes
; [filename] to appear in the Control Panel's Printer Configuration dialog
; box. A printer connected to [filename] directs its output into this file.
LPT1:=
LPT2:=
LPT3:=
COM1:=9600,n,8,1
COM2:=9600,n,8,1
COM3:=9600,n,8,1
COM4:=9600,n,8,1
EPT:=
FILE:=
LPT1.OS2=
LPT2.OS2=
```

For COM: ports, the values are baud rate, data parity, number of data bits, and number of stop bits. The LPT:, EPT:, and LPT.OS2 ports do not take values. The EPT: port is for particular IBM hardware ports configured as EPT:. You should use the LPTx.OS2 ports only if you are running Windows under OS/2 in the MS-DOS compatibility box and you are printing to the parallel port.

As the comment suggests, you can add a filename to the list. If you attach a printer to a filename, all output for that device is sent to the file. Thus, you might add a line at the end of the list:

```
c:\temp\myoutput.out=
```

27

> **Warning:** If you add a filename to the [ports] section, be sure to add it to the end of the list, not the beginning of the list. Control Panel assigns printers to ports on the relative position of the port in the list. If you add a line at the beginning, all other printers will become assigned to the wrong ports.

The FILE: port causes Windows to prompt you for the name of the output file each time you print. Figure 27.2 shows the dialog box you see when you print when this is the active port.

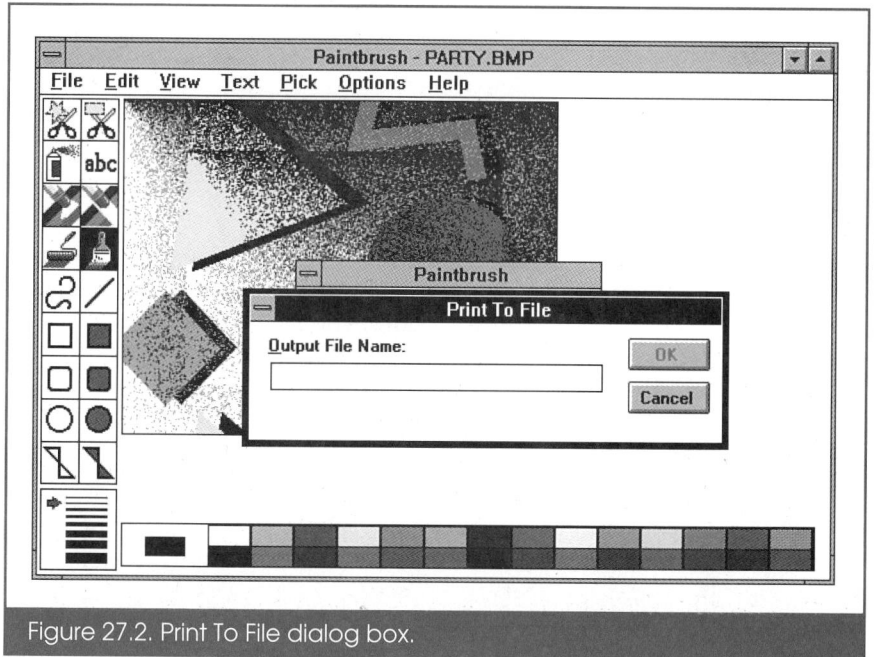

Figure 27.2. Print To File dialog box.

FontSubstitutes

FontSubstitutes tells windows that you want to use an unnamed or substitute font in place of one selected on the screen. For example, you might have installed the Windows 3.1 vector and stroke fonts included with Windows. After working with the fonts, you might find that you want to use the new MS Sans Serif font whenever you load a Windows 3.1 file that calls for Helv. You might also prefer to use the TrueType font over the standard Courier font. This feature is particularly useful if you are phasing out older Windows 2 and 3.0 rastor fonts in favor of stroke fonts, like TrueType and ATM. You can set your [FontSubstitutes] section to look like this:

```
[FontSubstitutes]
Helv=MS Sans Serif
Tms Rmn=MS Serif
Courier=Courier New
Times=Times New Roman
Helvetica=Arial
```

TrueType

This setting is used to document enabling TrueType:

```
TTEnable=1
```

Where 1 is on and 0 is off.

Fonts

The [fonts] section lists all the installed display fonts. Note that some of the installed fonts are TrueType fonts, new to Windows with Version 3.1. The keywords are the names of fonts, and the values are the names of the files that contain those fonts. These are maintained by the Fonts section of Control Panel.

A typical [fonts] section looks like this:

```
[fonts]
MS Sans Serif 8,10,12,14,18,24 (VGA res)=SSERIFE.FON
MS Serif 8,10,12,14,18,24 (VGA res)=SERIFE.FON
Symbol 8,10,12,14,18,24 (VGA res)=SYMBOLE.FON
Small (VGA res)=SMALLE.FON
Roman (Plotter)=ROMAN.FON
Modern (Plotter)=MODERN.FON
Courier 10,12,15 (VGA res)=COURE.FON
Script (Plotter)=SCRIPT.FON
Arial (TrueType)=ARIAL.FOT
Arial Bold (TrueType)=ARIALBD.FOT
Arial Bold Italic (TrueType)=ARIALBI.FOT
Arial Italic (TrueType)=ARIALI.FOT
Courier New (TrueType)=COUR.FOT
Courier New Bold (TrueType)=COURBD.FOT
Courier New Bold Italic (TrueType)=COURBI.FOT
Courier New Italic (TrueType)=COURI.FOT
Times New Roman (TrueType)=TIMES.FOT
Times New Roman Bold (TrueType)=TIMESBD.FOT
Times New Roman Bold Italic (TrueType)=TIMESBI.FOT
Times New Roman Italic (TrueType)=TIMESI.FOT
Symbol (TrueType)=SYMBOL.FOT
```

PrinterPorts

The [PrinterPorts] section lists all the printers you have installed in
Windows. You install printers in the Printers section of Control Panel.
A typical [PrinterPorts] section looks like this:

```
[PrinterPorts]
HP LaserJet III=HPPCL5A,LPT1:,15,45
PostScript Printer=PSCRIPT,COM2:,15,45
```

The format of these lines is

printername=drivername,port,notselectedtimeout,retrytimeout

The *printername* is the name of the printer that came from the installation. The *drivername* is the name of the driver file for this printer. The
port is the hardware port the printer is attached to. The two timeout
parameters tell Windows how many seconds to wait for a response from
a printer and how many seconds to keep trying to retransmit information to the printer if a transmission was initially unsuccessful.

Devices

This section is an artifact from Windows version 2 and is used only by programs written in Version 2. The device listed here is the active printer.

```
[devices]
PostScript Printer=PSCRIPT,COM2:
```

Keywords

Table 27.8 lists all the keywords normally found in the WIN.INI file in alphabetical order. Use this table to find the heading under which a keyword is found.

Table 27.8. Keywords in WIN.INI.

Keyword	Heading
ActiveBorder	[colors]
ActiveTitle	[colors]
AppWorkspace	[colors]
Background	[colors]
Beep	[windows]
BorderWidth	[windows]
ButtonFace	[colors]
ButtonShadow	[colors]
ButtonText	[colors]
COM1:-COM4:	[ports]
CursorBlinkRate	[windows]
Device	[windows]
DeviceNotSelectedTimeout	[windows]
Documents	[windows]
DoubleClickSpeed	[windows]
EPT:	[ports]
FILE:	[ports]

27

Keyword	Heading
GrayText	[colors]
GridGranularity	[Desktop]
Hilight	[colors]
HilightText	[colors]
IconSpacing	[Desktop]
iCountry	[intl]
iCurrDigits	[intl]
iCurrency	[intl]
iDate	[intl]
iDigits	[intl]
iLZero	[intl]
iMeasure	[intl]
InactiveBorder	[colors]
InactiveTitle	[colors]
iNegCurr	[intl]
iTime	[intl]
iTLZero	[intl]
KeyboardSpeed	[windows]
Load	[windows]
LPT1.OS2 and LPT2.OS2	[ports]
LPT1:-LPT3:	[ports]
Maximized	[Windows Help]
Menu	[colors]
MenuText	[colors]
MouseSpeed	[windows]
MouseThreshold1	[windows]
MouseThreshold2	[windows]
NetWarn	[windows]
NullPort	[windows]

continues

Table 27.8. Continued

Keyword	Heading
Pattern	[Desktop]
Programs	[windows]
Run	[windows]
s1159	[intl]
s2359	[intl]
Scrollbar	[colors]
sLanguage	[intl]
sList	[intl]
sLongDate and sShortDate	[intl]
Spooler	[windows]
sThousand	[intl]
sTime	[intl]
Swapdisk	[windows]
TileWallpaper	[Desktop]
TitleText	[colors]
TransmissionRetryTimeout	[windows]
Wallpaper	[Desktop]
WallpaperOriginX	[Desktop]
WallpaperOriginY	[Desktop]
Window	[colors]
WindowFrame	[colors]
WindowText	[colors]
Xl	[Windows Help]
Xr	[Windows Help]
Yd	[Windows Help]
Yu	[Windows Help]

Colors

When you use the [colors] section of Control Panel, you set the colors for the various items on the Windows screen. The [colors] section records those choices. Some settings you can make only by editing the WIN.INI file.

Each line in the [colors] section has the format

```
area=redvalue greenvalue bluevalue
```

27

The part of the screen that the colors apply to is called the area. The three color values are numbers between 0 and 255 that indicate the intensity of that color in the mix. For example

```
AppWorkspace=0 128 64
```

The color for the application workspace has 0% red intensity, 50% (128/255) green intensity, and 25% (64/255) blue intensity.

A typical [colors] section looks like this:

```
[colors]
Background=0 128 128
AppWorkspace=0 128 64
Window=255 255 255
WindowText=0 0 0
Menu=255 255 255
MenuText=0 0 0
ActiveTitle=0 64 128
InactiveTitle=193 193 193
TitleText=255 255 255
ActiveBorder=128 128 128
InactiveBorder=255 255 255
WindowFrame=0 0 0
Scrollbar=129 129 129
```

Table 27.9 lists the keynames and the items on the screen they refer to. Note that many of the items cannot be set in the [colors] section of Control Panel; you must add them in the WIN.INI yourself.

Table 27.9. Screen areas that can be colored.

Keyname	Screen Area	Set in Control Panel
ActiveBorder	Active windows border	Yes
ActiveTitle	Active windows title bar	Yes

continues

Table 27.9. Continued

Keyname	Screen Area	Set in Control Panel
AppWorkspace	Background for program	Yes
Background	Background for Windows	Yes
ButtonFace	Top of button	No
ButtonShadow	Shadow on button	No
ButtonText	Text on button	No
GrayText	Text that is dimmed	No
Hilight	Background for highlighted text	No
HilightText	Highlighted text	No
InactiveBorder	Inactive windows border	Yes
InactiveTitle	Inactive windows title bar	Yes
Menu	Menu bar background	Yes
MenuText	Menu text	Yes
Scrollbar	Scroll bar	Yes
TitleText	Title bar text	Yes
Window	Windows background	Yes
WindowFrame	Windows frame	Yes
WindowText	Windows text	Yes

Other Application Sections

Many applications write their own sections into the WIN.INI file. They use the information there to save and retrieve settings similar to the way Windows uses the file. For instance, Word for Windows lists converters you have selected, the Solitaire game keeps track of the last settings you use, the Clock program stores its format, and so on.

For example, after running the Solitaire and Clock programs, you might see the following lines at the end of your WIN.INI file:

```
[Clock]
iFormat=0
```

```
[Solitaire]
Options=9
Back=5
```

Advanced Configuration with the SYSTEM.INI File

The SYSTEM.INI file is similar to the WIN.INI file in that it consists of lines in groups. The entries in SYSTEM.INI are usually more related to your hardware than those in WIN.INI. Most of the entries are of interest only when your hardware and Windows do not interact correctly. A few entries are important, but the vast majority are rarely used and are included only if you have a particular hardware problem. Table 27.10 shows the headings in the SYSTEM.INI file.

Table 27.10. Headings in SYSTEM.INI file.

Heading	Use
[boot]	Hardware drivers and Windows dynamic link libraries
[keyboard]	Description of the keyboard
[boot.description]	Text used by Setup
[386Enh]	Settings for 386-enhanced mode
[standard]	Settings or standard mode
[NonWindowsApp]	Settings for running non-Windows programs
[mci]	List of drivers that use the multimedia command reference
[drivers]	List of alias names for device drivers

This section is arranged in the order in which the headings appear in the file, except that the [386Enh] section is described last because it is by far the longest. Within each heading, the keywords appear with the most important ones first. Most of the keywords are grouped because they refer to similar ideas.

Boot

The [boot] section lists the drivers and dynamic link libraries Windows uses when it starts. All the lines in this section are required. This section is filled in by Setup when you install Windows or change drivers. A typical [boot] section looks like this:

```
[boot]
386grabber=vga.gr3
286grabber=vgacolor.gr2
shell=progman.exe
network.drv=
language.dll=
fixedfon.fon=vgafix.fon
comm.drv=comm.drv
sound.drv=sound.drv
oemfonts.fon=vgaoem.fon
fonts.fon=vgasys.fon
mouse.drv=mouse.drv
keyboard.drv=keyboard.drv
display.drv=vga.drv
system.drv=system.drv
```

Each value in this section is the name of a file in the \system directory under the main Windows directory. It is very unlikely you will change any of the lines in this section (other than the shell= line) yourself. Because the drivers are often associated with a particular set of hardware features, it is much more likely you will use whatever Setup assigns.

Shell

You can tell Windows which program you want to be the "base" program with this line. This program must be a Windows program. When you quit from this program, you quit from Windows. Thus, it is common to name a program from which you can run other programs. The most common choice other than Program Manager (PROGMAN.EXE) is File Manager (WINFILE.EXE) as shown in the next example:

```
shell=winfile.exe
```

If you use a commercial or shareware replacement for Program Manager or File Manager, you might want to enter the name of that program here.

Warning: Be sure to enter the name exactly. If you give a name that does not exist, or the name of a non-Windows program, Windows will probably crash.

Other Boot Lines

Table 27.11 lists the other lines in the [boot] section. Again, it is unlikely you will change the names by editing SYSTEM.INI; instead, you will update them using Setup.

Table 27.11. Lines in the [boot] section.

Keyword	Meaning
286grabber	Device driver for screens of non-Windows programs running in standard mode
386grabber	Device driver for screens of non-Windows programs running in 386 enhanced mode
comm.drv	Serial port device driver
display.drv	Display device driver
fixedfon.fon	Name of fixed-width font file; this is used only by Windows version 2 programs
fonts.fon	Name of system font file
keyboard.drv	Keyboard device driver
language.dll	Dynamic link library that holds the language-specific code
mouse.drv	Mouse device driver
network.drv	Network device driver
oemfonts.fon	Additional font file for display
shell	Program to start Windows with (see previous section)
sound.drv	Sound device driver
system.drv	PC hardware device driver

Keyboard

The [keyboard] section has settings specific to the keyboard other than the name of the keyboard driver (which is given in the [boot] section). This section is useful if you have a nonstandard keyboard and you are having problems with Windows. A typical [keyboard] section looks like this:

```
[keyboard]
subtype=
type=4
oemansi.bin=
keyboard.dll=
```

The keyboard.dll= is the dynamic link library that contains the routines for non-U.S. keyboards. This is required for all keyboards other than standard U.S. keyboards so that Windows knows how to interpret key combinations. If the keyboard does not use the ANSI standard character set, you must specify the translation table in the oemansi.bin= line.

The type and subtype enable you to specify exactly how a keyboard differs from the expected driver. Almost every keyboard is of type 4, which has no subtype. Table 27.12 shows the types and subtypes.

Table 27.12. Keyboard types and subtypes.

Type	Description	Subtypes
1	IBM PC or XT (83 keys)	2: Olivetti M24 and AT&T 6300 type 301 keyboard 4: AT&T 6300 type 302
2	Olivetti ICO (102 keys)	1: Olivetti ICO used on M24 systems
3	IBM AT compatibles (84 or 86 keys)	
4	IBM enhanced (101 or 102 keys)	

Boot Description

This section is a list of names associated with the devices listed in the [boot] section. They are used by Setup (run from both Windows and MS-DOS) for displaying the names of the current setup.

The `[boot.description]` section for the previous `[boot]` section would look like this:

```
[boot.description]
keyboard.typ=Enhanced 101 or 102 key US and Non US keyboards
mouse.drv=Microsoft, or IBM PS/2
network.drv=No Network Installed
language.dll=English (American)
system.drv=MS-DOS or PC-DOS System
display.drv=VGA
```

27

These next settings do not directly affect Windows's operation. They are just strings of text. You can in effect add your own comments after = to make your day more interesting, or, if you were using a public machine, you could use this next example to display a warning to refrain from changing a setting. Try this if you have jokers working on your machine:

```
[boot.description]
keyboard.typ=Do not change any settings
mouse.drv=on this machine. It is owned
network.drv=by the Purchasing department.
language.dll=This message self destructs
system.drv=if tampered-with.
display.drv=            Signed, SYSOP
```

Standard

Windows's standard mode is fairly stable and requires little tuning. The four settings in this section are needed only in rare circumstances. A typical `[standard]` section looks like this:

```
[standard]
Int28Filter=10
NetHeapSize=8
PadCodeSegments=0
ReservedLowMemory=0
```

The `Int28Filter` specifies how many Int28 (hex) interrupts get passed outside of Windows when Windows is idle. This number is actually the inverse of the number passed. Thus, a value of 10 (the default) means that only 1 out of 10 is passed to other software that was running before Windows was loaded. Microsoft determined that this value is about the correct balance between sending too many Int28 interrupts (thus slowing down the PC) and sending too few (possibly causing some network and communications software to fail). You should change this only on the advice of a company whose hardware or software relies on Int28 interrupts.

If you are using a network, you can change the size of the pool of conventional memory used to buffer the network. The default for NetHeapSize is 8 kilobytes, but you can allocate more if it is necessary (at the expense of conventional memory available to other programs). Note that if you are not running a network, Windows does not use any of this memory, so there is not an advantage in changing this to 0.

Some very old 80286 chips (specifically, those of the B2 stepping) work better if code segments are padded with 16 bytes of null instructions. If your CPU is an 80286 in that stepping, you should set this value to 1. This slows down your system, so set this value to 1 only if your system hangs in standard mode.

The ReservedLowMemory line reserves conventional memory for programs other than Windows. It is included in SYSTEM.INI in case other programs might need it, but there are no known reasons to use it.

NonWindowsApp

This section describes how Windows handles non-Windows programs in standard mode. There are only three options. A typical [NonWindowsApp] section looks like this:

```
[NonWindowsApp]
SwapDisk=D:
NetAsynchSwitching=0
ScreenLines=27
```

SwapDisk

The SwapDisk line tells Windows where to put temporary swap files as you switch into and out of non-Windows programs. If you have more than one hard disk, you should specify the fastest disk, as long as it has more than 512K free on it. You can include a directory on that disk if you want, such as

```
SwapDisk=D:\SWAP
```

If you don't have this line in your SYSTEM.INI file, Windows looks for a TEMP or TMP environment variable and uses the disk and directory listed there. If you don't have these environment variables, Windows puts the swap files in the main Windows directory.

> **Tip:** If you enter an invalid disk or directory for the SwapDisk value, when you switch from a non-Windows program you see the error message
>
> ```
> Cannot return to Windows. Start Windows again.
> ```
>
> **Edit SYSTEM.INI** to change the value for SwapDisk and start Windows again.

NetAsynchSwitching

If you are on a network and a non-Windows program makes an asynchronous call to the NetBIOS on your PC, Windows normally does not enable you to switch out from the program. This is for safety because you have no idea when the response from the network will come or whether the response is complete. If you set the value in this line to 1, Windows enables you to switch away from your non-Windows program, but you must be very sure the program is not meant to receive any input from the network. If it does, the input will be lost and the program might crash.

ScreenLines

You can specify the number of lines for a text screen that non-Windows programs will see when they start with the ScreenLines line. For example, if you want all your non-Windows programs to think you have a 40-line monitor, you should include the line

```
ScreenLines=40
```

386Enh

The lines in the [386Enh] section control how Windows operates in 386-enhanced mode. The vast majority of these settings are of little interest to most PC users. They are only for specialized situations in which Windows needs assistance in determining your PC's setup so that it doesn't conflict with software and hardware.

A typical [386Enh] section looks like this:

```
[386Enh]
ebios=
display=*vddvga
EGA80WOA.FON=EGA80WOA.FON
EGA40WOA.FON=EGA40WOA.FON
CGA80WOA.FON=CGA80WOA.FON
CGA40WOA.FON=CGA40WOA.FON
device=*int13
device=*wdctrl
mouse=*vmd
network=*vnetbios,*dosnet
keyboard=*vkd
device=*vpicd
device=*vtd
device=*reboot
device=*vdmad
device=*vsd
device=*v86mmgr
device=*pageswap
device=*dosmgr
device=*vmpoll
device=*wshell
device=*BLOCKDEV
device=*PAGEFILE
device=*vfd
device=*parity
device=*biosxlat
device=*vcd
device=*vmcpd
device=*combuff
device=*cdpscsi
local=CON
FileSysChange=off
PermSwapDOSDrive=C
PermSwapSizeK=4709
```

Local

This line is a list of the devices that must be local to each virtual machine. A virtual machine is created for Windows itself as well as each DOS application you run under Windows. The default filled in by

Setup, CON, is the console device. The device name must be exact and match in case.

When you start a virtual machine, Windows copies each device listed here into the machine. That device then keeps a separate copy of its state for each machine. It is unlikely you will change this line because few other devices work properly in each virtual machine.

FileSysChange

This setting tells Windows whether File Manager will receive messages every time any other program creates, deletes, renames, or updates a file. Setting this to on causes File Manager to always have the most current data but causes Windows to run much more slowly.

Fonts

The four lines that have font-like names describe where non-Windows programs that display text in the EGA or CGA graphics modes can find them. The numbers in the name describe whether the fonts are for 40- or 80-character-wide screens.

Devices

As you can see from the example listing of the [386Enh] section (on the preceding page), the majority of lines have the device keyword or device-like keywords. In most cases, the values for these lines start with an asterisk, showing that the indicated driver is in the file WIN386.EXE in the \system directory under Windows's main directory. If you want to load a particular device driver, put that file's name in the line. For example, a replacement mouse driver might be indicated this way:

```
mouse=MDRV.DRV
```

In many cases, you have to add a device driver to your system. For instance, to run the MS-DOS CD-ROM extensions, you must include the LANMAN10.386 device driver (even if you are not running on a LAN). Include the line

```
device=LANMAN10.386
```

You also, of course, need to put that file in the \system directory under Windows's main directory. In this case, you can expand the file from the Windows distribution diskette.

Tip: After editing these lines in SYSTEM.INI, you get an error message when you start Windows in 386-enhanced mode, such as

```
Attempt to load duplicate device file that may be needed
to run in 386 enhanced mode. Run Setup again.
```

This indicates that you have duplicated a device statement. Remove one of the lines with a text editor and start again.

Useful Lines for (386Enh)

Some of the optional lines you can add to the [386Enh] section are used often and can help prevent Windows in 386-enhanced mode from crashing or acting erratically. This section describes those lines that have been found useful to many people. The section after this describes little-used lines. The lines in this section are

- ▲ EMMExclude
- ▲ VirtualHDIrq
- ▲ PagingDrive
- ▲ Paging
- ▲ MaxPagingFileSize
- ▲ MinUserDiskSpace
- ▲ IRQ9Global
- ▲ PerVMFiles
- ▲ VCPIWarning

EMMExclude

If you have device drivers or other programs loaded into the upper memory area (the memory between 640K and 1 megabyte), Windows often detects it and avoids using those areas. However, Windows is not always correct when it checks, and sometimes its checking can cause some devices to fail.

To prevent Windows from even looking in a particular location in memory, use the EMMExclude line with the range in hexadecimal. For example, if you have a device driver loaded at CC00 through CFFF, use the line

```
EMMExclude=CC00-CFFF
```

The EMMExclude line is one of the most common additions to the [386Enh] section, especially if you use memory managers that load device drivers into the upper memory area. These drivers, such as EMM386 with the NOEMS option and QuarterDeck's QEMM386, can move many programs to the upper memory area. If Windows does not see those programs, it might put other data over them and thus cause the driver (and possibly Windows) to crash.

VirtualHDIrq

Another common addition to the [386Enh] section is the VirtualHDIrq line. The line

```
VirtualHDIrq=off
```

takes care of most hard disk problems with Windows in 386-enhanced mode. If you see error messages such as

```
Cannot Read from Drive D:
```

or

```
Drive C: Not Ready Error
```

it is probably due to Windows bypassing MS-DOS in a way that causes the hard drive to work incorrectly. Setting the VirtualHDIrq to off causes Windows always to go through MS-DOS. This might slow down Windows a little bit (often by less than 5 percent), but it is always safer. For many hard disk drives and controllers, it is absolutely essential.

> **Tip:** Some non-Windows programs run slower under Windows unless you set VirtualHDIrq to off because of the way they access the hard disk. If you find that running a non-Windows program under 386-enhanced mode is noticeably slower than under standard mode, try setting VirtualHDIrq to off.

PagingDrive

This tells Windows the drive where Windows puts the 386-enhanced mode temporary swap files. You should set this to the fastest hard drive on your system, such as

```
PagingDrive=E:
```

Note that this drive must not be read-only. If you are running on a network, you should avoid setting this to a network drive because Windows becomes so slow, it is virtually unusable.

Warning: Because Windows writes the swap file to the root directory of the named drive, you must be sure that the root directory is not read-only. This is sometimes the case on particular networks.

Paging

If you want to prevent Windows from using a temporary swap file, you can set the value for this line to off. For example

```
Paging=off
```

Tip: A better way to prevent Windows from making a temporary swap file is to create a tiny permanent swap file. See Chapter 24, "Memory Configuration for Windows," for more information on temporary and permanent swap files.

MaxPagingFileSize and MinUserDiskSpace

You can control how much disk space (in kilobytes) Windows uses for temporary swap files. MaxPagingFileSize tells how much space can be used no matter how much space is left; MinUserDiskSpace tells how much space must be left.

For example, to prevent Windows from using more than about five megabytes for temporary swap files, use the line

```
MaxPagingFileSize=5000
```

To prevent Windows from leaving less than about two megabytes on the hard disk, use

```
MinUserDiskSpace=2000
```

IRQ9Global

If your PC hangs when Windows accesses a floppy disk for the first time, you should set the value for this line to `true`, such as

```
IRQ9Global=true
```

You can also prevent your system from hanging by reading from a floppy disk before running Windows, but this method does not always work.

PerVMFiles

When you run non-Windows programs that open many files, you might see a message from Windows that says

```
Insufficient file handles available.
Increase files= statement in config.sys to 30 or more
```

This message is incorrect because increasing the number of files in CONFIG.SYS won't affect this problem. Instead, you need to add a line in the [386Enh] of SYSTEM.INI, such as

```
PerVMFiles=100
```

The value can be up to 275. This setting gives each virtual machine (each non-Windows program) a specific number of private file handles.

VCPIWarning

Some non-Windows programs use a form of memory handling called *VCPI* or Virtual Control Program Interface. These programs are described in Chapter 20, "Other DOS Programs and Windows." You should not run VCPI programs in 386-enhanced mode. However, Windows doesn't prevent you from doing so after it has given you the warning. If you want to have Windows skip the warning about running VCPI programs, you can modify your SYSTEM.INI file and add the following line in the [386Enh] section:

```
VCPIWarning=false
```

27

Lines in (386Enh) Used by Networks

Chapter 28, "Networking and Communications," describes how to use Windows with networks. If you are running in 386-enhanced mode with a network, you might need to modify your SYSTEM.INI to make the network work well with your PC. The following lines are the ones you are most likely to add or modify.

TimerCriticalSection

Some networks require that only one program on an 80386 receive timer interrupts. If your network requires this, use the `TimerCriticalSection` line with a value of the number of milliseconds for a timeout. This forces Windows to go into a critical section around any timer interrupt and to wait for the specified time. For example, your network might require a line like

```
TimerCriticalSection=5000
```

NetAsynchFallback

If an asynchronous NetBIOS request fails, Windows generally drops the request, leaving the network program in an unpredictable state. Setting this value to `true` causes Windows to save the request in local memory and prevent other programs from continuing until the data is received.

```
NetAsynchFallback=true
```

NetAsynchTimeout

If you have `NetAsynchFallback` set to `true`, you can specify a timeout period (in seconds) for Windows to service the NetBIOS call. This can be specified as a decimal, such as

```
NetAsynchTimeout=2.5
```

NetDMASize

This setting tells Windows the minimum DMA buffer size for NetBIOS transport software, in kilobytes. Windows uses the larger of this setting and the `DMABufferSize` setting. The default is `0` for all systems other than MicroChannel systems, on which it is `32`. You might want to set the size higher than the default with a line like this:

```
NetDMASize=64
```

NetHeapSize

Windows normally allocates 12 kilobytes of conventional memory for the network data buffers. Use this line to increase or decrease this amount. Windows rounds this value up to the closest 4 kilobyte value. For example, to allocate 24 kilobytes, use

```
NetHeapSize=24
```

UniqueDOSPSP and PSPIncrement

Some networks identify programs and processes that are running by their starting address. This causes problems if your virtual machines start programs at the same virtual address in different virtual machines. To prevent this, set `UniqueDOSPSP` to `true`, and set the `PSPIncrement` to a small number that will be used as a space waster when new processes start. The `PSPIncrement` is the number of 16-byte blocks to waste. If your network requires these lines, you might use

```
UniqueDOSPSP=true
PSPIncrement=2
```

Other Lines for (386Enh)

Table 27.13 lists the other lines that can be included in the `[386Enh]`. The options in this table are described briefly in case any of them relate to your system. Unless specific hardware or software recommends that you use these options, they are probably unnecessary. The table is presented here to give a brief explanation of the other options available in case you are told to add lines to your `[386Enh]` section and you want some idea of what the line does.

Table 27.13. Options for the [386Enh] section.

NOTE: All numeric variables are displayed as *x*.
All true and false variables are displayed as T or F.

Keyword	Values	Description
AllVMsExclusive	(T/F)	Forces all non-Windows programs to run in full-screen mode if value is true.
AltKeyDelay	seconds	Tells how long to wait to process the Alt key.
AltPasteDelay	seconds	Tells how long to wait to paste characters after the key combination is pressed.
CGANoSnow	(T/F)	Causes Windows to avoid "snow" from appearing on CGA graphics monitors if value is set to true.
COMxAutoAssign	seconds	Is used when two programs are both trying to use the same COM port. Value of –1 means that Windows will prompt you to ask which program can use the port; 0 means that any program can use the port at any time; 1 to 1000 means that that number of seconds must pass before another program can use the port.
COMxBase	hex address	Gives address of the serial port. 3F8, 2F8, 2E8, or 2E0.
COMBoostTime	milliseconds	Specifies amount of time a program gets to process a character. Raise this value if the program is losing characters.

Keyword	Values	Description
COMxBuffer	size in bytes	Specifies size of the communications buffer.
COMxIrq	number	Gives interrupt line for the device 4, 3, 4, 3.
COMIrqSharing	(T/F)	Allows sharing of the interrupt line for COM1:/COM3: and COM2:/COM4:; false (except for MicroChannel and EISA machines, for which it is true).
COMxProtocol	XOFF / <blank>	Sets up XOFF as a break character. Set this to XOFF only if you are not transferring binary information.
DMABufferIn1MB	(T/F)	Puts the DMA buffer in conventional memory or upper memory area.
DMABufferSize	kilobytes	Specifies memory reserved for DMA buffers.
DualDisplay	(T/F)	Reserves memory for a second display at B000-B7FF.
EISADMA	(T/F), <channel>, <size>	Gives channel size for DMA channels. Set the value to false if you are running on an EISA system but Windows crashes often. You can specify a channel number and its size. The sizes are 8 (8-bit), 16w (16-bit as words), 16b (16-bit as bytes), and 32

continues

Table 27.13. Continued

Keyword	Values	Description
		(32-bit). 0,8; 1,8; 2,8; 3,8; 5,16w; 6,16w; 7,16w.
EMMInclude	range in hex	Specifies area of upper memory area to scan for extra memory.
EMMPageFrame	hex	Gives starting frame for 64K page frame.
EMMSize	kilobytes	Sets total amount available as expanded memory. Set this lower if you are running non-Windows programs that take all the expanded memory they can get (or change the program's PIF).
Global	device name	Specifies names of devices from CONFIG.SYS that need to be global.
HighFloppyReads	(T/F)	Converts DMA verify calls to E000-EFFF into floppy reads.
IgnoreInstalledEMM	(T/F)	Tells Windows to start even if the expanded memory manager does not work with Windows.
InDOSPolling	(T/F)	Prevents Windows from running other non-Windows programs if a TSR has its InDOS flag set.
INT28Critical	(T/F)	Tells whether a critical section is needed to handle INT28 (hex) interrupts.

Keyword	Values	Description
KeyBoostTime	seconds	Specifies time that a program gets to run in high priority when it gets a keystroke.
KeyBufferDelay	seconds	Specifies time to delay pasting keyboard input after the buffer is full.
KeyIdleDelay	seconds	Specifies time that Windows ignores idle calls after simulating a keystroke to a non-Windows program.
KeyPasteDelay	seconds	Specifies time to wait before pasting characters after a key has been pasted.
KeyPasteTimeout	seconds	Specifies time to allow a program to read input before switching to slow paste.
LPTxAutoAssign	seconds	Resolves conflict when two programs are both trying to use the same LPT port. A value of –1 means that Windows will prompt you to ask which program can use the port; 0 means that any program can use the port at any time; 1 to 1000 means that that number of seconds must pass before another program can use the port.
MapPhysAddress	hex	Gives addresses to preallocate physical page table entries and linear address space.

continues

Table 27.13. Continued

Keyword	Values	Description
MinTimeSlice	milliseconds	Specifies minimum time that a non-Windows program running in the background will run before other programs take over.
MouseSoftInit	(T/F)	Specifies whether to turn hard mouse initialization calls into soft calls.
NMIReboot	(T/F)	Specifies whether to reboot when a nonmaskable interrupt (NMI) is received.
NoEMMDriver	(T/F)	Prevents Windows from installing its expanded memory driver.
ReflectDosInt2A	(T/F)	Passes INT 2A signals to other programs.
ReservePageFrame	(T/F)	Creates EMS page frame space in conventional memory if no room in upper memory area.
SGrabLPT	port number	Routes all printer interrupts from this port in a non-Windows program to the main virtual machine.
SystemROMBreakPoint	(T/F)	Specifies whether the system ROM is in F000-FFFF.
SysVMEMSLimit	kilobytes	Sets the amount of expanded memory Windows can use. *0* prevents Windows

Keyword	Values	Description
		from using any expanded memory; –1 gives it all that it requests.
SysVMEMSLocked	(T/F)	Prevents Windows expanded memory from being swapped to the hard disk.
SysVMEMSRequired	kilobytes	Sets how much expanded memory must be free before Windows will run.
SysVMV86Locked	(T/F)	Prevents conventional memory in non-Windows programs from being swapped to the hard disk.
SysVMXMSLimit	kilobytes	Specifies maximum amount the XMS driver will allocate to non-Windows programs.
SysVMXMSLocked	(T/F)	Tells whether to prevent Windows extended memory from being swapped to the hard disk.
SysVMXMSRequired	kilobytes	Specifies how much extended memory must be free before Windows will run.
TokenRingSearch	(T/F)	Searches for a token ring adapter card on an AT-compatible machine.
TranslateScans	(T/F)	Translates keyboard scan codes to make them compatible with IBM.
UseInstFile	(T/F)	Causes Windows to look in the

continues

27

Table 27.13. Continued

Keyword	Values	Description
		INSTANCE.386 file for local data structures.
WindowKBRequired	kilobytes	Specifies amount of memory that must be free for Windows to start.
WindowMemSize	kilobytes	Specifies amount of conventional memory Windows will use for itself. −1 means as much as it wants.
WindowUpdateTime	milliseconds	Sets time Windows takes between screen updates for non-Windows programs.
WinExclusive	(T/F)	Tells whether Windows programs get all the CPU's processing time.
WinTimeSlice	number, number	Sets relative priority that Windows programs get in the foreground and background.
8042ReadCmd	command	Is used only by Everex Systems.
8042WriteCmd	command	Is used only by Everex Systems.

Configuring with Other Files

Although WIN.INI and SYSTEM.INI are the primary files you use to configure Windows, there are other files you can easily edit to change Windows settings. This section describes the other files you might edit or change with Windows programs.

Control Panel: CONTROL.INI

The CONTROL.INI file holds the descriptions of the color schemes and patterns you create with Control Panel. Sample lines from the CONTROL.INI file look like this:

```
[current]
color schemes=Windows Default
```

The [current] section gives the name of the current color scheme. The [color schemes] section describes each color scheme, including the ones you create. For each scheme, hexadecimal values of the blue, green, and red for each of the elements are listed. The order of the elements are

- ▲ Background for Windows
- ▲ Background for program
- ▲ Window's background
- ▲ Window's text
- ▲ Menu bar background
- ▲ Menu text
- ▲ Active window's title bar
- ▲ Inactive window's title bar
- ▲ Title bar text
- ▲ Active window's border
- ▲ Inactive window's border
- ▲ Window's frame
- ▲ Scroll bar

```
[color schemes]
Arizona=804000,FFFFFF,FFFFFF,0,FFFFFF,0,808040,C0C0C0,
FFFFFF,4080FF,C0C0C0,0,C0C0C0,C0C0C0,808080,0,
808080,808000,FFFFFF,0,FFFFFF
Black Leather
Jacket=0,C0C0C0,FFFFFF,0,C0C0C0,0,800040,808080,FFFFFF,
808080,808080,0,10E0E0E0,C0C0C0,808080,0,808080,
0,FFFFFF,0,FFFFFF
Bordeaux=400080,C0C0C0,FFFFFF,0,FFFFFF,0,800080,C0C0C0,
FFFFFF,FF0080,C0C0C0,0,C0C0C0,C0C0C0,808080,0,
808080,800080,FFFFFF,0,FFFFFF
```

```
Cinnamon=404080,C0C0C0,FFFFFF,0,FFFFFF,0,80,C0C0C0,
FFFFFF,80,C0C0C0,0,C0C0C0,C0C0C0,808080,0,
808080,80,FFFFFF,0,FFFFFF
Designer=7C7C3F,C0C0C0,FFFFFF,0,FFFFFF,0,808000,C0C0C0,
FFFFFF,C0C0C0,C0C0C0,0,C0C0C0,C0C0C0,808080,0,
C0C0C0,808000,0,0,FFFFFF
Emerald City=404000,C0C0C0,FFFFFF,0,C0C0C0,0,408000,808040,
FFFFFF,408000,808040,0,C0C0C0,C0C0C0,808080,0,
808080,8000,FFFFFF,0,FFFFFF
Fluorescent=0,FFFFFF,FFFFFF,0,FF00,0,FF00FF,C0C0C0,0,
FF80,C0C0C0,0,C0C0C0,C0C0C0,808080,0,808080,0,
FFFFFF,0,FFFFFF
Hotdog Stand=FFFF,FFFF,FF,FFFFFF,FFFFFF,0,0,FF,FFFFFF,
FF,FF,0,C0C0C0,C0C0C0,808080,0,808080,0,FFFFFF,
FFFFFF,FFFFFF
LCD Default Screen Settings=0,C0C0C0,C0C0C0,0,C0C0C0,0,800000,
C0C0C0,FFFFFF,800000,C0C0C0,0,C0C0C0,FFFFFF
LCD Reversed Dark=0,80,80,FFFFFF,8080,0,8080,800000,0,8080,
800000,0,8080,FFFFFF
LCD Reversed Light=800000,FFFFFF,FFFFFF,0,FFFFFF,0,808040,FFFFFF,
0,C0C0C0,C0C0C0,800000,C0C0C0,FFFFFF
Mahogany=404040,C0C0C0,FFFFFF,0,FFFFFF,0,40,C0C0C0,
FFFFFF,C0C0C0,C0C0C0,0,C0C0C0,C0C0C0,808080,0,
C0C0C0,80,FFFFFF,0,FFFFFF
Monochrome=C0C0C0,FFFFFF,FFFFFF,0,FFFFFF,0,0,C0C0C0,FFFFFF,
C0C0C0,C0C0C0,0,808080,C0C0C0,808080,0,808080,
0,FFFFFF,0,FFFFFF
Ocean=808000,408000,FFFFFF,0,FFFFFF,0,804000,C0C0C0,
FFFFFF,C0C0C0,C0C0C0,0,C0C0C0,C0C0C0,808080,0,0,
808000,0,0,FFFFFF
Pastel=C0FF82,80FFFF,FFFFFF,0,FFFFFF,0,FFFF80,FFFFFF,
0,C080FF,FFFFFF,808080,C0C0C0,C0C0C0,808080,0,
C0C0C0,FFFF00,0,0,FFFFFF
Patchwork=9544BB,C1FBFA,FFFFFF,0,FFFFFF,0,FFFF80,FFFFFF,
0,64B14E,FFFFFF,0,C0C0C0,C0C0C0,808080,0,808080,
FFFF00,0,0,FFFFFF
Plasma Power Saver=0,FF0000,0,FFFFFF,FF00FF,0,800000,C0C0C0,0,80,
FFFFFF,C0C0C0,FF0000,C0C0C0,808080,0,C0C0C0,
FFFFFF,0,0,FFFFFF
Rugby=C0C0C0,80FFFF,FFFFFF,0,FFFFFF,0,800000,FFFFFF,
FFFFFF,80,FFFFFF,0,C0C0C0,C0C0C0,808080,0,
808080,800000,FFFFFF,0,FFFFFF
```

```
The Blues=804000,C0C0C0,FFFFFF,0,FFFFFF,0,800000,
C0C0C0,FFFFFF,C0C0C0,C0C0C0,0,C0C0C0,C0C0C0,
808080,0,C0C0C0,800000,FFFFFF,0,FFFFFF
Tweed=6A619E,C0C0C0,FFFFFF,0,FFFFFF,0,408080,C0C0C0,
FFFFFF,404080,C0C0C0,0,10E0E0E0,C0C0C0,808080,
0,C0C0C0,8080,0,0,FFFFFF
Valentine=C080FF,FFFFFF,FFFFFF,0,FFFFFF,0,8000FF,
400080,FFFFFF,C080FF,C080FF,0,C0C0C0,C0C0C0,
808080,0,808080,FF00FF,0,FFFFFF,FFFFFF
Wingtips=408080,C0C0C0,FFFFFF,0,FFFFFF,0,808080,
FFFFFF,FFFFFF,4080,FFFFFF,0,808080,C0C0C0,
808080,0,C0C0C0,808080,FFFFFF,0,FFFFFF
```

The hexadecimal values are translated as blue, green, and red intensities from 0 to 255. For example, 804000 is

50% intensity blue (80 hexadecimal is 128 decimal; 128/255)

25% intensity green (40 hexadecimal is 64 decimal; 64/255)

0% intensity red

The custom colors in the [Custom Colors] section are described with the same blue, green, red style.

Warning: Note that the color combinations are described as blue, green, red, not the standard red, green, blue.

```
[Custom Colors]
ColorA=FFFFFF
ColorB=FFFFFF
ColorC=FFFFFF
ColorD=FFFFFF
ColorE=FFFFFF
ColorF=FFFFFF
ColorG=FFFFFF
ColorH=FFFFFF
ColorI=FFFFFF
ColorJ=FFFFFF
ColorK=FFFFFF
ColorL=FFFFFF
ColorM=FFFFFF
ColorN=FFFFFF
ColorO=FFFFFF
ColorP=FFFFFF
```

The [Patterns] section describes the standard patterns available, including any changes you have made to the patterns and new patterns you have added.

```
[Patterns]
(None)=(None)
Boxes=127 65 65 65 65 65 127 0
Paisley=2 7 7 2 32 80 80 32
Weave=136 84 34 69 136 21 34 81
Waffle=0 0 0 0 128 128 128 240
Tulip=0 0 84 124 124 56 146 124
Spinner=20 12 200 121 158 19 48 40
Scottie=64 192 200 120 120 72 0 0
Critters=0 80 114 32 0 5 39 2
50% Gray=170 85 170 85 170 85 170 85
Quilt=130 68 40 17 40 68 130 1
Diamonds=32 80 136 80 32 0 0 0
Thatches=248 116 34 71 143 23 34 113
Pattern=224 128 142 136 234 10 14 0
```

Program Manager: PROGMAN.INI

As you change and add windows in Program Manager, Windows updates the PROGMAN.INI file. It is unlikely you will need to edit the file yourself, but it is good to know how to in case some of the program groups become corrupted. A typical PROGMAN.INI file looks like this:

```
[Settings]
Window=64 48 576 384 1
SaveSettings=1
MinOnRun=0
AutoArrange=0
```

The Window values give the location of the upper-left and lower-right corners and the state of the Program Manager window when you start. The first two numbers are the coordinates of the upper-left corner (such as 64, 48 in the settings just shown) and the second two numbers are the coordinates of the lower-right corner (such as 576, 384 in the settings just shown).

The last number in the Window line tells the state of the window, as described in Table 27.14.

Table 27.14. State of Program Manager window on opening.

Number	Description
0	Closed
1	Normal
2	Minimized
3	Maximized

27

The SaveSettings value is 1 if the Save Changes option in the closing dialog box is checked and 0 if it is not. MinOnRun and AutoArrange are 1 if the **M**inimize On Use and **A**uto Arrange commands in the **O**ptions menu are selected and 0 if they are not.

```
[Groups]
Group1=C:\WINDOWS\ACCESSO2.GRP
Order= 2 3 4 5 1
Group2=C:\WINDOWS\GAMES1.GRP
Group3=C:\WINDOWS\WINDOWS1.GRP
Group4=C:\WINDOWS\NONWIND1.GRP
Group5=C:\WINDOWS\MAIN2.GRP
```

The Order= line is dedicated to the order in which group windows appear when tiled.

The [Groups] section lists each group used in the Program Manager window. Each keyword must be Groupx. The groups must appear in sequence without gaps.

Damaged or Missing Groups

If one of your group files is missing, you will see the error message shown in Figure 27.3. If one of your group files is damaged, you will see the error message shown in Figure 27.4. Both of these error messages indicate that you need to delete the .GRP file, remove the group from your PROGMAN.INI file and re-create it by hand.

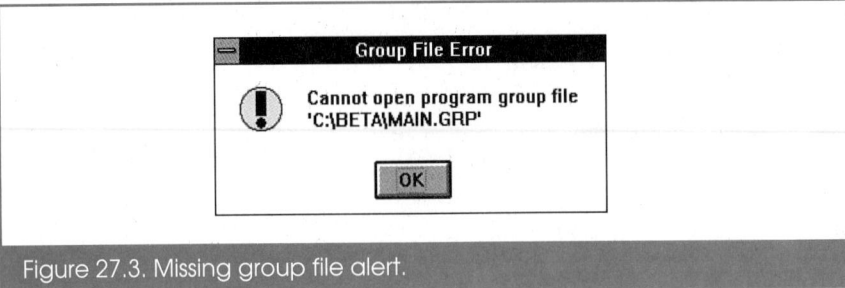

Figure 27.3. Missing group file alert.

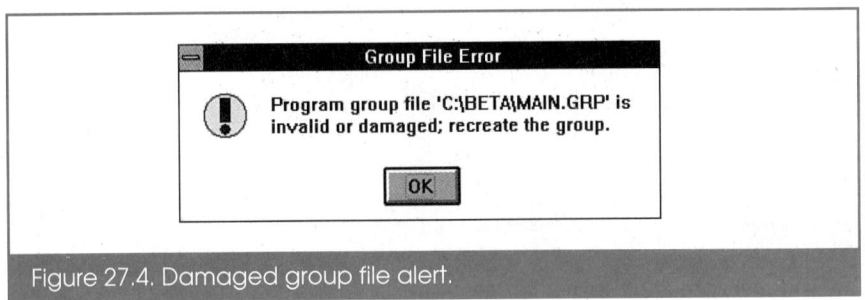

Figure 27.4. Damaged group file alert.

When you edit the PROGMAN.INI file, you must be sure that the groups named start at Group1 and are in sequential order. If the group you are removing is not the last group in the list, you must renumber the remaining groups.

 **Tip:** When you take a group out of your PROGMAN.INI file, you should be sure to delete the damaged group file (the .GRP file) from the disk so that you do not accidentally use it again later.

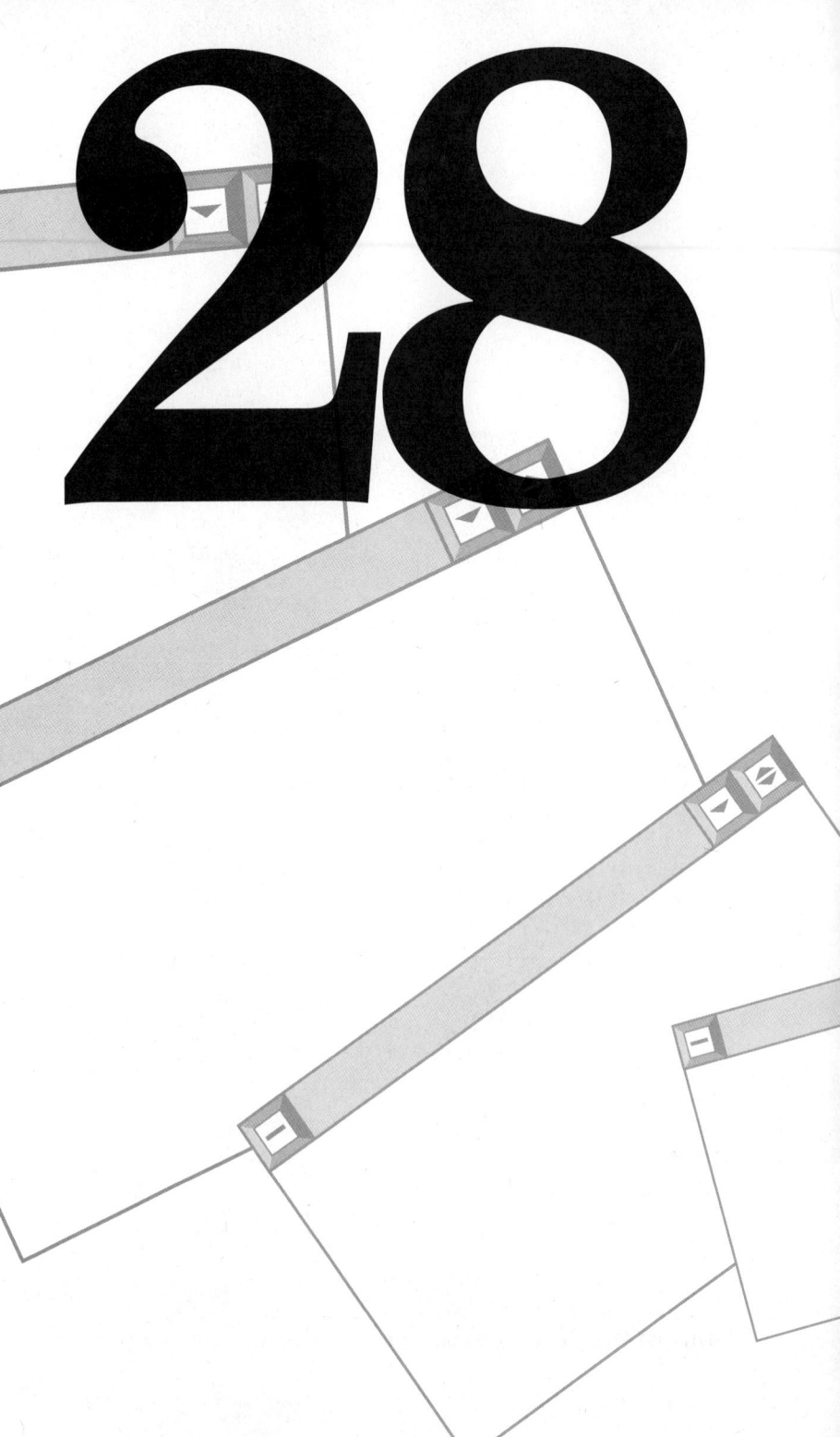

CHAPTER

28

Networking and Communications

Although you can run Windows on a stand-alone workstation in your own office or home you probably are going to want to communicate with some other computer. This communication may be on a regular basis, or it may be sporadic; the computers with which you communicate may be down the hall or on the other side of the world.

Computer communications is a big topic that has filled many books. This chapter is an overview of the most common types of communication between a PC and other computers. It explains how Windows works with communications, describes how to install Windows on a local area network (LAN), and discusses a few of the known oddities and abnormalities that come up with Windows and communications.

Networking Fundamentals

When talking about computer communications, you can run across several terms that often are used almost interchangeably, though they do have specific meanings. These terms include

▲ Data communications is the generic term for the exchange of bits between computers.

▲ Facsimile transmission (Fax) refers to sending or receiving data by fax machines or PCs equipped to send or receive data in the same format as that used by fax machines, whether the other machine is actually a fax or another computer pretending to be a fax.

▲ Connectivity is linking two computers, generally referring only to the hardware link between them.

▲ Interoperability or bridging is linking two computers in a way that the programs running on them can exchange data.

▲ Local area network (LAN) describes a group of computers, generally PCs, that are located in a limited area, perhaps within a building or a site, and linked with cable.

▲ Wide-area network (WAN) is a group of computers not close enough together to be linked with cable, so they are linked using any of a number of other methods: modems and dial-up telephone lines; telephone lines reserved for a connection between two computers ("leased lines"); satellites; microwave; or a public or private network specifically intended for data transmission (called "packet switched network," "public data network," or "X.25 network" after the communications methods used).

▲ Synchronous communication is linking between a PC and an IBM-compatible large computer, which requires a special type of communications method.

▲ Asynchronous communication: One computer using a modem and a telephone line to call up another, which could be a bulletin board, an on-line information service, or a minicomputer or main-frame.

▲ Enterprise Networking is linking an entire company, worldwide, using a combination of these methods.

For more detail on each of these, see the Glossary.

Purposes of the Local Area Network (LAN)

The type of communication most often associated with Windows is local area networking or "networking" for short. The network itself is referred to as a LAN.

Purposes of a LAN include

▲ Sharing data other users have created, such as reports or spreadsheets

▲ Sharing applications, including both commercially available programs such as Excel and WordPerfect, and user-developed programs

▲ Sharing network resources such as printers, data modems, fax modems, mainframe links, and plotters so that not all potential users of these devices have to have their own

▲ Communicating publicly or privately with other PC users by means of applications such as electronic mail and bulletin board systems

28

Types of LANs

Several types of networks actually fit under the umbrella term "LAN." These types of networks can be defined in three ways: by shape, or topology; by communications method, or protocol; and by the type of cabling used.

In terms of topology, the types of networks include

▲ Ring, a closed network with no "ends" where each machine on the network (known as a node) communicates with its neighbors

▲ Bus, a straight-line network with two ends

▲ Star, a network with one central node through which all messages travel

▲ Composite, star-shaped rings or star-shaped buses, which feature a central unit for configuration and setup but use a ring or a bus for the actual data transmission

Figure 28.1 shows an example of a ring topology and Figure 28.2 shows an example of a bus topology. These are the two most common network setups.

In terms of the communications method used, the two major types of networks include

▲ **EtherNet**, which transmits data at rates of up to 10 million bits per second. It generally uses the bus topology. It works by having each node "listen" before transmitting data to see whether the network is in use, and then transmitting the data. All the nodes have equal access to the network resource. Two nodes transmitting data simultaneously are known as a collision, and both nodes pause for a short time before trying again.

▲ **Token Ring**, which transmits data at rates of up to 4 million bits per second. An enhanced version transmits data at rates of up to 16 million bits per second. It generally uses the ring topology, as the name implies. It works by having an electrical signal, or token, constantly circulating from node to node on the network. A node cannot transmit data unless it has possession of the token. Consequently, as opposed to Ethernet, it is easier to determine a specific time within which a piece of data can be transmitted.

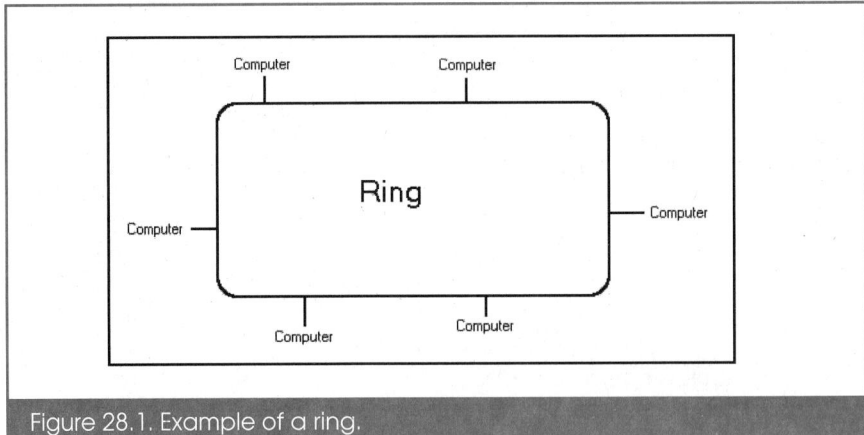

Figure 28.1. Example of a ring.

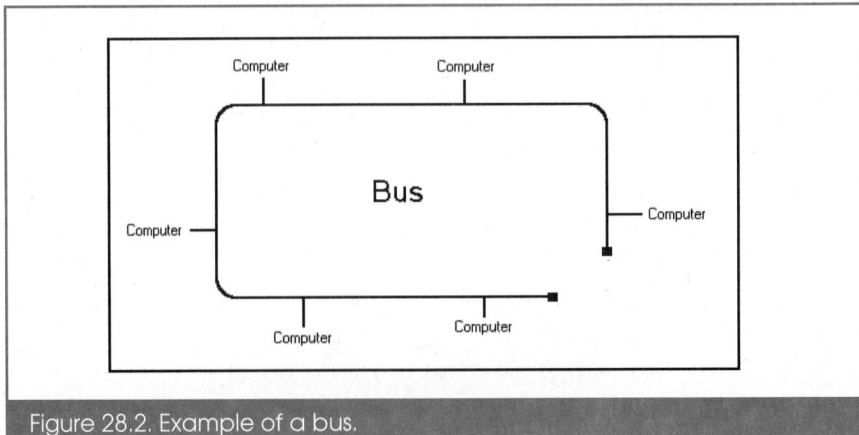

Figure 28.2. Example of a bus.

In terms of the cabling types used, the main types include

▲ Coaxial cabling, or coax, which is thick, expensive, and inflexible, but can transmit more data for longer distances than any other type of copper-based cabling.

▲ Thin coax, thinnet, or Cheapernet, which is a less thick, less expensive, and more flexible type of coax (it resembles cable TV wire) that cannot transmit as much data for as long a distance.

▲ Twisted-pair cabling, which comes in both shielded and unshielded forms. It is inexpensive and is often already available in quantity in your organization's walls in the form of extra telephone cabling.

▲ Fiber optic cabling, which is glass- or plastic-based and can transmit a great deal of data over great distances without error, but which is expensive and difficult to connect to.

Both EtherNet and Token Ring are available on all these forms of cabling. Because of its low cost and availability, many organizations are switching to unshielded twisted-pair cabling.

The Role of the Network Operating System

The LAN runs a piece of software called the network operating system or NOS. The role of this software is similar to that of Windows or DOS: It gives you access to network resources and functions, but across the entire network rather than just on your own PC.

The various types of network operating systems include

▲ NetWare, from Novell Inc., the most widely used network operating system

▲ LAN Manager, developed by Microsoft for use on OS/2 rather than DOS. It is sold directly to users by Microsoft and is also included in several other network operating systems from other vendors.

▲ 3+Open, developed by 3Com Corp., based on Microsoft's LAN Manager

▲ 3+, developed by 3Com Corp., a DOS-based network operating system

▲ PC LAN Program, developed by IBM

▲ Vines, developed by Banyan Systems, for Unix-based systems

▲ Network, developed by Microsoft and incorporated into several DOS-based network operating systems

Network Programming Interfaces

Programs that communicate with other programs on a LAN, whether you wrote them yourself or bought them, do so by means of one or more application programming interfaces (API). An API is an accepted standard for exchanging data between programs, so two vendors do not have to set up separate, incompatible communications protocols for every possible combination of their products.

The various types of interfaces include

▲ IPX/SPX, which is used with NetWare

▲ NetBIOS, which has been used with a wide variety of networks and is probably the most standard type

▲ Named "pipes," which is a high-performance interface but is only supported by LAN Manager-based network operating systems

▲ Advanced Program to Program Communication, or APPC, which was developed by IBM and is supported on its mainframes and minicomputers, as well as on PCs, but which is complicated to program

▲ Structured Query Language (SQL), which technically is not a communications protocol but a standardized method for accessing databases, either in a program or through user input.

Client/Server Computing

A term that often comes up these days in connection with LANs and Windows is client/server computing. This means that a computing task is divided into two parts: a specific part that is performed on your PC and a more general part that is performed on a network server.

For example, take an application that involves access to a large database. Without client/server computing, the entire database might have to be transmitted to a PC, at which point the user selects the relatively few records with the needed data. If the application were running on the server, however, the user might have terrible response time because every keystroke had to traverse the network before taking effect.

With client/server computing, the user interface and data request portion can be performed on a PC, whereas the actual database access can be performed on the server, with just those few needed records being transmitted back to the user.

The problem with client/server computing is it requires a new way of thinking about writing programs, not to mention actually having to write the programs themselves, often on a number of different machines. When you are developing new applications, it may make sense to think about whether this type of model might work for you.

Communicating with a Mainframe

Mainframes manufactured by IBM, and by other vendors that make their products compatible with IBM, use a different type of communications method than most other types of computers. Part of this is because mainframes were originally developed to communicate with remote terminals, and the concept of having to communicate with another device that might also have processing power was not considered at that time.

Because organizations set up huge applications based on mainframes, and mainframe programming is difficult, it is not possible to simply rewrite all those applications to support PC communication, even though that might seem more efficient. Such rewriting would also require that the entire user base be retrained.

Consequently, what most organizations do is use PC hardware and software that fools the mainframe into thinking that the PC is actually a dumb terminal. This fooling is known as terminal emulation, because the PC is emulating, or pretending to be, a particular kind of terminal. For communicating with IBM mainframes, PCs emulate IBM model 3270 terminals; for communicating with IBM minicomputers, PCs emulate IBM model 5250 terminals.

Normally, each PC would require the installation of hardware that can communicate with a mainframe by convincing it that the PC is a terminal. This hardware is called a terminal emulation board. In organizations with LANs where users do not have to stay connected to the mainframe or minicomputer all day, administrative staff can set up a gateway to the mainframe. What this means is that a certain number of terminal emulation boards are installed in the server, and the PCs on the network share these boards when necessary, rather than each PC having its own terminal emulation board.

Asynchronous Communications

An easy way to communicate with many types of computers is through a modem, communications software, and a standard telephone line. Chapter 12, "Terminal," discusses a simple way for you to communicate through a modem with the Terminal program that comes with Windows. The purpose of the modem is to translate the digital signals the PC uses into an analog signal that can be transmitted over the telephone line. A modem at the recipient's computer performs the reverse of the same function.

This form of communications is known as *asynchronous* because each computer transmits data when it is ready to, as opposed to communications where transmissions are synchronized by time. With asynchronous communication, you can call up many types of minicomputers, other PCs, bulletin boards (which are sources for free or cheap software, as well other uses), and commercial online information services such as CompuServe (which are also sources for both software and other uses, as well as for official or unofficial support from vendors).

Wide-Area Networks (WAN)

A wide-area network, or WAN, is a set of computers located in different geographical areas that is linked through a number of different methods. Many of these methods make use of a communications protocol known as X.25.

X.25 breaks up a message into a number of smaller parts, known as packets, and transmits each packet in the most efficient way at that time. For example, two packets going from San Francisco to New York may travel through different paths (perhaps one through Texas and one through Chicago) if the load on one of the links suddenly goes up. Because the user neither knows nor cares what path each packet takes, an X.25 network is generally depicted as a "cloud."

Another way to do wide-area networking is through store-and-forward. This method works for sending messages but not for direct connections to a remote machine. With store-and-forward, a message gets sent from machine to machine on a network until it reaches its destination. Generally, the message must carry its own path: It is as though, when writing a letter, you did not just give the recipient's address, but all the towns in between through which the letter passed.

REMOTE

Overview of Windows and Networking

Nothing about Windows inherently requires networking, and, in fact, little about Windows inherently is designed for networking. Nevertheless, the concepts of Windows and networking go together rather well.

With Windows, you can gain access to other resources on a network without having to be familiar with all the networking details. In the same way that Windows enables you to find files and run applications on your hard disk without having to type specific DOS commands, Windows gives you an easy-to-use way of finding files and running applications on the network.

The consistent Windows user interface allows developers and network administrators to stitch together different applications, including some that might run on a mainframe, minicomputer, or network server, in a way that is transparent to the users. Windows can also provide a user-friendly front end to old-style mainframe applications, making the applications easier to use without requiring a time-consuming rewrite.

One built-in aspect of Windows that is well-suited to networking is Dynamic Data Exchange, or DDE, described in Chapter 31, "Introduction to Windows Programming Elements" and Chapter 33, "Exchanging Data with the DDE." DDE is a form of interprocess communication that allows two applications, whether third-party- or in-house-developed, to exchange data and even link it so that when the data is changed in one place, it automatically changes in the other.

28

File Access Etiquette

If you are not accustomed to running on a network, you may not be aware of various fine points of network etiquette. Keep in mind that a network is a way for people to share certain resources; consequently, you need to be as careful of other people's needs when using network resources as you would using any other shared resource, such as the photocopy machine or the coffee maker.

For example, if you called up a file that you have the ability to modify (write access), your network operating system or application will most likely not allow any other user write access to that file. This is as it should be. If two people could simultaneously write to the same file, the system could, at best, be incorporating only one person's changes (the one who is saving the file last) or, at worst, saving a portion of each person's changes. Consider if one person could delete a file while somebody else is entering data in it?

If you are tying up a file by calling it with write access, you should try to limit the time that the file is unavailable to other users. Perhaps you could call it up with read access, which allows you to see the data but not change it, yet gives other users access to the data as well? Perhaps you could copy just the portion of the data you need, if you do not need the whole file. You certainly should not, say, go off to lunch or a meeting, leaving the file unaccessible.

If you are using a network operating system or applications that do not have the capability of keeping multiple users from writing to the file simultaneously, you need to be even more careful: You should manually check to make sure the file is not in use when you call it up, and you should let other users know that you are using the file.

E-Mail and Broadcast Etiquette

Another form of network rudeness of which you should be aware is that of being overly chatty. People often become annoyed with the office pest who wanders from cubicle to cubicle to gossip; similarly, networks can make it far too easy for coworkers to interrupt each other with trivialities.

If you are running Windows on a network, most likely you have a type of application known as electronic mail, or E-mail. E-mail is like an office memo, except that it is as easy to send a memo to everybody in the company as it is to send it to just one person. Networks, including one at IBM, have literally been shut down by the load of multiple-addressed E-mail messages.

When you send E-mail to multiple people, check the recipient list to make sure that everybody on the list needs to receive the message; for example, do the people in the Hong Kong office really need to know that somebody in the Iowa office is giving away kittens?

Broadcast messages are similar to E-mail. If E-mail is like an inter-office memo, broadcast messages are like the public-address system. These should be used even more sparingly than E-mail, as they pop up in the middle of users's applications and interrupt what they are doing. For example, if a user is running a job and a broadcast message pops up, the job halts until the user returns and clicks OK in the broadcast message's dialog box.

Tip: If you are running NetWare, you can enable and disable receiving broadcast messages with the Network Utilities menu, to which you can gain access by double-clicking the Network icon in Control Panel.

Network Drivers

The central point of interaction between Windows and your network operating system is the network driver. A driver is a piece of software that performs certain system-specific linking functions between two other pieces of hardware or software. For example, you also have drivers between your network adapter cards and your network operating system and between your monitor and your operating system.

28

Windows drivers are available for most of the major network operating systems: 3Com's 3+Open and 3+Share; Banyan's Vines 4.0; IBM's PC LAN Program; other network operating systems based on Microsoft's LAN Manager 1.x, 2.0, or 2.0 Enhanced; Microsoft's Network and network operating systems based on it; and Novell's NetWare, Version 2.01 or later.

Drivers between Windows and the network operating system may be written by Microsoft (because they are the developer of Windows), the network operating system vendor (which, in some cases, may be a different part of Microsoft), or even a third party such as the network operating system vendor.

Windows originally came with drivers for all supported networks. Later, the Supplemental Driver Library was released with updated (and much better) network drivers for Novell networks. If you are on a Novell network, be sure to use the newer drivers for more reliable network processing.

If you start Windows and it warns you that you are running outdated versions of your network operating system drivers, you need to get updated versions of these drivers from your network administrator. Always check with your network administrator when this warning appears.

Tip: Be sure that you use the most recent network drivers, regardless of the network you are running on. These are usually available through your network software salespeople. You can get even more up-to-date versions of drivers free through online sources such as CompuServe.

If you are running a network operating system not listed as officially supported, you need to start researching and experimenting. If you are lucky, your network operating system vendor may have developed its own driver; check with your vendor, their online support forum (if they have one), or a user group. You can also try the driver of some other network operating system with which they are supposed to be compatible.

Just because a driver exists for a network operating system does not mean that all network operating systems support Windows in the same way. Some networks (most notably Novell's NetWare and network operating systems based upon Microsoft's LAN Manager 2.0), support it more fully than others. In most cases, you will need to check with your network operating system vendor for specifics on how its product works with Windows.

Running Windows on Your Network

Each network operating system is different, and consequently Windows works differently with each one. To find out specifics, you need to check with your network operating system vendor, with the various informational files from Microsoft and your network operating system vendor, and with other users of Windows on your network operating system.

Certain generalities are true no matter what network operating system you are running. For example, it almost always works better to start your network first, and then run Windows, rather than starting Windows and then starting your network. There is rarely a good reason to start Windows before you start your network.

This is especially true when you wish to disconnect from your network; in some cases, stopping the network from within Windows 3.1 causes Windows to fail or act unpredictably. Novell's NetWare and network operating systems based on LAN Manager 2.0 are set up so that you can log on and off the network from within Windows. If you are accessing Windows from the network server, you cannot log off the network because that is where the files you are using are located. This is why many network administrators prefer to load and run Windows from each client machine.

Windows, Networks, and Security

Unless you live in a very small town, you do not go out and leave all your doors and windows unlocked. Similarly, when you leave your PC, you should not leave it logged in to the network. In addition to making your own applications, data, and other files vulnerable, you are making everything else attached to the network vulnerable, too. This possibility includes your corporate mainframe or your research-and-development machines.

Security is an important factor for both users and network administrators. Keep the following suggestions in mind.

▲ Back up your data frequently, both on an individual basis and from the server (one advantage of a network is that individual user's data can be backed up automatically on the server).

▲ Set up passwords for directories, network access, and so on.

▲ Make passwords nontrivial: not just your first name, for example.

▲ Do not make passwords so complicated you have to write them down on a note and stick it to your PC where any intruder can see it.

▲ Frequently change passwords.

▲ Limit access to files and directories to the minimum amount required. For example, do not allow write access to a file or directory when only read access is required. Write access to programs is seldom required.

▲ Do not put new software on the network without first checking it for viruses, especially freely available software from a user group or a bulletin board.

▲ Do not leave your PC logged to the network and unattended. The ease-of-use with Windows works for people trying to steal data, too.

▲ Never leave the PC logged in if you are the network administrator. In fact, network administrators should log in with their high-power capabilities only when they need to use them.

Tip: Depending on your network operating system, you may be able to change your password from within Windows. For example, with network operating systems based on LAN Manager 2.0, you can change your password by double-clicking the Network icon in Control Panel and then selecting Change Password.

Installing Windows on the LAN

The process of installing Windows on the network depends on how you have your LAN set up, the preferences of your company, and the security needed. In general, you will be installing it in one or more of these four ways.

▲ On a server, to be shared by other users on the network

▲ On your own PC, installed from the network server

▲ On your PC, installed from the Windows distribution diskettes but aware of the network

▲ On a diskless workstation

Deciding on Shared Windows Use

The first decision the network administrator needs to make is whether or not the LAN Windows users will run from the network server. If many of the network users are running Windows, it may make sense to install and run one copy of Windows on the network server. Users of the network then install only the personalized Setup files on their own PCs. This saves overall disk space, because only one copy of Windows is required. It also makes Windows easier to maintain, because only one copy needs to be modified when updates or changes occur. If users are running diskless workstations, or PCs without local hard disks, the only way they can run Windows is from the network server.

To install Windows on the network server, the server must have 5M to 6M of free disk space. Running Windows this way also means that the network administrator must take most of the responsibility for maintaining and upgrading Windows. Moreover, if the network goes down, users will not be able to run Windows from their individual PCs.

Do not expect local Windows performance to improve by installing it on the network. Windows runs best on the local workstation. Performance

may decrease because Windows has to keep going across the network to the server to gain access to Windows files. This problem is even worse with nondedicated servers, which are used for other purposes in addition to supporting the network, and on networks that have much traffic. For this reason, some network experts suggest that you not install Windows on a nondedicated network server unless centralized support is critical.

Installing Windows on a Server for Group Use

If you decide that you want users to run Windows from the network, the first step is to be sure to have one license for each user who will run Windows. You must have a license for each user who will run Windows from the network, just as you would have to have a license for each person who installed Windows on their local hard disk from a diskette. You can usually buy these from your local software dealer or your network vendor.

28

To begin installing Windows, perform the normal procedures for logging on to the network as a network administrator. You will not be using the normal Windows Setup procedure because Setup would modify AUTOEXEC.BAT and CONFIG.SYS files on the server. In order to gain complete control over the installation on a network server, we will perform the installation without the benefit of the Setup program.

Create a directory where Windows is located on your network. For example, you may want to set up a \windows network directory on the W: network disk drive.

Next, you need to convert the Windows distribution files into machine-readable form. To save space, most of the Windows files are shipped and stored on the diskettes in compressed form, which is a kind of code that makes the files smaller. (This is described in Chapter 2, "Installing Windows.")

To change the files from compressed form, you use the program called EXPAND.EXE, which you can find on Windows 3.1 Disk 2 (if you are using 5.25" diskettes). The EXPAND.EXE file itself is not compressed. The next step is to copy this program to the \windows subdirectory on the W: network directory.

```
COPY A:EXPAND.EXE W:\WINDOWS
```

(This assumes that your diskette drive is A:; the same assumption is made throughout the rest of this chapter.)

Expanding a file can be done only one file at a time, which is a laborious procedure. What you can do instead is write a little DOS program that goes through the diskettes automatically and expands each one in turn. Also, you need to rename some system files that Microsoft kept with different names. In addition, you set all the files in this directory to read-only so that no one accidentally modifies them.

To expand all the files from each diskette and perform the other tasks, use a text editor to create a file called EXPALL.BAT that contains the following:

```
A:FOR %%I IN (*.*) DO W:\WINDOWS\EXPAND %%I W:\WINDOWS\%%I
      RENAME W:\WINDOWS\*.SY$ *.SYS
      ATTRIB W:\WINDOWS\*.* +R
```

Tip: Remember to change A: or W:\windows when creating the program if your network setup is different.

To run the program, start by inserting Windows Disk 1 into drive A: and give the EXPALL command. When the EXPALL.BAT program finishes expanding all the files on Disk 1, install Windows Disk 2 in drive A: and run EXPALL.BAT on it. Continue this until all the files on all the Windows diskettes have been expanded.

When you have finished, make sure that the shared Windows directory does not contain any files named SYSTEM.INI or WIN.INI. These files need to be installed on each user's hard disk or personal directory on the network disk. They are not normally installed with the above procedure, but they may be there if you are reinstalling Windows over an existing copy that was installed incorrectly.

At this point you have finished the Windows server installation procedure and users can begin installing Windows on their PCs from the server (see "Installing Windows on Your Workstation from a Network Server" later in this chapter). If your organization is set up in such a way that users often run applications from the server, you should modify Windows to reflect this.

Installing Additional Programs Icons

You may recall from Chapter 5, "Program Manager," that Windows initially creates five program groups (Games, Main, Accessories, Windows Applications, and Non-Windows Applications) and that icons located in each of these groups represent the programs or documents that fall into that program group.

28

By modifying the Windows file SETUP.INF, you can indicate applications that should be included or not included in those program groups. This file is one of those copied to users's home directories, either on their own hard disks or on their directories on the network server, when users run the Windows SETUP/N program from their PC. This allows you to include icons for the programs of interest to all the networked Windows users .

Notice that you cannot use Notepad to edit SETUP.INF because the file is too long for Notepad to handle. You can use Write, but you have to be sure that you save the file in text-only mode.

> **Warning:** Before modifying the SETUP.INF file, make a copy of the original to which you can return in case of some sort of error with your modifications.

To add an application, edit the SETUP.INF file with a text editor. Locate the section called [progman.groups], as shown in Figure 28.3. Insert a new line under the appropriate group with a title of your choice, the pathname by which the application can be accessed, and, optionally, an icon filename and icon number, with each field delimited by commas. You can also add your own groups, if you wish.

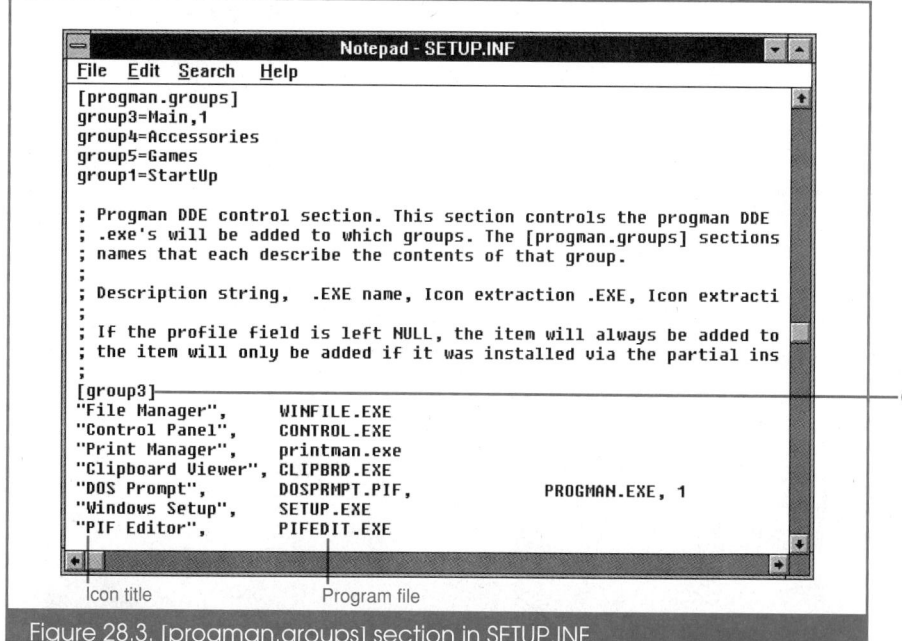

Figure 28.3. [progman.groups] section in SETUP.INF.

 **Tip:** To set the default so that user application files appear in their own directories rather than in the network directory that contains the application, refer to the application with the user's personal Windows directory rather than the network pathname. In other words, make an exclusive location for each user's application files. This is a must in the workplace where people leave and are transferred. If you don't know whose files are in the public domain on the server, you can never perform basic housekeeping. Eventually, even the largest of drives would be full of useless files.

An icon filename, as implied, is a file that contains one or more icons by which users can call up the application. Such a file may be included on the program diskette for the application. If an icon filename is not included or available, the application itself may provide the icon; if not, Program Manager provides one.

If the file contains more than one possible icon, you can select the one you prefer by including its icon number in the SETUP.INF file; the default is the first icon listed in the file. Figure 28.4 shows an example of adding a program icon to the Main window.

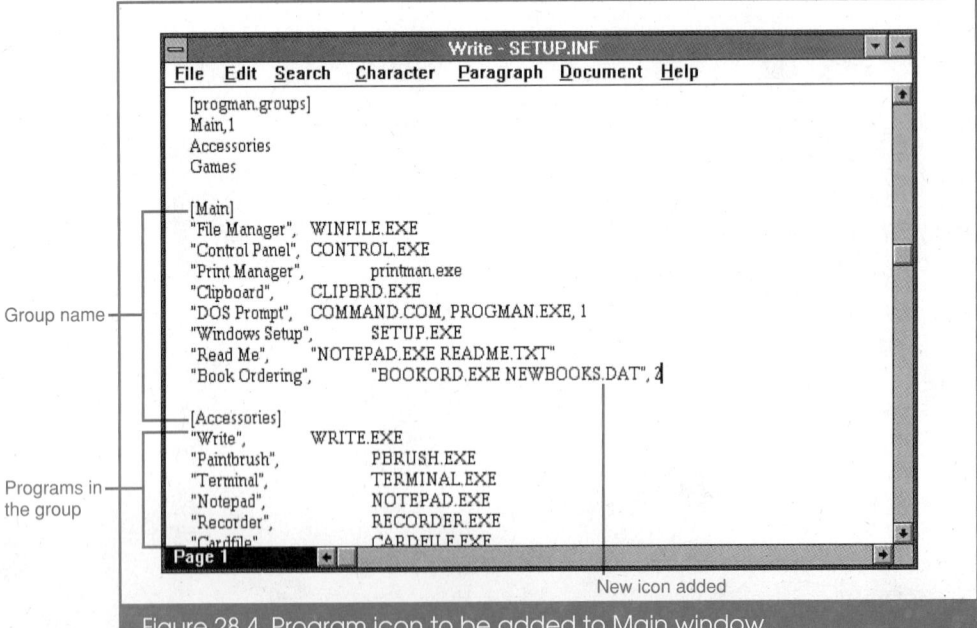

Figure 28.4. Program icon to be added to Main window.

Finally, locate the section [dontfind] in the SETUP.INF file and add a line containing the filename of the application that you just added to Program Manager. This keeps the new file from being referenced twice when the Setup program looks through the entire disk for files for which to make new icons.

Installing Additional Files for Each User

Another possible modification you can make to the SETUP.INF file at this point results in Windows copying additional SETUP files to the users' accounts when they install Windows on their systems. For example, you may wish to set up a file containing network application settings or program information files that is automatically copied to all Windows users.

Locate the section called [net] in the SETUP.INF file. To add a file, insert a line containing the diskette number (which is ignored, actually, so it can be any number), colon (:), filename, and an optional title that, if provided, Windows displays to the user when the file is copied to the directory at Setup time.

Figure 28.5 shows an example of adding a file, in this case "COMPANY.INF," to the files that get copied during a network setup to the user's main Windows directory. We use the name COMPANY.INF as an example of an INF file that is meant to be developed and pre-served for a particular company.

> **Tip:** The reason the diskette number is ignored is that it is only used when installing from diskettes. You are always installing from the network drive so Setup ignores the numbers.

Installing Windows on Your Workstation from a Network Server

The installation discussed in this section can only occur after your network administrator has installed a copy of Windows on the network server that is designed to be shared by users. You need to check with your network administrator to make sure this was done.

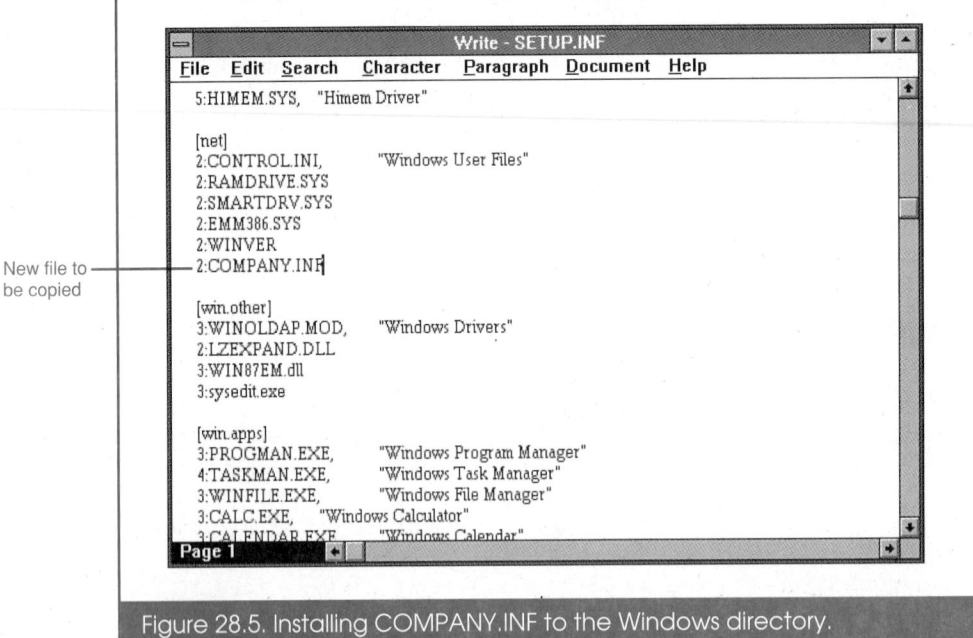

New file to be copied

Figure 28.5. Installing COMPANY.INF to the Windows directory.

While you are talking to your network administrator, find out the following information.

▲ The directory in which Windows is located on the network.

▲ The name of your personal directory on the network server. (You need this information if you are not installing Windows on your PC's hard disk or if your PC does not have a hard disk.)

▲ The make and model of your network printer, if any.

▲ Any special instructions or notes that your organization requires. For example, you may first need to install new network drivers to support Windows properly.

Perform your normal procedures for logging on to the network. Next, change to the directory where Windows is located on your network.

Then, at the MS-DOS prompt, give the command

```
SETUP  /N
```

With the SETUP command, you can personalize your copy of Windows. Windows does this by copying the files that make up the default Windows configuration file in your Windows directory. The /N modifier indicates to Windows that you are installing it from the network server and that Windows should not install copies of all its files on your local directory.

REMOTE

SETUP asks you where you want this directory located. You may want to put it either on your local hard disk or on your personal directory on the network server. This decision usually is up to the network administrator. Of course, if you have a diskless workstation, the decision is somewhat obvious. Because so many after-market products manipulate the INI files and even the way Windows uses its system files, it is advisable to install most of Windows locally. You will be limited by the speed of your client machine, but sooner or later the server may be bogged down too.

At this point in the installation, you need to refer to Chapter 2, "Installing Windows," to input the information Windows requires about the type of equipment you have and the type of network to which you are connected. Follow those directions for specifying Setup information.

During the installation, Setup also requires information about any network printers you have. Again, use the answers from your network administrator to answer these questions.

28

Installing Windows on a Diskless Workstation

If you are installing Windows on a diskless workstation, then, obviously, you do not have a hard disk on which to install your SETUP files. Consequently, when Windows asks you where these files should be installed, you should type the pathname for your personal directory on the network server.

Windows then creates files called CONFIG.WIN and AUTOEXEC.WIN that contain the new versions of your CONFIG.SYS and AUTOEXEC.BAT files. At this point, depending on whether you have write access to your boot directory, you may need to inform your network administrator to change these files for you. This is done as a precaution because automatically changing these files may affect other configuration options with your diskless workstation.

Configuring a Local Copy of Windows to Be Network-Aware

If you already have Windows set up on your system, you can make it aware of the LAN to which your PC is connected with the Setup program in Windows. This is in the Main window of Program Manager.

The Windows Setup program is shown in Figure 28.6. Give the Options Change System Settings command, which displays the dialog box shown in Figure 28.7.

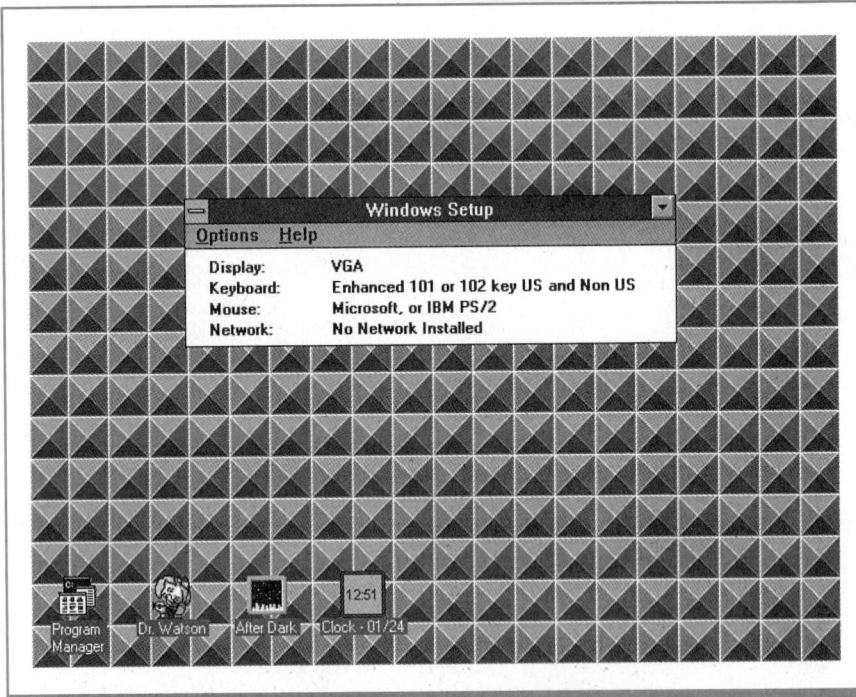

Figure 28.6. Setup program window.

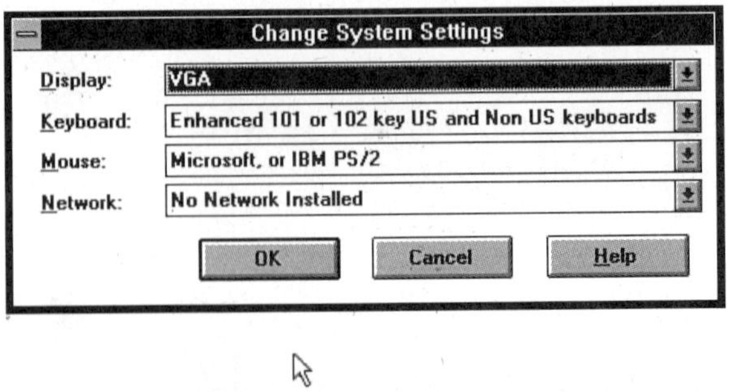

Figure 28.7. Change System Settings dialog box.

From the Network list, select the network operating system that your LAN uses. When the correct network operating system is highlighted, click the OK button. Windows then prompts you to insert the diskette that contains the network drivers for the network operating system you have selected, as shown in Figure 28.8. Windows copies the drivers to your Windows program directory and modifies the WIN.INI and SYS.INI files so that Windows is aware of your network connection when it starts up.

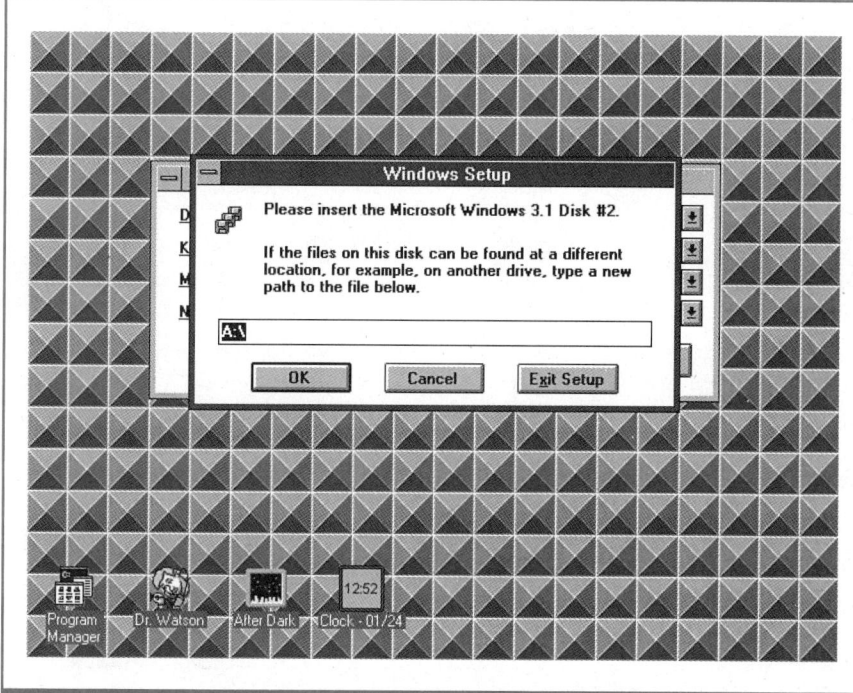

Figure 28.8. Windows requesting the network operating system driver.

When Windows has finished copying the drivers to your local directory, it will then display a dialog box with a **R**estart Windows button, shown in Figure 28.9. You can also opt to continue without restarting, but you must click the Restart button for the installation to take effect.

Performing Network Functions

Once you have Windows installed on your networked PC, whether you are running it locally or from the server, you can gain access to network resources through Windows. Accessing a network resource is not much different than accessing a local resource, such as a directory on your local hard disk or a locally attached printer. A network simply has more options.

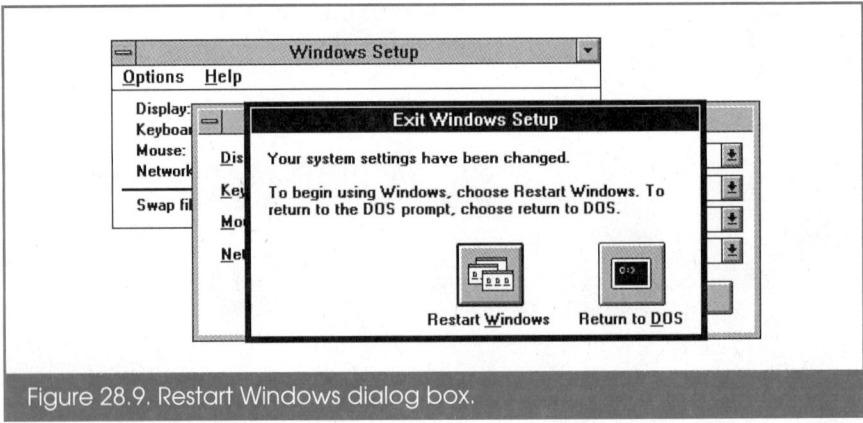

Figure 28.9. Restart Windows dialog box.

To find out the network resources to which you have access, log on to your local area network, start up Windows, and run the Control Panel program. There should be a Network icon on Control Panel.

Depending on how well your network operating system vendor has integrated its product with Windows, double-clicking the Network icon gives you a varying set of commands you can execute. For example, double-clicking the Network icon while running Novell's NetWare gives you the functions, shown in Figure 28.10, for attaching to or detaching from a file server and enabling or disabling broadcast messages.

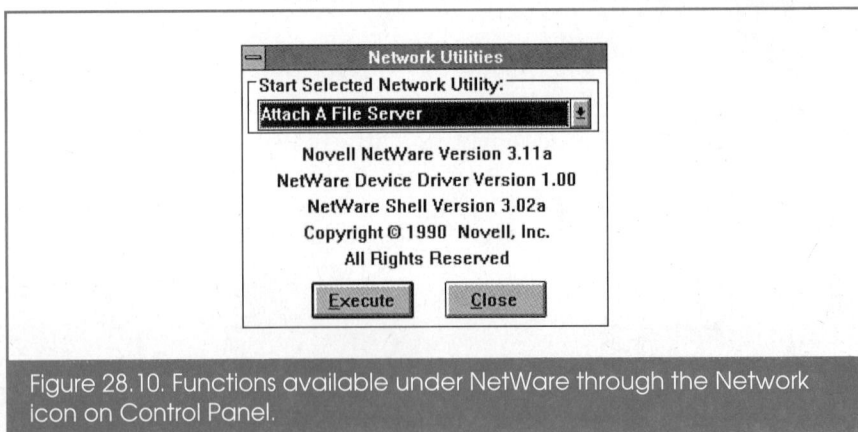

Figure 28.10. Functions available under NetWare through the Network icon on Control Panel.

> **Tip**: If you are running NetWare, and you have other network
> utilities you would like to be able to choose by double-clicking the
> Network icon in Control Panel, you can include them in the
> NETWORK.INI file. (As always, save a copy of this file before
> modifying it.) Edit the NETWORK.INI file from your favorite
> ASCII editor. Locate the heading called `[MSW30-UTILS]` and append
> lines to this section by typing the name of the command you wish
> to display in the Network Utilities menu, followed by an equal
> sign (=), followed by the name of the file you want the system to
> run when that function is selected.

28

Selecting a Network Server or Disk Drive

If you are running NetWare or a LAN Manager-based network operating system, you can attach to a network server using the Network icon
in Control Panel. To do this, double-click the Network icon, then select
Attach A File Server from the Network Utilities menu that comes up,
and click the Execute button.

When you do this, the network operating system and Windows work
together to show you a list of the available file servers to which you
have access, as shown in Figure 28.11. Alternately, you can type the
name of the file server in the area provided for that purpose.

Figure 28.11. Selecting a network server under NetWare.

After you have selected the file server to which you want access, you
will need to log onto it with your user name. Depending on your instal-

lation, you also may need to enter a password. After you have entered the appropriate information in these fields, click OK to connect to the selected network server.

Tip: If your network operating system supports this feature, it is a good idea to log on and off your network this way rather than from the DOS prompt, because logging off your network from within Windows may cause Windows to fail.

To detach from the network file server to which you are linked, select the Detach A File Server command from the Network Utilities menu and click the Execute button. When you do this, you get a dialog box as shown in Figure 28.12. Type the name of the network file server to which you no longer wish to be connected and click the OK button.

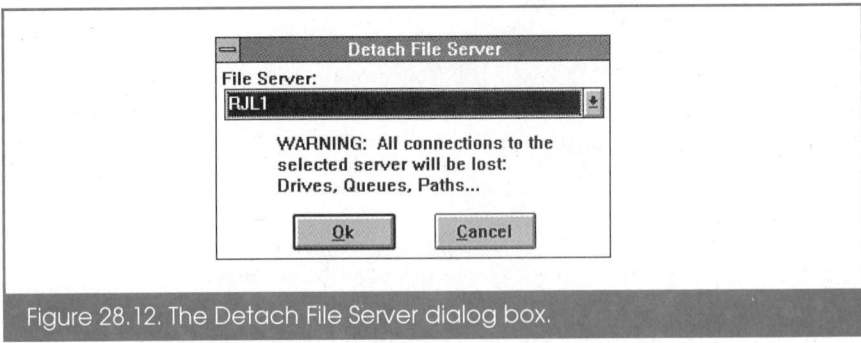

Figure 28.12. The Detach File Server dialog box.

Warning: If you are running Windows from a network file server, do not detach from that file server from within Windows.

Disk drives to which you are connected that are attached to network servers appear in File Manager, but the icons representing them look somewhat different, as shown in Figure 28.13. You can use these disk drives in the same way that you would use a local disk drive.

Figure 28.13. Network disk drive icons in File Manager.

To connect to a network volume, you first assign it a logical network drive letter. You can use any letters up through Z (Z:), meaning that you can connect to up to 26 network volumes. By default, the next available letter will appear in this field, but you can type over it if you prefer a different assignment.

> **Tip:** If your CONFIG.SYS file contains a `lastdrive=` statement, this could interfere with your ability to assign a logical drive letter. Such assignments result in an error message. LASTDRIVE denotes physical drive letters at the DOS level, and would not allow you to reassign the drive letter as a logical one from the network.

28

Once you assign a drive letter, you can either type the network path or click the Browse button to see a list of available network volumes, as shown in Figure 28.14. These disk volumes are listed by the network server to which they are attached and also show the directories defined for each volume. Depending on the security of your system, you may also need to type a password before you are allowed access to that network volume. Click the Connect button to set up your connection to the selected network drive.

Figure 28.14. Browse connections list.

Whenever you connect to a network disk drive to start a shared application, you should always refer to that disk drive by the same letter. In other words, if you refer to it as J: one time, you should refer to it as J: thereafter. This is because Windows keeps track of such things from one network session to another. If you are not consistent, Windows may

either not work at all, not work correctly, or perform poorly, especially if you have set up a network disk drive to work with an application that you can run from an icon in the Program Manager.

Being consistent with your disk drive letter assignments also makes the Connect Network Drive Previous listing more useful. If you click the Previous button, Windows shows all the network servers, volumes, and directories to which you have linked, as shown in Figure 28.15. That way, if you connect to a particular directory more than once, you can check the Previous list for it rather than having to track it down across the network again. You can choose one of the network drives in this list by clicking on Select. If you no longer want that network drive to be included in the Previous list, click Delete.

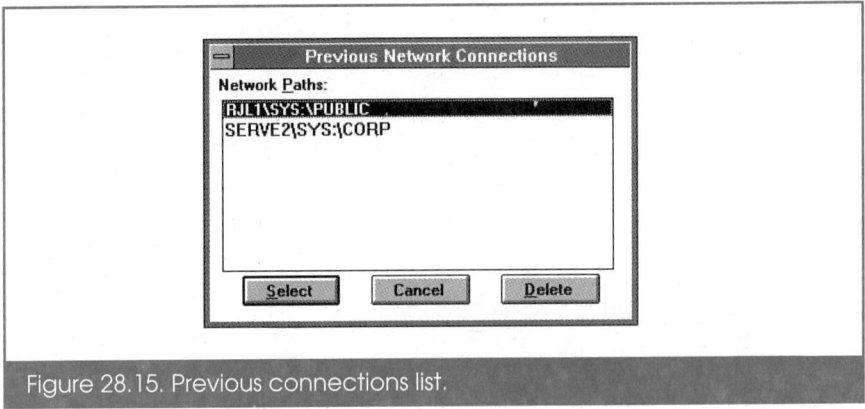

Figure 28.15. Previous connections list.

To keep from having a new network drive assignment added to the Previous list, click the Add to Previous List box in the Connect Network Drive menu.

To disconnect from a network drive, first make sure that it is not the Windows default drive, then click the Disconnect Net Drive command in the Disk menu of File Manager. This gives you the Disconnect Network Drive dialog box. Type the network drive to which you no longer want to be attached and then click OK.

Configuring Network Printers

To select and configure a network printer, you need to go through the Printers icon on Control Panel, rather than through the Network icon. When you double-click this icon, you get the standard Printers dialog box, except that it includes a Network button. Clicking this button

results in the Printers - Network Connection dialog box shown in
Figure 28.16. The dialog box shows you whatever network printer
connections are already set up. Setting up printers is covered in detail
in Chapter 26, "Printers and Fonts."

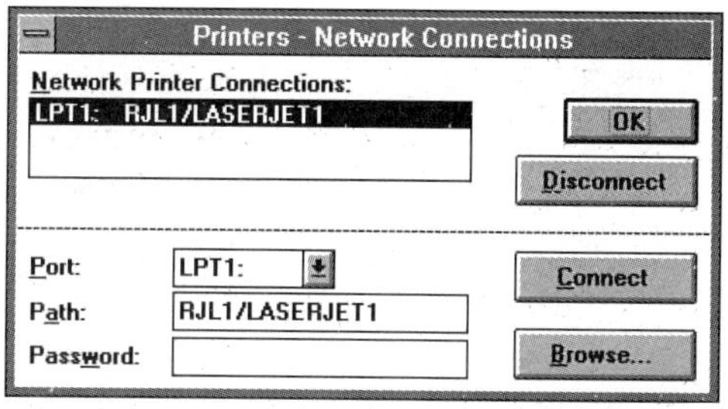

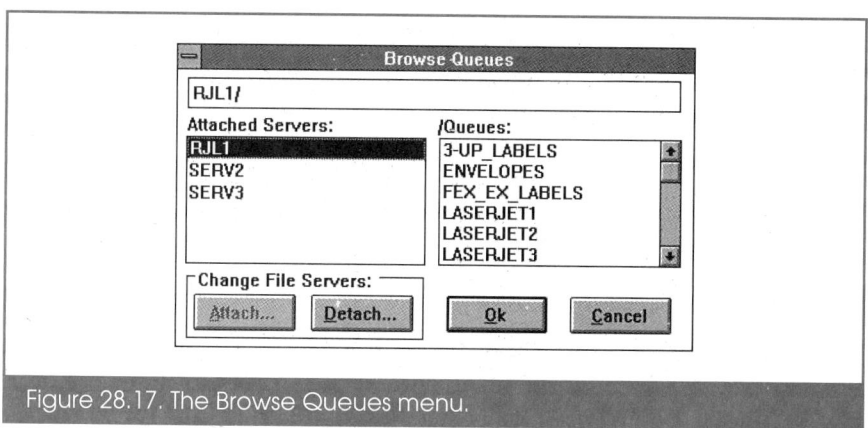

Figure 28.16. The Printers - Network Connections dialog box.

As with the Network Utilities menu available through the Network icon
of Control Panel, NetWare and LAN Manager-based network operating
systems allow you, by clicking the Browse button, to browse through a
list of possible network printers to which you can send jobs, as shown in
Figure 28.17. These printers are listed by the network server to which
they are attached.

Figure 28.17. The Browse Queues menu.

To connect to a network printer, you can either type the printer name
or select one of the printers displayed in the Browse Queue menu. You
may need to type a password. Then click the Connect button.

28

Tip: Whenever you connect to a network printer, you should always refer to that printer using the same port designation (LPT1:, LPT2:, etc.). Windows Control Panel keeps track of such things from one network session to another and associates certain printer configuration parameters with the port number. If you are not consistent, you may be trying to access a printer with the wrong set of configuration parameters, and the print job may either not work at all or produce incorrect output.

Depending on the capabilities of your network operating system, you may be able to use the Print Manager to check the load of a particular network printer before you send your print job to it. This list of print jobs assigned to a particular printer is known as that printer's *queue*. To check the load, double-click the Print Manager icon in Program Manager, and then give the View Selected Net Queue command, at which point Windows displays a dialog box with the print queue, as shown in Figure 28.18.

```
          PostScript Printer on RJL1/LASERJET1
1   AMUSCARIA -     15K        4:01 PM 5/29/1991
    SYSINI3.TXT



                        [ Close ]
```

Figure 28.18. A print queue dialog box.

To double-check the status of a network print queue, give the View Update Net Queues command from Print Manager. If you do not want Windows to check the print queues periodically, such as when network traffic is heavy, you can give the Options Network command from Print Manager. Windows then displays the Network Options dialog box shown in Figure 28.19. You can disable the periodic checks by clicking the Update Network Display box off.

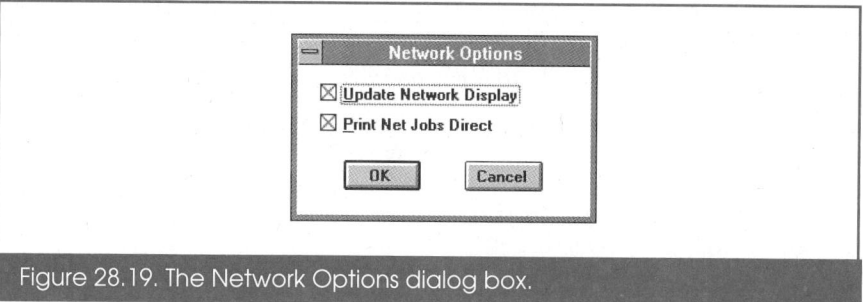

Figure 28.19. The Network Options dialog box.

If the View Other Net Queue command is selectable, you can look at the queues of network printers to which you are not attached. You can check the queues of multiple printers without having to attach and detach from each one individually. When you give the View Other Net Queue command, Windows displays a dialog box. Type the name of the network queue you wish to view in the Network Queue field, then click View. When you are finished, you can either type the name of another network queue to view or click Close to return to Print Manager.

Depending on the capabilities of your network operating system, you may get a pop-up window message when you have sent a print job to the network, confirming your print job.

To disconnect from a network printer and return control to the local printer (if any), click the Disconnect button.

Running Windows Applications on the LAN

In general, running applications from Windows while on a LAN is no different than running applications from Windows on a stand-alone PC. All you need to do is find the drive in which the application is located, connect to that drive, and run the application as you normally would.

You can also set up an icon for a network application in the same way that you would set one up for an application on your stand-alone PC. When you do this, you automatically receive a warning message from Windows.

The reason is related to the one mentioned earlier: Network disk drives should always be referred to by the same letter. The icon is set up to follow a specific path and displays an Invalid Path message if the drive name is incorrect. The Windows warning message is an indication that you might receive the Invalid Path message if you do not reference the network disk drive properly in the future.

> **Tip:** If you get "sharing violations" while trying to run an application that is on a shared network directory, use File Manager to make sure that the application files are set to read-only status. If they are not, use File Manager to change them to read-only.

> **Tip:** The issue of licensing applications for multiple users on a LAN is not yet resolved in the PC community, and vendors have developed several ways to do this. For example, your organization may have chosen to buy a license for 15 simultaneous users of a program, even though 25 users could potentially use the program. Consequently, if you are the 16th person trying to run the application, you will get an error message. You should report this to your network administration staff to help them decide whether your organization needs to modify its licensing arrangement.

Details of Particular Network Operating Systems

Because communications is a complex operation involving the coordination of multiple computers, operating environments, applications, and cabling, software anomalies are more likely to crop up in communications than under any other circumstance. Windows is no exception to this. Dozens of exception reports, notes, and warnings have already been released, and no doubt dozens more will appear as Windows and networks become more popular.

To find out about more recent quirks and problems, you can check the sources described below. Your network operating system vendor may have additional manuals or installation notes specifically for Windows. For example, Novell has published the *NetWare and Microsoft Windows Integration Book*, Novell part no. 164-000003001. Other vendors have published similar books.

> **Tip:** For the latest information on installation and running Windows on networks, be sure to talk to your network vendor. The instructions for installation have had many minor changes since Windows version 3.0 was released.
>
> Another good, up-to-date source of information on installing and maintaining Windows on a network is the Windows Resource Kit from Microsoft. This loose-leaf binder has the most current information on many topics, including how Windows handles networks.

28

Files on Disk

Table 28.1 lists the files that are installed in your main Windows directory when you install Windows. These contain valuable information on running Windows on a network. They are all text files and can be read using Notepad.

Because Windows and network information changes constantly, at least one person on your network should keep up on the latest information. The best way to do this is to subscribe to at least one of the online services and read the information there often. These services have many professionals who ask interesting questions and help each other with valuable information. Often, representatives from both Microsoft and the network vendors also participate.

Table 28.2 lists three large commercial services with active Windows and network discussions. In addition, the noncommercial Usenet system has many news groups that discuss Windows and networks. If you have access to Usenet (also called the Internet), you should find out how to read news and explore the COMP.IBMPC.WINDOWS news group. If you have access to the Internet itself, you may be able to download libraries of drivers and other information through the communications application known as *anonymous FTP*; the availability of such libraries is discussed in COMP.IBMPC.WINDOWS news group.

Table 28.1. Information files on disk.

File	Description
NETWORKS.TXT	Important information not included in the Windows User's Guide or online help, such as instructions for system administrators who are installing Windows on a network server, instructions for users sharing Windows on a network server, general notes on network behavior, running Windows on a diskless workstation, and network-specific notes.
3270.TXT	How to use specific non-Windows applications that allow your PC to emulate a 3270 terminal for communicating with an IBM or IBM-compatible mainframe.
README.TXT	Running Windows (not necessarily network-specific) information that was not available when the Windows User's Guide was printed.
PRINTERS.TXT	Information on using printers and fonts that will help you configure them to run with Windows, including information on networked printers.
SYSINI.TXT, SYSINI2.TXT, and SYSINI3.TXT	Procedures for advanced users on how to modify SYSTEM.INI settings.
WININI.TXT, WININI2.TXT	Procedures for advanced users on how to modify WIN.INI settings.

Networking Reference

Table 28.3 lists the network features of Windows that are available in each brand of network. Future versions of the network drivers (as well as future versions of the networks themselves) will probably include more of the Windows features.

Table 28.2. Commercial services with Windows information.

Service	Description
CompuServe	The advanced Windows user's forum (called WINADV) has two types of information: libraries of data such as new drives and hints from Microsoft on how to solve various problems. The discussions have both Windows users and Microsoft representatives to answer technical questions.
Byte Information Exchange (BIX)	The IBM.WINDOWS section includes information that is often more technical than CompuServe, which is a mixed blessing. This discussion has more network administrators and fewer users.
GEnie	The Windows forum on this system is similar to that available on CompuServe and BIX.

Table 28.3. Available functions for network operating systems.

Function List	Network Software Acronym								
	3+O	3+	LM1	LM2E	NW	PCLB	PCLE	MS	VIN
FILE MANAGER									
Connect Net Drive	x	x	x	x		x	x	[1]	x	x
Connect Net Drive/Browse						x	x			
Disconnect Net Drive	x	x	x	x		x	x	x	x	x
CONTROL PANEL									
Printers/Network/Connect	x	x	x	x		x	x	[1]	x	x
Printers/Network/Disconnect	x	x	x	x		x	x	x	x	x
Printers/Network/Browse				x		x				
PRINT MANAGER									
Display Net Queue	x			x		x	x	x	x	
View/Selected Net Queue	x	x	x	x		x	x	x	x	
View/Other Net Queue						x	x			
Display User Name Info	x	x	x	x		x	x	x	x	
Display Job Title				x		x				
Display Job Number	x	x	x	x		x	x	x	x	
Display Job ID		x		x		x	x	x	x	

continues

Table 28.3. Continued

| Function List | Network Software Acronym | | | | | | | | |
	3+O	3+	LM1	LM2E	NW	PCLB	PCLE	MS	VIN
Pause Local Net Jobs				x	x				
Resume Local Net Jobs				x	x				
Delete Local Net Jobs				x	x				
ADDITIONAL FEATURES									
On-Line HELP				x	x				
Server Attach/Detach (Login)				x	x				
Password Change			x	2					
Message Send				x	x				
Message Receive				x	x				
NetWarn Enable/Disable	x	x	x	x	x	x	x	x	x

[1] Indicates the function is available, but you cannot use the network names you are accustomed to. For example, the use of an internal network name is required.

[2] Other NetWare utilities such as 2 SYSCON can be installed in the NETWARE.INI file, which allows users to run these utilities through Control Panel.

Table Legend

Acronym	Full Product Name
3+O	3Com 3+Open
3+	3Com 3+
LM1	LAN Manager 1.X or 2.0 Basic
LM2E	LAN Manager 2.0 Enhanced
NW	Novell NetWare 2.10 or later
PCLB	IBM PC LAN Program Base Services
PCLE	IBM PC LAN Program Enhanced
MS	Microsoft Network
VIN	Banyan Vines

Serial Communications

One of the weakest links to your PC is the serial ports (also called the COM: or RS-232 ports). Compared to the parallel ports or network adapters you may have, the serial ports are slow, somewhat unpredictable, and difficult to diagnose when you have problems. Unfortunately, they are widely used by peripherals. All modems, many mice, and some printers connect through the serial ports.

Windows makes using serial ports easier than MS-DOS because you can use dialog boxes to check and change the settings for the ports, not commands that must be remembered and typed. You can also share serial ports among hardware devices better in Windows than you can in MS-DOS.

If you have only one serial port on your computer and you use it for a mouse, a 2400-baud modem, or a printer, you probably do not need to read this because it is likely that the port works fine for you. If you have two serial ports or you are using a high-speed modem, you may have problems using the serial port(s) with Windows. This next section will help you if you cannot get your serial ports to work correctly.

Serial Port Basics

28

A serial port is a connector on your PC that allows you to communicate with serial devices. These devices have similar connectors and are attached by a cable to your PC. In the early days of computers, the standard for serial port communications was not well-defined. Many devices still connect in non-standard ways to your PC. In order to hook a serial device to your PC, you must be sure you are using the correct cable, as defined by the manufacturer of the device.

Connectors

Most PCs come with one or two serial connectors. (If you have an internal modem, you do not need a serial connector for it because you plug it into the PC bus.) Check your PC manual for information on which of the many connectors on the back of your PC are the serial connectors.

The connectors for serial ports can be either male or female. Male connectors have pins, female connectors have holes. There are two types of serial connectors on the back of PCs: 9-pin male and 25-pin male. Both connectors have a slight "D" shape to them so that they can only be plugged in the correct way.

You can have up to four serial ports on your computer. They are called COM1:, COM2:, COM3:, and COM4:. If you are using an internal modem, it is assigned one of these port names. With most PCs you can configure the serial ports so that any particular connector can be associated with any of the four names. Thus, you might have a 25-pin connector as COM1: and a 9-pin connector as COM2:.

Warning: Most computers do not allow you to use both COM1: and COM3: at the same time, or COM2: and COM4: at the same time. See the section on troubleshooting later in this chapter for a description of this problem.

Warning: Do not confuse the serial connector with the parallel connector on your PC. A 25-pin serial connector on a PC is almost always male; a parallel connector is almost always female. Do not confuse a 9-pin serial connector with a monitor connector. A 9-pin serial connector on a PC is almost always male; a monitor connector is always female.

Communications Parameters

Once you are sure you have the correct cable for attaching your serial device to the PC serial port, you need to tell Windows the communications parameters to be used with the port. The parameters must match the parameters being used by the device with which you are communicating. If the parameters do not match, you will either not be able to communicate or the information being communicated will be garbled.

To set the communications parameters for your PC, use the Ports icon in Control Panel, as described in Chapter 7, "Control Panel." The dialog box for that icon is shown in Figure 28.20.

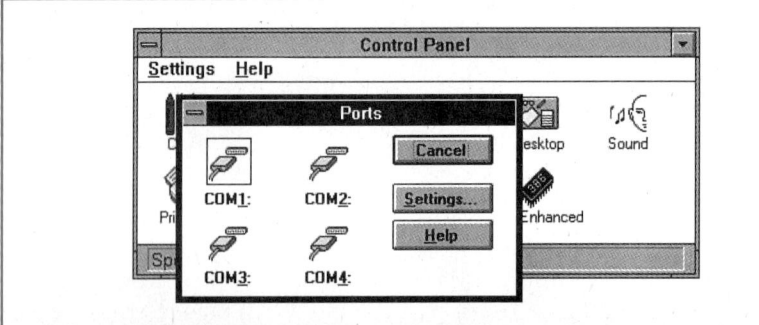

Figure 28.20. Ports dialog box.

To choose a port with the mouse, double-click the port's icon.

To choose a port with the keyboard, use the ←, →, ↑, and ↓ keys, then press the Alt-S keys or click the Settings button.

Tip: To set the options for more than one port at a time, use the Shift key to select multiple ports. You can duplicate the settings for one port with the mouse by dragging the icon of the source port on top of the icon of the destination port.

Warning: Many Windows programs that access the serial ports let you change the communications parameters from within the program. The Terminal program is a good example of this. If you are using such a program, use the parameter setting commands in that program, not in Control Panel. Programs that let you change the settings always override the settings you make in Control Panel.

28

Figure 28.21 shows the Settings dialog box.

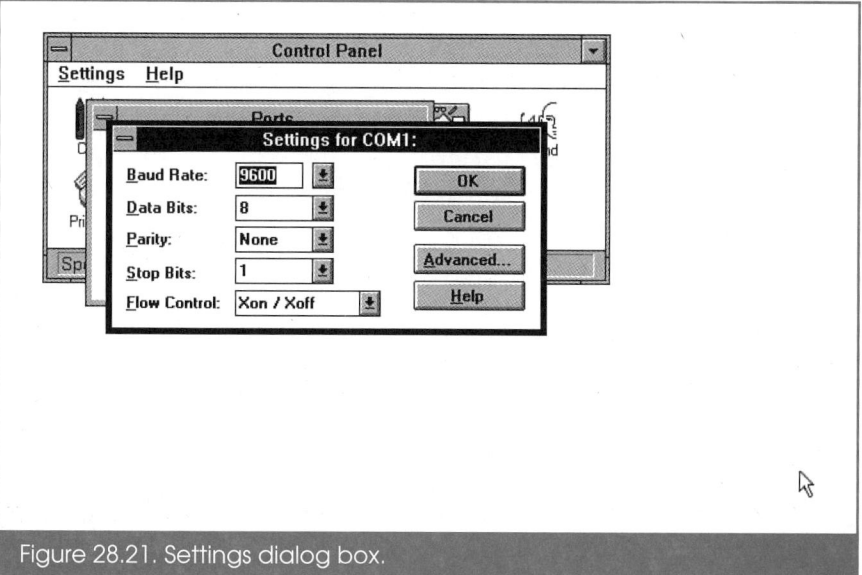

Figure 28.21. Settings dialog box.

Each serial port has five parameters that must be set.

▲ The baud rate is the speed of the serial port. The most common choices are 300, 1200, 2400, and 9600.

▲ The number of data bits is almost always 7 or 8.

▲ *Parity* is a method of adding an additional bit in order to allow the modem to check on the accuracy of the data being transferred. The parity is usually Even or None, although some older modems use Odd or Mark parity.

▲ A *stop bit* is a marker that indicates the end of transmission. The number of stop bits is 1 or 2 (1.5 is extremely rare).

▲ The flow control depends on the type of information you are transferring and is usually left set to None.

The baud rate depends on the capabilities of the hardware to which you are connecting. The two most common settings are

▲ 7 data bits, 2 stop bits, even parity

▲ 8 data bits, 1 stop bit, no parity

Flow control is only used when you are attached to a printer. If it is a PostScript printer, it may use Xon/Xoff flow control. Non-PostScript printers sometimes use hardware flow control (that is, they control flow through the cable), but most use no flow control.

Modems are special cases for the parameters. When you set the preceding parameters, you set them not for the modem you attach to your computer, but to the computer that you call from your modem. Thus, if you are calling a mainframe that uses 8 data bits, 1 stop bit, and no parity on its serial ports, you use those settings for your serial port.

Warning: Not all PCs can support all baud rates. If your PC has an 8086 CPU, it is unlikely to be able to work correctly at speeds faster than 2400 baud. Even if you have a fast CPU, your PC may not be able to support higher speeds for the serial port if you are running other software that takes a lot of processing time.

Selecting Ports

There can be up to four serial connectors on a PC. You have to tell the software you are using the port to which you have your hardware connected. For example, Figure 28.22 shows the dialog box from the

Printers icon of Control Panel that appears when you connect a port to
a printer. For a serial printer, choose the name of the port to which you
have attached your printer and click OK.

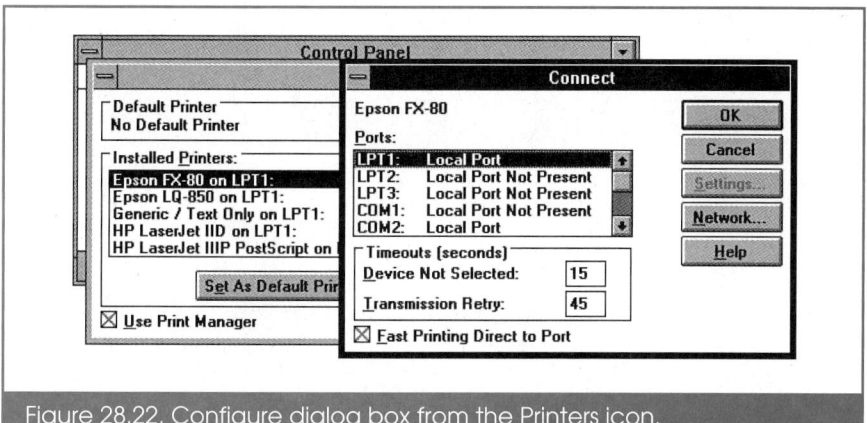

Figure 28.22. Configure dialog box from the Printers icon.

Other programs use different methods for choosing the port. For example, in Terminal you use the **S**ettings **C**ommunications command to
tell the program which port is your modem. As you can see from the
dialog box in Figure 28.23, you also use the command to set the communications parameters.

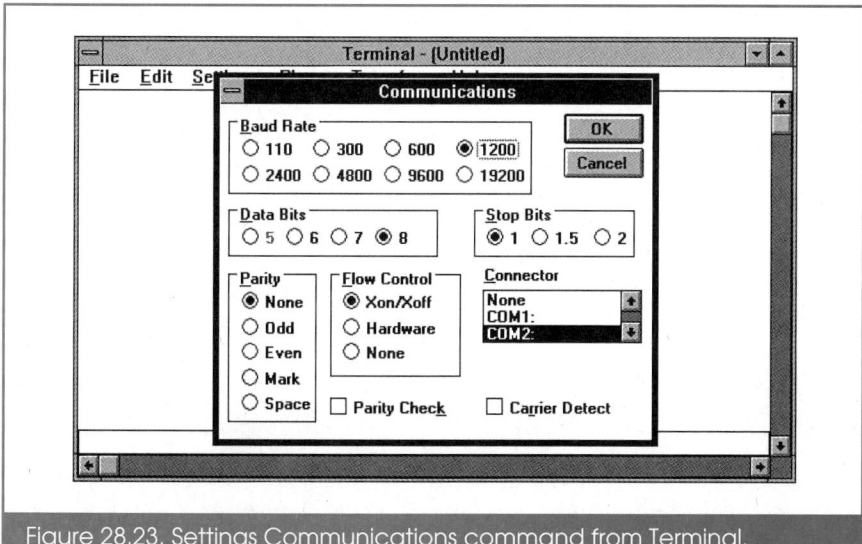

Figure 28.23. Settings Communications command from Terminal.

28

If you are running in 386-enhanced mode and have more than one program using the same serial port, be sure to tell Windows how to handle the device contention for that port. Use the 386 Enhanced icon in the Control Panel to call up the 386 Enhanced dialog box, shown in Figure 28.24. The settings for Device Contention are described in Chapter 7, "Control Panel."

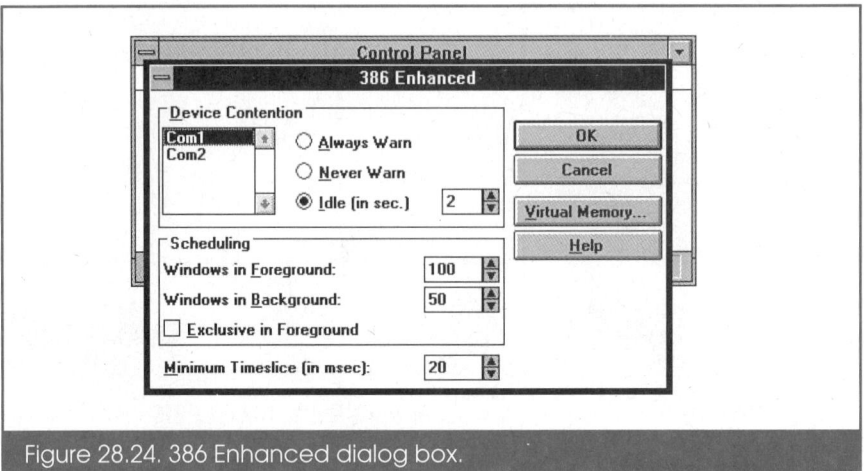

Figure 28.24. 386 Enhanced dialog box.

Problems with Serial Communications

As stated earlier, serial communications is one of the most trouble-prone aspects of using a PC. There is no absolute method for determining problems if you cannot get two serial devices to communicate correctly. This section outlines common problems and their solutions. Notice that some of these problems are only relevant if you are running in 386-enhanced mode.

Troubleshooting Checklist

This is a quick list of the questions you should ask if you have connection problems. It is in the approximate order of the most-frequent-to-least-likely problems.

▲ If the device is a printer, be sure you are using the cable the manufacturer supplied. Using the wrong cable is the most common serial printer problem.

▲ Be sure you are using the right communications parameters. If you know the baud rate but do not know the other parameters, use the two most common guesses first (7 data bits, 2 stop bits, even parity; 8 data bits, 1 stop bit, no parity). There are many other possible combinations and it is difficult to test them by guessing.

▲ If you are using two different serial devices at once, be sure they are on nonconflicting serial ports. This is described later in this chapter.

▲ If you are using a device on COM3: or COM4:, try connecting to COM1: or COM2: instead.

28

Conflicting Serial Ports

Although your PC can have up to four serial ports, some PCs can only use two at a time. In the low-level hardware, serial ports are controlled by interrupts. Interrupts are used by a device to stop a process or program so that the device can perform a task that can be performed only by interrupting the currently operating program. Control is normally returned by the interrupting device to the program that was executing when the interrupt occurred. There are only two interrupts for serial ports: IRQ 3 and IRQ 4. In almost every PC, both COM1: and COM3: use IRQ 4; COM2: and COM4: use IRQ 3. Thus, in most PCs, you cannot use COM1: and COM3: at the same time because they use the same interrupt (and likewise for COM2: and COM4:).

Newer PCs allow you to share interrupts. On those PCs, under Windows, it is acceptable to use both COM1: and COM3:, for example, because the newer hardware takes care of sharing the interrupt. PCs that conform to the EISA (Extended Industry Standard Architecture) and MCA (MicroChannel Architecture) standards allow interrupt sharing. If your computer supports interrupt sharing and you are running in 386-enhanced mode, be sure to add the following line to the [386Enh] section of your SYSTEM.INI file:

```
COMIrqSharing=true
```

(See Chapter 27, "Configuring with the WIN.INI and SYSTEM.INI Files" for more information.)

Problems with COM3: and COM4:

When running in 386-enhanced mode, it is likely you cannot get COM3: or COM4: to work correctly, if at all. You may see an error message such as the one shown in Figure 28.25. This message is incorrect; the problem is with the defaults that 386-enhanced mode uses for the ports.

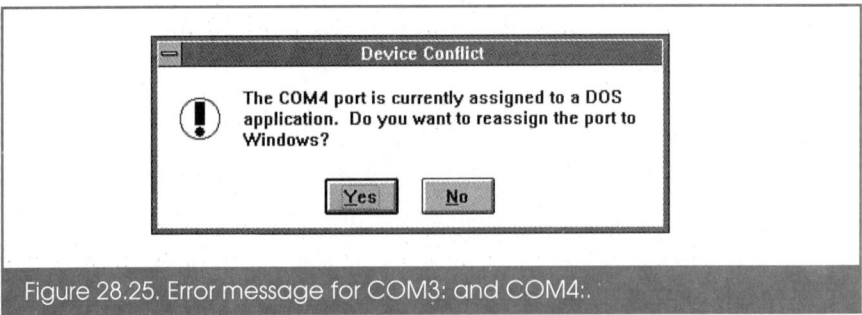

Figure 28.25. Error message for COM3: and COM4:.

Microsoft made an error when they set the defaults for some of the serial communications settings in 386-enhanced mode. Each serial port has a base port address that is used by the operating system for communication. If you are using 386-enhanced mode, you should include the following lines in the [386Enh] section of your SYSTEM.INI file:

```
COM1Base=3F8h
COM2Base=2F8h
COM3Base=3E8h
COM4Base=2E8h
```

The default settings for COM3Base and COM4Base were wrong for almost every computer, causing errors on those two serial ports.

In standard mode, COM3: and COM4: are sometimes unstable unless you have already used COM1: and COM2:. You should always use the lower-numbered serial ports first.

Losing Data When Using Non-Windows Programs and Serial Ports

If you lose data when you run non-Windows programs that access a serial port, you may have to use a lower speed for your device. Due to

the overhead of Windows, some non-Windows programs that run high-speed communications fine in MS-DOS may lose data when run in Windows. You should strongly consider using a Windows program instead of a non-Windows program.

If you are running in standard mode, edit the PIF for the program and select the Directly Modifies option for the serial port you are using. You can try this even if the program does not directly modify the serial port.

If you are running in 386-enhanced mode, try running in standard mode instead. This often clears up communications problems. If you do not want to change from 386-enhanced mode, before going to a slower speed or switching to Windows software, try the following:

▲ In the PIF for the program, be sure the Lock Application Memory option is selected in the advanced dialog box.

▲ Modify your SYSTEM.INI file on the COMxProtocol and COMxBuffer lines. COMxProtocol is only useful if you only send text data and your program supports Xon/Xoff handshaking protocol. COMxBuffer sets the size of the data buffer; try setting this to 1024 to see whether this prevents data loss.

28

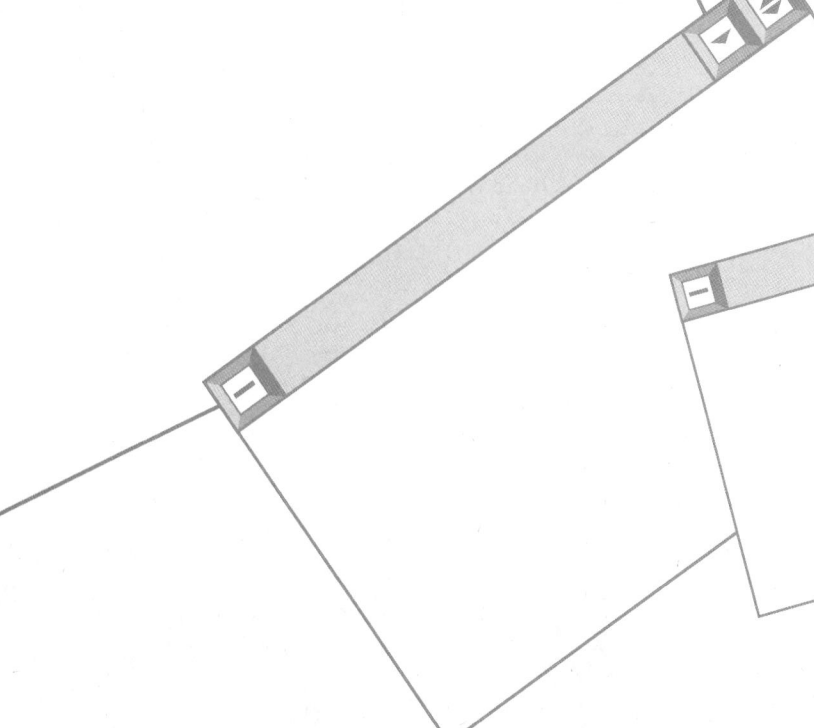

CHAPTER

29

Customizing Your Desktop

The whole concept behind Windows is to create an environment that is friendly, easily understandable, and organized. The creators of Windows decided to use the desktop concept because, at that time, most Windows buyers and users were perceived to be business personnel or people working within a business group of a company of some sort. The Windows desktop appears with a background pattern or bit map (wallpaper) on your screen. Everything Windows can display is presented on these two desktop backgrounds or their combination. Figure 29.1 shows minimized icons on a solid pattern desktop.

If you imagine your screen as being your actual desk, and everything on your desk as being objects that you would recognize every day, you begin to understand the concept underlying the Windows desktop.

Many of us would normally have writing instruments, a filing cabinet, a notebook, a clipboard, or an index card file at hand while performing the day's duties. In this way, the desktop metaphor really does work (personally, I can't wait for a trash can icon to show up in future versions of Windows).

Plain desktop

Minimized icons

Figure 29.1. Plain desktop with minimized icons.

The next comparison in the desktop metaphor is how you keep your desk organized while you use these tools. Enter Program Manager.

Program Manager (or one of its popular replacements) keeps your desktop objects (remember the clipboard?) where you can easily find them. You can do this in many different ways, of course. You are limited only by your concept of an organized desktop or work space.

Background Patterns

Believe it or not, if your system has the capability, you can configure your desktop to look like wallpaper or virtually any combination of colors. There are several wallpapers (bit maps) available with Windows 3.1. You can choose to display them in a fashion that fills the background of your desktop or you can, in some cases, just place them in the center of your screen (desktop) if you want something fancy, but don't want the full view. Figure 29.2 illustrates the WINLOGO.BMP wallpaper tiled on the desktop.

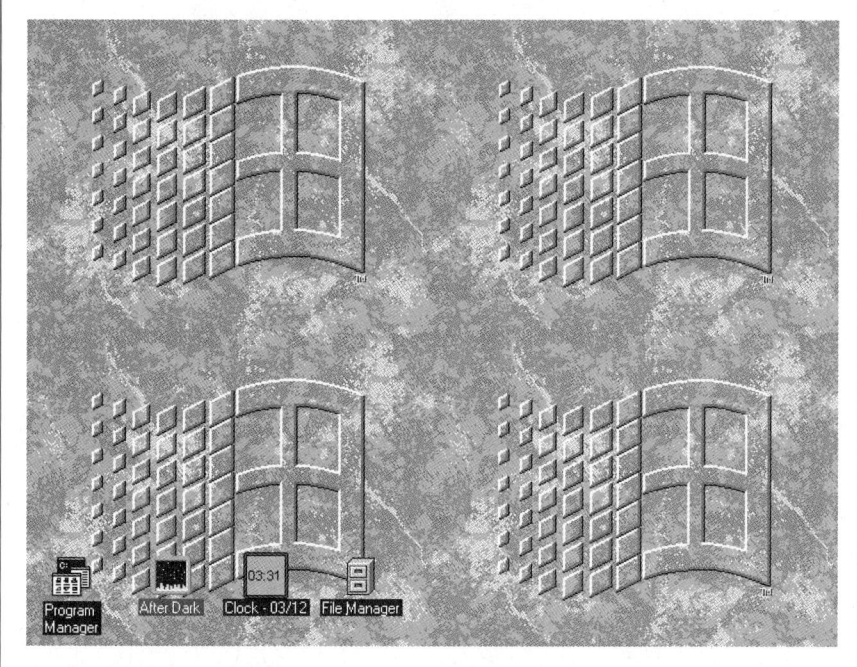

Figure 29.2. WINLOGO.BMP wallpaper.

Windows allows you to place background patterns on your desktop to make life more interesting. If you can imagine the background color as being the color of your work surface (that is, your desk), the wallpaper concept can be likened to placing a table cloth over your work surface.

If you just can't settle with plain old solid colors, try selecting a bit map from the Desktop section of Control Panel. Windows comes with several high-quality bit maps. Figure 29.3 shows the Desktop dialog box.

What You Get with Windows 3.1

There are several bit-map files from which to choose. These are some of them.

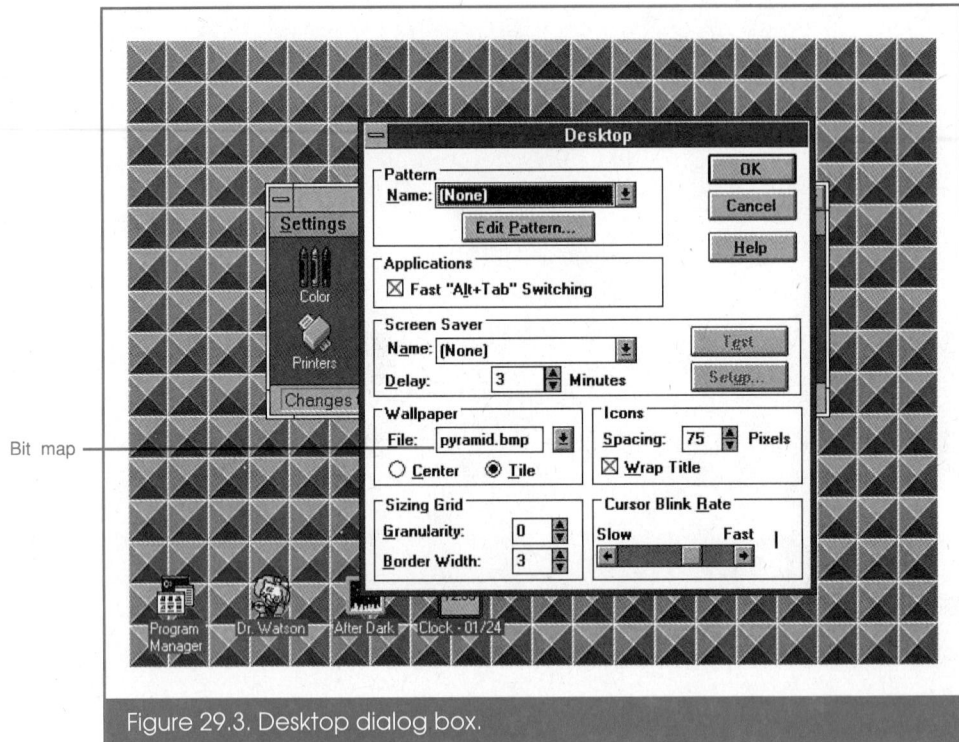

Bit map

Figure 29.3. Desktop dialog box.

▲ 256COLOR.BMP is made up of colorful spheres.

▲ ARCADE.BMP is a checkerboard pattern of mottled tiles.

▲ ARCHES.BMP is arches and aqueducts.

▲ ARGYLE.BMP is blue argyle.

▲ CARS.BMP is a parking lot stuffed with cars.

▲ CASTLE.BMP looks like mottled-grey bricks.

▲ CHITZ.BMP is fancy linear designs.

▲ EGYPT.BMP resembles a maze.

▲ FLOCK.BMP is a blue bird on a background.

▲ HONEY.BMP is a cross-section of a honeycomb.

▲ LEAVES.BMP is autumn leaves spread across the ground.

▲ MARBLE.BMP is cyan Venetian marble.

▲ REDBRICK.BMP looks like red bricks.

- ▲ RIVETS.BMP is made up of many small, interspaced rivets.
- ▲ SLASH.BMP is pebbled designs placed diagonally.
- ▲ SPOTS.BMP is a collection of floating bubbles.
- ▲ SQUARES.BMP is a lot of colorful squares.
- ▲ STEEL.BMP is a diamond-plate effect.
- ▲ TARTAN.BMP is the classic plaid-like design.
- ▲ THATCH.BMP is a latticework resembling chair caning.
- ▲ WINLOGO.BMP is the Windows 3.1 logo.
- ▲ XLBIG.BMP is large Excel logos.
- ▲ XLCUBES.BMP is a 3-D Excel logo in cube shape.
- ▲ ZIGZIG.BMP is made up of purple squiggles.

A Bit About Bit Maps

A bit map is a chart that is loaded into memory (typically from a bit-map file) and displayed on the screen for you to see. Each pixel (the tiniest dot your screen can display) represents a memory location in your computer's RAM. When you paint a bit map, you are filling in these dots with color. When you are painting in zoom-in mode with Paintbrush, you are painting individual pixels on a bit map. You can use Paintbrush to edit, change, or recolor any one of these bit maps to suit your individual taste if you like a particular pattern but dislike the colors in the pattern. Figure 29.4 shows the Desktop Pattern editing feature.

Windows uses a file format that's recognizable by the filename extension of .BMP. When you see a filename that ends with the extension of .BMP, it means that the file contains a bit map of an image suitable for display on your screen by Windows.

You can also review bit-map files using Paintbrush, the paint program that comes with Windows. Don't be alarmed if the image you see when using Paintbrush is just one segment of the image that Desktop arranges for display as desktop wallpaper. Windows tiles the screen (as it does with your program group windows) with the desired bit map until the screen is filled with the bit-map image.

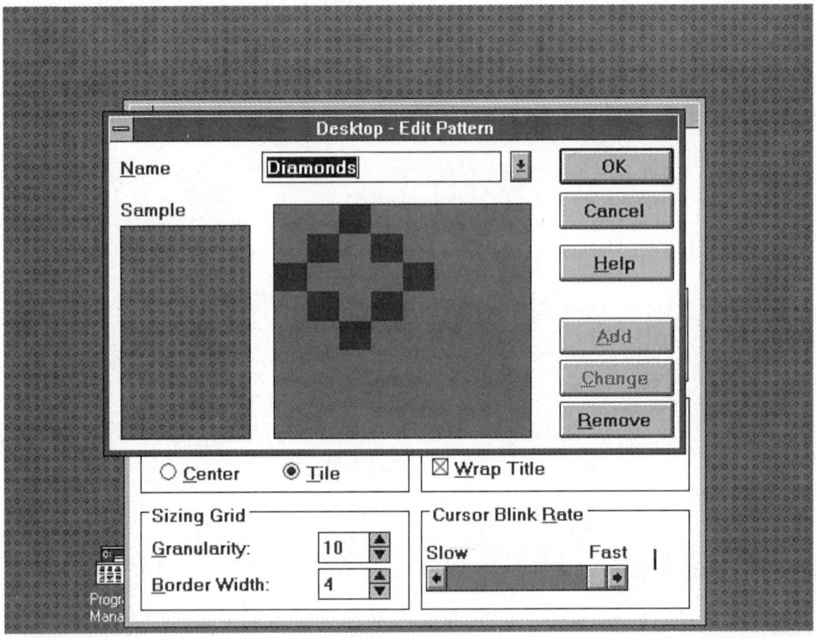

Figure 29.4. Editing the Diamonds desktop pattern.

Windows 3.1 also comes with a screen saver utility that you can modify to taste, called (cleverly enough) Screen Saver. Screen Saver is maintained from the Desktop section of Control Panel. You can, of course, install any of the many screen saver utilities offered for sale in shareware and commercial software channels. Figure 29.5 shows one of the screens available with the Windows 3.1 Screen Saver.

These purchased utilities manipulate and display bit maps to show screen images that can be static or moving. You can make your own bit maps and incorporate them into many of the popular screen saver utilities by using their built-in bit-map handling modules.

There are some bit-map designs that have become so popular they are included in virtually every screen saver package offered. Images such as fish in an aquarium, simulations of a vessel moving through a field of stars, and text messages moving across the screen have become commonplace as screen savers. These images are simply manipulated bit maps.

Figure 29.5. The Mystify screen saver.

29

The Good, the Bad, and the Ugly

Yes, we now have the power to make our eyesight degrade prematurely through the use of excessive color combinations and unreadble screen arrangements. On the up side, we have many more bit maps and other options to choose from. With the benefit of beauty comes the reality of what it takes to maintain it. This next section discusses some of the ins-and-outs of working with the user-definable screen enhancements that come with Windows 3.1.

The Memory Requirements

Most Windows consultants advise you not to use bit-map wallpaper if you are having memory shortage problems. Remember, a bit-map

image is the display of a bit map loaded into memory. If you have
chosen to display a bit map as wallpaper, the bit map has to stay in
memory, regardless of the tasks you perform or which programs you
use. If you have an 80286 machine with 1M of memory, the use of
wallpaper can be downright limiting.

Tip: If Windows displays an alert box warning you to close extra
windows to free memory, you may only need to remove a resident
bit map from memory to solve the immediate problem of low
memory resources. If you have loaded a bit map to be used as wallpaper, use Control Panel Desktop to select none in the wallpaper
drop-down list box provided. This removes the bit map from
memory and gets your system out of panic mode.

Hard Drive Hogs

Bit maps are really a lot of fun. Like anything, though, too much of a
good thing has an adverse effect. Bit maps can get very big. The bit
maps that come with Windows 3.1 take a total of about 264K. Some bit
maps can be up to 4M each, depending on the colors and the complexity. Therefore, you lose about a quarter of a megabyte to these pretty
pictures. This does not include other bit maps that you may have loaded
onto your system.

Many people experiment with background wallpaper and settle into
using just one, deleting the rest. You still have them for future use on
your installation diskettes, if you change your mind, and you free space
for other files. The more you pile onto your hard drive, the longer it
takes your drive to perform its work.

Tip: If you want to keep multiple bit maps on your hard drive, but
you don't plan to use them right away, you may want to compress
your bit-map files using any one of the popular file compression
utilities available. Bit-map (and most other graphic) files can often
be compressed to within 10 percent of their original size with no
side effects. You can compress files on floppies, too. This saves a
lot of space. This is the reason why Microsoft sent them to you in
compressed form. The only drawback to compressing bit-map files
is that you can't review the compressed file without expanding it
first.

The Phenomenon of Screen Clutter

Some people find the wallpaper bit maps that come with Windows distracting, simply from a standpoint of being too busy. When you are using a wallpaper bit map and you have multiple windows open, some things can definitely get lost on the screen. Figure 29.6 is an illustration of a screen that is definitely too busy.

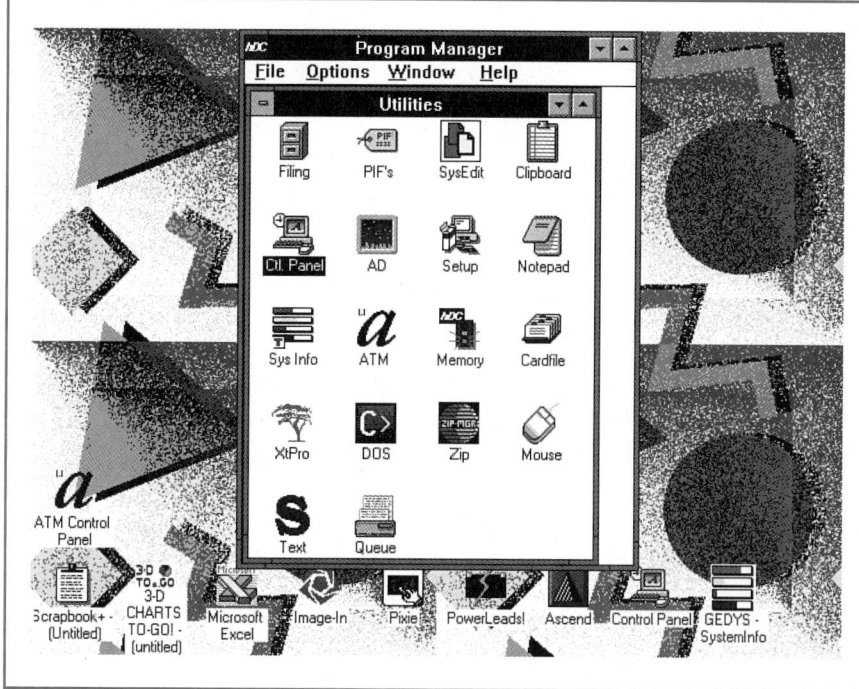

Figure 29.6. This screen is too cluttered to be of any real use.

29

If you keep font managers, spoolers, or other TSRs minimized (you may not have a choice) on your desktop, these icons can get lost. It's like finding your keys in a pile of desk rubble. You can cram too much on a display screen just as you can on a desk. Even the largest work surfaces become unmanageable when you demand too much from the available work space.

We really don't need to continually view all minimized icons, do we? Until Microsoft finds a way to keep minimized icons in a dedicated group that can itself be minimized, we all have to deal with the growing screen clutter along the base of our displays.

Tip: Keep your icon titles as short as possible. Not only does this reduce clutter, but your icons require agreement less space on your desktop and in your group windows. Windows 3.1 does allow the wrapping of icon titles. Use Control Panel Desktop to turn this feature on or off.

Color Combinations

You can manipulate all the colors on your screen by accessing the Colors utility (the icon looks like three crayons) found in the Control Panel Window. Figure 29.7 is an example of colors that do not contrast well enough to allow easy reading of the text.

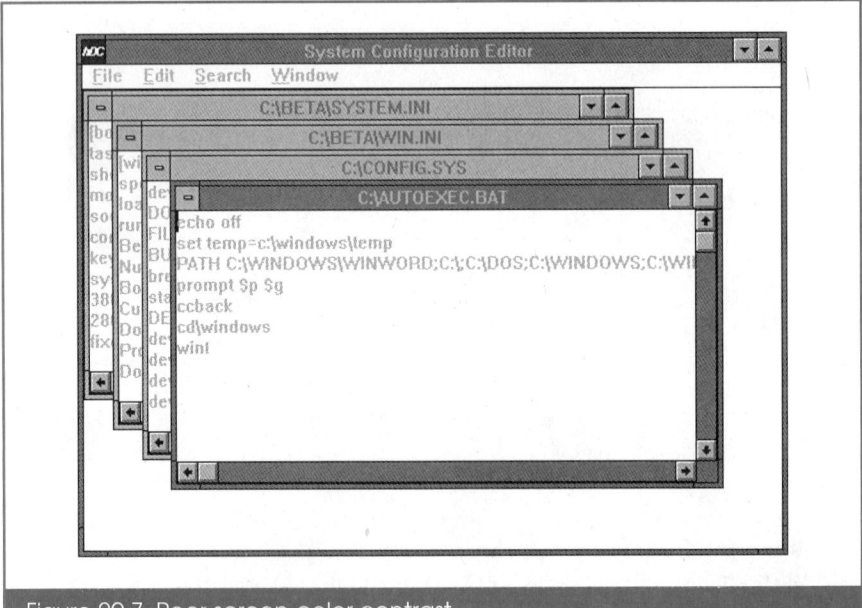

Figure 29.7. Poor screen color contrast.

It is generally advised that you select colors because they are pleasing from the standpoint of being easier on the eyes. High contrast color combinations can be very difficult to adjust to.

Depending on the lighting in your work area and the contrast level being delivered by the video hardware, color contrast can be tiring. If you must discern between characters and backgrounds of extremely similar (or extremely dissimilar) shades, your eyes have to work harder to do so.

Tip: Advice on how to ease the stress on your eyes when using computers can be obtained from the American Optometric Association at no charge. This organization publishes a pamphlet called "VDT User's Guide to Better Vision" that describes steps you can take to minimize long-term damage to your eyes if you use computers as part of your job. For a copy of this and other materials, you can call or write

> Communications Center
> The American Optometric Association
> 243 North Lindbergh Boulevard
> St. Louis, MO 63141
> (314) 991-4100 ext. 219

Many companies publish materials on this subject and make them available to employees for the asking.

See Chapter 7, "Control Panel," for more on selecting colors and wall-paper.

Getting Your System to Display More Stuff

This section talks about display resolutions and this business of seeing more on your screen at one time.

The 800x600 or Super VGA Mode

The Setup program can be run in two ways: One runs when you double-click the Setup icon from within Windows, and the other runs from the DOS prompt. Take a look at Chapter 25, "Changing Your Configuration." It's the easiest way to change how your monitor displays differing resolution levels from within Windows 3.1.

If your video card and monitor support high resolution mode, you can now change the way your system displays information entirely from within Windows with Version 3.1. Figure 29.8 shows the Program Manager window on a 640x480 resolution screen.

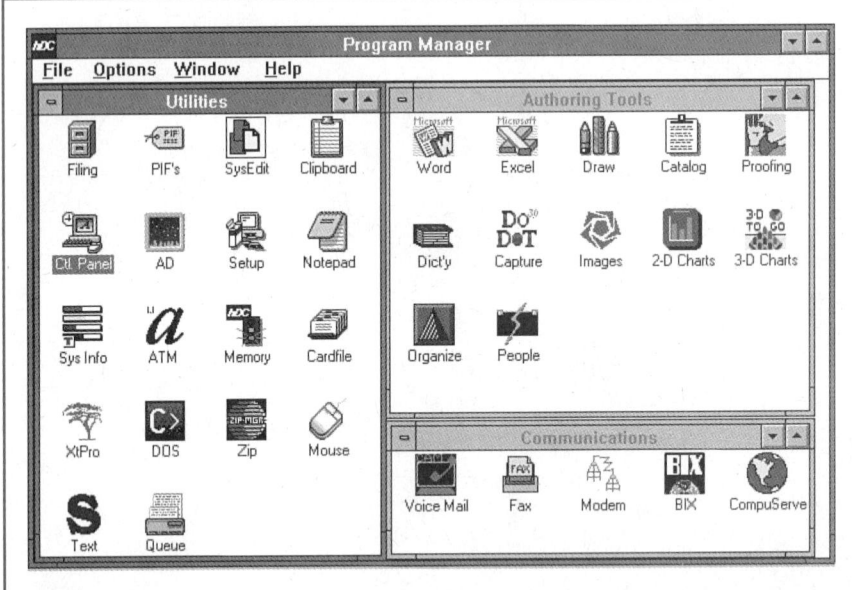

Figure 29.8. 640x480 resolution.

The benefit of working in a higher resolution mode is that you can get more on a screen at the same time. You can have more windows open, more icons in each window, and more text visible while editing a document if you go up one or two levels of resolution.

When you selected VGA from the Setup program as you installed Windows, a line in your SYSTEM.INI file was modified to reflect the name of the driver that would provide you with 640x480 resolution (if you have a VGA monitor).

If you were one of the many people who recently purchased a 1024 monitor, you may be able to get more on your screen than you are now. The two common modes above 640x480 are 800x600 and 1024x768. Figure 29.9 shows 800x600 resolution using the same image found in Figure 29.8. Notice the amount of gray background compared to the size of Program Manager.

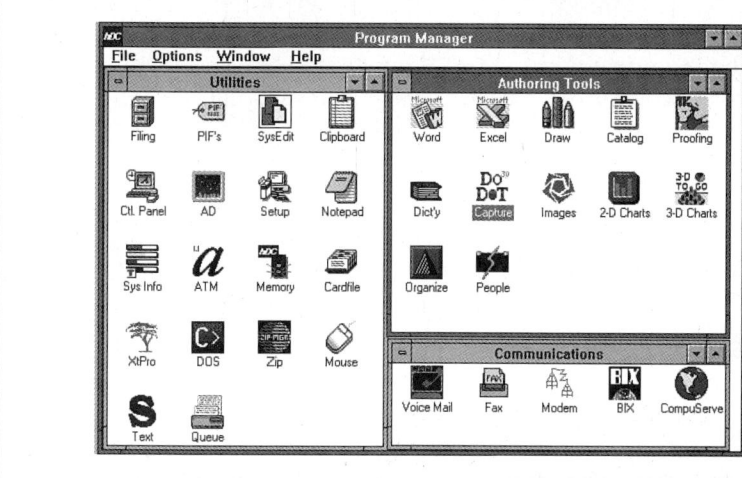

Figure 29.9. 800x600 resolution.

To use the 800x600 mode, your monitor must be of the multisync variety or a multiscanning monitor. The manual provided with your monitor should indicate if the monitor supports 800x600 resolution. Figure 29.10 shows the same image in 1024x768 resolution. Again, the Program Manager window is displayed on the gray desktop. Notice the size of this Program Manager window compared to the gray desktop.

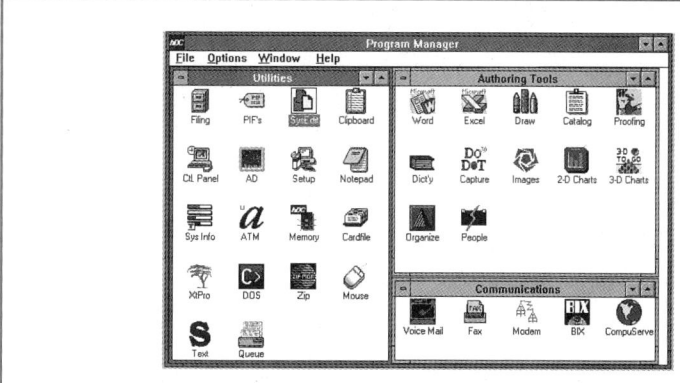

Figure 29.10. 1024x768 resolution.

If the video card supports the higher resolutions as well, the upgrade to 800x600 is simpler than some people realize. You may find you like

640x480 better, because colors may be more vivid, text may be more readable, and your screen refreshes somewhat faster; you can always go back to 640x480 if you choose. The Windows 3.1 800x600 screen driver is the fastest yet included with Windows. You may not recognize any decrease in speed when you use this driver.

Warning: It is always wise to make a backup copy of your SYSTEM.INI file before you amend it, just in case you make a mistake. Be very careful that you don't change anything else in the SYSTEM.INI file. One false move and Windows may not run at all.

If you are currently using 640x480, and your hardware is capable of 800x600 resolution, maybe you'd like to see what such higher resolution is all about. For you nuts-and-bolts types that refrain from doing things the easy way (in this case by using Windows Setup) here is a procedure for doing so from within Windows *without* using Setup.

1. Open Notepad.

2. Open the SYSTEM.INI file found in your Windows directory. This is the file you need to amend.

3. Scroll down through the [boot] section until this text appears:

   display.drv=vga.drv

   Figure 29.11 shows you what text to look for in the SYSTEM.INI file.

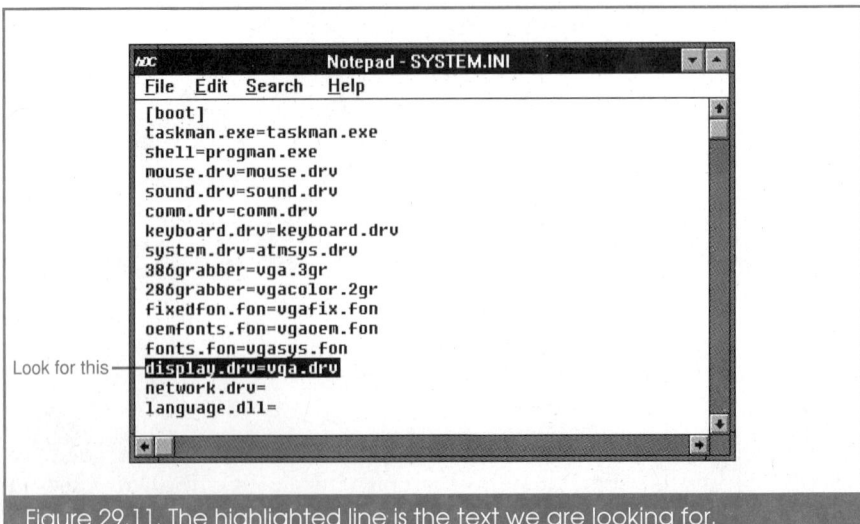

Figure 29.11. The highlighted line is the text we are looking for.

4. To see what your monitor looks like in 800x600, replace the text
   vga.drv with supervga.drv. Leave no spaces in this line of text. Do
   not make any other changes to the SYSTEM.INI file. Save the file
   and close Notepad.

5. Now, get out your Windows diskettes. Find the screen driver
   for 800x600 resolution. The file you need is SUPERVGA.DR_.
   Copy it to your windows\system subdirectory. Figure 29.12
   shows the highlighted filename after it is copied to the
   windows\system subdirectory using File Manager.

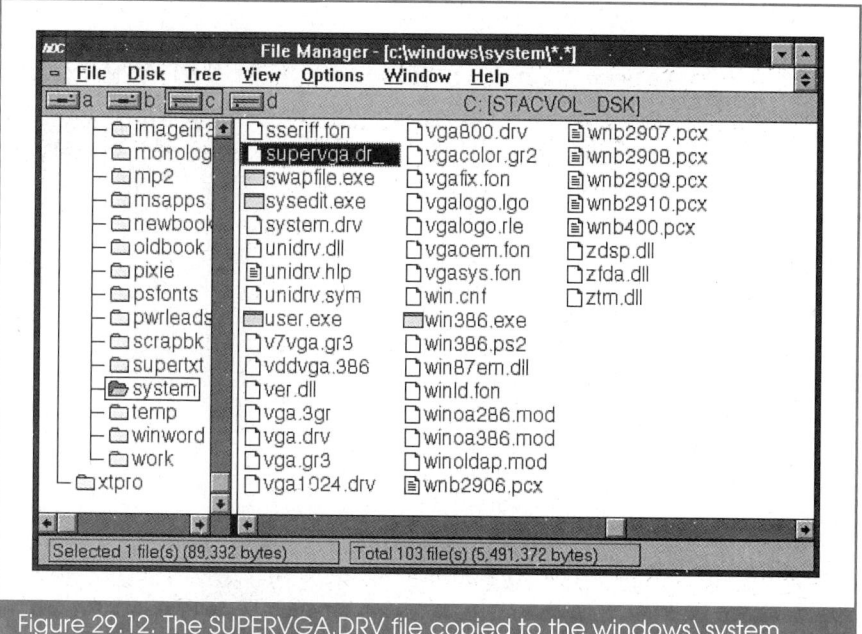

Figure 29.12. The SUPERVGA.DRV file copied to the windows\system
directory.

6. Because the files on your Windows 3.1 diskettes are in compressed form, you need to expand your driver before you can use
   it. You should find the file EXPAND.EXE on the same diskette
   that held the driver (.DR_) file that you just copied to the
   windows\system subdirectory. From the Windows floppy disk,
   copy EXPAND.EXE to the windows\system subdirectory.

7. Open either Program Manager or File Manager and select the **File**
   Run command. The next step is to expand the compressed driver

29

file. Type this in the text box provided, and then press the Enter key or the OK button.

```
EXPAND.EXE SUPERVGA.DR_ SUPERVGA.DRV
```

8. Windows should have shelled-out to DOS, and quickly completed the file expansion process. Your new driver is now ready to use.

9. Save your settings, then leave and restart Windows.

If you replaced the text vga.drv with supervga.drv, your screen now displays about 20 percent more than it did in 640x480 mode.

Of course, in packing more pixels onto the same size screen, Windows makes everything appear smaller in the higher resolution modes. You can now add more icons than you could in 640x480 mode and view more of your open windows.

If you want to change back to the 640x480 mode, just run this procedure again, but place display.drv=vga.drv where it was in the [boot] section of the SYSTEM.INI file, and you are all set.

Warning: If you have misspelled the driver name or anything else in the line of text in the SYSTEM.INI file, Windows beeps during the next startup and stall with the Windows logo still on the screen. If this happens, check your SYSTEM.INI file with a DOS-based text editor or use Setup from the DOS prompt to correct the error.

Warning: If you are wrong about your hardware's capabilities in rendering the Super VGA (800x600 and 1024x768) display mode capabilities, you may get unpredictable results when Windows restarts. In this case, use a DOS-based text editor to open the SYSTEM.INI file and reinsert the statement display.drv=vga.drv in place of your recent changes to fix the problem.

If you don't have a way to edit the SYSTEM.INI outside of Windows, use Windows setup from the DOS prompt as you did when you first installed Windows. Tell Setup you have a VGA monitor, and Windows takes care of the rest.

The 1024x768 Mode

If your monitor and card are capable of displaying 1024x768 pixels, you can install the driver that came with your video card the same way you installed the 800x600 driver with the procedure described previously. Check the documentation that came with the video card's Windows screen drivers. You can get a peek at what 1024x768 resolution looks like by identifying the driver intended for that resolution on the diskette(s) that came with the video card, and then substituting that driver for SUPERVGA.DRV using the procedure detailed earlier in this chapter.

29

CHAPTER

30

Windows for Advanced Users

This chapter provides perspectives on individual products that represent product categories in the marketplace.

Some of the products described in this chapter and Reference C, "Windows Product Directory," have not proved themselves fully acclimated to the Windows 3.1 environment. Many of the products were intended to run with Version 3.0 only and have not been updated for use with Version 3.1. At the time of this writing, these products could not be exhaustively tested for use with Windows Version 3.1. Most of the manufacturers contacted have verified that they are working to make their product(s) Windows 3.1 compatible. Get competent advice about a product's capability to run under Version 3.1 before purchasing a product for that use.

For a compendium organized by product type of software and hardware products for Windows, see Reference C, "Windows Product Directory."

What Are Utilities?

Since the early days of MS-DOS, there has been a big market for utilities, programs that help you in your regular work but do not really have a purpose of their own. There is still a huge demand for utilities that help make MS-DOS easier to use, such as file managers and so on.

Fortunately, Windows comes with many of its own utilities, such as Program Manager and File Manager, so the need for Windows utility software is less than it is for MS-DOS. Because many PC users think they might need utilities, however, a large market for them exists. The programs described in this chapter help you perform Windows tasks easier than you might without them.

There are literally hundreds of utilities available for Windows, and more are being produced every day. Because many of us get our most basic utilities from bulletin boards and other forms of public-access information retrieval systems, you must consider that files you load into your computer may contain viruses that can cripple your machine and/or network. It's a good rule of thumb to check floppy disks containing files in one floppy drive, with an antivirus utility in another floppy drive—before you copy it to any system.

This chapter gives you an overview of what you can expect from utilities and shows you some of the better utilities available. It shows you what some of the utilities look like when you are running them, so you can get a feel for what to expect when you look at utilities or buy the ones discussed here. For more information on Windows programs and utilities, see Reference C, "Windows Product Directory."

Many of these utilities are distributed as shareware, a method that allows you to try the software for free before you buy it. You can get shareware from computer networks like CompuServe, from local user groups or from friends. Unlike commercial software, it is all right for you to copy shareware and give it away.

However, if you use the software after you try it, you must pay for it. All shareware comes with instructions on how much the software costs and where to send your registration fee. You are on your honor to pay for shareware. Because most shareware is as sophisticated as commercial software, it is worth the fees that are requested, which are often under $50.

Warning: Before copying a program and giving it to a friend, be sure that it is, in fact, shareware. It is illegal to copy commercial software for any purpose other than making a backup copy. Copying software deprives companies of money for research and makes it less likely that the software will be improved in the future or that new and interesting programs will become available.

Program Manager Replacements

Because Program Manager is the base point of your work, getting comfortable with it will help you feel more comfortable with Windows. Chapter 5, "Program Manager," covers the ways that you can customize Program Manager in detail as well as giving examples of how you might arrange your workspace.

Program Manager is not the final word in convenient ways to start programs, however. Some people prefer to have access to icons that are not included with Windows. Some people prefer fewer icons and just program names; some people want both. Because of the variety of preferences of Windows users, many companies have created Program Manager replacements that perform the same basic task as Program Manager: They start programs for you. Most of these utilities include additional features that work within the interface of the program. Some combine the functions of both Program Manager and File Manager.

NewWave

30

Although Windows is plenty for most people, it can be made better. If you use more than one program at a time, you know that getting programs to transmit information back and forth takes a fair amount of work. If you have many tasks that require you to work in steps, even the batch programs described in Chapter 32, "Windows Programming Environments," may not be enough. NewWave is an environment that enhances Windows by making these things easier.

NewWave uses the concepts of objects to make describing and executing your tasks easier. An object is anything that has properties and tasks associated with it. Instead of running programs or dealing with files, you use objects which can be combinations of files, programs, actions, and associations. Figure 30.1 shows the main window for NewWave. Many programs now available know how to link into the NewWave environment, and NewWave knows how to deal with many (such as non-Windows programs) that do not.

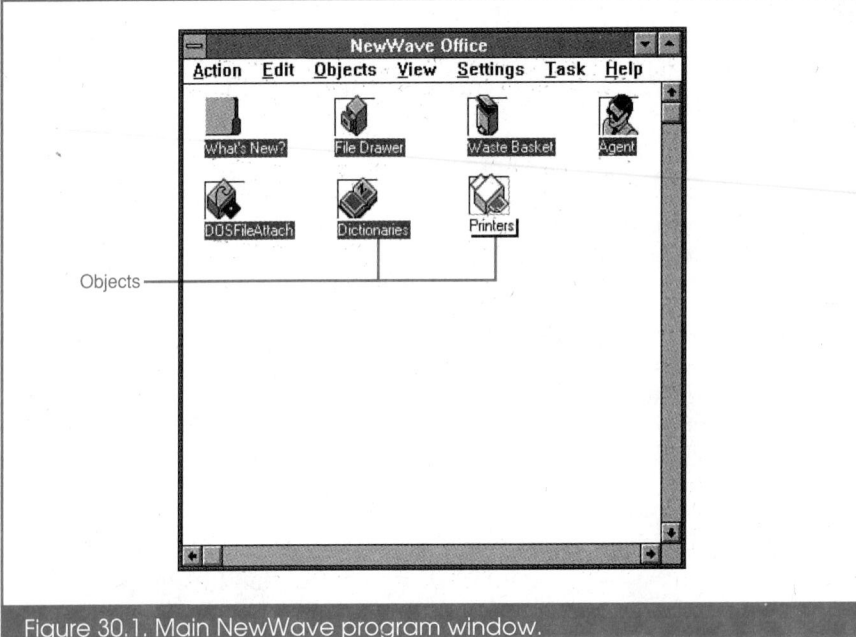

Figure 30.1. Main NewWave program window.

NewWave comes with a few of its own programs. NewWave Write is a word processing program that can be the center of your writing. It can link to any other NewWave object easily. The NewWave Write window, shown in Figure 30.2, looks much like any other word processor. However, it integrates information much better because it knows how to deal with tasks, such as electronically mailing a request to someone and incorporating the relevant part of their answer into a document.

One of the big advantages of using NewWave objects rather than individual pieces is that different people can "check them out" over a network. Because objects often represent work, the person doing the work simply takes the object to his or her PC and uses it. This prevents two people from accidentally using the same files at the same time. It also lets you control work flow more easily.

Another significant advantage of NewWave objects is that you do not need to worry where files are kept on a disk. If you move a file, NewWave allows you to reattach it within the object without having to change text files and so on. This file independence also helps when you clone objects, because you can start with the same files or replace them with new ones, making objects act like templates.

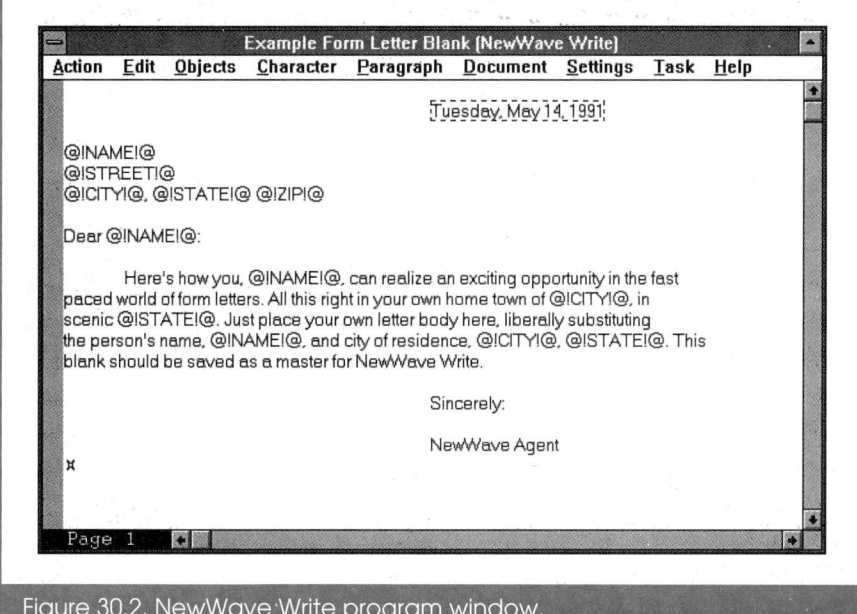

Figure 30.2. NewWave Write program window.

Hewlett-Packard
(800)752-0900

30

Aporia

For many, icons are the best way to work, and Aporia makes a desktop of just icons. There are no program groups, as in Program Manager, so you can move your icons wherever you want. Figure 30.3 shows a typical window in Aporia. The icons at the far right (such as Desk and Trash) come with Aporia, whereas the other icons are created for programs. Aporia refers to icons as "tools" because they help you perform tasks.

As you can see, Aporia also has a replacement in the form of trees and directory windows for File Manager. You can have multiple trees displayed so that you can see the directories of all your disks at the same time.

Each tool can be associated with a program and/or document. You can customize your icons and group them however you want. Creating tools is easy. For example, you can drag a program from a directory window onto the desktop to create a tool for that program. You do not need to use pictorial icons: You can use text only. You can set many preferences in Aporia, as shown in Figure 30.4.

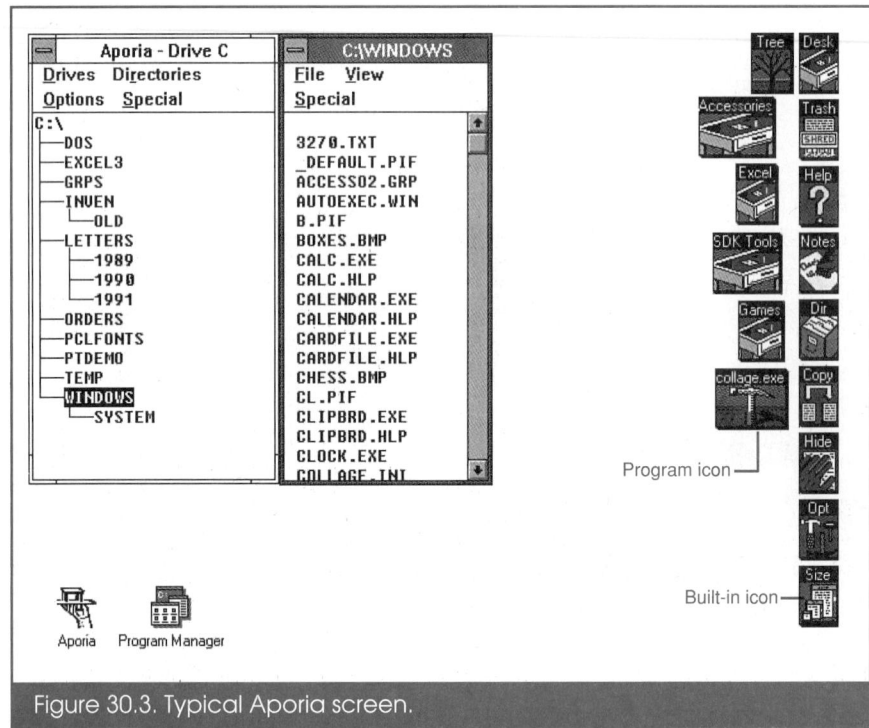

Figure 30.3. Typical Aporia screen.

Tools are kept in desktops. You can show all the tools easily by opening the desktop. Double-clicking the desktop hides them again. Aporia lays out your tools, so they do not obscure other tools; note how this is different from Program Manager where windows often overlap unless you take great pains to arrange them.

New Tools Inc.
P.O. Box 3269, Church Street Station
New York, NY 10008
(800)395-1532

Metz Desktop Manager

If you prefer long descriptive text to icons, Metz Desktop Manager makes a good replacement for Program Manager. As you can see from Figure 30.5, Desktop Manager does not use icons. Instead, you can give extensive

names (up to 38 characters) for each action and place these names any-where in one of the two windows available to you. You can also create your own windows, similar to program groups in Program Manager.

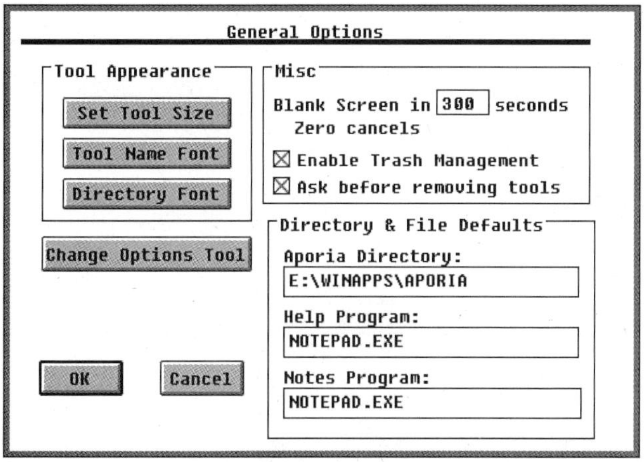

General Options

┌─Tool Appearance─┐ ┌─Misc────────────────────────┐
│ Set Tool Size │ │ Blank Screen in 300 seconds │
│   │ │   Zero cancels   │
│ Tool Name Font │ │ ☒ Enable Trash Management   │
│   │ │ ☒ Ask before removing tools │
│ Directory Font │ └─────────────────────────────┘
│   │ ┌─Directory & File Defaults──┐
│ Change Options Tool │ Aporia Directory: │
│   │ │ E:\WINAPPS\APORIA   │
│   │ │ Help Program: │
│   │ │ NOTEPAD.EXE   │
│   OK   Cancel │ │ Notes Program: │
│   │ │ NOTEPAD.EXE   │
└─────────────────┘ └────────────────────────────┘

Figure 30.4. Options dialog box.

30

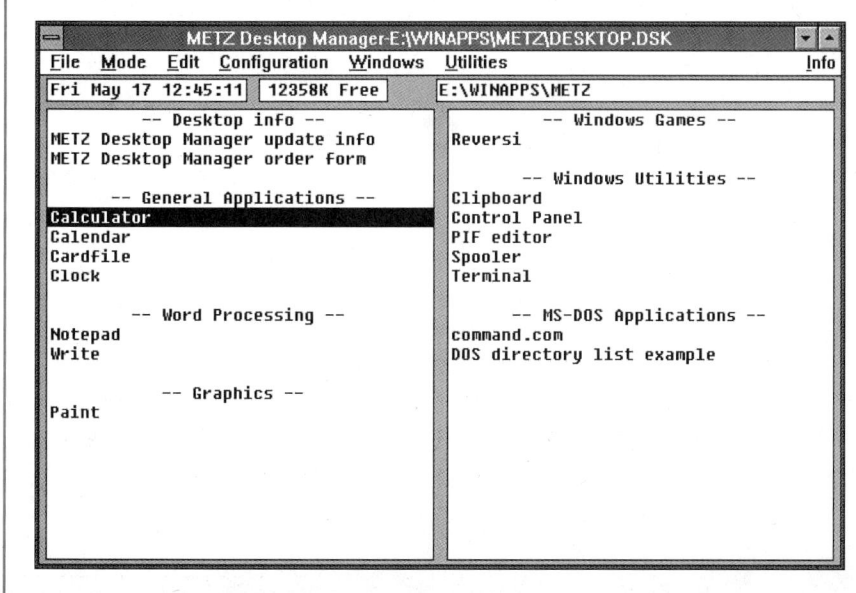

Figure 30.5. Initial screen for Metz Program Manager.

Each line has a text description, program name, optional parameters, and the default directory, as shown in Figure 30.6. The Select buttons enable you to search the disk for filenames to add in each entry. You can also duplicate lines quickly. Thus, customizing the windows for your own programs and documents is fairly painless.

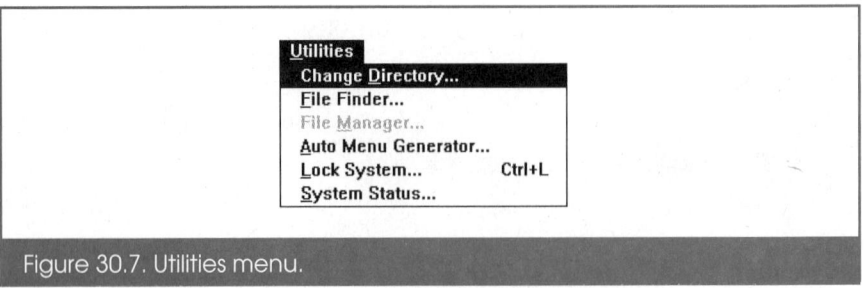

Figure 30.6. Parameters for each line.

There are also simple utilities, as shown in Figure 30.7. For example, with the **U**tilities **F**ile Finder command, you can look on any disk for a file with any name.

Figure 30.7. Utilities menu.

Metz Desktop Manager even has a small replacement for File Manager. With the Utilities File Manager command, shown in Figure 30.8, you can look at two parts of a directory tree and copy, move, rename, and delete files. If you don't use File Manager much, Desktop Manager will probably take care of 90 percent of your File Manager use.

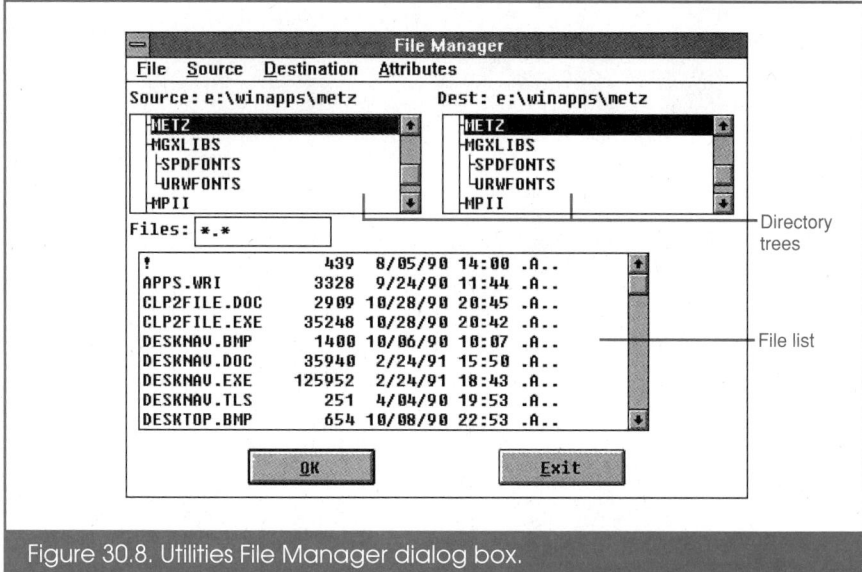

Figure 30.8. Utilities File Manager dialog box.

METZ Software
4018 148th Avenue NE
Redmond, WA 98052
(206)869-6292

30

Command Post

Command Post looks a great deal like File Manager, although its menus and many of its features are closer to Program Manager. Figure 30.9 shows a typical Command Post window.

Although the main screen lists the files in your directory, Command Post's power is in its menus. You can add and change the commands in any menu with the built-in command language. The language is very simple, and nonprogrammers can probably learn it in a few minutes. Figure 30.10 shows an example of the language.

Wilson WindowWare
2701 California Avenue SW, #212
Seattle, WA 98116
(800)762-8383

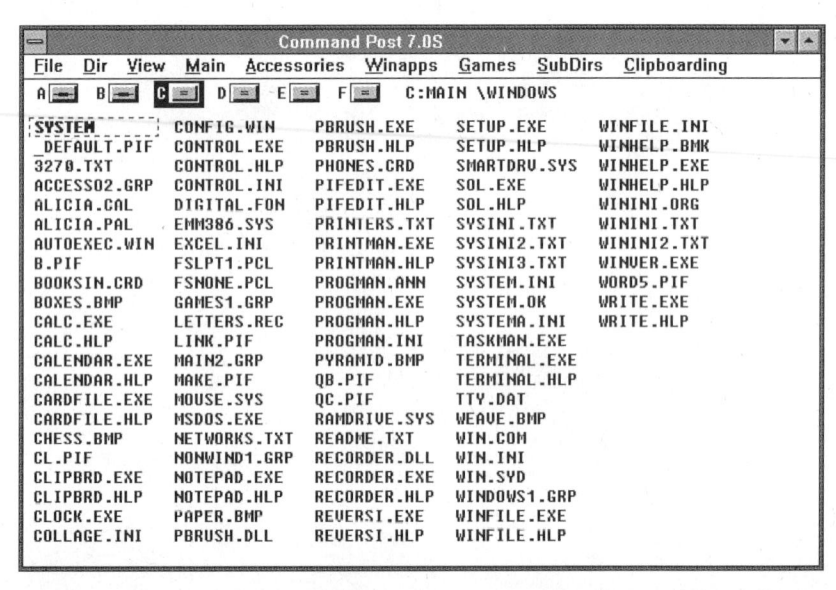

Figure 30.9. Main Command Post window.

Figure 30.10. Example of Command Post language.

WideAngle

Screen clutter is a major problem for most Windows users. If you have a few windows open, you have trouble navigating from one program to the other without going through Task Manager. Even then, you spend a lot of your time resizing windows so that they line up correctly.

WideAngle eliminates the need to wade through windows. It essentially gives you nine windows's worth of space by enabling you to move programs off screen and jumping to those subwindows quickly. Figure 30.11 shows an example of how you might set up your larger desktop with WideAngle. Even in this example, only five of the possible nine windows are used.

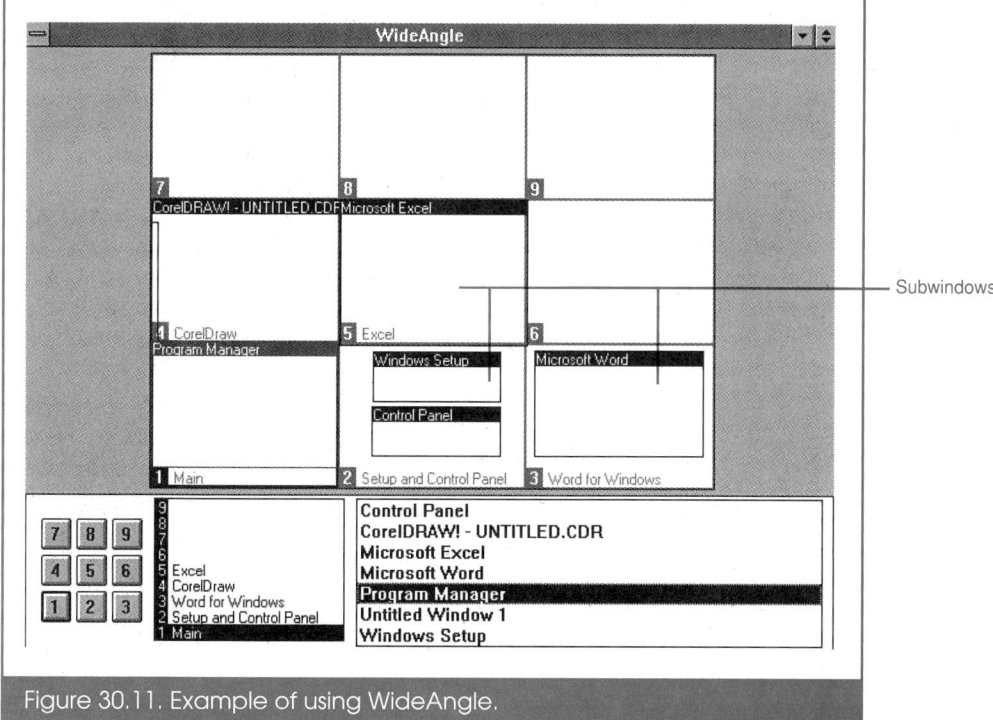

Figure 30.11. Example of using WideAngle.

Normally, WideAngle stays on your desktop as a small control panel, as shown in Figure 30.12. When you want to switch to a new window, you

30

simply click the associated button. You can move windows from one subwindow to another by dragging, as you normally would.

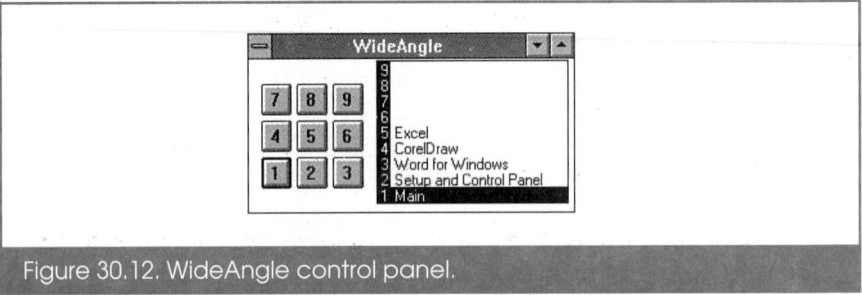

Figure 30.12. WideAngle control panel.

You can configure WideAngle to start all your programs in the correct windows when you start Windows. Although this starts Windows more slowly, it makes your workspace easier to handle. You will find many other uses for WideAngle, such as arranging your work into projects.

Inner Media Inc.
60 Plain Road
Hollis, NH 03049
(603)465-3216

File Manager Replacements

If you go back and forth to File Manager to perform tasks, such as looking at directories or copying files, you know that it can be tedious. The way that File Manager lays out windows can also be bothersome if you have specific ways you want to see your windows. Many companies have developed File Manager replacements to help make file management easier and quicker.

File F/X

Most people use File Manager to look at their directory tree and only one file list at a time. The File F/X uses this concept and always leaves both views fully visible, as you can see in Figure 30.13. The directory list always shows all information, so there is no need to resize either window.

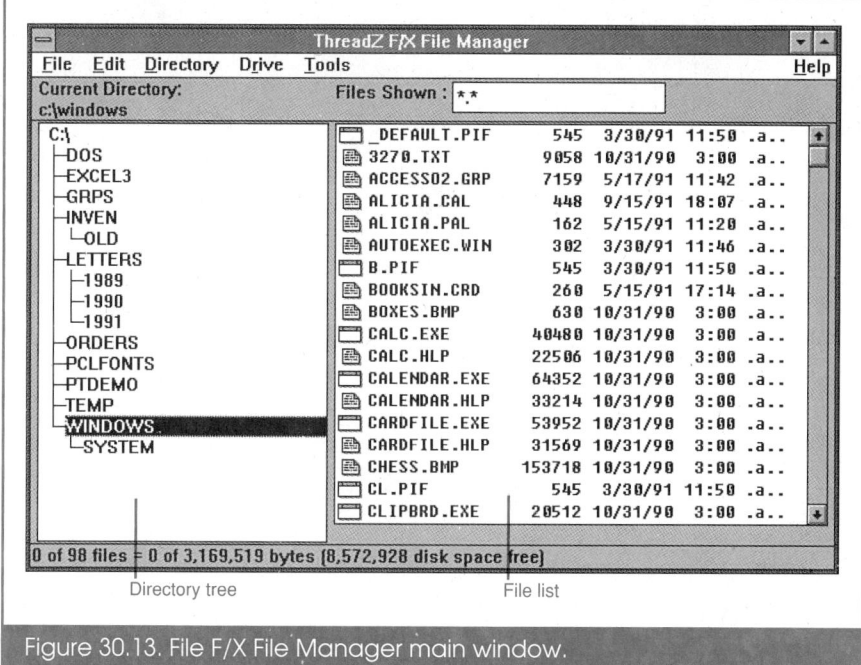

Figure 30.13. File F/X File Manager main window.

30

The File and Directory menus have all the options of File Manager. There are some useful additions, such as the Directory Status command, which tells you a great deal about the current directory, such as how much disk space the directory takes. This is shown in Figure 30.14. The Tools menu allows you to add any commands you regularly use so that you can start programs from the main window.

The File F/X package goes well beyond being a File Manager replacement, however. It also comes with two programs for searching: one for file names and one for text in files.

▲ The F/X Find program, shown in Figure 30.15, enables you to look through an entire disk or specific directories for files with certain attributes. In one command, you can specify many paths to search and can also limit the search by date. Once you have found files, you can run them with any associated program. For example, if you are searching for Write documents, the Run Using section automatically pops up WRITE.EXE so that you can select a file and run it immediately.

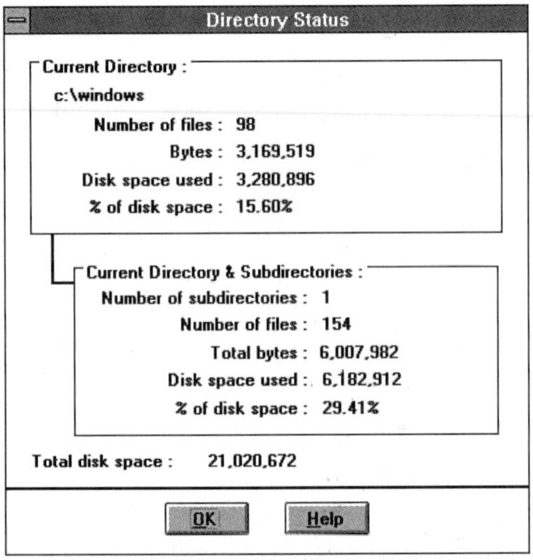

Figure 30.14. Directory Status command.

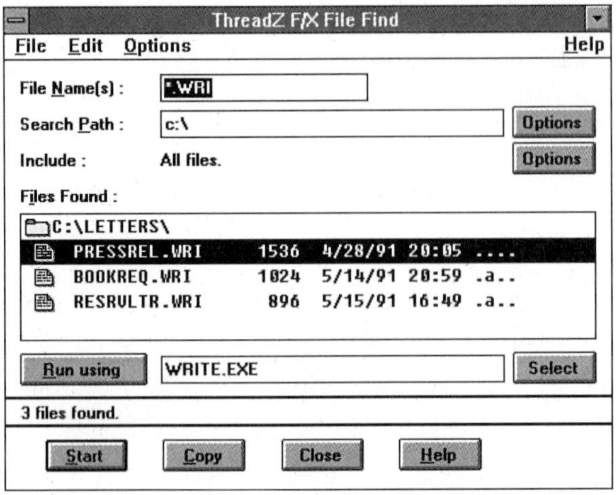

Figure 30.15. F/X File Find window.

▲ F/X Text Search is like F/X File Find in that you have a lot of flexibility in the search parameters, as shown in Figure 30.16. Note
that you can search for text in any type of file, not just text-only
files. When you find the document you want, you can run its associated program automatically.

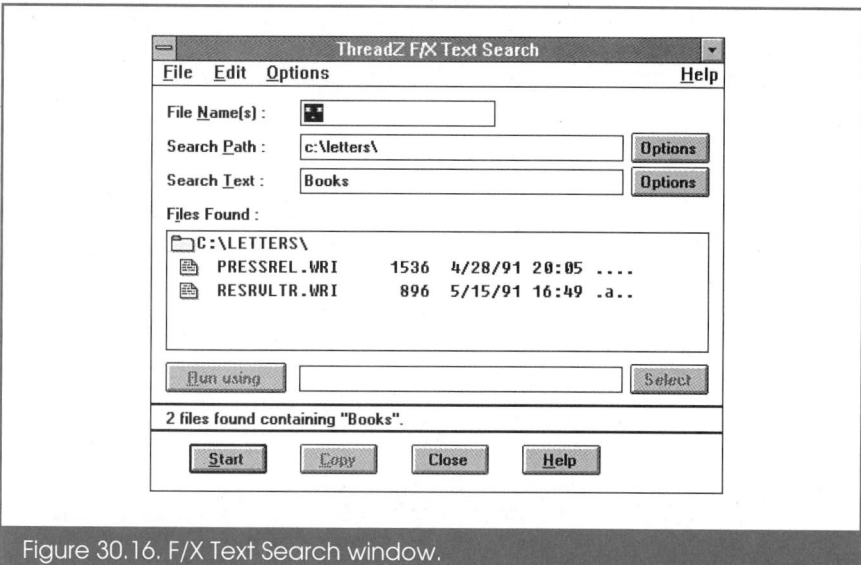

Figure 30.16. F/X Text Search window.

▲ F/X File Undelete undeletes files from your disk. It works like standard undeleting programs by looking for files recently deleted that have not been overwritten.

▲ ThreadZ Task Manager is like a cross between the Tools menu in the main F/X File Manager and Windows Task Manager. The Task Manager window is shown in Figure 30.17. After you run ThreadZ Task Manager, it replaces Windows Task Manager. For example, pressing Ctrl-Esc brings up the ThreadZ Task Manager.

30

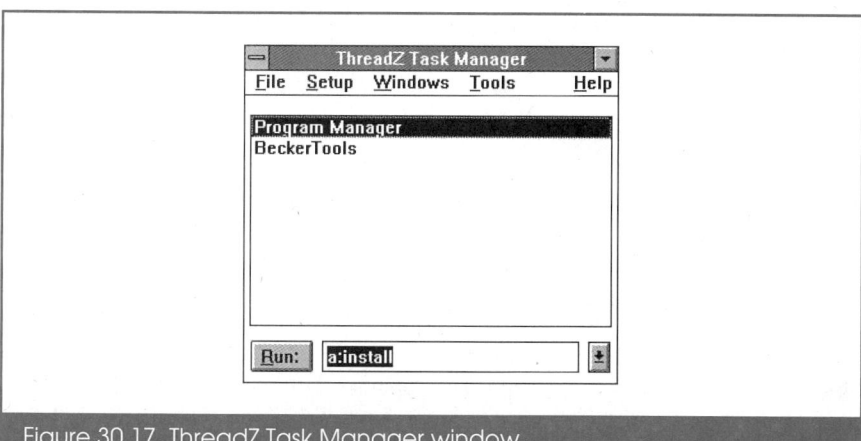

Figure 30.17. ThreadZ Task Manager window.

METZ Software
4018 148th Avenue NE
Redmond, WA 98052
(206)869-6292

BeckerTools

Because many file actions have a source and a destination, the
BeckerTools program window displays two directories at once, as shown
in Figure 30.18. In addition, most of the commands you normally give
from menus are also available as buttons. Like other File Manager
replacements, you can start programs from BeckerTools by double-
clicking them.

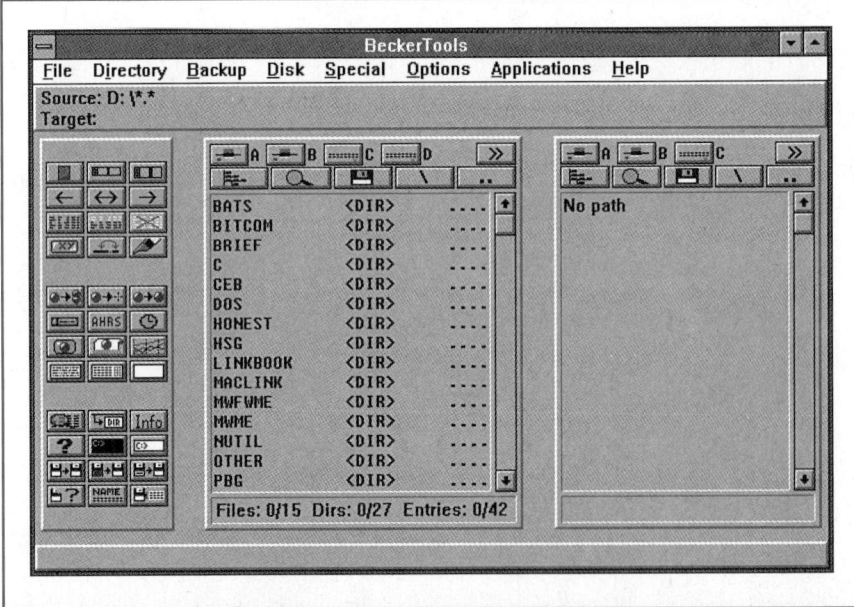

Figure 30.18. BeckerTools program window.

BeckerTools has a complete set of commands for handling disks, including one that lets you pack information onto diskettes in a very efficient
manner. Instead of copying files to the floppies and thereby leaving
blank space on diskettes, BeckerTools packs files and later unpacks
them.

You also get a great deal of flexibility on how files are shown on the screen. For example, Figure 30.19 shows the Directory Display Pattern command that you can use to choose the display for each panel.

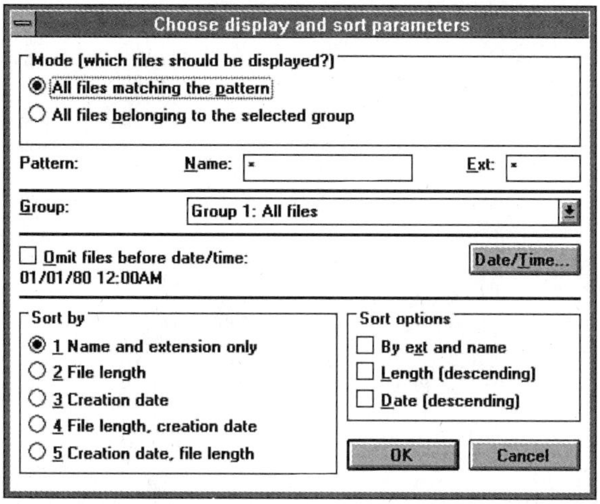

Figure 30.19. Directory Display Pattern dialog box.

Abacus
5370 52nd Street SE
Grand Rapids, ME 49512
(616)698-0330

File Shuttle Xpress

File Shuttle Xpress uses the same concept as F/X File Manager but adds the capability of transferring files from one PC to another. This is particularly useful for getting files from a laptop computer to your PC. The main window is shown in Figure 30.20. Most of the options are the same as in File Manager. You can customize the Applications menu to add your own programs.

The package allows you to connect two PCs through their parallel ports for file transfer. The other PC must be running File Shuttle Express, but it does not have to be running under Windows. The software comes with two versions of the program, the second of which has most of the same features but runs under regular MS-DOS.

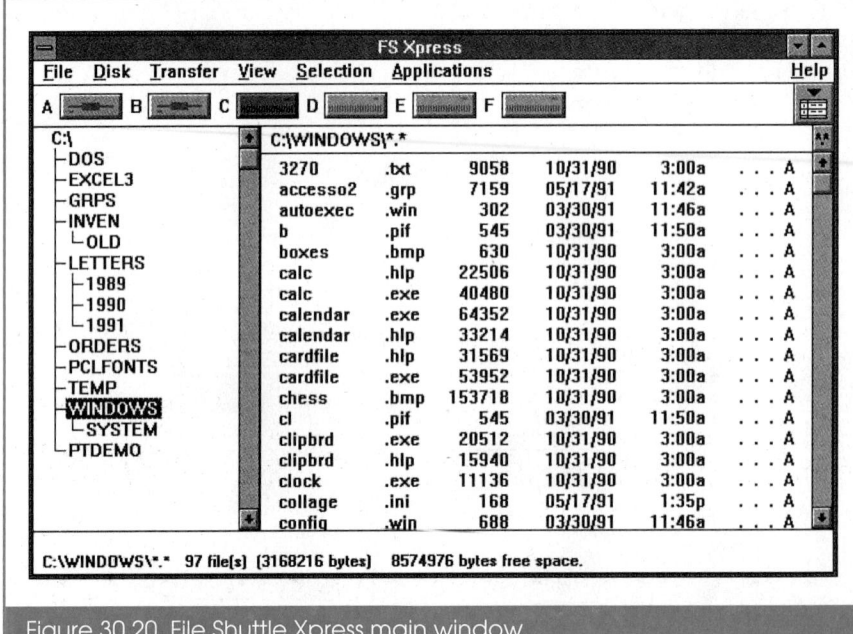

Figure 30.20. File Shuttle Xpress main window.

To transfer files, select them and give the **Transfer Send** command. As the files are sent, you see the dialog box shown in Figure 30.21. The transfer is very fast, usually around two megabytes a minute.

Figure 30.21. Transfer Send dialog box.

GetC Software Inc.
Box 8110-182
Blaine, WA 98230
(800)663-8066

FileApps

hDC takes a very different approach to file management with FileApps.
Instead of making a single program that handles all file management,
FileApps are "MicroApps" that launch from the control menu of any
program. You first run a program, like FileApps (and FirstApps,
described later in this chapter), that changes the standard control
menu to one that launches MicroApps from its own menus that extend
from the Program Manager control menu. Running one of these programs makes all the programs available at any time in any Windows
program without having to switch to another program, such as File
Manager. Figure 30.22 shows the new control menu with many hDC
programs loaded into it.

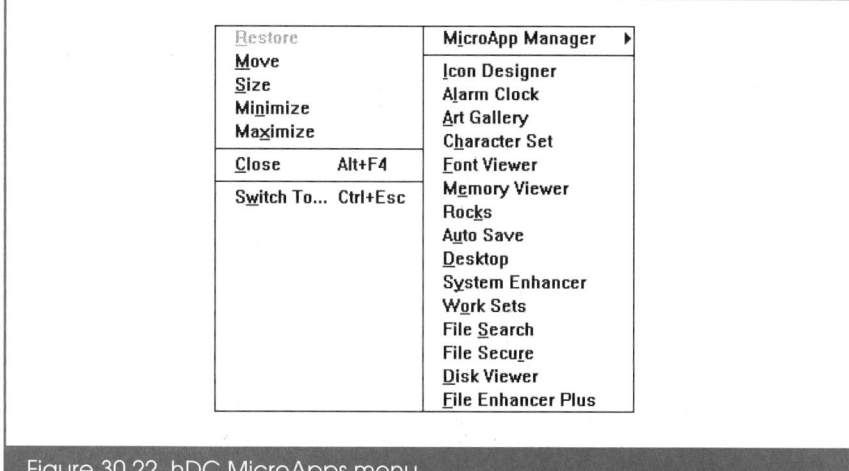

Figure 30.22. hDC MicroApps menu.

There are five FileApps programs.

▲ File Enhancer Plus is a menu with the common file commands
used in File Manager. These are shown in Figure 30.23. Note that
there is also an undelete command that works like many programs under MS-DOS.

30

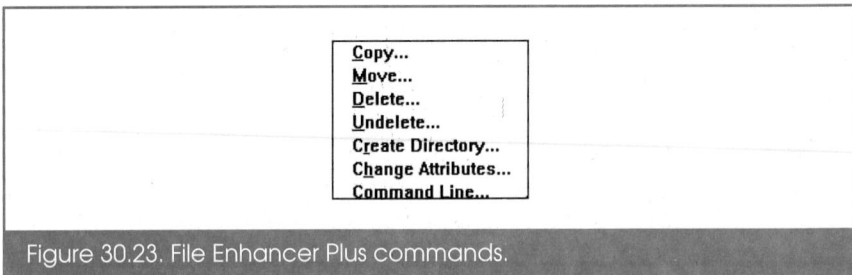

Figure 30.23. File Enhancer Plus commands.

▲ Disk Viewer gives you a graphical overview of your disk or directories, as shown in Figure 30.24. As you move the magnifying glass icon up and down, you can see a detail of the files on your disk.

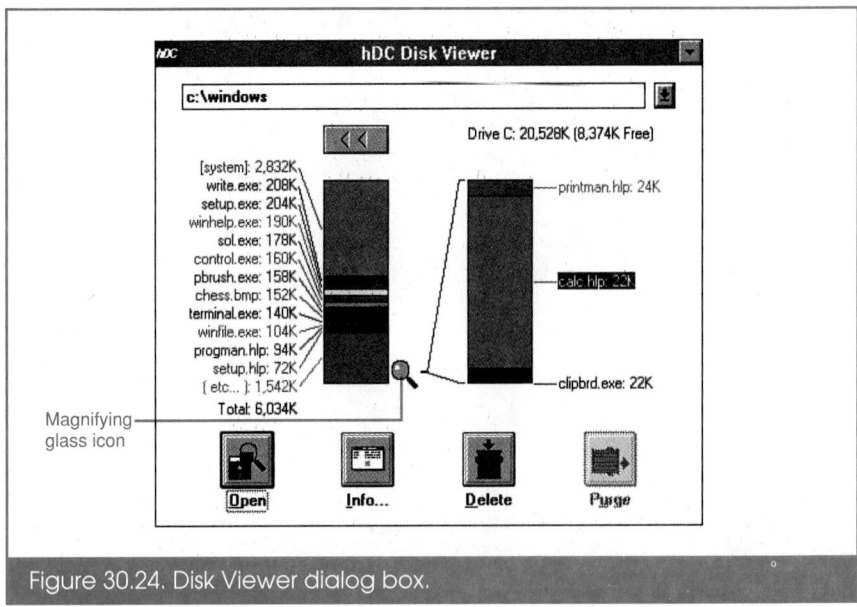

Figure 30.24. Disk Viewer dialog box.

▲ File Search enables you to look for files with particular file names or text strings in the files. You can specify where to look and even the date on the file. Figure 30.25 shows the options available for searching. The Find Files choice is a drop-down list with many common searches already included, such as *.txt and just documents. After you find the files, you can open or copy them by selecting their names from the list.

These features can be turned off and on with simple keystrokes or can be changed with the Access program, shown in Figure 30.27. The Adjust menu has commands for each feature.

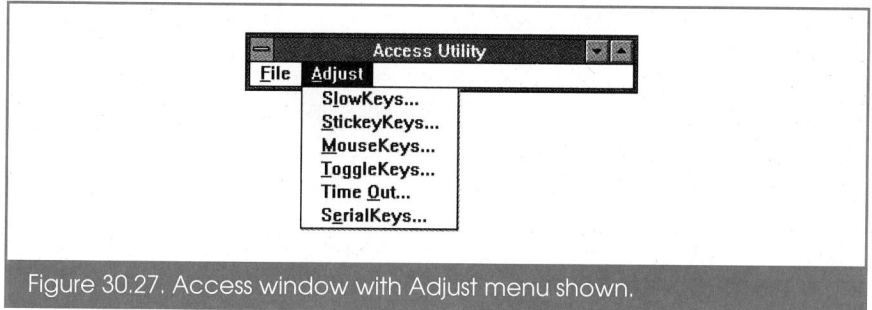

Figure 30.27. Access window with Adjust menu shown.

For example, the **Ad**just **SlowKeys** command is shown in Figure 30.28. Figure 30.29 shows the **Ad**just **S**tickeyKeys command.

Figure 30.28. SlowKeys Adjustment dialog box.

The Trace Access Pack comes in the Windows Supplemental Driver Library. These drivers are also available online on many services such as CompuServe. To order a copy of the Supplemental Driver Library, call Microsoft Customer Support at (800)426-9400.

30

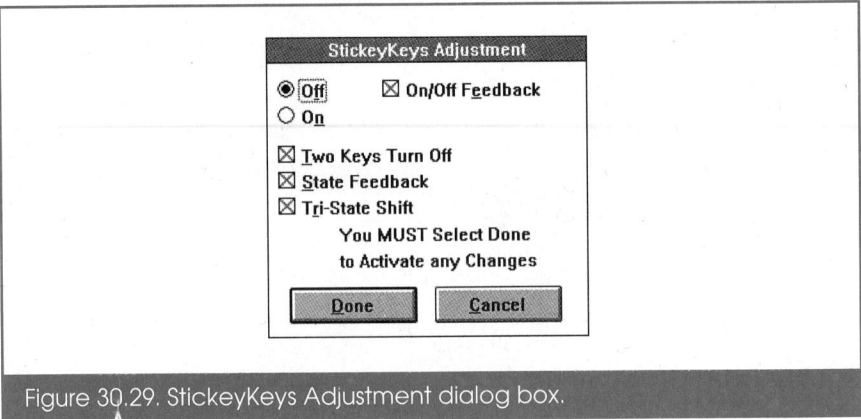

Figure 30.29. StickeyKeys Adjustment dialog box.

Information Software

Working with information management software is easier than it's ever been. All these products are part of the new generation of information software that does not require programming knowledge. With some of the best ones, you don't even have to know how to type. It's that easy!

ObjectVision's intuitive interface is destined to become the major player as a front-end for Borland's next generation of Windows database management products.

Lotus Notes is a pure information management package that allows the user to increase the size of images embedded in text for easier viewing.

Recent advances in attaching text to objects within images makes Thinx a unique solution to detail management.

ObjectVision

Many people find it difficult to organize the data they have available to them. You can use database management systems to create databases of rows and columns, as well as reports on summaries of that data, but going past a single database is usually difficult. ObjectVision is a simple Windows program that you can use to create forms for data entry and reports. You use standard Windows actions such as dragging and double-clicking to design your forms.

Each form you create with ObjectVision can contain multiple fields. Figure 30.30 shows a typical ObjectVision form. It looks like a standard form that you would fill in on paper.

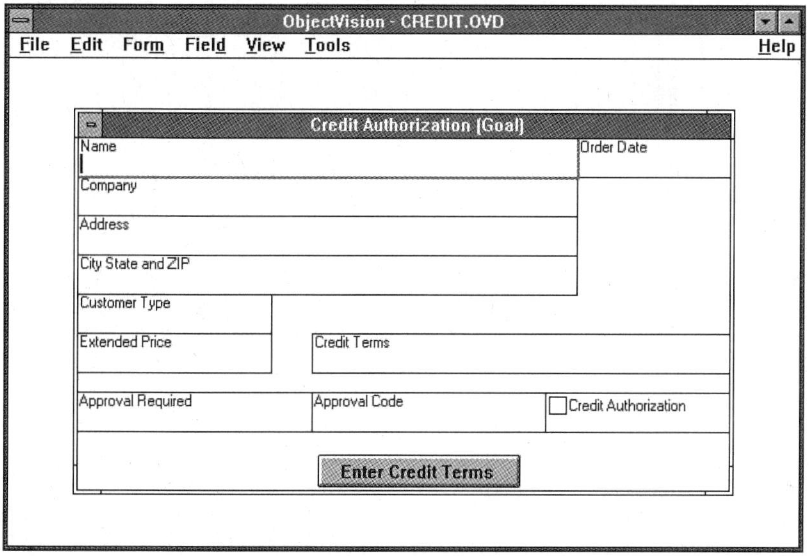

Figure 30.30. Typical ObjectVision screen.

30

As you know, on many forms you do more than fill in information: you often look up information for particular fields. For example, in the Approval Required field, there might be a chain of decisions to be made for credit approval. ObjectVision supports decision trees that show how a decision is made, possibly accessing another database in the meantime. Figure 30.31 shows a typical decision tree.

The great advantage of ObjectVision is that you can access data from a variety of databases, such as Borland's Paradox, dBASE-compatible files, plain text files, Btrieve files, and through *dynamic data exchange* (the ability to update a file created by another application from a file in the current application), as shown in Figure 30.32. Because you can read and write to these files, you can use ObjectVision as a Windows front-end for databases that might otherwise run only in MS-DOS.

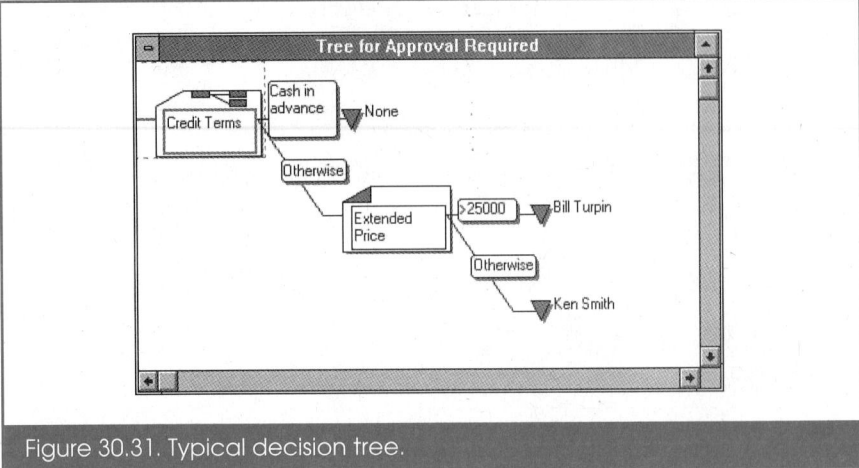

Figure 30.31. Typical decision tree.

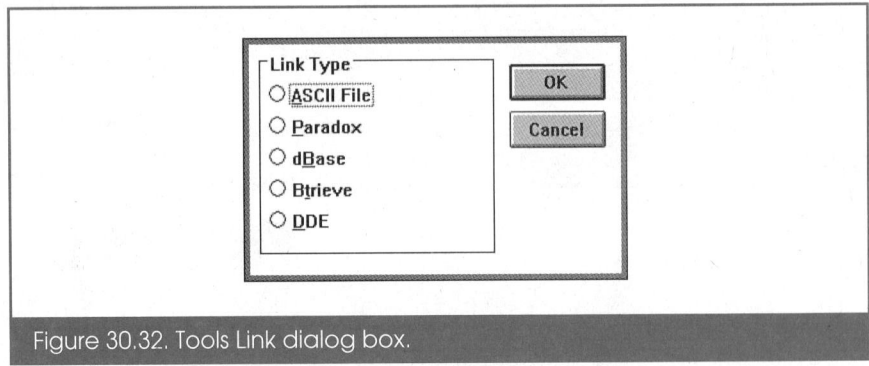

Figure 30.32. Tools Link dialog box.

Borland International
1800 Green Hills Road
Scotts Valley, CA 95067
(408)438-5300

Notes

If you work with many groups of people, you know how hard it is to coordinate projects or even communicate. Even with electronic mail, it is often difficult to share information in a structured fashion. Notes,

from Lotus, makes this type of group interaction much easier by integrating many types of work into a single program. It works particularly well for people who are scattered over a large area.

Notes works with other programs, so you can pass information in a variety of formats. The basic structure of a Notes document is a form. There are many views for the information in a particular form. For example, a field in one form may be a heading in a different form.

Notes also contains all the communications needed to support the software. Any updates to shared documents are Noted, or sent automatically to people who have requested updates as they occur, and documents can be duplicated where necessary on a network. Notes even comes with its own electronic mail that is seamlessly integrated with its other functions. Even laptop computers not hooked directly to the network can share information in a coherent fashion. Notes also supports dynamic data exchange and object linking and embedding, described in Chapter 33, "Exchanging Data with the DDE."

Lotus Development Corp.
55 Cambridge Pkwy.
Cambridge, MA 02140
(800)327-6148

30

Thinx

Most information systems keep pictures as pictures and handle all other information, such as numbers and text. With some database management systems you can have graphics in the same records as numbers and text, but they are not really related. Thinx is one of the first products to integrate pictures and numbers into one document.

For example, Figure 30.33 shows a Thinx layout of an office. It looks like a document from a standard drawing package, but it was made with Thinx! However, each symbol in the office layout has information associated with it. For instance, the large oval in the upper-left corner represents a conference table.

Each item in a layout can have as much data associated with it as you want. For example, if you double-click the conference table, you see the information associated with it, as shown in Figure 30.34. Note that you can modify the information or add to it in any way you want.

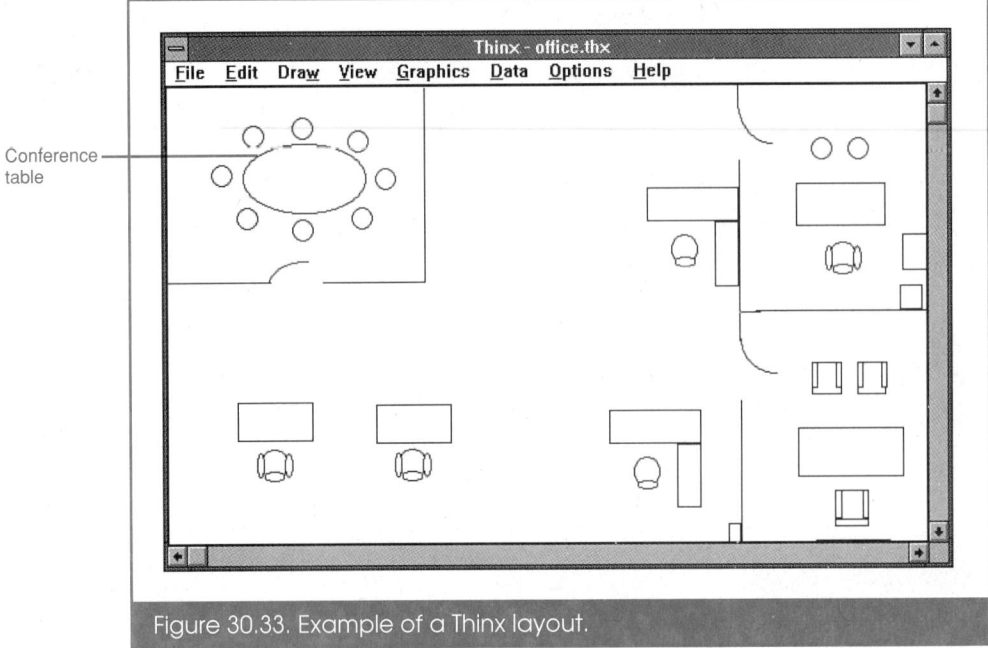

Figure 30.33. Example of a Thinx layout.

Figure 30.34. Information for the conference table.

After you create a document with various objects and enter the data for all the objects, you can combine the data in many ways. For example, you might want to know how much all the furniture in the office costs. You could create a formula, such as shown in Figure 30.35, that sums the cost of each item. You could also make formulas that find the most expensive item, the total number of chairs, and so on. Thinx also has a report generator.

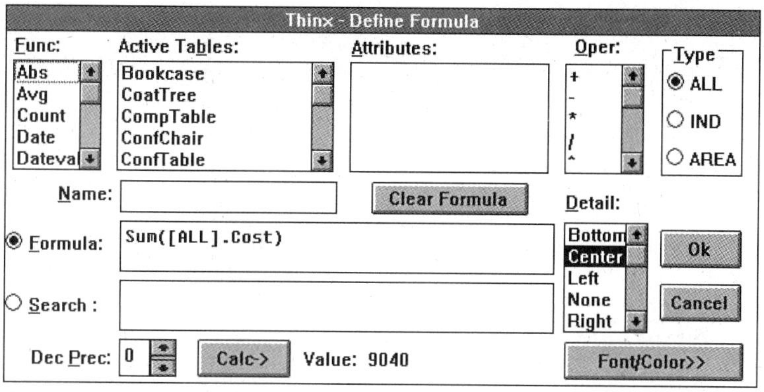

Figure 30.35. Equation for summing costs.

Thinx has a variety of uses. You could draw schematics for a machine and use it to produce a bill of materials. The information for an object can include dates, so you can produce a report about how long it will take to do something by looking for the last date in the drawing. If some data changes, such as the price of the conference table, you can quickly select all the objects, change the data accordingly, and then check the new total.

Bell Atlantic Corp.
13100 Columbia Pike
Silver Spring, MD 20904
(800)388-4465

30

Microsoft Resource Kit

The Microsoft Resource Kit (MRK) was devised to provide a hardcopy bank of undocumented data for Windows users. The original documentation that came with Windows 3.0 was well written but did not describe what was going on behind the scenes when the software was performing a task.

The volume is full of technical detail on the inner workings of Windows. A competent Windows glossary, trouble-shooting guide, Windows configuring guide, and character-based applications tips are all part of the MRK.

The package also includes diskettes with Windows utilities. Some of the programs contained on the diskettes are

hDC Memory Viewer	Memory usage is displayed in stacked bars within a dialog box.
Microsoft System Description	Hardware and device driver details are collected and presented for the purpose of troubleshooting via a company's tech support. This utility is character based.
Icon Draw	Icon creation tool.
Icon Tamer	Icon editing tool.
Icons	An Icon library for general use.
Windows 3.0 fish	An aquarium for your screen.
Microsoft Productivity Pack forWindows	Learning tools described elsewhere in this chapter.

Microsoft Corporation
One Microsoft Way
Redmond WA 98052-6399
(800)642-7676

Windows Screen Savers

If you leave a single image on a screen for a long time, that image will "burn" into the phosphors. If you have the same picture on the screen all the time, the phosphors in the screen become less effective at the places of most intensity and often leave a "ghost" of the image. This is less true of newer color monitors than of older monochrome monitors, but it can still be a problem.

Screen saving programs prevent this burning effect by changing the image on the screen when it is not in use. If you leave your computer on all the time, there are probably hours when you are not even looking at the screen. A screen saver dims or blanks the screen after a preset amount of inactivity. You can get the original screen back simply by moving the mouse or pressing a key on the keyboard.

Early screen saver programs just blanked the screen. This sometimes made it look like the computer had been turned off. Later screen savers

put a small message on the screen and moved that message around so that the message did not burn into the screen. In the past few years, the small images that screen savers leave have become much more complex and entertaining.

There are many Windows screen savers available, some for free. For example, there is a screen saver that comes with the Microsoft Entertainment Pack, which is described later in this chapter, and with the Metz Desktop Manager described previously. The most entertaining screen savers provide a wide variety of images. The most useful ones offer many options about what starts and stops the blanking process.

Intermission

Intermission lets you choose from over 30 different images and actions that appear on your screen when the screen is blanked. The dialog box for configuring Intermission is shown in Figure 30.36. You can specify a corner for the mouse to go into if you want to start the blanking immediately or to prevent the blanking from happening even after the elapsed time. You can also specify what actions stop the blanking and return your computer to your Windows screen.

30

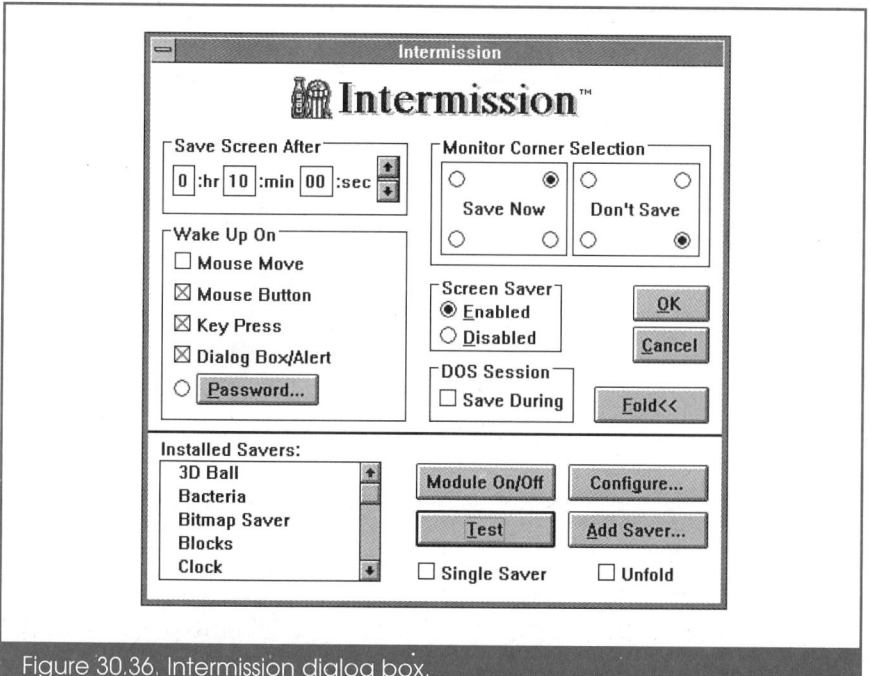

Figure 30.36. Intermission dialog box.

ICON Simulations
648 S. Wheeling Road
Wheeling, IL 60090
(708)520-4440

After Dark

After Dark has many of the same features but also some additional ones that make it more useful. For example, you can associate a password with your screen so that you have to give the password to get out of the screen saver. This prevents unauthorized people from seeing your screen or using your PC when you are gone. After Dark is also network compatible and the network system administrator can have his or her own screen password. Many of its screens are also pretty to watch, such as Flying Toasters, shown in Figure 30.37.

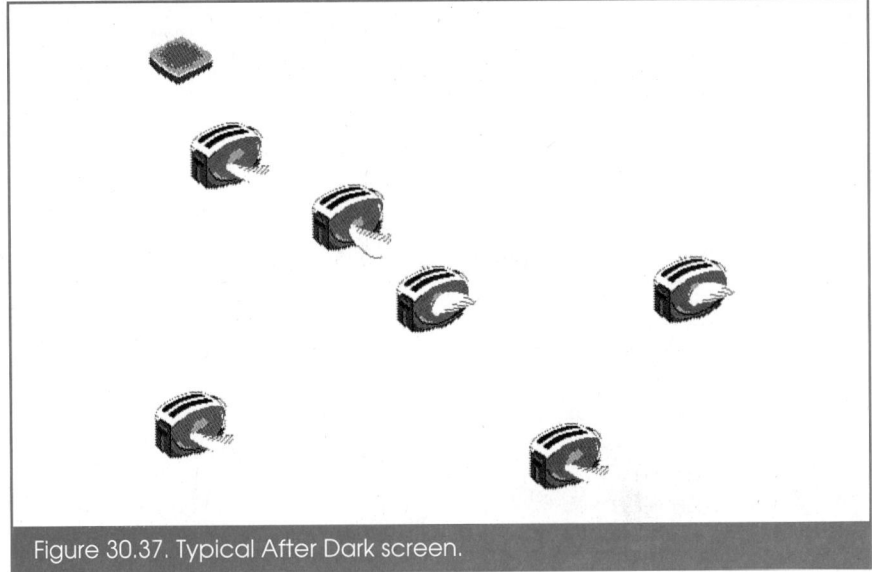

Figure 30.37. Typical After Dark screen.

Berkeley Systems
1700 Shattuck Avenue
Berkeley, CA 94709
(415)540-5535

Screenplay

Another screen blanker, Screenplay, puts up geometric patterns in bright colors. As you can see from the dialog box in Figure 30.38, you can control almost every aspect of how the patterns are produced.

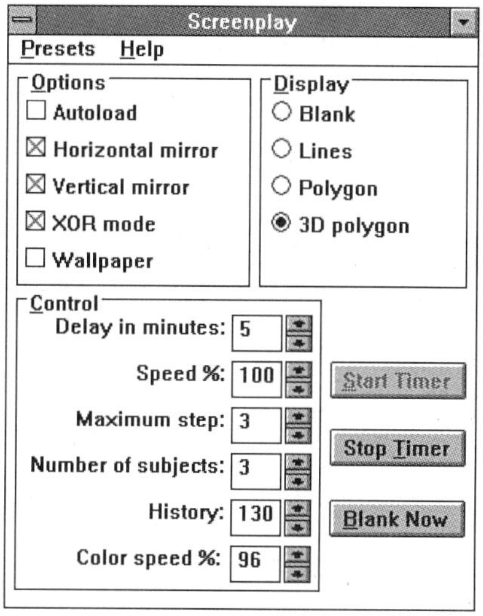

Figure 30.38. Screenplay dialog box.

Kamyan Software
1228 Robin Drive
Carol Stream, IL 60188

Utilities that Continually Monitor Status

Windows can give you minor status reports on memory, available disk space and remaining system resources. You can find products on the market that do this graphically, and real-time (What-You-See-Is-What's-Going-On). There is always a more slick approach to doing anything. It's a real education watching what goes on while programs execute, do their thing and then release memory (do they really?), and close. Here is one product that does just that.

30

One of the utilities that comes with a package called Windows Tools by Gedys is SystemInfo. This utility presents a dialog box on your screen that indicates

▲ System details

▲ Drive information

▲ Processor activity

▲ Mouse parameters

▲ Port assignment information

▲ Printer details

▲ Free system resources

The really interesting thing about this utility is that it displays some of this data in the form of horizontal bar charts that refresh continually. Even when the dialog box is minimized, the display continues to display miniaturized bar charts that monitor system status.

GEDYS
Rebenring 33
D-3300 Braunschweig, Germany

Network Software

Software designed for use on a network is becoming increasingly popular. Software intended to maximize the effectiveness of a network is the wave of the future with network administrators and managers alike. 1Team is one of the next generation of productivity enhancement products intended for network environments. This utility is designed to support the management of resources over a LAN.

Each user on the network is assigned a schedule. In this way, 1Team works as a project or task manager. A central manager can delegate tasks and schedule meetings for each user via the LAN. 1Team enables a manager to check on complex project and task completion status without calling expensive, nonproductive meetings.

Work-load balancing is supported across the entire staff. Each staff member updates the status of assigned tasks at their own computer. 1Team makes the data available to the manager instantly.

1Soft Corporation
P. O. Box 1320
Middletown CA 95461-1320

Mouse Utilities

Although many people are quite fond of the keyboard, others rely exten-
sively on the mouse. PC mice have two or three buttons, but most programs only use the left button for actions. If you are a mouse fan, you may
find that the right button (and middle button, if you have one) is wasted.

Right On

A small program called Right On helps you get much more use out of
the right button. With Right On, you can make clicking the right mouse
button take an action, such as producing a set of keystrokes or running
a program.

You load Right On when you first run Windows. As shown in Figure
30.39, you can indicate not only the action for a single right or middle
button, but for holding down combinations of the Shift, Ctrl, and Alt
keys with the right or middle button as well. You can also keep different templates for different sets of actions.

30

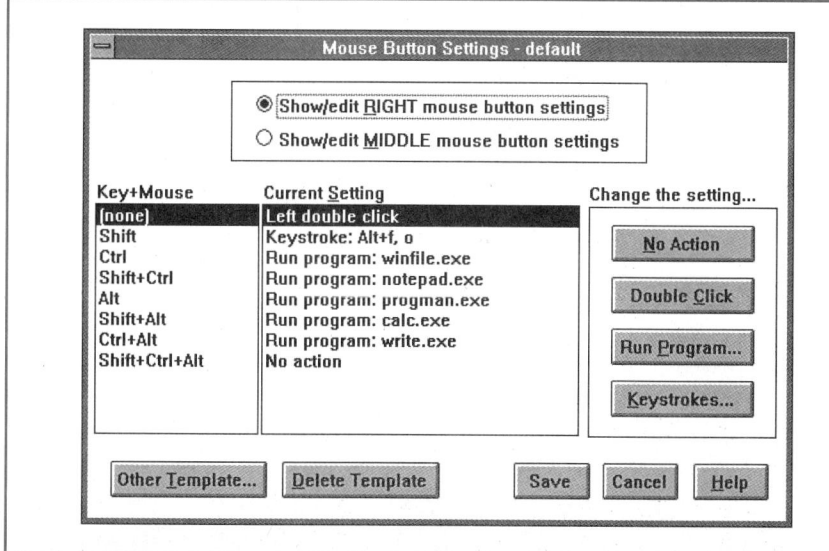

Figure 30.39. Mouse button settings for Right On.

For example, you can cause one of the actions to run any program you want. This is a handy way to bring up File Manager or Program Manager, for example. You can also specify as many as two keystrokes that perform an action, such as Alt-X to exit a program.

Magic Cursor

Another handy utility, Magic Cursor, makes finding the cursor on the screen easier. It allows you to make larger cursors or to make the cursor flash. If you have a Super VGA monitor, it is easy to lose the cursor on the screen. Most people sort of shake the mouse to see where the cursor appears on the screen.

Magic Cursor comes with many predefined cursors, as shown in Figure 30.40. The cursor in the upper-left is the same size as the normal cursor but has the distinctive shadow. The other cursors give you a much larger arrow or distinctive shape to find. You can also specify that all standard Windows cursors be automatically enlarged. Of course, some cursor shapes are not very well applied to some programs, for example, painting detailed drawings with a huge arrow for a cursor (pointer).

Figure 30.40. Magic Cursor dialog box.

Fanfare Software (Right On and Magic Cursor)
9420 Reseda Blvd., Suite 828
Northridge, CA 91324
(818)886-8787

Entertainment Pack

Microsoft's Entertainment Pack is a set of seven games and a screen blanker. The games are quite fun and you can spend hours of time on them. There really isn't much "utility" to the Entertainment Pack; in fact, you can say that it is an antiutility because it gets in the way of doing productive work.

All the games are meant to be played by yourself, although you can compete for scores in Tetris. The seven games are

- ▲ Tetris, the classic "falling tile" game

- ▲ Minesweeper, a game in which you look for mines. This game is included with Windows Version 3.1

- ▲ Cruel, a card solitaire game

- ▲ Golf, a popular card solitaire game

- ▲ TicTactics, standard three-dimensional tic-tac-toe

- ▲ Taipei, a mah-jongg game with many classical variations

- ▲ Pegged, a peg-jumping game

Figure 30.41 shows the window for Taipei, the most addicting of the thought games. Many people think that Tetris is the most addicting of the action games; it is shown in Figure 30.42.

Microsoft Corporation
One Microsoft Way
Redmond WA 98052-6399
(800)642-7676

30

Telecommunications

As you saw in Chapter 12, "Terminal," Windows is a good environment for communications. When you dial another system, it is useful to be able to switch back and forth through your terminal session and other programs. It is also convenient to be able to switch terminal settings with dialog boxes.

Advanced telecommunications software gives you many more features than this, however. Although Terminal can only remember one telephone number, most communications programs can keep a directory of as many numbers as you want. Each number can be associated with different communications settings. Most communications programs also handle a multitude of protocols for transferring binary files.

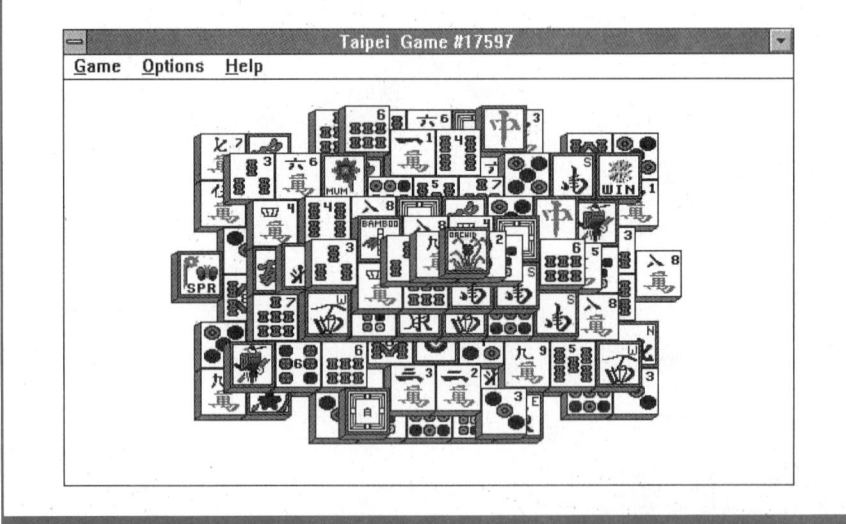

Figure 30.41. Window from Taipei.

In addition, many programs enable you to automate your work with macros. In telecommunications programs, these are usually called "scripts." Telecommunication script languages are like other macro languages in that you can create programs that take steps, check for particular output, and so on. For example, a typical telecommunications script would dial into an electronic mail service, look for new mail, save it, and send any outgoing mail. Another script might look on the corporate mainframe for a particular file, see whether it has been updated since you last looked and if it has, download a copy of it to your PC.

MicroPhone II

MicroPhone II, shown in Figure 30.43, has an advanced script language and many features to make using the program easy to use. In Figure 30.43, notice the buttons along the bottom portion of the screen. You can add buttons for any script. You can also execute scripts from the Script menu.

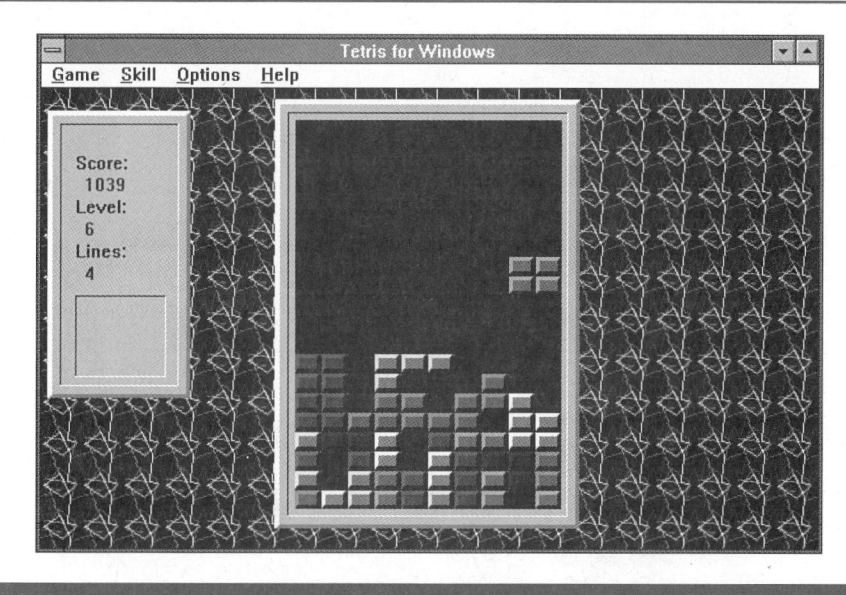

Figure 30.42. Window from Tetris.

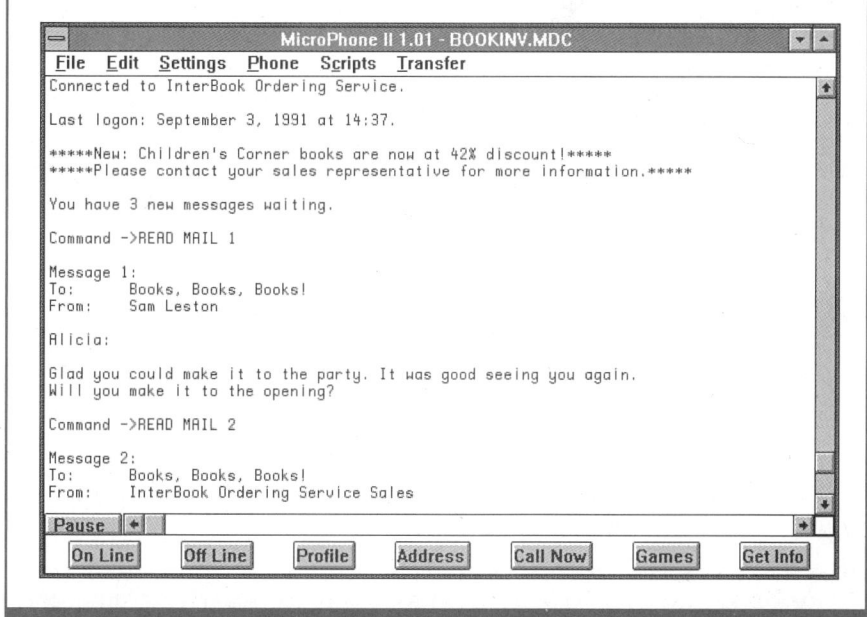

Figure 30.43. Main MicroPhone screen.

MicroPhone comes with scripts for many major network services. Scripts are in a language that resembles BASIC, as shown in Figure 30.44. You can create scripts by choosing from the lists at the bottom of the script creation window or type them yourself. You can also share scripts with the Macintosh version of MicroPhone.

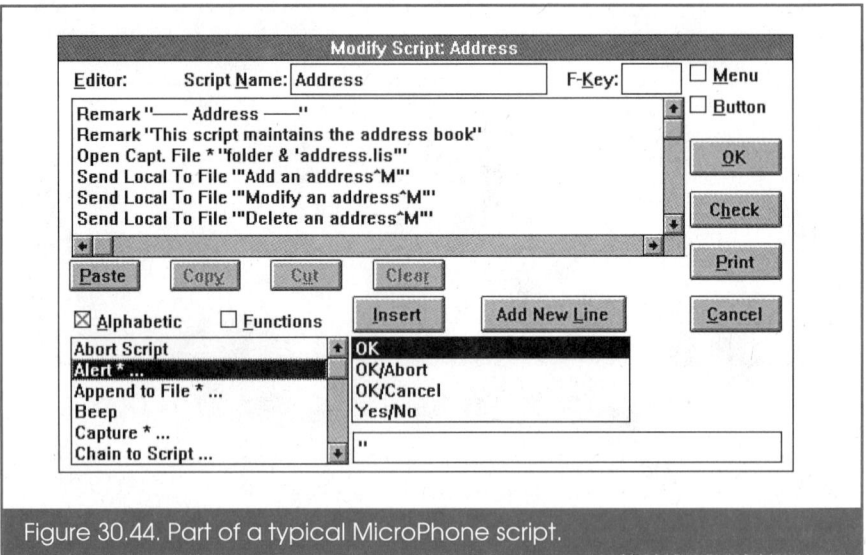

Figure 30.44. Part of a typical MicroPhone script.

Software Ventures Corp.
2907 Claremont Avenue, #220
Berkeley, CA 94705
(415)644-3232

DynaComm

DynaComm, shown in Figure 30.45, also has its own script language. In addition, it supports dynamic data exchange with other Windows programs so that you can integrate modem communications with other programs. A program such as Excel might make DDE calls to DynaComm to run a script that dials a remote computer, gets recent data, and sends that data back to Excel through DDE.

DynaComm is also known for its wide variety of terminal emulations. Figure 30.46 shows the extensive list of terminals that DynaComm can emulate. It also has a wide variety of binary transfer protocols, and you can view binary graphics files as they are received.

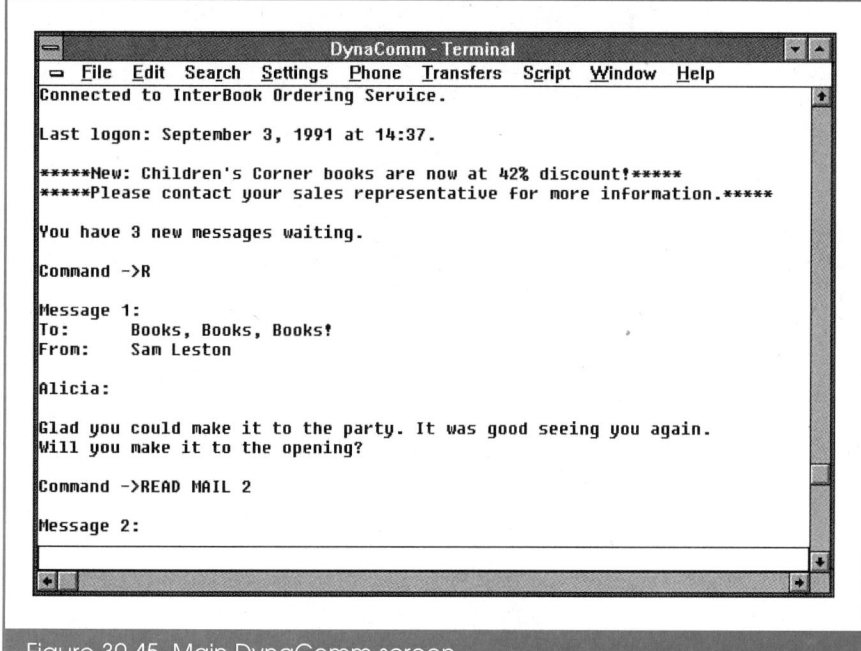

Figure 30.45. Main DynaComm screen.

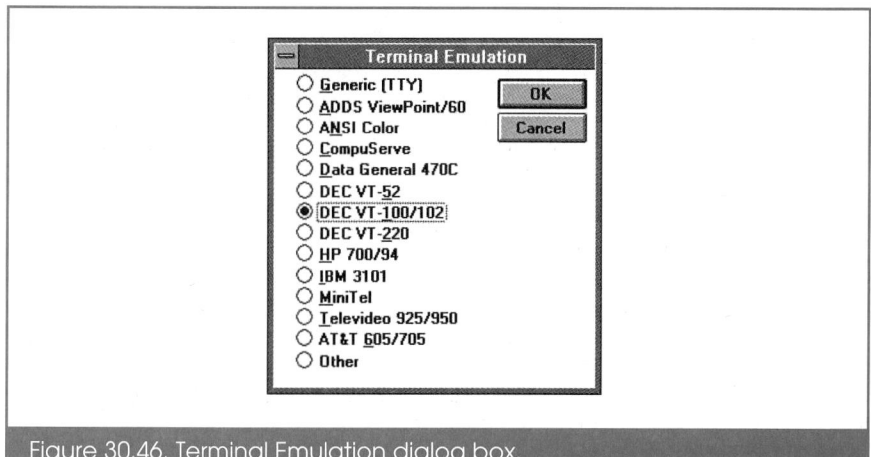

Figure 30.46. Terminal Emulation dialog box.

FutureSoft Engineering
1001 S. Dairy Ashford, #101
Houston, TX 77077
(713)496-9400

FAXit for Windows

Although not a purely communications-based package, FAXit for Windows is designed to operate FAX devices. All FAX devices include many of the required elements of a modem, so much so that when FAX boards and modems are integrated onto the same board, the cost is a great deal less than just a stand-alone FAX machine. In fact, combined 9600-Group III FAX and 2400-baud modem boards are now available for less than $125 via mail order sources. This is roughly 25 percent of the cost of a stand-alone FAX. Of course, you do get at least a scanner and often a phone built into the FAX machine designed to sit on your desktop.

FAXit works just fine with ATM (Adobe Type Manager) or Bitstream's FaceLift. You can FAX virtually any file right from Microsoft Paintbrush or Word for Windows by setting up a printer dedicated to sending output to a file. FAXit takes the file and converts it to a fax format before sending.

Alien Computing
38733 9th Street East, Unit R
Palmdale CA 93550
(805)947-1310

Graphics and Page Layout

As in every other product category, leaders (products) have emerged in Graphics and Page Layout that stand out because they try not to be all things to all people.

Arts & Letters

The Arts & Letters graphics package competes with the CorelDRAW! package described in Chapter 18, "CorelDRAW!." The programs have many features in common and each has its strong points. Arts & Letters' clip art library is much larger than CorelDRAW!'s and the art is much simpler. Arts & Letters is based more on adding your own customization to existing art than is CorelDRAW!, which emphasizes creating your own art. Figure 30.47 shows the main Arts & Letters window.

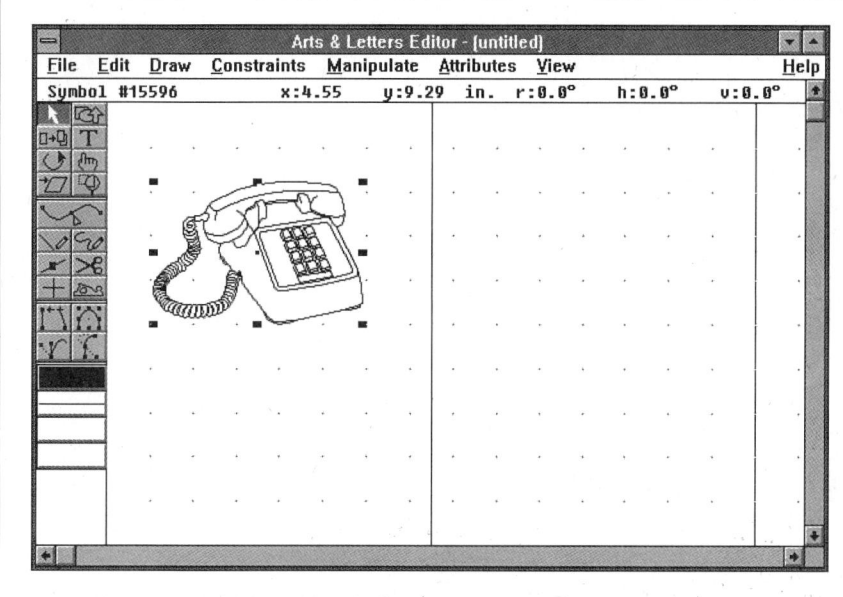

Figure 30.47. Main Arts & Letters window.

30

As you can see, Arts & Letters has many tools in its palette. These perform most of the same functions as the smaller palette of CorelDRAW!. Once you have a piece of clip art in your document, you can handle it as a single piece of art or break it into its individual pieces with the Draw Cut to Freeform command. You can then manipulate each part of a complex object individually.

Arts & Letters also is very good at making business charts much like spreadsheets in Excel. However, because you are already in a drawing environment, customizing those charts is much easier. Figure 30.48 shows the Draw Chart command where you enter the information for your chart. You can also enter the titles and specify the formatting in this command from the menus in the dialog box. A typical chart is shown in Figure 30.49.

The charts can even use other symbols for the bars. For example, you can use books as the symbols for the previous chart, as shown in Figure 30.50. To do this, you simply change the symbol number in the Draw Chart command.

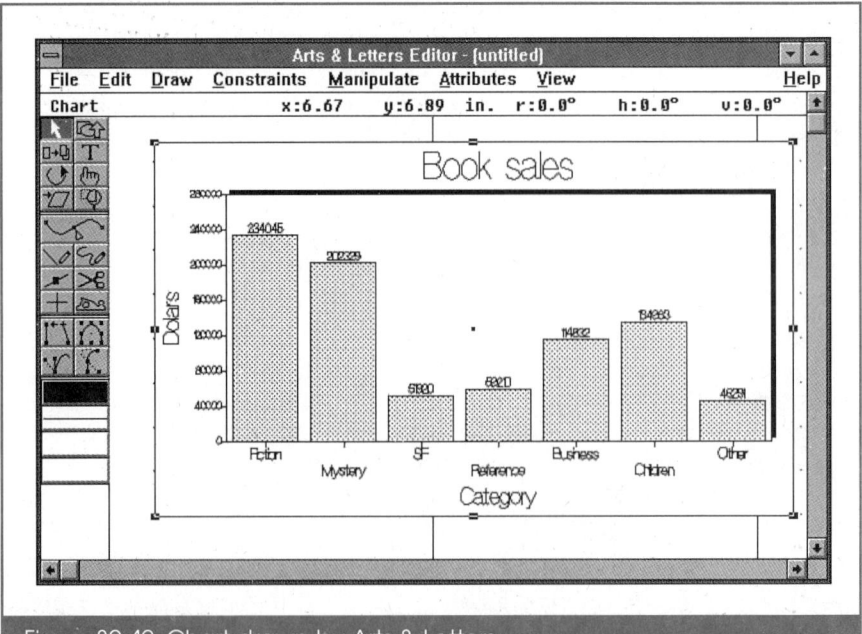

Figure 30.48. Draw Chart window.

Figure 30.49. Chart drawn by Arts & Letters.

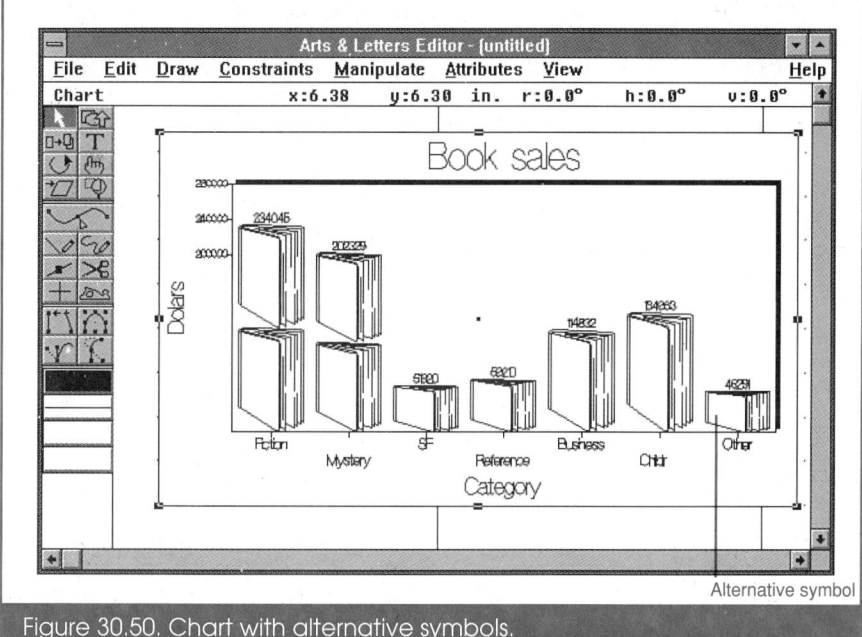

Figure 30.50. Chart with alternative symbols.

30

Computer Support Corp.
15926 Midway Road
Dallas, TX 75244
(214)661- 8960

PageMaker

Desktop publishing has made incredible strides since it was introduced about five years ago. Desktop publishing allows you to lay out pages of text and graphics with great flexibility. You can have multiple columns on a page, have text wrap around graphics, have floating headlines, and so on. A good page layout program must also give you exact mastery of the type so that you can control how letters look next to each other. PageMaker has always been at the forefront of the field, whether under Windows or on the Macintosh.

Figure 30.51 shows the PageMaker program window. You can have multiple documents open at one time. Each document consists of text blocks and graphics. The text blocks can be text that you type into PageMaker or "stories" that you import from other programs. You can import graphics from virtually any Windows program. The tool palette in the upper-right corner floats on the page so that you can put it wherever you are not working. The page icons at the lower-left tell you what page you are working on.

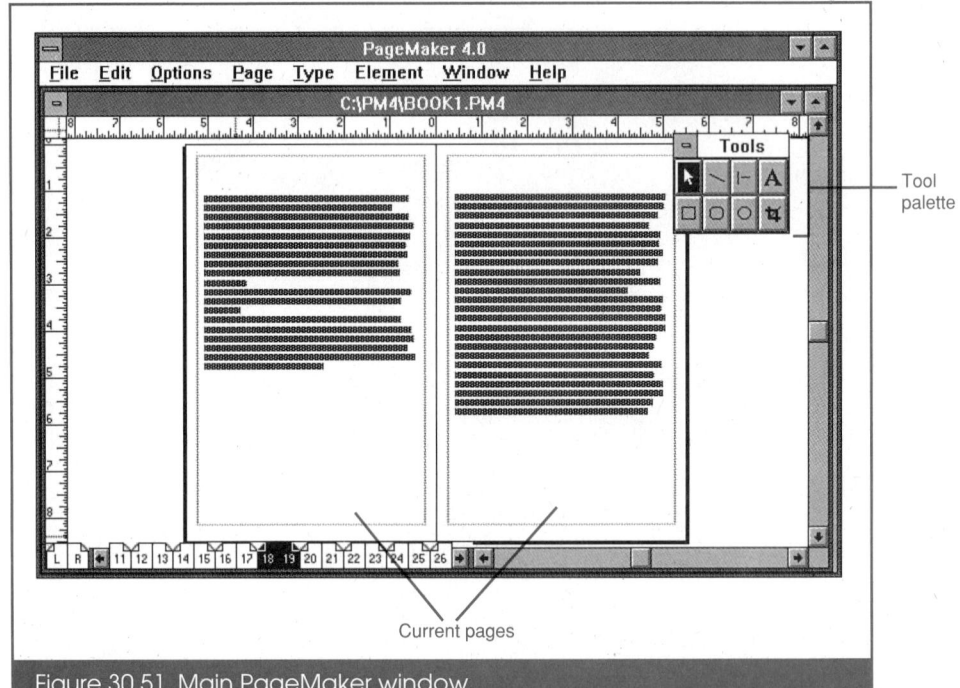

Figure 30.51. Main PageMaker window.

One of the popular concepts in PageMaker is the pasteboard. You can put bits of text and graphics around the outside of pages, like sticky notes you can use later. Thus, a document can have easily-accessible information that does not appear in the document.

Because type formatting is so important to page layout, PageMaker has an extensive array of formatting commands that can be applied to any text in a document. Figure 30.52 shows the Type menu, which controls text formatting. Note that you can also change paragraph formatting from this menu.

Like Word for Windows, in PageMaker, you use styles for paragraphs. You can control every aspect of the text within a style, as shown in Figure 30.53. If you base a style on another style, changes you make to the second style are automatically reflected in the first. For example, if you make all your headings based on a single heading style, you can change the font in that one style and have the font change for all headings in all styles.

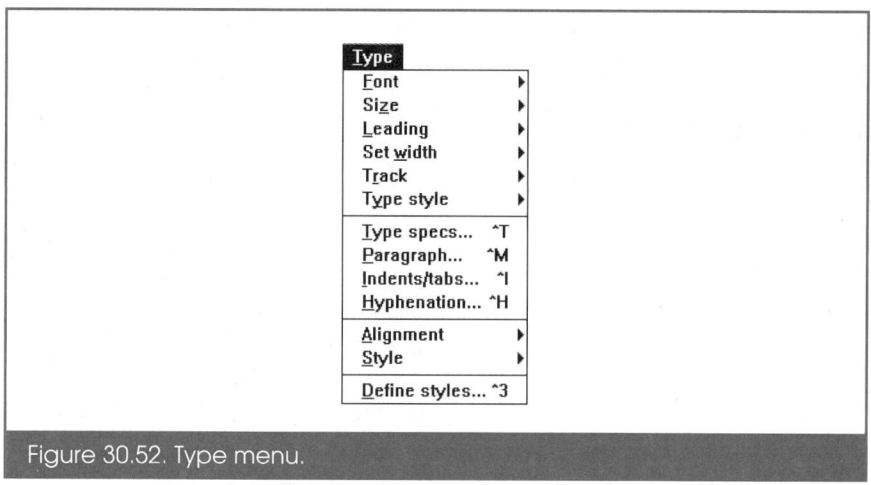

Figure 30.52. Type menu.

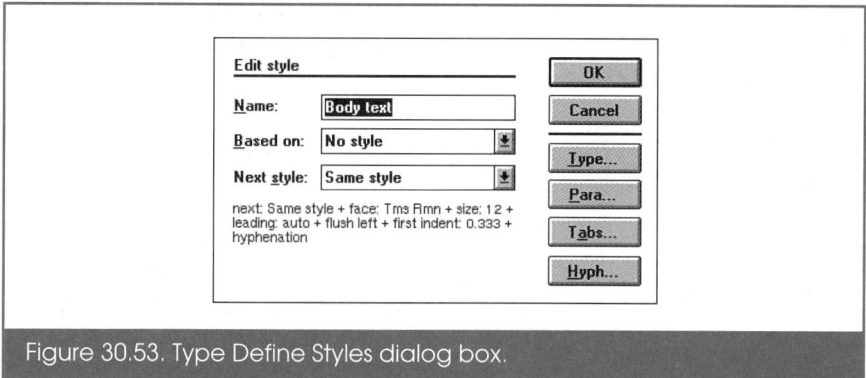

Figure 30.53. Type Define Styles dialog box.

30

Tables are always painful to produce in any program. PageMaker's table feature makes laying out tables much easier. The Table Editor program that comes with PageMaker, shown in Figure 30.54, is a full-featured table formatting program. You can vary the column width and row heights, format characters, and so on. When you move a table into a PageMaker document, you can later update the table in the Table Editor, and the information is automatically updated in your document.

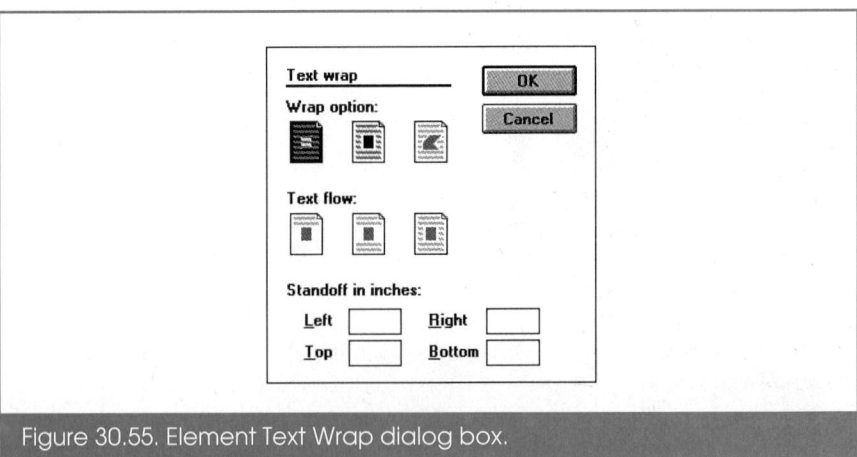

Figure 30.54. Table Editor program window.

Most page layout programs can wrap text around graphics. PageMaker provides choices for how it wraps, as shown in Figure 30.55. You can have text run under the graphic, stop at the rectangular borders around it, or wrap with the edge of the graphic. You can also tell PageMaker to stop when it reaches a graphic, to flow above and below it, or to flow around the sides.

Figure 30.55. Element Text Wrap dialog box.

Aldus Corp.
411 First Avenue South
Seattle, WA 98104-2871
(206)628-6594

Other Utility Software

Generally speaking, when a program is intended to do only very specific things, like manipulate hardware or perform simple tasks within or without other software packages, it is called a Utility. Utilities are available in shareware, public domain, and the private sector. The software utility is one category of software that is most likely to succeed or eventually be offered for sale in the conventional marketing channels.

System Engineer

Changing settings in your SYSTEM.INI file requires a fairly good knowledge of the technical aspects of Windows. Chapter 27, "Configuring with the WIN.INI and SYSTEM.INI Files," covers much of that information if you want a detailed tour of the file. On the other hand, if you just want to modify a few settings in the SYSTEM.INI file, you are much better off with the Windows System Engineer from the Windows Users Group.

30

Instead of your having to edit the SYSTEM.INI file, System Engineer enables you to use simple dialog boxes that relate to the various functions of the SYSTEM.INI file. For example, Figure 30.56 shows the dialog box for the 386-enhanced mode memory settings. Figure 30.57 shows the dialog box for 386-enhanced mode serial communications. As you can see, changing parameters here is significantly easier than wading through the SYSTEM.INI file by yourself.

The program also comes with extensive help for each option. You can search the help option for all related topics on particular problems.

WUGNET (National Windows Users Group Network)
P.O. Box 1967
Media, PA 19063
(215)565-1861

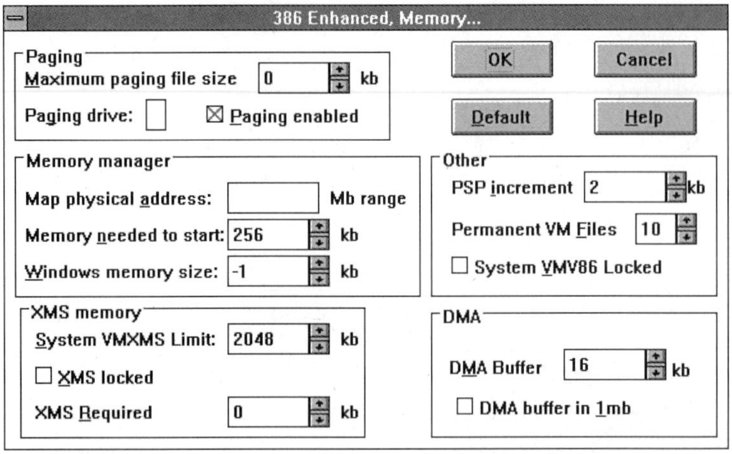

Figure 30.56. 386-enhanced mode memory dialog box.

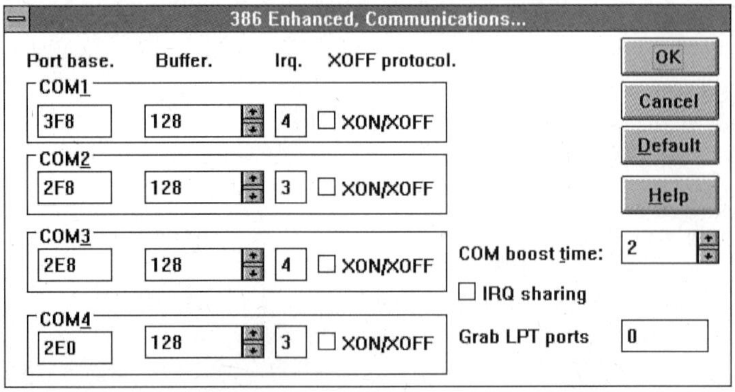

Figure 30.57. 386-enhanced mode serial communications dialog box.

FirstApps

As described previously, hDC makes "MicroApps" that you can run from a program's control menu. This prevents your having to use Task Manager or Program Manager to switch programs. The FirstApps package consists of nine small but useful programs that don't fit well into any category but come in handy at various times.

The FirstApps package includes programs such as

▲ *Memory Viewer*, which shows how the memory in your system is used. Figure 30.58 shows the Memory Viewer window. This is helpful when you get error messages about low memory, and you want to see what is using memory.

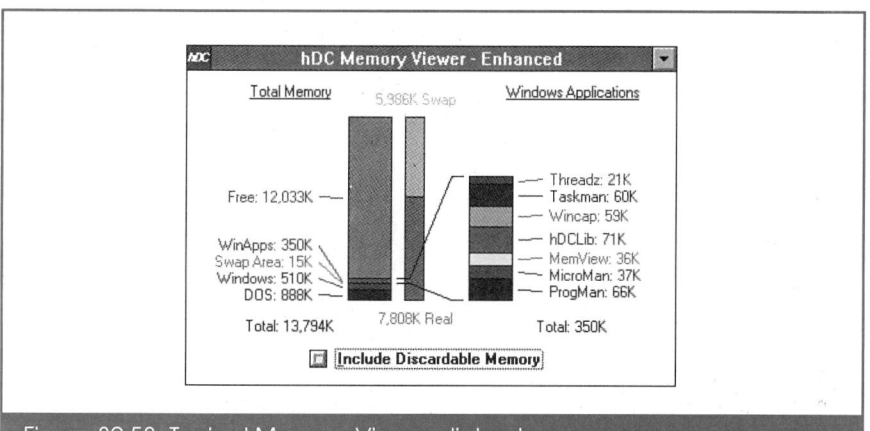

Figure 30.58. Typical Memory Viewer dialog box.

▲ *Desktop*, with which you can change the logo you see when you start Windows and the background. You also can include a screen saver. The logo and background are cosmetic changes, but make using Windows a bit more interesting. In fact, you can animate the background and even set it up as a desk calendar.

▲ *Auto Save*, which causes your Windows programs to save automatically your work every few minutes. You can tell it when to save (number of keystrokes entered or elapsed time) as shown in Figure 30.59.

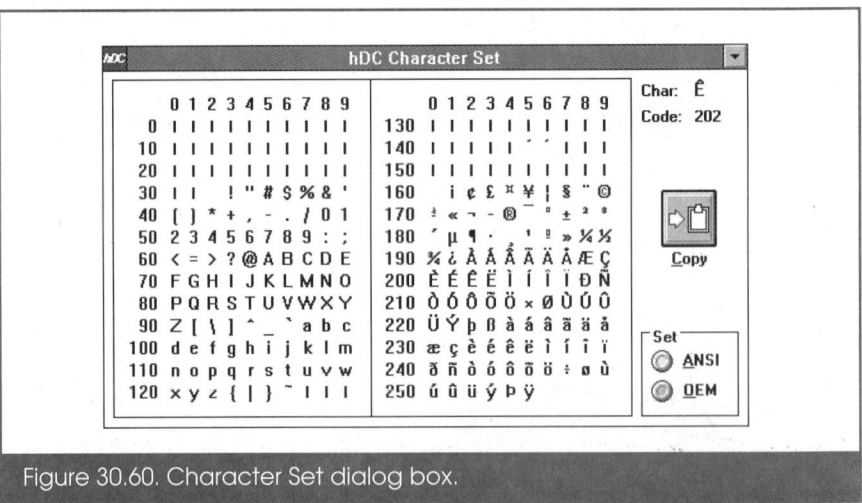

Figure 30.59. Auto Save dialog box.

▲ *Character Set*, which shows you all the characters available in each type of font, as shown in Figure 30.60. Instead of having to remember how to type a particular character in the high range, you can copy it to the Clipboard and paste it into your document.

Figure 30.60. Character Set dialog box.

▲ *Alarm Clock*, which enables you to set reminders to appear at the preset time. This is much handier than the Calendar program that comes with Windows, and you have period reminders as well as reminders at a set time and date.

hDC Computer Corp
6742 185th Avenue NE
Redmond, WA 98052
(206)885-5550

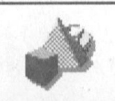

WinZip

A good method for giving yourself more space on your hard disk is to store in a compressed form files that you do not use often. You can typically save 50 percent of a file's space by compressing it, and many files can be compressed by over 80 percent. When you want to use the file, you uncompress it. The most popular method for compressing files is the shareware PKZIP and PKUNZIP from PKWARE, Inc. Files compressed with PKZIP are said to be zipped files. You can zip many files from your disk into a single compressed file.

If you use zipped files, it would be handy to be able to compress and uncompress them from within Windows. The WinZip program puts a friendly Windows interface on the PKZIP and PKUNZIP programs. Note that you already need to be using these programs to use WinZip. These two probably are some of the most popular shareware programs in the country.

Figure 30.61 shows a typical WinZip window. When you open a zipped file, WinZip displays the contents of the file including the dates. Use the View button to view text files in the zipped file without having to extract them. When you want to extract the files, you can select them from the list and click the Extract button.

30

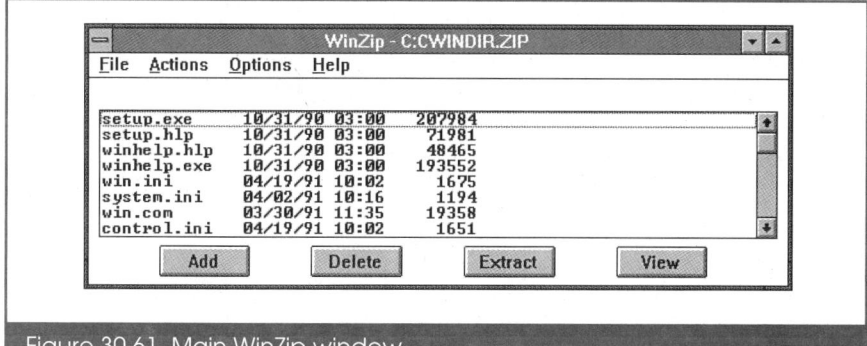

Figure 30.61. Main WinZip window.

You can also use WinZip to create the zipped files. The Actions Add command, shown in Figure 30.62, gives you a variety of methods for adding the files to an existing zipped file. You can update the contents with newer versions of files or add the files directly. You can also choose, with wildcards, the files you want to add individually or add a whole directory at a time.

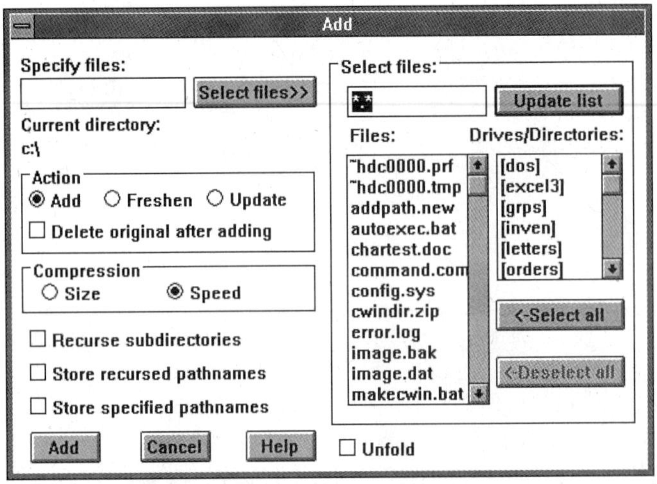

Figure 30.62. Actions Add dialog box.

Nico Mak
P.O. Box 919
Bristol, CT 06011

Scrapbook+

The Clipboard is only useful for holding one object at a time. There are times when you want to keep many things handy for copying and pasting, such as time when you are culling paragraphs from a report or creating many pieces of art for later use. You can keep these in Clipboard files, but they are difficult to use because you have to remember by name what each item is.

Scrapbook+ takes care of these problems by letting you paste as many things as you want into the scrapbook file. You can even keep multiple scrapbook files, for each project, for example. Figure 30.63 shows the main Scrapbook+ window. You can see the contents of each item in the file by scrolling through the list at the bottom of the window. As you can see, you can have both text and pictures in the same file.

You can use the tool palette in the upper-right corner of the screen to make pictures or subpictures of the information. For example, Figure 30.64 shows a bit-map image as the selected item. With the tools you

can copy just part of that image to the Clipboard (and if you wish, directly to Scrapbook+) so that you do not need to paste the entire image into your document.

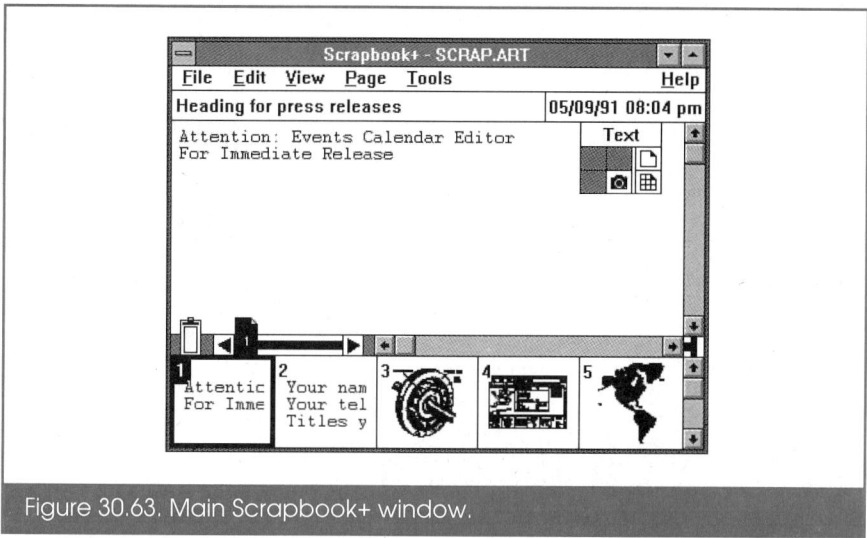

Figure 30.63. Main Scrapbook+ window.

30

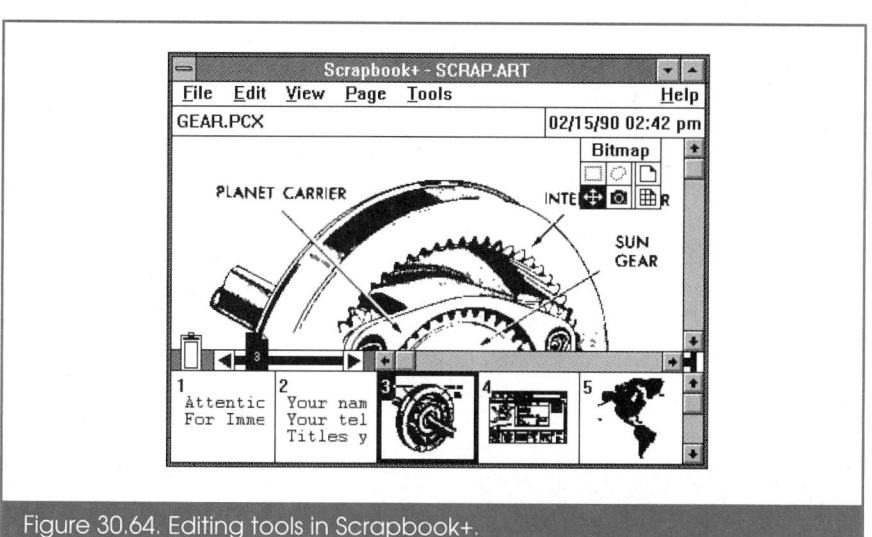

Figure 30.64. Editing tools in Scrapbook+.

If you have hundreds of files, being able to browse may not be sufficient for you. In this case, you can search for words in the information for each item. The item information is shown above the item in the main window. Figure 30.65 shows the Find Page command. This dialog box also lists all the types of information you can store in the Scrapbook+ file. Thus, you can use Scrapbook+ as a miniature database for things you want to include in any sort of Windows document.

Find Page		
Pattern:		Find
Include Formats		Cancel
☐ Bitmap	☐ Printer Bitmap	
☐ Picture	☐ Printer Picture	
☐ Text	☐ SYLK	
☐ TIFF	☐ CSV	
☐ PostScript	☐ DIF	
☐ Rich Text	☐ Custom	
Find Options		
☐ Search backwards through file.		
☒ Wrap-around search (at end of file).		Help

Figure 30.65. Find Page dialog box.

Eikon Systems Inc.
989 E. Hillsdale Blvd., Suite 260
Foster City, CA 94404
(415)349-4664

Productivity Pack

Because you are reading this book, you are clearly interested in understanding Windows. A book like this is great for learning at your own speed. Others may want the computer to teach them. Microsoft's Productivity Pack is a good method for beginners to learn Windows and to troubleshoot their system.

The Productivity Pack has three major parts.

▲ Learning Windows is an interactive tutorial for beginners on how to perform various tasks. It uses cute characters from history to teach lessons on Windows basics, such as shown in Figure 30.66.

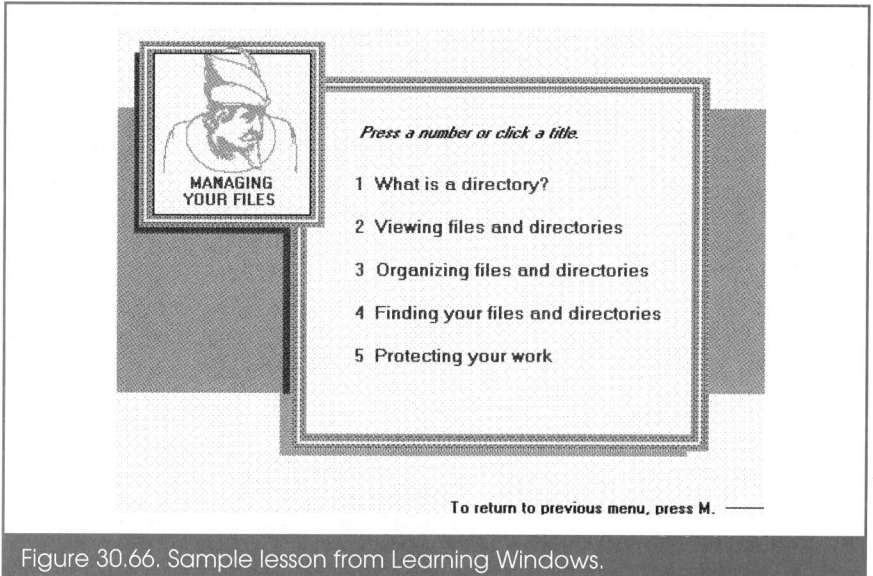

Figure 30.66. Sample lesson from Learning Windows.

30

▲ Quick Troubleshooter runs under the Windows help system to assist you in finding basic problems with your system. It is shown in Figure 30.67.

▲ Working Smarter is a help guide to using Windows features to make your work easier (such as arranging Program Manager windows). It is shown in Figure 30.68.

Other Advanced Programs

The term "Advanced Programs" does not denote a superior product, but a specialty product that has outgrown the label of "utility" by virtue of its complexity and functionality.

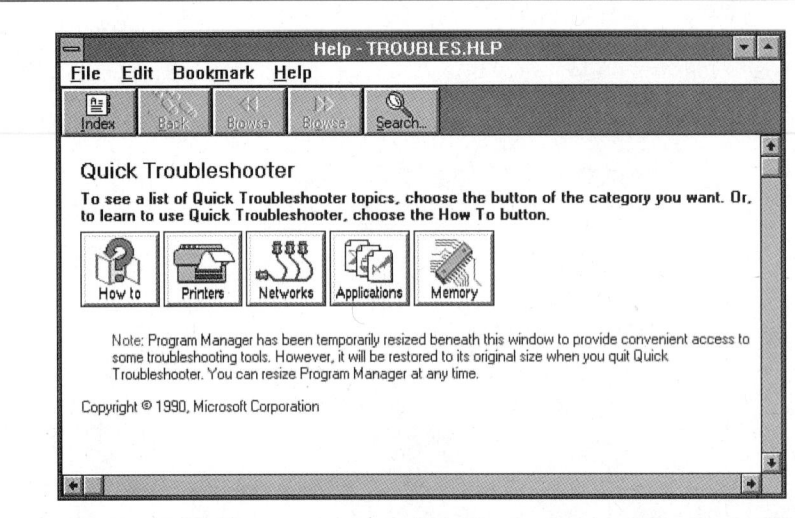

Figure 30.67. Quick Troubleshooter main screen.

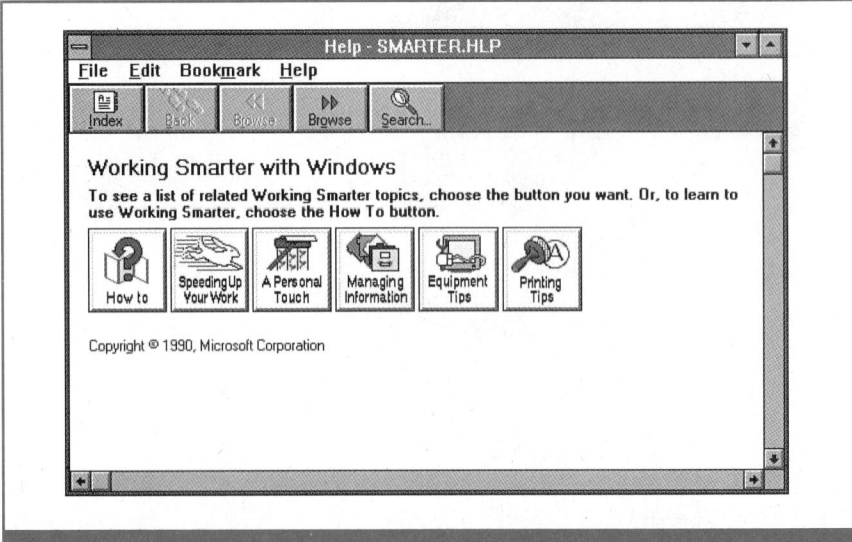

Figure 30.68. Working Smarter main screen.

WinSleuth

If you need to know more about what is happening in your PC, WinSleuth can probably tell you. Figure 30.69 shows typical information you can get from WinSleuth. It tells you about your hardware, network, device drivers, ports, and so on.

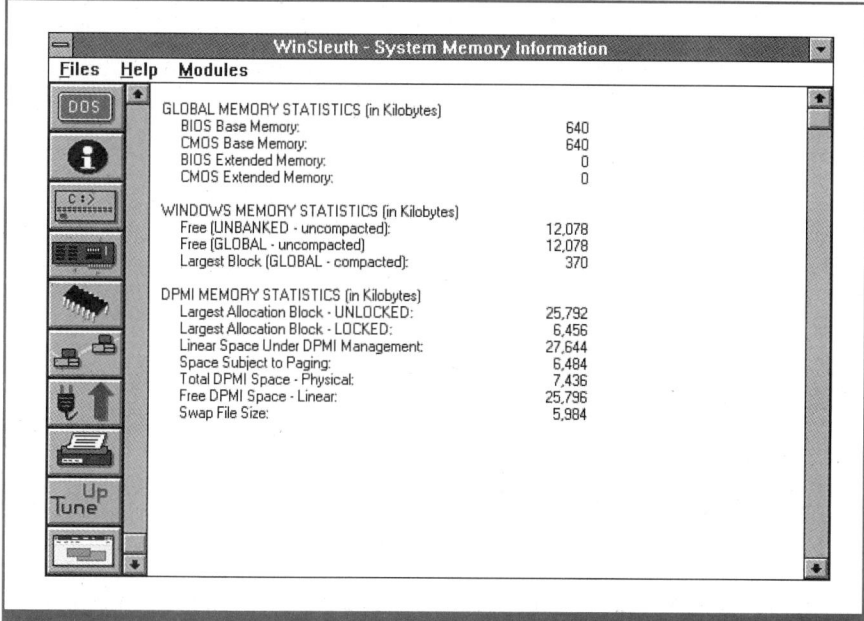

Figure 30.69. Information from WinSleuth.

WinSleuth also comes with System Sleuth Analyzer, which is a general diagnostic program that runs under MS-DOS. System Sleuth Analyzer reports much of the same information as WinSleuth but in a different layout.

You can use these programs if you have general problems with your computer that you cannot resolve. They are useful for finding conflicting memory interrupts, network problems, and so on.

Dariana Technology
6945 Hermosa Circle
Buena Park, CA 90620
(714)994-7400

30

Tempo

The Recorder, described in Chapter 13, "Other Accessories," is a bare-minimum macro recorder. If you want to have more control over your system, you need more flexibility and a more advanced interface. Tempo provides those while remaining a simple program. Figure 30.70 shows the Tempo window.

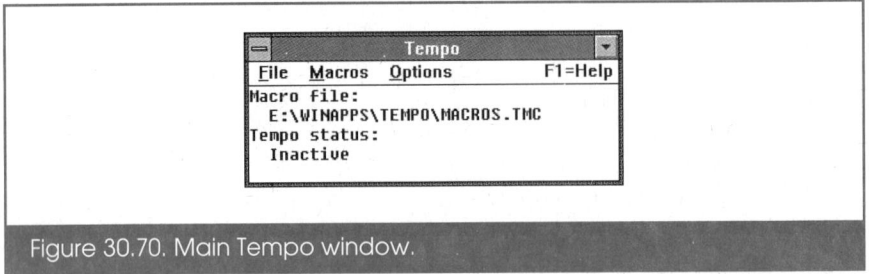

Figure 30.70. Main Tempo window.

As with the Recorder, most of what you want to record in Tempo is just keystrokes. You can tell Tempo what you want to record with the Options Recording command, shown in Figure 30.71. You can easily turn off recording mouse moves, or if you want to record them, you can specify that they are relative to the window rather than to the screen. Recordings relative to the window are much more likely to be correct than ones relative to the screen, because if the window is at a different position on the screen when you run your macros, the objects in it have moved with it.

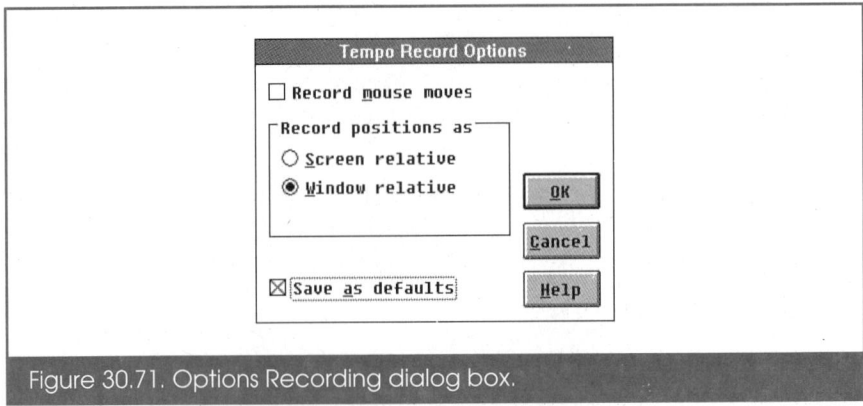

Figure 30.71. Options Recording dialog box.

Another advanced feature is your ability to stop the macro recording and make decisions based on the contents of the Clipboard. For example, assume that you are controlling a spreadsheet program and you want to perform one action if the cell you are looking at has a particular value. You copy that cell to the Clipboard and give the Macros Control command in Tempo, shown in Figure 30.72. You then set the comparison and tell Tempo which other macro to branch to if the comparison is true. You can also loop based on the value of the Clipboard.

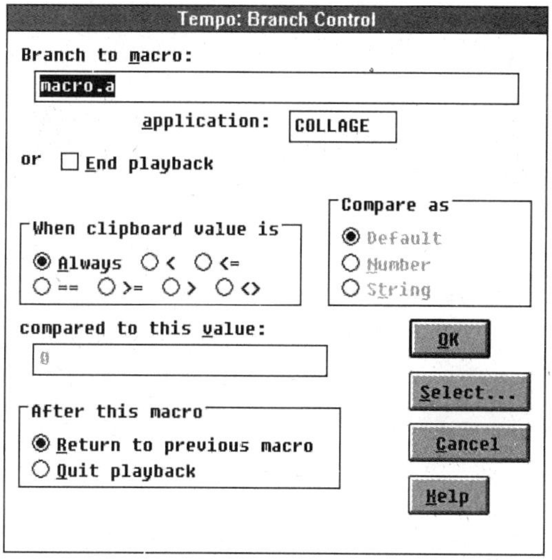

Figure 30.72. Macros Control window.

Affinity Microsystems
1050 Walnut Street, Suite 425
Boulder, CO 80302
(303)442-4840

Icon Management Programs

The most memorable part of the Program Manager program is its icons. Each Windows program comes with its own built-in icons. You can also get sets of additional icons from many sources. Most people leave program icons as they come from the manufacturer but often want unique icons for their documents.

Icon Designer is an hDC MicroApp that you can use to design your own Program Manager icons. It comes with over 100 icons and makes it easy to design your own. The program, shown in Figure 30.73, can also extract icons from other Windows programs so that you can modify them as well.

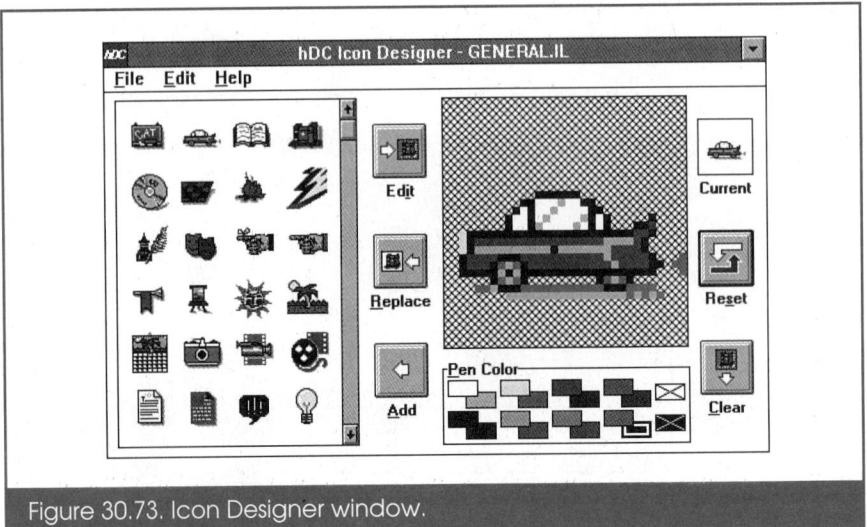

Figure 30.73. Icon Designer window.

hDC Computer Corp
6742 185th Avenue NE
Redmond, WA 98052
(206)885-5550

What Comes with DOS 5.0?

Even though the utilities that come with MS-DOS 5.0 are not designed to run as true Windows programs, some are important to the operation of Windows.

If you are running a version of DOS that is lower than 5.0, it's time to take the plunge. Without getting into the overall benefits of 5.0, here are a few of the utilities included:

SHARE.EXE   Allows multiple applications within Windows to access the same data file at the same time. Not required when using contemporary LAN programs.

FASTOPEN.EXE	Saves the addresses of programs on disk to a portion of memory so that DOS does not have to read the entire disk when it looks for the same file a second time.
MEM.EXE	Shows memory configuration.
EQUIP.EXE	Displays current hardware configuration and some memory details.
LOADHIGH	Preceding the name of a driver or TSR in the AUTOEXEC.BAT file with this command causes DOS to load the driver into the upper memory area rather than into conventional memory. Makes more memory available to some Windows programs.
DEVICEHIGH	Does the same thing as LOADHIGH, but does it from the CONFIG.SYS file.

Read your application documentation before using these DOS commands. Programs have variable natures when running in high memory and under Windows at the same time.

See Reference C, "Windows Product Directory," for highlights of these and other products for Microsoft Windows.

30

VII

Windows Programming

P
A
R
T

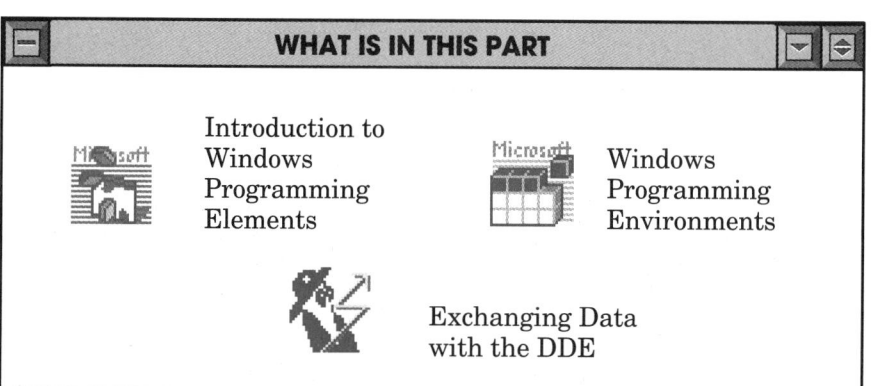

WHAT IS IN THIS PART

Introduction to Windows Programming Elements

Windows Programming Environments

Exchanging Data with the DDE

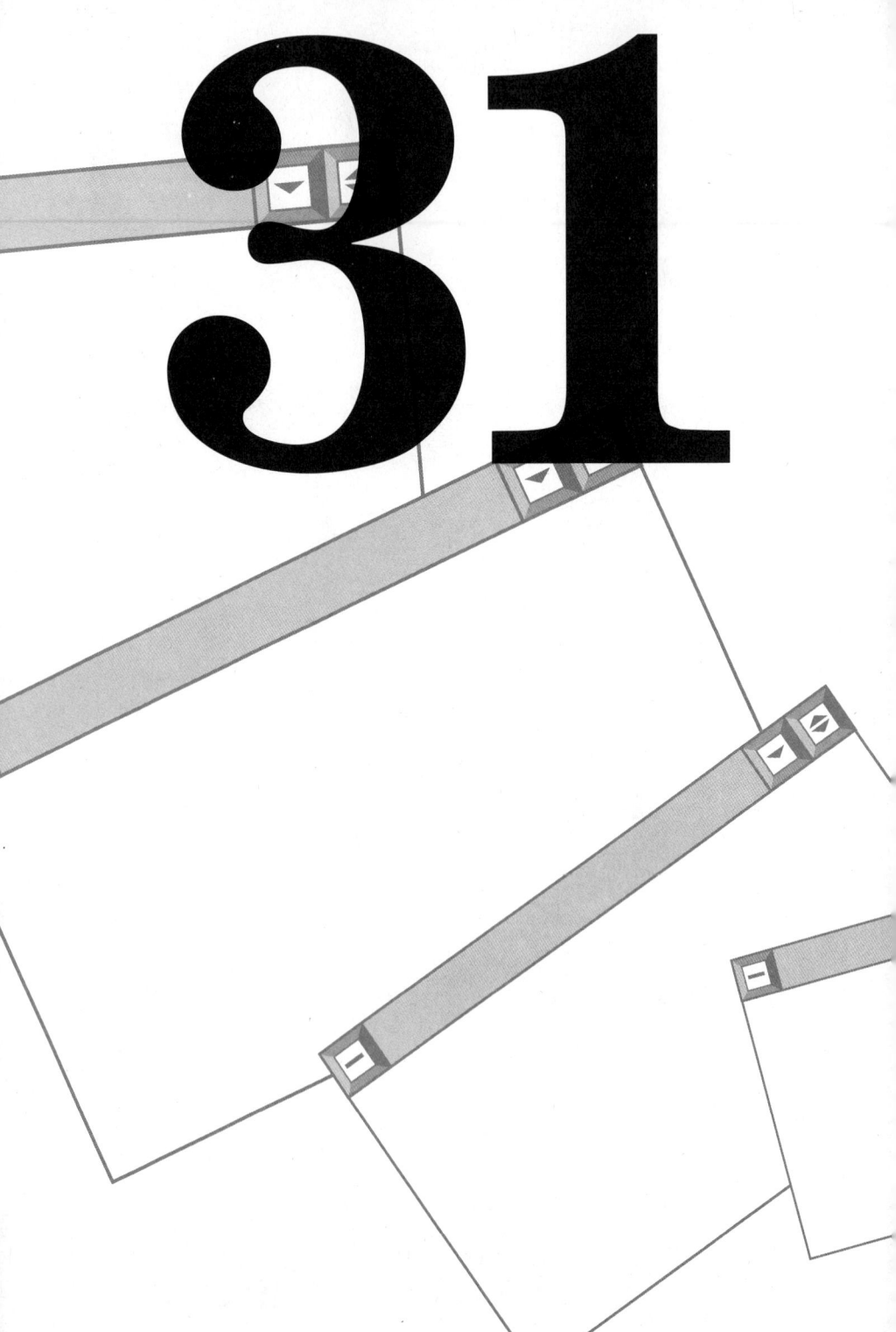

CHAPTER

31

Introduction to Windows Programming Elements

Programming for Windows is not like it was in the "Good Old Days." Windows programming is more global, or object-oriented, than traditional programming ever was. But then again, Windows programs keep track of more detail like window positions and foreground/background information for programs running under Windows. That's the reason the old school of procedural programming can't really exist in this world of juggling resources against multiple requests for attention from the computer.

Object-Oriented Versus Procedural Programming

Windows programs are significantly different from regular DOS programs. If you are familiar with general programming concepts, you may be interested to learn about the differences. Procedural programming relies on stepping the machine through line-by-line code. The code interprets variables created to provide contextual support.

Object-oriented programming is based on events. Each event or set of conditions is in effect surrounded by many variables that define conditions that exist. In the area of screen painting and window management alone, there are probably more variables to juggle at any one time than there are in many procedural applications *on the whole*. This difference alone makes Windows programs much more dynamic in nature.

For the sake of clarity, try on this example for size. When you write a simple batch file program to format a double-sided diskette or you just add to an existing AUTOEXEC.BAT file, you are writing a simple procedural program. The lines of "code" do not check with all of the other things going on in the environment, such as noting when the user moves windows or minimizes programs to icons. Procedural programming tries to do only one thing at a time. This is one of the major reasons why DOS- or character-based programs run so much faster than Windows programs.

Procedural programs get to do one thing at a time. Remember the old joke about walking and chewing gum at the same time? Try running Windows 3.0 on an 80286 that runs at less than 10 megahertz with 1 megabyte of memory and you'll get a feel for how much more of a struggle (or is it juggle?) it is for a system to review every variable many times each second. You'll need caffeine pills at times to stay awake. The only thing apparent to the average user is how well Windows performs on their particular computer. Object-oriented programs really want more horsepower because of how much they try to do in order to shine.

The user (who generally doesn't care how programs are written) perceives this difference as being one of power. From many a novice programmer's standpoint, it's this sense of power and control that makes the Windows environment unique and appealing. It's for these inspired individuals that this chapter describes how Windows programs are constructed and how they interact with Windows.

Multitasking

Windows programs are also fundamentally different because Windows is a multitasking environment. Multitasking means that several programs, or *processes*, can be going on at the same time. They do not run at the same time literally: The CPU can only execute one instruction at a time. Windows divides the system resources, however, so it appears that several programs are running at the same time.

There are two types of multitasking systems: preemptive and nonpreemptive. With a preemptive system, a scheduler equally allocates the CPU time to the various concurrent processes, modified by a system of priorities so that more important tasks get more time. For instance, a particular process has been allocated 24 milliseconds; at the end of that period, the operating system saves the state of the process's environment, and switches to the next process. When the time comes for the initial process to be active again, the operating system restores the state of the machine and the process continues as if nothing had happened.

With nonpreemptive multitasking systems, the operating system does not switch out a process when its time allotment has expired. Instead, it waits for the process to actively yield control. If a process gets into a loop and is unable to yield control, the operating system never regains control and all other processes will cease. Windows doles out resources instead of letting an application take all of the resources it needs indefinitely.

Windows is a nonpreemptive system. Therefore, Windows programs must be written in a special way so that Windows can frequently regain control.

Messages

Another major difference between Windows programs and regular DOS programs is in the use of messages. Windows sends messages to indicate that one of several types of events has occurred (for example, a key has been pressed or the mouse has been moved) or to request a program to take a certain action (for example, repainting a window or quitting).

Windows programs run in a loop, alternately waiting for the next message from Windows and responding to it. This is known as the *message loop*. For example, if you press the mouse button within the area controlled by the program, the next message Windows sends to that program is that the mouse button has been pressed. When you release the button, Windows sends another message. As you move the mouse, Windows sends a stream of messages, constantly updating the program with the current location of the mouse.

Suppose you have two programs running on your Windows desktop. One program is the foreground program and the other is the background program. If you click the button in the area controlled by the background program, Windows sends the message to the background

program instead. It may also send a lot more messages, such as a message to the foreground program indicating it is no longer the foreground program and a message to the background program telling it to repaint any part of its windows that had been covered up by the foreground program.

Not all messages are retrieved through the main message loop. In some cases, Windows bypasses the message loop and calls a function within your program directly.

Operating System Calls

Another difference between Windows programs and regular DOS programs is in the way they interface with the operating system. The operating system (DOS) provides many services to programmers such as reading the keyboard and handling files. Windows programmers must ask Windows to perform many of the tasks they would have otherwise requested from DOS. These requests are passed through library functions that are provided with the programming environment.

There are two reasons why Windows programmers do not make so many direct operating system calls. First, DOS is not a multitasking operating system, so Windows must handle sharing the available resources. For example, if two programs were sending data to the printer at the same time, the data would be mixed up and produce a very strange printout consisting of a combination of both documents. By asking Windows to print instead of asking DOS to print, programmers can avoid this untidy result. Windows keeps the two sets of data separate and only prints the second document when the first has been printed.

Second, DOS was not designed to handle more than 640K of memory. Windows uses a method of getting around this limitation that ensures each program can access all the memory in the computer. Because Windows manages this memory allocation method, programmers ask Windows to take care of operating system functions.

Icons

Icons are small graphic images that have representational meaning. Two types of icons are used in Windows programs. The first is the icon that represents an application and is displayed when you minimize an

31

application or when an application is represented in a group box on the Program Manager screen. The second type of icon is displayed in dialog boxes: the hand icon and the exclamation point used in warning messages.

Displaying Icons

When you create a window, you can specify the name of an icon and attach it to the window, so that when the window is minimized Windows displays the icon. You can also include an icon in dialog boxes by specifying the icon's name and the position in which to display it.

Special Icons

Some icons serve special system purposes. For instance, when you use the Clock program in Windows and the window is minimized, the icon representing the Clock program is a small clock that continues to display the time. Clearly, this is not a regular icon. There is a way you can tell Windows not to display an icon when a window is minimized but to continue to send messages to the window. In this way, you can keep the application active while it is minimized, and display text and graphics in the tiny minimized window or icon. You tell Windows to manipulate an icon through programming techniques when the application is written. Minimizing a program window to an icon does not always mean the program has stopped completing tasks.

Other programs that use icons to continue to display changing information when the program is minimized are communications programs. Displaying file transfer status, like the time remaining for a file transfer in progress are also popular uses for special icons.

Creating a Windows Program

To create an executable file in a compiled-language program for DOS, the procedure is to write one or more source files, compile them into object files, and link the object files with one or more library files. Creating a Windows program is similar except there are two more stages.

Resource Files

In addition to source files for a program, there are *resource files*. Resource files contain data such as icons that will be added to the executable file. You create one main resource file, with the extension .RC. This file can be specified further to include other files, such as icon files with the extension .ICO and bit-map files with the extension .BMP.

There are two stages to adding resources to the executable file. First, the main resource file with the extension .RC is compiled using the resource compiler (RC.EXE) into a file with the extension .RES. Second, RC.EXE is invoked again to add the resources to the executable file.

The Module Definition File

The big difference between creating a DOS executable file and a Windows executable file is that for Windows, you must also write a module definition file, with the extension .DEF. This file gives instructions to the linker. When you run most DOS programs, the whole program is loaded into memory at once. Under Windows, however, sometimes only part of a program is loaded initially, and other parts are loaded as they are needed. One of the jobs of the module definition file is to tell the linker how to organize the components of the program so that they can be brought into memory in the most efficient manner. Frequently used parts of the program can be defined as PRELOAD so that they are loaded into memory as soon as the program starts. Others can be defined as LOADONCALL so that they will be loaded only when needed.

Another job of the module definition file is to define the links between the program and Dynamic Link Libraries (DLLs). DLLs contain functions that can be called from within a program but do not form part of the program itself. They are similar to operating system calls, many of which are contained within the Windows DLLs that form part of Windows itself. Unlike operating system calls, however, DLLs are called by name rather than through interrupts. DLLs are also supplied by Microsoft and third party vendors to perform specialized functions, like providing libraries of only icons, as in the case of MORICONS.DLL that comes with Windows 3.1.

If you call a function by name from within your program and the linker cannot find a function with that name in any of your object modules or libraries, it gives you an error message such as Unresolved external reference. When you call external functions from within a Windows program, you can specify these functions within the module definition file as IMPORT functions so that the linker does not give you this message and constructs the executable file in such a way that it can find the external functions when the program is run. This is what is meant by dynamic linking.

This process works in the other direction also. Sometimes Windows functions are not just called by your program, but actually call functions within your program themselves. For example, you can write a function to handle printer errors, and tell Windows to call that function when a printer error occurs. Any of your functions that can be called by Windows (known as callback functions) must be defined within the module definition file as EXPORT functions.

Types of Windows

There are many types of windows that Windows programs can paste on the screen for the user's benefit. Happily enough, there seems to be a movement on the part of Microsoft to limit the number of the types of dialog boxes that can be used by developers when creating applications.

Dialog Boxes

Dialog boxes are windows that appear to provide some temporary interaction with the user. The simplest type of dialog box is the one that provides a warning message together with an icon of a hand or an exclamation point. This dialog box asks the user to press a button marked OK or to choose between buttons marked OK and Cancel. Windows provides a MessageBox() function that you can use to display this type of box. You tell Windows the type of icon, the text to display, and which buttons to display. Windows displays the box, waits for the user to make a selection, and returns a number indicating which button was pressed. Figure 31.1 shows a simple message box.

More complicated dialog boxes can contain a number of "controls" such as radio buttons, scrolling list boxes, and text entry fields. Radio buttons are often used to select between a number of options when only one may be in use. When one button in a group is turned on, the others turn off. For example, a communications program only runs at one baud rate at a time. A dialog box could display a radio button for each baud rate from 300 to 9600, and the user selects only one of these. Check boxes are used to indicate options that can only be either on or off.

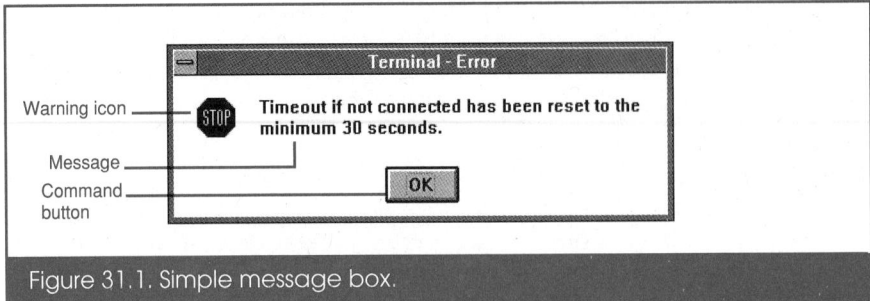

Figure 31.1. Simple message box.

One of the most common types of dialog box is the one that prompts you for the name of a file to open. A list of files matching a wildcard specification such as *.DOC appears, and you scroll through the list to pick a file or change the directory or type the name of another file or directory path. Figure 31.2 shows this type of dialog box.

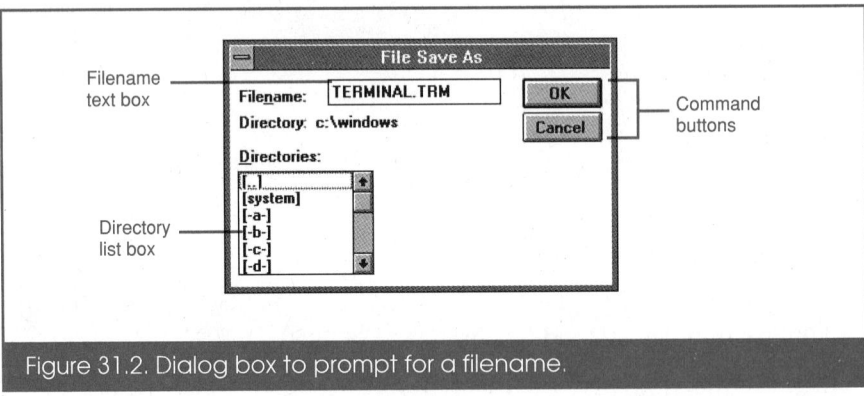

Figure 31.2. Dialog box to prompt for a filename.

Figure 31.3 shows a dialog box with radio buttons and check boxes to cover setting parameters for a communications program.

Programming this type of dialog box is more complicated, but fortunately a utility program that comes with the Software Developer's Kit from Microsoft, SDKDialog, is provided with the SDK to make the process simpler. Most other programming environments also have similar dialog-creation programs. SDKDialog enables you to design the dialog box, and offers a tool kit from which you can select tools such as radio buttons, check boxes, and list boxes.

Once you have designed your dialog box, SDKDialog saves it in a file that you include in your resource file. The dialog box becomes a resource that you can call from your program. When you ask Windows to display the box, you provide Windows with a *callback* function, which

Windows calls as the user interacts with the dialog window. This enables your program to keep track of events affecting that window. When data entry is complete, your program can ask Windows for the contents of text fields entered by the user, which radio buttons were pressed, and so on.

31

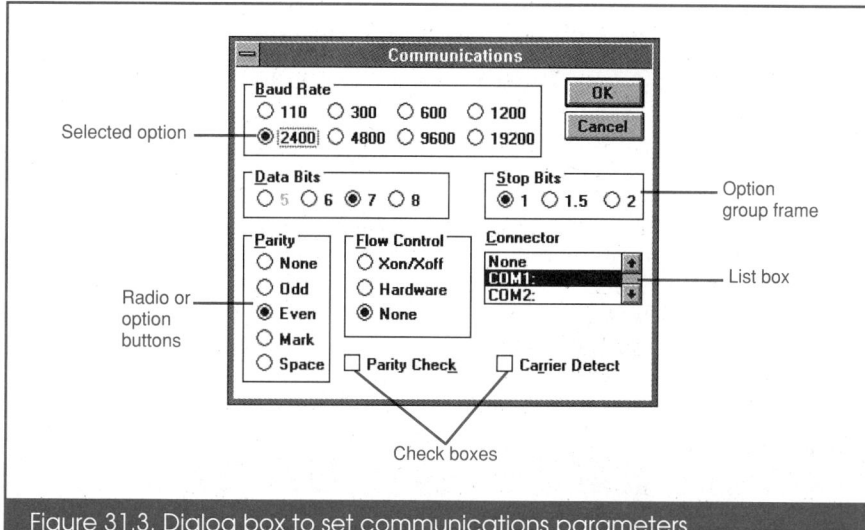

Figure 31.3. Dialog box to set communications parameters.

Menus

Menus in Windows are the lists of available options that appear across the top of a window, together with their associated submenus that pull or drop down when an item is selected. For example, the Options menu and the options are displayed when using the Program Manager.

Menus are resources and are defined within a program's resource file. The programmer lists each option, with the names of the choices to display and a unique number for each item. When the user chooses a menu item from the menu bar, Windows displays a pull-down submenu if there is one. When the final choice has been made, Windows sends a message to the program indicating the number of the item that was chosen.

You may have noticed that sometimes when you pull down a menu, one of the choices has a check mark next to it indicating the option currently selected. It is up to the programmer to tell Windows which items to check, using the `CheckMenuItem()` function. The programmer can also tell Windows to display certain choices in gray, indicating that the choice is not currently available.

Menus can also be altered while the program is running: Items can be
added, deleted or changed. In this way the menus can reflect the
options currently available.

Graphics

If you want to display an image in a Windows program, you can either
construct the image out of graphics primitives such as lines and curves,
or you can instruct Windows to display a bit map. A bit map is the
binary representation of a chart that defines the pixels that make up an
image.

Bit maps for Windows programs are generally created using the
SDKPaint program that comes with Windows SDK and produces files
with the extension .BMP. They can also be hard-coded into a program
by defining all the bits within the program itself, or constructed at run
time by the program using graphics primitives. You can also create bit-
map files with the Paintbrush program. Bit maps can be multicolor or
monochrome; the term *monochrome* means single-color, but not necessarily black and white.

Once you have created a bit-map file using a paint program such as
SDKPaint or Paintbrush, you declare the bit-map file in your resource
file. This causes the bit map to be added to your program by the resource compiler. Then your program can refer to the bit map by name
and display it in a window using a *device context* for the window. Bit
maps can be displayed in different colors (if you have a color monitor),
rotated, and superimposed on one another. There are some complicated
instructions for Windows on how to deal with superimposing bit maps:
whether any pixel in the new bit map should be added to the pixel
already in that location, whether it should replace the existing pixel,
and so on.

A problem with bit maps is that they are dependent on the *aspect ratio*
of a display device. The aspect ratio is the number of pixels per inch
on the display in the vertical direction compared to the number of
pixels per inch in the horizontal direction. Because aspect ratios differ
from display to display, if you create an image on one screen, such as
a VGA, it may not look right on a different screen, such as an EGA.
It may look stretched in either the vertical or horizontal direction. You
can ascertain from Windows the aspect ratio of the display device in
use when the program is run, and ask Windows to stretch the image

appropriately, but the results may not be very good. The best solution is to create bit maps for each type of display; you run the risk, however, of users running your program on a display for which you did not plan.

Fonts

31

Many fonts are available for Windows, either included with the package or supplied as third-party add-ons. You may want to create your own font, either for sale as a separate item or to meet a specialized need in a particular program. You can create fonts with the FontEdit program that is supplied with SDK. Other programming environments come with their own font editors.

To use FontEdit, you start by specifying the name of an existing file, which FontEdit loads. You specify the size of the font and certain other attributes. FontEdit approximates a font in the size that you requested and displays enlarged versions of the individual characters, which you can edit on a pixel-by-pixel basis. Usually extensive editing is required to produce an acceptable result.

Once you are satisfied with the font, you tell FontEdit to save it in a file. The file has the extension .FON. It is not yet in a format in which it can be used. Before the font is used, it must be incorporated into a program, or more likely, incorporated into a font file with the extension .FNT. These files can contain one or more fonts and are actually DLLs (dynamic link libraries). As discussed earlier in this chapter, DLLs contain code and resources that can be shared by one or more programs. To create a .FNT file, you create a dummy program with the .FON files as its resources and then link the program as a DLL.

Resources

A distinct difference between Windows programs and other DOS programs is in the use of resources. Resources are objects such as icons, menus, and dialog boxes that are incorporated into Windows programs. They are generally created using special programs such as SDKPaint, which generates icons and other graphics, and SDKDialog, which creates dialog boxes. Once you have created the resource, you add it to your Windows program using the resource compiler program, RC.EXE. Some programming environments come with other programs for creating and editing resources. Resources are not used when creating DOS programs.

Creating Windows

Every Windows program must have at least one main window. Creating this window is one of the first things a Windows program must do. Once you have created the main window, you can create other windows that are child windows of the main window (such as document windows) or child windows of other child windows. In this way, there is a hierarchy of windows, with each window other than the main window having a parent and some windows having children. When a window is moved or closed, its child windows are moved or closed with it.

A window to a programmer is not quite the same thing as a window to a user. A dialog box is a type of window, but a button is also a window. If a dialog box contains buttons, those buttons are child windows of the dialog box. When you click a button within a dialog box, a message indicating the key click is initially sent to the window that is the button.

Window Classes

Each window you create must belong to a specific *class*. The class defines certain properties of the window and also specifies which function within the program or within Windows is responsible for maintaining the window. Some classes are predefined by Windows, and others are defined specifically for a particular program. Table 31.1 shows the predefined window styles.

Table 31.1. Predefined window styles.

Type	Description
Button	An image of a button that you can "press" with the mouse
Edit	A window in which you can enter text
Static	A window containing text or simple graphics
Listbox	A window containing a list of items from which the user can choose
Combobox	A combination box containing an edit box or a static control together with a list box, typically used for selecting a file name from a list of files in a directory
Scrollbar	A window that works like the scroll bar in a standard window

31

As you can see, there are predefined window classes for the standard controls used for interacting with users. The advantage of using predefined window classes is that Windows handles many of the functions. For example, if an Edit control is used, Windows handles moving the cursor, inserting and deleting characters, and so on. You can request Windows to return to your program the string of characters entered. If a button is used, Windows displays the button in its pressed state when the user clicks it and sends a message to the program that the button has been pressed.

Other classes are defined by the programmer using the Windows `RegisterClass()` function. The following are some of the attributes you can specify for a class of windows:

▲ The class name

▲ The function within your program that processes messages for the window

▲ The type of cursor to display

▲ The icon to display when the window is closed

▲ The background brush (color and pattern)

Each class is given a name. For example, in writing a solitaire program, you could specify a class of window within your program to represent playing cards and call that class `card`. When you want to display a new card, you instruct Windows to create a window with the class `card`, and the new window will have the properties associated with that class.

Other Window Attributes

In addition to specifying a class for a new window, you specify other attributes. These include

▲ The size of the window

▲ The initial position

▲ The title to appear in the title bar, if there is one

▲ The window's parent

▲ The menu to appear in the window, if any

▲ The window style

The style specifies many of the attributes of the window, including

▲ The type of border, if any

▲ Whether there are scroll bars (horizontal or vertical)

▲ Whether there is a title bar

▲ Whether there is a minimize box

▲ Whether the window is initially active when it is created

Classes and Program Instances

You know you can run more than one copy of a program at the same time under Windows. Each copy is known as an *instance*. When a program starts, it can find out whether other instances of the same program are currently running. If it finds out that it is not the first instance, it does not need to define any classes it uses because the primary instance of the program has already registered the new class types with Windows. The new instance of the program can skip the part of the code that defines those classes.

Manipulating Windows

Once you have created a window, you can manipulate it in many ways. You can move it to a new location, change its size, or temporarily hide it. You can scroll areas within the window. You can change the window's title or its background color. You can also write text or draw images within the window, as you will see in the next section.

Your program also receives messages associated with that window, for example that the cursor has entered its area or that the user is manipulating the scroll bar. You also receive a message from Windows from time to time to repaint a part of the window that might have been temporarily covered up by another window.

The Graphics Device Interface

The part of Windows that handles output to a graphics device is known as the GDI (*Graphics Device Interface*). Graphics devices include video cards (such as the one that sends output to your monitor), printers, and plotters. Output in this context refers to both text and graphics; because text in Windows is bit-mapped, displaying text is considered to be a graphical operation. Even if a particular printer cannot display graphics, it is still controlled through the GDI.

GDI and Device Drivers

When you install Windows, or modify your installation using Control Panel, device drivers, with the extension .DRV, are installed into your Windows System directory. These drivers contain code for actually controlling the devices, but you do not have to write directly to the device drivers: The GDI acts as an interface between the program and the drivers. The flow of control is, therefore, program to GDI to driver to device.

GDI Functions

GDI includes a large number of functions you can call to control graphics devices. These include

▲ Displaying or printing text

▲ Selecting colors, fonts, and brushes

▲ Displaying or printing bit maps

▲ Displaying or printing lines, ellipses, and polygons

These functions are described later in this chapter.

Device Contexts

A *device context* describes a number of settings for a given device. These include the background color, the currently selected brush, and the coordinates of the area that are available to the program. Before a program can write to a device it must first obtain from Windows a device context for that device. Windows returns a *handle* to the device context, and the program uses this handle for subsequent output to the device. A handle is a number that the program uses to refer to the object.

It is the use of device contexts that enables multiple programs to share a device; for example, you might be running a drawing program in one part of your screen and a word processor in another part. You might tell the drawing program to change the background color for the drawing; you would not want the same operation to change the background color of the text document. By using a drawing program device context, that program will be prevented from changing parts of the screen that do not belong to it.

Pens and Brushes

To output text or graphics to a graphics device, you use a pen or a brush. The pen is used for text and lines and describes the thickness and color of text and lines that are drawn. An application can either use one of the stock pens provided by Windows (Black, Null and White) or you can create one using the CreatePen() function. With CreatePen() you can specify the line style, the thickness of the line, and the color.

The dashed and dotted styles cannot be used if the line is greater than one pixel wide; they also are not suitable for text. The Insideframe style displays a second line inside the frame of graphics primitives such as squares and circles. The default pen automatically allocated to a device context is a black solid pen, one pixel thick.

You can draw with a brush as well as a pen. You can also use a brush to fill areas. Windows provides a set of predefined brushes (black, dark gray, gray, hollow, light gray, null and white) and you can also specify your own in a similar way to pens. A solid brush is created using (you guessed it!) the CreateSolidBrush function. All you specify is the color. You can also specify a hatched brush. These contain regular patterns of lines within the patterns painted using the brush.

Color

When you want to display text or graphics you must specify a color value unless you want to use the defaults (black for a pen, white for a brush). All colors are constructed by varying amounts of red, green and blue light. In Windows, you specify a color by giving a value that specifies each of these components. This value is known as a COLORREF, and is constructed using the macro RGB(redval, greenval, blueval) where redval, greenval, and blueval specify the amounts of each color to include. In this scheme, black is RGB(0, 0, 0), indicating no amounts of any color, and white is RGB(255, 255, 255) indicating maximum amounts of each color.

Problems can come from the limitations of certain output devices. For example, some video cards can display thousands of different colors, but only 256 at any one time. The colors currently in use are specified using a hardware palette stored on the card itself. You might think at first that there is no problem there: You simply limit the number of colors your program uses to no more than 256. Remember, however, that other programs might be running at the same time; they may be trying to display additional colors on the screen in another window.

The combined number of different colors in use between your program and any other programs running at the same time might be more than 256. Windows has to do some very clever manipulation to ensure that the limits are observed; if a program tries to add more colors than the device can support, Windows starts to approximate colors, replacing some colors with the nearest color already available.

For greater accuracy, your program can create a logical palette by giving Windows a list of colors it wishes to use. When you handle colors in this way, Windows can display the foreground window using colors from that logical palette, and in that way can ensure that your wishes for that window are respected. Then background windows are displayed using the closest available approximations if not enough colors are available in the device's palette.

If this all sounds complicated, it is. There are even further complications, because RGB values are not absolute definitions of colors, but only relative to the characteristics of a particular device. In other words, pure red (RGB(255, 0, 0)) on one device may not look exactly like pure red on another device. A true device-independent graphics device interface should probably take this into account.

It may not be critical for many applications, but it can be quite important. If you created a picture on your screen using carefully chosen colors, you would be disappointed if it looked quite different when printed on a color printer. Unfortunately, this probably will be the case. With color display and printing, what you see is rarely what you get.

Displaying and Printing Text

You can instruct Windows to display text in a window by specifying the string to print, the device context, and the coordinates. You can also choose the color and the style of the text by specifying a pen and a font. We already discussed pens and colors earlier.

All screens in Windows are bit-mapped. A complication of using bit-mapped screens for text is that you have to specify the coordinates of where you want the text to appear in units that relate to the device in question (normally pixels), rather than in terms of rows and columns of text characters. Because Windows can use proportional fonts, where the characters are not all the same width, displaying successive strings of text is not very straightforward. The point at which each string ends depends on the width of each character in the string for the particular font in use.

Fortunately, Windows provides functions to provide this proportional font information and to compute the length of the string as actually written. Windows can also handle foreign character sets such as Kanji (the Japanese pictographs) in which the character displayed may occupy more than one byte within the string. If your program is to be used internationally, you may need to take this into account.

Fonts

One of the strengths of Windows is its capability to display text in many different styles and sizes. This applies not only to the screen, but also to printers and other output devices, subject to the limitations of each device. Programmers who want to take advantage of this capability have three choices.

▲ Use a stock font

▲ Ask the user to select a font

▲ Use a specially created font

Stock Fonts

Because users can install their own fonts, programmers cannot know exactly which fonts are available. For many applications, this is not important. A programmer might not consider it necessary, for example,

to let the user choose the font in which to display data in a database program. When offering a choice of font is not important, a programmer can ask Windows to use a stock font. You can request Windows to use one of the following stock fonts shown in Table 31.2.

Table 31.2. Stock fonts.

Font	Description
System	The font used by Windows to display text such as menu bar options and window titles. It is the only font that is guaranteed to be available.
ANSI Fixed	Fixed-pitch font based on the ANSI character set.
ANSI Variable	Variable-pitch font based on the ANSI character set.
Device Default	Windows uses the default font for the device in question, usually built into the device's memory.
OEM Fixed	Windows uses a fixed-pitch font based on the character set used by the particular system. For example, with VGA systems, Windows uses the character set built into the VGA adapter.

Choosing from Available Fonts

With many programs, users have the ability to select a font in which to display text. This is typically a menu bar option. When the user chooses this option, a list of available typefaces appears, and beside it is a list of font sizes.

When you want to offer this option to the user, you must first ask Windows for a list of fonts that are available on the individual system. Windows returns a list of available fonts, which you then instruct Windows to display in a list box. For a font to be available, it is not sufficient that it is present on the disk. The font must have been installed through Control Panel or specifically loaded by a program.

Logical Fonts

You can also use a function call that asks Windows to select a font matching certain specifications such as size and family type. Windows searches the list of available fonts and chooses the nearest match. To

some extent, Windows can modify fonts to make a closer match. For example, if an underlined font is requested Windows can add the underlining to each character. Windows can also create a font in a new size, but only by doubling the size of an existing font. Windows does not create intermediate font sizes. For this reason, Windows does not always provide a font that is exactly the size you requested.

Loading Fonts

As described earlier, you only can use fonts that are actively available. This means that they have been installed using Control Panel or are specifically loaded by a program. To load a font in this way, you must specify within your program the name of a file that contains the font. This is generally a special font file, with the extension .FNT. Fonts can also be incorporated into program files, although this is officially discouraged. To load the font, you use the AddFontResource() function.

Once loaded, you can make a font available to other Windows programs that happen to be running at the same time by telling Windows to publish the font. Windows sends a message to any other programs indicating that the new font is available. The other programs may or may not take advantage of this message.

Drawing

You may want to display pictures in your Windows program. There are two ways in which you can do this. One is by displaying bit maps, which define every pixel in the image.

The other way is by drawing the image using graphics primitives. These are instructions to Windows to draw objects. You first select a pen (it can have varying thicknesses, or you can draw dots and dashes) in the device context. You can also specify a color. The following are some of the objects you can draw:

▲ Lines

▲ Rectangles and rounded rectangles

▲ Ellipses

▲ Arcs

▲ Pies

31

You draw a line by specifying the device context and using the MoveTo() and LineTo() functions. You move the pen to the starting position by specifying the horizontal and vertical coordinates and then telling Windows to draw a line to another specified position.

You draw a rectangle by specifying the device context as well as the coordinates of the top-left and bottom-right corners. For rounded rectangles, you also specify the starting and ending points of the ellipse used to draw the rounded corners.

You draw an ellipse by specifying the device context and the coordinates of a rectangle that the ellipse would fit into.

You draw an arc by specifying the device context, the coordinates of a rectangle containing the circle that the arc forms part of, and the starting and ending points for the arc itself.

Pies are wedges cut out of a circle, such as the shape of a slice of pizza. They are drawn in the same way as arcs.

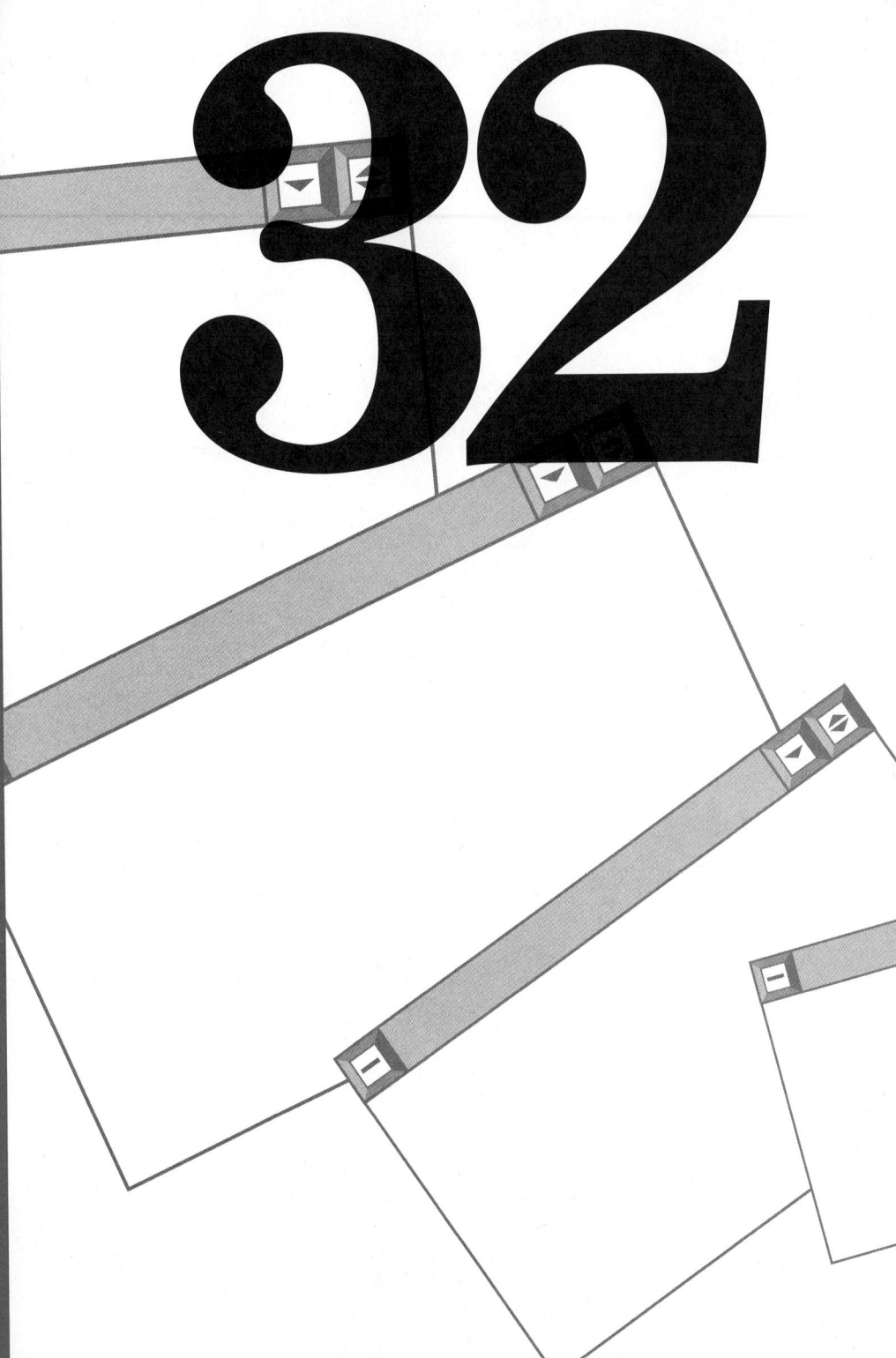

CHAPTER

32

Windows Programming Environments

Most PC users shy away from anything labeled "programming" because they have an image of programming as arcane and time-consuming. Ten years ago this was true, but it is no longer. Programming environments are available for all levels of users, from beginning to advanced. Even with the low-level tools, you can create useful Windows programs literally in minutes.

All programs described throughout this book were written in a programming environment. Most were written in Microsoft C with a special Windows add-on called the "Software Development Kit," or SDK for short. Until Windows 3.0 was released, this was about the only way to write real Windows programs. Since the release of Versions 3.0 and 3.1, however, dozens of additional programming environments and tools have been made available for Windows.

If you are interested in tools for creating Windows applications, see Reference C, "Windows Product Directory," for more information on these and other products for Windows.

Why You Should Program

If you read Chapter 31, "Introduction to Windows Programming Elements," you learned about the many parts that make up a Windows program. As the introduction to that chapter emphasized, you do not need to understand those parts to program in many programming environments. All you really need to understand is what you want your program to do and how you want it to look. The elements described in Chapter 31 are important to programmers using some languages but unimportant to most other programmers.

Everybody has something they wish Windows would do that it doesn't presently do. It might be something simple, like the ability to run one program and then automatically run another one, such as if you always run Excel after running Word for Windows. You might want something more advanced, such as a program that looks in a text file on the network for particular information and if it is there, changes the file with new information.

Of course, you can perform actions such as these by yourself by hand. However, one of the main reasons for owning a computer is to automate repetitive processes. The programs you use in Windows already help you to do that, but you might want more.

Introduction to Programming Environments

A programming language is different from a programming environment. The language is just the low-level way of communicating what you want; the environment is the situation in which you communicate it. English is a language, but you can communicate in environments such as on the stage, in books, on television, and so on. Thus, for one programming language, there can be many environments. Of course, some environments are easier to communicate in than others.

In the early days of PCs, there were many programming languages, such as BASIC, C, and FORTH. The environments for these languages were fairly primitive, making it seem that programming in the language itself was hard. Over time, more languages became available and there was more competition among language developers, which caused them to improve the languages and, more importantly, the environments.

As environments improved, companies started developing environments that took the tedium and pain out of programming. The companies realized that many more people would program if they didn't have to think about the low-level details of the computer or the language. Programming environments today are so much better than even five years ago that many people who would have never survived writing their first program can now produce simple programs easily.

Simultaneous to this improvement in environments, many PC programs started sporting their own macro languages. Macro languages are pretty much like other programming languages and are often patterned after such popular programming languages as Pascal. Programs such as WordPerfect and 1-2-3 came with macro languages to help you automate tasks within the program. Later, some programs started coming with macro languages that even helped control other programs.

32

New Languages

A few companies noticed that many people who thought they couldn't program were writing macros just fine. The companies also noticed that millions of people were writing MS-DOS batch programs. These people didn't feel intimidated by the macro or batch language because it wasn't packaged as "programming." Clearly, there was an opportunity to create languages and environments that didn't seem like programming but in fact were.

The result was the creation of two types of simplified programming environments: the instant program and the batch system.

▲ A simplified programming environment is one in which you associate actions with objects on the screen such as buttons and menus. You can display information and graphics easily. The programming language is much less complex than standard programming languages, and the environment helps prevent you from making mistakes.

▲ A batch system enables you to run a series of programs in sequence. It also enables you to control the way the programs are run and enables you to get and give information as the program is running.

The first popular simplified programming environment was HyperCard on the Macintosh. Apple gave HyperCard so much publicity that many software companies came out with competing environments for the Macintosh and the PC. These environments make creating and modifying programs almost as easy as using drawing packages.

Languages, Environments, and Windows

Languages for MS-DOS had fewer requirements than languages for Windows. Under MS-DOS, your program could have any user interface you wanted. Under Windows, you must conform to the Windows user interface guidelines and provide things like scrollable windows. You must also follow the design rules described in Chapter 31.

Programming environments can make your programs run under Windows in two ways: They can force you to write all the code that implements the rules, or they do all that work for you. Surprisingly, there are reasons for both methods. Forcing programmers to enter all the code gives programmers much more power to add nonstandard features to their programs, which you can't do if all the low-level instructions (like handling drive operations and data transfers from a port to a device) are hidden. Of course, if you want only the standard Windows features, you can write programs significantly faster if you don't have to deal with the low-level instructions.

Choosing an Environment

If you are new to programming, you should start with one of the simplified environments or batch languages described in the next few sections. Because programming involves learning the language and the programming environment, and understanding how programs interact with Windows, you are best off starting with the less flexible but easy environments. You can always switch if you feel you have outgrown one of the environments.

Many millions of people have experimented with programming in BASIC on the PC. If you have learned BASIC, you can certainly start creating programs with Visual Basic. If you feel more adventurous and want to create programs with less of a "safety net," you can probably

32

learn C or Pascal. Although the environments for these programs are not quite as friendly as for the easier languages, you probably will not find them too difficult.

If you are a serious programmer but haven't tried programming in Windows, you should feel comfortable in any of the environments described in this chapter. Note that the object-oriented programming (OOP) environments are quite different from traditional sequential languages. However, the time you spend learning to use an OOP environment will most likely save you even more time in constructing a full-blown program.

Simplified Environments

In a simplified environment, you might never see the underlying commands that normally go with creating a program. You put together programs from menus and palettes of tools. The "work" of a program often can also be programmed simply by selecting from menus and dialog boxes. If you start with a premade program, such as one that you were given by a coworker or that you got from an information service, you can modify it to your own tastes just as easily.

Simplified environments usually have their own associated languages. These languages are much easier to use than standard programming languages because the market for these environments usually consists of people with less interest in programming. The languages are much more tolerant of errors and often help you as you do whatever programming you need.

ToolBook

Asymetrix, the developers of ToolBook, made an early arrangement with Microsoft to distribute a sample ToolBook program with Windows Version 3. That piqued many people's interest enough to look at the ToolBook environment. They found that creating programs with ToolBook is, in fact, very easy.

ToolBook programs consist of "books" with many pages. As you navigate through the program, you are actually viewing different pages. You can interact with pages because they have buttons, lists, and other Windows items. You can show pages one at a time or let the user specify the pages by choosing items on the current page. The pages can also have their own animation and sound.

Thus, to program in ToolBook, you simply choose what information you want to show (and its layout and so on) and how you want the user to see it presented. You also decide what kind of information you want from the user. Advanced ToolBook programming can do much more than this, but most ToolBook programs really just describe what is shown on the screen and how to get from page to page.

Figure 32.1 shows the ToolBook programming environment. It is just a blank page, waiting for you to put items on it. The tool palette has items such as buttons and text fields, as well as standard drawing tools. The indicator in the lower-left corner shows you what page number you are on.

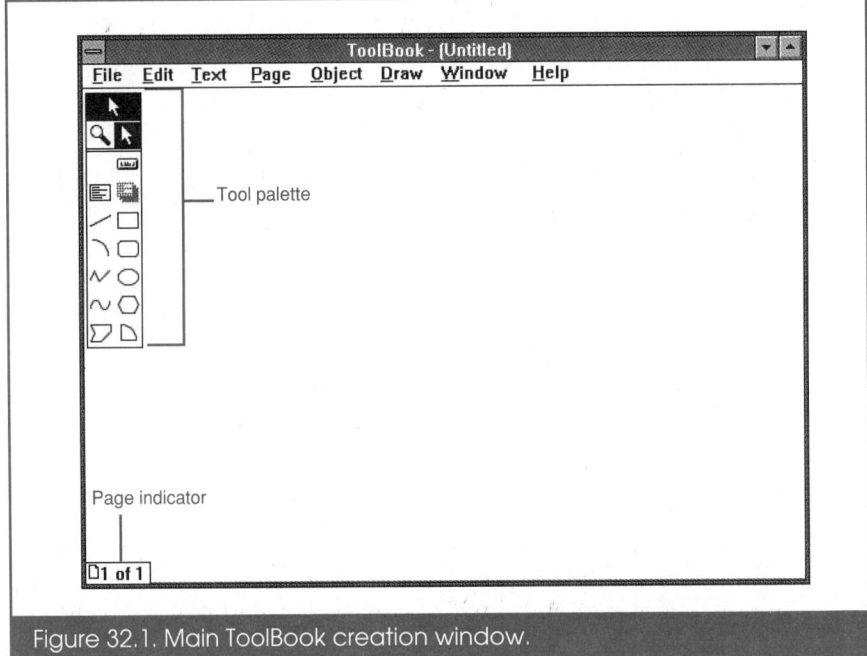

Figure 32.1. Main ToolBook creation window.

ToolBook creates the programs for most of the common items you use. If you want to create your own scripts, the language is fairly easy. Figure 32.2 shows a typical ToolBook script.

Asymetrix
110 110th Ave. NE, #717
Bellevue, WA 98006
(206)637-1500

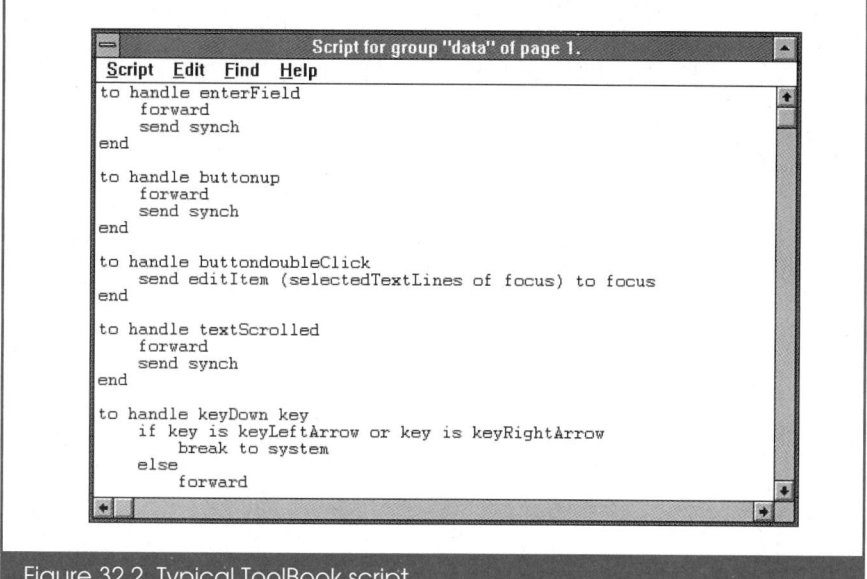

Figure 32.2. Typical ToolBook script.

32

Plus

Plus uses many of the same concepts as ToolBook. Rather than books, Plus uses "stacks"; pages are called "cards." This terminology is taken from Apple's HyperCard. In fact, Plus can read stacks created in HyperCard and use them as a base for stacks that you write. The procedure you use to create programs is the same: You add active elements such as buttons and text fields to cards in a stack.

Plus has many advantages over ToolBook. It runs on many operating systems, not just Windows. You can move your Plus stacks to OS/2 and to the Macintosh, so one stack can be used in many different parts of a company. It also handles multimedia elements such as sound and animation better.

Figure 32.3 shows the Plus program creation window. The tool palette is at the top of the window, under the menu bar. The menus help you specify how each object you put in your stack reacts and what card the user sees next.

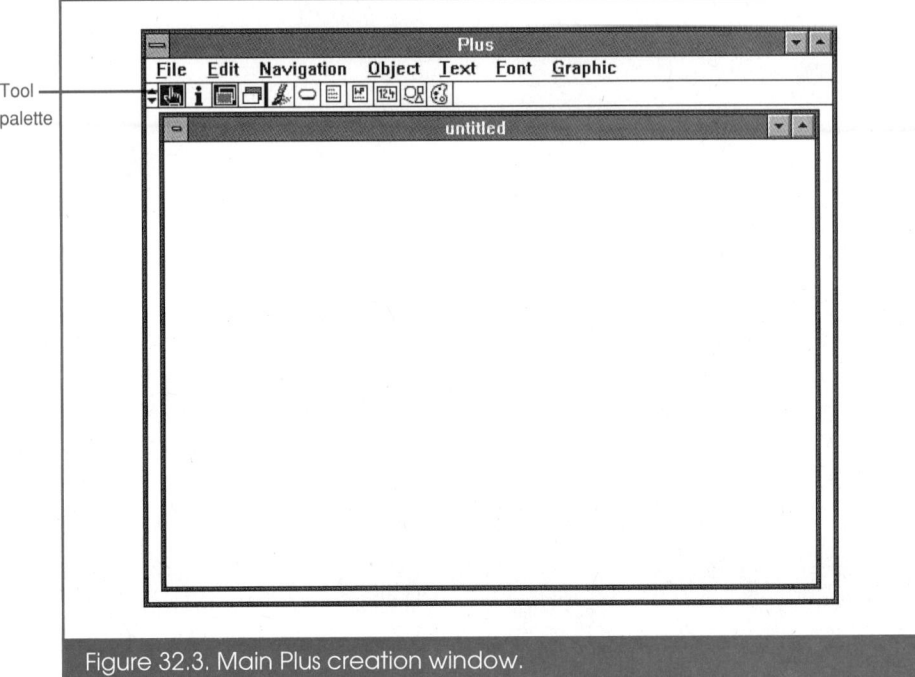

Figure 32.3. Main Plus creation window.

The scripting language in Plus is called PPL, for Plus Programming Language. It is patterned after HyperTalk, the HyperCard programming language. A typical PPL script is shown in Figure 32.4.

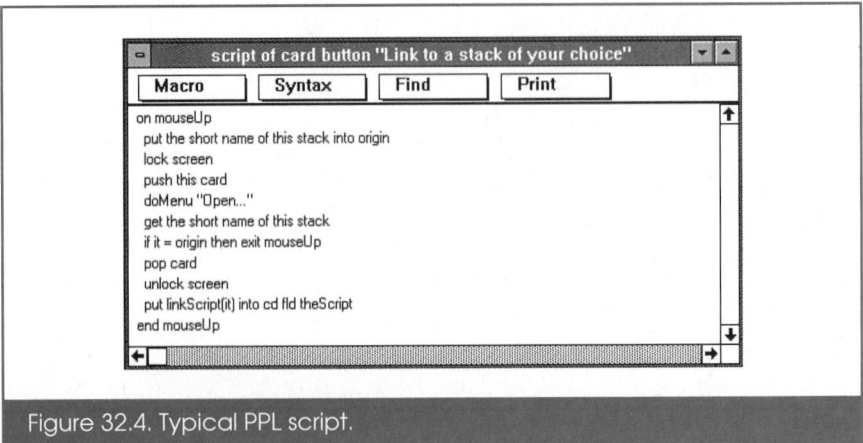

Figure 32.4. Typical PPL script.

Spinnaker Software
201 Broadway
Cambridge, MA 02139
(800)826-0706

Batch Languages

32

Batch languages enable you to automate Windows tasks that involve more than one program. They also enable you to control programs by sending them keystrokes and mouse movements. You can imagine a batch language as a control center for Windows. Just like you take actions when you run programs, you can tell a batch program to take those actions for you.

The advantage of having a batch program is that you can automate tasks so that they run without you. In this sense, batch languages are like macro processors such as Recorder (covered in Chapter 13, "Other Accessories"). For instance, assume that one of the things you do every week is generate a table from a database management system and send it by electronic mail to your bookkeeping firm. A batch program can handle a task like this easily.

Batch programs under Windows have additional challenges. For example, many people run non-Windows programs and use the information from those programs in their work with Windows. A batch program has to be able to interface with non-Windows programs. The tasks you want to automate are often not completely deterministic: You need to decide things after looking at results. Batch programs need a way to present information to you and enable you to direct them in their next steps.

The elemental programming parts of a batch language are commands that give instructions (such as running programs or sending keystrokes), commands that involve the user interface (such as those that put up dialog boxes or change menus) and commands for choosing things. They are usually fairly easy to follow, especially if you are at all familiar with BASIC. They mimic the BASIC language in some ways, and they are generally easy to write.

> **Tip:** There is no clear line between batch programs and BASIC-like languages. They both perform similar tasks. The next section in this chapter describes BASIC environments.

Batch programs are written with text editors, usually Notepad. Note that batch languages do not have environments like other languages. You write the programs in a text editor, and you run them from a dialog box. There really isn't much else to the environment.

WinBatch

WinBatch is a rich language for creating batch programs. This language has simple commands for activating and running programs as well as sending keystrokes to programs. Figure 32.5 shows part of a typical WinBatch program. Note how much of the program consists of comments so that you can follow a program written by other people. The program shown here activates Notepad and gives the **F**ile **O**pen command but replaces the Filename field with *.* rather than *.TXT so that you can open any file.

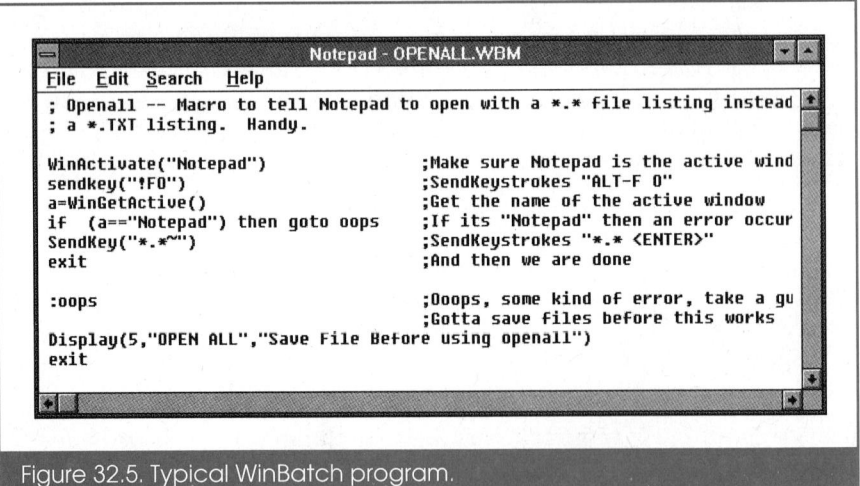

Figure 32.5. Typical WinBatch program.

Wilson WindowWare
2701 California Ave. SW, Suite 212
Seattle, WA 98116
(800)762-8383

Bridge

The Bridge system enables you to make sophisticated batch files that control Windows. Softbridge Microsystems, the developers of Bridge, also wrote the Recorder program that comes with Windows. The Bridge program comes in different levels. If you are developing complete batch systems, you can use Bridge to create programs that other people can use for a licensing fee. The lowest level enables you to create your own batch programs that can control your environment and communicate with MS-DOS programs.

Figure 32.6 shows an example of a Bridge program that starts an MS-DOS session and sends commands to it. It then receives the information and closes the MS-DOS window.

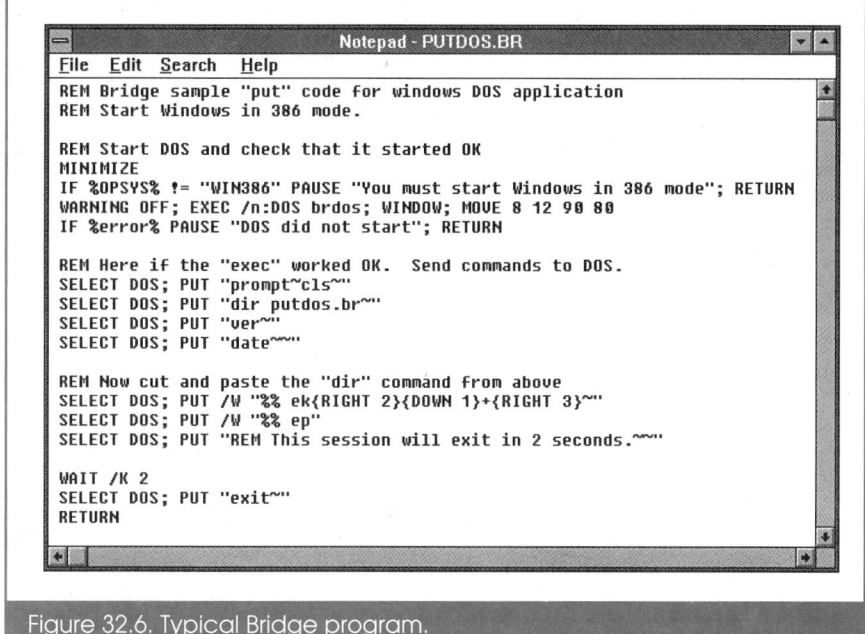

```
Notepad - PUTDOS.BR

File   Edit   Search   Help

REM Bridge sample "put" code for windows DOS application
REM Start Windows in 386 mode.

REM Start DOS and check that it started OK
MINIMIZE
IF %OPSYS% != "WIN386" PAUSE "You must start Windows in 386 mode"; RETURN
WARNING OFF; EXEC /n:DOS brdos; WINDOW; MOVE 8 12 90 80
IF %error% PAUSE "DOS did not start"; RETURN

REM Here if the "exec" worked OK.  Send commands to DOS.
SELECT DOS; PUT "prompt~cls~"
SELECT DOS; PUT "dir putdos.br~"
SELECT DOS; PUT "ver~"
SELECT DOS; PUT "date~~"

REM Now cut and paste the "dir" command from above
SELECT DOS; PUT /W "%% ek{RIGHT 2}{DOWN 1}+{RIGHT 3}~"
SELECT DOS; PUT /W "%% ep"
SELECT DOS; PUT "REM This session will exit in 2 seconds.~~"

WAIT /K 2
SELECT DOS; PUT "exit~"
RETURN
```

Figure 32.6. Typical Bridge program.

Softbridge Inc.
125 CambridgePark Dr.
Cambridge, MA 02140
(800)955-9190

ObjectScript

ObjectScript is a simplified environment that is somewhat like a batch language. Unlike batch languages, you construct programs in a visual fashion like a simplified environment. ObjectScript differs from the simplified environments in that most of its power is in the controlling of other Windows programs. It also has many features that make it almost like a development language. For example, you can access dBASE files from within a program. You can also make two-dimensional tables like spreadsheets.

ObjectScript has its own editing environment, shown in Figure 32.7. Because ObjectScript is like a simplified environment, a script is associated with an object on the screen (like a button); it is not an entire process like other batch programs.

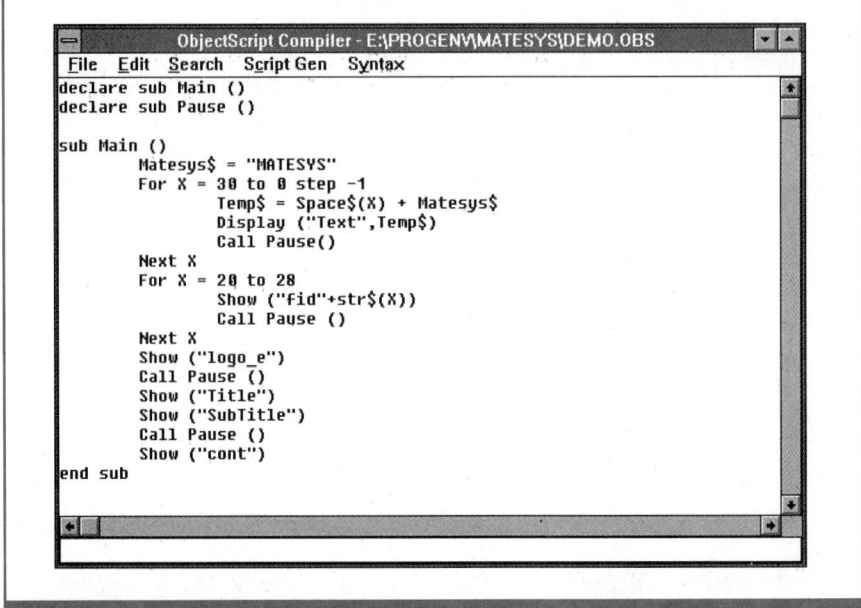

Figure 32.7. Typical ObjectScript program.

MateSys
3 Bethesda Metro Center, Suite 700
Bethesda, MD 20814
(800)777-0545

BASIC Languages

BASIC (Beginner's All-Purpose Symbolic Instruction Code) has been the most popular microcomputer language for almost 15 years. Almost every personal computer has come with BASIC free, which has given BASIC a huge audience. Even though most advanced applications are no longer developed using BASIC, it's often the first exposure to programming languages for many people.

As programming languages go, BASIC is fairly good for beginners. The structure of a BASIC program is easy to follow, the essential parts of the language are easy to remember, and the programs usually run as expected. It has major limitations if you are doing serious programming, but it is still used by tens of thousands of business programmers. Dozens of good books on how to learn BASIC are available.

The BASIC language has evolved with the PC. There are many variations on the BASIC language, but by far the best-known one is Microsoft's BASIC. Originally, BASIC could only put characters on a screen in sequential order. Later, you were able to make the characters appear anywhere on the screen. Next, graphics were added so that you could draw shapes, display pictures, and change the color of the screen (primitive sound was added as well). After that, Microsoft improved BASIC so that it was easier to program by letting you structure your programs more freely.

Windows presents interesting challenges to a programming language. For instance, in MS-DOS, you always know the screen size; in Windows, you do not know how large the window is because the user might have resized it. In Windows, you can write text in many different fonts, so placement of characters differs depending on the font. BASIC was never designed to handle things like dialog boxes or menus. And so on.

Visual Basic

Visual Basic is the next step in the evolution of BASIC. Using simple commands, you can control the Windows environment in such ways as making menus and creating dialog boxes. The main part of the programming language is the same Microsoft BASIC that millions of people have learned. Visual Basic can create programs for both Windows and OS/2.

One of the advantages of using Visual Basic over other Windows programming environments is how easy it is to design the user interface. Using the Visual Basic tool palette, the programmer can design custom windows for programs in a matter of minutes.

Figure 32.8 shows the Visual Basic programming environment. You can create, edit, and run programs from the environment as well as debug them. After you are done creating and testing your program, you can turn it into an executable file that you can sell or give away freely.

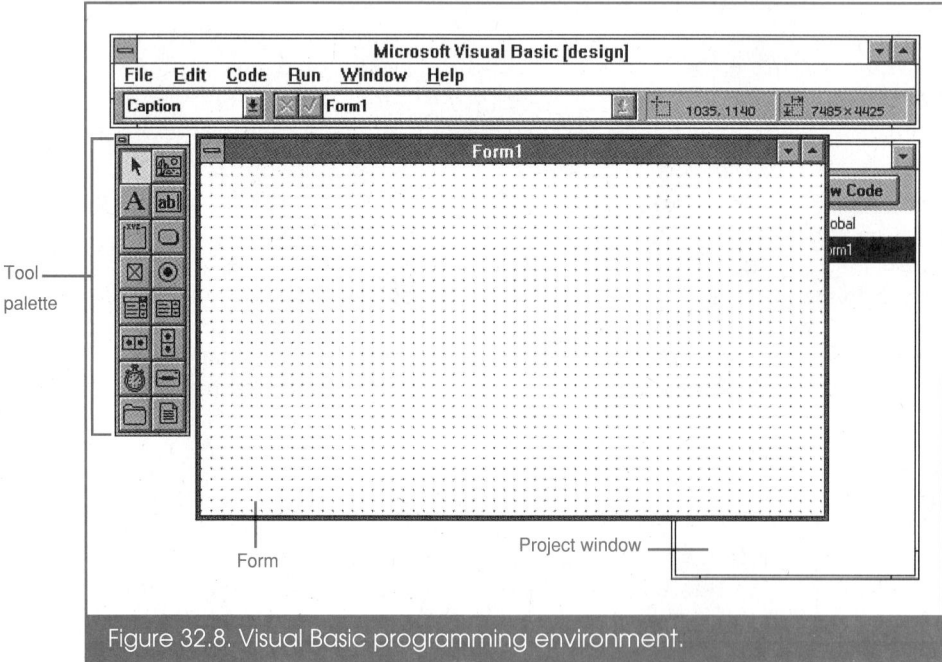

Figure 32.8. Visual Basic programming environment.

Visual Basic uses the concept of a project for the programs you write. Because you might have many files for one program, you need a way to organize them and know what is in your program. Figure 32.9 shows a typical project window. Breaking up a project into separate parts makes it easier to develop other programs because you can reuse the parts you built before.

The BASIC programming language in Visual Basic is pretty much like standard BASIC. However, since Visual Basic is an event-driven language, it has special ways of dealing with objects and events. The code looks much like code from standard BASIC. For example, Figure 32.10 shows the code for the directory list of a Save As command.

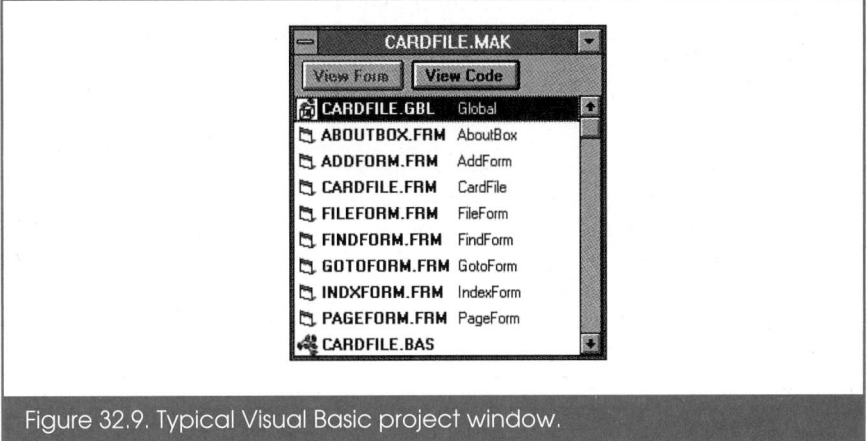

Figure 32.9. Typical Visual Basic project window.

```
Sub Dir_DirectoryList_Change ()

    ' Make the current directory that of Dir_DirectoryList.
    '
    ChDir Dir_DirectoryList.Path

    ' Display the new path
    '
    Lbl_CurrentDirectory.Caption = Dir_DirectoryList.Path

    ' Notifiy the File Listbox of the path change
    '
    File_FileList.Path = Dir_DirectoryList.Path

    UpDate_FileSpec SaveFileDlg

End Sub
```

Figure 32.10. Typical Visual Basic program.

Realizer

Like Visual Basic, Realizer enables you to create Windows items like menus and dialog boxes with single BASIC commands. It also has access to other Windows programs that are running so that it can be

used to control them. The programming environment, shown in Figure 32.11, enables you to write and run programs. You can also step through a program to look for errors and look at the variables you use.

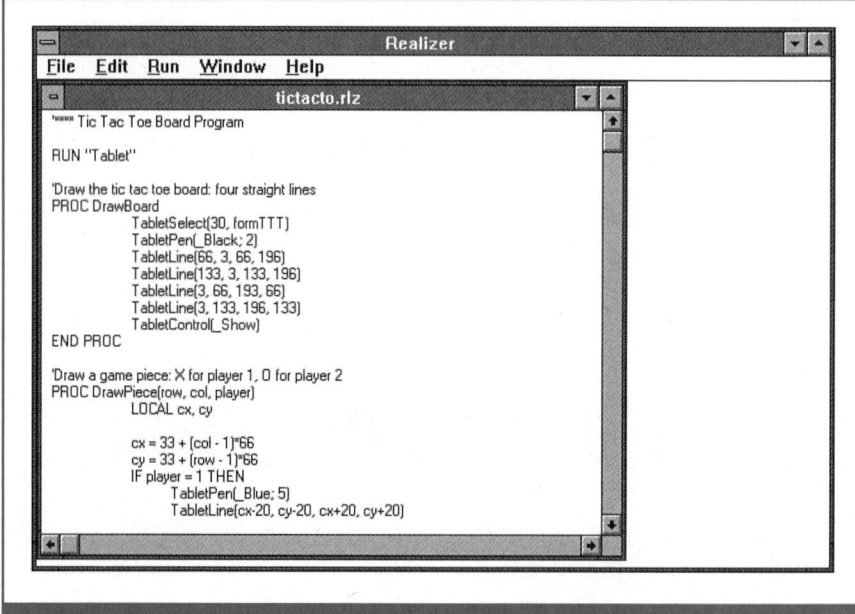

Figure 32.11. Realizer programming environment.

Realizer also has many additional features that go way beyond standard BASIC. You can read and write files in many formats (such as Lotus 1-2-3 and Excel files), use tools for making spreadsheets and charts from within programs, design a dialog box on-screen and turn it into programming steps, make text-editing windows, and animate pictures. For example, the program in Figure 32.12 shows the few lines needed to set up a spreadsheet. Figure 32.13 shows the result.

Because Realizer does not require the user to buy a run-time module in order to run Realizer programs, you are able to write programs and give them away to people who do not have Realizer. This makes Realizer a great environment for a midlevel programmer to create sophisticated Windows programs that can be sold or given away.

Within Technologies
8000 MidAtlantic Dr.
Mount Laurel, NJ 08054
(609)273-9880

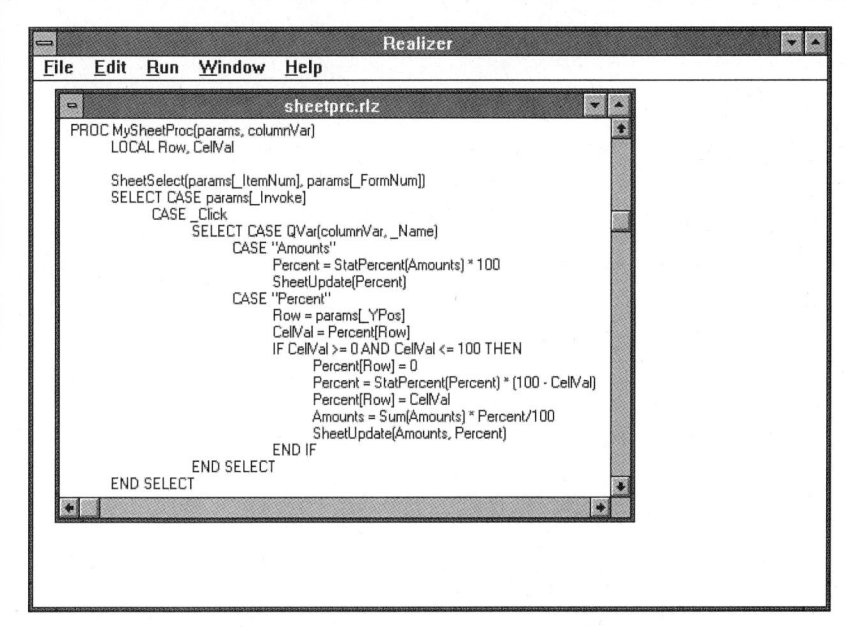

Figure 32.12. Program to set up a spreadsheet.

32

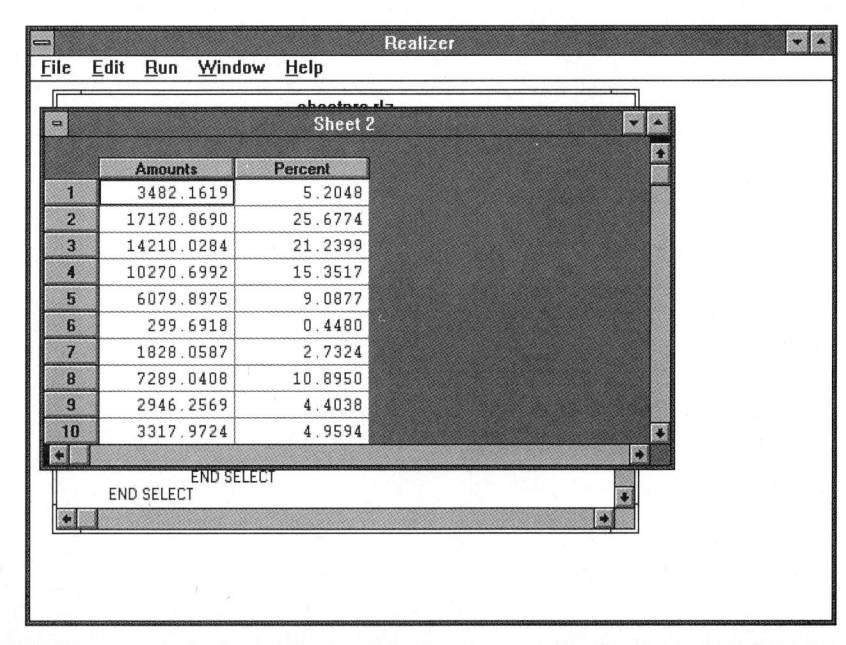

Figure 32.13. Spreadsheet object.

C and C++

After BASIC, C is the most popular programming language. In fact, at least three-quarters of all commercial MS-DOS and Windows programs are written in C or C++, which is a derivative of C. C is considered to be a much better professional programming language than BASIC for many reasons:

▲ It gives you more control over the computer. You can program "closer to the chips" if you want to.

▲ The programming environments for C are much better for creating large programs. It is easier to create programs in parts and combine them later.

▲ C handles memory much better than BASIC.

▲ C programs are more compact than the equivalent BASIC programs.

Note that these arguments might have been valid five years ago but are not as valid anymore. BASIC has moved ahead rapidly, and although some of these arguments might still be valid, BASIC programming is fairly good.

Microsoft C and the SDK

For a long time, the only viable programming environment for creating professional Windows programs was Microsoft C with the addition of the Microsoft Windows Software Development Kit, commonly known as the SDK. Microsoft C is a popular MS-DOS development environment that includes many tools such as an editor, a debugger, programs for keeping the many parts of a large program in order, and so on. The SDK gave many C programmers a good start on Windows programming.

Figure 32.14 shows part of a typical C program for Windows. The extensions for programming for Windows in C are described in Chapter 31, "Introduction to Windows Programming Elements." Almost all the extensions are simply more function calls and predefined variables.

The SDK comes with a version of Windows which has special features that aid in program debugging. This gives you flexibility in determining when the program is making Windows calls and when it encounters Windows-specific problems.

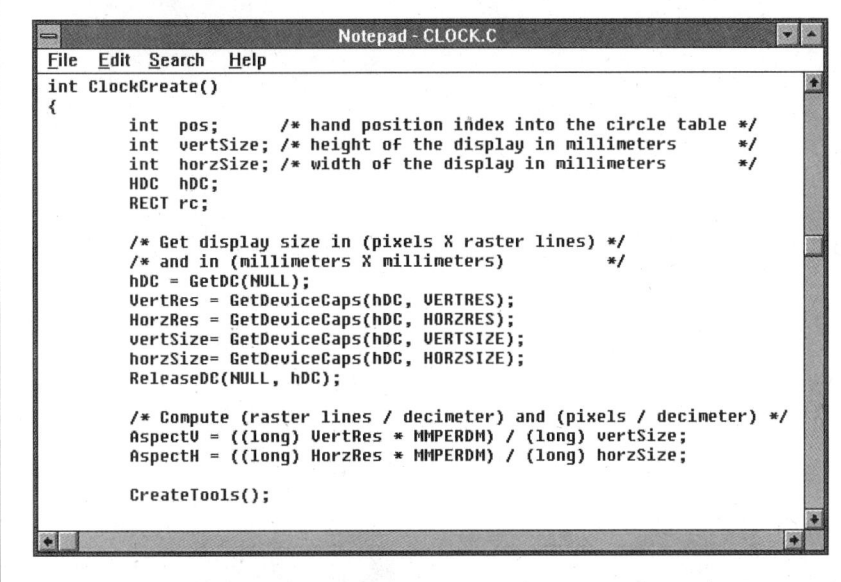

```
                    Notepad - CLOCK.C
 File  Edit  Search  Help
int ClockCreate()
{
        int  pos;      /* hand position index into the circle table */
        int  vertSize; /* height of the display in millimeters      */
        int  horzSize; /* width of the display in millimeters        */
        HDC  hDC;
        RECT rc;

        /* Get display size in (pixels X raster lines) */
        /* and in (millimeters X millimeters)          */
        hDC = GetDC(NULL);
        VertRes = GetDeviceCaps(hDC, VERTRES);
        HorzRes = GetDeviceCaps(hDC, HORZRES);
        vertSize= GetDeviceCaps(hDC, VERTSIZE);
        horzSize= GetDeviceCaps(hDC, HORZSIZE);
        ReleaseDC(NULL, hDC);

        /* Compute (raster lines / decimeter) and (pixels / decimeter) */
        AspectV = ((long) VertRes * MMPERDM) / (long) vertSize;
        AspectH = ((long) HorzRes * MMPERDM) / (long) horzSize;

        CreateTools();
```

Figure 32.14. Part of a typical C program.

Other tools in the SDK help you create parts of a Windows program that you need to create a finished product. These include

▲ SDKPaint, shown in Figure 32.15, enables you to create icons, cursors, and bit maps. You then use these resources in your program and call them from your C code.

▲ The Dialog Editor enables you to create dialog boxes by placing elements. It then saves these so that you can call the dialog box from your program directly. The window for the Dialog Editor is shown in Figure 32.16.

▲ The Font Editor, shown in Figure 32.17, enables you to add new fonts for your program. Most programs use the fonts that come with Windows, but you might want a unique font.

▲ A special debugger that requires a second monitor enables you to run your program under Windows and have the debugger in the second window. This is often better than debugging directly in Windows, especially in the early stages of a program when it often can crash Windows.

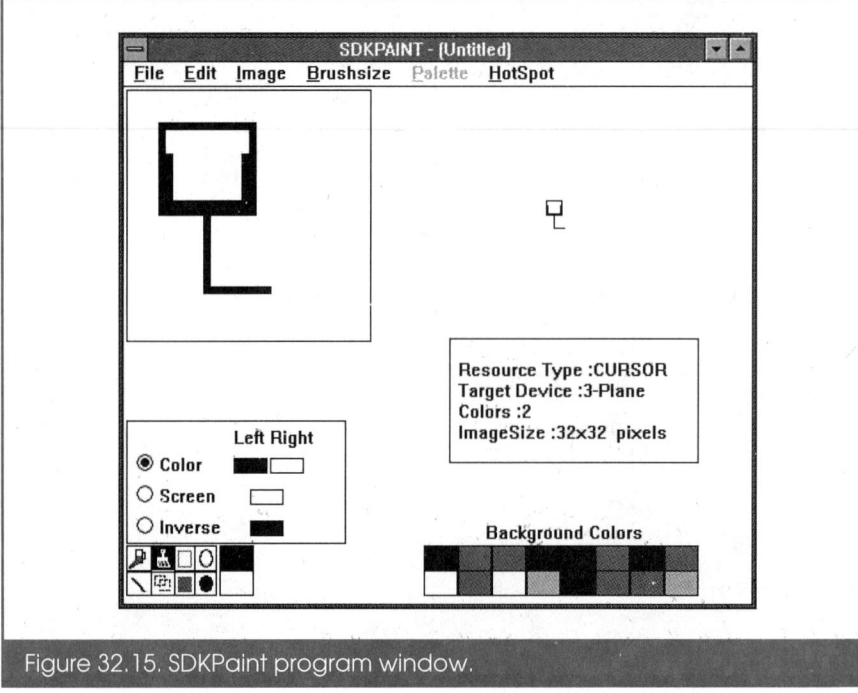

Figure 32.15. SDKPaint program window.

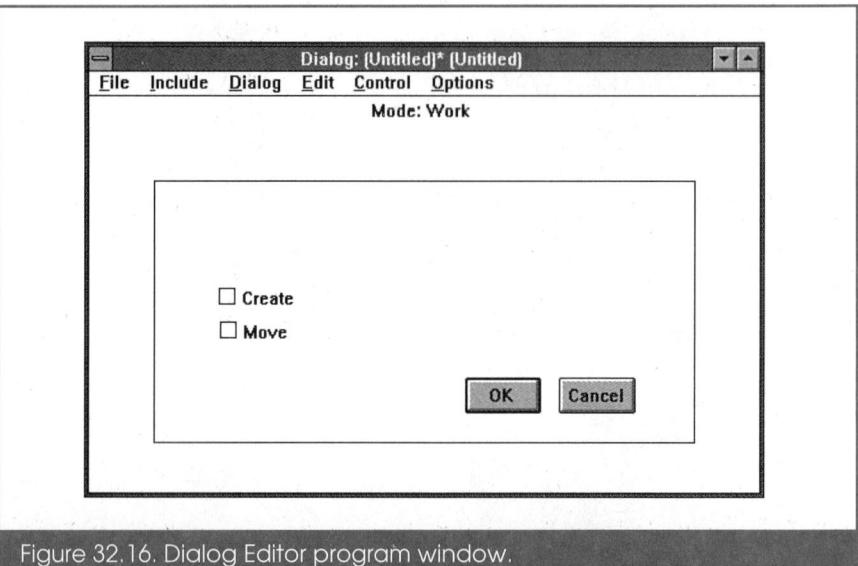

Figure 32.16. Dialog Editor program window.

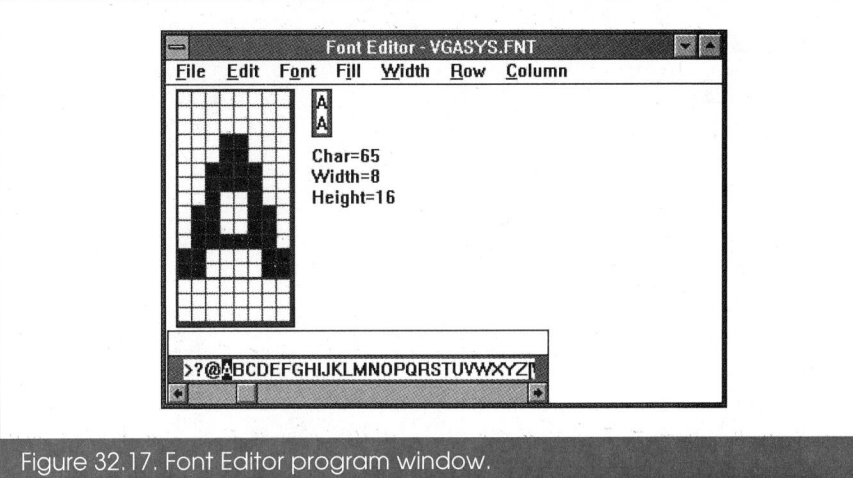

Figure 32.17. Font Editor program window.

32

▲ Spy, shown in Figure 32.18, enables you to watch the messages that get sent to the program's window. This is useful for checking whether your Windows program is sending the right messages.

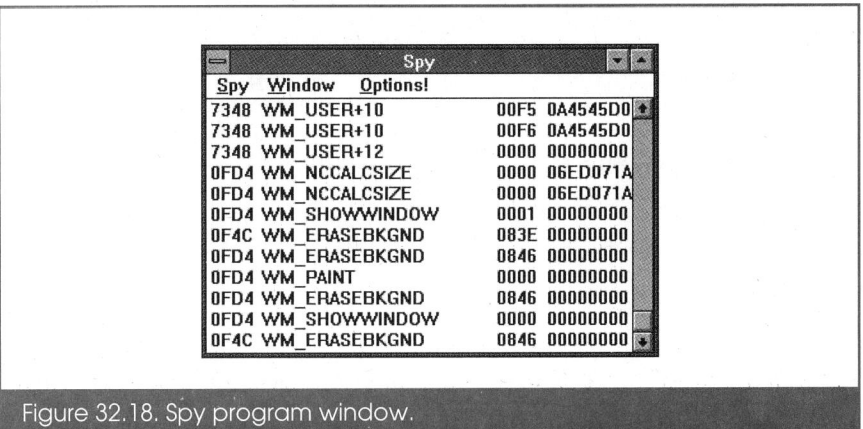

Figure 32.18. Spy program window.

▲ The Heap Walker, shown in Figure 32.19, enables you to look in the Windows memory area to see how your program is affecting global memory. You also can often see what caused your program to crash by analyzing the memory contents.

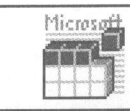

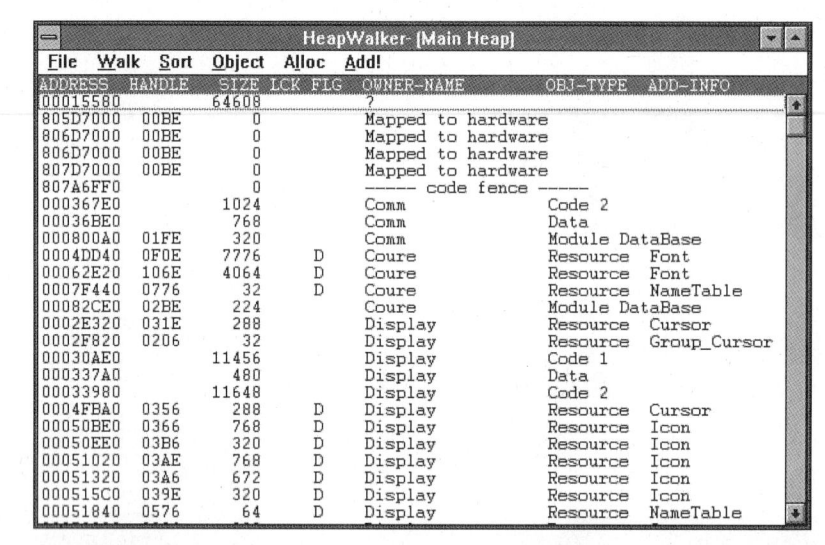

Figure 32.19. Heap Walker program window.

▲ Profilers help you determine how much time parts of your program spend doing certain tasks. You can use the profilers to make your programs run faster by finding time-wasting sections and removing them.

The SDK, together with the many tools that are normally part of Microsoft C, give a very full set of tools for the C programmer. For example, Microsoft C comes with the popular QuickC program for creating small C programs quickly. Future versions of QuickC will run under Windows and help developers create and debug programs in the native C environment.

Borland C++

The most popular alternative to Microsoft C and the SDK is the Borland C++ package. C++ is an object-oriented variation of C, meaning that you can create more structured programs which have parts that are easier to reuse. In fact, the Borland C++ package is both a C compiler and a C++ compiler.

Borland C++ generates Windows programs through the use of special header files. It comes with the Resource Workshop and the Microsoft resource compiler, so you can create programs as easily as with the SDK.

The Borland C++ environment is fairly friendly. Figure 32.20 shows an example of a program in the programmer's platform. The program uses a character-based user interface that is similar to Windows with pull-down menus, Alt-key shortcuts, mouse interface, and so on. You can see that even the document windows have a control box in the upper-right corner. You use this environment most of the time when you develop programs because you can compile them right from the menus.

32

```
 ≡  File  Edit  Search  Run  Compile  Debug  Project  Options    Window  Help
┌[■]═══════════════ \PROGENV\BORLANDC\EXAMPLES\TODOWIN.CPP ═══════════2═[↑]┐
│     Window *cur = Window::winList;                                        ▲
│                                                                          
│     //  look up the handle in our Window list                            
│     while( cur != 0 && cur->hWnd() != hWnd )                             
│         cur = cur->nextWin;                                              
│                                                                          
│     //  normal dispatching                                               
│     if( cur != 0 )                                                       
│         return cur->dispatch( msg, wParam, lParam );                     
│                                                                          
│     //  if we're inside CreateWindow( ), assume that the message is for us
│     if( inCreate != 0 )                                                  
│         {                                                                 
│         inCreate->hWindow = hWnd;                                        
│         return inCreate->dispatch( msg, wParam, lParam );                ▓
│         }                                                                 
│                                                                          
│     //  otherwise, pass it on to windows                                 ▼
│     return DefWindowProc( hWnd, msg, wParam, lParam );                   
└─╪══ 145:1 ═══◀■══════════════════════════════════════════════════════════┘
 F1 Help  F2 Save  F3 Open  Alt-F9 Compile  F9 Make  F10 Menu
```

Figure 32.20. Typical view of Borland C++ environment.

You can create the Windows-specific features such as menus and dialog boxes in your program, or you can create them with the Resource Workshop that comes with Borland C++ and then link the resources with your program. When you tell the environment you are creating a Windows program, it knows to compile automatically and include the resources you make with the Resource Workshop with your program. Thus creating a Windows program is a one-step (and very fast) process.

Figure 32.21 shows the initial screen for the Resource Workshop.

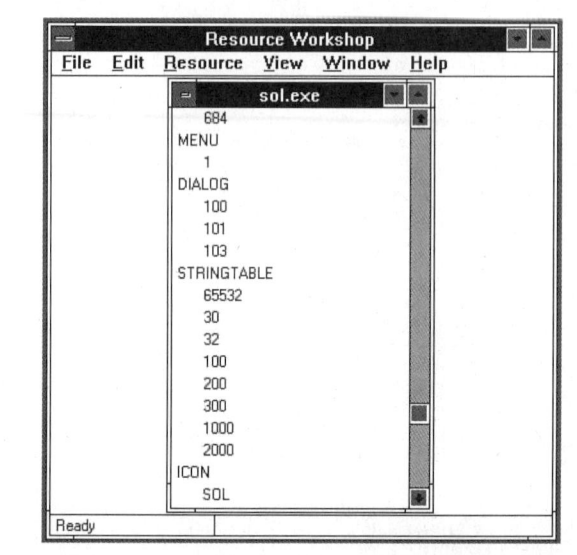

Figure 32.21. Initial Resource Workshop program window.

You can use the Resource Workshop to create the Windows resources you need for your programs, including:

▲ Keyboard acceleration keys are key combinations such as Ctrl-Ins for **E**dit **C**opy. You do not need to use this for Alt keys, which are defined in the menu editor.

▲ A single editor, called the Paint editor, is used to edit and create bit maps, cursors, fonts, and icon resources. Using the Paint Editor, you can create and edit bit maps for pictures you might use in your program. The drawing environment is quite complete, as shown in Figure 32.22. You can also import bit maps from Paint-brush or other paint programs.

▲ Drawing cursors with the Paint Editor is also fairly easy, as shown in Figure 32.23. You can create large and small cursors or start with the Windows standard cursors.

▲ The dialog editor, shown in Figure 32.24, gives you much flexibility not only in choosing dialog items to include but also in making it easy to line up items with each other. You do not have to eyeball anything because you can select groups of items and align them with each other or with the edge of the dialog box.

▲ Icons are edited in a similar fashion as cursors because they are stored in a similar fashion internally to Windows.

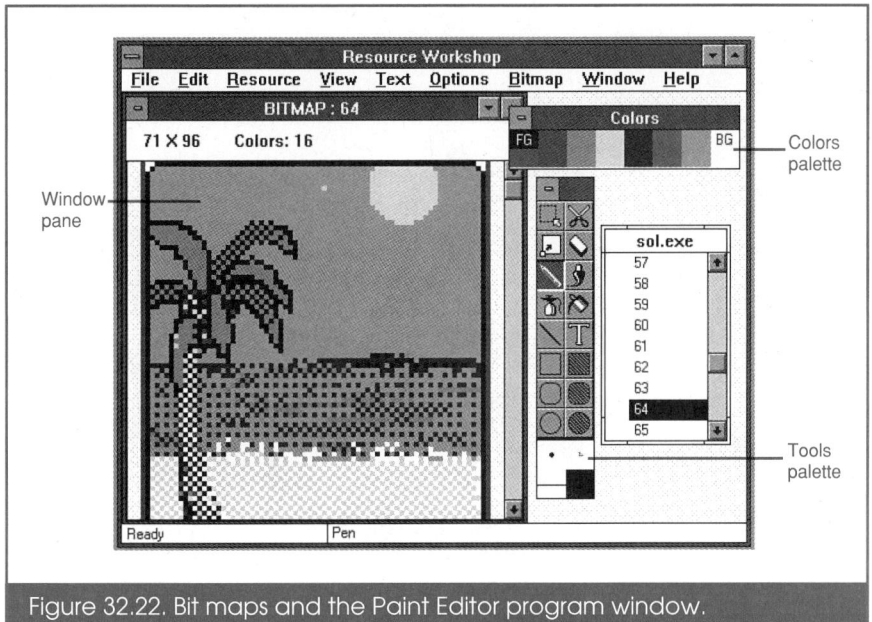

Figure 32.22. Bit maps and the Paint Editor program window.

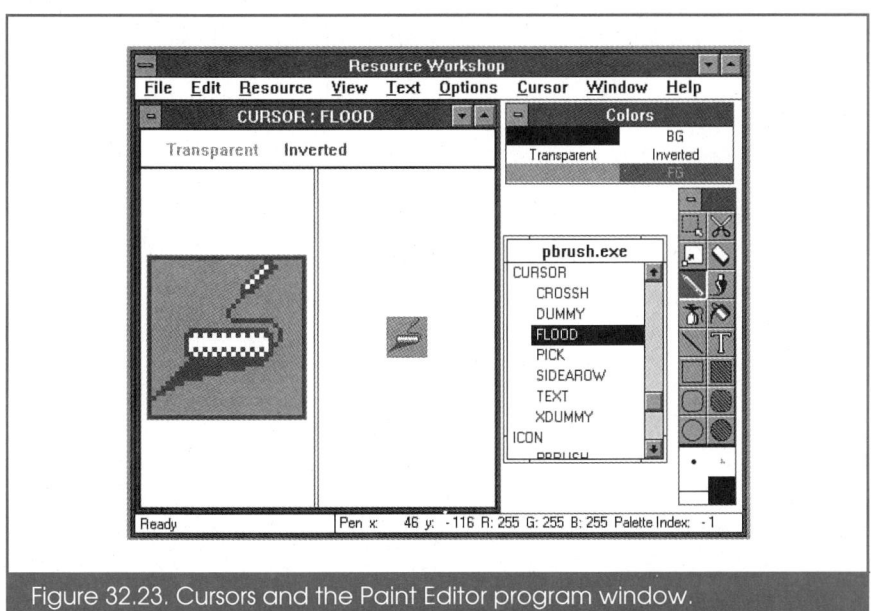

Figure 32.23. Cursors and the Paint Editor program window.

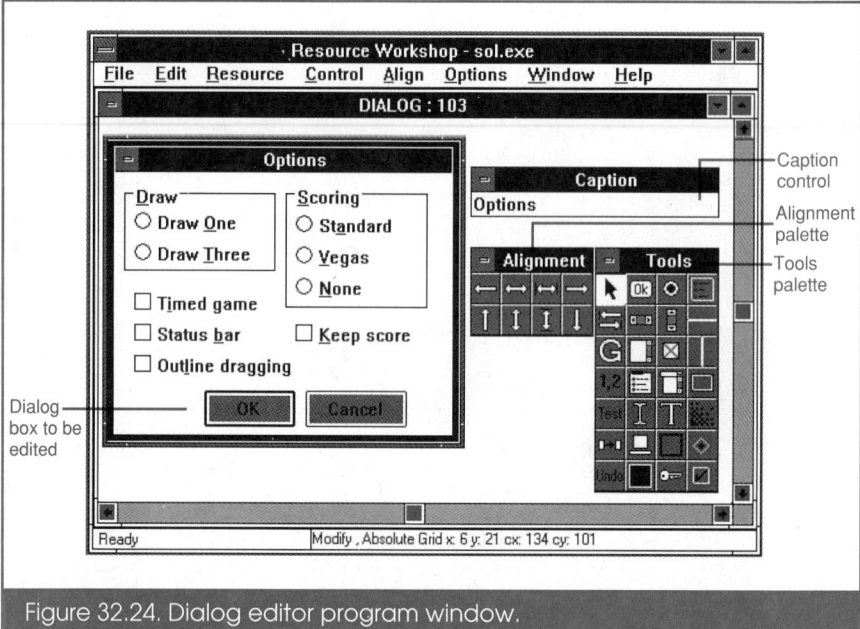

Figure 32.24. Dialog editor program window.

▲ Building menus is easy because you can start with menus from other programs. The menu editor, shown in Figure 32.25, gives you complete control over how your menus work. It also has a built-in test window so that you can see how your menus will look in your finished program.

▲ You can also create string resources, which are text that you want to display or read in your program. The string editor is shown in Figure 32.26. Most programmers simply include this directly in their programs. However, if you keep your strings as separate resources, you can later find and change them much more easily. For example, if you wanted to make a French version of your program, you would be able to translate the strings in one place instead of searching through all your program files.

The advantages of programming in C++ for Windows are many. Because the Windows interface is very object-oriented, using an object-oriented programming language gives you more flexibility to create interesting additions. In C++, objects come as parts of classes, which are general ways of dealing with objects. Some software companies sell premade classes of Windows objects to make programming easier. For example, Blaise Computing provides the Win++ Class Library for Borland C++. Classes and their role in object-oriented programming are covered in Chapter 31, "Introduction to Windows Programming Elements."

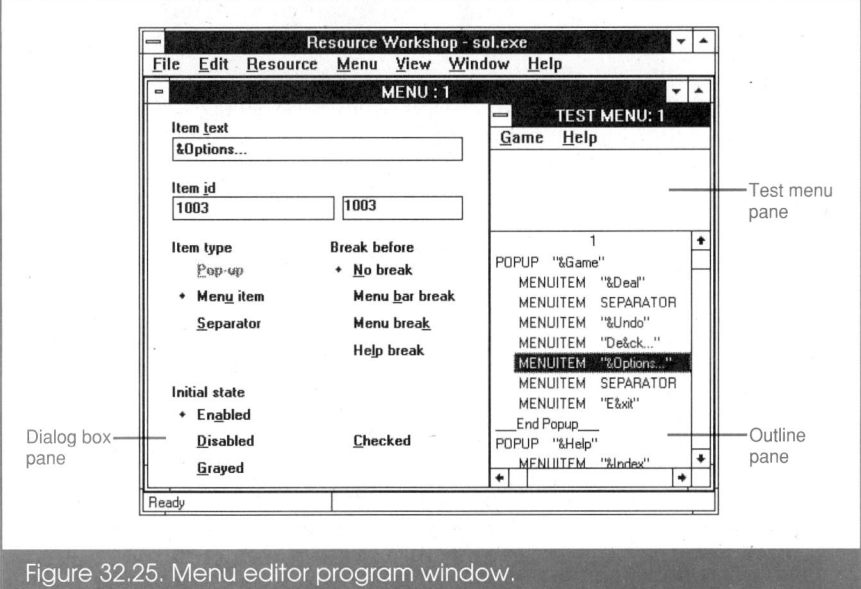

Figure 32.25. Menu editor program window.

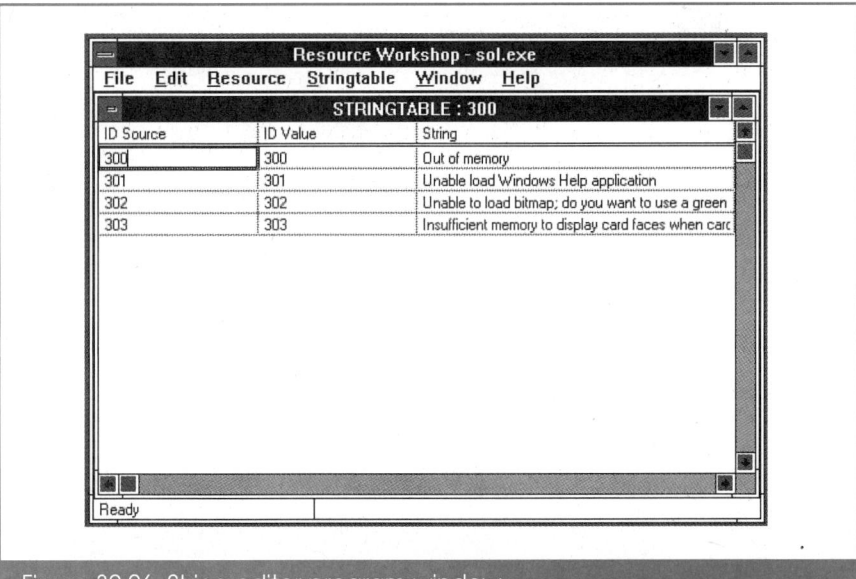

Figure 32.26. String editor program window.

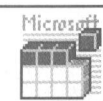

Borland and Microsoft have always been major competitors in the C programming market. Whether you are writing for MS-DOS or Windows, you will find both environments are easy platforms for writing serious programs. Many people prefer Borland products, saying they run faster and have better support. On the other hand, many people prefer Microsoft because they are closest to MS-DOS and Windows.

Pascal

For reasons that are hotly argued in the programming community, Pascal has become a base language for graphical interfaces like the Macintosh and Windows. Borland's Turbo Pascal for Windows is a complete object-oriented environment that enables you to create Windows programs easily. The Pascal language is much like C, although it has advantages for object-oriented programming.

Figure 32.27 shows part of a typical Pascal program in this environment. You can compile, run, and check your programs from the main environment window.

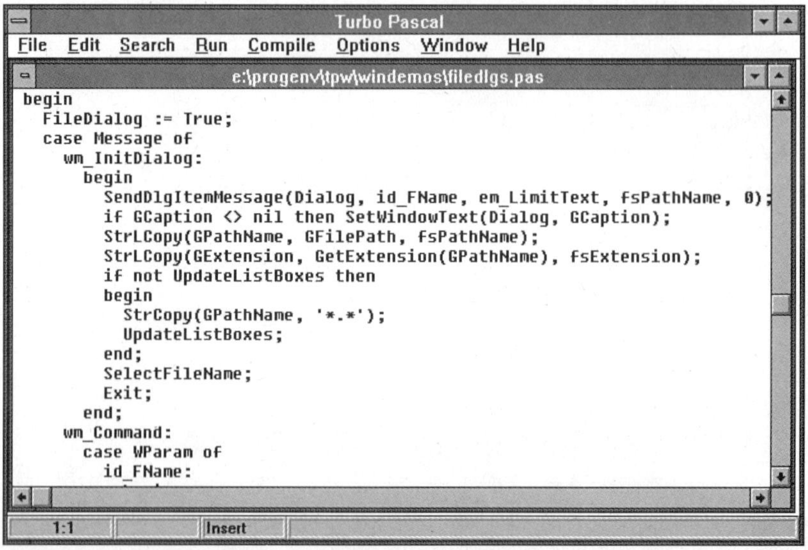

```
Turbo Pascal
File   Edit   Search   Run   Compile   Options   Window   Help
                    e:\progenv\tpw\windemos\filedlgs.pas
begin
  FileDialog := True;
  case Message of
    wm_InitDialog:
      begin
        SendDlgItemMessage(Dialog, id_FName, em_LimitText, fsPathName, 0);
        if GCaption <> nil then SetWindowText(Dialog, GCaption);
        StrLCopy(GPathName, GFilePath, fsPathName);
        StrLCopy(GExtension, GetExtension(GPathName), fsExtension);
        if not UpdateListBoxes then
        begin
          StrCopy(GPathName, '*.*');
          UpdateListBoxes;
        end;
        SelectFileName;
        Exit;
      end;
    wm_Command:
      case WParam of
        id_FName:

1:1              Insert
```

Figure 32.27. Main Turbo Pascal program window.

Turbo Pascal comes with the ObjectWindows set of objects and classes to get you going with object-oriented programming. These enable you to create full Windows programs quickly. You can even run standard text-mode Pascal programs with the CRT object. If you already have many Pascal programs you want to translate, you can use this as a start, then build in the Windows interface.

Borland International
1800 Green Hills Rd.
Scotts Valley, CA 95067
(408)438-5300

32

Other OOP Languages

Both C++ and Pascal can be used as object-oriented programming (OOP) systems. As explained earlier, many programmers think OOP systems are best for developing for Windows because you can reuse objects that you create more easily than with standard programming techniques. Because the user interface is more apparent in Windows programs than with regular text-based MS-DOS programs, this can be a big advantage when you are creating full-sized programs.

The programming world is much larger than BASIC, C, and Pascal, although these three languages make up a huge portion of the commercial market. Some language developers have extended other OOP languages to work with Windows. Smalltalk, one of the first OOP languages, has two major implementations for Windows: Objectworks and Smalltalk/V. Both of these systems run on many platforms other than Windows, such as the Macintosh and UNIX systems.

Objectworks/Smalltalk

The Objectworks/Smalltalk environment is shown in Figure 32.28. Note that the windows are different than those of standard Windows. You can use the Smalltalk language to define any type of object, including those used in windows and dialog boxes. You can also use the standard objects from Windows if you want.

Smalltalk programs are fairly easy to follow. Figure 32.29 shows part of a typical Smalltalk program in Objectworks/Smalltalk. Note that ParcPlace also sells a version of Objectworks for C++.

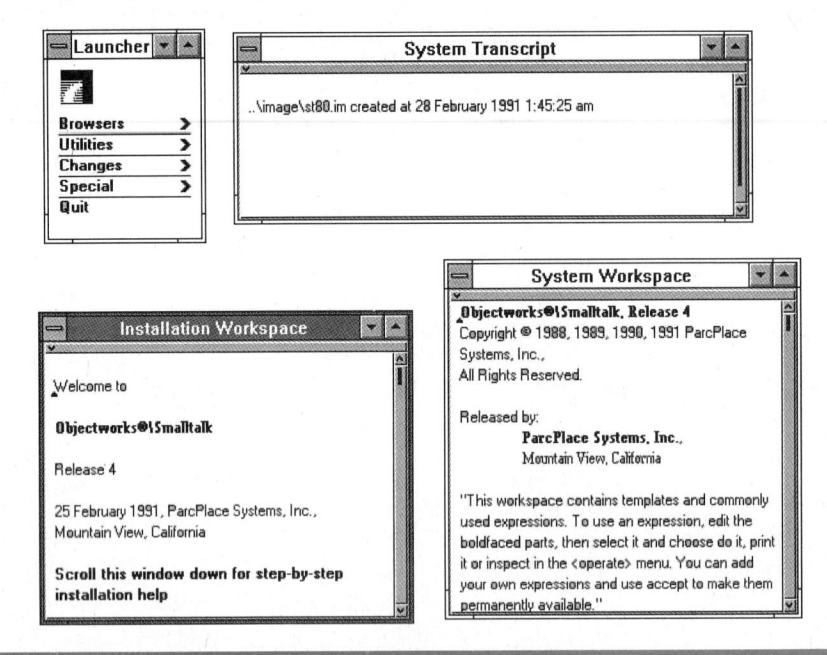

Figure 32.28. Objectworks initial screen.

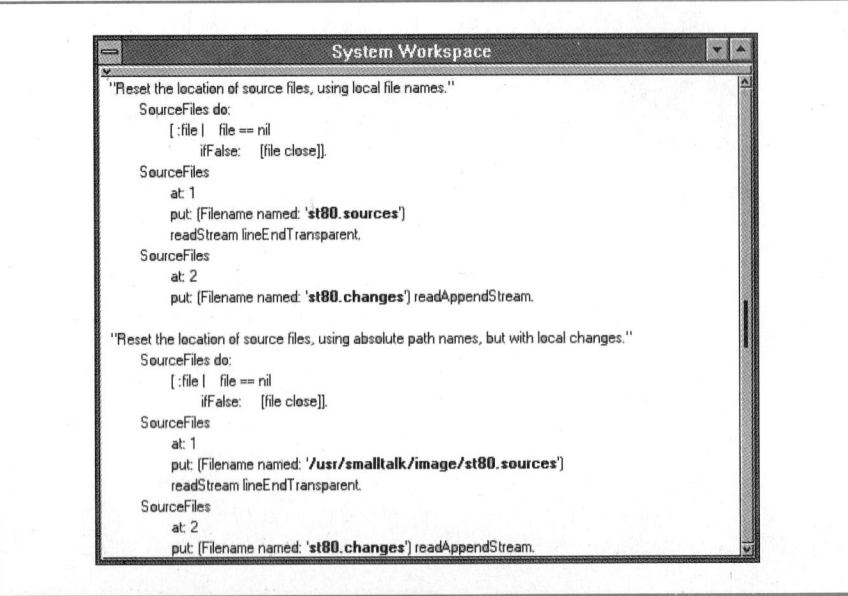

Figure 32.29. Typical Smalltalk program.

ParcPlace Systems
1550 Plymouth St.
Mountain View, CA 94043
(415)691-6700

Smalltalk/V

This low-cost programming environment is one of the most used OOPs in the world. You can create programs in Smalltalk/V for Windows more quickly than a programming language like C++ and move them to the OS/2 Presentation Manager. In addition, you can distribute the results of your programming freely. Figure 32.30 shows a typical view of the Smalltalk/V environment.

32

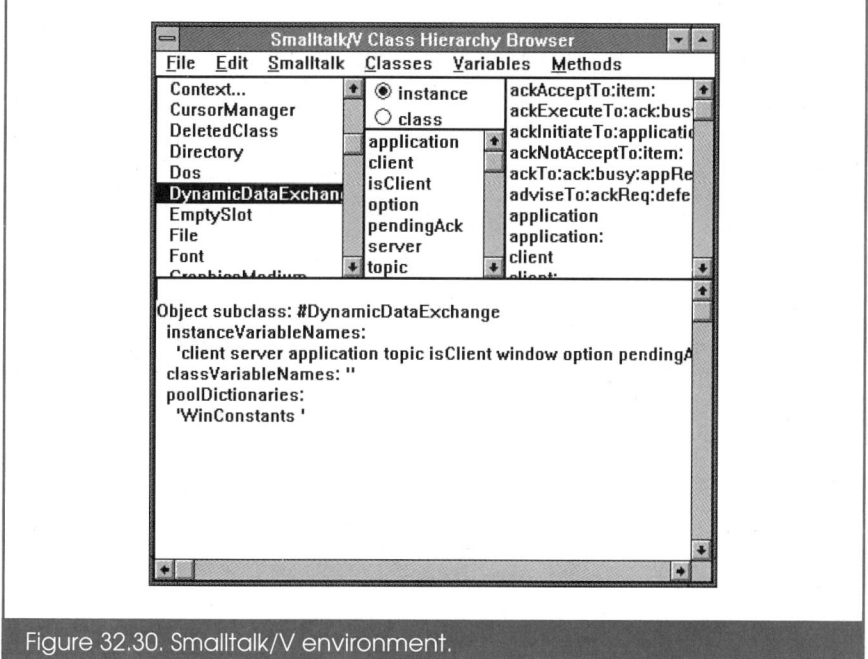

Figure 32.30. Smalltalk/V environment.

Digitalk
9841 Airport Blvd.
Los Angeles, CA 90045
(213)645-1082

Actor

Unlike the Smalltalk environments, Actor is based on a C-like language. However, Actor is not C or C++. The environment is like other OOP environments in that you can create code incrementally and reuse objects easily. It also comes with the Whitewater Resource Toolkit and a very complete object library for Windows. It has internal memory management so that you can run large Actor programs on small PC systems. Figure 32.31 shows sample Actor code.

```
Editor: e:\progenv\actor\act\queen.act
 File  Edit  Search  Doit!  Inspect!
/* Set up the display board with its scaling, brushes for drawing. */
Def init(self,w,s,l,t | colorSet)
{ width := w;
  vScale := s;
  hScale := vScale * 2;
  left := l; top := t;
  wBrush := stock(WHITE_BRUSH);
  bBrush := stock(BLACK_BRUSH);
  gBrush := stock(GRAY_BRUSH);
}!!

/* Return a boolean indicating proper color for a cell. */
Def color(self,c,r)
{ ^((r+c) bitAnd 1 = 0);
}!!

Def drawCell(self,c,r)
{ Call Rectangle(hdc,
    left + c * hScale,
    top + r * vScale,
    left + (c+1) * hScale,
```

Figure 32.31. Part of a typical Actor program.

Whitewater Group
1800 Ridge Ave.
Evanston, IL 60201
(708)328-3800

KnowledgePro

KnowledgePro is another OOP that uses its own language as a base for the system. Figure 32.32 shows the KnowledgePro environment. Like other OOPs, KnowledgePro comes with tools that help you create programs without having to write code. Although there are objects for

standard Windows functions, KnowledgePro's strongest area is in information display. It is easy to create hypertext systems using the information objects supplied with the package.

32

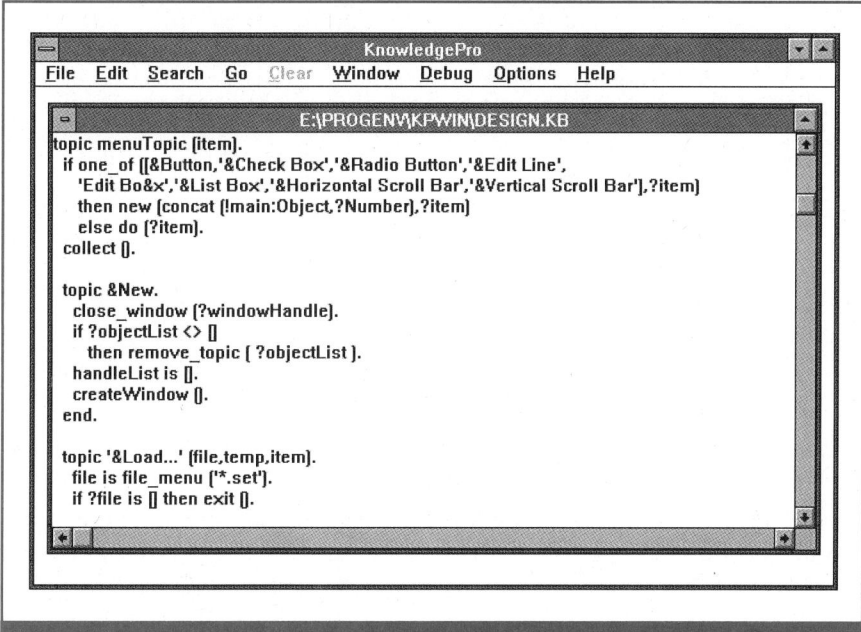

Figure 32.32. KnowledgePro program window.

Knowledge Garden
473A Malden Bridge Rd.
Nassau, NY 12123
(518)766-3000

There are many other languages and tools for Windows programming. Almost every major computer language now has a Windows version available. Refer to Reference C, "Windows Product Directory," for more information on development languages and tools.

Programming Development Tools

CASE (Computer-Aided Software Engineering) and Prototyping tools have really come into their own as we have entered the '90s. With some

exception, these specialty products are intended almost exclusively for the professional applications developer. CASE tools are designed to help the developer maintain facets of the application development process itself. CASE tools can play a role in the actual programming of the application, and also support the management of the development process itself. CASE and Prototyping tools typically serve several of these functions:

▲ Overall project management tools (task/timeline tracking)

▲ Resource allocation tracking (manpower hours, for example)

▲ Application documentation development

▲ Work process flowcharting

▲ Application testing on hardware that simulates a PC

▲ Standardized methods evaluation

▲ Project level tracking from alpha to beta to version release

▲ Map complex system module relationships

Prototyping tools and aids can help the developer build the concept of the application. Some developers even test it when it reaches various stages of completion. These tools typically help you build a mock-up of the actual application.

A developer would typically collect a set of requirements for an application (what it's supposed to do) and build what amounts to a shell of the finished application (what it would look like). When done, you can navigate between menus, push buttons, and so on, but the application does nothing else yet.

The developer then demonstrates the product to the end user as it seems to work before actual application development begins. Many customer objections are born of problems with the look of the interface or work flow layout, so clearing up these potential problems before you start a major programming project can reduce the number of changes made at the end of the project.

The benefit can be a drastically shorter product development cycle. The key to the recent success of prototyping products is that they reduce a development team's wasted effort by helping to clarify the real requirements for the application.

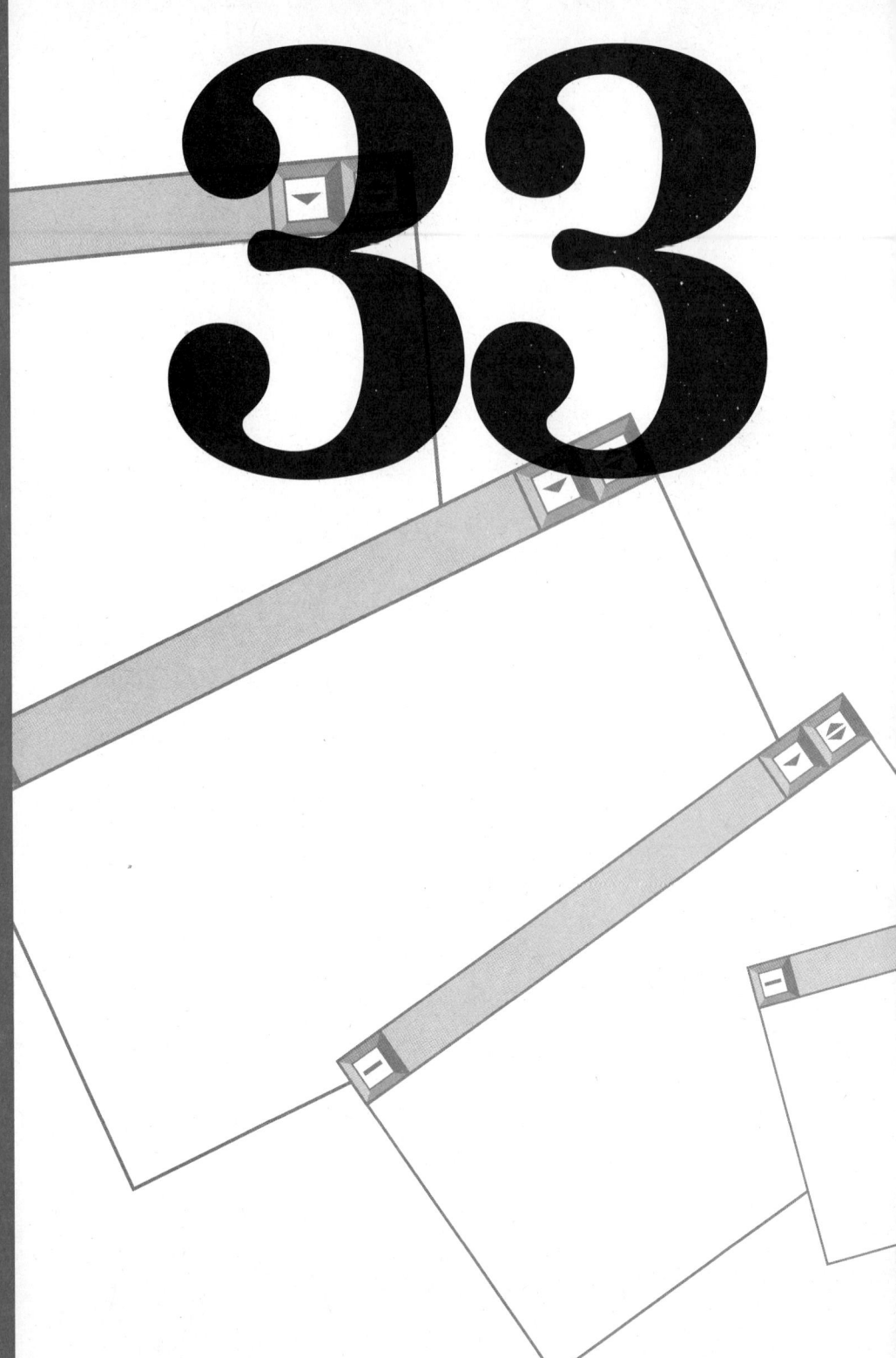

CHAPTER

33

Exchanging Data with the DDE

Dynamic Data Exchange (DDE) is a protocol in Windows that allows programs to communicate with one another, exchange commands and data, and in effect, control each other. This means the functionality of one program can be added to another so that eye-popping custom programs can be put together with minimal effort. The term *Client*, refers to the application that is accepting data, and the term *Server*, means the application that created the data.

Both programs in a DDE conversation must be loaded into RAM, and both must be Windows programs designed to employ DDE. Not all Windows programs have been designed to do so. Maybe a couple hundred of the 1,500 Windows programs out there have some DDE functionality. Again, it has to be a Windows program: there is no way DDE can work with DOS programs running in Windows. As long as those two conditions are satisfied, the uses are endless.

Examples include

▲ Real-time tracking of stock, bond, or commodity prices. Using a Windows communications package with a DDE, you can link to a Windows spreadsheet such as Microsoft Excel, perhaps with custom front-end graphics composed with one of the programming environments described in Chapter 32, "Windows Programming Environments."

▲ Greatly enhancing word processors.

▲ Linking CAD (Computer-Aided Design) programs to a database. This can be done with workstation networks, with the database on the server and the CAD on the client. With DDE both the CAD program and the database can be in the same machine.

▲ Linking documents with data. You can include a graph that was actually generated by another program. The graph can be changed to match the original data.

▲ Creating a PC-to-mainframe mail system using a Windows communications package tied to a code converter.

DDE had been built into previous versions of Windows, but only became practical—and popular—with the introduction of Windows 3.0. Windows 3.0 defeated the PC's 640K-RAM ceiling and finally made loading multiple programs realistic. Previous versions of Windows like 2.0 used extended memory as a disk cache, and all code still had to run within the 640K limit.

DDE is based on the message-passing system inherent within Windows itself. Windows is event driven, with code segments from various programs (more specifically, processes) responding to messages from other programs within the system, or to outside events such as mouse movements or keyboard input. Windows performs its multitasking on the basis of these messages. DDE is a method of accessing this messaging system from the user level.

Types of DDE

There are three types of DDE that the user is likely to encounter: Paste-Link, macro languages, and spreadsheet functions.

Paste-Link

Paste-Link is a facility that resembles the use of the Windows Clipboard. You select data you want to share with another application and then copy it to the Clipboard so that it can be pasted into another application. In the program where you are going to use the data, you then choose the Paste-Link, rather than the standard Clipboard Paste command, to insert the data. With a "hot" link, data is updated in the second program the moment it changes in the first. With a "warm" link you are notified of a change, but no update is made. In a "cold" link updates are made only on request.

Microsoft often uses the example of a figure in a Windows Word document being linked to a chart in Excel. The chart is then paste-linked back to the document as an illustration on the page, and the chart is updated as you change the number.

33

Macro Languages

Macro languages of major Windows programs such as Word for Windows and Excel provide DDE commands. This is the functionality that interests systems integrators and power users. You must understand that the protocol of DDE commands includes a three-tiered data structure: program, topic, and item. If you are addressing cell R1C1 of an Excel spreadsheet named "MYSALES," for example, Excel is the program, MYSALES is the topic, and R1C1 is the item.

This structure appears to be quite intuitive when used with Excel, but proves to be less so with other programs. With IBM Current, for instance, you get a long list of topics, each of which has a list of possible items, and each has specific parameters, options, and syntax that Current needs to see before it can react meaningfully to a DDE message.

You have to know the DDE syntax of the "server" program before you can extract data from it with a "client" program. Additionally, some programs operate only as clients and some only as servers, and a few are bidirectional.

Spreadsheet Functions

Spreadsheet functions are embodied in the remote reference formulas you can use within a Microsoft Excel cell. If the cell contains

```
='STOCK'¦'NYSE'!IBM
```

the link is to a program named STOCK, a topic named NYSE, and an item named IBM.

Object Linking and Embedding

In early 1991, Microsoft announced its commitment to a "document-centric" approach to office integration (apparently meaning office automation's version of object-oriented programming) based on an enhancement of the DDE protocol called Object Linking and Embedding (OLE).

Linking is the Paste-Link described earlier. Embedding, however, is a new concept that has already been put into a few software packages and is appearing in more applications as OLE becomes more established.

Embedding is the capability of using one program from within another. For example, Microsoft implemented graphing in its PowerPoint package using embedding. You elect to insert a graph, and that launches the graphing module (another Windows program). Later, that module exits back to PowerPoint. This is very different from linking in that you are not just linking a picture of the graph you created, but also the data behind it and the program that created it. Using embedding, double-clicking the graph invokes the original program with the original data for possible revision.

Some programmers say linking is better and some say embedding is better, but they are really just two separate implementations of DDE. With linking you have the original object (the data item) in another file, and that makes sense if you want the data to have a common source, as when there are a lot of users using the same data.

Using DDE

Windows works on the basis of internal messages. There are nine preset internal messages dealing with DDE, shown in Table 33.1.

Table 33.1. DDE internal messages.

Message	Description
INITIATE	Initiates a DDE conversation
TERMINATE	Halts a conversation
ACK	Acknowledges a DDE message
REQUEST	Asks a server for data
DATA	Transmits data
ADVISE	Asks that a server update data as it changes (sets up a hot link)
POKE	Sends unrequested data
EXECUTE	Sends a command to a program
UNADVISE	Stops hot link updating

The way these are displayed to the user varies with the program. When using Paste-Link, the user does not deal with them on any level. Everything is handled internally by the program. When using macro languages, the user often has access to the message structure. For instance, to contact an Excel spreadsheet with the macro language of Lotus's Ami Pro word processor, you use these commands:

```
ChannelID = DDEInitiate("Excel" "Mysales")
DDEExecute(ChannelID, "[[calculate.now()]]")
Result = DDEReceive$(ChannelID, "R1C1")
DDETerminate(ChannelID)
```

The first command sends the initiate message to the program (Excel) with the topic Mysales (that is, Excel loads a spreadsheet named Mysales). ChannelID is necessary because a program can have many DDE conversations going at one time. The second command sends a command to Excel, in this case to calculate the spreadsheet. The third command receives the value of Excel spreadsheet cell R1C1 into the Ami Pro Result variable. The fourth command terminates the DDE conversation.

Programs generally exchange data in the same formats that they support with the Windows Clipboard. DDE commands must conform to the syntax expected by the receiving program.

Problems with DDE

As for complaints about DDE, they fall into two broad areas: performance and compatibility. In terms of performance, you can't use DDE to move large blocks of data. A DDE channel is certain to choke on 64K of data and with certain programs, may choke on less. (Of course, the idea is usually to have the other program process the raw data and just send the final results.) Many programmers complain also that you can't use DDE for precise real-time control situations due to the unpredictable actions of the Windows message handling loop.

Networking is another area of concern. DDE messages can be sent over a network just like any other data, but on arrival, their internal "handles" (names) won't necessarily have any meaning to the new machine. Although some people have configured Windows DDE for use on a network, there is very little commercial software that allows it.

VIII

Windows
References

PART

P
A
R
T

WHAT IS IN THIS PART

  Windows
        Command
        Reference

  Windows Product
        Directory

  MS-DOS 5.0
        and Windows

  General Windows
        Information

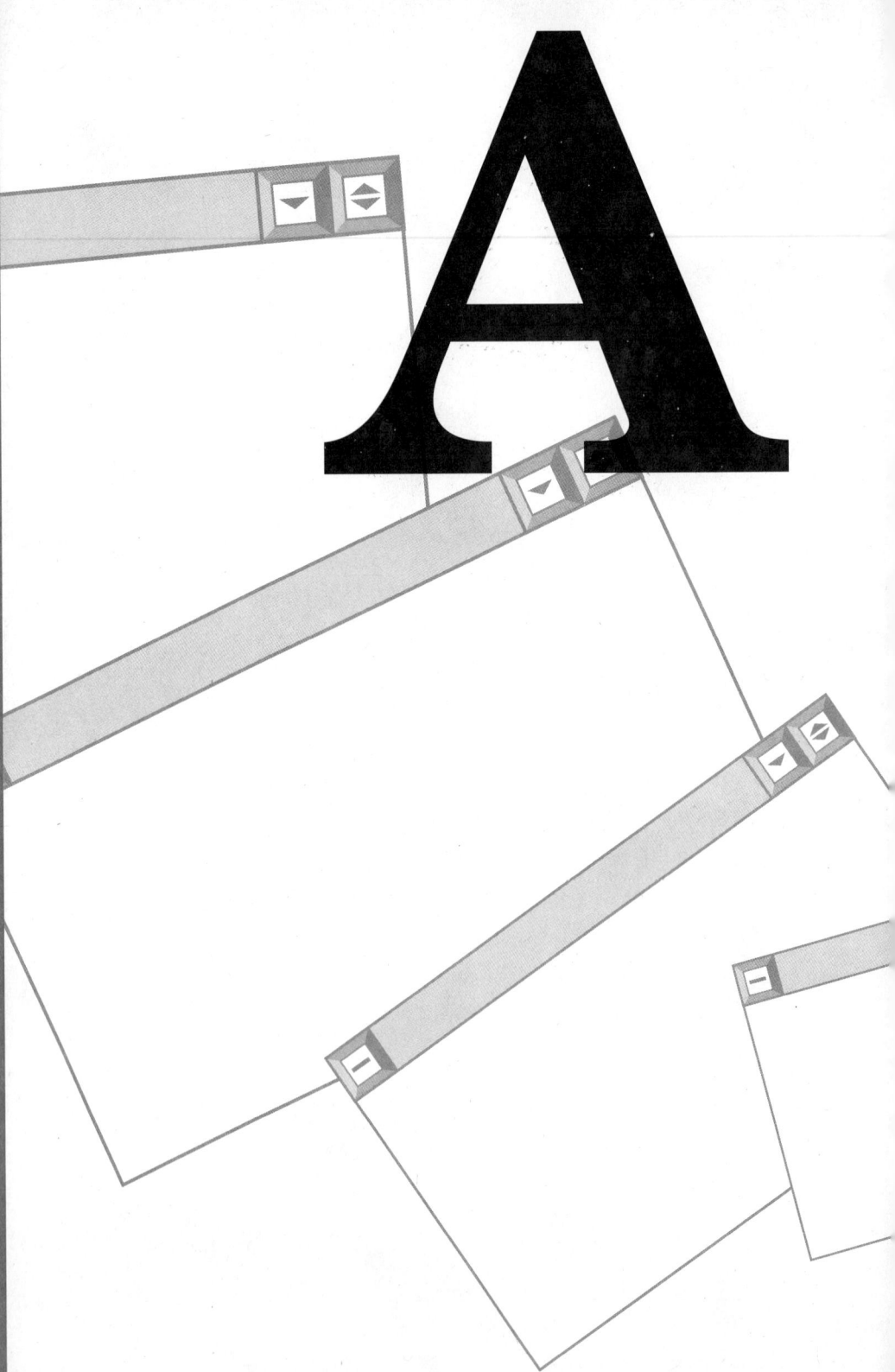

REFERENCE

Windows Command Reference

This reference section contains keystroke and keystroke combinations common to Windows and most Windows applications.

General Keys

The keys listed in this section generally work in all Windows programs, although some are specific to Program Manager and programs that use similar keys.

← →↑↓	Moves a window after selecting the **M**ove command from the control menu, or changes the document's size after you have selected the **S**ize command. These keys also enable you to move between menus and commands within a menu.
Alt-Backspace	Gives the **E**dit **U**ndo command.
Alt-Enter	Switches a non-Windows program between running in a window and a full screen mode.

Alt-Escape	Cycles through all programs that are running, whether they are windows or icons.
Alt-F4	Exits from a program.
Alt-hyphen	Opens the control menu in a document window.
Alt-Print Screen	Copies the contents of an active window onto the Clipboard.
Alt-spacebar	Opens the control menu in a program menu.
Alt-Tab	Moves to the next program, restoring it to normal size if it has been reduced to an icon.
Backspace	Deletes the area to the left of the cursor one space at a time.
Ctrl-Esc	Brings up the Task List dialog box.
Ctrl-F4	Closes a window.
Ctrl-Insert	Gives the **E**dit **C**opy command.
Ctrl-Tab	Cycles through all open documents whether they are windows or icons.
Delete	Deletes the area to the right of the cursor one space at a time.
F1	Enables you to view a program's **H**elp index.
Print Screen	Copies the screen contents onto the Clipboard.
Shift-Delete	Gives the **E**dit **C**u**t** command.
Shift-F1	Transforms the cursor into a question mark so that a specific command, screen element, or key can be selected.
Shift-Insert	Copies the Clipboard's contents onto a document at the insertion point.

Keys for Manipulating Dialog Boxes

←→↑↓	Moves between options in a group, up or down in a list, or to the left or right in a text box.
Alt-↓	Opens a drop-down list box.
Alt-↓, Alt-↑	Chooses items in a drop-down list box.

Alt-N	Moves to the item whose title has an underlined letter N.
Backspace	Deletes one space at a time to the left of the cursor.
Ctrl-/	Chooses all items in a list box.
Ctrl-\	Cancels all selections, leaving only the active item.
End	Moves to the last item in a list box, or to the last character in a character box.
Enter	Chooses a selected item and activates the specified command button.
Esc or Alt-F4	Closes a dialog box without following through on any commands.
Home	Moves to the first item in a list box or to the first character in a text box.
Page Up, Page Down	Scrolls up or down one box of data at a time in a list box.
Shift-Tab	Moves to the previous item.
Shift-↑, Shift-↓	Extends the selection in a list box.
Shift-End	Extends the list box selection to the last character.
Shift-Home	Extends the selection in a list box to the first character.
spacebar	Chooses or cancels a specified item in a check box or a list box.
Tab	Moves to the next item.

A

Using a Mouse with Windows

The actions listed in this section generally work in all Windows programs, although some are specific to Program Manager and programs that use similar mouse actions. They are organized by action.

| Begin a program | Double-click the icon or filename. |
| Bring a program or a document to the foreground | Click the window. |

Exit a program	Double-click the program's control menu icon.
Maximize a window	Click the maximize button, the upward-pointing arrow located on the right end of the title bar.
Minimize a window	Click the minimize button, the downward-pointing arrow located on the right end of the title bar.
Move a window	Drag its title bar.
Move between programs	Click the window of the program you want to work in.
Resize a window	Drag its borders.
Restore a maximized arrow window to its original size	Click the restore button, the double-headed located on the right end of the title bar.
Restore a minimized program to a window	Double-click its icon, or double-click the desktop to bring up the Task Manager dialog box.
Select a command from a menu	Click the menu and then click the chosen command.
Show Task List	Double-click the desktop.

Program Manager Reference

These keystrokes and keystroke combinations can be used when you are running Program Manager.

File Menu

File **N**ew	Enables you to create a new program group or add a program to a program group.
File **O**pen	Runs an icon. If no icon is selected, it opens a window.
File **M**ove	Enables you to move the selected icon into another group.
File **C**opy	Copies an icon from one program group to another.
File **D**elete	Removes a program from a program group or a whole program group from the Program Manager file. This does not delete the program from your hard disk.

File **P**roperties	Enables you to change the name of a group icon or change the icon itself. It also enables you to add a document to a program item or use the **B**rowse command to find a program.
File **R**un	Enables you to start a program that is not already part of a program group. This command also can be accessed in the File Manager **F**ile menu.
File E**x**it Windows	Enables you to exit Windows with the option of saving your most current program-group window layout.

Options Menu

Options **A**uto Arrange	Repositions program icons automatically every time you change the dimensions of a program-group window.
Options **M**inimize on Use	Reduces the Program Manager window to an icon automatically when you start another program.
Options **S**ave Settings on Exit	Saves window screen addresses and other variables to .INI files.

Window Menu

Window **C**ascade	Arranges windows into a stack, fanned out so that the each window's title bar is visible.
Window **T**ile	Arranges the windows and reduces their size so that they fit across the desktop.
Window **A**rrange Icons	Neatly arranges the icons. This works only in the active window. To arrange all your icons, choose the **A**rrange Icons command, close all your group windows, then open them again.
Window **1,2,3...9**	Brings up a list of all open documents that can be selected for rapid activation.

File Manager Reference

These keystrokes and keystroke combinations can be used when you are running File Manager.

File Menu

File **O**pen	Opens a directory window or a document associated with an application, or begins an application.
File **M**ove	Moves one or more directories or files to a destination directory from a source directory.
File **C**opy	Copies one or more directories or files to a destination directory from a source directory.
File **D**elete	Erases one or more directories or files.
File **Ren**ame	Enables you to rename a file or directory.
File Properties	Sets or changes file attributes.
File **R**un	Enables you to open a document or begin an application.
File **P**rint	Prints a text file.
File **A**ssociate	Associates a document with an application so that the application automatically starts when a document is opened.
File **C**reate Directory	Makes a new directory.
File Searc**h**	Searches for a directory or a file.
File **S**elect Files	Opens the file selection dialog box.
File E**x**it	Enables you to close all the File Manager windows and quit from File Manager.

Disk Menu

Disk **C**opy Disk	Copies the contents from one diskette to another.
Disk **L**abel Disk	Enables you to create or change volume labels for hard drives and diskettes.
Disk **F**ormat Disk	Formats a floppy diskette.
Disk **M**ake System Disk	Formats a floppy diskette and adds the operating system's files.
Disk **S**elect Drive	Opens a dialog box with a list box for selection of available drives.

Tree Menu

Tree Expand One Level	Expands one level of a collapsed directory.
Tree Expand **B**ranch	Expands an entire collapsed directory.
Tree Expand **A**ll	Expands all the branches in the Directory Tree window.
Tree Collapse Branch	Collapses all the directory levels beneath a specified directory in the Directory Tree window.
Tree **I**ndicate Expandable Branches	Marks folders with a plus (+) sign to indicate that the folder (directory) contains subdirectories.

View Menu

A

View **Tr**ee and Directory	Lists the names of files and directories in the open window.
View **Tr**ee Only	Displays only directory information in the open window.
View Directory **O**nly	Displays only the files in the currently selected directory.
View Sp**l**it	Presents a movable vertical bar that enables the user to size directory-versus-file display space.
View **N**ame	Alphabetizes the display of files by filename.
View **A**ll File Details	Displays file attributes, file size, file creation date, and file creation time.
View **P**artial Details	Opens a dialog box enabling you to specify which displayable file details are desired.
View **S**ort by Name	Sorts file display in order of filename.
View Sort **by** Type	Sorts file display in order of file extension name.
View Sort by Si**z**e	Sorts file display in order of file size.
View Sort by **D**ate	Sorts file display in order of file creation/update date.
View By File **T**ype	Opens a dialog box enabling you to specify the type of file (extension name(s)) to be displayed.

Options Menu

Options **C**onfirmation	Tells which warning messages you do or do not want to see.
Options **F**ont	Opens a dialog box that enables you to change or review information relative to the desired screen and/or printer font.
Options **S**tatus Bar	When on, enables you to view the status bar at the bottom of the File Manager window. When off, removes the status bar from view.
Options **M**inimize on Use	Automatically minimizes File Manager to an icon whenever you begin an application.
Options Save Settings on **E**xit	Preserves settings you changed in the current File Manager session.

Window Menu

Window **N**ew Window	Opens a new window to be viewed. Allows concurrent viewing of multiple drives and\or directories.
Window Cascade	Arranges windows into a stack so that only the title bar is visible for each window.
Window **T**ile	Arranges and reduces the windows so that each one is visible and nonoverlapping.
Window **A**rrange Icons	Arranges Windows and icons to suit you.
Window **R**efresh	Updates the current directory or the Directory Tree window.
Windows [windows list]	Makes any window foremost in view by selecting an available window from the list.

Control Panel Reference

These keystrokes and keystroke combinations can be used when you are running Control Panel.

Settings Menu

Settings **C**olor	Enables you to modify color schemes for items on the screen.
Settings **F**onts	Enables you to input and remove fonts.
Settings **P**orts	Modifies the specifications of serial port settings.
Settings **M**ouse	Defines specifications when using the mouse, including setting the functions of the left and right buttons.
Settings **D**esktop	Enables you to make specifications concerning the desktop.
Settings **K**eyboard	Enables you to set the speed of a key repeating itself when held down.
Settings **P**rinters	Enables you to install and remove a printer and modify its options.
Settings **I**nternational	Enables you to change the international settings.
Settings **D**ate/**T**ime	Enables you to set the date and time of the computer's clock.
Settings D**r**ivers	Enables you to install, remove, and configure drivers.
Settings **S**ound	Enables you to associate different sounds with system and application events such as the default beep.
Settings 386 Enhanced	Sets various parameters for 386-enhanced mode.
Settings **N**etwork	Enables you to modify the options for your network links.
Settings E**x**it	Closes the Control Panel window and quits from Control Panel.

A

Auxiliary Programs Reference

These keystrokes and keystroke combinations can be used when you are running the programs included with Windows 3.1. You'll probably notice that many programs sold on the open market also respond to these common keystroke combinations. Microsoft has used these keystroke combinations in their common interface standards, also called the SUA or Standard User Interface.

Calculator

These keystrokes and keystroke combinations can be used when you are running Calculator.

Edit Menu

Edit **C**opy	Enables you to copy the number onto the Clipboard.
Edit **P**aste	Pastes information to the Calculator. If there are equations on the Clipboard, it solves them.

View Menu

View **S**cientific	Displays the scientific calculator.
View **St**andard	Displays the standard calculator.

Calendar

These keystrokes and keystroke combinations can be used when you are running Calendar.

File Menu

File **N**ew	Starts a new calendar document.
File **O**pen	Opens a calendar document that exists on your disk.
File **S**ave	Saves the current calendar document.
File **S**ave **A**s	Saves the current calendar document on disk, enabling you to change its name or name a new file.
File **P**rint	Prints appointments.

File Page Setup	Enables you to specify the margins and add headers and footers as they will appear on the printed appointment.
File Print Setup	Enables you to choose the printer on which to print, as well as change the settings for that particular printer.
File Exit	Closes the active document and quits from Calendar. Enables you to save a file before quitting if the file is unsaved.

Edit Menu

Edit Cut	Erases text from a document and puts it onto the Clipboard.
Edit Copy	Copies text from a document and puts it onto the Clipboard.
Edit Paste	Pastes a copy of the Clipboard contents at the indicated point or replaces specified text.
Edit Remove	Deletes all entries from a specified range of days.

A

View Menu

| View Day | Displays the day view. |
| View Month | Displays the month view. |

Show Menu

Show Today	Displays the current day in the month or the day view.
Show Previous	Enables you to view the previous day in the day view or the previous month in the month view.
Show Next	Displays the next day or month, depending on whether you are in the day view or the month view.
Show Date	Locates a date in the day or the month view.

Alarm Menu

Alarm Set	Enables you to set and turn off an alarm.
Alarm Controls	Enables you to set the alarm to sound up to 10 minutes before a specified time, and enables you to turn the alarm's sound off or on.

Options Menu

Options **M**ark	Marks and unmarks selected days in the month view.
Options **S**pecial Time	Enables you to specify and erase special times in an appointment day.
Options **D**ay Settings	Enables you to define the specifications for the day view.

Cardfile

These keystrokes and keystroke combinations can be used when you are running Cardfile.

File Menu

File **N**ew	Starts a new file.
File **O**pen	Opens a file that exists on your disk.
File **S**ave	Saves the current file.
File Save **A**s	Saves the current file on disk, enabling you to change the name or name a new file.
File **P**rint	Prints the top card in a file.
File Print All	Prints the entire file.
File Page Setup	Enables you to specify the margins and add headers and footers that will appear on the printed cards.
File **Pr**int Setup	Enables you to choose the printer on which to print, as well as change the settings for that particular printer.

| **F**ile **M**erge | Merges the cards from another file into the active file. |
| **F**ile E**x**it | Closes the active file and quits from Cardfile. |

Edit Menu

Edit **U**ndo	Reverses the last typing or editing action.
Edit Cu**t**	Erases text or a picture from a card and puts it onto the Clipboard.
Edit **C**opy	Copies text or a picture and puts it onto the Clipboard.
Edit **P**aste	Copies the contents of the Clipboard onto a card.
Edit Past **L**ink	Inserts the contents of the Clipboard.
Edit Paste **S**pecial	Selects the format of the inserted data.
Edit **I**ndex	Enables you to modify the index line of the top card of the file.
Edit **R**estore	Reverses all the modifications made on a card if it is still the top card of a file or if the file hasn't been saved.
Edit Te**x**t	Changes back to text mode.
Edit Pictu**r**e	Enables you to paste and move a picture on a card.
Edit Lin**k**	Changes the appearance of the link.
Edit **O**bject	Starts the application from which the linked object was acquired.
Edit In**s**ert Object	Opens a dialog box to allow selection of other applications that support linking. Choosing an application from the list causes Windows to open the application for use.

A

View Menu

| **Vi**ew **C**ard | Enables you to view the entire card. |
| **Vi**ew **L**ist | Lists the indexes in alphabetical order. |

Card Menu

Card **A**dd	Adds a new card to a file.
Card **D**elete	Erases a card.
Card Du**p**licate	Duplicates a card.
Card **A**utodial	Dials a telephone number on the chosen card.

Search Menu

Search **G**o To	Moves a card to the top of the file.
Search **F**ind	Locates text on cards in a file.
Search Find **N**ext	Repeats the most recent search.

Clipboard Viewer

These keystrokes and keystroke combinations can be used when you are running Clipboard Viewer.

File Menu

File **O**pen	Opens a Clipboard file.
File Save **A**s	Saves the current Clipboard contents in a file.
File E**x**it	Closes the current Clipboard window and quits from the Clipboard program.

Edit Menu

Edit **D**elete	Erases the contents of the Clipboard.

Display Menu

Display **A**uto	Enables you to view the contents of the Clipboard in its original format.
Display [format name]	Displays format name of current Clipboard contents.
Display **O**wner Display	Enables you to view the contents of the Clipboard in the originating application's format.

Display **T**ext	Displays Clipboard contents in draft format (system font) without formatting codes visible.
Display **L**ink	Updates a linked application with the contents of the Clipboard.
Display **OEM** Text	Displays the contents of the Clipboard using OEM text font.

Clock

These keystrokes and keystroke combinations can be used when you are running Clock.

Settings Menu

Settings **A**nalog	Displays an analog clock.
Settings **D**igital	Displays a digital clock.
Settings Set **F**ont	Enables the user to select a display font from the list of available fonts. Shows sample text.
Settings **N**o Title	Causes Clock to omit the display of the window title.
Settings **S**econds	Causes Clock to omit or include a display of seconds.
Settings Date	Causes clock to omit or include a display of the date.
Settings A**b**out Clock	Displays information about the Clock program.

Notepad

These keystrokes and keystroke combinations can be used when you are running Notepad.

File Menu

File **N**ew	Starts a new text document.
File **O**pen	Opens a text file that exists on your disk.
File **S**ave	Saves the current document.

A

File Save **A**s	Saves the current document on disk, enabling you to name a new file or change the name of an existing file.
File **P**rint	Prints the file.
File Page Setup	Defines the margins and enables you to insert headers and footers that will appear on the printed document.
File **P**rint Setup	Enables you to choose the printer on which to print, as well as change the settings for that particular printer.
File E**x**it	Closes the active file and quits from Notepad. Enables you to save the document before leaving Notepad.

Edit Menu

Edit **U**ndo	Reverses the last editing or formatting action.
Edit **C**ut	Moves text from a document onto the Clipboard.
Edit **C**opy	Copies selected text from a document onto the Clipboard.
Edit **P**aste	Copies the contents of the Clipboard and pastes it in a document at the insertion point, or as a replacement for selected text.
Edit Delete	Erases specified text from a document.
Edit Select **A**ll	Selects the entire file.
Edit Time/**D**ate	Inserts the current time and date to the text file.
Edit **W**ord Wrap	Wraps the lines of text.

Search Menu

Search **F**ind	Looks for specified words or characters in a text file.
Search Find **N**ext	Repeats the most recent search.

Paintbrush

These keystrokes and keystroke combinations can be used when you are running Paintbrush.

File Menu

File **N**ew	Begins a new drawing.
File **O**pen	Opens an existing drawing.
File **S**ave	Saves the current drawing.
File Save **A**s	Saves the current drawing, enabling you to change the formatting options for saving the drawing or view information about the drawing.
File Page Se**t**up	Enables you to specify the placement of margins and add headers and footers that will appear on the printed drawing.
File **P**rint	Enables you to print a drawing.
File **P**rint Setup	Enables you to choose the printer on which to print and change the settings for that particular printer.
File E**x**it	Closes the active drawing and quits from Paintbrush.

A

Edit Menu

Edit **U**ndo	Reverses the last drawing or formatting action.
Edit Cut	Removes the selected area from the drawing onto the Clipboard.
Edit **C**opy	Copies the selected area onto the Clipboard.
Edit **P**aste	Places the contents of the Clipboard into the upper-left corner of the drawing.
Edit C**o**py To	Saves the selected area into another file.
Edit Paste **F**rom	Enables you to retrieve a cut-out from a file and puts it in a flexible box in the upper-left corner of the drawing.

View Menu

View Zoom **I**n	Enlarges a selected part of the drawing so that you can make changes one pixel at a time.
View Zoom **O**ut	Returns an enlarged drawing to its normal size, or displays an entire drawing that is larger than the area that can be viewed in the window.

View **V**iew Picture	Removes everything except for the drawing so that it is the only thing that can be viewed on the screen.
View **T**ools and Linesize	Takes the tools and linesize box out of view from the window.
View **P**alette	Takes the palette out of view from the window.
View **C**ursor Position	Enables you to view the position of the cursor as an x,y coordinate.

Text Menu

Text **N**ormal	Removes text attributes.
Text **B**old	Makes selected text bold.
Text **I**talic	Makes selected text italic.
Text **U**nderline	Makes selected text underlined.
Text **O**utline	Outlines selected text, using the currently selected background color.
Text **S**hadow	Creates a shadow behind selected text, using the currently selected background color.
Text **F**onts	Opens a dialog box allowing change of font style, size, and attributes.

Pick Menu

Pick Flip **H**orizontal	Flips the selection from side to side.
Pick Flip **V**ertical	Flips the selection from top to bottom.
Pick **I**nverse	Inverts the colors in the selection.
Pick **S**hrink+Grow	Modifies the size of the selection.
Pick **T**ilt	Tilts the selection.
Pick **C**lear	Makes the area within the original cut-out the background area color when you choose the **S**hrink+Grow or **T**ilt commands.

Options Menu

Options **I**mage Attributes	Enables you to define the settings for the new drawing.
Options **B**rush Shapes	Modifies the shape of the brush tool.
Options **E**dit Colors	Enables you to make custom colors.
Options **G**et Colors	Retrieves color palettes with custom colors you have saved.
Options **S**ave Colors	Saves color palettes.
Options **O**mit Picture Format	Limits the number of formats for pictures available to other applications when pasting a picture from the Clipboard.

PIF Editor

File Menu

File **N**ew	Begins a new PIF file with the standard settings.
File **O**pen	Opens a PIF file that exists on your disk.
File **S**ave	Saves the current PIF file.
File Save **A**s	Saves the current PIF file that already exists on disk, with the option of renaming a file or creating a name for a new file.
File E**x**it	Closes the active PIF file and quits from PIF Editor.

Mode Menu

Mode **S**tandard	Shows the Standard Mode settings dialog box.
Mode **3**86 Enhanced	Shows the 386 Enhanced settings dialog box.

Print Manager

These keystrokes and keystroke combinations can be used when you are running Print Manager.

View Menu

View Time/Date Sent	Enables you to turn the time-and-date display on or off.
View Print File Size	Gives you the option of using the file-size display.
View Refresh	Refreshes queue information. Especially useful for viewing network queues that might have changed since the last review.
View Selected Net Queue	Update the selected network printing queues.
View Other Net Queue	Shows the queues for other network printers, if available.
View Exit	Exits Print Manager.

Options Menu

Options Low Priority	Gives Print Manager few resources.
Options Medium Priority	Gives Print Manager a medium amount of resources.
Options High Priority	Gives Print Manager most resources.
Options Alert Always	Continuously shows a message box whether the Print Manager window is active or not.
Options Flash If Inactive	Alerts you to an incoming message from Print Manager if its window is inactive.
Options Ignore If Inactive	Ignores incoming messages from Print Manager if its window is inactive or reduced to an icon.
Options Network Settings	Enables you to change settings for a network printer.
Options Network Connections	Enables the user to select network printing devices for review.
Options Printer Setup	Enables the user to change printer settings.

Recorder

These keystrokes and keystroke combinations can be used when you are running Recorder.

File Menu

File **N**ew	Starts a new macro file.
File **O**pen	Opens a macro file that exists on your disk.
File **S**ave	Saves the current macro document.
File Save **As**	Saves the current macro document on disk, enabling you to change the filename or name a new file.
File **M**erge	Merges two different macro files.
File **Ex**it	Closes the active macro file and quits from Recorder.

Macro Menu

Macro **R**un	Runs a macro.
Macro Re**c**ord	Starts macro recording.
Macro **D**elete	Erases a macro.
Macro **P**roperties	Enables you to modify a macro's specifications.

Options Menu

Options **C**ontrol+Break Checking	Prevents a Ctrl-Break from stopping a macro.
Options **S**hortcut Keys	Prevents Recorder from detecting shortcut keys.
Options **M**inimize on Use	Reduces the Recorder window to an icon automatically on starting a macro.
Options **P**references	Enables you to modify the default specifications for recording a macro.

Solitaire

These keystrokes and keystroke combinations can be used when you are running Solitaire.

Game Menu

Game **D**eal	Begins a new game.
Game **U**ndo	Reverses your last action.
Game Dec**k**	Enables you to choose another design on the backs of the cards.
Game **O**ptions	Enables you to select different game options.
Game E**x**it	Quits from Solitaire.

Minesweeper

These keystrokes and keystroke combinations can be used when you are running Minesweeper.

Game Menu

Game **N**ew	Starts a new game.
Game **B**eginner	Game starts with the smallest mine field.
Game **I**ntermediate	Game starts with a larger mine field.
Game **E**xpert	Game starts with the largest mine field.
Game **C**ustom	Enables settings to be customized.
Game **M**arks	Leaves marks.
Game Color	Displays game in color or monochrome.
Game Best **T**imes	Displays best times for the three levels of ability.
Game E**x**it	Exits Minesweeper.

Terminal

These keystrokes and keystroke combinations can be used when you are running Terminal.

File Menu

| **F**ile **N**ew | Opens a new configuration file. |
| **F**ile **O**pen | Opens an existing configuration file. |

File **S**ave	Saves changes to the active configuration file.
File Save **A**s	Saves a new or existing configuration file under a new name.
File **Pr**int Setup	Enables you to choose the printer on which to print, as well as change the settings for that particular printer.
File **E**xit	Closes the active file and quits from Terminal.

Edit Menu

Edit **C**opy	Copies specified text from the window onto the Clipboard.
Edit **P**aste	Transfers the contents of the Clipboard to the remote computer.
Edit S**e**nd	Transfers selected text to the remote computer.
Edit Select **A**ll	Selects all text in the window and scroll buffer.
Edit Cl**e**ar Buffer	Deletes the contents of the scroll buffer.

A

Settings Menu

Settings Phone **N**umber	Specifies the options for dialing the remote computer.
Settings **T**erminal Emulation	Enables you to set the terminal emulation type.
Settings Terminal **P**references	Enables you to set options for terminal actions.
Settings Function **K**eys	Enables you to specify the actions of the function keys.
Settings Te**x**t Transfers	Specifies the options for sending text files.
Settings **B**inary Transfers	Sets the binary transfer protocol.
Settings **C**ommunications	Defines the communications parameters.
Settings Mo**d**em Commands	Defines modem commands.
Settings Printer **E**cho	Prints incoming text and keystrokes.

Settings **Ti**mer Mode	Enables you to time your work session in Terminal.
Settings Show/Hide **F**unction Keys	Enables you to hide the function keypad and the timer.

Phone Menu

Phone **D**ial	Dials the modem to make a connection.
Phone **H**angup	Hangs up the modem.

Transfers Menu

Transfers **S**end Text File	Delivers a text file.
Transfers **R**eceive Text File	Starts receiving a text file.
Transfers **V**iew Text File	Displays a text file before sending or receiving it.
Transfers Send **B**inary File	Delivers a binary file.
Transfers Receive Binary **F**ile	Starts receiving a binary file.
Transfers **P**ause	Pauses the transfer of a text file.
Transfers Re**s**ume	Restarts a text file transfer after a pause.
Transfers St**o**p	Ends a transfer of a text or a binary file.

Write

These keystrokes and keystroke combinations can be used when you are running Write.

File Menu

File **N**ew	Starts a new document.
File **O**pen	Opens a document that already exists on your disk.

File **S**ave	Saves the current document with the changes you have made.
File Save **A**s	Saves the current document on disk, enabling you to change the filename, directory, and file format.
File **P**rint	Prints the active document.
File **P**rint Setup	Enables you to choose the printer on which to print, as well as change the settings for that particular printer.
File **R**epaginate	Repaginates a document and displays the page breaks on the screen.
File E**x**it	Closes the active document and quits from Write.

Edit Menu

Edit **U**ndo	Reverses the last typing, editing, or formatting action.
Edit Cu**t**	Moves the selected text or graphics from a document onto the Clipboard.
Edit **C**opy	Copies the selected text or graphics onto the Clipboard.
Edit **P**aste	Copies the contents of the Clipboard at the indicated point, or replaces a selection in a document.
Edit Paste Sp**e**cial	Displays the format of the Clipboard data.
Edit Paste **L**ink	Links and pastes data in the Clipboard to an open Write file.
Edit Lin**k**s	Changes information related to a link.
Edit **O**bject	Starts the application that originated the linked data.
Edit **I**nsert Object	Opens a dialog box to allow selection of OLE supporting applications. Selecting an application causes Windows to open the application. A link is established during this process.
Edit **M**ove Picture	Enables you to move a picture horizontally.
Edit **S**ize Picture	Enables you to modify the size of a picture.

A

Find Menu

Find Find	Locates text in the document.
Find Repeat **Last** Find	Enables you to repeat the last search without having to open the **Find F**ind dialog box.
Find Replace	Locates and changes text.
Find Go To Page	Goes to a specified page in the document.

Character Menu

Character Re**g**ular	Enables you to change the character style to regular.
Character **B**old	Makes the character bold.
Character **I**talic	Makes the character italic.
Character **U**nderline	Underlines selected text.
Character Su**p**erscript	Places text higher on the line.
Character Subscript	Places text lower on the line.
Character **R**educe Font	Decreases the font size to the next smaller size.
Character **E**nlarge Font	Enlarges the font size to the next larger size.
Character **F**onts	Enables you to select and/or modify a font.

Paragraph Menu

Paragraph **N**ormal	Makes the paragraph formatting single-spaced and aligned with the left margin.
Paragraph **L**eft	Aligns the selected paragraphs with the left margin.
Paragraph **C**entered	Aligns the selected paragraphs with the center between the left and right margins.
Paragraph **R**ight	Aligns paragraphs with the right margin.
Paragraph **J**ustified	Aligns paragraphs with the margins on each side of the page.
Paragraph **S**ingle Space	Modifies the line spacing to single-spaced.
Paragraph **1** 1/2 Space	Modifies the line spacing to 1 1/2 lines.

Paragraph **D**ouble Space	Modifies the line spacing to double-spaced.
Paragraph **I**ndents	Enables you to define the left, right, and first line indentations for a paragraph.

Document Menu

Document **H**eader	Enables you to create a header that will appear in your printed document.
Document **F**ooter	Enables you to create a footer that will appear in your printed document.
Document **R**uler On	Shows the ruler at the top of the window so that you can modify paragraph formatting and tabs with the mouse.
Document **T**abs	Enables you to set tabs for the entire document.
Document **P**age Layout	Enables you to set the starting page number, define the margins, and choose one of the two measurement systems used in Write.

A

Packager

These keystrokes and keystroke combinations can be used when you are running Packager.

File

File **N**ew	Starts a new Package.
File **U**pdate	Updates the Package and the file.
File **I**mport	Displays the application icon and file information.
File **S**ave Contents	Saves the contents of file information to the file.
File **E**xit	Exits Packager.

Edit

Edit **U**ndo	Nullifies changes made since the last save.
Edit **C**ut	Removes and places the contents of the active window onto the Clipboard.

Edit Copy	Places the contents of the active window onto the Clipboard.
Edit Delete	Removes the highlighted information from the active window.
Edit Paste	Places the contents of the Clipboard into the active window.
Edit Paste Link	Links data in the Clipboard to Packager.
Edit Copy Package	Copies icons and files to the Clipboard.
Edit Links	Changes link information.
Edit Label	Changes an icon's text label.
Edit Command Line	Enables you to include a command line within an icon to open other applications or files from that single icon.
Edit Object	Opens the application that originated the data in the content window.

SysEdit

These keystrokes and keystroke combinations can be used when you are running SysEdit.

File

File Save	Prompts the user to save changed files.
File Print	Prints the file in the active window.
File Print Setup	Enables printers and settings to be changed.
File Exit	Exits SysEdit.
File About	Displays information about the SysEdit program.

Edit

| Edit Undo | Enables you to nullify your changes. |
| Edit Cut | Removes data from the file and places it onto the Clipboard. |

Edit Copy	Copies selected data to the Clipboard.
Edit Paste	Places Clipboard contents into the active file window.
Edit Clear	Removes selected data from the active file window.
Edit Select All	Selects all text within the active file window.

Search

Search Find	Seeks one occurrence of data in the active file window.
Search Next	Seeks all occurrences of prompted data in the active file window until the end of the file is found.
Search Previous	Seeks all occurrences of prompted data in the active file window until the beginning of the file is found.

A

Window

Window Tile	Causes all file windows to share the application window space equally.
Window Cascade	Causes all file windows to overlap each other. Only the active file window is foremost and visible.
Window Arrange Icons	Causes any minimized window icons to neatly arrange at the bottom of the SysEdit work area.
Window [windows list]	Provides a list of the windows currently displayed by SysEdit. A check mark is displayed to indicate the active file window.

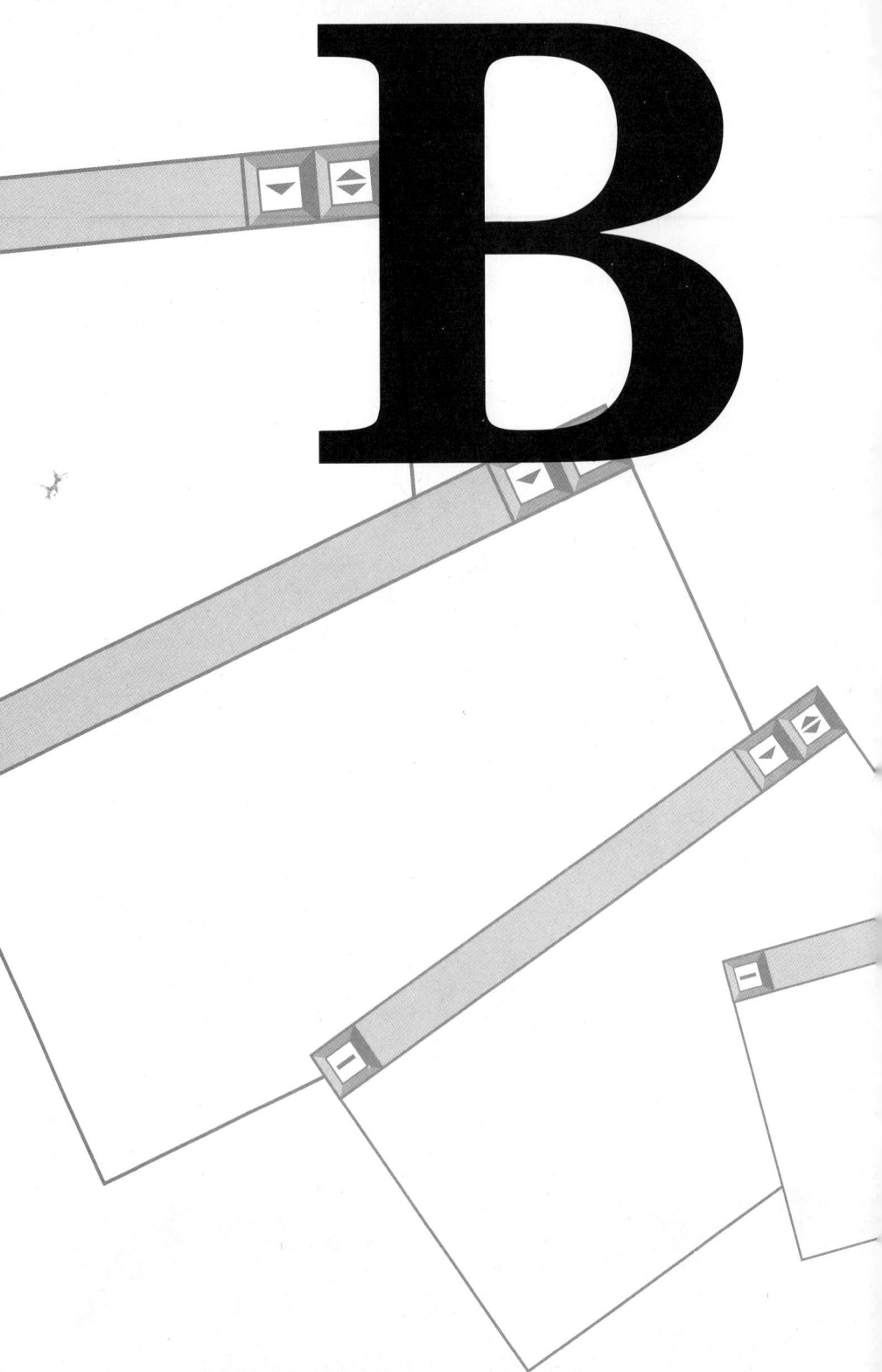

REFERENCE

B

MS-DOS 5.0 and Windows

When you run Windows, it doesn't really seem as though MS-DOS (*MicroSoft Disk Operating System*) 5.0 is there at all. Of course, unlike OS/2, Windows operates on top of or in conjunction with DOS. DOS is a group of programs that convert instructions delivered by a human into instructions that a machine can understand. You can think of DOS as something of an interpreter for Windows. Today's Windows cannot operate computer hardware all by itself.

A Brief History

The first version of DOS was developed for the IBM Personal Computer (PC). The first PC was a simple machine by today's standards, but it was a powerful thing to behold compared to its contemporaries. Your interpreter then, as now, was DOS. DOS Version 1.0 supported floppy drives that could read one side only, about 160K of space for each floppy. Version 1.1 could recognize a disk drive that used a 320K drive.

In 1983 a new version of the PC was released by IBM and along with it a new version of DOS. PC-DOS (the IBM flavor) Version 2.0 allowed a fixed disk to reside in the PC, now called an XT (for *Extended*

Technology). With Version 2.0 you could use diskettes formatted to 360K. Version 2.0 also offered batch files, the capability of clearing the screen, and programs intended to support the new hard drive implementation. IBM PC-DOS Version 2.1 was released in 1984. Some folks still use DOS 2.1 today.

Version 3.0 increased the stakes in diskette capacity. You could format and use a high-density diskette with 1.2M (megabytes) of storage space if you had an IBM AT (*Advanced Technology*) machine. Subsequent versions of 3.0 offered many refinements and added utility in being able to work with newer, add-on output devices.

Version 3.3 enabled the user to partition one physical disk drive into several logical ones. This gave the user the ability to set up *logical* or separate drive partitions (electronic dividers) on one hard drive unit. Each logical partition could have a drive letter and had to be 32M or less in size.

Versions 4.0 and 4.1 of DOS were not readily accepted by the public. The only saving grace as far as the average user was concerned was Version 4's capability of addressing a logical or physical hard drive of more than 32M. DOS 4.0 gave the user the ability to partition a hard drive as large as two gigabytes (two thousand megabytes) into four logical drives of 536M each.

The next section of this chapter concerns the most recent release of MS-DOS, Version 5.0.

MS-DOS 5.0 Files

Because this is a book about Windows 3.1, we talk about only files that are direct enhancements to Windows 3.1 performance.

Most of the files that come with DOS 5.0 diskettes must be decompressed or expanded. DOS does this during the install process. The compressed files have an underscore in place of the last letter (the third character) of the filename extension.

When you install DOS 5.0, you create a set of 360K destination or usable diskettes that contain the DOS files in their decompressed states.

Note: Although most command-line entries and examples in the following sections are capitalized, you are not required to use either uppercase or lowercase letters at the command line in order for your commands to work properly.

DOS Commands You Don't Use with Windows

For the sake of clarity, we'll look first at the DOS functions relevant to the operation of Windows that cannot be performed from within Windows (for example, FORMAT.EXE).

APPEND

APPEND is one of the few DOS functions or commands that definitely should not be invoked before loading Windows. APPEND allows programs to open data files in directories as if the files were in the current directory.

CHKDSK(/F)(/V)

CHKDSK looks for fragmented allocation units on a disk or a drive. Windows 3.1 does not enable you to run CHKDSK in any form while you are in a Windows session. You must leave Windows to use CHKDSK. This program converts lost chains to files that can be deleted by using the /F switch after the program name. If CHKDSK reports any fragmented space on the disk, it asks you whether you want to convert it to files. Answer Y if you are about to compress your hard drive. You might lose data if you use the /F switch, but use the switch if you are about to compress the disk. Using the /V switch provides a running update of the files as they are checked. When CHKDSK has finished its conversion (if any), look in your root directory for files that have a filename extension of .CHK. Review the files to determine their value, then delete them if they are not required.

   Example: CHKDSK /F /V

Special Commands for Your AUTOEXEC.BAT File

This section is dedicated to DOS version 5.0. If you are interested in optimizing Windows, you must run DOS 5.0. In any event, these topics represent improvements to your system's overall operating performance, improvements that will be reflected while using and not using Windows.

LOADHIGH

If you type the word LOADHIGH before a program name in a batch file, the named program is loaded into the upper memory area between 640K and 1024K rather than conventional memory. Because conventional memory is the most precious of all memory areas, it is wise to use this command as often as you have drivers and other smaller files to load. TSRs (*T*erminate and *S*tay *R*esident programs), mouse drivers, and software intended to operate in the background are prime considerations for usage of the LOADHIGH command. This example shows how you can save conventional memory space by loading a mouse driver into the upper memory area.

> Example: LOADHIGH MOUSE.COM

Note: You must have first installed extended and expanded memory managers for this command to work. Place the DOS=HIGH,UMB command in your CONFIG.SYS file prior to the LOADHIGH command. See the CONFIG.SYS section in this chapter for more on DOS=HIGH,UMB.

PATH

DOS uses the PATH statement as a logical choice on its file-finding missions. Consider the WIN program name as an example. When you type the filename WIN, DOS looks first in the directory that is currently accessed, it looks in the directories named in the PATH=

statement in your AUTOEXEC.BAT file. If DOS still does not find WIN, it then tells you the file does not exist.

The system environment is established using this command. This command is in essence a statement that directories named after the PATH command are *public,* or available to all programs in the system. Unless you place the name of a subdirectory in the PATH command statement, other programs do not know what other files exist on your drive(s).

Because most applications need DOS at one time or another, most people add the name of their DOS directory as the first directory after the syntax PATH=. DOS checks for your filename in each subsequent directory in the PATH statement. If you are running two versions of the same software, it is best to omit one of the directory names from the PATH statement, or DOS might find the named file in the first directory it sees, but that file would not be the file that you want to run.

> **Tip:** Place your *most frequently used* directory names immediately after the PATH= statement. Put your Windows directory name second after the DOS directory names to slightly speed up Windows execution times.

B

> **Tip:** If you don't want files to be publicly available to any calling program, simply omit the directory name from the PATH statement.

SET TEMP

The SET TEMP command is used to tell DOS that when a condition exists, take a particular action to a named place on a drive. For example, for Windows users who operate in 386-enhanced mode, DOS needs to know where to put temporary swap files created by DOS applications while they are running in a window. Use the SET TEMP statement to name the directory where you want these files placed. Otherwise, they show up in your root directory.

Example: SET TEMP=C:\WINDOWS\TEMP

> **Tip:** You should already have a directory named TEMP to accommodate Windows. When you name a directory in the SET TEMP statement, temporary files created by DOS applications get stored there. These almost always are junk files that serve no purpose as soon as the application closes. If you use the directory for only that purpose, it's easy to occasionally erase the entire contents of the directory without risk of deleting valuable files by mistake. This maintenance needs to be done periodically, so why not make it more foolproof?

SHARE

The SHARE command allows multiple applications to access one file between them at the same time and have DOS arbitrate between them to keep the file from being corrupted. If you are running Windows on a network, it is not advisable to run SHARE, because most network software does its own arbitrating. To run SHARE from your AUTOEXEC.BAT file, use this statement:

Example: SHARE.EXE

If you want to load SHARE into the high memory area to free conventional memory (you must be running EMM386.EXE and HIMEM.SYS to do this), add this statement:

Example: LOADHIGH SHARE.EXE

If you lack the space in the upper or high memory area to use the LOADHIGH statement, see INSTALL in the CONFIG.SYS section of this chapter for more on loading SHARE.

A few examples of how these command files and command line options appear in sample AUTOEXEC.BAT files can be found in the section of this reference entitled "Useful Sample Files."

The CONFIG.SYS File

The CONFIG.SYS file is used to tell your system special things about your system. CONFIG.SYS loads device drivers and reserves space in system memory for information processing. Let's look at the entries found in the CONFIG.SYS file that directly affect Windows operation.

BUFFERS=

The BUFFERS command sets the amount of RAM (*R*andom *A*ccess *M*emory) that DOS sets aside for data transfer to and from disks. The value of 15 is a good starting value to use before you experiment with lower values. If you are using SMARTDRV, make sure this statement appears in one of the first three lines in your CONFIG.SYS file.

> Example: BUFFERS=15

If you are running Windows and are using SMARTDRV and your BUFFERS value is higher than this recommended value (15), you are effectively allocating memory twice to do the same thing, which slows down system performance. If you have installed SMARTDRV, you can use a value in the BUFFERS= statement as low as 1.

It's best to experiment with this value until you believe you are getting the maximum speed.

If you have not installed SMARTDRV, use this statement:

> Example: BUFFERS=30

DEVICE=

For Windows to access extended memory and utilize SMARTDRV.EXE when moving data to and from Windows applications, you must have the DEVICE= <driver name> in your CONFIG.SYS file. This statement loads any installable device driver or a file that is treated by DOS like a device driver (like HIMEM.SYS) into the operating system.

> Example: DEVICE=DRIVER.SYS

DEVICEHIGH=

This statement loads an installable device driver in the upper memory area. You can free the space the driver normally would occupy in conventional memory if you have invoked EMM386.EXE and HIMEM.SYS first, and use this statement. Some DOS programs try to access only the same old memory addresses located below 640K, even though Windows can give them entire megabytes of memory to work with. To avoid this problem, load programs and devices into your upper memory area (640k to 1024k) to make sure that you have as much memory space available below 640k as you can arrange.

This is how the DEVICEHIGH statement should be used:

    Example: DEVICEHIGH=*DRIVER.SYS*

DEVICEHIGH SIZE=

If you use the DEVICEHIGH command, and your driver allocates additional memory *after it is loaded,* you might want to specify how much memory it can take while it performs its tasks. In general, device drivers such as SMARTDRV and RAMDRIVE should not be loaded into the upper memory area. Doing so causes unpredictable results such as system lockup. You can control how much memory a driver can take by first issuing the DOS MEM command to see how much room you have to work with.

    Example: MEM /C

This little utility shows you what is occupying memory space in both the conventional and the upper memory areas. If you first load your device driver using the DEVICE= statement, you can run MEM /C to see how much space it takes. Look at the size of the file in bytes and hex. Write down both values. If MEM says you have enough space in the upper memory area (UMA) to load your driver high, then use the DEVICEHIGH statement rather than DEVICE.

If your driver takes more space than is available in the UMA during the normal course of its duties, you may encounter problems. If the driver takes yet more UMA memory space by design, allocate the space it can occupy in the *upper memory area* by placing the hex value you wrote down earlier after the DEVICEHIGH SIZE statement.

    Example: DEVICEHIGH SIZE=39E0 MOUSE.SYS

Now you have told your system to give the device only enough room in the upper memory area to operate. The driver will have to get any additional memory for its purposes from conventional memory.

DOS=(<HIGH>,<UMB>)

Utilizing the upper memory area for the storage and operation of device drivers and programs frees memory for Windows to use for other things. With HIMEM.SYS running, you can load part of DOS 5.0 into the high memory area, freeing some conventional memory for programs. DOS also maintains a link to the upper memory area with the same statement. To accomplish this, you must place this statement into your CONFIG.SYS file after the HIMEM.SYS entry. This is the statement:

Example: `DOS=HIGH,UMB`

EMM386.EXE

EMM386.EXE is the expanded memory manager offered with MS-DOS 5.0. It makes memory available to applications that can use expanded memory. You tell EMM386 how much memory is available by using a *command line switch* like this:

Example: `DEVICE=EMM386 1024`

If your system has only 1024K of memory, use EMM386 to take advantage of the memory area formerly dedicated for device drivers and hardware management. You should use this command line switch if you have 1024K of system memory.

Example: `DEVICE=EMM386 NOEMS`

If your system has more than 1024K of memory, you might want EMM386 to dole out memory above 1024K, up to your system's memory limit. If you want EMM386 to access space in the upper memory area as well as make memory available (in this case, 1024K) for applications that can use expanded memory (like Lotus 1-2-3 for DOS), use this command line switch.

Example: `DEVICE=EMM386 1024 RAM`

B

FASTOPEN

Because Windows is a true multitasking environment (in 386-enhanced mode), you will often call up the same files over and over during the course of a normal work session.

FASTOPEN stores the location of files that you have used since you powered up the machine. FASTOPEN improves access times if you are accessing filenames that are not located in more than one place on your hard drive. If you are using two versions of Windows, for example, you should not use FASTOPEN because the program retains the address of the filename *when last used.* If you run the Windows 3.1 Print Manager and then run Windows 3.0 and print a file using its Print Manager, FASTOPEN loads the filename PRINTMAN.EXE from your Windows 3.1 directory, not the currently used version's directory. It remembers where the file is so that your hard drive does not have to waste time seeking the filename each time you need it. Therefore, filenames that are found in several places on your hard drive (such as SETUP.EXE or INSTALL.EXE) may be "remembered," and the wrong copy of the file may be opened by FASTOPEN. You can invoke FASTOPEN when you boot up your system by including a line in your AUTOEXEC.BAT file that looks like this:

> Example: FASTOPEN

You can load FASTOPEN and place its filename storage area in expanded memory with this command line:

> Example: FASTOPEN/X

You can use expanded memory rather than conventional memory for both the filename cache and the program itself by using this command line:

> Example: LOADHIGH FASTOPEN/X

See INSTALL in the CONFIG.SYS section of this chapter for more on loading FASTOPEN.

Note: You must first place the DOS=HIGH,UMB command line in your CONFIG.SYS file for the LOADHIGH command to work. See the CONFIG.SYS section in this chapter for more on DOS=HIGH,UMB.

> **Warning:** Do not run a disk compaction or compression program while FASTOPEN is invoked, because you might lose critical data. Reboot the system from a floppy that does not load an expanded memory manager, disk caching program or FASTOPEN before disk compaction is attempted.

FCBS=

This section applies to the running of older DOS programs in a window. The FCBS statement allows older applications to open many files simultaneously and *keep* them open. Without the FCBS statement, DOS may close data files opened earlier in the session if it runs out of FCBS (*File Control BlockS*). A file control block is a data segment that stores information about a file. Most contemporary applications have no need for the FCBS statement. If you are experiencing difficulty using applications that cannot seem to keep many files open, place this statement in your CONFIG.SYS file.

Example: FCBS=20

Unless you really need the FCBS statement in your CONFIG.SYS file, don't include it.

FILES=

The FILES= statement tells your system how many files can be open at any given time. For best results when running Windows, use this statement.

Example: FILES=30

HIMEM.SYS

HIMEM.SYS manages the memory area known as the upper memory area. The UMA exists between 640K and 1024K. The space traditionally is reserved by DOS for device drivers, ROM instructions, and display

B

operation. Because there usually is some space left over, DOS 5.0 enables you to place device drivers and TSRs in the UMA as well. This frees conventional memory for your applications. Do not load HIMEM.SYS into the UMA with the DEVICEHIGH command, or you might experience unpredictable results. If you have at least 1024K of memory, place this statement in your CONFIG.SYS file.

Example: DEVICE=HIMEM.SYS

INSTALL

The INSTALL statement in your CONFIG.SYS file loads TSRs into conventional memory. If you load a TSR, such as FASTOPEN or SHARE, with the INSTALL statement, it will occupy slightly less space in conventional memory than it will without using the INSTALL statement. If you have no more space in the upper memory area for TSRs, use the INSTALL statement.

Example: INSTALL=FASTOPEN

RAMDRIVE.SYS

RAMDRIVE.SYS is a DOS utility program that creates and manages a logical disk drive located in your system's RAM. RAMDRIVE is a TSR, so it's always there, taking up space. It will create a disk as large as your free memory capacity. A RAM drive is infinitely faster than many hard drives, in that the access times normally are less than one millisecond. Most modern hard drives *boast* an average access time of about 15 milliseconds. This attribute alone makes RAM drives very tempting, especially if you use a graphical user interface such as Windows.

RAMDRIVE fools your system into believing that there is another disk drive out there in your memory. You can treat it just like any other drive. Copy files to it, run programs from it, and save it periodically to your hard drive.

If you don't save the contents of a RAM disk to permanent media such as a real hard drive, you risk losing the contents of the drive if and when the system powers down. If you are in an area where the power is less than totally reliable, you might want to forego the use of a RAM drive. Fortunately, now you can purchase a UPS (*U*ninterruptable

Power Supply) to get around power problems so that using a RAM disk is potentially rewarding. Always name a RAM drive with the *next available* drive letter. For example, let's create a 4M (one M is 1024K) RAM disk using the next statement.

Example: `DEVICE=RAMDRIVE.SYS 4096`

If you have room for a RAM disk and RAMDRIVE in expanded memory (memory located beyond 1024K), you can place both in expanded memory using this statement.

Example: `DEVICE=RAMDRIVE.SYS 4096 /A`

SMARTDRV.SYS

SMARTDRV is a disk cache program for your hard drive. Your system must have extended or expanded memory to use SMARTDRV. A cache is a dedicated storage area in memory. SMARTDRV allows your system to get and save data without remaining linked to a hard drive while the process occurs. SMARTDRV saves the data you send to the hard drive to the cache first, so that when you next ask for it, you get it from the cache (memory) and not the hard drive. The cache saves data to the drive at its best speed while freeing you to go on with your work.

B

If you have at least 4M of memory, you should be using SMARTDRV. The program really needs one to two megabytes of RAM in order to be effective. Unless you work with file sizes of more than 2M, don't assign more than 2M of space to SMARTDRV. The returns diminish after that point because SMARTDRV does not effectively use more than 2M.

This cache can give you an effective average access time of about one-half millisecond to about three milliseconds. If your hard drive has an average access time of 15 milliseconds, your system can be about five times faster during the data storage and retrieval process with SMARTDRV.

For optimal performance, you should assign a minimum and a maximum memory allocation to SMARTDRV. Don't set the minimum below 256K and don't set the maximum above 2M. This is an example of a very effective allocation of memory (2M) for a system with 8M of total system memory:

Example: `DEVICE=SMARTDRV 2048 1024`

STACKS

DOS allocates space in memory for the processing of internal tasks called *interrupts*. You can save memory by making a statement in your CONFIG.SYS file that effectively reduces this allocation to zero. Windows does not benefit from the allocation of memory via the STACKS statement. If you are using DOS 3.3 or later and are running primarily Windows applications, use this statement in your CONFIG.SYS file.

Example: STACKS=0,0

Useful Sample Files

Sometimes it's a lot easier to use commands if you have an example to look at while you're doing so. We've included a few sample files in text to make the job of working with DOS a little easier.

A Sample AUTOEXEC.BAT File

```
echo off
mkdir d:\temp
set TEMP=d:\temp
PATH=C:\;C:\DOS;C:\WINDOWS;C:\WINDOWS\SYSTEM;C:\XTPRO;C:\PKWARE
loadhigh CCBACK
loadhigh c:\mouse\mouse
prompt $p $g
cd\windows\winword
copy *.* d:\
cd\beta
win
```

Looking at the commands in order, you can see that this AUTOEXEC.BAT file does the following:

1. Renders the batch file commands invisible.

2. Makes a directory on a RAM disk established when the CONFIG.SYS file was loaded.

3. Tells DOS that any temporary files Windows applications make should be stored on the RAM disk and therefore be erased during power-down.

4. Lists the directories that you want all programs to have access to, in the order of the most actively accessed directories.

5. Loads your background fax/voice mail board driver into upper memory, freeing that much conventional memory for applications.

6. Loads a mouse driver so that the mouse works in non-Windows applications.

7. Creates a prompt made up of the current drive letter followed by a colon, a backslash, the current directory name, a space, and the > symbol.

8. Changes directories to that of a favored, but slower, word processor.

9. Copies all word processor application files to the RAM disk.

10. Makes the Windows directory the current directory.

11. Loads Windows 3.1.

A Sample CONFIG.SYS File

```
FILES=30
BUFFERS=1
lastdrive=d
break=on
stacks=0,0
device=himem.sys
DEVICE=EMM386.EXE 5120
DOS=HIGH,UMB
device=smartdrv.exe 2048 1024
device=ramdrive.sys 3072 /a
```

Looking at the commands in order, you can see that this CONFIG.SYS file does the following:

1. Allows DOS to open 30 files at any given time.

2. Assigns the minimum buffers because SMARTDRV is being used in conjunction with Windows; therefore, no additional disk drive buffering is needed.

3. Tells the operating system that there are four drives or that the last addressable drive is called drive D.

4. Asks DOS to check for the Ctrl-Break keystroke combination to interrupt non-Windows programs on demand more quickly.

5. Effectively negates the STACKS function. Windows does not need the STACKS statement included. STACKS will, however, assign an unwanted default value unless you tell it otherwise.

6. Installs HIMEM.SYS as the extended memory manager of choice.

7. Runs EMM386.EXE expanded memory manager and gives it 5120K of memory to work with.

8. Tells DOS to load part of itself into extended memory and to allow other programs to be loaded into extended memory as well.

9. Installs SMARTDRV.EXE as the preferred disk cache program and gives it a maximum of 2048K and a minimum of 1024K with which to work.

10. Causes RAMDRIVE.SYS to load itself and create a 3M RAM disk named drive D, both in expanded memory.

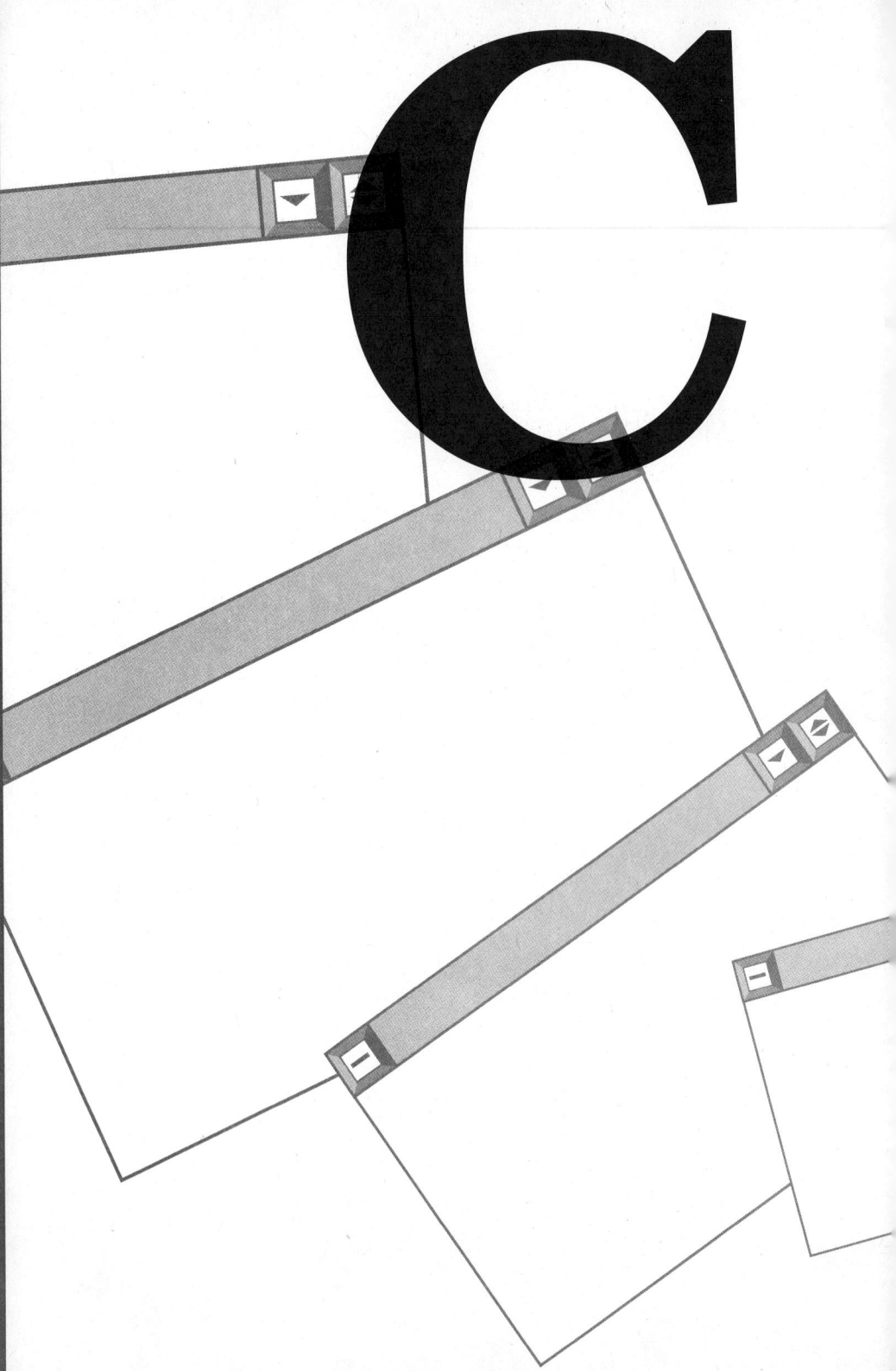

REFERENCE

C

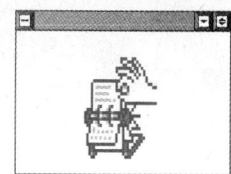

Windows Product Directory

The Windows Product Directory is a collection of products that is designed to run under Windows Version 3.0 or higher. The directory is provided not to advertise products but to help the Windows user become more aware of what is out there for solutions.

The lion's share of the products included in this directory are graphical in nature. Nongraphical (non-Windows) products are included because they directly enhance the performance of the Windows environment or products designed to run under Windows.

Most of the makers of the products in this directory graciously provided their time, support, and in many cases, their products to aid the creation of this directory.

The text and figures included in the directory are intended to do the following:

▲ Impart the look and feel of the interface

▲ Illustrate an example of work you might perform while using the product

▲ Convey the utility or features of the product

All the figures in this directory are captured screens from the actual product. Slide show, demonstration, and graphics files created for the sole purpose of marketing the product have been avoided. What-You-See-Is-What-You-Get!

How to Use This Directory

This section of the book is made up of categories or types of products grouped together to form some semblance of organization. It's probably easier to check the product index before you look for a particular product. For example, if you were looking for material on the subject of Word Processors, you should check the index to see which ones are covered in this section.

Because it is impossible to cover over 2000 Windows products in a book like this one, we have tried to focus on several categories, with some categories containing only one product. The idea is to let you know that products of this sort are available and to give you a feel for what they can do.

If you are looking for a detailed product directory for Windows products, we recommend Whitefox Communication's "Windows Shopper's Guide." It is not inexpensive, but the collection of detail about products and companies that produce these products makes it unrivaled in its field. You'll get more than your money back via the knowledge that you have made an informed choice when you select your next Windows software package.

The Product Categories that we have included are

Accounting
Application Development
Artwork Design
Batch File Development
Business Analysis
Calculators
Charts and Graphs
Communications
Computer-Aided Negotiations
Contact/Lead Management
Database Management Systems
Desktop Publishing
Entertainment
File Compression
File Conversion

File Manager Replacements
Font Management
Forms Processing
Hard Disk Management
Icon Development
Image Management
Information Managers
Integrated Software
Mapping
Memory Management
Multimedia
Personal Finance Management
Pointing Devices
Presentation Management
Print Manager Replacements
Program Manager Replacements
Project Management
Publications
Screen Capture
Screen Savers
Spell Checkers
Spreadsheets
Tax Preparation
Text Editors
Training Aids
Utilities
Word Processing

Accounting

This category covers the area of Accounting. The general accounting
packages are geared to the small business.

ACCPAC Simply Accounting: Computer Associates

ACCPAC Simply Accounting is the right accounting software package
for the small-business professional. This system includes a competent
tutorial that takes you through all the processes you might encounter
in the normal course of keeping track of your operating finances.

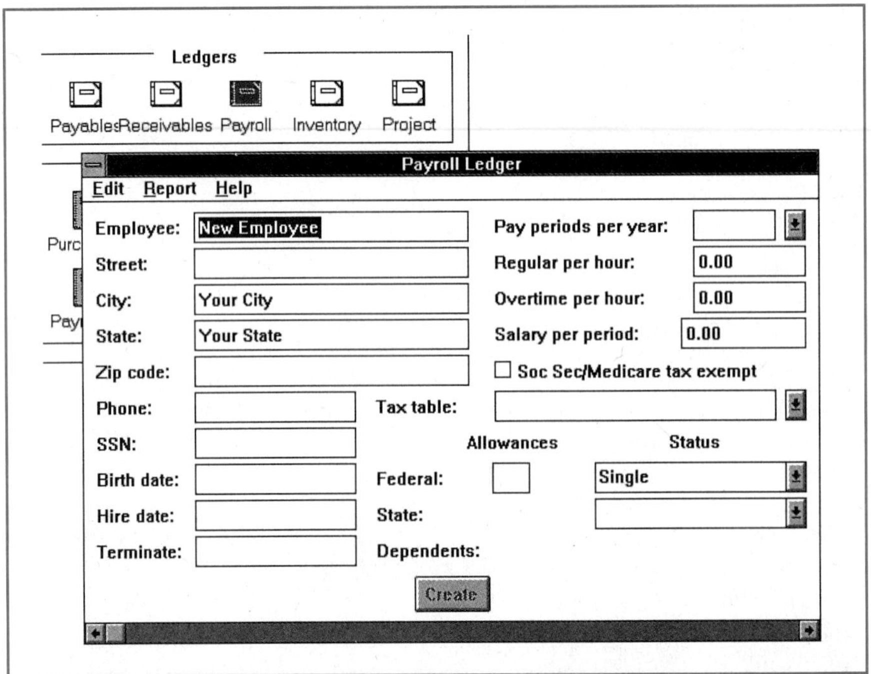

Ledgers

Payables Receivables Payroll Inventory Project

Payroll Ledger

Edit Report Help

Employee:	New Employee
Street:	
City:	Your City
State:	Your State
Zip code:	
Phone:	
SSN:	
Birth date:	
Hire date:	
Terminate:	

Pay periods per year:

Regular per hour: 0.00

Overtime per hour: 0.00

Salary per period: 0.00

☐ Soc Sec/Medicare tax exempt

Tax table:

Allowances   Status

Federal: Single

State:

Dependents:

Create

Figure C.1. ACCPAC Simply Accounting.

Some of the more outstanding features of ACCPAC Simply Accounting include the following:

- ▲ Employee records management
- ▲ Complete payroll accounting
- ▲ General ledger
- ▲ Job costing
- ▲ Receivables and payables
- ▲ Inventory control
- ▲ Password protection

ACCPAC Simply Accounting is designed to make the task of tracking expenses virtually effortless.

Computer Associates International Inc.
1240 McKay Drive
San Jose CA 95131-9990
Voice: (408)432-1727
Fax: (408)432-0614

Application Development

Application Development (AD) means several different things. For example, some AD packages just build a front end for an SQL server; some AD packages are designed to generate complete source code for vertical applications. There are even AD products that are made specifically for the IS professional. These ADs create EIMs or Executive Information Managers dedicated to managing many subordinates on a Local Area Network. This truly could be the beginning of the paperless office we were all promised back in the 70s.

Actor: The Whitewater Resource Group

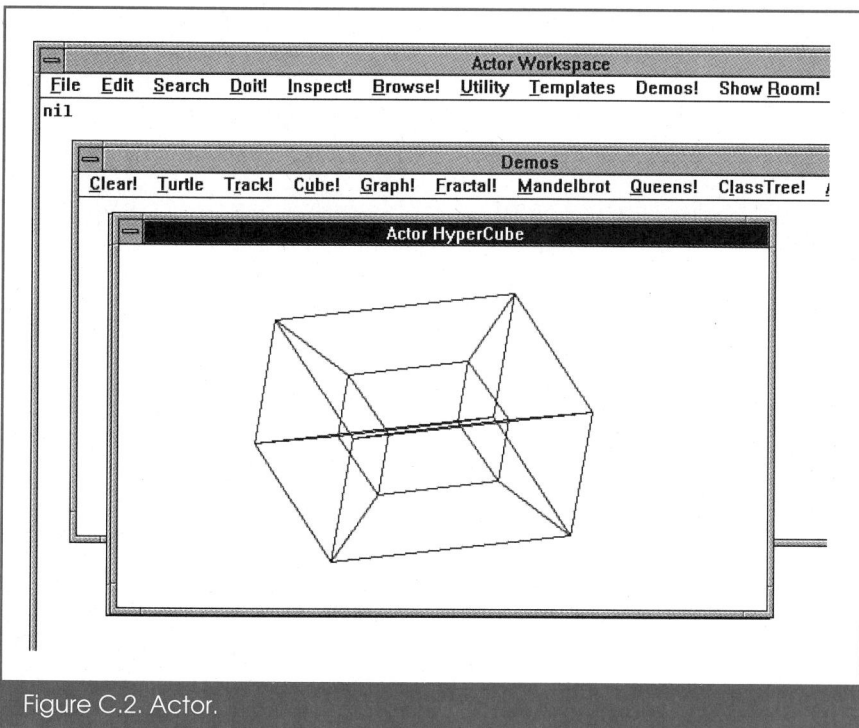

Figure C.2. Actor.

Actor is a complete Windows application development system that enables you to create stand-alone executables without a great deal of programming experience. Actor has its own programming language that is fairly easy to learn, even for the novice. You can integrate existing C code into any Actor application. It's DDE compatible, linkable to any of the popular databases, and comes with debugging tools to make the creating process more stress-free.

Some of the database products that can be utilized by Actor include the following:

▲ BTrieve

▲ DBVista

▲ Oracle

▲ Paradox

▲ SQL-Server

The Whitewater Group
1800 Ridge Avenue
Evanston IL 60201
Voice: (708)328-3800

Borland C++: Borland

Borland C++ is a professional-level compiler and debugger intended to provide you with the ability to write either Windows or DOS applications. Borland C++ provides a programming environment that makes all the functions, features, and utilities available to you without leaving the programming environment. A project manager is provided, along with the ability to write Windows applications utilizing DDE (Dynamic Data Exchange), DLLs (Dynamic Link Libraries), and the MDI (Multiple Document Interface).

This product compiles both C and C++ code. It includes the Whitewater Resource Kit so that you can visually create windows, list boxes, icons, and so on, rendering the Microsoft SDK (Software Development Kit) unnecessary for the creation of Windows applications.

This product contains everything you need to write Windows applications.

Borland International Inc.
1800 Green Hills Road
Scotts Valley CA 95067-0001
(408)438-5300

Bridge Toolkit: Softbridge

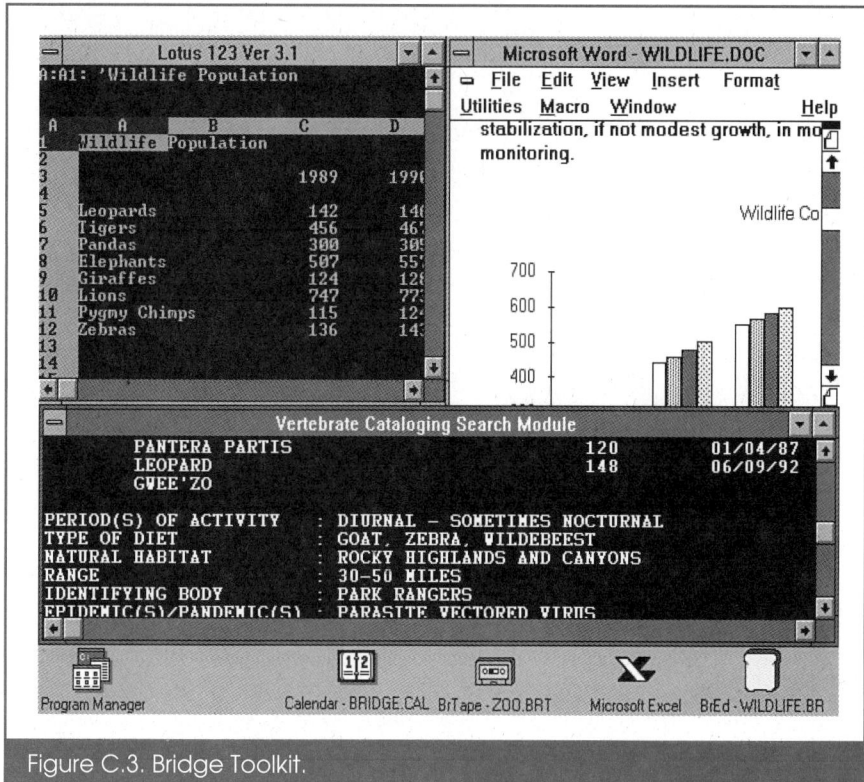

Figure C.3. Bridge Toolkit.

The Bridge Toolkit enables you to seamlessly integrate DOS and Windows application information. This product creates DDE links between Windows and non-Windows applications so that a wide cross-section of data-intensive applications from either world can access and share data that could not previously be orchestrated. The Bridge Toolkit can transparently use a communications package to link remote systems so that personnel can work with information.

This product builds its own menuing systems so that learning to share data between Windows and DOS is not a recurring, daily event.

Softbridge Technologies Group
125 Cambridge Park Drive
Cambridge MA 02140
Voice: (800)955-9190
Fax: (617)864-7747

Case W: Caseworks

Case W: is different from most code-generating application development products. First you build the interface (or the part of the application that the user sees), then you prototype it by actually running the interface, animated by Case W: before the code is even generated. This feature enables developers to present a prototyped product to a client before a major investment in time and resources is made by the developer.

If the client approves of the prototype, the developer can then pursue the development of the application with a higher degree of confidence—and the product is more likely to meet the end requirement sets of the client.

Caseworks
1 Dunwoody Park, Suite 130
Atlanta GA 30338
Voice: (404)399-6236
Fax: (404)399-9518

Choreographer: GUIdance Technologies

Choreographer is an application interface creation tool that can be ported between Windows and OS/2. This product is very simple to use—so much so that an end user can generate an application's look and feel and present that interface to programmers without any technical knowledge of programming.

The programmers then can build the underlying code without wasting valuable time with the interface requirements.

Choreographer also supports the following:

▲ DDE

▲ 3270/EHLLAPI

▲ LU 6.2/APPC

▲ SQL

▲ C

▲ Cobol

C

GUIdance Technologies Inc.
800 Vinial Street
Pittsburgh PA 15212
Voice: (412)231-1300
Fax: (412)231-2076

Guild: Expert Ease Systems

This development tool compiles the 32-bit code for an interface for use
with Windows, OS/2, and Motif (Unix). Guild is primarily an interface
design and creation tool. It produces state-of-the-art objects that
incorporate full three-dimensional windows, menus, and controls. This
product is intended for the professional developer requiring high-
quality interfaces. These are some of Guild's features:

▲ Accepts integration of C code

▲ Provides debugging support

▲ Includes full internal testing facility

▲ Has high-level development language

▲ Provides B-tree database

Expert-EASE Systems Inc.
1301 Shoreway Road
Belmont CA 94002
Voice: (415)593-3200
Fax: (415)595-8158

Liana: Base Technology

Liana utilizes a C-like, object-oriented programming language that is
used to create Windows applications. Liana's language is high-level and
interpreted. By using an interpreter, Liana is able to reduce your
learning curve. You don't need to be familiar with C or C++, but any
background is useful because Liana's language is very similar.

Some of Liana's features include the following:

▲ Printing both text and graphics

▲ Sound generation

▲ No memory management skills required

▲ Does not require the Windows SDK

▲ Icons are embedded in the executable EXEs

▲ Bit-map file conversion utility is included

▲ Screen capture utility is included

▲ The Help system is a mirror of the manual

Base Technology
1543 Pine Street
Boulder CO 80302
Voice: (303)440-4558

LightShip: Pilot Executive Software

LightShip is an Executive Information System development tool. Experience with programming is definitely not required. LightShip is designed to enable you to build applications that can display information from any ASCII text file or DDE-compliant Windows application.

LightShip can create charts and graphs from data displayed by LightShip.

The information that LightShip displays can be the following:

▲ .PCX graphics file

▲ ASCII text file

▲ Windows DDE

▲ Clipboard-based

Pilot Executive Software
40 Broad Street
Boston MA 02109
Voice: (617)350-7035

MetaDesign: Meta Software

MetaDesign is a sophisticated diagramming tool for designing and editing complex system models. You can use MetaDesign to create any sort of simple or elaborate visual organizational aids.

The product also creates the following:

- ▲ Flow charts
- ▲ Simulation analysis models
- ▲ Technical documentation
- ▲ Source code documentation
- ▲ Brainstorming diagrams
- ▲ Network diagrams

Meta Software Corporation
150 CambridgePark Drive
Cambridge MA 02140
Voice: (800)227-4106
Fax: (617)576-0519

MultiScope Debugger: Multiscope

This product is designed for the application development professional. MultiScope Debugger can find flaws in programming code written in these languages:

- ▲ IBM C/2
- ▲ IBM Pascal/2
- ▲ IBM Macro Assembler/2
- ▲ Microsoft C
- ▲ Microsoft Fortran
- ▲ Microsoft Macro Assembler
- ▲ Microsoft Pascal
- ▲ Microsoft Basic
- ▲ Logitech/MultiScope Modula-2

Multiscope Inc.
1235 Pear Avenue, Suite 111
Mountain View CA 94043
Voice: (415)968-4892
Fax: (415)968-4622

ObjectVision: Borland

ObjectVision is a visual programming tool that enables nontechnical professionals to create interactive business applications. ObjectVision enables you to create Windows applications by mapping out the flow of information rather than by stepping through lines of code. You actually draw a chart of how the application's organization, and ObjectVision creates the code to create the application.

The creation process consists of using a flow-chart-like drawing utility to create segments of the application. You connect the segments by drawing lines between the segments or objects. If you have used a simple line drawing program, you will have no trouble using ObjectVision.

ObjectVision supports the following database formats:

▲ ASCII

▲ BTrieve

▲ dBASE

▲ Paradox

Borland International Inc.
1800 Green Hills Road
Scotts Valley CA 95067-0001
Voice: (408)438-8400

ProtoView: ProtoView

ProtoView is a screen development product. It enables you to interactively create dialog boxes, all manner of text boxes and fields, windows, buttons, and so on. ProtoView excels at creating prototyped applications. It generates code to support the interface and objects you create.

Some of ProtoView's features include the following:

▲ ViewPaint paints windows and the source code

▲ ProtoGen creates and codes windows and menus

▲ ProtoView DLL includes 175 functions

ProtoView Development Corp.
353 Georges Road
Dayton NJ 08810
Voice: (908)329-8588
Fax: (908)329-8625

Artwork Design

Sooner or later even the most reluctant of us are forced to draw a picture of something. Paintbrush is really great at making bit-map files; you can cut and paste your way through the process. Eventually, you will graduate to the need for handling elements of your images as objects, stretching and reversing them, or manipulating them in other ways. For that sort of stuff, you'll need a full-fledged art design tool.

Arts & Letters Graphics Editor: Computer Support Corporation

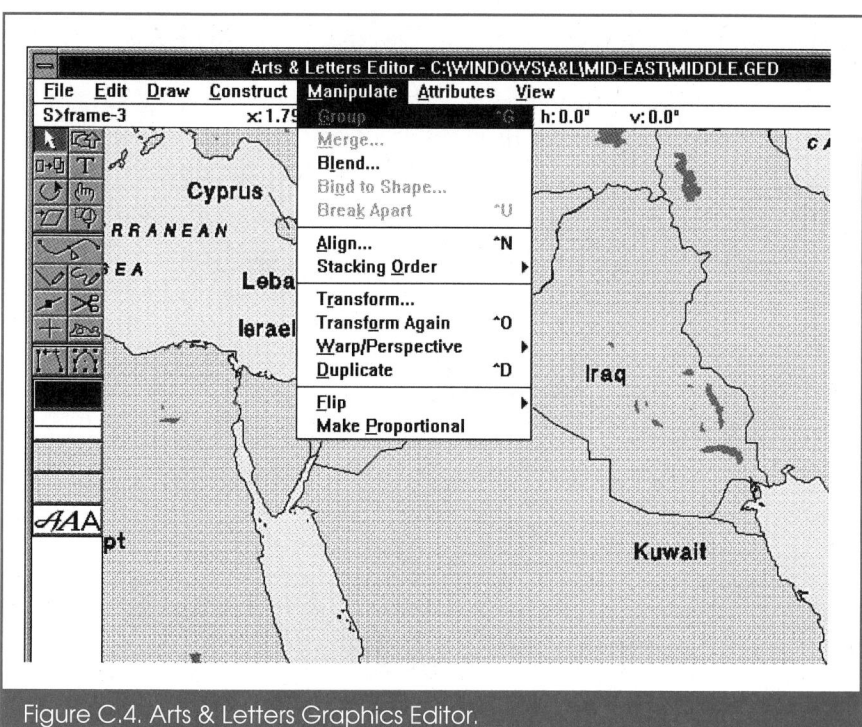

Figure C.4. Arts & Letters Graphics Editor.

Arts & Letters Graphics Editor gives you the power to create freehand illustrations, signs, and charts. It comes with the largest library of clip art for any product of its kind. You can redraw custom clip art and insert it into a document to create special visual effects in desktop publishing or newsletters.

Some of the product's other features include the following:

▲ Imports and exports a large array of file types

▲ Creates bar and pie charts

▲ Can convert and manipulate postscript clip art

Computer Support Corporation
15926 Midway Road
Dallas TX 75244
Voice: (214)661-8960
Fax: (214)661-5429

Batch File Development

Making batch files to automate a process that needs to happen again and again (like a nightly file transfer over a modem to the same destination) can really save time and trouble. Batch files actually automate procedures that are redundant for us people. Better your computer should suffer!?

WinBatch: Wilson WindowWare

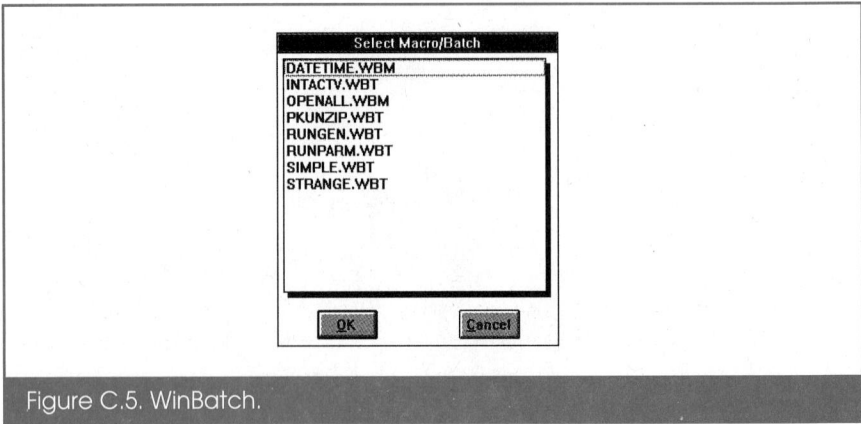

Figure C.5. WinBatch.

WinBatch is batch file language processing tool. Designed primarily for the task-oriented professional, WinBatch can overcome many of the perceived shortcomings of Windows.

C

Here are some of the things WinBatch can do:

- ▲ Read and write strings to .INI files
- ▲ Manage windows
- ▲ Display text in a message box
- ▲ Run multiple programs from an icon
- ▲ Transparently move data to and from the Clipboard
- ▲ Use if-then logic to execute actions
- ▲ Send keystrokes to any Windows application
- ▲ Record keystroke sequences as macro translations

Wilson WindowWare
2701 California Ave. SW #212
Seattle WA 98116
Voice: (800)762-8383
Fax: (206)935-7129

Business Analysis

Modeling information gleaned from several spreadsheets can be a cumbersome job. If you create models, simulations, or projections for review or analysis, you will appreciate business analysis tools that take the spreadsheet program past the point of the conventional one- or two-dimensional model.

CA-Compete!: Computer Associates

CA-Compete! is a data analysis and presentation tool. Useful for a variety of decision-making processes, CA-Compete! affords the collection and assimilation of multiple spreadsheets to create a three-dimensional model that can be analyzed. "What if" analysis supports the creation of dynamic simulation models to support critical business decisions.

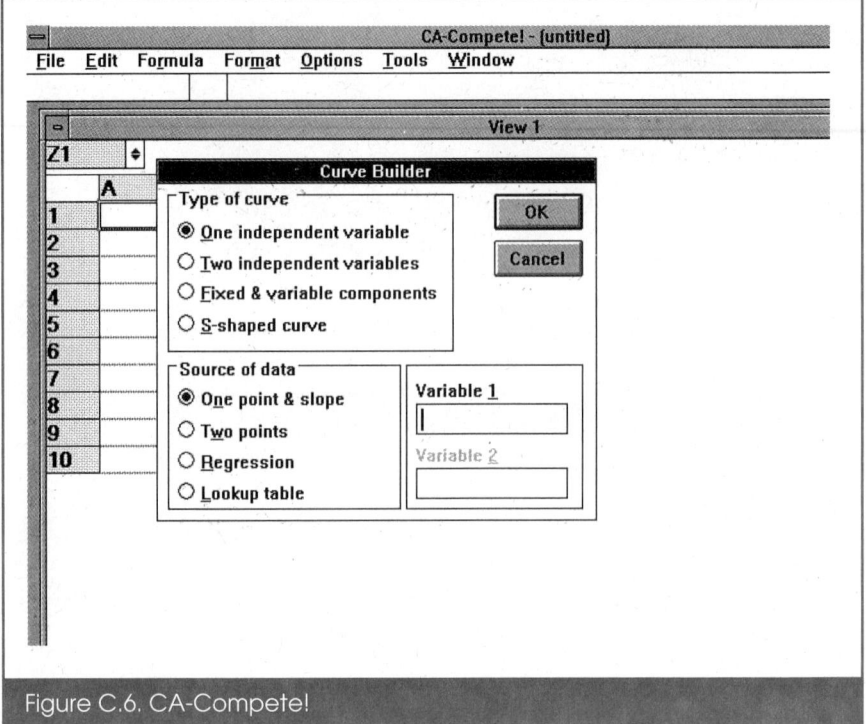

Figure C.6. CA-Compete!

Other features of CA-Compete! include the following:

▲ Results forecasting

▲ Profitability model determination

▲ Investment decision analysis

▲ Acquisition analysis

▲ Activity-based costing detail

▲ Goal-targeting support

Computer Associates
711 Stewart Avenue
Garden City NY 11530-4787
Voice: (800)645-3003

Calculators

If you've ever wished you could get a computerized version of your HP calculator, you're in luck! Here's a product that can keep calculator batteries off your grocery list.

C

MacroCalc: Anderson Consulting & Software

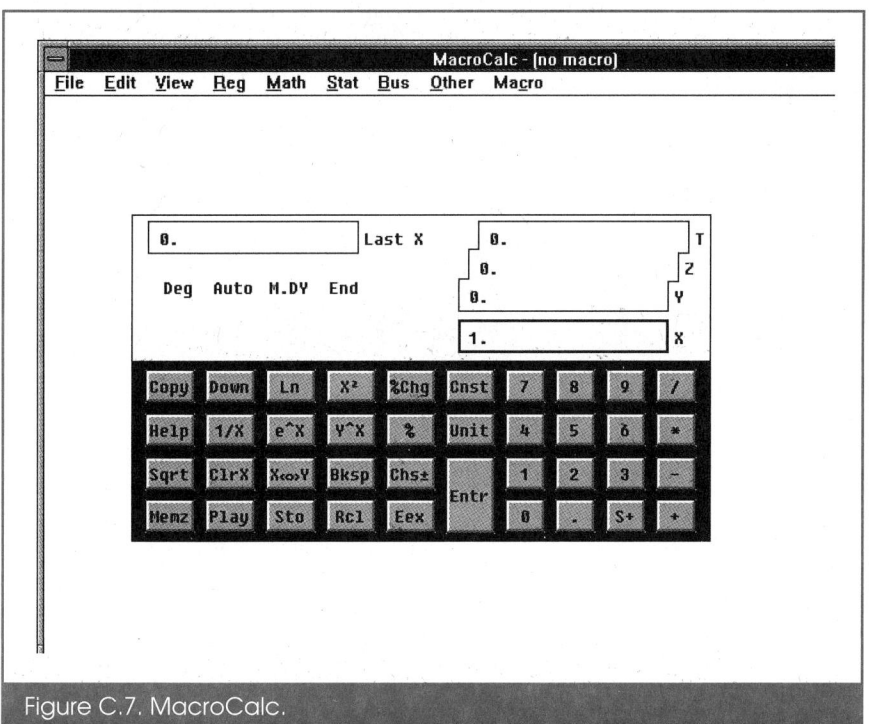

Figure C.7. MacroCalc.

MacroCalc is an extensive, powerful calculation program. Used in several environments because of its flexibility, MacroCalc can perform many calculation tasks better than most products. This product specializes in calculation tasks, so its power and flexibility are almost exponential compared to the calculators that come with Windows or personal information managers.

Some of the features of MacroCalc include the following:

▲ 243 operations

▲ 27 constants

▲ 3290 unit conversions

▲ Context-sensitive help

▲ Numerical analysis

▲ Macro keystroke recording

▲ Visual "Tape" provides audit trail

▲ 13 keyboard layouts from which to choose

Anderson Consulting and Software
C-7-3 Cascade Drive
P. O. Box 40
North Bonneville WA 98639
Voice: (800)733-9633
Fax: (509)427-5380

Charts and Graphs

Charting and Graphing software has become very specific in some cases. You can now buy products that make only organizational charts, for example. The recent popularity of three-dimensional charting has caused a boom in charting and graphing software in general.

ABC Flowcharter: Roykore

ABC Flowcharter provides an easy way to make elaborate flow charts from within Windows. All displays are true WYSIWYG. It supports 30 popular symbols, and it also comes with drivers for the most common printers in use today. You actually can create chart sizes of up to 100x100 inches.

More features of ABC Flowcharter include the following:

▲ Displayed rulers to help organize charts

▲ Automatic or manual routing of lines

▲ Full color capabilities for proof presentations

▲ 32 patterns and background shading

▲ Import graphics and insert as objects

▲ All your favorite font managers are supported

▲ Multidimensional charting links objects to charts

Roykore
2215 Filbert Street
San Francisco CA 94123
Voice: (415)563-9175

C

CA-Cricket Graph!: Computer Associates

CA-Cricket Graph! is a charting and graphing tool for anyone who wants to present information graphically. You can construct very pleasing backgrounds for charts, and you also can import a bit-map image to present as a background for your graphs. CA-Cricket Graph! is a competent tool for the serious information presentation professional as well as for the business practitioner who requires high-quality, appealing presentation materials that can be printed on paper or transparencies.

These are other features of CA-Cricket Graph:

▲ Imports data from spreadsheets and text files

▲ Directly accesses database information

▲ Comes with Windows 3.0 runtime

▲ Requires an 80286 or higher

▲ Includes 30 days of free telephone support

Computer Associates
711 Stewart Avenue
Garden City NY 11530-4787
Voice: (800)645-3003

Communications

If you've been around PCs for any great length of time, you probably remember what a thrill it was to upgrade from 300-baud to 1200-baud modems. These days, modems are the basis for several combo cards. Some of them even take messages, FAX in and out, forward calls and FAXes, and make your calls (delivering messages) in your absence.

Complete Communicator:
Complete PC

The Complete Communicator is a hardware communications solution
that provides complete compatibility with the telecomputing world.
Voice mail, fax, and modem are incorporated onto a true one-slot board
for your personal computer. Complete background operation is supported for all three functions. You can assign as many as 9999 mail-
boxes.

Features of the Complete Communicator are the following:

▲ 9600-baud Group III send/receive fax

▲ 2400-baud MNP 5, V42 modem

▲ Bitcom modem software provided

▲ Compatible with FAXit for Windows

▲ Use included voice messages or record your own

▲ Converts many file formats to fax format

▲ Use included fax cover sheet or create your own

The Complete PC
1983 Concourse Drive
San Jose CA 95131
Voice: (408)434-0145
Fax: (408)434-1048

MicroPhone II for Windows:
Software Ventures

MicroPhone II is a communications program that operates under
Windows. The PC version is very similar to the very successful Macintosh version. It offers intuitive interfaces and logical menu choices to
support the most demanding communications user.

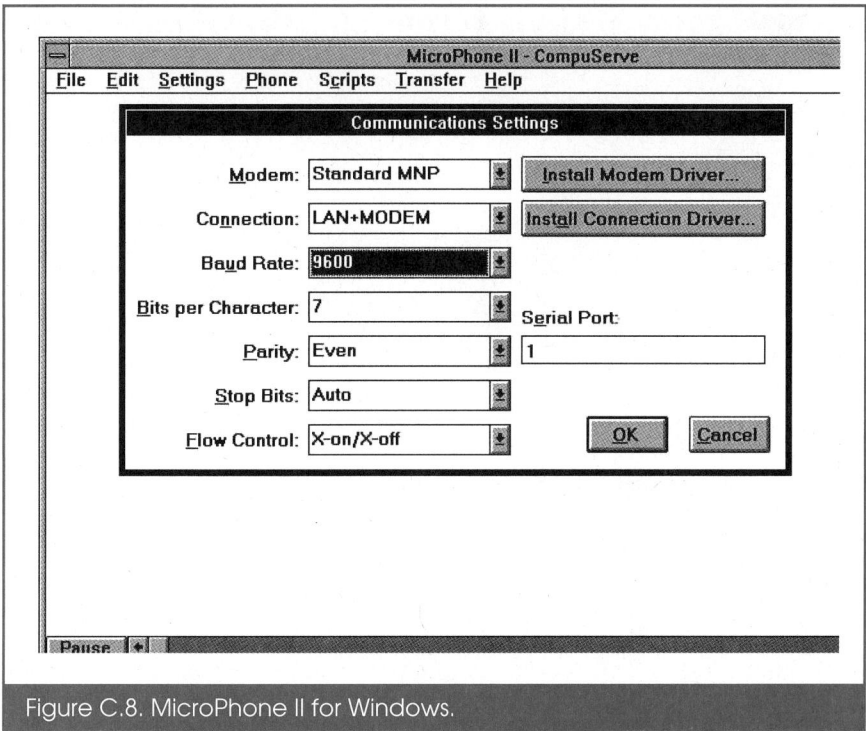

Figure C.8. MicroPhone II for Windows.

Features of MicroPhone II for Windows include the following:

▲ Graphical script support

▲ Autoinstallation of included scripts for popular BBSs

▲ Full ZMODEM and CRC checking facilities

▲ Icon library

▲ Interface library of BBSs

▲ Hardware device drivers included

▲ Background script execution

Software Ventures
2907 Claremont Avenue Suite 220
Berkeley CA 94705
Voice: (510)644-3232

Computer-Aided Negotiations

Computer-Aided Negotiations is a budding field for expert system developers. If you have ever had to keep track of complex scenarios and manage multiple sets of variables, these products can help keep your negotiating position sound.

Negotiator Pro: Beacon Expert Systems

Negotiator Pro is the tool of choice for completing successful negotiations. The product's knowledge base incorporates the power of more than 129 published reference works to provide the user with a base of experience that would not normally be available to the average user. Negotiator Pro recognizes the elements of interest and position in a negotiation process and supports the user in finding common-ground solutions to what can become an adversarial situation.

The features of this rule-based system are the following:

▲ Keeps track of the valid points for each party

▲ Aids in brainstorming creative options

▲ Assesses negotiator profiles

▲ Aids in construction of complete negotiation plan

Beacon Expert Systems
39 Gardner Road
Brookline MA 02146
Voice: (617)738-9300
Fax: (617)734-3308

Contact/Lead Management

Telephone dialers made lists, spreadsheets dialed, and databases posted reminders on your screen. If you were one of the many people who had to keep track of people and maintain contact with them, you probably had to make a spreadsheet, dialer, or DBMS do something it was not intended to do. Now you can get products that are designed to help you keep the art of contact management in your delivery and the science of contact management in your computer!

PowerLeads: Pyramid Data

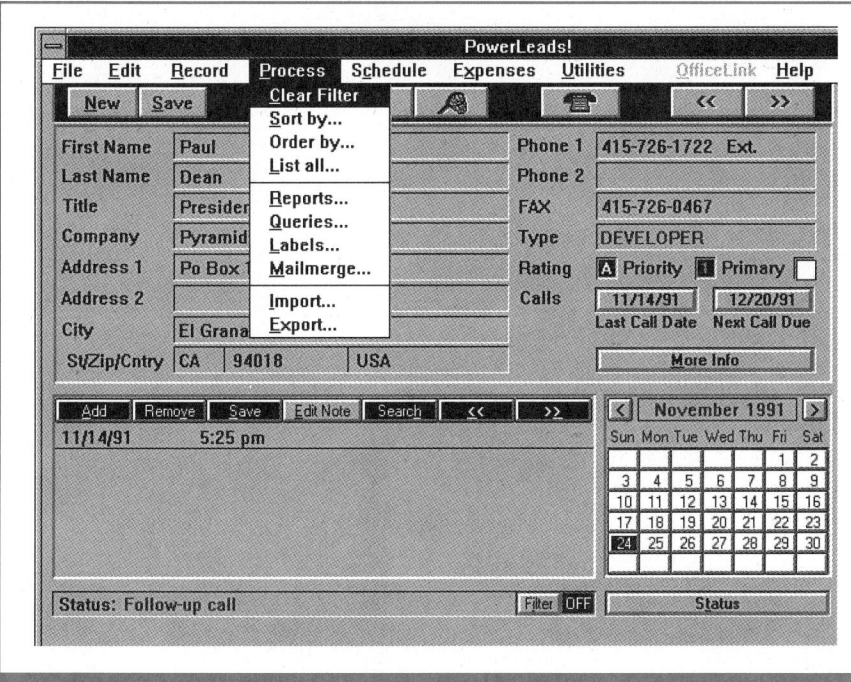

Figure C.9. PowerLeads.

PowerLeads is a sophisticated relational database intended to support extensive contact management tasks. Complete detail regarding a company, its key employees, and products can be assembled in files for fast access. You can look up the profile of a company based on a query of a key employee's name while you are conversing with the individual on the phone. You can store personal information such as birthdays of the key business personnel of your favorite accounts or clients.

This product schedules calls, appointments, and to-do lists. You can add unlimited pages of notes.

Other features of PowerLeads include the following:

▲ Tracks expenses such as length of calls, rentals, and so on

▲ Fully customizable

▲ Provides 26 different reports

▲ Auto data and time stamps your notes

- ▲ Scheduler auto-dials your contacts
- ▲ Prints eight label formats

Pyramid Data Inc.
100 E. William St. Suite 100
Carson City NV 89701
Voice: (800)972-7972

Database Management Systems

Database Management Systems (DBMSs) are becoming more powerful and easier to use. The Windows environment has its share of modern, fast programs able to store and process information.

Anthora: Exxitus/Evolution Trading

Anthora is a relational database management system. This product supports the single user as well as multiuser environments. Anthora works with files utilizing the delimited ASCII format that has become the world standard.

A list of Anthora's features includes the following:

- ▲ Browse multiple databases
- ▲ An unlimited number of open files of all types
- ▲ Graphical report writer
- ▲ Functions and commands simulate x-BASE syntax
- ▲ Create and modify your own screens
- ▲ Utilizes bitmaps and metafiles
- ▲ Structured programming language similar to C

Exxitus/Evolution Trading
7206 NW 32st Street
Miami FL 33122
Voice: (305)593-1516
Fax: (305)593-9106

C

Desktop Publishing

The field of Desktop Publishing (DTP) has changed considerably in the last few years. Now you can buy a word processor that does most of the tasks of the traditional high-end products. If you don't have to make complicated documents, there are now small, nimble, and easy-to-use DTP products that are almost as easy to learn and use as Windows Write!

Microsoft Publisher: Microsoft

Microsoft Publisher is a complete page layout tool that provides everything you need to create multiple-page documents. You can review clip art before you insert it into a document. Microsoft Publisher is intended to be a simplified alternative to elaborate desktop publishing systems.

This is a list of features:

▲ Button bar combines drawing and text tools

▲ Complete preview facility

▲ Imports text from most major word processors

▲ Includes a competent word processor

▲ Font effects generator enhances text

▲ Manipulate borders to create visual effects

Microsoft Corporation
One Microsoft Way
Redmond WA 98052-6399
Voice: (800)426-9400

Entertainment

The field of games and entertainment grows with the rest of the world of computing. Games, too, specialize and excel at what they do.

Casino Pak I: Moon Valley Software

Casino Pak I is a collection of Las Vegas-style card games. For the dedicated card player, this product offers Poker, Keno, and Blackjack with full betting options. The screens are user-definable.

Casino Pak I includes these features:

- ▲ Selectable arcade sounds
- ▲ Save current games for later play
- ▲ Percentage tracking of hands played in Poker
- ▲ Play 1, 2, 4, or 6 decks in Blackjack
- ▲ Tracks hands won, lost, and pushed in Blackjack
- ▲ Vary speed animation of ball in Keno

Moon Valley Software
107 East Paradise Lane
Phoenix AZ 85022
Voice: (602)375-9502

File Compression

If you are sending files via modem or the mail, you should be using a file-compression utility. Not only do such utilities save connect time on long distance calls made with your modem, they save diskette cost by making files smaller.

PKLITE Professional Package: PKware

PKLITE Professional Package is the latest in this file compression technology company's offerings. This utility compresses executable files to reduce file size up to 40 percent. PKLITE makes the process transparent to the user.

Executables that have been compressed using PKLITE can be run without being expanded first. You simply run the compressed .EXE or .COM file as you would normally. The compressed file expands itself and then runs as normal, without any additional input or syntax knowledge by the user.

C

PKWARE Inc.
9025 Deerwood Drive
Brown Deer WI 53223
Voice: (414)354-8699
Fax: (414)354-8559

File Conversion

With all the file formats to contend with, it helps to have a way to
convert file formats into one your favorite software can use.

ImPort: Zenographics

Zenographics ImPort is a file translation utility intended for users of
technical drawing and graphics design software. This product allows
the conversion of the popular CAD file formats so that the files can be
utilized by desktop publishing and painting software.

ImPort also comes with SuperPrint, a print manager replacement that
can greatly accelerate print spooling operations. SuperPrint also drives
color laser printers and plotters. ImPort converts files as shown in
Table C.1.

Table C.1. Import conversions.

Converts From	Converts To
.PIC	.CGM
.DFX	Windows Metafile
.ADI	Windows Clipboard
.RND	Aldus Metafile
.CGM	Printer Device

Zenographics
4 Executive Circle
Irvine CA 92714
Voice: (714)851-6352

File Manager Replacements

If you are not happy with File Manager, you can always get a replacement.

Prompt: Access Softek

Prompt is a File Manager replacement. As well as providing the usual file organizational support, this product enables you to view many different file formats without calling up a paint or a database application. Designed primarily as a hard disk housekeeping tool, Prompt will satisfy the most demanding File Manager evacuee.

File formats that can be viewed with Prompt include the following:

▲ HPGL

▲ CGM

▲ PCX

▲ DBF

▲ TIF

▲ WKS

▲ WRI

▲ DOC

▲ WordPerfect

Access Softek
3204 Adeline Street
Berkeley CA 94703
Voice: (415)654-0116

Font Management

You can now have as many fonts on hand as your computer's hard drive space and your computer's memory capacity will allow.

Adobe Type Manager: Adobe Systems

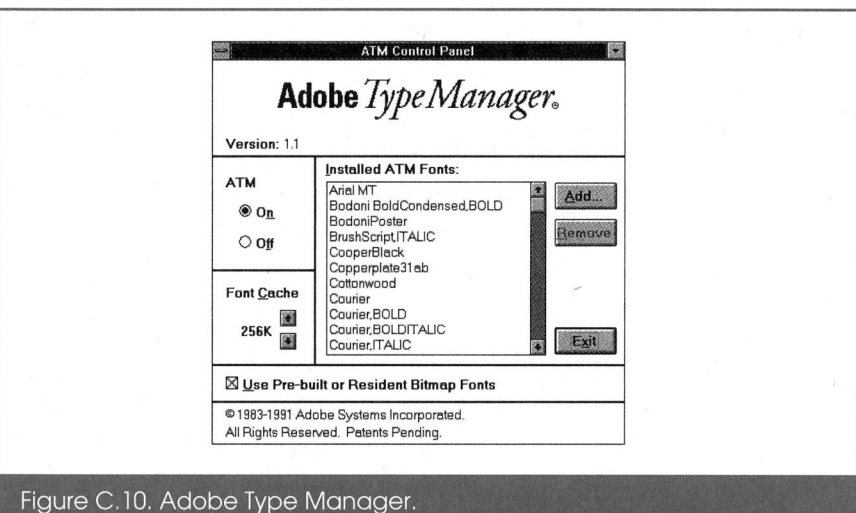

Figure C.10. Adobe Type Manager.

The Adobe Type Manager (ATM) is a font-management utility that produces matching on-the-fly fonts for your screen and printer. ATM uses outline font technology to create complete libraries of font sets for installation with or without your Windows fonts. The installation is simple and quick.

ATM produces PostScript quality fonts while operating as a RAM-resident utility. As soon as they are installed, ATM fonts appear with your other installed fonts from within any application. The ATM starter set includes 13 popular outline fonts. Other add-on font sets are available from Adobe. They include the following:

▲ Type Set 1

▲ Type Set 2

▲ Type Set 3

▲ Plus Pack

Adobe Systems
1585 Charleston Road
P.O. Box 7900
Mountain View CA 94039-7900
Voice: (800)344-8335

Forms Processing

For those of us who manage vast amounts of information that must be collected on paper, there are now solutions that integrate forms and the manipulation of the data they collect.

FormsBase: Xerox

FormsBase is a forms-management system that can use forms as a front end for its database management system. Unlike conventional forms creation tools, FormsBase is a complete office solution to data management.

As well as offering forms creation facilities, FormsBase uses your forms as data-entry templates. Data collection forms can look exactly like your data-entry screens.

Other FormsBase features include the following:

▲ Imports popular image files

▲ Imports spreadsheet and database files

▲ Offers shading and slick borders

▲ Exports to popular Windows programs

▲ Prints forms with data, forms only, or data only

Xerox Corporation
360 North Sepulveda Boulevard
El Segundo CA 90245
Voice: (800)445-5554

Hard Disk Management

As the information on your hard drives becomes more critical to your business and life in general, the need for properly maintained equipment and data backup tools becomes more evident.

Distinct Back-Up is a Windows-based file backup utility. Distinct Back-Up can back up your files in the background, or schedule the backup to occur during low use periods. This product enables you to save selected directories or groups of files in "projects" so that only critical data files are backed up.

Distinct Back-Up: Distinct

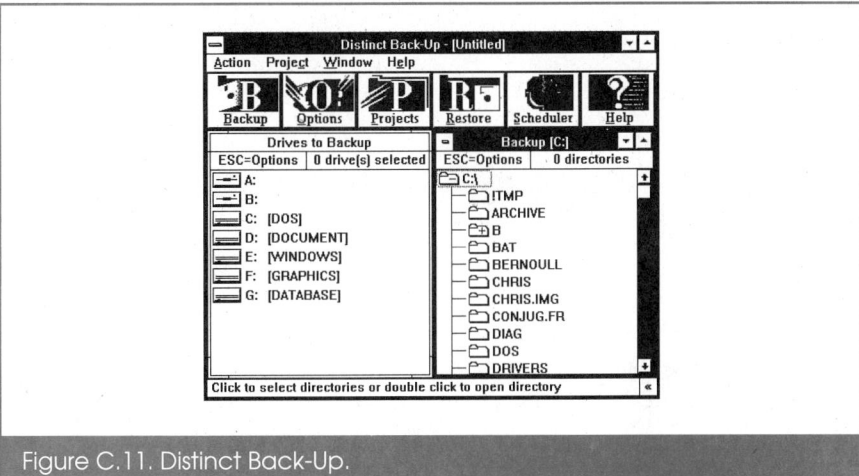

Figure C.11. Distinct Back-Up.

Distinct Back-Up also offers these unique features:

▲ Graphic and text file viewer

▲ Can back up only highlighted files

▲ Runs totally in the background

▲ Lightning-fast storage device access

▲ Bit-by-bit verification of saved data

▲ Extensive on-line help

▲ Password protection

Distinct Corporation
P. O. Box 3410
Saratoga CA 95070
Voice: (408)741-0795
Fax: (408)741-0781

PC Tools: Central Point Software

Central Point Software's PC Tools is a heavyweight hard disk management facility that can deal with just about any problem your hard drive throws at you. It compresses all drive types to improve drive performance, it restructures corrupted files, and it even rebuilds your hard drive's file allocation tables.

These are just some of PC Tools' features:

- ▲ Hard disk diagnostics and repair facilities
- ▲ Competent shell improves visual organization
- ▲ Virus protection
- ▲ Interleave optimization
- ▲ Screen blanker with password protection
- ▲ Full LAN support
- ▲ Safe disk formatter
- ▲ Appointment scheduler and integrated PIM
- ▲ Telecommunications and Fax support

Central Point Software Inc.
15220 NW Greenbrier Parkway
Beaverton OR 97006
Voice: (503)690-8090

Icon Development

Do icons leave you tired of the same old, same old? Making and editing icons can be fun with one of the many icon editing tools available.

hDC Icon Designer: hDC Computer Corporation

hDC's Icon Designer is a full-featured facility adept at creating icons of any color combination or design. This product builds libraries of icons that can be used by Program Manager as you would any independent icon file. You build or draw the icon of your choice and save it to a library file. This library file contains all the icons you make with Icon Designer.

To substitute a newly designed icon from Program Manager, use the File Properties command, and click the Change Icon button. Type the name of your Icon Designer library file and press the Enter key. Select the desired icon and save.

You can permanently replace the icons in executable (.EXE) files with Icon Designer as well.

hDC Computer Corporation
6742 185th Avenue NE
Redmond WA 98052
Voice: (800)321-4606
Fax: (206)881-9770

C

Image Management

Ever wonder just how "they" got that interesting image to look the way it does in your magazines and publications? Image management tools have come a long way.

Image-In Professional: Image-In

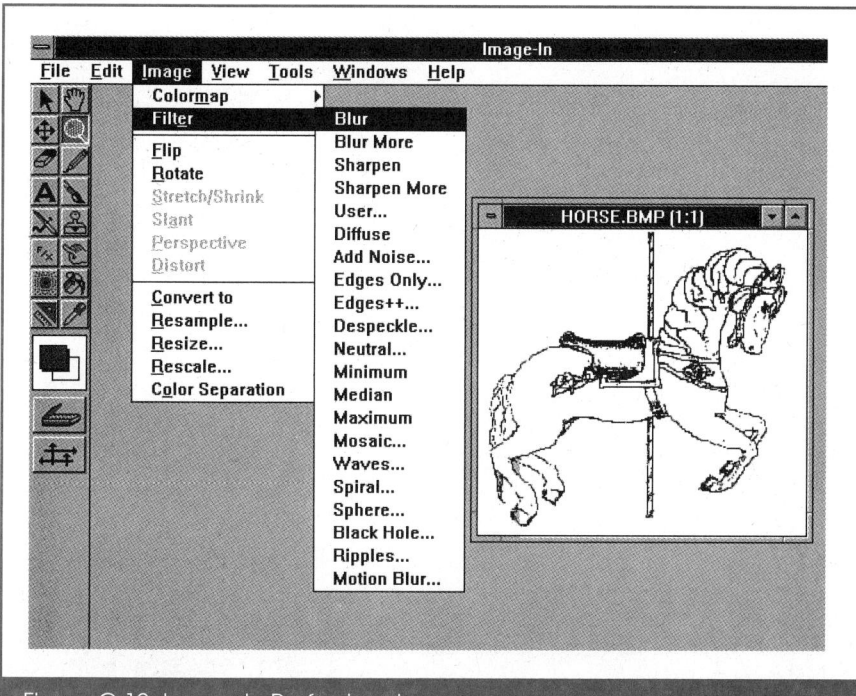

Figure C.12. Image-In Professional.

Image-In Professional is a prepress image manipulation product. This product offers 24-bit true-color processing for any user who wants to work with an image in either color or monochrome. Image-In Professional gives you gray component, under color removal, and press gain compensation editing ability. You also can control the size, density, and pressure of tools such as the paint brush, air brush, pencil, and others. It supports popular 24-bit, high-end professional color-imaging boards.

Image-In imports these file formats:

▲ .TIF

▲ .EPS

▲ .PCX

▲ .BMP

▲ .GIF

▲ .TGA

▲ .MSP

▲ .IMG

Image-In Incorporated
406 East 79th Street
Minneapolis MN 55420
Voice: (800)345-3540
Fax: (612)888-3665

Information Managers

Today, we have PIMs (Personal Information Managers), EIMs (Executive Information Managers) and HIMs (Home Information Managers). Some of them work with paper systems that keep you organized when you're away from your machine.

Ascend: NewQuest Technologies

Ascend is a personal productivity product intended to provide users with the ability to organize many facets of their personal and professional lives.

C

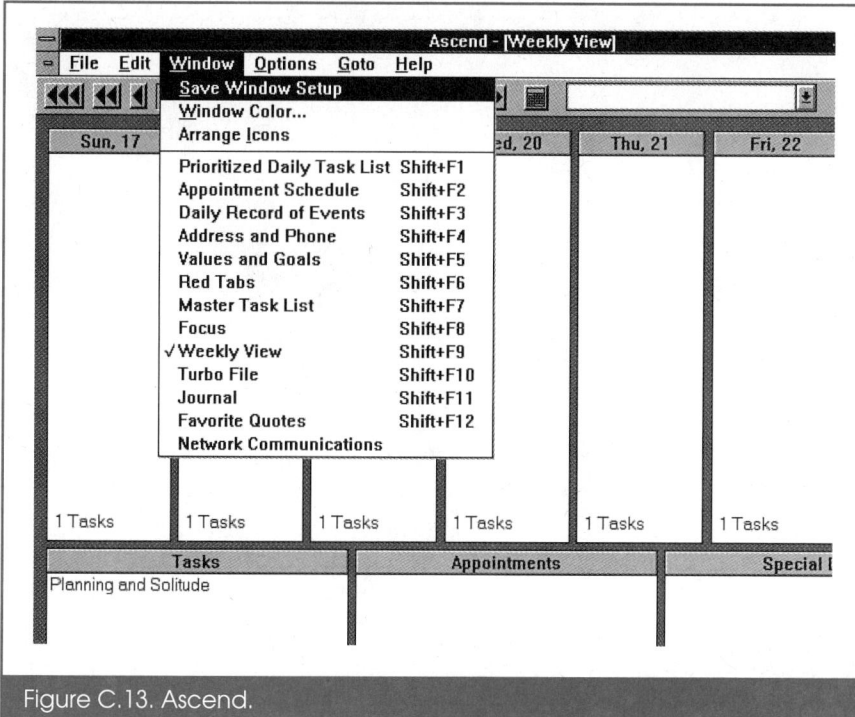

Figure C.13. Ascend.

This product comes complete with a daily planner that holds hard copy for up to one year in the most popular format. Ascend also comes with video and audio media that train and inform the user on the subjects of organization and goal attainment through solid time-management techniques.

The software that comes with Ascend offers these and other features:

▲ Prioritized daily task management

▲ Appointment scheduler

▲ Address and phone book, with dialer

▲ Values and goals tracking

▲ Weekly view to check future commitments

▲ Library of motivational quotes

NewQuest Technologies
2550 South Decker Lake Blvd.
Salt Lake City UT 84119
Voice: (800)877-1814

Integrated Software

There always will be a need for software that does everything for almost everybody. This kind of product is referred to as "integrated." Integrated softward usually includes a word processor, spreadsheet, and database, but some vary from the norm.

Microsoft Works: Microsoft

Microsoft Works is a product that includes a spreadsheet program, a charting and graphing program, a database, a word processor, and a label generator, all from a common interface. Unlike its DOS-based sister product, this graphical version is intended to run exclusively under Windows 3.0 or higher.

The word processor has a large spell checker and thesaurus. You can draw on your documents (create a logo, and so on) from within the word processor. You also can combine spreadsheets and drawings into your documents.

Microsoft Corporation
One Microsoft Way
Redmond WA 98073-9717
Voice: (800)426-9400

Mapping

Sophisticated mapping software has become popular in very specific work places. These vertical market products can often be tailored to entire industries.

GeoGraphix Exploration System: GeoGraphix

The product is a professional geographical mapping facility. Intended primarily for geological and geophysical professionals, GeoGraphix Exploration Systems provides these tools for the spatial presentation of data:

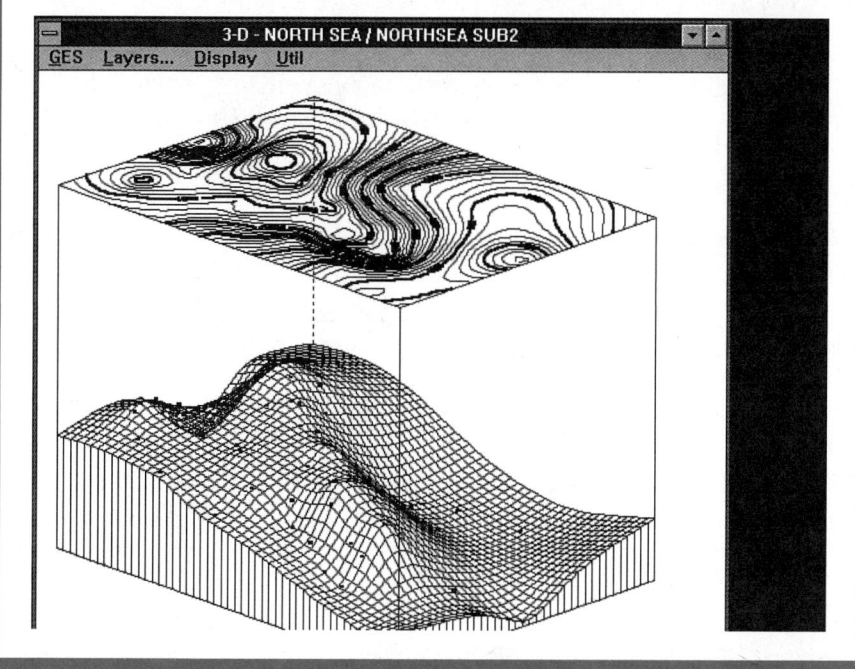

Figure C.14. GeoGraphix Exploration System.

▲ Petrophysical analysis

▲ Construction of posted basemaps

▲ Locates wells on a three-dimensional mapped terrain

▲ Imports geophysical survey data into the model

▲ Exacting surface modeling and contouring

▲ Supports the determination of reservoir volumes

GeoGraphix
1860 Blake Street, Suite 900
Denver CO 80202
Voice: (303)296-0596
Fax: (303)292-1143

Memory Management

Maximizing system memory is one of the most elusive goals of the ardent Windows user. There are products out there that make this process a "No-Brainer."

386MAX: Qualitas

386MAX is a product intended to automate and optimize the management of your system's total memory management resources. This product checks what you have to work with for memory hardware. It then looks at what you say you need loaded by virtue of what you have included in your CONFIG.SYS and AUTOEXEC.BAT files.

Your high memory area is not a contiguous block of memory. It is broken into small pieces of space that vary in size. 386MAX measures startup memory requirements and places each device driver and so on into a free space in memory where it occupies as much of the block of free space as possible.

The result of this memory-tailoring process is that previously under-utilized space on your system is rendered accessible. You don't have to load as much of these drivers and TSRs into conventional memory.

This product also offers smaller and faster SMARTDRV.EXE, HIMEM.SYS, and EMM386.EXE replacements for the benefit of Windows users.

Qualitas Inc.
7101 Wisconsin Avenue, Suite 1386
Bethesda MD 20814
Voice: (800)676-7386

Multimedia

Combining sound, moving video, and your responses with computers is called multimedia. When these products are used for training purposes, they can actually converse with the user and train more specifically on weak points identified by the user as the training commences.

C

Icon Author: AimTech

IconAuthor is a multimedia application creation tool that utilizes visual rather than syntactical means of making fully interactive applications. This product builds your system by enabling you to create a flowchart-like model of the desired application to support simplified visualization of your created program.

You can create animated programs, incorporate live or prerecorded video and audio, present bit maps and images as backgrounds for your screens, and manipulate color pallets to author applications with a very polished look and feel.

IconAuthor supports all the popular video animation hardware.

AimTech
20 Trafalgar Square
Nashua NH 03063
Voice: (800)289-2884
Fax: (603)883-5582

SuperVideo Windows: New Media Graphics

SuperVideo Windows is a complete hardware/software solution for your video presentation needs. This product offers full motion video, stereo audio, and graphics overlay capabilities. NTSC and full-frame PAL video can be viewed within a window, with full stereo sound.

You can save displayed images to many popular file formats. A digital real-time NTSC/PAL video processor offers luminescence filtering, automatic color control, and automatic gain control. Video images may be scaled to any size horizontally or vertically.

When used in conjunction with a multimedia software authoring product, this hardware/software product family renders high-quality multimedia applications.

New Media Graphics
780 Boston Road
Billerica MA 01821-5925
Voice: (508)663-0666
Fax: (508)663-6678

Personal Finance Management

These products will usually print checks, track investments, and even suggest avenues of making your money work harder for you.

Balance Point: Moon Valley Software

Balance Point is a personal and small business financial management program. You can work with as many as six accounts at one time. This product supports detailed budget reporting, charting, portfolio management, receivable/payables, and check writing processes.

Balance Point sports an icon palette so that you don't have to use pull-down menus to perform the most frequent tasks. You can keep track of credit cards, personal and business checking, and assets/liabilities.

Moon Valley Software
107 East Paradise Lane
Phoenix AZ 85022
Voice: (602)375-9502

Pointing Devices

Mice are taking over the world. If you don't have one now, you will want one as you continue to use Windows applications.

Microsoft Mouse: Microsoft

The Microsoft Mouse is still the most popular mouse on the market today. Its small size and high mass give the heavy-handed user a pointing device that does not move as readily as other, lighter mice. The mouse is housed in a glossy white plastic case. This mouse is of the two-button variety, suitable for use with most Windows applications.

This product has feather-touch microswitches under its buttons, giving it the distinction of having the best "action" in the business. The Microsoft Mouse is available in either bus or serial port versions.

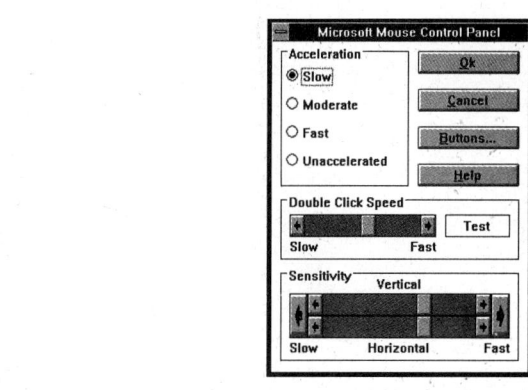

Figure C.15. Microsoft mouse Control Panel.

Microsoft Corporation
One Microsoft Way
Redmond WA 98073-9717
Voice: (800)426-9400

Presentation Management

Preparing for a slide show or other form of presentation can be a time-consuming process in the days and weeks before the presentation. As always, there are products designed to help.

Powerpoint for Windows: Microsoft

Powerpoint for Windows is a presentation management tool that specializes in the creation of presentation materials. With this product, the user can create overheads and slides quickly and easily. As soon as you create your materials, you can transfer them in file format to a national presentation materials company that will turn your files into the highest-quality hard copy and send it back to you by courier or mail.

You can process text and graphics from within Powerpoint with its word and graphics editors. It includes clip art for insertion into your presentation materials.

Microsoft Corporation
One Microsoft Way
Redmond WA 98073-9717
Voice: (800)426-9400

Print Manager Replacements

If you are disillusioned with Print Manager, as in the case of most
Windows utilities, there are products that claim to do it faster, better,
or just plain smarter.

SuperPrint: Zenographics

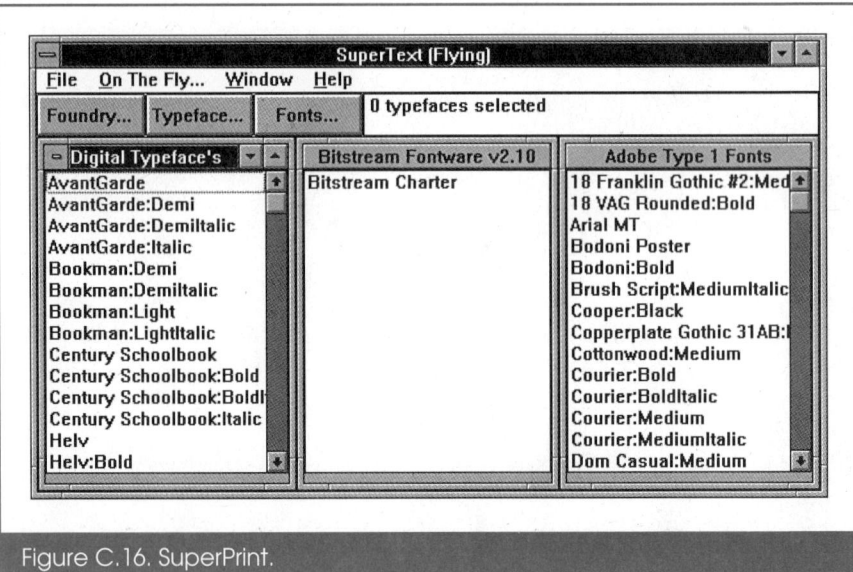

Figure C.16. SuperPrint.

SuperPrint actually is three products in one. Sold in a bundle and
labeled as SuperPrint, this might be one of the best values in Windows
software today.

The first product is SuperText, a font management utility. This module
of the product can produce on-the-fly, scalable outline fonts that print
exactly as you see them on the screen. SuperText handles with ease all
fonts produced by the top five font makers.

SuperQue, the second part of this bundle, replaces Print Manager. It spools and prints your output with greater speed than Print Manager.

SuperDriver is the last of the products included in the package. It replaces your printer driver to give you improved graphics output. SuperDriver also supports many high-end printing devices. The end result is that SuperDriver provides better color-to-gray scale mapping and dithering control than Print Manager, giving you improved hard copy.

Zenographics
4 Executive Circle
Irvine CA 92714
Voice: (714)851-6352

Program Manager Replacements

Even Program Manager can be usurped by a newcomer. Most products intended to replace PM do so in their own unique and sometimes strikingly-graphical way.

Power Launcher: hDC Computer Corporation

Power Launcher is a companion product to your favorite shell. This product provides a multitude of services.

Power Launcher does the following:

▲ Supports the building of enhanced menu commands

▲ Creates and manages custom menus

▲ Records macros from startup to exit

▲ Creates a virtual desktop for your display

▲ Launches applications

▲ Makes hot-key assignments

▲ Customizes your toolbar

▲ Automates redundant tasks and functions

▲ Performs tasks using a timer

hDC Computer Corporation
6742 185th Avenue NE
Redmond WA 98052
Voice: (800)321-4606
Fax: (206)881-9770

Project Management

Keeping track of complex projects and multiple tasks is the job of the Project Management software product. These packages usually offer Gantt and Pert charting so that you can organize variables occuring over a period of time.

Microsoft Project: Microsoft

Microsoft Project is designed to manage simple and complex projects. This product creates Gantt charts to show tasks spread out over time, PERT charts to show the relationship of tasks, and outlines to organize your projects.

Data is entered in a standard spreadsheet format to make the process familiar and easy. You can manage many small subprojects under one umbrella project, and manage the subprojects individually. Microsoft Project tracks resources and automatically levels them as tasks are completed. You can lay out projects on a department task basis or let this product reassign resources as they become available.

Microsoft Project handles plotters of sizes A through E. The product utilizes data from the most popular spreadsheet and database as well.

Microsoft Corporation
One Microsoft Way
Redmond WA 98073-9717
Voice: (800)426-9400

Publications

All special user groups have magazines. Windows users are no exception.

The Windows Shopper's Guide: WhiteFox Communications

The Windows Shopper's Guide is a complete reference source for information about products intended to run with or under Windows. Laid out in a catalog format, this publication categorizes each product and displays information about it in detail. The Windows Shopper's Guide is published by the same people who created Microsoft's "Windows Shopping" booklet, included with each copy of Microsoft Windows. This distinction is where any similarity ends.

The Windows Shopper's Guide provides images and details on more than 1100 products, many of which are represented by screen shots of the interface or in the case of hardware items, illustrations of the products themselves. This product is a must for professional specifiers and computer industry practitioners.

Other features of the Windows Shopper's Guide include the following:

- ▲ DDE compatibility index
- ▲ Advertiser's index
- ▲ Product index by product name
- ▲ Product index by manufacturer's name
- ▲ Manufacturer's address listing

WhiteFox Communications Inc.
P. O. Box 7125
Beaverton OR 97007-7125
Voice: (800)669-5612
Fax: (503)645-8642

Windows Magazine: CMP Publications

Windows Magazine is a monthly publication for the Windows user. This product features articles and interviews with persons who shape the future of the GUI. Regular inclusions include the following:

- ▲ Publisher's Column
- ▲ From the Editor's Desk
- ▲ What's Inside
- ▲ Letters

▲ News in Brief

▲ New Products

Software and hardware are reviewed, breakthrough products are analyzed, and coming industry events are profiled.

CMP Publications Inc.
600 Community Drive
Manhasset NY 11030
Voice: (516)562-5000
Fax: (516)562-5833

Screen Capture

If taking snapshots of images on your computer screen is part of your calling, you will want a dedicated screen capture utility.

DoDot: Halcyon Software

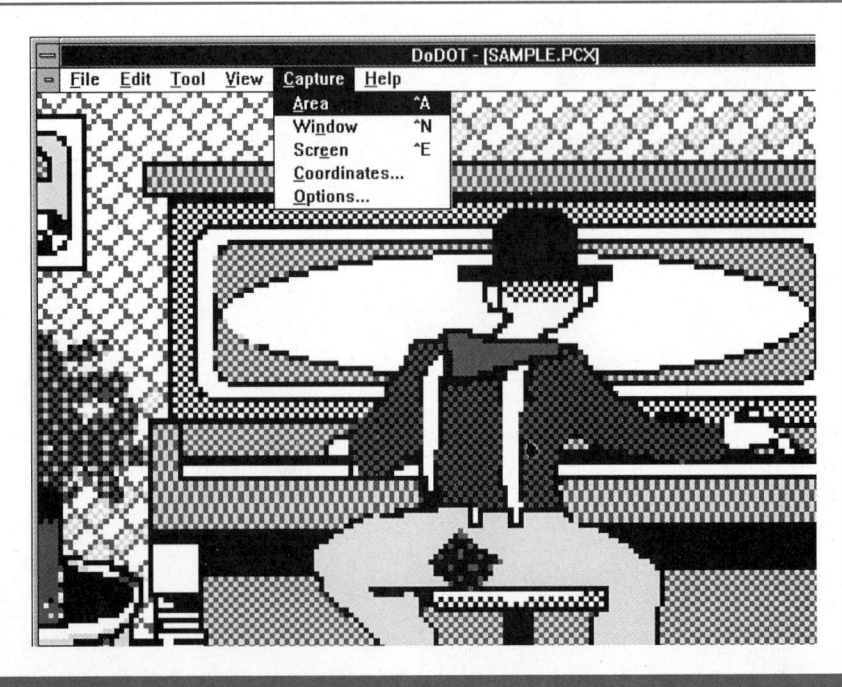

Figure C.17. DoDot.

DoDot is a multipurpose image-processing utility for Windows. This product is first and foremost a screen capture utility. It saves captured screens in various formats.

Some of DoDot's other features include the following:

- ▲ File format conversion
- ▲ Captured image printing
- ▲ Image viewing
- ▲ Image processing including dithering, palette editing, and color separation

Halcyon Software Inc.
10297 Cold Harbor Avenue
Cupertino CA 95014
Voice: (408)984-1464
Fax: (408)984-1499

Screen Savers

Screen Savers can prolong the life of your monitor and can make computing a lot more fun! In a nut shell, Screen Saver utilities don't allow an image to stay on your screen for more than a specified period of time. You decide how long that period is. These programs paste moving images on your monitor like swimming fish or fireworks when your system is idle.

After Dark: Berkeley Systems

After Dark is a slick screen saver utility. This product, first developed for the Mac, offers many interesting options for the user. The purpose of this product is to provide users with a way to keep their monitor screens from getting a condition called "burn-in." If your system runs unattended for more than two hours each day, you should be using some sort of screen saver.

This product offers 35 different animated screen designs, including Flying Toasters. This maker sells neckties (emblazoned with flying toasters) in the catalog that comes with the After Dark product.

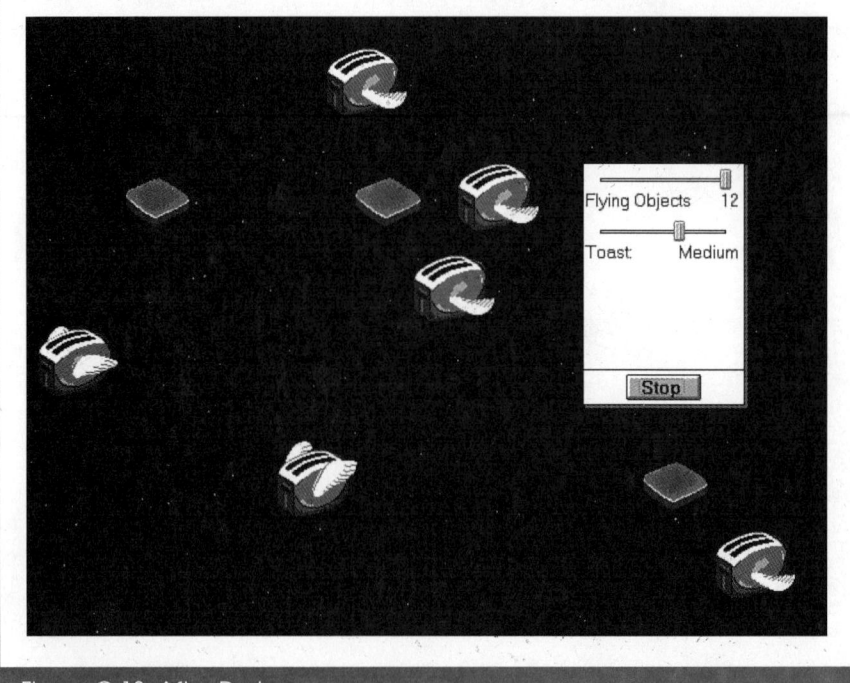

Figure C.18. After Dark.

After Dark also sports the following:

- ▲ Password protection
- ▲ Company logo display option
- ▲ Programmable hot keys

Berkeley Systems Inc.
1700 Shattuck Ave.
Berkeley CA 94709
Voice: (415)540-5535

Spell Checkers

Some software products are designed to work with text, but have no
dedicated spell checker. Therefore, software has been created to serve
this purpose.

Windows Spell: Palsoft

Windows Spell is an easy-to-use spell checker with a dictionary of more than 130,000 words. This product is designed to provide document quality enhancement value to pages of text created with Windows Write, PageMaker, and other Windows-based products that do not have a built-in spell checking utility.

This product can check and correct spelling in one document while you work with another if your computer supports multitasking. It checks documents while minimized to an icon and flashes that icon if it finds a spelling error.

Windows Spell also checks spelling on the Windows Clipboard. You can create professional or specialized dictionaries.

Palsoft
4455 South Padre Island Drive, Suite 43
Corpus Christi TX 78411-4417
Voice: (512)854-8788
Fax: (512)853-1541

Spreadsheets

Keeping track of and working with piles of numbers is the job of the spreadsheet application. Most spreadsheets sold today make charts and graphs, too.

Excel: Microsoft

Microsoft Excel is a spreadsheet creation tool. This product finds its roots in the version created for the Mac. Because of its high level of acceptance and the lack of competition, Excel is now the most popular spreadsheet management program designed for Windows.

Excel offers three-dimensional charts, line drawing, and object drawing for those who need to create graphical spreadsheets as part of a presentation. This product also utilizes extensive macro support. You can build your own spreadsheet application by using Excel's menu and dialog box creation tools.

You also can format spreadsheets in full colors that can be output to a color printing device. Excel includes an add-on product to handle database files, and Solver, a way to solve problems that have changing variables.

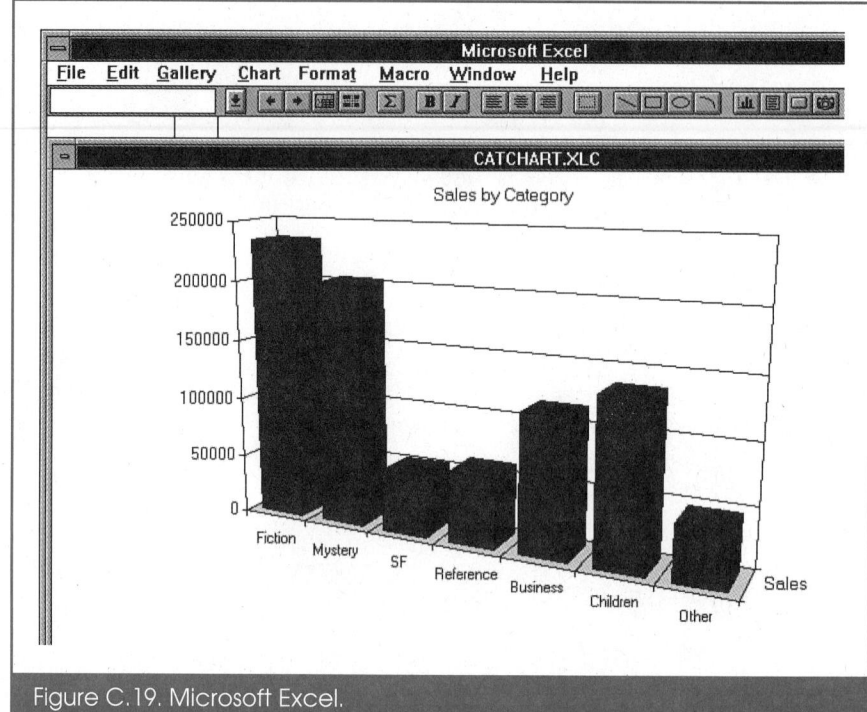

Figure C.19. Microsoft Excel.

Microsoft Corporation
One Microsoft Way
Redmond WA 98073-9717
Voice: (800)426-9400

Tax Preparation

Your taxes need not be left to the professional. If you have Windows, you can do your own taxes with the same software the pros use to do theirs.

Taxview Professional Edition: Softview

Taxview Professional Edition is the tax preparation product for the tax preparation professional. This product offers flexibility for the user by supporting federal and state tax laws. The maker sends an update disk for each impending tax season to keep the application current.

Some of the forms and states supported include the following:

- ▲ 1040
- ▲ 1065
- ▲ 1120
- ▲ 1120S
- ▲ E / F
- ▲ CA, CT, IL, MA, NJ, NY, OH, VA
- ▲ Plan

Softview
1721 Pacific Avenue, Suite 100
Oxnard CA 93033
Voice: (805)385-5000

Text Editors

Programmers don't have to use Notepad when they begin to program from inside the Windows environment. Specialized editors offer macro command languages and key reassignments to make even the most stalwart DOS-based programmer comfortable when working in Windows.

SpeedEdit: Bradford Business Systems

SpeedEdit is a comprehensive software system designed to provide great capability with minimal complexity. Every effort is made to maintain compatibility with many different computers. The power and flexibility of this product make it a choice of many professional programmers.

SpeedEdit is fully customizable. With more than 150 built-in editing functions, this product can improve the productivity of anyone who spends a great deal of time writing source code. Several languages are supported. One of the most unique features of this product is its capability to work with files on a remote host system. For developers, maintenance of programs installed at an end-user site can be performed without costly site visits.

Bradford Business Systems Inc.
23151 Verdugo Drive, #114
Laguna Hills CA 92653
Voice: (714)859-4428

Training Aids

These products make the job of learning easier and therefore more successful. Some of these products can help you learn foreign languages. A few even read files of text to you so that you can hear it the way the intended listener will hear it.

Monologue: First Byte

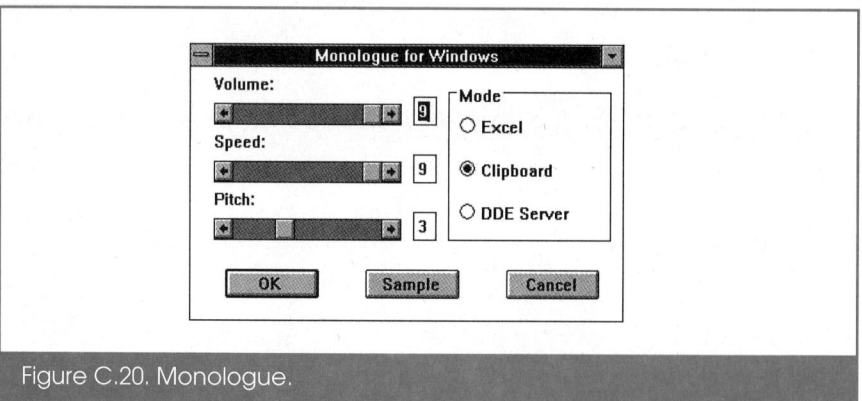

Figure C.20. Monologue.

Monologue is a speech synthesis product that can read any block of pronounceable text over your system's speaker or an external audio system. This product can proofread materials for ease of assimilation testing.

Writers can use this product to test how their material sounds to the reader. Software Developers can add speech to their applications by using the DDE to access Monologue's speech synthesis utility.

You can control the tone and speed of the speech. The manufacturer claims that speech quality is enhanced if you load Monologue into a RAM disk before using it.

This product essentially reads any text copied onto the Windows Clipboard. The size of the Clipboard is the only constraint as to how long Monologue speaks for any specified length of time.

First Byte
P. O. Box 2961
Torrance CA 90509
Voice: (800)556-6141

C

Utilities

Utilities are products that perform specific functions. By definition, they are not related to any particular application, but provide a service of some sort to many applications.

OSFrame: Playroom Software

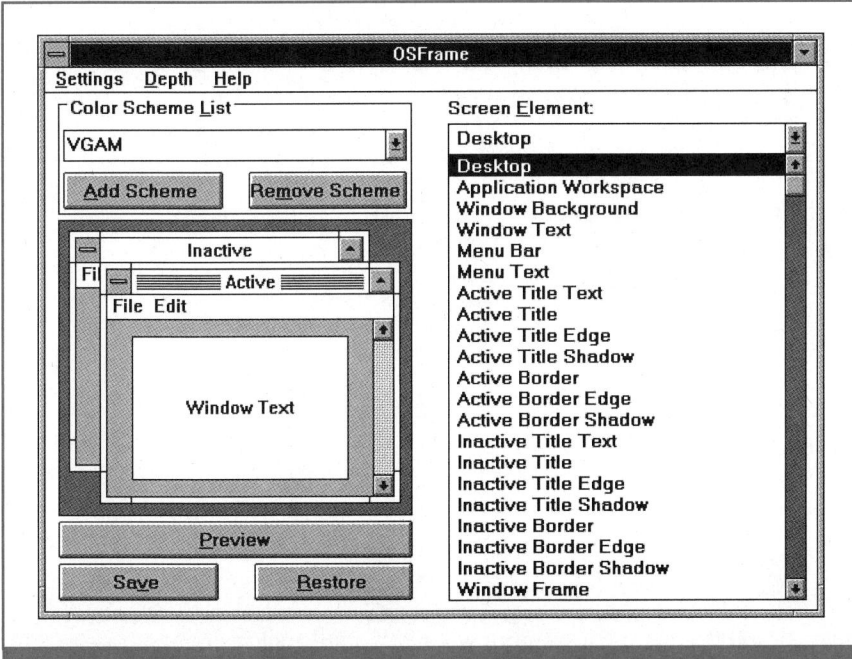

Figure C.21. OSFrame.

OSFrame is a screen enhancement product for Windows. This product effectively supersedes the Control Panel Color program to increase screen configuration flexibility.

OSFrame enables you to add three-dimensional effects to virtually every object bar, border, and button of every GUI application you run under Windows. This product also makes Windows appear as other GUIs. As a transitional aid for people migrating from another GUI to the Windows environment, this feature is not only a lot of fun, but it is also a necessary aid.

One of the best features of this product is its capability to change just about every aspect of screen objects in the Windows environment. You can color border shadows, make them slightly three-dimensional or very three-dimensional, and control the colors of aspects of buttons such as the control menu button and the minimize and maximize buttons.

Playroom Software
7308-C East Independence Boulevard, Suite 310
Charlotte NC 28227
Voice: (704)536-3093

Word Processing

If Windows Write does not exactly leave you singing in the shower, you can choose from many products that offer both simplicity and/or elaboration...to fit your particular needs.

Word for Windows: Microsoft

Microsoft Word for Windows has undergone major changes since its inception. This product offers state-of-the-art features and utilities that users now demand. Features such as spell checking, grammar checking, thesaurus, easier envelope creation, and macro management are standard fare in the latest version of Microsoft Windows.

This product is intended for the small- and large-document creator. Full outline capabilities have been a feature of the past and the present version, making Word for Windows a powerful tool for users generating large documents and publications.

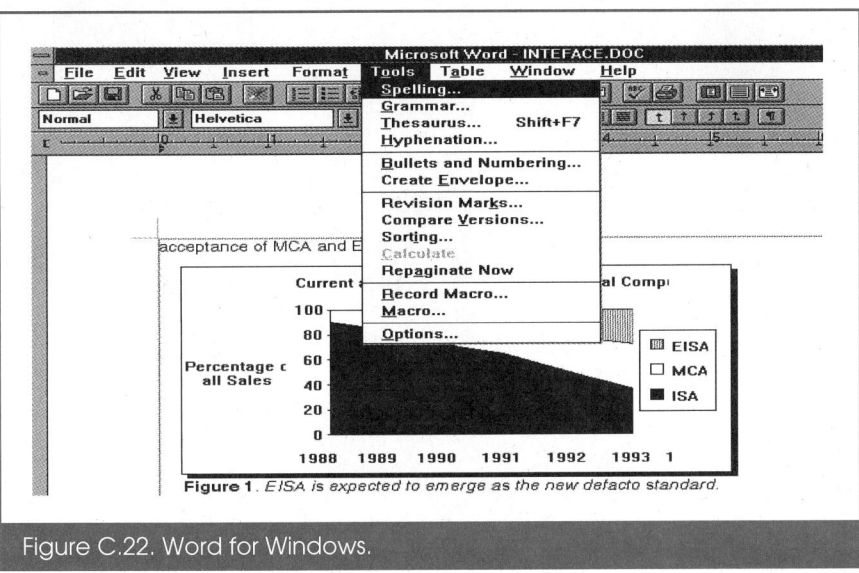

Figure C.22. Word for Windows.

Other features of Word for Windows include the following:

▲ Use of frames is supported

▲ Three-dimensional graphing is invoked via the button bar

▲ A paint application is invoked via the button bar

▲ Many files' formats can be imported and exported

▲ Bulleted lists can be created by clicking an icon

▲ Numbered lists are built with a click of an icon

Microsoft Corporation
One Microsoft Way
Redmond WA 98073-9717
Voice: (800)426-9400

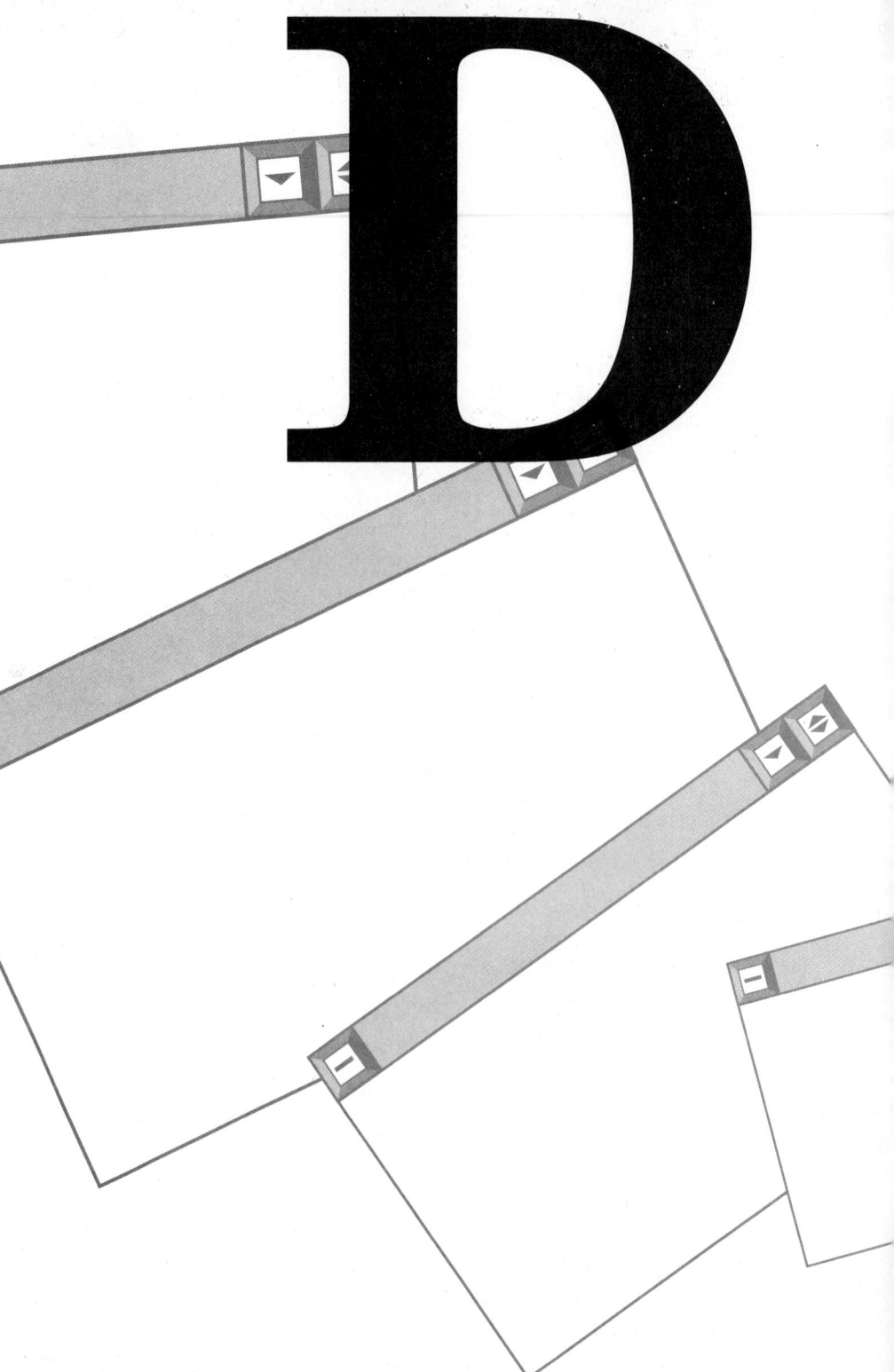

REFERENCE

D

General Windows Information

Windows's popularity has created the need for a variety of information sources. Some of the services listed in this chapter are aimed at a particular level of user, but most are aimed at all Windows users.

Magazines

The most common source of information for most users is magazines. There are many excellent magazines that specialize in the PC market. These often have regular Windows columns and review Windows software.

The popular magazines with good general Windows coverage include the following:

- ▲ *PC* Magazine
- ▲ *PC World*
- ▲ *PC/Computing*

PART VIII ▲ WINDOWS REFERENCES

These usually are available on the newsstand.

If you want lots of Windows-specific information, you probably want *Windows and OS/2* Magazine. Although smaller and less flashy than the general PC magazines, *Windows and OS/2* Magazine doesn't waste your time with the non-Windows programs that still make up the large majority of the PC market. If it isn't on your newsstand, you can reach the magazine at 1101B Eugenia Place, Carpenteria CA 93013; (805)566-1282.

Information Networks

Computer services usually provide two important ways of getting information about Windows. They all charge some sort of fee, although they seem to set their fees in their own intrinsic fashions. Check with each service before you join to learn what you will be charged and how they come up with the numbers.

▲ In forums, you discuss Windows and related topics. You can ask questions, give answers to problems you have encountered and overcome, or just listen to the discussion so that you know what the important topics are.

▲ In file areas, you can download new programs, device drivers, and so on. Some of these files are free, and some of them are shareware (in which you are supposed to pay for the program if you use it). Some files are not programs but are information about Windows, such as collected tips about particular topics.

There are literally hundreds of computer services in the United States, most of them small. The larger networks include CompuServe and Prodigy.

Most of the large services have active discussions of Windows. Smaller bulletin board systems usually also have discussions, but because they have fewer people in the discussions, it is often more difficult to get good information from them.

Contact telephone numbers for the largest services are listed in Table D.1.

1184

Table D.1. Phone numbers for large information services.

Service	Phone Number
CompuServe	(800) 848-8990
Prodigy	(800) 776-0836
GEnie	(800) 638-9636
Delphi	(800) 544-4005
The WELL	(415) 332-4335
Channel 1	(617) 864-0100

D

User Groups

Local PC user groups often have Windows special interest groups (SIGs). See your local computer newspaper for information on finding a PC user group in your area.

There is a national Windows user group called WUGNET (National Windows User Group Network). WUGNET offers a wide variety of services to members, including a bimonthly journal, reference services, consulting, and so on. The group is geared toward business and advanced users, although novices certainly can get a great deal of benefit from their services.

WUGNET (National Windows User Group Network)
P.O. Box 1967
Media PA 19063
(215)565-1861

Glossary

386-enhanced mode	One of the Windows operating modes. It requires an 80386 or higher CPU.
accelerator key	A keyboard shortcut for a command. For example, Shift-Delete is an accelerator command for the Edit Cut command.
activate	To bring a window to the front and make it active.
active printer	The printer that will be used by programs.
active window	The window that is currently being used.
adapter segment	Another name sometimes used for the upper memory block area.
Advanced Program-to-Program Communication	A communications standard defined by IBM. The APPC standard is intended to allow multiple users to share the processing of programs.
alert message	A critical warning, confirmation, or information message that appears in a dialog box.

ANSI	A standard for the ordering of characters within a font. For more information, see Chapter 26, "Printers and Fonts."
API	See Application Programming Interface.
APPC	See Advanced Program-to-Program Communication.
Application Programming Interface (API)	A set of interface functions available for applications.
ASCII characters	A subset of the ANSI character standard described in the preceding definition.
ASCII file	Same as text file.
associate	Links a document with the program that was used to create it so that both can be opened with one command.
attribute	A property or characteristic.
background operation	A job being performed by a program when another program is in the active window.
Basic Input/Output System	A program that usually resides on a ROM-based storage device in your PC that handles instructions to and from the system bus.
Bezier	A mathematically constructed curve, such as that used in drawing programs.
binary file	Any file that contains characters other than text.
BIOS	See Basic Input/Output System.
bit map	A screen page in memory.
Calculator	A program that comes with Windows and enables you to perform standard or scientific operations.

Calendar	A program that comes with Windows and enables you to record your appointments by date and time.
Cardfile	A program that comes with Windows and enables you to record information cards and sort through them using their index lines.
cascade	To arrange all the windows so that they are neatly stacked, with only the title bars showing behind the active window.
cascading menu	A submenu that drops down when a command is given.
character-based	Usually used when referring to non-Windows applications. Character-based applications display information using the ASCII character set, or characters normally found on the keyboard.
check box	A dialog box item that takes an off or on value.
clicking	Quickly pressing and releasing the mouse button.
Clipboard	Holds one piece of information for use in a program or to pass information between programs.
Clock	A program that comes with Windows and gives you the option of viewing the time in either analog or digital mode.
collapse	To hide additional directory levels below the selected directory level.
color pattern	A color selection that is made up of two other colors.
command button	A dialog box item that causes an action when clicked.
control menu	A menu that exists in every window and enables you to modify its parameters or take global actions.

G

Control Panel	A program that comes with Windows and enables you to make settings for many Windows actions, such as changing network, keyboard, and international settings.
conventional memory	Memory located in the first 640K.
CPU	Central processing unit. An example of a CPU is the Intel 80386 CPU.
current window	The window which you are currently using and which is in front of all other open windows.
cursor	The representation of the mouse on the screen. It may take many shapes.
database	A file or group of related files that are designed to hold recurring data types as though the files were lists.
DDE	See Dynamic Data Exchange.
default button	The command button that is activated when you press Enter in a dialog box.
desktop	The screen area on which the windows are displayed.
desktop pattern	A bit map that decorates your desktop. You can select one of Windows's patterns or create your own.
device driver	A file that provides data about a device that is connected to, but not part of, the original motherboard of the computer.
dialog box	A box that appears on your screen to give or ask for information.
document window	The window in which a document appears.
double-click	To press the mouse button twice in rapid succession while keeping the mouse still between clicks.

drag	To move an object on the screen from one place to another by clicking it with the mouse and pulling it to where you want it to be.
drop-down list	A dialog box item that shows only one entry until its drop-down arrow is clicked.
Dynamic Data Exchange (DDE)	A feature of Windows that allows programs to communicate and actively pass information.
EMM386.EXE	A file that enables you to emulate expanded memory.
expanded memory	Memory that conforms to the LIM 4.0 standard for memory access.
extended memory	Memory that can be accessed by Windows past the first megabyte in your system.
File Manager	A program that comes with Windows to help you manage files.
font	A description of how to display a set of characters.
foreground operation	The program in the active window.
group window	A window within Program Manager that shows all the programs in one group.
Help	A program that gives you information about how to run Windows and Windows programs, including how to use the Help program.
HIMEM.SYS	A program that lets Windows access all your RAM memory.
I-beam	The shape the cursor takes in the area of a window where text can be entered.
icon	A small graphic symbol seen in Program Manager and used to represent a program or a document.

G

inactive	An open window that is not currently in use.
insertion point	A flashing vertical line that shows where text will be inserted.
keyboard shortcut	A combination of keystrokes that initiates a menu command without dropping the menu down.
list box	A dialog box item that shows all available options.
macro	A sequence of keyboard strokes and mouse actions that can be recorded so that their play back can be activated by a single keystroke or keystroke combination. The Recorder program can be used to create a macro.
maximize button	The button in the upper-right corner of a window that has an arrow pointing up. When clicked, it enlarges a window to its maximum size.
menu	A list of available command options.
menu bar	Located under the title bar, it displays the names of all the available menu lists.
menu command	A word or a phrase in a menu that, when selected, activates a function.
menu title	A title for a group of commands that, when selected, enables you to view all the commands.
minimize button	The button in the upper-right corner of a window that has an arrow pointing down. When clicked, it reduces the window to an icon.
mouse pointer	The symbol that displays where your next mouse click will occur. The mouse pointer symbol changes according to the context of the window or the dialog box in which it appears.

non-Windows program	A program not designed to be used specifically in Windows. Most non-Windows applications or programs are character-based in nature.
Notepad	A program that comes with Windows and enables you to view and edit text files.
option button	A dialog box item that enables you to choose only one of a group of choices.
Paintbrush	A Windows drawing program.
permanent swap file	A file that gives Windows more effective and faster memory in 386-enhanced mode.
PIF	A file that provides Windows with the information it needs to know in order to run a non-Windows program.
PIF Editor	A Windows program that enables you to specify how a non-Windows program is started and how it utilizes Windows's capabilities.
Print Manager	A Windows program that controls the printing for all Windows programs. Its print spooling capabilities enable you to work with other Windows programs while a document is in the process of being printed.
printer driver	A Windows program that tells programs how to format data for a particular type of printer.
Program Manager	The main Windows program that enables you to start programs.
program swap file	Used to hold all the information for an application after you switch away from it.
program window	A window that contains a program and its documents.
raster font	A font in which characters are stored as pixels.

G

real mode	One of Windows 3.0's three modes. This mode was intended to support the 8086 and 8088 family of processors. Real mode was discontinued with the release of Windows Version 3.1.
Recorder	A Windows program that records and plays back macros.
Restore button	Located in the upper-right corner of a window or in the control menu, it restores a window to the size it was before being maximized.
Reversi	A Windows board game program based on the game of Othello. Reversi was discontinued with the release of Windows Version 3.1.
scroll arrow	Located at either end of a scroll bar, it can be clicked to scroll up or down.
scroll bar	Displayed at the bottom and/or right edge of a window when the window's contents aren't completely visible.
scroll box	A small box located in the scroll bar that shows where the visible window is located in relation to the entire document, menu, or list.
select	To specify a section of text or graphics for initiating an action. To select also can be to choose an option in a dialog box.
shortcut key	A keystroke or key combination that enables you to activate a command without having to enter a menu.
SMARTDRV.SYS	A program that speeds disk access.
Solitaire	A Windows game program based on the card game Solitaire.
standard mode	One of two operating modes of Windows 3.1.

stroke font	A font that can have its size greatly altered without distorting the font.
SYSTEM.INI	The file that contains hardware-specific information used when you start Windows.
Task List	A dialog box that displays all the programs running and enables you to switch among them.
Terminal	A Windows communication program.
text box	A space in the dialog box where text or numbers can be entered so that a command can be carried out.
text file	A file with only text characters in it.
tile	To reduce and move windows so that they can all be seen at once.
title bar	The bar at the top of a program or a document window that shows you what its title is. The control menu and the maximize and minimize buttons can be accessed in the title bar.
vector fonts	A set of lines that connect points to form characters.
virtual memory	The use of permanent media to simulate additional RAM.
WAN	Wide Area Network, as opposed to a LAN, or Local Area Network.
wide area network	A network designed to accommodate users over a wide area, using the phone system to replace interconnecting cabling.
WIN.INI	The file that contains information about all your software settings, used when you start Windows.

G

Product Index

Index

I

I

I

1215

I

F

I

I

H

I

I

O

program information files (PIFs),
  655-670, 673-678, 680-688
Program Manager, 8-9, 89, 91,
  103-104, 1193
    desktop, 105, 930
    File menu, 1082-1083
    files, 131
    help, 95
    icons, 625
    layouts, 129-131
    Options menu, 1083
    programs, 91
      running, 111-113
    replacements, 949-954, 957-958
    windows, 104
      arranging, 109-110
program manager replacement
  software, 1169
program swap files, 1193
program switching
    386-enhanced mode, 683-685
    standard mode PIFs, 666-670
program windows, 68-69, 1193
programming, 1035-1036
    development tools, 1067-1068
    dialog boxes, 1020
    environments, 1036-1041, 1043
      Actor, 1066
      KnowledgePro, 1066-1067
      Objectworks/Smalltalk, 1063-
        1065
      Pascal, Turbo, 1062-1063
      Smalltalk/V, 1065
    events, 1014
    files
      module definition, 1018-1019
      resource files, 1018
    interfaces, networks, 888
    languages
      BASIC, 1036
      C, 1036, 1052, 1055, 1057-
        1058, 1060, 1062
      C++, 1052, 1055, 1057-1058,
        1060, 1062
      FORTH, 1036
      Pascal, 1037

    Realizer, 1049-1050
    Visual Basic, 1047-1049
    messages, 1015-1016
    multitasking, 1014-1015
    object-oriented, 1013-1016, 1039
    procedural, 1013-1016
    Windows programs, 1017-1019
programs
    activating, 93
    additional, 13
    background, 91
    background execution, 678
    communication between, 9, 10
    disk caching, 727-730
    DOS, 623-652
    drawing, 558
    exclusive execution, 680
    extended memory, 651
    foreground, 91
    graphics-based, 624
    inactive, 91
    installation, 30-41
    instances, 1026
    launching, icons, 111
    linking, 9, 10
    loading as icons, 825-826
    memory-resident, 624, 716
    non-Windows, 623-627, 1193
      icons, 122
      passing data, 639-642
      switching from, 650-651
    paint, 558
    protected-mode, 644-645
    running, 46-47, 149
      at startup, 826
      from icon, 111
      from keyboard, 111
      mimimized, 112
      Program Manager, 111-113
    Setup, 30
    setup, 752
    simultaneous running, 7-8
    starting from File Manage, 149
    switching between, 92-94, 639
    TSR (Terminate and Stay
      Resident), 624, 636-638, 716

I

I

I

I

I

I

Sams—Covering The Latest In Computer And Technical Topics!

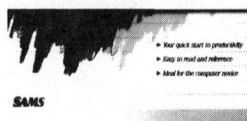

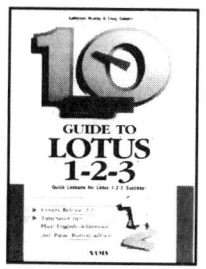
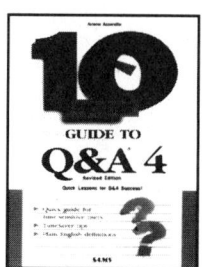

Turn to Sams For Complete
Hardware and Networking Information